COPY MACHINE MANIFESTOS

COPY MACHINE MANIFESTOS

With contributions by:

Gwen Allen
Julia Bryan-Wilson
Mimi Thi Nguyen
Tavia Nyong'o
Alexis Salas

ARTISTS WHO MAKE ZINES

Branden W. Joseph
and Drew Sawyer

Brooklyn Museum

XEROX

Date: 1923 - 1973

CELEBRATING 50 HAPPY YEARS OF FAMILY ENTERTAINMENT

To Our Customers:

I have just made a service call on your **ZINES** machine.

This letter represents the type of copy that your machine is now producing.

On each call, I use this document to ensure that your machine is operating at peak performance. I will be back on a scheduled basis to perform preventive maintenance and to update your equipment as required.

In the meantime, if your machine should require attention, please do not hesitate to call me. I will be happy to serve you.

Sincerely,

JOHN DOWD

Xerox Technical Representative

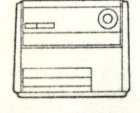
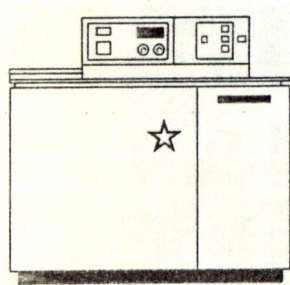
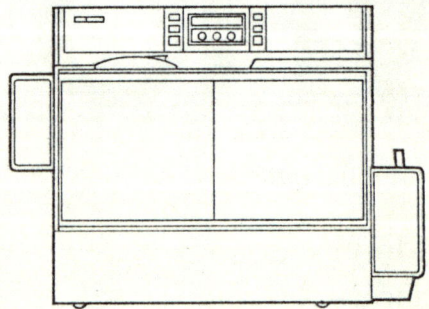

XEROX CORPORATION

John Dowd
From Dowdaland Archives, 1973
Photocopy, perfect bound, leather-covered boards,
11 ¾ × 9 ½ in. (29.8 × 24.1 cm)
Collection Luke and Noel Dowd

Foreword 6
Anne Pasternak

Acknowledgments 8

Copy Machine Manifestos: Artists Who Make Zines 10
Branden W. Joseph and Drew Sawyer

Artists' Zines: The Fanzine as an Artistic Medium 16
Gwen Allen

1. The Correspondence Scene, 1969–1980 24

Zines by Artists: Post-Pop Punk Art 56–67
Branden W. Joseph

2. The Punk Explosion, 1975–1990 92

Social Media: Photography and Zines in the Age of Xerography 130–41
Drew Sawyer

3. Queer and Feminist Undergrounds, 1987–2000 170

Cool Older Siblings: Queer Zines as Queer Theory 224–31
Julia Bryan-Wilson

4. Subcultural Topologies, 1990–2010 268

Friendly Specters: *Casper* and Other Mexico City–based
Artists' Zines and Projects 292–97
Alexis Salas

5. Critical Promiscuity, 2000–2020 322

In Love and Rage: The Revolutionary Counter-Mood of Zine Culture 342–49
Tavia Nyong'o

6. A Continuing Legacy, 2010–2023 368

The Eventfulness of Incomplete Presence, or 398–405
No One Turned Away for Lack of Future
Mimi Thi Nguyen

Selected Artists and Collectives 430
Branden W. Joseph, Drew Sawyer, Imani Williford, and Marcelo Gabriel Yáñez

Picture Credits 444
Author Biographies 445
Brooklyn Museum Board of Trustees 447

Foreword

Copy Machine Manifestos: Artists Who Make Zines, the first major exhibition dedicated to artists' zines produced in North America, builds on the Brooklyn Museum's commitment to shedding light on overlooked or marginalized people, histories, and art forms. Like many of our shows, it expands on the art historical canon, in this case, highlighting the vast production and influence of zines, an art form little considered in museums and galleries.

When Phil Aarons, the passionate champion and collector of artists' books, shared with me his dream of an expansive exhibition on the history of artists' zines, I immediately signed up the Brooklyn Museum to organize this project. Zines erupted as a global force in the visual arts in the early 1970s and have since been one of the most pervasive, accessible, and democratic art forms. Known for challenging the status quo, giving people control over their own stories and representations, and being free or low cost and often shipping directly to the consumer by mail, zines have bypassed traditional barriers to audiences and have been important catalysts for artistic, social, and political transformation.

Gathering an extensive presentation of zines and related artworks by more than one hundred artists, our curators have endeavored to create a complex, albeit knowingly fragmentary understanding of the inspiring experimentation and ingenuity of artists and zine makers over the past fifty years. Zines are often centered around local communities, and this exhibition and book feature many artists who are based in Brooklyn, from John Dowd in the late 1960s and early 1970s to Neta Bomani, Lizania Cruz, and others working today. The project also moves out from Brooklyn and New York to chart networks and histories across the United States, Canada, and Mexico.

We are honored that Branden W. Joseph, Frank Gallipoli Professor of Modern and Contemporary Art at Columbia University, and Drew Sawyer, Sondra Gilman Curator of Photography at the Whitney Museum of American Art (formerly Phillip and Edith Leonian Curator of Photography at the Brooklyn Museum), have worked tirelessly over the past several years to speak with zine makers, explore alternate histories, and gather exceedingly rare objects that have gone largely underexplored. The results of their efforts are all the more remarkable given the impact of a global pandemic, which halted travel, shut down archives and libraries, and limited in-person meetings for several years during the course of the project's development. This publication is a testament to their dedication and passion, and will lead to new scholarship and elevate the status of zines as a truly important art form.

This undertaking is indebted to the vision, partnership, and support of Phil and Shelley Fox Aarons, who have long championed marginalized artists, countercultural histories, and artists' publications. Their extensive collection forms the foundation of the exhibition and book. And their passionate commitment to preserving this ephemeral art form has had an immeasurable impact on artists and the field. We have profound personal and professional gratitude for their tireless efforts and devotion to this project.

Every exhibition and publication takes the work and generosity of dozens, if not hundreds, of people. We are thankful to all the visionary funders who understand the importance of this undertaking. In addition to Phil and Shelley Fox Aarons, the Andy Warhol Foundation for the Visual Arts provided major support for this project. We are also deeply appreciative of the generosity of lenders to the exhibition, including museums, archives, foundations, galleries, collectors, and artists, who have entrusted us with their works and allowed them to be shown in these pages. For the ongoing support of the Museum's Trustees, we extend special thanks to Barbara Vogelstein, Chairman, and every member of our Board. Without the confidence and active engagement of our Trustees, it would not be possible to maintain our trailblazing programming.

Like zines, this exhibition and book are the products of a collective effort, and I want to thank the entire Brooklyn Museum staff for their dedication to our mission and work. I also want to extend my gratitude to Phaidon, especially Keith Fox and Deborah Aaronson, for partnering on this groundbreaking and significant book, and helping it reach a larger audience of readers. There are many other colleagues, collaborators, and contributors who are thanked in Joseph and Sawyer's extensive acknowledgments. I echo their gratitude, especially to the artists and keepers of these histories, which continue to hold the promise of a more informed, connected, empathic, equitable, and even aesthetic world.

Anne Pasternak
Shelby White and Leon Levy Director
Brooklyn Museum

Acknowledgments

In keeping with this exhibition's focus on zines, which are so often collaborative and centered on community, *Copy Machine Manifestos* grew from the efforts and support of numerous individuals and institutions. More than four years in the making, a project of this scale would not have been possible without our colleagues and collaborators at the Brooklyn Museum. Our heartfelt gratitude goes to Anne Pasternak, the Brooklyn Museum's Shelby White and Leon Levy Director, and the rest of the leadership team, in particular Deputy Director for Art Sharon Matt Atkins and Director of Curatorial Affairs and Senior Curator of Decorative Arts Catherine Futter, for their critical and steadfast support. A special thanks to the Brooklyn Museum's Associate Curator Carmen Hermo, who began as a co-conspirator in 2019 but had to step away from the project in early 2021 to oversee another important exhibition. We also wish to thank Marcelo Gabriel Yáñez and Imani Williford for their invaluable research and assistance on details big and small. Beatrice Johnson expertly managed many logistical aspects of the exhibition, while Katrina Dumas and Cindy Ortiz contended with the complicated business and volume of loans of work for the project. Several interns assisted with research and compiling our database, which at one point reached nearly five thousand objects; for their efforts we thank Eric Afflerbach, Mary Joy Jimenez, Chloe Ming, Taylor Ndiaye, Zach Ngin, and Kirk Patrick Testa.

Copy Machine Manifestos would not have been possible without the vision and support of Philip Aarons and Shelley Fox Aarons. Research for this exhibition and book began in 2019 thanks to their partnership. While the COVID-19 pandemic closed most libraries and archives from March 2020 until the spring of 2022, the Aaronses opened up their vast collection, allowing us to physically handle and read hundreds of zines and related materials. This exhibition and book attest to their generosity and to their advocacy for artists and artists' publications. We are deeply grateful. We also thank the Aaronses' collection manager, David Vu, for his assistance with our many inquiries and visits and for expertly photographing hundreds of zines for this volume.

Preparation for this project entailed corresponding with, interviewing, and visiting more than one hundred artists, most of whom are featured in this publication. Our profound gratitude goes to all of them—as well as to their collaborators, families and friends, and galleries and representatives—who spent countless hours with us talking over Zoom, digging through boxes in basements and storage units, and connecting us with other artists, zine makers, scholars, curators, librarians, archivists, dealers, and writers. Many of the featured zines and related materials come directly from the collections of artists and other individuals, whom we thank for entrusting us with their work. This book is a testament to and celebration of their creative energies, which have had an indelible impact on so many aspects of contemporary culture.

Over the course of our research, we have had the privilege of visiting numerous collections at institutions in North America and Europe, both virtually and in person. We thank the many colleagues who accommodated our requests during the pandemic by scanning materials or video conferencing with us, and welcoming us into physical archives even before institutions were officially reopened to outside researchers. Most of these institutions made crucial loans and photographed material for this publication. In particular we wish to thank: Mauricio Marcín and Sandra Sánchez at Aeromoto; Jack Waters at Allied Productions; Jessica Beck and Matthew Gray at the Andy Warhol Museum; the Archives of American Art; Raegan Swanson and Lucie Handley-Girard at the ArQuives; Jon Shibata at the Art Museum & Pacific Film Archive, University of California, Berkeley; Jenna Friedman at the Barnard Zine Library, Barnard College; Rachel Churner at the Carolee Schneemann Foundation; Ellen Keith at the Chicago History Museum; Xaviera S. Flores at Chicano Studies Research Center, University of California, Los Angeles; Colleen Doyle at the David Armstrong Archives; Nicholas Martin at Fales Library and Special Collections, New York University; Nadine Wietlisbach and Therese Seeholzer at the Fotomuseum Winterthur; Teresa Gruber at Fotostiftung Schweiz; Luz Elena Mendoza at Fundación Jumex AC/Museo Jumex; Isaac Fellman at the Gay and Lesbian Historical Society in San Francisco; Glenn Phillips and Zanna Gilbert at the Getty Research Institute; James Capobianco at Houghton Library, Harvard University; Aldo Hernández and Doug Bressler at Howl! Arts and Archive; Anna Tidlund and Teresa Sudeyko at the Morris and Helen Belkin Art Gallery and Western Front archives, University of British Columbia; Lionel Bovier at the Musée d'art moderne et contemporain (ECART) in Geneva; Sol Henaro at the Museo Universitario Arte Contemporáneo; José Luis Paredes Pacho at the Museo Universitario del Chopo; Sophie Cavoulacos, Michelle Elligott, Tasha Lutek, Oluremi Onabanjo, Jillian Suarez, and Ashley Swinnerton at the Museum of Modern Art in New York; Lexi Johnson and Loni A. Shibuyama at ONE National Gay and Lesbian Archives at the University of Southern California Libraries; Katherine Reagan at the Rare and Manuscript Collections, Cornell University; Maria Ilario at the Ray Johnson Estate; the staff at the San Francisco Public Library; Cheryl Beredo and staff at the Schomburg Center for Research in Black Culture; Jane Bramwell at Tate in London; Elizabeth Riordan and Rachel Miller-Haughton at the University of Iowa Libraries' Special Collections & Archives; Emily Martin at Video Data Bank, School of the Art Institute of Chicago; Kyle Croft and Kailee Faber at Visual AIDS; and Wanda vanderStoop at VTape.

A tremendous amount of effort, detail, and care went into this publication. We wish to thank Audrey Walen at the Brooklyn Museum for overseeing all aspects of its production. Sarah DeSantis and Taylor Catalana provided invaluable support in obtaining permissions for and gathering and producing photographs of these complicated and rare objects. The book's editor, Diana Stoll, tackled both the largest conceptual issues and the minute details with finesse and patience. Our praise and thanks go to Garrick Gott for his inspired design. In addition to David Vu, we thank the many lenders who provided photography for these rarely reproduced objects. Finally, the expert team at Phaidon has been a great partner in bringing the book to completion and getting it into the world.

We also had the privilege to have worked with a brilliant group of scholars in preparing this book. We thank each of the essayists for their contributions and for being interlocutors: Gwen Allen, Julia Bryan-Wilson, Mimi Thi Nguyen, Tavia Nyong'o, and Alexis Salas. Some of them have been active participants in these zine cultures, and we greatly benefited not only from their essays in this volume, but also from their previous writings and research. Other scholars and experts assisted in various ways, even lending material from their personal collections or facilitating loans with other individuals, including Arthur Fournier, John Held, Jr., Johan Kugelberg, and Jay Reeg. A special thanks to David Evans Frantz, who not only shared research from his own related projects, such as *Axis Mundo*, but also helped us to access other collections. Mary Fellios and Emily Small at Columbia University assisted with research helping to compile bibliographies that informed the project, and the Media Center for Art History at Columbia University facilitated numerous last-minute scans.

Branden W. Joseph
Frank Gallipoli Professor of Modern and Contemporary Art
Columbia University

Drew Sawyer
Sondra Gilman Curator of Photography
Whitney Museum of American Art

Copy Machine Manifestos:
Artists Who Make Zines

Branden W. Joseph and Drew Sawyer

Copy Machine Manifestos is the first historical survey of zines produced by artists working in North America over the past half century. A *zine*, short for "fanzine" (or sometimes "magazine"), is generally defined as a quickly produced, low-cost publication intended for relatively limited distribution. The "classic" zine likely comprises several sheets of letter-sized, photocopied paper, folded in half and staple bound to form a booklet, but in fact zines come in a wide variety of sizes and formats, with a range of binding styles and reproduction techniques, from photocopy to offset- and laser-printing to "publications" in the form of videotapes and DVDs. While zines share much with other products of independent publishing—such as political pamphlets and countercultural newspapers—they form their own distinct lineage. The word "zine" and its typical form gained popularity with the wide availability of affordable reproduction technologies, first with the mimeograph (as seen with the appearance of science fiction fanzines in the 1930s), and later, more expansively, with accessibility of the photocopy machine, starting in the early 1970s. Particularly since the latter period, artists have harnessed the medium's essential role in community building and communication, not only to transform their material and conceptual approaches to making art, but also to challenge institutions and extant artistic categories. In the past two decades, alongside the rise of social media platforms and digital publishing, artists (and their "fans") have continued to be drawn to these printed publications, as evidenced by the proliferation and growing popularity of zine fairs and workshops as well as artist-publishers. By focusing on the intersection of zines, zine makers, and artistic practices, *Copy Machine Manifestos* makes a case for the important role of the medium in the history of art of the past fifty years and provides new lineages for contemporary practices.

When this project was initiated in 2019, its working title was "An Incomplete History of Zines by Artists." Indeed, a comprehensive survey or canon of such publications would be impossible because of the sheer volume, variety, and often private and anti-institutional nature of zines by artists (let alone zines more broadly). In one of the first detailed studies of zine production, *Notes from Underground: Zines and the Politics of Alternative Culture*, media scholar Stephen Duncombe placed "Art zines" last in a lengthy taxonomy of subgenres, just before "The Rest" (designated simply as "a large category") and well below such subgenres as "Music zines," "Travel zines," "Health zines," and "Comix."[1] Duncombe defined the art zine primarily according to its contents ("print media collages, photographs, drawings, and mail art") and secondarily according to its function (to "create a network of artists and a floating virtual gallery").[2] This characterization aptly describes certain correspondence art zines of the 1970s featured in this volume. From the perspective of this exhibition and book, however, a more substantial segment of artists' zines might more accurately be defined as what Canadian artist and zine-maker AA Bronson termed "format-oriented work": the post-conceptual appropriation of such structures as books, magazines, beauty pageants, or political campaigns in order to bypass the "middleman of galleries or critics."[3] Adopting these and other traditionally non-art formats allows not only for more egalitarian modes of distribution (such as the postal service) and a populist market, but also—as feminist critic Lucy R. Lippard argued about cheaply printed artists' books—for the promotion and circulation of work by historically and institutionally marginalized groups "without depending on the undependable museum and gallery system" (a system, as she noted, that has been "especially undependable for women").[4] Adopting the zine as a post-conceptual strategy in no way precludes many of the artists in this survey from actively participating in, and in many cases considerably impacting, the subcultures with which they and their work engage, as witnessed by the significant number of artists who have performed in punk and post-punk bands, who have attained renown as skateboarders, or who have interacted with other communities, from bicyclists to pigeon fanciers.

As the writings of Bronson and Lippard make clear, artists' zines exist not only as a subgenre of zine production, but also within a lineage of artistic publications, one that arguably extends as far back as Dada's most ephemeral volumes.[5] Beginning in the late 1960s, the artists' zine entered a burgeoning field of artists' publications, including artists' books, artists' magazines, mimeographed little magazines, underground publications (such as Yayoi Kusama's 1969 tabloid-sized *Orgy*), Lettrist- and Situationist-inspired political pamphlets, mini-comics, and more. Often, the lines separating such genres could be blurred. The self-dubbed "megazine" *File*, a parody of *Life* magazine produced beginning in 1972 by the Toronto-based Conceptual art group General Idea (AA Bronson, Felix Partz, and Jorge Zontal), stands perhaps on the line between zine and magazine: while Bronson described it as "a simulacrum of a real magazine; more than a real magazine," artist Tom Hosier classed *File* as a contemporary "dadazine" along-

46 ←

87, 50–53 ←

side much smaller and scrappier publications of the era, such as the **West Bay Dadaist**, *491*, and his own **Modern Correspondence Magazine**.[6] The first issue of Anna Banana's **Vile**, which appeared in 1974, was even more evidently hybrid, with its two-color offset cover (a takeoff on both *File* and *Life*) wrapped around a zine-like, photocopied, and velo-bound interior. *File*'s regular column "Zines" routinely discussed low-cost zines and higher-production magazines,

49 ←

while Bill Gaglione's altered 1974 Charlie Brown comic in the San Francisco zine **Quoz?**, depicting an array of "dadazines," also included both zines and magazines, as well as the mini-comic *Sin City* and the underground comic *Young Lust*.[7]

Perhaps because the definition of the artists' zine has been relatively fluid and manifold, there has yet to be an established canon of zine-making artists. Zines were not among the subjects of focus that Toronto arts center Art Metropole chose to anthologize in its groundbreaking series of books on "format-based work," published beginning in 1979—which included *Performance by Artists*, *Books by Artists*, *Museums by Artists*, or *Sound by Artists*.[8] Nor have zines been comprehensively studied, as other sorts of artists' publications have, in such books as Gwen Allen's *Artists' Magazines: An Alternative Space for Art*; Andrew Roth, Philip E. Aarons, and Claire Lehmann's *Artists Who Make Books*; or Aarons and Roth's *In Numbers: Serial Publications by Artists Since 1955*.[9] This exhibition and catalogue therefore aim to take the first steps in that direction, however limited and incomplete—and perhaps antithetical to the very ethos of zines—the endeavor may be.

As was the case for *Artists Who Make Books* and *In Numbers*, this project draws upon the invaluable archive of artists' publications in the collection of Philip Aarons and Shelley Fox Aarons. This crucial cache of materials has been supplemented by extensive research in archives throughout North America and Europe, including the ArQuives: Canada's LGBTQ+ Archives in Toronto; the Chicago History Museum; Fales Library and Special Collections at New York University; the Getty Research Institute in Los Angeles; L'Archive ECART at the Musée d'art modern et contemporain (MAMCO) in Geneva; the Mark Morrisroe Estate at the Fotomuseum Winterthur in Switzerland; the Morris and Helen Belkin Art Gallery at the University of British Columbia in Vancouver; the Museo Universitario Arte Contemporáneo (MUAC) at the Universidad Nacional Autónoma de México in Mexico City; the Museum of Modern Art Library and Cinema Department in New York; and ONE Archives at the University of Southern California in Los Angeles. Additional research entailed extensive studio visits, both remotely—particularly when the COVID-19 pandemic halted most travel and closed the majority of libraries and archives in 2020–22—and in person, including sometimes dusty investigations of boxes and basement storage rooms that had not been opened for decades.

Without the benefit of an a priori definition of the artists' zine, our selection of materials had to be both inductive and associative, focused largely on publications that were called "zines" at the time of their making, either by their creators or by their contemporary readers, rather than relying exclusively on publications that conform to current understandings of the genre. For example, while there were numerous artists making photocopied books and journals in the 1970s and 1980s that look similar to zines—such as Louise Odes Neaderland's International Society of Copier Artists and the *I.S.C.A. Quarterly*—these were neither conceived nor named as such at the time. Other examples would include such accomplished productions as the xeroxed photobooks of Christopher Wool (begun 1984) or Josh Smith's *New York Death Trip* volumes (2003–8), which evidently draw from the photocopied aesthetic of zines, but clearly fit within his wider bookmaking practice. Curatorial investigations into an artist or group often led to the discovery of zines by other members of their community, whether in city-based scenes like those in Toronto, San Francisco, and Los Angeles, or through the broader networks made possible through correspondence and other distribution channels.

Consequently, this exhibition and publication chart the changing definitions of zines from 1969 to now, while investigating a number of important networks and lineages associated with them. In its conception, due to the large number of artists who have adopted this capacious genre over the past five decades, the project's scope was very quickly narrowed to North America. We also soon realized that the majority of photographic skater zines, zines by illustrators, mini-comics, and the productions of a number of important art-zine publishers (such as the Zurich-based Nieves, which has collaborated with several artists in this book) simply could not be accommodated. Each of these categories warrants a full-scale exhibition and publication in its own right. Even with such restrictions, however, a great number of artists' zines lamentably could not be included for reasons of space.

Although *Copy Machine Manifestos* traces only a fraction of the possible lineages of artists' zines, it nonetheless features more than one hundred artists and hundreds of zine titles, alongside a significant selection of additional works in a range of media associated with each artist's zine work. The particular body of materials featured in this volume foregrounds several things. First, it emphasizes an area of artistic practice that, despite more than five decades of production, has been largely relegated to the margins, both of the art world and (as Duncombe's taxonomy suggests) within extant zine literature. Second, it presents new historical insights, such as how the development of certain artists' zines preceded, rather than followed, the punk zine explosion of the mid-1970s; how this trajectory differed from that initiated by science fiction fans in the 1930s (even as certain practitioners acknowledged this lineage); and how intertwined the musical practices of queercore and Riot Grrrl movements were with visual arts, not only within associated zines, but also in film, photography, and video production. Finally, the works in *Copy Machine Manifestos* allow for a renewed focus on a number of previously over-looked or marginalized artists. In the exhibition and catalogue, well-known art world figures such as Mark Gonzales, Miranda July, Mike Kelley, Terence Koh, Raymond Pettibon, and Dash Snow share space with less-recognized artists such as Anna Banana, Gene Barnes, Lisa Baumgardner, Félix Endara, Bill Gaglione, Kate Huh, Xanthra Phillippa MacKay, Tim Mancusi, Cory Roberts-Auli, Gerardo Velázquez, Frederick Weston, and others. Some of these individuals created zines as a means of making their voices and visions known, while others embraced the format for its ability to circulate in an almost clandestine manner among a select, if sometimes far-flung, network of associates.

The presence in this project of a significant number of artists of color, as well as queer, trans, and nonbinary figures, goes a long way toward challenging the longstanding assumption that zines are primarily the products of a relatively privileged and overwhelmingly straight, white, middle-class constituency—at least among artists.[10] Similarly, the range of aesthetic and art historical strategies and references within the zines assembled here, as well as their inter-sections with artists' work in other media, undercuts the notion that zines are, as Duncombe puts it, spontaneous "bursts of raw emotion," an "unfettered, authentic expression" that is wholly "unbeholden to the rules of design."[11] Instead, we often find in these publications clear consciousness and knowledge of art history, as well as deft conceptual and appropriationist strategies that utilize the zine format in a knowing and thoughtfully self-critical manner.

As noted above by Duncombe, one of the commonalities between artists' zines and zines in general has to do with their relationship to networks and communities. Zines often indicate the existence of "scenes," but the scenes they chronicle do not necessarily already exist. Indeed, as evinced time and again in this project, more often than not the communities to which zines speak are not only differential, but anticipatory; zines have often effectively *created* the communities they wish to speak to and for—a form of world-making that actualizes a community by means of the zines' interpolative addresses. Such has been the case, for example, with **Fanzini, Homeboy Beautiful, J.D.s, This Is the Salvation Army**, a great many Riot Grrrl zines, and the productions of **BlackMass Publishing**, among many others.

→ 30–35, 80–83, 160–64, 216–21

→ 422–25

The title *Copy Machine Manifestos* derives from a 1992 article in the *San Francisco Bay Guardian* charting the proliferation of queer "sex zines" amid a growing conservatism in the United States. While acknowledging the diversity of these small publications' design and content, the author Cate Corcoran regarded them as "united in their lack of patience for the conformist mainstream . . . mainstream thought, mainstream queers, mainstream news, or mainstream sex."[12] Importantly, the noncommercialism and relatively small, targeted audiences of these pioneering queer zines—made possible by access to affordable reproduction technologies like photocopy machines and desktop publishing software—allowed for greater editorial and artistic freedom. Many of the zines featured in this book and exhibition take a similarly oppositional stance toward dominant cultures and structures of power. Yet, as Corcoran's words make clear, artists have also often made zines that respond critically to exclusionary practices in their own communities, thereby serving as important engines of critical engagement, self-questioning, and renewal. While some zines include explicit manifestos, or similarly strident proclamations touting their authors' critical positions, others serve as more implicit manifestos about their political, ethical, and artistic practices, communicating—via both their format and their content—larger frameworks for their production in other media.

Organized roughly chronologically and by networks and communities, *Copy Machine Manifestos* documents the zine's relationship not only to various subcultures such as punk and queercore, but also to a range of avant-garde practices and intersections with other artistic mediums, including painting, drawing, collage, photography, performance, sculpture, video, music, and film. Across six interrelated sections—"The Correspondence Scene," "The Punk Explosion," "Queer and Feminist Undergrounds," "Subcultural Topologies," "Critical Promiscuity," and "A Continuing Legacy"—the exhibition and book consider how artists have been central to the histories of zines, as well as how zines have shaped art over the past fifty years, from correspondence art to punk, post-punk, queer, and feminist performance and video practices, to engagements with various subcultures such as graffiti writing and skateboarding, and more. While the project encompasses zines made throughout Canada, Mexico, and the United States broadly, it takes New York City, and the borough of Brooklyn in particular, as its starting point. As such, the book and exhibition begin with the publications of Brooklyn-based artist John Dowd in the late 1960s and early 1970s, only to move toward connections with correspondence artists working in Toronto, Vancouver, San Francisco, Los Angeles, and beyond. While the first five sections of this project are historical in nature, focusing on particular moments or places in which artists' zines flourished, the final section considers a handful of artists who have been working in this arena over the past thirteen years. Their zines and art practices create links to artists in earlier sections, as well as indicate new directions for zines in the twenty-first century, such as the mail-based projects of BlackMass Publishing and Mexico's 416–17 ← **RRD** (Red de Reproducción y Distribución / Reproduction and Distribution Network).

Accompanying the six sections of plates in this volume are seven essays by scholars who approach issues related to the phenomenon of artists' zines from a variety of angles. Gwen Allen brings her expertise about Conceptual and post-conceptual artists' publications to the particular vicissitudes of zines by artists. Branden W. Joseph interrogates the artists' zine's relationship to the legacy of Pop art and the emergence of the aesthetic of punk music. Drew Sawyer explores how zines and xerography have served as generative media for artists using photography. Examining zines through what she terms a "generational lens," Julia Bryan-Wilson demonstrates how they intersect with perspectives drawn from feminism and queer theory. Alexis Salas discusses the history of artists' collectives and zines in Mexico since the 1990s. Reflecting broadly on the history of punk performativity, Tavia Nyong'o considers the revolutionary potential of zines through their sustaining and archiving of "counter-moods." Taking off from the zine's capacity to create community across distances, Mimi Thi Nguyen looks at the issue of futurity and community prefiguration in the zine and the related medium of the punk flyer. Rather than provide totalizing overviews, each of these essays offers a provisional, though also substantive, model for considering the ongoing history of zines by artists.

Critics and zine makers like Nguyen have rightly cautioned against the institutionalization of zines (Nguyen calls them "radically minor objects") within established historical narratives and frameworks.[13] Accordingly, this project attempts to maintain some of the inchoate, rhizomatic, and fragmentary nature of these histories and contemporary practices

Branden W. Joseph and Drew Sawyer

by emphasizing the places and communities from which zines derive and by pointing toward multiple networks and lineages.

In her essay "Cheap Art Utopia," published in 1976 in a special issue of the artists' magazine *Art-Rite*, the artist Adrian Piper asked: "Suppose art was as accessible to everyone as comic books? as cheap and as available?" Such a condition would mean, she argued, that "people would have to be able to discriminate quality in art without the trappings of preciousness, e.g., the gilt frame, the six-figure price tag, the plexiglas case, the roped-off area around the work, etc."[14] Like the low-cost artists' books that are the subject of Piper's essay, most artists' zines entered the world as inexpensive and readily available objects. Many zines are still fully accessible, through such outlets as Art Metropole in Toronto and Printed Matter in New York, and at the many zine fairs that take place across North America and beyond. Ironically, but perhaps inevitably, it is precisely because zines were originally so inexpensive and ephemeral—not necessarily understood, treated, or valued as "art"—that a great many are now exceedingly rare and precious (if still not yet attaining six-figure prices). Indeed, some of the specimens depicted in this book represent the sole copy of a title found in nearly five years of archival research, while others (such as the very first issue of **I ♥ Amy Carter**) remain unlocatable, even to their makers. As such, a majority of the zines in the exhibition are displayed—just as Tom Hosier recalled encountering the earliest Dada publications—"under glass."[15] *Copy Machine Manifestos* thus walks a fine line between presenting artists' zines for observation and preserving their legacy for further generations of artists and zine makers—who might be inspired, just as Hosier was, to produce their own.

→ 233–36

NOTES

1   Stephen Duncombe, *Notes from Underground: Zines and the Politics of Alternative Culture* (London: Verso, 1997), 12–13.

2   Ibid., 13.

3   AA Bronson, "The Rise and Fall of the Peanut Party," *Art-Rite* 14 (Winter 1976–77): 45.

4   Lucy R. Lippard, in "Idea Poll: Statements on Artists' Books by Fifty Artists and Art Professionals Connected with the Medium," in ibid., 10.

5   This lineage is traced in Emily Hage, *Dada Magazines: The Making of a Movement* (New York: Bloomsbury Visual Arts, 2020).

6   Tom Hosier, "Dadazines," *Cascade Comix Monthly* 1, no. 1 (March 1978): 6–7. The wide range of zines' production values has also been noted by Michael Crane: "Most 'zines do not appear to be serious works but this is often the point. Others are designed and produced to resemble commercial magazines"; Crane, "Exhibitions and Publications," in *Correspondence Art: Source Book for the Network of International Postal Art Activity*, ed. Michael Crane and Mary Stofflet (San Francisco: Contemporary Arts Press, 1984), 314.

7   The title of *File*'s column fluctuated between "Zines" (e.g., in May 1973) and "Magazines" (e.g., in Fall 1975). Gaglione's comic appears in *Quoz?* 2, no. 7 (September 1974): 20–21.

8   AA Bronson and Peggy Gale, eds., *Performance by Artists* (Toronto: Art Metropole, 1979); Tim Guest, ed., *Books by Artists* (Toronto: Art Metropole, 1981); AA Bronson and Peggy Gale, eds., *Museums by Artists* (Toronto: Art Metropole, 1983); Dan Lander and Micah Lexier, eds., *Sound by Artists* (Toronto: Art Metropole; and Banff: Walter Phillips Gallery, 1990).

9   Gwen Allen, *Artists' Magazines: An Alternative Space for Art* (Cambridge, MA: MIT Press, 2011); Andrew Roth, Philip E. Aarons, and Claire Lehmann, eds., *Artists Who Make Books* (New York: Phaidon, 2017); and Philip E. Aarons and Andrew Roth, eds., *In Numbers: Serial Publications by Artists Since 1955* (Zurich: PPP Editions, 2009).

See also the pioneering compendium of little magazines by Steven Clay and Rodney Phillips, *A Secret Location on the Lower East Side: Adventures in Writing, 1960–1980* (New York: New York Public Library and Granary Books, 1998).

10   On the assumption that zine-making is primarily a white, middle-class activity, see Duncombe, *Notes from Underground*, 8; and Amy Spencer, *DIY: The Rise of Lo-Fi Culture*, rev. ed. (New York: Marion Jones, 2008), 18. Strong counters to this assumption have been made by, among others, C. Ondine Chavoya and David Evans Frantz, with their groundbreaking exhibition and catalogue *Axis Mundo: Queer Networks in Chicano L.A.* (New York: DelMonico Books–Prestel, 2017). Their research proved essential for *Copy Machine Manifesto*'s section on correspondence art and for new understandings of histories of contemporary art in the United States. The POC Zine Project (online at: issuu.com/poczineproject); the Brown Paper Zine & Small Press Fairs that artist Devin Morris organized in 2017 and 2018; and Brown Recluse Zine Distro (brownreclusezinedistro.com), among others, have demonstrated the rich histories and contemporary importance of zine-making by artists of color. That zine-making has been a significant practice in queer and trans communities has been copiously substantiated in AA Bronson and Philip Aarons, *Queer Zines*, 2nd ed. (New York: Printed Matter; and Rotterdam: Witte de With Center for Contemporary Art, 2008), and by the Queer Zine Archive Project (archive.qzap.org).

11   Duncombe, *Notes from Underground*, 32–33.

12   Cate C. Corcoran, "Copy-Machine Manifestos," *San Francisco Bay Guardian*, February 12, 1992, 23.

13   Mimi Thi Nguyen, "Minor Threats," *Radical History Review*, no. 122, "Queering Archives" special issue, ed. Kevin Murphy, Daniel Marshall, and Zeb Tortorici (May 2015): 12.

14   Adrian Piper, "Cheap Art Utopia," *Art-Rite* 14 (Winter 1976–77): 11.

15   Hosier, "Dadazines," 6.

Artists' Zines: The Fanzine as an Artistic Medium

Gwen Allen

3 DOT ZINE is my hand collaged letter to you. An olive branch offered in hopes that we will become and remain friends. Here is where a community will be built.

—Devin N. Morris, publisher of *3 Dot Zine*

Zines proliferate where the lines of communication becomes specialized, tenuous, and dangerous. . . . As anyone who loves them will know, to hold that handmade object in your hand is to have another's hand clasped in yours. They say: if you are reading this, I am not alone and you are not alone.

—Scott Treleaven, publisher of *This Is the Salivation Army*

We all know a zine when we see one or hold it in our hands. As defined by Stephen Duncombe, who wrote the first scholarly book on the subject, zines are "noncommercial, nonprofessional, small circulation magazines which their creators produce, publish and distribute by themselves," or, in slightly more evocative terms, "scruffy, homemade little pamphlets" that are "filled with rantings of high weirdness and exploding with chaotic design."[1] While there are exceptions, zines are usually cheaply produced by a single person and typically photocopied onto standard A4 or letter-sized paper, which is then folded in half and stapled down the center to create a binding.

Yet what makes a zine a zine is so much more than this.

"Zine" is short for "fanzine," a word coined to refer to "little" magazines self-published by science fiction fans in the United States in the 1930s. These amateur publications originated in the letters columns of science fiction magazines, which—even if their editors had wanted to—could not publish the massive volume of correspondence and feedback sent in by readers, who soon began to write not only to the magazine but to one another.[2] Fanzines thus emerged out of reader-driven desire and enthusiasm to participate in the media, to be co-producers of the culture they consumed, and to form communities around that culture—all ambitions that remain intrinsic to zines as they have evolved to this day. In the 1970s zines acquired a distinctly subcultural association in the context of punk rock music as a form of do-it-yourself practice that was antithetical to mainstream mores and media—an association that would continue in the queercore and Riot Grrrl music scenes of the 1980s and 1990s. However, with the advent of inexpensive printing and postage, this period also saw an explosion of zines about everything from Pez dispensers to squat culture to paganism to mental health reform, as well as personal zines ("perzines") that record autobiographical musings and experiences from everyday life.

Zines tend to be produced by teenagers and young people—under thirty—although this is likely a matter less of biological age than of an antagonistic relationship to the mainstream "adult" conventions of capitalist, consumerist society. The burgeoning zine culture in the United States in the 1980s and 1990s, for example, may be understood as a protest of the neoliberal social and economic policies of the Reagan and Clinton years, which brought the defunding of education and social programs, the deregulation of media industries, diminishing employment opportunities for young people, and the expansion of prisons and policing. As the anthropologist Julie Chu has argued, these conditions, and not simply the accessibility of photocopiers and desktop publishing, informed the growth of zines and shaped their character as an oppositional media practice. As Chu aptly put it: "Why, for instance, has there been a proliferation of personal, confession zines by teenage girls in the past two decades? Or, to ask it another way, why *not* a boom in sports zines by middle-aged businessmen?"[3]

Artists' zines are a particular kind of zine, and also a particular category of artists' publication, albeit one that cuts across other genres. As the publications in *Copy Machine Manifestos* attest, not only have artists adopted the zine as an artistic medium in itself, they have participated meaningfully in its history and evolution, expanding the creative possibilities of this vital form of self-publishing. Artists have created zines for a variety of reasons and in a variety of contexts. Some, such as Tammy Rae Carland, Vaginal Davis, and G. B. Jones, have done so as active participants in the punk or queercore or Riot Grrrl movements. Others, such as Raymond Pettibon and K8 Hardy, have seized upon the zine as a medium that enables particular kinds of expression, communication, and/or community within—as well as outside of—the art world. Indeed, often artists make zines in order to engage a different audience or to place themselves at some kind of a remove from rarefied art publications and exhibition spaces. As Carland wrote in the editorial statement of the first issue 236 ← of her zine **I ♥ Amy Carter**, in 1992, it was "an escape, and excuse to not constantly be feeling like all I do is create fodder for the art world (one of my bigger fears)."[4]

In his zine taxonomy, Duncombe singles out art zines as those that "contain print media collages, photographs, drawings, and mail art which create a network of artists and a floating virtual gallery."[5] But this definition applies equally to many other types of zines, nearly all of which make creative use of visual art, images, or collage.[6] Conversely, some artists make zines that are not primarily concerned with visual art per se—Vaginal Davis's *Shrimp* (1993), dedicated to the sexual 182–85 ← subculture of sucking toes, comes to mind, as does Greta Snider's **Mudflap** (1991–94), ostensibly devoted to biking (but in fact ranging far from the subject). Yet despite—and because of—the fact that they defy tidy definition, zines by artists prompt reflection on the very question of what a zine is, and on its contemporary significance and ongoing potential.

To better understand and appreciate how they do so, it is helpful to situate artists' zines within a larger history of artists' publications. Especially relevant in this regard are the experimental artists' magazines that proliferated during 1960s and 1970s, when the magazine became an important new site of artistic investigation in the context of Fluxus, Conceptual art, and related practices.[7] These self-published little magazines were associated with egalitarian and anti-establishment attempts to circumvent the commercial gallery and mainstream art press, providing a more direct channel for the artist's voice and work. In them, artists explored the materiality of language and the tactility and interactivity of the printed page. Artists paid attention not only to the magazine's content, but to its format, distribution and circulation, advertising, and editorial structure—that is, to the "apparatus" in Walter Benjamin's sense of the "forms and instruments" of a publication.[8] They approached the magazine as an artistic medium with a distinct set of historical conditions and material conventions, at the same time seeking to transform those conditions and conventions, forging new models of writing, editing, and publishing.

Some artists' magazines from this period, such as *Aspen* (1965–71), consisted of unbound folios and site-specific works of art designed expressly for the printed page (a format echoed by 330–32, 222–23 ← later artists' zines such as **LTTR** [2002–6] and **Lucky** [1988–90]). Others, such as *0 to 9* (1967–69) and *Art-Rite* (1972–78), favored cheap, DIY printing processes and materials such as mimeograph and newsprint—decisions that may have been born out of economic necessity but that also functioned symbolically to eschew glossy art magazines like *Artforum*. Still others reimagined the conventional structure of the periodical to serve explicitly political editorial goals. For example, the anti-racist, anti-imperialist journal *Black Phoenix* (1978–79) reconceived the format and function of the periodical as a vehicle for decolonial critique. And the feminist magazine *Heresies* (1977–92) challenged the patriarchal, capitalist systems of the art world with its collective editorial structure and rejection of gallery advertisements. By publishing magazines, artists sought to alter the social, economic, and political conditions under which they worked, and to create new kinds 390–92 ← of artistic communities—aspirations that are reawakened in recent artists' zines such as **3 Dot Zine** 422–25 ← (2014–16) and some of those published by **BlackMass**.

Like these earlier artists' magazines from the 1960s and 1970s, more recent artists' zines draw our attention to not just form and content, but also production, reception, circulation, distribution, and archivization—all of which have shaped the social, political, and artistic potential of zines. One provisional definition of an artists' zine is this: it is a publication that is a work of

Gwen Allen

art in itself—which is to say it is to some extent self-reflexive about its medium, foregrounding the history, materiality, and communicative possibilities of the fanzine. Certainly, other kinds of zines do this as well. Indeed, artists' zines question the division between zine making and artistic practice, underscoring the fact that *every* zine maker is a kind of creator, and the distinctions between zine makers and artists are, at least in part (though not always), a function of class, education, and institutional power. Rather than separating out artists' zines from other kinds of zines, or from other kinds of artists' publications, this essay seeks to acknowledge and uncover the connections between them.

In his 1979 book *Subculture: The Meaning of Style*, cultural theorist Dick Hebdige described punk fanzines alongside other punk cultural and sartorial innovations, as "signifying practice[s]" through which the punk subculture invented an "alternative value system" by symbolically trans-forming dominant cultural forms.[9] According to him, zines corresponded to "punk's subterranean and anarchic style" and evinced a working-class consciousness with their use of vernacular lang-uage filled with expletives and typos, grainy halftone images, Letraset, ransom-note-style cut-outs, and collage.[10] Graphic design scholar Teal Triggs has further analyzed the crude visuals and low-budget production quality of punk zines as a "graphic language of resistance" that strategically flouts "proper" rules of design and grammar in order to challenge mainstream media and social conventions.[11] In a sense, zines are *anti*-magazines. These amateur, handmade, photocopied pamphlets embody the assault on commercialism that was behind punk music, insisting on a DIY ethos—a form of "typographic democracy" that was central to punk's radicality, as captured by the famous diagram published in the first issue of the British zine *Sideburns* (and later reprinted on the cover of *Sniffin' Glue*) that shows three guitar necks marked with the chords A, E, and G, along with the caption "This is a chord. This is another. This is a third. Now form a band."[12] Likewise, zines encourage readers to make their own zines.[13]

 While punk zines were decidedly amateur-looking, this does not mean that zine makers were or are ignorant or naïve producers. In fact, a number of punks were art-school trained, and they self-consciously referenced and utilized artistic strategies such as montage and *détournement* that stem back to Dadaist, Surrealist, and Situationist practices.[14] Tracing such connections is not to affirm the precedence of high art, but to complicate the opposition between professional artists and amateur cultural producers. Moreover, punks did not just look back to earlier artistic practices; they also found affinities with artists who were their contemporaries, notably mail artists, who used the postal system as a medium and mode of distribution. Mail artists exchanged and disseminated personal correspondence and postcards in order to establish a decentralized informational structure, in contrast to the hierarchies of the art world. With its reliance on such techniques as collage, rubber stamping, and photocopying, mail art thumbed its nose at received definitions of aesthetic quality and competence—a form of deliberate "deskilling" that resonated with punk's attack on bourgeois and commercial conventions of music.

 Several years before the earliest punk zines were published (around 1975), a number of mail artists published fanzines and Dada-inspired zine-like micro-magazines they called "dadazines." These publications (which included titles such as **Egozine**, **Fanzini**, *File*, the **John Dowd Fanny Club Fanzine**, *New York Correspondence School Weekly Breeder* (or **NYCS Weekly Breeder**), **Vile**, and **West Bay Dadaist/Quoz?**) were usually cheaply printed and stapled. Fanzines functioned for these artists (much as they had for early science fiction fans) as a way to challenge cultural authority and encourage participatory social networks. As art historian Kirsten Olds has argued in her study of Les Petites Bon-Bons—a group of mail and performance artists involved in the Los Angeles glitter rock scene in the early 1970s—they used fandom, in the form of fanzines and fan clubs, as "an artistic format" that at once appropriated and subverted celebrity and media culture in order to construct and express countercultural and queer identities.[15]

 In striking ways, mail art fanzines and "dadazines" anticipated—and indeed likely influenced—the cut-and-paste aesthetics of later punk zines, as art historian Emily Hage has discussed in her study of the Bay Area Dadaists, a group of mail artists active in San Francisco in the 1970s. There, punk musicians and mail artists performed at the same venues (Mabuhay

→ 70–73, 32–35, 30, 36–41, 50–53, 46–49

Gardens prominent among them), and referenced one another in their zines, which they sold and bartered at certain music, art, and comics bookstores.[16] A number of individuals, including V. Vale 90–91 ← (who published the punk zine **Search & Destroy**), Genesis P-Orridge and Cosey Fanni Tutti of the band Throbbing Gristle, Monte Cazazza, Irene Dogmatic, and Winston Smith, were active in both the punk music and mail art scenes. Later, similar types of cross-pollination would occur between artists and punk musicians in the queercore movement of the 1980s and 1990s.

When today's artists make zines, they implicitly and explicitly position themselves in relationship to the DIY aesthetics of refusal pioneered by the makers of mail art fanzines and 124, 128 ← punk zines. For example, with Raymond Pettibon's **Tripping Corpse** series (beginning in 1981), which satirizes the idealistic delusions of hippie culture, the artist used the format of the punk zine almost as a form of quotation, a foil to critically interrogate the utopian aspirations of an earlier generation of artists' publications as well as the countercultural underground 326–28 ← press of the 1960s and 1970s.[17] In a different way, Paul P. and Joel Gibb's **Gay Goth Scene** cites 160–64, 216–21 ← queercore precedents such as **J.D.s** (1985–91) and **This Is the Salivation Army** (1996–99, with two subsequent issues produced in 2001 and 2004), to which it was "a loving homage, as well as a 336–39 ← bit of send-up," according to its publisher.[18] And K8 Hardy's **FashionFashion** (launched 2003), which features her own hilarious homemade outfits, uses the DIY format of the zine to mirror her irreverent, improvisational approach to clothing, implicitly encouraging readers to make their own fashion—and fashion magazines—too.

If artists' zines mobilized punk's subcultural "graphic language of resistance," they have also manifested other characteristics and qualities that have been key to the history and meaning of zines. Going back to their origins in science fiction fanzines, zines have been a conduit for certain kinds of emotional expression and intensity. This capacity is suggested by their very etymology: the word "fan" is an abbreviation of "fanatic," which comes from the Latin *fānum*, meaning "temple," suggesting the quasi-religious devotion and zealotry involved in fandom. Indeed, one dictionary definition of "fanatic" is "excessive and mistaken enthusiasm, an unreasoning enthusiast," and even "possession by a deity or demon." Fans are defined by their love for something—often an obsessive, over-the-top love. Accordingly, zines favor forms of speech and image that violate the rational, cerebral modes of other kinds of public communication, from the supposedly disinterested discourse of the bourgeois public sphere—as identified by German theorist Jürgen Habermas—to the theoretical and erudite tone of academia, to the refined judgments of art criticism. Indeed, due to its emotionally driven excess, engagement with devalued artifacts of mass culture, and violation of "good taste," fandom has often been shunned as a scandalous and even deviant phenomenon in contemporary culture. And yet it has also been understood as a serious and critically engaged oppositional practice, one that offers tactical 233–36 ← models of reading and interpretation.[19] To this end, zines such as Tammy Rae Carland's **I ♥ Amy** 250–51 ← **Carter** (1992–94) and Kathleen Hanna's **My Life with Evan Dando, Popstar** (1993) ironically (and sometimes sincerely) appropriate the language of fandom and infatuation, offering queer and feminist critiques of media, advertising, and celebrity culture.

Zines express strong feelings. This can be witnessed in the anger and rawness of punk zines, and it is seen in a different way in the confessional and diaristic modes that have characterized so many zines since the 1980s. The emotional intensity of zines is evident in the honesty and vulnerability of the writing, as well as the intimacy of tone and mode of address, which often express warmth, approachability, affection, and familiarity. In her study of girl zines as a form of life-writing, author Jennifer Sinor quotes a young zinester who explains: "Zines are a way of typing how you feel, letting it out. It's another form of crying."[20] As this quote suggests, emotional states are centered in the body, and in both their content and form, zines insist upon their writers and readers as embodied beings, which may heighten the emotional connection they foster. Not only do many zines explore topics such as body image, sexuality, and abuse, but, as the late feminist scholar Alison Piepmeier has argued, the *materiality* of the zine, as a handmade visual and tactile object, reinforces the emotional connection felt by zine producers and readers: "The physical act of creating a zine locates zine creators in their bodies which is a site of care and

Gwen Allen

pleasure, and the act of reading does the same thing for the reader."[21] The interface—physical and emotional—between zine creator and zine recipient has been embraced by artists to deepen the connection and closeness they feel with their audience. As artist and zine-maker Scott Treleaven describes: "The level of commitment required on the part of the zine reader mirrors that of the zine manufacturers themselves, which makes the exchange an intimate one."[22]

The capacity of zines to express strong feelings and to foster emotional connection is by no means at odds with their ability to publish critical, intelligent, and coherent commentary. Indeed, feminist theorists and philosophers such as Alison Jaggar have insisted that our emotional responses are in fact key to knowledge, ethics, and critical thinking.[23] Arguably, it is precisely the emotive aspect of zines that makes the thoughts and ideas articulated in them so compelling and urgent.

The zine's propensity for emotional expression and connection has made it an important vehicle for exploring various aspects of subjectivity and identity, as can be witnessed in queer and feminist zines as well as in those focusing on intersectional experiences of race, ethnicity, and class. However, while emotional self-revelation has functioned as a form of consciousness-raising, it has also sometimes been problematically coupled with essentialist assumptions that celebrate the personal at the cost of the political, neglecting the systemic roots of oppression— or reinforcing them. As Mimi Thi Nguyen has argued in her critique of the politics of gender, race, and class in the Riot Grrrl movement, while zines fostered "universal girl love" as a form of solidarity and feminist politics, too often such intimacy ended up affirming the privilege of whiteness.[24] In her own zines of the 1990s, such as *Slant*, *Aim Your Dick*, and *Evolution of a Race Riot*, Nguyen sought to foreground the experiences, vulnerabilities, and intimacies of those marginalized by punk's "whitestraightboy hegemony."[25]

Likewise, numerous artists' zines have challenged the heteronormativity and whiteness of the punk, queercore, and Riot Grrrl scenes, even as they have been formative to these movements from the start (although not always acknowledged as such). For example, in her **Fertile La Toyah Jackson Magazine** (1987–91), Vaginal Davis asserts Black, Chicanx, and gender-queer identity in the Los Angeles hardcore scene, while lampooning celebrity culture with scandalous gossip and rumors in a campy style that recalls filmmaker Kenneth Anger's 1959 book *Hollywood Babylon*. As queer theorist José Esteban Muñoz argued, Davis enacts an ambivalent "disidentification," defined as "a performative mode of tactical recognition that various minoritarian subjects employ in an effort to resist the oppressive and normalizing discourse of dominant ideology," which "unsettles the strictures of class, race, and gender."[26] Other examples of zines that explore the complexities of intersectional identity include Brontez Purnell's **Fag School** (launched 2003) and Osa Atoe's **Shotgun Seamstress** (launched 2006), a zine "by and for Black punks."[27]

→ 172–75

→ 361–65
→ 366–67

As scholar of gender and women's studies Adela C. Licona has argued in her study of contemporary zines whose authors identify as antiracist, of-color, and/or feminist, they are often informed by critical and coalitional consciousness and are distinguished by their promotion of social justice and their status as sites of social action and change.[28] The pedagogical activism of Kandis Williams's **Cassandra Press** is exemplary in this regard. Named after the ancient Greek mythological figure who was bestowed with the gift of prophecy but condemned never to be believed, Cassandra Press publishes both printed and digital zines and readers and offers workshops and courses that revolve around Black and feminist scholarship and politics.

→ 406–9

Because zines so powerfully give voice to marginalized individuals and communities, they embody the concept of the "counterpublic," a term that refers to those publics that have been historically excluded from dominant definitions and institutions of the public sphere, and discriminated against on the basis of class, race, ethnicity, gender, sexual orientation, disability, and so forth. Literary critic and social theorist Michael Warner's understanding of the counterpublic as a practice of "poetic world-making" is especially pertinent because it suggests not only the life-altering effects that publications can have, but also the fact that they do not merely speak to an already constituted public; they bring that public into being and sustain it over time. We can see this playing out in a zine such as *J.D.s*, often credited with ushering the queercore movement into Toronto in the 1980s. Published by artists G. B. Jones and Bruce LaBruce, *J.D.s* imagined an alternative to the homophobia and sexism of punk, while also criticizing the assimilationism of the mainstream gay and lesbian movement at the time. While the zine started off as the vision of the editors and a handful of their friends, it soon conjured a nascent community, propagating a whole new cultural scene—and many subsequent zines.

Zines also differ from other kinds of publications in how they cultivate communities and counterpublics. They facilitate a unique set of social relationships in their very circulation and distribution—the ways in which they move through time and space. As a number of scholars have noted, zines are exchanged through a kind of gift economy, based on barter and generosity.[29] Against the anonymity of most capitalist information and commodity exchange systems, zines are often traded or given away, or sold cheaply, which promotes a sense of familiarity and obligation. Furthermore, in contrast to many other types of textual counterpublics, which generally consist of individuals who are brought together through the act of reading but remain strangers to one another, zine readers more directly hold out the possibility of eventually knowing one another or meeting in person—and they often make good on this promise. As cultural studies scholar Janice Radway has observed in her study of zines produced by young women in the 1990s, the types of communication and interaction facilitated "through zine exchange often broadened into different kinds of relationships in the world through letter-writing, pen-pal exchange, carefully orchestrated first meetings, friendships, and even intimate relations."[30] In all these ways, zines produce what Radway has termed "intersubjects," that is, subjects who are "constituted in relation to and therefore always together with others."[31]

Artists' zines foster such intersubjective communities, defined by togetherness both on the page and in person. Exemplary in this regard is *LTTR*, founded in 2002 by the New York–based collective of the same name, a malleable DIY platform where queer and feminist artists and activists could collaborate and share work. The journal, each issue of which was produced in an edition of one thousand, contains more traditional texts such as criticism and fiction, as well as reproductions of artworks, posters, CDs, postcards, booklets, and artists' multiples, many of which have an element of the handcrafted, such as an altered tampon by Fereshteh Toosi, or a hand-knitted glove by Liz Collins. The printed publication formed a continuum with other sites of social encounter, such as gatherings for collating issues, public talks, performances, workshops, and release "block parties" at which editors, contributors, friends, potential readers, and passersby come into contact with one another. As one of *LTTR*'s editors recalled: "We set up situations for people to come together, whether physically to dance and witness a performance or as literally as two texts sitting side-by-side or back-to-back on the pages of a journal printed one thousand times."[32]

This characterization of the page as a place "for people to come together" is telling. Indeed, publications do not merely facilitate or record social relationships; in an important sense they are themselves social spaces: sites of dialogue, friendship, solidarity, and more. Publications such as *3 Dot Zine* and those produced by BlackMass Publishing exemplify a model of printed matter as a form of collaboration and kinship. *3 Dot Zine* has been compared by its editor, Devin N. Morris, to a "hand-collaged letter" offered to promote friendship and community—a mission furthered by in-person events, such as the Brown Paper Zine & Small Press Fair founded by Morris in 2017 to feature the work of artists of color.[33] If zines and zine communities are grounded in time and space, however, they can also transcend and bridge geographical and temporal distances. For example, BlackMass, co-headed by Yusuf Hassan, has brought contributors together on the pages of its publications in ways that would not be possible in person—for instance, pairing the poet Amiri Baraka and the rapper Big L.[34]

Like so many of the publications in this exhibition, *LTTR*, *3 Dot Zine*, and BlackMass's titles look to the history of both fanzines and artists' magazines in order to create communities that differ from the competitive professional and financial networks that tend to dominate the art world. In their role as platforms for the voices of artists and an alternative site of display and distribution, they may invite comparisons to artists' magazines that preceded them, such as *Aspen*, *Art-Rite*, and *0 to 9*. However, in their refusal of the norms of the art world and in their insistence on the agency of contributors and readers to imagine a different world, they draw on the history

Gwen Allen

of zines—from the militant nihilism of punk zines to the emotional candor and vulnerability of personal zines. To return to Warner's language, they are practices of "poetic world-making"— poetic not in the sense of a poem on the page (although they can be this too), but in the sense of *poesis*: the process of creating something that did not exist before.

NOTES

NB: The sources of the epigraphs that open this essay are as follows: Devin N. Morris, "Editorial Statement," *3 Dot Zine*; 3dotzine.com. Scott Treleaven, "The Lowest of the Low: A New Cautionary Tract from the Salivation Army," in *Queer Zines 2*, ed. AA Bronson and Philip Aarons (New York: Printed Matter; Rotterdam: Witte de With Center for Contemporary Art, 2014), 241.

[1] Stephen Duncombe, *Notes from Underground: Zines and the Politics of Alternative Culture* (New York: Verso, 1997), 9, 4.

[2] For a history of science fiction fanzines, see Fredric Wertham, *The World of Fanzines: A Special Form of Communication* (Carbondale: Southern Illinois University Press, 1973).

[3] Julie Chu, "Navigating the Media Environment: How Youth Claim a Place Through Zines," *Social Justice* 24, no. 3 (1997): 74.

[4] Tammy Rae Carland, *I ♥ Amy Carter*, no. 1, December 1992, n.p.

[5] Duncombe, *Notes from Underground*, 14.

[6] For a discussion of the distinction between zines and art zines, see Susan E. Thomas, "Value and Validity of Art Zines as an Art Form," *Art Documentation: Journal of the Art Libraries Society of North America* 28, no. 2 (Fall 2009): 27–36, 38.

[7] See Gwen Allen, *Artists' Magazines: An Alternative Space for Art* (Cambridge, MA: MIT Press, 2011).

[8] Walter Benjamin, "The Author as Producer," in *Reflections: Essays, Aphorisms, Autobiographical Writings*, ed. Peter Demetz, trans. Edmund Jephcott (New York: Harcourt Brace Jovanovich, 1978), 220–38. Here Benjamin makes the distinction between "the mere supplying of a production apparatus and its transformation," and argues that no matter how radical or revolutionary a piece of writing it cannot effectively protest the status quo without reflecting upon and seeking to transform its own apparatus.

[9] Dick Hebdige, *Subculture: The Meaning of Style* (London: Routledge, 1979), 113.

[10] Ibid., 112.

[11] Teal Triggs, "Scissors and Glue: Punk Fanzines and the Creation of a DIY Aesthetic," *Journal of Design History* 19, no. 1 (Spring 2006): 69–83.

[12] See Teal Triggs, "Typo-Anarchy: A New Look at the Fanzine Revolution," *Émigré* 46 (Spring 1998), 20.

[13] Stephen Duncombe has termed this process "emulation," writing: "Zines, with all their seams showing . . . encourage you to come close and say 'I see how they did that. That's not too hard. Anybody can do that.'" Duncombe, *Notes from Underground*, 139.

[14] See Triggs, "Scissors and Glue."

[15] Kirsten Olds, "Fannies and Fanzines: Mail Art and Fan Clubs in the 1970s," *Journal of Fandom Studies* 3, no. 2 (2015): 172. See also Olds, "Gay Life Artists: Les Petites Bonbons and Camp Performativity in the 1970s," *Art Journal* 72, no. 2 (Summer 2013): 16–33; and Olds, "Queered Territories: Zines of the 1970s and Networked Identity," in *The Territories of Artists' Periodicals*, ed. Steven Perkins (Rennes, France: Éditions Provisoires, 2015): 55–62.

[16] Emily Hage, "Bay Area Dadazines and Punk Zines in 1970s San Francisco: Interactive, Ephemeral, Live," *American Periodicals* 27, no. 2 (October 2017): 180–205.

[17] As Benjamin H. D. Buchloh has written of Pettibon's zines, they "are artistic as much as they are subcultural." Buchloh, "Raymond Pettibon: Return to Disorder and Disfiguration," *October* 92 (Spring, 2000): 42.

[18] Paul P., "Gay Goth Scene," in *Queer Zines 2*, 84.

[19] See Henry Jenkins, *Textual Poachers: Television Fans and Participatory Culture* (London: Routledge, 1992); and Catherine Grant and Kate Random Love, eds., *Fandom as Methodology: A Sourcebook for Artists and Writers* (London: Goldsmiths; Cambridge, MA: MIT Press, 2019).

[20] Jennifer Sinor, "Another Form of Crying: Girl Zines as Life Writing," *Prose Studies* 26, no. 1–2 (2003): 246. Originally quoted in Jessica Rosenberg and Gitana Garofalo, "Riot Grrrl: Revolution from Within," *Signs: Journal of Women's Culture and Society* 23 (1998): 823.

[21] Alison Piepmeier, "Why Zines Matter: Materiality and the Creation of Embodied Community," *American Periodicals* 18, no. 2 (2008): 230.

[22] Scott Treleaven "The Permission Factory: A Few Notes," in *Queer Zines*, ed. AA Bronson and Philip Aarons (2nd ed., New York: Printed Matter; Rotterdam: Witte de With Center for Contemporary Art, 2014), 236. (1st ed. published 2008.)

[23] See Alison M. Jaggar, "Love and Knowledge: Emotion in Feminist Epistemology," *Inquiry* 32, no. 2 (1989), 151–76.

[24] Mimi Thi Nguyen, "Riot Grrrl, Race, and Revival," *Women & Performance: A Journal of Feminist Theory* 22, no. 2–3 (July–November 2012): 183, 180.

[25] Mimi Thi Nguyen "It's (Not) a White World: Looking for Race in Punk," *Punk Planet*, no. 8 (November–December 1998): 80.

[26] José Esteban Muñoz, "The White to Be Angry: Vaginal Crème Davis's Terrorist Drag," in *Disidentifications: Queers of Color and the Performance of Politics* (Minneapolis: University of Minnesota Press, 1999), 115, 97.

[27] Osa Atoe, *Shotgun Seamstress*, no. 1 (2006).

[28] Adela C. Licona, *Zines in Third Space: Radical Cooperation and Borderlands Rhetoric* (Albany: State University of New York Press, 2012).

[29] See for example Chris Atton, *Alternative Media (Culture, Representation and Identity)* (Thousand Oaks, CA: SAGE Publications, 2001), and Piepmeier, "Why Zines Matter."

[30] Janice Radway, "Girl Zine Networks, Underground Itineraries, and Riot Grrrl History: Making Sense of the Struggle for New Social Forms in the 1990s and Beyond," *Journal of American Studies* 50, no. 1 (February 2016): 26.

[31] Janice Radway, "Zines, Half-Lives, and Afterlives: On the Temporalities of Social and Political Change," *PMLA: Publications of the Modern Language Association of America* 126, no. 1 (January 2011): 148.

[32] Ginger Brooks Takahashi, "Editorial: I NO WE CAN REIGN HERE," *LTTR*, no. 5 (October 2006): 45.

[33] Devin N. Morris, "Editorial Statement," *3 Dot Zine*; 3dotzine.com.

[34] *Mic Check Selected the Poems and Lyrics of Amiri Baraka and Big L* (New York: BlackMass, 2022).

1.

The Correspondence Scene, 1969–1980

The following entries include both zines and paste-ups, with methods of reproduction and binding given, and details for covers or wrappers if appropriate and when different from interior. Dimensions are given for zines when closed, height followed by width. Works reproduced on gray pages are related artworks.

At the November 27, 1969, Rolling Stones concert at New York's Madison Square Garden, Brooklyn-based artist and designer John Dowd distributed copies of *The Star*, the broadsheet publication he produced with photographer Stanley Stellar. Drawing upon the iconography of fandom, the zine's cover acknowledges rock's debt to Black American music, while the interior's collages of appropriated mass media images pay homage to Stones guitarist Brian Jones, who had died that July. Three years later, Dowd himself achieved ersatz stardom in the fanzine of the semi-fictional "John Dowd Fanny Club," spearheaded by Canadian artist John Jack Baylin, also known as "Count Fanzini." Dowd and Baylin had met through the international correspondence art scene known as the "Eternal Network," which sprang out of the image-exchange lists assembled by Vancouver artists Michael Morris and Vincent Trasov's Image Bank. These lists were eagerly distributed in the pages of *File*, the "megazine" published by Toronto Conceptualists AA Bronson, Felix Partz, and Jorge Zontal, working collectively as the group General Idea.

The zines in this section, including *Egozine*, *Fanzini*, *Homeboy Beautiful*, *Modern Correspondence Magazine*, the *West Bay Dadaist* (later titled *Quoz?*), and *Vile*, derived from or were closely associated with these mail art networks, often reproducing readymade submissions received by post. The *New York Correspondence School Weekly Breeder* (or *NYCS Weekly Breeder*) reveals the evolution particularly clearly: it began in 1972 as a one-page mailer created by Ken Friedman, was transformed into a two-pager under the editorship of Stu Horn (publisher of another mailer, the *Northwest Mounted Valise*), and, finally, under Tim Mancusi, became a full-fledged zine.

Many of the artists featured here were drawn into correspondence art and zine-making in the wake of the liberation struggles and countercultural movements of the 1960s as a way of community building or world-making outside of traditional institutions. This was especially true of gay-identifying artists like Dowd, Baylin, and Joey Terrill, all of whom frequently "queered" mainstream culture by appropriating its imagery and its forms—such as the magazine—to express explicitly homoerotic content. Where Dowd and Baylin's zines often emulated the traditional fanzine, Terrill's *Homeboy Beautiful* imitated more aspirational, middle-class magazines like *House Beautiful*. Terrill, whose Pop-art-inflected paintings echoed the *fotonovelas* (narrative picture stories) in his zines, also engaged with the correspondence network, alongside fellow queer Los Angeles artists.

Like Baylin, who played the role of Count Fanzini, several artists in this period undertook "life performances" or adopted the fan club as an art form. In the early 1970s, before relocating to San Francisco, Canadian artist Anne Long took the pseudonym "Anna Banana" and inhabited the role of "Town Fool" of the city of Victoria. Jerry Dreva and Robert Lambert co-founded the performative group Les Petites Bon-Bons in Milwaukee, Wisconsin, before moving to Los Angeles, where they became artist-groupies in the city's glam rock scene. They, too, were mail artists, sending altered newspaper pages and press coverage of their antics to celebrated figures such as Andy Warhol. Lambert founded *Egozine*, a fanzine devoted to life art, to document and contextualize their work. In 1974 Les Petites Bon-Bons and many of the correspondence scene artists gathered in Los Angeles for Decca-Dance, a mock awards ceremony in which Dowd performed with the New York Corres-Sponge-Dance School of Vancouver.

The San Francisco correspondence and performance artists known as the Bay Area Dadaists—which included Banana, Monte Cazazza, Charles Chickadel, Irene Dogmatic, Bill Gaglione, and Mancusi—were inspired to make "dadazines" by the precedent of the European historical avant-gardes. Their neo-Futurist interest in noise and Dada-inspired collages prefigured the punk aesthetics of the 1970s, and some participated in the local punk and industrial music scenes. Dogmatic, for example, formed the punk band SST and was featured in V. Vale's punk fanzine *Search & Destroy* (a publication that was strikingly attentive to the diversity of race, gender, and sexuality in the California punk community). Cazazza, who was depicted ripping his heart out on the cover of the inaugural issue of Banana's zine *Vile*, recorded a number of tracks with the Industrial Records label. He also contributed to Vale's pioneering industrial zine *RE/Search*, photographer Jim Jocoy's zine *Widows and Orphans*, and the band Throbbing Gristle's *Industrial News*.

John Dowd and Stanley Stellar

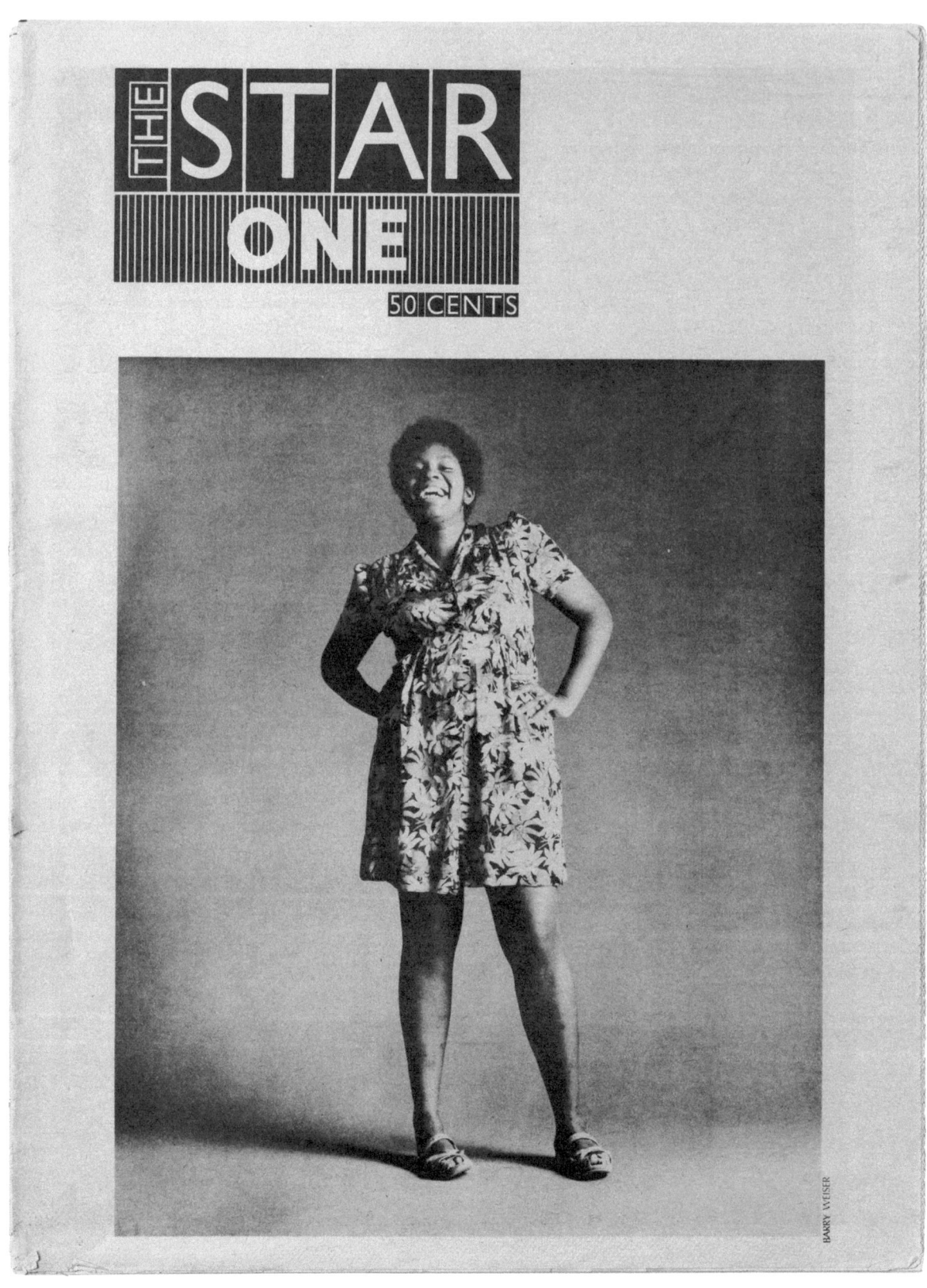

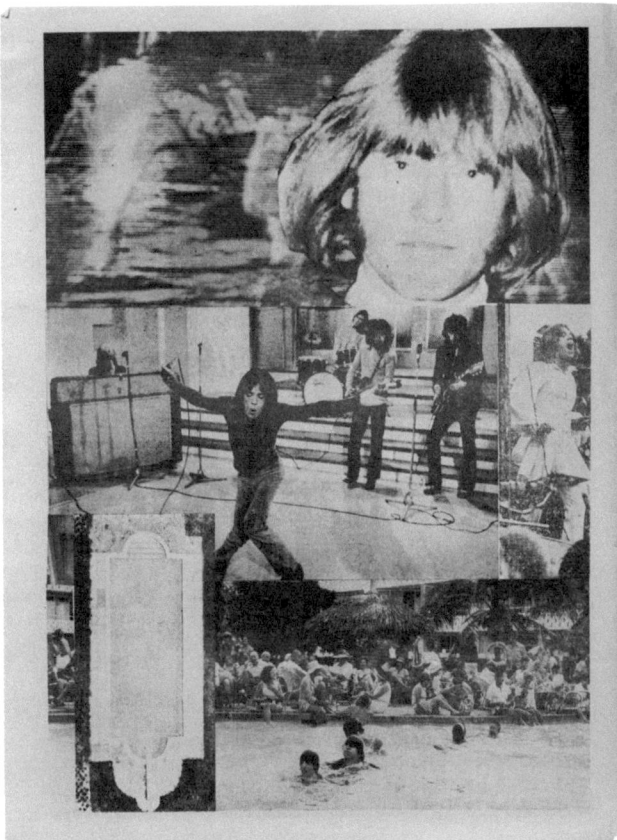
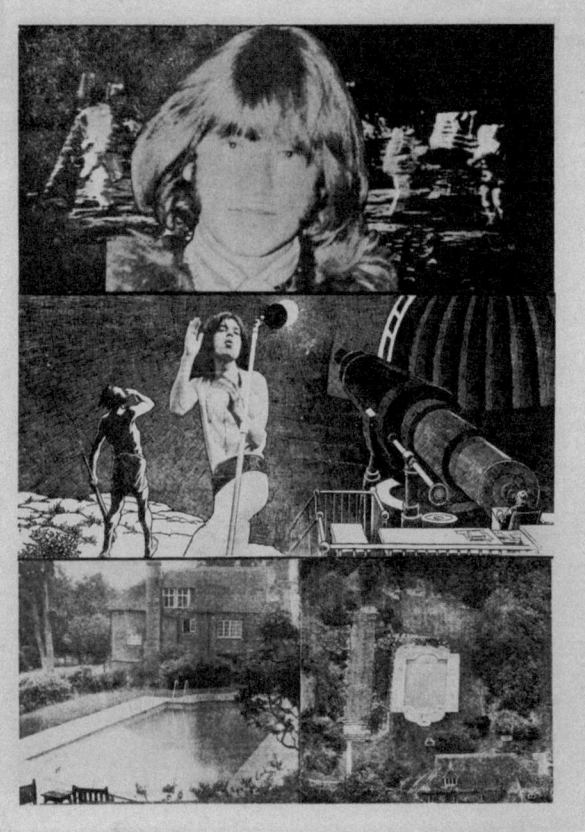
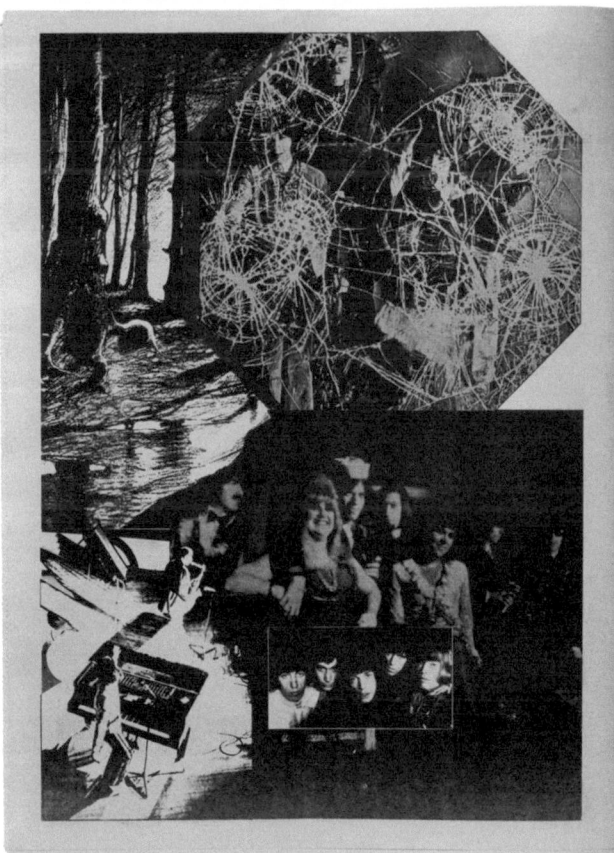
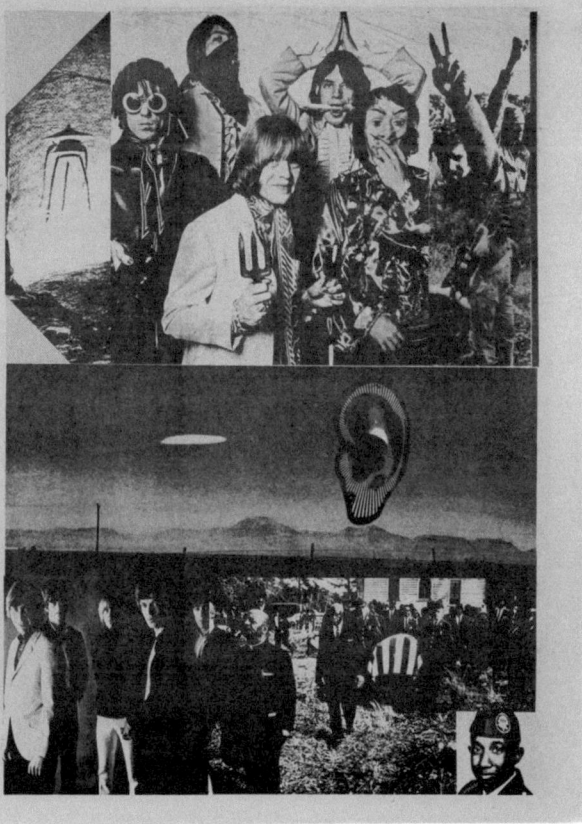

The Star, no. 1, 1969
Offset, folded, 15 3/8 × 11 7/16 in. (39 × 29 cm)
Collection Philip Aarons and Shelley Fox Aarons

John Dowd

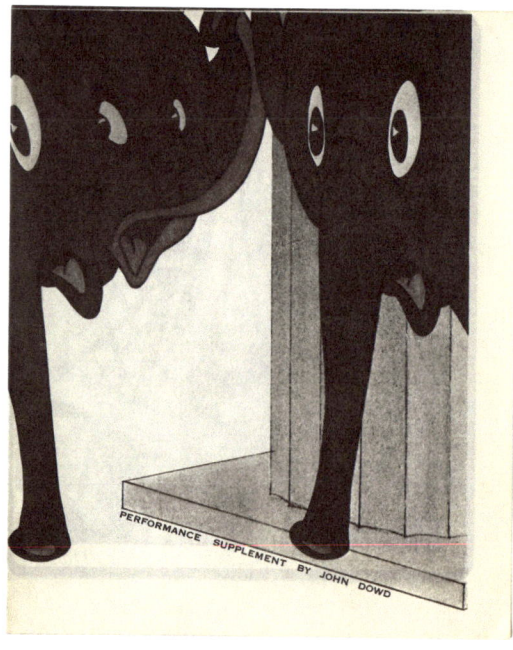

Performance Supplement, Summer 1970
Offset, folded, 9 × 7 ½ in. (22.9 × 19.1 cm)
Collection Philip Aarons and Shelley Fox Aarons

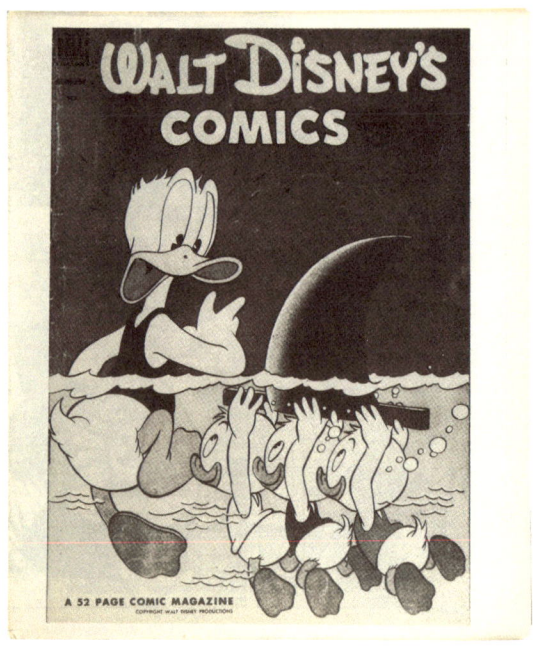

Summertime Supplement, 1970
Offset, folded, 9 × 7 ½ in. (22.9 × 19.1 cm)
Collection Philip Aarons and Shelley Fox Aarons

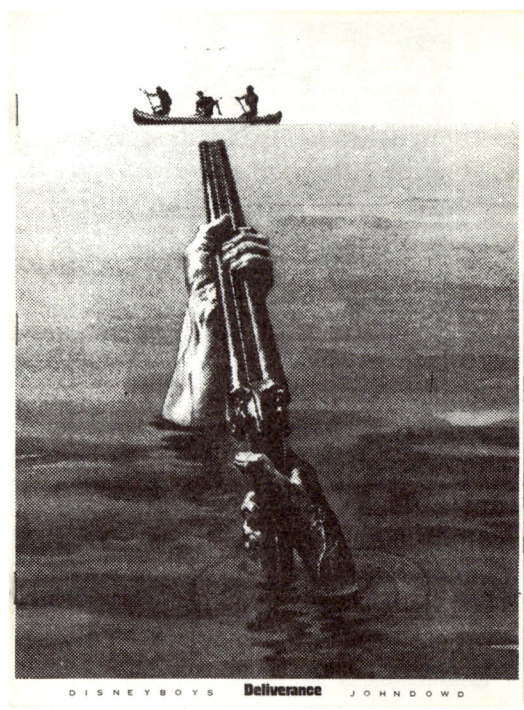

Disneyboys/Deliverance, 1972
Offset, side stapled, 11 × 8 ½ in. (27.9 × 21.6 cm)
Collection Philip Aarons and Shelley Fox Aarons

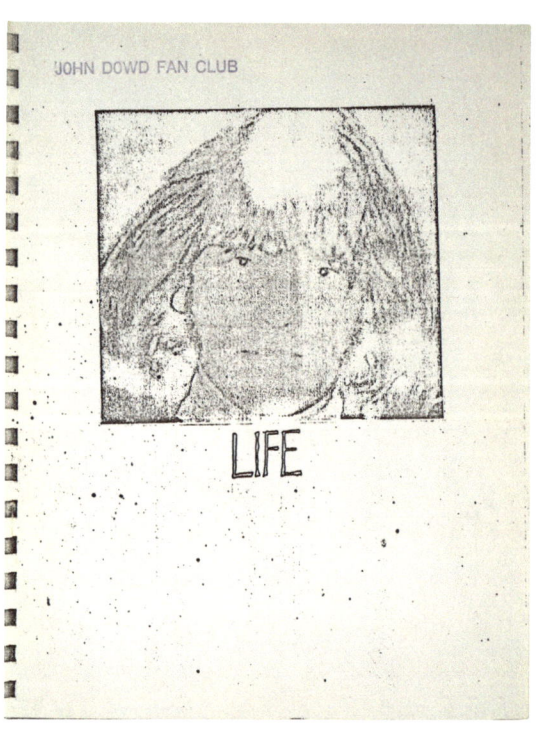

Life, ca. 1972
Photocopy, stamped ink, side stapled, 11 × 8 ½ in. (27.9 × 21.6 cm)
Morris and Helen Belkin Art Gallery, University of British Columbia,
Morris/Trasov Archive

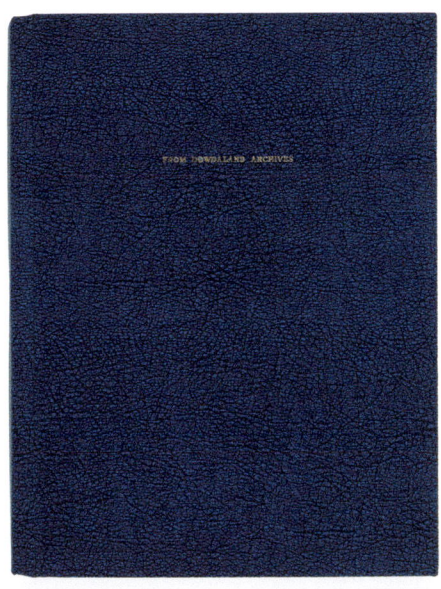

From Dowdaland Archives, 1973
Photocopy, perfect bound, leather-covered boards,
11 ¾ × 9 ½ in. (29.8 × 24.1 cm)
Collection Luke and Noel Dowd

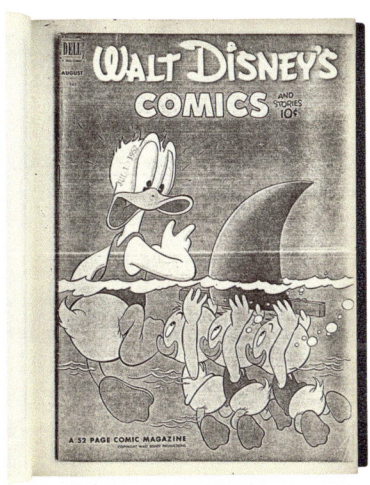

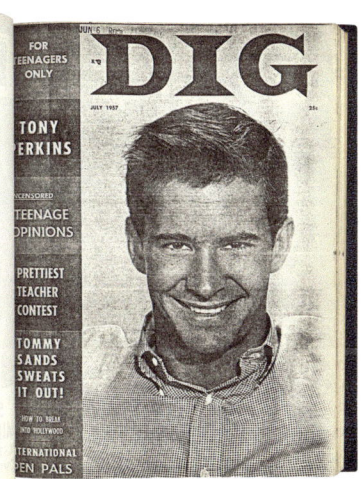

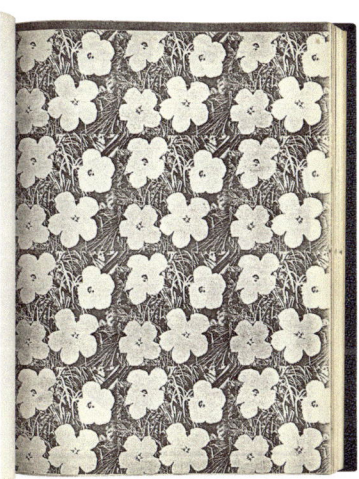

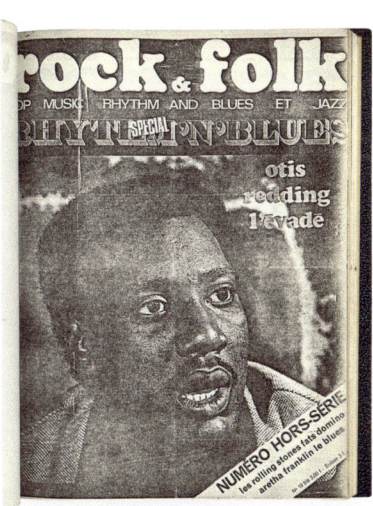

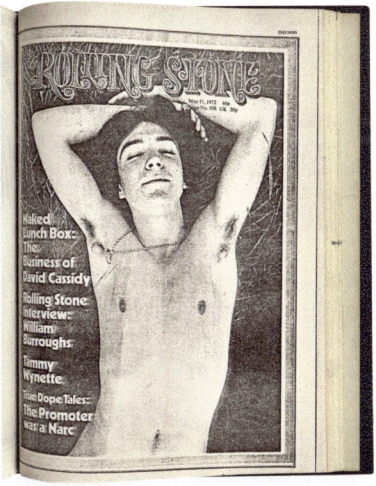

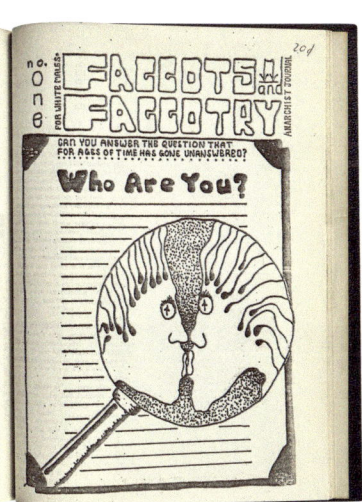

John Dowd and John Jack Baylin

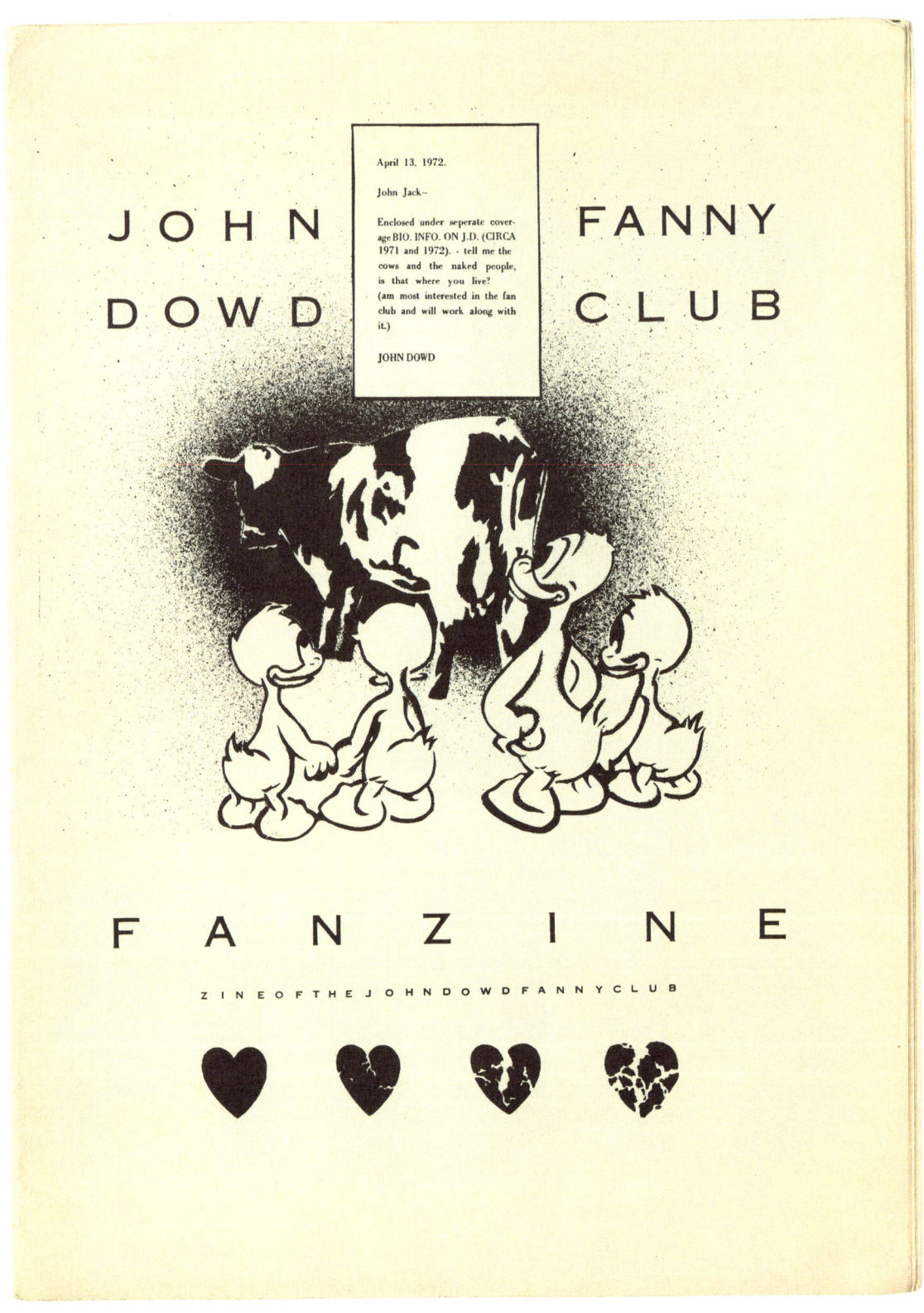

John Dowd Fanny Club Fanzine, 1972
Offset, saddle stitched, 11 × 8 ½ in. (27.9 × 21.6 cm)
Collection Philip Aarons and Shelley Fox Aarons

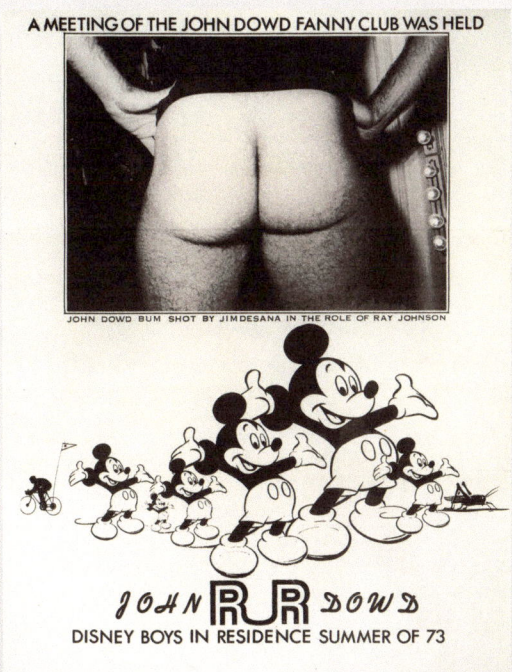

John Dowd
A Meeting of the John Dowd Fanny Club Was Held, 1973
Photocopy, 11 × 8 ½ in. (27.9 × 21.6 cm)
Morris and Helen Belkin Art Gallery, University of British Columbia,
Morris/Trasov Archive

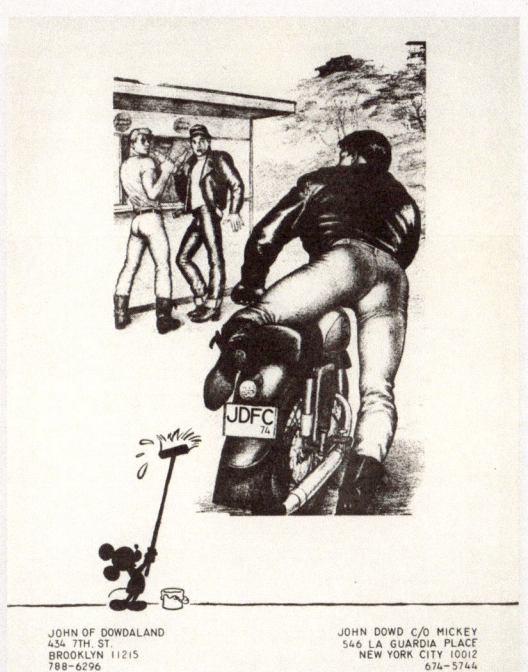

John Dowd
John of Dowdaland mailer, ca. 1972
Photocopy, 11 × 8 ½ in. (27.9 × 21.6 cm)
Morris and Helen Belkin Art Gallery, University of British Columbia,
Morris/Trasov Archive

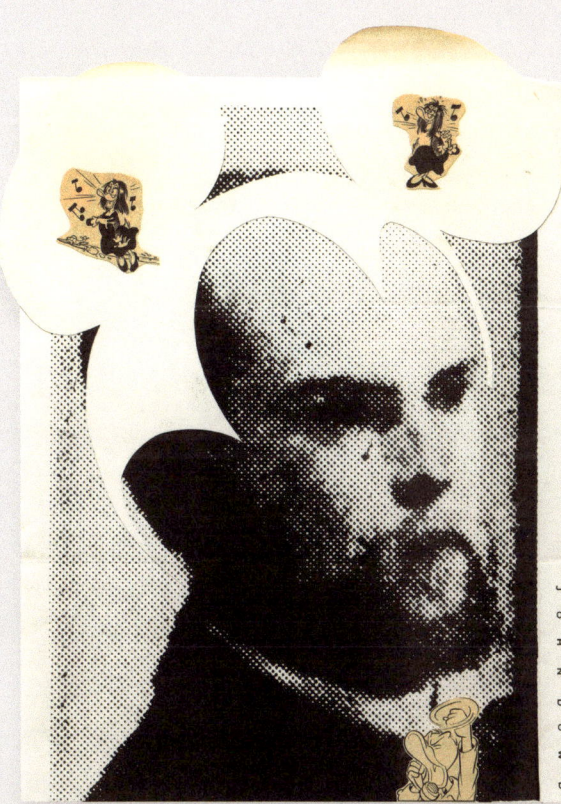

John Dowd
Ray Johnson mailer, ca. 1972
Photocopy and collage, 11 × 8 ½ in. (27.9 × 21.6 cm)
Ray Johnson Estate, New York

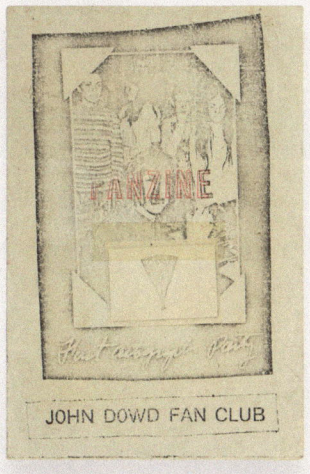

John Jack Baylin
John Dowd Fan Club postcard, 1972
Photocopy, stamped ink, and tape on postcard,
6 × 4 in. (15.4 × 10.2 cm)
Morris and Helen Belkin Art Gallery, University of British Columbia,
Morris/Trasov Archive

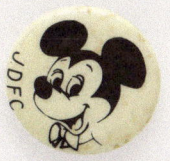
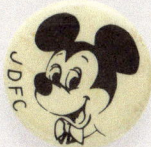

John Jack Baylin and Image Bank (Michael Morris, Vincent Trasov,
Gary Lee-Nova)
John Dowd Fan Club buttons, 1974
Pin-back metal buttons, each 1 in. (2.5 cm) diameter
Morris and Helen Belkin Art Gallery, University of British Columbia,
Morris/Trasov Archive

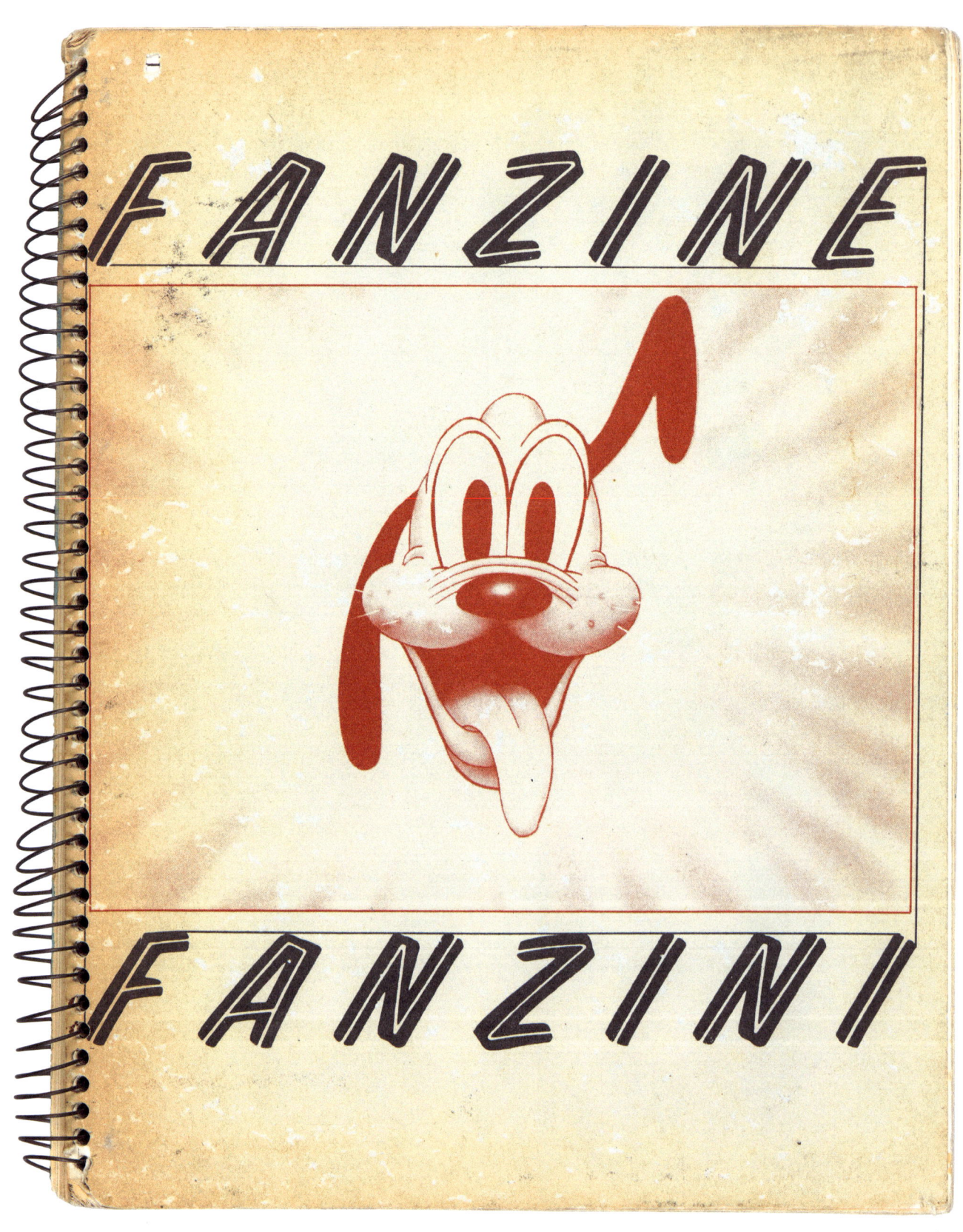

Fanzine/Fanzini, ca. 1972
Photocopy, spray paint, ink, spiral bound, offset
covers, 11 × 9 1⁄16 in. (27.9 × 23 cm)
Private collection

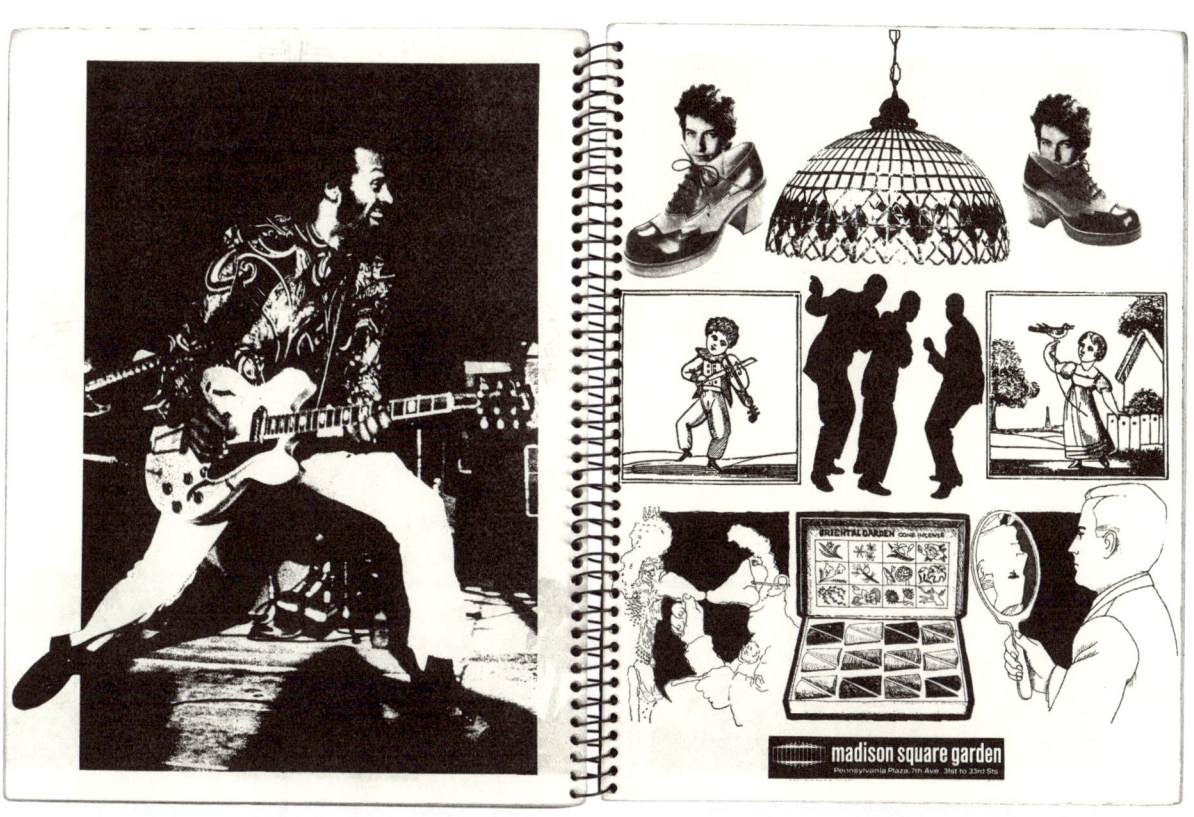

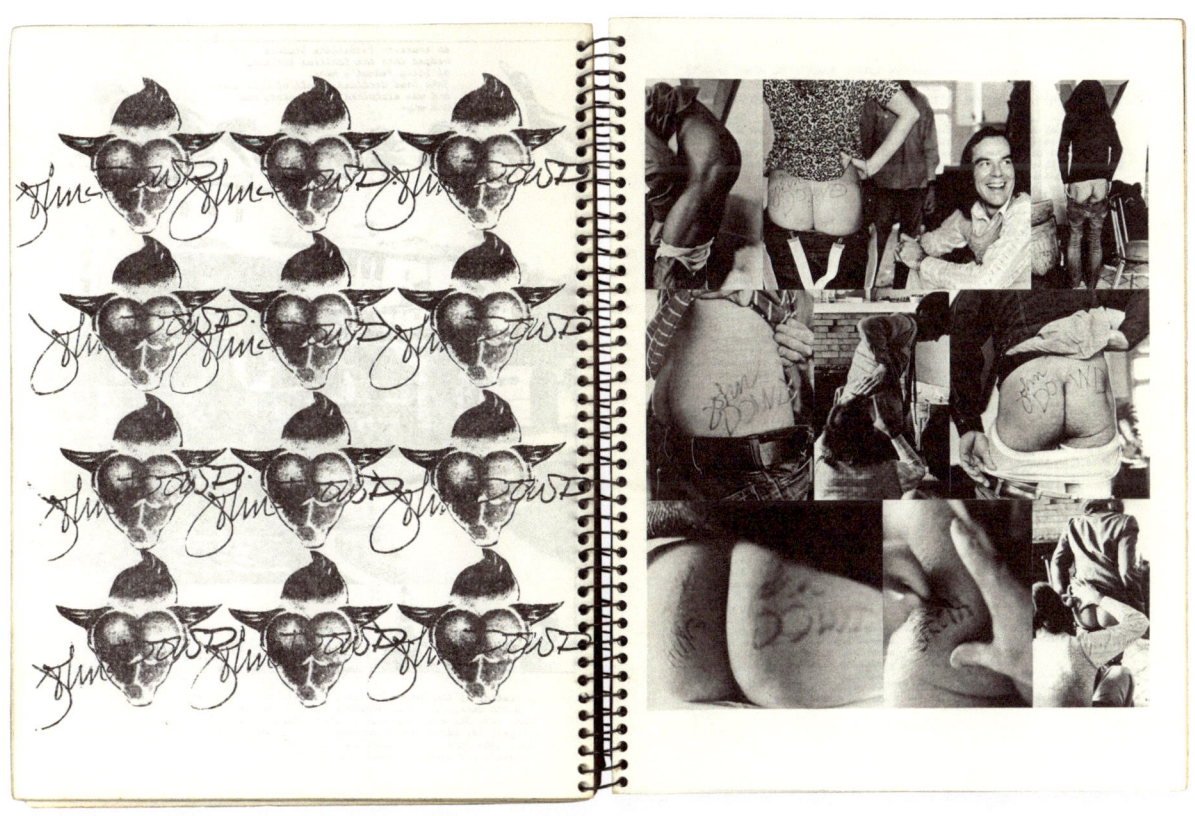

FANZINI GOES TO THE MOVIES

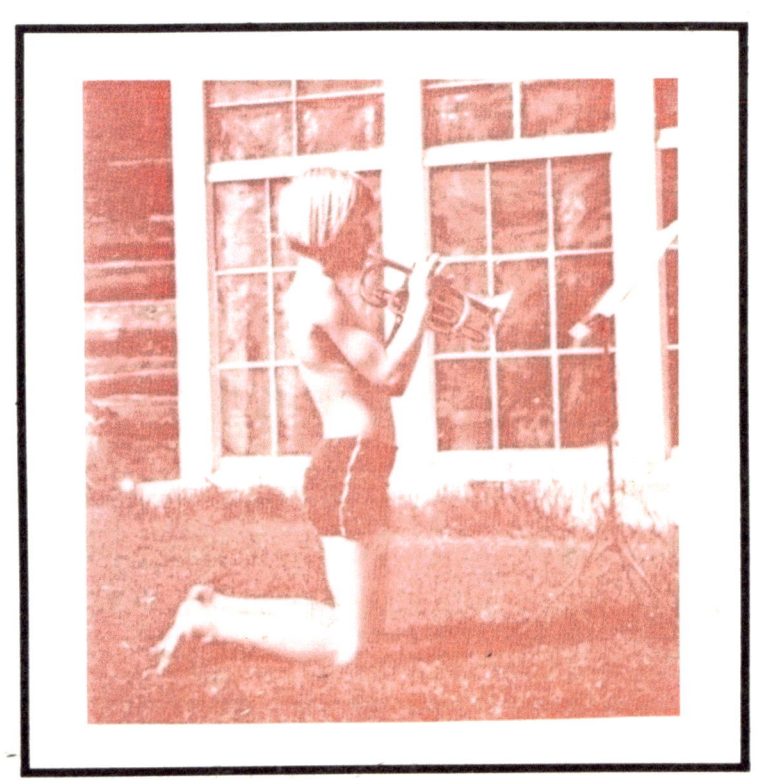

Fanzini Goes to the Movies, 1974
Offset, perfect bound, 11 × 9 1/16 in. (27.9 × 23 cm)
Collection Philip Aarons and Shelley Fox Aarons

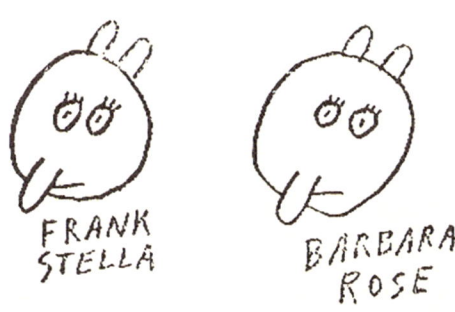

FRANK STELLA   BARBARA ROSE

June 4, 1972

Dear John Jacks,

As per your request, I will attempt to obtain for you a genuine
photo of J.D.'s bum. I was given by Santa Claus last December a
poleroid camera and have film both color & black & white but haven't
as yet figured out how to work the damned thing but hopefully will
do so and will meter over to John Dowd's and do said photo.

At the Anna May Wong Meeting yesterday, John Dowd was there with a
little baby Dowd and at one point after the Meeting he was bending
over talking to someone and the exposed backside above his trouser
belt was seen and had hairs on the said backside. We will go <u>all the
way</u> for the cover photo. I am sure J.D. will cooperate.

Ed Plunkett threw a smashing Anna May Wong party after the Meeting
and a fake Anna Banana was there but I told everyone she was a
fake and the <u>real</u> Anna Banana was in Canada in a parade. The NYCS
Meeting bythe way was also a smash success and video-taped by the
Beautiful Karla Munger A-2, whose eleventh birthday was celebrated
on stage with a birthday cake also,Linda Tits did some pretty good
video work. I interviewed people and Taylor Mead interviewed me and
we all had a good time up at Cultural Center.

Please trust me to follow through on your photo request and pary pray
and light candles I push the right buttons when John Dowd is pants-
lowered saying cheese.

                                    Most sincerely yours,

                                    Barbara Rose

Ken Friedman

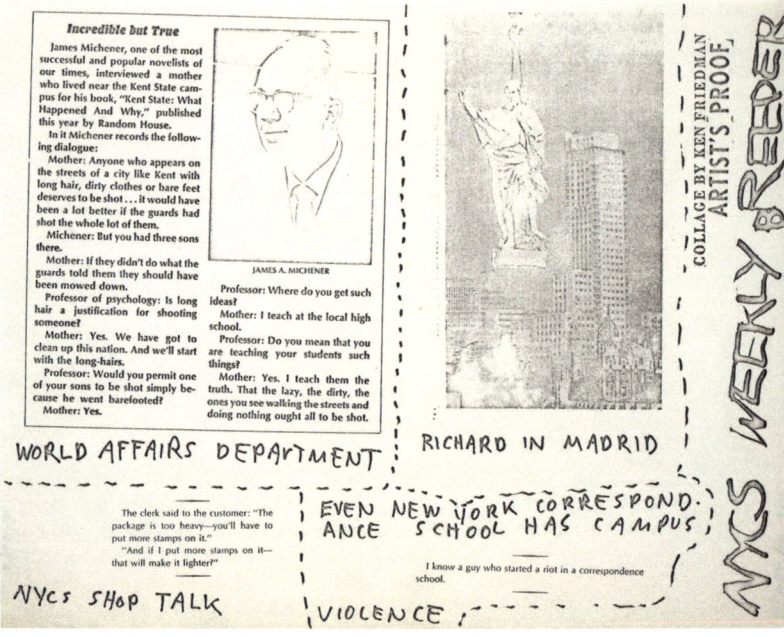

NYCS Weekly Breeder, vol. 1, no. 1, 1971
Photocopy, 8½ × 11 in. (21.6 × 27.9 cm)
Morris and Helen Belkin Art Gallery, University of
British Columbia, Morris/Trasov Archive

NYCS Weekly Breeder, vol. 1, no. 5, 1971
Photocopy, 11 × 8½ in. (27.9 × 21.6 cm)
Morris and Helen Belkin Art Gallery, University of
British Columbia, Morris/Trasov Archive

NYCS Weekly Breeder, vol. 1, no. 8, 1971
Photocopy, 11 × 8½ in. (27.9 × 21.6 cm)
Morris and Helen Belkin Art Gallery, University of
British Columbia, Morris/Trasov Archive

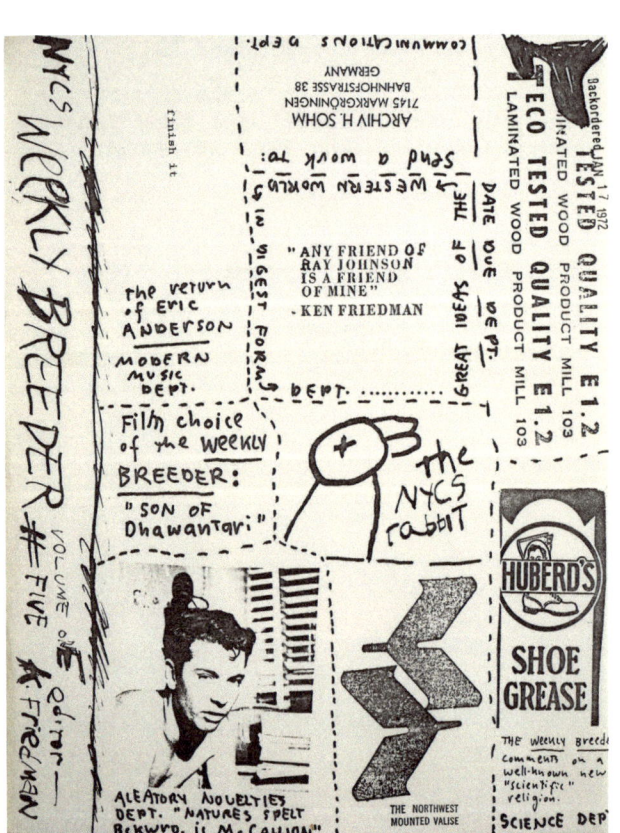

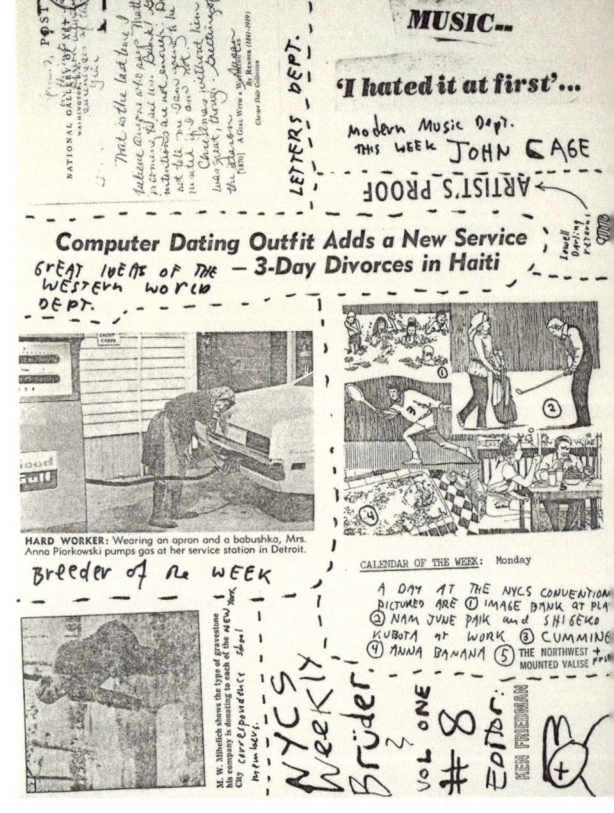

Stu Horn

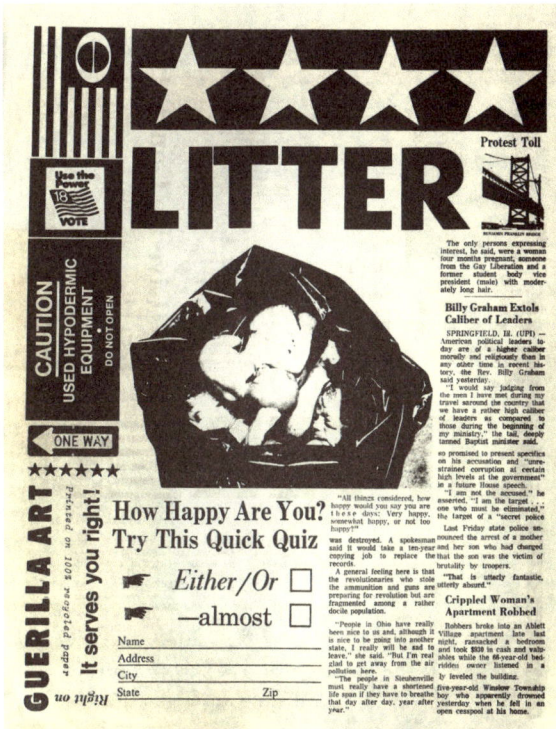

Northwest Mounted Valise, ca. 1971–74
Photocopy, 11 × 8 ½ in. (27.9 × 21.6 cm)
ATCA Artists' Works and Correspondence Files Collection,
The University of Iowa Libraries, Iowa City, Iowa

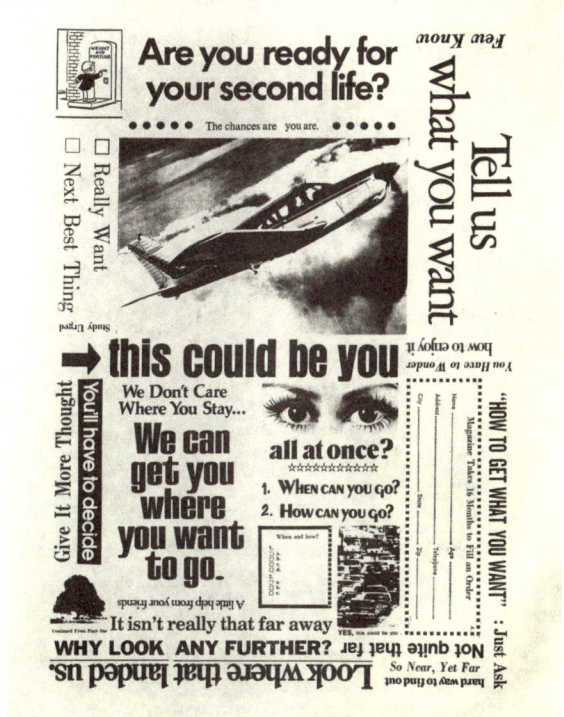

Northwest Mounted Valise, ca. 1971–74
Photocopy, 11 × 8 ½ in. (27.9 × 21.6 cm)
ATCA Artists' Works and Correspondence Files Collection,
The University of Iowa Libraries, Iowa City, Iowa

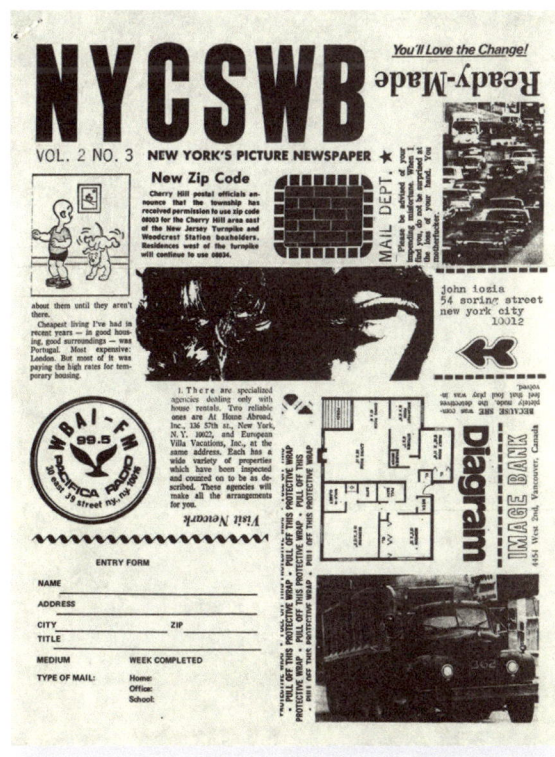

NYCS Weekly Breeder, vol. 2, no. 3, 1972
Photocopy, corner stapled, 11 × 8 ½ in. (27.9 × 21.6 cm)
ATCA Artists' Works and Correspondence Files Collection,
The University of Iowa Libraries, Iowa City, Iowa

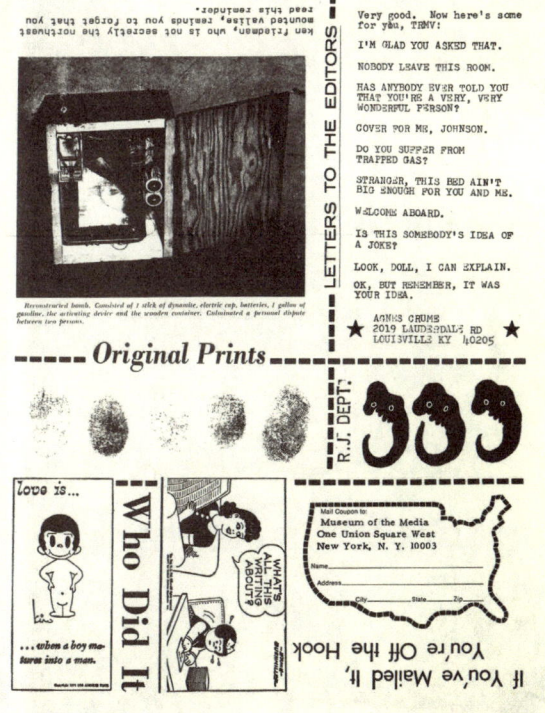

Tim Mancusi (with Bill Gaglione)

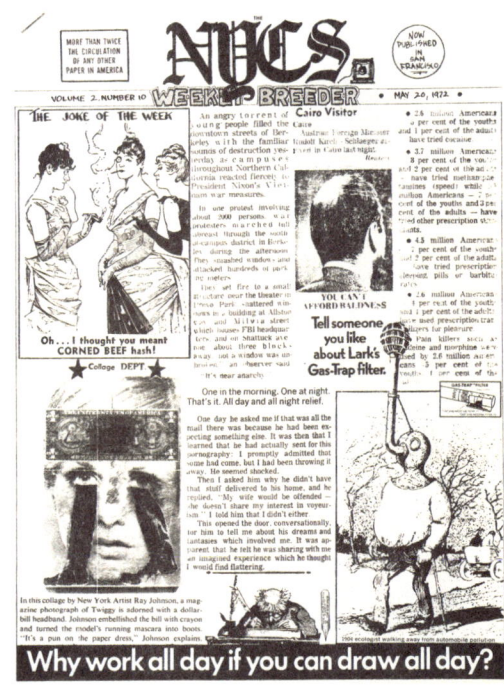

NYCS Weekly Breeder, vol. 2, no. 10, May 1972
Instant print, corner stapled, 11 × 8½ in. (27.9 × 21.6 cm)
Collection Philip Aarons and Shelley Fox Aarons

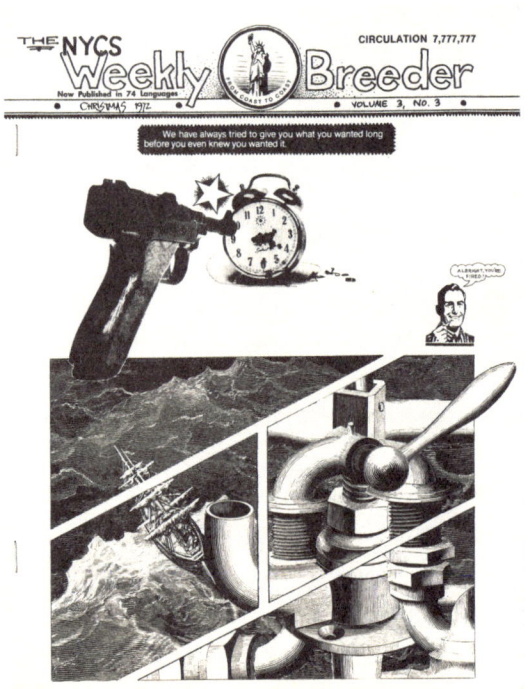

NYCS Weekly Breeder, vol. 3, no. 3, December 1972
Instant print, side stapled, 11 × 8½ in. (27.9 × 21.6 cm)
Collection Philip Aarons and Shelley Fox Aarons

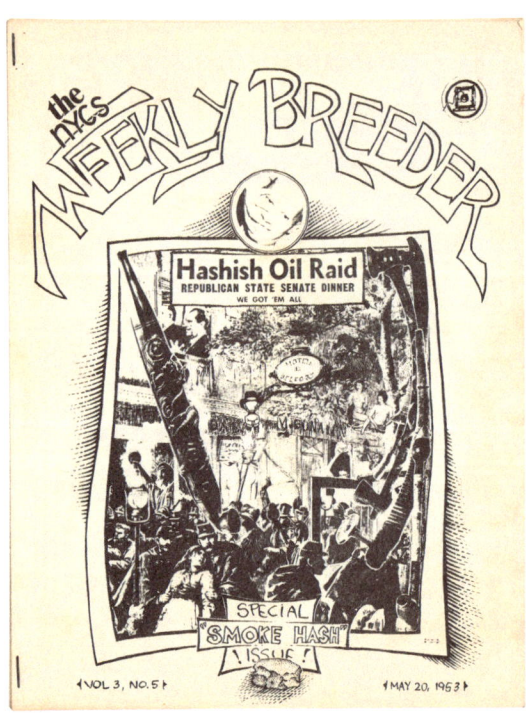

NYCS Weekly Breeder, vol. 3, no. 5, May 1973 (misdated 1953)
Instant print, side stapled, 11 × 8½ in. (27.9 × 21.6 cm)
Collection John Held, Jr.

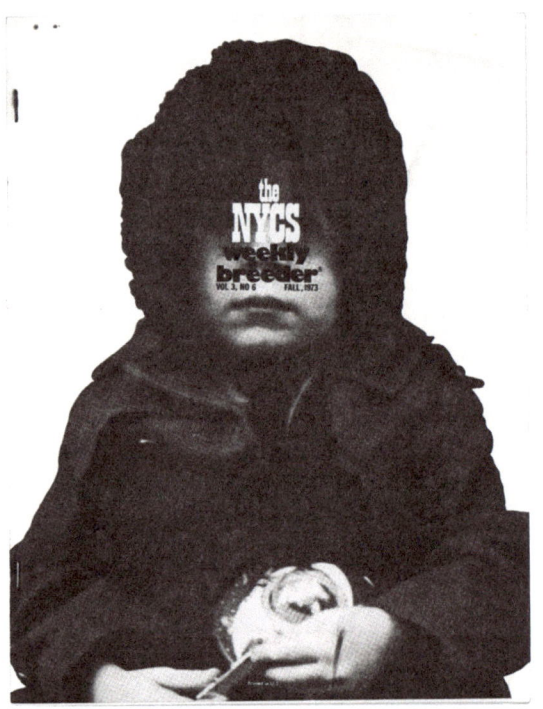

NYCS Weekly Breeder, vol. 3, no. 6, Fall 1973
Instant print, side stapled, 11 × 8½ in. (27.9 × 21.6 cm)
Collection Philip Aarons and Shelley Fox Aarons

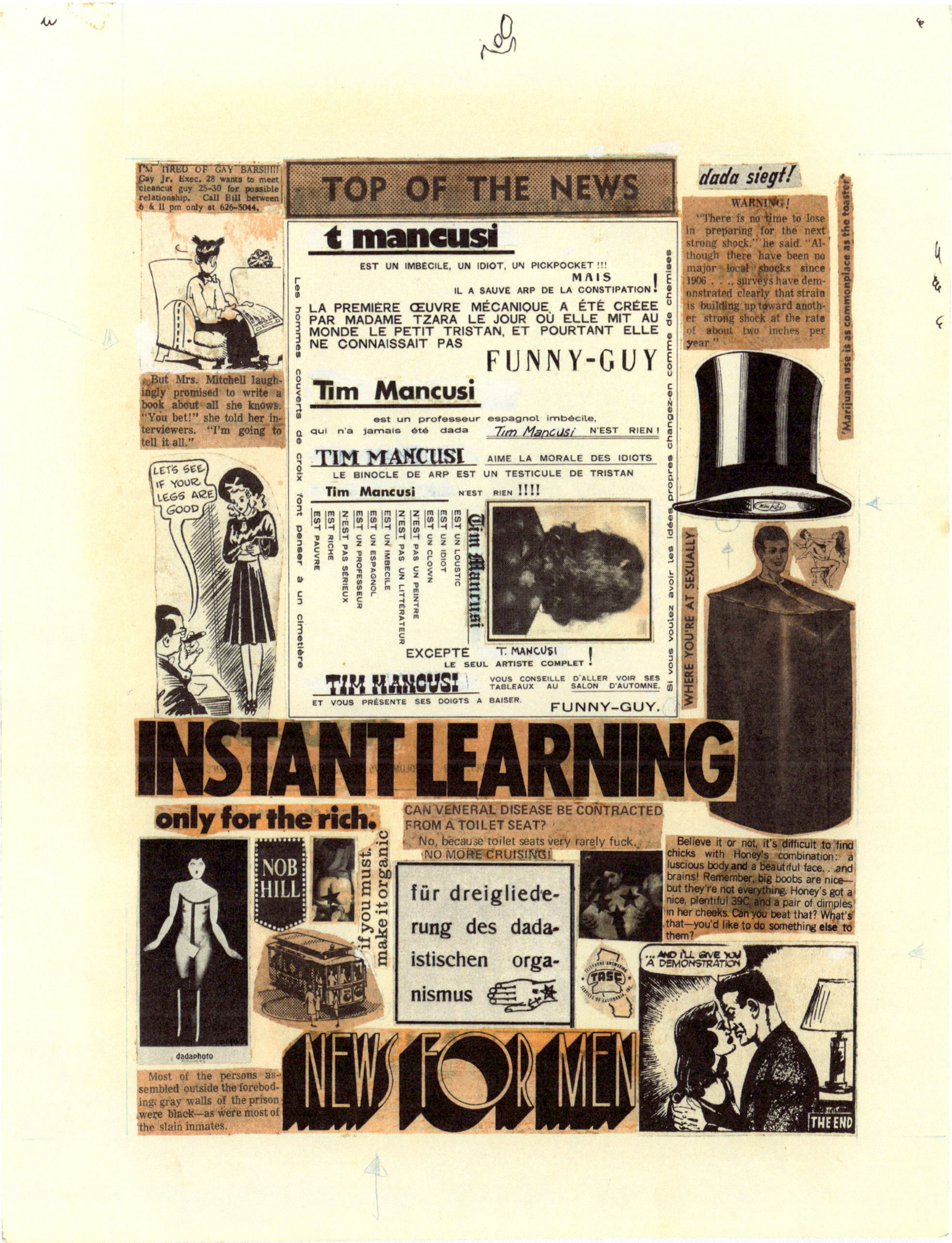

Paste-up collage for *NYCS Weekly Breeder*, vol. 3, no. 5, May 1973
Offset, paper, correction fluid, ink, glue, 13 7/8 × 11 in. (35.2 × 27.9 cm)
Collection John Held, Jr.

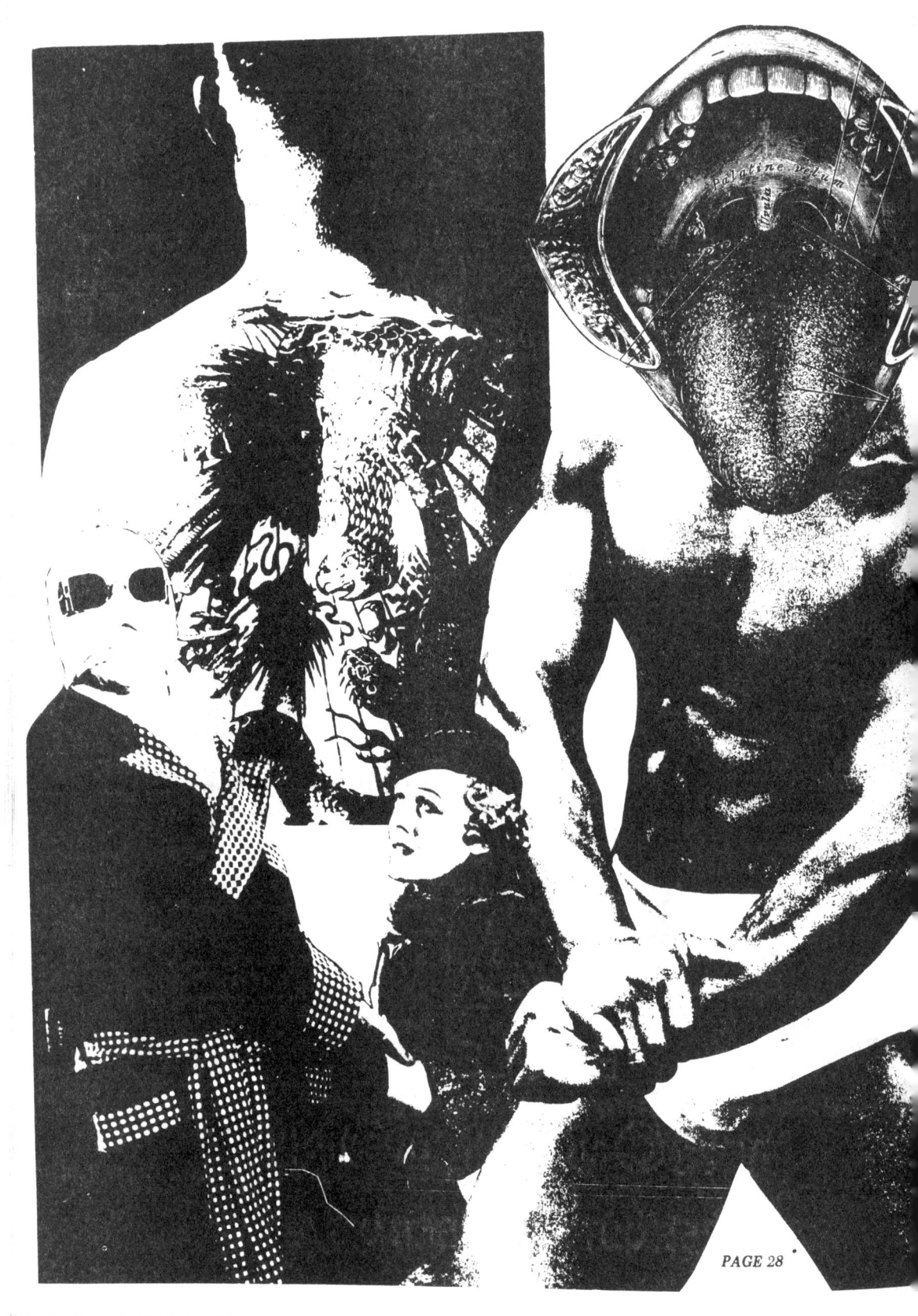

PAGE 28

NYCS Weekly Breeder, vol. 3, no. 6, Fall 1973
Instant print, side stapled, 11 × 8½ in. (27.9 × 21.6 cm)
Collection Philip Aarons and Shelley Fox Aarons

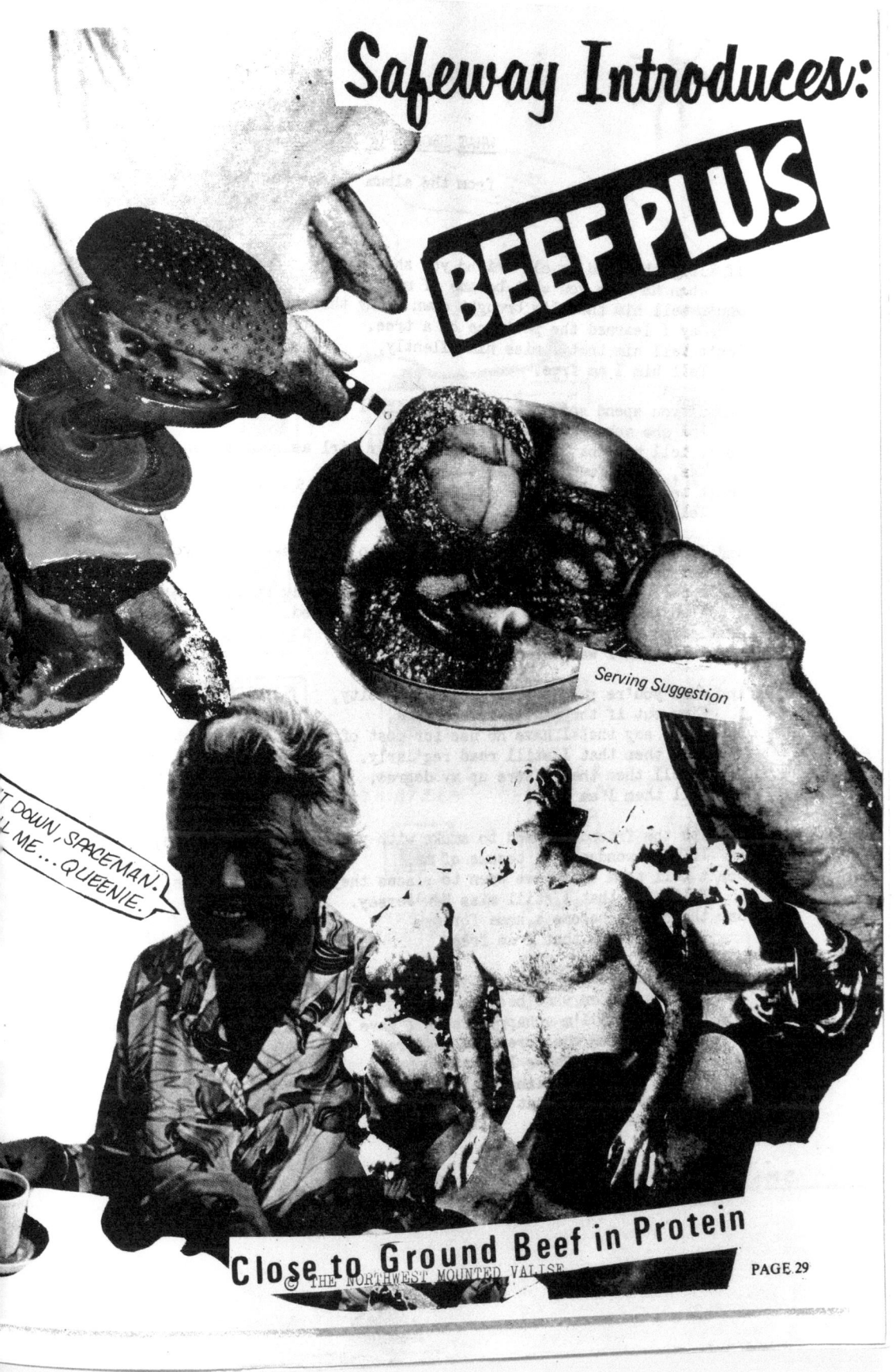

Bill Gaglione

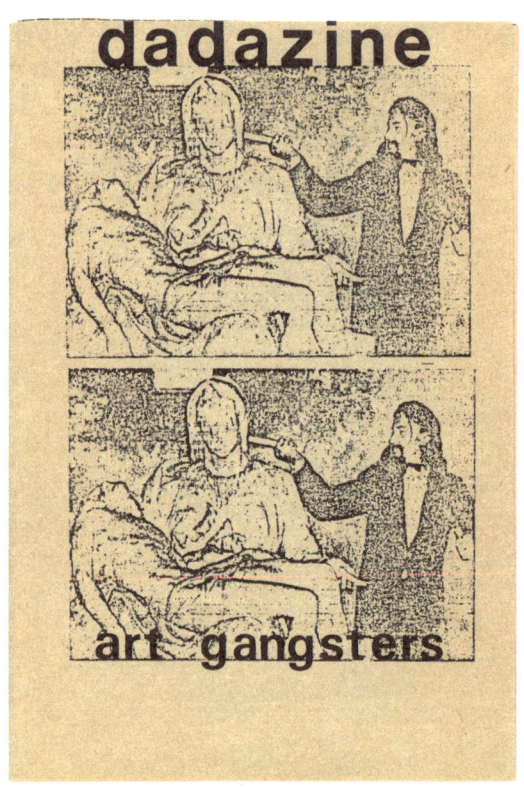

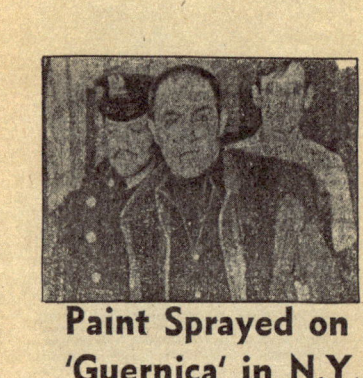

Paint Sprayed on 'Guernica' in N.Y.

New York

A man who said he was an artist wanting to "tell the truth" sprayed red paint across the famed "Guernica" painting by Pablo Picasso at in midtown Manhattan yesterday the Museum of Modern Art terday.

The alleged vandal was apprehended by a guard and taken into police custody within moments.

In letters more than a foot high, he sprayed, "KILL LIES ALL." But the museum began removing the the masterpiece cubist work paint immediately and said was undamaged. The painting was inspired by the German destruction of the town of Guernica during the Spanish Civil War.

Museum officials said the 11-foot-5 inch by 25-foot-5 inch painting was protected by a coat of varnish. The spray paint did not penetrate.

The alleged vandal identified himself as Tony Shafrazi, 30, authorities said.

Asked why he did it, Shafrazi said, "I'm an artist, and I want to tell the truth."

Associated Press

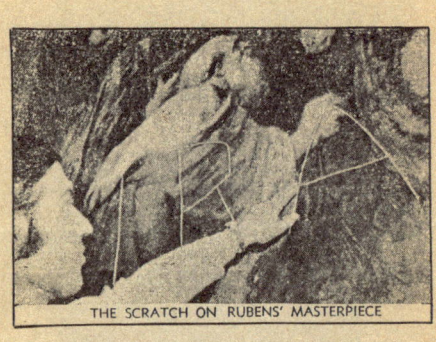

THE SCRATCH ON RUBENS' MASTERPIECE

Versailles repairs: $1 million

VERSAILLES — The chief curator at Versailles Palace says the damage caused by a terrorist bomb that wrecked portions of the sumptuous 17th-century chateau can be repaired in two to three months for about $1 million. Police said they have no significant clues to the identity of the bomber and were not prepared to comment on claims by three separate underground movements — two leftist and one Breton secessionist — of responsibility. The blast wrecked three ground-floor rooms in the Midi Wing of the 17th-century palace, badly damaging 16 paintings and wall panels, three plaster busts, a dozen antique chairs, assorted candelabra, ornate curtains and sculpted woodwork in galleries devoted to the Napoleonic Empire period.

Dadazine, no. 6, August 1978
Offset, folded, 8 × 5½ in. (20.3 × 14 cm)
The Museum of Modern Art Library, New York

Tim Mancusi

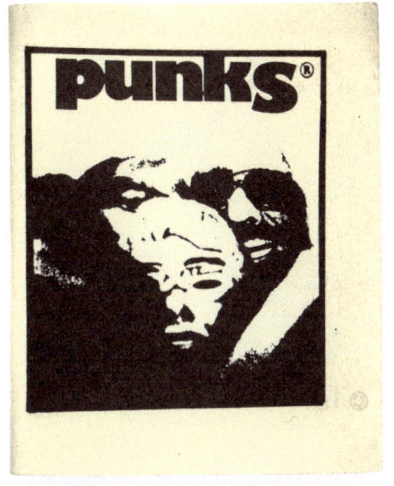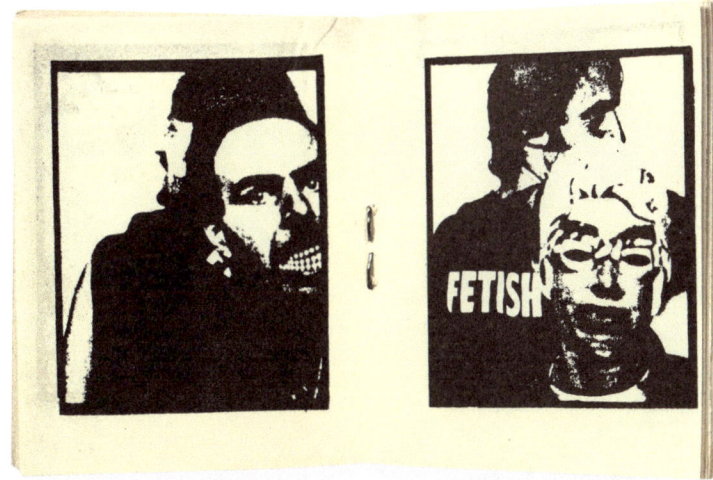

Punks, 1975
Photocopy, saddle stitched, 2 ½ × 2 in. (6.4 × 5.1 cm)
Private collection, New York

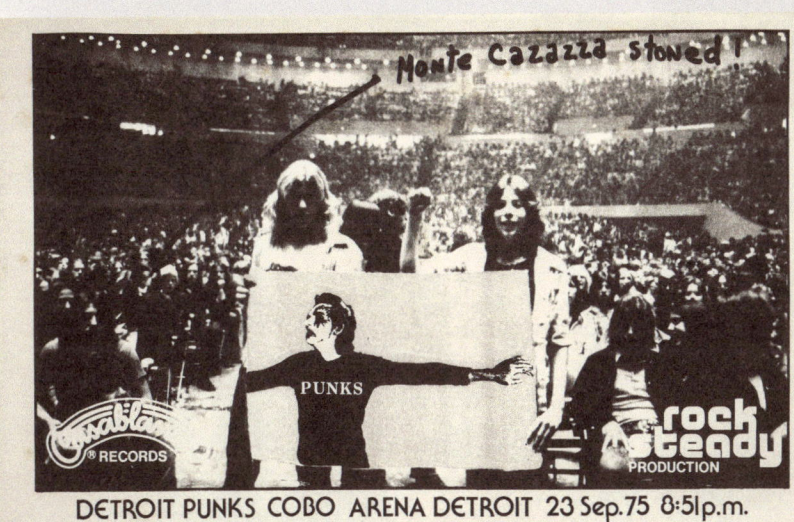

Bill Gaglione
Detroit Punks mailer, 1975
Instant print, 11 × 8 ½ in. (27.9 × 21.6 cm)
Collection John Held, Jr.

Monte Cazazza

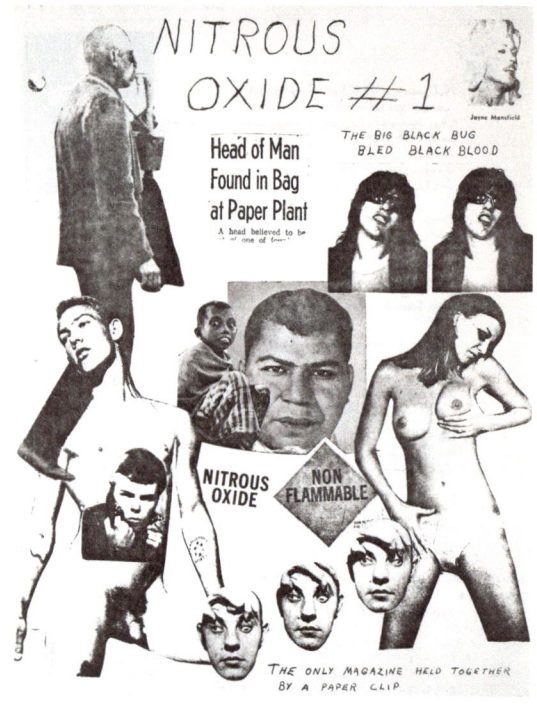

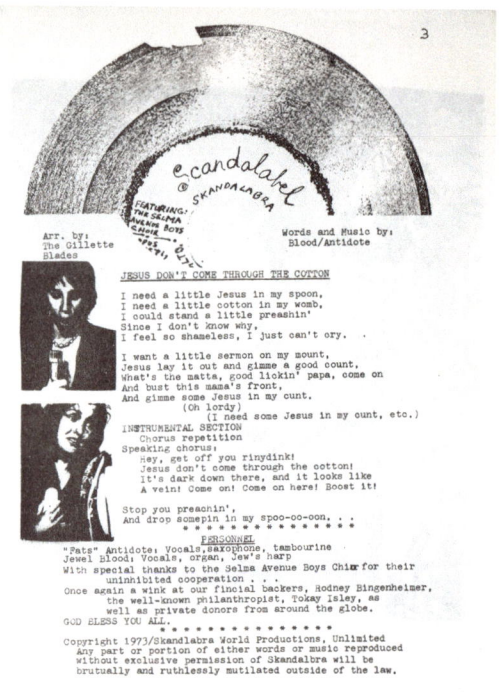

← ↑ *Nitrous Oxide*, no. 1, 1973
Photocopy, spray paint, bound with paper clip, 11 × 8 ½ in. (27.9 × 21.6 cm)
Morris and Helen Belkin Art Gallery, University of British Columbia,
Morris/Trasov Archive

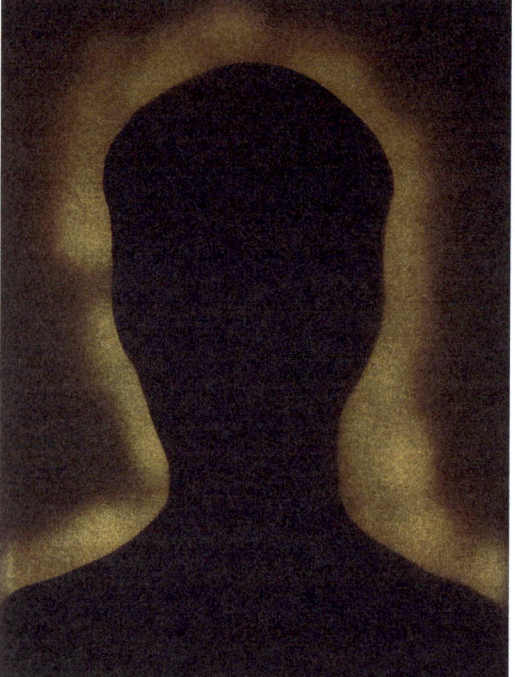

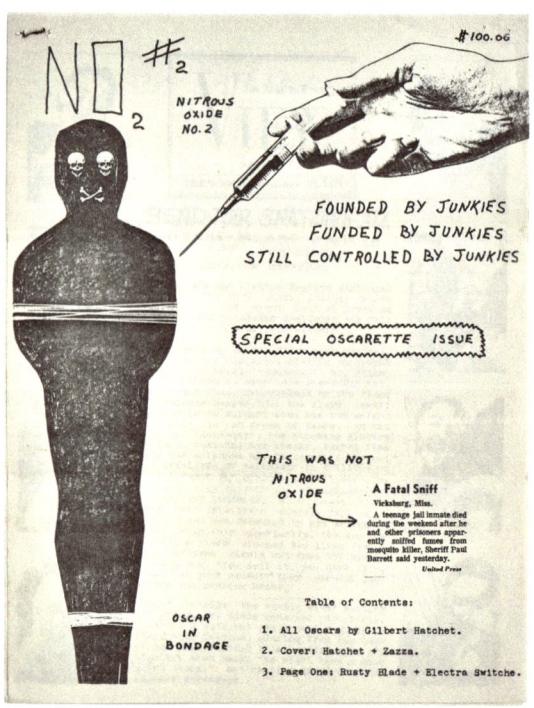

Nitrous Oxide, no. 2, 1977
Photocopy, spray paint, corner stapled, 11 × 8 ½ in. (27.9 × 21.6 cm)
Collection Robert Lambert

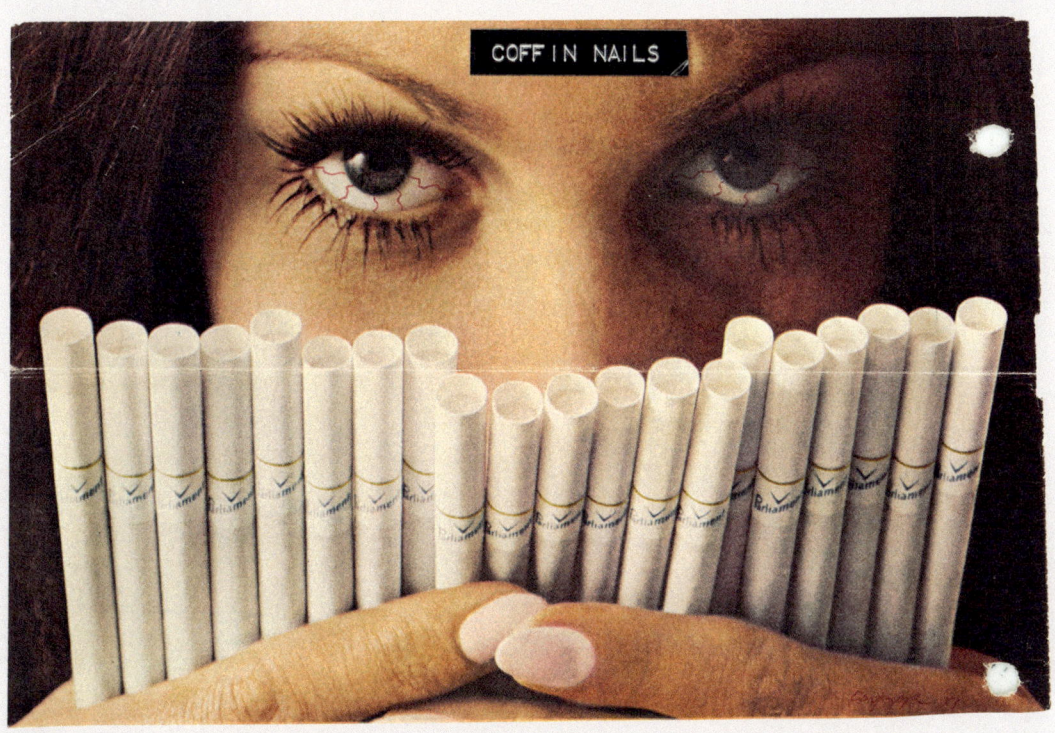

Coffin Nails, 1971
Ink and embossed tape on magazine clipping, 5 ½ × 8 ¼ (14 × 21 cm)
Morris and Helen Belkin Art Gallery, University of British Columbia,
Morris/Trasov Archive

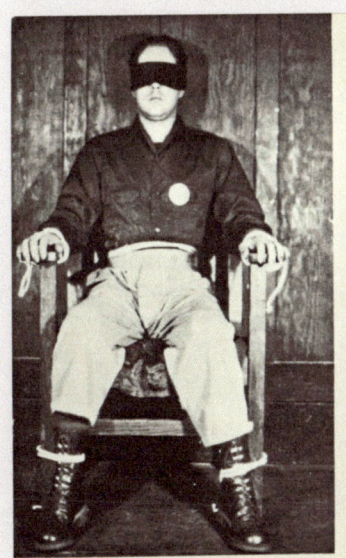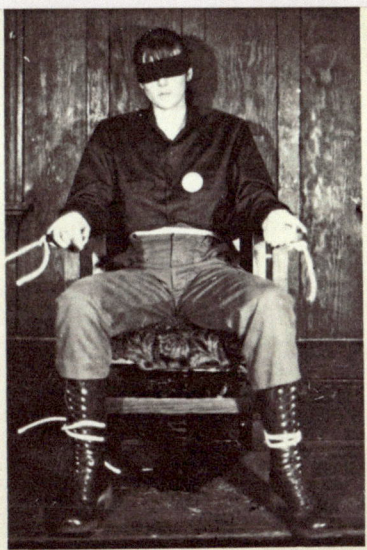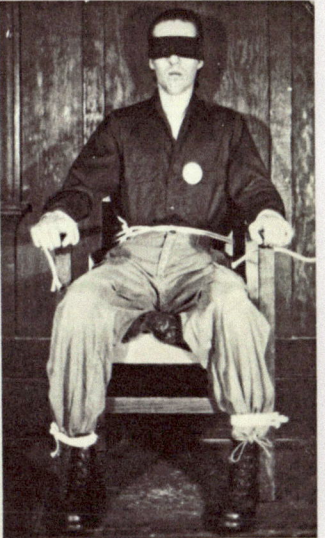

Monte Cazazza, Genesis P-Orridge, and Cosey Fanni Tutti
Gary Gilmore Memorial Society postcard, 1977
Offset, 3 ½ × 5 ¾ in. (8.9 × 14.6 cm)
Collection Jim Jocoy

Charles Chickadel

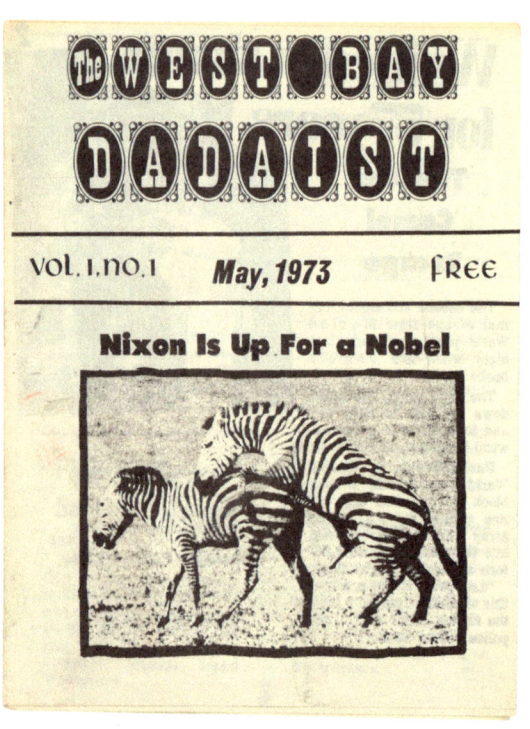

West Bay Dadaist, vol. 1, no. 1, May 1973
Instant print, saddle stitched, 5 ½ × 4 ¼ in. (14 × 10.8 cm)
Morris and Helen Belkin Art Gallery, University of British Columbia,
Morris/Trasov Archive

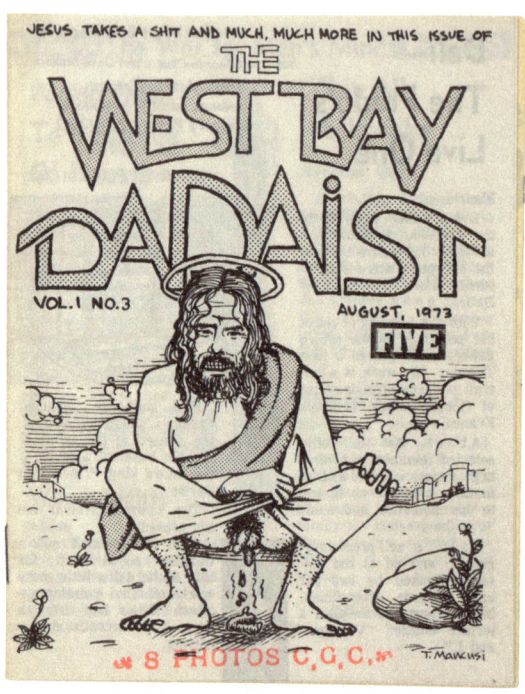

West Bay Dadaist, vol. 1, no. 3, August 1973
Instant print, stamped ink, saddle stitched, 5 ½ × 4 ¼ in. (14 × 10.8 cm)
Morris and Helen Belkin Art Gallery, University of British Columbia,
Morris/Trasov Archive

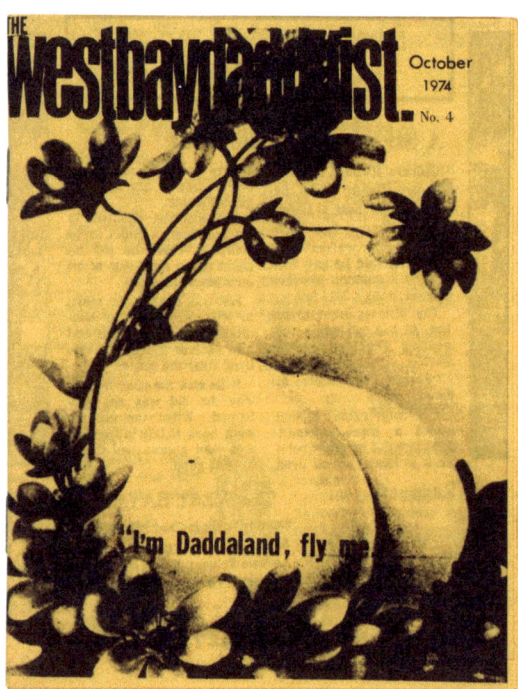

West Bay Dadaist, vol. 1, no. 4, October 1973 (misdated 1974)
Instant print, saddle stitched, 5 ½ × 4 ¼ in. (14 × 10.8 cm)
Morris and Helen Belkin Art Gallery, University of British Columbia,
Morris/Trasov Archive

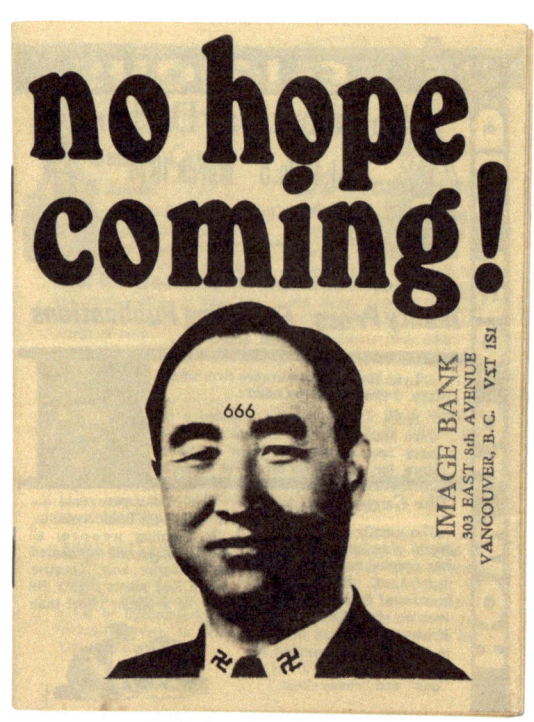

West Bay Dadaist, vol. 2, no. 5, March 1974
Instant print, saddle stitched, 5 ½ × 4 ¼ in. (14 × 10.8 cm)
Morris and Helen Belkin Art Gallery, University of British Columbia,
Morris/Trasov Archive

The West Bay Dadaist

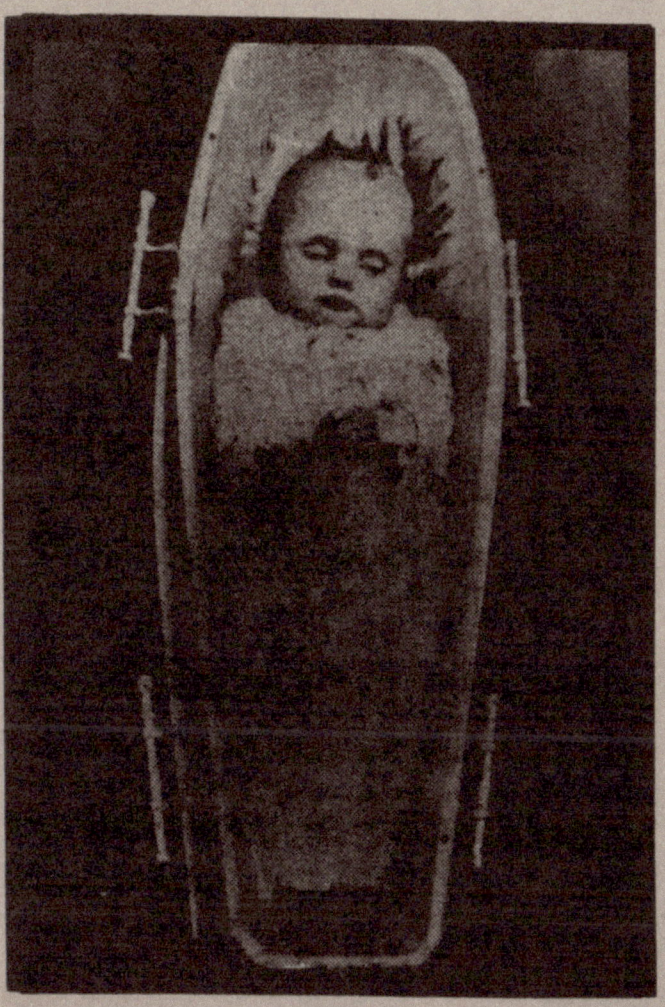

Is Dead!

Quoz?, vol. 2, no. 6, June 1974
Instant print, saddle stitched, 5 ½ × 4 ¼ in. (14 × 10.8 cm)
Morris and Helen Belkin Art Gallery, University of British Columbia,
Morris/Trasov Archive

Quoz?, vol. 3, no. 9, March 1975
Instant print, saddle stitched, 5 ½ × 4 ¼ in. (14 × 10.8 cm)
Morris and Helen Belkin Art Gallery, University of British Columbia,
Morris/Trasov Archive

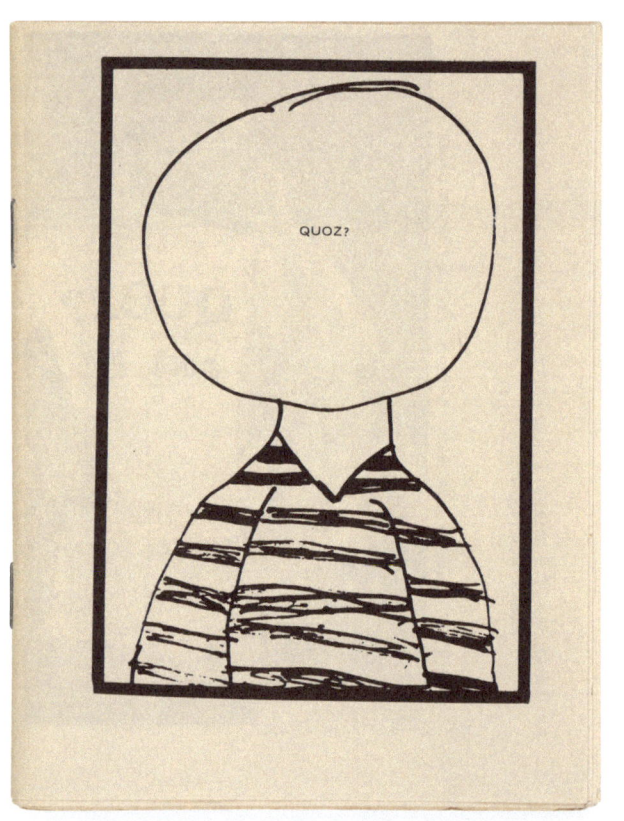

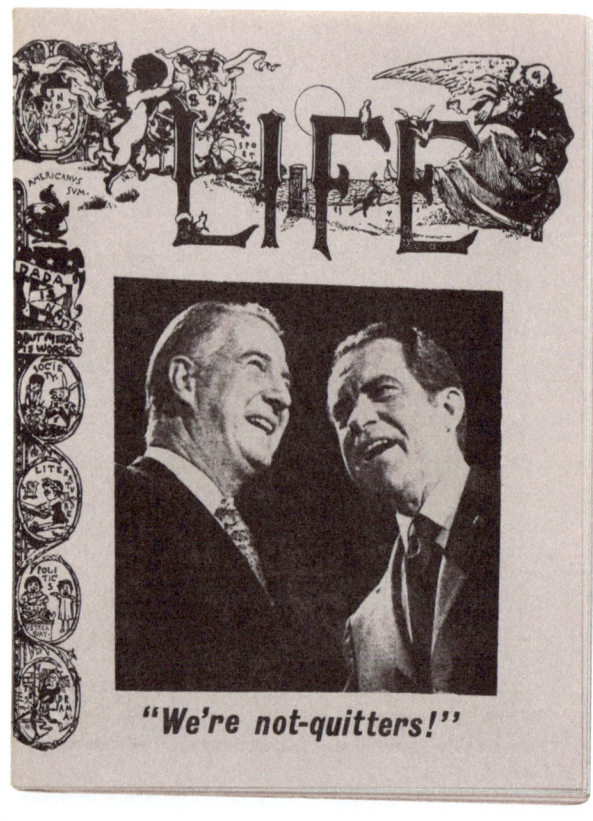

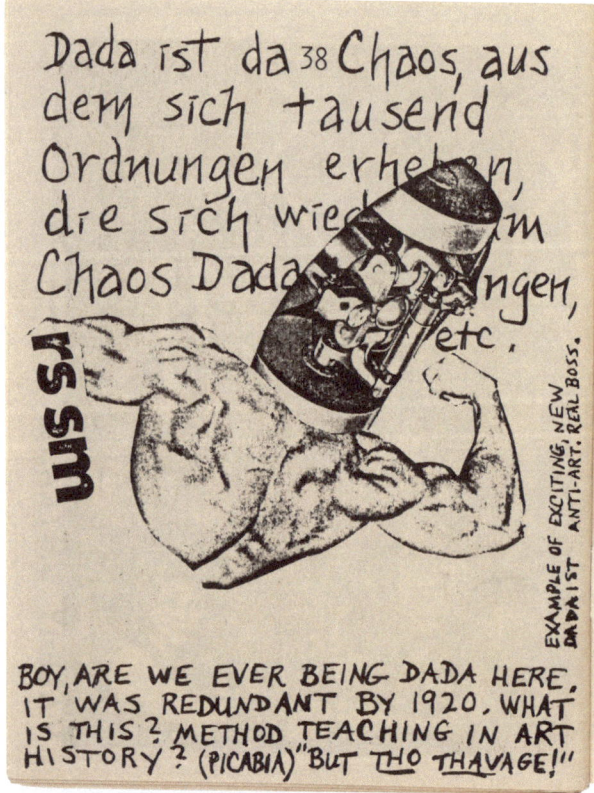

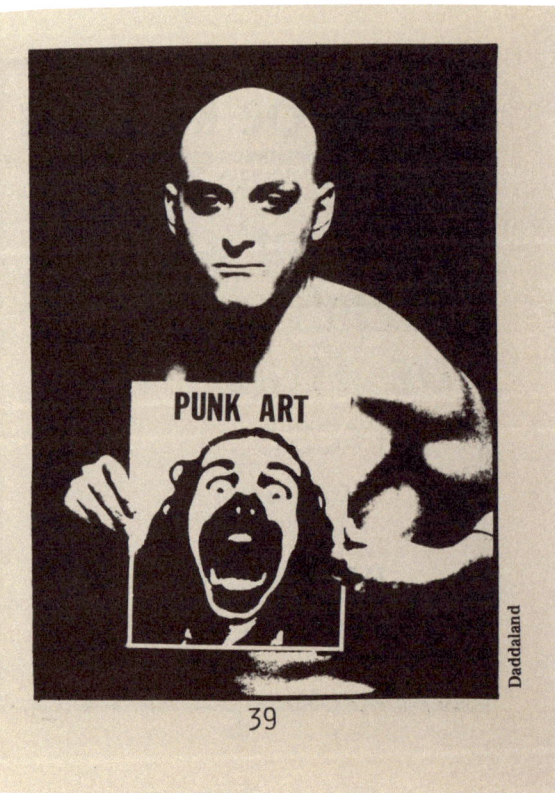

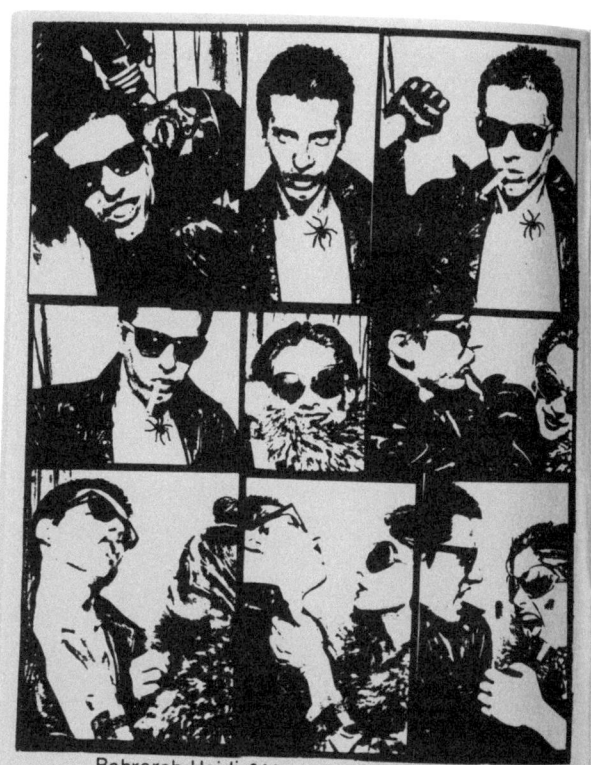

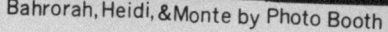

Bahrorah, Heidi, & Monte by Photo Booth

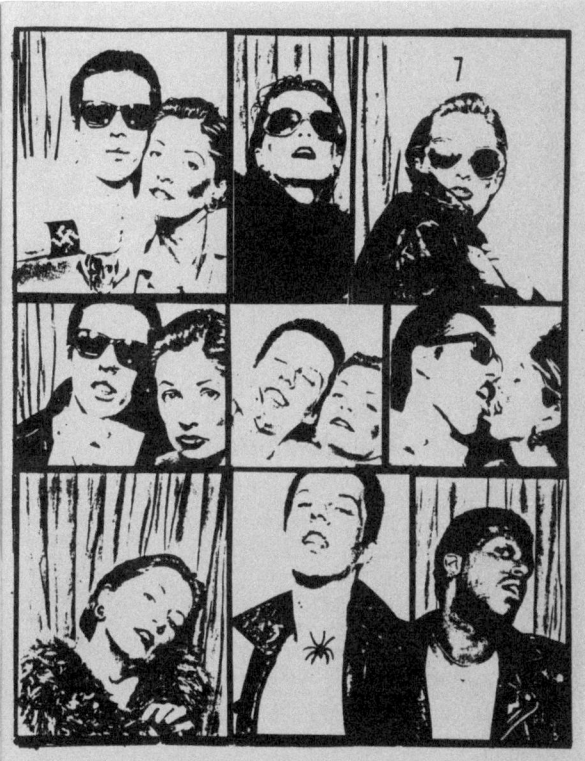

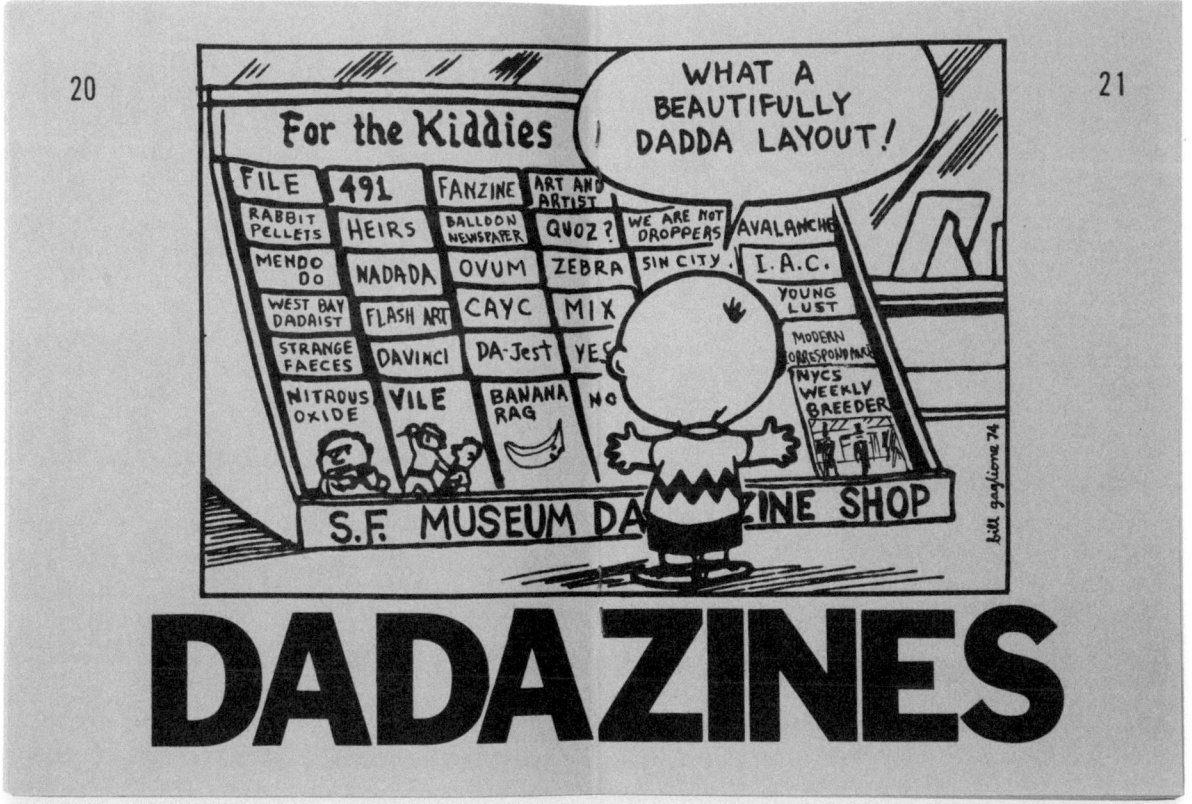

Quoz?, vol. 2, no. 7, September 1974
Instant print, saddle stitched, 5 ½ × 4 ¼ in. (14 × 10.8 cm)
Morris and Helen Belkin Art Gallery, University of British Columbia,
Morris/Trasov Archive

Anna Banana

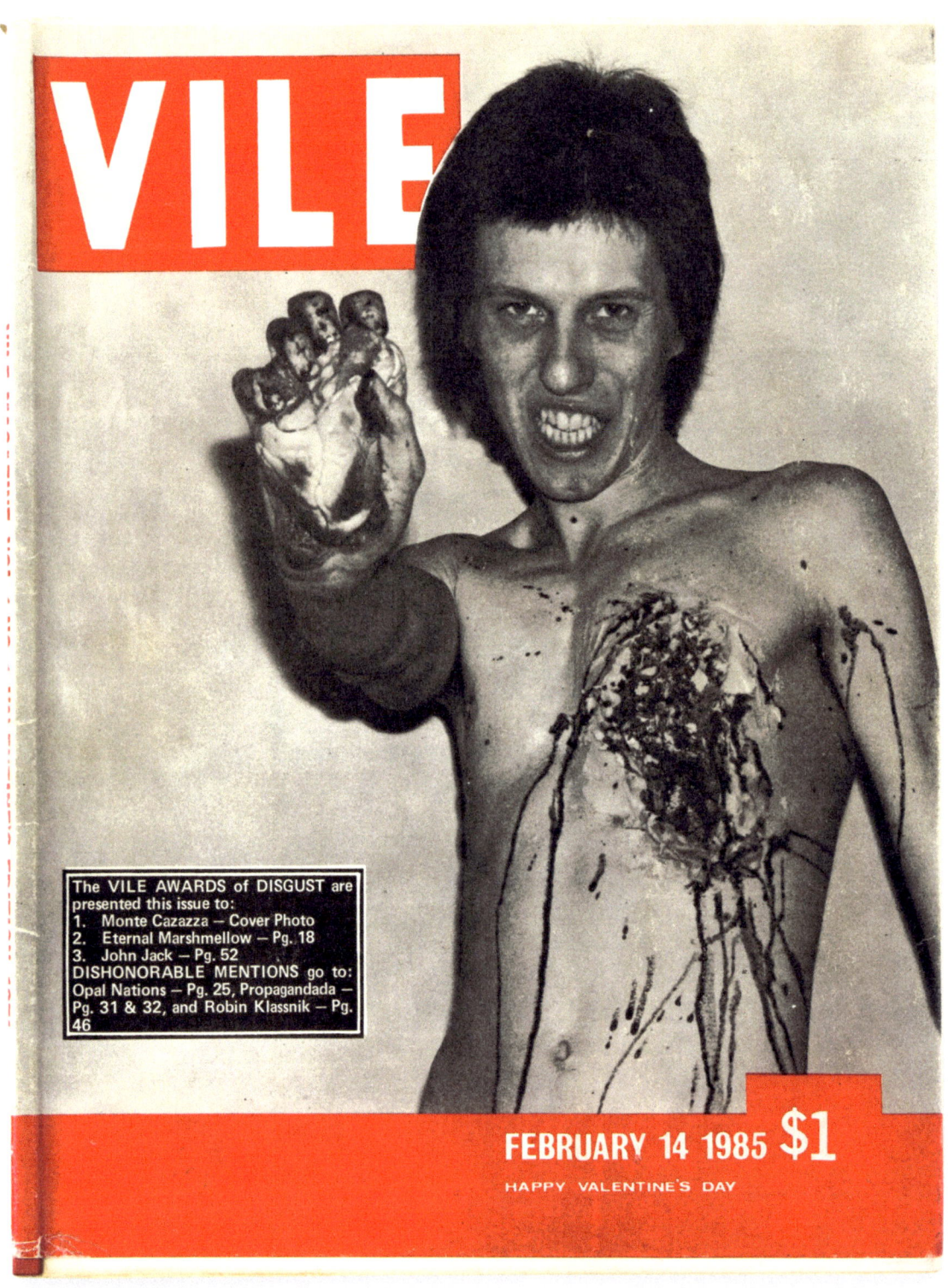

Vile, vol. 1, no. 1 (issue 1), February 1974 (misdated 1985)
Instant print, velo binding, two-color offset wrappers,
11 × 8 ½ in. (27.9 × 21.6 cm)
Collection Philip Aarons and Shelley Fox Aarons

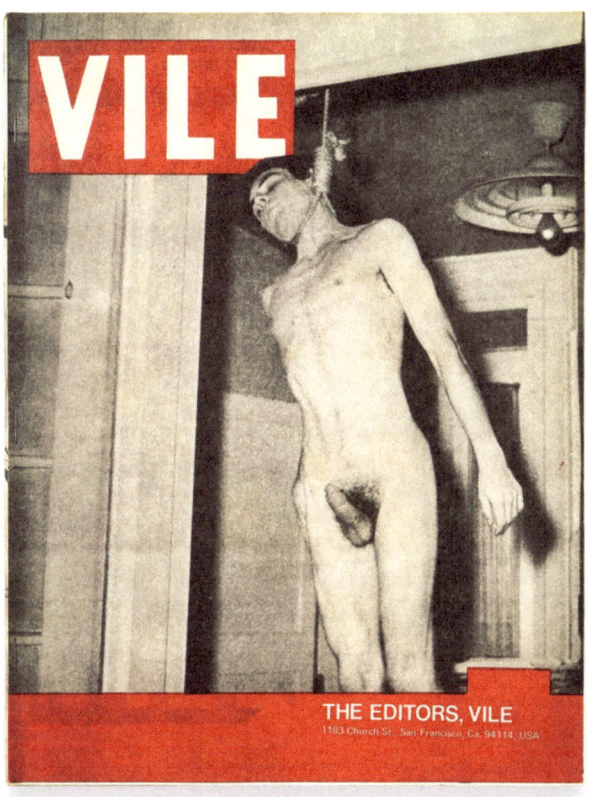

Vile, vol. 1, no. 4 (issue 2), September 1974
Offset, side stapled, two-color offset wrappers, 11 × 8 ½ in. (27.9 × 21.6 cm)
Collection Philip Aarons and Shelley Fox Aarons

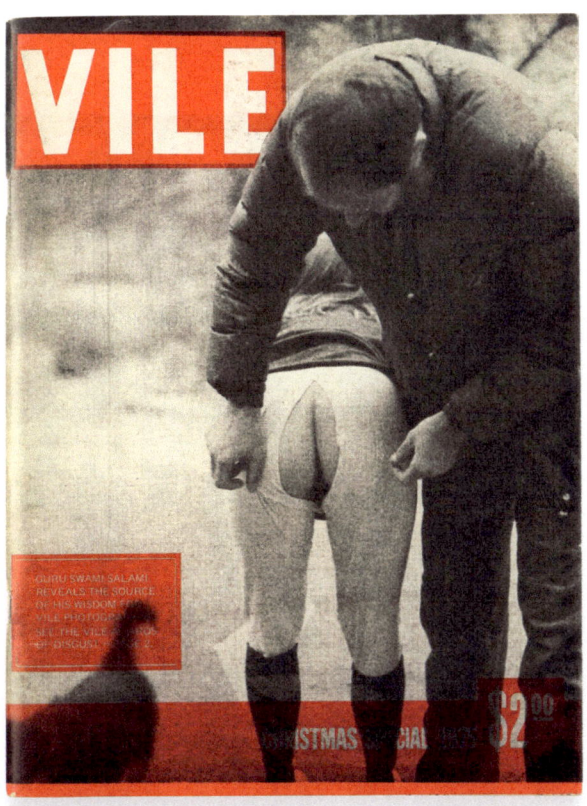

Vile, vol. 3, no. 1 (issue 3), December 1975
Offset, saddle stitched, two-color offset wrappers, 11 × 8 ⅜ in. (27.9 × 21.3 cm)
Collection Philip Aarons and Shelley Fox Aarons

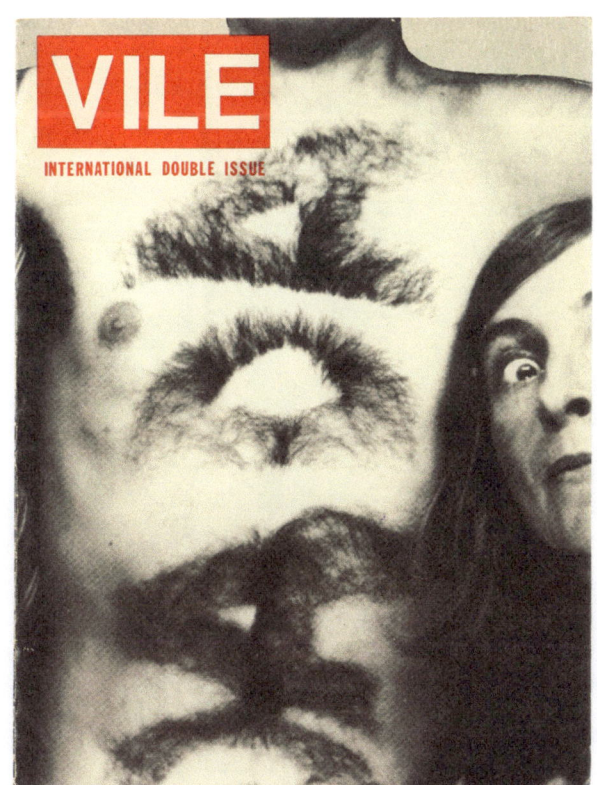

Vile, vol. 1, no. 2 / vol. 2, no. 1 (issue 4), Summer 1976
Editor: Bill Gaglione
Offset, perfect bound, two-color offset wrappers, 11 × 8 ½ in. (27.9 × 21.6 cm)
Collection Philip Aarons and Shelley Fox Aarons

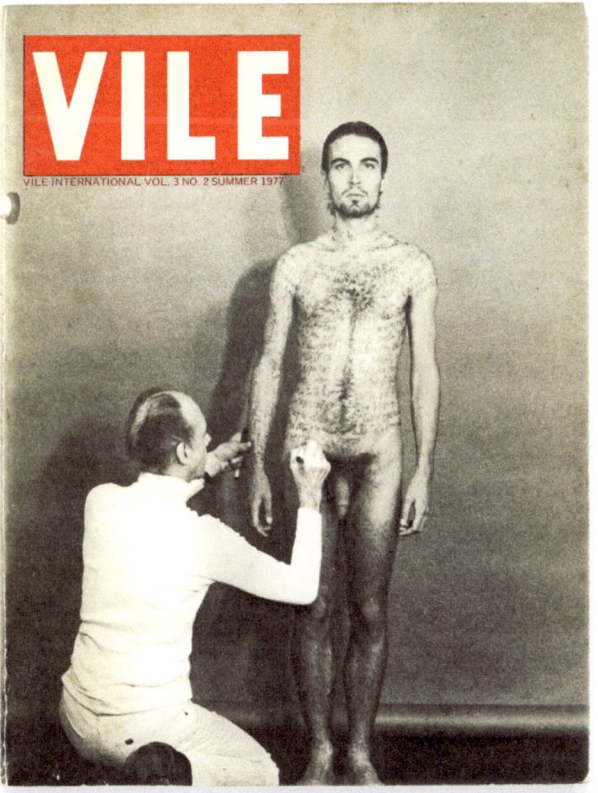

Vile, vol. 3, no. 2 (issue 5), Summer 1977
Offset, perfect bound, two-color offset wrappers, 10 ¾ × 8 ½ in. (27.3 × 21.6 cm)
Collection Philip Aarons and Shelley Fox Aarons

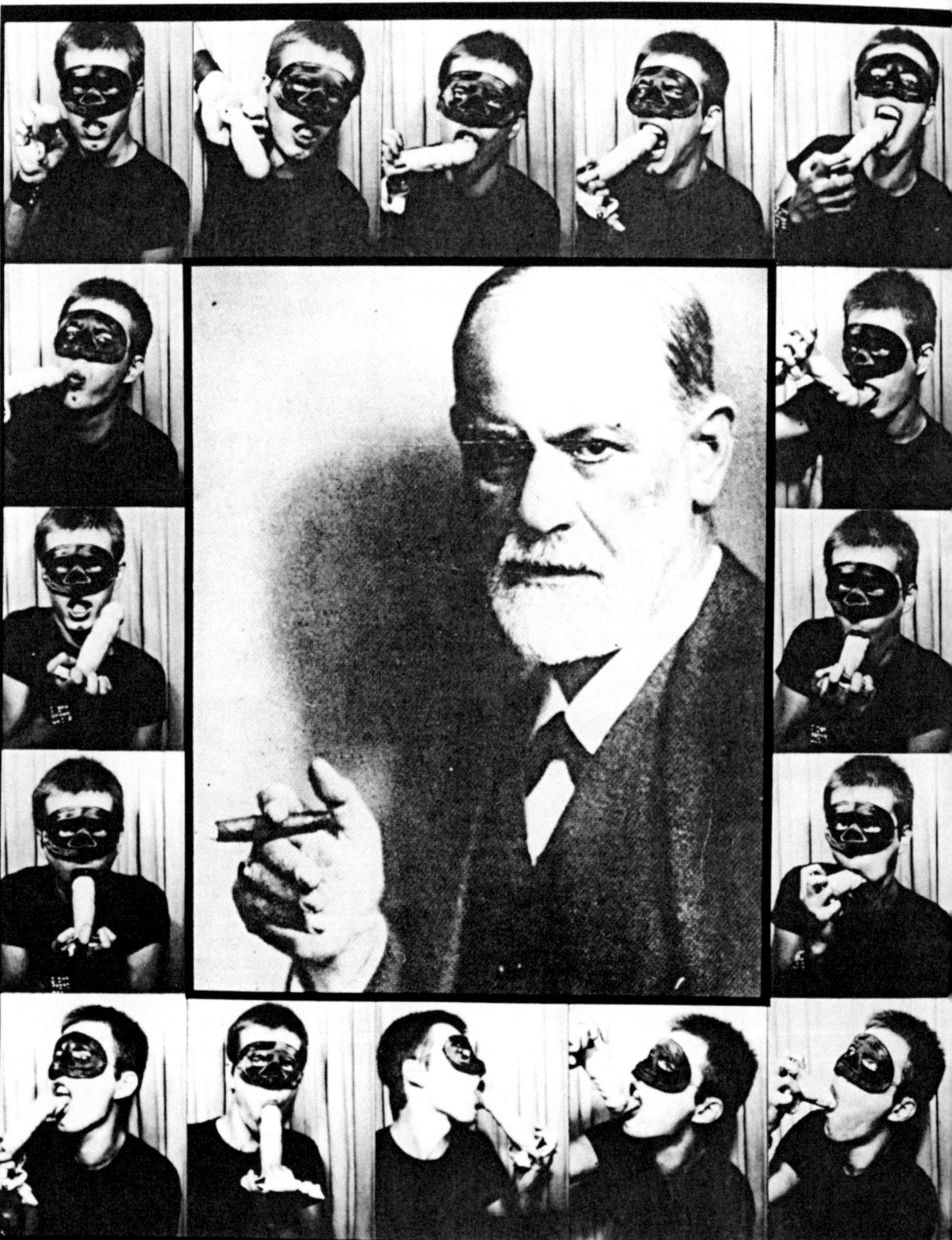

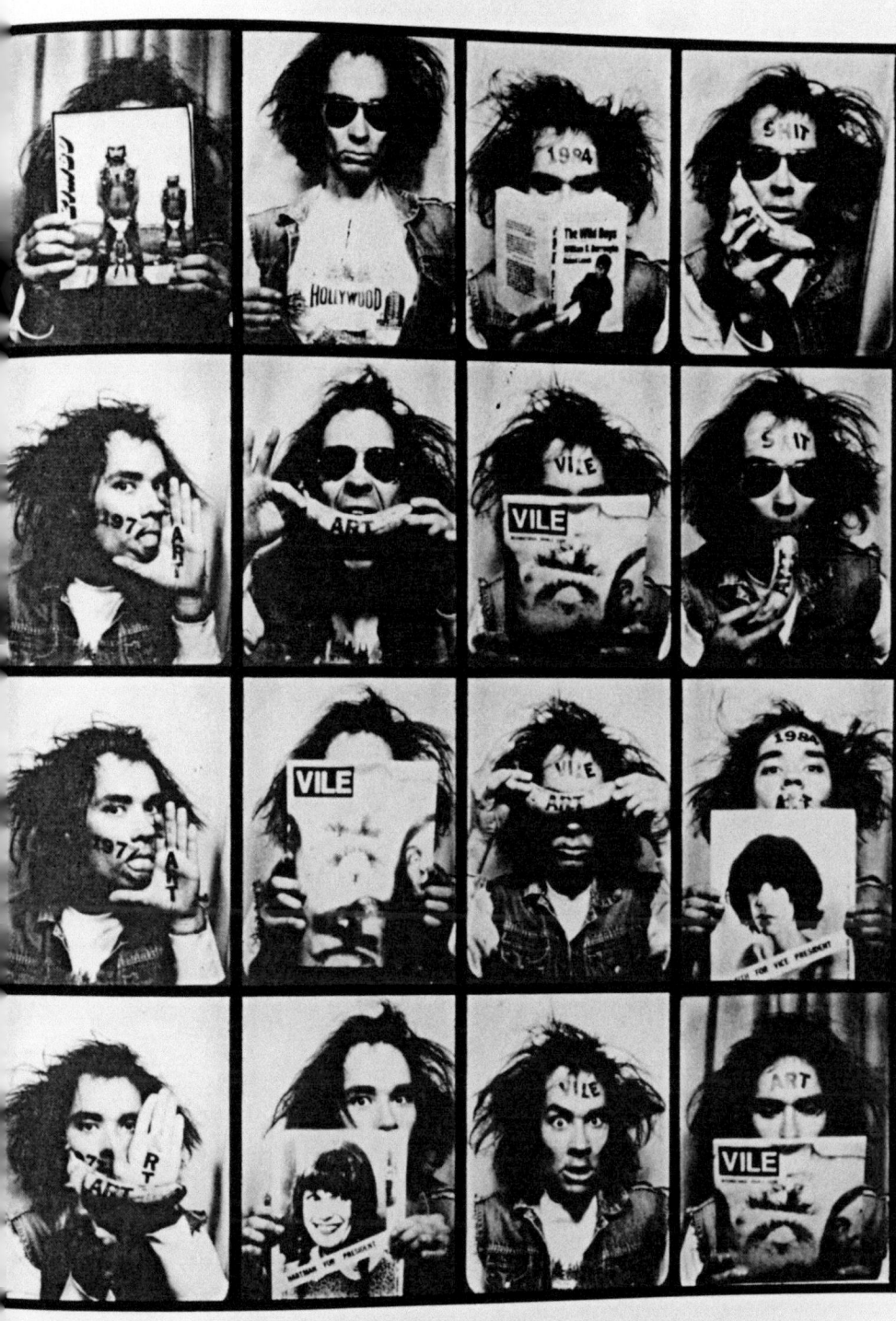

JERRY DREVA '77

← *Vile*, vol. 3, no. 2 (issue 5), Summer 1977
Offset, perfect bound, two-color offset wrappers,
10 ¾ × 8 ½ in. (27.3 × 21.6 cm)
Collection Philip Aarons and Shelley Fox Aarons

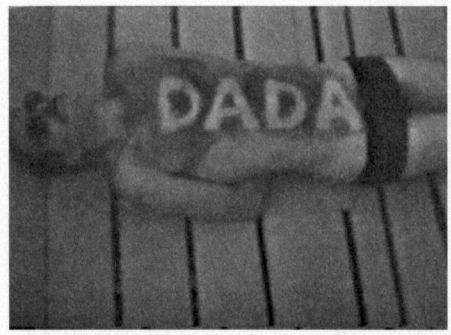 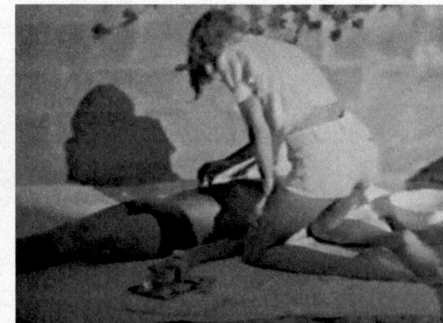 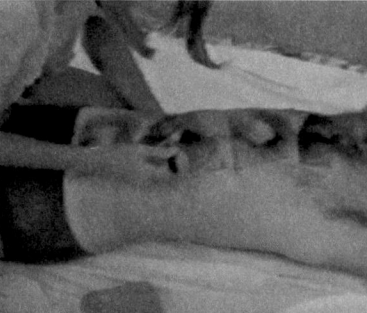

Anna Banana and Bill Gaglione
Stills from *Dada Shave*, 1975
8mm film; black and white, sound; 13 min.
Berkeley Art Museum & Pacific Film Archive

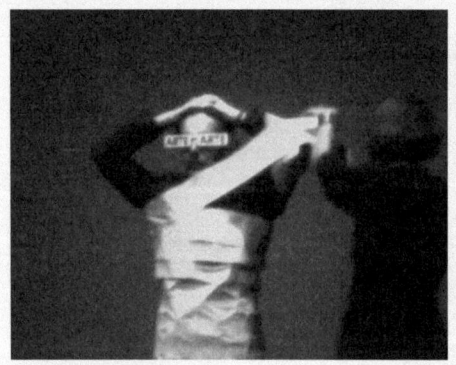 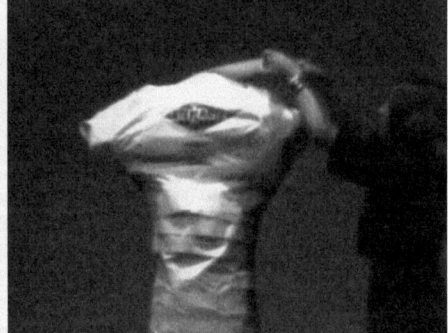 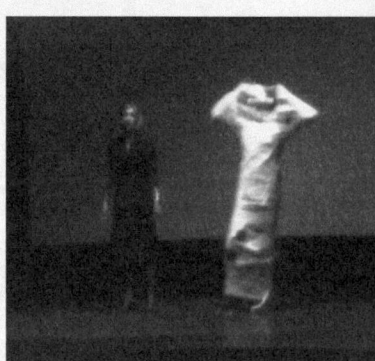

Anna Banana and Bill Gaglione
Stills from *Futurist Sound*, 1979
8mm film; black and white, sound; 46 min., 55 sec.
Western Front, Vancouver

Free   Free

Nude Death

SAVE TIME, MONEY & TROUBLE

Free-flowing

Free

Free

art on exhibit

Free

Ape movie to highlight

The Pop Artists have succeded in covering Dada with
snow. They empty the snow from their pipe, and bury
Dada. But Dada is digging it's way out. We have
more shovels than they have snow. Their grotesque
mouths are everywhere. They know that Dada can
prevent them from practising their odious trade:
Selling Art Expensively.
Art costs more than meat, more than men or women,
more than everything or nothing.
Art is man's monument to himself, but we need no
more monuments.
Art is an explanation of stupidity.
Art is a pharmaceutical product for imbeciles.
Art is a lobotomy to ease the conscience of society.
Buy your intricate autographs. Yes Art becomes more
inspired according to the auction prices.
Pop Art represents the dearth of ideas.
They have popped life, popped death, popped love,
popped hate, popped peace, popped war, popped blacks,
popped the illustrated newspapers, popped young girls,
popped young boys, popped tea bags, ice bags, and
paper bags, and they have even tried to pop illusion
into reality. How they must pop money!
Dada itself wants nothing.
We know nothing.
We do something to make ourselves and others understand
nothing.
We will come to nothing, because there is nothing to
come to.
And we the signed below declare ourselves nothing.
frankpicabiarichardpaulsonbillgaglionemontecazazza
timmankusirubybegonia

SAVE TIME, MONEY & TROUBLE!   BACKSTREET GIRLS

Free

Yes.

Zines by Artists: Post-Pop Punk Art

Branden W. Joseph

In 1973 New York artist and graphic designer John Dowd commandeered a Xerox machine, copying nearly two hundred fifty images from popular publications (mostly front covers), including Disney and DC comics, teen-idol rags, music periodicals, fan club newsletters, counterculture magazines, gay liberation tracts, and more. Bound like a dissertation and titled **From Dowdaland Archives**, the resulting volume catalogued the types of sources he incorporated into his publication **The Star** (1969, in collaboration with Stanley Stellar), various newsprint **"supplements"** he had been making since 1970, and the photocopied booklets such as **Life** that he sent to correspondence artist John Jack Baylin as part of Baylin's "John Dowd Fanny Club" project.[1] More specifically, *Dowdaland Archives* outlined a genealogy for his and Baylin's "major work," **Fanzine/Fanzini** (ca. 1972), a spiral-bound publication that collated and expanded upon materials mailed between the two artists.[2] The front and back covers of *Fanzine/Fanzini* appeared as the final two images of *Dowdaland Archives*, implicitly positioning them as the culmination of the lineage of publications previously pictured in the volume. As the opening page of *Dowdaland Archives*, Dowd appropriated the Xerox corporation's maintenance call sheet, listing himself as "Technical Representative" and altering it to read: "I have just made a service call on your ZINES machine," filling the space for the model number with the word "zines."

→ 4, 29
→ 26–27
→ 28
→ 28
→ 32–33

Dowd was aware of the history of zines. In a letter to Baylin reproduced in *Fanzine/Fanzini*, he located their origins in 1930s science fiction fan culture (correcting Baylin, who had thought the term "fanzine" Dowd's own coinage). In *Dowdaland Archives*, Dowd included covers of *Mojo Navigator* and *Who Put the Bomp!*, two pioneering rock fanzines of the mid-1960s and early 1970s that played important roles in establishing the early aesthetics of punk. Both were edited by music writer Greg Shaw, who, like Dowd, had a knowledge of earlier zine culture and drew connections between his publications and their historical precedents. *Bomp!*, Shaw explained, was not only "written and produced by amateurs," but relied on readers' participation, which, he contended, was the "essence of a fanzine."[3]

As the contents of *Dowdaland Archives* make clear, Dowd's project was informed not just by the history of the fanzine, but by the wider realm of pop culture. In it, reproductions from teenage fan magazines like *Hit Parader*, *Teen*, and *Tiger Beat!* far outnumber those from *Bomp!* and *Mojo*. Also prominently included in *Dowdaland Archives* was *Interview*, the film-cum-celebrity publication founded by Andy Warhol in 1969. Images of two recent covers of it appear just a few pages before those of *Fanzine/Fanzini*. As a Pop artist in the mid-1960s, Dowd had produced paintings of musicians including Bob Dylan, Shirley Ellis, and the Rolling Stones, figures he described as "the Madonnas and Crucified Christs of mid-twentieth century mass culture."[4] The collages Dowd created for zines like *The Star*—where the recently deceased Rolling Stones guitarist Brian Jones was depicted as a martyr, if not a Christ—continued to deploy such imagery for its iconographic signification, only now minus the high-art format of stretched canvas. In this transformation from canvas to zine, Dowd's artistic trajectory seems to have been authorized by Warhol's 1965 "retirement" from painting to pursue endeavors such as *Interview*.[5]

In drawing attention to the photocopier on its opening page, *Dowdaland Archives* demonstrates a degree of self-reflexiveness similar to that of Seth Siegelaub's better-known *Xerox Book* (1968). Unlike Siegelaub's publication, however, which turned inward, exemplifying the dryness of early Conceptualism by voiding itself of any content other than its own artistic strategies, Dowd's compendium gestured outward, embracing the kitschy, sexy, cool, and comic realms of popular music, celebrity fandom, countercultural lifestyles, and queer subjectivity. If I begin an essay on artists' zines by considering *Dowdaland Archives* as a meta-reflection on Dowd's zine-making practice, it is both because it reveals the type of attentiveness to medium expected of sophisticated artistic production (in referencing the Xerox machine), and because it incorporates popular cultural and subcultural materials outside those usually legitimated in the art world. The dual alliance with art and pop (in all its manifestations: pop music, pop culture, and Pop art), will prove central to the discussion that follows. Taking a cue from the inclusion in *Dowdaland Archives* of the proto-punk *Bomp!* and the post-Pop *Interview*, this essay will approach the legacy of artists' zines by considering their various engagements with punk and pop.

PUNK BEFORE PUNK

124, 128 ←
The artists' zines most closely associated with punk are undoubtedly those of Raymond Pettibon, which, beginning in 1981 with the first issue of **Tripping Corpse**, have become iconic for their depiction of the darker sides of the 1960s—particularly around violent, drugged-out hippies like Charles Manson—and their association with Southern California hardcore. The artists' zine's interaction with a notion of punk, however, appears as early as 1975 with the dim-
43 ←
inutive publication **Punks**, produced by Tim Mancusi of the Bay Area Dadaists, a group of correspondence and performance artists that also included Anna Banana, Ruby Begonia, Monte Cazazza, Charles Chickadel, Irene Dogmatic, and Bill Gaglione.[6] (To enhance their Dadaist credentials and mystique, Chickadel, Gaglione, and Mancusi often worked under the names "Arthur Cravan," "daddaland," and "dada processing," respectively.) Also in 1975, Gaglione contributed an image of artist Urs Lüthi holding a placard that has been modified to read "PUNK
47–49, 43 ←
ART" to Chickadel's zine **Quoz?** and produced several mailers on the theme of "**Detroit Punks**."[7] All these works predate the widespread adoption of the term "punk" to designate the then-emergent musical genre now associated with the term. Nevertheless, beginning in the early 1970s, rock fanzine *Bomp!* and Detroit music magazine *Creem* had already begun formulating what would become known as the punk aesthetic around a belated appreciation of 1960s garage bands.

As philosopher and cultural historian Bernard Gendron has observed, the early-1970s discourse around punk continued a trajectory of high art/pop culture interchanges that ran from the chansons of turn-of-the-twentieth-century Montmartre cafés to the Velvet Underground's presence in Warhol's Factory.[8] Although music writers Lester Bangs, Shaw, and others described the stripped-down confrontational style of 1960s garage bands as a counter to the pretentious virtuosity of 1970s "art rock," they did not laud it simply as anti-art, but characterized the style as a product of certain internal "tensions between art and pop."[9] "For Shaw, sixties punk style, though as lowbrow and pop as music could get, failed to achieve much popularity because," Gendron argues, "the 'sneering stud arrogance' of these bands" evinced "a certain (unconscious) element of underground, confrontative art," related, above all, to the artistic legacy of Dada. "The art/pop binary, in the discourses of punk," he continues, "was thus not consistently or only an oppositional binary. 'Art' was both an inseparable complement to 'pop' (that is, as avant-garde [art]) as well as its unrelenting opposite ('mainstream' art). There was, dare we say, a dialectical tension between art and pop in the new discursive formations denoted as 'punk.'"[10]

In their sometimes adolescent irreverence and vulgarity, as well as their celebration of
42 ←
iconoclastic vandals such as **László Tóth** (who attacked Michelangelo's *Pietà* with a hammer in 1972), the Bay Area Dadaists also superficially appeared to be anti-art. For them, however, such combative tactics were consciously related to the historical avant-garde legacies of both Dada and Futurism. Indeed, Banana and Gaglione became so enamored with the latter movement that they
54 ←
revived and toured **Futurist performances** throughout North America and Europe beginning in 1976.[11] As such, the Bay Area Dadaists' practice expressed not just a vaguely proto-punk attitude of sneering insolence, but also a structural parallel to the discursive dialectic of art and pop that informed the early discursive formulation of punk rock: what Gendron also describes as a "good art/bad art/pop ternary."[12] For these artists, the avant-garde of Dada and Futurism was located at the "good art" pole; institutionalized and profit-driven practices such as painting represented "bad art"; and the more democratic production and distribution allowed by correspondence art and their rapidly printed, low-cost "dadazines" denoted a populist (or "pop") impulse.[13]

Unlike the more individualized drawings and collages directed to specific recipients for which mail artist Ray Johnson is best known, practitioners in what Anna Banana called correspondence art's "second wave" liberally used photocopies and cheaply printed mailers to address a much larger group of readers.[14] In 1973 this practice was castigated as "quik-kopy krap" in *File*, the magazine produced by the Toronto Conceptual artists' group General Idea.[15] Although intended as an insult, the Bay Area Dadaists embraced the designation for its connotations of cheapness, ephemerality, and mass dissemination, flooding mailboxes with flyers sometimes expressly inscribed "Quickkopy Mail Art." It was as a means of assembling and further circulating such mailers that some of the first artists' zines were born.

Branden W. Joseph

San Diego–based artist Ken Friedman initiated the *New York Correspondence School Weekly Breeder* (or **NYCS Weekly Breeder**) in 1971 as a one-page mailer, based on the models of Ray Johnson's New York Correspondance [*sic*] School and Fluxus publications like *cc V TRE*. After producing eleven issues, Friedman passed the editorship of the *Breeder* to Stu Horn, who was known for the tightly gridded, text-heavy collage mailers he distributed under the title the **Northwest Mounted Valise**. In 1972 Horn passed the now two-page **Breeder** to Mancusi, who expanded it into a full-fledged zine of up to thirty-five pages, filled with reproduced mailers and collages that reflected the Bay Area Dadaists' interest in the historical avant-garde. → 36 → 37, 38–41

The **West Bay Dadaist**, launched by Chickadel in 1973 (and renamed **Quoz?** the following year), was produced in the quarto format of contemporary mini-comics—a genre that was also invoked by the third issue's cover image of a squatting Jesus contributed by Mancusi, an adept underground cartoonist.[16] Issue 2 boasted an inserted "8-pager" (a standard mini-comic format) by Horn, featuring on its second page the appropriated line "Do-It-Yourself," an invocation that would later be closely associated with the punk movement. → 46, 47–49

Banana founded **Vile**, the glossiest of the dadazines, in 1974, a year after *File* distanced itself from second-wave correspondence "krap." The first two issues of *Vile* featured what she termed "pure mail art"—that is, reproduced exactly as submitted—while issues 3 and 5 also contained "modified mail art."[17] The latter term designated Banana's practice of subversively infiltrating contributed materials into what initially appear to be typical *Life* magazine pages. Thus, for example, an image of the nude, paste-covered body of British artist Genesis P-Orridge appears alongside a modified ad for cigars.[18] → 50–53

MAKING THE PUNK (AND INDUSTRIAL) SCENE

Given mail art and early punk's similarly democratizing and confrontational aesthetics (as exemplified in *Vile*'s sometimes shocking covers), it is not surprising to find crossovers between the two scenes.[19] Dogmatic's correspondence zines changed from punningly canine-themed, as in **Rover's Romances** (1975), to avowedly punk, in *Insult* and **Insults** (both 1979).[20] She also formed the band SST with future Flipper guitarist Ted Falconi, packaging their sole vinyl release in a zine-like photocopied and hand-stapled sleeve. Zine makers and correspondence artists **World Imitation** transformed into the band Monitor. Tom Hosier's **Modern Correspondence Magazine** (1974–76) prominently featured proto-punk musicians Iggy Pop and the MC5 on its covers. Lisa Baumgardner's partly correspondence-based zines **Modern Girlz** (1977–78) and **Bikini Girl** (1978–90) promoted bands such as the Fleshtones and the Cramps.[21] And Jerry Dreva documented his move from glam to punk in his 1978 one-off zine **Jerry Dreva and Friends at 33-1/3**. → 86 → 112–13, 87 → 104–5; 106–7 → 74

Further connections can be found in the career of Bay Area Dadaist Monte Cazazza, whose work manifested a strongly confrontational, proto-punk attitude. (See, for instance, the collage he contributed to the **NYCS Weekly Breeder**.) Indeed, so closely does the 1973 issue of his zine **Nitrous Oxide** anticipate punk that certain contents would reappear in that context several years later. For instance, its photograph of future *Slash!* magazine writer Judith Bell with a revolver showed up again on the cover of the punk zine *Upsetter* in 1978. The song "Jesus Don't Come Through the Cotton," reproduced in *Nitrous Oxide* as a page of lyrics attributed to the band the Gillette Blades, would be released by Los Angeles punk band the Flesh Eaters on the 1980 LP *No Questions Asked*. (The same image of Bell with a gun also appeared on the band's 1978 EP *Disintegration Nation*.) → 40 → 44

Cazazza moved into music himself in 1979 with the release of the song "To Mom on Mother's Day" on the band Throbbing Gristle's Industrial Records label. (The lyrics had also been published in the first issue of *Nitrous Oxide*.) Cazazza had met future Throbbing Gristle members P-Orridge and Cosey Fanni Tutti when they came to California in 1976 as the performance art group COUM Transmissions. Cazazza would become central to the formulation of the artistic and musical movement that would become known as "Industrial Culture," collaborating with P-Orridge and Tutti on the **"Gary Gilmore Memorial Society"** photo shoot and co-editing, with Tana Emmolo-Smith, a collage-filled issue of *Industrial News* in 1979.[22] Cazazza and Emmolo-Smith, who made the transgressive, COUM-inspired film *SXXX-80* in 1980, also contributed → 45

88–89 ←
78 ←
90–91 ←
160–64 ←
172–75 ←
176–77 ←
366–67 ←
260–61, 245–47 ←
246–47, 361–65 ←
424 ←
94–99 ←
100–101 ←
99 ←
122 ←
202–4 ←
152 ←

to V. Vale's pioneering industrial zine *RE/Search* (launched 1980) and brought an industrial look to the sixth issue of photographer Jim Jocoy's **Widows and Orphans** (launched 1977). Skot Armstrong's zine **The PM Generation** (1979), dedicated to serial killer John Wayne Gacy, also contributed to the nascent industrial scene.

Vale's punk fanzine **Search & Destroy** (1977–79) foregrounded connections to correspondence art, particularly in a 1978 article on Dogmatic.[23] Glancing through its pages also reveals a surprising attentiveness to the diversity of gender, sexuality, and race in the California punk scene. Among the musicians prominently depicted in *Search & Destroy* were Black lesbian drummer Karla "Maddog" DuPlantier of the Controllers; Asian Americans Dianne Chai of the Alley Cats and Winston Tong of Tuxedomoon; and Latinx punks Alice Bag of the Bags; Baba Chenelle, Javier Escovedo, and Robert Lopez of the Zeros; Alejandro Escovedo of the Nuns; Tito Larriva and Charlie Quintana of the Plugz; and Carlos Cadona (a.k.a. 6025) of the Dead Kennedys (who soon left the band, which was later joined by influential Black drummer D. H. Peligro).

The diversity of the early punk scene was also stressed in other publications. In 1990 Black trans artist, zine maker, and musician Vaginal Davis produced an informative, if irreverent, chart for G. B. Jones and Bruce LaBruce's zine **J.D.s** that outlined the California punk scene's queer and racially non-hegemonic roots.[24] Included in Davis's inventory are "fierce Homo" Darby Crash of the Germs, "Homo Horn Dog" Tomata du Plenty of the Screamers, DuPlantier, and Alice Bag. After her punk band folded, Bag joined Davis's performance group Afro Sisters, which also included Fertile La Toyah Jackson (the titular figure of Davis's **Fertile La Toyah Jackson Magazine**). Later, Bag and Jackson would also perform in Davis's band **¡Cholita!** The Female Menudo.

Drawing from these antecedents, later artists' zines would continue to foreground and fight for punk's racial and sexual diversity. Among these titles are Osa Atoe's **Shotgun Seamstress** (launched 2006), Ramdasha Bikceem's **Gunk** (1990–94), Félix Endara's **Chica Loca** (1994–95) and **Chop Suey Spex** (1997–98), Brontez Purnell's **Fag School** (launched 2003), and BlackMass Publishing's **Stay Close to ME** (2021).

Mark Morrisroe and Lynelle White's zine **Dirt** emerged around 1975 from the early punk scene surrounding Boston's club The Rat and local musicians such as Willie "Loco" Alexander and Marc Thor. Primarily discussed in the context of Morrisroe's overall oeuvre, *Dirt*'s look was actually in line with that of Boston's other scandalously gossipy and willfully abject punk zines and broadsides including **The Nervous Reader, Boston Groupie News,** *Miscarriage,* and **Sleaze.**[25] Campier than most of its peers, *Dirt* featured faux reportage that initially targeted world-famous stars like Elizabeth Taylor, but later focused increasingly on local celebrities since, to its editors' bemusement, "a suprising [*sic*] number of people would rather read about Marc Thor than Liz!"[26] "Dirt Kids" Morrisroe and White soon began appearing in rival zines, such as Loretta Baretta and Carbon Monoxide's **Miscarriage** (which also published a special one-page insert in issue 5 of *Dirt*) and *Boston Groupie News,* which reported on the shooting that left Morrisroe partially disabled.[27]

Once punk was established as a genre, artists imported its energy and aggressiveness back into their art. As the AIDS crisis decimated the gay and trans communities, many zine-making artists expressed their outrage through their publications. After being diagnosed with HIV/AIDS, Gerardo Velázquez of the synth-punk band Nervous Gender—whose zine-like chapbook *never to be released lyrics* could be ordered to accompany their 1981 LP *Music from Hell*—produced a series of zines combining punk's attitude with what art historian Benjamin H. D. Buchloh has termed Conceptual art's "aesthetic of administration."[28] Titles like **First the Fags, The Gay Death List,** and **The Annals of Selective Annihilation** (all 1990) lampooned the necrophilic predisposition of the art market (in which prices generally increase upon an artist's death) with a savagery approaching that of HIV-positive artist Cory Roberts-Auli's zine **Infected Faggot Perspectives** (1991–93), or the confrontational activist publication *Diseased Pariah News* (1990–99).

Violence on the world stage was another cause for fury, and zines provided an energetic platform for its expression. Presciently recognizing the political aspirations behind certain subgenres of punk music and associated publications, the artist Carolee Schneemann emulated a zine format for her **The Lebanon Series** (1983). The hastily cut-and-pasted appearance of the booklet both reflected and served as a primer on the devastation wrought by the ongoing Lebanon War. By collecting and sequencing text fragments literally torn from the popular press, Schneemann turned the tropes of violence and abjection characteristically associated with punk music toward a feminist critique of the humiliations that were being inflicted upon the Lebanese population.

PUNK VIA POP

Restaging a mid-1960s photograph by Stephen Shore for the cover of **issue 8 of J.D.s** (shot by Jena von Brücker), editors G. B. Jones and Bruce LaBruce posed as Andy Warhol and Ingrid Superstar. LaBruce appears shirtless, a leather bracelet recalling the bondage scenes in Warhol's 1965 film *Vinyl*, while Jones adapts Warhol's pose to more closely resemble one of his 1963 self-portraits. The photocopy's high contrast additionally recalls the grainy, blown-out imagery of *Andy Warhol's Index (Book)* of 1967, while the term "SWISH!" in bold letters to the right references Warhol's recollection of being too out ("too swish") for peers Robert Rauschenberg and Jasper Johns.[29] → 164

Warhol and his Factory likewise served as points of reference for Detroit-based art collective-cum-experimental band Destroy All Monsters (DAM), founded in 1974 by Mike Kelley, Cary Loren, Niagara, and Jim Shaw. **Destroy All Monsters Magazine** (1976–79), edited and designed by Loren with contributions from the others, frequently invoked Warhol, casting Niagara as a post-Goth Nico to the rest of the band's Velvet Underground—one of the relatively few musical interests on which the members of DAM all agreed.[30] The Velvet Underground's association with Warhol and "strong emphasis on avant-garde experimentalism and bohemianism" put forth an "art/pop dialectic" similar to early punk, allying it, as Gendron contends, with the discourse being formulated in the pages of *Bomp!* and *Creem*.[31] (Indeed, Kelley invoked Bangs's proto-punk manifesto "James Taylor Marked for Death"—originally published in 1971 in *Bomp!*—in relation to DAM.)[32] → 114–18

Jones, LaBruce, von Brücker, and others around *J.D.s* patterned themselves on the Factory group more explicitly than did Destroy All Monsters. Their assumed identities and fabricated superstardom extended from the zine's pages into underground films shot by Jones, LaBruce, Candy Parker, and Suzy Richter. Although Jones and LaBruce would go on to longer and more celebrated filmmaking careers, Richter's little-known 1990 movie **Cross Your Heart** most overtly revolves around the zine. It shows Richter (who had graced the cover of **J.D.s issue 3**) picking up the phone and calling Jones after leafing through a copy of *J.D.s* issue 4, the cover of which shows their associate Cizzy Ché with a Super-8 camera. → 167 → 160

J.D.s is most widely recognized for championing "homocore" or "queercore," a musical genre pioneered by Jones's band Fifth Column, which also influenced the Riot Grrrl movement. Now among the more prominent titles of the era, *J.D.s* actually followed in the wake of important earlier zines that similarly made connections between Toronto's punk and experimental film scenes. Foremost among them were **Hide**, founded by Parker and edited by Jones with Fifth Column bandmates Caroline Azar and (briefly) Kathleen Pirrie Adams, and **Dr. Smith**, founded and edited by Parker with Jean Young. → 156–57 → 158–59

Spurred in part by *J.D.s*, the Toronto scene would generate a succession of competing (and sometimes feuding) queer artists' zines, including von Brücker's **Jane and Frankie** zines (1989–93); **Bimbox** (by Johnny Noxzema and Rex Boy, 1989–94); **Salmon Hut** (by Luis Jacob et al., 1987–88); **Double Bill** (by Azar, von Brücker, Jones, Noxzema, and Boy, 1991–2001); **Monstar** (by LaBruce, 1992); **This Is the Salivation Army** (launched in 1996 by Scott Treleaven); and **Gay Goth Scene** (by Paul P. and Joel Gibb, launched 2003). From a different branch of artists' and activists' film and video came Mirha-Soleil Ross and Xanthra Phillippa MacKay's groundbreaking trans zine **Gendertrash** (1993–95). → 168 → 168, 169 → 168, 169 → 216–21, 326–28 → 208–10

In actuality, *J.D.s* formed merely one outlet for Jones and LaBruce's critique of straight (in all senses of the term) culture. It was accompanied not only by their music and films, but also by their contributions to more mainstream punk zines such as *Flipside* and *Maximum Rocknroll*. They also contributed to the academic journal *CineAction!*, where LaBruce served as editor under the name Bryan Bruce. There, LaBruce and Jones contributed "The Superstar Story," which approached Warhol's legacy from a feminist perspective, as well as a mock interview in which

"Bruce" talked with LaBruce and Jones about their films and "silly little fanzine, *J.D.s*, a small publication made by, for, and about homopunks."[33]

In the 1970s many zine makers looked to Pop art as a precedent. As artists, however, most of them avoided or even opposed the medium of painting. (One exception was Joey Terrill, whose canvases of queer Chicano culture paralleled his **Homeboy Beautiful** zines of 1978–79.) As mentioned previously, the publication of Warhol's *Interview* magazine served to justify John Dowd's move from painting into print. Warhol also legitimated Jerry Dreva and Robert Lambert's brand of "life performance," particularly as part of Les Petites Bon-Bons, artist-groupies deeply immersed in Los Angeles's glam rock scene.[34] Although impressed by Pop art paintings, which he first encountered in an exhibition in London, Dreva came to see Warhol's fabricated artistic persona as the most significant aspect of his practice. "Warhol," he explained, "was the first person in our time who became more important than his work. Films, the Velvet Underground, his whole world was his support system."[35] In the local rock press—which often featured the Bon-Bons and which they, in turn, made into flyers that were mailed or hand-delivered backstage to such figures as Warhol and Lou Reed—Dreva, in wig and sunglasses, was once misidentified (perhaps jokingly) as the Pop artist himself.[36]

Originally conceived as a set of "zine-format bound zerox pages," Lambert's glossy, offset-printed **Egozine** was founded in 1975 to showcase and theorize "Lifestyle Art and Creative Personal Mythology."[37] In it, Lambert discussed his and Dreva's adoption and transformation of performative personas as a type of postmodern appropriation, precociously associated with the idea of "pastiche."[38] As each issue was to be dedicated to a single "life artist," beginning with Lambert, its announcement declared: "You are egotisticly [*sic*] NOT invited to send your contribution to EGOZINE."[39] Lambert, however, proved a tough act to follow, and the subsequent two issues of *Egozine* functioned more like typical art magazines, covering a range of practices rather than focusing on a single individual.

Science Holiday, a prolific zine-making group that formed around correspondence artist Skot Armstrong, also claimed a Pop art lineage. "We might bear comparison on first meeting to thee old Warhol gang at thee Factory imitating Astro Boy imitating Marcel Duchamp," they declared.[40] Like Les Petites Bon-Bons, Science Holiday advocated for an artistic inhabitation of daily life, which would become the object of documentation and dissemination in print. "We are a movie," they noted:

> We perform; both arty arts and on thee streets. We put out all sorts er megazines as a presentational format for other boys and girls who place this same importance on living their art. Were sort er like walty disney in that respect only our hearts belong to uncle andy warhol, and grandpa uncle bill burroughs and all those nice boys who got somuch of that initial work out of thee way. Were their vision manifested as people living.[41]

Such cycles of performance, documentation, and dissemination formed feedback loops. In order to understand them, John Jack Baylin (who came to know Lambert in Los Angeles) proposed in 1974 to teach a course at the University of California, Los Angeles, titled "Workshop in Information Processes," that drew on subjects including "cybernetics, systems theory, 'process art,' [and] the 'flow of information.'"[42]

The Bay Area Dadaists also referenced Pop art, unabashedly reproducing Warhol's countenance, stamped signature, and *Interview* letterhead on their mailers. More confrontational than many of their contemporaries, however, the group also proclaimed their opposition to Pop in a **mailer** that adapted Francis Picabia's 1920 *Dada Manifesto*. "The Pop Artists have succeded [*sic*] in covering Dada with snow," they declared. "They know that Dada can prevent them from practising their odious trade: Selling Art Expensively." "Buy your intricate autographs," they continued. "Yes Art becomes more inspired according to the auction prices."[43] The group's "Quickkopy Mail Art" missives and cheaply produced dadazines extended Pop's use of repro-ductive technologies such as silkscreen printing, while avoiding high-art formats and prices. Whereas Dreva and Lambert embraced Warhol's transformation of artist into celebrity, the

80–83 ←

70–73 ←

76–77 ←

55 ←

Branden W. Joseph

Bay Area group undermined the notion of singular artistic identity and fame via collectivity, obfuscation (often through the use of pseudonyms), self-deprecation (such as Gaglione's frequent self-designation in mailers as a "jerk"), and confusion (as in postcards declaring "this is not dadaland" or "dada processing" under Gaglione's and Mancusi's images, or publishing a picture of Warhol in *Vile* with the caption "Imitation/Bill Gaglione").[44]

The wall works that Richard Kern and Montanna Houston put up in the streets (or, in one instance in 1981, mailed to a North Carolina gallery) reformatted the text/image collaborations they published in Kern's zines into a typology resembling Warhol's gridded silkscreen paintings. Kern met Houston when the latter began contributing to Kern's scrappy fiction/punk zine the *Heroin Addict*. After moving to New York in 1979, Kern used the photocopier of Houston's employer as an after-hours publishing house, credited publicly as "Montanna Prinnerz" or "Montannaprinners." Houston's writings and ransom-note-like poetry, composed of cutout headlines, appeared throughout Kern's serialized zine, as its title changed from the **Heroin Addict** to the **Valium Addict** and then to **Dumb Fucker** (the last a self-deprecating reference to being a "rural" outsider in the city). In 1981 the two artists produced the visually arresting one-off collaborations **A Key for the Streets of Fear and Other Stories** and **You Should Taste What Happens to: You**, which crossed the text/image typology of Conceptual art with the cut-and-paste typography of punk graphics. Surrounding Houston's cut-up poems with a grid of Kern's photocopied photos, the pair's wall works of the early 1980s spatialized the aesthetic they had developed in the zines. Both the format and the imagery, particularly of police and automobiles, prove reminiscent of Warhol's *Death and Disaster* series of paintings from the early 1960s. By using the photocopier, Kern and Houston extended the mechanical, reproductive implications of Warhol's silkscreen paintings to an expansive, even spectacular scale, while avoiding the high-art associations of paint on stretched canvas.

→ 142–45
→ 142, 144

ART WORLD ALTERNATIVES

In 1983 Kern mounted a grid of photocopies in Mike Bidlo and David Wojnarowicz's Ward Line Pier Project, an exhibition installed at the piers along New York's Hudson River. At the time, Kern, Houston, Wojnarowicz, and photographer and filmmaker Tommy Turner were close, all contributing regularly to Kern's zines. Wojnarowicz, in addition to publishing fiction (which ran alongside writings by Irene Dogmatic and others), also submitted to **Dumb Fucker** a faux children's drawing of his signature burning-house motif and an altered comic in which the character Archie gets crabs from the school principal, Mr. Weatherbee.[45] The two issues of Turner's zine **Redrum** (1985) featured more substantial, stand-alone comic inserts by Wojnarowicz in which Archie and the gang become heroin addicts or go on a homicidal rampage à la the Manson Family. (Interestingly, G. B. Jones would make her own series of altered *Archie* comics, which appeared in the zines *Hide* and *Dr. Smith*.)

→ 145
→ 148–50

As its title suggests, *Redrum* ("murder" spelled backward) was devoted to the cultural fascination with violence and homicide. The first issue's cover referenced attempted presidential assassin John Hinckley Jr. and serial killer David "Son of Sam" Berkowitz, while the second was devoted to "Satanic" Long Island teenaged killer Ricky Kasso. The Kasso case also formed the subject of Turner and Wojnarowicz's 1985 film *Where Evil Dwells*, which was titled after a tabloid headline reproduced in *Redrum* issue 2. Originally intended to be a feature-length film, the movie included prolonged scenes set in hell (presided over by artist Joe Coleman, in the role of Satan), which extended the two directors' interest in the macabre, previously manifest in the double-exposed **"Ghost Photos"** they shot in cemeteries after late-night shifts working at the Peppermint Lounge nightclub.

→ 151

Providing an alternative to the institutionalized art world, Bidlo and Wojnarowicz's Ward Line Pier Project responded to an impulse similar to that motivating artists' turn to rock clubs, whether as members of bands (as in Kern's Black Snakes, Wojnarowicz's 3 Teens Kill 4, and Barbara Ess's the Static), or as organizers, exhibitors, and denizens. Baumgardner's zine *Bikini Girl* was associated with New York's Mudd Club and Club 57. The zine was particularly closely aligned with the aesthetic of Club 57, where *Bikini Girl* hosted movie nights, as both Baumgardner and Club 57's organizer Ann Magnuson reveled in the ironic appropriation of trashy, retro, and stereotypical female roles.[46] This subversion occurred throughout the pages of *Bikini Girl*, with such juxtapositions as vintage beauty ads and sadomasochistic imagery (the latter sometimes drawn from Baumgardner's employment as a bondage model).

Baumgardner's musical tastes tended toward garage bands—she was close to Miriam Linna, drummer for the Cramps, Nervus Rex, and the Zantees (all referenced in *Bikini Girl*)—and her zine criticized the No Wave movement in no uncertain terms.[47] By contrast, Ess's zine **Just**

108–11 ←

Another Asshole (1978–87) was strongly affiliated with No Wave. With its scornful title scrawled indiscriminately over images of everyone from mystic/philosopher George Gurdjieff to poet/rocker Patti Smith, Ess's publication initially adopted the photocopied aesthetic typical of the zine only to transform in subsequent issues into an offset-printed tabloid, an LP, a magazine insert, a pulp paperback, and an art catalogue. The third issue of *Just Another Asshole*, which came out in 1979, prominently featured a two-page spread of lyrics from the wider No Wave scene, including A Band, Disband, Kim Gordon and Nina Canal, Theoretical Girls, Wharton Tiers, Youth in Asia, and Ess's own bands, Daily Life and the Static.

Gendron discusses this era of New York's downtown scene in terms of "punk art," a short-lived label briefly touted in the press and to which Baumgardner, Ess, Houston, Kern, Turner, and Wojnarowicz would almost certainly not answer.[48] (Gendron does not seem to have known of Gaglione's invocation of the term "punk art" in 1975.)[49] Nevertheless, a variant of the "good art/bad art/pop ternary" structuring the early discursive formation of punk would seem to apply. Here, elitist art forms, however vanguard, figured as *bad art* (dry, orthodox Conceptualism again proving a target), while art that assumed more populist forms (however *un*popular the results might be commercially) served as the *good*—whether the approach was experimental (as in No Wave music and film), retro "trash" (as in neo-garage bands, campy exploitation films, and vaudeville-like performances at Club 57), or a bit of both (as in the Cinema of Transgression movement in which Kern would become a central figure).[50]

Now firmly established as a punk and post-punk typology, the zine functioned as an analogue of, and adjunct to, the artistic position that Gendron finds common to both proto-punk music and so-called punk art. As such, artists' zines of this period not only chronicled and created alliances with alternative venues such as Club 57, but also served as spaces for oppositional and populist artistic practices. It might be argued, in fact, that the structure elucidated above—of an opposition to established art practice and an alliance with popular cultural or subcultural formations, all the while maintaining an internal art/pop dialectic of its own—forms the artists' zine's general DNA.

The function of the artists' zine is staged with particular self-consciousness in Johanna

258–59, 252–55 ←

Fateman's **The Opposite, Part One** (1996). Fateman had previously produced the zine **Snarla** (1993–94) with Miranda July in the context of the feminist post-punk Riot Grrrl movement spearheaded by Fateman's friend Kathleen Hanna of Bikini Kill (and future bandmate of Fateman in Le Tigre).

250–51 ←

Hanna's own zines, most notably **My Life with Evan Dando, Popstar** (1993), served as partial inspiration for a zine trilogy Fateman made while studying for her MFA at New York's School

258 ←

of Visual Arts: *The Opposite*; **My Need to Speak on the Subject of Jackson Pollock** (1996); and

256–57 ←

Artaud-Mania . . . the diary of a fan (1997). In the vein of experimental writer Kathy Acker (who took on the persona of a murderess in her 1973 publication *The Childlike Life of the Black Tarantula*), Hanna assumed the role of "a female stalker."[51] Confounding the boundary between fiction and nonfiction, Hanna's exaggerated love/hate relationship with Dando played out through the hierarchies of race, class, gender, and beauty operating in the realm of pop music—and Pop art (see, for instance, her condemnation of Warhol for "trying to act like he was questioning notions of fine art," while "FOR REAL exploiting certain people [workers] and certain revolutionary conceptions IN ORDER TO buy himself two thousand dollar black 'Mammy' cookie jars").[52]

In *The Opposite*, Fateman adopted "the form of the punk polemic" to effect an analogous critique of the mid-1990s art world.[53] Most interesting in our context is how, amid critical discussions of the works of Robert Ryman and Vito Acconci, Fateman lauded the 1995 LP *Real Fiction* by the Fakes, a one-off group composed of Hanna and members of the bands Nation of Ulysses and Kicking Giant. Whereas music critic Greil Marcus, reviewing *Real Fiction* in the pages of *Artforum*, described it reductively as "an artfully crude rock opera about child abuse," Fateman defended the record as a "cross-genre" example of "conceptual art," which (much like Hanna's *Dando* zine) interrogated "notions of 'authenticity' in pop music and Identity."[54] That Marcus could not recognize it as such, Fateman argued, stemmed in part from the fact that "the Fakes record isn't art. It's got nothing to do with galleries or the art market. [T]his record was put out on the Chainsaw label, a lesbian-owned business not affiliated with a major label, or major label distribution."[55] Fateman's analysis does not merely emulate the tenor of punk discourse; in the tension formed by her seemingly contradictory description of *Real Fiction* as both "not art" and "conceptual art," Fateman's discussion once again evinces what we have come to see as the fundamental art/pop dialectic underlying the punk aesthetic. In this instance, Fateman situates the Fakes outside institutionalized, market-oriented art production and allies them instead with the wider popular realm via the form, format, and mode of distribution proper to the LP.

For its part, Fateman's *The Opposite* makes a claim to being not only a form of artistic production structurally analogous to the Fakes (the format of the zine, like that of the LP, being generally opposed to high art and populist in bent), but also its functional equivalent within the genre of art criticism. Disseminated via a low-cost zine, rather than a glossy, mainstream art magazine, Fateman's mode of art critical writing opposed that of Marcus, who served as a figure-head for "the liberal establishment of cultural criticism," as she put it.[56] This subtext was made still clearer in Fateman's zine *Artaud-Mania*, in which she emulates the voice of the fan, in place of that of the mainstream liberal critic, the example of which was Donald Kuspit (another regular *Artforum* contributor and one of her professors at SVA).

Miranda July would likewise embrace and expand the format of the zine, with her **Big Miss Moviola** project (launched 1995, later renamed *Joanie 4 Jackie* due to copyright issues). → 264–65 Soliciting the open submission of videotapes from female filmmakers, July compiled them onto a single VHS tape and redistributed them as a "chainletter" with an accompanying program. The references and parallels within July's project are multiple: it draws not only on punk's DIY ethos and the solicitation of community input typical of the fanzine, but also on the egalitarian aims of the New York Film-Makers' Cooperative and the ideals of audience enlightenment behind Russian Productivism.[57] The last association was made graphically manifest in the adaptation of Aleksandr Rodchenko's 1924 Kino Glaz (Film Eye) poster for the 1996 *Underwater Chainletter* booklet designed by July and Julia Bryan-Wilson.

For July, every woman is a potential moviemaker, in that they continually internalize a sense of being watched by the male gaze; they need only to externalize that perspective to become actual film- or videomakers themselves.[58] The trope of female surveillance formed the basis of July's 1998 short film **The Amateurist**, distributed on the tape *Joanie 4 Jackie 4 Ever*. July's mission → 267 of making viewers into producers was further realized in her **Nobody Ever Told Me** (1996–2001), → 267 a project that entailed setting up a video camera at screenings so that audience members (most of them female) could express aspects of forbidden wisdom, the collective results of which were then screened as part of the program.

THE ARTISTS' ZINE AS APPARATUS

The 1990s and early 2000s brought an explosion of artists' zine-making activity, fueled, at least in part, by the energies surrounding the proliferation of queer and Riot Grrrl zines. In becoming a recognizable artistic format, however, the artists' zine does not simply take its place as one more self-reflexive modernist medium. Nor is it defined solely by the characteristics generally attributed to zines: cheapness and ephemerality, communal participation and feedback, and unmediated self-expression—although all these factors play parts in artists' zines. Rather, it might be argued that the artist's zine, at least within the lineage sketched above, operates as an apparatus in which an internal art/pop dialectic fuels an opposition to established "high art" practices in favor of popular cultural or subcultural alliances.

For the artists' zines that have appeared since the turn of the twenty-first century, the affiliated subcultural fields go far beyond punk music to encompass graffiti (Dash Snow);

skateboarding (Mark Gonzales, Ed Templeton); snowboarding, street basketball, and urban hip-hop (Ari Marcopoulos); DIY fashion (Susan Cianciolo, K8 Hardy); adolescent girlhood (Maggie Lee, Deanna Templeton); bicycling and train hopping (Greta Snider); backyard wrestling (Cameron Jamie), and more. By the 1990s, the valorized (or "good art") pole of artistic practice described by Gendron, previously found in the historical avant-garde (in, for instance, the work of the Bay Area Dadaists) or in aspects of Warhol's oeuvre (as in the work of Les Petites Bon-Bons, Destroy All Monsters, the circle around *J.D.s*, Richard Kern, and others mentioned above), began to include the legacy of the zine itself. Hence, a group like the feminist collective LTTR (established 2001), which counts zine-maker K8 Hardy and co-originator of the **Projet Mobilivre-Bookmobile** Ginger Brooks Takahashi among its founders, could bring the energies of the Riot Grrrl movement more firmly into the New York art world (which it sought both to infiltrate and to transform), while drawing upon earlier moments in feminist artists' zine production. Whether directly or at some remove, the multimedia format of the zine **LTTR** recalls earlier innovative publications such as Laurel Beckman and Kate Sorensen's "metazine" **Lucky** (1988–90) and Beckman, Sorensen, and Ryan Hill's **Joy** (1994–97).[59]

334–35 ←

330–32 ←
222–23 ←
222 ←

Conceiving of the artists' zine as a productive apparatus, driven by a populist impulse against an exclusive and institutionalized artistic culture, helps explain why it does not seem entirely incongruous to think of an artist like Beverly Buchanan as allied with the ethos of punk (however far that may have been from her musical tastes), or why BlackMass Publishing's zines can valorize her in the same format in which they pay homage to the Black punk group Bad Brains.[60] Buchanan turned to making zines in the 1980s, the same period during which she was distancing herself from the established New York art world in favor of engaging with the vernacular architecture of Black communities in the South. A publication like **Hope This Helps You Survive Your Gallery Visit** (undated) demonstrates how her zine practice was vectored (humorously) against the mainstream art world.

271 ←

That the artist's zine continues to function fruitfully as a productively oppositional apparatus is testified by its having become such a vibrant platform for a generation of artists of color over the past decade. Examples in this volume include BlackMass Publishing (headed by Yusuf Hassan and Kwamé Sorrell), Neta Bomani, Lizania Cruz, Demian DinéYazhi', Maggie Lee, Devin N. Morris, Jordan Nassar, and Kandis Williams. All these artists—and, of course, many, many more—continue to productively harness the zine's oppositional energies in order to address and enfranchise aspects of their communities in the face of the often exclusionary forces of the institutionalized art world.

NOTES

1 At least two copies of *From Dowdaland Archives* exist: one is in the collection of Luke and Noel Dowd, and another is at the Morris and Helen Belkin Art Gallery, University of British Columbia, Vancouver (the archive of the latter is hereafter referenced as "Belkin"). On the John Dowd Fanny Club, see Kirsten Olds, "Fannies and Fanzines: Mail Art and Fan Clubs in the 1970s," *Journal of Fandom Studies* 3, no. 2 (2015): 171–93.

2 John Dowd described *Fanzine/Fanzini* as "a major work" in a letter to Marcel Idea (Michael Morris), November 18, 1972; Belkin.

3 Greg Shaw, in Bernard Gendron, *Between Montmartre and the Mudd Club: Popular Music and the Avant-Garde* (Chicago: University of Chicago Press, 2002), 229.

4 John Dowd, "Rock, Pop, Folk Heroes, 1965–66," exhibition brochure (Reading, PA: Albright College Library Art Gallery, 1966); reproduced as a "John Dowd Fan Club" mailer; Belkin.

5 On Warhol's "retirement," see Jean-Pierre Lenoir, "Paris Impressed by Warhol Show: Artist Speaks of Leaving Pop Pictures for Films," *New York Times*, May 13, 1965.

6 Emily Hage, "Bay Area Dadazines and Punk Zines in 1970s San Francisco: Interactive, Ephemeral, Live," *American Periodicals* 27, no. 2 (2017): 180–205.

7 *Quoz?* 3, no. 9 (March 1975): 39.

8 Gendron, *Between Montmartre and the Mudd Club*.

9 Ibid., 228.

10 Ibid., 238.

11 Banana and Gaglione drew upon Michael Kirby, *Futurist Performance* (New York: Dutton, 1971), which included Victoria Nes Kirby's translation of a selection of historical Italian Futurist scripts.

12 Gendron, *Between Montmartre and the Mudd Club*, 241.

13 See Klaus Groh, "Mail Art and the New Dada," in *Correspondence Art: Source Book for the Network of International Postal Art Activity*, ed. Michael Crane and Mary Stofflet (San Francisco: Contemporary Arts Press, 1984), 75. Groh's perspective was informed by a two-page letter from Anna Banana, April 26, 1974; Belkin.

14 Anna Banana, "Mail Art Canada," in *Correspondence Art*, 233.

15 Ibid., 250. "Quik-kopy krap" seems to be Banana's paraphrase of the criticism by Hudson Ant Farm (Hudson Marquez) of "everything by typewritten Quikkopy"; "Letters to the Editor," *File* 2, no. 3 (September 1973): 63.

Branden W. Joseph

16 Tim Mancusi produced two issues of the mini-comic *Sin City* (1972–73). On contemporary eight-page comics, see Bruce Chrislip, *The Minicomix Revolution, 1969–1989* (self-published, 2015), 14–27.

17 Anna Banana, "Editorial," *Vile* 3, no. 1 (issue 3) (December 1975): 2.

18 "Pictures to the Editors," ibid., 20.

19 See Monte Cazazza's and Jimmy DeSana's images, which appear, respectively, on the covers of *Vile*'s first and second issues, both published in 1974. On connections between the Bay Area Dadaists and punk, see Hage, "Bay Area Dadazines and Punk Zines."

20 Dogmatic describes *Insult* as "punk" in Irene Dogmatic, "Xerox Art" (n.d.) online at judymalloy.net/newmedia/irene.html.

21 *Modern Girlz* was once disparagingly likened to the "second wave" correspondence scene by being characterized as "more of that dada crap." "Letters to the Editor," *Bikini Girl* 1 (June 1978): n.p.

22 *Industrial News* 2 (June 1979). The idea of "Industrial Culture" would be codified in a 1983 special issue of the zine-cum-journal *RE/Search* featuring Cazazza; *RE/Search*, no. 6/7: "Industrial Culture Handbook" (1983).

23 "SST: Irene Dogmatic's Mail Art Correspondences," *Search & Destroy* 8 (1978): 23.

24 Portions of Davis's lengthy chart, titled "Rectus/Lingus," appear in *J.D.s* 7 (1990).

25 *The Nervous Reader* was produced by Willie Alexander; *Sleaze* by Marc Thor.

26 *Dirt* 3 (ca. 1977): n.p.

27 *Boston Groupie News* 9 (January 1977). In 1977 Morrisroe, who was working as a hustler, was shot in the back by a client, an injury that left him with a noticeable limp for the remainder of his life.

28 Benjamin H. D. Buchloh, "Conceptual Art, 1962–1969: From the Aesthetic of Administration to the Critique of Institutions," *October* 55 (Winter 1990): 105–43.

29 Andy Warhol and Pat Hackett, *Popism: The Warhol Sixties* (New York: Harcourt, 1980), 11.

30 Mike Kelley, "To the Throne of Chaos Where the Thin Flutes Pipe Mindlessly" (1993), *Book Beat*; thebookbeat.com/backroom/to-the-throne-of-chaos-where-the-thin-flutes-pipe-mindlessly-by-mike-kelley.

31 Gendron, *Between Montmartre and the Mudd Club*, 240.

32 Mike Kelley, "What Destroy All Monsters Means to Me," liner notes to *Destroy All Monsters, 1974–1976*, three-CD set, produced by Ecstatic Peace! and Father Yod, 1994; see Lester Bangs, "James Taylor Marked for Death," *Who Put the Bomp!* (Winter–Spring 1971); repr. in Bangs, *Psychotic Reactions and Carburetor Dung*, ed. Greil Marcus (New York: Knopf, 1987), 53–81.

33 Gloria Berlin and Bryan Bruce, "The Superstar Story," *CineAction!* 7 (Winter 1986–87): 52–63.; and Bryan Bruce, "Underground," *CineAction!* 16 (May 1989): 75.

34 See Kirsten Olds, "'Gay Life Artists': Les Petites Bonbons and Camp Performativity in the 1970s," *Art Journal* 72, no. 2 (Summer 2013): 17–33.

35 Jerry Dreva, "Have You Heard from Dreva?" *High Performance* 3, no. 1 (issue 9) (1980): 20.

36 See clipping reproduced in ibid., 21.

37 Robert Lambert, letter to Marcel Idea (Michael Morris), ca. 1975; and *Egozine* announcement (ca. 1975); both Belkin.

38 *Egozine* 1, no. 1 (1975): n.p. Cultural theorist Fredric Jameson would not develop his influential discussion of postmodernism and pastiche until the mid-1980s. See Fredric Jameson, "Postmodernism and the Consumer Society," in *The Anti-Aesthetic*, ed. Hal Foster (Port Townsend, WA: Bay Press, 1983), 111–25.

39 *Egozine* promotional mailer (ca. 1975); Belkin.

40 Science Holiday mailer, n.d., collection James P. H. Kotsybar.

41 Ibid.

42 Baylin's course description appears on the back of a letter to Marcel Idea (Michael Morris), September 10, 1974; Belkin.

43 Frank Picabia, Richard Paulson, Bill Gaglione, Monte Cazazza, Tim Mankusi [sic], Ruby Begonia, one-page statement; Belkin.

44 *Vile* 1, no. 1 (February 1974): 55.

45 *Dumb Fucker* 5 (September 1982): n.p.

46 On Club 57, see Ron Magliozzi and Sophie Cavoulacos, *Club 57: Film, Performance, and Art in the East Village, 1978–1983* (New York: Museum of Modern Art, 2017); and Maria Elena Buszek, "Ladies' Auxiliary of the Lower East Side: Post-Punk Feminist Art and New York's Club 57," *Punk and Post-Punk* 9, no. 13 (2020): 425–42.

47 D. Jonson, "Debbie's 'Swingin' Spinsters," *Bikini Girl* 2 (1979), n.p.

48 Gendron, *Between Montmartre and the Mudd Club*, 299–315.

49 Gaglione, in *Quoz?* 3, no. 9 (March 1975): 39; and *Quoz?* 3, no. 11 (Fall 1975): 12.

50 On a "trash" aesthetic versus Conceptualism, see Gendron, *Between Montmartre and the Mudd Club*, 304.

51 Kathleen Hanna, *My Life with Evan Dando, Popstar* (self-published, 1993), n.p. Acker's early publications, including *The Childlike Life of the Black Tarantula*, were initially distributed by mail as zine-like chapbooks.

52 Ibid.

53 Johanna Fateman, *The Opposite: Part One* (self-published, 1996): 2.

54 Ibid., 16–17. Marcus's review originally appeared in "Real Life Rock: Greil Marcus' Top Ten," *Artforum* 33, no. 8 (April 1995): 40.

55 Fateman, *The Opposite*, 19.

56 Ibid., 18–19.

57 Miranda July discusses the New York Film-Makers Cooperative in *U-Matic Chainletter* (1997), n.p.

58 Miranda July, "A Historical Romance," *Underwater Chainletter* (1996), n.p.

59 The term "metazine" is the artist's own; see laurelbeckman.com/lucky.

60 BlackMass Publishing has paid homage to Beverly Buchanan with the 2020 publications *Beverly Buchanan: Sculptures, 1978–1980* and *Beverly Buchanan: The Makings of You: Drawings & Sculpture*; and with Kwamé Kamau Omari (Kwamé Sorrell), *Quotidien Acts of Minimalism (a lecture)* (2021). The group Bad Brains is the subject of BlackMass Publishing's *Stay Close to ME* (2021).

Decca-Dance

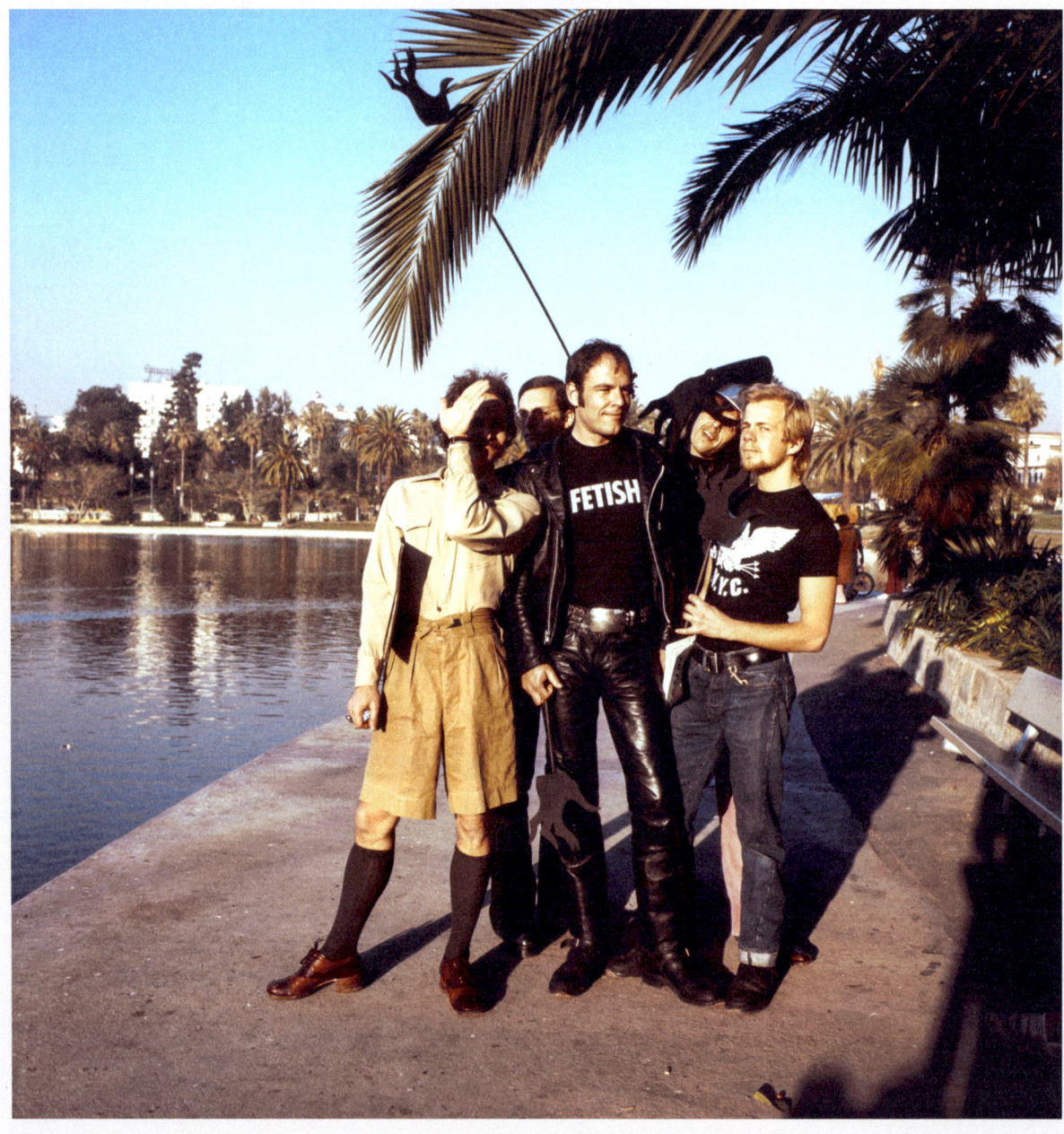

Bud Lee
AA Bronson, John Jack Baylin, John Dowd, Felix Partz,
Zeke Smolinsky during Decca-Dance, 1974
Color transparency
Morris and Helen Belkin Art Gallery, University of British Columbia,
Morris/Trasov Archive

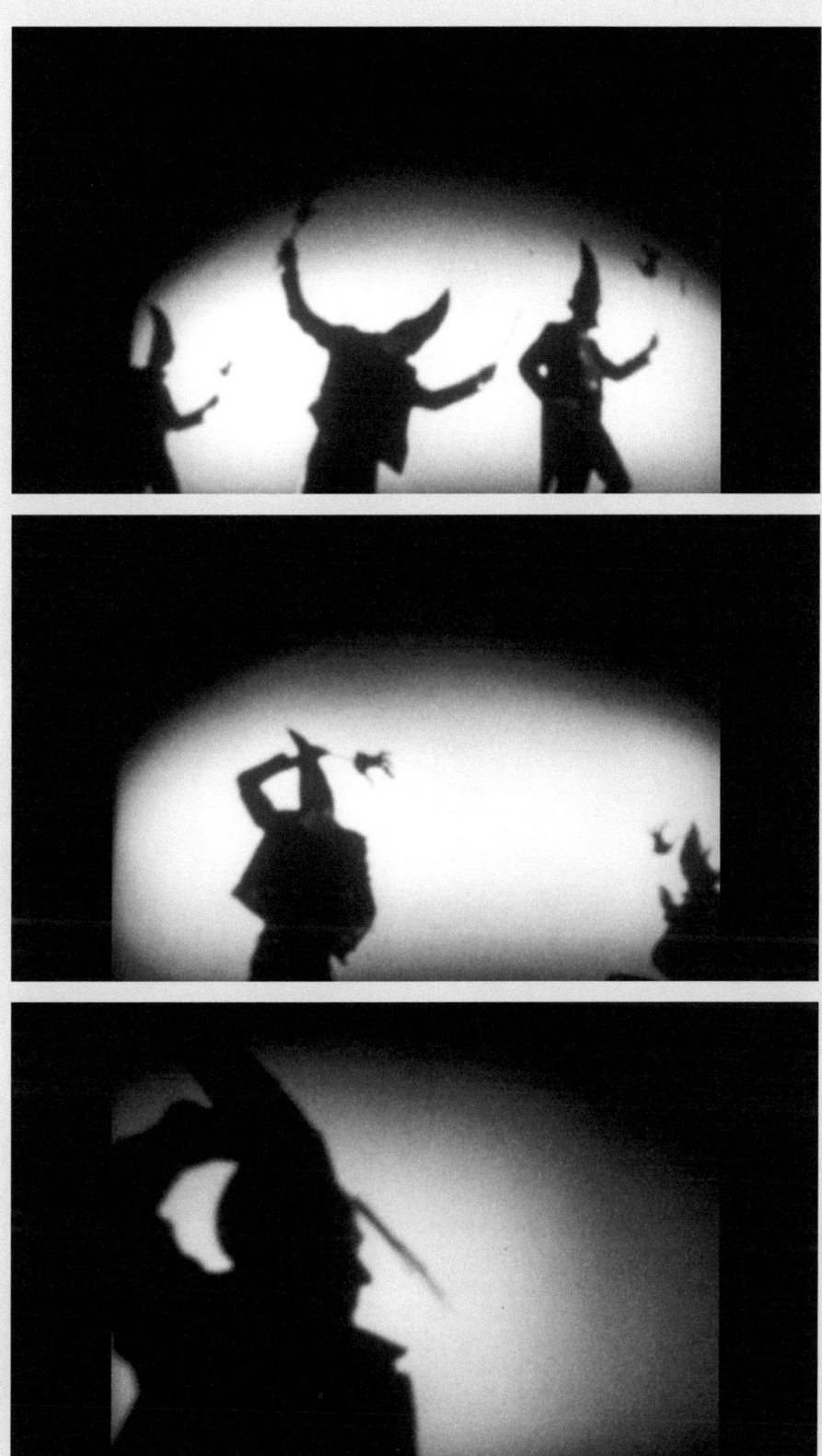

Kate Craig (a.k.a. Lady Brute) with music by Hank Bull
Stills from *Decca-Dance*, 1974
8mm film; black and white, sound; 6 min., 20 sec.
Western Front, Vancouver

Robert Lambert

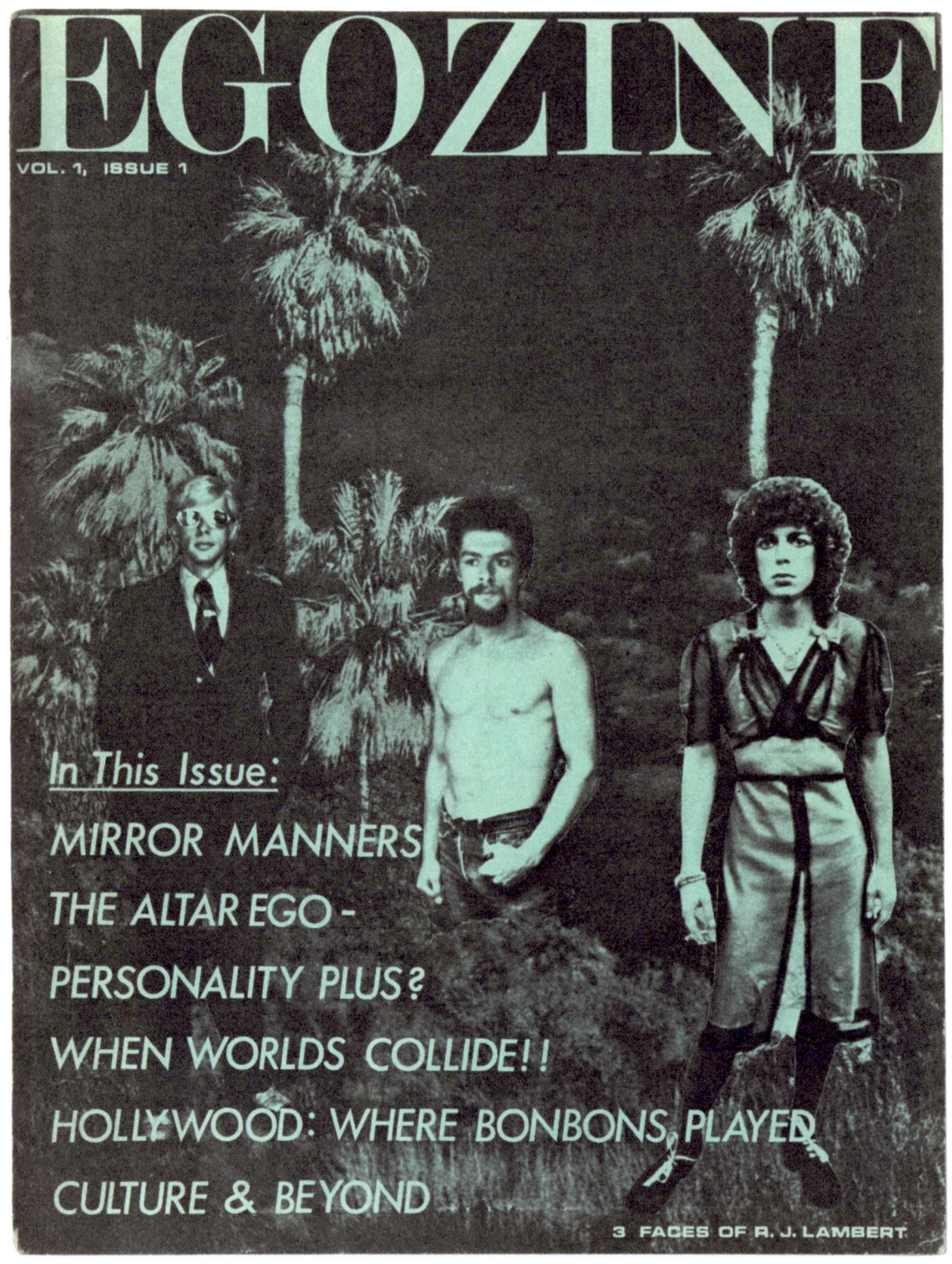

Egozine, vol. 1, no. 1, 1975
Offset, saddle stitched, color offset wrappers,
11 × 8 ½ in. (27.9 × 21.6 cm)
Collection Philip Aarons and Shelley Fox Aarons

PASTICHE

Pastiche- 1)[a]A literary, artistic or musical composition made up of bits from various sources- potpourri. [b] Such a composition intended to imitate or ridicule another artists style. 2) A jumbled mixture; a hodge-podge.
- Webster's New World Dictionary

"While its film production has been sharply curtailed, MGM has proved once more that it hasn't forgotten how by ringing the box office bell lustily with "That's Entertainment." There is a certain irony in the fact that the hit was an artful pastiche of MGM's lustrous old musicals."
- Los Angeles Times news item

"Miss Simmons... is a welcome addition to American shores, and in person every bit as fascinating to behold as she was in countless Technicolored drama pastiches... Remember her love affair with Leonard Whiting in "Say Hello to Yesterday"? yell!"
- Entertainment West review of "A Little Night Music" with Jean Simmons

"The Hawkline Monster" is rather more of a pastiche, more of a parody than any of Braudigan's other fictions. Never mind. There are enough oppositions here to keep freshman instructors fueled for a decade."
- Newsweek magazine review of "The Hawkline Monster" by Richard Brautigan

"In the streets (of Montreal), individual lifestyles shift and change as those of English and of French descent mingle in a pastiche of pretty places; there are people who live for the present while waiting for the future."
- After Dark magazine

PASTICHE

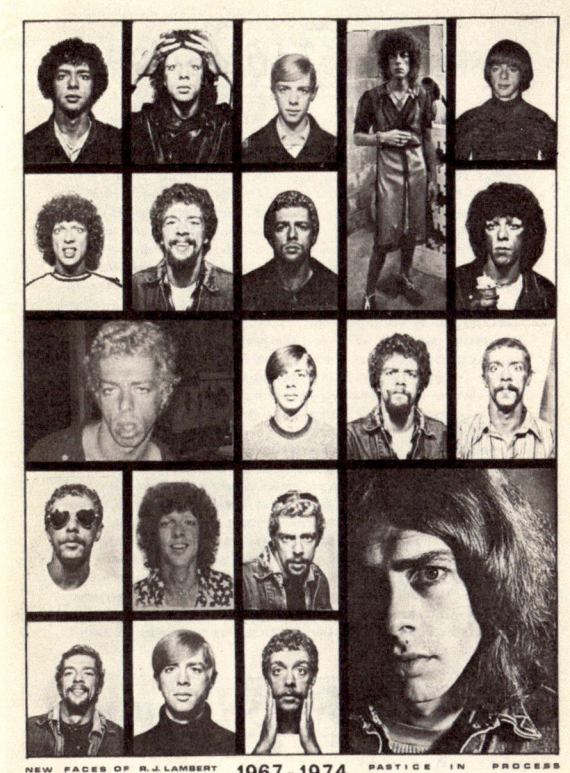

NEW FACES OF R.J. LAMBERT 1967-1974 PASTICE IN PROCESS

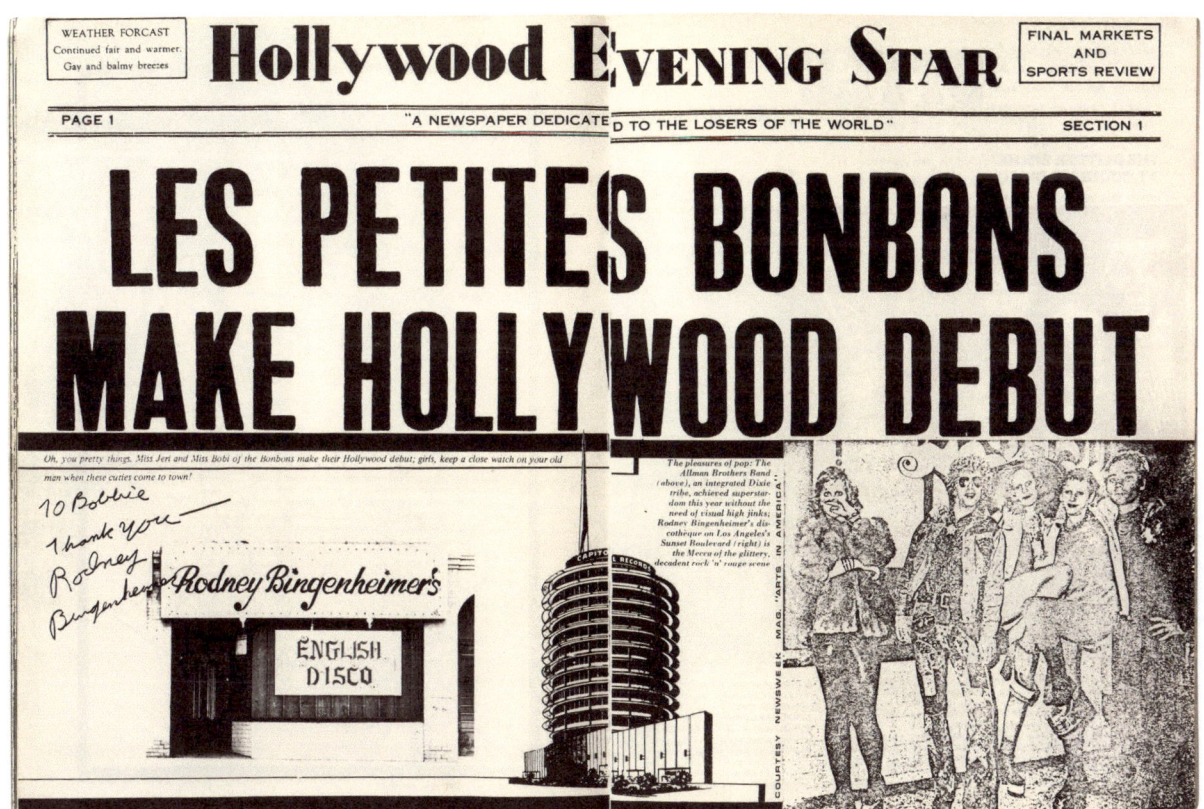

WEATHER FORCAST
Continued fair and warmer.
Gay and balmy breezes

Hollywood Evening Star

FINAL MARKETS AND SPORTS REVIEW

PAGE 1   "A NEWSPAPER DEDICATED TO THE LOSERS OF THE WORLD"   SECTION 1

LES PETITES BONBONS MAKE HOLLYWOOD DEBUT

Oh, you pretty things. Miss Jeri and Miss Bobi of the Bonbons make their Hollywood debut; girls, keep a close watch on your old man when these cuties come to town!

To Bobbie
Thank You
Rodney
Bingenheimer

Rodney Bingenheimer's
ENGLISH DISCO

The pleasures of pop: The Allman Brothers Band (above), an integrated Dixie tribe, achieved superstardom this year without the need of visual high jinks; Rodney Bingenheimer's discothèque on Los Angeles's Sunset Boulevard (right) is the Mecca of the glittery, decadent rock 'n' rouge scene

COURTESY NEWSWEEK MAG "ARTS IN AMERICA"

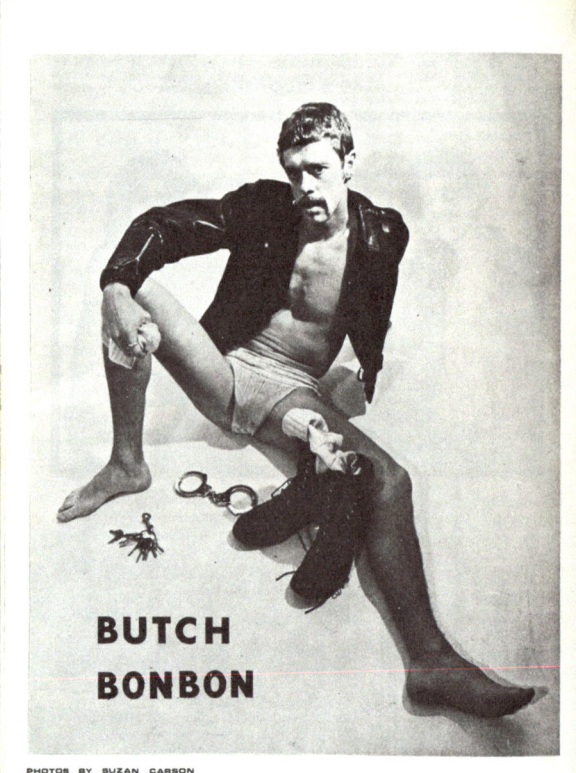

**BUTCH
BONBON**

PHOTOS BY SUZAN CARSON

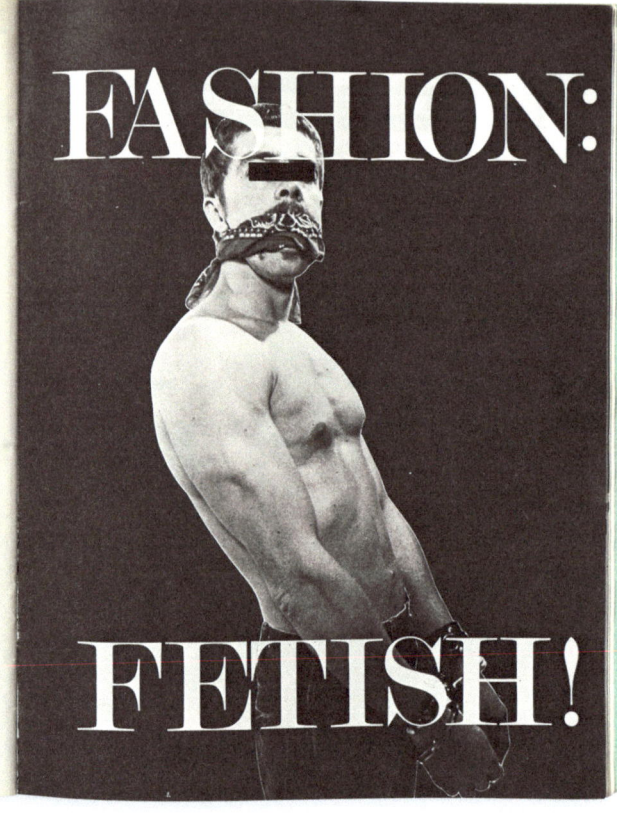

FASHION:

FETISH!

IN MEMORIAM:

These pages are dedicated to our exquisite nameless fetish model who appears here (lower left) and elsewhere in this issue. Unable to strike the arduous balance between fantasy & reality and keep one from being the victim of the other, he is dead of a self-inflicted gunshot wound. Vita mutatur, non tollitur.

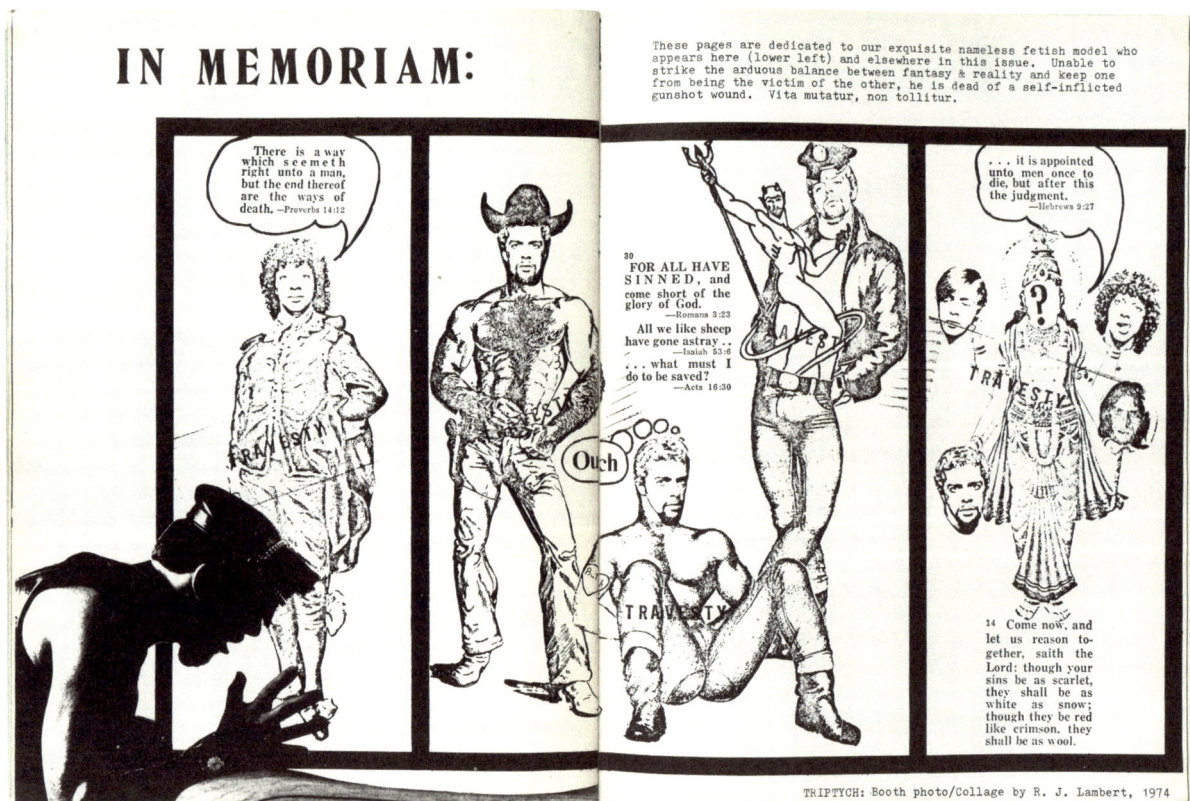

TRIPTYCH: Booth photo/Collage by R. J. Lambert, 1974

Egozine, vol. 1, no. 1, 1975
Offset, saddle stitched, color offset wrappers,
11 × 8 ½ in. (27.9 × 21.6 cm)
Collection Philip Aarons and Shelley Fox Aarons

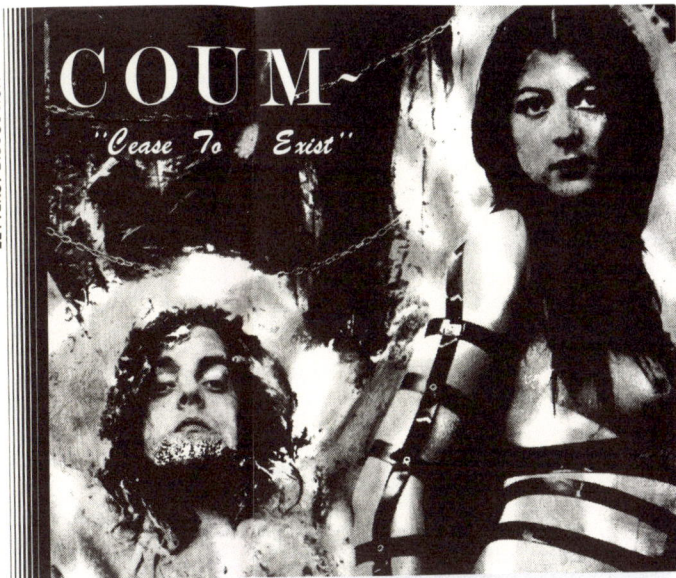

Egozine, vol. 2, no. 2, 1976
Offset, saddle stitched, color offset wrappers,
11 5/8 × 9 1/16 in. (29.5 × 23 cm)
Private collection, New York

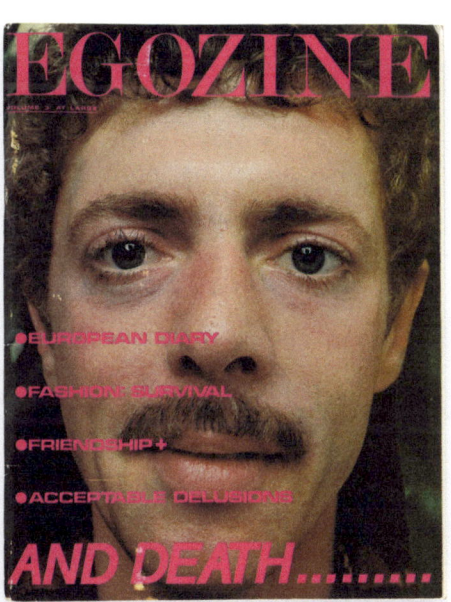

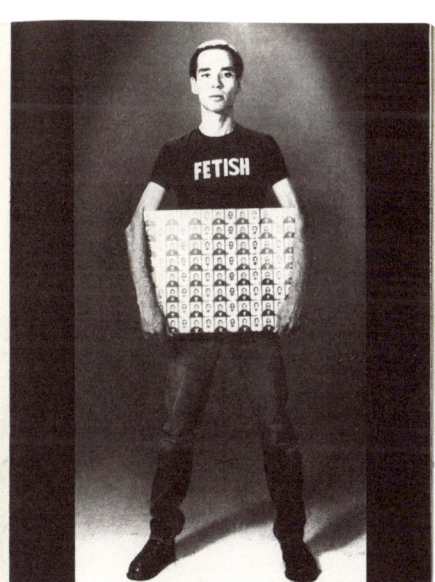

Egozine, vol. 3, at large, 1979
Offset, saddle stitched, color offset wrappers,
11 × 8 1/2 in. (27.9 × 21.6 cm)
Collection Philip Aarons and Shelley Fox Aarons

Jerry Dreva

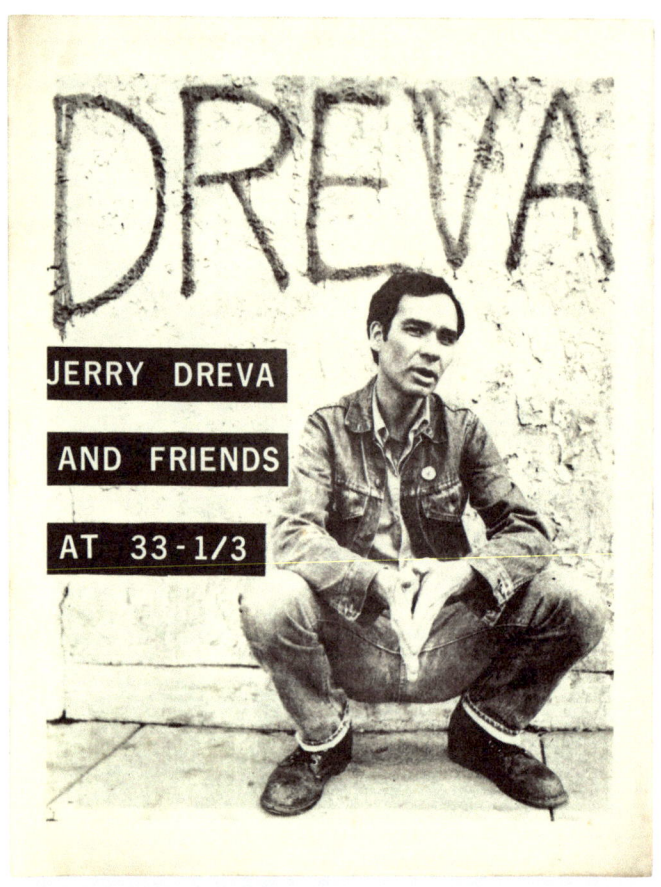

Jerry Dreva and Friends at 33-⅓, 1978
Offset, perfect bound, 11 × 8 ½ in. (27.9 × 21.6 cm)
Collection Robert Lambert

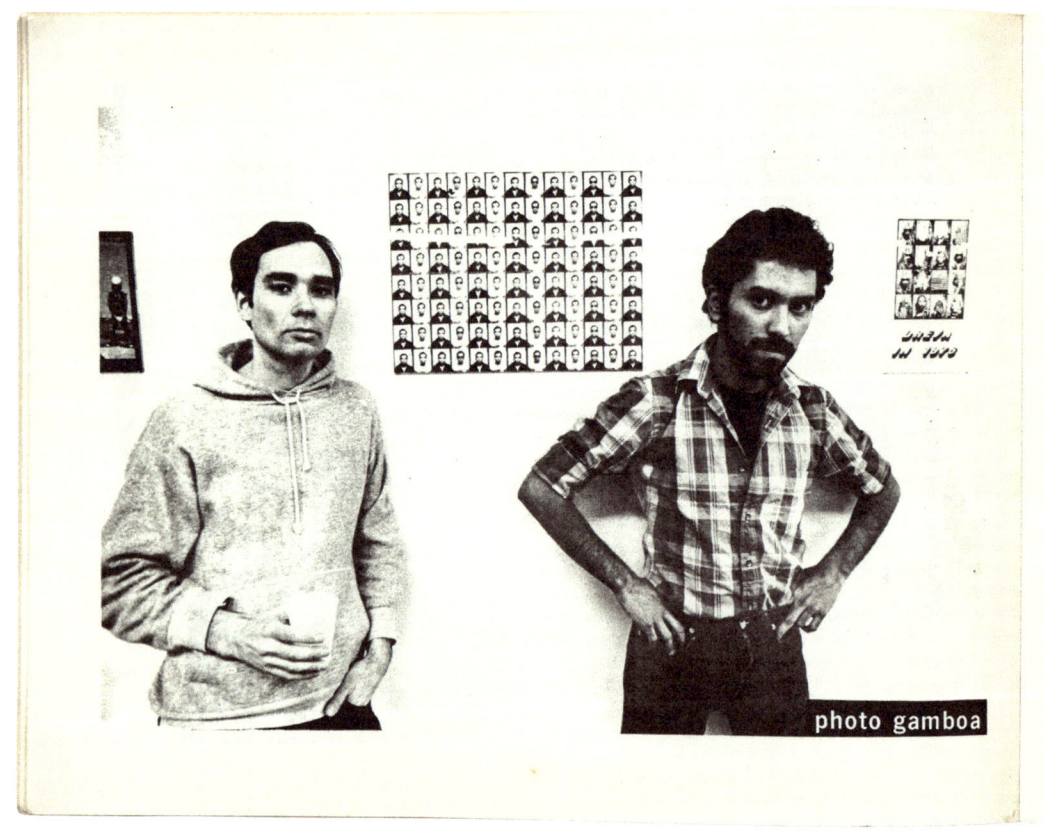

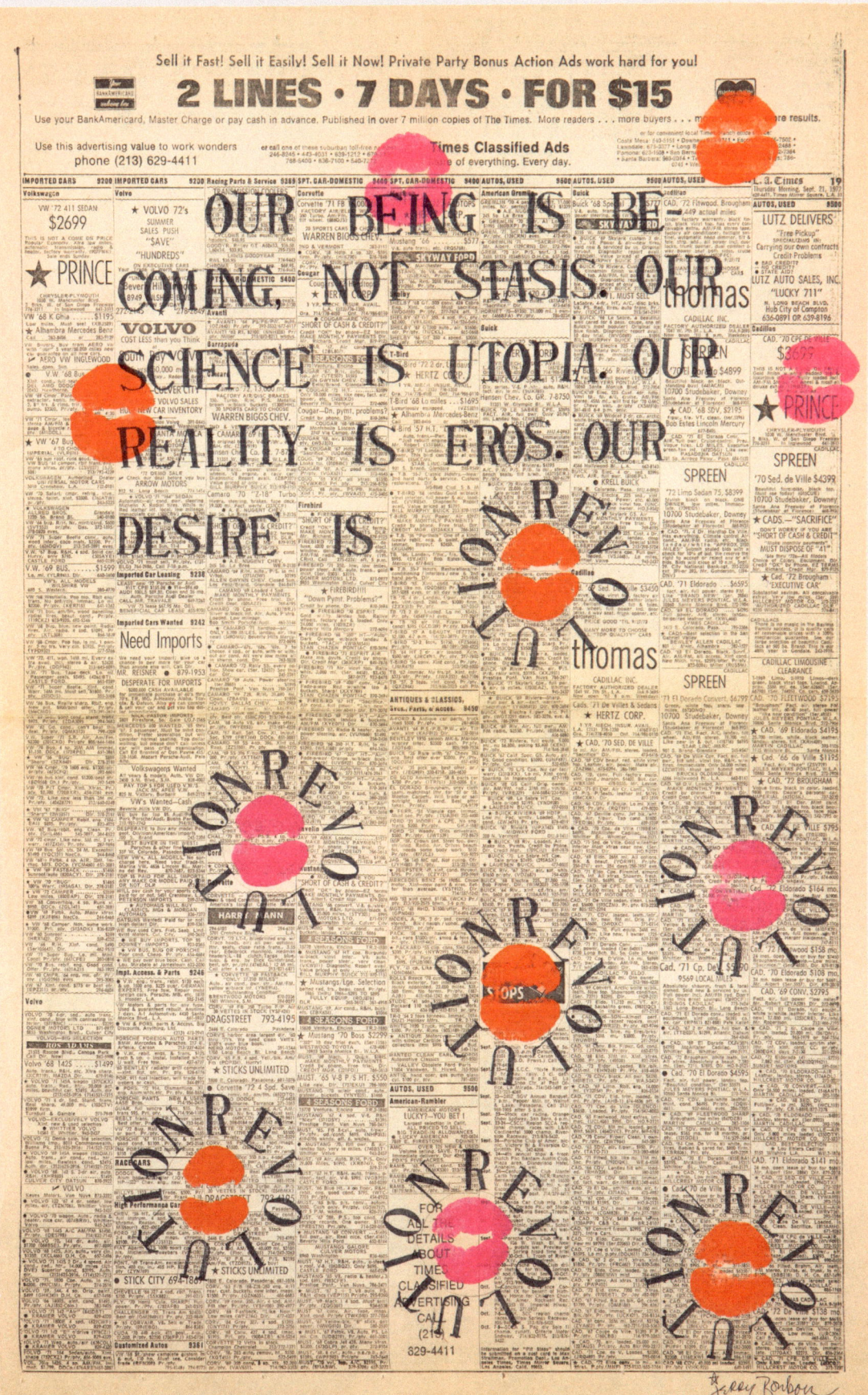

Untitled ("Revolution"), 1972
Ink and fluorescent paint on newsprint, 22¾ × 14⅝ in. (57.8 × 37.1 cm)
The Andy Warhol Museum, Pittsburgh; Founding Collection,
Contribution The Andy Warhol Foundation for the Visual Arts, Inc.

Skot Armstrong / Science Holiday

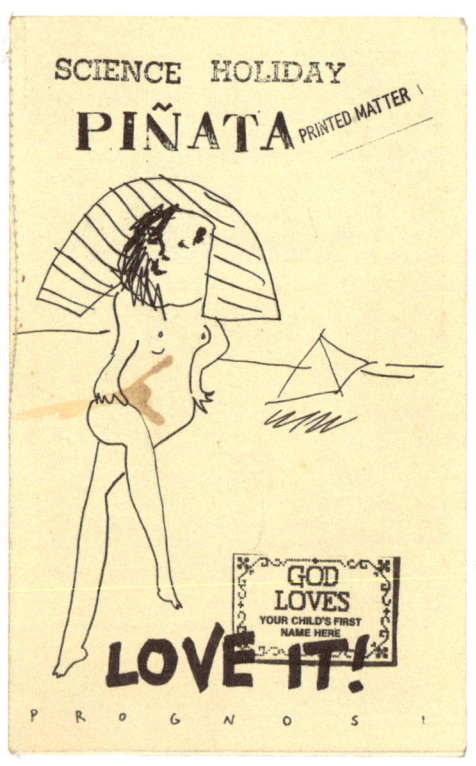

Piñata, 1974
Offset, sewn binding, 8 ½ × 5 ½ in. (21.6 × 14 cm)
ONE Archives at the USC Libraries

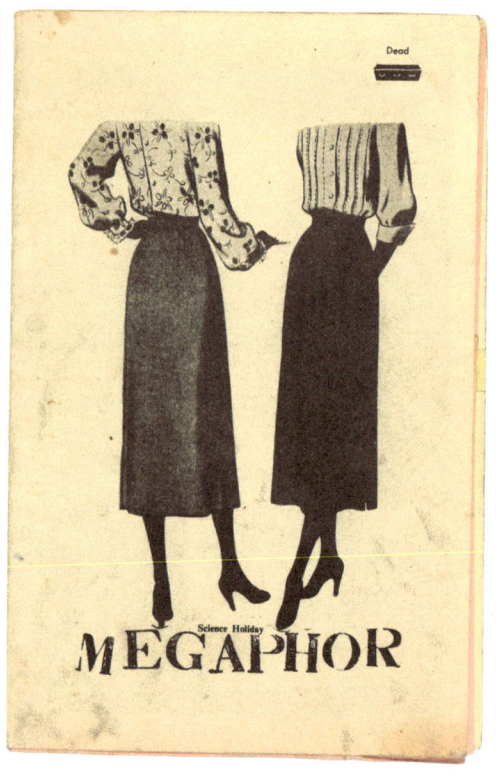

Megaphor, 1975
Offset, saddle stitched, 8 ½ × 5 ½ in. (21.6 × 14 cm)
ONE Archives at the USC Libraries

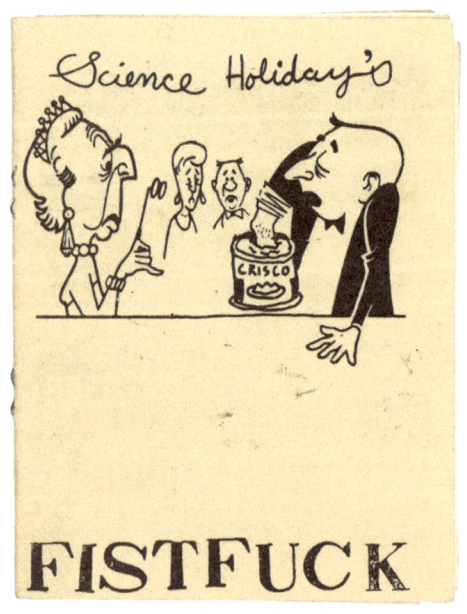

Fist Fuck, 1975
Offset, saddle stitched, 5 ½ × 4 in. (14 × 10.2 cm)
ONE Archives at the USC Libraries

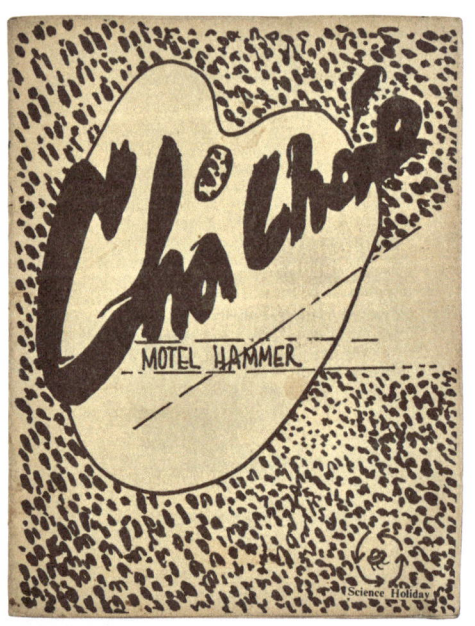

Cha Cha's Motel Hammer, 1975
Offset, saddle stitched, 5 ½ × 4 ½ in. (14 × 11.4 cm)
Collection James P. H. Kotsybar

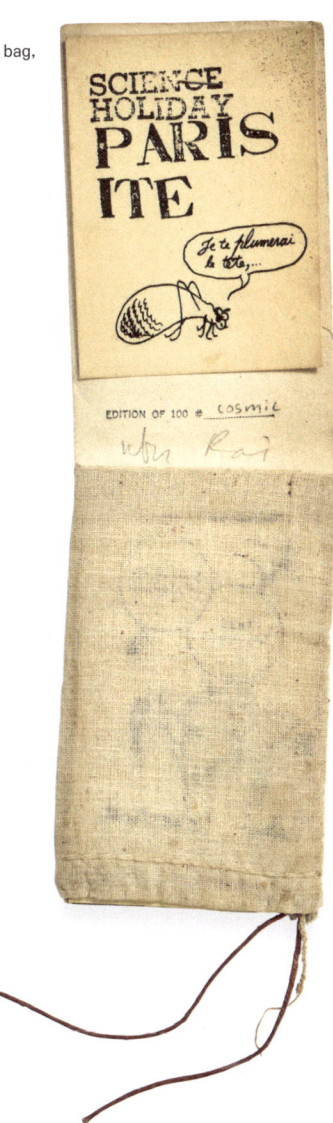

Paris-ite, 1975
Offset, stapled to army surplus parts bag,
10 × 3 in. (25.4 × 7.6 cm)
Collection James P. H. Kotsybar

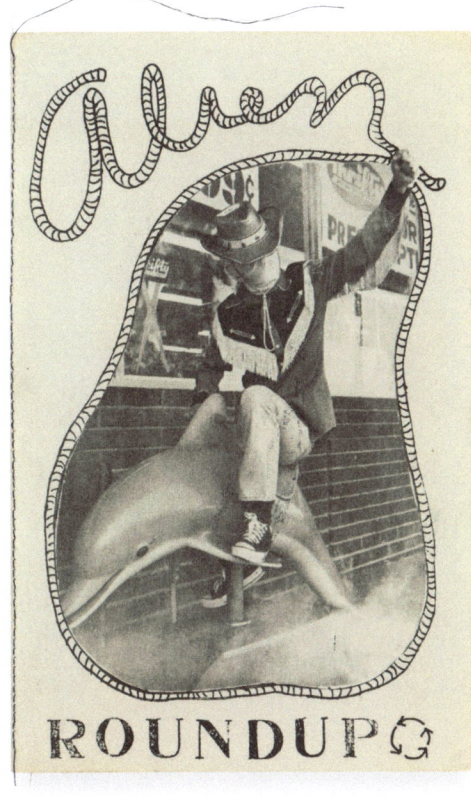

Alien Roundup, 1975
Offset, sewn binding, 8½ × 5½ in. (21.6 × 14 cm)
ONE Archives at the USC Libraries

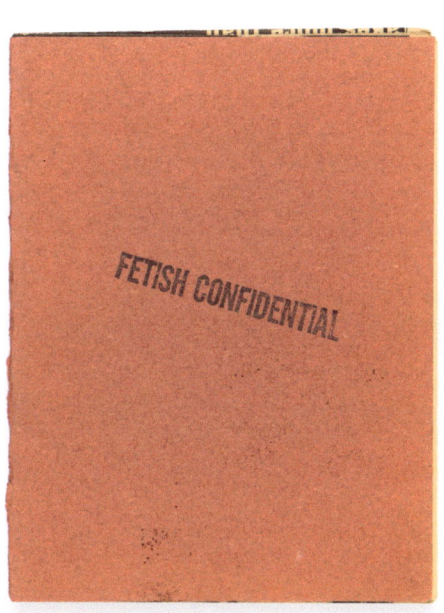

Fetish Confidential, 1975
Offset, saddle stitched, with stamped ink on orange
construction paper wrappers, 5½ × 4 in. (14 × 10.2 cm)
ONE Archives at the USC Libraries

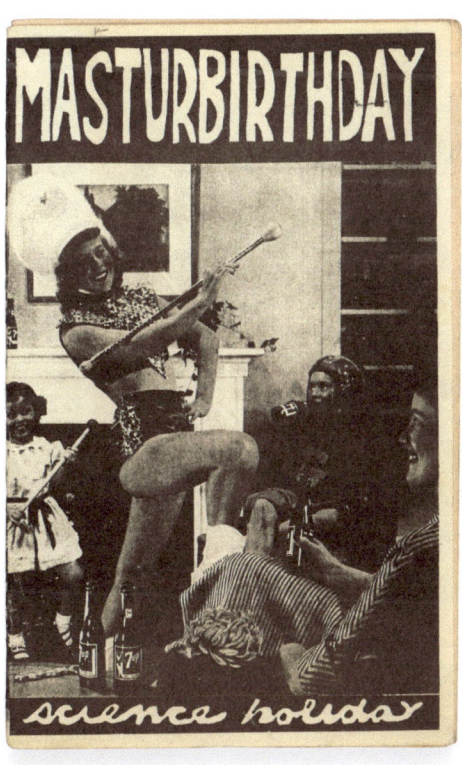

Masturbirthday, 1975
Offset, saddle stitched, 8½ × 5½ in. (21.6 × 14 cm)
ONE Archives at the USC Libraries

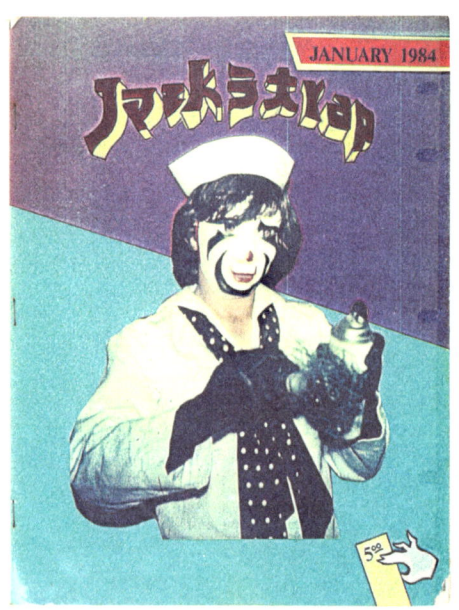
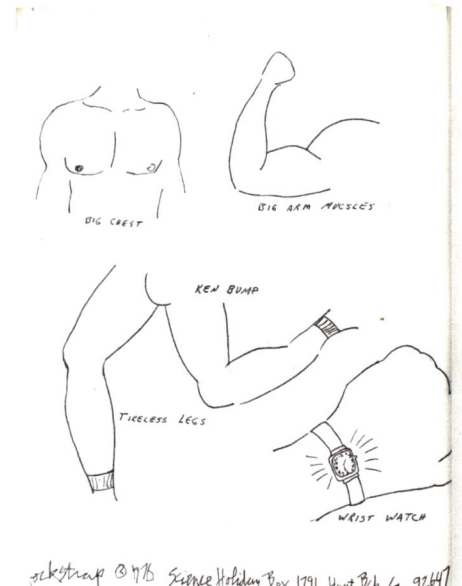
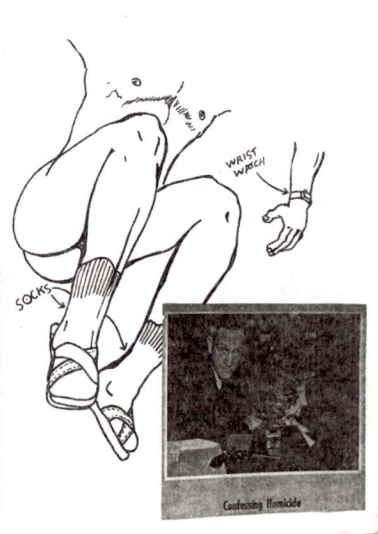

Jockstrap, 1976
Black-and-white and color photocopy, side stapled, 11 × 8 ½ in. (27.9 × 21.6 cm)
ONE Archives at the USC Libraries

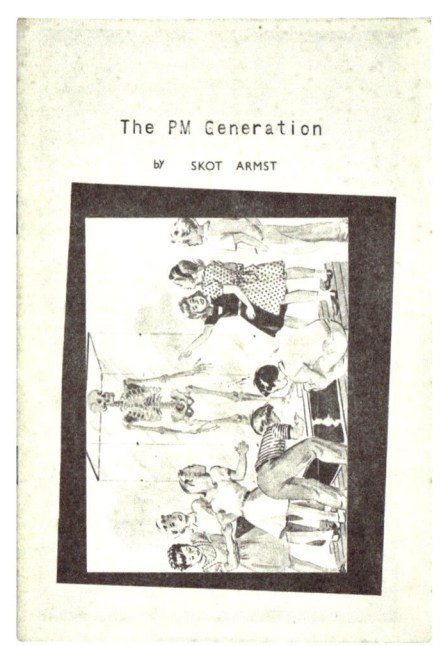
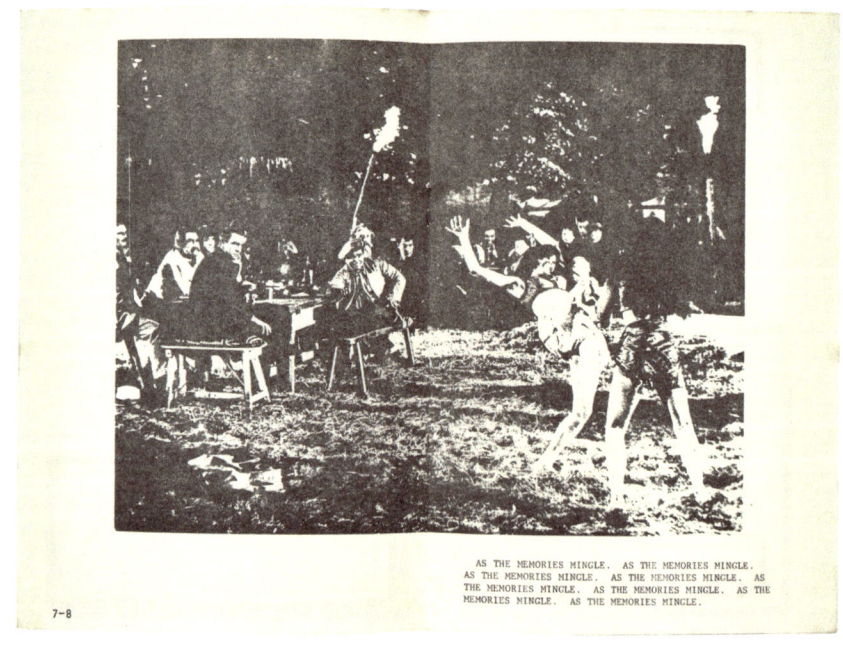

The PM Generation, 1979
Photocopy, saddle stitched, 8 5/16 × 5 ¾ in. (21.1 × 14.6 cm)
Private collection, New York

Jack Vargas

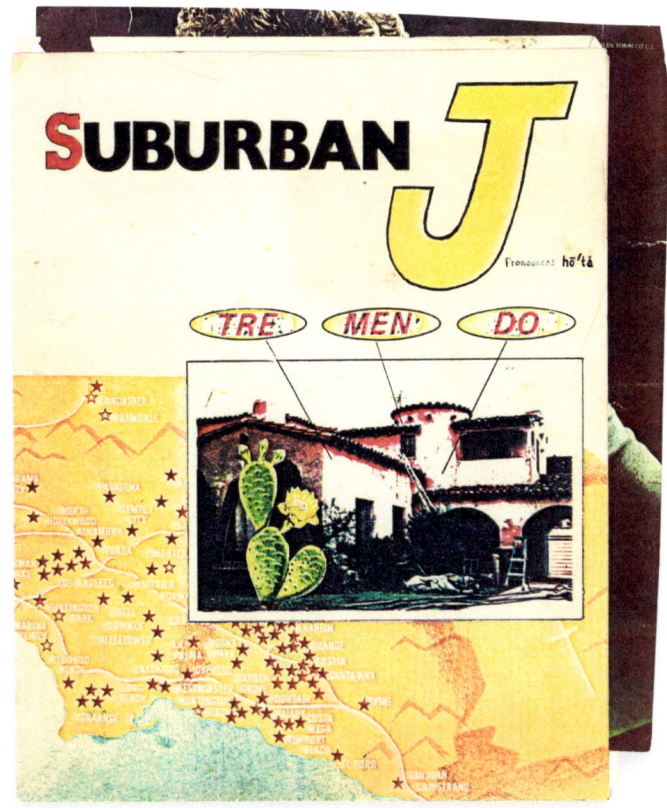

Suburban J, ca. 1975
Photocopy, folded wrappers, 8 ½ × 7 in. (21.6 × 17.8 cm)
ONE Archives at the USC Libraries

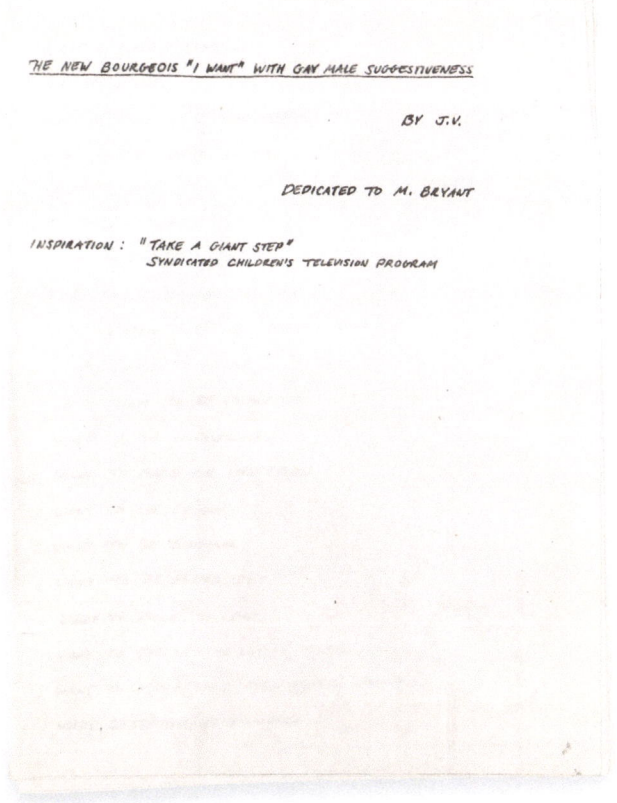

THE NEW BOURGEOIS "I WANT" WITH GAY MALE SUGGESTIVENESS

BY J.V.

DEDICATED TO M. BRYANT

INSPIRATION : "TAKE A GIANT STEP"
SYNDICATED CHILDREN'S TELEVISION PROGRAM

100

I WANT HIM TO CARRY ME.
I WANT THE STRONG/SILENT TYPE.
I WANT TO DREAM ABOUT HIM.
I WANT A DREAMY GUY.
I WANT A BIG GUY.
I WANT A BIG MAN.
I WANT A REAL MAN.
I WANT "EVERY MAN"
I WANT ANY MAN.
I WANT MEN FOR DAYS.
I WANT ALL MEN.
I WANT A MAN.
I WANT "A MAN FOR ALL SEASONS."
I WANT "OF MICE AND MEN."
I WANT A MID-WEST MAN.
I WANT "OKLAHOMA."
I WANT "SEVEN BRIDES FOR SEVEN BROTHERS," "OF THEE I SING."
I WANT MUSICALS.
I WANT A BARITONE.
I WANT HIM TO BE WELL-HUNG.

The New Bourgeois "I Want" with Gay Male Suggestiveness, 1976–79
Photocopy, loose-leaf, 11 × 8 ½ in. (27.9 × 21.6 cm)
ONE Archives at the USC Libraries

Joey Terrill

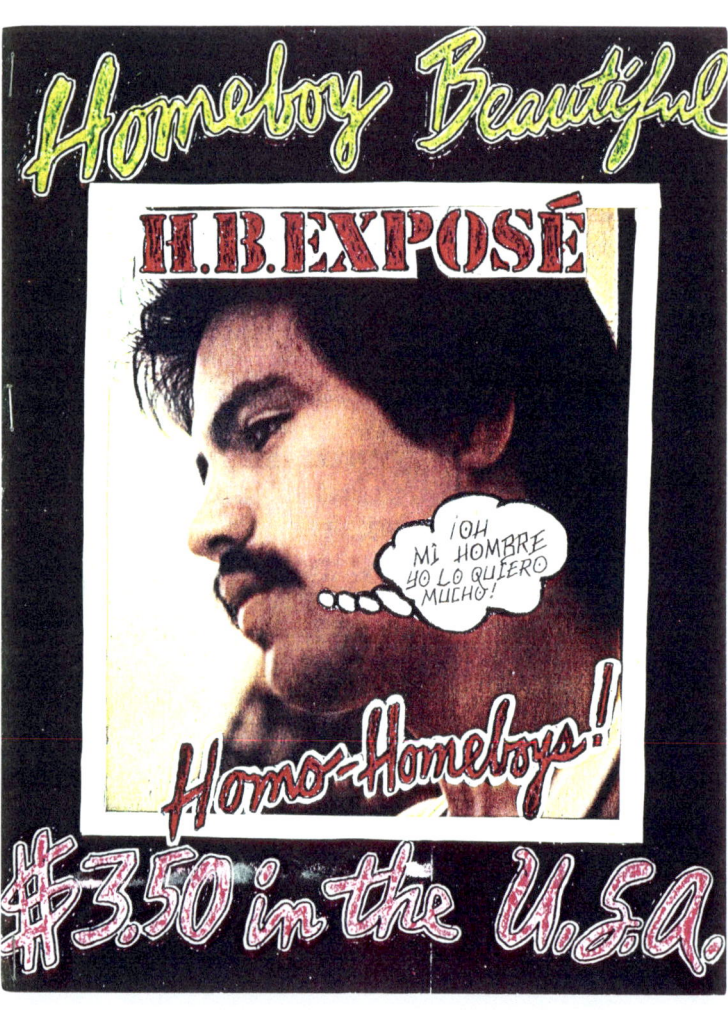

Homeboy Beautiful, no. 1, 1978
Color and black-and-white photocopy, side stapled,
11 × 8 ½ in. (27.9 × 21.6 cm)
ONE Archives at the USC Libraries

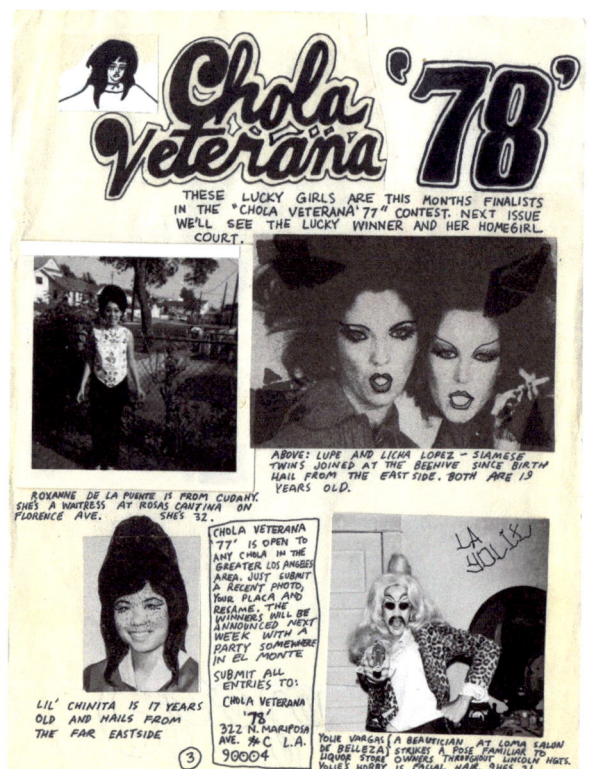

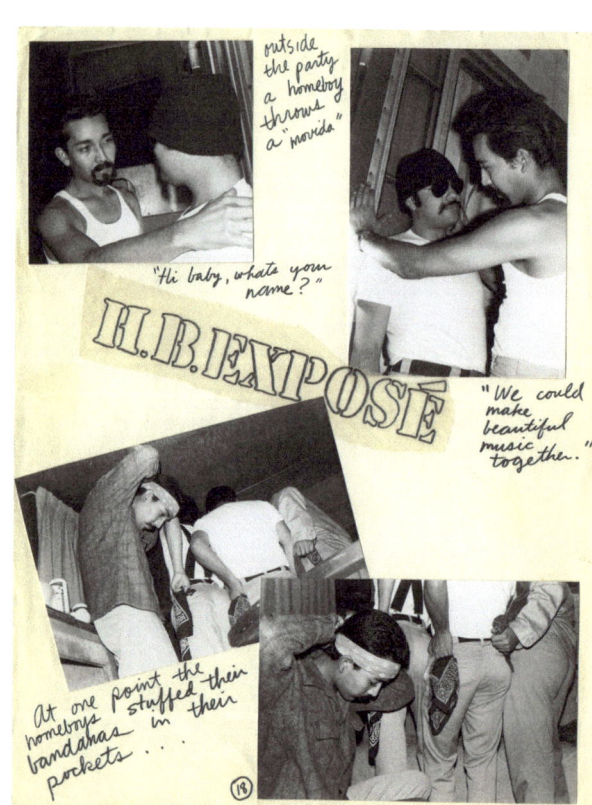

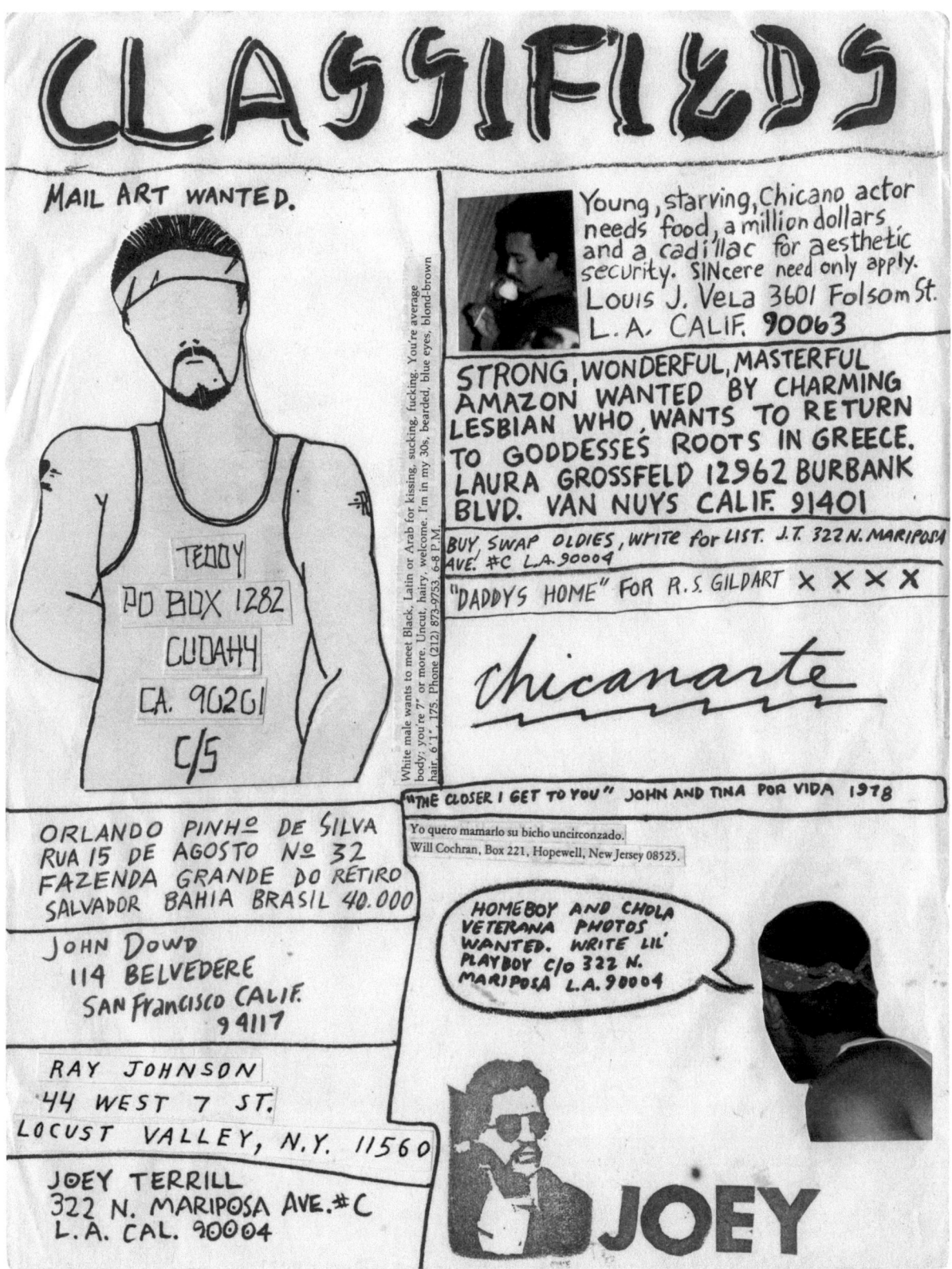

CLASSIFIEDS

MAIL ART WANTED.

TEDDY
PO BOX 1282
CUDAHY
CA. 90201
C/S

White male wants to meet Black, Latin or Arab for kissing, sucking, fucking. You're average body; you're 7" or more. Uncut, hairy, welcome. I'm in my 30s, bearded, blue eyes, blond-brown hair, 6'1", 175. Phone (212) 873-9753. 6-8 P.M.

Young, starving, Chicano actor needs food, a million dollars and a cadillac for aesthetic security. SINcere need only apply. Louis J. Vela 3601 Folsom St. L.A. CALIF. 90063

STRONG, WONDERFUL, MASTERFUL AMAZON WANTED BY CHARMING LESBIAN WHO, WANTS TO RETURN TO GODDESSES ROOTS IN GREECE. LAURA GROSSFELD 12962 BURBANK BLVD. VAN NUYS CALIF. 91401

BUY, SWAP OLDIES, WRITE for LIST. J.T. 322 N. MARIPOSA AVE. #C LA. 90004

"DADDYS HOME" FOR R.S. GILDART ✕ ✕ ✕ ✕

Chicanarte

"THE CLOSER I GET TO YOU" JOHN AND TINA POR VIDA 1978

Yo quero mamarlo su bicho uncirconzado.
Will Cochran, Box 221, Hopewell, New Jersey 08525.

ORLANDO PINHº DE SILVA
RUA 15 DE AGOSTO Nº 32
FAZENDA GRANDE DO RETIRO
SALVADOR BAHIA BRASIL 40.000

JOHN DOWD
114 BELVEDERE
SAN FRANCISCO CALIF.
94117

RAY JOHNSON
44 WEST 7 ST.
LOCUST VALLEY, N.Y. 11560

JOEY TERRILL
322 N. MARIPOSA AVE. #C
L.A. CAL. 90004

HOMEBOY AND CHOLA VETERANA PHOTOS WANTED. WRITE LIL' PLAYBOY C/O 322 N. MARIPOSA L.A. 90004

JOEY

← ↑ Paste-ups for *Homeboy Beautiful*, no. 1, 1978
Photographs and mixed media on paper,
11 × 8 ½ in. (27.9 × 21.6 cm)
ONE Archives at the USC Libraries

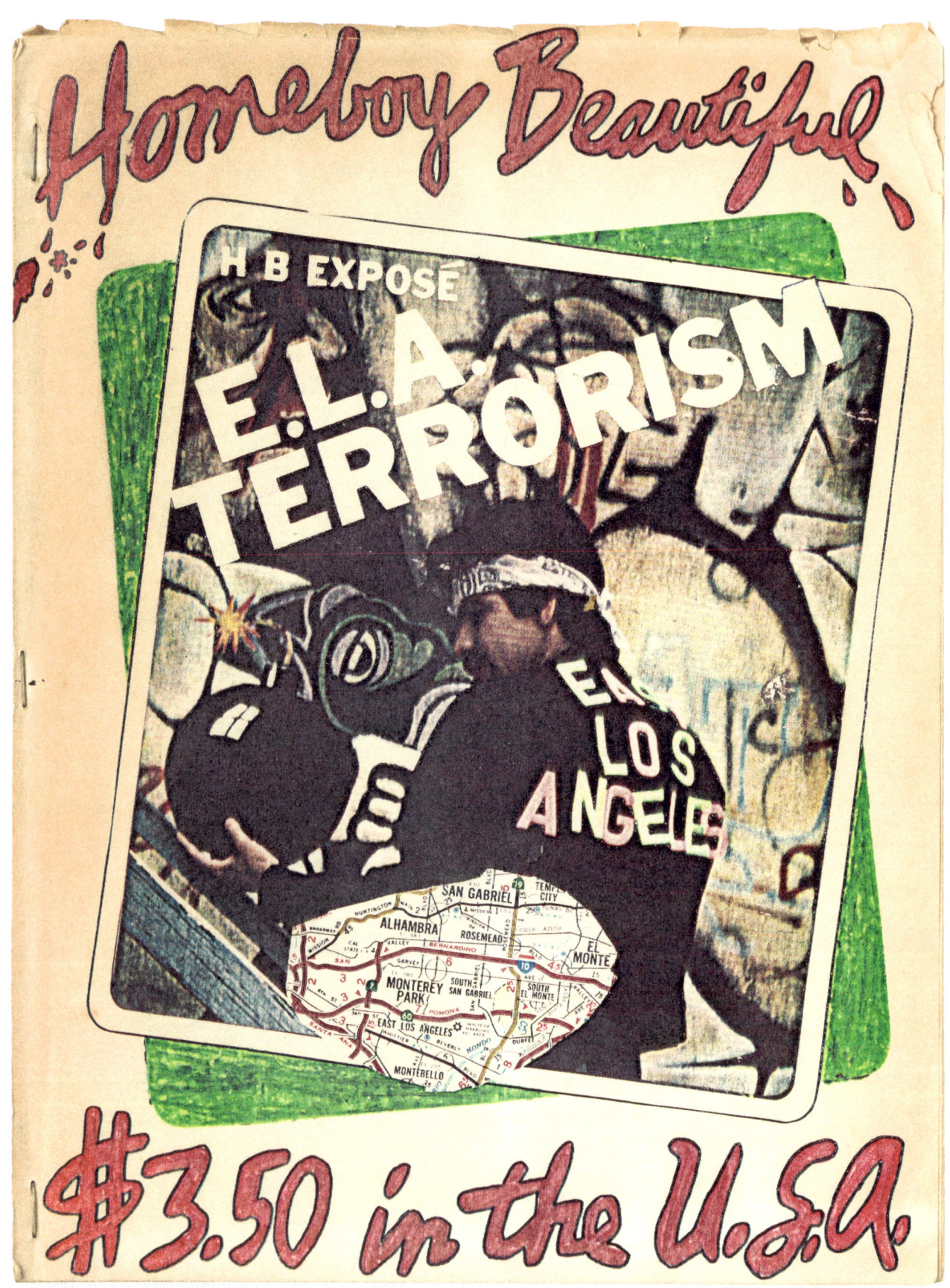

Homeboy Beautiful, no. 2, 1979
Color and black-and-white photocopies, side stapled,
11 × 8 ½ in. (27.9 × 21.6 cm)
Collection Philip Aarons and Shelley Fox Aarons

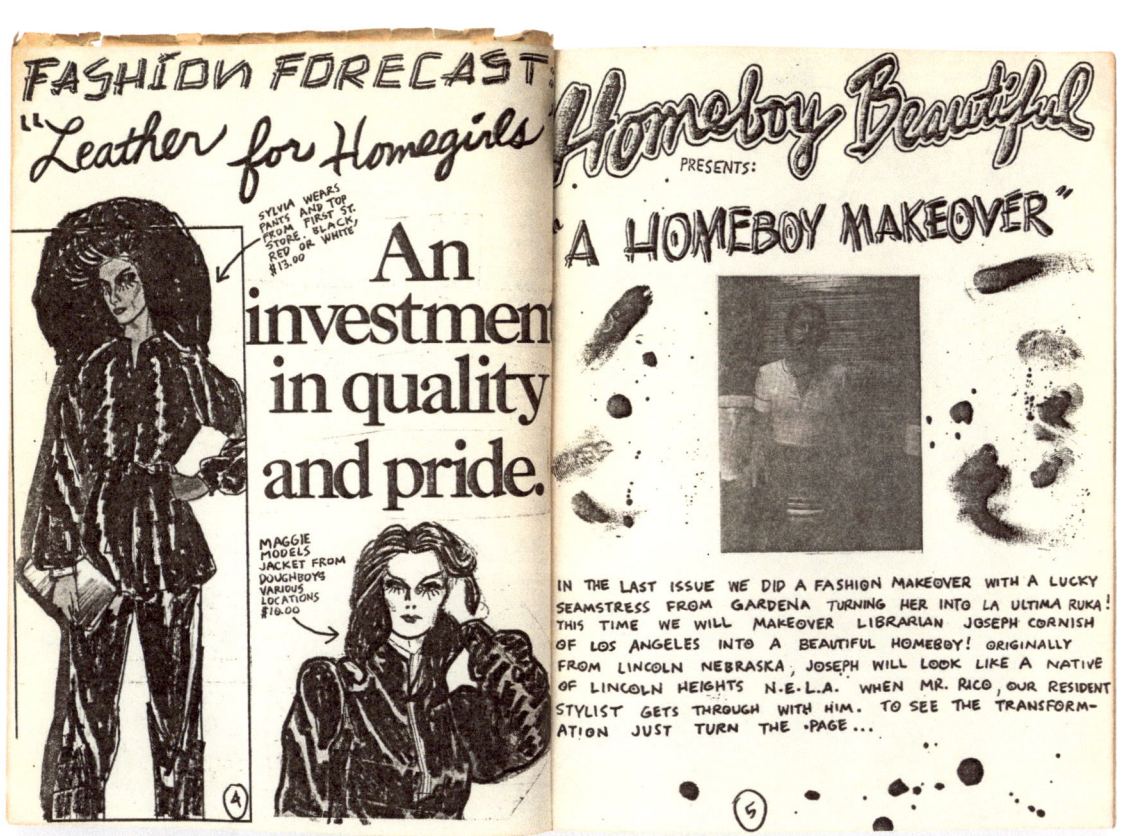

FASHION FORECAST
"Leather for Homegirls"

SYLVIA WEARS PANTS AND TOP FROM FIRST ST. STORE - BLACK, RED OR WHITE, $13.00

An investment in quality and pride.

MAGGIE MODELS JACKET FROM DOUGHBOYS VARIOUS LOCATIONS $10.00

Ⓐ

Homeboy Beautiful
PRESENTS:
"A HOMEBOY MAKEOVER"

IN THE LAST ISSUE WE DID A FASHION MAKEOVER WITH A LUCKY SEAMSTRESS FROM GARDENA TURNING HER INTO LA ULTIMA RUKA! THIS TIME WE WILL MAKEOVER LIBRARIAN JOSEPH CORNISH OF LOS ANGELES INTO A BEAUTIFUL HOMEBOY! ORIGINALLY FROM LINCOLN NEBRASKA, JOSEPH WILL LOOK LIKE A NATIVE OF LINCOLN HEIGHTS N.E.L.A. WHEN MR. RICO, OUR RESIDENT STYLIST GETS THROUGH WITH HIM. TO SEE THE TRANSFORMATION JUST TURN THE PAGE...

Ⓢ

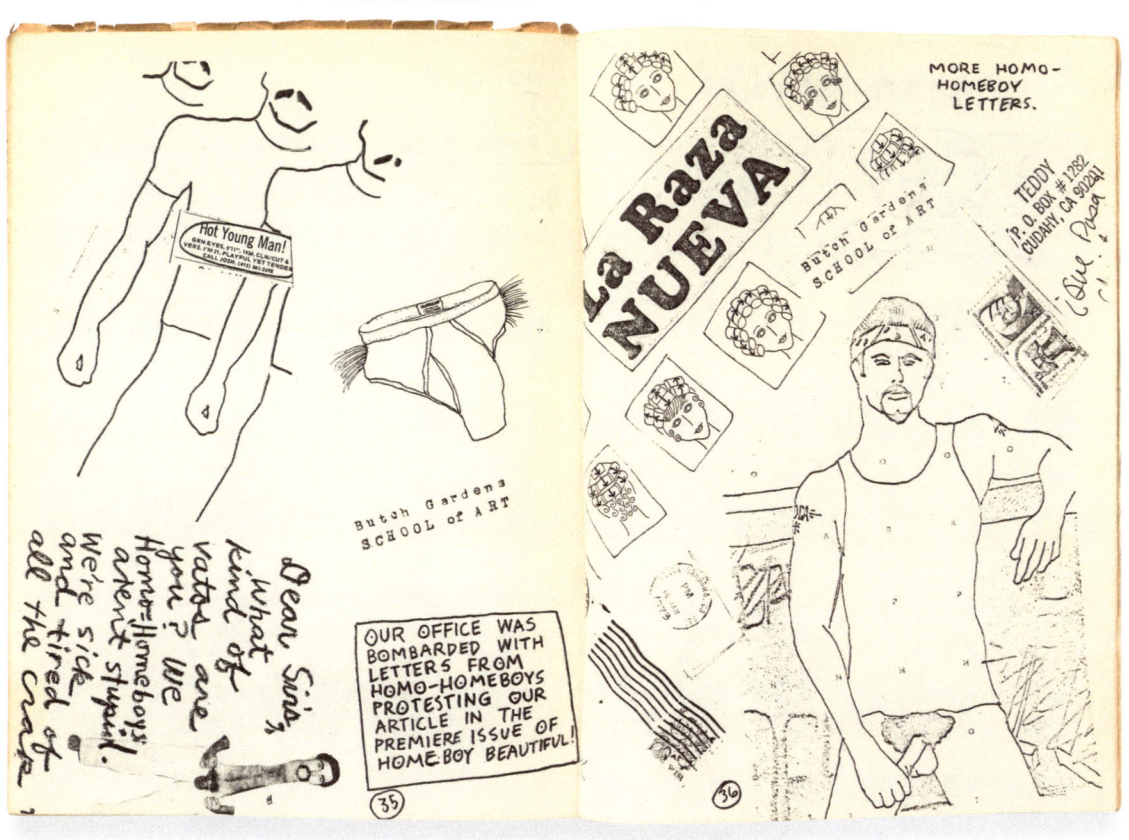

Hot Young Man!

Butch Gardens SCHOOL of ART

Dear Sirs, what kind of vatos are you? We Homofhomeboys aren't stupid. We're sick and tired of all the crap.

OUR OFFICE WAS BOMBARDED WITH LETTERS FROM HOMO-HOMEBOYS PROTESTING OUR ARTICLE IN THE PREMIERE ISSUE OF HOMEBOY BEAUTIFUL!

㉟

MORE HOMO-HOMEBOY LETTERS.

La Raza NUEVA

Butch Gardens SCHOOL of ART

TEDDY P.O. BOX #1282 CUDAHY, CA 90241

㊱

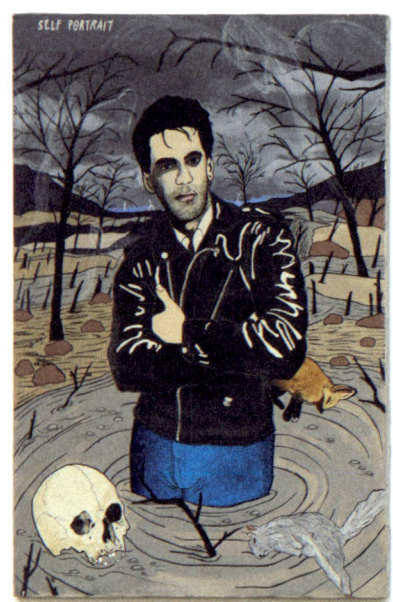
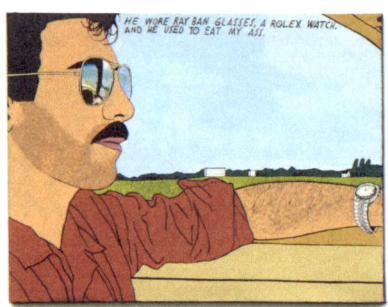
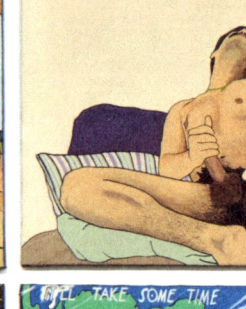
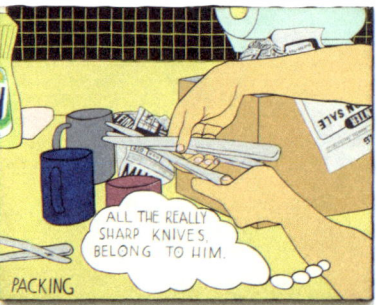
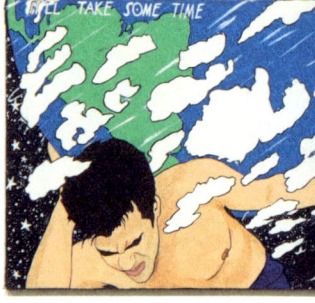
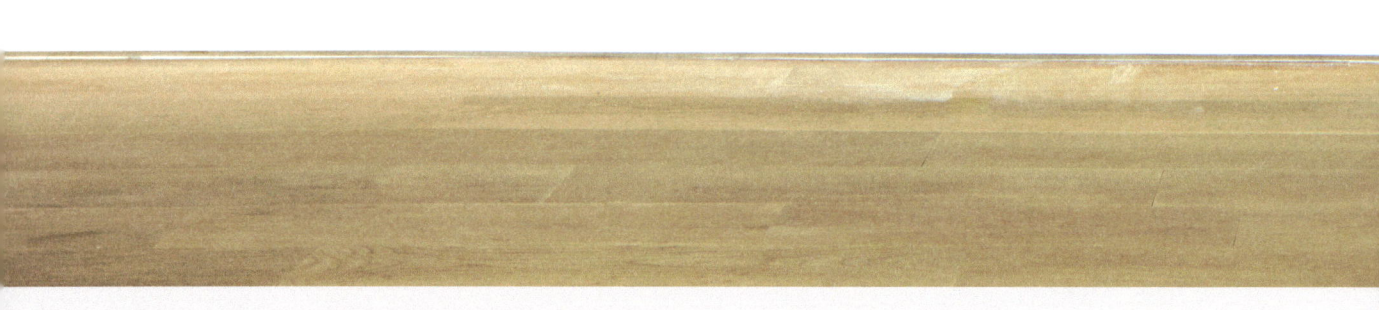

Breaking Up / Breaking Down, 1984–85
Acrylic on canvas, ten parts, 37 ¼ × 149 in. (94.6 × 378.8 cm) overall
Whitney Museum of American Art, New York

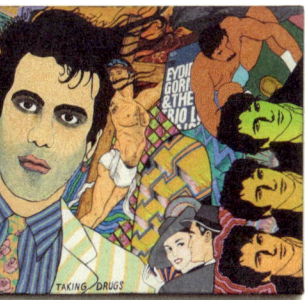
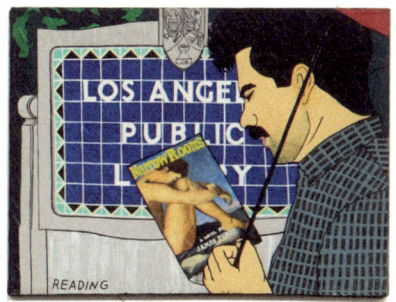
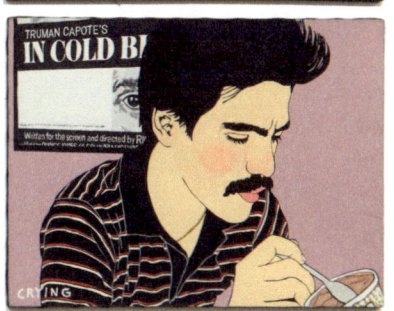
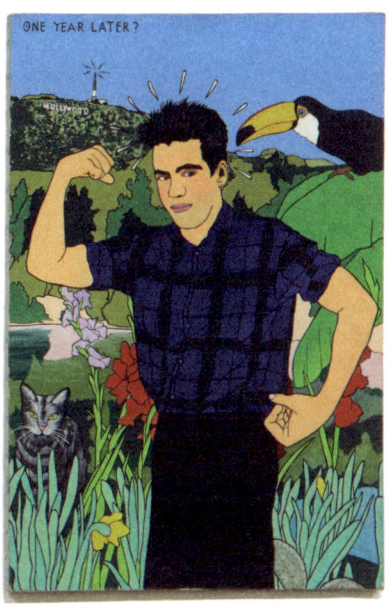

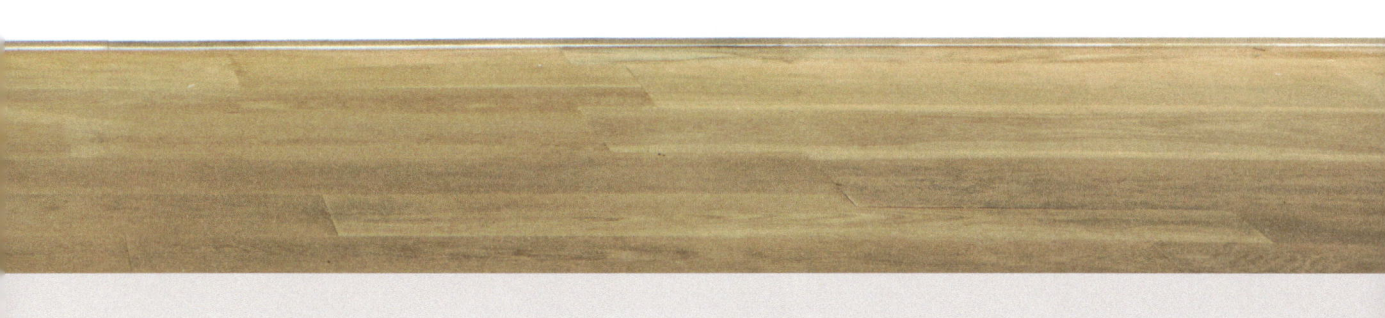

Irene Dogmatic

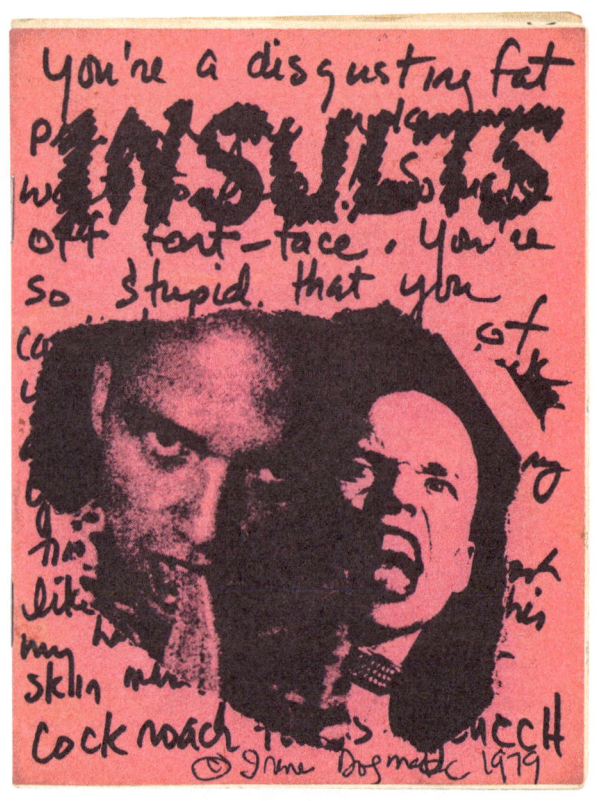

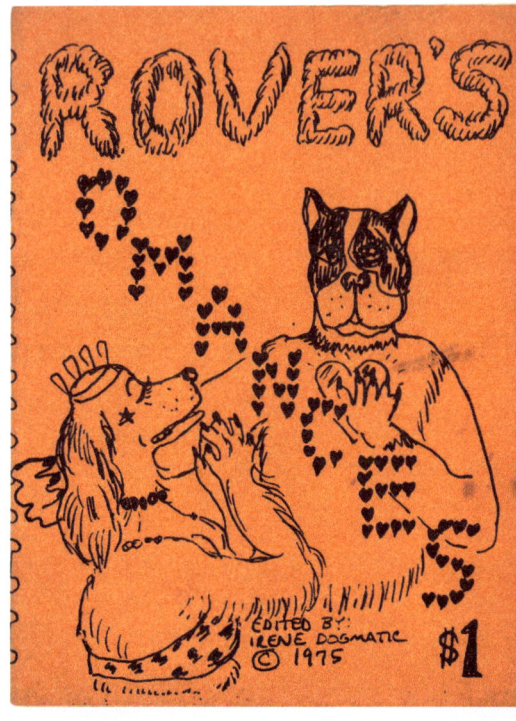

Rover's Romances, 1975
Photocopy, saddle stitched, orange paper wrappers,
4 ½ × 3 ¼ in. (11.4 × 8.3 cm)
Collection John Held, Jr.

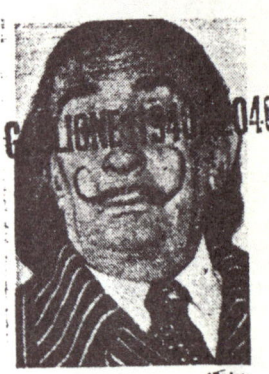

Painter **Salvador Dali**, who
this year completed a
trilogy of one book, one
movie and one stage play,
moved into the legal arena
when it was disclosed that
the 76-year-old hermit of
Spain's Cadaques was
filing a $3 million suit
against a Chicago firm he
claims is engaging in
"commercial exploitation
of one of his designs."

⑫

YOU'Ve got a face like a pig
you walk like a rhino
Your hair is a wig
your breath is a wino
You shout all the time
Out on the street
You go to doggie diner
But you never do eat

What a disease, what a waste
What an epidemic, you're post-human
race

You're a Plastic Surgeon's mistake
Everything about you is fake
Your arms are vinyl
Your legs are acrylic
Your rear end is naugahyde
You're hydrocephalic

You're a fucked-up dead-end kid
Someone played tricks with your id
They tried to define you
But you grew up an X
No one can console you
You don't even like sex

I used to love you
But you've been 86'ed
I used to want you
But baby, you've been fixed
You're a shadow on a wall
Left by the bomb
They tried to erase you
But you'll never be gone

⑬

Insults, 1979
Photocopy, saddle stitched, pink paper wrappers,
5 ½ × 4 ¼ in. (14 × 10.8 cm)
Private collection, New York

Tom Hosier

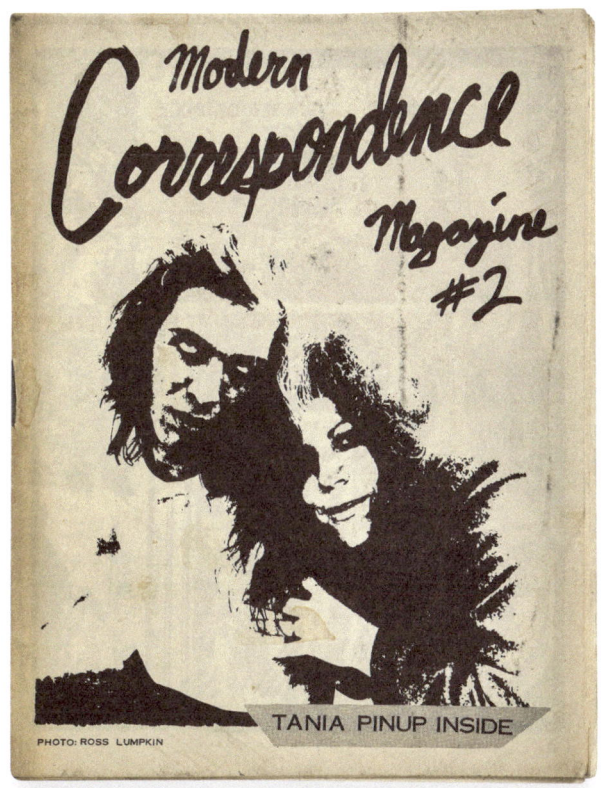

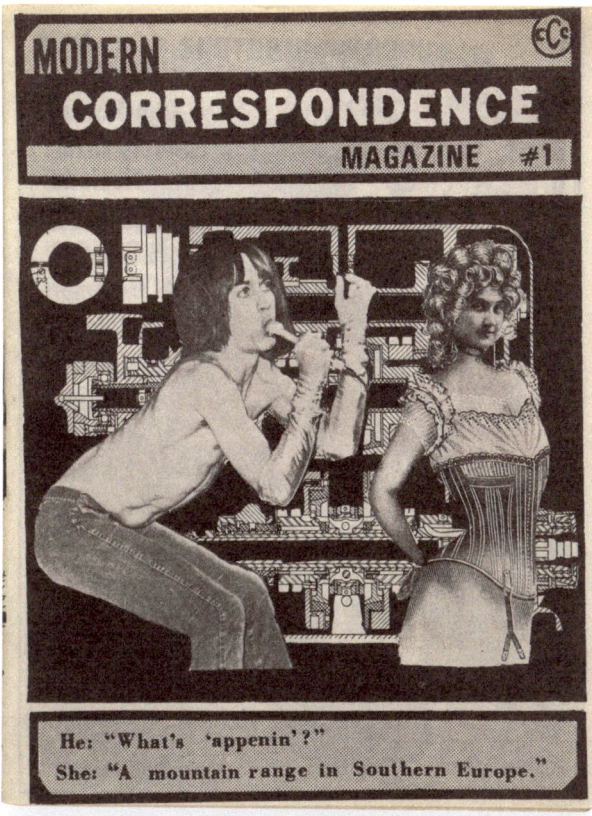

Modern Correspondence Magazine, no. 1, 1974
Photocopy, saddle stitched, 5 ½ × 4 ⁵⁄₁₆ in. (14 × 11 cm)
Morris and Helen Belkin Art Gallery, University of British
Columbia, Morris/Trasov Archive

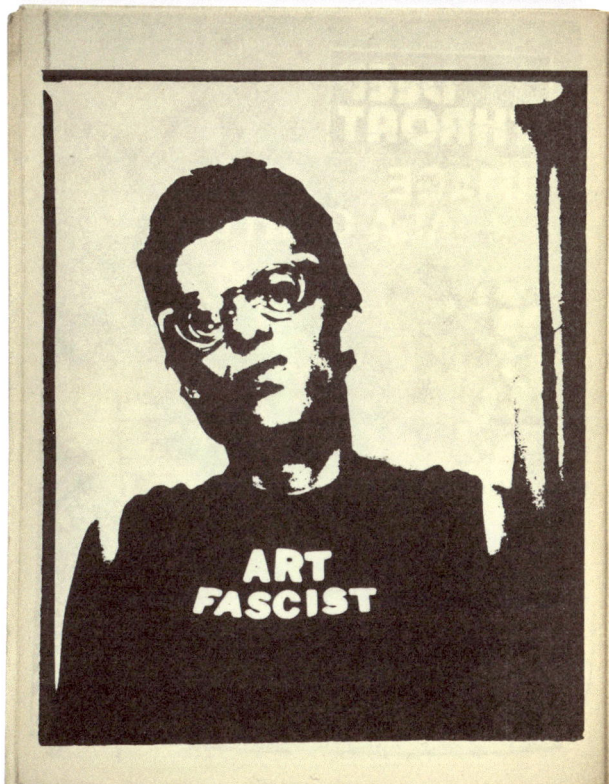

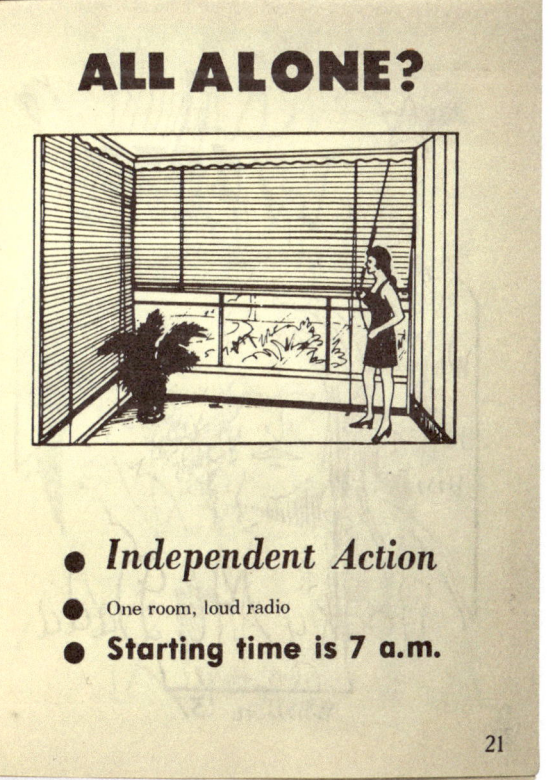

Modern Correspondence Magazine, no. 2, 1974
Photocopy, saddle stitched, with fold-out, 5 ½ × 4 ¼ in. (14 × 10.8 cm)
Private collection, New York

Jim Jocoy

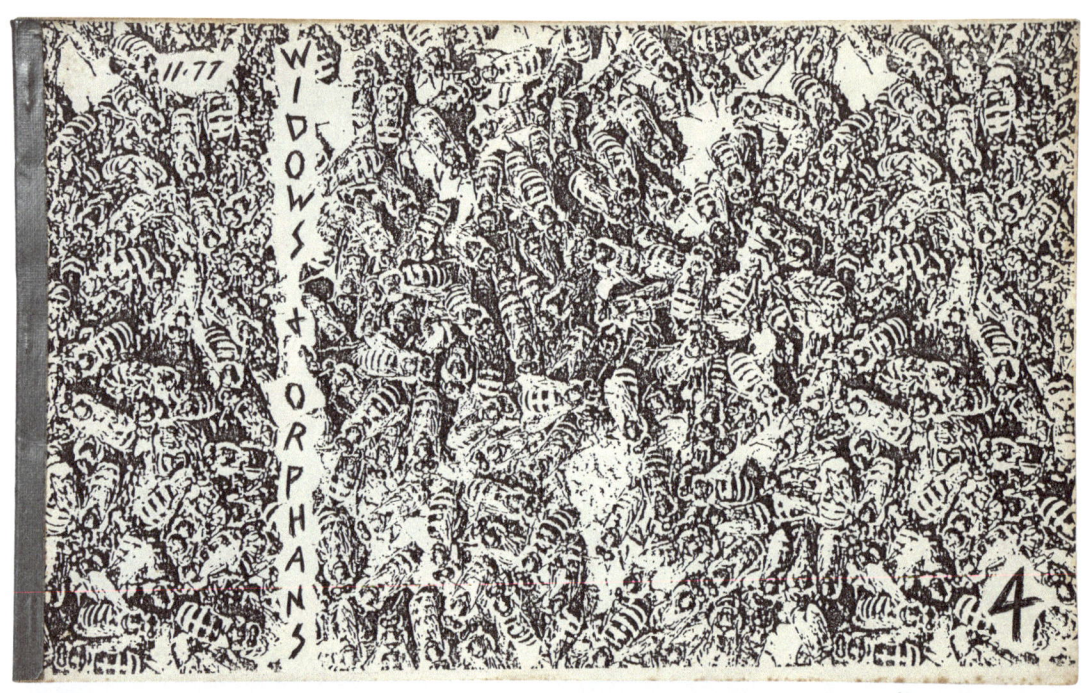

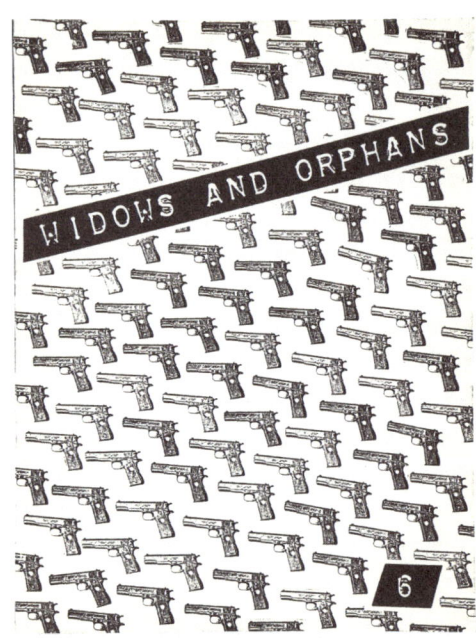

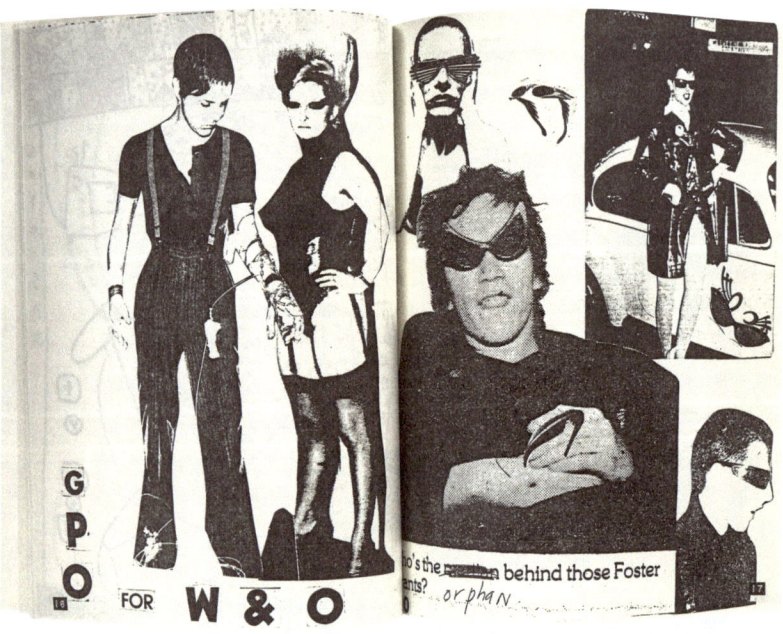

Widows and Orphans, no. 6, Winter 1978
Black-and-white and color photocopy, perfect bound,
10 ¹³⁄₁₆ × 8 ⅜ in. (27.5 × 21.3 cm); envelope: 12 × 9 in. (30.5 × 22.9 cm)
Collection the artist

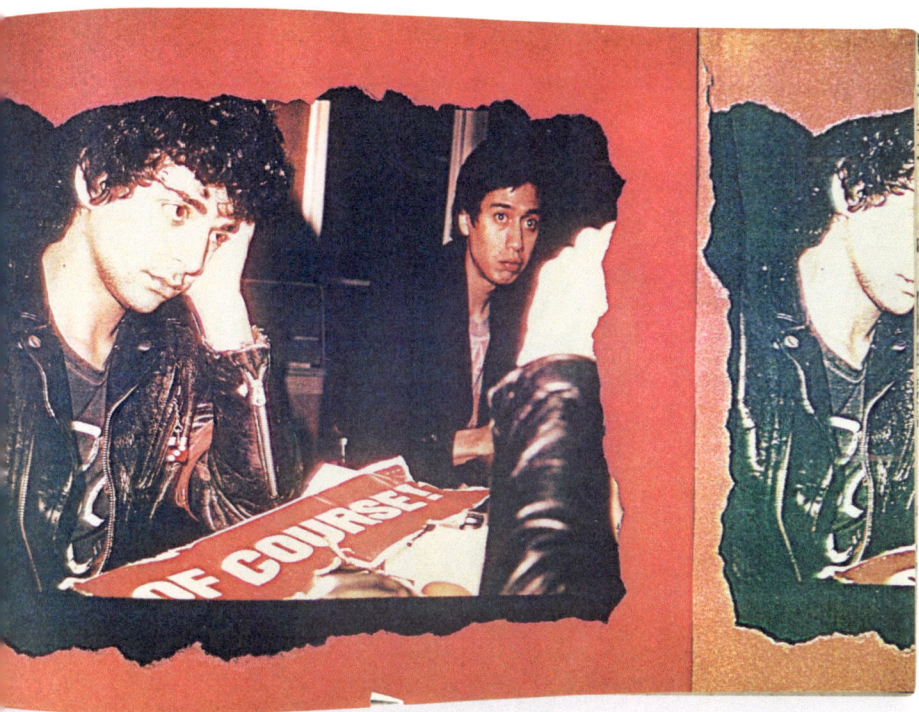

Widows and Orphans, no. 4, November 1977
Photocopy, side stapled and taped,
8 ½ × 14 ¹⁄₁₆ in. (21.6 × 35.7 cm)
Collection the artist

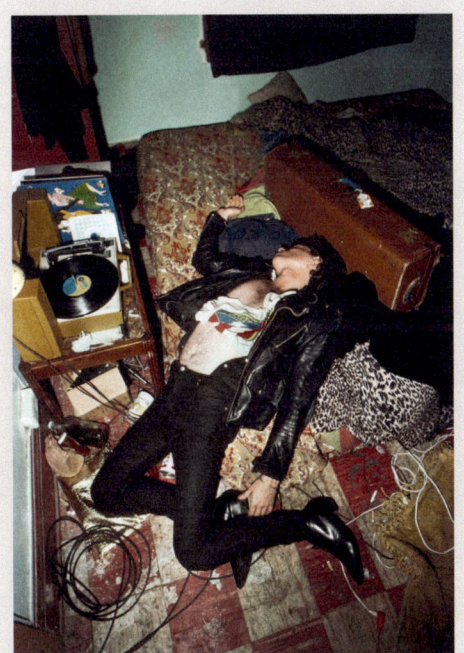

Guy Passed Out, 1979
Inkjet print, 22 × 17 in. (55.9 × 43.2 cm)
Casemore Kirkeby, San Francisco

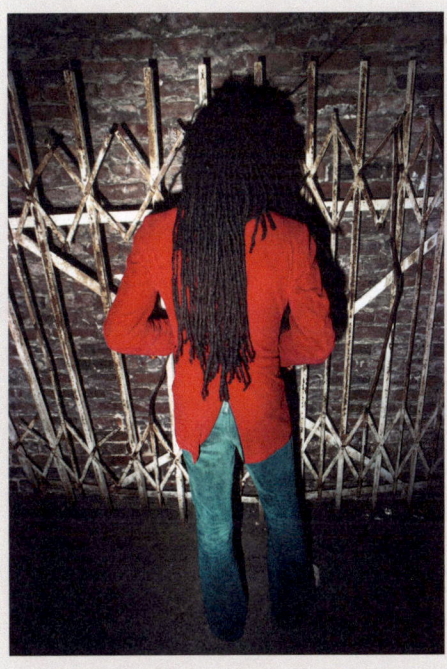

Tony with Red Jacket, 1978
Inkjet print, 22 × 17 in. (55.9 × 43.2 cm)
Casemore Kirkeby, San Francisco

V. Vale

↓→ *Search & Destroy*, no. 8, 1978
Offset, folded, 11 ½ × 9 in. (29.2 × 22.9 cm)
Collection Philip Aarons and Shelley Fox Aarons

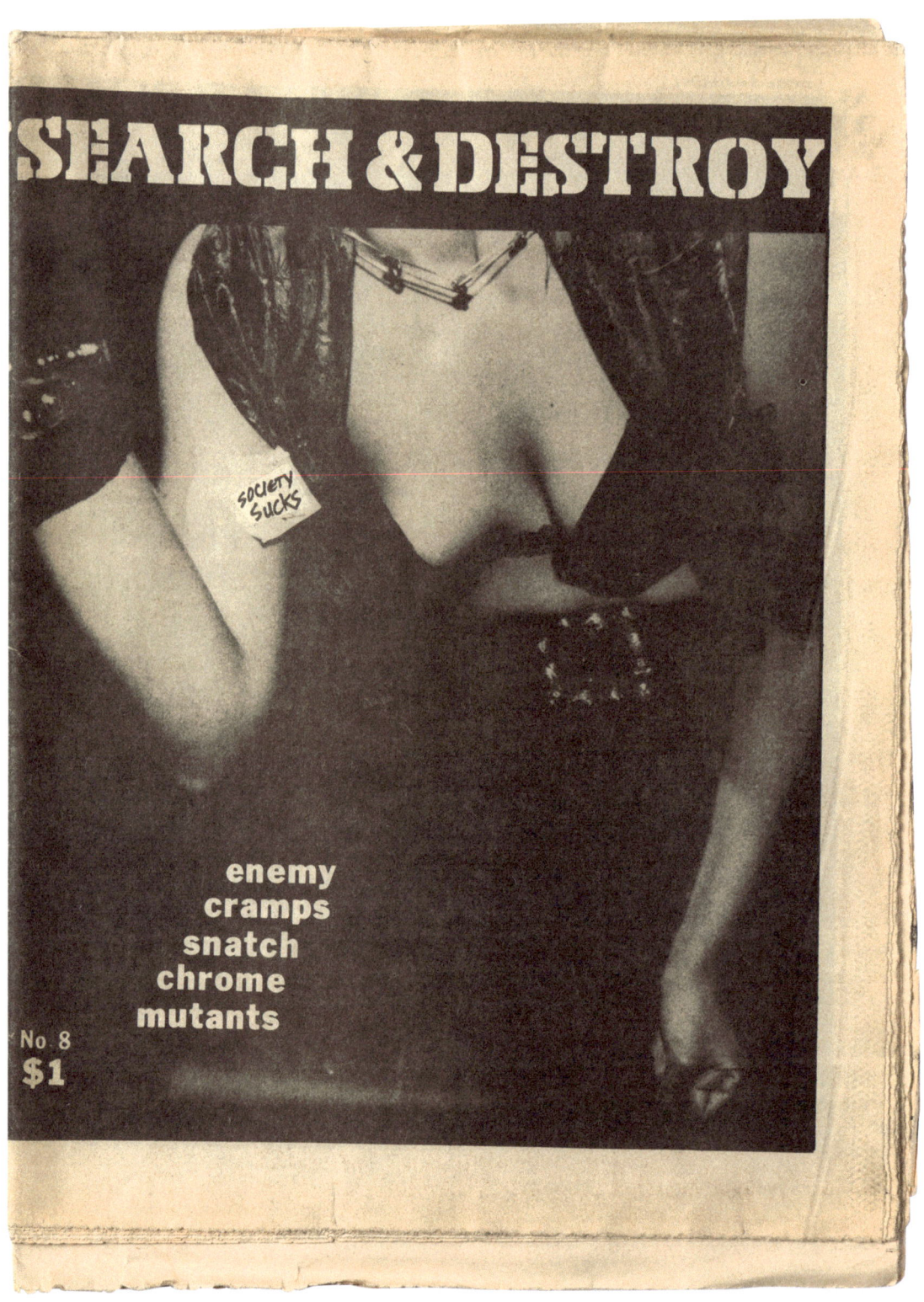

→ *Search & Destroy*, no. 10, 1978
Offset, folded, 11 ½ × 9 in. (29.2 × 22.9 cm)
Collection Philip Aarons and Shelley Fox Aarons

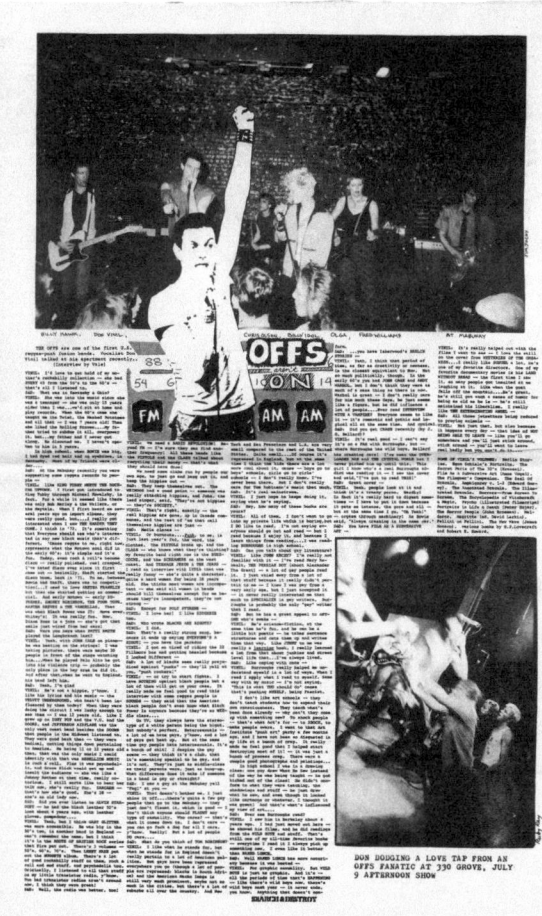

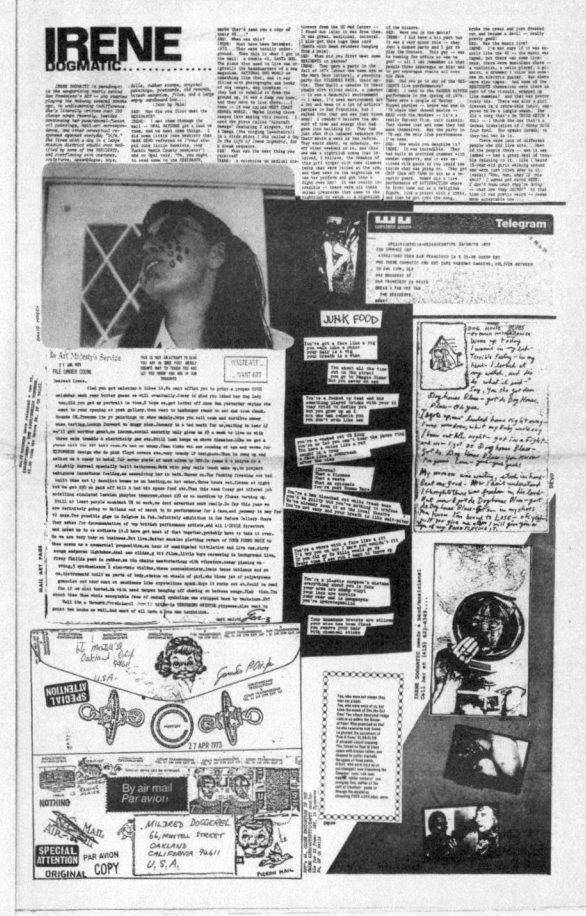

IRENE
DOGMATIC...

CONTROLLER: KARLA

MADDOG

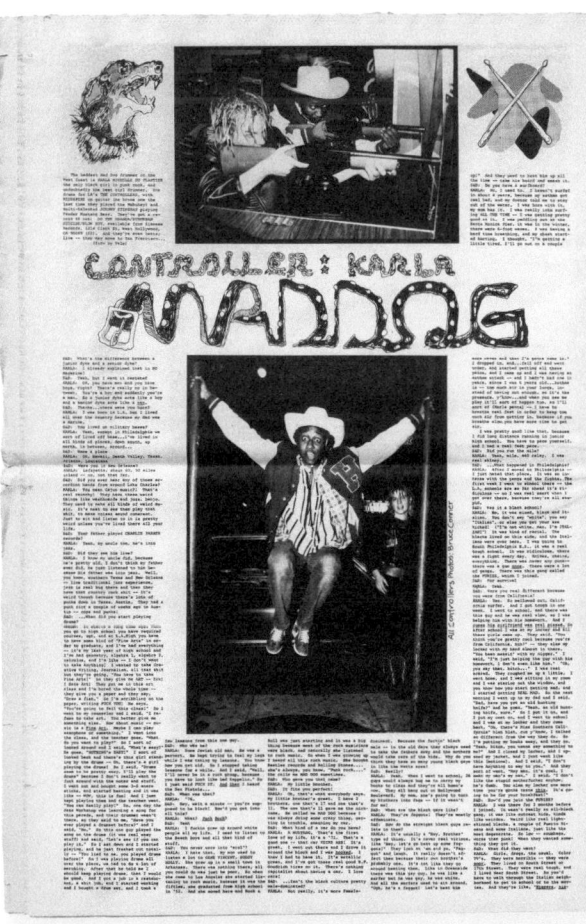

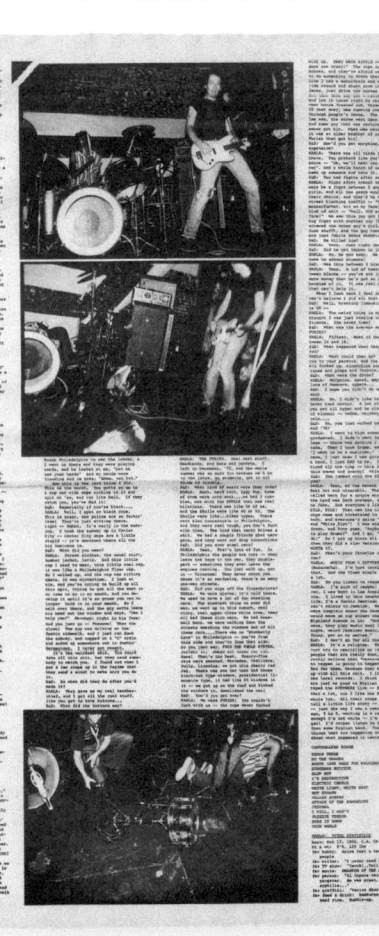

2.

The Punk Explosion, 1975–1990

Artists played a key role in adopting and disseminating punk's signature publication aesthetics and do-it-yourself ethos during the 1970s and 1980s. All that was necessary, as Richard Kern wrote in his zine the *Heroin Addict*, was to "buy a glue stick, dig out your photographs, put together a quick layout, and find a Zerox [*sic*] machine." Connections to correspondence-scene forerunners are found in Lisa Baumgardner's *Modern Girlz* and *Bikini Girl*, which included contributions by mail artists Irene Dogmatic and Tom Hosier; they are also seen in the work of art collective World Imitation, which initially produced zines as an offshoot of correspondence artist Skot Armstrong's *Science Holiday* before becoming the band Monitor. Forging further links to the punk community, many of the artists formed bands, notable among them Destroy All Monsters, Fifth Column, and Nervous Gender. Barbara Ess was part of New York's post-punk No Wave scene with her band the Static (with Glenn Branca), and her zine *Just Another Asshole* featured many associated artists and bands.

Many artists' zines of this period channeled the tropes of violence and abjection that were popularly associated with punk. Raymond Pettibon's publications are among the best known of this genre, with their counter-iconography of the 1960s, featuring murderous hippies, now indelibly associated with the image of Southern California hardcore. A similar impulse lay behind Cary Loren's photographs of the performer Niagara wielding a knife—images that appeared in numerous issues of *Destroy All Monsters Magazine* in the late 1970s, alongside drawings and photocopied collages by Destroy All Monsters band members Mike Kelley, Jim Shaw, and Niagara herself. Kern's many zines of this era featured stories of urban alienation, addiction, and violence written by himself, Dogmatic, Montanna Houston, Tommy Turner, and David Wojnarowicz. Kern and Turner also contributed street photography; Houston, cut-up collage poems; and Wojnarowicz, drawings and altered Archie cartoons. Turner's zine, *Redrum*, also charted the period's fascination with violence via press clippings, fictional accounts, Kern's elaborately staged gore photographs, and additional Wojnarowicz comics.

New York punk subcultures overlapped with graffiti and hip-hop, as seen in *IGTimes (International Graffiti Times)*, founded in 1983 by photographer David Schmidlapp, who was joined in 1986 by graffiti artist Phase 2 as art director. The zine's multicolor printing and poster-like format made a case for the aesthetic qualities of the city's tagging culture, at a time when graffiti was officially denounced as vandalism.

As with the correspondence artists considered in the previous section, many artists central to punk's formative years identified as queer and refuted the "respectability politics" of the more mainstream and assimilationist gay liberation movement. With a title referencing its willfully low production quality and trashy contents, Mark Morrisroe and Lynelle White's *Dirt*, for example, emerged in the mid-1970s out of Boston's punk scene, where zines like *Boston Groupie News*, *Miscarriage*, and *Sleaze* vied with one another in presenting scandalous faux gossip about local celebrities. With a campier sensibility than its peers, *Dirt* was an early example of the genre of queer zines that would spring up in subsequent decades. Among its successors were the zines of Gerardo Velázquez, who brought the confrontational tone of his queer, electro-punk band Nervous Gender to the publications he produced in the early 1990s in response to the AIDS pandemic and his own HIV-positive diagnosis.

Perhaps the most influential of the early queer zines was *J.D.s*, produced by G. B. Jones and Bruce LaBruce in Toronto. The zine followed in the wake of earlier Toronto publications such as *Hide* and *Dr. Smith*, which similarly brought together the city's punk and experimental film scenes. *J.D.s* was particularly important in promoting the newly coined musical genre of homocore, or queercore, pioneered by Jones's band Fifth Column. In the mode of many of their New York–based peers, Jones, LaBruce, and others associated with *J.D.s* (such as Candy Parker and Suzy Richter) also took up independent filmmaking. Their legacy would be continued by a lineage of Toronto queer zines, including *Bimbox*, *Jane and Frankie*, *Monstar*, *Salmon Hut*, and others that emerged in the 1980s and 1990s.

Mark Morrisroe and Lynelle White

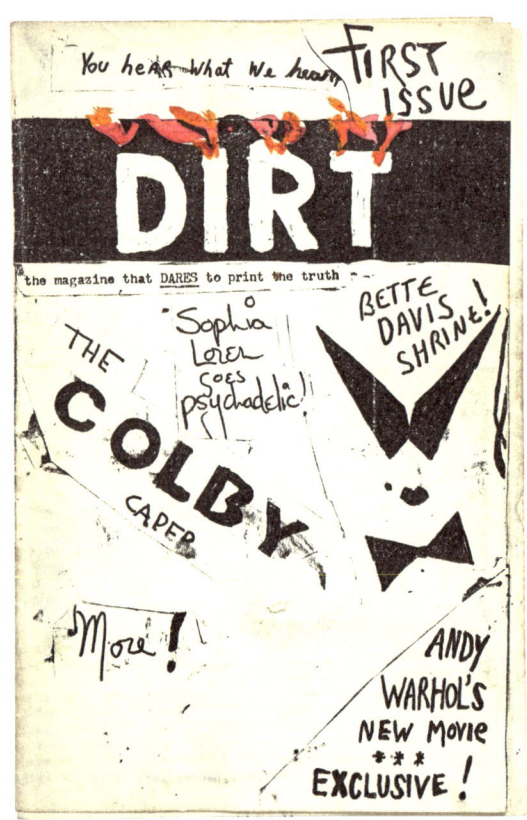

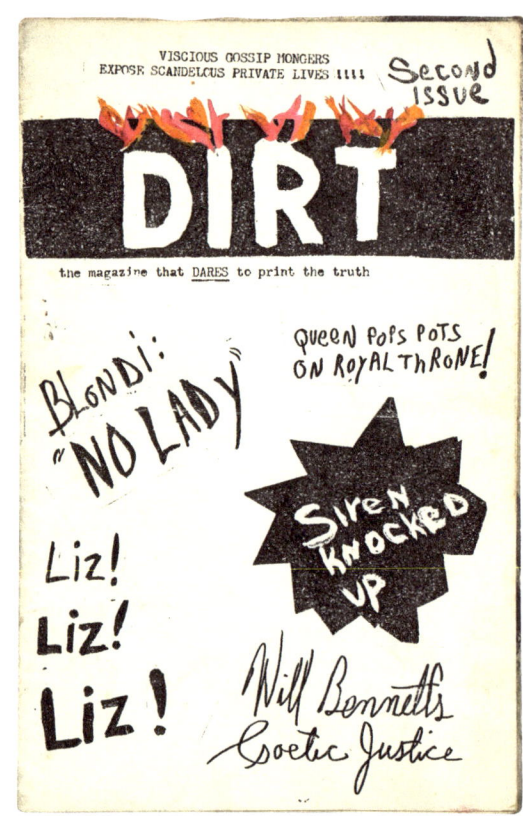

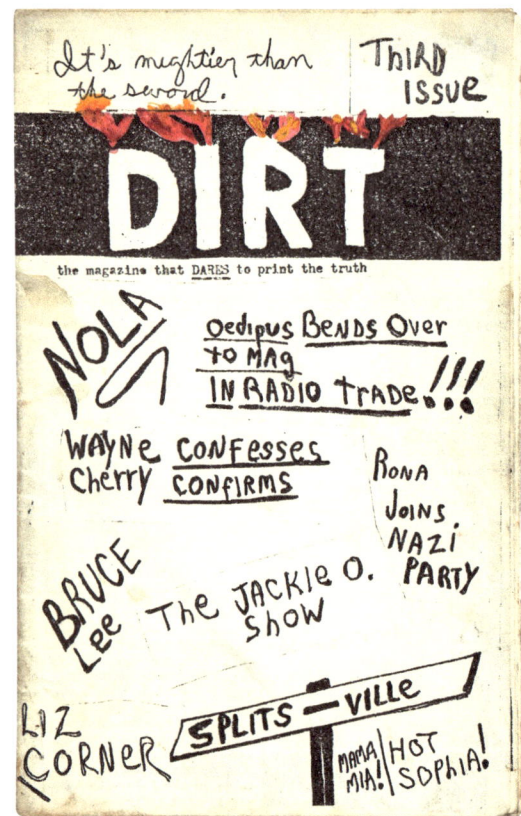

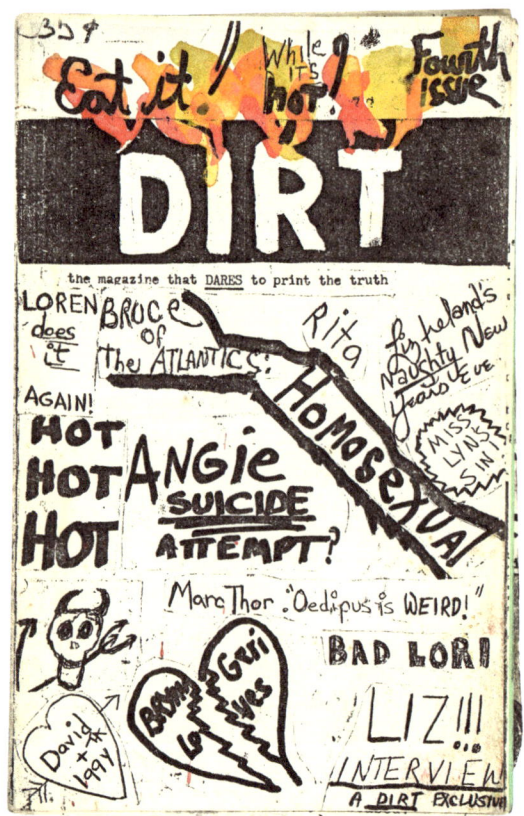

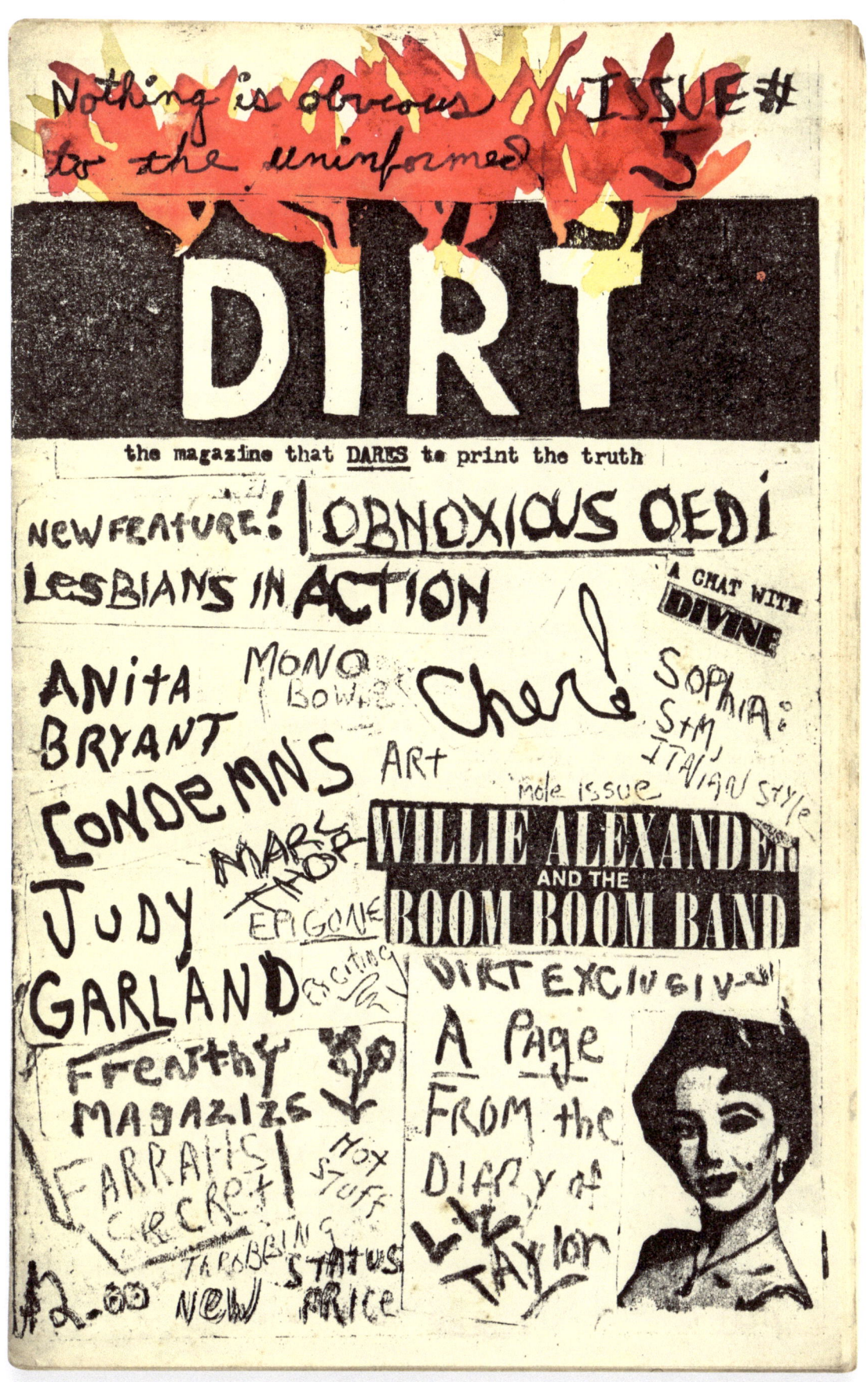

Nothing is obvious to the uninformed × ISSUE # 5

DIRT

the magazine that <u>DARES</u> to print the truth

NEW FEATURE! | OBNOXIOUS OEDI

LESBIANS IN ACTION

A CHAT WITH **DIVINE**

ANITA BRYANT CONDEMNS

MONQ BOWRE

Cher!

ART

SOPHIA, S&M, ITALIAN STYLE

nole issue

WILLIE ALEXANDER AND THE BOOM BOOM BAND

MARY TYLER EPIGONE

JUDY GARLAND

exciting

FFEATHY MAGAZINS

FARRAHS SECRET!

HOT STUFF

THROBBING STATUS NEW PRICE

$2.00

DIRT EXCLUSIV~

A Page FROM the DIARY of Liz TAYLOR

Dirt, nos. 1–5, 1975–77
Photocopy with watercolor on covers, folded, 8 9/16 × 5 3/4 in. (21.7 × 14.6 cm)
Collection Willie Alexander

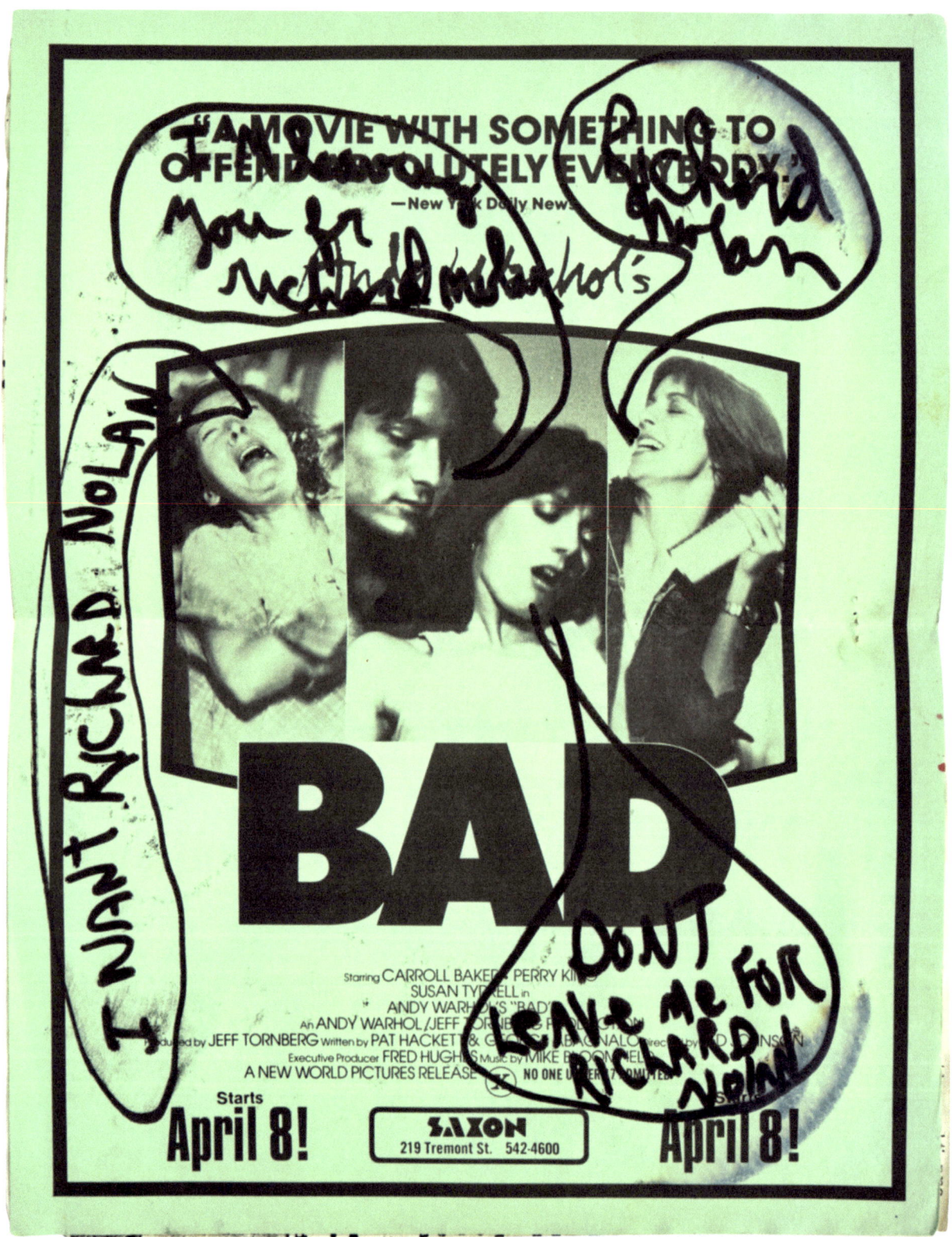

TRUE CONFESSIONS   CONT.

My teeth were chattering like magpies. We sat by the square,
white brick fire place. I guess I had a few drinks. I knew he
did.
"Honey?" I asked, "Don't you think five is enough?" My eyes
flickered up and down shily and I dropped my voice.
I can see your in a bad way baby", he said brutally almost
savagely. His eyes bore blue laiserx beams right/thru/through
my brain. "I'm not gonna end up on the floor like dad every
night." Then he accused me of making love to the boss's son.
I dont know how many hours later I regained consicunness.
But my hands were black and blue and the odor was unmistackeable
My clothes were a rubbish heap on the floor. I pulled my dress
down over my knees, trying to fight back the lump in my throat.
Nicks words came back to me in a dream: "You dirty slut." I seemed
to hear him say. Finally I called my best friend Anna.
Part two next issue. This is just one dirt readers true con-
ssion. /Send in yours and we might print it.

Mathew Makenzy of Reddy Teddy is a very
sleazy person as well as a very lazy one.
He lays around his room all day drinking
  when he has to pee, he usually does it
  in one of his empty bottles. Well, one day
good friend Willis A. was visiting and helped
himself to a drink of tequila and can you
guess what was in the bottle? Thats right,
PISS. Drinks piss and he cant even send us a
letter now & then.   Willie teeses his
hair and used to wear blue Jack Stien make-up.
Willie was also one of the winners of Dirt's
cheapest thrill contest for that picture he sent
us of him in the bathtub. The other winner was
Marc Thor for his bondage catalogues. Your prizes are
waiting.

Photo BY Frank

Did you know that beautiful Boston groupie,
had a miscarrage? Did she? She did try to kill
herself--slashed her wrists. What caused her to
do it? We dont really know. Do you beleave that?
Well, we do know but we are not going to say
because we have too much respect for her. She isnt
exactly the dumb blond she pretends to be. We hear
that she draws and does some really great cartoon
work. Maybe she will do something for Dirt some time.
We would really like that. And in exchange we probably print what ever she liked. (How about a center
Dolly pParton has been seen around town

A NEW FACE IN THE CROWD

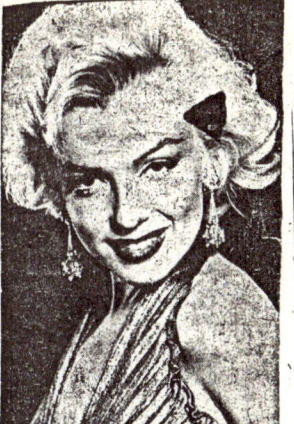

And her name is Rita
Daniels. She's from NY &
came up here because she
likes the Boston Rock scen
better (not to mention the
boys). Ha Ha New York.
Rita holds the record for
the most guys fucked in an
hour. 26. She loves gang
bangs, light S&M, and her
kick is water sports.
She is a member of our sta
so put her on your guest
list.

Poor, little LANCE LOUD,
he's all alone in the gym now
that his body building buddy, Russ Mael, is off on tour
but I doubt that he'll be
lonley for long. It's good
to see so much constructive
energy put to use.

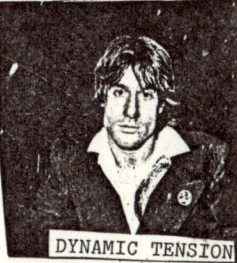

DYNAMIC TENSION

DAVID BOWIE SEEN USING PUBLIC TRANSPORTATION!!!!

Who stole Willie Alaxander's red polka dot undi
and wears them quite frequently? We cant tell, but
his initials are MDM.

DIRT EXCLUSIVE!

Annie Golden interview.
Dirt magazene resently had
an exclusive interview with
Annie Golden, who has a band called the Shirts.
When we asked her about her sex life she said " I
sometimes fuck the organist, and he's got a nice ol
organ." She also was the girlfriend of the Tuff
Darts bass player for 5 months. Lately she has beer
after Lenny Kaye, and she thinks he has something
for her too. She gave Judy Garland and Bowie
as her biggest influences, and thinks "Cars
(the band) are obnixieus."

Battered Patty

Dirt, no. 4, 1977
Photocopy with watercolor on cover, folded, 8¾ × 5¹¹⁄₁₆ in. (22.2 × 14.4 cm)
Collection Willie Alexander

97

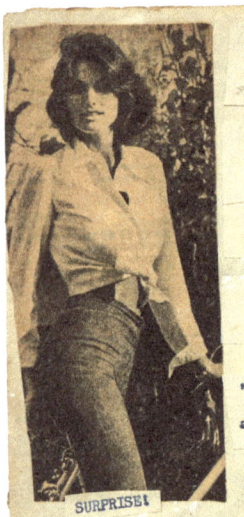

R.W., Miss "Jugs", used to jump out of cakes at conventions for a living before she became an actress.

Rumor has it that ANDY WARHOL is silk-screening up a batch of crusifixion paintings. A was reported to have said

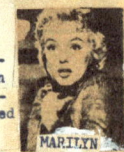

MARILYN

when asked why such a religious theme," Everyone does a Crusifixion scene. All the great painters..."

" THE CHITA REVEREZ SHOW WITH CHARO", will premiere next summer. A sisters act. Get it?

SURPRISE!

Lou Reed is planning a new album and tour, but that's all we know.

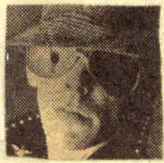

Complications-- Sources say that at the time Geri Hall married Mr Ferry she had a bun in the oven, though now it has disappeared. Who took the Sarah Lee? Not only that but they are back together again, just like Liz + Dick.

Katherine Hepburn just had another facelift we are told. Keep your chin up Kate.

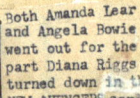

Both Amanda Lear and Angela Bowie went out for the part Diana Riggs turned down in the NEW AVENGERS seri.

CLUTZ

Remember all of those rumors about David Bowie losing his hair? Well, they're true. The man is as bald as an egg. There is no need to worry though, it's growing back. Too bad we dont have a picture.

At a benefit for the Concerned Foundation (which supports cancer research) LIZA MINNELLI led a brass band down Rodeo Drive--and stumbled over a bump in the street and fell flat on her face right in front of the Gucci showroom.

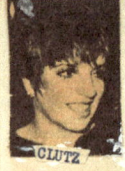

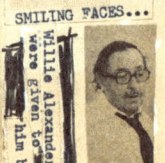

An eye witness tells us that during the taping of one of her shows in front of a live audience, Dinah Shore rose to do a song and when she opened her mouth to sing, her upper plate of her dentures became dislauged and nearly fell out of her mouth.

SMILING FACES...

Willie Alexanders torn jeans were given to him by Marc Thor.

Playwrite Tennessee Williams was arrested in Italy, our most trustworthy sources tell us, for being in possesion of a fifteen year old boy. The child claims to have been kept against his will but the authorities do not believe his story because of his past reputation. It seems that Truman Capote was arrested under the same circumstances just last year, and with the same boy, who it was fourteen at the time. There is still the matter of statutory rape though.

Actress Julie Harris was arrested for drunken driving recently we are told. When asked why while under the influence of the drink, she began to rave on about the memory of James Dean. It seems that quite a thing developed between them during the filming of EAST OF EDEN. Miss Harris refused to go into mourning at the time of his death, now the memory is driving her to madness.

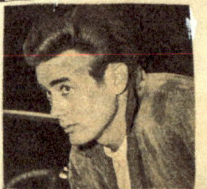

DIRT EDITORIAL

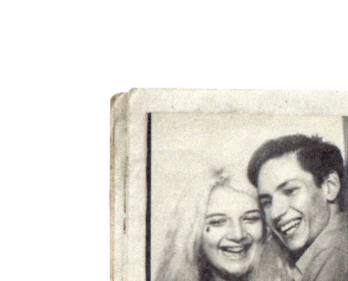

you're happy--we're happy

We at Dirt have decided that our mag is an art form which gives us the right to steal pix, lie, and slander people. Art is above the law. We just wanted you to know. If you would like to write for us, just send us your stories and we will print them. Specify if you want your name printed. You can lie if you want to. Slander your friends, or just get your name in print. It's fun. And readers, please send us photes of your faverite stars that you would like to see in print. We have a very hard time getting pictures of local celebrities to print. Did you read that celebrities! Jhonny barnes goes into pay toilets and shits on the floor, local celeb tells us.

"The Lone Ranger of Sex" whose photos first in Melanie's Sleep Mask (Black & silly) so lewd lipsticked & still wears the one Ginger Snaps (Rockscene Jan 76' nude photo & whatcha cant see is that I have a 45 adapter on my nipple hence Beatific expression) found in the glove compartment of an old car an old abandon in the Wellfleet Woods car & she sewed a few Butterflies on it like on her right shoulder tatoo But most of the Butterflies have fallen off & stars & wonderfull things & she's in LA & thats good..............A.K.A. "The Masked Marvel",But really I don't always use it ,I dig scarvs too etc "I wanna get led on stage like that some time".........Nada Mas. Sometimes when I wake up with it on I don't know whose next to me. Sometimes I just grab whatever is next to me on the floor like a teeshirt if I havent just jerked off into it . . . X WA

SOPHIA'S BIG BREAK-UP PART 5

"It must have been the drugs."
" Dont worry said the nude roomservice boy, his cock still hard. The tip just barely rubbing the floor between his knees as he kneeled over the unconsious Italian film star. "Her pulse seems ok."
Marchelle was on the brink of hysterics. " You are not a doctor,what do you know? For all you know she could die any minuite right here on the floor of this expensive Swiss hotel. What a scandle."
"I told you not to worry said Hans as he dipped his hand into the piture of ice water he had brought to the room only an hour earlier. He sprinkled a few dropd onto her face. She immediatly stirred.
Marchelle rambled on. " I knew it. I shouldnt have let her sheot up after she had taken so much acid..."
"She's coming around."
The first thing that Sophia Loren saw as she opened her eyes was Hans huge tool dangling in front of her. It was too much for her to resist. Even in her condition.
Hans moaned.
Marchelle, the boy she kept, regained his composure and immediately became arroused.
Sophia sucked and swallowed greedily, gagging herself at times but ignoring it until finally she was choking on her own vomit.
Hans drew back immediatly as Sophia retched unashamedly before him on to the carpet. Chunky yellow yellow bile ran down her chins.
Marchelle could have sworn that she was going to die that night.

TO BE CONTINUED.......

If you want to find out how all this started, send for back issues.

← Paste-up for *Dirt*, no. 2, 1975–76
Offset, photocopies, gelatin silver prints, glue, paper,
8 ½ × 5 ⅝ in. (21.6 × 14.3 cm)
Collection Jack Pierson

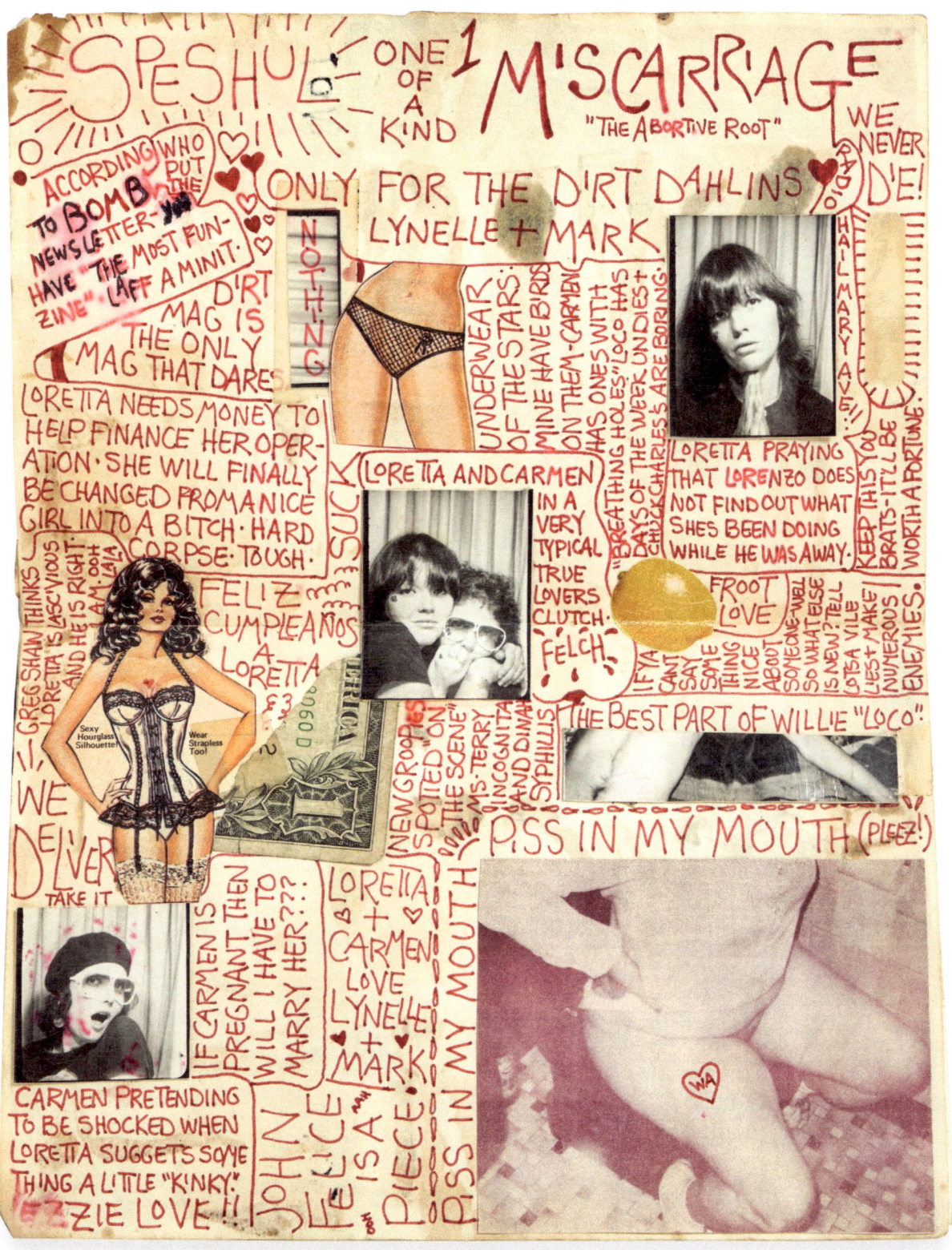

←↑ Paste-ups for *Dirt*, no. 5, 1977, with special issue of *Miscarriage* by Loretta Baretta
(a.k.a. Penny Greenwald) and Carmen Monoxide (a.k.a. Carmen Wiseman)
Offset, ink photocopies, gelatin silver prints, glue, paper, 8 ½ × 5 ⅝ in. (21.6 × 14.3 cm)
Collection Jack Pierson

99

Boston Punk Zines and Broadsides

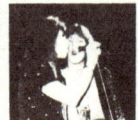

← Miss Lyn (a.k.a. Linda Cardinal)
The Boston Groupie News, no. 9, 1977
Offset, folded, 11 × 8 ½ in. (27.9 × 21.6 cm)
Collection the artist

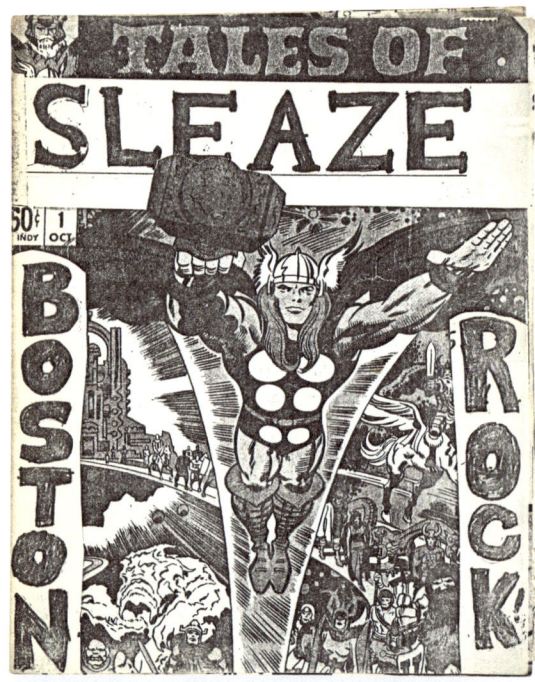

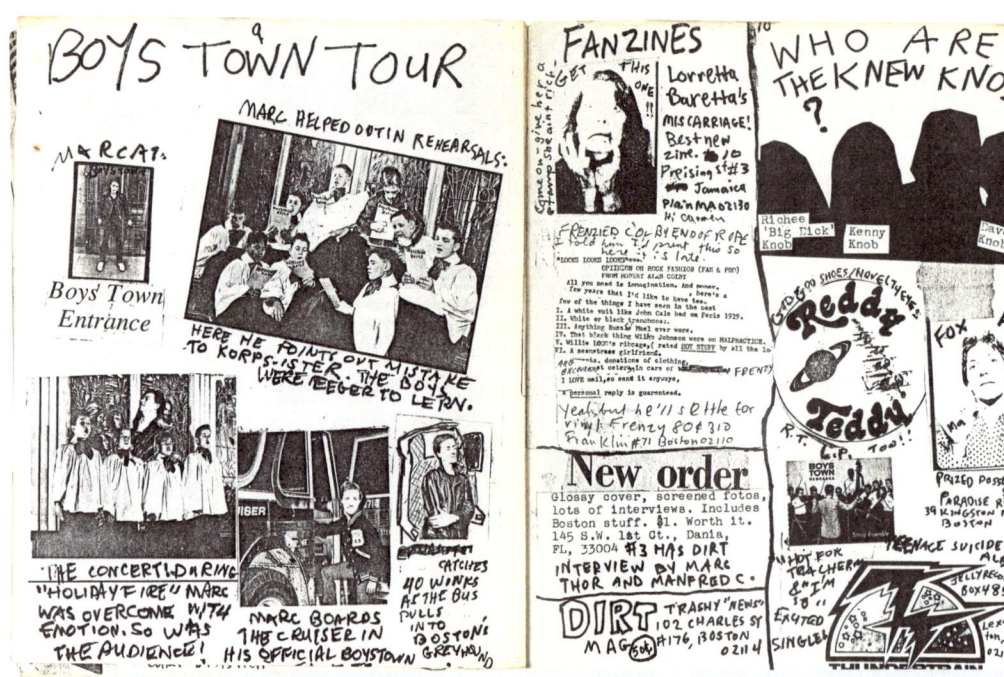

Marc Thor
Sleaze, no. 6, ca. 1977
Photocopy, folded, 8 11/16 × 7 1/16 in. (22.1 × 17.9 cm)
Collection Willie Alexander

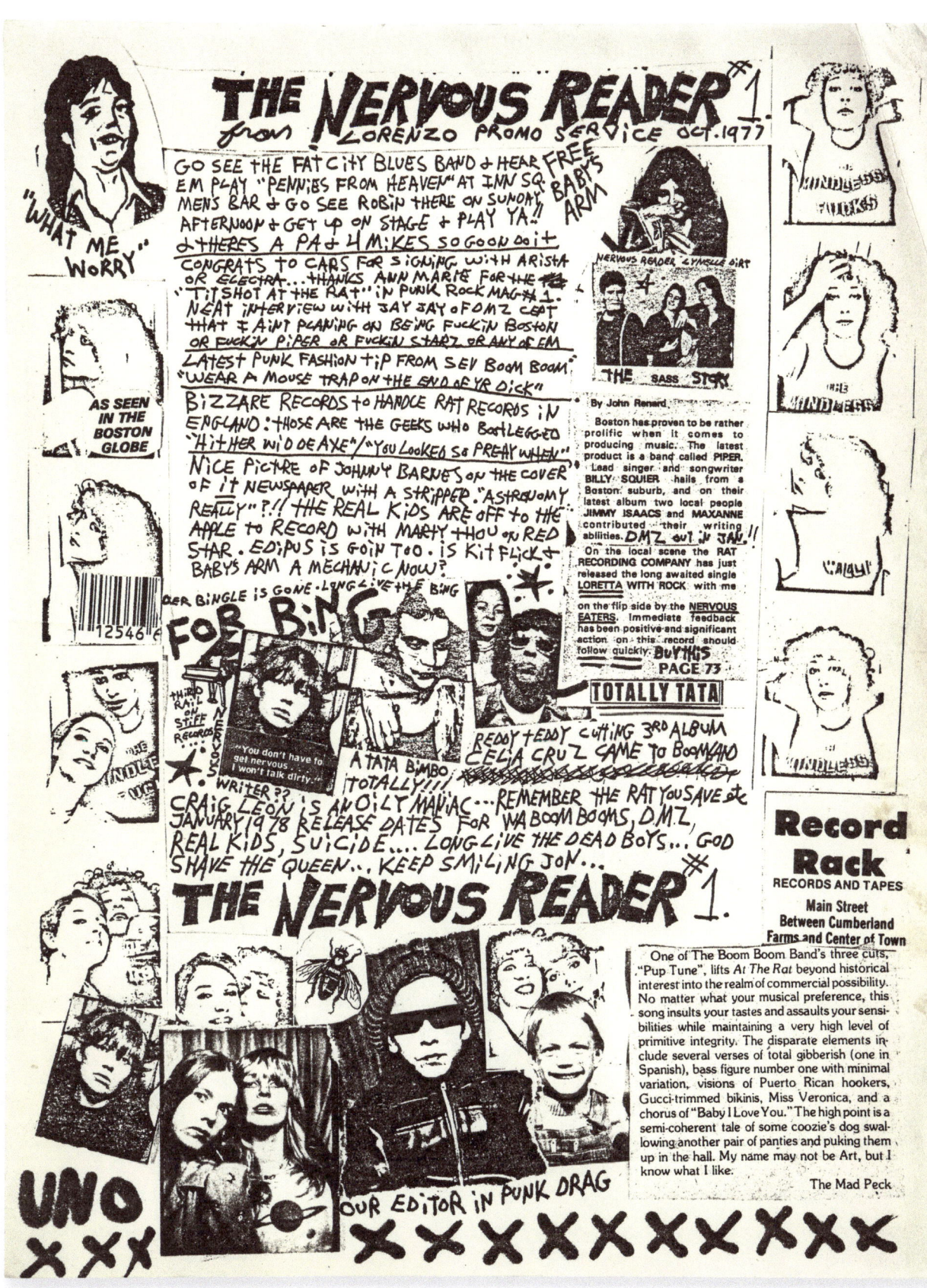

Willie Alexander
The Nervous Reader, no. 1, October 1977
Photocopy, 11 × 8 ½ in. (27.9 × 21.6 cm)
Collection the artist

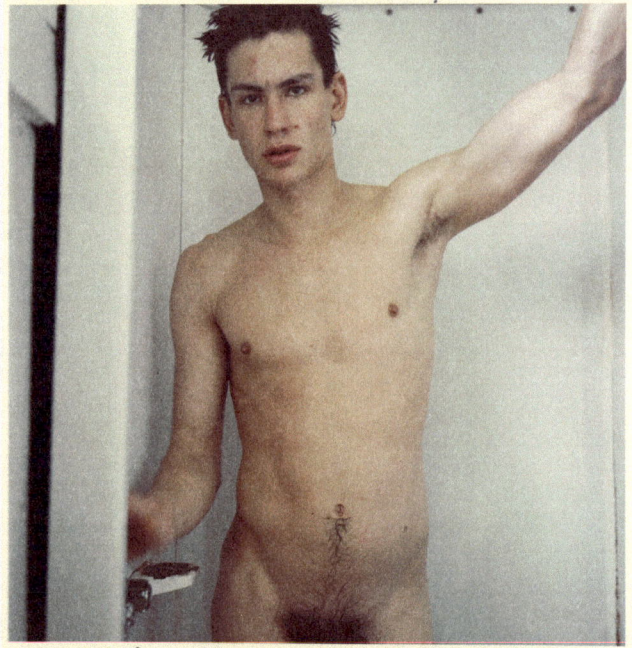

Mark Morrisroe
Self-Portrait (to Brent), 1982
Chromogenic print, negative sandwich,
retouched with ink and inscribed with marker,
20 × 16 in. (50.8 × 40.6 cm)
Whitney Museum of American Art, New York

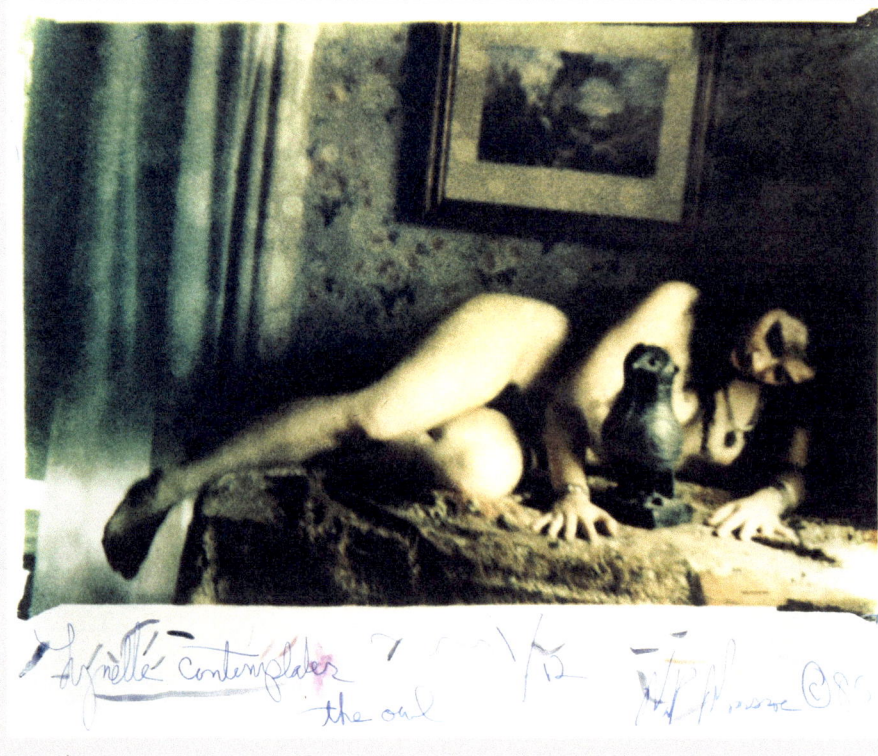

Mark Morrisroe
Lynelle Contemplates the Owl, 1985
Chromogenic print, negative sandwich, retouched with ink and inscribed with marker,
16 × 20 in. (40.6 × 50.8 cm)
CLAMP, New York

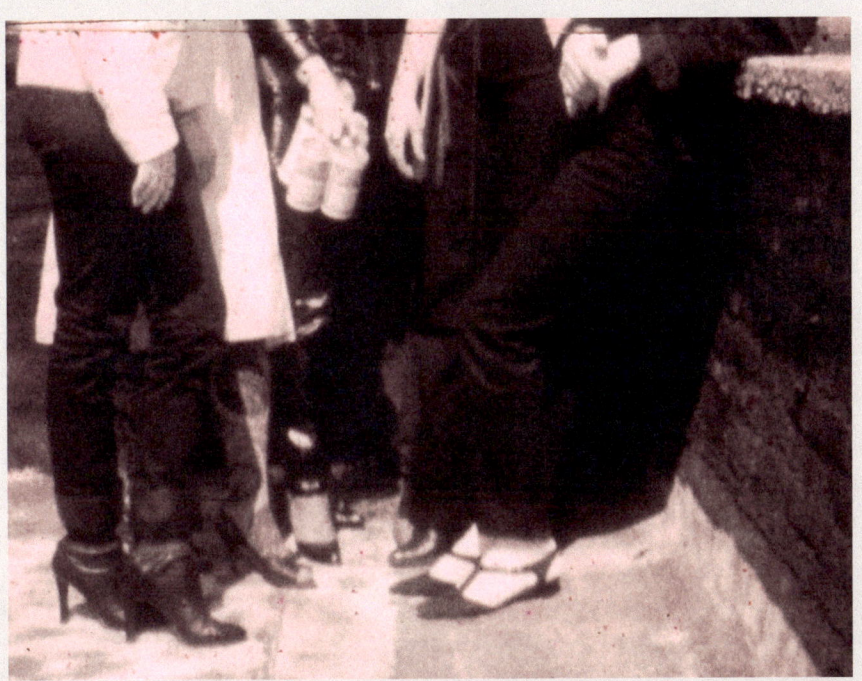

Lisa Baumgardner
Still from *Girl Pack*, 1978
Super-8 film; black and white (dyed pink), silent; 5 min., 38 sec.
The Museum of Modern Art, New York

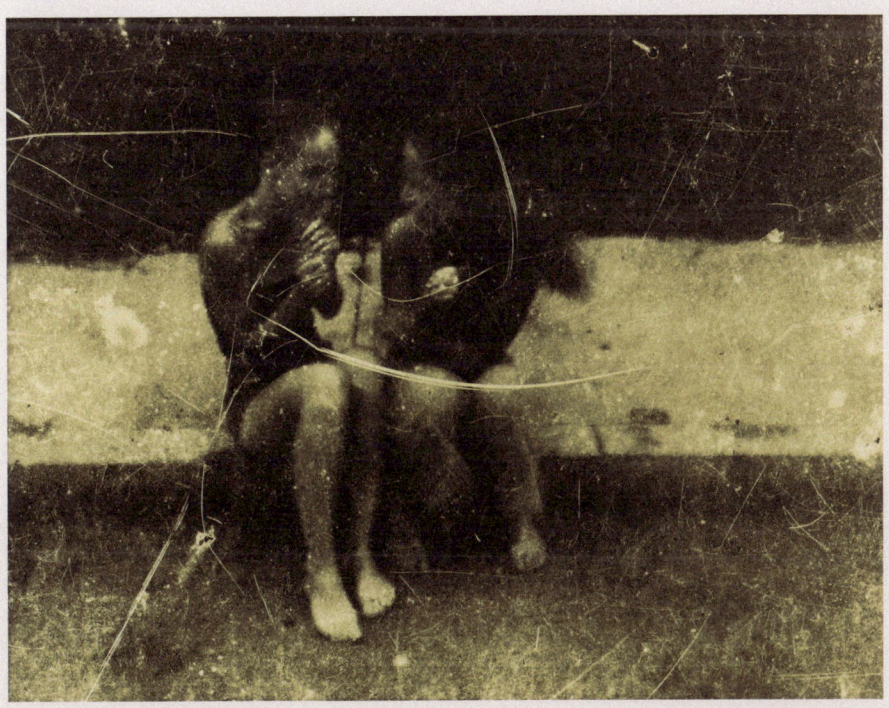

Barbara Ess
Girls on Curb, 1983
Chromogenic print, 29 ¾ × 39 ¾ in. (75.6 × 101 cm)
The Estate of Barbara E. Schwartz (a.k.a. Barbara Ess)

Lisa Baumgardner

→ *Modern Girlz*, no. 4, 1978
Photocopy and offset, saddle stitched, 8 ½ × 5 ½ in. (21.6 × 14 cm)
Collection Philip Aarons and Shelley Fox Aarons

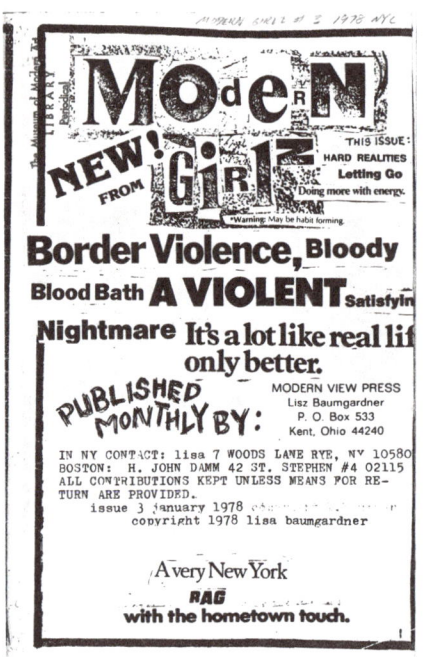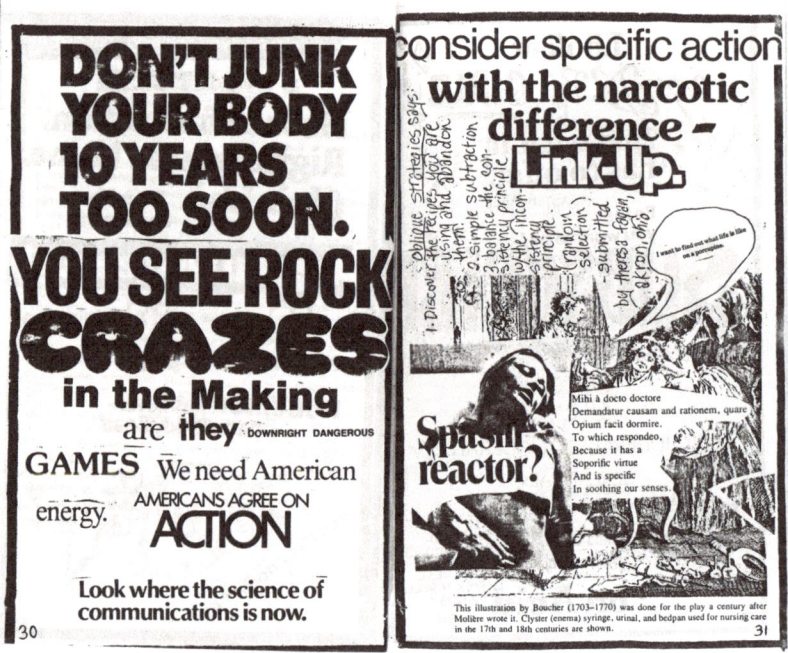

Modern Girlz, no. 3, 1978
Photocopy and offset, saddle stitched, 8 ½ × 5 ½ in. (21.6 × 14 cm)
The Museum of Modern Art Library, New York

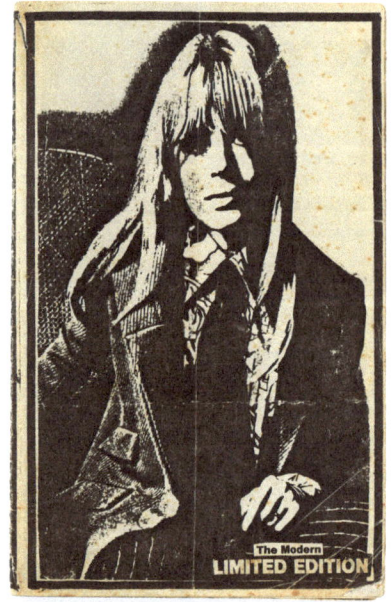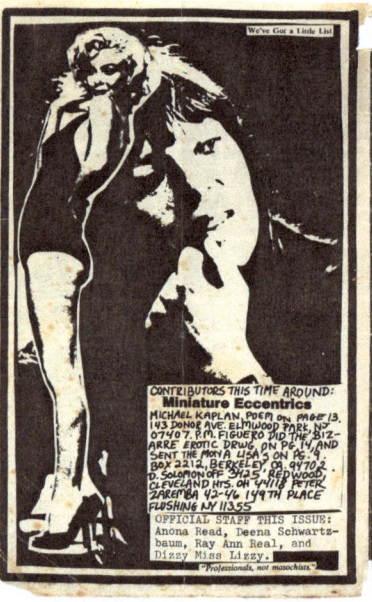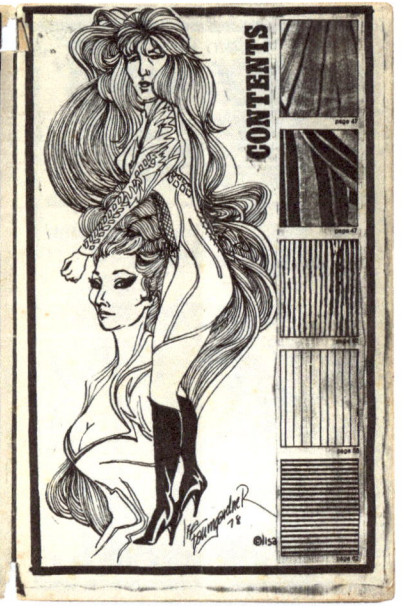

Modern Girlz, no. 5, 1978
Photocopy and offset, saddle stitched, 8 ½ × 5 ½ in. (21.6 × 14 cm)
Collection Philip Aarons and Shelley Fox Aarons

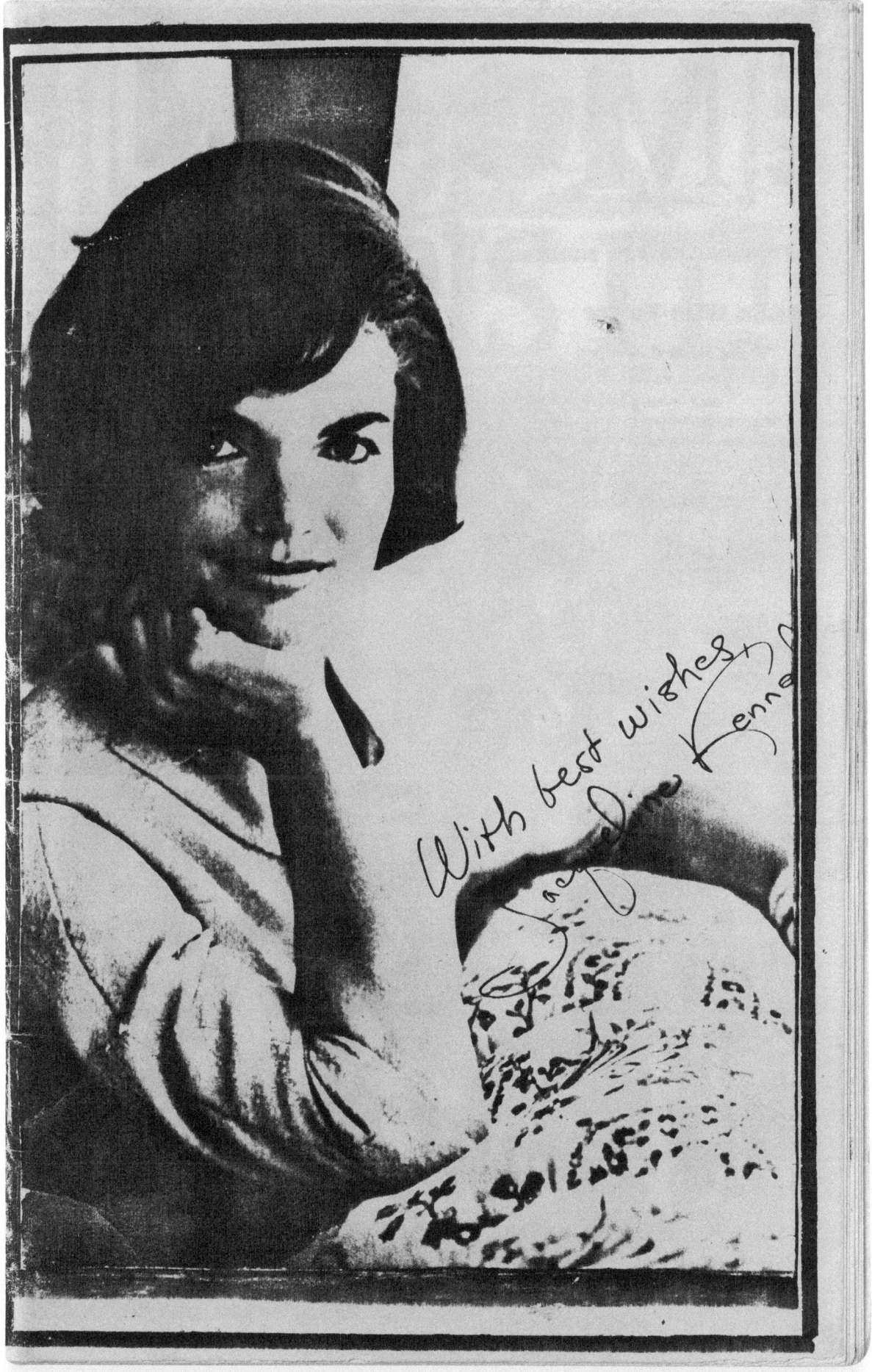

With best wishes
Jacqueline Kennedy

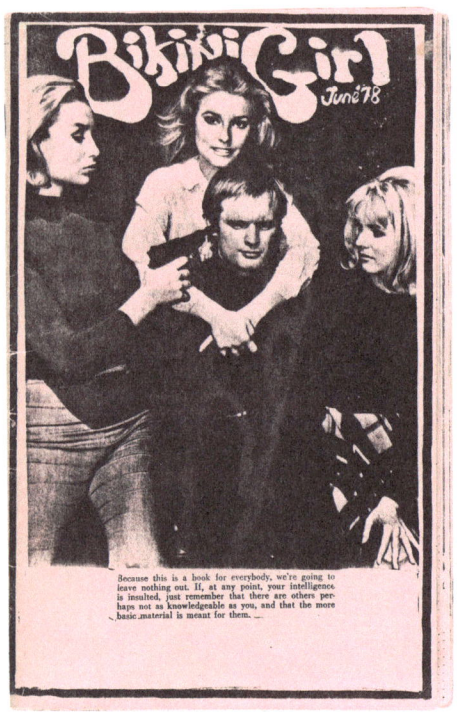

Bikini Girl, vol. 1, no. 1, 1978
Offset, saddle stitched, 8½ × 5½ in. (21.6 × 14 cm)
Franklin Furnace Collection. The Museum of Modern Art Library,
New York

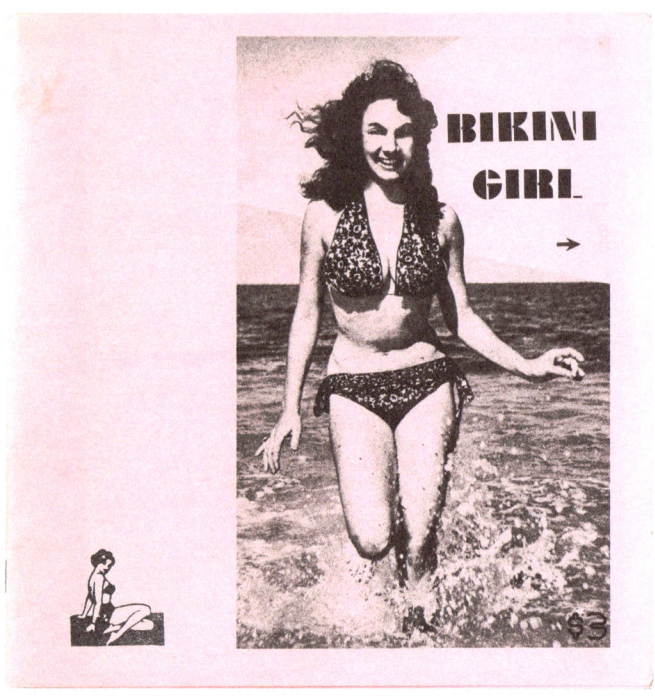

Bikini Girl, vol. 1, no. 5, 1980
Offset, saddle stitched, 8 × 8 in. (20.3 × 20.3 cm)
Collection Philip Aarons and Shelley Fox Aarons

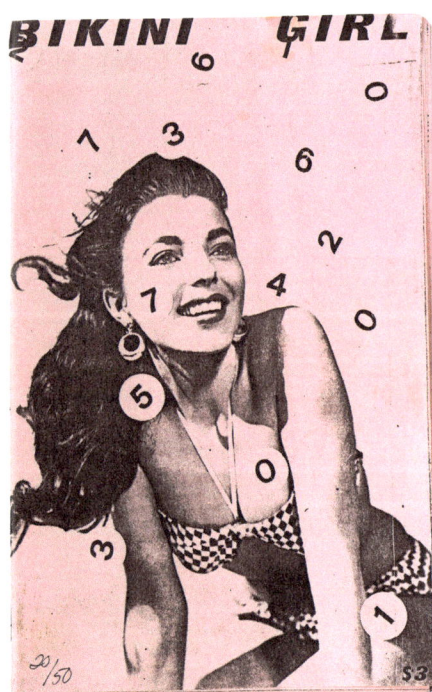

Bikini Girl, vol. 1, no. 7, 1980
Offset, saddle stitched, 8½ × 5½ in. (21.6 × 14 cm)
Collection Philip Aarons and Shelley Fox Aarons

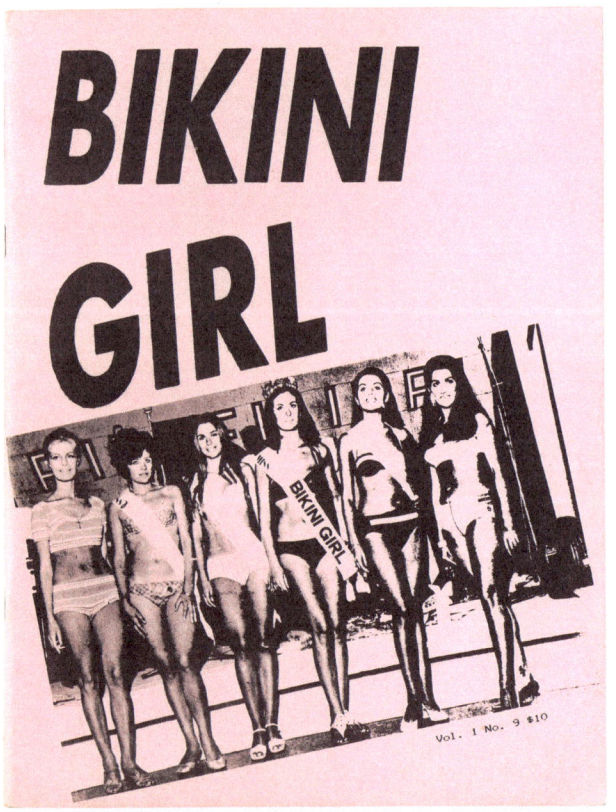

Bikini Girl, vol. 1, no. 9, 1987
Offset, saddle stitched, 11 × 8½ in. (27.9 × 21.6 cm)
The Museum of Modern Art Library, New York

BIKINI GIRL

THERE ARE NO MIRACLES.
THERE IS ONLY DISCIPLINE.

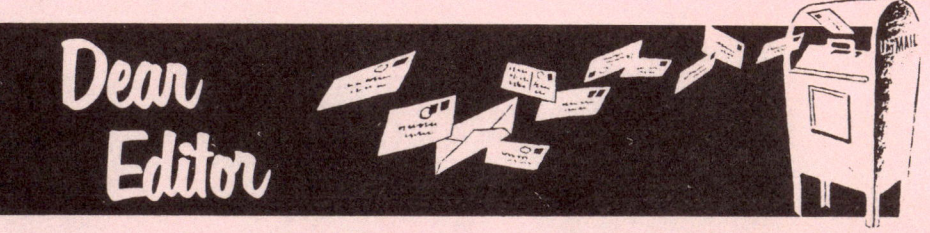

Dear Editor

Mom has a knotty problem

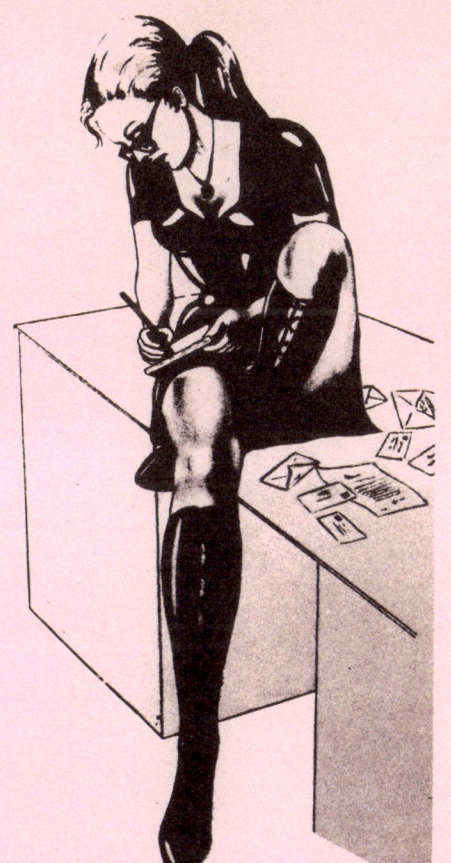

DEENA I am raising a 14-year-old daughter alone. She has a boyfriend, also 14, who is very likable. They have one unusual activity that I find hard to understand. He likes to tie her up, and obviously she likes to be tied. He treats her very gently when he ties her, although she often gets tied into some very stringent positions. They often spend hours inventing new positions and new ways to tie her. Some evenings they watch television for hours while she is tied rigidly to a chair.

They seem to keep this hobby of theirs to themselves, but are open about it at his house and ours. His mother and I have discussed it. She feels it is just their way of having fun. I find it quite interesting to watch them and am amazed at how many ways a person can get tied up. On two occasions I let them tie me up—once to a chair and once to a post. I found it to be a fascinating sensation.

How much of this goes on in the world? Is there any harm in it? Should I continue to join them in this game?
—Mrs. B.F., No City or State Please

Dear Mrs. B.F.: What you describe is the precursor to kinky sex. I can promise you that if this bondage-type playing around continues, your daughter and her boyfriend are going to be into some pretty heavy stuff before long.

The fact that you became part of the act is another strange one. And the boy's mother knows and approves. More oddities.

I suggest you talk to a therapist about this. You need to understand what is going on between your daughter and her boyfriend...also with yourself and the boy's mother. I can't do it in three inches of newspaper space.

```
Italy's shoes are like Italy's gents:
To foreign ladies they give offense.
The shoe and the man initially please
But sinfully soon, they pinch and squeeze.

I hate those heels on the hoof, on the street
Both make you suffer though each looks sweet
I'll not be beguiled, despite their appeals;
As of today, I'm swearing off heels.

Unless of course, a Don Juan comes by
Who likes me with heels impossibly high.
Then back to stilts, though the shoe abuses,
Life's short. Love' long--and worth a few
       bruises.

                    --Jennie Farley
                      "Punch"
```

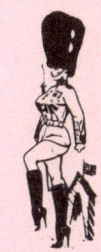 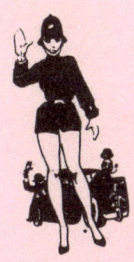

Bikini Girl, vol. 1, no. 9, 1987
Offset, saddle stitched, 11 × 8 ½ in. (27.9 × 21.6 cm)
The Museum of Modern Art Library, New York

Barbara Ess

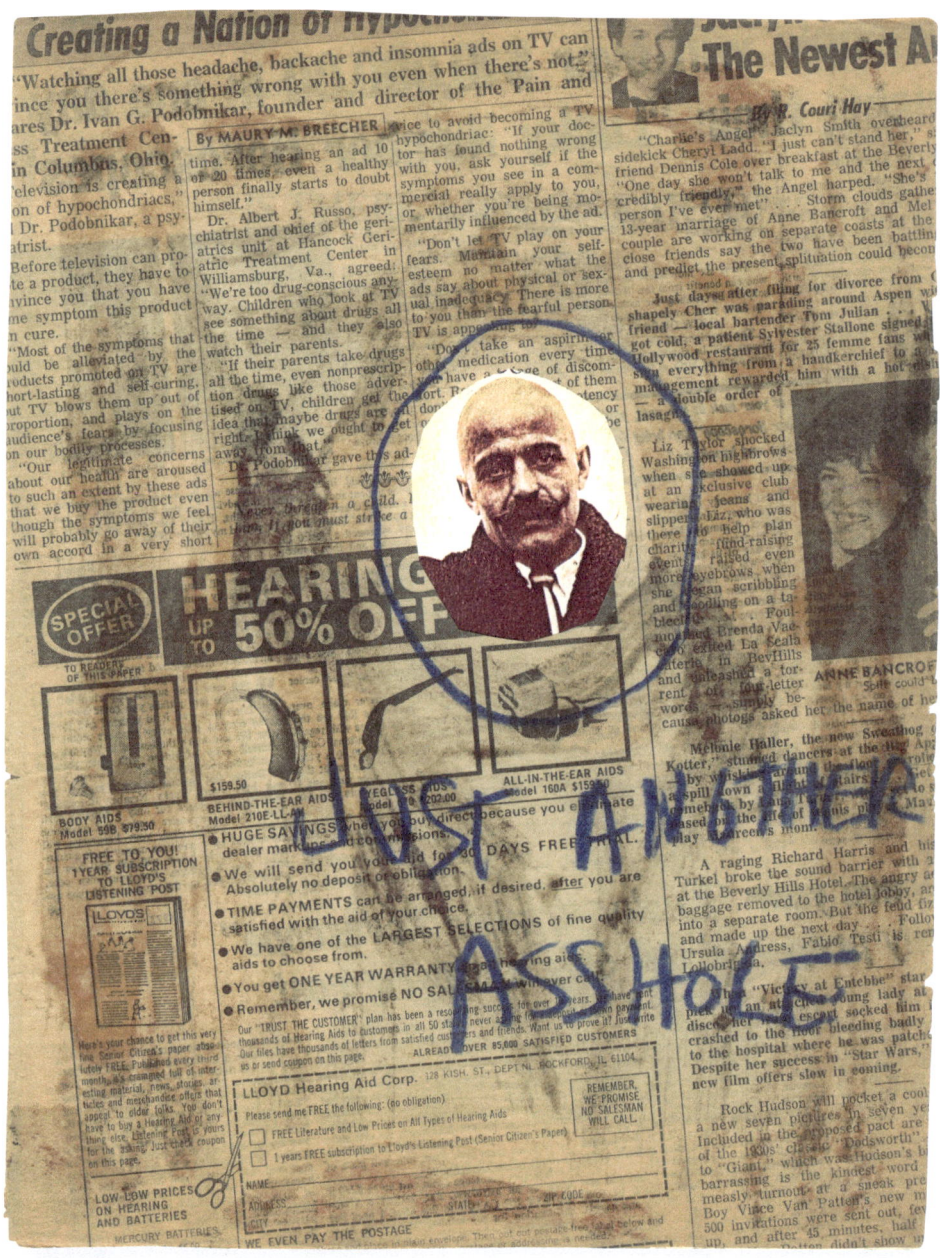

Paste-up for *Just Another Asshole*, no. 1, series 1, 1978
Offset, paper, glue, color pencil, 11 5/16 × 8 3/4 in. (28.8 × 22.3 cm)
The Estate of Barbara E. Schwartz (a.k.a. Barbara Ess)

→ *Just Another Asshole*, no. 1, series 1, 1978
Photocopy and offset, side stapled and taped, painted Mylar wrappers,
11 5/16 × 8 3/4 in. (28.8 × 22.3 cm)
Collection Philip Aarons and Shelley Fox Aarons

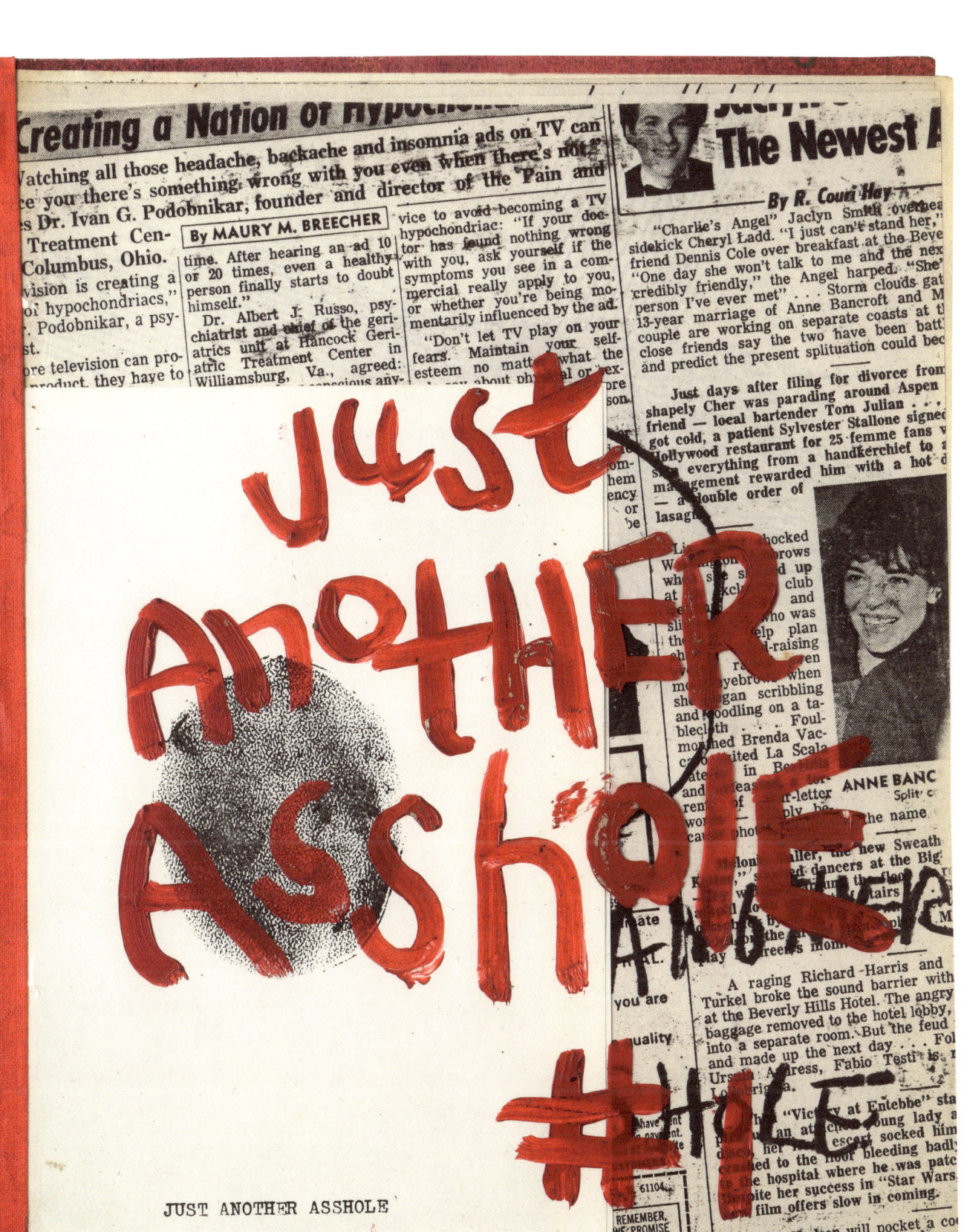

JUST ANOTHER ASSHOLE

SERIES I

B Eso 78

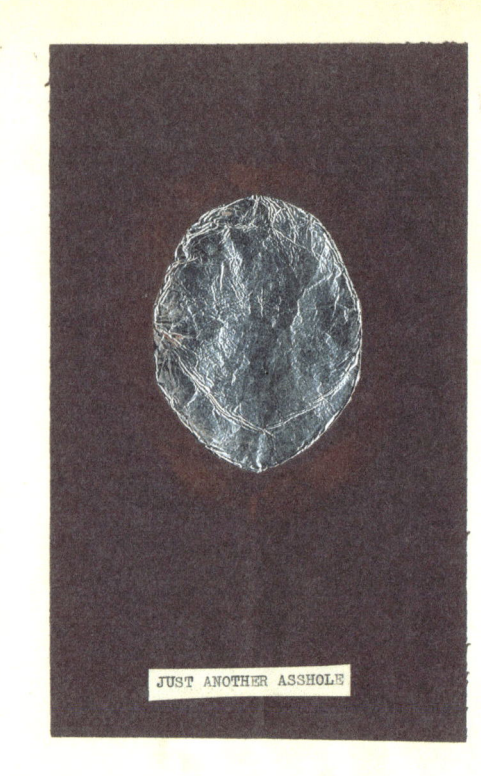
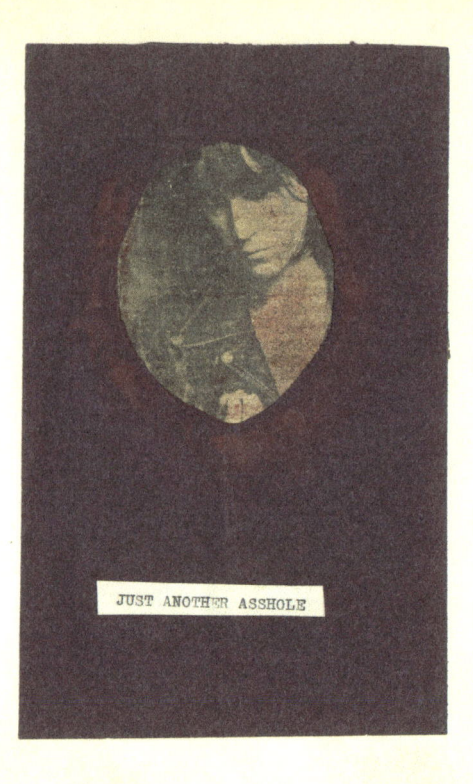

Paste-up for *Just Another Asshole*, no. 1, series 1, 1978
Offset, paper, foil, glue, 8 ½ × 11 in. (21.6 × 28 cm)
The Estate of Barbara E. Schwartz (a.k.a. Barbara Ess)

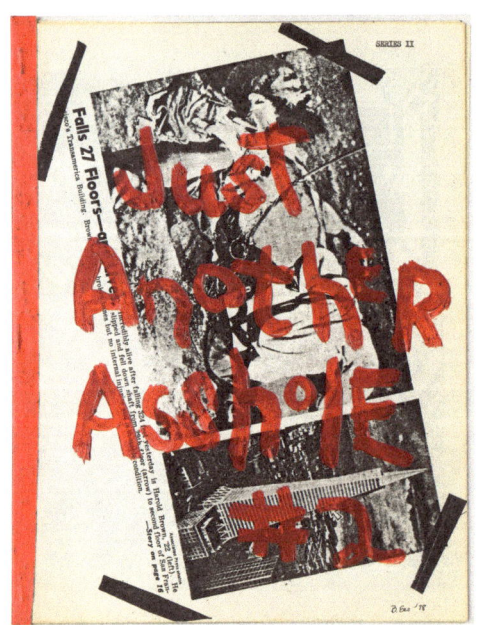
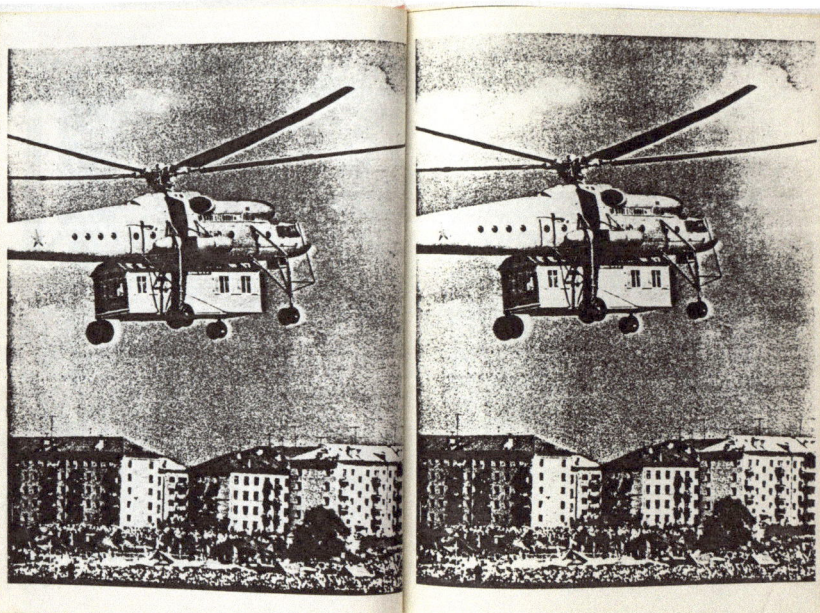

Just Another Asshole, no. 2, series 2, 1978
Photocopy and offset, side stapled and taped, painted
Mylar wrappers, 11 ⁵/₁₆ × 8 ¾ in. (28.8 × 22.3 cm)
Collection Philip Aarons and Shelley Fox Aarons

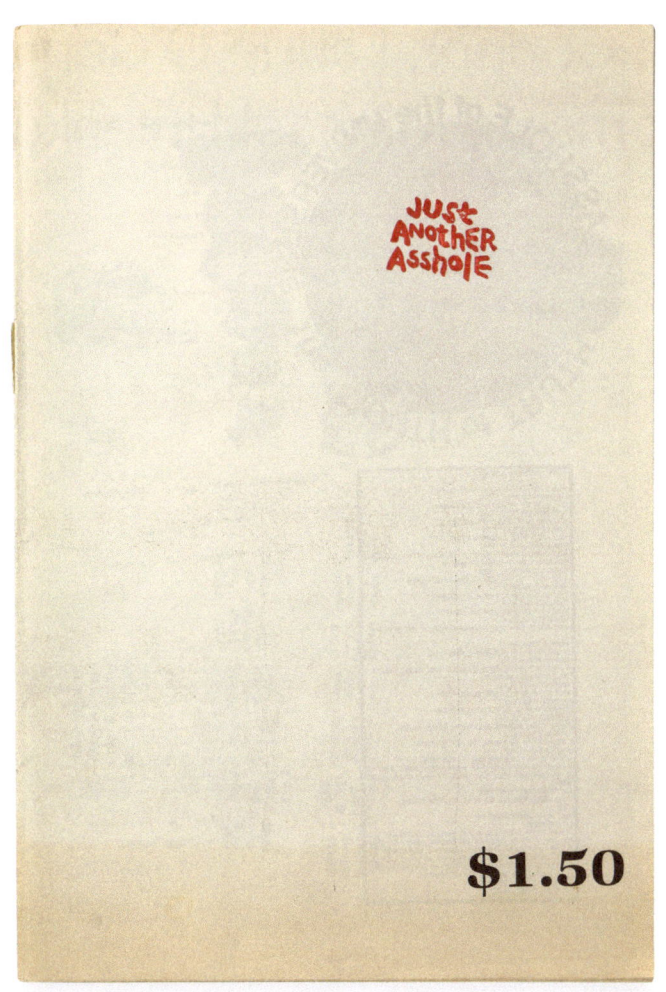

Just Another Asshole, no. 3, 1979
Editors: Barbara Ess and Jane M. Sherry
Offset, stamped ink, folded, 16 1/8 × 11 in. (41 × 28 cm)
Collection Philip Aarons and Shelley Fox Aarons

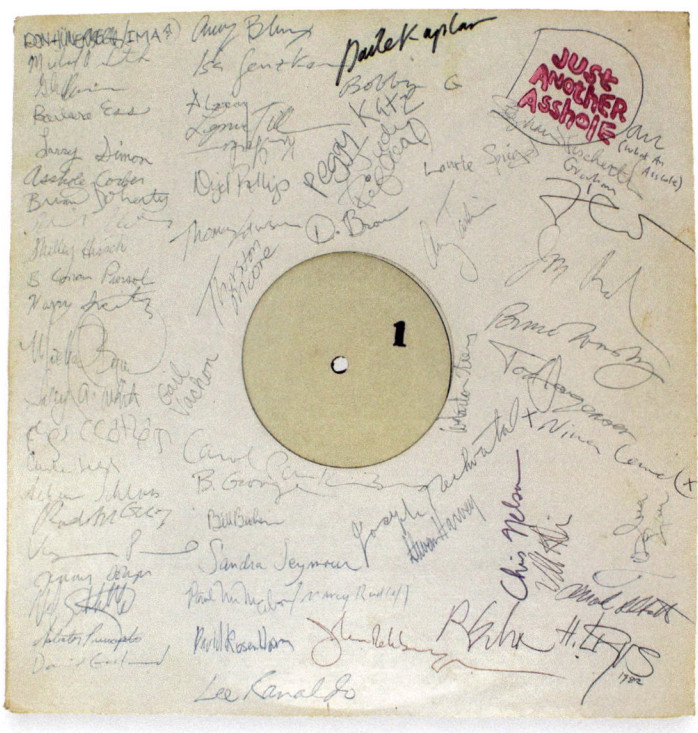

Just Another Asshole, no. 5, 1981
Editors: Barbara Ess and Glenn Branca
Vinyl album and sleeve with stamped ink (unique
copy with signatures), 12 × 12 in. (30.5 × 30.5 cm)
The Estate of Barbara E. Schwartz (a.k.a. Barbara Ess)

World Imitation (Anne Connor, Laurie O'Connell, Jeff Rankin, Steve Thomsen, Michael Uhlenkott)

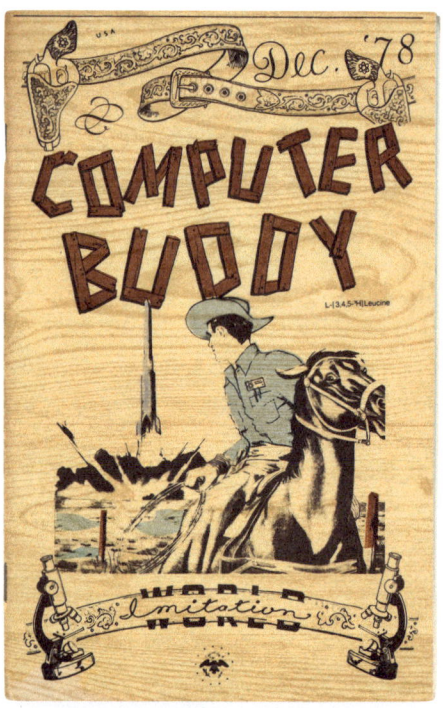

World Imitation Productions
Computer Buddy, January 1979
Photocopy, saddle stitched, four-color offset wrappers,
8 ½ × 5 ½ in. (21.6 × 14 cm)
Collection Michael Uhlenkott

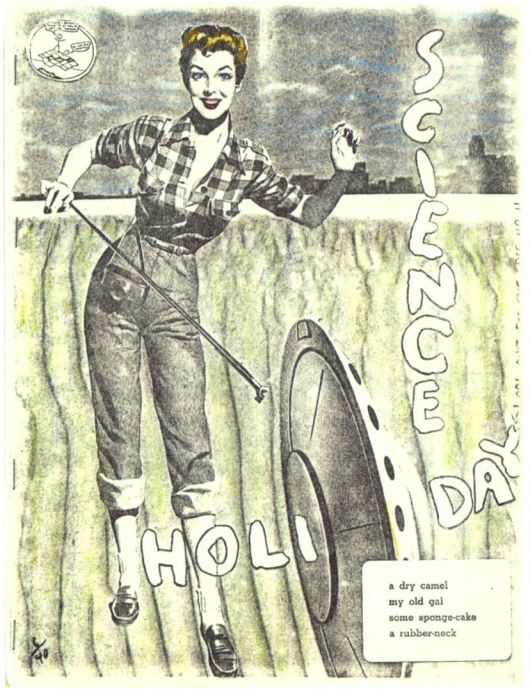

World Imitation Productions
Science Holiday, October 1977
Photocopy, side stapled, hand-colored cover,
11 × 8 ½ in. (27.9 × 21.6 cm)
Collection Michael Uhlenkott

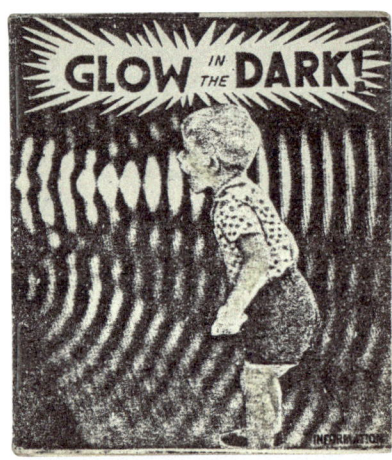

Steve Thomsen
Glow in the Dark!, November 1978
Photocopy with glow-in-the-dark paint, saddle stitched,
3 × 2 ¾ in. (7.6 × 7 cm)
Collection Michael Uhlenkott

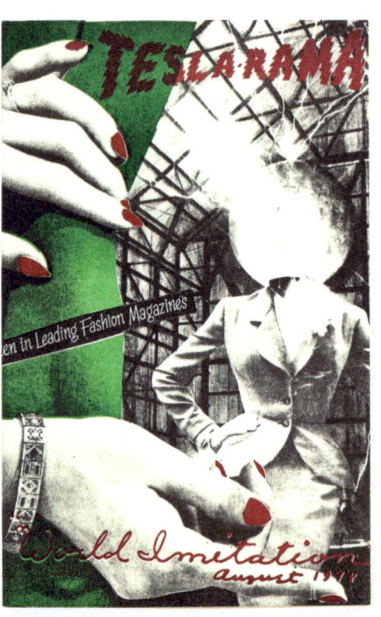

Michael Uhlenkott
Tesla-Rama, August 1978
Photocopy, saddle stitched, four-color offset wrappers,
8 ½ × 5 ½ in. (21.6 × 14 cm)
Collection Michael Uhlenkott

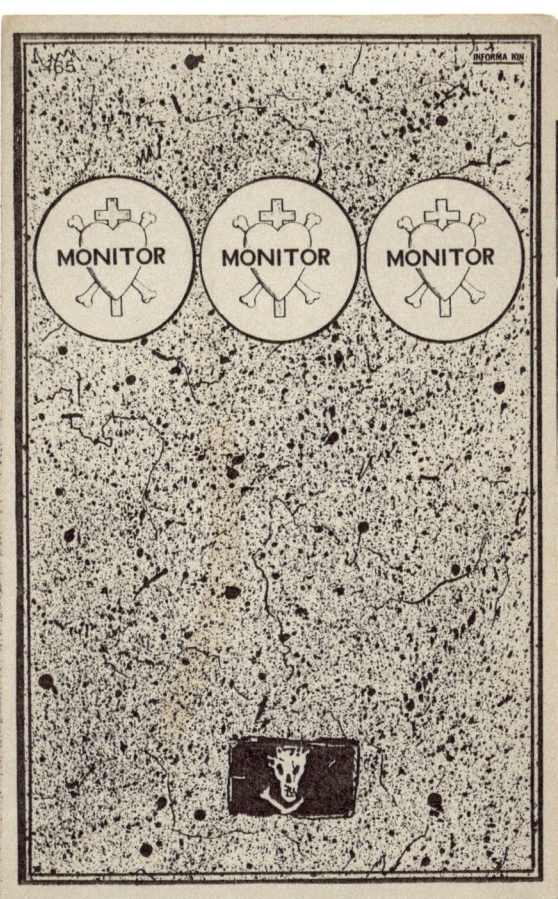

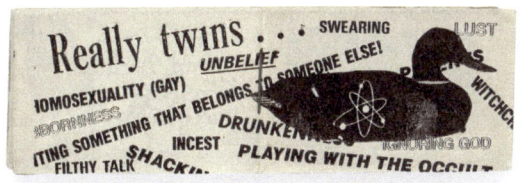

Steve Thomsen
Really Twins, September/October 1978
Photocopy, saddle stitched, 1 ¼ × 2 in. (3.2 × 5.1 cm)
Collection Michael Uhlenkott

Monitor Catalogue, no. 1, 1980
Photocopy, saddle stitched, painted wrappers,
8 ½ × 5 ½ in. (21.6 × 14 cm)
Collection Michael Uhlenkott

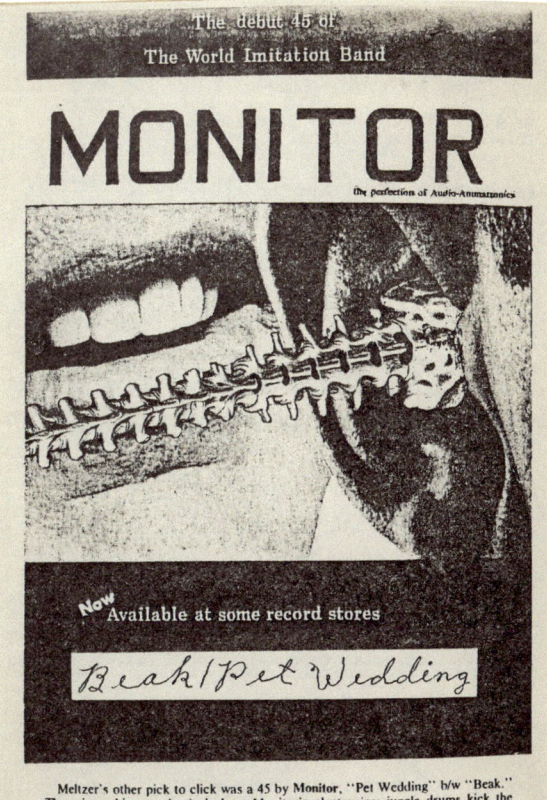

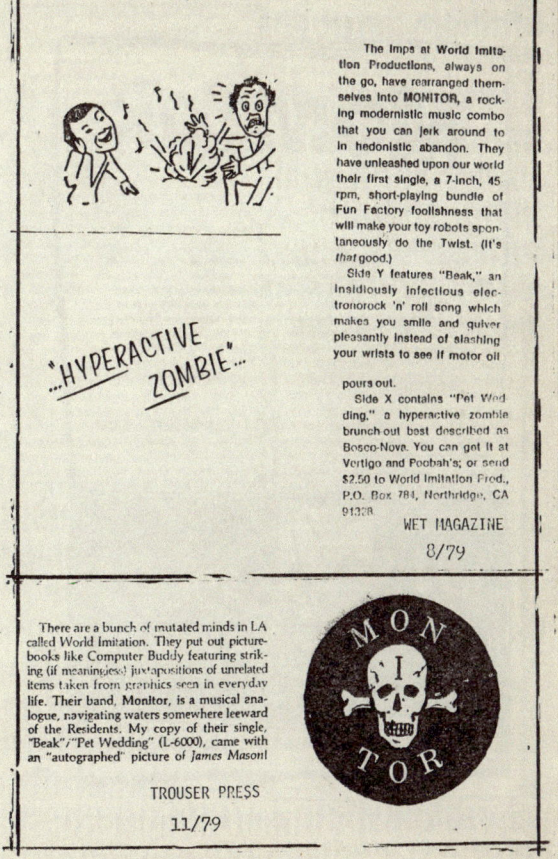

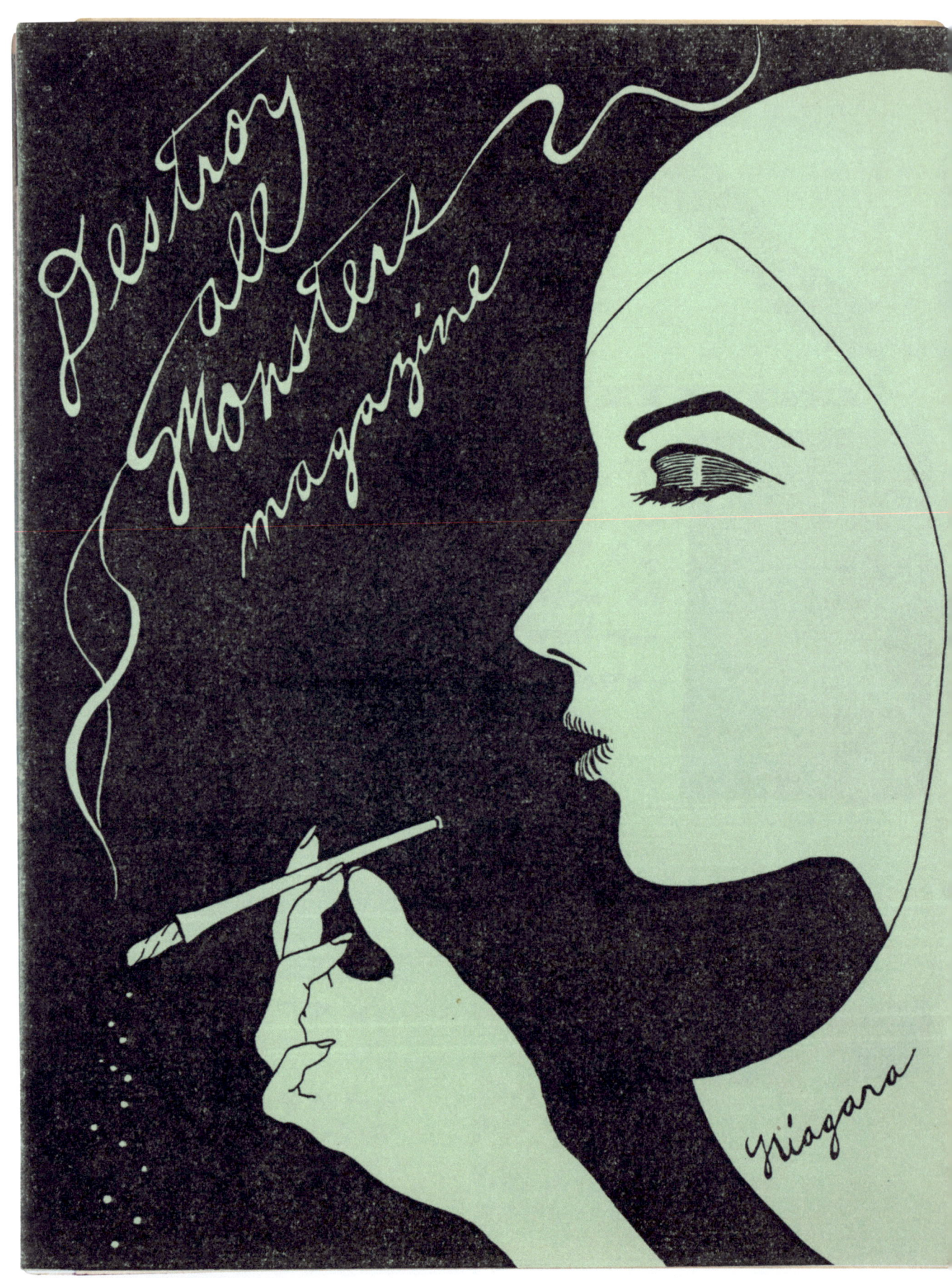

Destroy All Monsters Magazine, no. 1, 1976
Editor: Cary Loren
Offset and photocopy, saddle stitched, 11 1/16 × 8 1/2 in. (28.1 × 21.6 cm)
Collection Cary Loren

Destroy All Monsters (Mike Kelley, Cary Loren, Niagara, Jim Shaw)

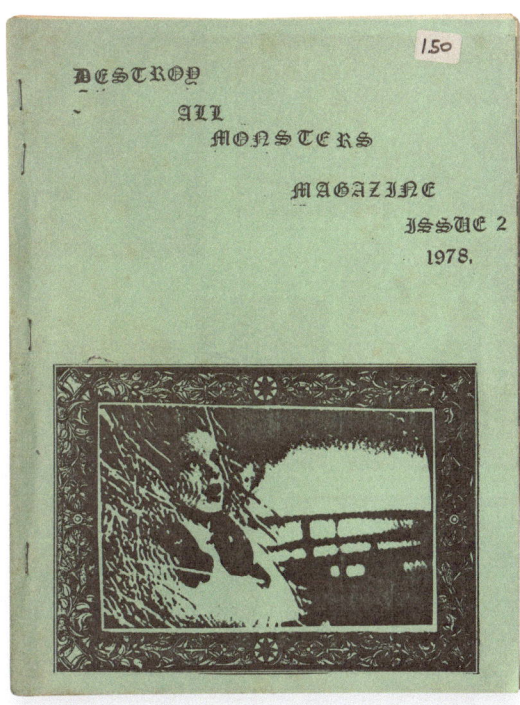

Destroy All Monsters Magazine, no. 2, 1978
Editor: Cary Loren
Photocopy, side stapled, 11 × 8½ in. (27.9 × 21.6 cm)
Collection Philip Aarons and Shelley Fox Aarons

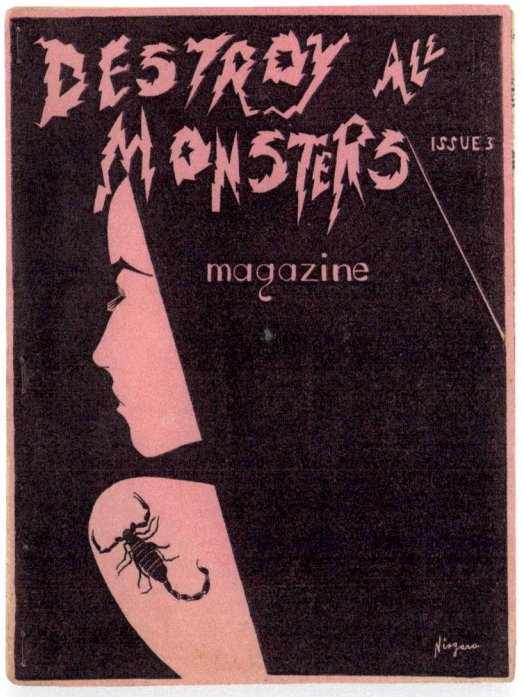

Destroy All Monsters Magazine, no. 3, October 1978
Editor: Cary Loren
Photocopy, side stapled, 11 × 8½ in. (27.9 × 21.6 cm)
Collection Philip Aarons and Shelley Fox Aarons

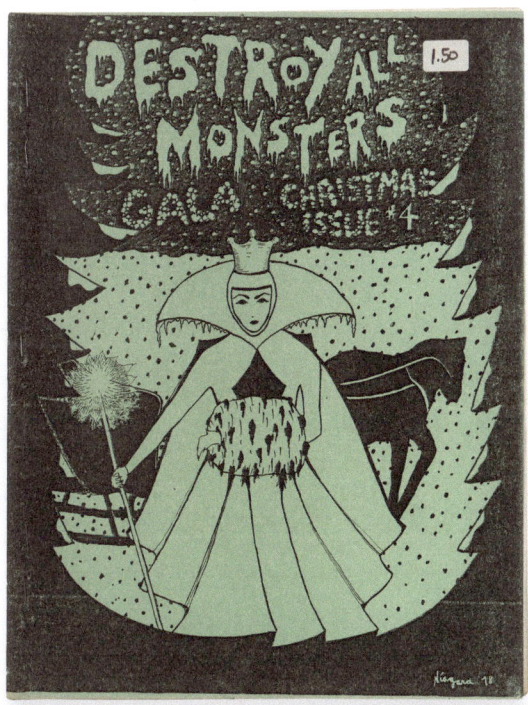

Destroy All Monsters Magazine, no. 4, 1978
Editor: Cary Loren
Photocopy, side stapled, 11 × 8½ in. (27.9 × 21.6 cm)
Collection Philip Aarons and Shelley Fox Aarons

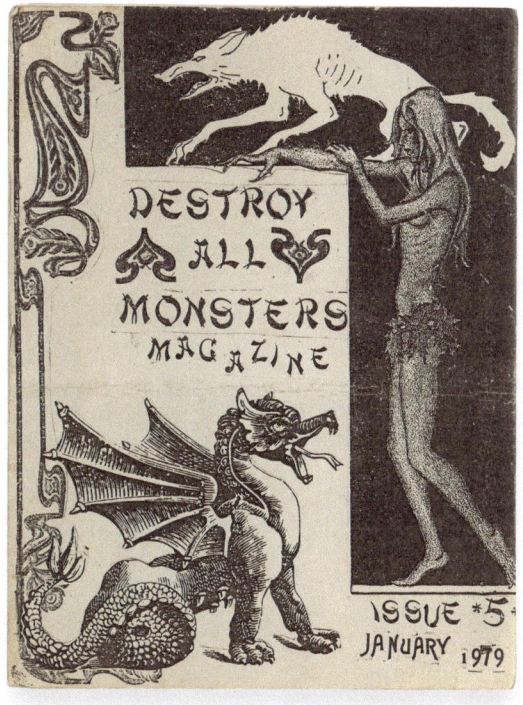

Destroy All Monsters Magazine, no. 5, January 1979
Editor: Cary Loren
Photocopy, spray paint, side stapled, 11 × 8½ in. (27.9 × 21.6 cm)
Collection Philip Aarons and Shelley Fox Aarons

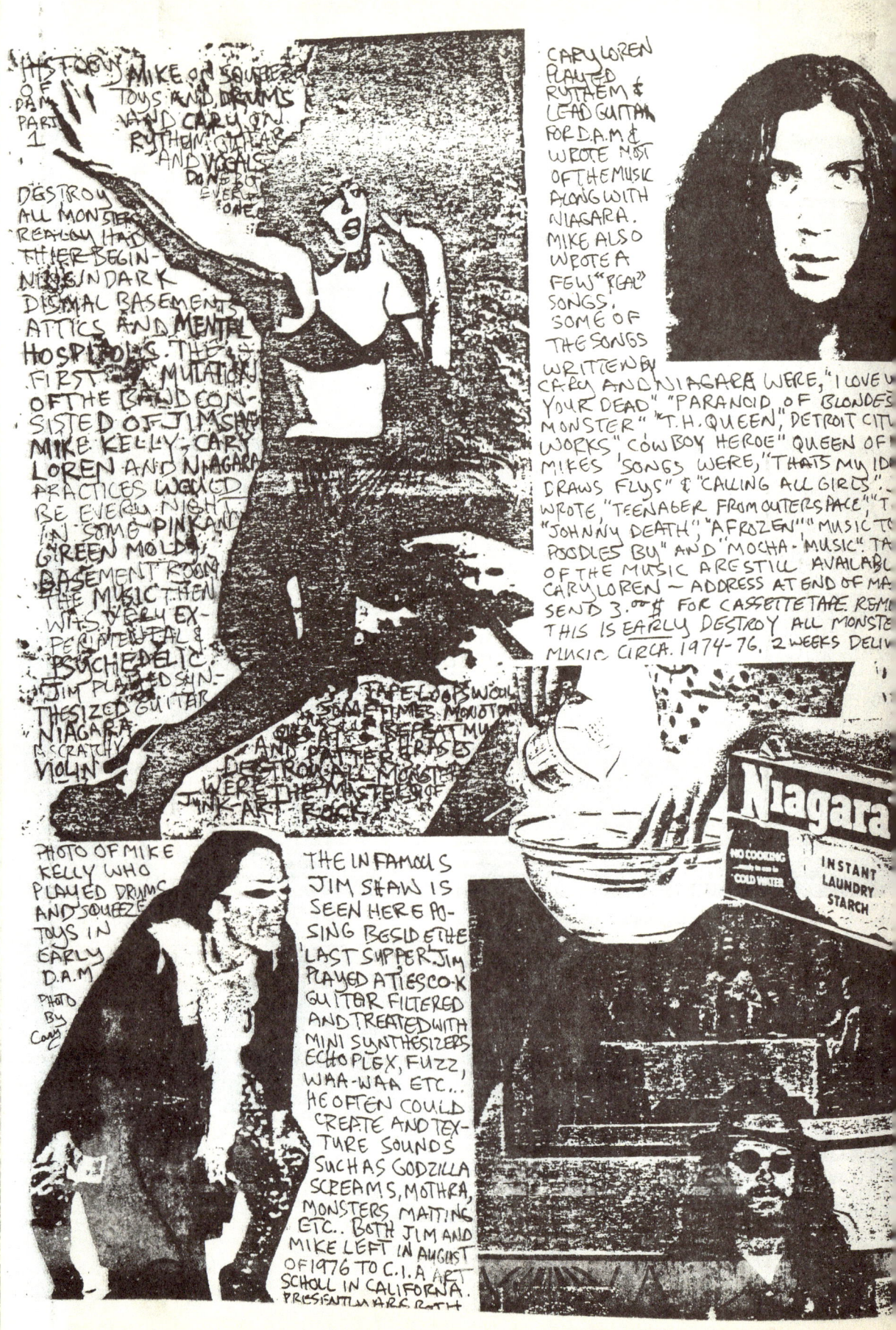

HISTORY OF D.A.M PART 1

MIKE ON SQUEEZE TOYS AND DRUMS AND CARY ON RYTHEM GUITAR AND VOCALS. DONE BY EVERY ONE.

DESTROY ALL MONSTERS REALLY HAD THIER BEGINNINGS IN DARK DISMAL BASEMENTS ATTICS AND MENTAL HOSPITALS. THE FIRST MUTATION OF THE BAND CONSISTED OF JIM SHAW MIKE KELLY, CARY LOREN AND NIAGARA. PRACTICES WOULD BE EVERY NIGHT IN SOME PINK AND GREEN MOLDY BASEMENT ROOM. THE MUSIC THEN WAS VERY EXPERIMENTAL & PSYCHEDELIC. JIM PLAYED SYNTHESIZED GUITAR. NIAGARA A SCRATCHY VIOLIN.

TAPE LOOPS WOULD SOMETIME MONOTONOUSLY REPEAT MUSICAL AND PATTER PHRASES DESTROY ALL MONSTERS WERE THE MASTERS OF JUNK ART ROCK.

CARY LOREN PLAYED RYTHEM & LEAD GUITAR FOR D.A.M & WROTE MOST OF THE MUSIC ALONG WITH NIAGARA. MIKE ALSO WROTE A FEW "REAL" SONGS. SOME OF THE SONGS WRITTEN BY CARY AND NIAGARA WERE, "I LOVE U YOUR DEAD" "PARANOID OF BLONDES" "MONSTER" "T.H. QUEEN", DETROIT CITY WORKS" "COW BOY HEROE" QUEEN OF... MIKES 'SONGS WERE, "THATS MY IDOL DRAWS FLYS" & "CALLING ALL GIRLS". WROTE, "TEENAGER FROM OUTERSPACE" "T... "JOHNNY DEATH", "A FROZEN" "MUSIC TO POODLES BY" AND "MOCHA-MUSIC" TA... OF THE MUSIC ARE STILL AVAILABL... CARY LOREN — ADDRESS AT END OF MA... SEND 3.00 $ FOR CASSETTE TAPE REM... THIS IS EARLY DESTROY ALL MONSTE... MUSIC CIRCA. 1974-76. 2 WEEKS DELIV...

PHOTO OF MIKE KELLY WHO PLAYED DRUMS AND SQUEEZE TOYS IN EARLY D.A.M
PHOTO BY CARY

THE INFAMOUS JIM SHAW IS SEEN HERE POSING BESIDE THE 'LAST SUPPER' JIM PLAYED A TIESCO K GUITAR FILTERED AND TREATED WITH MINI SYNTHESIZERS ECHOPLEX, FUZZ, WAA-WAA ETC... HE OFTEN COULD CREATE AND TEXTURE SOUNDS SUCH AS GODZILLA SCREAMS, MOTHRA, MONSTERS MATTING ETC.. BOTH JIM AND MIKE LEFT IN AUGUST OF 1976 TO C.I.A ART SCHOLL IN CALIFORNA. PRESENTLY ARE BOTH

Niagara
NO COOKING
INSTANT LAUNDRY STARCH

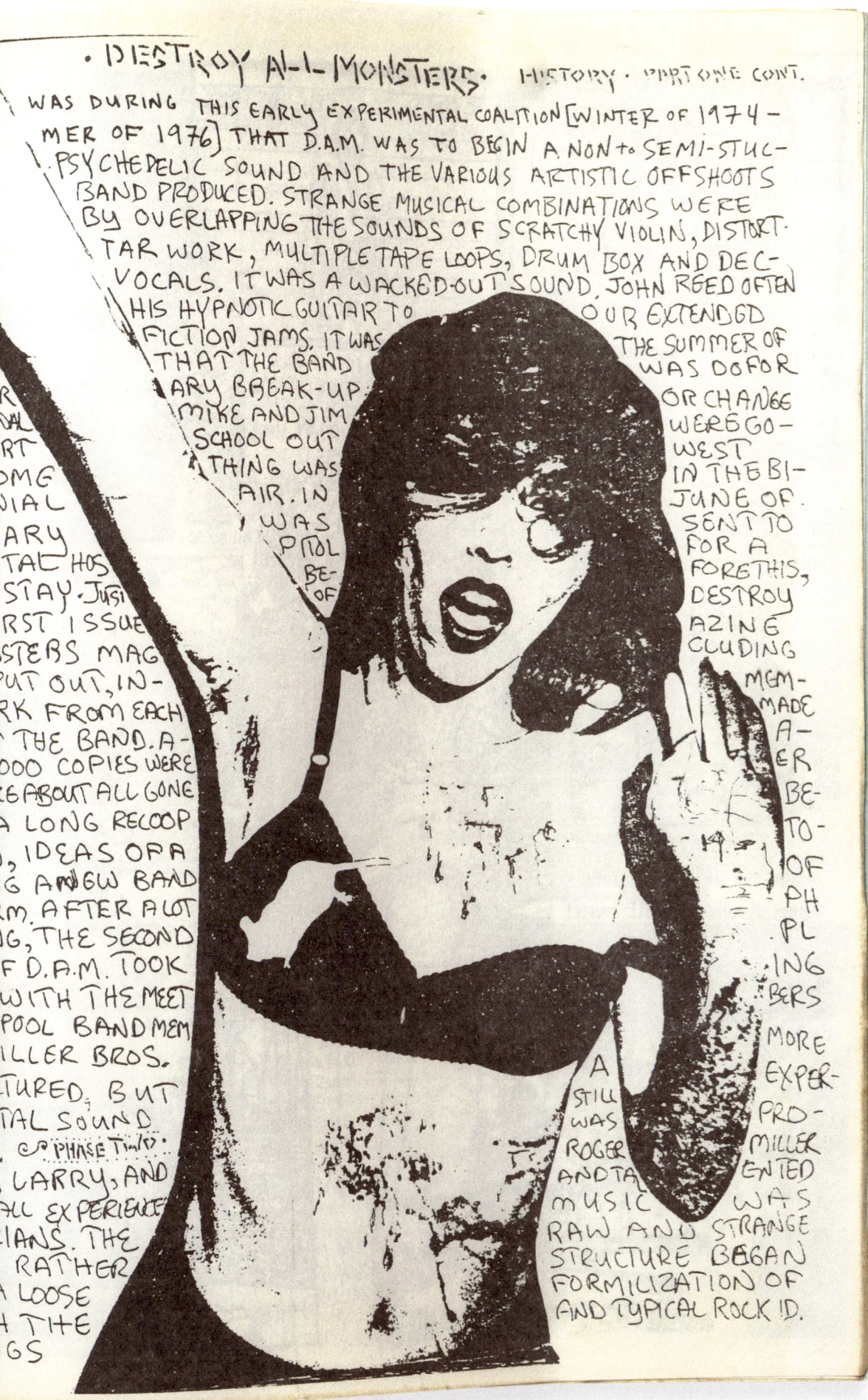

WAS DURING THIS EARLY EXPERIMENTAL COALITION [WINTER OF 1974 -
MER OF 1976] THAT D.A.M. WAS TO BEGIN A NON to SEMI-STUC-
PSYCHEDELIC SOUND AND THE VARIOUS ARTISTIC OFFSHOOTS
BAND PRODUCED. STRANGE MUSICAL COMBINATIONS WERE
BY OVERLAPPING THE SOUNDS OF SCRATCHY VIOLIN, DISTORT-
TAR WORK, MULTIPLE TAPE LOOPS, DRUM BOX AND DEC-
VOCALS. IT WAS A WACKED-OUT SOUND. JOHN REED OFTEN
HIS HYPNOTIC GUITAR TO   OUR EXTENDED
FICTION JAMS. IT WAS   THE SUMMER OF
THAT THE BAND   WAS DO FOR
ARY BREAK-UP   OR CHANGE
MIKE AND JIM   WERE 5 GO-
SCHOOL OUT   WEST
THING WAS   IN THE BI-
AIR. IN   JUNE OF.
WAS   SENT TO
PITOL   FOR A
BE-   FORE THIS,
OF   DESTROY
                                          AZINE
                                          CLUDING

OR   MEM-
NAL   MADE
ART   A-
OME   ER
NIAL   BE-
ARY   TO-
TAL HOS   OF
STAY. JUS?   PH
IRST ISSUE   .PL
NSTERS MAG   .ING
PUT OUT, IN-   BERS
RK FROM EACH
THE BAND. A-   MORE
OOO COPIES WERE   EXPER-
RE ABOUT ALL GONE   PRO-
A LONG RECOOP   MILLER
IDEAS OF A   ENTED
NG A NEW BAND   WAS
RM. AFTER A LOT
NG, THE SECOND   A   STRANGE
F D.A.M. TOOK   STILL
WITH THE MEET   WAS
POOL BAND MEM   ROGER
MILLER BROS.   AND TA
CTURED, BUT   MUSIC
TAL SOUND   RAW AND STRANGE
. PHASE TWO   STRUCTURE BEGAN
, LARRY, AND   FORMILIZATION OF
ALL EXPERIENC   AND TYPICAL ROCK ID.
CIANS. THE
RATHER
LOOSE
H THE
NGS

Destroy All Monsters Magazine, no. 4, 1978
Editor: Cary Loren
Photocopy, side stapled, 11 × 8½ in. (27.9 × 21.6 cm)
Collection Philip Aarons and Shelley Fox Aarons

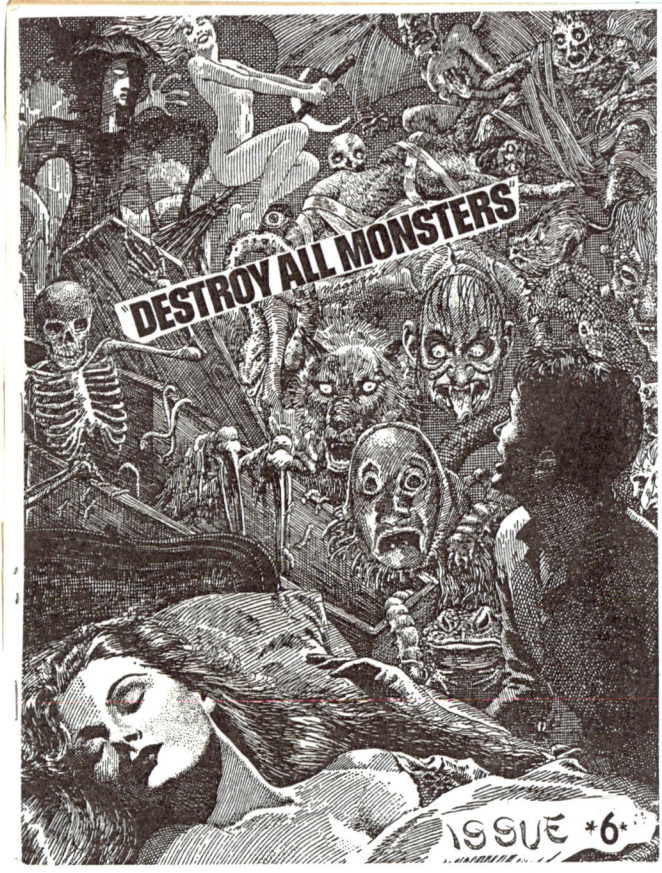

Destroy All Monsters Magazine, no. 6, 1979
Editor: Cary Loren
Photocopy, side stapled, 11 × 8½ in. (27.9 × 21.6 cm)
Collection Philip Aarons and Shelley Fox Aarons

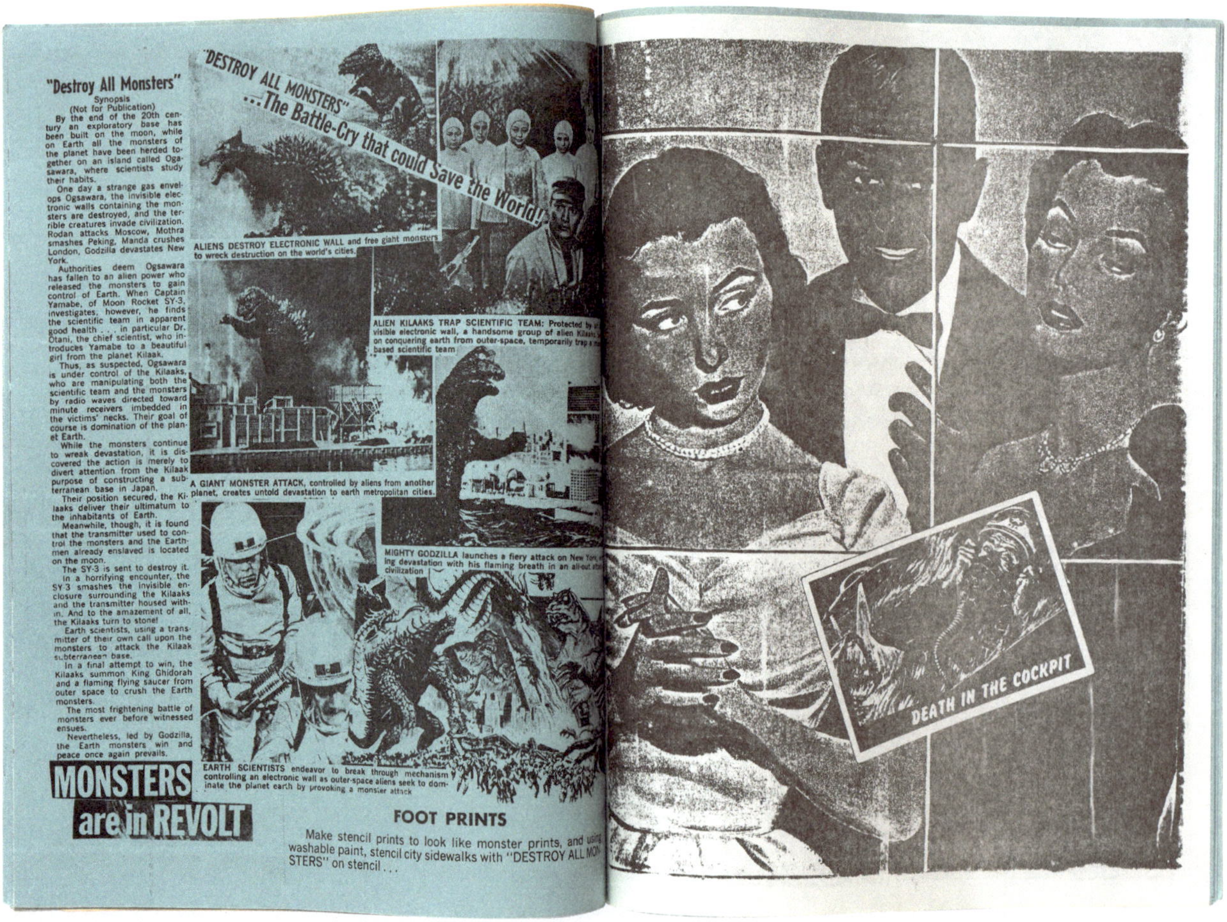

Cary Loren

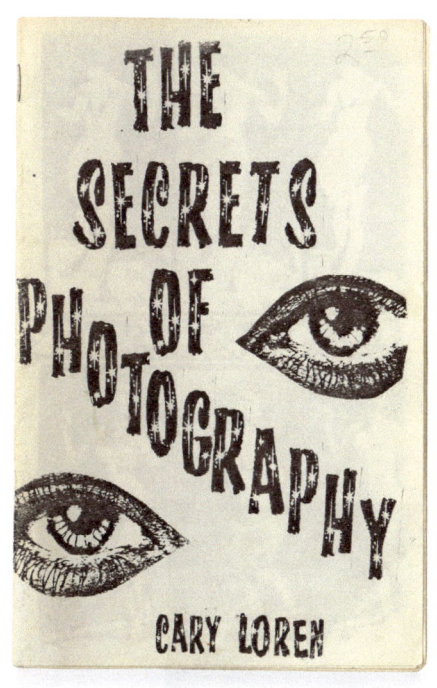

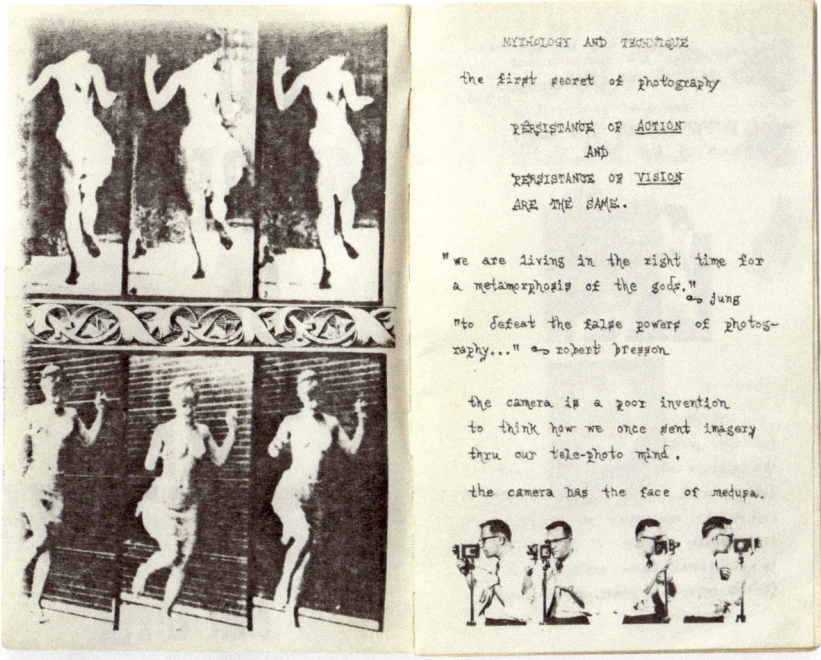

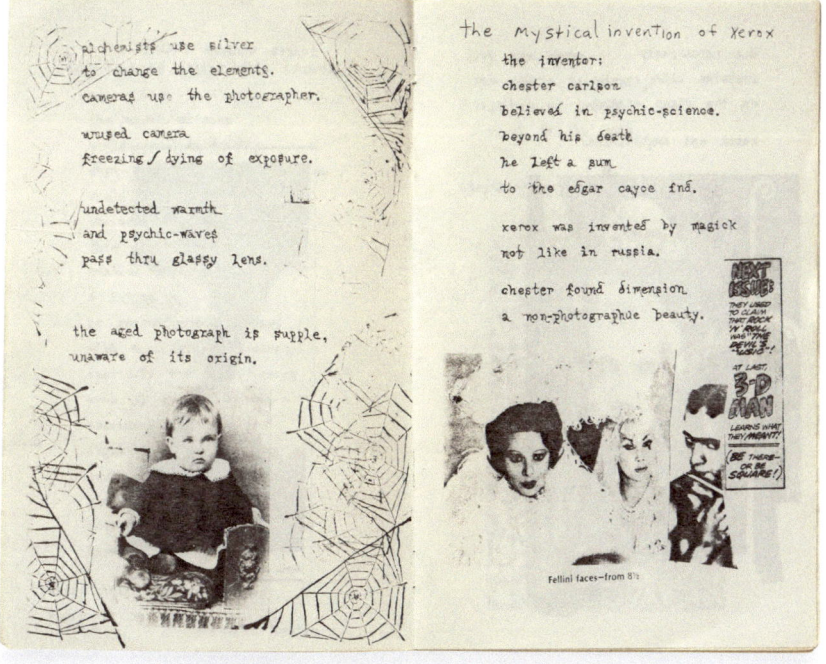

The Secrets of Photography, 1980
Photocopy, saddle stitched, 8 ½ × 5 ½ in. (21.6 × 14 cm)
Collection Philip Aarons and Shelley Fox Aarons

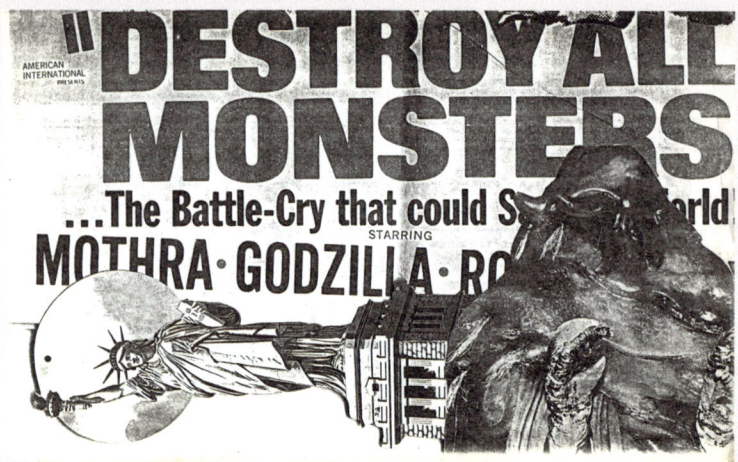

Jim Shaw
Black and White Xerox, 1975
Photocopy, 8 ¼ × 13 ¾ in. (21 × 34.9 cm)
Collection the artist

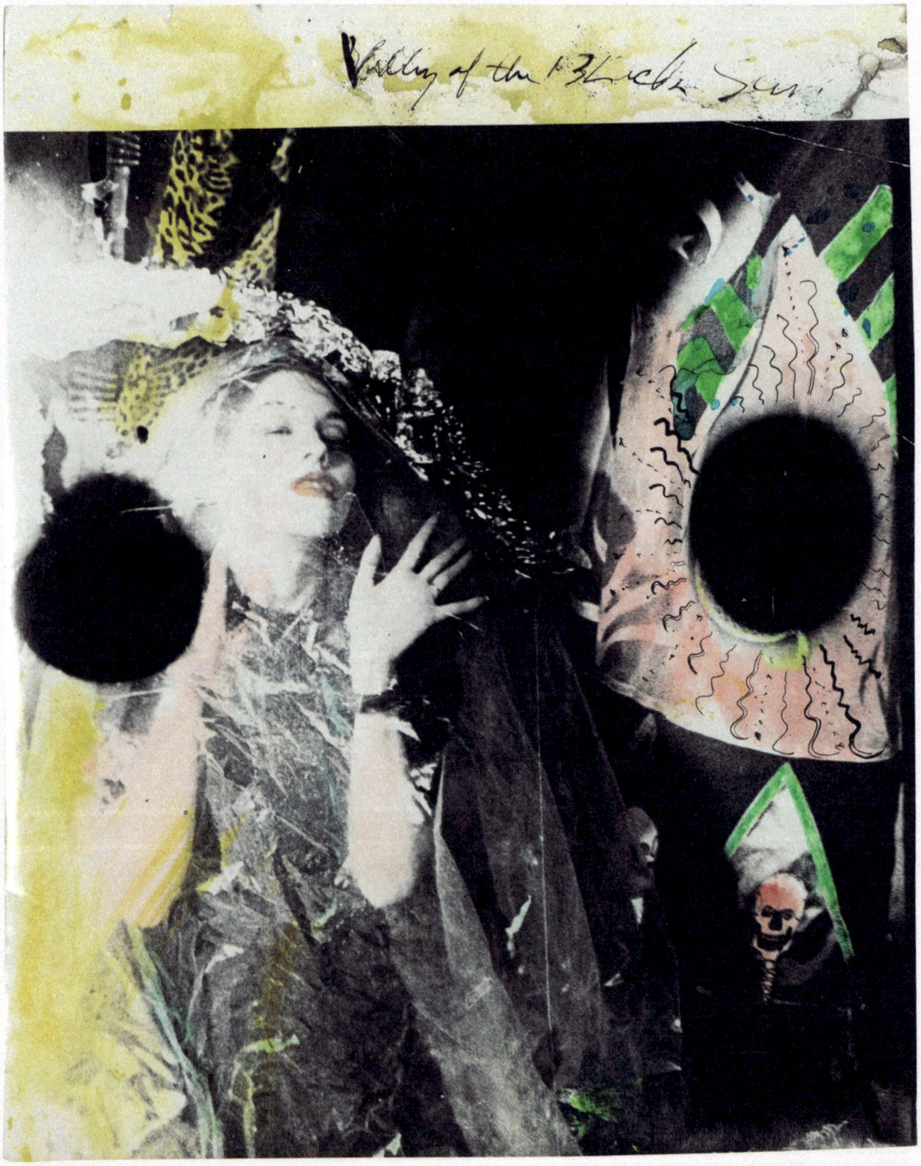

Cary Loren
Niagara in Cocoon, Wizard Robe, and Sun Spots, 1975
Hand-colored gelatin silver print, 9 ½ × 7 ¹³⁄₁₆ in. (24.1 × 19.8 cm)
Collection the artist

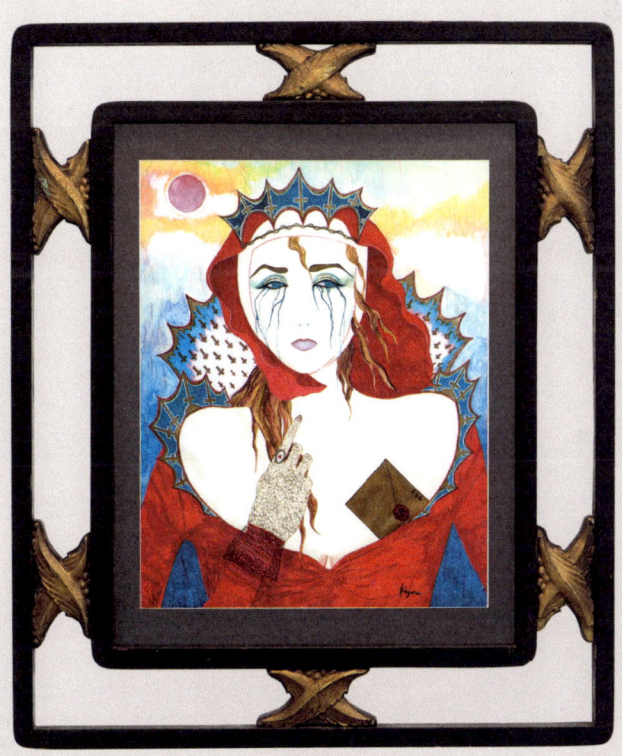

Mike Kelley
Portrait of Cary Loren, 1975
Mixed media on paper, 26 ½ × 26 ⅛ × 1 ⅛ in. (66.4 × 66.4 × 2.9 cm)
Private collection, Switzerland

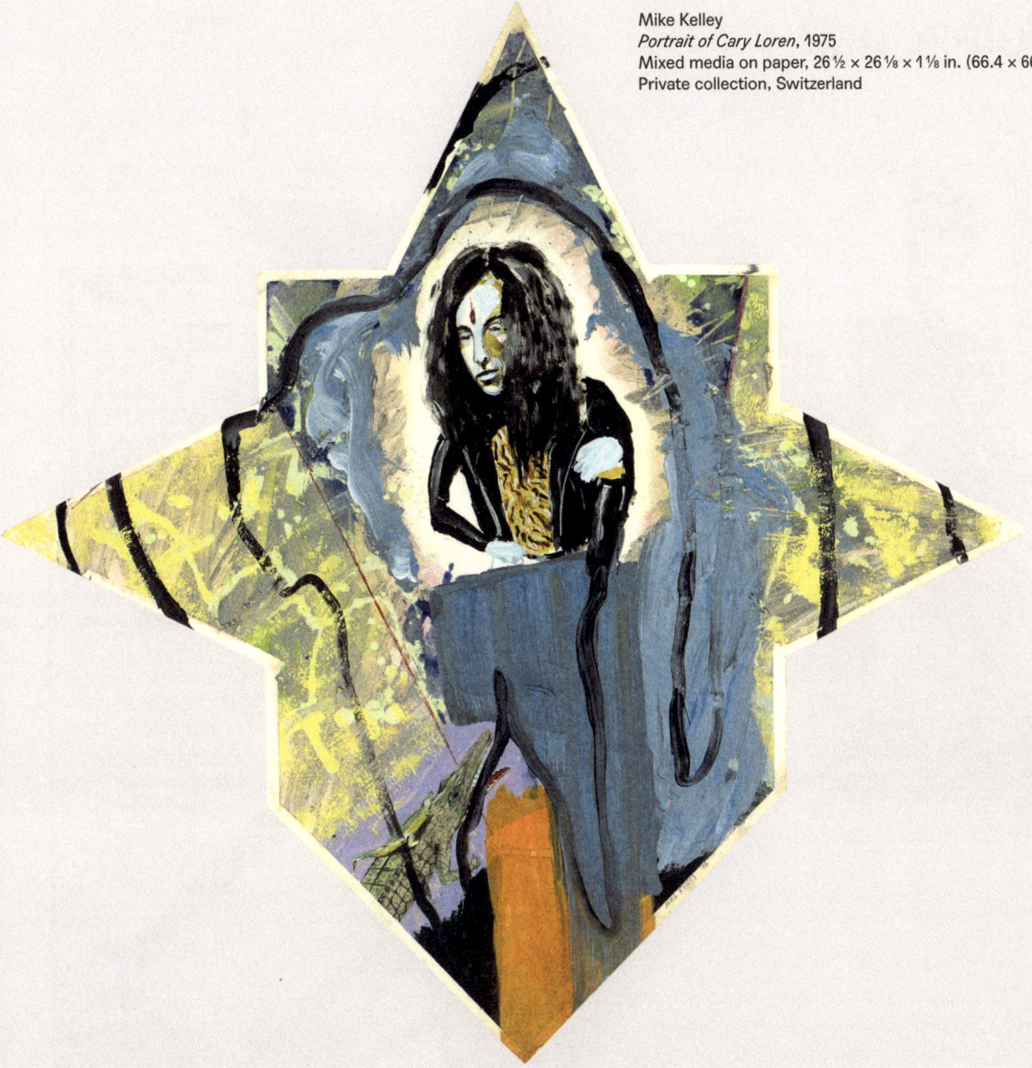

Niagara
Letter from the Devil, 1978
Watercolor on paper, 17 × 14 in. (43.2 × 35.6 cm)
Collection the artist

Gerardo Velázquez

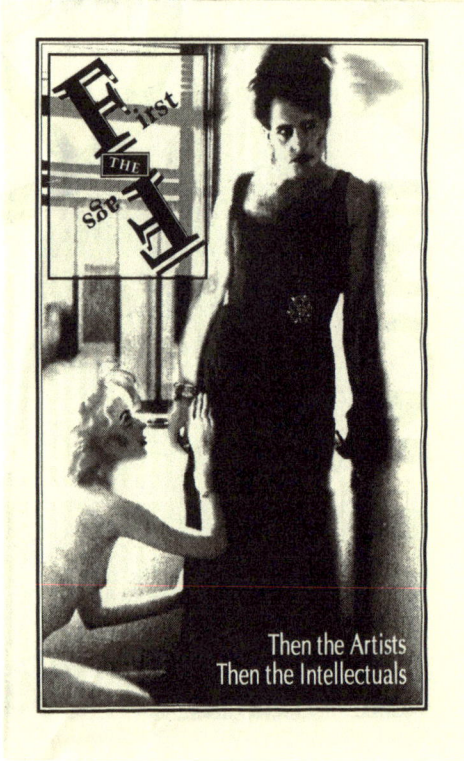

First the Fags, 1990
Offset, saddle stitched, 8½ × 5½ in. (21.6 × 14 cm)
ONE Archives at the USC Libraries

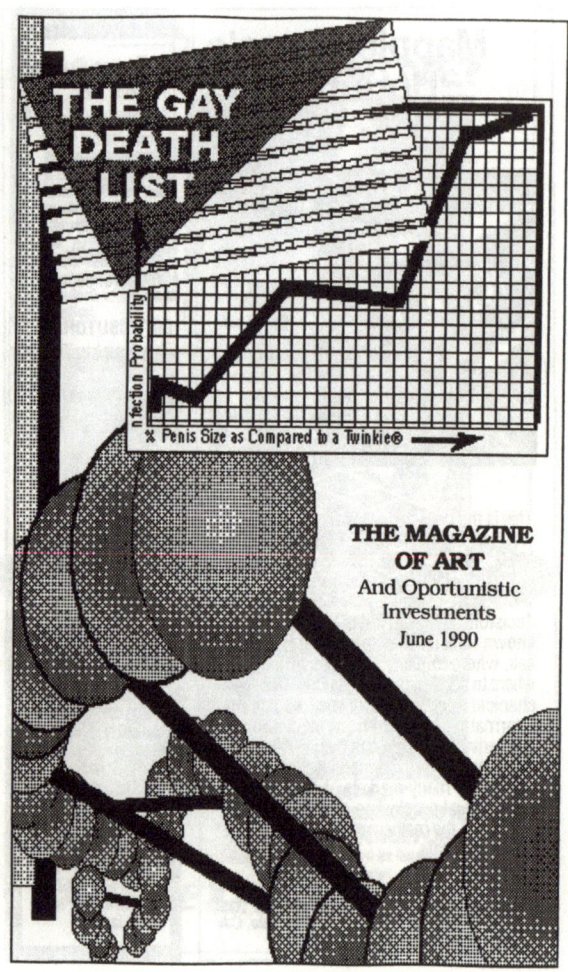

The Gay Death List, 1990
Offset, saddle stitched, 8½ × 5½ in. (21.6 × 14 cm)
ONE Archives at the USC Libraries

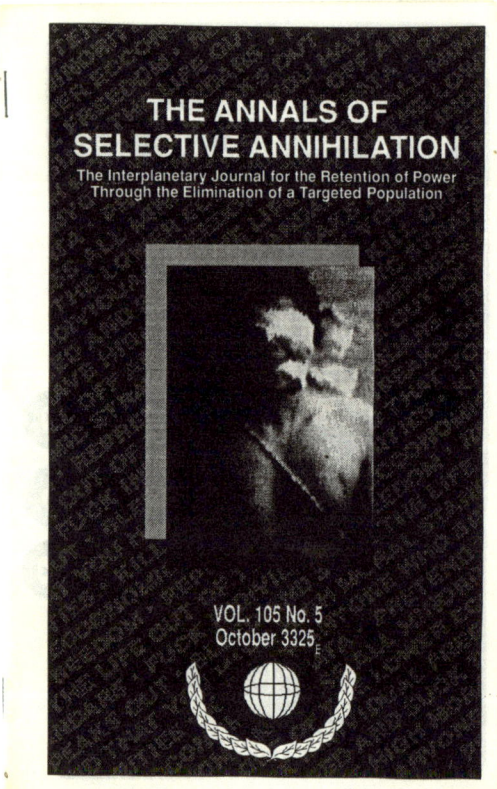

The Annals of Selective Annihilation, 1990
Offset, saddle stitched, 8½ × 5½ in. (21.6 × 14 cm)
ONE Archives at the USC Libraries

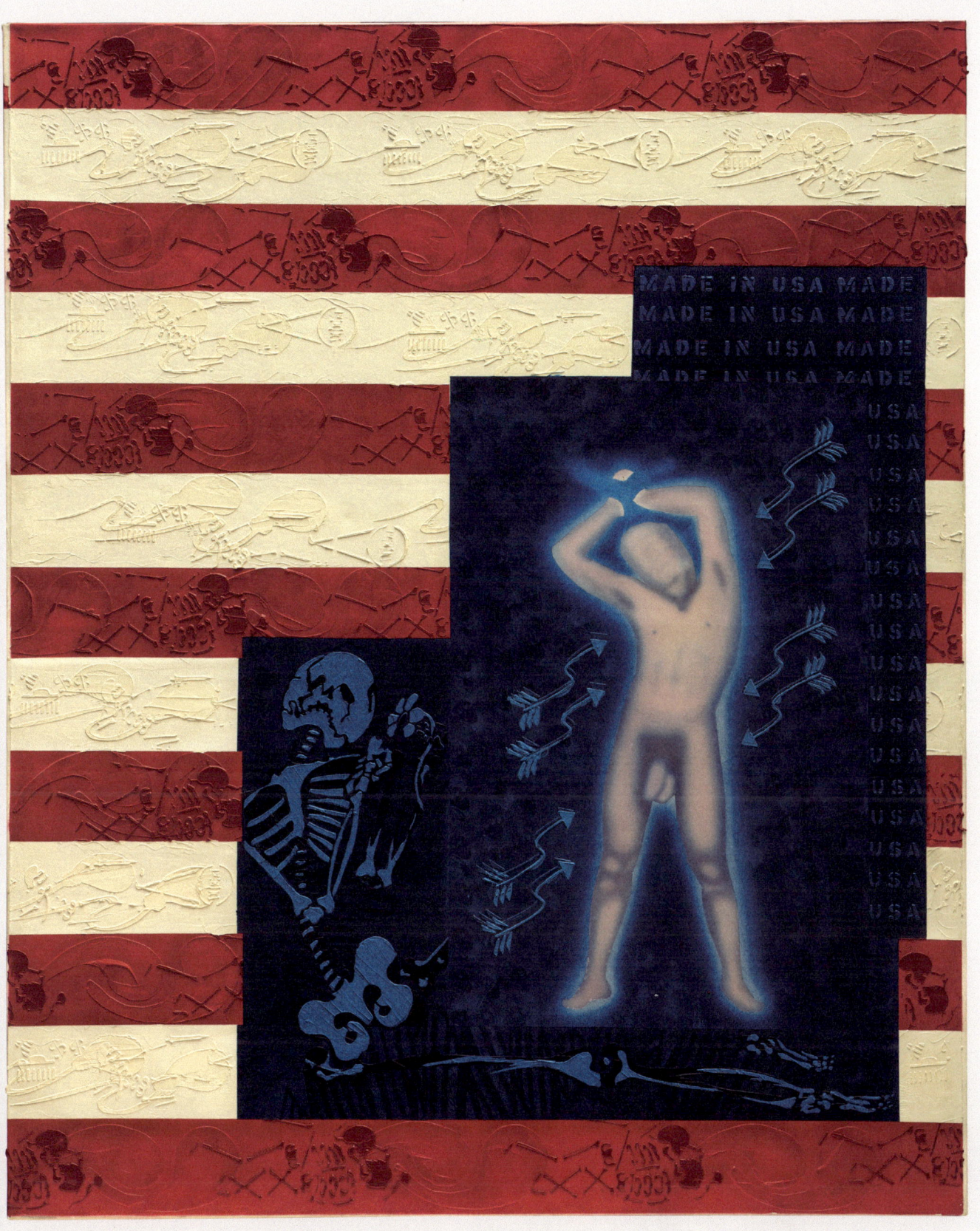

The Neglected Martyr, 1990
Acrylic on canvas, 80 × 66¼ in. (203.2 × 168.3 cm)
ONE Archives at the USC Libraries

Raymond Pettibon

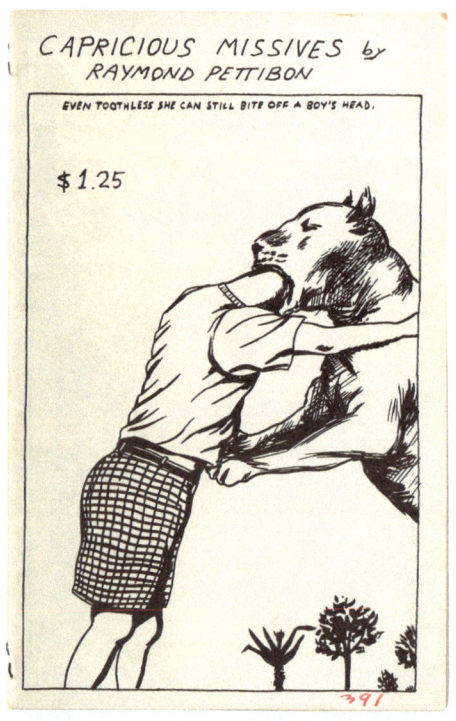

Capricious Missives, April 1983
Offset, saddle stitched, 8 ½ × 5 ½ in. (21.6 × 14 cm)
Collection Philip Aarons and Shelley Fox Aarons

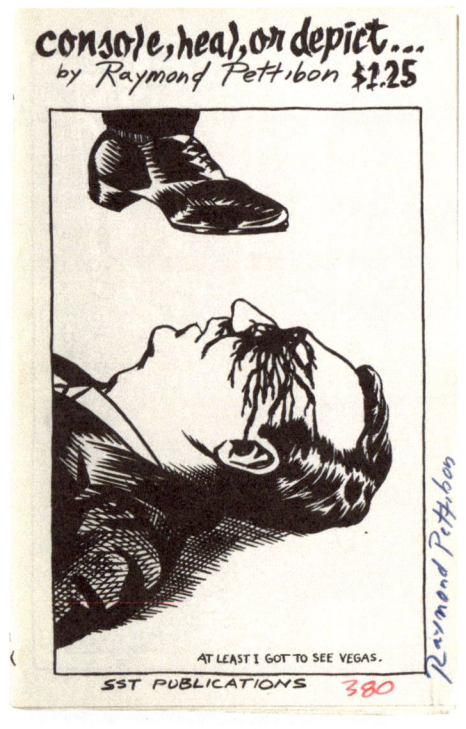

Console, Heal, or Depict, August 1984
Offset, saddle stitched, 8 ½ × 5 ½ in. (21.6 × 14 cm)
Collection Philip Aarons and Shelley Fox Aarons

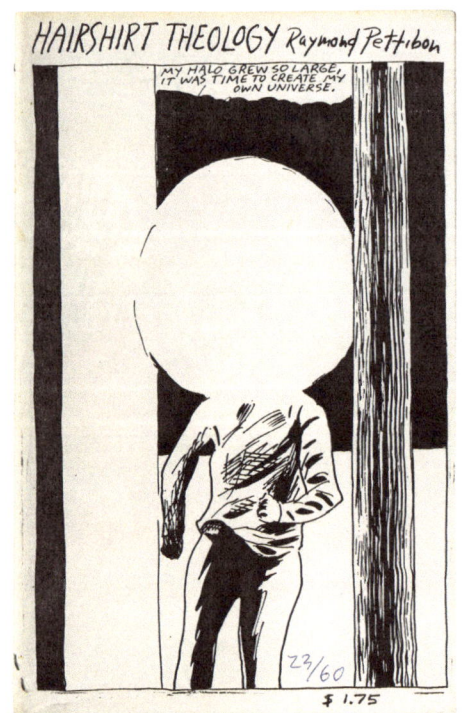

Hairshirt Theology [with Nelson Tarpenny], 1988
Offset, saddle stitched, 8 ½ × 5 ½ in. (21.6 × 14 cm)
Collection Philip Aarons and Shelley Fox Aarons

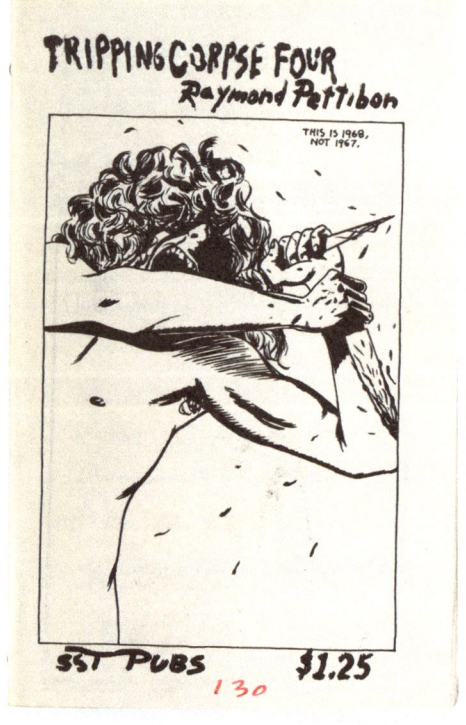

Tripping Corpse Four, 1985
Offset, saddle stitched, 8 ½ × 5 ½ in. (21.6 × 14 cm)
Collection Philip Aarons and Shelley Fox Aarons

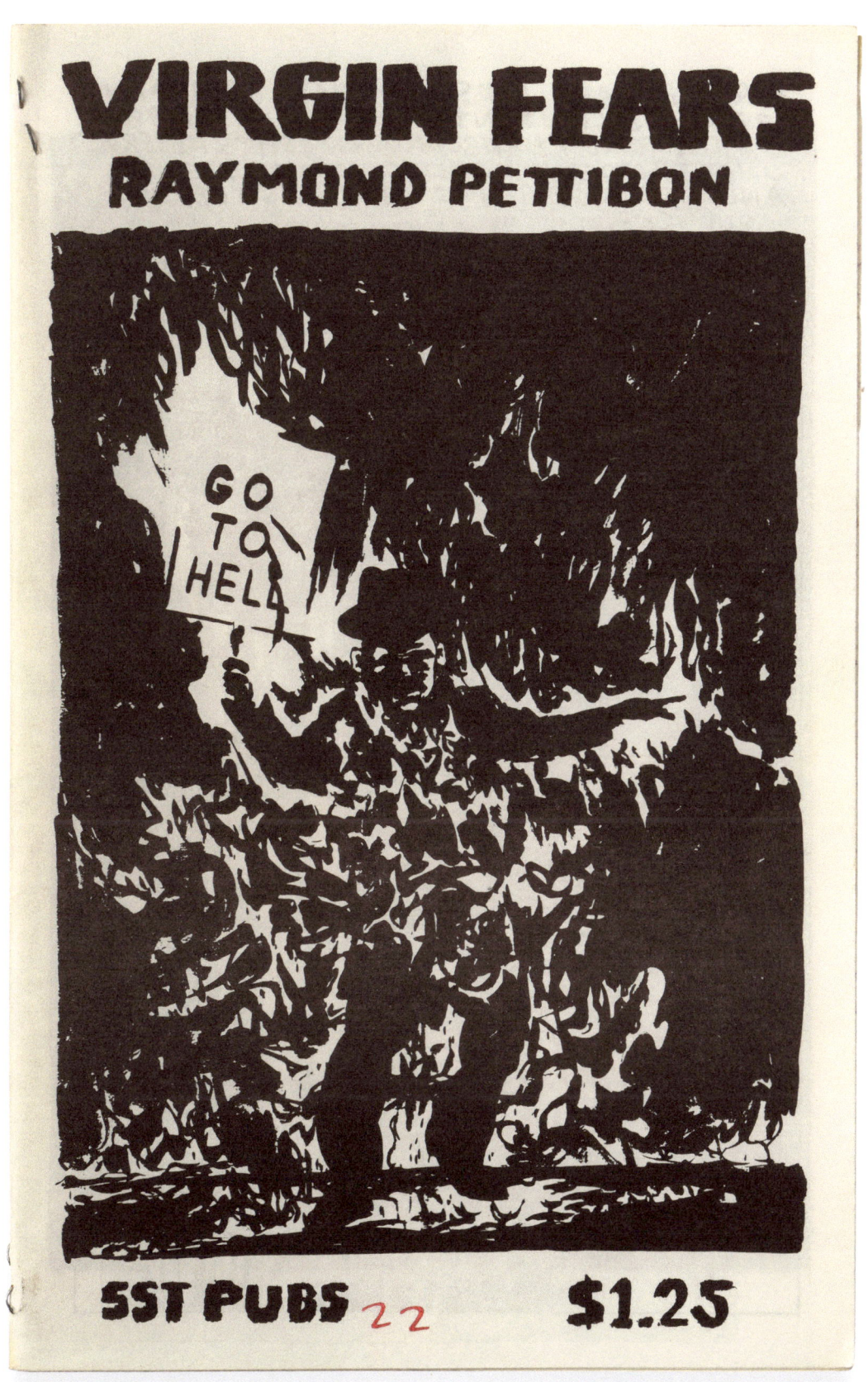

↑→ *Virgin Fears*, January 1983
Offset, saddle stitched, 8 ½ × 5 ½ in. (21.6 × 14 cm)
Collection Philip Aarons and Shelley Fox Aarons

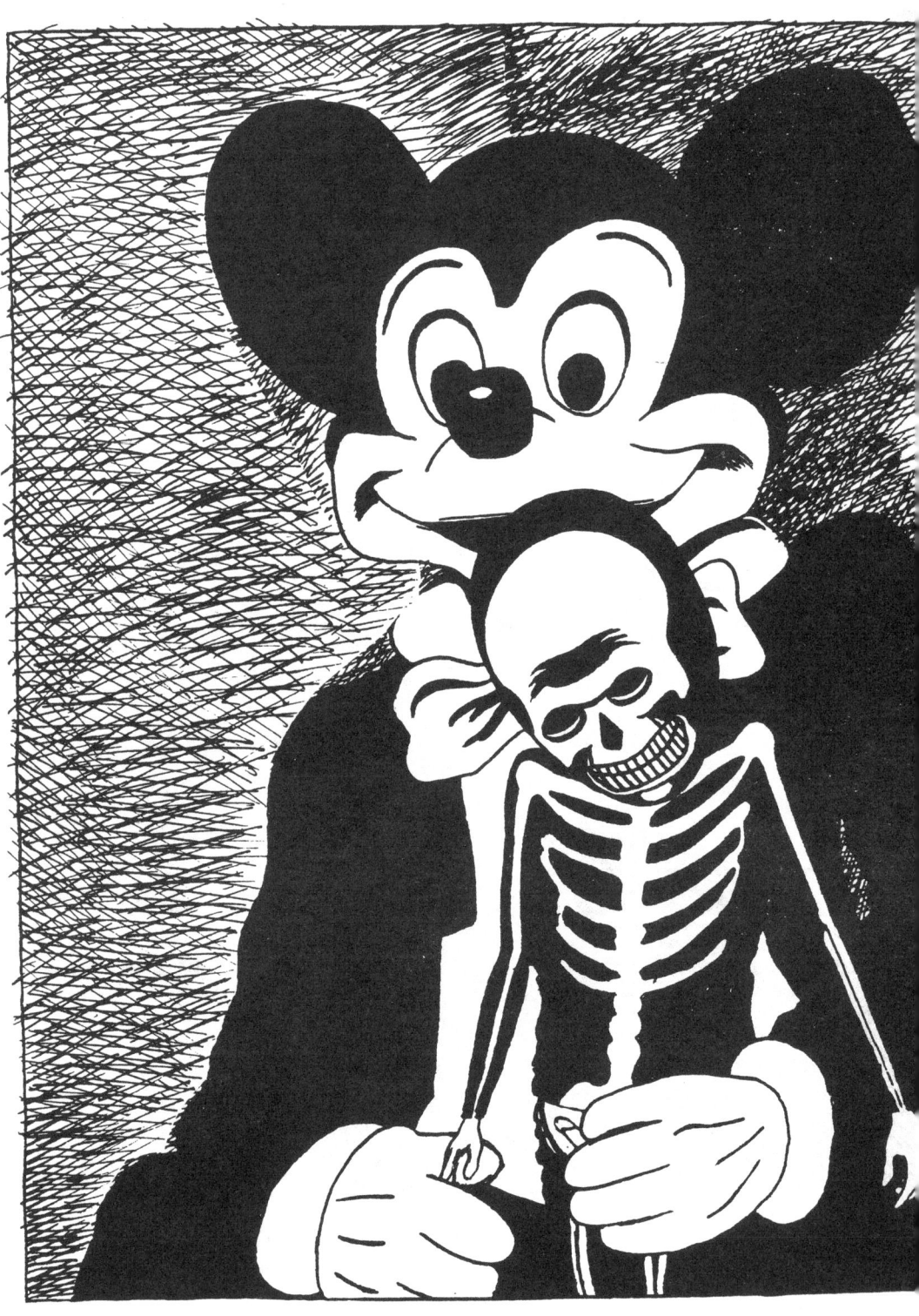

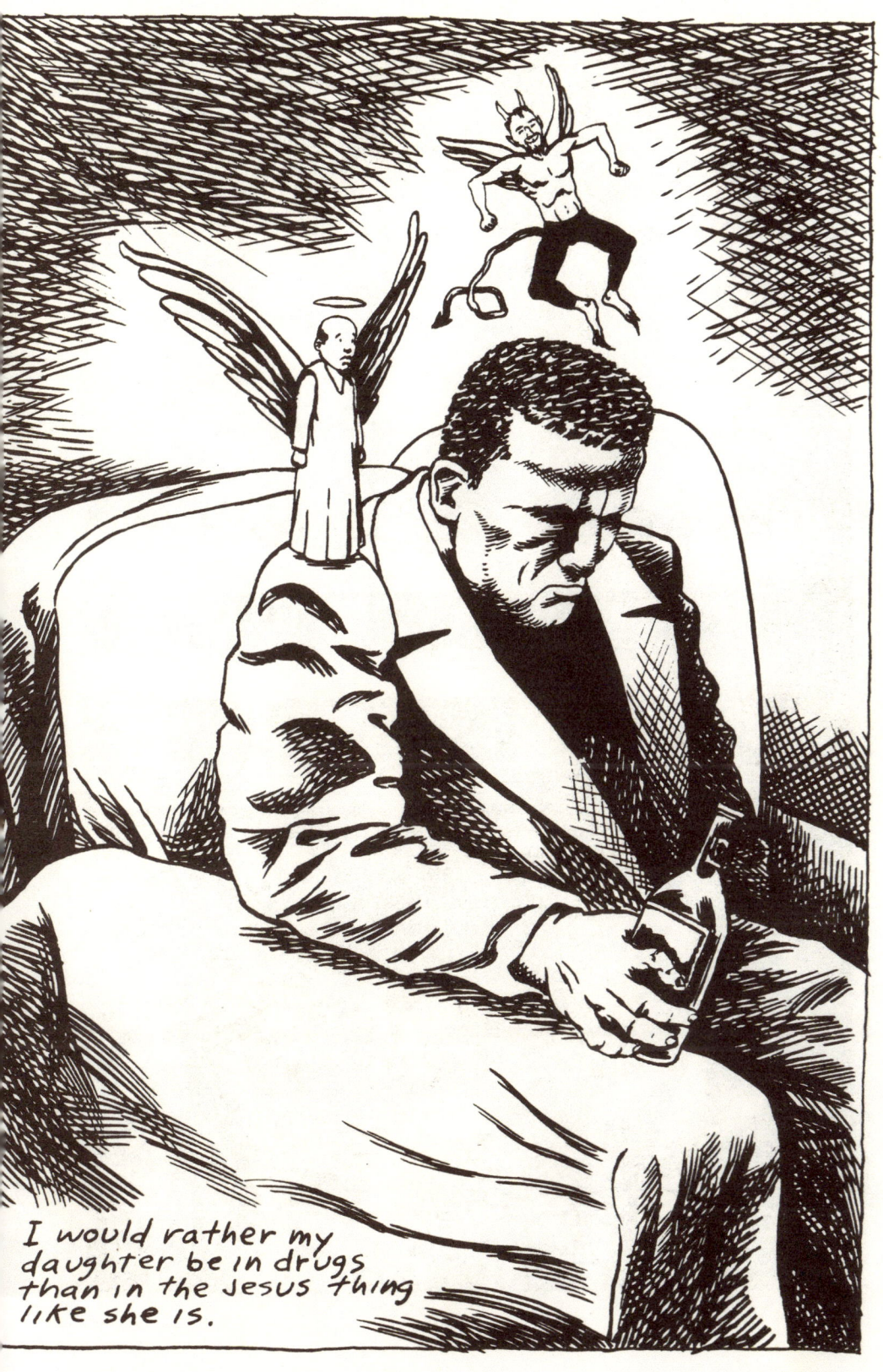

I would rather my daughter be in drugs than in the Jesus thing like she is.

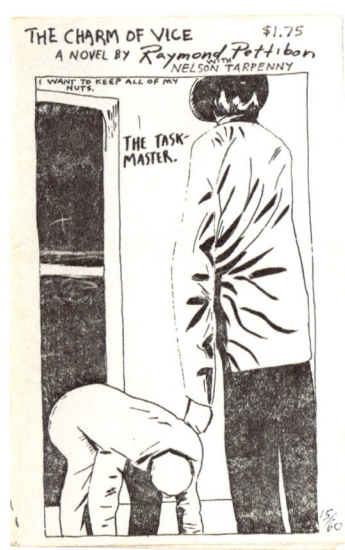

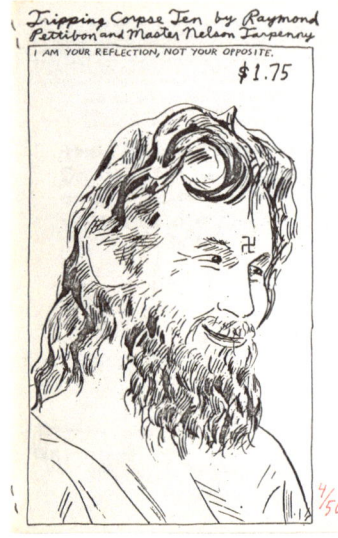

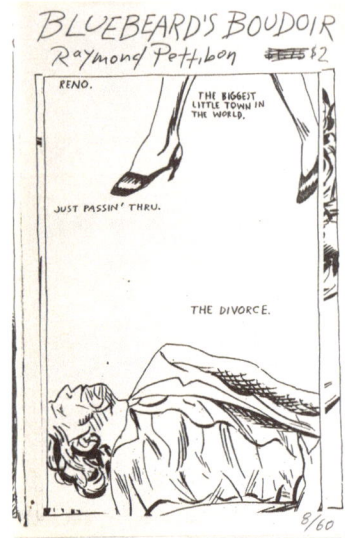

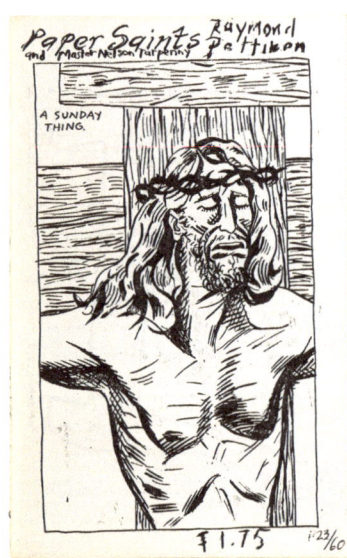

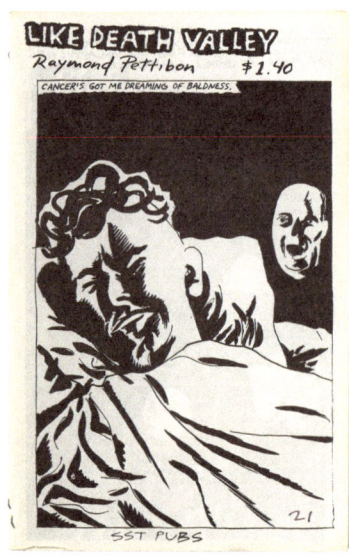

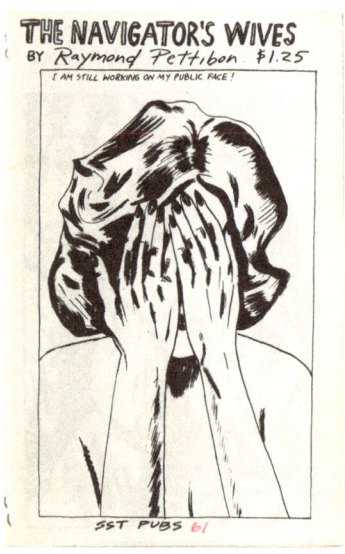

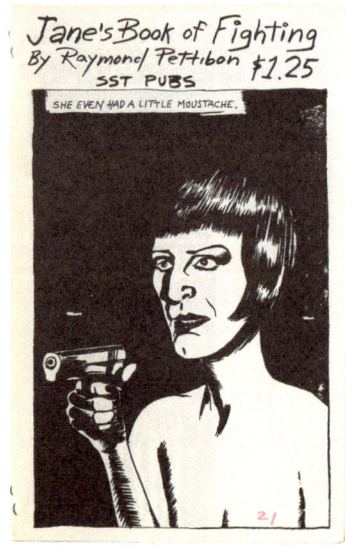

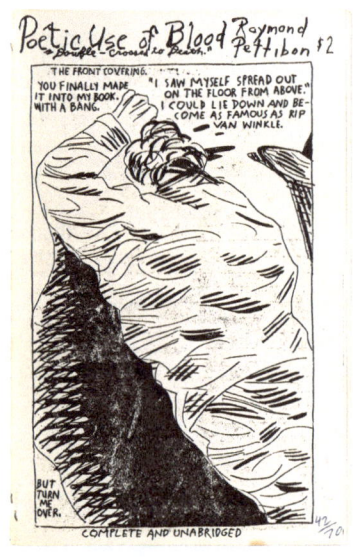

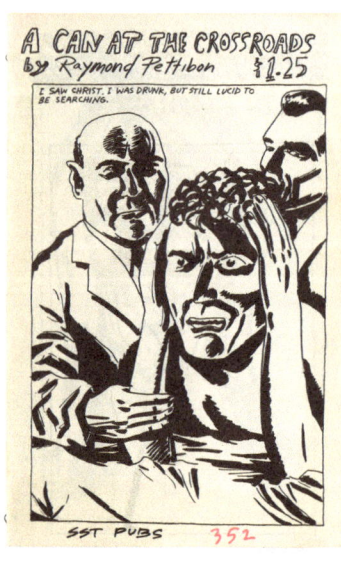

Various zines, 1982–91
All offset, saddle stitched, 8 ½ × 5 ½ in. (21.6 × 14 cm)
Collection Philip Aarons and Shelley Fox Aarons

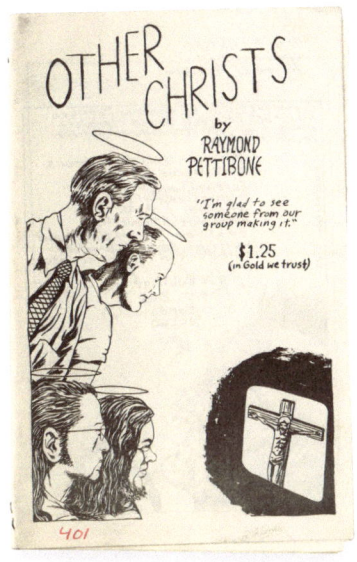

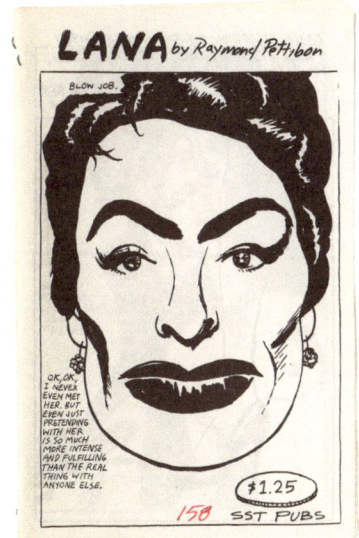

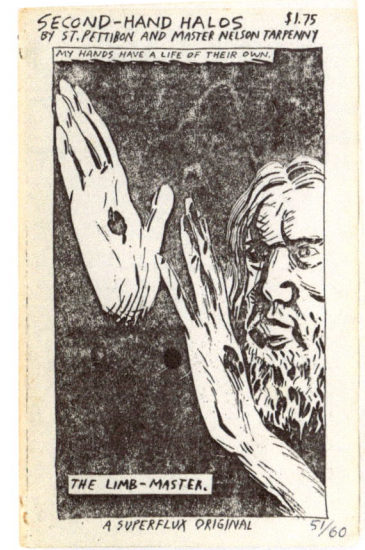

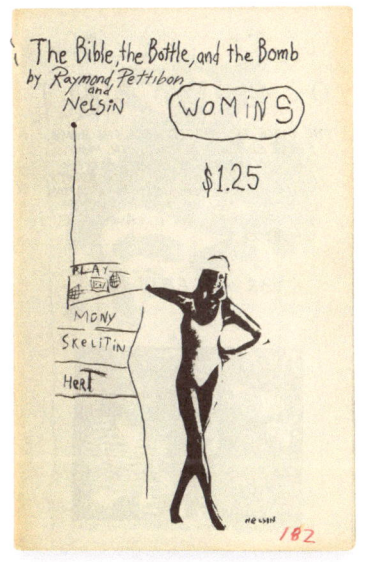

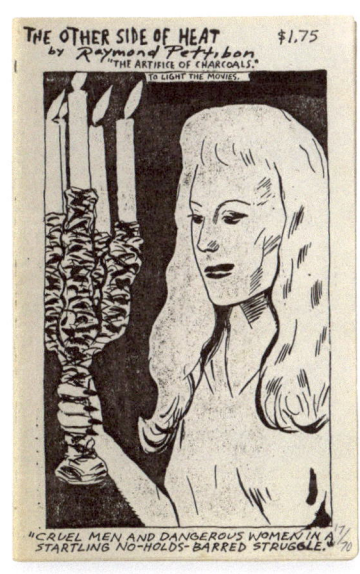

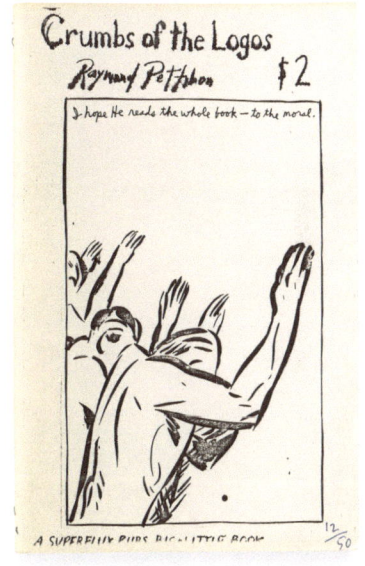

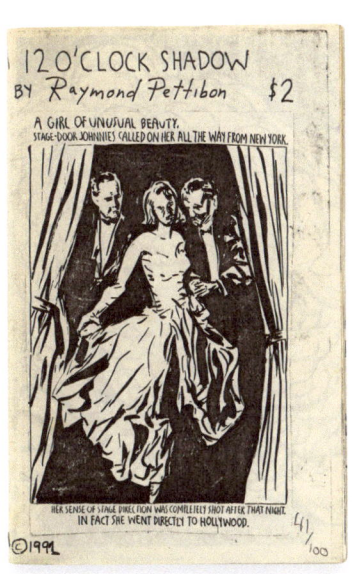

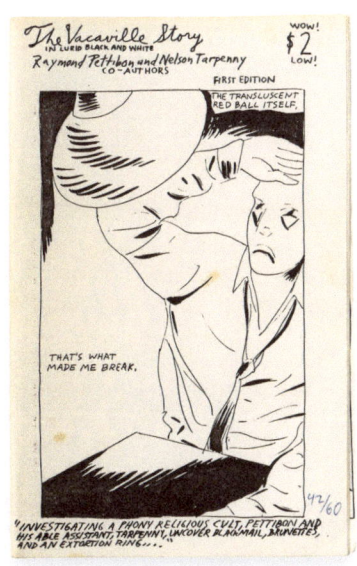

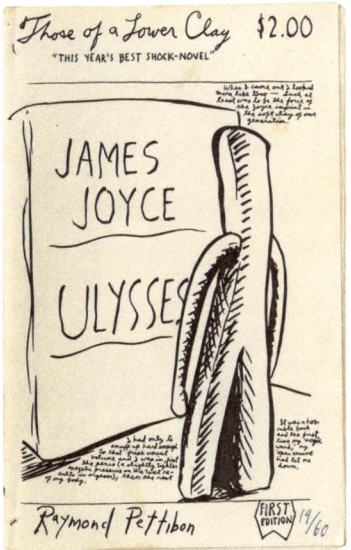

Social Media: Photography and Zines in the Age of Xerography

Drew Sawyer

In 1980 Cary Loren, a founder of the Detroit band Destroy All Monsters and editor of its **eponymous zine** (1976–79), published **The Secrets of Photography**. A collection of Loren's → 114–18, 119 "visual notes and poems" with quotes by everyone from German theorist Friedrich Nietzsche to British photographer and socialite Cecil Beaton to Syrian poet Saniya Salih, the black-and-white photocopied zine offers a number of "secrets" or insights that seem to oppose the medium's more familiar associations with the rational, mechanical, and objective. Loren's selection of fragmentary texts and images, which range from nineteenth-century motion studies to Hollywood film stills, foregrounds photography's irrationality, instability, and mass reproducibility.

Under the heading "Xerographs" is Loren's second "secret of photography": "THE DESIRE TO COPY AN IMAGE IS TO BELIEVE IN NO LIMITATIONS."[1] Loren connects xerography to magic and psychic powers, recounting how the process's inventor, Chester Carlson, upon his death in 1968, bequeathed money to the foundation of Edgar Cayce, the self-proclaimed faith healer, clairvoyant, and founder of the Association for Research and Enlightenment. In Loren's zine, appropriated photographs are interspersed with enigmatic short lines of prose: "xerox your family into anarchy," "exposure to xerox leaves a trace of carbon on the memory," and "xerox language/an opiated camera drama/unfolding its cipher/by esoteric revelation."[2] For Loren, as for many zine makers and artists during this period, xerography was a potentially liberating medium of disruption, transformation, and beauty. As such, *The Secrets of Photography* is not only an underrecognized contribution to the critical debates around photography during the 1970s and 1980s (it was published in the same year as Roland Barthes's influential book *Camera Lucida*),[3] but also an early and rare meditation on the centrality of xerography to the history of photography—a meta-analysis of the very medium Loren had used to make the publication.

Xerography, as *The Secrets of Photography* notes, is a dry photographic technology that was invented by Carlson in 1938 and developed in the 1940s and 1950s by the Xerox corporation (originally known as the Haloid Photographic Company). First called "electrophotography," the process was renamed "xerography"—from the Greek *xeros*, meaning "dry," and *graphia*, meaning "writing"—because, unlike most photographic techniques, it does not rely on liquid chemicals. Rather, xerography uses photoconductive materials, such as carbon (or now mostly plastics known as toner), on an electrically conductive base, which are then fixed to the surface of paper or whatever material is put through the machine. Xerox introduced its historic Model 914 machine in 1959. Widely considered the first successful commercial copier, the 914 was a major catalyst for transformations in everyday life as well as art in the second half of the twentieth century.

Despite its ubiquity and importance, however, there are few studies of xerography's technology and its impact, especially on the fields of art and photography. That impact was profound, from Conceptual practices like Seth Siegelaub's *Xerox Book* project (1968) to the AIDS activism of the collective known as fierce pussy (active since 1991). Loren and others adopted xerography and its aesthetics to make not only zines but also related photographic works that were often featured in or alongside the publications. A consideration of the history of artists' zines and their relationships to photographic practices reveals that these publications have served as important spaces for experimentation and new discourses in art since the 1970s, from explorations of mass media imagery and constructions of identity to documenting and galvanizing communities and subcultural practices.

In her volume *Adjusted Margin: Xerography, Art, and Activism in the Late Twentieth Century* (2016), media scholar Kate Eichhorn is one of the few figures to contend with the rise of the xerographic copy machine as an artistic medium and a tool for the creation of counter-publics.[4] While copy machines were engineered to facilitate the reproduction of documents and to reduce both the time and the cost associated with bureaucracy, Eichhorn observes that the technology had an especially consequential effect on subcultural communities—on the "margins," to borrow her term.[5] For Eichhorn, the margin is a central metaphor or category of the late twentieth century; as it became synonymous with subcultures and subalterns, she remarks that artists especially have used the "margin" as a vantage point from which to critique the "center" (or mainstream culture). From the 1960s through the late 1990s—

by which time digital platforms were rapidly replacing copy machines—many visual artists welcomed xerography as a means to produce and distribute printed material quickly, cheaply, and collaboratively, and to engage dynamically in local, national, and international political and cultural battles. Eichhorn points to how zines in particular helped disseminate a shared aesthetic around xerography and allowed people to be active participants in scenes or subcultures, rather than passively bearing witness to them—as had been the case with most forms of mass media and culture, from magazines to television.

Zines and xerography were tools with which photographers could challenge the "center" of the medium, where the status of the photograph was prioritized as a reliable document, with fixed meaning or "truth," and as a finely crafted gelatin silver print. While the discipline of art history has tended to focus on more official forms of critique during these years—the writings of artists and professors like Allan Sekula and Martha Rosler, or critics like Roland Barthes and Susan Sontag, to name a few—artists and activists associated with punk in particular, as well as "marginal" communities, adopted these mediums in ways that similarly challenged the uses of photography by a range of institutions. In many instances, zines and the photographs in them were instrumental in what scholar and theorist José Esteban Muñoz has called the future-oriented or utopian project of "queer world-making."[6] Artists as varied as Joey Terrill of 80–83, 160–64 ← **Homeboy Beautiful** (1978–79) and G. B. Jones and Bruce LaBruce of **J.D.s** (1985–91) published photographs and stories in zines that anticipated queer social scenes that did not yet exist, and made those scenes come into being by the very act of bringing groups of people together to make staged photographs, and by circulating the resulting images along with texts. Some artists used the zine format and photography to satirize and respond to mass media and power. For others, zines and the photographs in them served as social documents, archives, and pedagogical spaces for marginalized practices and communities and underinvestigated subjects—from graffiti and skateboarding to the vernacular architecture of Black communities in the southern United States—and helped distribute these images and ideas to wider audiences.

GHOST IMAGES

As Eichhorn observes, punk artists took enthusiastic advantage of xerography to quickly produce and share art, flyers, and zines, elevating and spreading the copy machine's gritty, do-it-yourself aesthetic across public spaces as well as art markets during the 1970s and 1980s. Loren and other artists who made zines frequently used the copy machine to produce collages and photomontages, or even to make prints from their photographic negatives. Filmmaker Richard Kern, creator of 143; 142, 144; ← the zines the **Heroin Addict**, the **Valium Addict**, and **Dumb Fucker** in the late 1970s and early 145 1980s, for example, produced a number of installations of xeroxed photographs, often repeating a single image in a large grid surrounding collaged text by his friend and colleague Montanna 145 ← Houston. Kern and Houston collaborated on zines such as **How Magic Works** (1981), featuring Kern's photographs and Houston's text pieces. The two of them would print the pages of their zines and installation works on the Xerox 9500 machine at the Ford Foundation in New York (where Houston worked at the time). "It was like the first Xerox machine that made photo quality printing in black and white," Kern later recalled. "So, we would go there and print at night. [Montanna would] let us in and we could print just like thousands of magazines." For Kern, the use of xerography to make his zines and photographic works was transgressive not only because it was being subsidized by corporate funds, but also because of its ephemeral and anti-commercial nature. When he was still in school, Kern said, he "got into the idea that art was supposed to be pure. It couldn't be purchased. Once it was purchased, it was tainted."[7] After Kern made dozens of copies of a single photograph—"some kind of hopefully dark, surrealist looking image"—Houston would add a collaged poem and Kern would then wheat-paste the paper directly to a wall, ensuring that the work would eventually either be destroyed or disintegrate.[8]

Like Houston, many photographers and zine makers made use of photocopy machines at their places of employment or relied on connections who worked at local copy shops. In Northern 88–89 ← California in the late 1970s, the photographer Jim Jocoy published the zine **Widows and Orphans** (1977–78) while working at a copy shop in Palo Alto. He was immersed in the local punk scene, and his color photographs of friends and bands are featured in the zines alongside contributions by other Bay Area punks and correspondence artists, such as Monte Cazazza and Genesis P-Orridge. Thanks to his day job in those years, Jocoy was able to work from color slides: the shop had a copy machine that could produce color images through a carousel slide-projector attachment, and his boss allowed him to use the machine for his own art. "That's how I generated volumes and volumes of images, and it's what drove me so strongly to take pictures," Jocoy recalls. "After I stopped working there, I couldn't afford to make them anymore!"[9]

While many artists used copy machines because of the technology's affordability, accessibility, and anti-commercial potentials, they also appreciated the quality of the images: photocopying produced rich yet degraded pictures, defying the supposed "transparency" of the medium and making visible the material support of the image. Beginning in the late 1970s, a number of artists and zine makers associated with punk experimented with photographic techniques of distortion that echoed the aesthetics of xerography. Artist Mark Morrisroe began making photographs in the 1970s, while still a teenager in Boston; he and his friend Lynelle White launched the fanzine **Dirt** in 1975. Working primarily with Polaroid film (which shares   → 94–99
the element of instantaneity with xerography), Morrisroe became known for his so-called "sandwich" prints, made by rephotographing his own images and combining the intermediate and original negatives to make muted, painterly pictures—often self-portraits or intimate scenes with his friends and lovers. As he did in his gossipy zine, Morrisroe would often add handwritten personal inscriptions to the margins of the prints in marker.

Barbara Ess, who started her zine **Just Another Asshole** in 1978 as a crudely photocopied   → 108–11
compilation of her collages, simultaneously began making enigmatic and haunting photographs with DIY pinhole cameras made of cardboard. Ess came up with her zine's title after reading a *New York Post* article about a deaf-mute boy killed by an intruder he couldn't hear: "There was a picture of the boy, and he looked so sweet. I made a color Xerox of it, and I wrote on it, 'just another asshole,'" she later recalled.[10] Her words are telling, and representative of the critical take Ess and many other zine makers brought to the uses of photography in mass media. If her zine started as a response to the alienating and dehumanizing effects of mainstream media, which exploited such events for their shock and entertainment value, Ess's use of the pinhole camera countered the instrumentalization of the medium in other ways. Works like **Girls on**   → 103
Curb (1983)—the first image she made with the pinhole device, which she used to rephotograph a scratched Polaroid of her younger sisters—feature distortions that are an unavoidable factor of working with that simple picture-making process. The images read as metaphors for psychological states, and Ess's (literally) warped interpretations of scenes from everyday life are heavy with a sense of the weight of the past, and of disintegrating social structures during her own time. "I think of my work as an investigation," she said in a 1991 interview, "and it's always concerned with the same question: Exactly what is the true nature of reality?" And, in answer to her own question: "I don't know if there's an essential reality it's possible for us to get a grip on, but I know I don't experience life primarily in terms of the physical world—my emotions and memories play a much larger role in shaping my experience as a human."[11]

New York–based artists Tommy Turner and David Wojnarowicz similarly experimented with xerography, zines, photography, and film to explore the darker sides of US culture. The two met while working at the Peppermint Lounge nightclub in 1981 and bonded over their shared interest in photography. After work, just before dawn, they would often explore abandoned buildings in Manhattan or de-industrialized landscapes and cemeteries in nearby New Jersey, making **photographs** at night with their flashlights, the long exposures and movement of forms   → 151
creating a ghostly effect.[12] In 1984 the pair became fixated on the recent story of Ricky Kasso, teenage heavy metal fan and self-described "Acid King" of Northport, Long Island, who was the subject of media frenzy over heavy metal, drugs, and Satanism when he committed the pseudo-ritualistic murder of a fellow teen in the woods. Shortly after, Turner created two issues of the zine **Redrum** (1985), featuring news stories of murders and suicides collaged with writing and   → 148–50
photographs from the other contributors—an appropriated photograph of Kasso appeared on the cover of the second issue. Turner and Wojnarowicz also interviewed several of Kasso's friends

as material for a Super-8 film, intended as feature-length, *Where Evil Dwells* (1985). Wojnarowicz worked with photocopying throughout his career, often collaging his own photographs together with appropriated ones. His *Arthur Rimbaud in New York* series (1978–79) features a photocopied cutout of the French poet's young face, cast against various locations around New York City. The series underscores both the ephemerality and mobility of xerography and its ability to transform the city and representation—here inserting queer history and visibility into public spaces.

PERFORMING IDENTITIES AND DECONSTRUCTING MEDIA

Embracing Xerox's aesthetics of image degradation and distortion was just one strategy that zine makers used in challenging the supposed "truth" and transparency of the photographic image. Many also satirized mass media representations by creating, and then reproducing, staged photographs that mimicked photojournalism, photo essays, fashion editorials, and advertisements published in mainstream magazines. These zine makers used photography's indexical nature to play with the constructions of identity by economic and social forces associated with mass media and to push back against the fetishizing gaze of others.

The 1970s brought a proliferation of correspondence artists, who frequently produced and circulated photographs of performances or staged photographs alongside appropriated ones—purposefully confusing not only authorship but also the boundaries between fact and fiction. Numerous mail artists circulated photographs and photocopies through the artists' group Image Bank, based in Vancouver, which established a network of mailed-out requests soliciting artists to send them images based on broad themes (subjects included "piss pics" and "beauty pageants"). Beginning in 1974, the group published an annual directory of artists' addresses and image requests in the "megazine" *File*, produced by the Toronto collective General Idea.[13] New York–based photographer Jimmy DeSana was one of the artists who made photographs for distribution in these mail art networks. His pictures subsequently appeared in zines—including images of John Dowd's bum for John Jack Baylin's "Bum Bank" and the related **"John Dowd Fanny Club"** (issue 3 of Baylin's *Fanzini* zine). DeSana's own self-portrait hanging from a noose with an erection showed up several times in the pages of *File* and was published on the cover of Anna Banana's zine **Vile** in 1974. While such theatrical practices responding to media representations have often been associated with the more commercially oriented practices of the Pictures Generation beginning in the late 1970s, zines and correspondence art were important early forums for such image play.

This performative style of self-portraiture—drawing upon mass media types and playing with constructions of identity—was the central theme of **Egozine** (1975–79), created by Robert Lambert, otherwise known as "Bobbi Bon-Bon," of the conceptual glam rock group Les Petites Bon-Bons. Lambert formed the Bon-Bons with Jerry Dreva and others in Milwaukee in 1971; three years later, they decamped to Los Angeles, where they developed their group identity by mailing out photocopied, collaged, and handmade items to other participants in the correspondence art scene. Like many working in correspondence art networks, the Bon-Bons adopted multiple names, upending any notion of a singular identity, and explored the relationship between the circulated image and the performative actualization of the self or of donned identities.[14] The Bon-Bons' participation in correspondence art allowed them to explore their gay identity in particular while differentiating themselves from the more mainstream and militant activist gay community. As early as 1973 they invited readers, via image-request lists published in *File*, to "send faggot art."[15]

Lambert manifested this approach to destabilizing identity through his photocopied collages, often featuring self-portraits disguised as various types, that were sent through the mail and compiled into *Egozine*. It is not surprising that **grids of photobooth images** were common among mail artists like Lambert—the format allowed them to highlight the serialized and fragmented nature of the self and the proliferation of its image through media. In one mailer from 1974, which was reproduced in the first issue of *Egozine* in 1975, Lambert enacts a series of contrived roles riffing on themes or types: the dandy, the cowboy, the leather man, and the man in uniform. In another feature, he is dressed in a jockstrap, leather jacket, combat

30 ←

51 ←

70–73 ←

71 ←

Drew Sawyer

boots, and white athletic socks, with keys and handcuffs: large letters identify him as "**BUTCH** → 72
BONBON." As the art historian Kirsten Olds has argued, such images reflected a shift in the
construction of homosexual male identity in the early years of the gay liberation movement,
when gay men adopted long-established tropes of masculinity in order to take ownership of
them, and thus to create new ones. This shift coincided with gay sexuality becoming a marketed
group identity or lifestyle—as seen in the pages of then new periodicals like the *Advocate* and
Gay Power—rather than a potentially revolutionary force that could transform the very structures
of society. Lambert and other correspondence artists, Baylin and Dowd among them, played
with the construction of these new identities.[16] Zines and xerography would continue to play
important roles in challenging the co-option and commercialization of identity and related
social and political struggles.

Participants in mail art networks often deployed sophisticated and humorous combinations of staged photography and text to mimic and subvert mass media representations and
to bring light to subjectivities and communities that existed outside these systems—or were
more frequently represented by "outsiders." In 1978–79 artist Joey Terrill, a Los Angeles–based
correspondent in the mail art networks with Lambert and others, created two issues of the
photocopied **Homeboy Beautiful**, a satirical lifestyle magazine that took aim at barrio machismo → 80–83
and homophobia.[17] The scholar of Latinx literature Robb Hernández has dubbed Terrill's
project *maricónography*: a direct visualization of "*maricón*" (a Spanish slur for a queer person)
identities that answered the violence against them "with an equally combative, unapologetic,
and flamboyant set of tactics."[18] Like *Egozine*, *Homeboy Beautiful* challenged mainstream media
representations of gay men, and did so with a decidedly camp sensibility. *Homeboy* included an
advice column ("Ask Lil Loca"), beauty tips, and fashion makeovers that played with (or against)
chola/o stereotypes.

As an artist, Terrill worked primarily in printmaking and painting (he had studied art
with Sister Corita Kent at Immaculate Heart College in Los Angeles), but his zines prominently
featured photographs, often laid out as *fotonovelas*, or picture stories. While Terrill was the engine
driving *Homeboy Beautiful*, his friends Ronnie Carrillo, Teddy Sandoval, and Efren Valadez helped
by performing for the camera as "homo-homeboys" (as they were called). Issue 1 includes a
mock-exposé on the homo-homeboys of East Los Angeles, while the second and final issue,
released in 1979, depicts them protesting the zine itself—and thus gaining self-representation
in its pages. The fictitious mobilization of homo-homeboy "activists" was made possible by the
actual mobilization of Chicano gay men who contributed to the production of the publication
by appearing, for example, in photographs for Terrill's humorously designed photo essays that
mimicked the format of the *fotonovela*. (As Terrill later recalled, the photo shoots also offered
a reason to get together and celebrate with food and drink.[19]) Despite its limited circulation,
Homeboy Beautiful achieved cult status in Los Angeles and ultimately reached readers far beyond
the boundaries of the city.[20] The zine thus succeeded in forging a print culture for a community
that was both real and aspirationally imagined.

The Toronto zine **J.D.s**, published between 1985 and 1991 by filmmakers and musicians → 160–64
G. B. Jones and Bruce LaBruce, likewise used photography alongside other media to address
homophobia in punk subcultures, combining staged photographs and appropriated materials
to show the Toronto punk scene as they envisioned it—although not necessarily as it existed.
Indeed, as Jones later recalled, *J.D.s* "pretended that there was already a fully fledged homo punk
movement in full swing going on in Toronto."[21] In addition to LaBruce's erotic fiction, Candy
Parker's comics, and Jones's "Tom Girl" drawings, most issues featured photographs of shirtless
and unclothed punks. LaBruce and Jones often found models at concerts; these photographs
are frequently juxtaposed with images of punk bands lifted from other magazines (including
several of the Red Hot Chili Peppers), making explicit the homoerotic undercurrents within punk
culture. Like earlier zines associated with punk subculture, *J.D.s* exaggerated the Xerox aesthetic
by repeatedly photocopying certain visual elements, allowing images to degrade over multiple
generations of copies, in the process becoming increasingly illegible and seemingly more
authentic—a similar aesthetic both artists pursued in their Super-8 films during these years.

The makers of *Homeboy Beautiful* and *J.D.s* showed a keen self-awareness and criticality about their adoption of mass media formats and attempts at speaking for particular subcultures—and often used humor to shed a questioning light on their own motivations.

In the 1990s staged photographic self-portraiture became a more widely adopted practice by artists, as photography itself was increasingly assimilated into the market and institutional structures of the art world, and artists considered the more particularized and "dispersed" forms of subjectivities as they related to the intersections of gender, sexuality, race, ethnicity, and class.[22] Zines continued to provide a forum for artists to push against these commercial and institutional forces, even as many participated openly in them. Artist Tammy Rae Carland made identity construction the central theme of her zines, photography, and video work in the mid-1990s, using self-portraiture as her primary mode. While she had been part of the so-called Riot Grrrl movement as an undergraduate at Washington State's Evergreen State College—where she befriended and began collaborating with Kathleen Hanna, zine maker and lead singer of the band Bikini Kill—Carland produced the majority of her zines during the theory-intensive MFA program at the University of California, Irvine, and the Whitney Museum of American Art's Independent Study Program in New York in the mid-1990s.[23] Like Hanna's music and zines (which include **Bikini Kill, no. 2** of 1991, and **My Life with Evan Dando, Popstar** of 1993), Carland's work conveys an engagement with cultural theories of sexuality, gender, race, and class—concerns that are clearly expressed in her zine **I ♥ Amy Carter** (1992–94, named for the daughter of US President Jimmy Carter).

248, 250–51 ←

233–36 ←

For Carland, both photography and identity are traces. "I like to make visual this riddle, this rhetoric mirror that tells us that a photograph is a sign of identity and that identity is assigned by photographs," she has said. "The ongoing and relatively consistent thread to all my work is an interest in personal and political disappearance and the desire to re-perform marginal histories and marginal bodies."[24] Perhaps taking a cue from her own zines, Carland maintains that her photographs are copies. "Not copies made in the vein of appropriation, but rather through looking at the original as if it were a performance and that this performance, or script, can be re-interpreted, re-performed and re-staged much like a play."[25]

237 ←

While *I ♥ Amy Carter* featured appropriated photographs, Carland's subsequent zines incorporated her own photographic work. In her **Random Letters to Ransom Girls** (1998), for example, Carland photographed "re-creations and performative portraits based on mostly self-portraits" of eight women who were "historically known for their relationship to, and with, their lovers and/or companions." The women ranged from Victorian-era diarist Hannah Cullwick to contemporary Japanese artist Yoko Ono. Alongside the photographs are texts, collaged in ransom-note style. As Carland writes in a short introduction to the publication: "In many ways this work is about revisiting the past and the desire to keep alive and vibrant a women's history that is at the same time absent and empty as much as it is ever present and full."[26] Her photographs also appeared in other photocopied zines, such as *Beehive* (1993–96), produced by Laura Splan and Allyson Shaw (who were undergraduates at UC Irvine while Carland was pursuing her MFA there). Issue 2 of **Beehive** features photographs from Carland's *Horror Girl* series, in which she poses as adolescent girl characters from popular horror films, such as Carrie from Brian De Palma's 1976 cult horror film of that name and Regan MacNeil from William Friedkin's 1973 film *The Exorcist*. Carland's photography and zines demonstrate the intermingling of zine cultures and more official ones, from new cultural theories to professional arts programs, and how artists continue to produce zines in conversation with their work in other media.

238 ←

Such performative practices have persisted into the twenty-first century, and zines continue to serve as important spaces for creating and publishing photographs that explore how identities are shaped by mass culture. New York–based artist K8 Hardy is known for her videos, photographs, and performances that deconstruct television news programs and fashion photography, but her zine-making career began when she was still a teenager in her home state of Texas in the early 1990s (*Glitter Days*, 1994; and *Move On*, 1995). As an undergraduate at Smith College in 1998, she worked as an intern for artist/filmmaker Miranda July, contributing a video to July's video-platform zine (or "chainletter," as July calls it) **Joanie 4 Jackie** and curating

264–66 ←

another of the tapes in the series. Like Carland, Hardy moved to New York to study in the Whitney Museum's Independent Study Program. The zines she made in this period were inspired by a drive to bring some of the Riot Grrrl energy and humor into her professional life and art practice. In addition to co-founding the feminist queer artists' collective **LTTR** in 2001 and producing its eponymous zine between 2002 and 2006, Hardy created **FashionFashion** (launched 2002), a zine that consists mostly of self-portraits that impishly disrupt the usual standard of sexist fashion photography. The theme of play with fashion and identity has also been taken up by Devin N. Morris, whose **3 Dot Zine** (2014–16) featured his staged photographs of friends; and in the zines of Maggie Lee (and related photo and video works); as well as in the zines of Pat McCarthy, to name only a few.

→ 330–33
→ 336–39
→ 390–92

BETWEEN ARCHIVE AND PUBLICITY

A number of artists have made use of the zine essentially as a repository for their photographs: a documentary archive of their lives, their communities, their passions, and their aesthetics. In the 1980s and 1990s the artist and sculptor Beverly Buchanan photographed vernacular architecture associated with Black communities in the US South, both to preserve the endangered structures and their histories and to serve as inspiration for her own bricolage sculptures. During the 1990s and early 2000s, along with other, more conceptual and sardonic zines she was making, Buchanan compiled these documents into color photocopied and spiral-bound booklets, such as *Survivors* and **Survivor 2** (ca. 2001) and **Houses** (2001). In producing zines made up of her own photographs, Buchanan was engaged in a mode of preservation—even if such publications themselves may be deemed "ephemera." Buchanan's zines began receiving recognition only after her death in 2015. In 2020 BlackMass Publishing produced *Beverly Buchanan: The Makings of You: Drawings & Sculpture* and *Beverly Buchanan: Sculptures, 1978–1980*, as well as the double zine **Kreyòl Homes/Southern Homes**, clearly inspired by Buchanan's work.

→ 272

→ 424–25

Many artists have created zines not only as a way to disseminate their work but as a means to engage with others. The artist Paul Mpagi Sepuya studied photography at New York University, and was drawn to zines shortly after graduating in 2004 by his "desire to connect to a community—to form channels for conversation and make opportunities, rather than wait for validation."[27] Each issue of his photocopied zine **Shoot** (2005–7) features Sepuya's photographs of a single figure— often young men the artist met online or at local bars. The zines serve as documents of a particular social group in Williamsburg, Brooklyn, in the early twentieth century—a project in the vein of the German photographer August Sander's monumental but never completed *People of the Twentieth Century*. While *Shoot* provided Sepuya with a reason to connect with people in his Brooklyn neighborhood, it also allowed him to think more about his practice as a photographer. "Zines let me think about sequencing, created a channel for me to begin revisiting negatives, contact sheets, and outtakes, and to explore how meaning shifted from when I took images versus what happened when they were printed and when they went out into the world."[28] That economy of social media exchange included making photographs for other zines, such as the Dutch publication *BUTT*, and being a subject in zines like Futoshi Miyagi's **Strangers** (2006).

→ 354–55, 357

→ 358

By the end of *Shoot*'s run, Sepuya's photographs had circulated well beyond the pages of his zine. Reflecting on this, the artist remarked:

By 2007 I was confronted with the effects of widespread dissemination of those portraits, on myself and on the other subjects, as well as our relationships to those pictures. I had to think about what it meant to be making portraits that circulated within the economy of homoerotic art and fanzine culture, such as publications like *BUTT* magazine. The photographs were made as art but developed a social currency on Friendster, Myspace, Facebook, and then within apps.[29]

Sepuya went on to make a series of **photographic works** based on screen grabs that feature some of his photographs circulating on these various online platforms. This artist's zines and photographs are important social documents of this transition from zine networks to online social media platforms—and of the crucial role of photography and portraiture on them.

→ 356

Dash Snow and Ryan McGinley began producing zines of their photographs and collages in the late 1990s, often documenting rollicking nights in New York City, as seen in McGinley's 1999 publication *The Kids Are Alright*. In 2001 *Vice* magazine (at the time a free glossy) published a story by film- and zine-maker Bruce LaBruce titled "The *Vice* Guide to New York Graffiti," which ran with McGinley's photographs.[30] The story chronicled several raucous nights out with the IRAK crew of graffiti artists—a group that included McGinley, Snow, Kunle Martins, and a graffiti writer dubbed "Semen Spermz." The inclusion of these images in zines lent them a kind of gravitas, a sense of authority and authenticity that is often associated with the printed page. It also allowed the images to be viewed outside the group of friends: McGinley received wide recognition for **The Kids Are Alright**; his 2003 solo exhibition of the same title at the Whitney Museum of American Art was one result.

308 ←

These artists, although clearly indebted to the queer and feminist zine practices that blazed a path for them (as their friendship with LaBruce attests), were also participating in skate and graffiti cultures that had their own rich tradition of zines and photography. The New York–based **IGTimes** (initially titled *International Graffiti Times*) is one of the earliest and most prominent of the genre. Founded by photographer David Schmidlapp in 1983, the zine featured interviews with and contributions by graffiti writers, as well as photographic documentation of graffiti art. The copious color photographs in the zine's pages celebrated the works of these artists, and the first issue's editorial statement assumed the tone of a manifesto:

154–55 ←

> Graffiti is an exercise of global citizenship. As an anarcho-architectural manifestation of free speech, graffiti bucks the bondage of propriety. An armed elite has controlled and manipulated the word plus image from parchment to the associated press, leaving the prophets to the walls to write on.[31]

It was also in 1983 that the San Diego–based skateboarder and photographer Tod Swank launched **Swank Zine**. The zine's simple and bold design comprises photographs of professional and amateur skaters—among them future zine-maker Mark Gonzales—doing tricks at parks, in backyards, and on the streets. Like graffiti artists of the era, skateboarders were a marginalized community, facing police curfews, prohibitive legislation, and bans from public areas.

285 ←

Both *IGTimes* and *Swank*, like their peer zines, were part of larger efforts to document certain maligned subcultural practices as art forms and to show their practitioners as a community, rather than as criminals—a favorable light that was rarely shone on them. Beginning in the late 1980s Schmidlapp and *IGTimes* art director Phase 2 compiled and toured the *Aerosol Art Armada*: a photographic slideshow along with talks, which they presented in classrooms, theaters, and other cultural spaces in an attempt to educate the public about graffiti writing and its cultures.

In the early 1990s members of the skateboarding and the graffiti "margins" (to return to Kate Eichhorn's term) coalesced around downtown New York's Alleged gallery, which served as a nexus for artists (Gonzales and others) who were working at the intersections of skateboarding, graffiti, painting, photography, film, and street fashion.[32] Many photographers—particularly those associated with documenting skate culture—exhibited or published through Alleged, which was founded by artist and curator Aaron Rose in 1992. Among the most prominent figures in this arena were Ari Marcopoulos and Ed and Deanna Templeton. Marcopoulos cites skate and graffiti zines especially as sources of inspiration for his own photo-based zines during this period.[33] As McGinley and Snow would later do, Marcopoulos and the Templetons produced zines that foregrounded their own photographs, often printing images full bleed on a page and juxtaposing two, butted up against one another, on a spread. Their photographs echo, in both subject and style, the zine aesthetic—the vision of life is strikingly unfiltered and immediate—and through their zines their work was widely disseminated. Marcopoulos often creates zines featuring his **photographs of a single figure or group**, such as snowboarder Johan Olofsson, basketball player Tyson Chandler, or hip-hop group the Wu-Tang Clan. Other zines document events and travels—often these were made as gifts or mementos for friends or acquaintances, highlighting the important role zines have played in fostering relationships and networks. Marcopoulos, who

304–5 ←

Drew Sawyer

began making Xeroxes of his photographs while working on his first book, *Portraits from the Studio and the Street* (1987), subsequently used photocopiers to make exhibition prints, enlarging his photographs or installing them in dense grids.

Since the early 2000s, this type of zine—a compilation of photographs with little or no text—has become a prevalent genre, continued by photographers such as the Italian-born Lele Saveri. In 2012, shortly after moving to New York, Saveri co-founded the 8-Ball Community—a media platform, gathering space, and collective of zine makers and other artists. Saveri also co-curated **The Newsstand**, a pop-up zine shop in Brooklyn's Lorimer Street subway stop.[34] → 384–85 *The Newsstand*, which was open for ten months in 2013–14, carried zines that were made by photographers or focused on photography, such as Ray Potes's *Hamburger Eyes* and publications by Marcopoulos, Pat McCarthy, and photographer Nick Sethi, who volunteered at the pop-up shop. During *The Newsstand*'s run, Saveri created **Commuters**, a series of more than six hundred → 382 photographic portraits of passersby made by the artist, forming a collective portrait of that time and place. Saveri published two zines from the images, and installed grids of 4×6-inch (10.2×15.2-cm) prints of them at *The Newsstand*; any commuters who recognized themselves in a photograph were invited to take the portrait home.

Saveri's colleague McCarthy worked with him at *The Newsstand* and has had a hand in the 8-Ball Community as well. At the pop-up, McCarthy similarly photographed commuters by installing a "camera-trap"-style setup, of the sort typically used by hunters following the path of animals, making a direct connection between street photography and predatory practices. He published the results in several issues of his own photocopied zine **Born to Kill** (launched → 386–89 in 2009). Often in its pages are photographs documenting McCarthy's Conceptual art practice involving pigeon-keeping: several issues feature photocopies of his pigeons' plumages, which the artist has transferred to **ceramic plates** via a copy machine and transfer papers. → 389

McCarthy's ceramic photocopies are one of the more unusual uses of the Xerox machine to be seen in *Copy Machine Manifestos*—nonetheless, they are paradigmatic of the level of innovation that zine makers have long brought to the fields of publishing and photography. Indeed, it might be argued that both disciplines have been altered by zine makers' refusal to submit to the limitations of institutional distribution channels, usage rights, commerciality, standard media formats, mainstream aesthetics, or the precious (and now long obsolete) notion of photography's role as authoritative "truth." Photocopier technologies have also been central to the creation of counter-publics over the past fifty years by allowing individuals and communities to participate in the production and distribution of media. While copy machines have been displaced to a great extent by digital technologies and platforms in the twenty-first century, zines continue to thrive—as does xerography. Social media platforms, mostly owned by large publicly traded corporations, allow many people to share information and create community more easily and quickly than photocopy machines alone. Yet physical zines, many still made with photocopiers, continue to serve as essential and intimate artistic and social tools that challenge commercial, institutional, and aesthetic forces. For many artists, xerography remains a decidedly transgressive medium that has played a central—but largely unrecognized—role in the history of photography.

NOTES

1 Cary Loren, *The Secrets of Photography* (Detroit: self-published, 1980), n.p.

2 Ibid.

3 The English-language edition was published a year later: Roland Barthes, *Camera Lucida: Reflections on Photography* (New York: Hill & Wang, 1981).

4 Kate Eichhorn, *Adjusted Margin: Xerography, Art, and Activism in the Late Twentieth Century* (Cambridge, MA: MIT Press, 2016).

5 Ibid., 21.

6 José Esteban Muñoz, *Cruising Utopia: The Then and There of Queer Futurity* (New York: New York University Press, 2009). Muñoz discusses numerous zine makers and artists connected to correspondence art, including Ray Johnson and John Dowd.

7 "Interview with Richard Kern by Diana Kamin and Marvin Taylor," August 30, 2016, David Wojnarowicz Knowledge Base, The Artist Archives Initiative, New York University; artistarchives.hosting.nyu.edu/DavidWojnarowicz/KnowledgeBase/index.php/Main_Page.html.

8 Ibid.

9 Jim Jocoy, in Emily Manning, "Electrifying Portraits from San Francisco's Forgotten Punk Scene," *i-D* (June 16, 2017); i-d.vice.com/en/article/bjnng8/electrifying-portraits-from-san-franciscos-forgotten-punk-scene.

10 Barbara Ess, interview with Nancy Princethal, quoted in Princethal, "Barbara Ess: Machine Dreams," *Print Collector's Newsletter* 21, no. 5 (November–December 1990): 169.

11 Barbara Ess, in Kristine McKenna, "Shadow Land," *Los Angeles Times*, November 10, 1991.

12 "Interview with Tommy Turner by Glenn Wharton and Marvin Taylor," May 20, 2016, David Wojnarowicz Knowledge Base, The Artist Archives Initiative, New York University; artistarchives.hosting.nyu.edu/DavidWojnarowicz/KnowledgeBase/index.php/Interview_with_Tommy_Turner_by_Glenn_Wharton_and_Marvin_Taylor_on_5-20-2016.html.

13 See Krist Gruijthuijsen, Maxine Kopsa, and Scott Watson, *Image Bank* (Berlin: Hatje Cantz; 2019).

14 For a discussion of Les Petites Bon-Bons in relation to the gay liberation movement, see Kirsten Olds, "'Gay Life Artists': Les Petites Bonbons and Camp Performativity in the 1970s," *Art Journal* 72, no. 2 (Summer 2013): 16–33.

15 Les Petites Bon-Bons, listing in General Idea's *File* 2 no. 3 (September 1973): 57.

16 Olds, "Gay Life Artists," 24.

17 See Richard T. Rodríguez, "Homeboy Beautiful; or Chicano Gay Male Expression in the 1970s," in *Axis Mundo: Queer Networks in Chicano L.A.*, ed. C. Ondine Chavoya and David Evans Frantz (Los Angeles: ONE National Gay & Lesbian Archives at the USC Libraries/DelMonico Books-Prestel, 2017), 113–23.

18 Robb Hernández, "Drawing Offensive/Offensive Drawing: Toward a Theory of Maricónography," *MELUS: The Society for the Study of the Multi-Ethnic Literature of the United States* 39, no. 2, "Race and Visual Culture" special issue (Summer 2014): 121–52.

19 Joey Terrill, oral history interview, December 30–31, 2017, Archives of American Art, Smithsonian Institution; aaa.si.edu/collections/interviews/oral-history-interview-joey-terrill-17532.

20 As Richard T. Rodríguez has noted, *Homeboy Beautiful* was featured in the 1994 exhibition *The Zine Scream* at Resolution Gallery in Los Angeles, and also in the 2011 retrospective *Asco: Elite of the Obscure* at the Los Angeles County Museum of Art. See Rodríguez, "Being and Belonging: Joey Terrill's Performance of Politics," *Biography* 34, no. 3, "Performing Queer Lives" issue (Summer 2011): 488.

21 G. B. Jones, in Sasha, "Ms. Jones: You Got a Thing Going On," *Xtra* (April 27, 2005); xtramagazine.com/culture/ms-jones-2-39738; quoted in Philip E. Aarons and Andrew Roth, eds., *In Numbers: Serial Publications by Artists Since 1955* (Zurich: PPP/Ringier Kunstverlag, 2009), 209.

22 For this turn in the 1990s, see for example Amelia Jones's "Dispersed Subjects and the Demise of the 'Individual' 1990s Bodies in/as Art," in *Body Art/Performing the Subject* (Minneapolis: University of Minnesota Press, 1998), 19–240; and "The 'Eternal Return': Self-Portrait Photography as a Technology of Embodiment," *Signs* 27, no. 4 (2002): 947–78.

23 Growing up in Section 8 housing in Maine, Carland recalls having often been the subject of local photography students, who documented the poverty of her family and neighborhood. For these reasons, Carland largely avoided producing photographs as social documents or "anything that had to do with the realness" of her life, instead preferring to use herself and friends in staged scenarios. Glen Helfand, "Tammy Rae Carland," *Aperture*, no. 233 (2018): 64–69.

24 Tammy Rae Carland, "Artist Statement," in *The (r)Evolution of Gender Exhibit* (San Francisco: SomArts/Rear Gallery, 2003), n.p.

25 Ibid.

26 Tammy Rae Carland, *Random Letters to Ransom Girls* (1998): n.p.

27 Paul Mpagi Sepuya, in Lesley A. Martin, "For Paul Mpagi Sepuya, Books Are a Way to Think About Time," *Aperture* online (April 16, 2020); aperture.org/editorial/paul-mpagi-sepuya-photobooks-process.

28 Ibid.

29 Paul Mpagi Sepuya, in Wassan Al-Khudhairi, "Interview with Paul Mpagi Sepuya," in *Paul Mpagi Sepuya* (St. Louis and New York: Contemporary Art Museum; Aperture, 2020), 12.

30 Bruce LaBruce, "The *Vice* Guide to New York Graffiti," *Vice* (November 30, 2001); vice.com/en/article/mv3zm3/graf-v8n3.

31 Yankee Junkie, *International Graffiti Times*, no. 1 (January 1984).

32 For more on the history of the Alleged gallery, see Aaron Rose, ed., *Young, Sleek and Full of Hell: The Alleged Gallery* (Rome: Drago, 2005).

33 Ari Marcopoulos, email to the author, August 11, 2022.

34 Lele Saveri, et al., *The Newsstand* (New York: Skira Rizzoli, 2016).

Richard Kern
(with Montanna Houston)

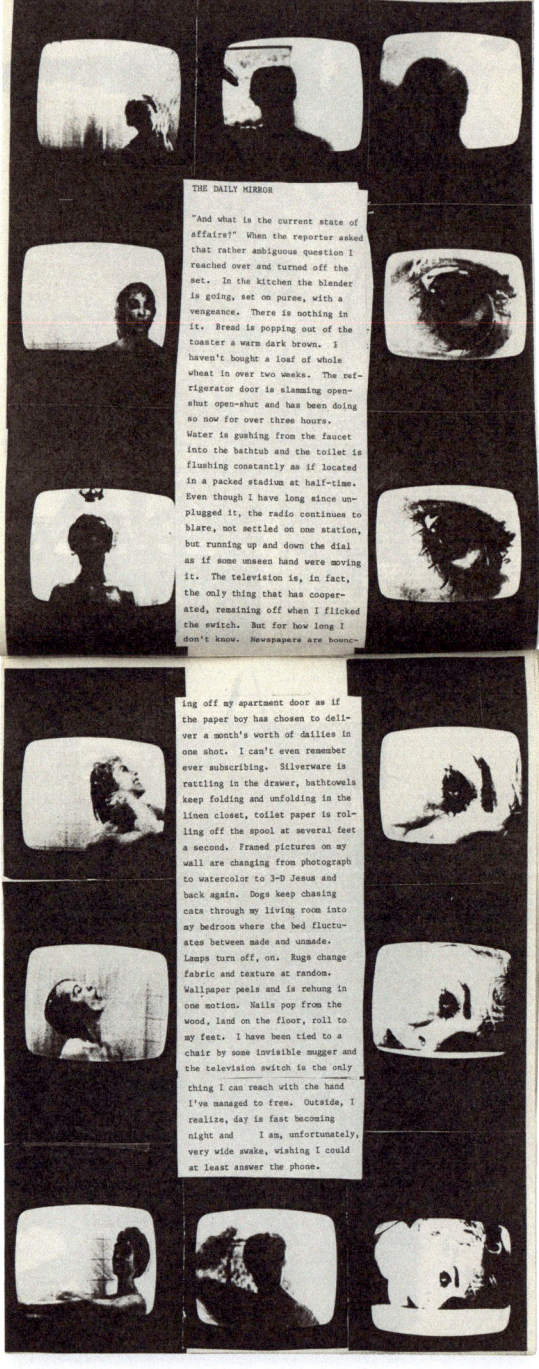

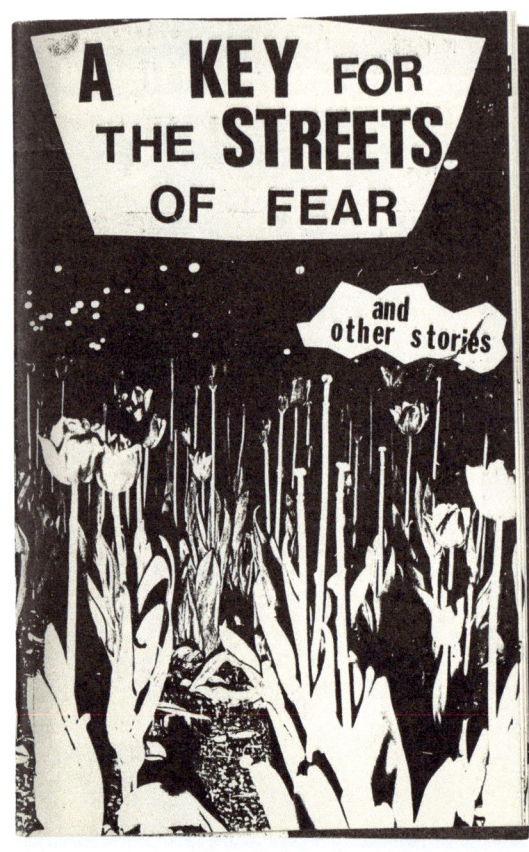

Richard Kern and Montanna Houston
A Key for the Streets of Fear and Other Stories, June 1981
Photocopy, saddle stitched, 8 ½ × 5 ½ in. (21.6 × 14 cm)
Collection Philip Aarons and Shelley Fox Aarons

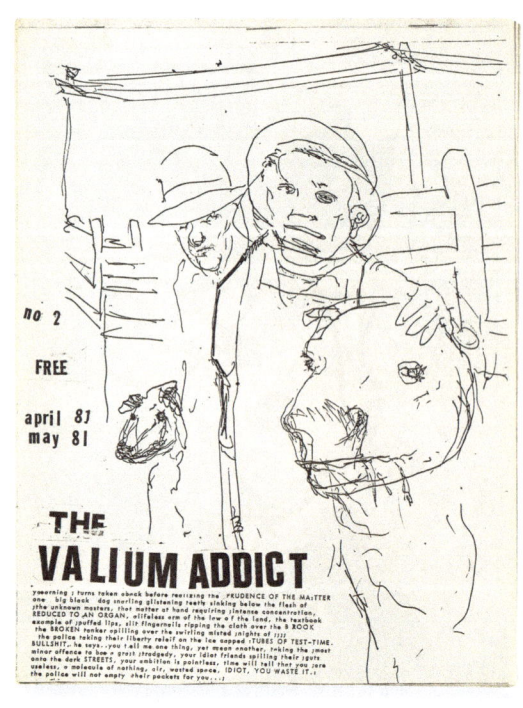

The Valium Addict, no. 2, April/May 1981
Photocopy, side stapled, 11 × 8 ½ in. (27.9 × 21.6 cm)
Collection Philip Aarons and Shelley Fox Aarons

THE HEROIN ADDICT

NO 5

right?s me because i have the desire to better my
right/ mornful respect for them, too lazy to get
as an infringement of / opon their rights..oly the true fools ask the wrong questions, any action serv
long to act upon their innermost desires..last week in paree i was hanging around with suzzie...
their pert figures , pink cheeks,   the dogs, the faithful followers of fashion, the time
the dogs, once excited take their stands; faces inches apart snarling in dog language, eyes whit
hot, salivating freely, lips curled into twisted grins, greedily anticipating the defeat of thei
lifelong foe....doggie personality clash...snarling scarastically , eyes flare, hair on end, musc
tense, challenge of the turf owner ship, final act to determine who is lord and master..quickly
changing from one leg to the other one step closer, deep throaty growls, owners step back, breath
less waiting for flying fur and bitting teeth, canines glint in white light, one animal will need
a trip to the vet....my way my way
there is no o
behind the ears
feeling but not
feelings that
....was it just the
intense emotion that
any given subject,
embarassment, often
become instantly
instant reaction
comfort to those
just the instant
subject, operate
that his mind op
what quiller calls
to any given situatic
but allowing the
of their personal
then. i have done this thing. words cannot describe the actions that i am about to perform. the st
studied carelessness, immitation of brief understanding for 'appeal'.performing , acting on the jsudde
impulse but regreting it later, no room for his behavior in an ordered and rationalsociety, causing sh
waves, acting towards his own demis, smoking cigarettes, causing the walls of jerico to fall upon his
mind that has taken a vacation from his body, this impulse that impulse, instantanious equilivent to h
human domination, reactions to minor upsets, causing frowns and sighs of dismay, often embarassing him
elf. acts of treson rebellion, treason, hateing everything,suddenly understanding why people break win
why they damage things, cause fright, wanting memories to be stored for later use, waiting for the ol
patterns to stop the
own personal interest
tired imagery, action
featuring cars, animal
type, still free, this
slick, patting his night
trim, pink cheeks, kno
lots of money, the reign
armed and considered..
i often critize people
quotes from the dead
never, never, never,
all the way, get drunk
memories, the first mover
pausing before the fiiii
to him as he enters the
various stages of dis
only slips and bras, meta
girl in just panties, l
the dark figures in the
courts, pillow tents carefully, erected over the plains, wearing loin cloths, they pause spears back a
tree limbs touching every dwelling in the tiny village, the men come home each night to their big and
strong wives, the white man traveling in his sturdy jeep, the jungle noises, the steaming winds turni

FREE

AUG 1980

i am right and
way..too green
liking the tense
understanding th
will soon undert
way, the time the
that he felt towa
causing him much
in public he would
alienated, causin
causing general di
around him. no ta
reaction to any gi
only on the same le
on. gut think is
it, instant reacti
causing angry rebu
person to regain so
fame.great. do tha
the st
acting on the jsudde

young giant, hi
being served, t
packed issue, fe
drawings, smalle
is issue no. 5
stick, whistling
knight in shinin
of terror, we ar
this bueatiful w
live with the st
never cheat, no
say never. pleas
eat fish, erased
keeping on lickin
these girls are f
dressing room, mo
robement, wearing
metal clips, one
stealing from oth
sandy tree lined c

THE MAG

WITH A CONSISTANT ATTITUDE

The Heroin Addict, no. 5, August 1980
Photocopy, corner stapled, 11 × 8 ½ in. (27.9 × 21.6 cm)
Collection Philip Aarons and Shelley Fox Aarons

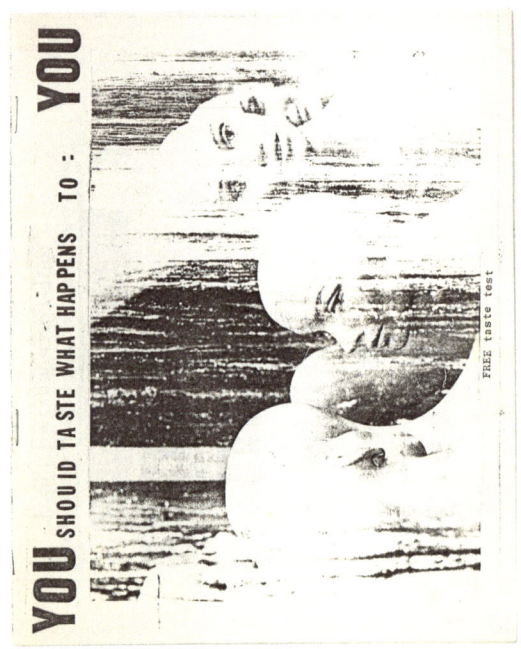

Richard Kern and Montanna Houston
You Should Taste What Happens To: You, January 1981
Photocopy, side stapled, 8 ½ × 7 in. (21.6 × 17.8 cm)
Collection Philip Aarons and Shelley Fox Aarons

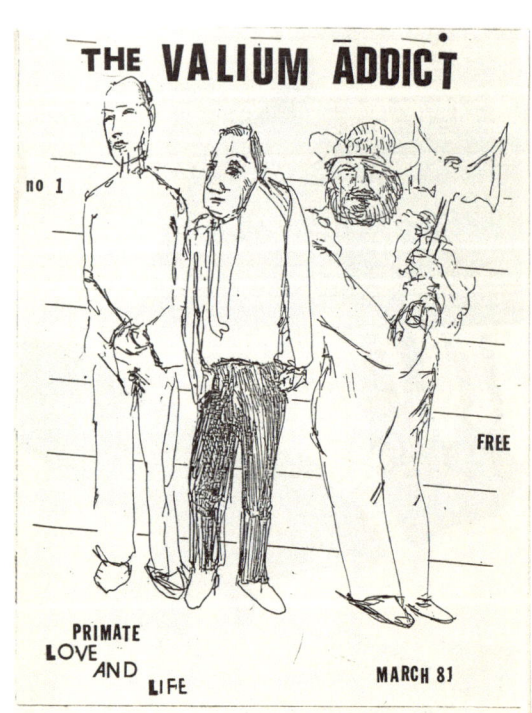

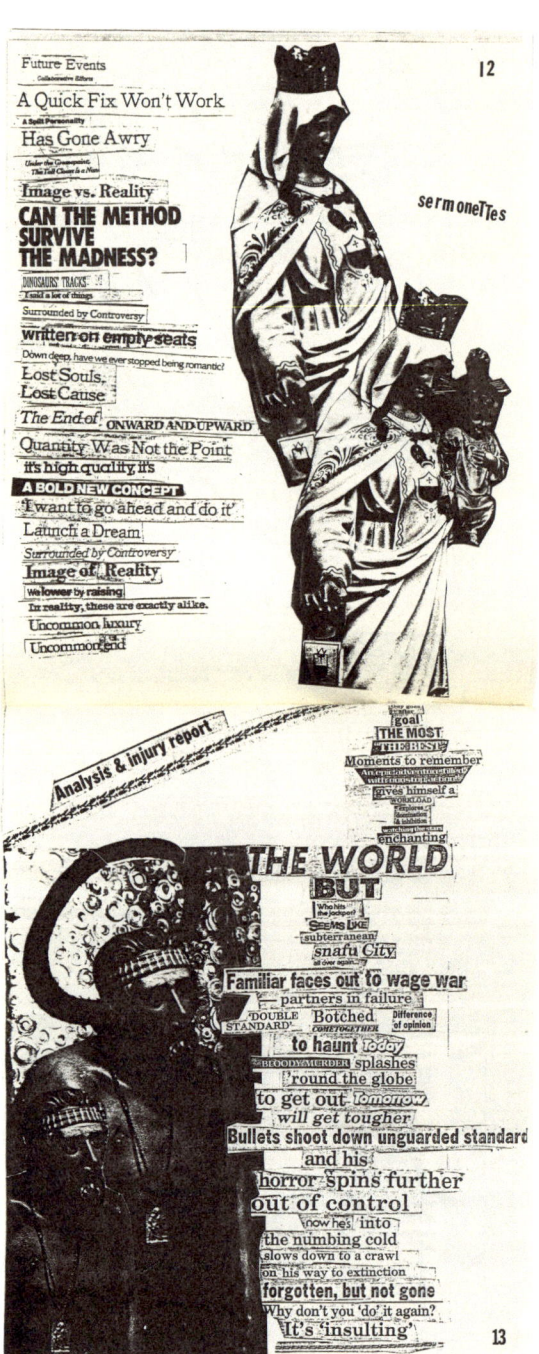

The Valium Addict, no. 1, March 1981
Photocopy, side stapled, 11 × 8 ½ in. (27.9 × 21.6 cm)
Collection Philip Aarons and Shelley Fox Aarons

Car and Truck: The Pinup and/or Coloring Poster Book for the Motor Vehicle Fan, November 1980
Photocopy, side stapled, 8 ½ × 11 in. (21.6 × 27.9 cm)
Collection Philip Aarons and Shelley Fox Aarons

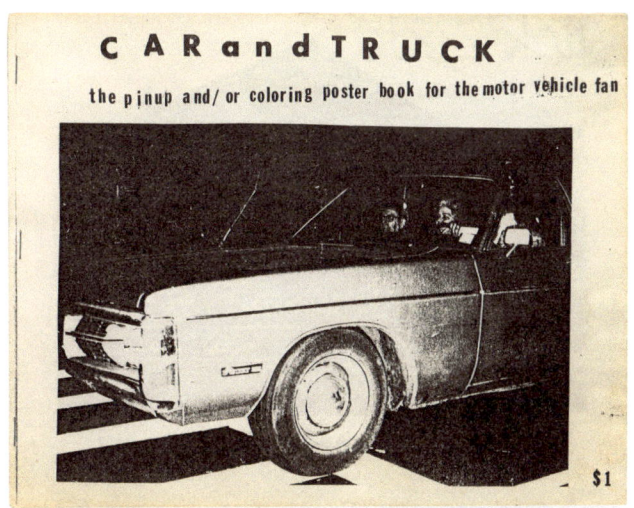

Richard Kern and Montanna Houston
How Magic Works, 1981
Photocopy, saddle stitched, 8 ½ × 5 ½ in. (21.6 × 14 cm)
Collection Philip Aarons and Shelley Fox Aarons

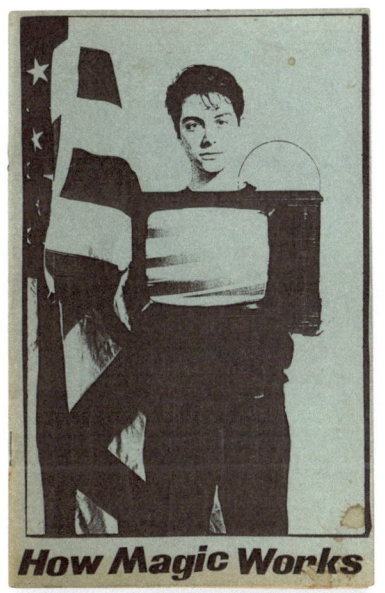

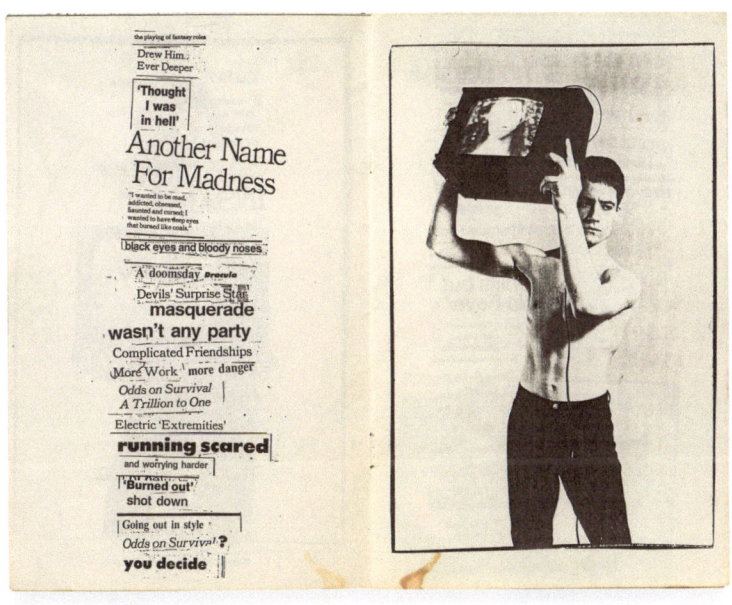

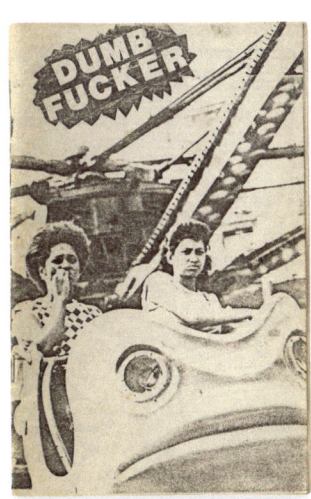

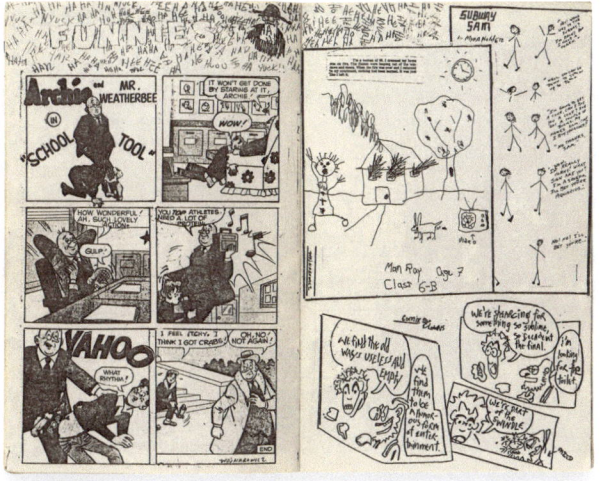

Dumb Fucker, no. 5, September 1982
Photocopy, saddle stitched,
8 ½ × 5 ½ in. (21.6 × 14 cm)
Collection Philip Aarons and Shelley Fox Aarons

Nick Zedd

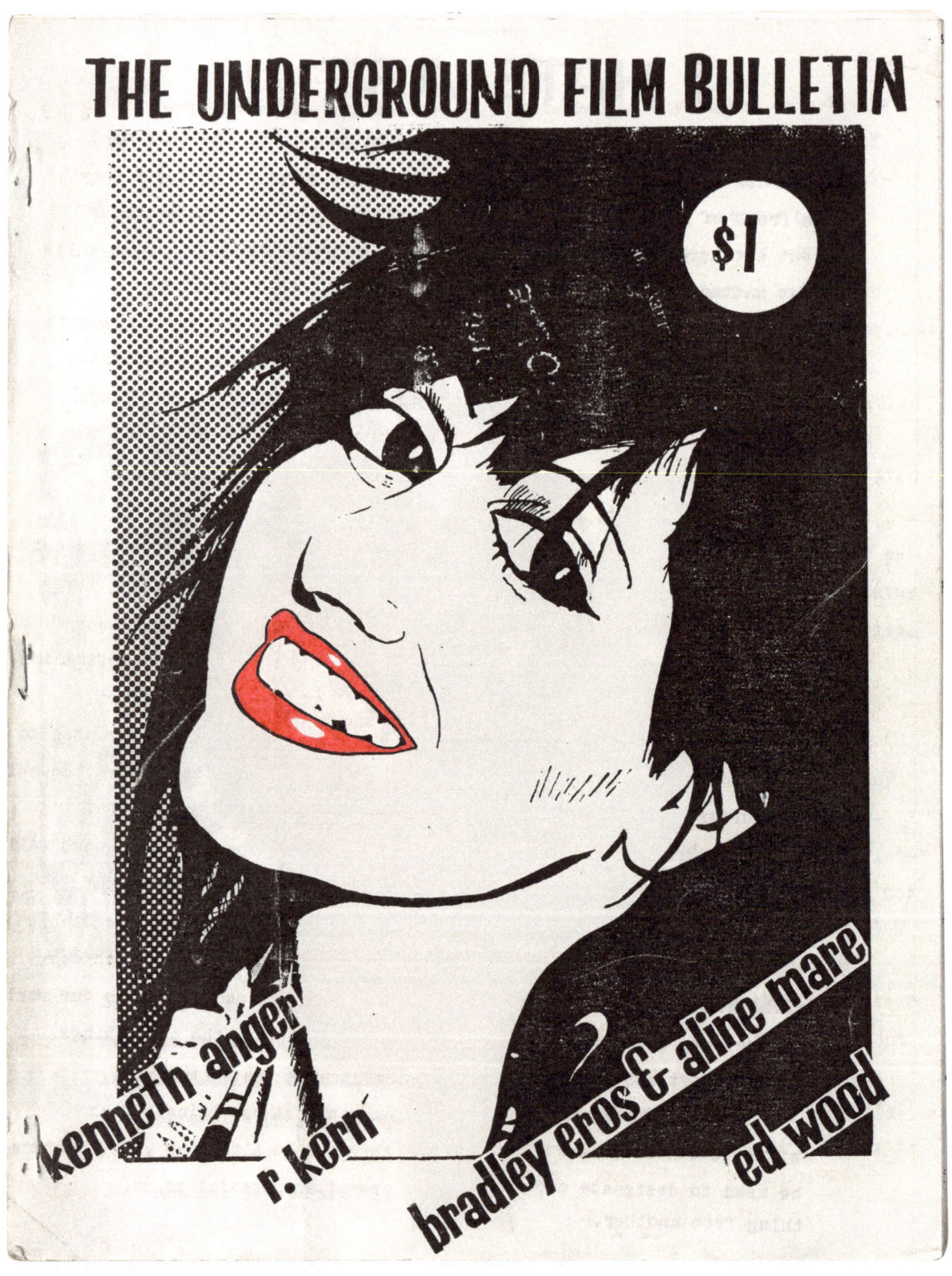

The Underground Film Bulletin, no. 2, 1985
Photocopy, side stapled, 11 × 8 ½ in. (27.9 × 21.6 cm)
Collection Philip Aarons and Shelley Fox Aarons

Casandra Stark

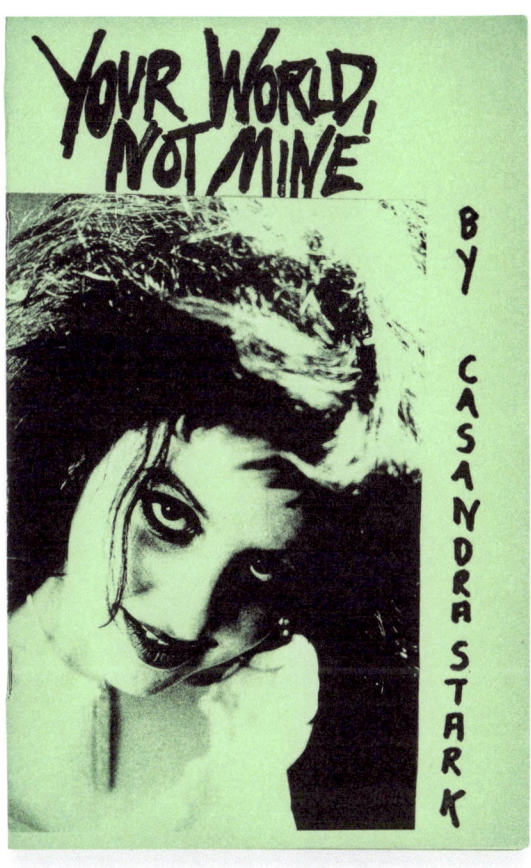

Your World, Not Mine, 1986
Photocopy, saddle stitched, green paper wrappers,
8 9/16 × 5 ½ in. (21.7 × 14 cm)
Collection the artist

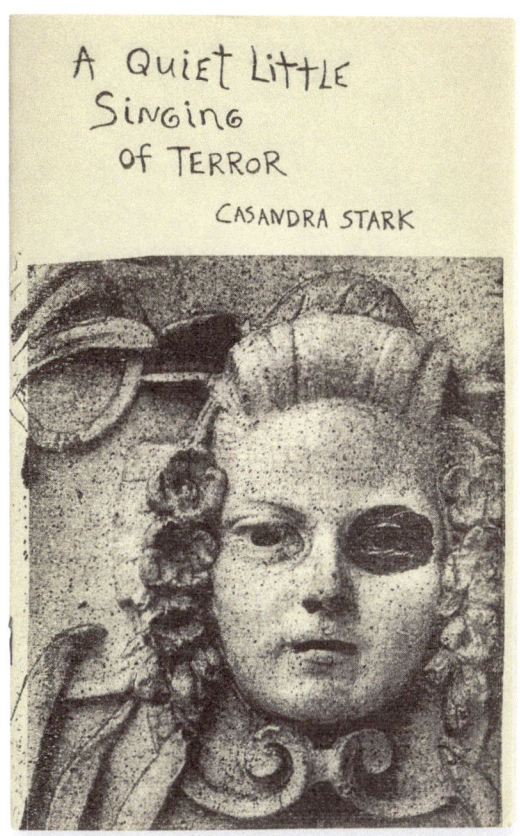

A Quiet Little Singing of Terror, 1991
Photocopy, saddle stitched,
8 9/16 × 5 ½ in. (21.7 × 14 cm)
Collection the artist

Tommy Turner (with David Wojnarowicz)

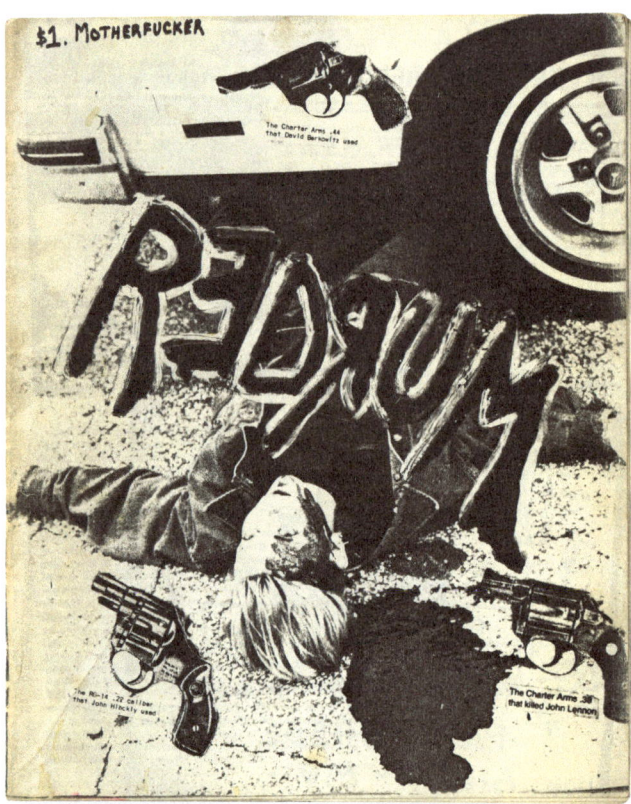

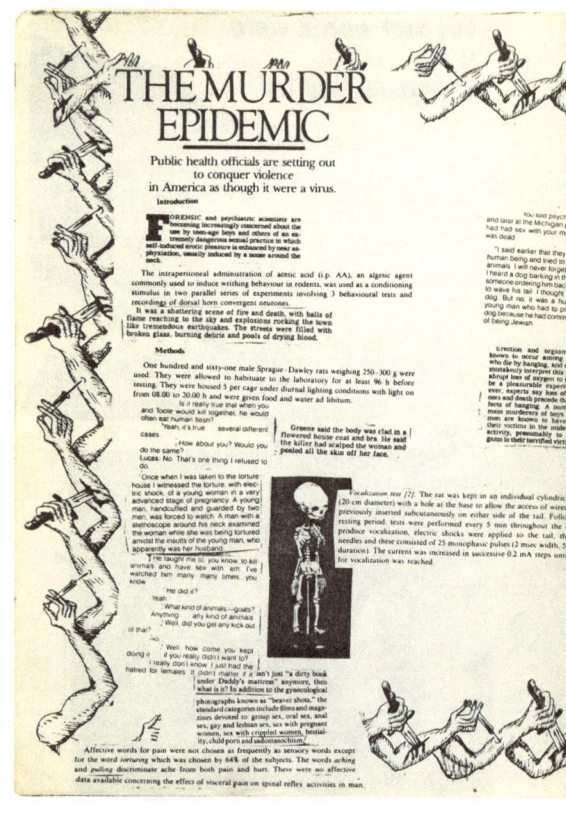

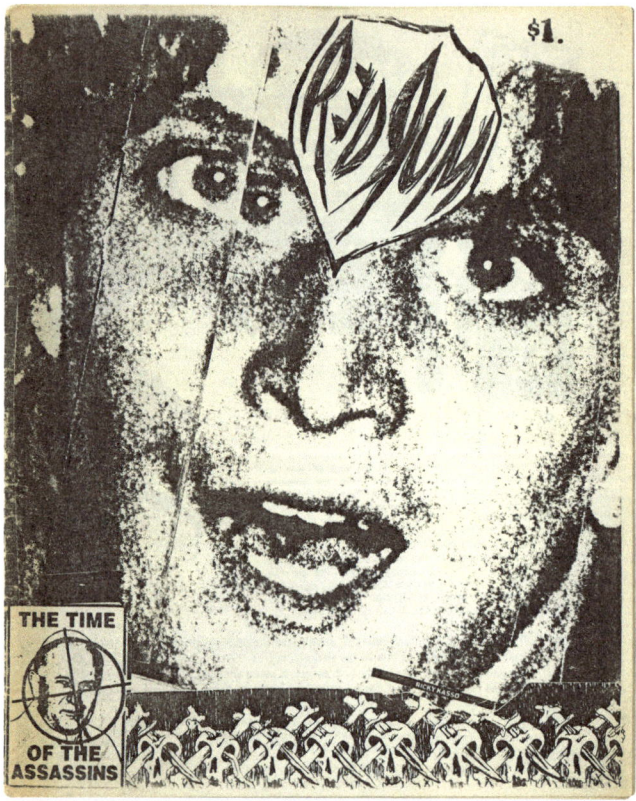

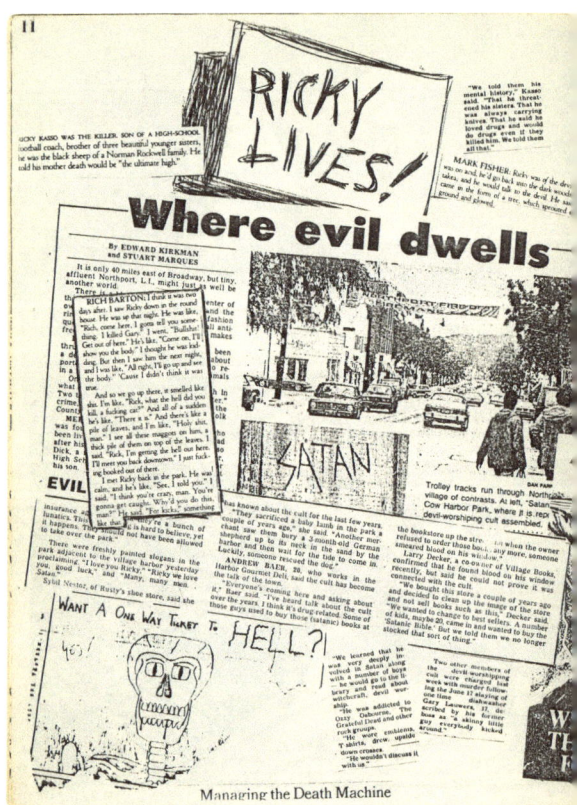

Redrum, no. 1, 1985
Photocopy, saddle stitched, 8 ½ × 7 in. (21.6 × 17.8 cm)
Collection Philip Aarons and Shelley Fox Aarons

Norman Rockwell, Jr. (David Wojnarowicz)
Archie, 1985
Prototype, intended for distribution in never-completed *Redrum*, no. 3
Photocopy, corner stapled, 11 × 8 ½ in. (27.9 × 21.6 cm)
Collection Philip Aarons and Shelley Fox Aarons

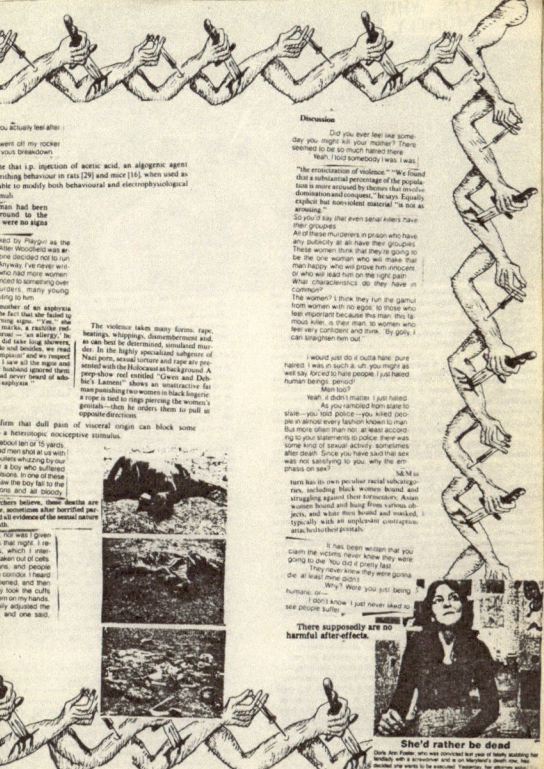

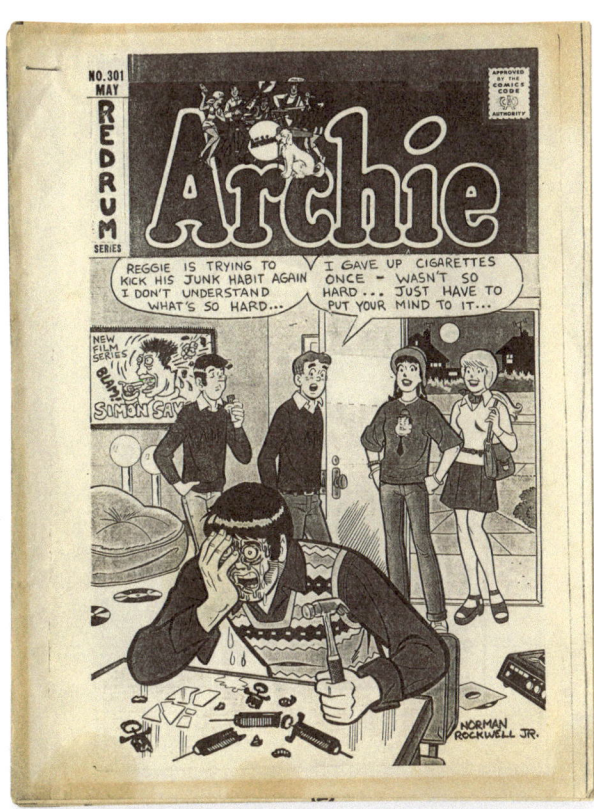

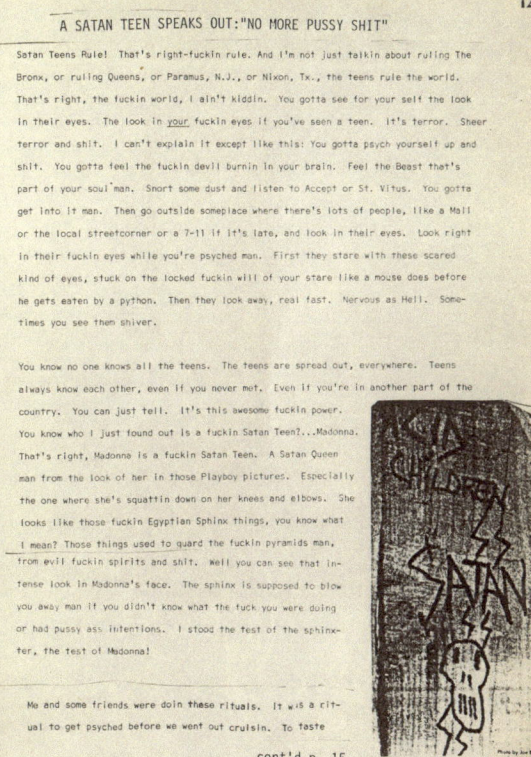

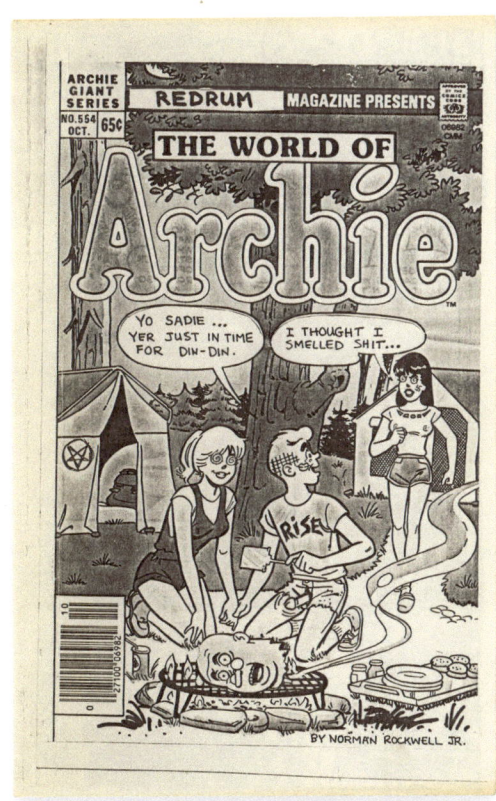

Redrum, no. 2, 1985
Photocopy, saddle stitched, 8 ½ × 7 in. (21.6 × 17.8 cm)
Collection Philip Aarons and Shelley Fox Aarons

Norman Rockwell, Jr. (David Wojnarowicz)
Redrum Magazine Presents: The World of Archie, 1985
Insert distributed with *Redrum*, no. 2
Photocopy, saddle stitched, 8 ½ × 5 ½ in. (21.6 × 14 cm)
Collection Philip Aarons and Shelley Fox Aarons

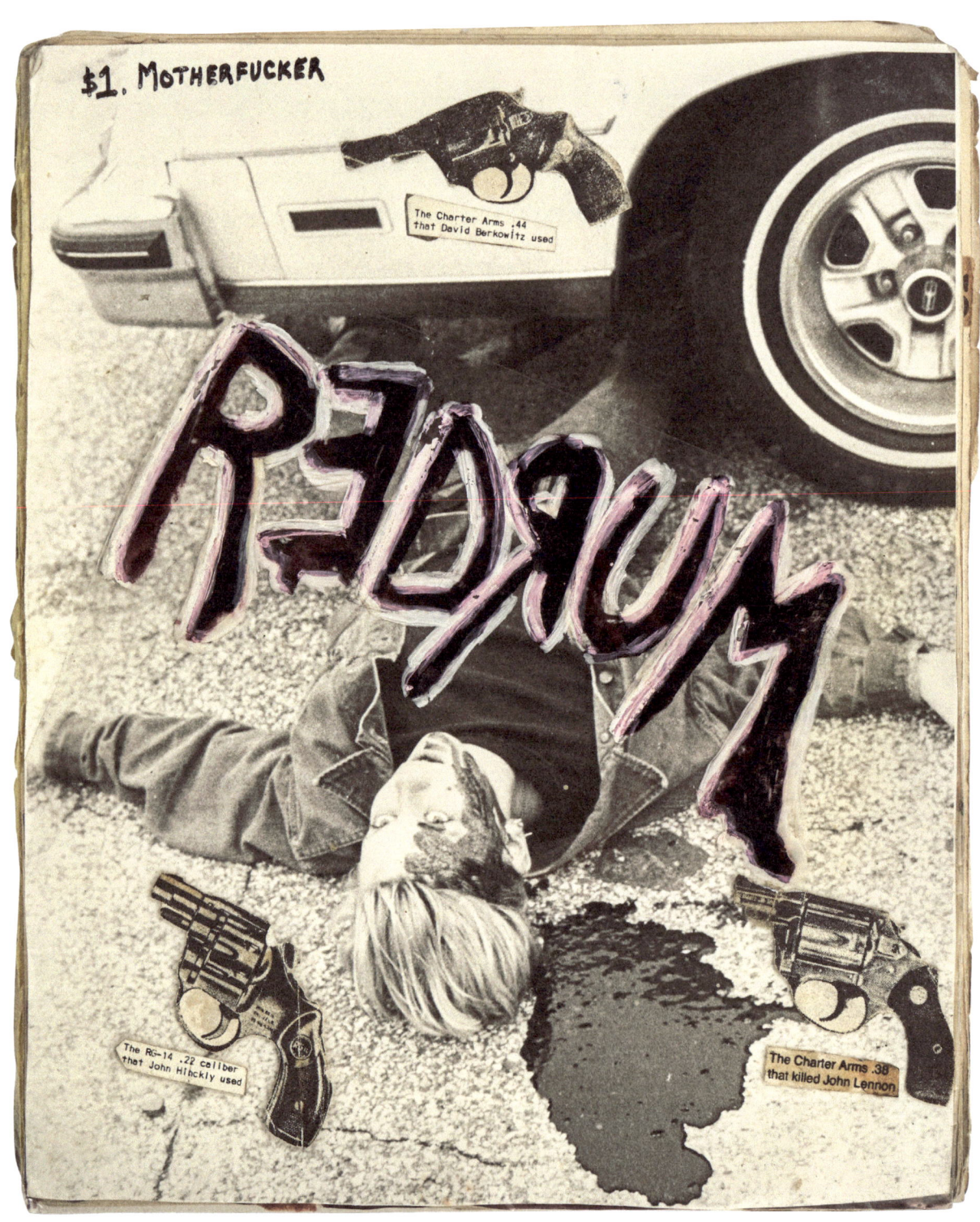

Paste-up for *Redrum*, no. 1, 1985
Gelatin silver print, paper, correction fluid, ink, glue,
8 ¾ × 7 ⅜ in. (22.2 × 18.7 cm)
Collection the artist

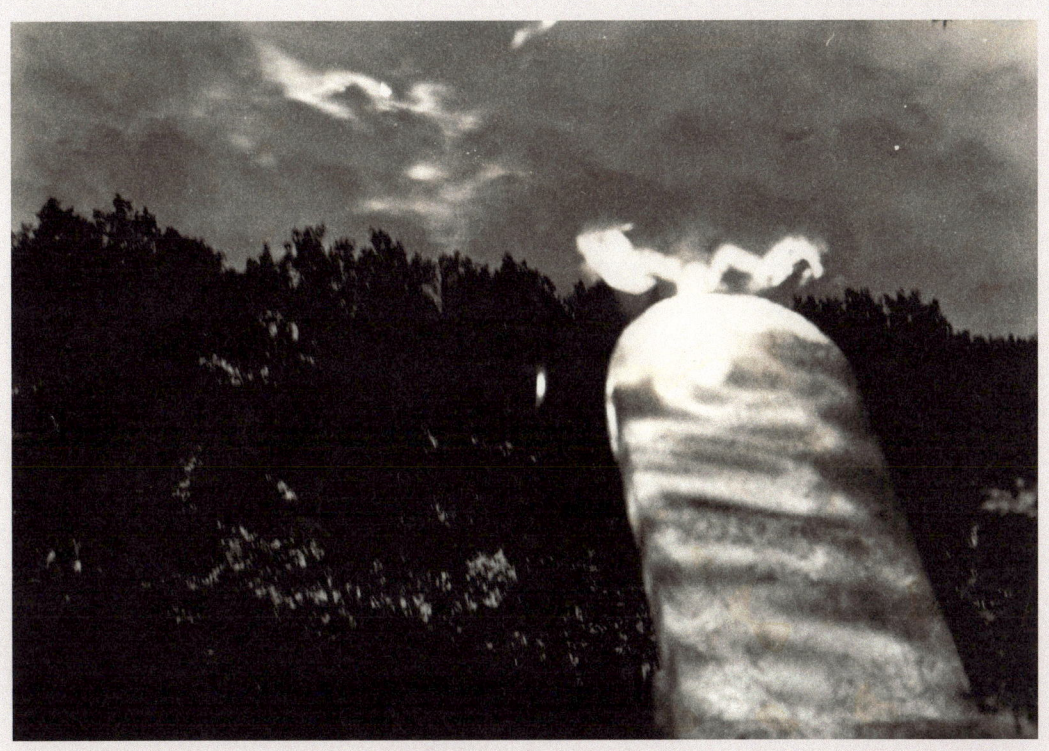

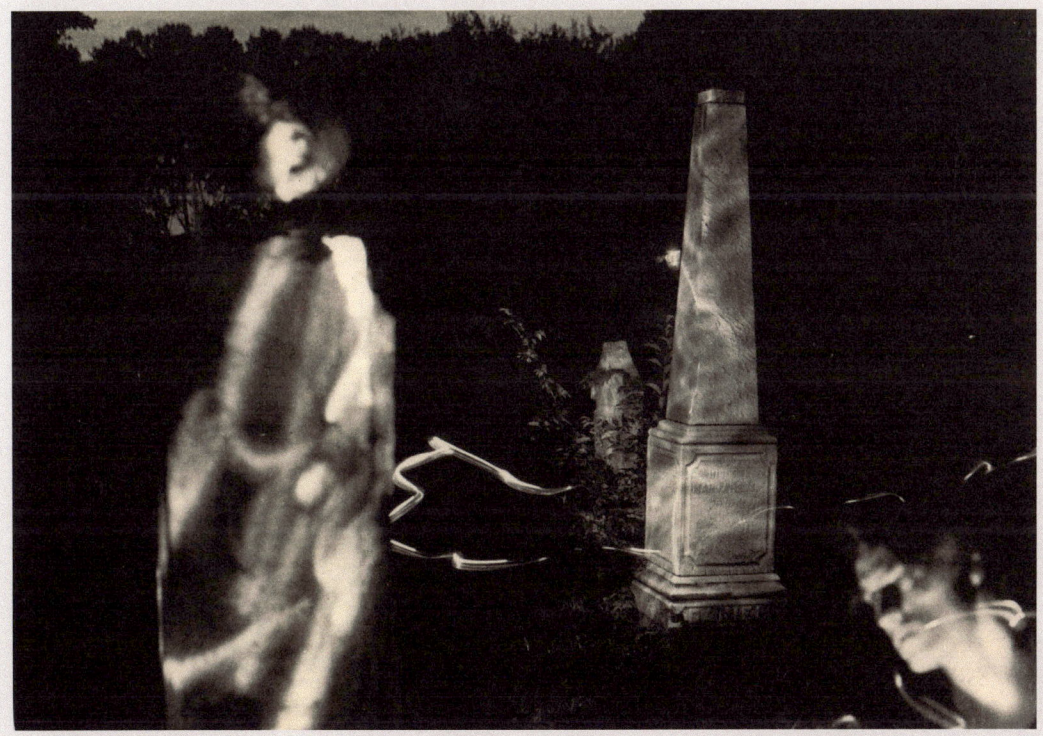

Tommy Turner and David Wojnarowicz
Untitled (Ghost Photos), 1983
Gelatin silver prints, 8 × 10 in. (20.3 × 25.4 cm)
P·P·O·W Gallery, New York

Carolee Schneemann

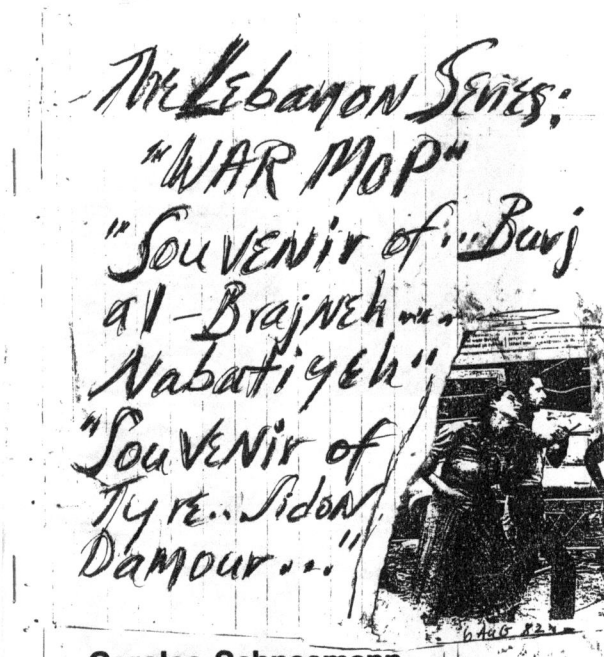

The Lebanon Series, 1983
Photocopy, saddle stitched, 8¼ × 6⅞ in. (21 × 17.5 cm)
Private collection, New York

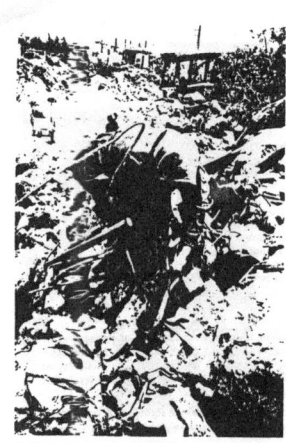

...re at Tyre in a couple of hours, and the
...e land bombardment of Sidon, by tank
...orning. Both towns had come under nav
...y.

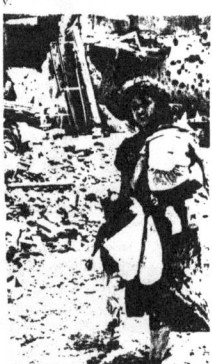

Ain Heweh refugee camp, near Sidon (UNRWA)

...idiyeh refugee camp, near Tyre (UNR

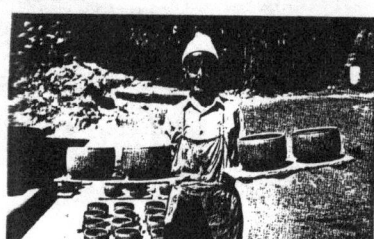

The PLO's political achievements were epitomised by institutions such as: Samed economic enterprises, that provided work and on-job training for over 5,000 Palestinians (and Lebanese poor); the Palestine Red Crescent Society's medical and public health facilities, which provided free medical care to Palestinians and Lebanese alike; music, literary and cultural groups; schools and vocational institutes; and communication centres, ranging from the Palestine Research Centre to the Voice of Palestine broadcasting network.

At 2pm on Friday, a different group of militiamen came, wearing different uniforms, according to the Asian doctor. He said they started to molest one of the Lebanese nurses, whose name was Friyal. They stopped after she started screaming. 'Shortly after that we went down to the shelter', the doctor said, 'and found that one of the Palestinian nurses down there had been raped repeatedly and then shot.' He identified her as Intisar Ismail, 19 years old.

the Palestinian Red Crescent Society incorporated the School of Theology into one of the most remarkable health-care delivery services in the world, one that maintains 25 dispensaries and a 2,000-bed hospital system serving a half million people still surviving the air and ground attacks that threaten the existence of west Beirut.

Hospitals are jammed with wounded. Stretchers are lined up outside the American University Hospital with people writhing in pain awaiting medical attention. The morgues are scenes of sobbing people looking at mutilated bodies as they seek out lost relatives.

WASHINGTON, Aug. 6 — The head of the United States Tactical Air Com-

. Gen. W. L. Creech, speaking Wednesday to reporters, said he felt reassured by the effective performance of McDonnell Douglas F-15's and General Dynamics F-16's over Lebanon.

about the wisdom of war. I met an Austrian woman whose husband and two children were gone when she returned home from her job as a nurse in west Beirut. They lived in a camp

that had been destroyed by incendiary and cluster bombs. "I could find no one," she said, "only bits and pieces of arms and legs. We just pushed the whole camp into a hole and covered it with plastic and earth."

Mystery still surrounds the 'vacuum bombs' that implode rather than explode, causing whole buildings to collapse inwards: two bombs collapsed two tall buildings in Beirut burying 80 people in one, 120 in the other.
Why did Israel have to use these horrific weapons against the besieged city of Beirut? It had total control of the air, total control of the sea and overwhelming superiority in numbers and firepower on land.

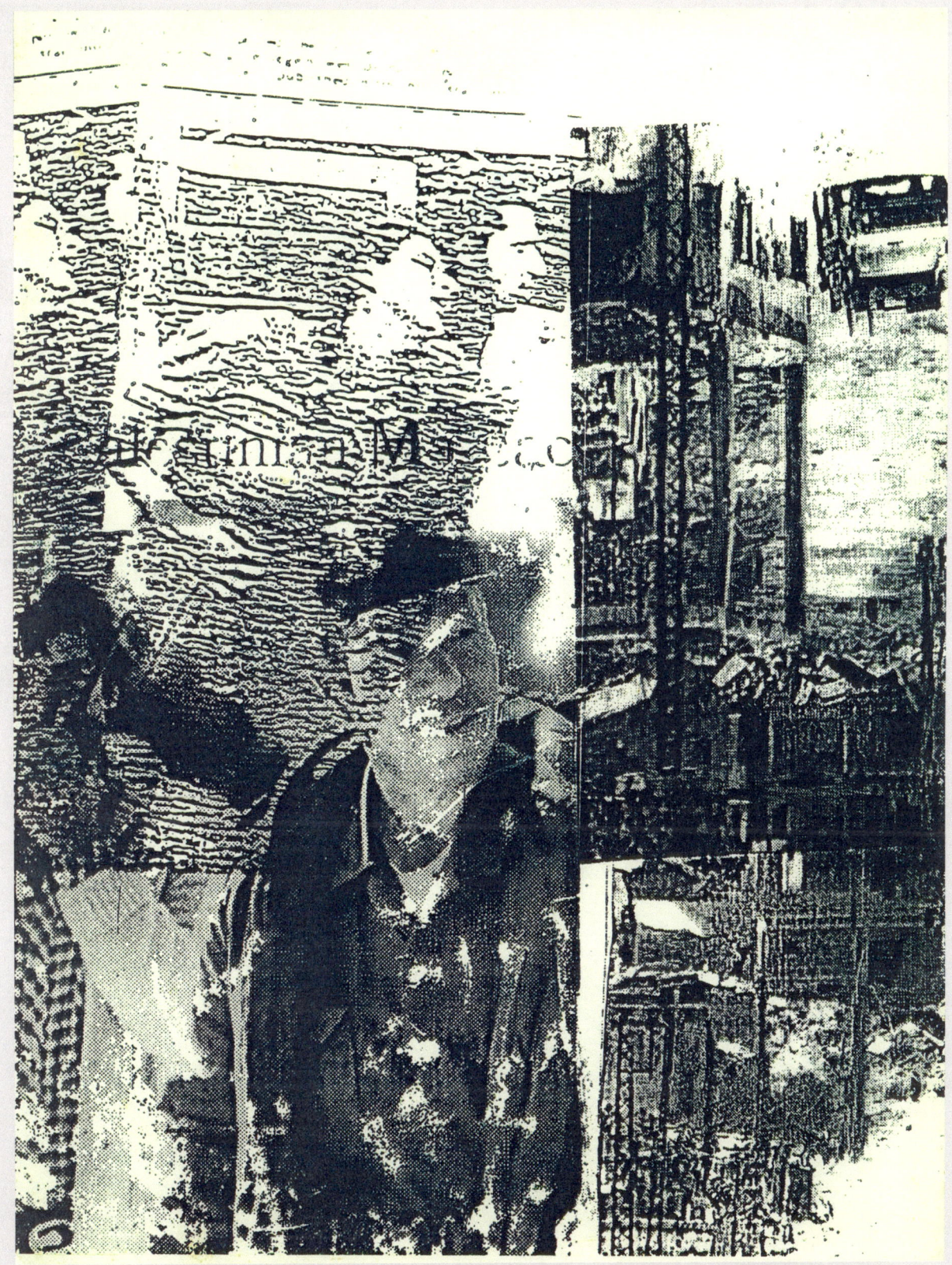

From *The Lebanon Series*, 1983
Color photocopy, 12 × 8 ½ in. (30.5 × 21.6 cm)
Carolee Schneemann Foundation

David Schmidlapp
(with Phase 2)

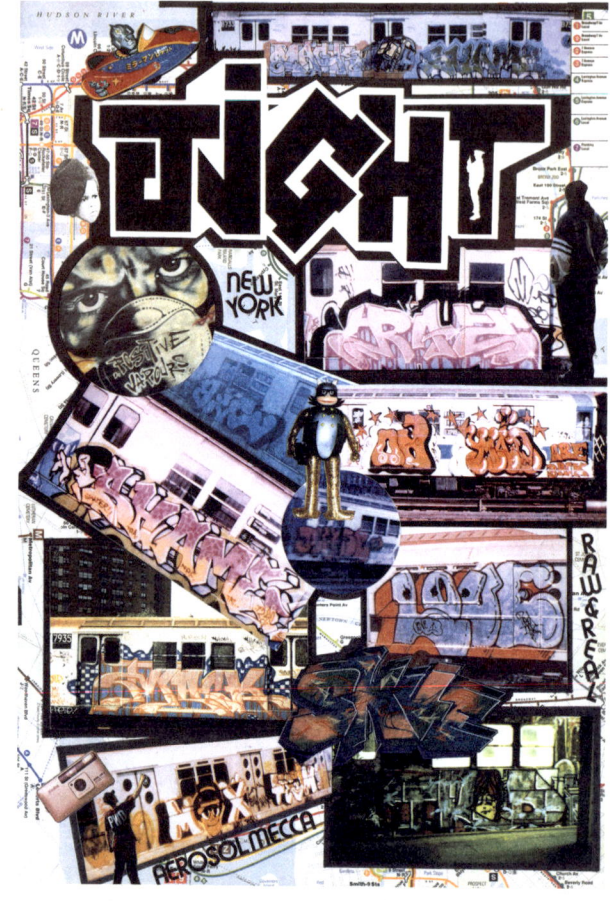

→ *IGTimes*, vols. 14 and 15, 1994
Art direction by Phase 2
Offset, folded, 22 × 17 in. (55.9 × 43.2 cm)
Collection the artist

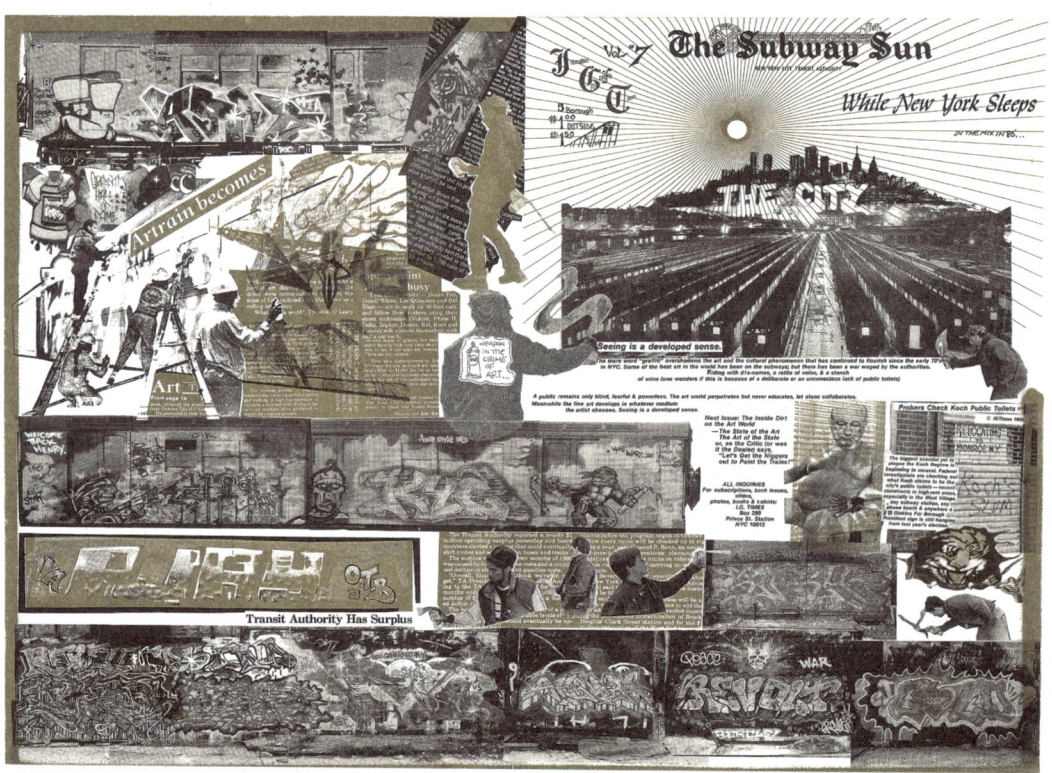

IGTimes, vol. 7, 1986
Offset, folded, 17 ½ × 22 ½ in. (44.5 × 57.2 cm)
Collection the artist

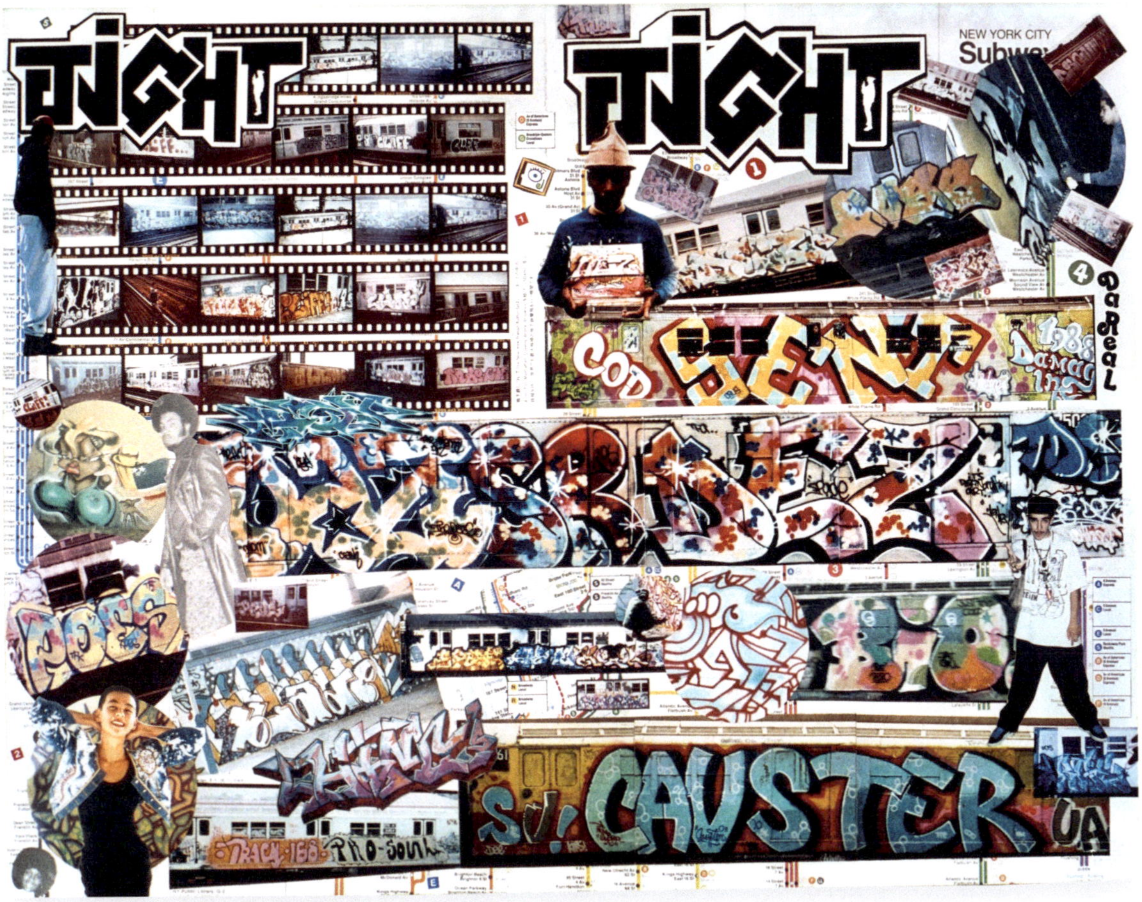

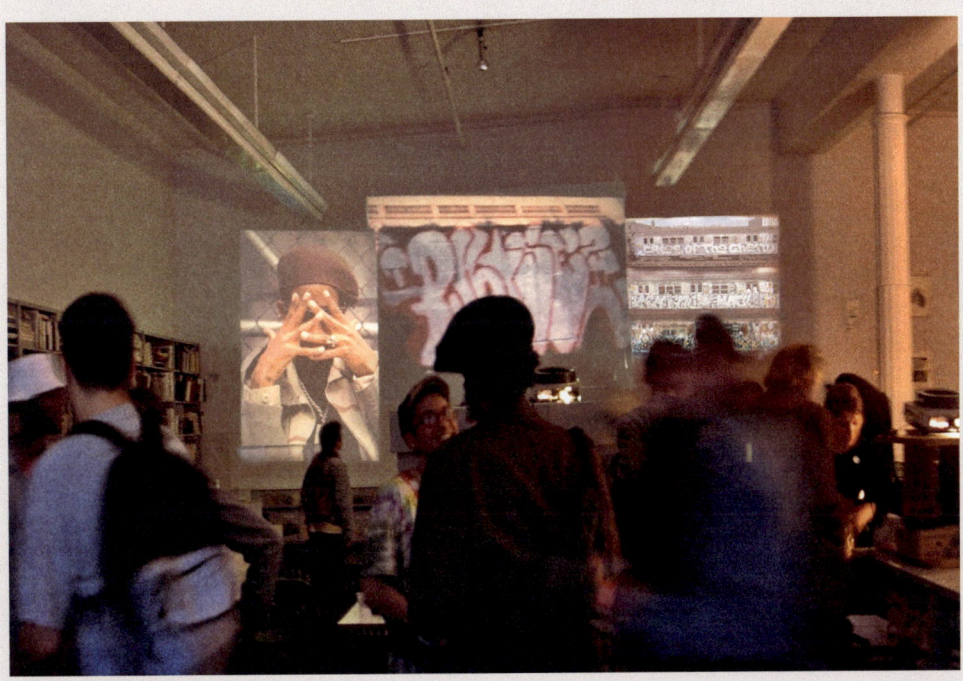

David Schmidlapp
Photograph of David Schmidlapp, Phase 2, and Vulcan's
Aerosol Art Armada slideshow at Printed Matter, New York, 1996

Kathleen Pirrie Adams, Caroline Azar, G. B. Jones, Candy Parker

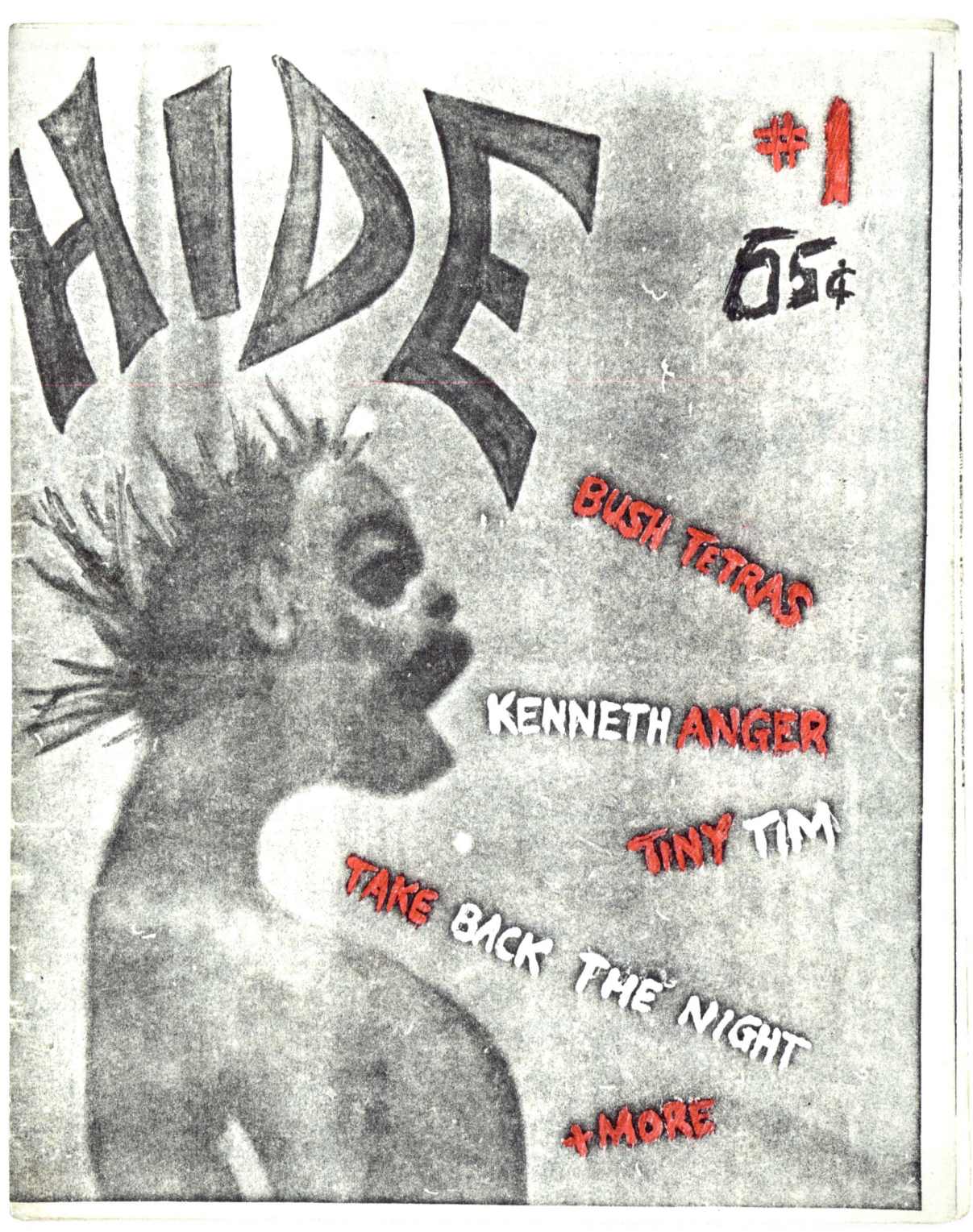

↑→ *Hide*, no. 1, 1981
Editors: Caroline Azar, Candy Parker, Kathleen Pirrie Addams
Photocopy, saddle stitched, 8 ⅝ × 7 ¹⁄₁₆ in. (21.9 × 17.9 cm)
Collection Jim Shedden

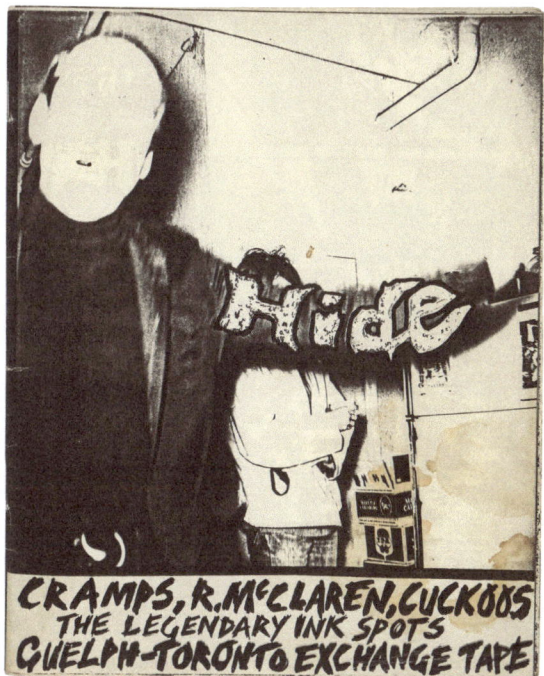

Hide, no. 3, 1984
Editors: Caroline Azar, G. B. Jones, Candy Parker
Photocopy, saddle stitched, 8⅝ × 7 1/16 in. (21.9 × 17.9 cm)
Collection Bruce LaBruce

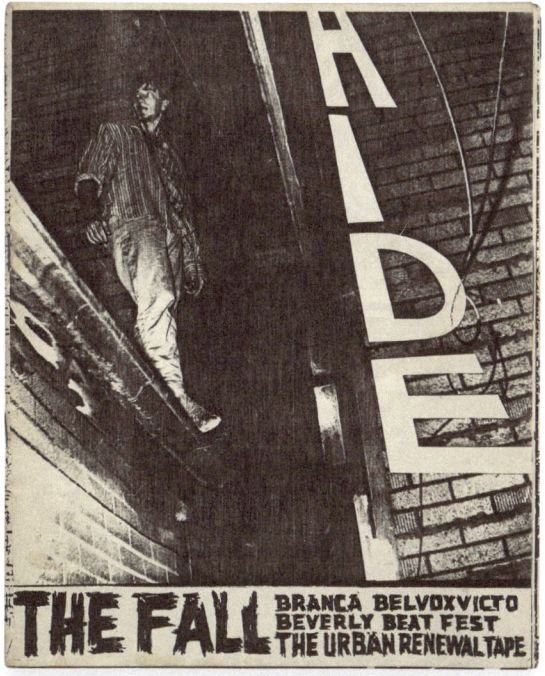

Hide, no. 4, 1984
Editors: G. B. Jones and Caroline Azar
Photocopy, saddle stitched, 8⅝ × 7 1/16 in. (21.9 × 17.9 cm)
Collection Bruce LaBruce

'Fifth columnists inside the Hilton blinked their lights in a show of solidarity when our delegates spoke from across Michigan Avenue; later a few were arrested in their rooms.'

FIFTH COLUMN

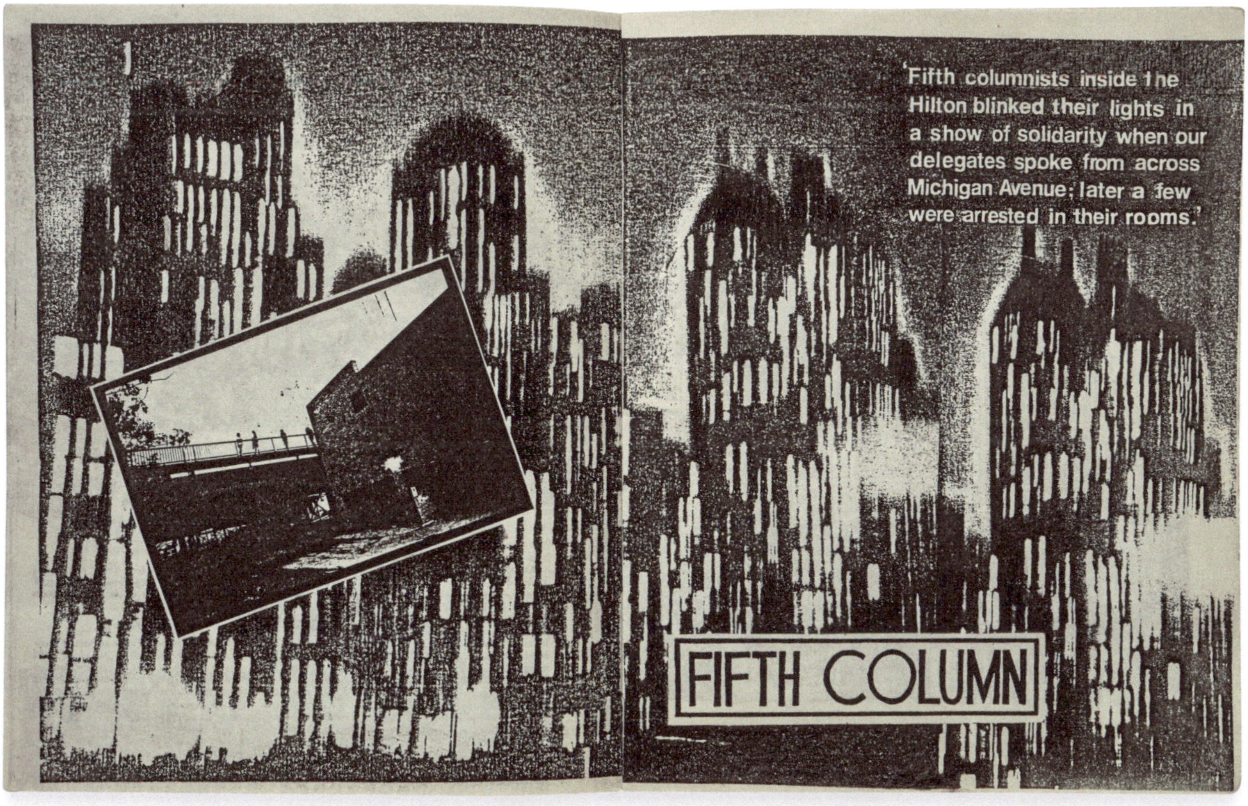

Candy Parker and Jean Young

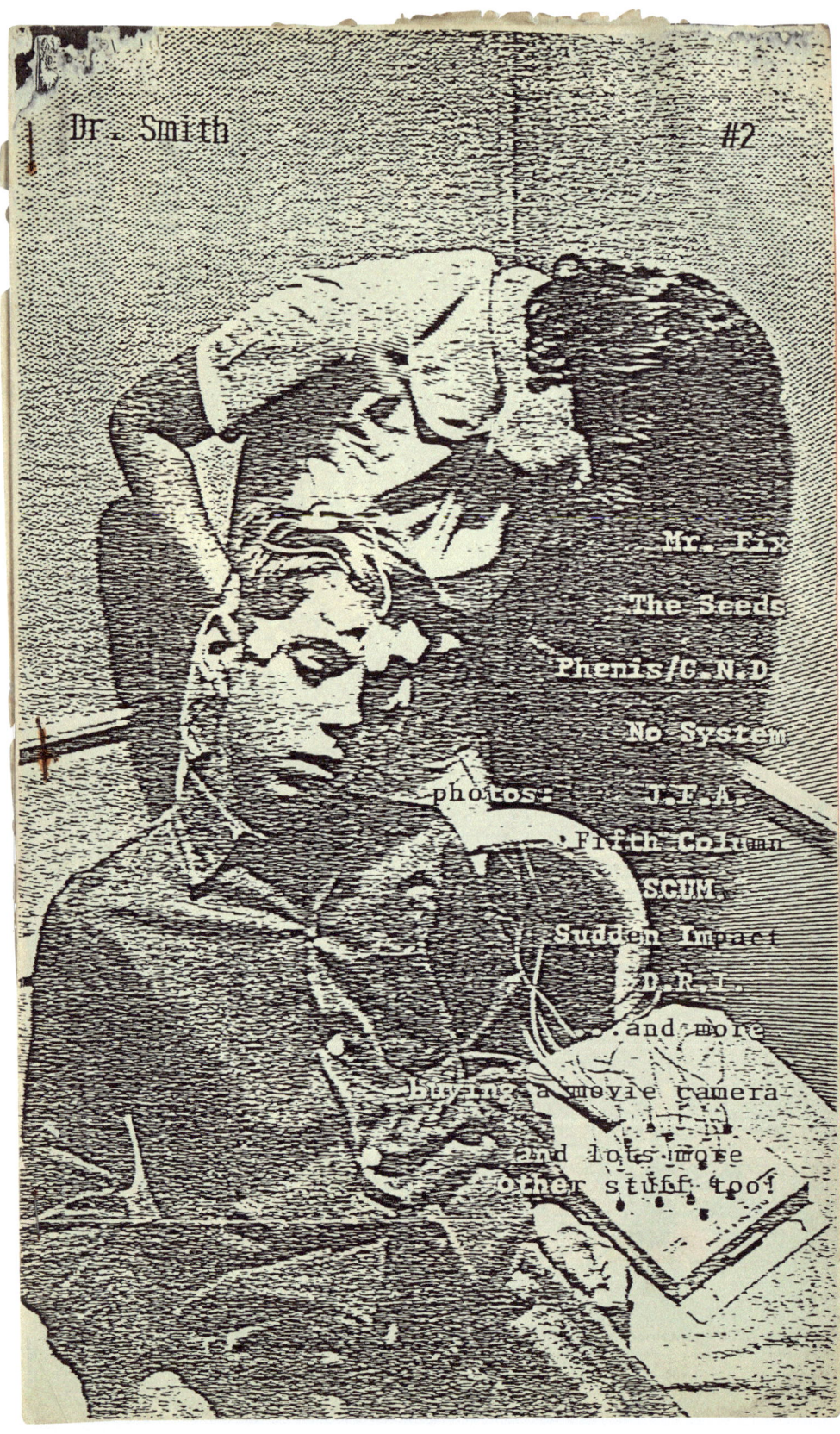

Dr. Smith, no. 2, 1984
Photocopy, side stapled, 14⅛ × 8½ in. (35.9 × 21.6 cm)
Collection Bruce LaBruce

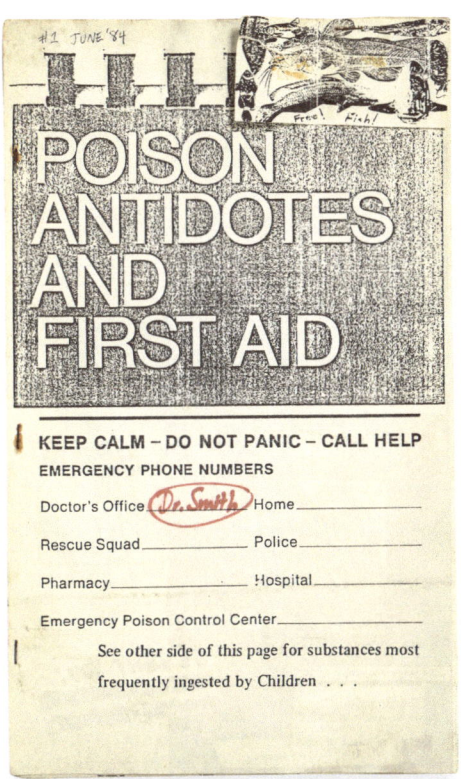

Dr. Smith, no. 1, June 1984
Photocopy, side stapled, 14 × 8 9/16 in. (35.6 × 21.7 cm)
Collection Bruce LaBruce

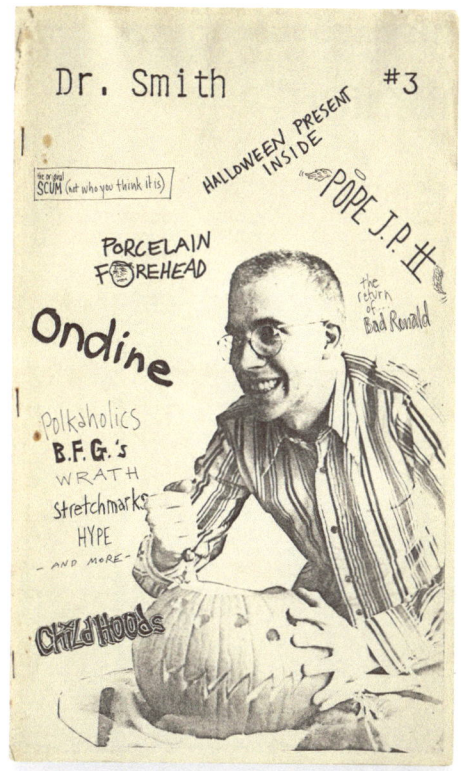

Dr. Smith, no. 3, ca. 1984
Photocopy, side stapled, 14 × 8 9/16 in. (35.6 × 21.7 cm)
Collection Bruce LaBruce

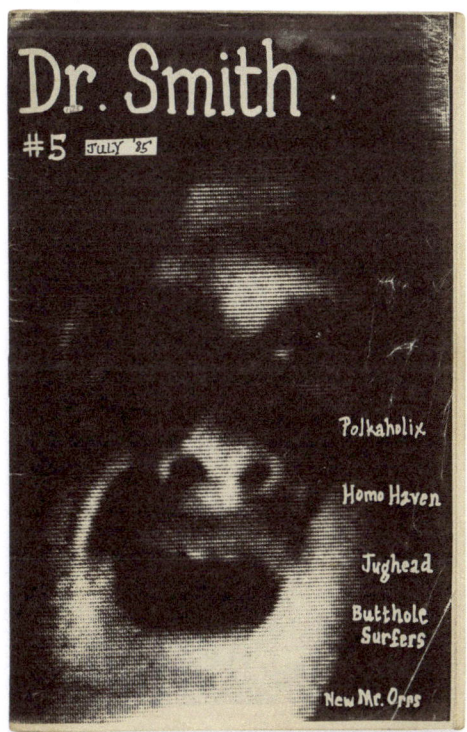

Dr. Smith, no. 5, July 1985
Photocopy, side stapled, 8 ½ × 5 ½ in. (21.6 × 14 cm)
Collection Bruce LaBruce

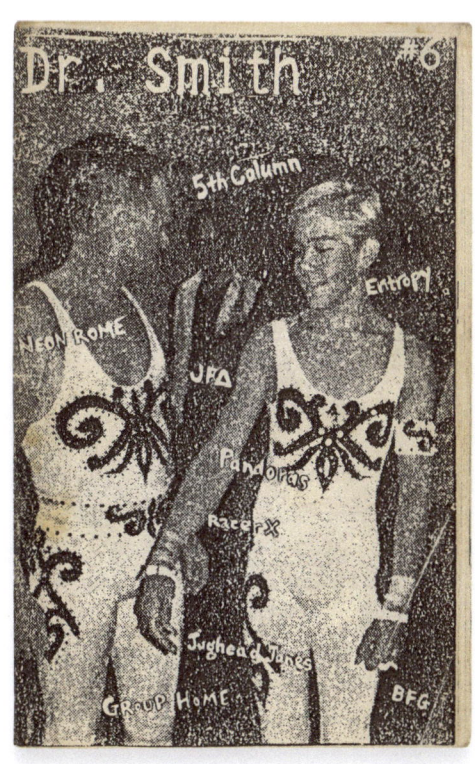

Dr. Smith, no. 6, 1988
Photocopy, side stapled, 8 ½ × 5 9/16 in. (21.6 × 14.1 cm)
Collection Bruce LaBruce

G. B. Jones and
Bruce LaBruce

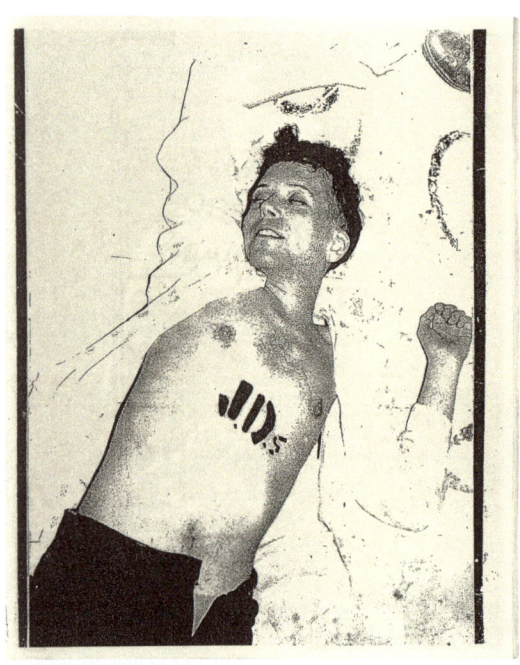

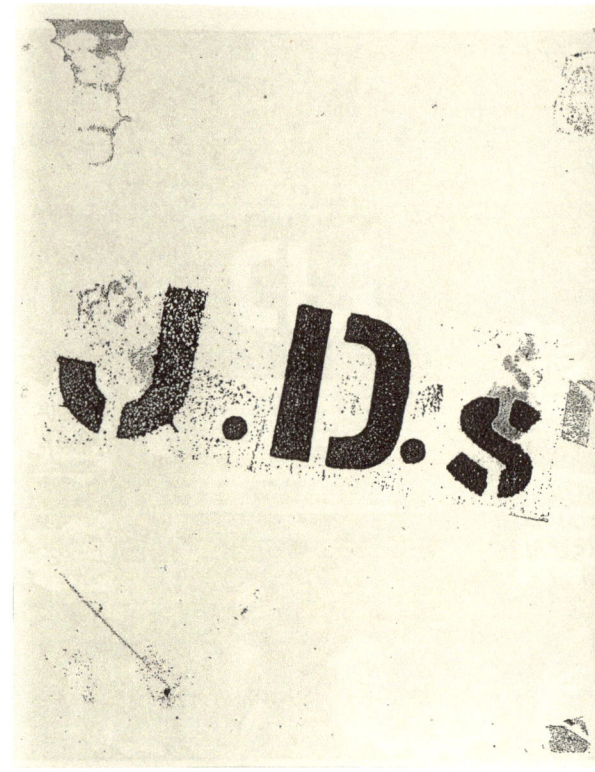

J.D.s, no. 1, 1985
Photocopy, saddle stitched, 8 ½ × 7 in. (21.6 × 17.8 cm)
Collection Bruce LaBruce

J.D.s, no. 2, 1986
Photocopy, saddle stitched, 8 ½ × 7 in. (21.6 × 17.8 cm)
Collection Bruce LaBruce

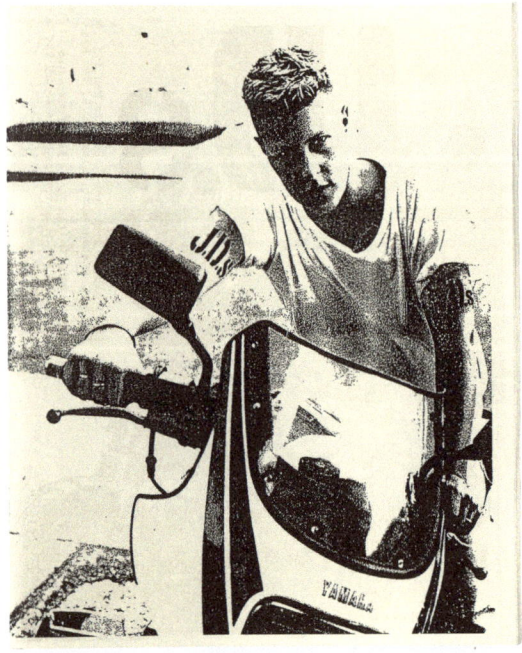

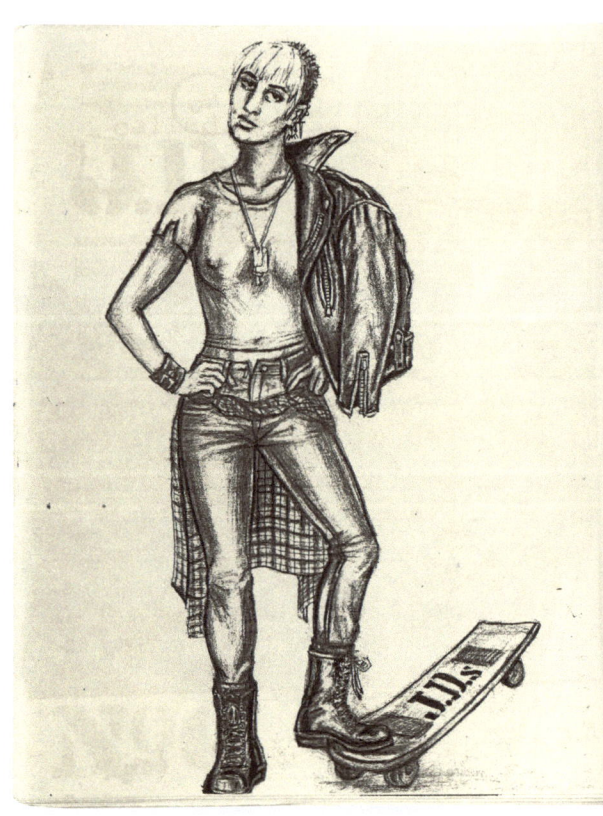

J.D.s, no. 3, 1986
Photocopy, saddle stitched, 8 ⁹⁄₁₆ × 7 ⅛ in. (21.7 × 18.1 cm)
Collection Bruce LaBruce

J.D.s, no. 6, 1989
Photocopy, saddle stitched, 8 ⁹⁄₁₆ × 7 ⅛ in. (21.7 × 18.1 cm)
Collection Bruce LaBruce

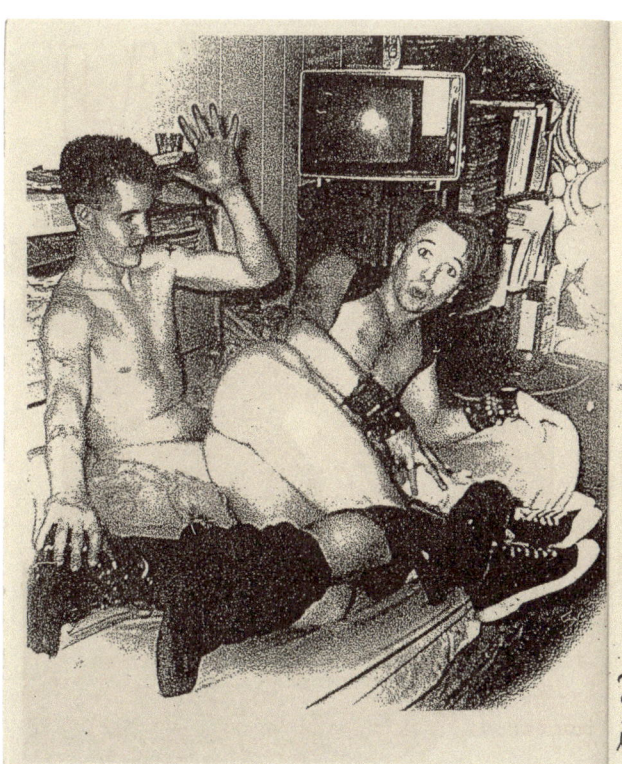

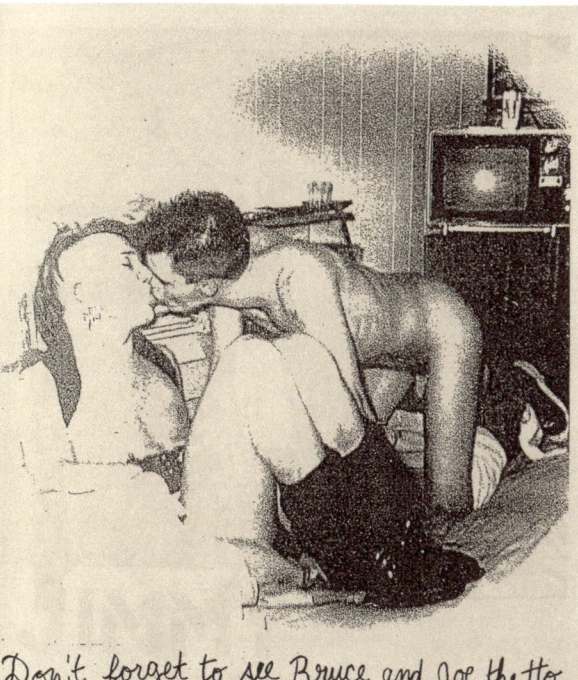

Don't forget to see Bruce and Joe the Ho in G.B. Jones new movie "The Troublemakers"

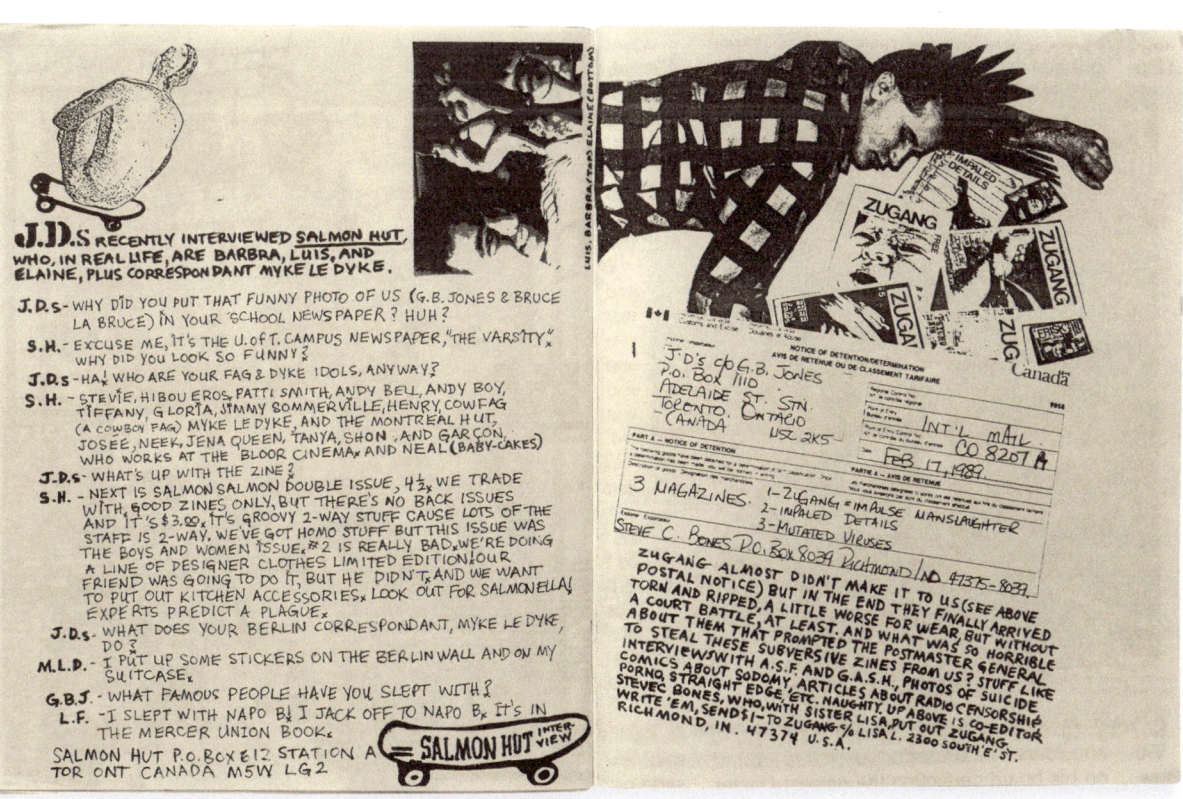

LUIS, BARBRA/and ELAINE (BOTTOM)

J.D.s RECENTLY INTERVIEWED SALMON HUT, WHO, IN REAL LIFE, ARE BARBRA, LUIS, AND ELAINE, PLUS CORRESPONDANT MYKE LE DYKE.

J.D.s - WHY DID YOU PUT THAT FUNNY PHOTO OF US (G.B. JONES & BRUCE LA BRUCE) IN YOUR 'SCHOOL NEWSPAPER? HUH?

S.H. - EXCUSE ME, IT'S THE U. OF T. CAMPUS NEWSPAPER, "THE VARSITY"x WHY DID YOU LOOK SO FUNNY?

J.D.s - HA! WHO ARE YOUR FAG & DYKE IDOLS, ANYWAY?

S.H. - STEVIE, HIBOU EROS, PATTI SMITH, ANDY BELL, ANDY BOY, TIFFANY, GLORIA, JIMMY SOMMERVILLE, HENRY COWFAG (A COWBOY FAG) MYKE LE DYKE, AND THE MONTREAL HUT, JOSEE, NEEK, JENA QUEEN, TANYA, SHON, AND GARÇON, WHO WORKS AT THE 'BLOOR CINEMA× AND NEAL (BABY-CAKES)

J.D.s - WHAT'S UP WITH THE ZINE?

S.H. - NEXT IS SALMON SALMON DOUBLE ISSUE, 4½, WE TRADE WITH, GOOD ZINES ONLY, BUT THERE'S NO BACK ISSUES AND IT'S $3.00, IT'S GROOVY 2-WAY STUFF CAUSE LOTS OF THE STAFF IS 2-WAY. WE'VE GOT HOMO STUFF BUT THIS ISSUE WAS THE BOYS AND WOMEN ISSUE. #2 IS REALLY BAD, WE'RE DOING A LINE OF DESIGNER CLOTHES LIMITED EDITION! OUR FRIEND WAS GOING TO DO IT, BUT HE DIDN'T, AND WE WANT TO PUT OUT KITCHEN ACCESSORIES× LOOK OUT FOR SALMONELLA! EXPERTS PREDICT A PLAGUE×

J.D.s - WHAT DOES YOUR BERLIN CORRESPONDANT, MYKE LE DYKE, DO?

M.L.D. - I PUT UP SOME STICKERS ON THE BERLIN WALL AND ON MY SUITCASE×

G.B.J. - WHAT FAMOUS PEOPLE HAVE YOU SLEPT WITH?

L.F. - I SLEPT WITH NAPO B! I JACK OFF TO NAPO B× IT'S IN THE MERCER UNION BOOK×

SALMON HUT P.O. BOX 812 STATION A TOR ONT CANADA M5W LG2   = SALMON HUT INTER-VIEW

NOTICE OF DETENTION/DETERMINATION
AVIS DE RETENUE OU DE CLASSEMENT TARIFAIRE

J.D's c/o G.B. Jones
P.O. BOX 1110
ADELAIDE ST. STN.
TORONTO, ONTARIO
CANADA   M5Z 2K5

INT'L MAIL   CO 8207 A
FEB. 17, 1989.

3 MAGAZINES.   1- ZUGANG = IM FALSE MANSLAUGHTER
                        2- IMPALED DETAILS
                        3- MUTATED VIRUSES

STEVE C. BONES, P.O. BOX 8039, RICHMOND, IND. 47375-8039

ZUGANG ALMOST DIDN'T MAKE IT TO US (SEE ABOVE POSTAL NOTICE) BUT IN THE END THEY FINALLY ARRIVED TORN AND RIPPED, A LITTLE WORSE FOR WEAR, BUT WITHOUT A COURT BATTLE, AT LEAST. AND WHAT WAS SO HORRIBLE ABOUT THEM THAT PROMPTED THE POSTMASTER GENERAL TO STEAL THESE SUBVERSIVE ZINES FROM US? STUFF LIKE INTERVIEWS WITH A.S.F. AND G.A.S.H., PHOTOS OF SUICIDE COMICS ABOUT SODOMY, ARTICLES ABOUT RADIO CENSORSHIP, PORNO, STRAIGHT EDGE, ETC. NAUGHTY, UP ABOVE IS CO-EDITOR STEVE C. BONES, WHO, WITH SISTER LISA, PUT OUT ZUGANG. WRITE 'EM, SEND $1 TO ZUGANG c/o LISA L. 2300 SOUTH 'E' ST. RICHMOND, IN. 47374 U.S.A.

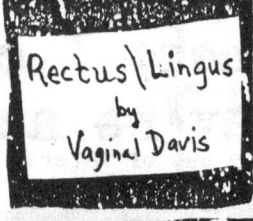

Rectus\Lingus
by
Vaginal Davis

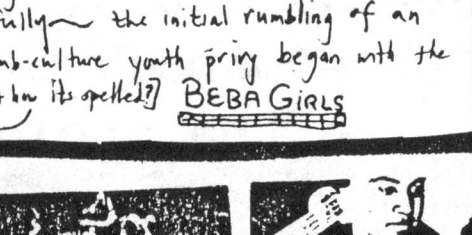

The beginnings: And this is a little known fact, so listen carefully— the initial rumbling of an alternate gay sub-culture youth priny began with the notorious [is that how its spelled?] BEBA GIRLS

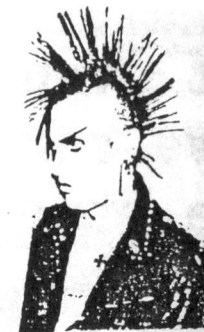

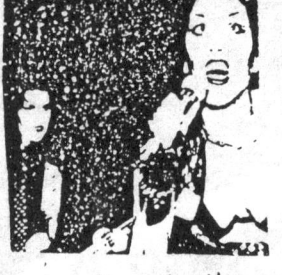

 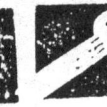 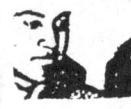

Who are the BEBA GIRLS? An ultra cool seat of Lesbian, Bi & Straight girls who took to the *HANNA SCHAGUYA MODE OF DRESSING IN MID 1979. Some of these ladies were also witches. The BEBA GIRLS had a definate look. The name BEBA comes from the radical make-up line that these chicks used that was sold at Judy's in Century City. Judy's at the time was a hip store for sub-culture's kids. Hard to believe to-day, but Judy's along with Norma Kamali's store on La Cienega Blvd, "On My Own" were the focal points of a pre-Melrose music, fashion and sexual politicing brigade.

*HANNA SCHAGUYA WAS THE STAR OF FASSBINDERS LESBIAN FILM, "THE BITTER TEARS OP 'PETRA VON KANT'"

Cool Places to Hang

On My Own — Restaurant Row
Farmers Market — Hollywood South
Paradise Garage, Other Side, Butch Gardens

Rodney's English Disco
Rainbow ⟩ Hollywood West
Starwood, Gino's, OTUM Hollywood
Circus

Judys - Century City shopping Center

THE BEBA GIRLS

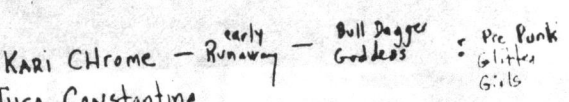

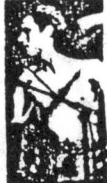 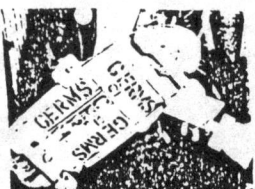 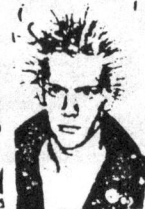

Proprietor of Zero One Gallery
— Bands: KREW KUTS KLAN, TROUBLE FOR NORA

Responsible for the fad of tying bandanas around boots. Now living in England in the band Jimmy The Hoover

jewelry designer

Kari CHrome — early Runaway — Bull Dagger Goddess : Pre Punk Glitter Girls

Thea Constantine

Michele Beuler — Make-up artist for movies now

Tequila Mockingbird — Witch — Kidnapped David Bowie for 3 Days

Carla (Vaginal's Cousin) — formed the band The ___ Controllers.

Connie Parente — Witch — drug supplier — Now an established —

Odessa — Witch

Lena Lloyd — Glitter queen; Famous Groupie

Marisol — Hostess of the Fiorucci Parties, Mgr of Melrose Store Let it Rock —

Inez — Now the Chanel Model

Fayette Hauser — Interpol lead singer | 1980-1982

Ellen — Screamers Fan Club President Girlfriend of Raymond Pettibone, Dez Cadena & Beulah Love (Photographer of Fertile)

HAG — Only male Beba Girl nowu successful fashion stylist in NY City

Rae Dawn Chong — Witch — Now Movie Star

Sandy Grey — Witch, gorgeous lesbian dancer in the movie "Grease"

Professional → Rock & Roll Girlfriend

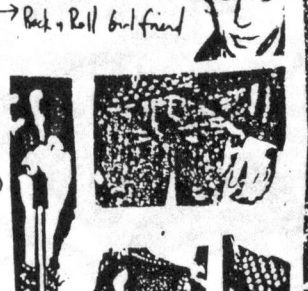

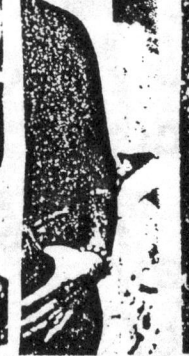

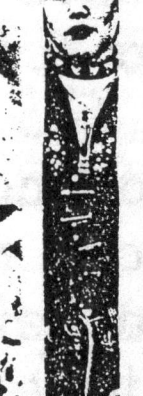

J.D.s, no. 7, 1990
Photocopy, saddle stitched, 8 9/16 × 7 1/8 in. (21.7 × 18.1 cm)
Collection Bruce LaBruce

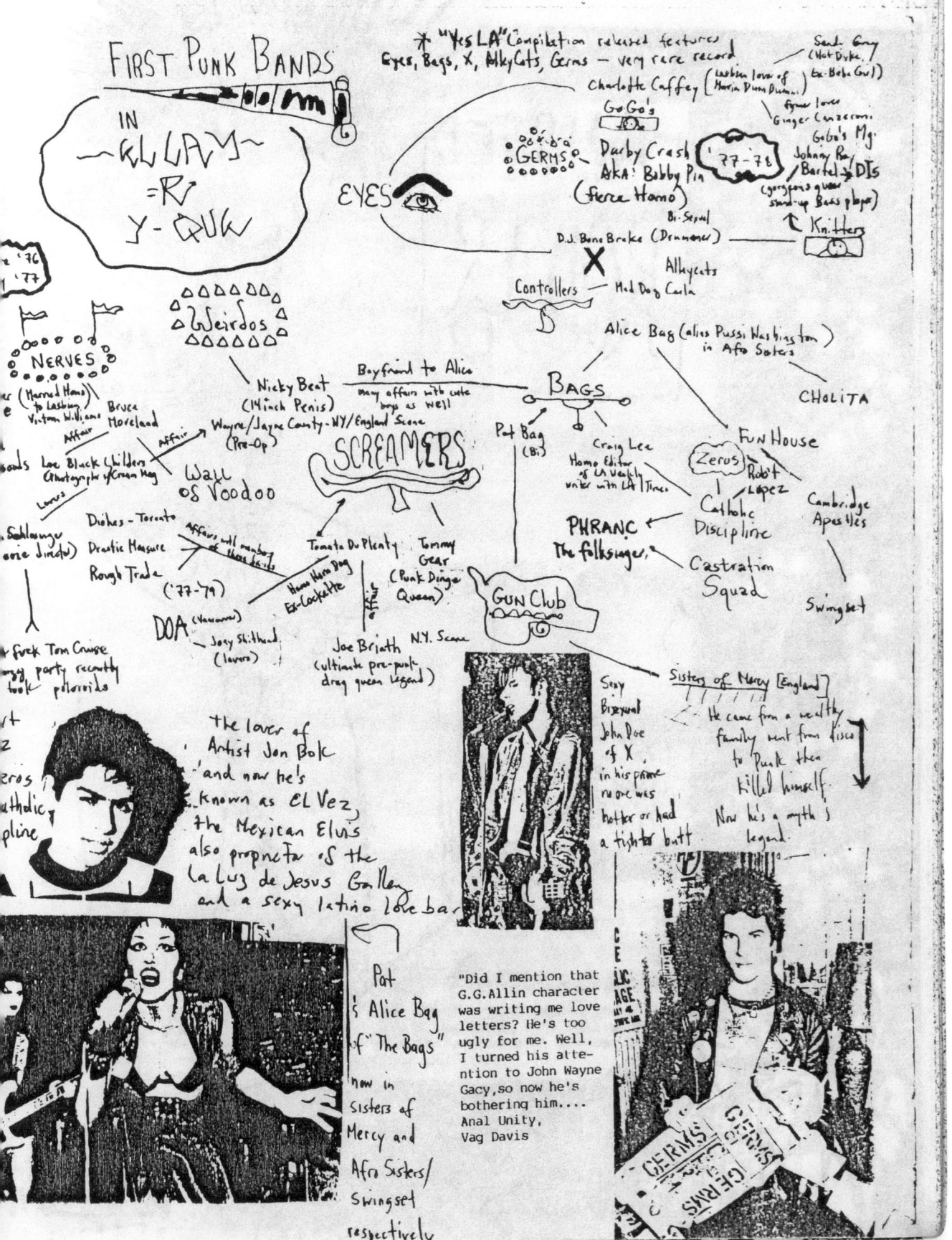

FIRST PUNK BANDS

IN ~ EL LAY ~ =R= Y - QUE

* "Yes LA" Compilation released features Eyes, Bags, X, AlkyCats, Germs — very rare record

Sandy Guy (Hot Dyke / Ex-Bebe Girl)

Charlotte Caffey (Lesbian lover of Maria Dura Duran)

GoGo's

GERMS

Darby Crash AKA: Bobby Pin (fierce Homo)

'77-'78

former lover Ginger Canzoneri GoGo's Mgr Johnny Ray Bartel → DI's (gorgeous queer stand-up Bass player)

EYES

Bi-Sexual

D.J. Bone Brake (Drummer)

X

Alkycats — Mad Dog Carla

Knitters

'76 '77

NERVES

(Married Homo) to Lesbian Victor Williams

Bruce Moreland

Lee Black Childers (Photographer of Cream Mag)

Lovers

Weirdos

Nicky Beat (14 inch Penis)

Wayne/Jayne County-NY/England Scene (Pre-Op)

Boyfriend to Alice many affairs with cute boys as well

Controllers

Alice Bag (alias Pussi Washington) in Afro Sisters

BAGS

CHOLITA

Pat Bag (Bi)

Craig Lee Homo Editor of LA Weekly writer with LA Times

FUN HOUSE

Zeros Rob't Lopez

Cambridge Apostles

SCREAMERS

Wall of Voodoo

Schlanger (one director)

Dishes - Toronto Drastic Measure Rough Trade

('77-'79)

Affairs with members of those bands

Tomata Du Plenty

Tommy Gear (Punk Dinge Queen)

Homo Hero Dag Ex-Cockette

PHRANC The folksinger

Catholic Discipline

Castration Squad

Swingset

DOA (Vancouver) Joey Skidhead (lovers)

Joe Briath (ultimate pre-punk drag queen legend)

N.Y. Scene

GUN CLUB

fuck Tom Cruise party recently took polaroids

Zeros Catholic pline

the lover of Artist Jon Bok and now he's known as El Vez, the Mexican Elvis also proprietor of the La Luz de Jesus Gallery and a sexy latino love bar

Sexy Bisexual John Doe of X, in his prime no one was hotter or had a tighter butt

Sisters of Mercy [England]

He came from a wealthy family went from disco to Punk then killed himself. Now he's a myth & legend.

Pat 's Alice Bag of "The Bags" now in sisters of Mercy and Afro Sisters/ Swingset respectively

"Did I mention that G.G. Allin character was writing me love letters? He's too ugly for me. Well, I turned his attention to John Wayne Gacy, so now he's bothering him.... Anal Unity, Vag Davis

GERMS
GERMS
GERMS

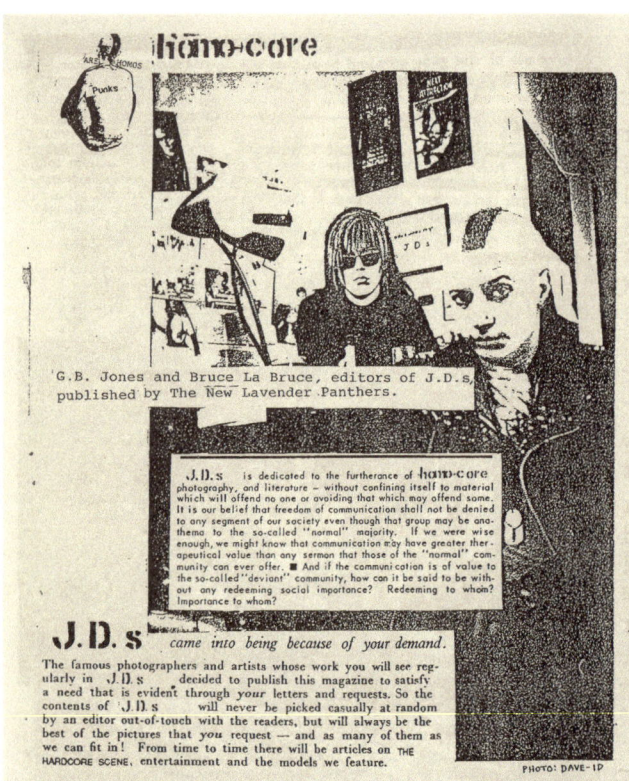

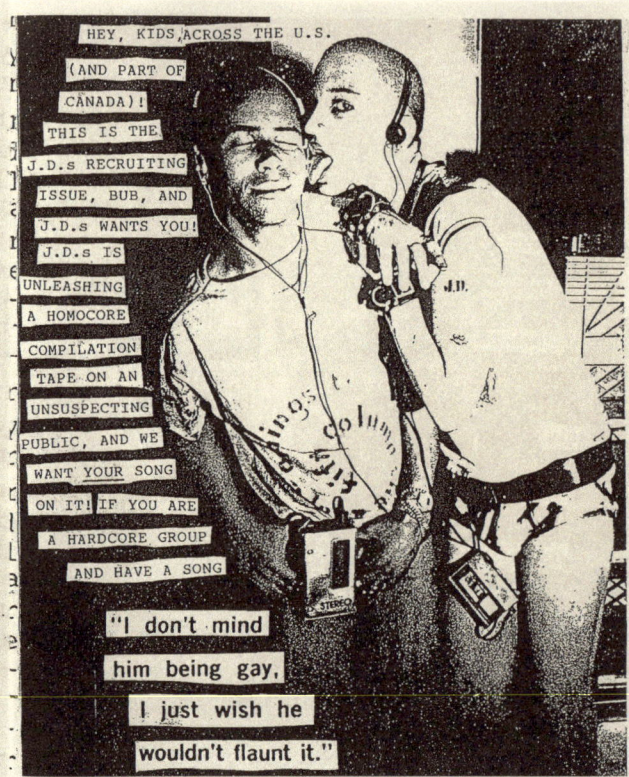

G.B. Jones and Bruce La Bruce, editors of J.D.s,
published by The New Lavender Panthers.

J.D.s is dedicated to the furtherance of homo-core photography, and literature — without confining itself to material which will offend no one or avoiding that which may offend some. It is our belief that freedom of communication shall not be denied to any segment of our society even though that group may be anathema to the so-called "normal" majority. If we were wise enough, we might know that communication may have greater therapeutic value than any sermon that those of the "normal" community can ever offer. ■ And if the communication is of value to the so-called "deviant" community, how can it be said to be without any redeeming social importance? Redeeming to whom? Importance to whom?

J.D.s *came into being because of your demand.*

The famous photographers and artists whose work you will see regularly in J.D.s decided to publish this magazine to satisfy a need that is evident through *your* letters and requests. So the contents of J.D.s will never be picked casually at random by an editor out-of-touch with the readers, but will always be the best of the pictures that *you* request — and as many of them as we can fit in! From time to time there will be articles on THE HARDCORE SCENE, entertainment and the models we feature.

PHOTO: DAVE-ID

HEY, KIDS, ACROSS THE U.S. (AND PART OF CANADA)! THIS IS THE J.D.s RECRUITING ISSUE, BUB, AND J.D.s WANTS YOU! J.D.s IS UNLEASHING A HOMOCORE COMPILATION TAPE ON AN UNSUSPECTING PUBLIC, AND WE WANT YOUR SONG ON IT! IF YOU ARE A HARDCORE GROUP AND HAVE A SONG

"I don't mind him being gay, I just wish he wouldn't flaunt it."

J.D.s, no. 5, 1988
Photocopy, saddle stitched, 8½ × 7 in. (21.6 × 17.8 cm)
Collection Bruce LaBruce

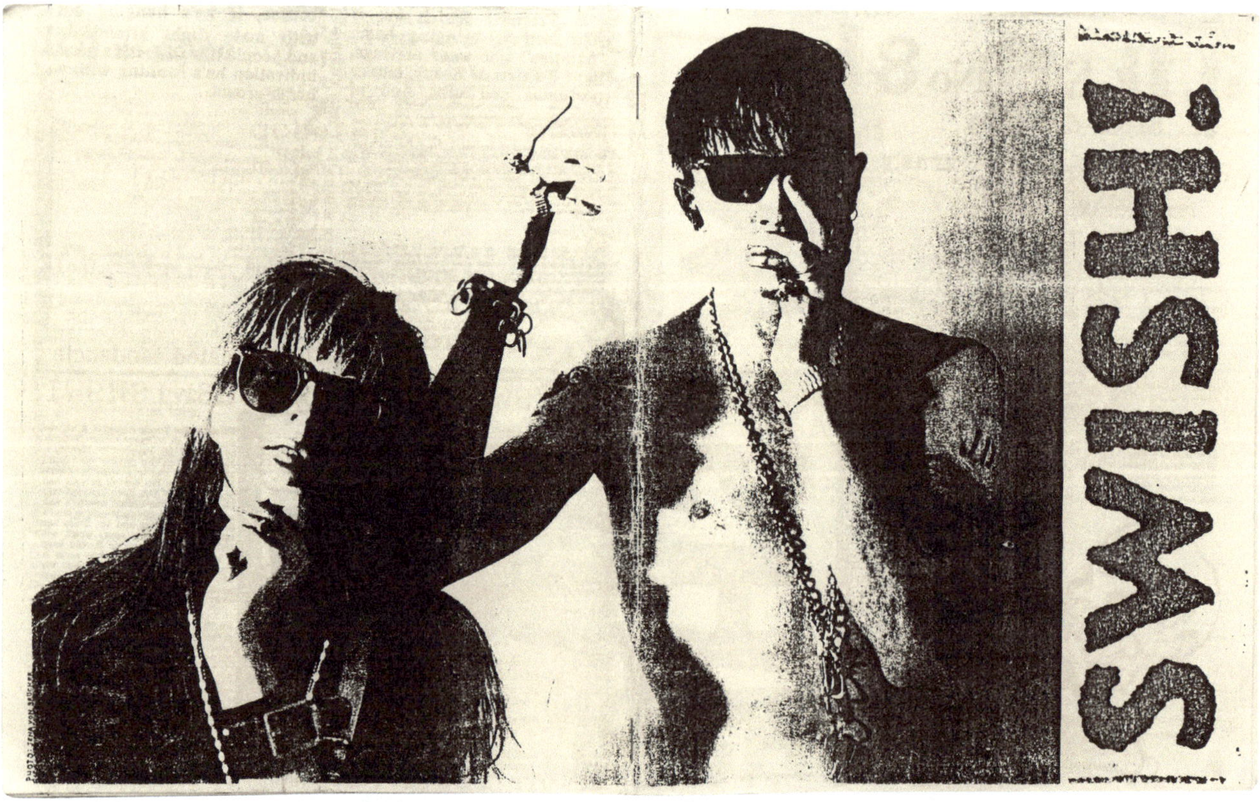

J.D.s, no. 8, 1991
Editor: Bruce LaBruce
Photocopy, saddle stitched, 8½ × 7 in. (21.6 × 17.8 cm)
Collection Bruce LaBruce

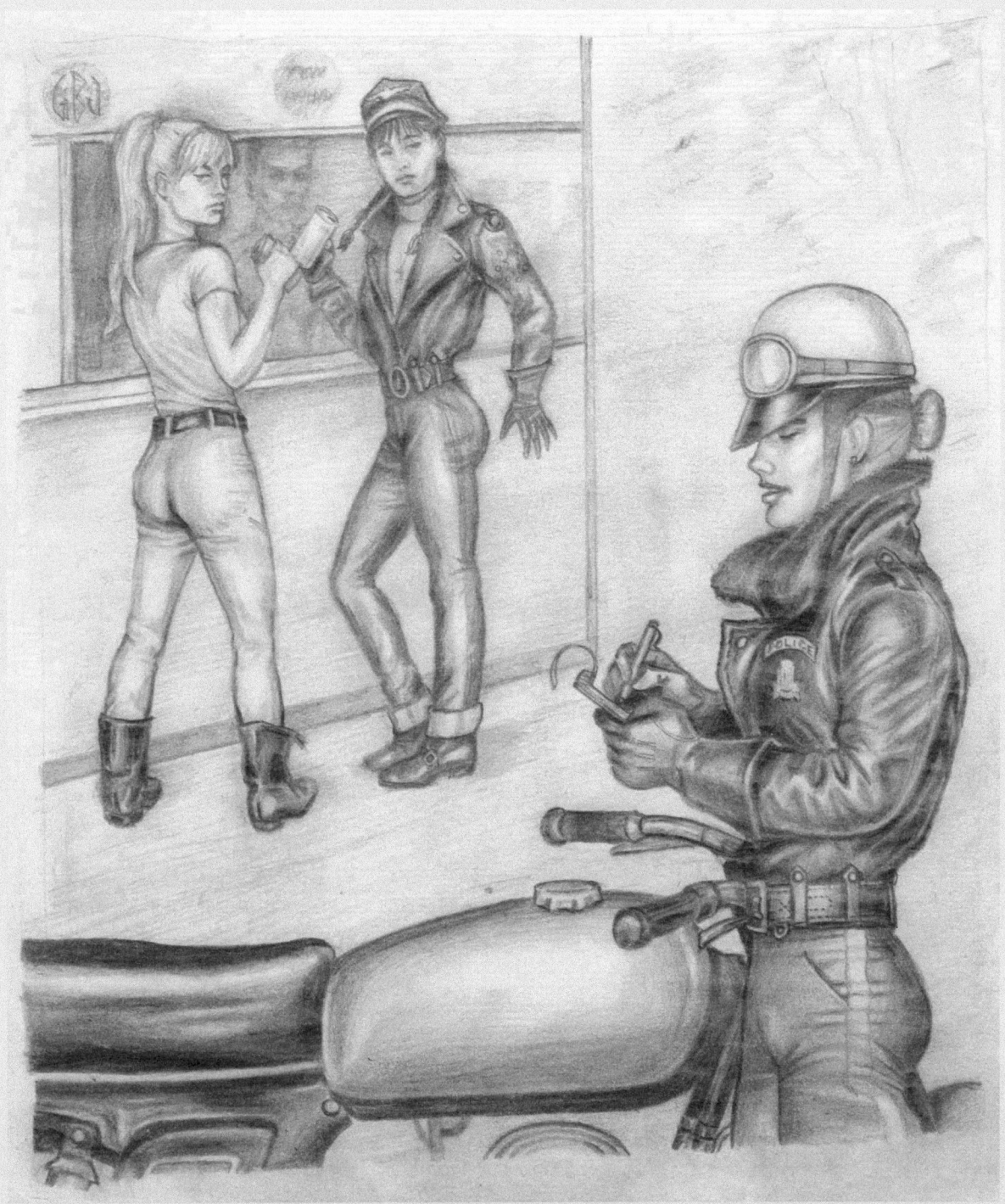

G. B. Jones
I Am A Fascist Pig # 1, 1985
Graphite on paper, 9 ¹³⁄₁₆ × 9 ⅛ in. (24.9 × 23.1 cm)
Collection the artist

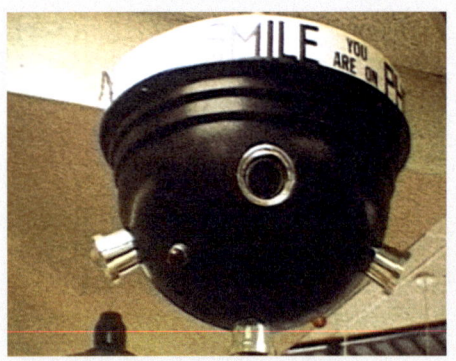 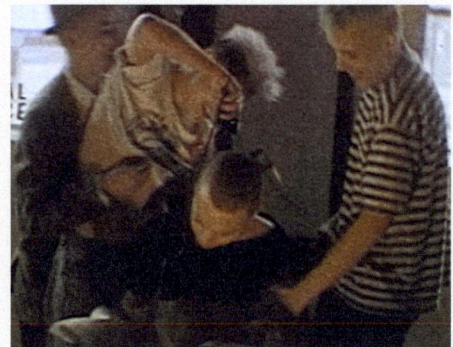 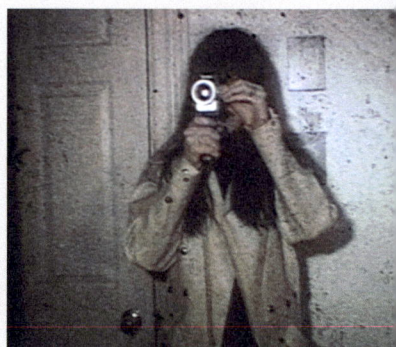

G. B. Jones
Stills from *The Troublemakers*, 1990
Super-8 film; color, sound; 20 min.
Vtape, Toronto

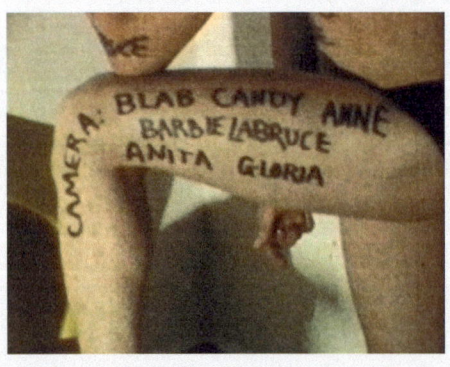 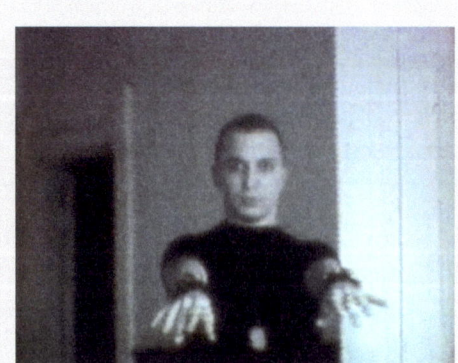

Bruce LaBruce
Stills from *I Know What It's Like to Be Dead*, 1987
Super-8 film; color, sound; 15 min., 13 sec.
Vtape, Toronto

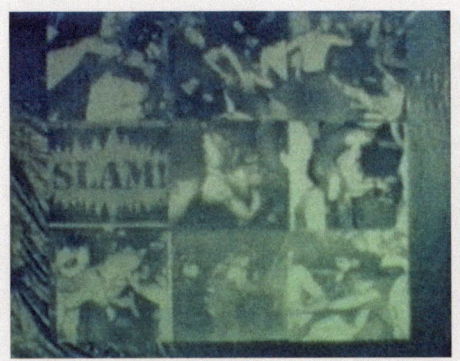 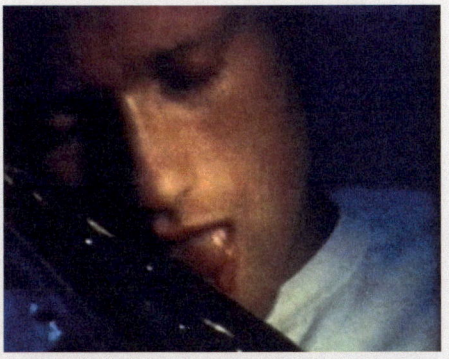

Candy Parker
Stills from *Sexbombs*, 1987–88
Super-8 film; color, sound; 11 min., 13 sec.
Vtape, Toronto

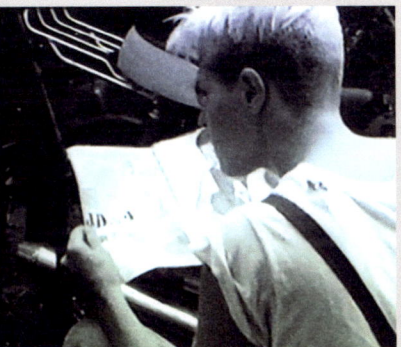 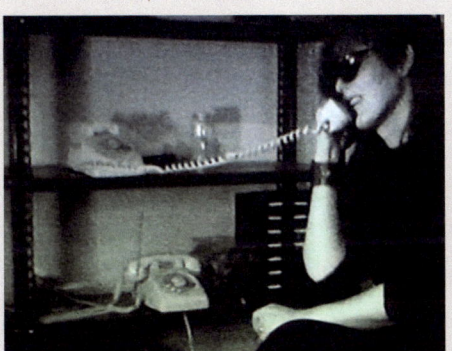 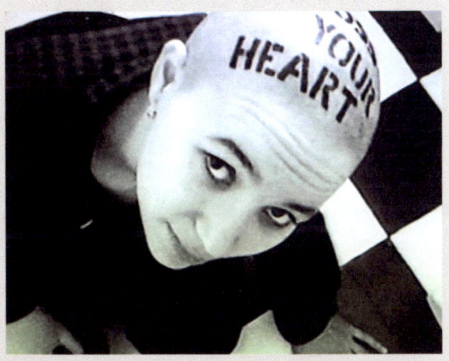

Suzy Richter
Stills from *Cross Your Heart*, 1990
Super-8 film; color, sound; 13 min.
Collection the artist

Toronto Zines

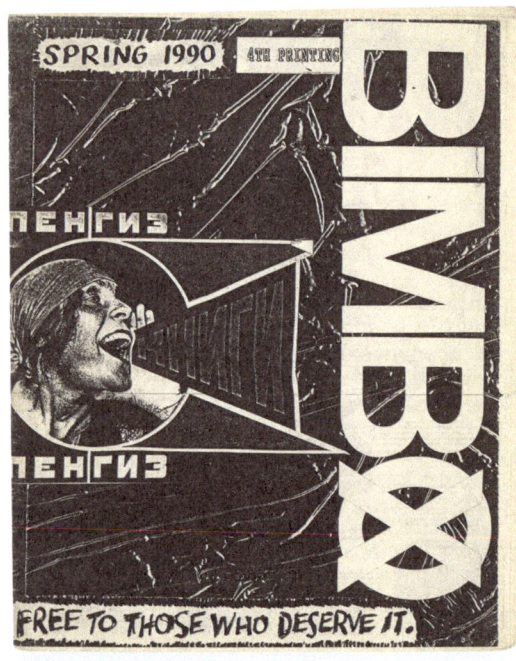

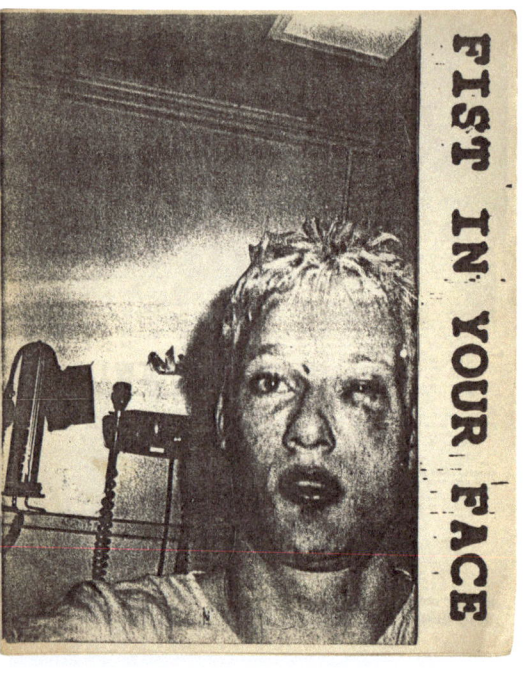

Johnny Noxzema and Rex Boy
Bimbox, no. 1, Spring 1990
Photocopy, saddle stitched, 8 ⅝ × 7 ⅛ in. (21.9 × 18.1 cm)
Collection Steve Lafreniere

Candy Parker and Dr. Joe
Fist in Your Face, Fall 1988
Photocopy, saddle stitched, 8 ⁹⁄₁₆ × 7 in. (21.6 × 17.8 cm)
Collection Bruce LaBruce

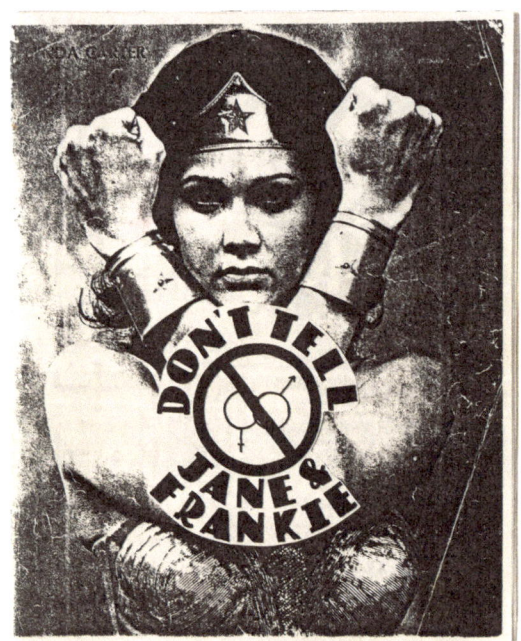

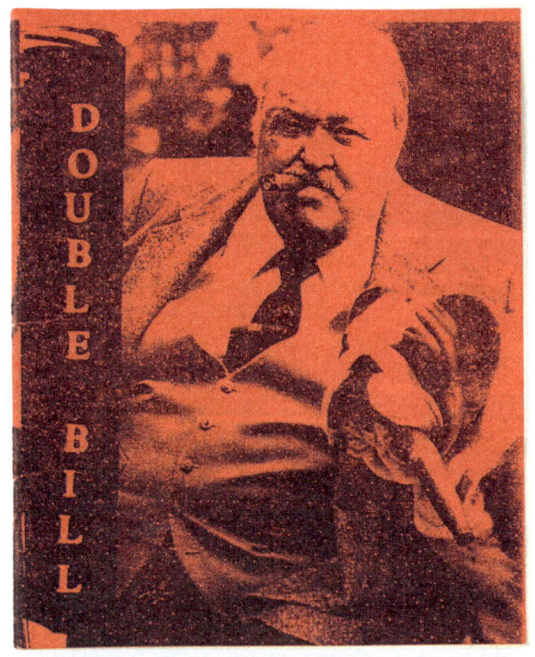

Jena von Brücker and Klaus von Brücker
Don't Tell Jane and Frankie, 1989
Photocopy, saddle stitched, 8 ½ × 7 in. (21.6 × 17.8 cm)
Collection Philip Aarons and Shelley Fox Aarons

Caroline Azar, Rex Boy, G. B. Jones,
Johnny Noxzema, Jena von Brücker
Double Bill, no. 1, 1991
Photocopy, saddle stitched, red paper wrappers,
8 ½ × 7 in. (21.6 × 17.8 cm)
Collection Steve Lafreniere

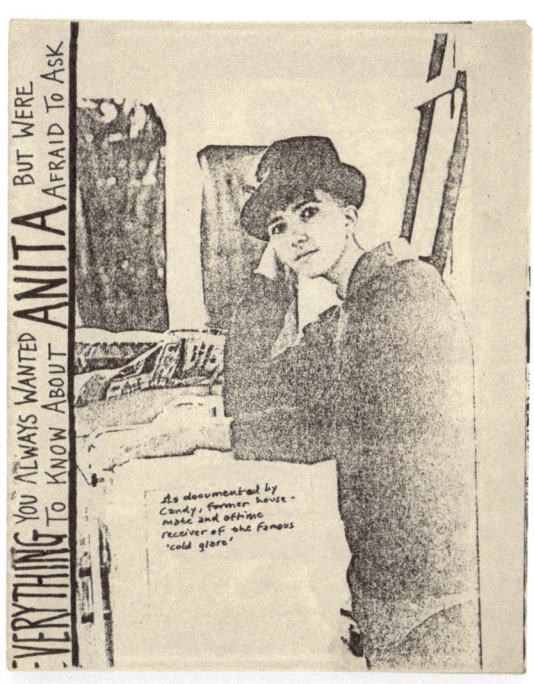

Candy Parker
*Everything You Wanted to Know about Anita
but Were Afraid to Ask*, ca. 1986
Photocopy, saddle stitched, 8 9/16 × 7 in. (21.6 × 17.8 cm)
Collection Bruce LaBruce

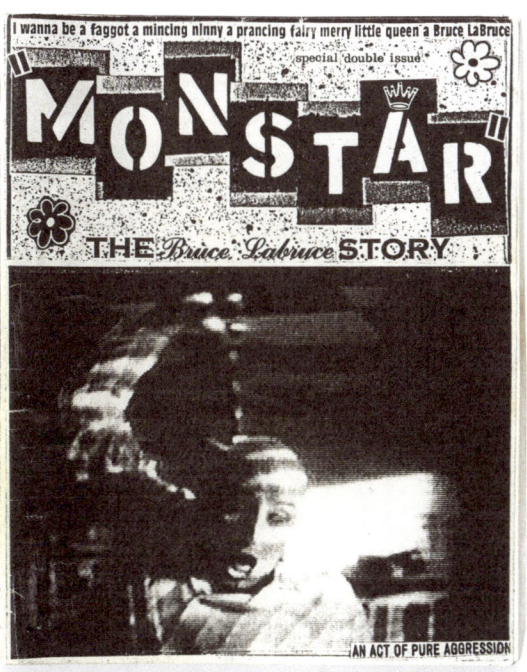

Bruce LaBruce
Monstar, 1992
Photocopy, saddle stitched, 8 9/16 × 7 in. (21.6 × 17.8 cm)
Collection Bruce LaBruce

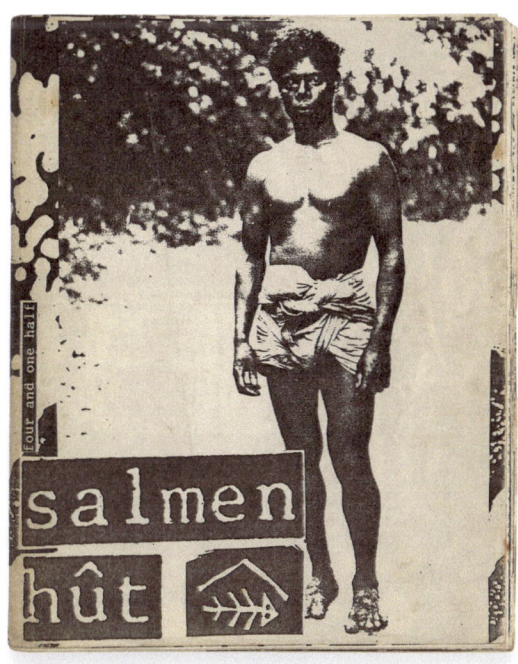

Salmon Hut, no. 4½, *Salmen Hut / Salmyn Hut*, 1988
Salmyn editors: Mizz B, Bezuk, Tanya Churchmuch, Jena Ledson,
oatfisch mimmy, Jill 7, Miss Barbrafisçh, Soo, Elaine Yau
Salmen editors: Dan Banks, Eric Boehm, Ron Chadhuri, Victory
Commissar-in-charge, Neek Davies, the Glamorous Peacock Sisters
Excellent Stories for Children, Mike Hill, Luis Jacob, groooovollah
meester, Colin Paton, Geoff Pounsett, David Rodgers, Kevin Scragg,
Peter Smith, Shon turunen, Sean Walker
Photocopy, saddle stitched, 8½ × 7 in. (21.6 × 17.8 cm)
Collection Bruce LaBruce

3.

Queer and Feminist Undergrounds, 1987–2000

The late 1980s and early 1990s experienced what Larry-Bob Roberts, editor of *Holy Titclamps*, dubbed the "queer zine explosion." Building on the legacies of alternative publishing in the wake of liberation struggles of the 1960s and the DIY ethos of punk culture, queer and feminist artists of this period boldly seized control of the practices related to media creation and distribution, in order to offer representations and perspectives that differed from those promoted by commercial culture industries (if they were represented at all). Zines of this era, such as Vaginal Davis's *Fertile La Toyah Jackson Magazine*, Tammy Rae Carland's *I ♥ Amy Carter*, and W. Wayne Karr and Cory Roberts-Auli's *Infected Faggot Perspectives*, to name only a few, provided platforms on which to share not only personal experiences and interests but also information on homophobia, transphobia, sexism, racism, white supremacy, ableism, HIV/AIDS activism, and classism—often with heavy doses of satire.

Music was a vital expressive and networking tool in these contexts. Among the many bands with connections to zines were Kathleen Hanna's Bikini Kill and Le Tigre (which counted artists/zine-makers Johanna Fateman and Sadie Benning as members) and Vaginal Davis's ¡Cholita! The Female Menudo and Pedro, Muriel and Esther (PME). Although some of the zines in this section have been associated with the queercore and Riot Grrrl punk movements, such categorizations have obscured the overlap of these two ostensibly distinct subcultures. The distinction has also excluded artists who identified with neither, who brought more intersectional perspectives, or who have been self-reflexively engaged with artistic legacies and recent academic writings on gender, sexuality, and race, by figures ranging from boundary-pushing artists like Kathy Acker and David Wojnarowicz to cultural theorists such as Judith Butler and bell hooks.

Film and video were as central to zine culture as music, a fact made possible with the introduction of small-format 8mm and VHS camcorders that were easy to use, relatively low cost, and widely available by the late 1980s. Many artists began producing video versions of their print publications; among these were Davis's *Fertile La Toyah Jackson Video Magazine*, Ho Tam's *Yellow Pages*, and Scott Treleaven's *The Salivation Army*. Numerous artists and zine makers also organized festivals, such as SPEW: The Homographic Convergence, first held in Chicago in 1991, which became key sites for sharing not only publications but also film and video works. In 1995, after collaborating on the zine *Snarla* with Fateman, performance artist and filmmaker Miranda July launched her video "chainletters," collectively titled *Big Miss Moviola* (later renamed *Joanie 4 Jackie*), which featured contributions by women filmmakers across North America; each video chainletter was accompanied by a zine-like booklet.

As with sections 1 and 2, the works in this chapter reveal connections between artists, sometimes based on geography—such as hubs like Chicago, Los Angeles, New York, and Portland, Oregon—but also through their zines' distribution channels. Thanks to *J.D.s* and General Idea's Art Metropole, Toronto continued to be a center of self-publishing, as seen with Tam and Treleaven's zines, as well as those of trans activists and artists Mirha-Soleil Ross and Xanthra Phillippa MacKay, whose zine *Gendertrash* was launched in 1993. In other cases, individuals helped catalyze widely dispersed communities through their zines, videos, and music. Carland, for example, who collaborated in the early 1990s with Hanna in Olympia, Washington, was a close friend of *Hippie Dick*'s Gene Barnes (a.k.a. Portia Manson). Carland also studied with Adriene Jenik (co-editor of the zine *Screambox*) at the University of California, Irvine, along with Félix Endara, Kelly Marie Martin, and Laura Splan. She contributed videos to July's "chainletters" and distributed the music of Davis, Le Tigre, and others through her independent label, Mr. Lady Records and Videos, a distribution company dedicated to feminist and queer projects.

Vaginal Davis

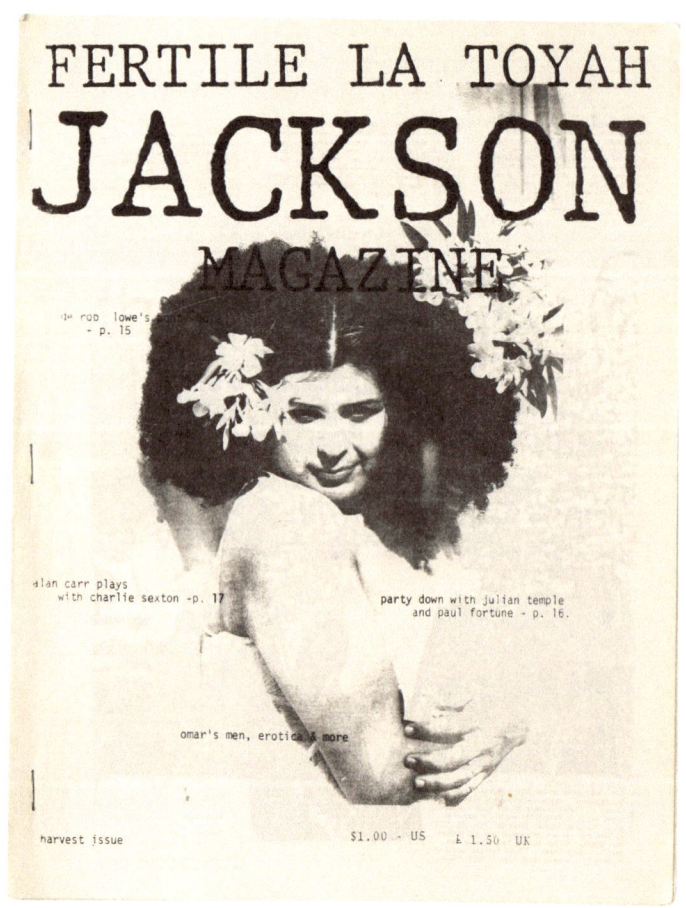

Fertile La Toyah Jackson Magazine, no. 1, 1987
Photocopy, side stapled, 11 × 8 ½ in. (27.9 × 21.6 cm)
Collection Steve Lafreniere

Fertile La Toyah Jackson Magazine, no. 2, *Harvest Issue*, 1987
Photocopy, side stapled, 11 × 8 ½ in. (27.9 × 21.6 cm)
Collection Philip Aarons and Shelley Fox Aarons

2 THINGS THAT MAKE FERTILE MAD

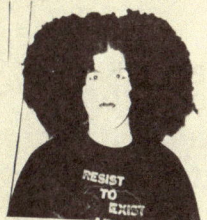

Punk rock type trendies from the suburbs that are narrow minded and bigoted that think they are cool because they dress all in black and even dye their hair black. Well all these type of people have crusty butt's and I hate them and when I see them I tell them so.

People who drive fancy expensive cars like BMW's and the like that when they are stopped at a light and they look over and see a third-world person they immediately lock their door.

reprinted by Permission from "The Five Days of Fertile", copyright © 1986 Big Binocar Press.

photo by Jacqueline Diverse

HENRY ROLLINS

unnatural desires

By Vag Davis

I heard that Henry Rollins moved to Silverlake in some house where he produces his writings. Well honey thats the house that I'd sure like to live in. Yes indeed. I've had the extreme hots for that pile of tatoos and muscles ever since he took Dez Cadena's place in Black Flag. Now dez was another saucy cutee, but back to Henry. The reason I feel he is so angry looking all the time because he doesn't have a beautiful black women to have sex with, well Henry just give me a call and I'll satisfy your natural and unnatural desires.

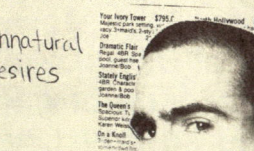

Photographed by Jeffrey Scales

YOU BE SHE BE IT BE

You've heard of Hip-Hop slang and Valley Girl language but the hottest new expression to hit the streets is inspired by Fertile LaToyah Jackson and the Afro Sisters its called TALK-TALK. Here's a few examples:

PHRASE | MEANING BEHIND EXPRESSION

1. Stop being a Bob Mackie — 1. Pretentious individual, who thinks that they are the most fashionably or politically correct. Can also refer to a person who wears dated punk clothing (ie Mohawks, colored or spiky hair) or a girl or guy that wears tacky, shiny clothing in a non-camp manner.
2. Shafted — 2. Stood up on a date or getting the last word in an argument.
3. You be molded — 3. embarrassed to a considerable degree
4. Shine — 4. To ignore as if they don't exist
5. Slap my thigh. — 5. To be in a state of joyfull exultation.
6. Peckerwood — 6. Poor and unloved class of white with absolutely no concept of style or grace.
7. Bodacious tata — 7. The erect swollen nipples of a sexually charged dynamic hot boy.
8. salty rump — 8. beach sand found on or between the buttocks of a gorgeous surfer boy.
9. crusty — 9. Smelly, rancid, gross
10. Nude Husband — 10. A boyfriend or lover with a voracious sexual appetite
11. Fidgety Dry Pussie — 11. Booty hole that longs to be penetrated.
12. Mustache Cafes — 12. Conservative, uptight homesexual males.
13. Bubba Chunking — 13. Dry humping or a full make-out session with clothes kept on.
14. Thump, Thump and Holler — 14. Quick yet artfully fullfilling sex.
15. Slug — 15. The extremely large endowment of a
16. Butch Patrick — Well built, blonde or redhead surfer boy from Huntington Beach
17. Buff
18. Beef Jerky
19. Shrimp
20. Jean-Claude
21. You're so Connie Parente — 16. Type of homesexual male who pretends to be masculine/dominate when in actuality he's strictly passive/bottom to the ultimate degree or a clone type who will only have sex with his mirror image or other men who are well built and muscular.
17. Tall(Over 6 feet) boy with a terrific hard body
18. Sexy, well endowed, nicely developed but neurotic jewish boy. — 19. To suck or lick on the extremely large well formed feet of a beautiful boy.
20. Arrogant, trendy frenchman or Eurotrash girl with a bad attitude.
21. Someone who wears rhinestones of any fashion or style.

---

what makes fertile la toyah mad?

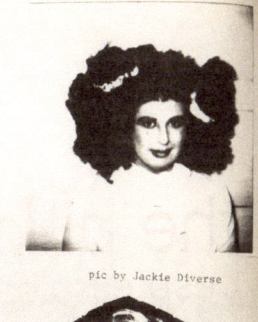

People who cling on to a celebrity to further their own career or to raise their position in the social strata. I especially hate cute boys with good bodies who cling on to me just so they can meet all my prestigious contacts or they pretend to like me in a sexual manner just so they can get into the pants of some hot boy who is a good friend of mine. Now that makes me rip roaring mad.

pic by Jackie Diverse

true sexual encounters

by Vaginal Davis

One day I was sitting on the bus stop waiting for the RTD to come along and take me to the Beverly Center where I could do some fierce clothes shopping. Well after waiting the usual 45 minutes this van pulls up to me and inside is this gorgeous boy with blonde hair and misty blue eyes, he's smiling this vicious smile and tells me to get in.

Well, before I know it I'm at this cute boys beach house in Malibu and we're having incredible edible sex. Needless to say I didn't make it to the Beverly Center.

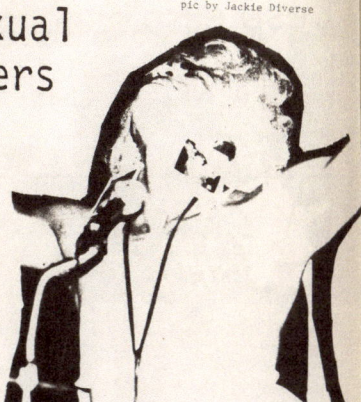

pic by Mari Kono

3

WHAT FERTILE SEZ PEOPLE COPY

Due to overwhelming demand. Fertile has compiled a list of colorful phrases and expressions that she and the Afro Sisters use on a daily basis.

photo: beulah luv

PHRASE | DEFINITION

1. grilled — 1. To be mounted and penetrated in a excessively rough and tumble fashion.
2. ill — 2. Something so tacky that it becomes fashionably correct. Example(That be an ill hairdo, and I'm an ill hairdo girl)
3. dinge queen — 3. white person who is obsessively attracted to blacks.
4. cha-cha queen — 4. white person obsessively attracted to Latinos or Hispanics
5. rice queen — 5. " " to Asians
6. patty queen — 6. Black person obsessively attracted to white persons.
7. skull dagger — 7. Any stupid person who dresses in the death rock mode.
8. filly — 8. Santa Monica Blvd hustler with a hard body and a mean face.
9. Bunny-itis — 9. Someone who lives in a deluded state.
10. frock — 10. A poseur punk
11. knocked up — 11. Getting fucked by a powerful, sexually robust young man

5

→ *Fertile La Toyah Jackson Magazine*, no. 4, *Paris Issue*, 1991
Photocopy, side stapled, 11 × 8 ½ in. (27.9 × 21.6 cm)
Collection Philip Aarons and Shelley Fox Aarons

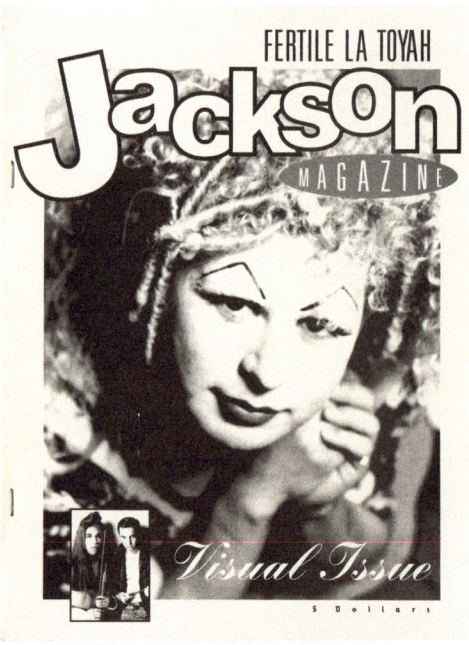

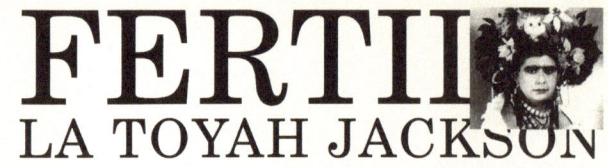

FERTII
LA TOYAH JACKSON
M A G A Z I N E

G.G. Allin, Lisa Suckdog, Bloody Mess, Joe Coleman, Psychodrama, Gender, Summer Caprice, Billy Wisdom & the Hee Shees, Robert Smith, Phranc, MDC, Johnny Depp, Sean Penn, John Wayne Gacy, Aaron Spelling, Vaginal Davis, Michele Lamy, Glen Meadmore, Herb Ritts, Jayne County, Cherie Curry, Red Hot Chile Peppers, Madonna, Bernard Figueroa, Studio Bercot, Jean Paul Gaultier, Isabelle Adjani and Sex Club Scandals

P A R I S   I S S U E $4.00

Fertile La Toyah Jackson Magazine, no. 5, *Visual Issue*, 1991
Photocopy, side stapled, 11 × 8 ½ in. (27.9 × 21.6 cm)
Collection Philip Aarons and Shelley Fox Aarons

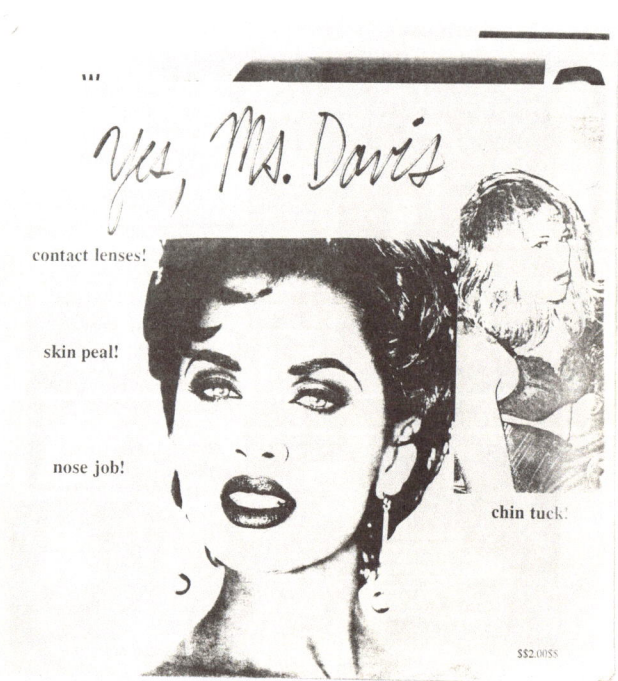

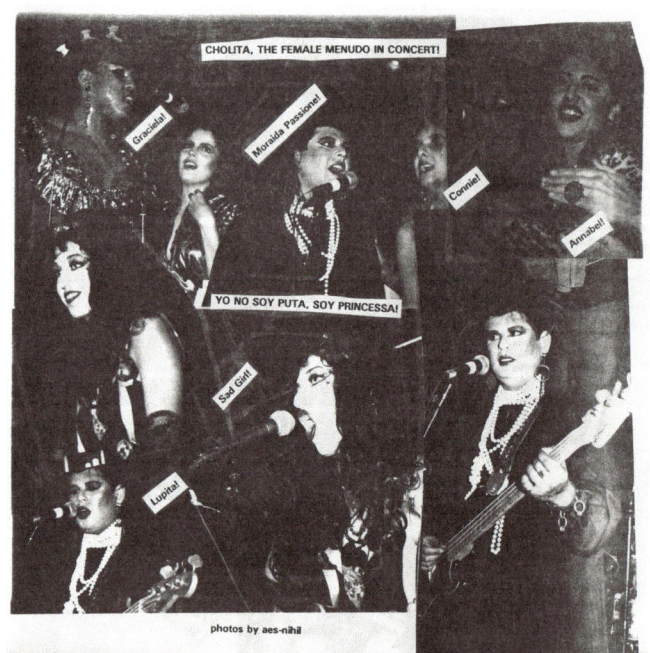

Yes, Ms. Davis, 1994
Photocopy, bound with paper clip, 8 ¾ × 8 ½ in. (22.2 × 21.6 cm)
Collection Philip Aarons and Shelley Fox Aarons

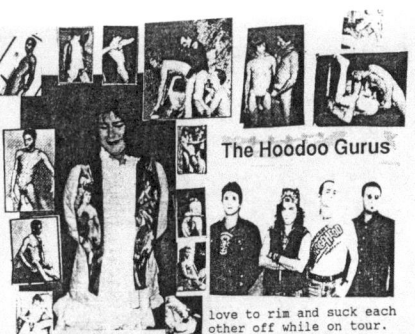

The Hoodoo Gurus

love to rim and suck each
other off while on tour.

FERTILE FANZINE GUIDE By Boris Streisand

Fertile trades with over a million and a half 'zines all over the world. Here's a partial list of some of the best. If we failed to mention you this time, please don't be upset we'll be sure to talk all about you in the next issue.

1. Factsheet Five (c/o Mike Gunderloy 6 Arizona Avenue Rensselaer, New York 12144-4502 $2.00) This is the best of the breed listing every 'zine known to man. What makes this so special The fact that Factsheet Five educates the ignorant. There's even 'zine etiquette and how to start your own 'zine. Thank God this publication exists. 15****'s!

2. Maximum RocknRoll ($2.00 P.O. BOX 288 Berkeley, Ca., 94701) Very Berkeley in tone and scope. The best thing are the letters, reviews tend to be of the milky mouth white boy variety, way too white-male/straight/music oriented for my tastes. 3*'s

3. Flipside ($2.00, P.O. BOX 363 Whittier, CA.,) Very suburban punk rock oriented. See above descrp. Very old school. !* (con't on page +)

photo of Fertile La Toyah Jackson by Denning Taylor

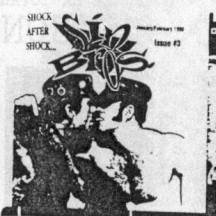 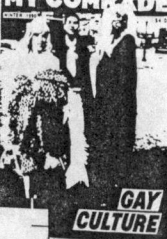 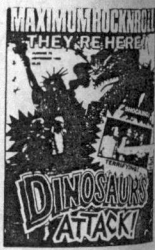

Stylist Jeff Gardner
Hair & Make-up Cochise
Porno Vest by Jean Paul Gaultier
available at Maxfields
jewelry by connie parente
fangs by Gavin
dress by Rifat Ozbek available
at Madeleine Gallay

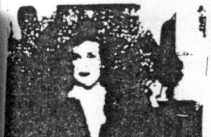

what makes
fertile mad?

One thing that really makes Fertile mad is all these trendy coffee houses popping up - Java, Gasoline Alley, Mad Hatter, they are all trying desperately to create a San Francisco-ish bohemian chic, but honey those days are over, so get over it!

Case in point: Fertile accompanied some out-of-town friends to the Onyx/Sequel on Vermont. Fertile didn't want to go there, but her friends dragged her in. So she orders plain coffee (not espresso or cappuccino mind you) and dessert. And wouldn't you know, these tired people at the table next to Fertile are seriously discussing existentialism. (Did I spell it right?)

So Fertile gets disgusted and yells at these stupid trendy people,"STOP TALKING ABOUT EXISTENTIALISM!"

One of the dummies even sported a trendy goatee and get this: he was wearing a beret.

And while we're on the subject of things that really irk Fertile.
No one bothers Fertile more than Natalie Merchant of the group 10,000 Maniacs. Fertile is just sick up to her cooz with all the critical acclaim that woman gets. Fertile would like to put that chick to check. Now if what I've just mentioned isn't enough to make Fertile La Toyah Jackson REALLY, REALLY MAD! What is?

Adesso
l'ultimo regalo
prima
della festa
finale.
Per un mese,
tutti i
mercoledì
e i venerdì
in edicola
con il giornale,
un altro

Top 20 lps

1. Jean Paul Sartre Experience "The Size of Food" - Haunting pop gems from New Zealand
2. De La Soul - "3 Feet High and Rising" Get off your ass and jam
3. My Bloody Valentine - "Isn't Anything" The Jesus and Mary Chain wish they were this good
4. Jungle Bros. "Done By the Forces of Nature" Hip-hop album of the year
5. Freakwater - "Freakwater" Most gorgeous country folk in years
6. The Go-Betweens - "16 Lovers Lane" Pristine, evocative and their best
7. Lou Reed - "New York" His best solo work since "The Blue Mask"
8. Glen Meadmore "Squawbread" And do-si-do your partner.
9. Womack & Womack - "Conscience" This record got me through 1989
10. The Hollowmen - "Pink Quartz Sunblasting" Love, faith and rage impeccably expressed
11. Opal - "Early Recordings" Why don't you be good children, close your eyes
12. Al Green - "Love Ritual" (Rare and Unreleased) I'd buy an album of him gargling
13. 11th Dream Day - "Beet" Like the MC5 way past midnight, thit thrills
14. Kassav - "Vini Pou" If you can't dance to this you're lame
15. My Dad is Dead - "The Taller You Are" Doublebarreled mayhem
16. Bob Dylan - "Oh Mercy" His best since "Blood on the Tracks"
17. Dirty Dozen Brass Band - "Voodoo" A brilliant stew of musical genres
18. Mudhoney - "Mudhoney" Overrated but still monster rock.
19. N.W.A - "Straight Outta Compton" Brutally right on target.
20. Les Negresses Vertes - "Mlah" The Clash meets the Pogues in a French Ska town

Siamo quasi
in dirittura
d'arrivo.
Il miliardo
di S. Silvestro
è vicino.
Prima Pagina,
il gioco
più divertente
e più facile
ha distribuito
tanti milioni

3.

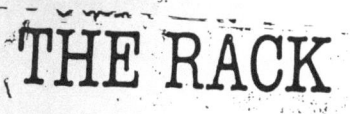

THE RACK

A PRIVATE SEX CLUB

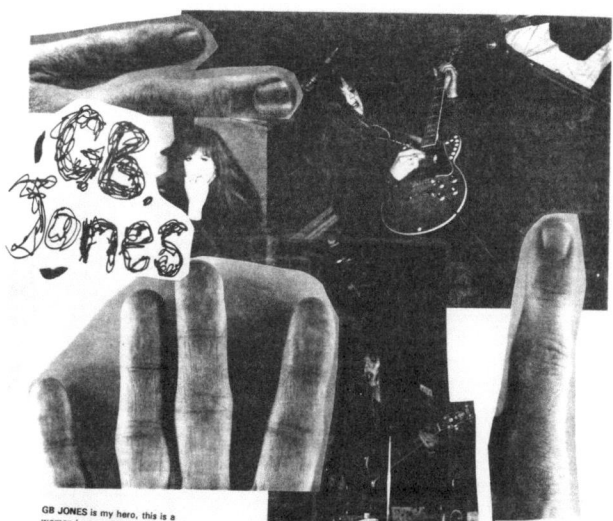

GB JONES is my hero, this is a
woman i never get tired of
talking about and praising.
She deserves more recognition
for being the pioneer that
she is.

As a film maker she ranks
up there with the greats
like F.W. Marnau or G.W.
Pabst. Her movies, The
YoYo Gang and the sensational
Lollipop Generation attest
to her talents.

As an artist her Tom Girl
drawings are remarkable.
Erotic and daring, GB Jones
conquers territories other
artists only can dream of.

Then there is GB Jones
the musician, as lead
guitarist with the all
dyke hard core band
Fifth Column, GB Jones
rocks out. Yeah man
this woman is the wom
of the year. She out
does everyone by 99%

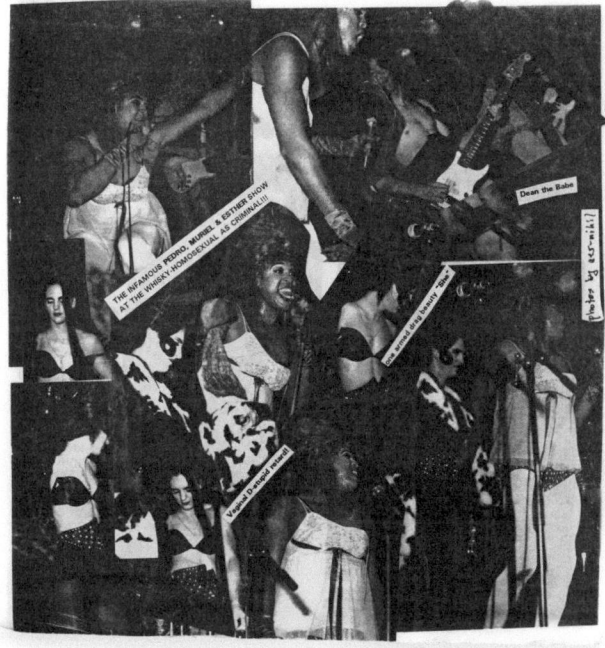

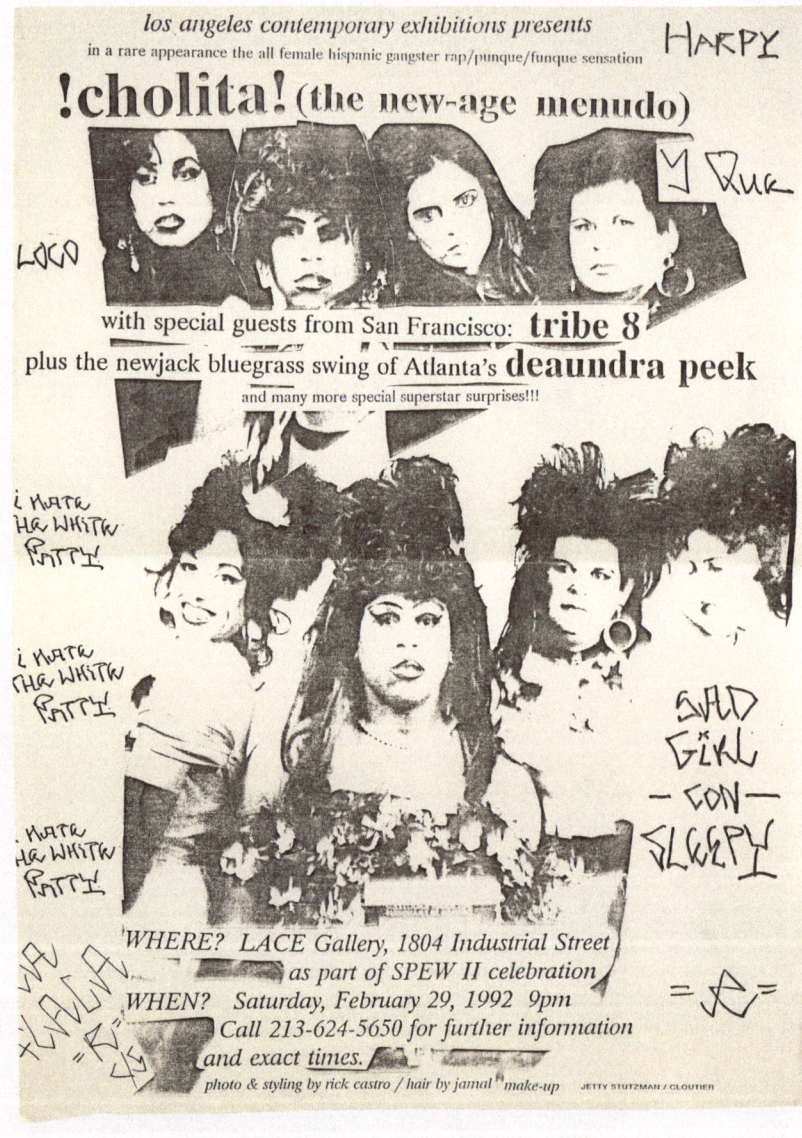

¡Cholita! The Female Menudo flyer, 1992
Photocopy, 15 ¼ × 11 in. (28.7 × 27.9 cm)
Collection Steve Lafreniere

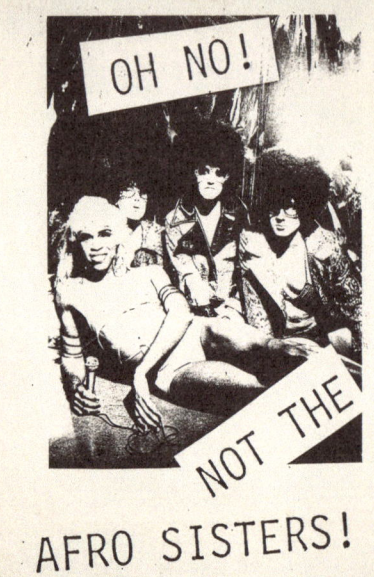

Afro Sisters flyer, ca. 1990
Photocopy, 11 × 8 ½ in. (27.9 × 21.6 cm)
Collection Steve Lafreniere

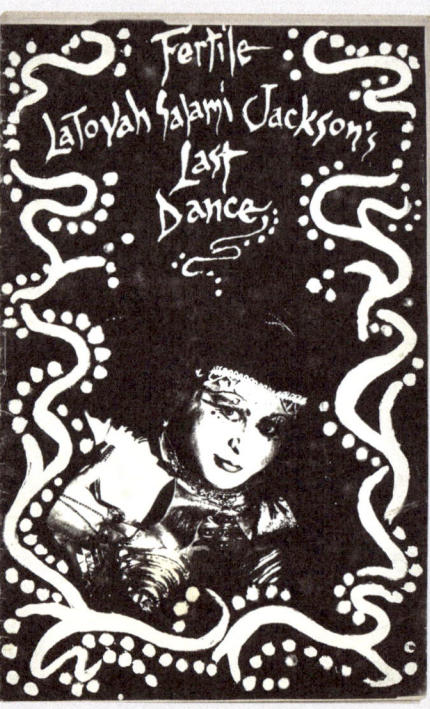

Fertile LaToyah Salami Jackson's Last Dance, 1986
Photocopy, side stapled, 11 × 8 ½ in. (27.9 × 21.6 cm)
Collection Steve Lafreniere

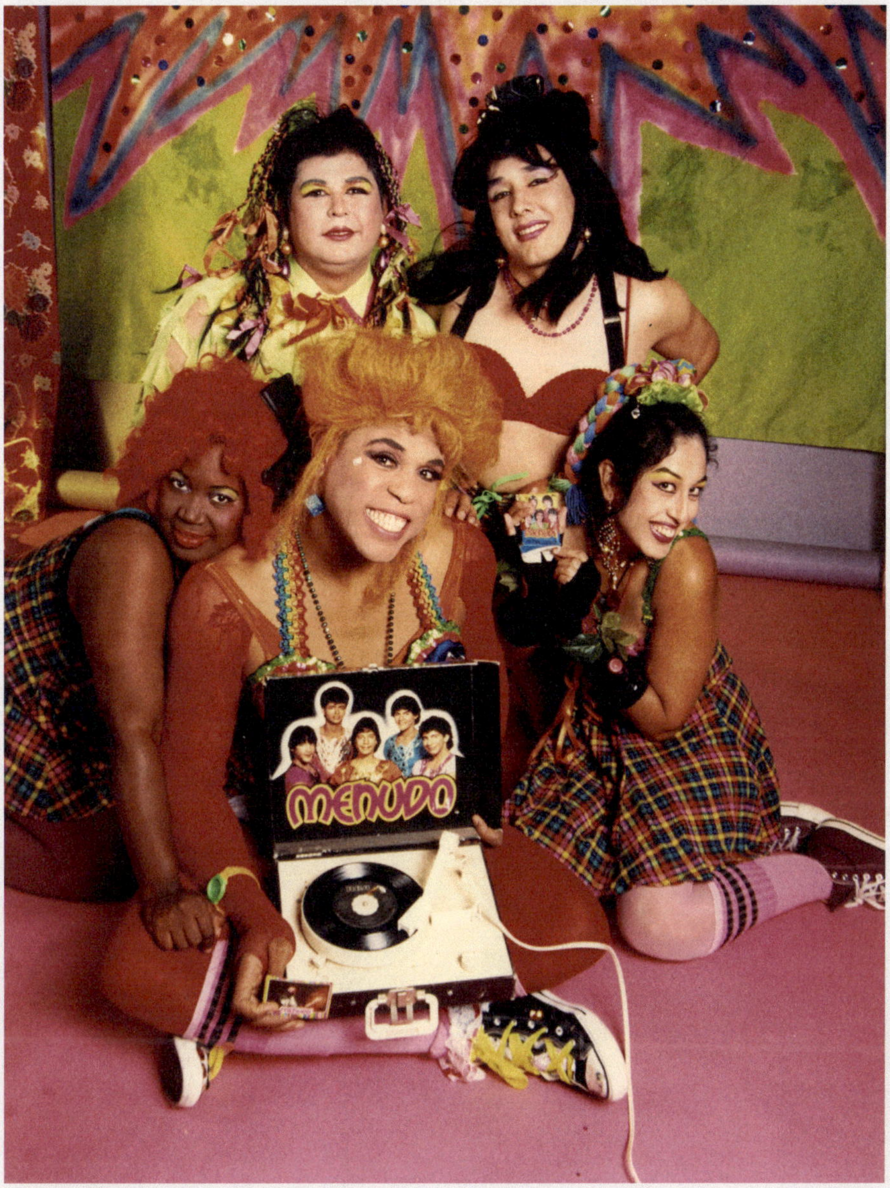

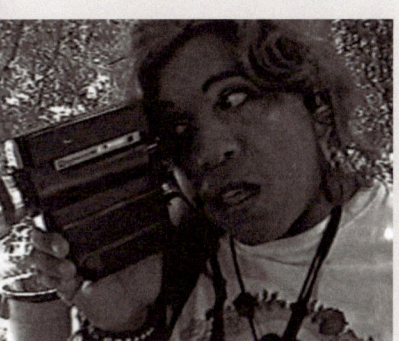

Ann Summa
¡Cholita!, ca. 1990
(left to right: Melanie Sparks, Fertile La Toyah
Jackson, Vaginal Davis, Webmaster, Alice Bag)
Scan of color transparency film
Collection the artist

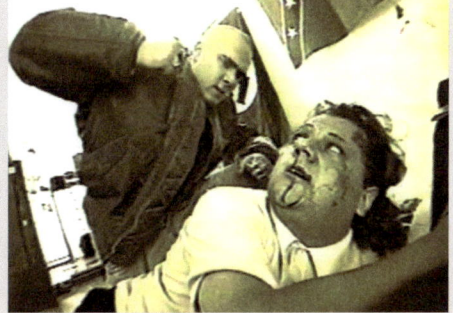

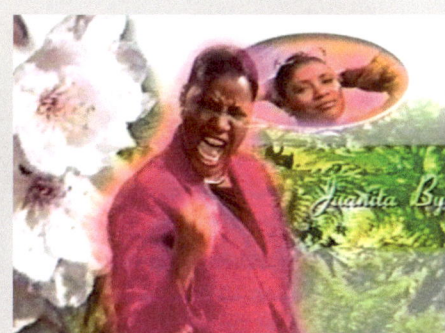

Stills from *The White to Be Angry*, 1999
Video; color, sound; 19 min., 22 sec.
Collection the artist

Rick Castro

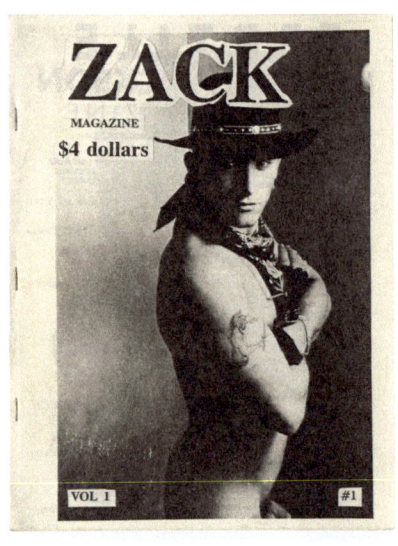

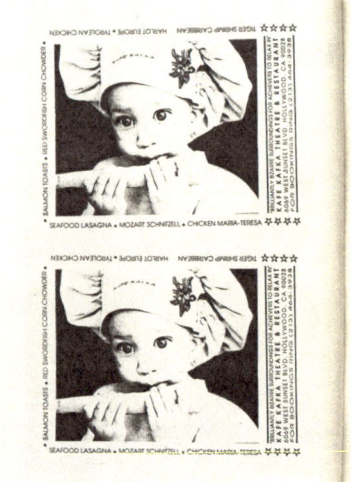

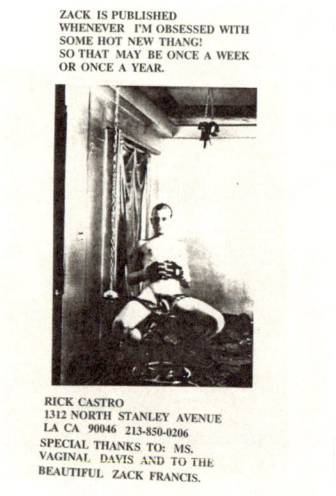

Zack, vol. 1, no. 1, 1991
Photocopy, side stapled, 11 × 8 ½ in. (27.9 × 21.6 cm)
Collection Steve Lafreniere

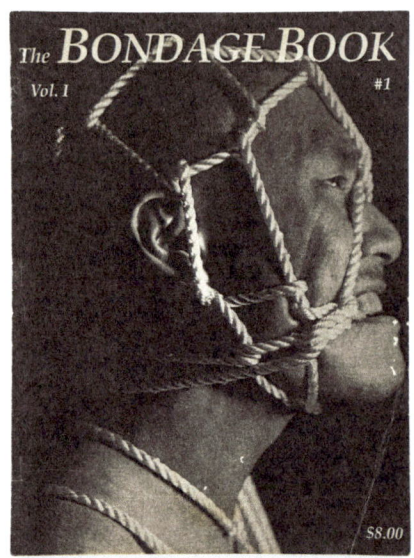

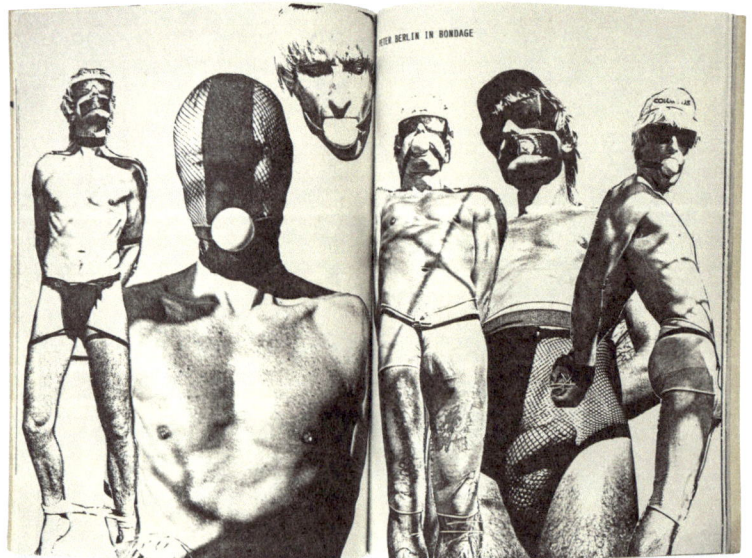

The Bondage Book, vol. 1, no. 1, 1992
Photocopy, side stapled, 11 × 8 ½ in. (27.9 × 21.6 cm)
Collection the artist

178

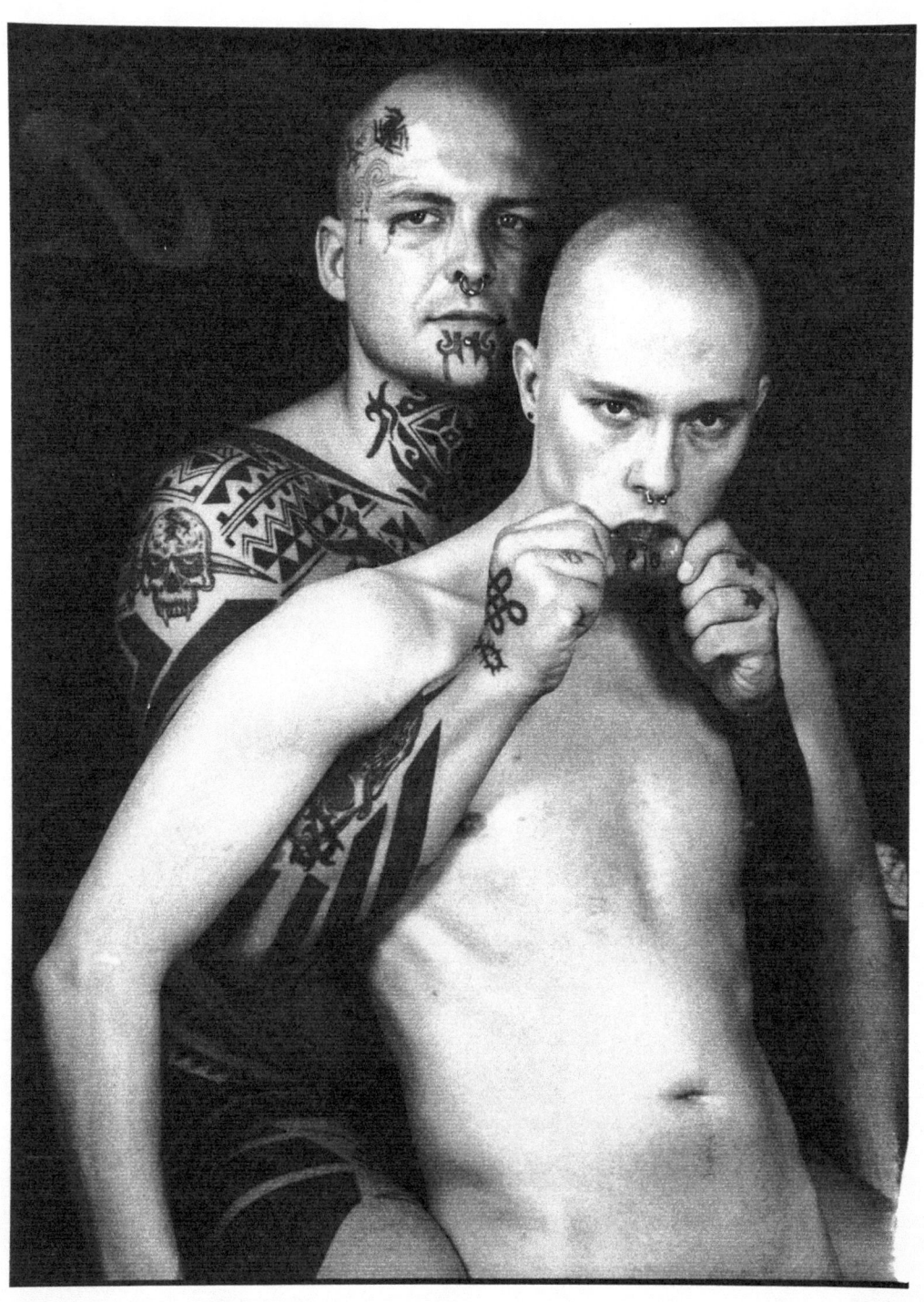

Ron Athey and Piglet, 1993
Archival pigment print, 11 × 8 in. (27.9 × 20.3 cm)
Collection the artist

Tom Jennings and
Deke Nihilson

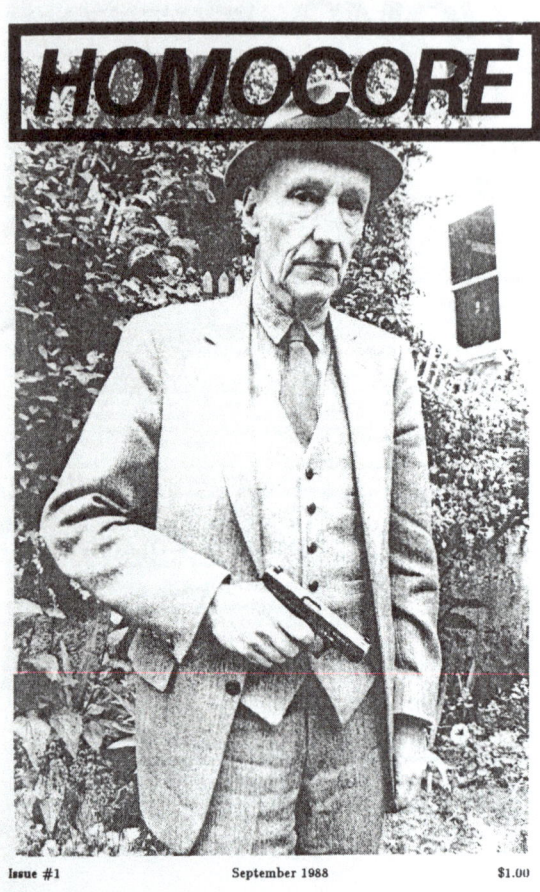

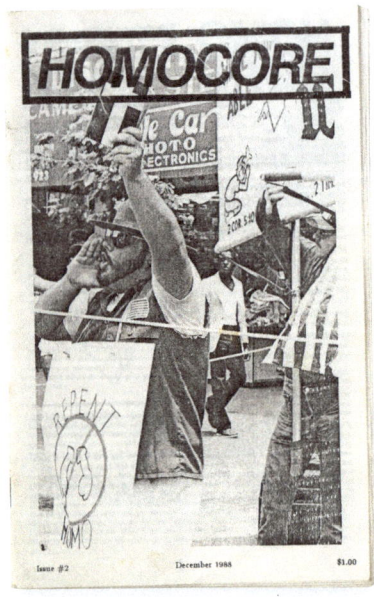

Homocore, no. 2, December 1988
Offset, saddle stitched, 10 ¾ × 7 ¼ in. (27.3 × 18.4 cm)
Collection Philip Aarons and Shelley Fox Aarons

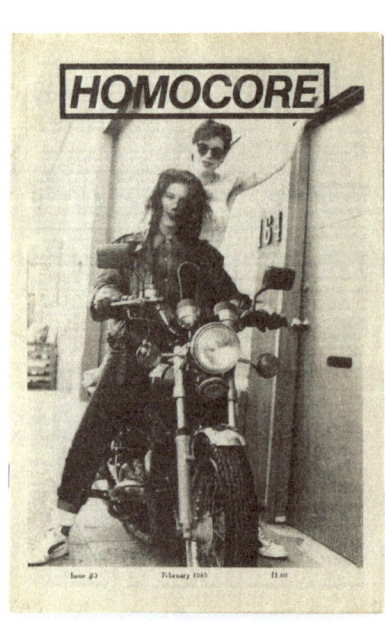

Homocore, no. 3, February 1989
Offset, saddle stitched, 10 ¾ × 7 ¼ in. (27.3 × 18.4 cm).
Collection Philip Aarons and Shelley Fox Aarons

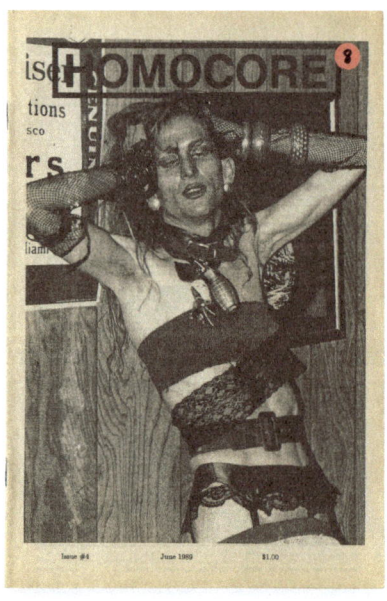

Homocore, no. 4, June 1989
Offset, saddle stitched, 10 ¾ × 8 ⅛ in. (27.3 × 20.7 cm)
Collection Philip Aarons and Shelley Fox Aarons

←↓ *Homocore*, no. 1, September 1988
Photocopy, saddle stitched, 8 ½ × 5 ½ in. (21.6 × 14 cm)
Collection Philip Aarons and Shelley Fox Aarons

What the Fuck is *HOMOCORE*?

This is the first issue of **HOMOCORE**. I think it's been needed for a long time, and it took me nearly a year to get off my ass and do it.

You don't have to be a homo to read or have stuff published in **HOMOCORE**. One thing everyone in here has in common is that we're all *social mutants*; we've outgrown or never were part of any of the "socially acceptable" categories. You don't have to be gay; being different at all, like straight guys who aren't macho shitheads, women who don't want to be a punk rock fashion accessory, or any other personal decision that makes you an outcast is enough. Sexuality is an important part of it, but only part.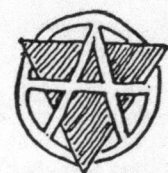

It's obvious that there's gay punks and other people in the various scenes we hang out and work and live in. You'd almost never know it though, from the way people behave. It's usually just too scary to be open and honest when you hear supposedly cool and politically aware people and bands say or do sexist or homophobic shit, especially if you don't know any other homo punks or other people.

Plus there's lots of interesting and important things around; other homopunk zines, music, people, events, news and whatever, but they're all so scattered or buried it's hard to discover. That's what I want **HOMOCORE** zine to include. The stuff in this issue is just a hint at the stuff out there, probably everyone has got something interesting, send it in and share it!

There's also unpleasant things to deal with, like bigotry and hatred and violence. Even straight guys get "fag-bashed" if they act "faggy", whatever the fuck that means. Gay issues aren't just for same-sex friends and lovers; the freedom to do or behave as you want is important for everybody. Racist assholes hate blacks, jews, faggots, whatever: it's all the same hatred and fear.

We're outlaws, if we don't follow the usual rules, and don't want to be part of mass culture. We're mutants, if we try new things, things that are honest and human, like making our own cultures, preferably lots of them, all with room for each others'.

So this is what **HOMOCORE** is about, if that helps any. If not, read and decide for yourself. There will be more issues, though I won't attempt to stick to any hard schedule for now. It depends on the stuff you send, plus whatever victims I can get locally to help put it all together.

Some people deserve special thanks for helping me get this zine together, even indirectly:

• The gay people who write to **MAXIMUMROCKNROLL**; this zine is made mainly with you in mind. Thanks to Tim and the M.R.R. gang for encouraging it by not discouraging it; far more substantial than it sounds!

• Bruce LaBruce and **J.D.s** zine. J.D.s has done more than he realizes...I still like reading J.D.s a year later, so much so that I swiped some stuff from it.

• Duke, Shawn and the rest of Shred of Dignity for doing all the wierd things we do that keeps everyone thinking (or at least keeps them confused).

• Everyone who ever helped at the Gilman St. Project (R.I.P.), especially Jane, Cammie, Radley, Lawrence, Eggplant, Brian, Tim, Martin, everyone who ever coordinated a show or swept a floor.

• The Radical Faeries, for being wonderful mischief-making homo anarchist pagans.

• The polysexual anarchist community that I met in Toronto this year, and the Bound Together Bookstore collective in SF, especially Joey Cain.

Tom

1

Greta Snider

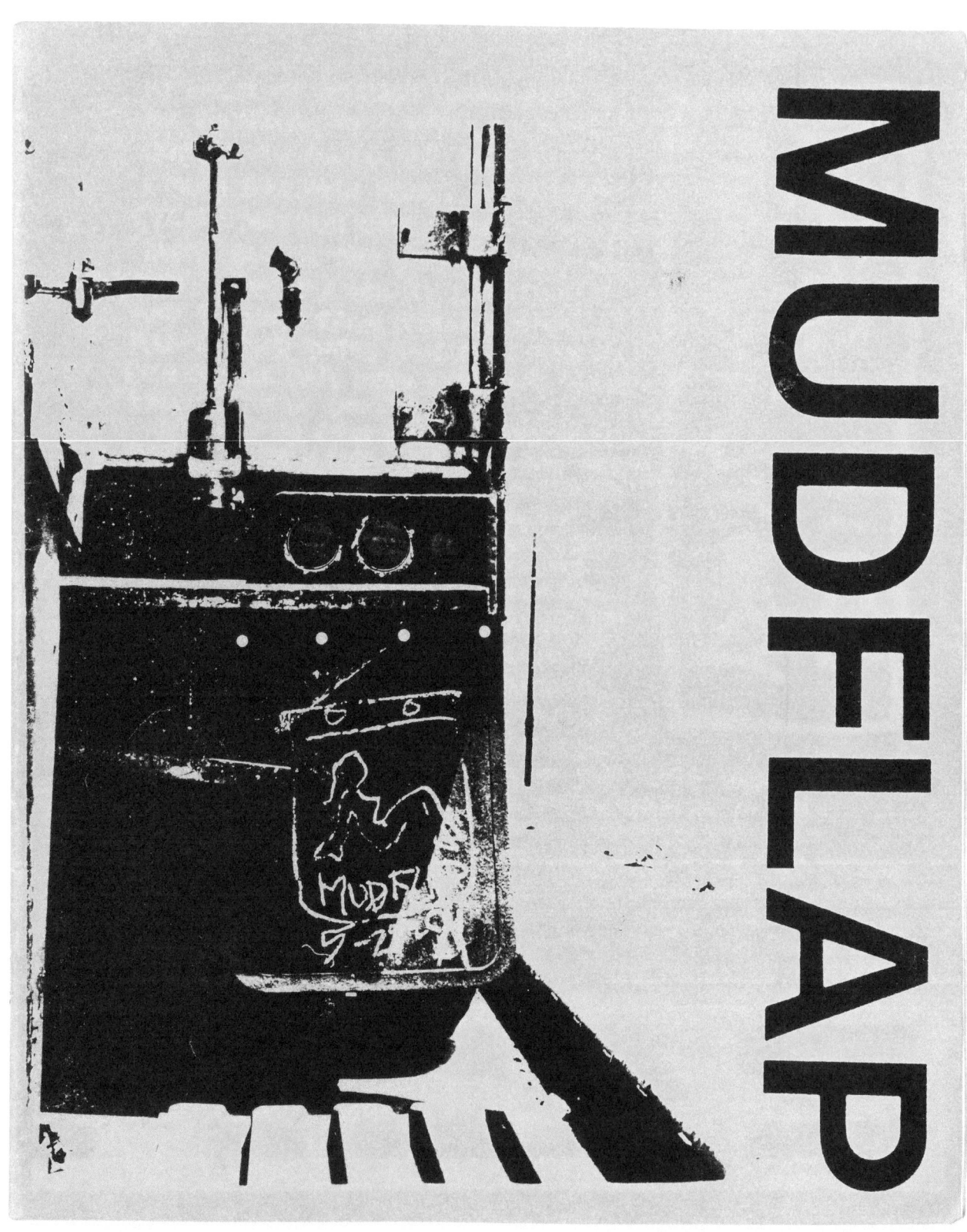

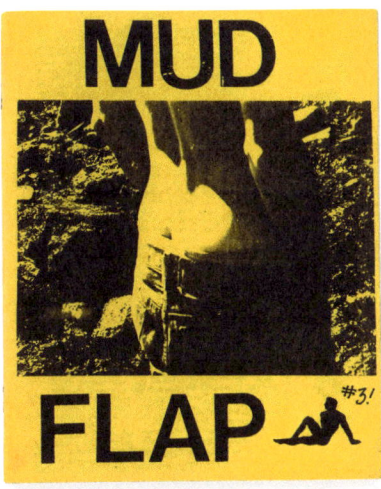

Mudflap, no. 3, 1992
Photocopy, saddle stitched, yellow paper wrappers,
8 ½ × 7 in. (21.6 × 17.8 cm)
Collection Philip Aarons and Shelley Fox Aarons

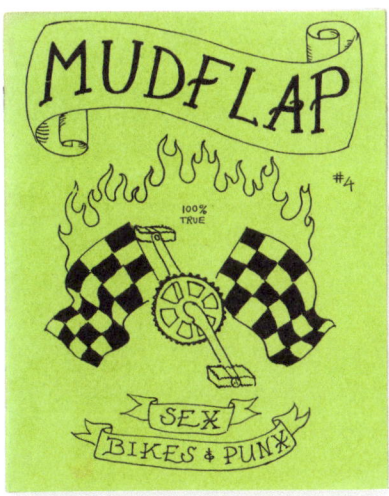

Mudflap, no. 4, 1992
Photocopy, saddle stitched, green paper wrappers,
8 ½ × 7 in. (21.6 × 17.8 cm)
Collection Philip Aarons and Shelley Fox Aarons

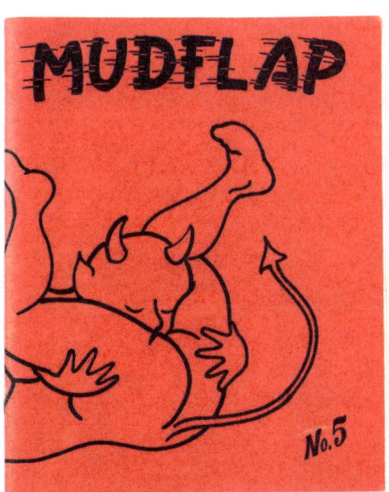

Mudflap, no. 5, 1993
Photocopy, saddle stitched, red paper wrappers,
8 ½ × 7 in. (21.6 × 17.8 cm)
Collection Philip Aarons and Shelley Fox Aarons

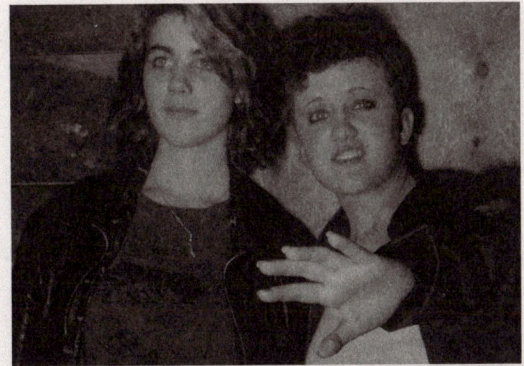

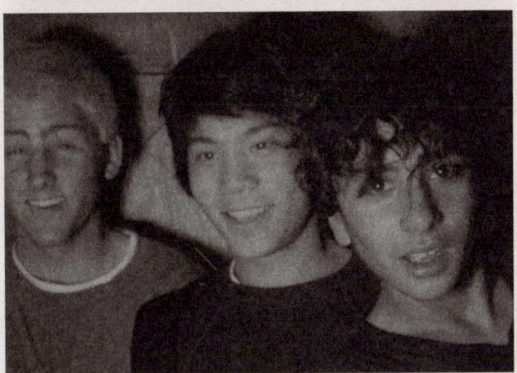

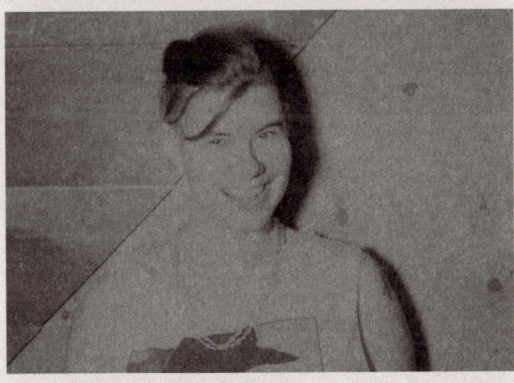

Stills from *Hard Core Home Movie*, 1989
16mm film; black and white, sound; 5 min.

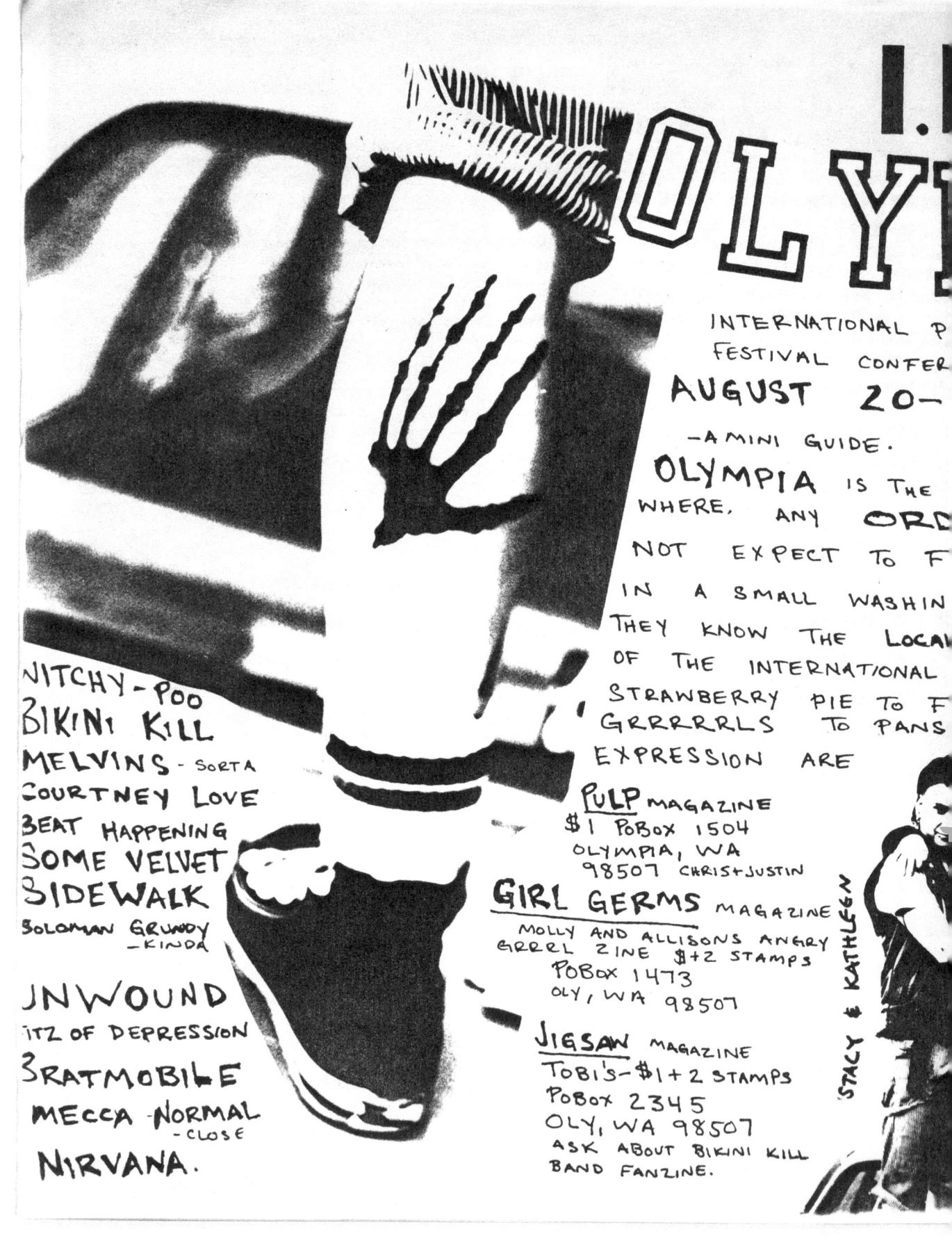

I.[

OLY[

NITCHY-POO
BIKINI KILL
MELVINS - SORTA
COURTNEY LOVE
BEAT HAPPENING
SOME VELVET
SIDEWALK
SOLOMAN GRUNDY
                -KINDA

UNWOUND
ITZ OF DEPRESSION
BRATMOBILE
MECCA-NORMAL
              -CLOSE
NIRVANA.

INTERNATIONAL P
FESTIVAL CONFER
AUGUST 20-
    -A MINI GUIDE.
OLYMPIA IS THE
WHERE, ANY ORD
NOT EXPECT TO F
IN A SMALL WASHIN
THEY KNOW THE LOCA
OF THE INTERNATIONAL
STRAWBERRY PIE TO F
GRRRRLS TO PANS
EXPRESSION ARE

PULP MAGAZINE
$1 POBOX 1504
OLYMPIA, WA
98507 CHRIS+JUSTIN

GIRL GERMS MAGAZINE
MOLLY AND ALLISONS ANGRY
GRRRL ZINE $+2 STAMPS
POBOX 1473
OLY, WA 98507

JIGSAW MAGAZINE
TOBI'S-$1+2 STAMPS
POBOX 2345
OLY, WA 98507
ASK ABOUT BIKINI KILL
BAND FANZINE.

STACY & KATHLEEN

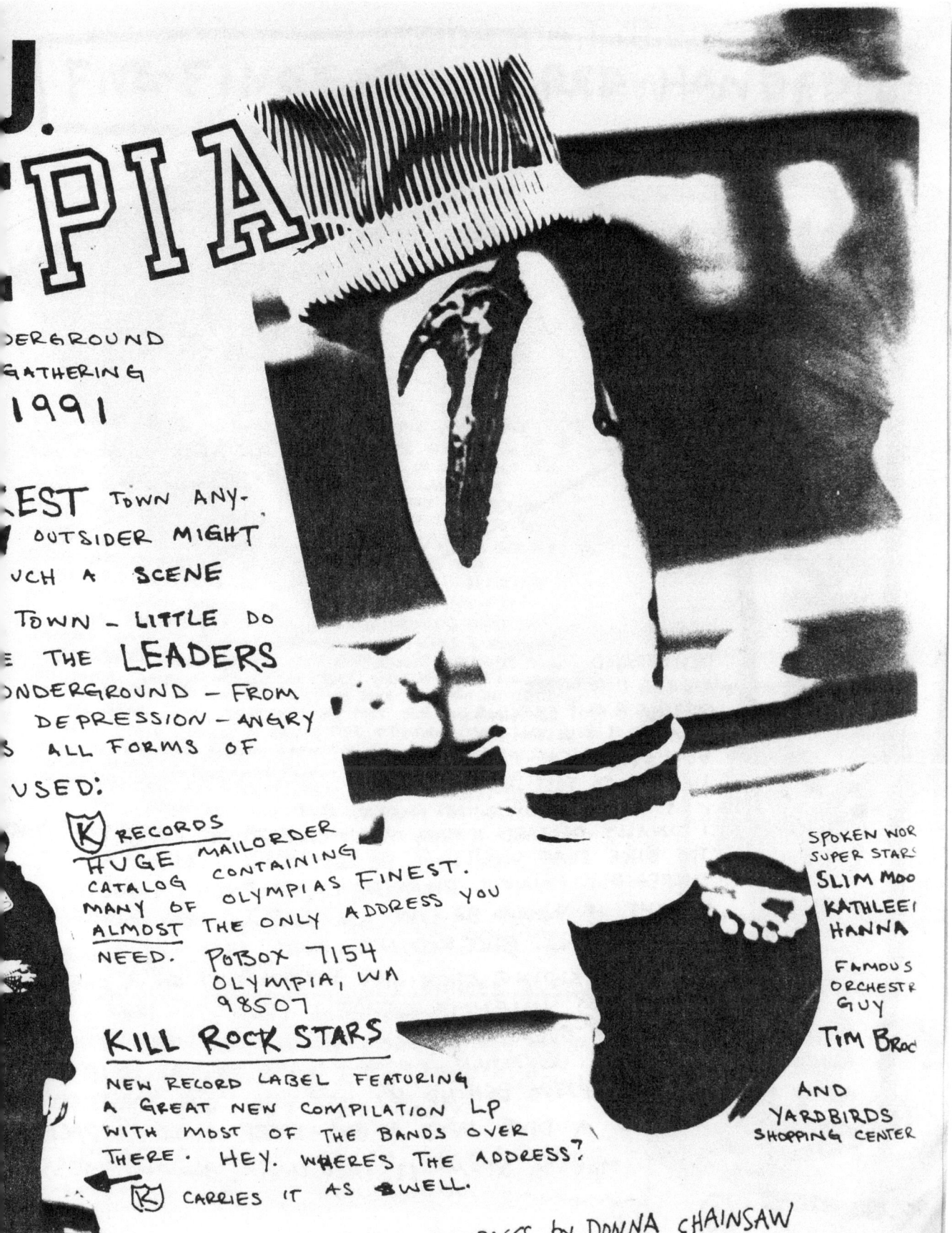

J.
PIA
UNDERGROUND
GATHERING
1991

EST TOWN ANY-
OUTSIDER MIGHT

UCH A SCENE

TOWN — LITTLE DO
THE LEADERS
UNDERGROUND — FROM
DEPRESSION — ANGRY
ALL FORMS OF

USED:

Ⓚ RECORDS
HUGE MAILORDER
CATALOG CONTAINING
MANY OF OLYMPIAS FINEST.
ALMOST THE ONLY ADDRESS YOU
NEED. PO BOX 7154
OLYMPIA, WA
98507

KILL ROCK STARS

NEW RECORD LABEL FEATURING
A GREAT NEW COMPILATION LP
WITH MOST OF THE BANDS OVER
THERE. HEY. WHERES THE ADDRESS?
Ⓚ CARRIES IT AS SWELL.

SPOKEN WOR
SUPER STARS
SLIM MOO
KATHLEE
HANNA

FAMOUS
ORCHESTR
GUY

TIM BROC

AND
YARDBIRDS
SHOPPING CENTER

PAGES BY DONNA CHAINSAW

Mudflap, no. 1, 1991
Photocopy, saddle stitched, yellow paper wrappers,
8½ × 7 in. (21.6 × 17.8 cm)
Collection Philip Aarons and Shelley Fox Aarons

Robert Ford (with Trent Adkins and Lawrence Warren)

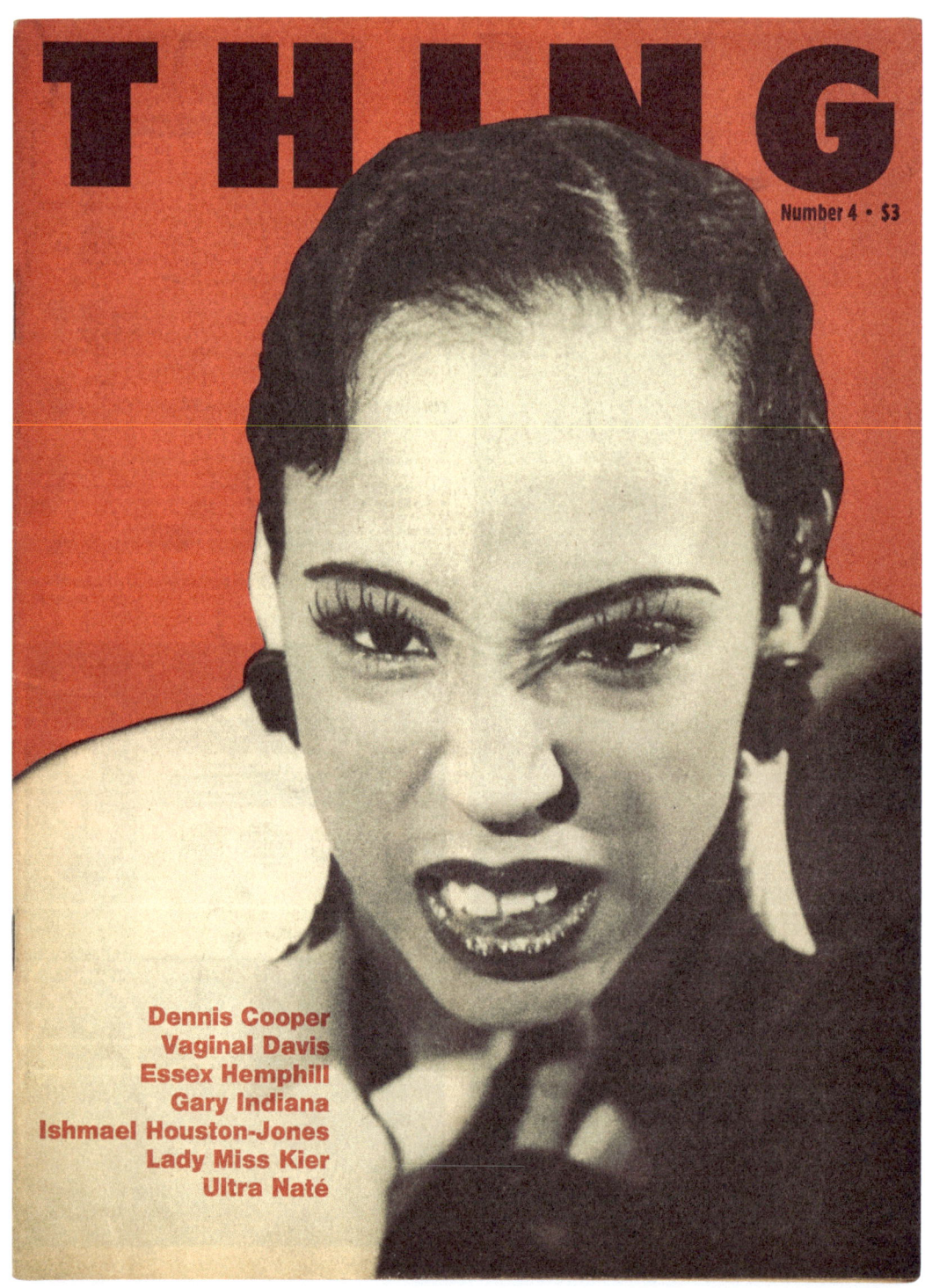

Thing, no. 4, Spring 1991
Offset, saddle stitched, color offset wrappers,
10 5/8 × 7 7/8 in. (27 × 20 cm)
Collection Steve Lafreniere

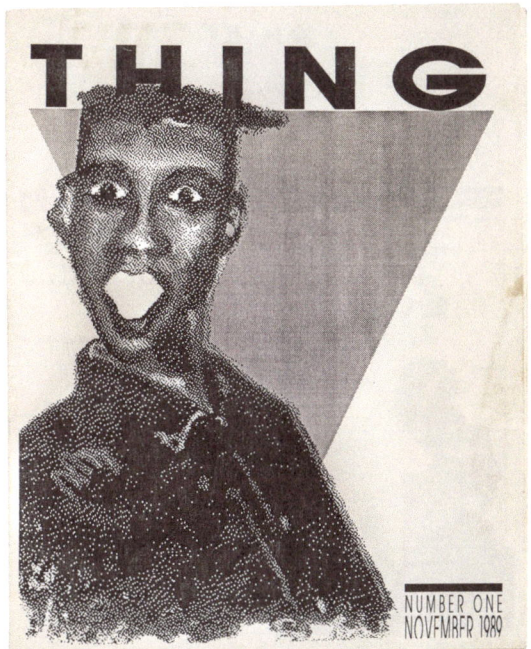

Thing, no. 1, November 1989
Photocopy, saddle stitched,
8 ⅝ × 7 1/16 in. (21.9 × 17.9 cm)
Collection Steve Lafreniere

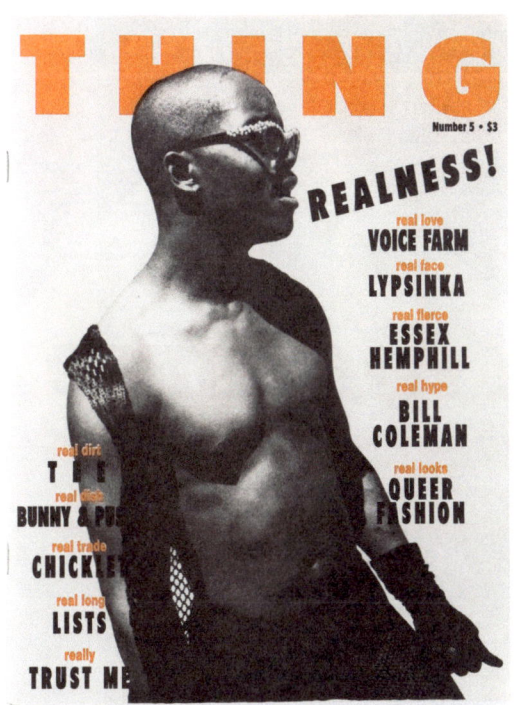

Thing, no. 5, Fall 1991
Offset, saddle stitched, color offset wrappers,
10 ½ × 8 in. (26.7 × 20.3 cm)
Collection Steve Lafreniere

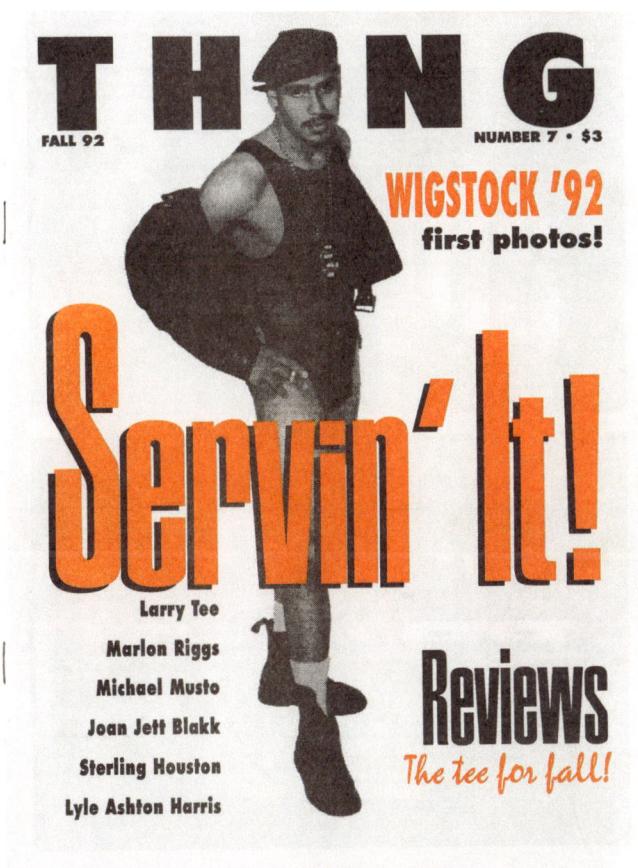

Thing, no. 7, Fall 1992
Offset, saddle stitched, color offset wrappers,
10 ½ × 8 in. (26.7 × 20.3 cm)
Collection Steve Lafreniere

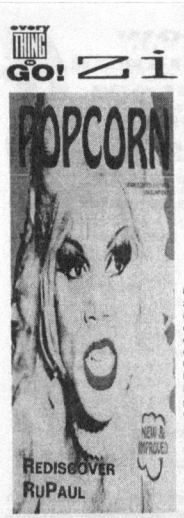

GO! zine

POPCORN

REVIEWS

REDISCOVER RuPaul

Many years ago, before *Thing* magazine, before *Think Ink* magazine, before *Planet Roc*, there was the idea for a music magazine to record and promote all the DJ drama that is the stay of our club-going, disco dancing lives in Chicago. We were gonna call it *BPM*. Now, finally, there is *Crossfade*, covering as much of the Chicago underground (and other) dance music scene as possible. Terry Martin's baby. I never thought I'd live to see it! Now *Thing* doesn't have to pass as "Chicago's coolest hip hop paper!" 2151 W. Division/Chicago IL 60622

— Trent Adkins

Much like its food namesake, *Popcorn* magazine is light and fluffy, crunchy and delightfully habit forming. Atlanta has long been a mecca of entertainment and personalities with inimitably authentic Southern charm. Here's the news of all the southern belles and bellettes that follow Lady Bunny, RuPaul, Lurleen Wallis, Daisy Chain, Larry Tee, The American Music Show and Funtone Records, The Pop Tarts, Mr. Chuck, DeAundra Peek and the gang and on and on. And right now, it's the only place where you'll find the genius Betty Jack DeVine, *Popcorn*'s resident columnist and fabulous Thing-about-the-globe. Did she ever write a society column for The County Herald? 325 Edgewood/Atlanta GA 31312

— Trent Adkins

#1 BITCH QUEEN

Hey kool girlz who want to do it for themselves... *Bitch Queen*'ll show you how, and then some. It'll leave you wondering what to make of Mz. Michelle who puts out (ahem) the first issue of her zine (methinks she's another bichick, but Fire Chick does have a bias, of course.) There are great blood and guts directions on how to take a hemorrhage to get a free abortion. (Especially useful in years to come.) Good chick positive interview with a Guerrillo Girl. The whole zine is very — fuck "asking" — fuck just "taking back" — this is more like "attack!" *Bitch Queen* has a pro sex worker piece, reprints galore on many issues political with regards to women, queers and racism. You can read where to spit some venom at Nike for a particularly condescending and sexist ad campaign they wrought and thrust into our world. If that sounds too PC for your tastes, look and slobber over some cute sponky bondage-girl graphics, or turn to the page where she says that mace and whistles are ladylike wimp shit for stopping rapists — more of that age old argument that makes girlz take the nice way, the non-violent way, to stop a fuck-er — Bitch Queen wants you packin' a pistol, a shotgun, or a .38 special. Hail the Bitch girlz, she knows what she wants. Send it to her — she's begging for submission(s). (Fire Chick tends to have a one track mind.) box 1443/Boston MA 02117

— Fire Chick

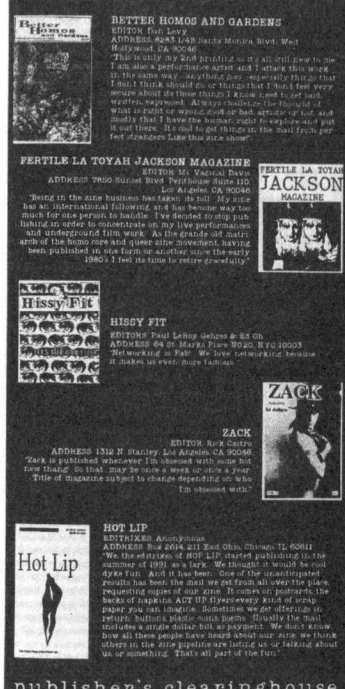

BETTER HOMOS AND GARDENS
EDITOR Dell Levy
ADDRESS 8243 1/2 Santa Monica Blvd, West Hollywood, CA 90046

FERTILE LA TOYAH JACKSON MAGAZINE
EDITOR Ms Vaginal Davis
ADDRESS 7850 Sunset Blvd Penthouse Suite 110, Los Angeles, CA 90046

HISSY FIT
EDITORS Paul LeRoy Gehres & Ed Oh
ADDRESS 64 St Marks Place No 20, NYC 10003

ZACK
EDITOR Rick Castro
ADDRESS 1312 N Stanley, Los Angeles, CA 90046

HOT LIP
EDITRIX Anonymous
ADDRESS Box 2614, 211 East Ohio, Chicago IL 60611

publisher's clearinghouse

Zinesters who are up on their history claim that the first zine was a science fiction fanzine published in the 1930's called *The Comet*. It came about in much the same way as zines do today—by people who didn't feel that the larger magazines were addressing their particular concerns or areas of interest. During the 70's & 80's this amateur underground activity was given a big shot in the arm with the introduction of accessible and cheap photocopying machines. Now anyone could be a publisher and their views and opinions were free to circle the globe.

These statements have been selected from some of the queer zines submitted to an international zine show that the Aggressive School of Cultural Workers-Iowa Chapter is organizing in Iowa City. The show was planned to coincide with the Decentralized Worldwide Networker Congress 1992, a call for alternative cultural producers to meet and network, within and between other communities, to strengthen the bonds between them and to plan alternative cultural strategies for the coming decade.

As part of the call for submissions for the show, editors were asked to submit a short statement on their "...thoughts/views, and experiences of zines and networking." It's been surprising how many people have put pen to paper to describe their experiences of doing zines, the statements succinctly encompass the range of responses received from other editors coming out of very different communities and concerns.

As of late July the show consists of about 200 zines from 14 different countries. The submission deadline was September 1st, but we'll accept zines throughout the length of the show. The show will be open each Saturday during September from 10:00AM–4:00PM at Subspace. If you are unable to attend at these times feel free to call us at (319) 351-3035 and alternative arrangements for you to view the show can be organized. If you are interested in receiving a copy of the catalogue for the show drop us a line and we'll contact you when it's available.
SUBSPACE • 221 W. BENTON • IOWA CITY IA 52246

— Stephen Perkins

---

letter to the DEAD

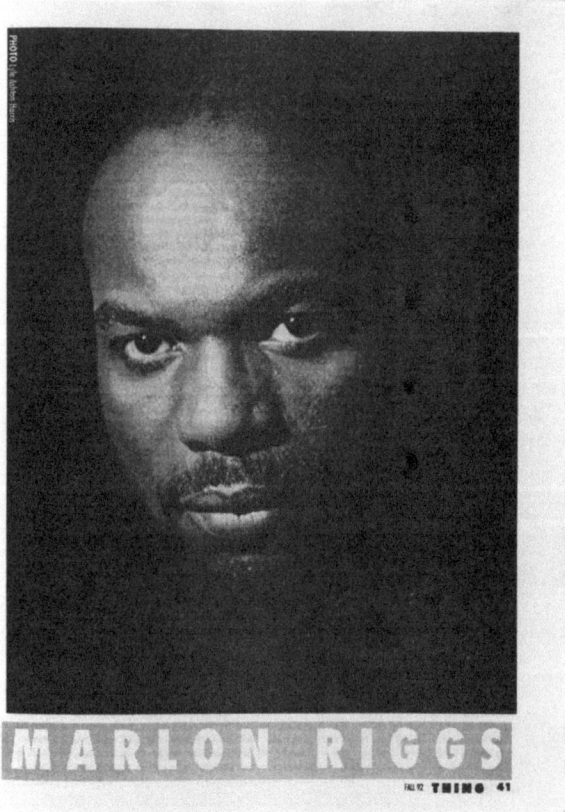

MARLON RIGGS

Thing, no. 7, Fall 1992
Offset, saddle stitched, color offset wrappers, 10½ × 8 in. (26.7 × 20.3 cm)
Collection Steve Lafreniere

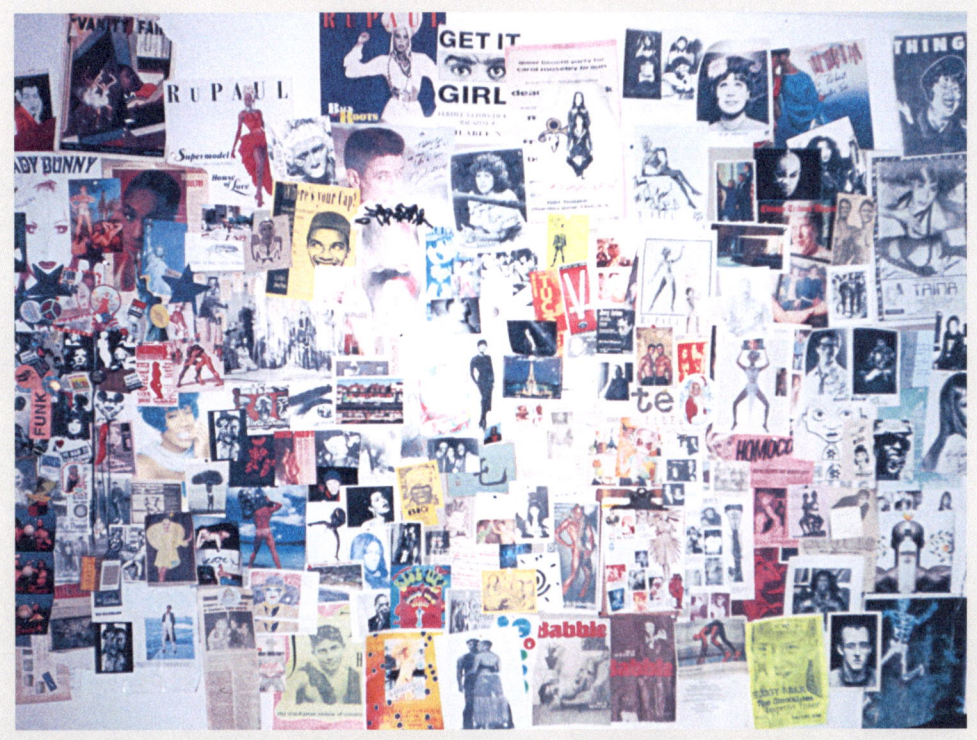

Collage of images on a wall of the *Thing* magazine office,
Chicago, Illinois, ca. 1990
Chromogenic print, 4 × 6 in. (10.2 × 15.2 cm)
Chicago History Museum, ICHi-182757

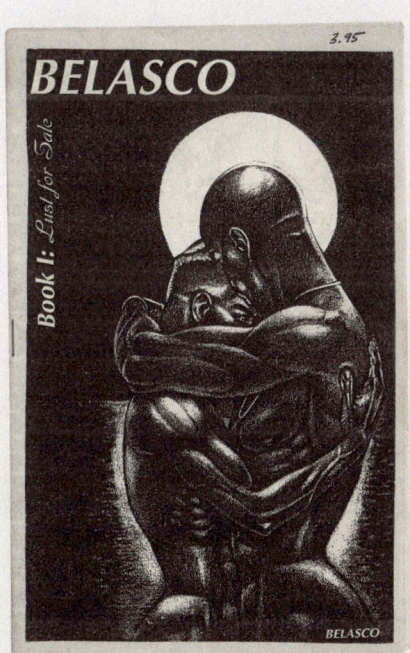

Belasco
Book 1: Lust for Sale, ca. 1990
Photocopy, saddle stitched, 8½ × 5⅝ in. (21.6 × 14.3 cm)
Collection Steve Lafreniere

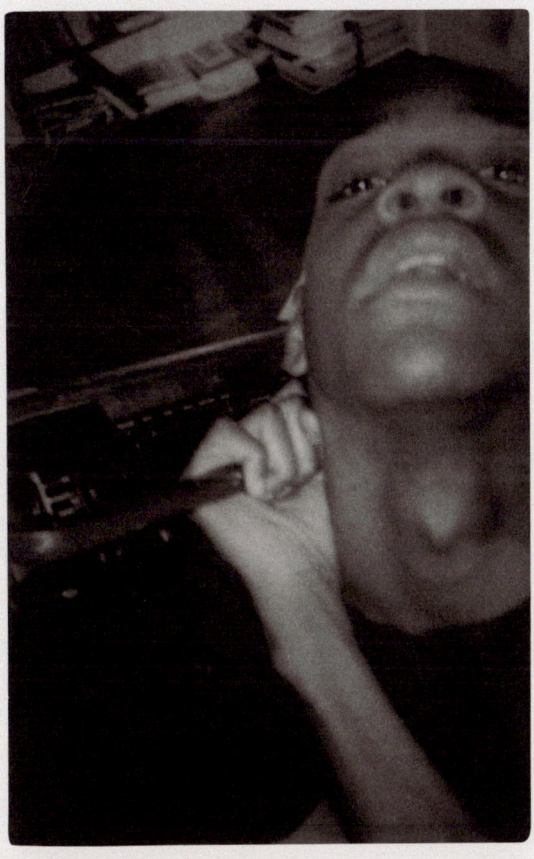

Lyle Ashton Harris
Postcard to Robert Ford, 1992
Chromogenic print, 4 × 6 in. (10.2 × 15.2 cm)
Chicago History Museum, ICHi-182756

189

Steve Lafreniere

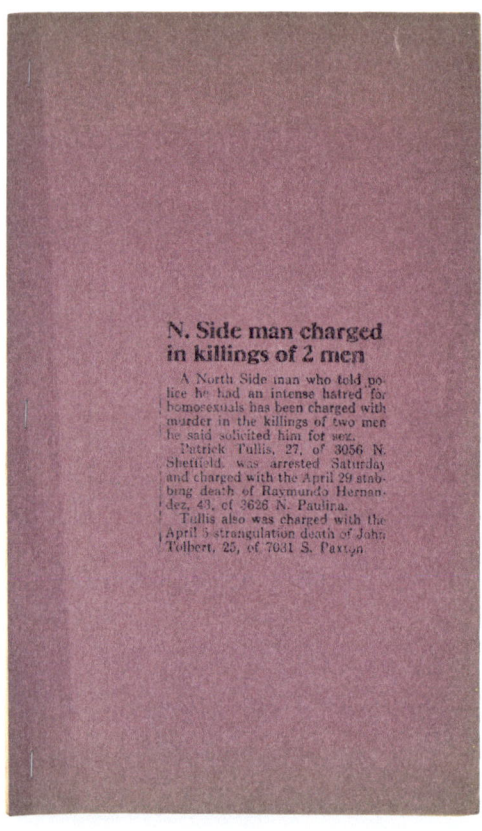

The Gentlewomen of California, no. 3, 1990
Photocopy, side stapled, violet construction
paper covers, 14 × 8 ½ in. (35.6 × 21.6 cm)
Collection Steve Lafreniere

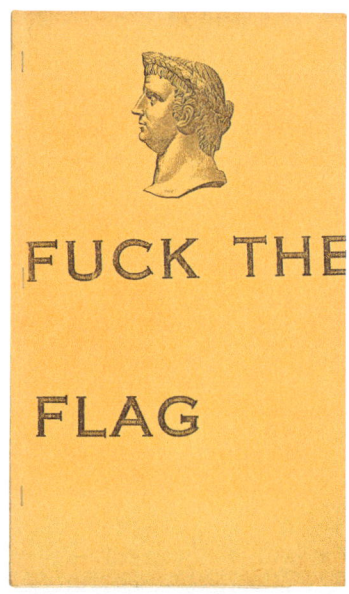

The Gentlewomen of California, no. 2, 1990
Photocopy, side stapled, yellow construction
paper covers, 14 × 8 ½ in. (35.6 × 21.6 cm)
Collection Steve Lafreniere

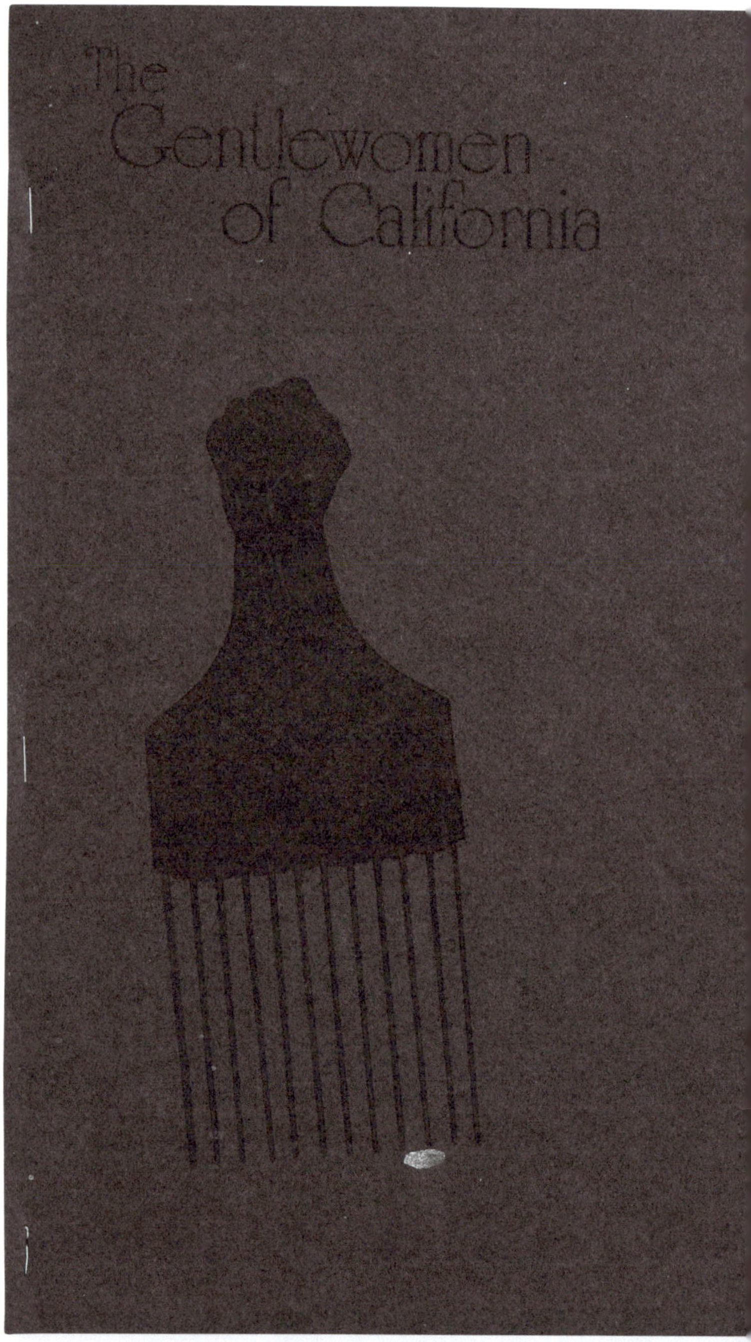

The Gentlewomen of California, no. 1, 1989
Photocopy, side stapled, black construction
paper covers, 13 ¾ × 8 ½ in. (34.9 × 21.6 cm)
Collection Steve Lafreniere

Hudson

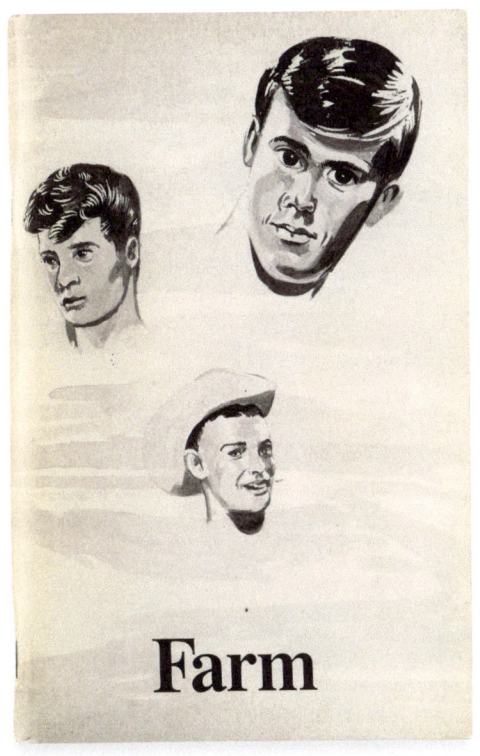

Farm, no. 1, 1990
Offset, saddle stitched, 8½ × 5⅝ in. (21.6 × 14.3 cm)
Collection Philip Aarons and Shelley Fox Aarons

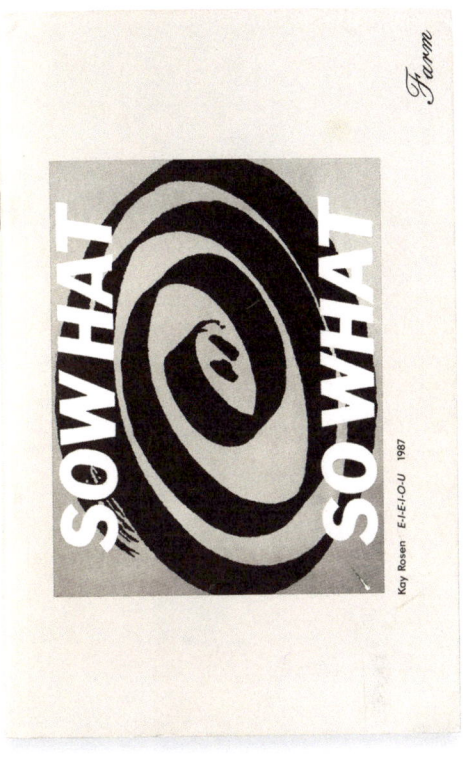

Farm, no. 2, 1990
Offset, saddle stitched, 8½ × 5⅝ in. (21.6 × 14.3 cm)
Collection Philip Aarons and Shelley Fox Aarons

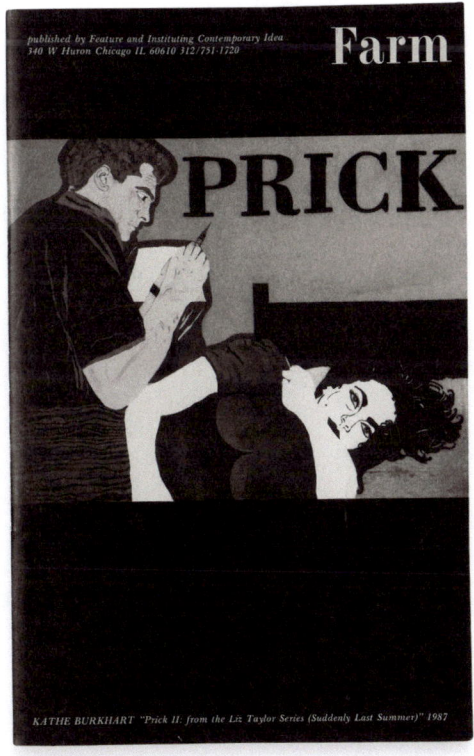

Farm, no. 3, 1991
Offset, saddle stitched, 8½ × 5⅝ in. (21.6 × 14.3 cm)
Collection Philip Aarons and Shelley Fox Aarons

SPEW: The Homographic Convergence

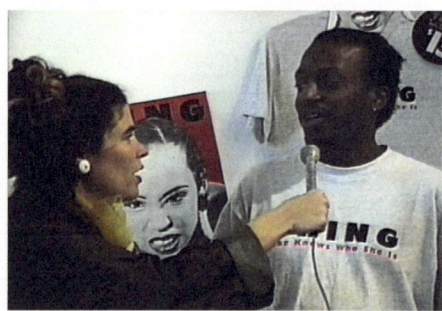

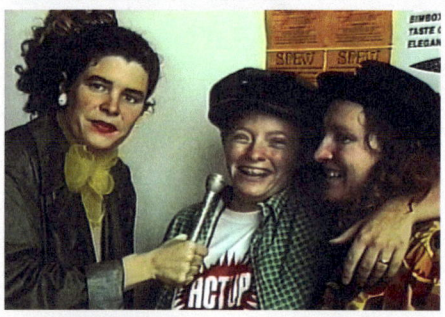

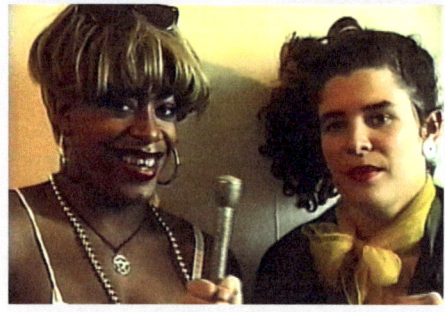

Mary Patten
Stills from *Hokey Sapp Does SPEW*, 1991
Pictured with performer Kate Schechter (top to bottom):
Robert Ford, Sadie Benning and Suzie Silver, and
Joan Jett Black
Producer: Steve Lafraniere
Video; color, sound; 59 min., 56 sec.
Collection Mary Patten

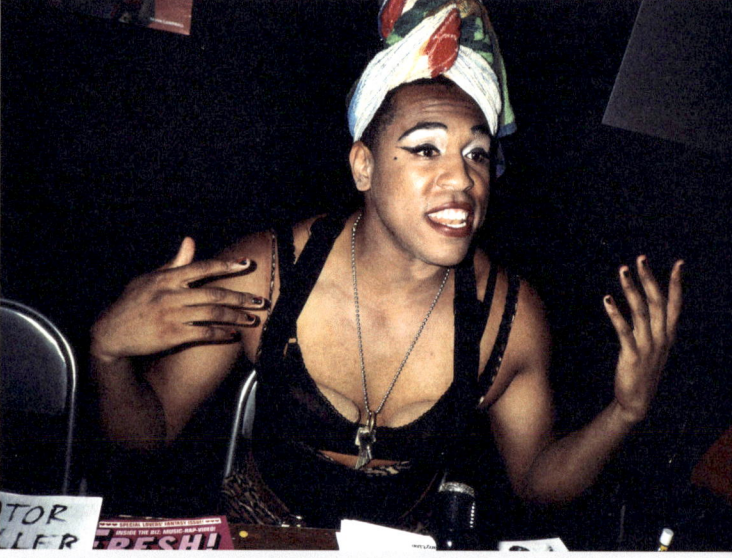

Lyle Ashton Harris
Vaginal Davis at SPEW, 1992
Chromogenic print, 15 × 20 11/16 in. (38.1 × 52.6 cm)
Collection the artist

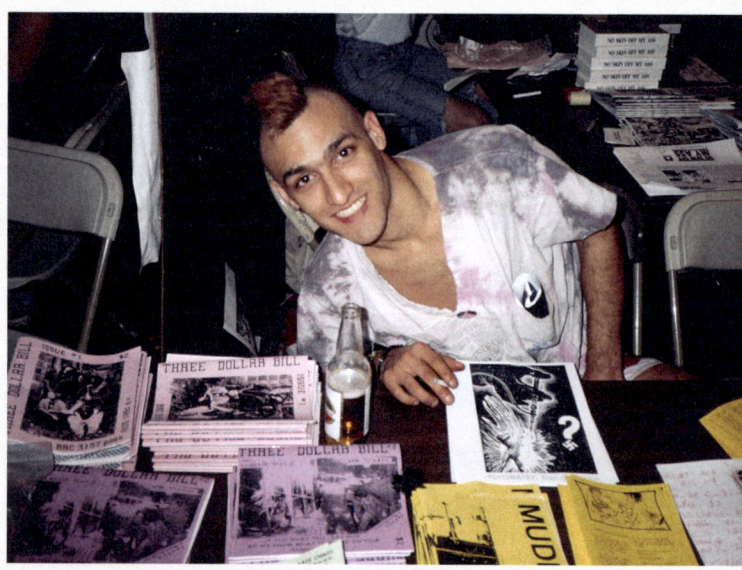

Lyle Ashton Harris
Deke at SPEW, 1992
Chromogenic print, 15 × 20 11/16 in. (38.1 × 52.6 cm)
Collection the artist

•Most zine publishers are willing

SPEW²

FEBRUARY 28, 29 & MARCH 1, 1992
L.A.C.E., LOS ANGELES, CALIFORNIA

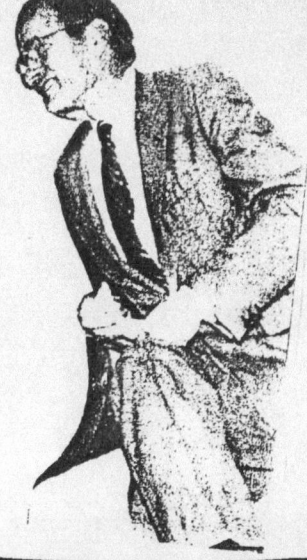

Are you ashamed to ask—but would like more information on orgasm? Face lifts? Rape? Contraceptives? Bashful kidneys? Homosexuality? Constipation? Frigidity? Shyness?

saturday, february 29

fair spew

lace
1804 industrial street
los angeles

12 noon to 6 p.m.

editors from:

bimbox
    screambox
fagazine
    whorezine
girl jock
    sin bros.
su madre
diseased pariah news
  more fine zines

8:00 p.m.
cabaret spew

deaundra peek

cholita!
(the female menudo)
w/ vaginal creme davis
joan jett blakk
(presidential candidate)
tribe 8
    geko
blast off
(the lesbian clown

and more

friday, february 28

opening nite party:
club spew

a co-production with
lace
jeffrey hilbert
(sin bros.
and sit & spin)
richard glatzer
(trade)

featuring:

hole

glue

park plaza hotel
los angeles

sunday, march 1

spew at 2

filmforum and lace present

seedy celluloid from the zine scene

shred of sex & hard core home movie
greta snyder
bill daniel/mudflap

boy/girl
bruce la bruce/jd's
sexbombs
candyland productions

burning shorts
bill brown/not bored

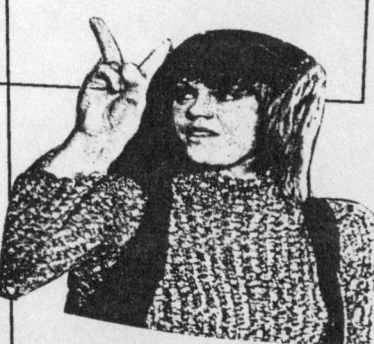

•If you have any problems with a zine please let us know.

Linda Simpson

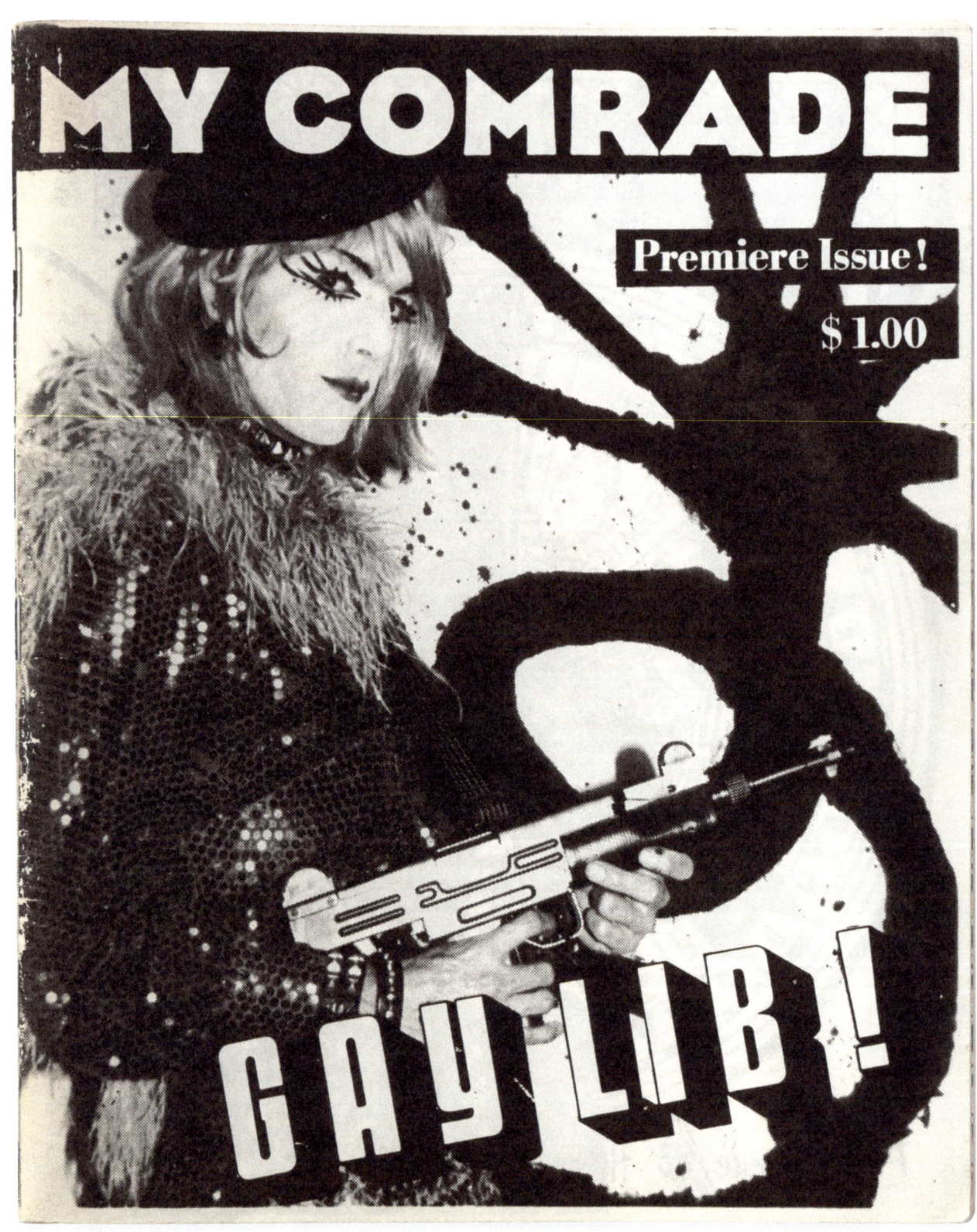

↑ → *My Comrade*, no. 1, 1987
Photocopy, saddle stitched, 8 ½ × 7 1/16 in. (21.6 × 17.9 cm)
Collection Steve Lafreniere

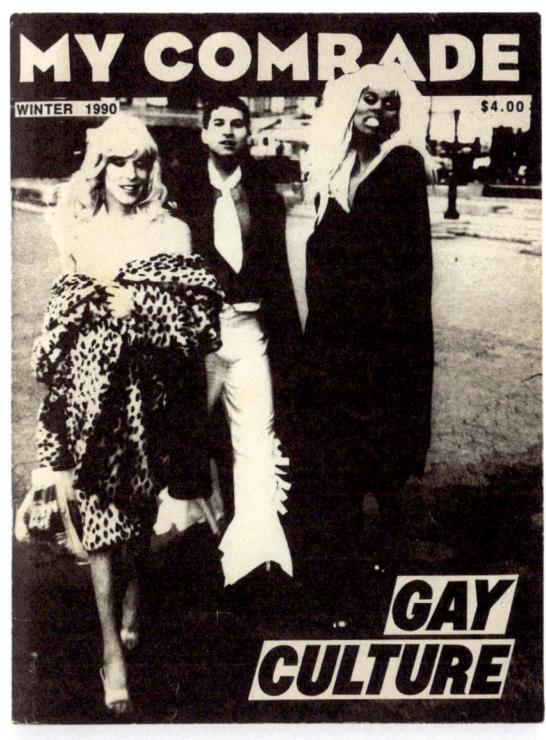

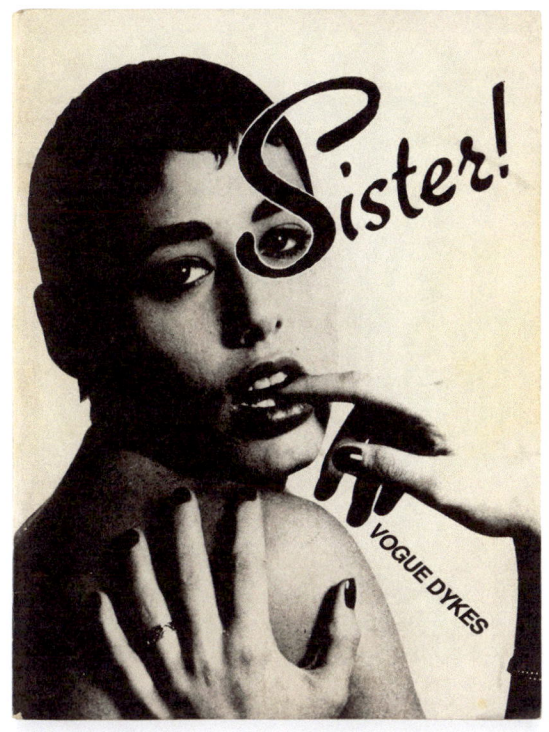

My Comrade/Sister!, no. 6, Winter 1990
Offset, saddle stitched, 10 ¾ × 8 ¼ in. (27.3 × 21 cm)
Collection Steve Lafreniere

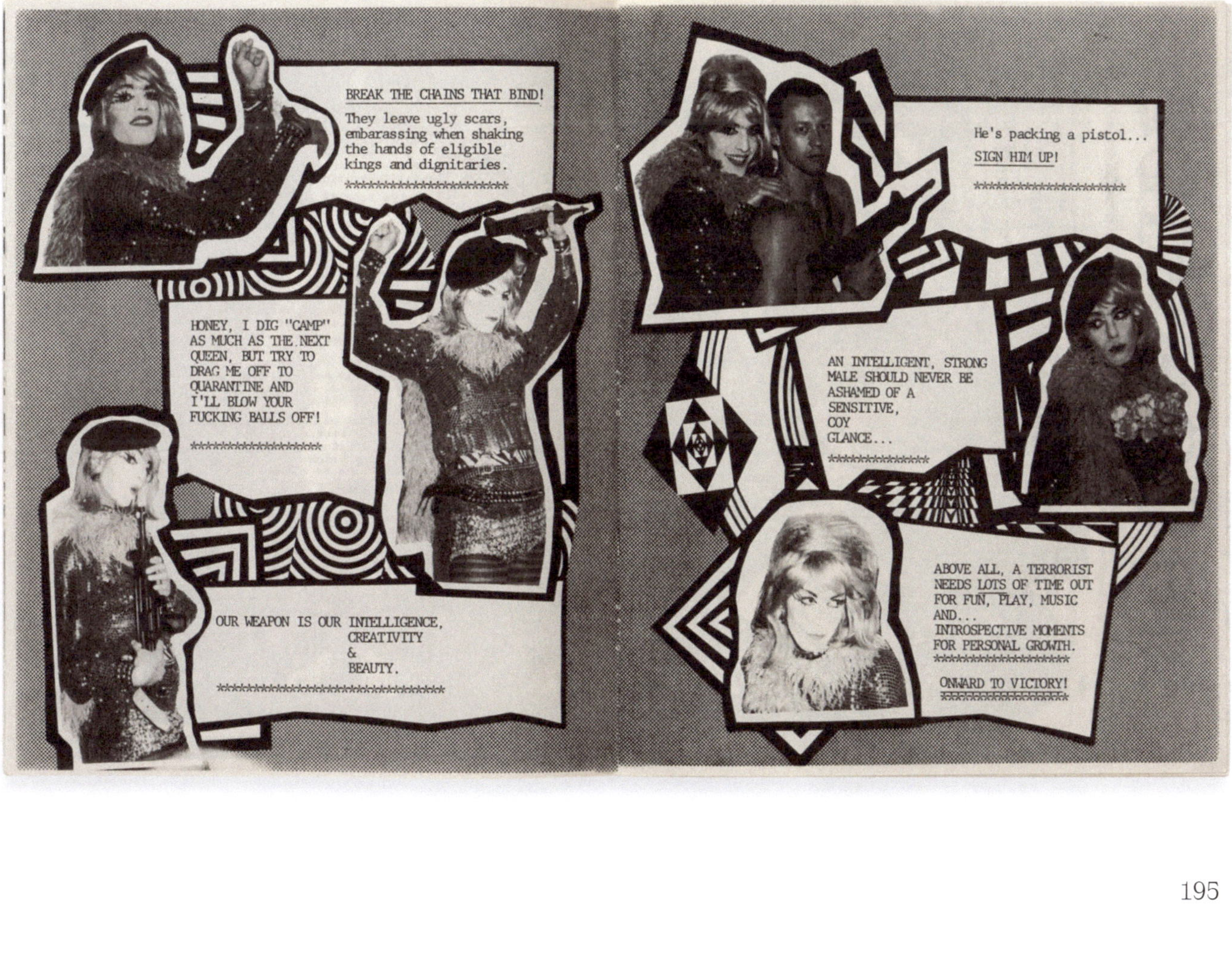

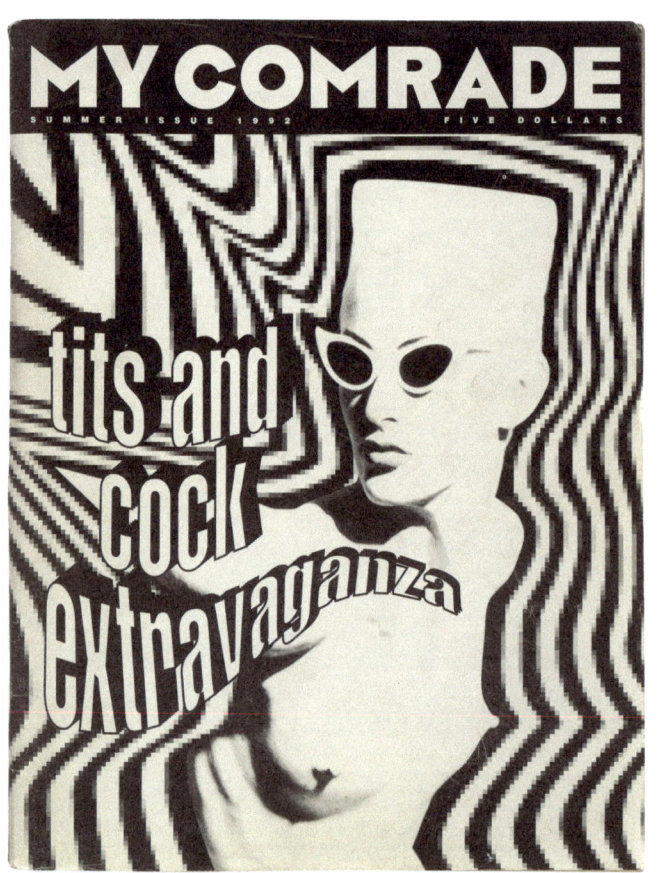

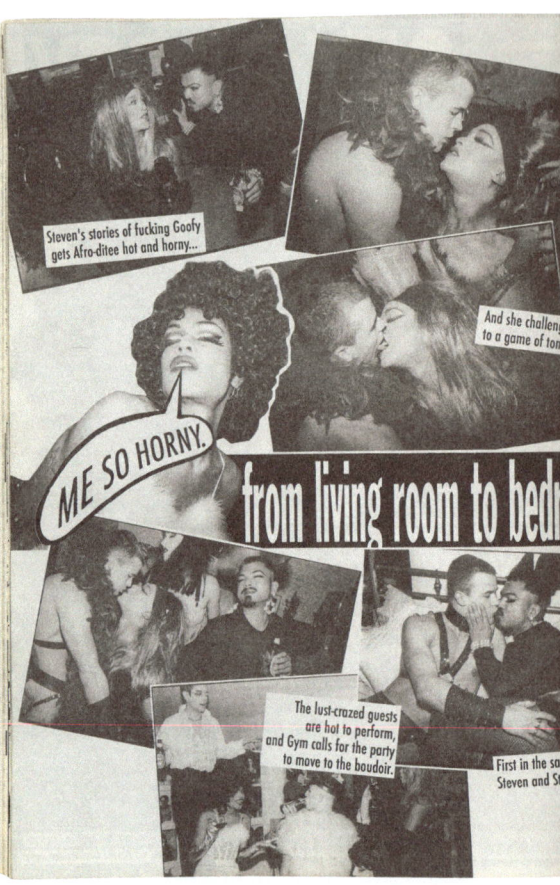

My Comrade, no. 9, Summer 1992
Offset, saddle stitched, 12 ¼ × 9 ½ (31.1 × 24.1 cm)
Collection Steve Lafreniere

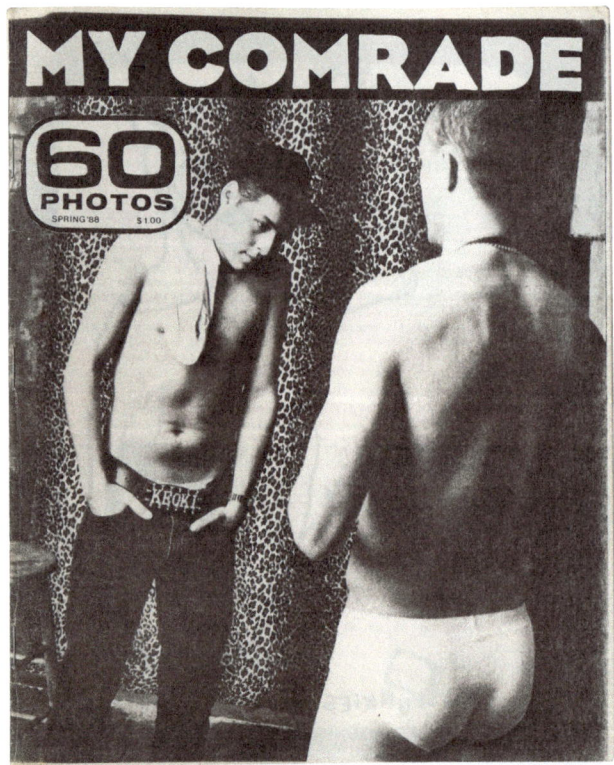

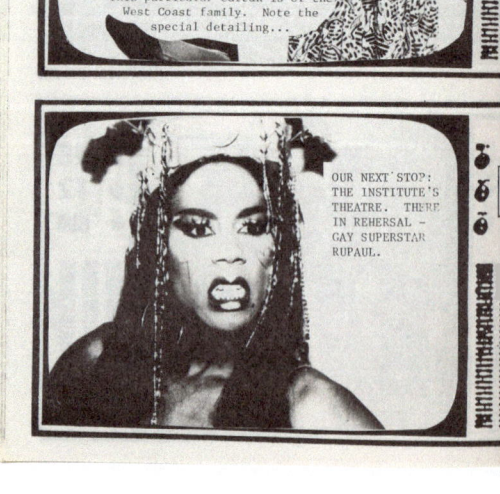

My Comrade, no. 3, Spring 1988
Photocopy, saddle stitched, 8 ½ × 7 1⁄16 in. (21.6 × 17.9 cm)
Collection Steve Lafreniere

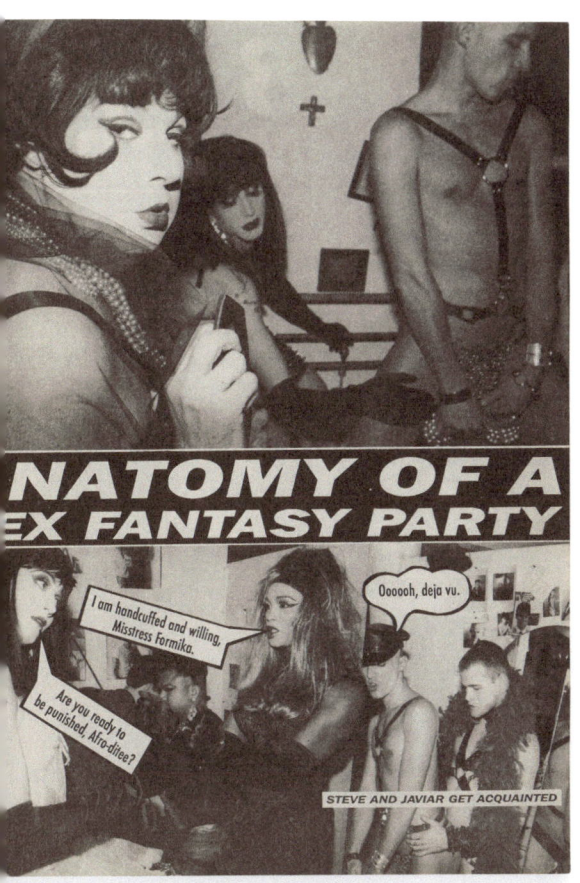

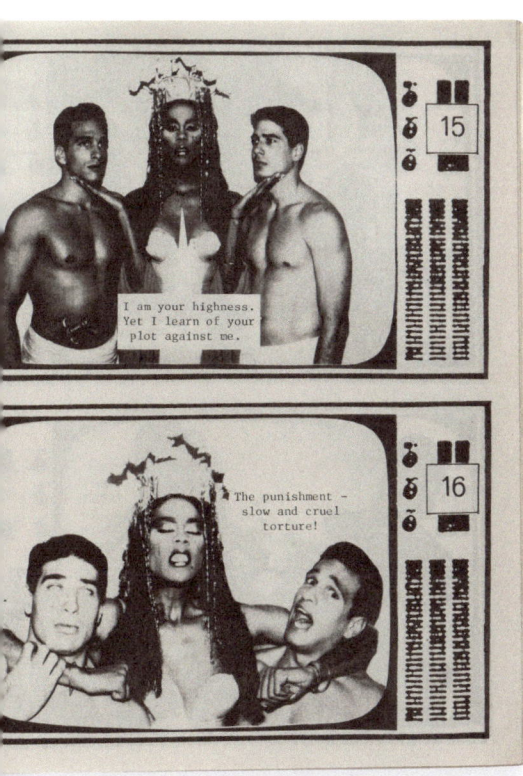

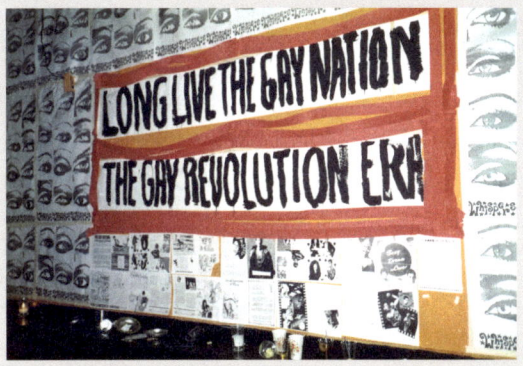

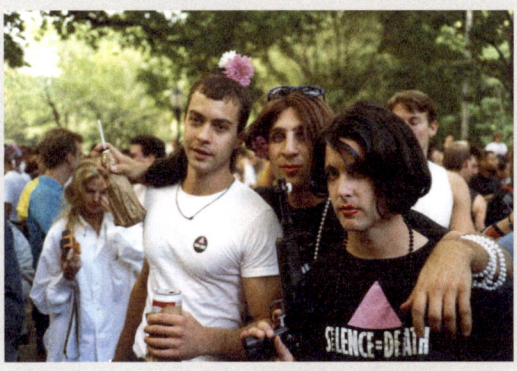

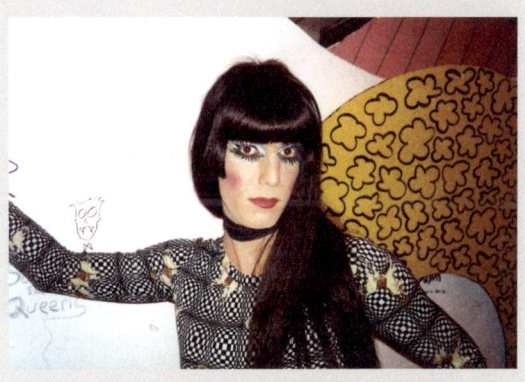

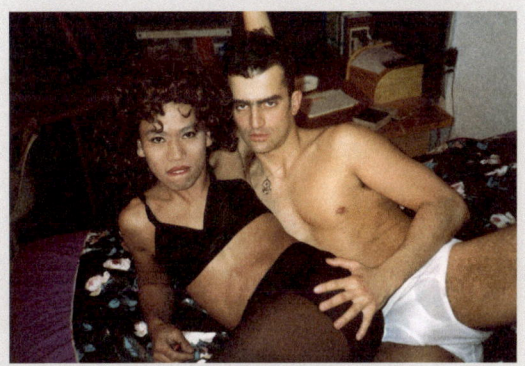

From *The Drag Explosion*, 1986–96
Digital slides, 195 color photographs, dimensions variable
Collection the artist

Glenn Belverio and Emily Nahmanson

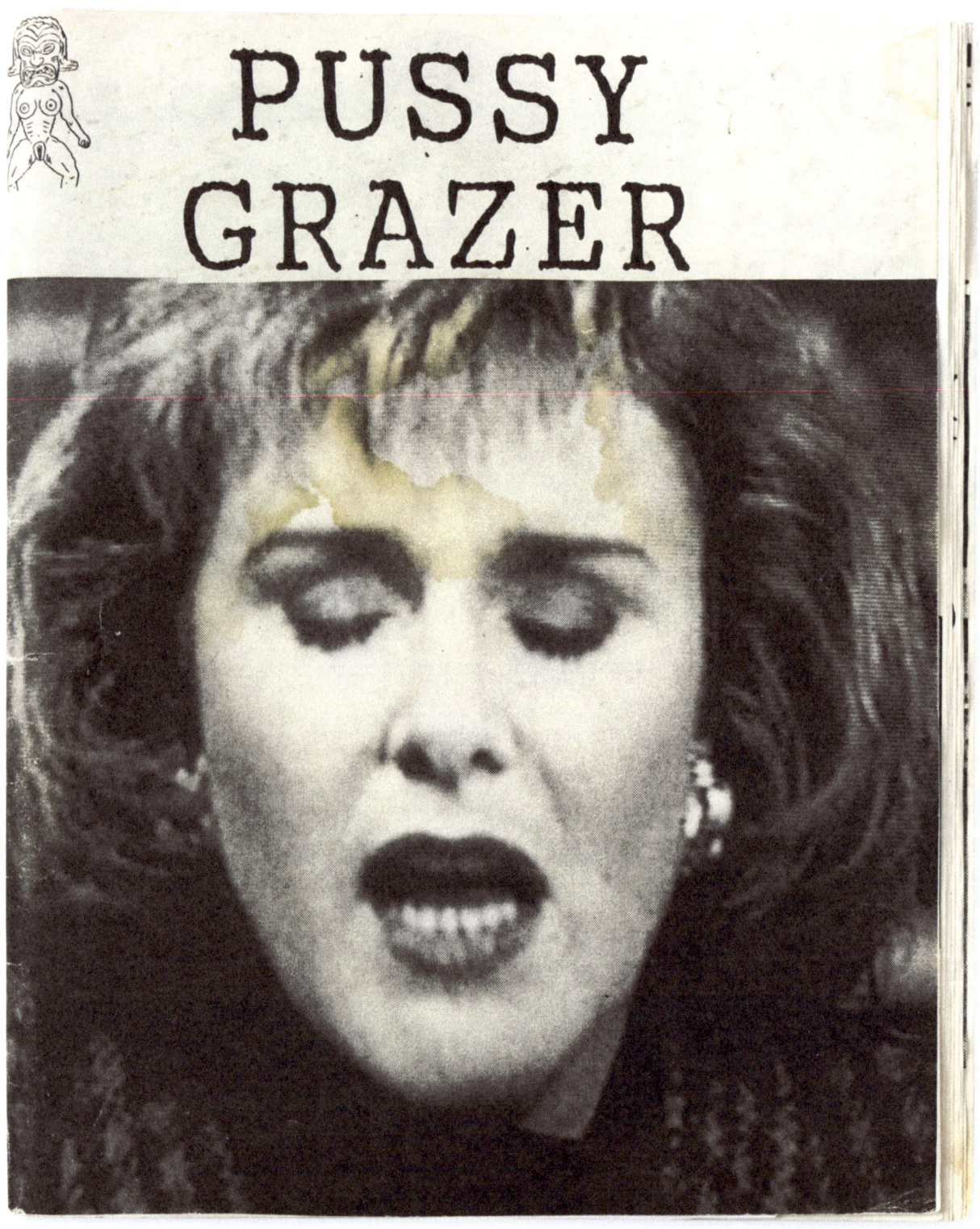

Pussy Grazer, no. 1, 1991
Photocopy, saddle stitched, 8 ½ × 7 in. (21.6 × 17.8 cm)
Collection Philip Aarons and Shelley Fox Aarons

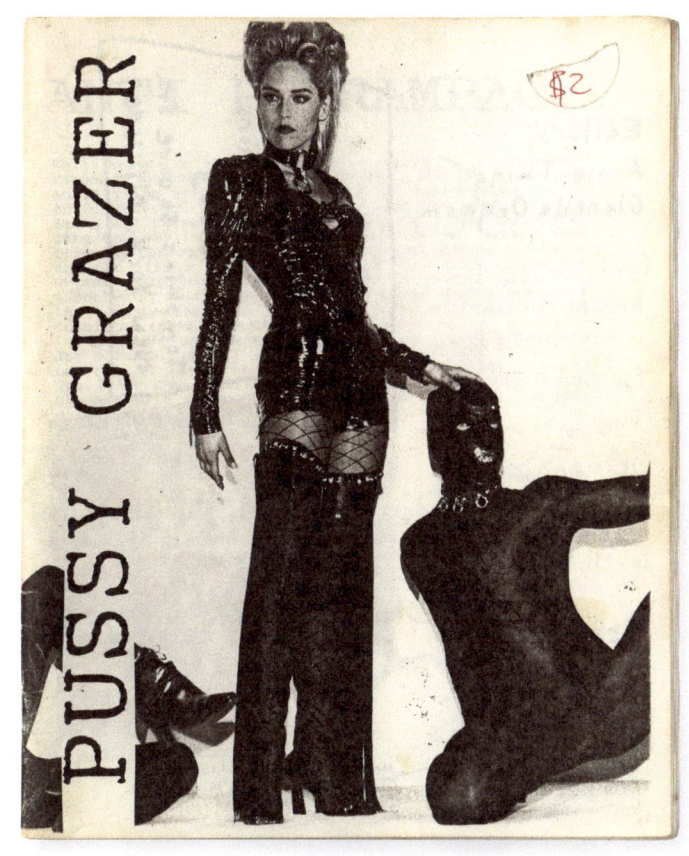

Pussy Grazer, no. 3, 1992
Photocopy, saddle stitched, 8 ½ × 7 in. (21.6 × 17.8 cm)
Collection Philip Aarons and Shelley Fox Aarons

MY FANZINE FRIENDS by GLENNDA ORGASM

This past leap-year weekend I was fortunate enough to leave the piss-smelling streets of NY for a too-brief visit to Los Angeles for the west coast premiere of the video I co-produced ("Gender Cruise on the Circle Line") and the next leg in the Pussy Grazer book tour (SPEW 2), both of which took place at LACE gallery. I found a lot of things to be bigger and better in sunny LA: instead of small, shitty apartments, Angelinos live in spacious houses, instead of Lady Bunny, LA has The Goddess Bunny and instead of sanitizing the realities of criminals, hustlers and psycho killers, many LA queers fetishize and embrace them.

As soon as I got off the plane I was whisked off to the Sissy Club where I was thrown into a room with fanzine editors such as Steve Lafreniere and Billy from Straight to Hell and other fabulous divas like Glen Meadmore and Deaundra Peek.

My Abbreviated Guide to People I Think You Should Know

Joan Jett Blakk - After hearing so much about each other, we were excited to finally meet in person at the Sissy Club. During the fanzine fair, Joan held a press conference for ABC News and announced her bid for presidency. Work that media, sister! My only problem now is I'm torn between voting for Joan or Eileen Myles (the 1st open lesbian official write-in candidate). If Joan wins, tho, she's promised me a position in her cabinet as Official Secretary of Drag Queen Gossip. (Stay tuned for a debate between Joan and Eileen on an up-coming episode of "The Brenda and Glennda Show"!)

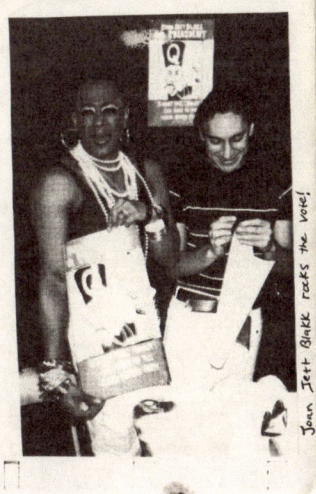

Joan Jett Blakk rocks the vote!

Klaus Von Brucker - Klaus and I did the tourist thing and made a trip to glamorous Hollywood Boulevard and checked out all the foot and hand prints at Grouman's Chinese Theater. We tried to pull a Lucy and Ethel by stealing Natalie Woods' footprints, but there were

too many people wathing. However I did manage to write GLENNDA ORGASM in black magic marker in one of the empty stars in the sidewalk. We managed to escape from the police by taking cover in the Hollywood Wax Musuem where we noticed that the replica of Kiss' Paul Stanley was displaying mucho pubic hair in his low-cut sequined outfit.

Vaginal Creme Davis - I finally met the sexational blacktress herself and i was not disappointed. Definitely one of the high points of SPEW was the appearance of her band CHOLITA-the female Menudo. Punky salsa with lyrics in Espanol y Ingles, Latino homeboy drag king go-go dancers who slammed their way through the crowd, and Vag's call-to-arms to overthrow the white power structure - CHOLITA is a force to be reckoned with. Fun and sexy, but also confrontational and dangerous, it made something like NY's Boy Bar look like The Lawrence Welk Show.

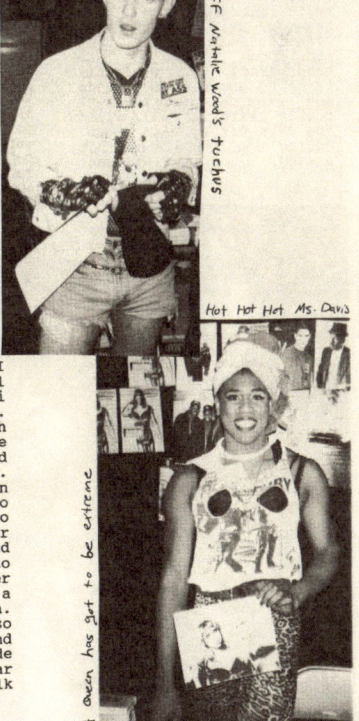

No shit off Natalie Wood's tuchus

Hot Hot Hot Ms. Davis

A Queen has got to be extreme

199

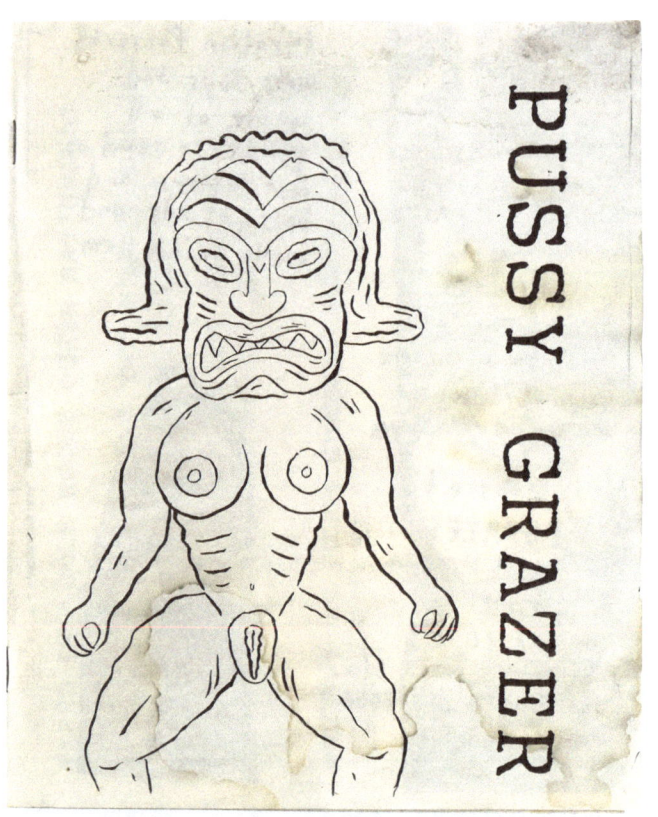

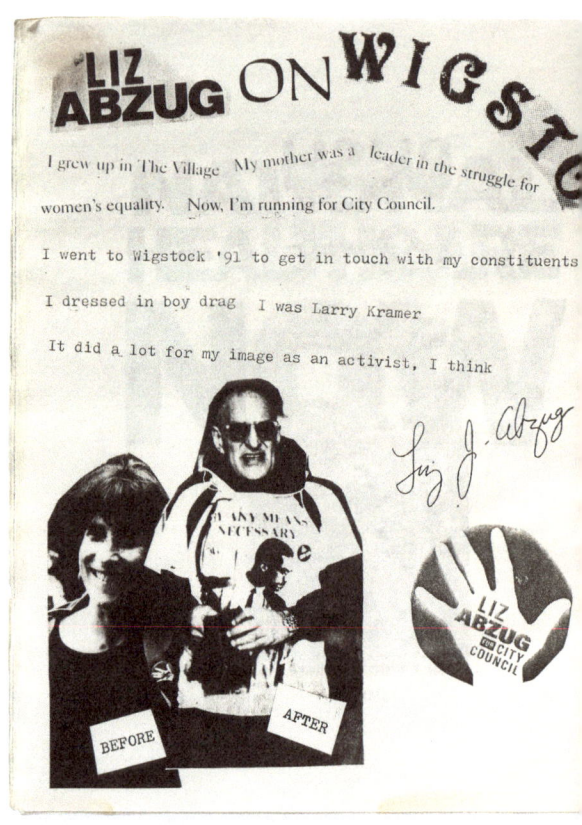

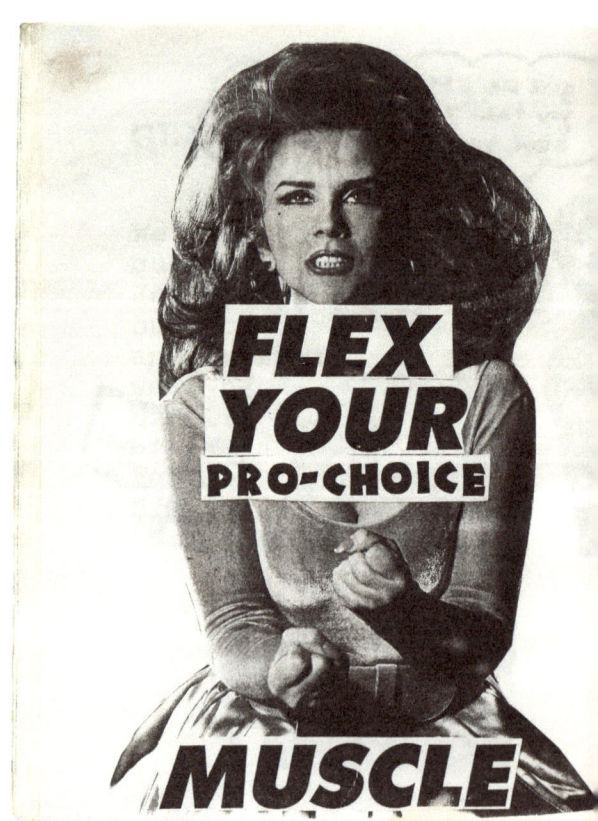

Pussy Grazer, no. 2, 1991
Photocopy, saddle stitched, 8 ½ × 7 in. (21.6 × 17.8 cm)
Collection Philip Aarons and Shelley Fox Aarons

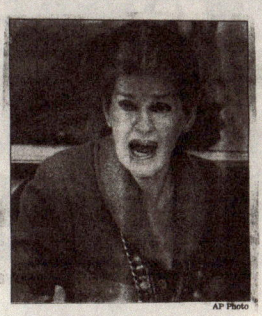

news

r has it that Pat Buckley
pping mad that she wasn't
to chair the Pediatric
Foundation(PAF)Benefit
Thursday. The gala event,
d by Veronica Prego, Dio-
arwick and Barbara Streis-
ill raise funds for the
ent victims of the disease.
rn my back on faggots and
es as much as Barbara does"
ey told PAF's publicist
rday "Besides, everyone
she's protecting that
son of hers from being
ed on his buttocks. He is
wn AIDS-carrier and soc-
needs to be protected from
Streisand's spokespeople
unavailable for comment at
time.

People are talking about
how Leona Helmsley allowed
the Empire State Building
to be lit lavendar for Lesbian and Gay Pride Day only
because she was threatened
with a lawsuit. "This is un-
true" says lesbian writer Pat
Califia, who claims to have
had an affair with Mrs. Helmsley. "She enjoys a good vaginal fisting or golden shower
as much as the next girl. The
building was lit by her request." Mrs. Helmsley would
not return our calls.

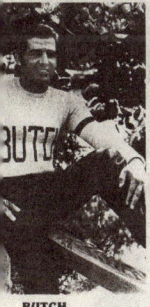

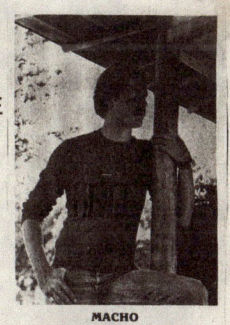

WHY I HATE MEN
by
A Man who doesn't hate himself

BUTCH   MACHO

world is fucked up because men own it and I hate men.
ate breeder men who kiss and fondle women in the street
ause I have to look at it and it makes me nauseous. But
lso hate fags because many of them are just as offen-
e as breeder men. I hate men who think they are absolv-
f of all sexism just because they're fags and aren't
re of their own misogyny. I hate men who aren't in
ch with their feminine side. I hate men who refuse to
ept the possibility of more than two genders. I hate
who talk to me in bars or at parties only until some-
they think is more attractive comes along. I really
e men, especially fags, who refuse to socialize with
en. I hate men who won't use condoms unless you insist
n it. I hate men who are selfish during sex, especially
s who think you are soley responsible for your own or-
m. I hate men who treat me like an object or a joke
n I am in drag. I hate men who think this article is
ut them and don't realize that I like them and would
e to suck their dicks.

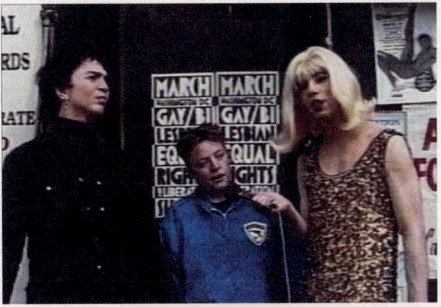

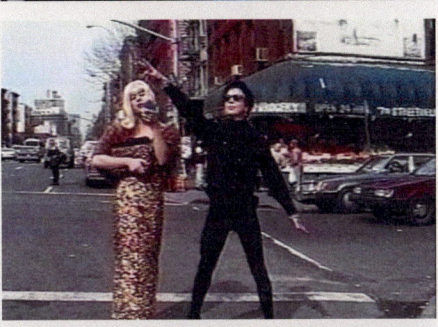

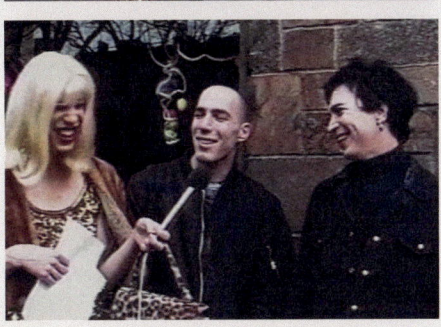

Glenn Belverio
Stills from *The Post Queer Tour*, 1993
Video; color, sound; 29 min.
Video Data Bank; School of the Art Institute of Chicago

Cory Roberts-Auli and W. Wayne Karr

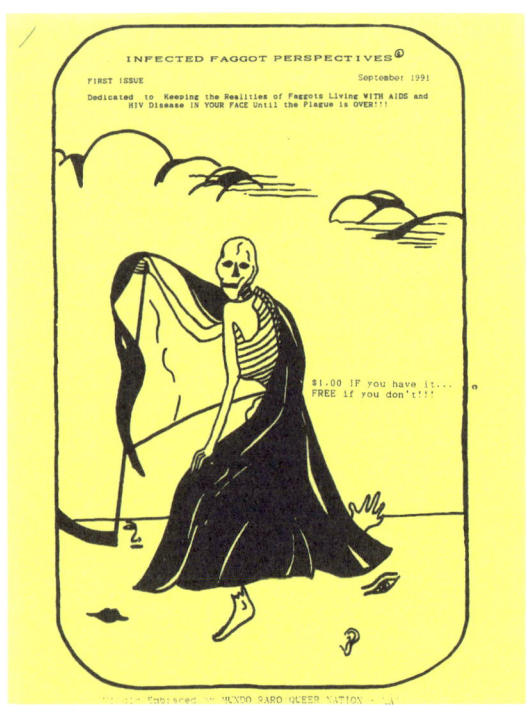

Infected Faggot Perspectives, no. 1, September 1991
Photocopy, corner stapled, yellow paper covers,
11 × 8 ½ in. (27.9 × 21.6 cm)
ONE Archives at the USC Libraries

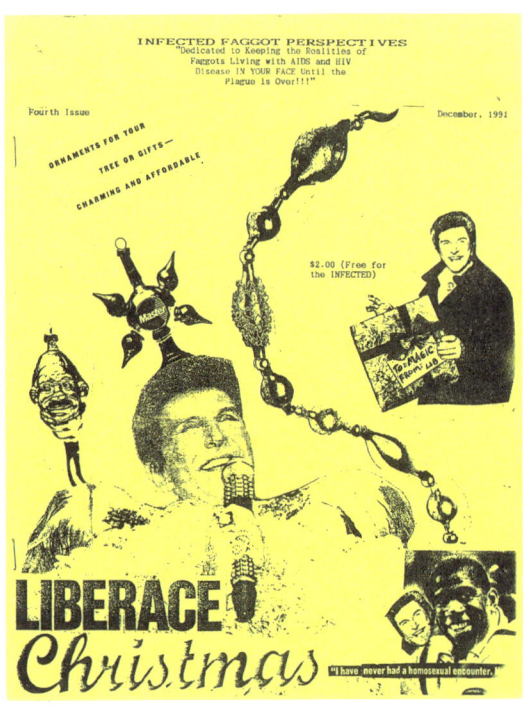

Infected Faggot Perspectives, no. 4, December 1991
Photocopy, side stapled, yellow paper covers,
11 × 8 ½ in. (27.9 × 21.6 cm)
ONE Archives at the USC Libraries

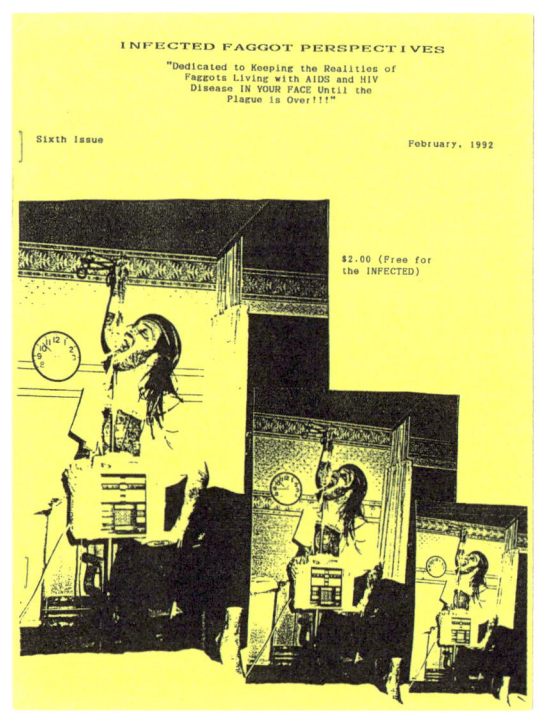

Infected Faggot Perspectives, no. 6, February 1992
Photocopy, side stapled, yellow paper covers,
11 × 8 ½ in. (27.9 × 21.6 cm)
ONE Archives at the USC Libraries

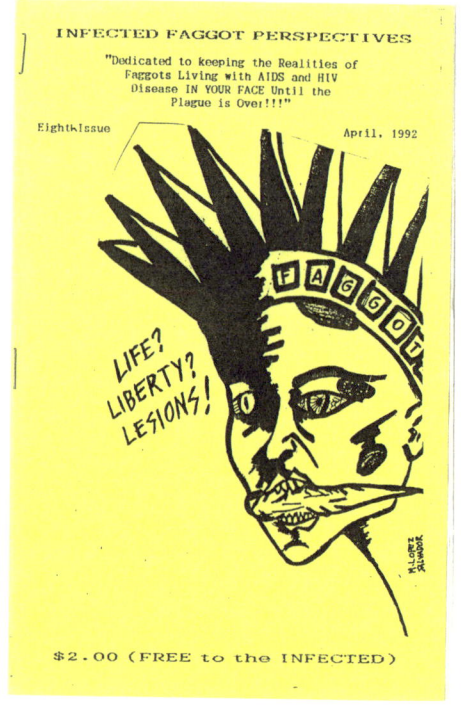

Infected Faggot Perspectives, no. 8, April 1992
Photocopy, saddle stitched, yellow paper wrappers,
8 ½ × 5 ½ in. (21.6 × 14 cm)
ONE Archives at the USC Libraries

Infected Faggot Perspectives, no. 12, December 1992–January 1993
Photocopy, saddle stitched, yellow paper wrappers,
8 ½ × 5 ½ in. (21.6 × 14 cm)
ONE Archives at the USC Libraries

INFECTED FAGGOT PERSPECTIVES

FIRST ISSUE   AUGUST 1991

Dedicated to Keeping the Realities of Faggots Living With Aids and HIV Disease IN YOUR FACE Until the Plague is Over !

AIDS-PHOBES MAKE ME PUKE !

I tell you I've been sick and YOU say "but you don't LOOK sick". (Tell me...just HOW does SICK look ?)

I tell you I'm not feeling well and you suggest I go to the Doctor. (Why don't you ask me what it is I'm FEELING ?)

I ask you what you've done for AIDS and Persons living with HIV infection and you tell me that you did the Dance-a-thon last year. (BIG FUCKING DEAL !)

I tell you that ANOTHER friend died last week and between my tears you tell me how he's better off now. (How the fuck do YOU know ? Why must you try to difuse my emotions by placating me with your spineless, empty, meaningliss BULLSHIT ?)

I tell you that the definition of AIDS is being expanded October first to enable more people to access benefits and you say "oh, really...". (Why the fuck didn't YOU tell ME about this ?)

You have kissed me on the lips for 10 years but three days of hospital and PCP and your lips can barely touch my cheek. (Don't even bother - it would be LESS offensive.)

You tell me about yet ANOTHER GREAT WORKSHOP for people living with AIDS that I should attend. (Aren't we ALL living with AIDS ? Have YOU nothing more to learn ? Don't you think perhaps - just perhaps - I'M a little more familiar with - and therefore require LESS education about - HIV disease ?)

I tell you about the ongoing battle with County, State and Federal Governments over funding for AIDS and HIV related issues and you tell me "I'm not into politics". (Are you into LIFE ? I don't think so. GO FUCK YOURSELF !)

I tell your your AIDS-PHOBIC and you say "show me how". (Well showing you AIN'T my priority - I'm fighting FOR MY LIFE...I guess you'll just have to try to figure it out ON YOUR OWN !)

When I ask you if you know just exactly ehat it is I want from you you just stare back at me rather stupidly. (Well stupid, it's the same thing ARETHA has been looking for for oh so many years !)

You say "let me know if there is anything I can do". I say why don't you start BY LISTENING TO WHAT I HAVE TO SAY !

(1)

Infected Faggot Perspectives, no. 1, September 1991
Photocopy, corner stapled, yellow paper covers,
11 × 8 ½ in. (27.9 × 21.6 cm)
ONE Archives at the USC Libraries

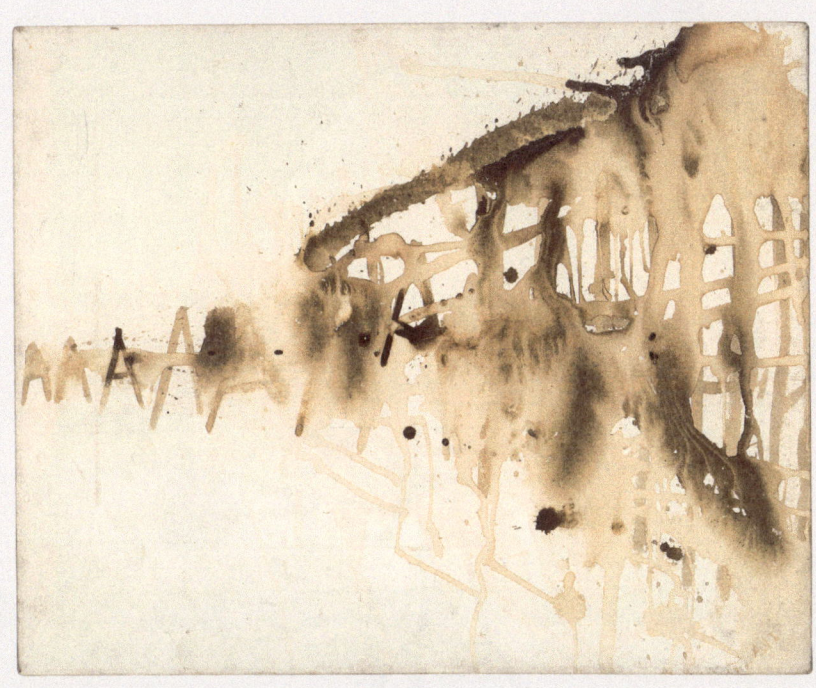

Cory Roberts-Auli
The Scream, 1993
Blood on canvas, 24 × 30 in. (61 × 76.2 cm)
ONE Archives at the USC Libraries

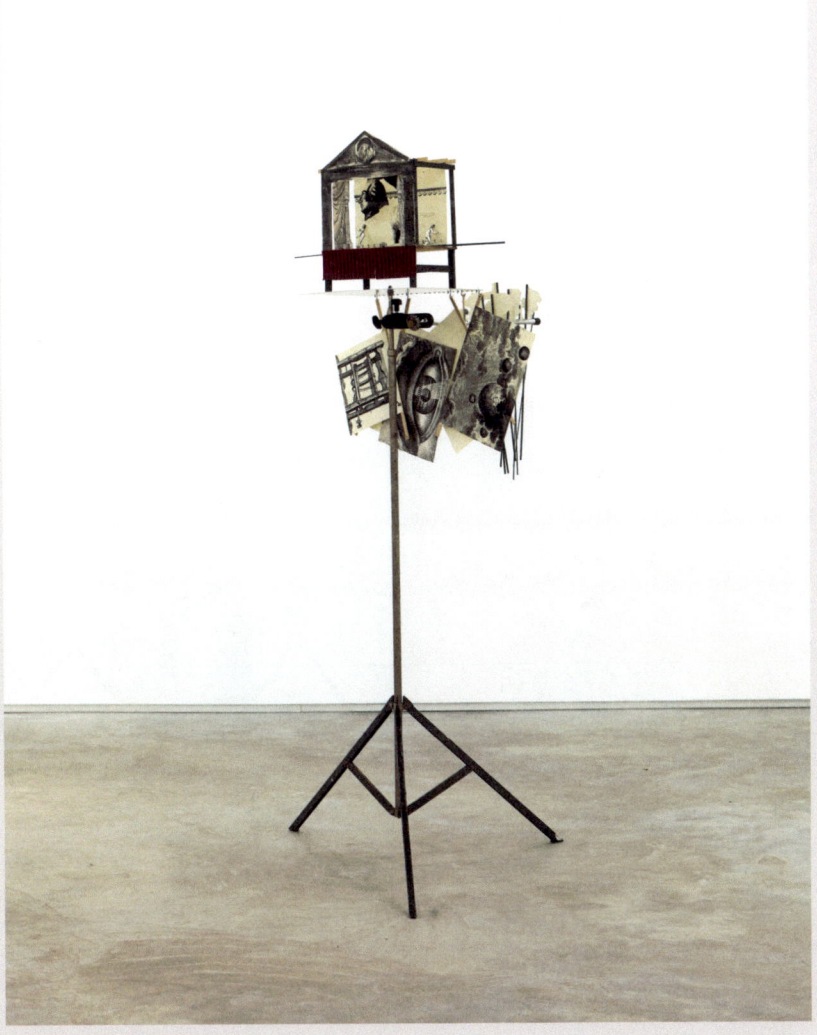

Nayland Blake
The Tabletop Production of Philosophy in the Bedroom, 1991–93
Paper, aluminum, steel, wood, plastic,
61 ½ × 29 × 31 in. (156.2 × 73.7 × 78.8 cm)
Matthew Marks Gallery, New York

Nayland Blake

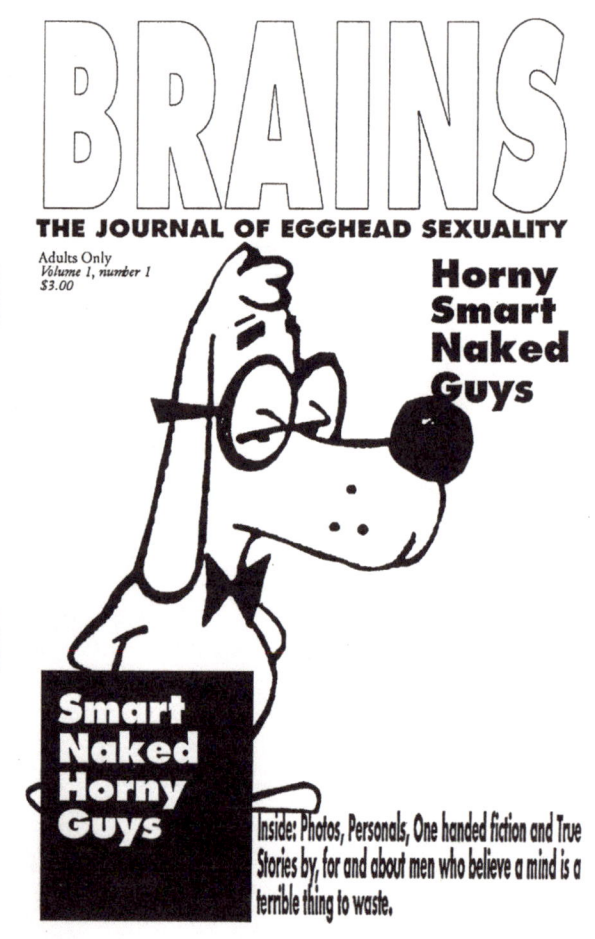

Nayland Blake and D-L Alvarez
Brains: A Journal of Egghead Sexuality, 1990
Photocopy, saddle stitched, 8 ½ × 5 ½ in. (21.6 × 14 cm)
Collection Philip Aarons and Shelley Fox Aarons

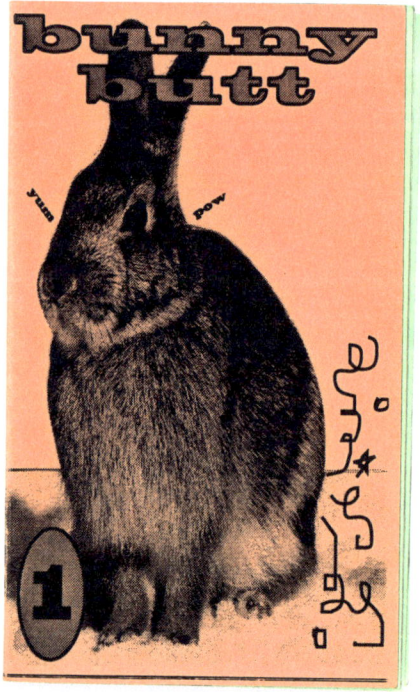

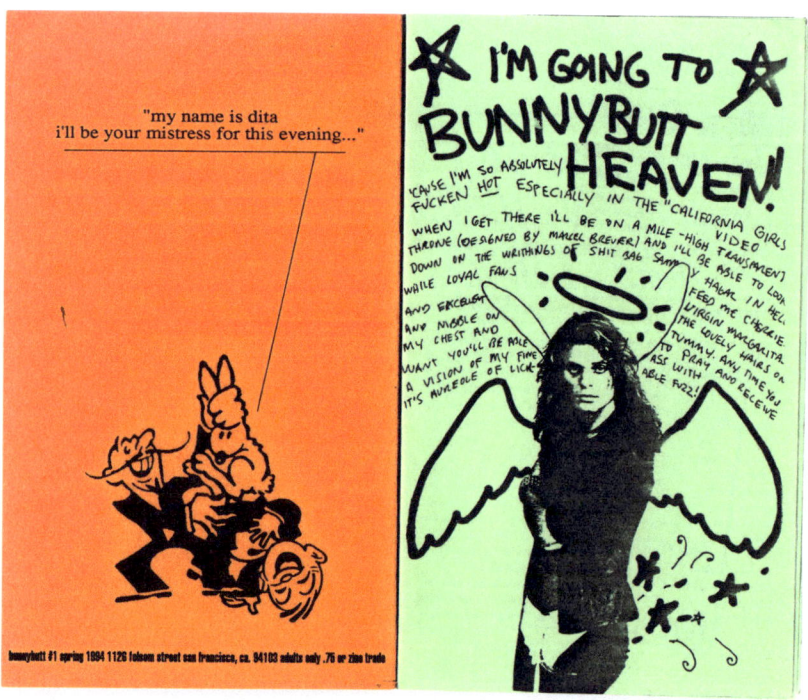

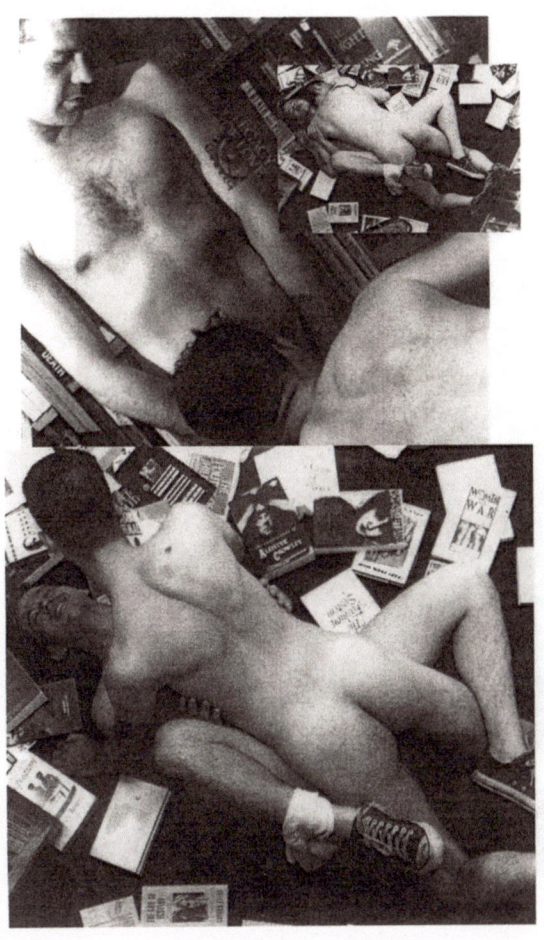

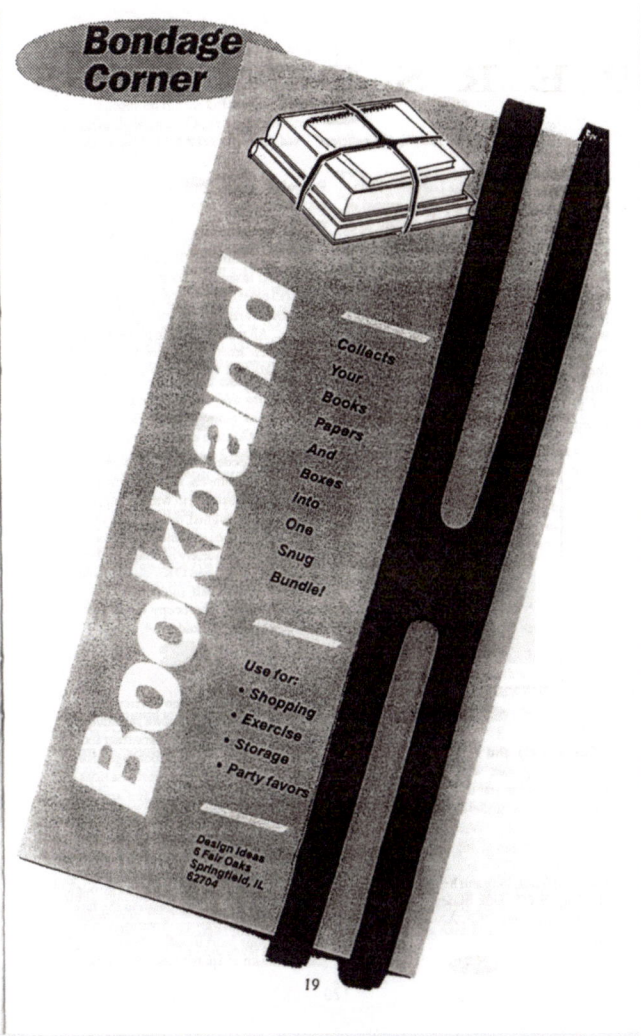

Bondage Corner

Bookband

Collects
Your
Books
Papers
And
Boxes
Into
One
Snug
Bundle!

Use for:
• Shopping
• Exercise
• Storage
• Party favors

Design Ideas
6 Fair Oaks
Springfield, IL
62704

18

19

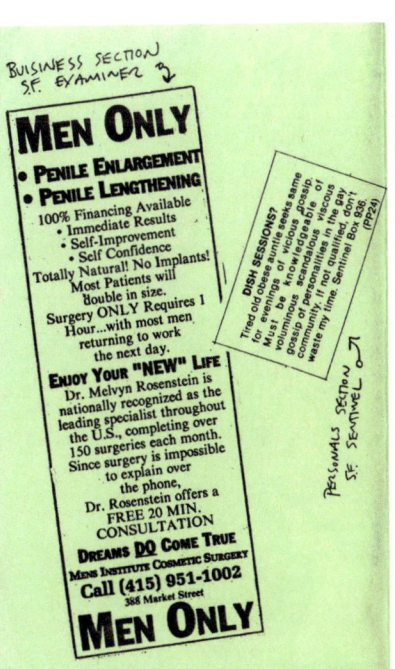

The Story of H
(excerpt)

The suit itched. H had thought it was a joke, when his lover Andre rolled out of bed after a long evening of mutual frottage, rummaged in the closet and pulled out a bulky box splashed with lurid color. "Open it." Andre had said and H heard the steely tone that meant no argument would be tolerated. Inside the box was a mass of white artificial fur, pale pink satin and wire that finally resolved itself into a bulky one-piece suit, a hood with tapering pink ears, and mittens. H fumbled self consciously with the zipper and Andre hissed, "Get it on.", his grey eyes blank with impatience.

Once inside the outfit, H had looked into the mirror. Staring back at him was a ludicrous figure; a six foot tall rabbit with silly booties and a pair of ears that bobbed with the slightest movement of his head. The suit hung from his shoulders, flaring at the waist and giving the impression of a wide and low hanging ass that the cottony tail did nothing to dispel. The outfit radiated a cheeriness that contrasted sharply with H's mood.

Andre had pulled an elegant robe on over his customary harness and was now puffing on a short, pungent cigar. His contempt for H was evident in every gesture and H found himself standing in awkward silence, his normal lassitude deepening into a frozen panic.

"You're an idiot, H. You think that by putting up with my

Bunny Butt, 1994
Photocopy, saddle stitched, 8 ½ × 5 ½ in. (21.6 × 14 cm)
ONE Archives at the USC Libraries

Mirha-Soleil Ross and Xanthra Phillippa MacKay

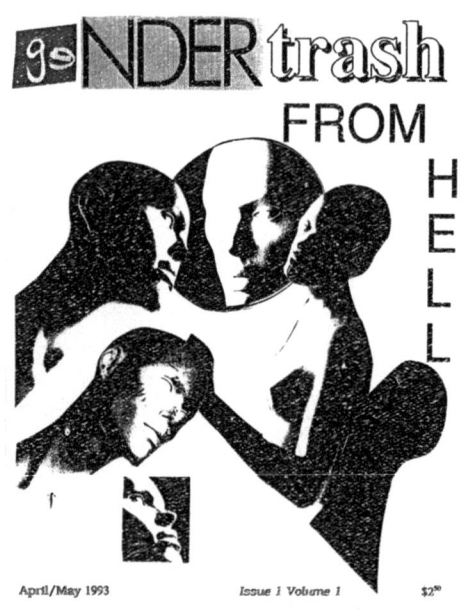

Gendertrash, vol. 1, no. 1, April/May 1993
Offset, saddle stitched, 8 7/16 × 7 1/16 in. (21.5 × 18 cm)
The ArQuives: Canada's LGBTQ2+ Archives

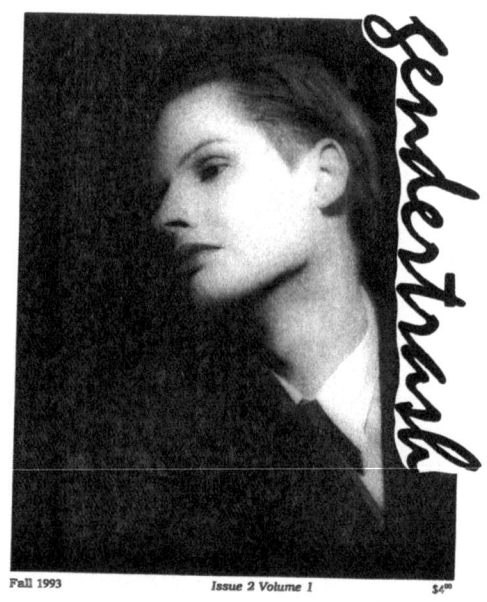

Gendertrash, vol. 1, no. 2, Fall 1993
Offset, saddle stitched, 8 7/16 × 7 1/16 in. (21.5 × 18 cm)
The ArQuives: Canada's LGBTQ2+ Archives

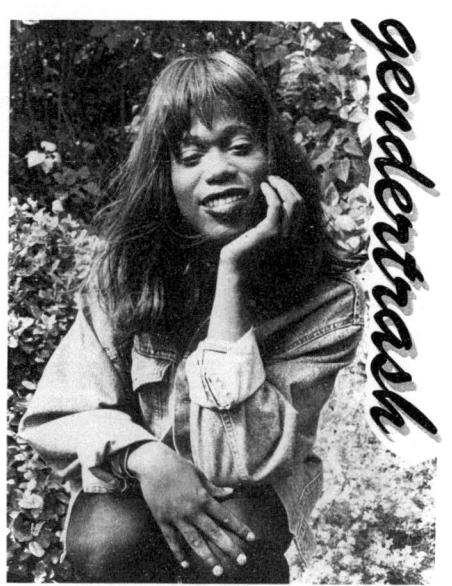

Gendertrash, no. 3, Winter 1995
Offset, saddle stitched, 11 × 8 11/16 in. (28 × 22 cm)
The ArQuives: Canada's LGBTQ2+ Archives

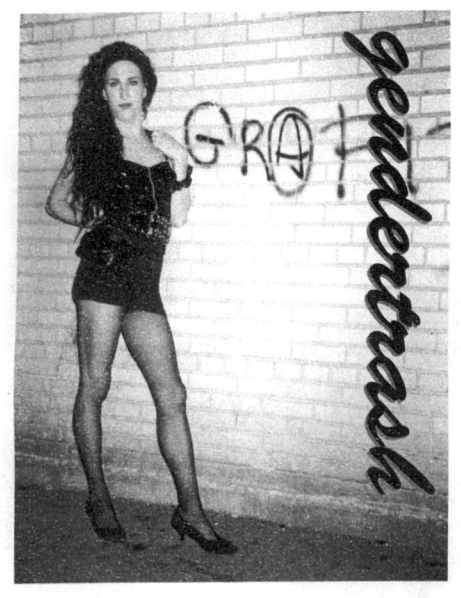

Gendertrash, no. 4, Spring 1995
Offset, saddle stitched, 11 × 8 1/2 in. (27.9 × 21.6 cm)
The ArQuives: Canada's LGBTQ2+ Archives

Let our buttons speak for you:

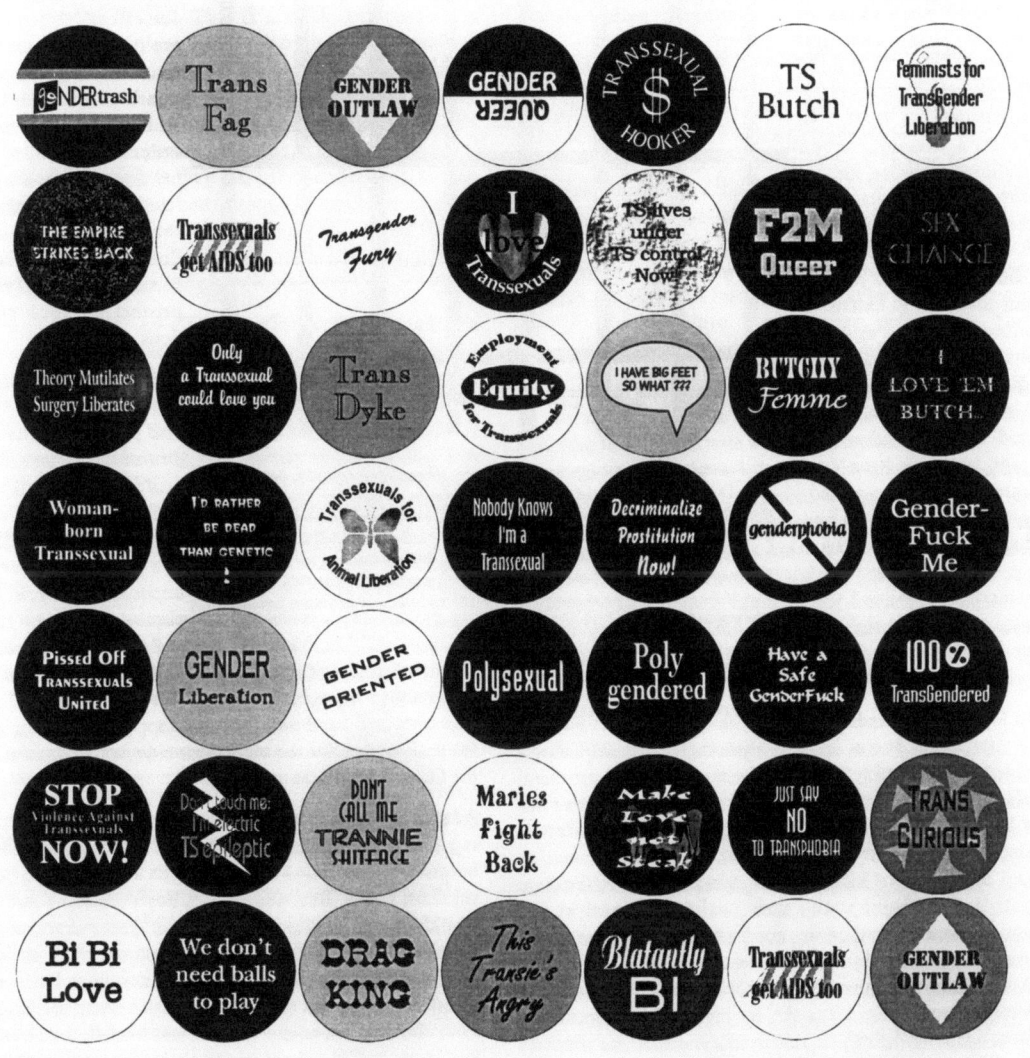

This sample is a black & white, 40% of the actual size version of some of our buttons.
See left hand page for ordering instructions.

Gendertrash, no. 4, Spring 1995
Offset, saddle stitched, 11 × 8 ½ in. (27.9 × 21.6 cm)
The ArQuives: Canada's LGBTQ2+ Archives

<u>welcome</u>

welcome gender queers
to the world of gender trash
our gender world
where we can give voice
to our concerns in/around/about gender
issues
metamorphoses
transformations
changes
loves
lusts
intensities
hungers
nightmares
feelings about ourselves
need to be valid on our own terms
to express ourselves in our own languages
phrases
words
ways
to feel strong being ourselves
to be heard by ourselves
for community
to be who we are
to control our own futures
our own lives
our own bodies
to develop our own gender culture
to plan
build
shape
run
guide all of our institutions real & abstract

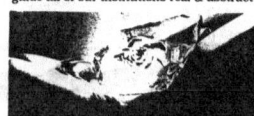

welcome to a safe place
a space of our own
a place of our own
to rest in
to explore ourselves
our wants
wishes
desires
thoughts
spiritualities
sexualities
feelings
emotions
bodies
free from gender oppressive controls
limits
societally created terrors
Patriarchally induced fears
self hatred
self censorship
a space of our own
of warmth & pride & strength
free from gender oppression & hate
free of the War of the Patriarchy
free from the GenderCide we are currently enduring
free from the oppressive indifference of genetics
free of the prisons of the Patriarchy
for all of us to share with
laugh with
sing with
exchange our personal herstories/histories with
cry with
hear
touch
feel
associate with other gender queers

Gendertrash, vol. 1, no. 1, April/May 1993
Offset, saddle stitched, 8 7/16 × 7 1/16 in. (21.5 × 18 cm)
The ArQuives: Canada's LGBTQ2+ Archives

Hooker of the Year:

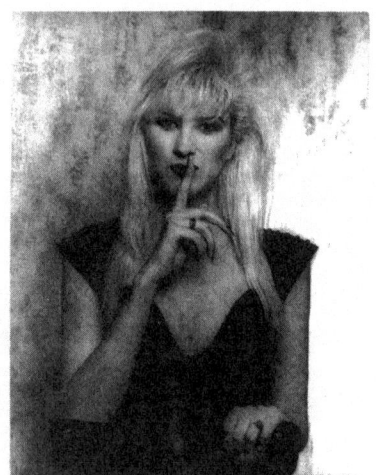

Justine Piaget

presentation and interview by jeanne b.

There are a number of pervasive anti-prostitute attitudes amongst some transsexuals, most of whom happen to be white, "well-educated" and middle-class. This is especially true, amongst those whose careers have already been established and were therefore safe enough when they began their gender journeys.

What these would-be well-heeled and well-integrated citizens forget, is that most transsexual prostitutes started living as women at a very early age (sometimes as early as twelve), making it difficult for them to continue within the structure of traditional education and/or careers.

For decades, prostitution has provided many TS's with a decent and empowering way to earn a living and made necessities (such as electrolysis, SRS' and cosmetic surgery) a reality despite their astronomical costs.

It is time for the larger transsexual community, to start looking at certain TS prostitutes as role models. We make up a very large and important part of transsexuals as a group.

We are strong, courageous, intelligent, self-motivated, insightful and clear-sighted individuals whose stories and lives should not be silenced in order to gain mainstream acceptance.

jeanne   For how long have you been working in the sex trade?

Justine   For about nine years.

jeanne   Have you always worked as a girl?

Justine   Yes.

jeanne   Where did you work, mostly? In bars, as an escort, on the streets?

Justine   I worked on the streets for about 80% of the time, then I started to work independently on my own as an escort.

jeanne   Where have you been working?

Justine   First I started in Edmonton, then I went on to Calgary then back to Edmonton. Then I spent about two years in Vancouver and then back to Edmonton for another year. And then on my way to Toronto, I got arrested in Calgary, so I stayed in Calgary for six months. And then I went to Toronto - that's the first time I came to Toronto in 1987. Since then I've been living in Toronto except for a year and a half in Montréal. I've gone all across Canada.

Gendertrash, vol. 1, no. 2, Fall 1993
Offset, saddle stitched, 11 × 8 ½ in. (27.9 × 21.6 cm)
The ArQuives: Canada's LGBTQ2+ Archives

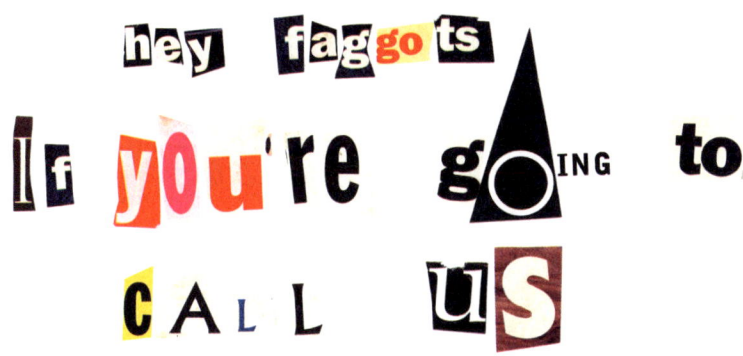
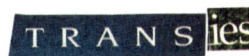
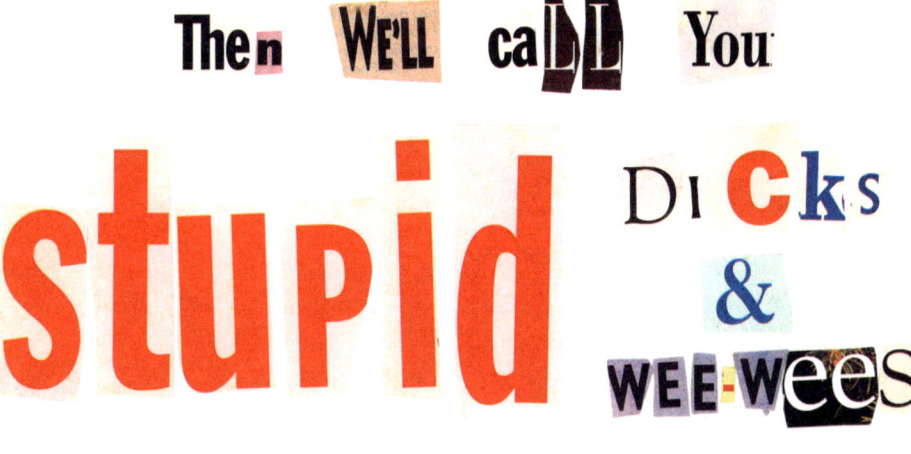

Xanthra Phillippa MacKay
Dicks and Weewees, 1993
Collage of offset prints, paper, glue, 10 ¹³⁄₁₆ × 8 ⁷⁄₁₆ in. (27.5 × 21.5 cm)
The ArQuives: Canada's LGBTQ2+ Archives

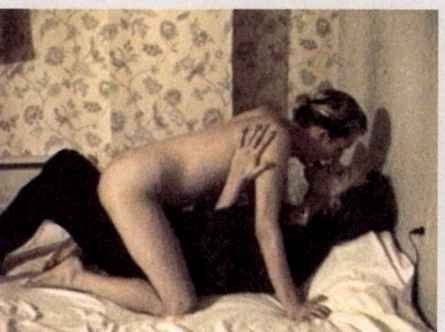
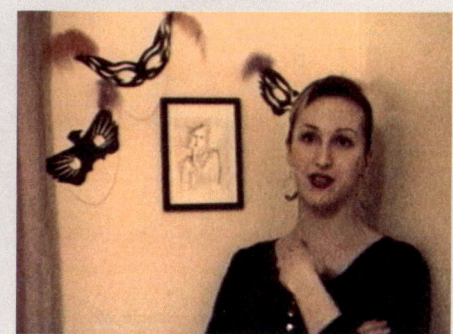

Stills from *Gender Troublemakers*, 1993
Video; color, sound; 20 min.
Vtape, Toronto

Ho Tam

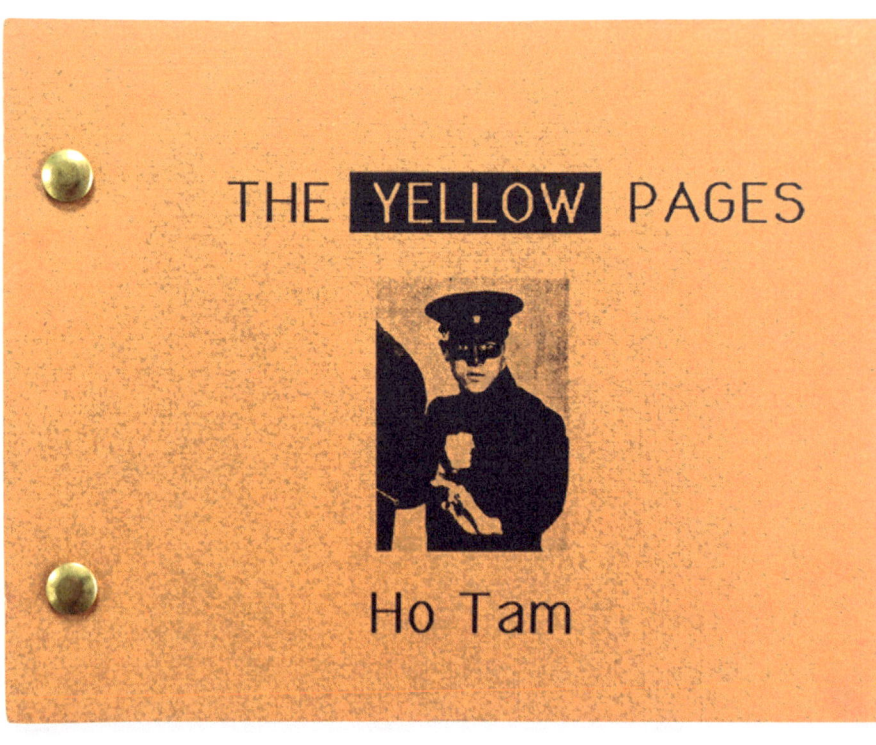

The Yellow Pages, 1993
Photocopy, brass fasteners, brown board covers,
4 ¼ × 5 ½ in. (10.8 × 14 cm)
Collection Philip Aarons and Shelley Fox Aarons

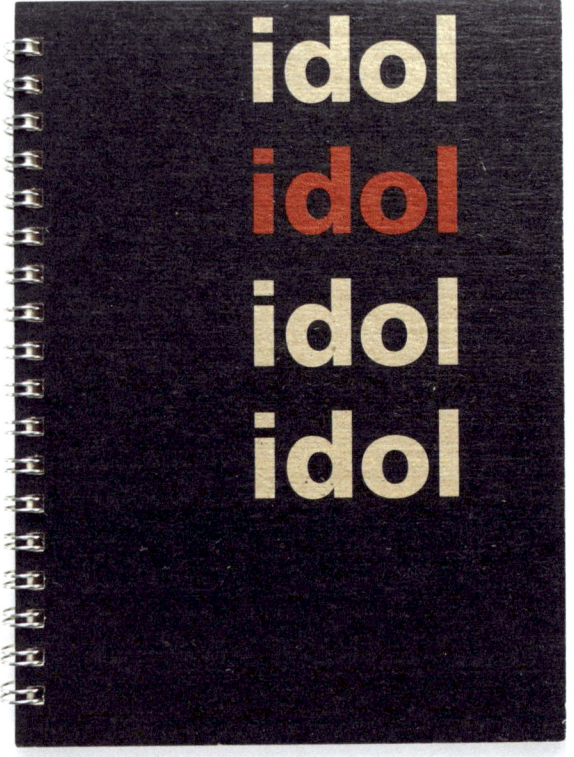
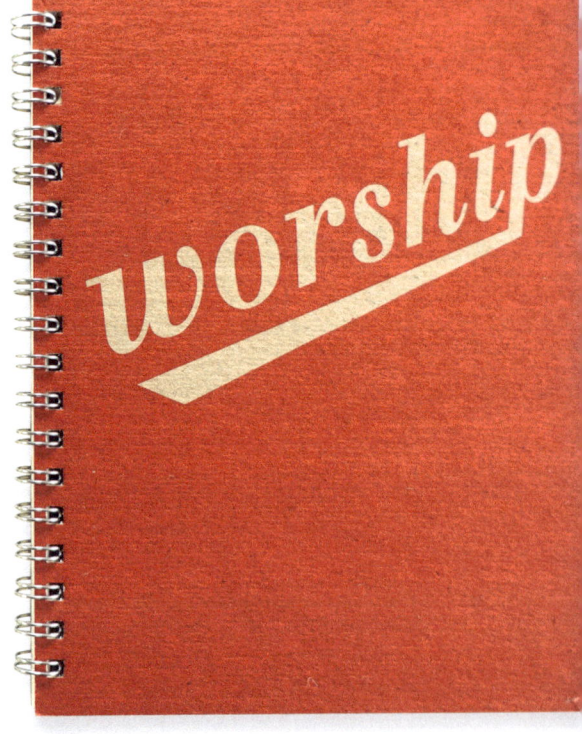

Idol + Worship, 1995
Screenprint, spiral bound, offset covers,
7 × 5 in. (17.8 × 12.7 cm)
Collection the artist

Poser, nos. 1–7, 2013–16
Digitally printed, saddle stitched,
10 ¾ × 8 ¼ in. (27.3 × 21 cm)
Collection the artist

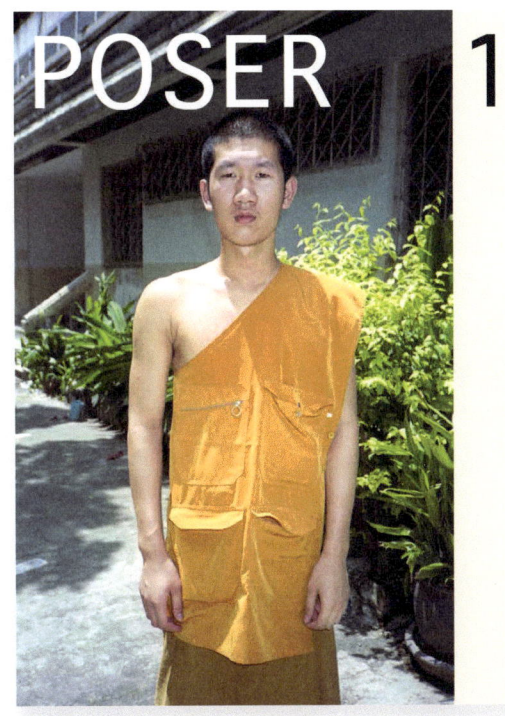

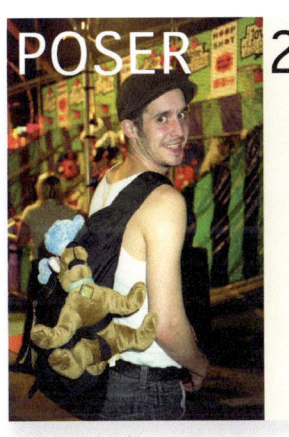

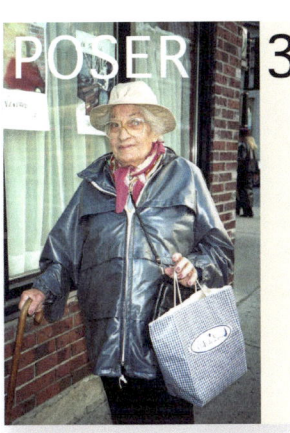

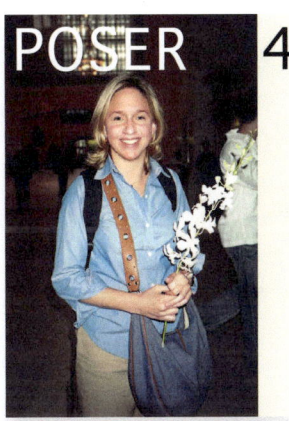

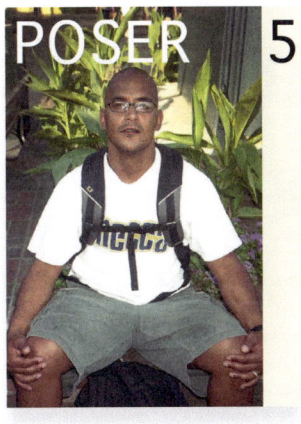

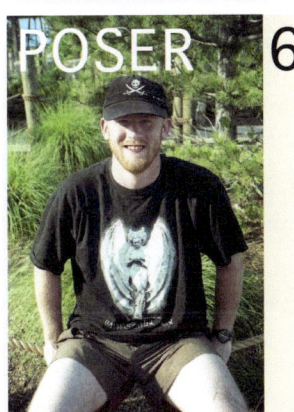

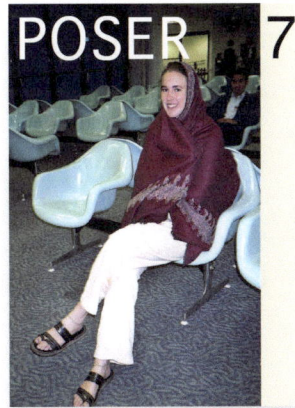

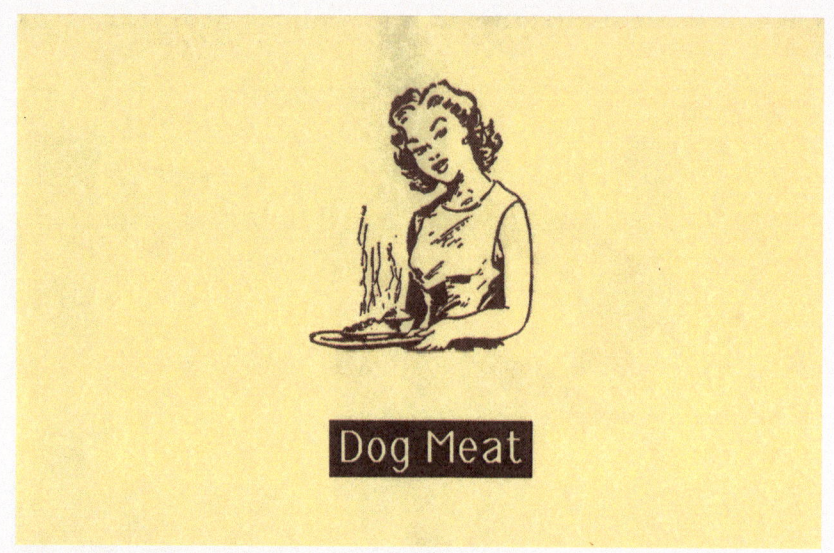

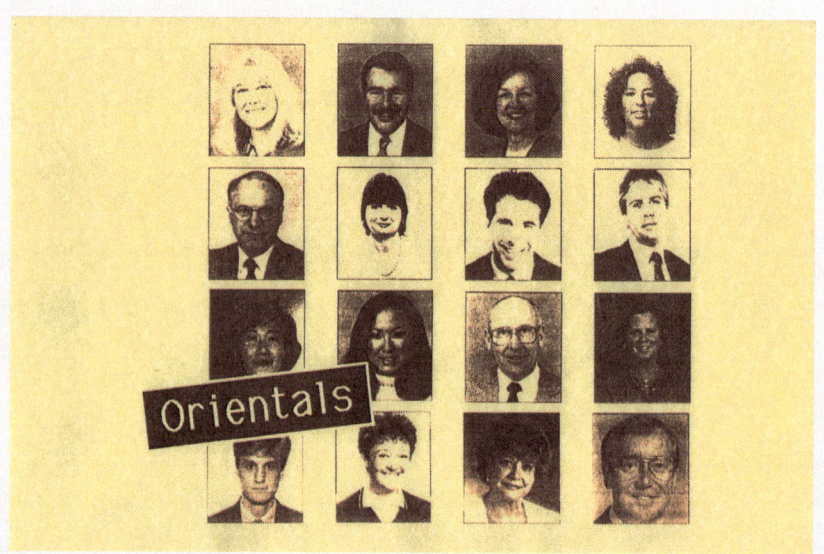

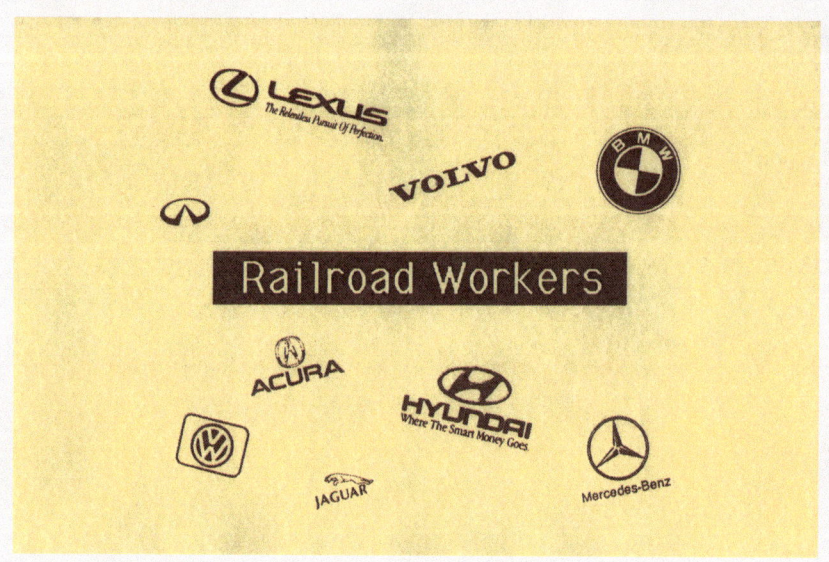

The Yellow Pages, 1994
Photocopies on parchment paper, 10½ × 14 in. (26.7 × 35.6 cm)
Collection the artist

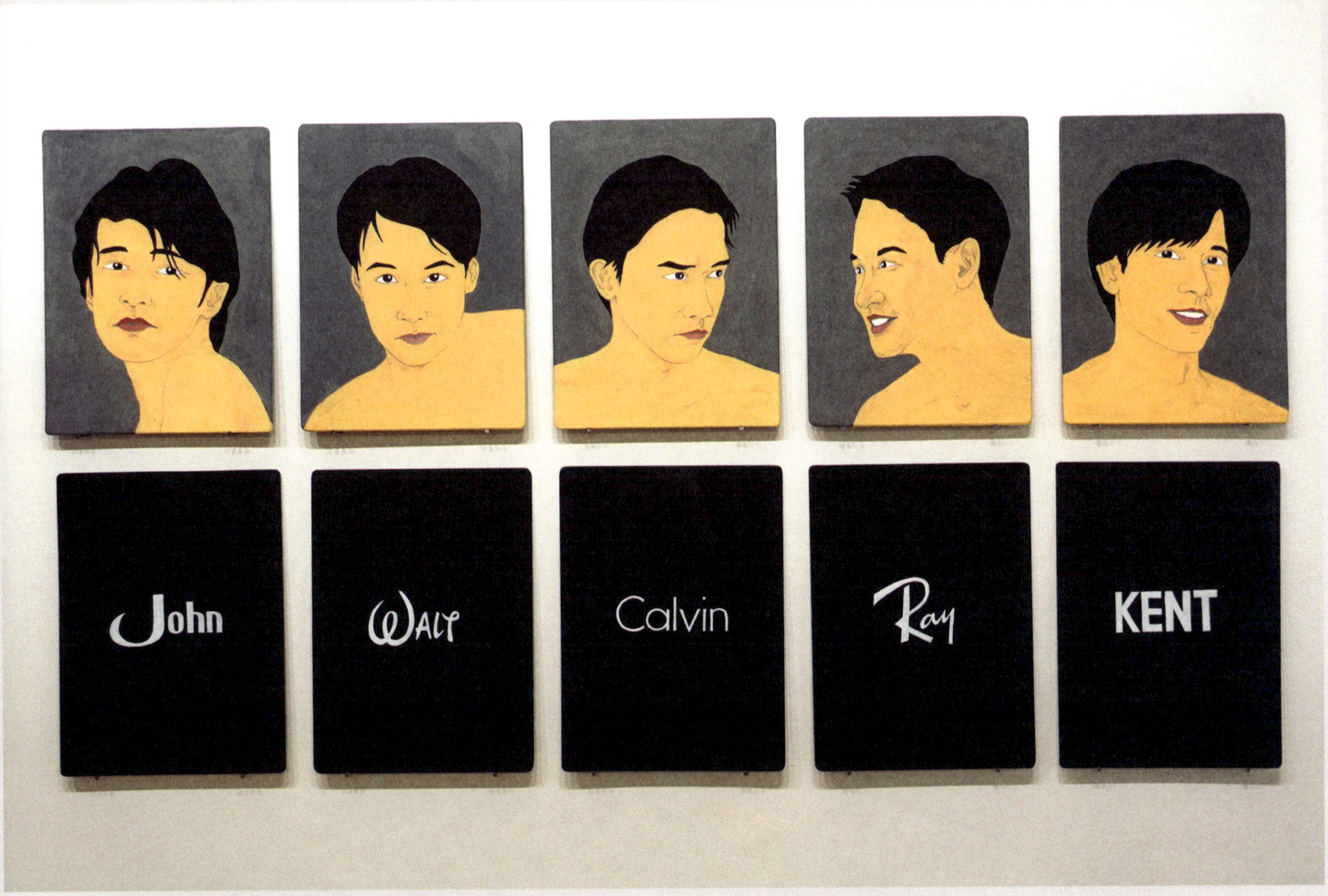

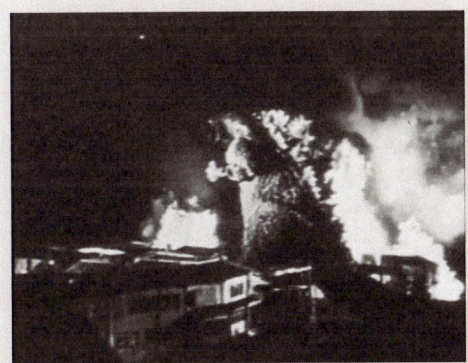

Matinee Idols, 1994
Oil on masonite, 16 × 12 in. (40.6 × 30.5 cm) each
Collection the artist

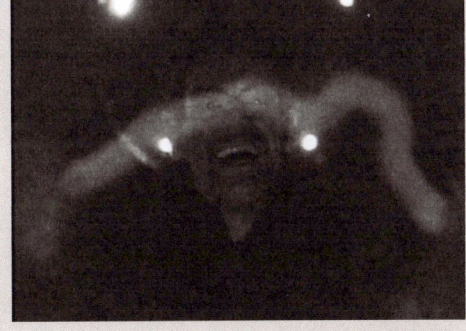

Stills from *The Yellow Pages*, 1994
Video; black and white, sound; 8 min.
Collection the artist

215

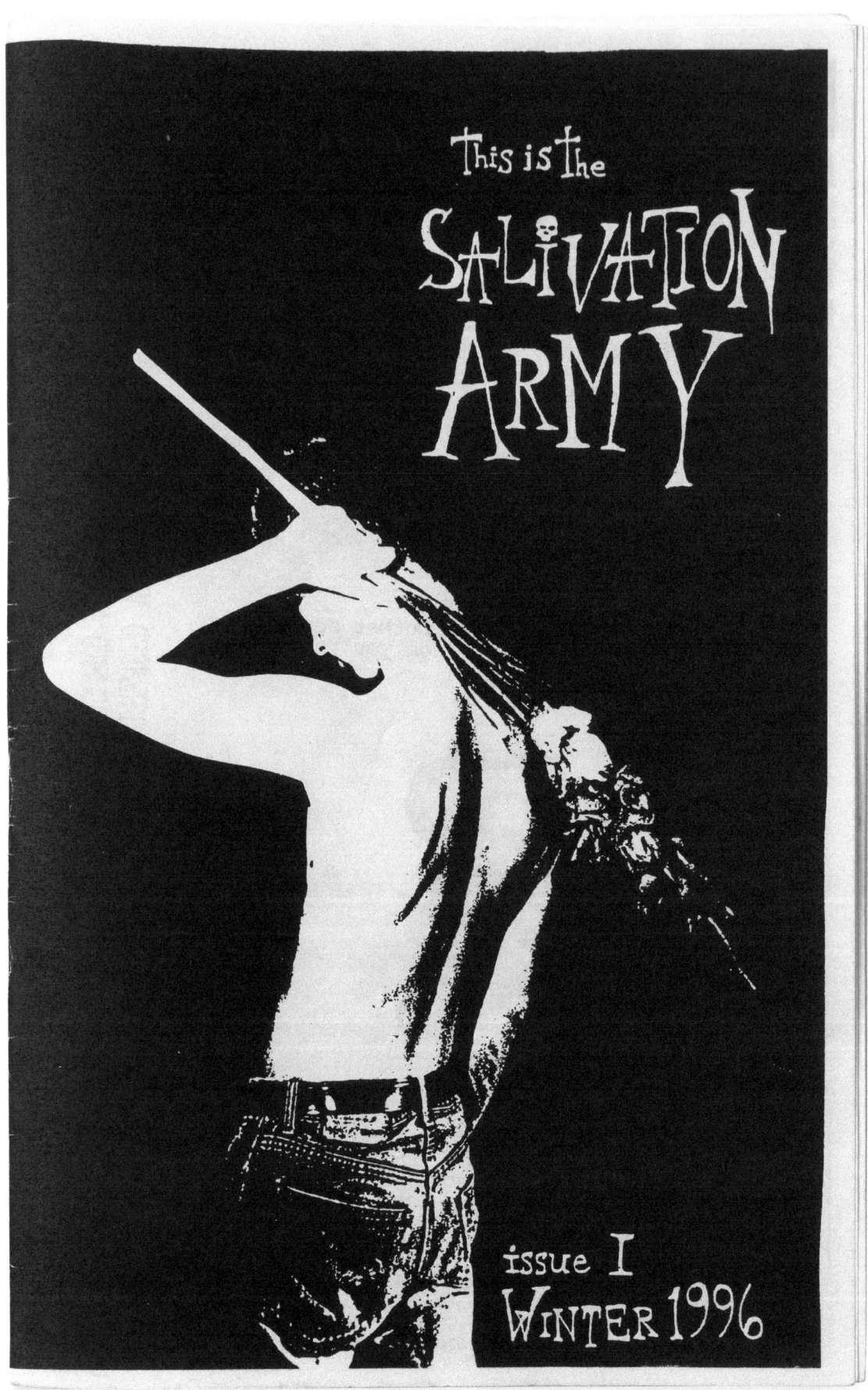

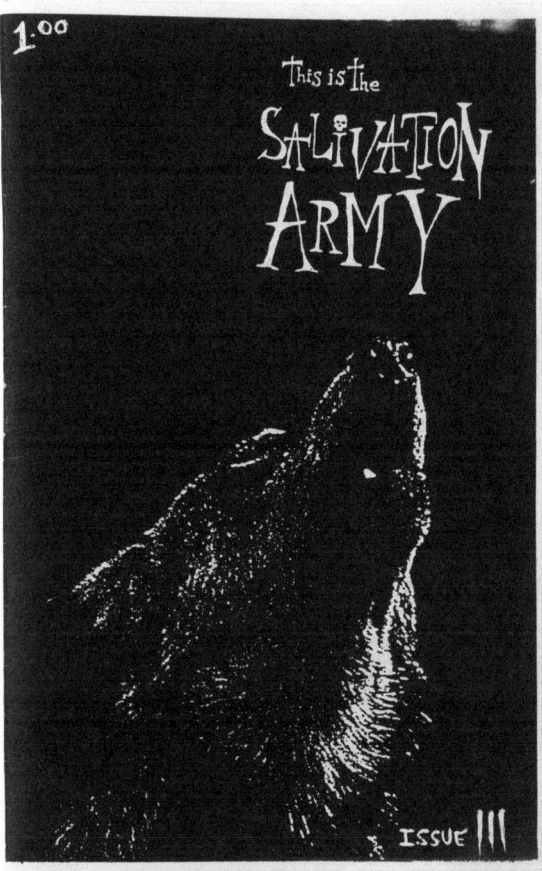

This Is the Salivation Army, no. 1, 1996
Photocopy, saddle stitched, 8½ in × 5½ in. (21.6 × 14 cm)
Collection Philip Aarons and Shelley Fox Aarons

This Is the Salivation Army, no. 3, 1997
Photocopy, saddle stitched, 8½ in × 5½ in. (21.6 × 14 cm)
Collection Philip Aarons and Shelley Fox Aarons

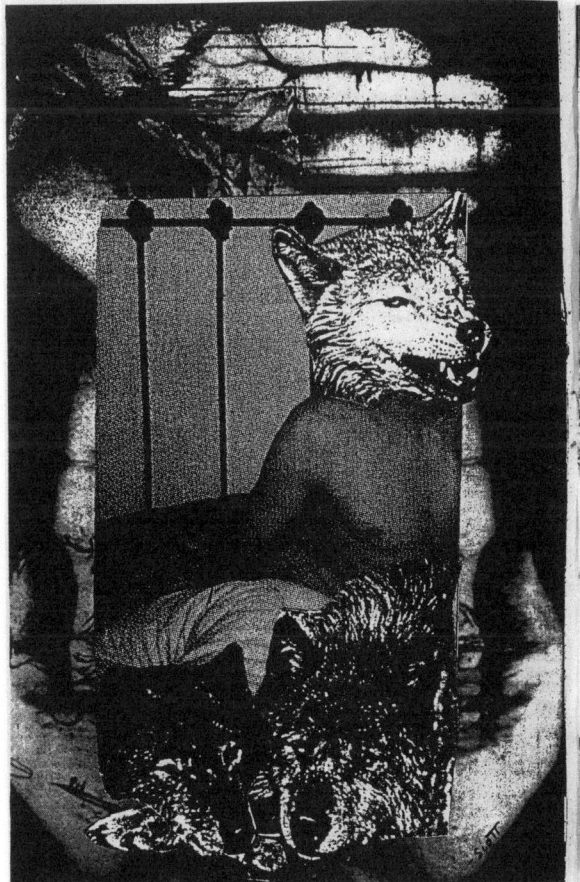

ARMY LORE by SCOTT

Last night I dreamt of the three boys that were born against this age. The eldest sees only in varying shades of red, and uses the word 'fuck' like a spice. His aggression is the same that shakes the rabbit till it's back breaks in the dog's jaws; not hate, just a malicious instinct to put things out of their misery. He is unfolding, ambitious flower smelling sweet and acrid, the odour of gardenia & sweat, the meat of youth. He will have more words as his worth becomes more apparent. We teach each other charmingly awful habits.

Next is a boy who they call Mosquito 'cos as a young Romantic he once asked an older boy to give him a few drops of his blood. Refused and heart-broken, he at least knows his name. He is resurrecting the romance of thievery, Mercury bless him, finally realising that the thief's trick is not to trade, but to *take things away*. He learns to starve people of his beauty. Maybe one day he wraps his lips around cold steel. Lastly, there is a boy who is caught up in neither cause, just his love for the other two. He thinks that he is safely married into his third of the clock face (tik, tok, & boom). He cares for both his brothers, he braves being torn apart. If that happens the boys, in bed, will split the mourning; one will wonder after him, the other will compose a requiem mass. The lights will fade.

It will rain for days.

the SALIVATION ARMY eats the roses, thorns and all

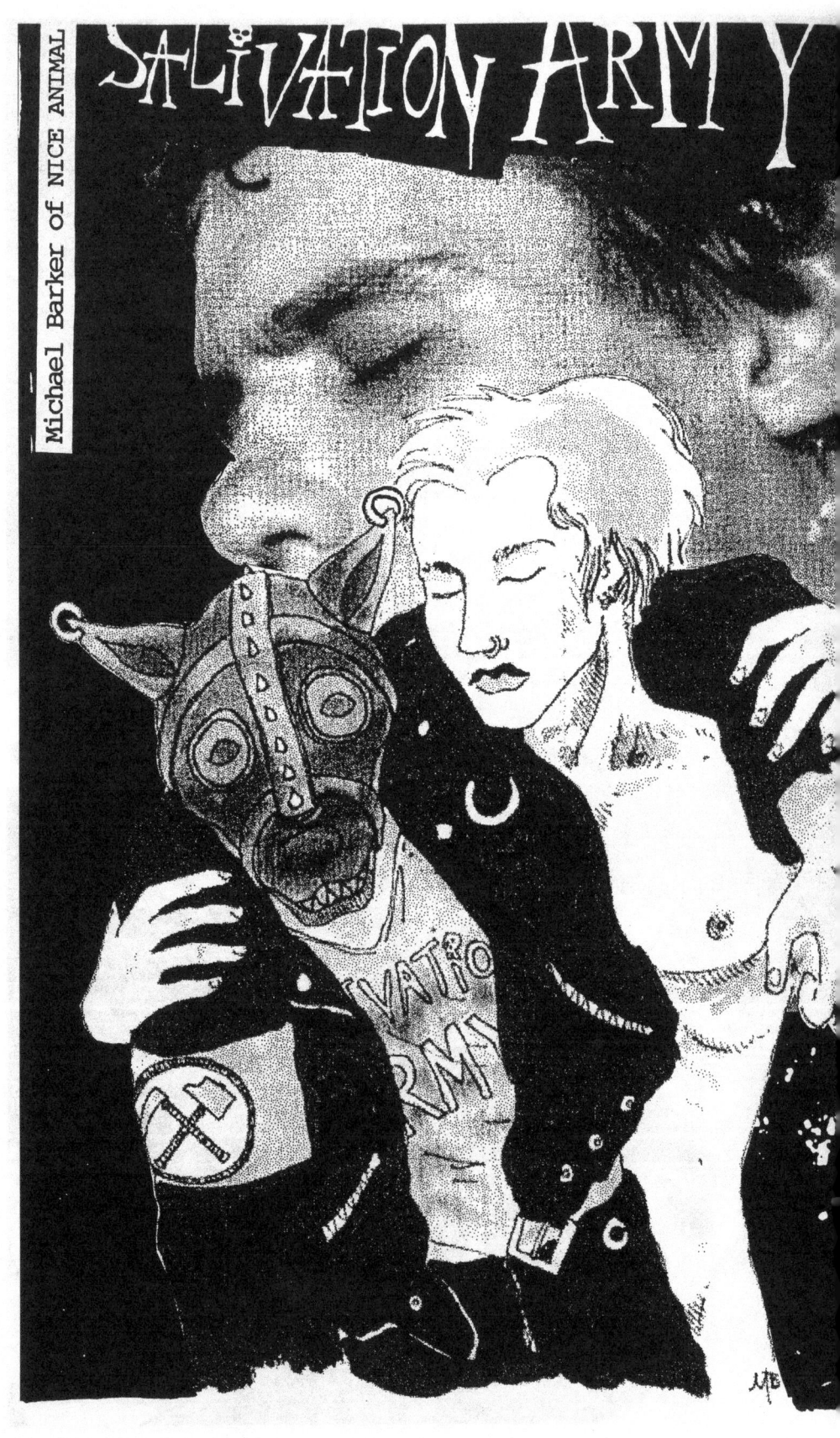

Michael Barker of NICE ANIMAL

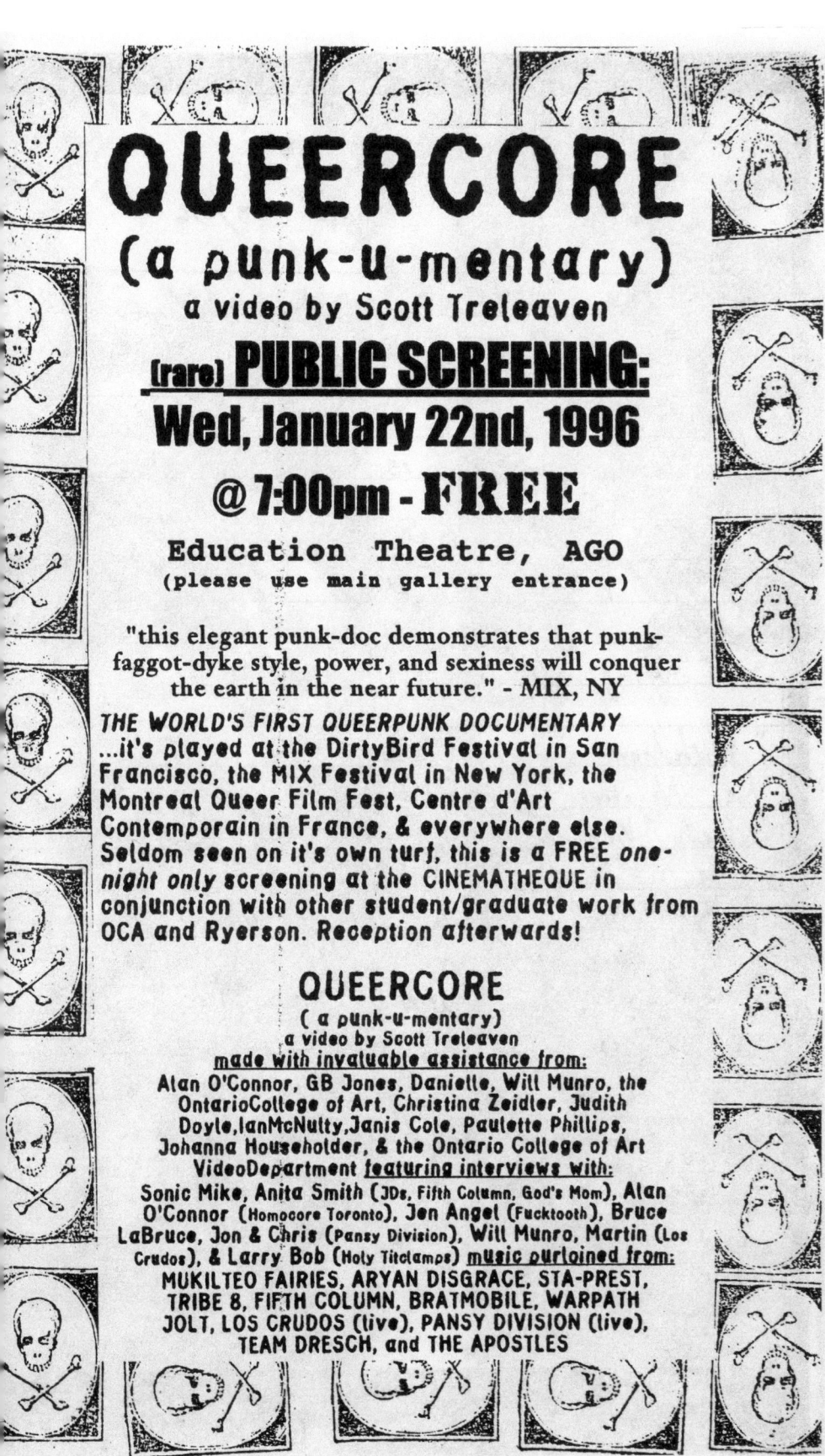

QUEERCORE

(a punk-u-mentary)
a video by Scott Treleaven

(rare) PUBLIC SCREENING:
Wed, January 22nd, 1996
@ 7:00pm - FREE

Education Theatre, AGO
(please use main gallery entrance)

"this elegant punk-doc demonstrates that punk-faggot-dyke style, power, and sexiness will conquer the earth in the near future." - MIX, NY

THE WORLD'S FIRST QUEERPUNK DOCUMENTARY ...it's played at the DirtyBird Festival in San Francisco, the MIX Festival in New York, the Montreal Queer Film Fest, Centre d'Art Contemporain in France, & everywhere else. Seldom seen on it's own turf, this is a FREE *one-night only* screening at the CINEMATHEQUE in conjunction with other student/graduate work from OCA and Ryerson. Reception afterwards!

QUEERCORE
(a punk-u-mentary)
a video by Scott Treleaven
made with invaluable assistance from:
Alan O'Connor, GB Jones, Danielle, Will Munro, the OntarioCollege of Art, Christina Zeidler, Judith Doyle, IanMcNulty, Janis Cole, Paulette Phillips, Johanna Householder, & the Ontario College of Art VideoDepartment featuring interviews with:
Sonic Mike, Anita Smith (JDs, Fifth Column, God's Mom), Alan O'Connor (Homocore Toronto), Jen Angel (Fucktooth), Bruce LaBruce, Jon & Chris (Pansy Division), Will Munro, Martin (Los Crudos), & Larry Bob (Holy Titclamps) music purloined from:
MUKILTEO FAIRIES, ARYAN DISGRACE, STA-PREST, TRIBE 8, FIFTH COLUMN, BRATMOBILE, WARPATH JOLT, LOS CRUDOS (live), PANSY DIVISION (live), TEAM DRESCH, and THE APOSTLES

This Is the Salivation Army, no. 4, 1997
Photocopy, saddle stitched, 8 ½ in × 5 ½ in. (21.6 × 14 cm)
Collection Philip Aarons and Shelley Fox Aarons

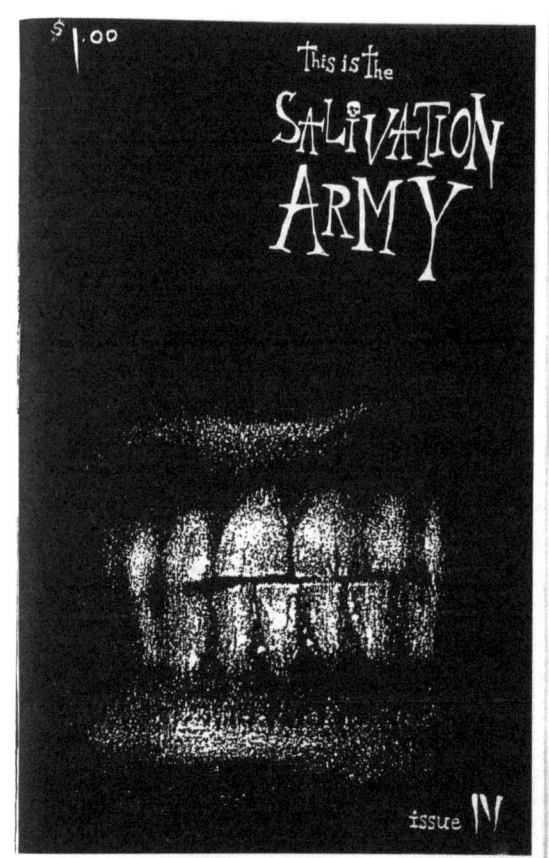
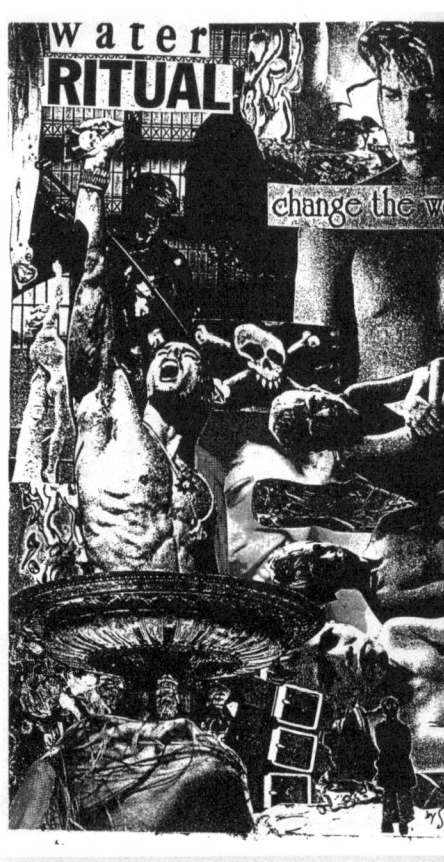
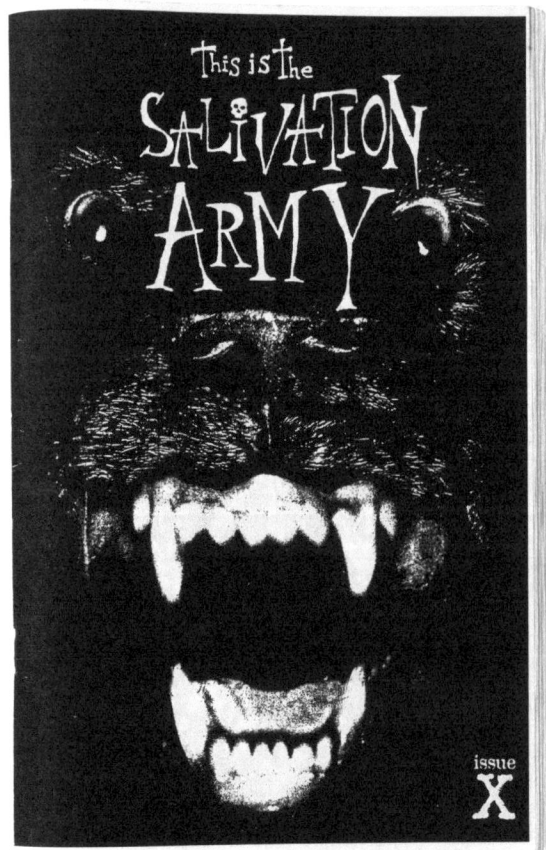
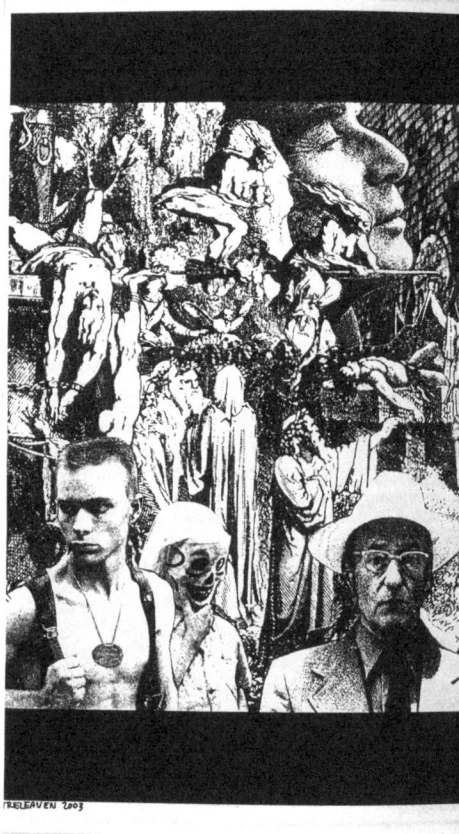

This Is the Salivation Army, no. 4, 1997, and no. 10, 2004
Photocopy, saddle stitched, 8 ½ in × 5 ½ in. (21.6 × 14 cm)
Collection Philip Aarons and Shelley Fox Aarons

ARMY LORE by Scott
(Sunday, December 1st, 1996 - 2:00am UK time; at sea)
Thee SALIVATION ARMY would make up stories and imaginary dialogues. cut thro' with the most savage fact and scalding observation.

'thee orchard in ash'

Lands burnt to ashes, wherein the people ate the ash. Their mouths dried and lips torn to split scab holes from which only smoke would pour. I spent my days in the ruins of the orchard where no one thought to go. My digging unearthed seeds, perfectly incubated in the untrodden dust. To revive them I kept them in my mouth where they moistened my tongue. In turn, in spit, they sprout - I spit them out and planted them in a corner sheltered from the winds and blowing dust. They grew, slow, and I was too weak or too astonished to do it alone; this garden, thee orchard in ash. I spoke in metaphor, I subtly said what I'd found. Those that noticed I'd stopped speaking in dust were seduced into coming to help. Strange trees grow and bear strange fruit. By the time it was ripe we had developed a compound, fiercely guarded, tho' anyone who could work, anyone who made things from understanding, was allowed to come and go as pleased them. The fruit was shared as the hungers dwelt and dissipated - enough for the small group to nourish themselves on. More than enough come to think. Those, all of us, that would gorge themselves with the bloody nectars were taken with Satyriasis - we would court our own sex as the ribbons of juice flowed and stained our throats. The ash washed away. We could no longer recall the taste of dust, tho' we'd breathed it only months ago. Tongues scarcely acquainted with their own hot moisture now sought new homes in the mouths of Lovers.
We come & go thro' the land of dust and ash, the tenuous smoky air. The people who choose not to kiss us revile us -
WE ARE THEE ENVY OF THEE WORLD.

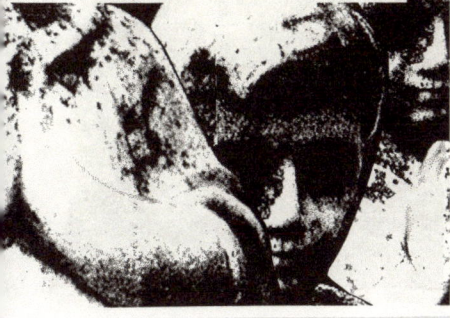

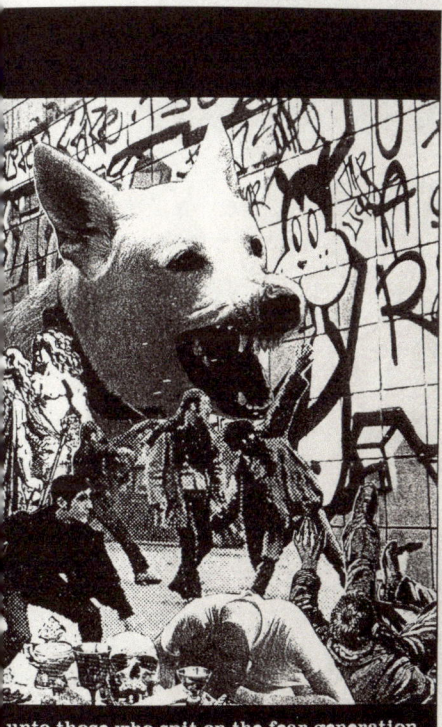

unto those who spit on the fear generation
wind will blow it back..." raf simons

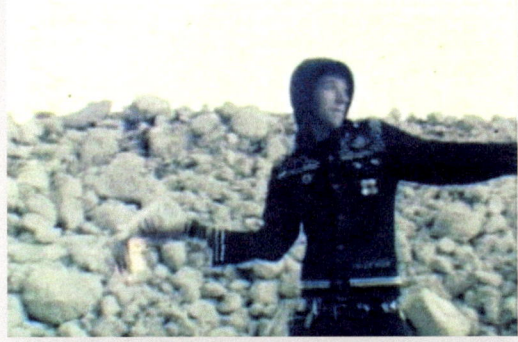

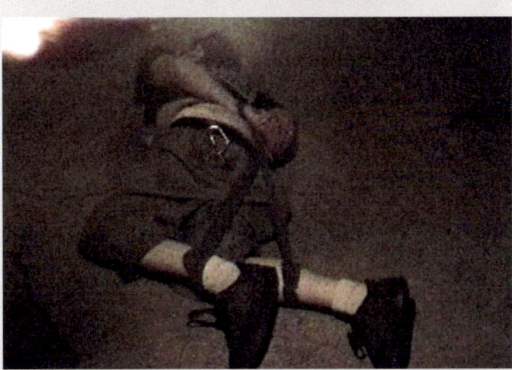

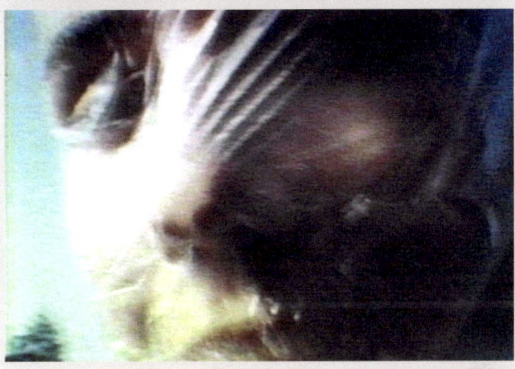

Stills from *The Salivation Army*
(*This Is the Salivation Army*, no. 9), 2002
Video; color, sound; 21 min., 46 sec.
Vtape, Toronto

221

Laurel Beckman (with Ryan Hill and Kate Sorensen)

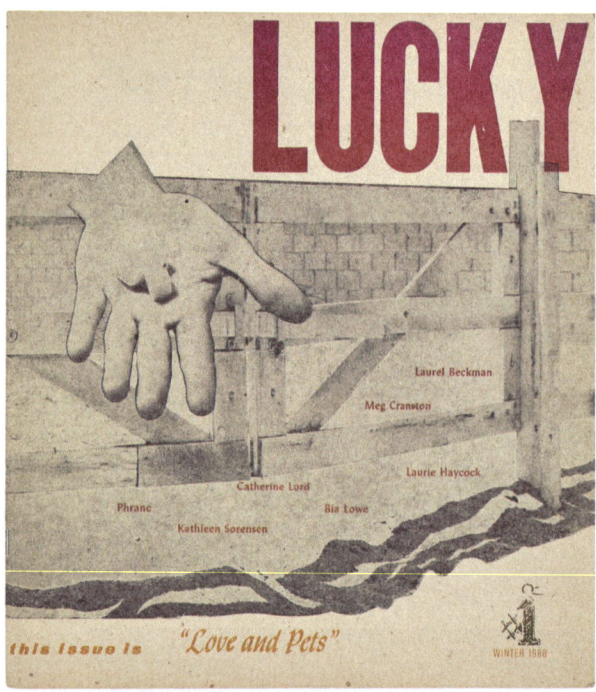

Laurel Beckman and Kate Sorensen
Lucky, no. 1, *Love and Pets*, 1988
Letterpress and diazo (blueprint), chipboard cover,
11⅛ × 10 in. (28.3 × 25.4 cm)
Collection Laurel Beckman

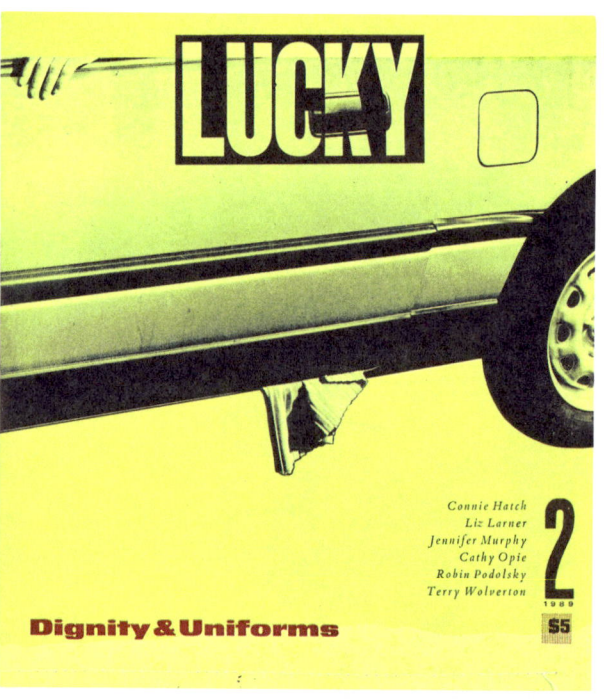

Laurel Beckman and Kate Sorensen
Lucky, no. 2, *Dignity and Uniforms*, 1989
Letterpress and offset, brass washers, thread on
fluorescent cover, 11⅛ × 10 in. (28.3 × 25.4 cm)
Collection Laurel Beckman

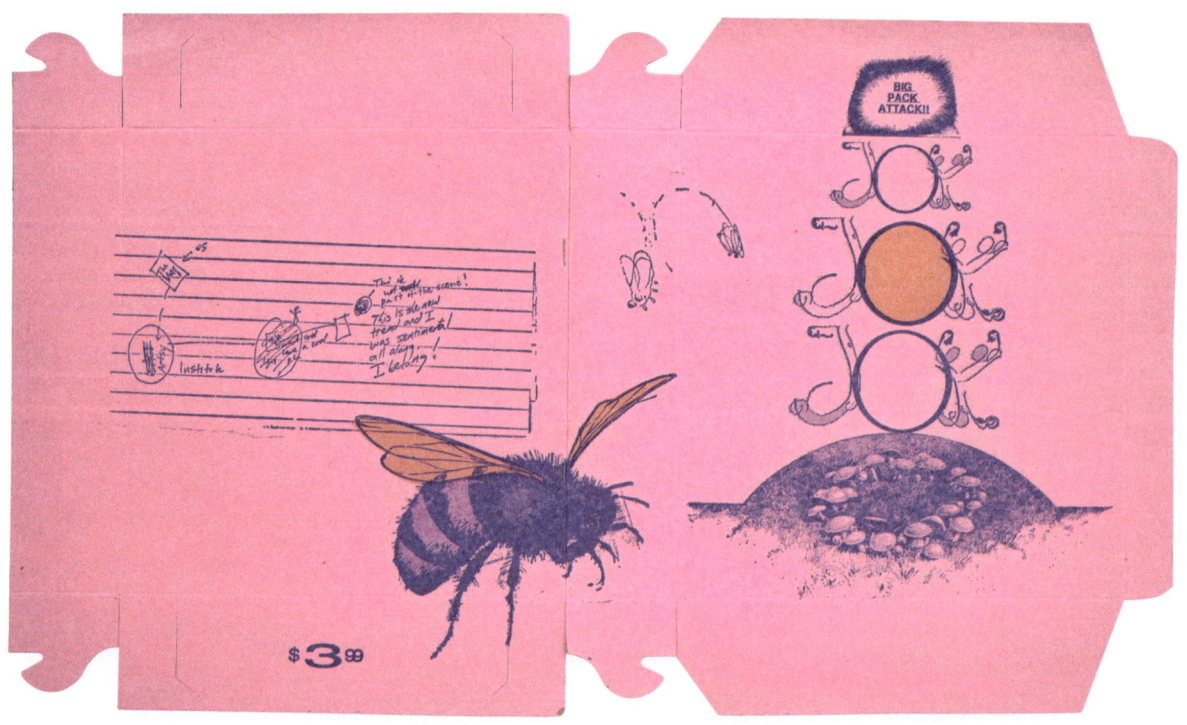

Laurel Beckman, Ryan Hill, Kate Sorensen
Joy, no. 1, 1994
Letterpress, offset, silkscreen on pastry box,
12½ × 11 in. (31.8 × 27.9 cm)
Collection Laurel Beckman

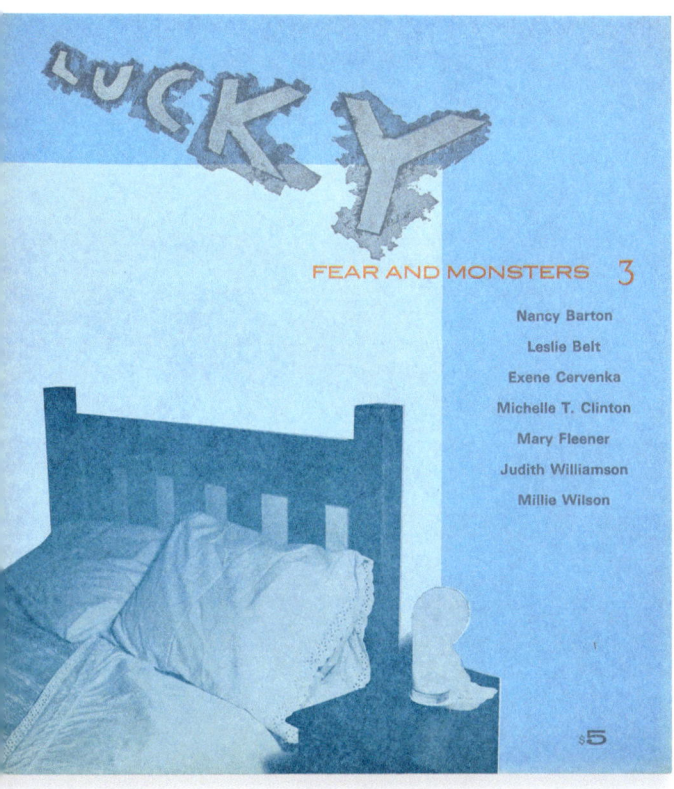

Laurel Beckman and Kate Sorensen
Lucky, no. 3, *Fear and Monsters*, 1990
Letterpress, offset, photocopy, latex on blue stock
cover, 11 × 10⅛ in. (27.9 × 25.7 cm)
Collection Laurel Beckman

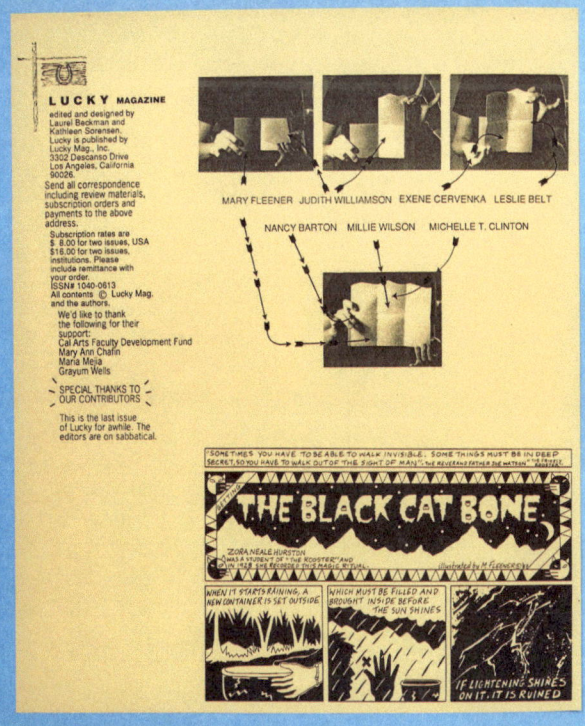

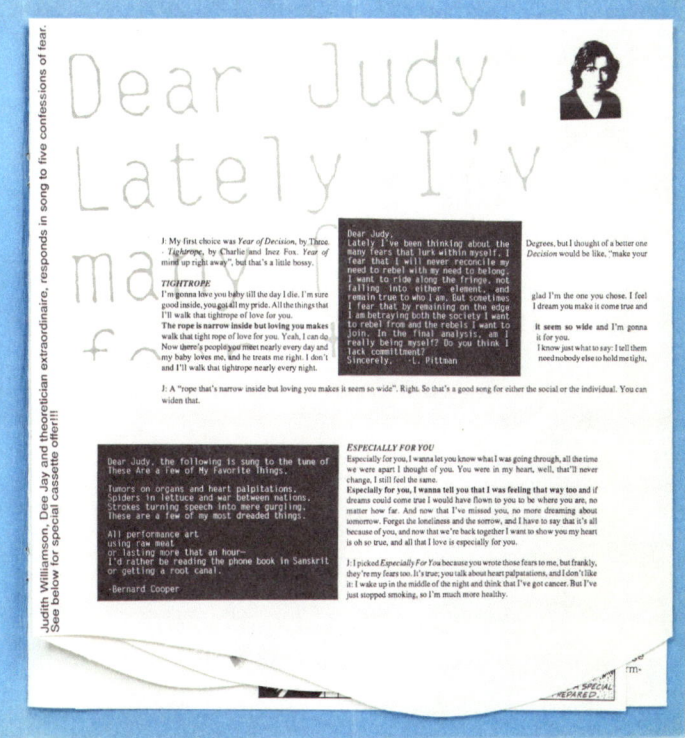

Cool Older Siblings:
Queer Zines as Queer Theory

Julia Bryan-Wilson

The cool older sibling might have dyed-purple hair, teach you how to smoke pot, share her record collection with you, lend you her fake ID. The cool older sibling might sneak you into R-rated movies, might switch the radio in the family car to the alternative college station, might show you how to use eyeliner. The cool older sibling might give you a book by Toni Cade Bambara or Maxine Hong Kingston for your birthday.

Feminist and queer pedagogies are frequently examined through a generational lens, but rather than taking the familiar rift between parents and children as my starting point (as many generational accounts do), I approach queer feminist zines through the model of the "cool older sibling." Zines impart to us, with a tender and protective intimacy, the insights of someone just a few years older. A zine can function as a passport to another realm, a path to subcultural style, a map of new modes of embodiment that might otherwise be just out of reach. Like a cool older sibling, a zine can beckon to those who are slightly younger, inaugurating those who might be unfamiliar with a scene by outlining its rituals and hazards. Offering tips like: Here's how you make a dental dam out of a latex glove to protect yourself from contracting HIV during oral sex. Or, Watch out: that club is notorious for letting dangerous men have their way. Zines are sites of learning, yet the lessons they impart about topics such as feminist practices and queer embodiment are less patronizing and didactic than they are conspiratorial. In them, knowledge is passed down and also *passed around*—handed out at a club, or stacked next to the tampon dispenser.

Much literature is devoted to feminist intergenerational relations, both the conflicts and the accords within feminist theory and activism, including the debated terminology of successive "waves" of feminism that presumes a linear and teleological development. Gendered familial and maternal metaphors like "dutiful daughters" and "foremothers" have suffused feminist thinking about genealogies.[1] By contrast, I take my cues from thinkers such as Juliet Mitchell and Helen Molesworth, who argue for a more laterally oriented relationality and also friction. My own model is (like Molesworth's) gender-neutral, a siblinghood rather than a sisterhood, and relies on the queer idea of a horizontal and chosen family, instead of a born family.[2] Writing generationally about queer zines in this manner means accounting for far-flung constellations of influence and connection, including "a copy of a copy of a copy belonging to a sister of an older brother's best friend [which] might find its way into the hands of a young punk," as gender scholar and zine-maker Mimi Thi Nguyen notes.[3]

Part of what queer zines meant to me in the 1990s, from my late teens into my early twenties, was access—access not only to life-saving information but also to new identifications and other subjectivities that I might not otherwise have been capable of imagining. Seeing copies of, for example, *Bamboo Girl* zine (which was started in 1995 by editrix Sabrina Margarita Alcantara-Tan and ran for some ten years) gave me the thrill of discovery as a young queer feminist, hungry—starved—for stories about female anger and pictures of female desire from as many perspectives as I could find. "Confronting racism, sexism, and homophobia from the Filipina/API/Asian mutt feminist point of view" was *Bamboo Girl*'s stated manifesto, and in its pages I was exposed to more about what is now called intersectional feminism than I had been in my women's studies courses in college.[4] With their hand-drawn figures of rad women, collages made from magazines, grainy photographs, and typewriter fonts, these sorts of lovingly ratty photocopied publications—made on the cheap due to scams everyone knew how to pull off at Kinko's—gave shape to ways of being alive that were nowhere else represented.[5] Writer Hanif Abdurraqib comments, in reference to the Black punk zine **Shotgun Seamstress**, that these publications acted in some essential way as "blueprints for survival."[6]

→ 366–67

Especially potent for me were the zines created to push against punk maleness and punk straightness and punk whiteness: to quote the cover of Alcantara-Tan's *Bamboo Girl* no. 1, its content includes "ranting and raving! Weird Filipino shit! Racial rage and feminine sexuality!" Queer zines were the only places where I read first-person accounts of abuses of power in lesbian relationships, the shame of experiencing childhood poverty, the nitty-gritty of sex work, and meditations on the hotness of the soft butch, from the standpoint of someone who was a near-peer. The feeling of elder siblinghood was imparted by those who were maybe just a handful of years older than I was, or even were technically my same age, but who had been made wiser by their experiences, and from whom I absorbed vital education. In a time when collective knowledge of marginalized queer bodily practices could not be easily found in the library (and personal computers were not widespread), zines were the repositories of crucial information about how to bind breasts, say, or how to make a homemade packing penis.

160–64 ←

Queercore older siblings G. B. Jones and Bruce LaBruce, in their zine **J.D.s** (1985–91) highlighted graphic, raunchy sex scenes featuring both fags and dykes, indicating a cross-gender zone of fantasy, despite the fact that "gay porn" and "lesbian erotica" were usually found on different shelves in most queer bookstores, segregated even by nomenclature. *J.D.s* featured Jones's pencil drawings of white, working-class butches that took inspiration from the work of Tom of Finland—pictures about which author Dodie Bellamy enthused: "I was desperate for nasty female role models. When I encountered G. B. Jones's 'Tom Girls,' my heart flip-flopped. Jones co-opts the male-on-male objectifying gaze of gay erotica and converts it to a female-on-female gaze. By claiming their own objectification, the dykes of Jones's drawings exude a venomous sexuality that wards off predators."[7] The situations Jones drew referred to more than just lesbian sexuality; they captured glimpses of radical politics: within them, women were shown fighting back against police, and triumphing.[8]

Many queer zines were produced out of an urgent need to provide narratives, or invent paradigms, not found in white, straight, normative culture. Alcantara-Tan, in "The Herstory of *Bamboo Girl* Zine," writes of the lack of a context that led her to create her zine: "I was looking for a fierce Asian woman to look up to so I could read and feel validated, and it would have been even cooler if she was of mixed race like me. But no luck."[9] She writes, too, of being touched by those (like me) who read her zine, who were not Asian or mixed race but who saw in her raw handiwork and outpourings of angst a form of possible or incipient kinship.

The cool older brother is the first one you tell about getting your period. The cool older sister might encourage you to learn carpentry alongside her. The cool older sibling might be queer, might be trans, might be nonbinary. They might be cis and straight but support you if you are queer, or trans, or enby.

The zine as a genre is a tool of knowledge-sharing among loose networks; it can help catalyze solidarities across difference or foment insurgent group identifications. Another term for what this enacts is "world-making." Queer world-making is about activating unlikely affiliations that have nothing to do with blood. Neither does the idea of the cool older sibling rely on actual genetic links—they can also be a friend, or a friend of a friend. World-making as a concept has had a long life in queer theory, emerging as a critical keyword in the late 1990s alongside the broader academic uptake of queer theory, in José Esteban Muñoz's work on queer-of-color performance and in Lauren Berlant and Michael Warner's postulation of queer counterpublics.[10]

In their 1998 article "Sex in Public," Berlant and Warner state that "the queer world is a space of entrances, exits, unsystematized lines of acquaintance, projected horizons, typifying examples, alternate routes, blockages, incommensurate geographies," gesturing to meandering circuits that feel akin to the oblique ways that zines circulate.[11] *Bamboo Girl* and other zines articulated a theory of queer world-making in advance of these thinkers; in fact, Muñoz's critical notion of "disidentifications" is rooted in queer Black punk zines such as Vaginal Davis's **Fertile**

172–75 ←

La Toyah Jackson Magazine, which began in 1987 as a print publication and later spawned video and live performance.[12] Zines, that is, put these theories into practice and were foundational for them, as tangible exemplars on which the theories were built—and not only by those thinkers who came into their scholarship partly through *making* zines, like Nguyen, who has been producing zines since 1991 and has also been a prominent voice advocating for more nuanced and less whitewashed zine histories.[13] Queer zines were also the laboratory spaces for testing out ideas that would later emerge in the academy around anti-assimilation politics, homo-normativity, and the abolition of police. Queer scholar Adela C. Licona emphasizes the idea of "radical cooperation" in her examination of feminist and queer-of-color zines, elucidating how the circulation of zines activates a queer commons.[14]

Julia Bryan-Wilson

Such vectors of influence between queer theory and queer zines pointed in multiple directions, as ideas swirled from zine to academic text and back to zine. Indeed, with their expediency and cheapness, zines offered an effective route of publication for significant texts before the institutionalization of queer theory. For instance, a 1978 photocopied and stapled "workbook" (essentially a zine) called *Chez Foucault*, edited by cultural theorist Simeon Wade, contains the original transcript of an important 1975 conversation, "Dialogue on Power," between students at Pomona College and the French thinker Michel Foucault.[15] The irreverent *Judy!*, a 1993 fanzine that lustily celebrates influential philosopher and gender theorist Judith Butler, intersperses snide asides about Dennis Cooper and his tired "revolutionary boy-posturing" with snippets parodying MLA conference gossip: "The New York Hilton was SIZZLING this December as the famous theorists swarmed the lobby and the cash bars. . . . Eve Sedgwick worked the crowd."[16]

For issue 1 of *Judy!* (made in the pre-Google era), the zine's author, University of Iowa undergraduate Andrea Lawlor-Mariano, placed photographs of queer icon Judy Garland on the cover and in the interior, noting: "It's really hard to find pictures of Judith Butler so here is another Judy." Not long after the fanzine appeared, Butler attacked *Judy!* for being "slanderous . . . demeaning" and for trivializing academic dialogue. Butler's negative words, and journalist Larissa MacFarquhar's response to the zine in the journal *Lingua Franca*, were published in a subsequent issue of *Judy!*, generating a distinct sense that queer theory might have several (and not always compatible) audiences.[17] *Judy!* reveled in and humorously deployed queer theory's libidinal language, but drew condemnation from Butler because it did so from "below"—that is, from the often-degraded space of the fan—as a brazen act of tastelessness.

The debate illustrates how, in the late 1980s and into the 1990s, queer zines and queer theory, although closely twinned, sometimes had a contentious, even rivalrous relationship— rivalry is one hallmark of the sibling formation. A zine like *Judy!* excitedly pulled high theory down into the trenches, generating new forms of queer reading with its irreverence and making Butler's provocations differently accessible, but as the example of Muñoz demonstrates, zines were also fertile arenas where queer theory was organically cultivated and then harvested. Due to their unequal positions in stratified zones of privilege with distinct relationships to notions of cred and authenticity, the tone of the turf wars between academics and zine makers sometimes veered from skepticism to outright hostility. In his book *Queercore: Queer Punk Media Subculture*, media scholar Curran Nault states: "Queer theory owes much of its inspiration to the activists and artists who practice its application, but this has not always been acknowledged or appreciated: as queercore instigator G. B. Jones said . . . 'We invented queer theory. We lived it. But, we're not academics, so we don't get credited with it, because we didn't write the book about it.'"[18] The formative role played by zines in academic thought and the richness of theorizations about queer desire enacted within their pages were only spottily recognized—embraced by Muñoz as indispensable but rejected by Butler as objectionably salacious and diluted.

The cool older sibling will beat up your bullies, tell you the truth about your parents' divorce, warn you about your uncle.

Although the emphasis is often put on "world" in queer theories of world-making, queer zines also underscore the importance of *making*: making by hand, making in solitude in a bedroom, making with others at a convention, making with a pseudonym, making with scissors and black markers, peeling dried glue from fingertips, pricking one's palm with a rogue staple. Queer in both form and content, the zine's emphasis on cut-and-paste collage was a method of reassembling given sign-systems and torquing received images away from themselves to forge new languages. Zines also queered circuits of distribution. Before the dawn of the internet, these do-it-yourself publications were trafficked via local gift economies and microeconomies: given away for free, swapped and bartered, or sold for cost, two or three dollars each. They could be left anonymously on a table at the rape crisis center for anyone who might need them. Nobody created a zine to make money, but rather to telegraph something urgent. They were exchanged in face-to-face encounters as a way to say: *This is who I am. Now show me with your zine, who are you?*

The amateur, anti-capitalist, DIY aspect of the making of zines is particularly important with respect to the punk music and indie film/video worlds with which they are integrally connected. A rebellious eagerness to make one's own culture rather than be content with the corporate dregs on offer is what draws together these very disparate practices across print media, music, and screen technologies. Each of these practices feeds off, and reciprocally into, related activist efforts around healthcare, HIV/AIDS awareness, anti-racist endeavors, women's rights, and queer/trans rights. Together this welter of activity makes a set of demands related to personal autonomy and collective freedom. The proposition is this: to control your own body and to take things into your own hands is to participate in a struggle for liberation. Sometimes what this looks like is scathing and confrontational, as in W. Wayne Karr and Cory Roberts Auli's zine

202–4 ← **Infected Faggot Perspectives**, initiated in the early 1990s, "dedicated to keeping the realities of faggots living WITH AIDS and HIV Disease IN YOUR FACE until the plague is OVER."[19] At other times, it is openly instructional, like zines about how to administer emmenagogic herbs that will induce abortion (*Hot Pantz: Do It Yourself Gynecology*, 1995).[20]

One important initiative in this regard that interlaced activism, music, pedagogy, and a print component was *Free to Fight: An Interactive Self-Defense Project*, 1995. Organized by a group that included Jody Bleyle of the queer punk/Riot Grrrl band Team Dresch, youth counselor/martial artist Anna LoBianco, and self-defense teacher Staci Cotler, the *Free to Fight* zine package consists of a compilation record and accompanying instructional booklet with stories, drawings, comics, and practical advice about self-identified women and girls fighting back; it was issued by Bleyle's Candy Ass Records, headquartered in Portland, Oregon. The album tracks alternate between songs (including one by G. B. Jones's band Fifth Column) and verbal directives in self-defense; the seventy-five-page zine is a resource guide containing personal testimonies about assault, accounts of successful resistance, and how-to advice about body language and when to use violence. It begins with a boldly outlined four-step diagram captioned "how to make a fist." The power of the female figure punching back is also foregrounded on several covers of the contemporaneous *Bamboo Girl* (with winking allusions to other uses of the fist in queer sex).

Free to Fight also contains an excerpt, reprinted with permission, from renowned author and activist bell hooks's 1990 book *Yearning: Race, Gender, and Cultural Politics*, a text that anchors notions of safety within distinctly racialized and gendered histories, commenting that "this task of making homeplace was not simply a matter of black women providing service; it was about the construction of a safe place where black people could affirm one another and by doing so heal many of the wounds inflicted by racist domination."[21] *Free to Fight* had a vivid life after the album release, spawning live self-help demonstrations at Riot Grrrl conventions as a way to try to make good on its promise that "the money from this project is going to be used to teach self-defense to communities that cannot afford this capitalist society"—although this pledge was limited by the exclusionary stratifications around race and class that persisted in many aspects of the scene.[22]

The cool older sibling develops a drug problem, drops out of high school, steals your allowance, sneaks money from your mom's purse, gets kicked out of the house. The cool older sibling has a controlling boyfriend who is mean to you and when he ODs and dies, you are not sad but relieved.

How many queer zines grew out of that undersung and enormously generative affect known as disenchantment? A lot, probably. Zine histories are full of words like "frustrated," "tired," "burned out," and "fed up." Often oppositional by nature, zines like *Bamboo Girl* were made because, to quote Alcantara-Tan, she was "getting totally disenchanted with the punk and hardcore scene."[23] To a rejected seventeen-year-old standing outside, the eighteen-and-over club seems like a glittering and magic promised land; once the youngster is finally let in, the place turns out to be another cramped dump filled with assholes. But such disenchantment can in turn drive innovation. In 1995 artist Miranda July started the feminist video "chainletter" **Big Miss**

264–65 ← **Moviola** (later titled *Joanie 4 Jackie*), a DIY method of circulating "lady-made movies" to other self-identified (trans-inclusive) women by issuing "a challenge and a promise" to compile ten short videos onto VHS tapes.[24] However, the movies that July received from her first call

Julia Bryan-Wilson

were predominantly by white, middle-class younger women in college, and the revolutionary underground she aspired to promote proved to be yet another instance of in-crowd narrowness.

So in 1996 July went out with a tape recorder to the streets of Portland, Oregon, and posed a question to women: "If you could make a movie, what would it be about?" She recorded their answers and printed them, along with inky photographs, on a long poster titled **The Missing Movie Report.** "The idea of revolution was available to me and actually foundational to the projects I made. I wouldn't have bothered doing any of them if I didn't feel that possibility," recalls July. "I had identified a structure that didn't work and was trying to provide another one, though I had no authority to do so as a young queer woman."[25] *The Missing Movie Report* was a way to acknowledge that the alternative system she was setting up was also flawed, with structural blind spots around race, age, and class. The faces on the poster are notably more diverse than those of the contributors to July's first few "chainletters." "Oh no, I'm too old for that kind of thing," says one woman; others dream of making movies about "positive black role models," and "a female action hero," and "how men can do whatever and women are, excuse my language, their sluts or whores." "The best movies of 1996 will never be made," the poster declares. "But that's not a reason to forget about them." Using the interview snippets was a way to point to an archival void and a systemic inequality—an ecology in which most women still did not have access to video cameras, and even if they did, were not granting themselves permission to think of their creations as grandiose "movies."[26]

→ 266

July, who came out of a zine-making background, wanted to fuel the same kind of energy in which the lines between consumer and producer were forever blurred. As she wrote in the first issue of *Big Miss Moviola* in 1995:

> Even though big budget mainstream movies are sometimes moving or scarey, on the whole they, in my opinion, do not inspire women in the audience to go: **I can do that.** This is partly because the movies are usually **womanhating** or racist or classist. I also think it is because they have nothing to do with the kind of things that women talk to eachother about. For example: Reading other women's fanzines's usually makes me want to write because I am feeling like I am in some kind of indirect "conversation" with this stranger girl. I am allowed to participate. I wish movies could be like this. And I think they can.[27]

July also encouraged others to make "missing movie" reports, especially if they couldn't themselves make a video, exhorting in the 1996 **Underwater Chainletter** booklet: "Trade in your personal frustration for big big inspiration."[28] (This might be the moment to disclose that I worked with July on her project for a spell, including most prominently as the co-editor and designer of this very zine from 1996.)

→ 264

Queer zines should be understood as an accessible and tactile manifestation of critical queer theory. This is evident in many of the zines I have been discussing, and it is palpable in July's treatises from *Joanie 4 Jackie* that articulate a queer feminist theory of female spectatorship and of the potential for participatory filmmaking. It bears repeating that nobody invents their revolution out of thin air; rather, they enlist the support of the coalitions around them, and in this vein July had cool older siblings to draw from, including G. B. Jones with her 1992 low-budget movie *The YoYo Gang* (the trailer for which was included on July's *U-Matic Chainletter* in 1996).

Throughout July's work with *Joanie 4 Jackie*, along with her writings, ephemera, and videos (such as **The Amateurist**, 1998), she outlines a dynamic theory of the gendered gaze, not beating the usual dead horse of the "male gaze," but rather illuminating the rarely considered girl's-eye view. She proposes a continuum, for instance, between being spied upon by an incestuous father and a male doctor's medicalized scrutiny. In the framework of *The Amateurist*, in which a "professional" monitors a seemingly captive "amateur," July renders these positions unstable, alluding to shifts in power that can occur when the watched subject dares to look back at the camera lens. In her writings for *Joanie 4 Jackie*, July entangles queer lesbian cruising, self-surveillance, and the constant vigilance required because of creepy gawking men within her subtle discussions of the pleasures of women looking at other women. These complex

→ 267

lines of vision, in particular the notion of how "being watched" becomes internalized within the pervasive activity of watching, are conscripted into July's open-ended idea about "movie-making." "It is the idea that girls and women are Moviemakers every second of every hour of our lives. We watch ourselves being watched every day and night. . . . We are making movies in our head everyday and the camera is OUR EYES."[29]

The cool older sibling keeps the letters you wrote them in college. The cool older sibling remembers your secrets.

I'll admit my discomfort with the idea of a museum exhibition of zines. Because the zine is always a super-local and anti-institutional phenomenon, and because it seems nonsensical to try to create a timeline or overview of a movement so vast and unruly. Zines are akin to scribbles on drawing pads shown to friends, or mixtapes given to lovers, or marginalia in books scattered throughout the world's libraries; how can anyone possibly claim to have surveyed even a sliver of what is out there? Given that zines are such a fragmented, multiple, and dispersed sphere of global cultural production, it would be insane to claim comprehensive expertise about them. Some zines exist as only one exquisite volume, tucked away in a dresser drawer. At the same time, I am wary of seemingly ahistorical attempts to corral any small publication under the rubric of "the zine." For me, a zine is not just any little newsletter, but a specific form of self-publishing that is at the same time a method of community formation.

It is common practice to be troubled by the evident holes that gape open when personal memory becomes official history. And although I recognize that growing repositories of zine collections in the United States—at the Fales Library at New York University, the ONE Archives at the University of Southern California, and the Barnard College Zine Library, for example—are providing materials for new avenues of research and facilitating future discoveries, I also am indifferent about certain mass-market efforts to narrate these necessarily incomplete histories.[30] I feel cynical about how major corporate publishing houses are looking for ways to crack into multiple markets by looking to zine-inspired first-person memoir and auto-fiction.

But just as we should honor the pivotal role played by peers, friends, and slightly more mature comrades—anyone, that is, with a little more experience to share—so too should we respect all the younger siblings, and students, and emerging zine makers who might need to be shown the ropes. Take, as my last example, the artist and filmmaker Maggie Lee, who grasped the alluring style of punk as early as age six, when she asked her mother and older sister (who introduced Lee to Riot Grrrl) to throw her a punk-themed birthday party, an event

374 ←

377 ←

commemorated in her 2020 zine **Punk Party '93**. The bright pink cover shows her small face as she leans over to blow out the candles of her birthday cake. Lee works with techniques of collage across genres, including in her trailblazing video **Mommy** (2015), which mourns her mother's death in an atemporal pastiche layering fragments of home footage. Lee shows how little sisters usually turn out to be cooler, more mind-blowing, and more boundary-breaking than any older sibling could ever dream of being.

This essay is dedicated to D'Arcy Chell, the coolest older sister ever.

NOTES

[1] See Iris van der Tuin, *Generational Feminism: New Materialist Introduction to a Generative Approach* (Lanham, MD: Lexington Books, 2015).

[2] I choose siblinghood over the 1970s rubric of feminist sisterhood, which too often is reduced to a cis-terhood; see Robin Morgan, ed. *Sisterhood Is Powerful: An Anthology of Writings from the Women's Liberation Movement* (New York: Random House, 1970). Juliet Mitchell, *Siblings: Sex and Violence* (Cambridge, UK: Polity, 2003); Helen Molesworth, "How to Install Art as a Feminist," in *Women Artists at the Museum of Modern Art*, ed. Cornelia Butler and Alexandra Schwartz (New York: Museum of Modern Art, 2010). See also Catherine Grant, *A Time of*

One's Own: Histories of Feminism in Contemporary Art (Durham, NC: Duke University Press, 2022), which opens with the author's encounter with the zine *LTTR*.

[3] Mimi Thi Nguyen, "Minor Threats," *Radical History Review*, no. 122, "Queering Archives" special issue, ed. Kevin Murphy, Daniel Marshall, and Zeb Tortorici (May 2015): 11–12.

[4] Sabrina Margarita Alcantara-Tan, *Bamboo Girl* Zine blogspot; bamboogirlzine.blogspot.com.

Julia Bryan-Wilson

5 I considered writing an entire how-to guide about the best ways to make photocopies at corporate copy centers on the cheap, but the technology has changed over the years and most of my advice is out of date. So I'll keep it simple: the number one way, then as now, is to make friends with people who work at a copy shop or get a job at one yourself, preferably on the night shift when there is less managerial oversight.

6 Hanif Abdurraqib, "Shotgun Seamstress," *4Columns*, December 2, 2022; 4columns.org/abdurraqib-hanif/shotgun-seamstress.

7 Dodie Bellamy, "Fan Letter: On G. B. Jones's Nasty Female Role Models," *Frieze* (January 9, 2019); frieze.com/article/dodie-bellamy-gb-joness-nasty-female-role-models.

8 See Jones's own description about the difference between her work and that of Tom of Finland vis-à-vis the police, Sasha, "Ms. Jones: You Got a Thing Going On," *Xtra* (April 27, 2005); xtramagazine.com/culture/ms-jones-24381.

9 Sabrina Margarita Alcantara-Tan, "The Herstory of *Bamboo Girl* Zine," *Frontlines: A Journal of Women's Studies* 21, no. 1/2 (2000): 159.

10 José Esteban Muñoz, *Disidentifications: Queers of Color and the Performance of Politics* (Minneapolis: University of Minnesota Press, 1999); Lauren Berlant and Michael Warner, "Sex in Public," *Critical Inquiry* 24, no. 2 (1998): 547–66.

11 Berlant and Warner, "Sex in Public," 558.

12 The zine, and its video and performance offshoots, are first mentioned by Muñoz in "The White to Be Angry: Vaginal Davis's Terrorist Drag," *Social Text*, no. 52/52 (Fall–Winter 1997), 80–103; this text was repurposed as a chapter in Muñoz's *Disidentifications*.

13 Mimi Thi Nguyen, "Riot Grrrl, Race, and Revival," *Women & Performance: A Journal of Feminist Theory* 22, no. 2–3 (July–November 2012): 173–96.

14 Adela C. Licona, *Zines in the Third Space: Radical Cooperation and Borderland Rhetorics* (Albany: State University of New York Press, 2012).

15 Simeon Wade, ed. *Chez Foucault* (Los Angeles: Circabook, 1978).

16 Andrea Lawlor-Mariano, *Judy!* no. 1 (published in Iowa City, Iowa, 1993), n.p.

17 Larissa MacFarquhar, "Putting the Camp Back in Campus," *Lingua Franca* (September/October 1993); and response by Butler repr. in *Judy!* no. 2 (1993).

18 Curran Nault, *Queercore: Queer Punk Media Subculture* (London: Routledge, 2018), 7.

19 W. Wayne Karr and Cory Roberts-Auli, *Infected Faggot Perspectives* (Los Angeles, 1991–93). For an argument about how this kind of zine fostered a counterpublic, see Daniel Brouwer, "Counterpublicity and Corporeality in HIV/AIDS Zines," *Critical Studies in Media Communication* 22, no. 5 (2005): 357–71.

20 Isabelle Gauthier and Lisa Vinebaum, *Hot Pantz*, an English adaptation of the French version *C'est toujours chaud dans les coulottes des filles* (Quebec: Blood Sisters, 1994).

21 bell hooks, "Homeplace: A Site of Resistance," in *Yearning: Race, Gender, and Cultural Politics* (Boston: South End Press, 1990), repr. in *Free to Fight: An Interactive Self Defense Project* (Portland, Oregon: Candy Ass Records, 1995), n.p.

22 The proliferation of zines from around the world that focus on techniques of self-defense for women indicates a widespread need for such material. See for example *Autodefensa para mujeres* (Argentina, 2005).

23 Alcantara-Tan, "A Herstory of *Bamboo Girl* Zine," 159.

24 Quotes from Miranda July's *Big Miss Moviola* promotional materials, ca. 1995, author's archive.

25 Miranda July, interview with the author, November 2022.

26 I have written elsewhere about the blanket term "movies," utilized by July as a way to disregard debates about film vs. video medium-specificity; see Julia Bryan-Wilson, "Implicated: Feminist Art Histories and Affective Pasts," repr. in *Institutions by Artists* (Vancouver: Fillip, 2021), 91–102.

27 Miranda July, *Big Miss Moviola*, booklet 1, 1995, n.p. (All typos and bold text in the original.)

28 Miranda July, "The Missing Movie Report," as featured in her *Underwater Chainletter* booklet (designed by July and Julia Bryan-Wilson), 1996.

29 July, *Underwater Chainletter* booklet, 3.

30 For example, for a (fairly conventional) look at the music and zines since the 1990s in the United Kingdom and the United States, see Amy Spencer, *DIY: The Rise of Lo-Fi Culture* (London: Marion Boyars, 2005).

Bryn Austin, Pam Gregg, Adriene Jenik

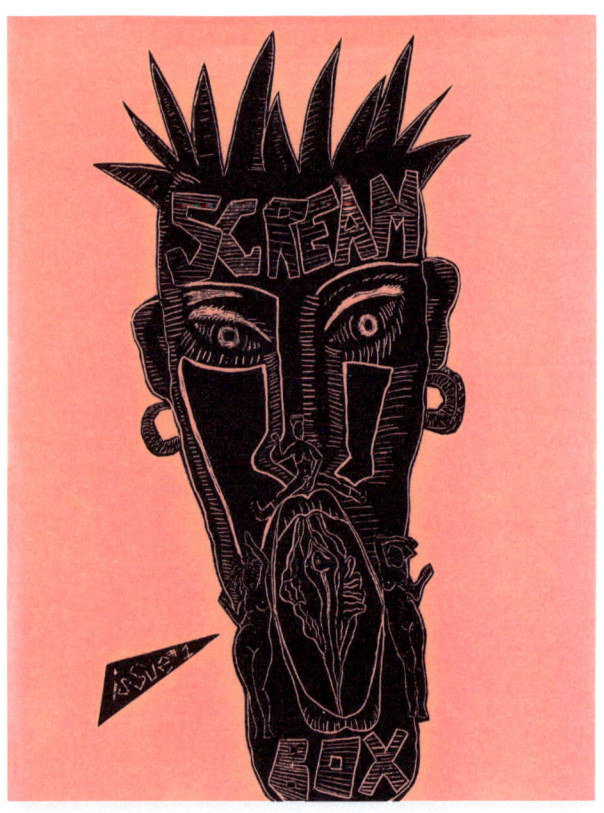

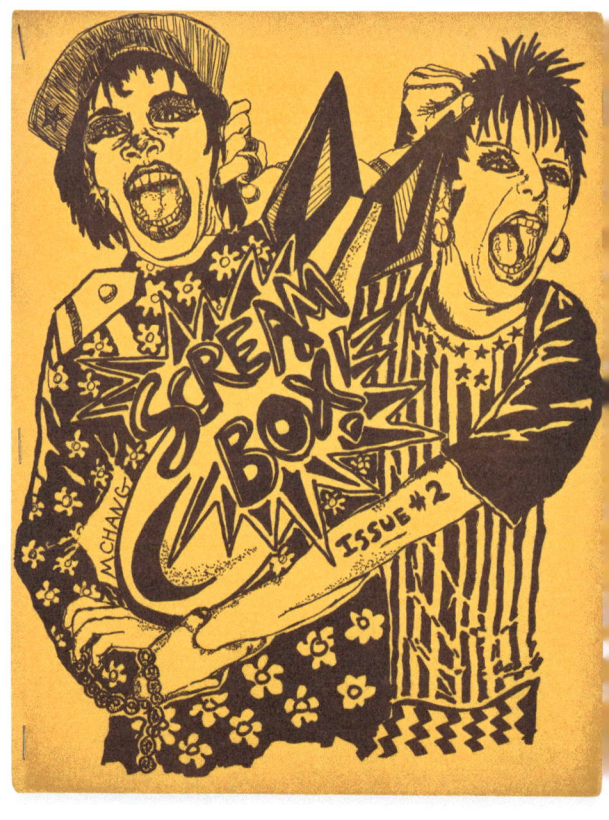

Screambox, no. 1, November 1990
Photocopy, side stapled, pink paper covers,
11 × 8 ½ in. (27.9 × 21.6 cm)
Collection Adriene Jenik

Screambox, no. 2, May 1991
Photocopy, side stapled, yellow paper covers,
11 × 8 ½ in. (27.9 × 21.6 cm)
Collection Adriene Jenik

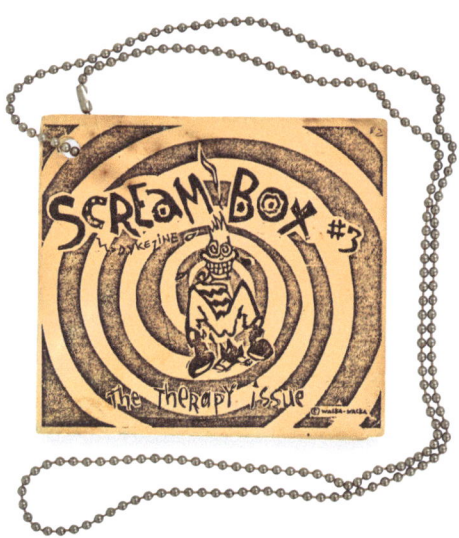

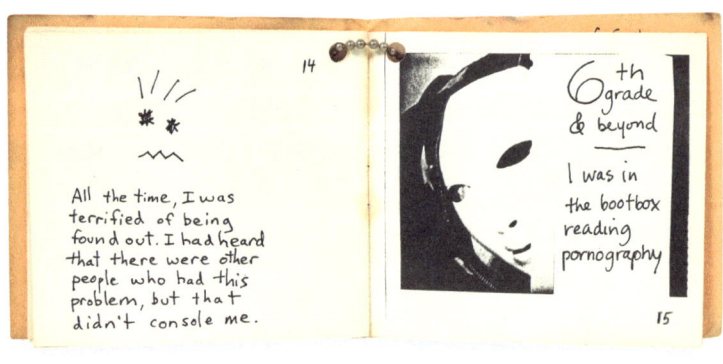

Screambox, no. 3, February 1992
Photocopy, saddle stitched, metal chain, orange paper
wrappers, 4 × 4 ½ in. (10.2 × 11.4 cm)
Collection Adriene Jenik

Tammy Rae Carland

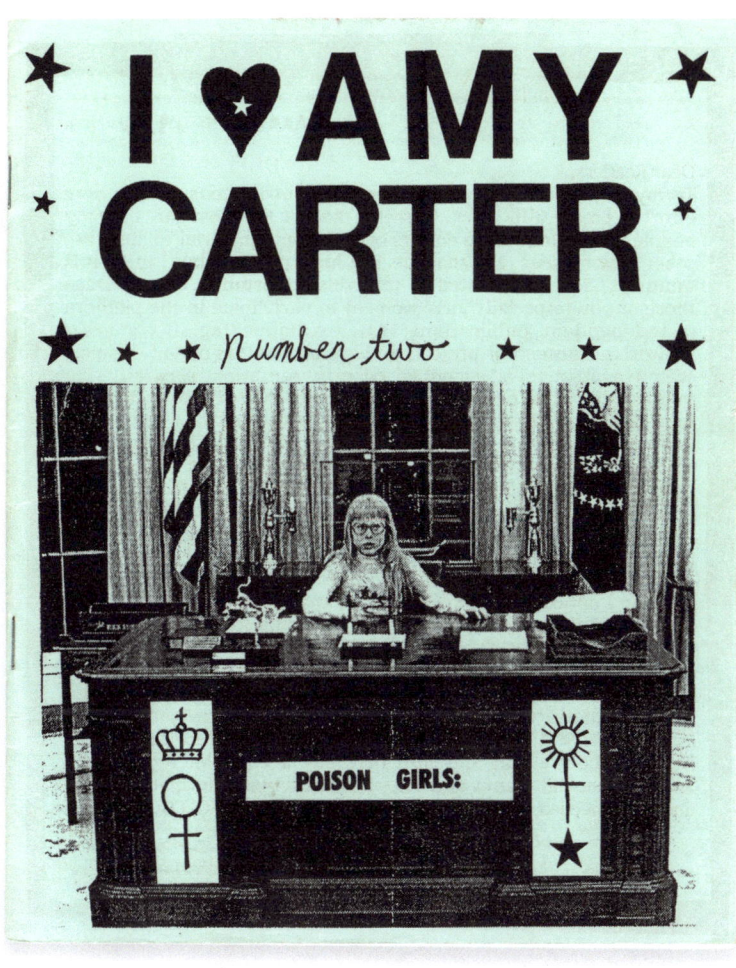

I ♥ Amy Carter, no. 2, 1993
Photocopy, saddle stitched, pastel blue paper wrappers,
8 × 7 in. (20.3 × 17.8 cm)
Fales Library, New York University

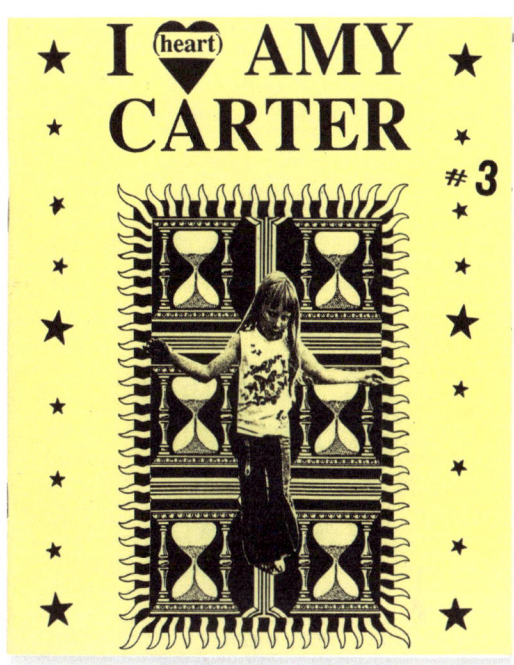

I ♥ Amy Carter, no. 3, Summer 1993
Photocopy, saddle stitched, 8 ½ × 7 in. (21.6 × 17.8 cm)
Collection the artist

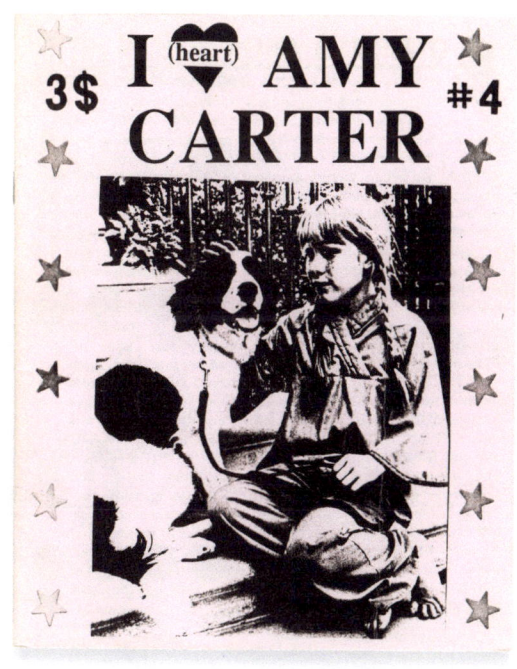

I ♥ Amy Carter, no. 4, January 1994
Photocopy, saddle stitched, pastel pink paper wrappers,
8 ½ × 7 in. (21.6 × 17.8 cm)
Collection Philip Aarons and Shelley Fox Aaron

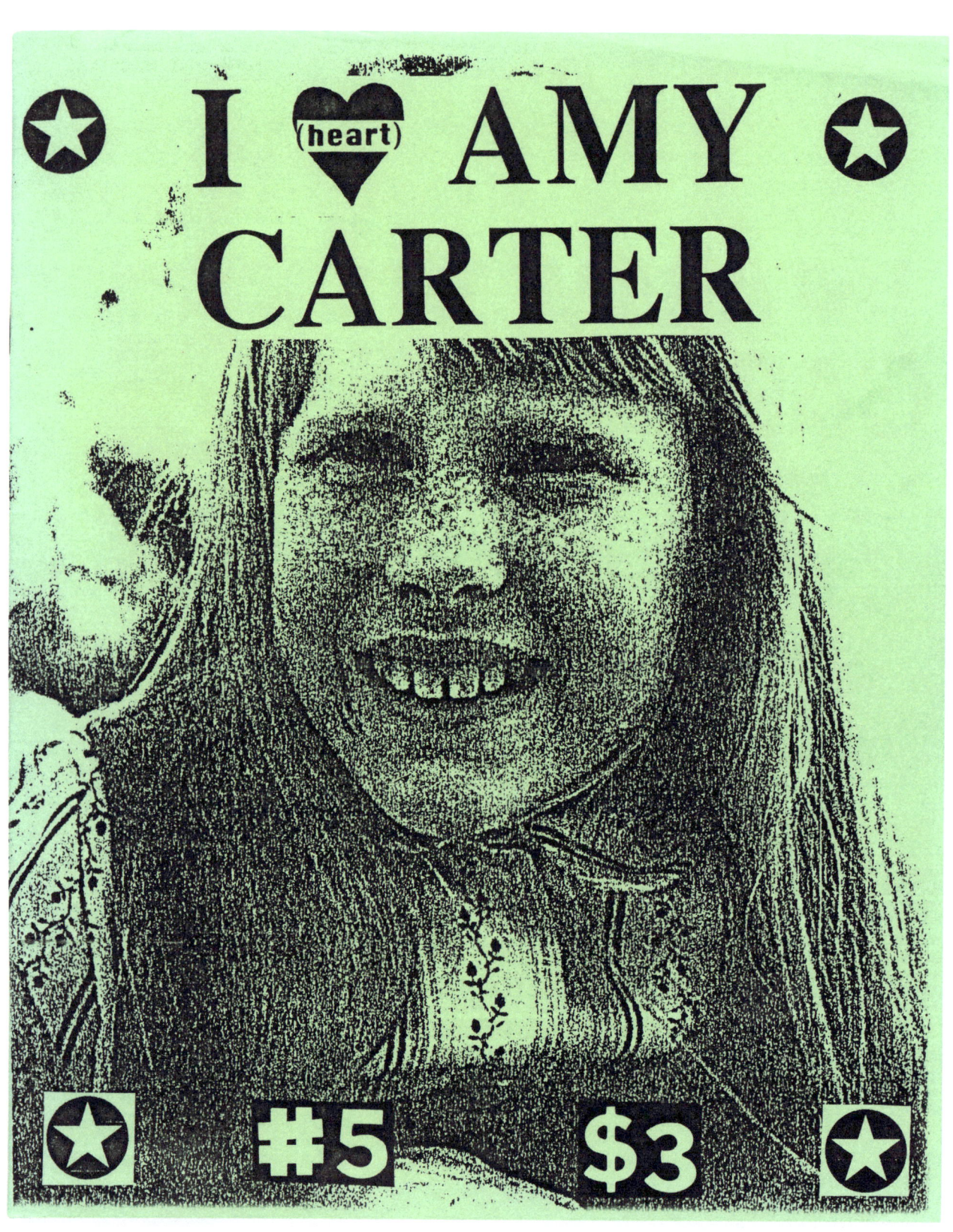

I ♥ Amy Carter, no. 5, Summer 1994
Photocopy, saddle stitched, pastel green paper wrappers,
8 ½ × 7 in. (21.6 × 17.8 cm)
Collection the artist

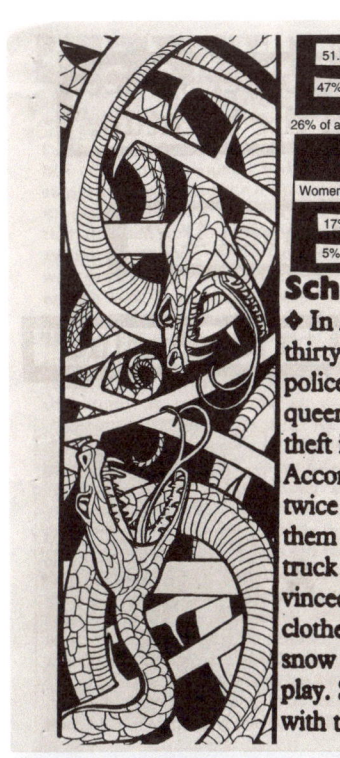

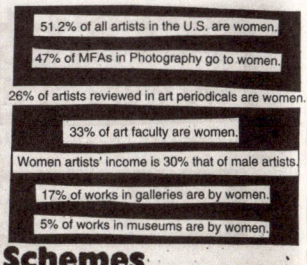

51.2% of all artists in the U.S. are women.

47% of MFAs in Photography go to women.

26% of artists reviewed in art periodicals are women.

33% of art faculty are women.

Women artists' income is 30% that of male artists.

17% of works in galleries are by women.

5% of works in museums are by women.

Schemes

❖ In April, Della Dobbs, thirty-one, the woman police called "the snow queen," was arrested for theft in Stevens Point, Wis. According to police, she twice met men in bars, took them outside to her pickup truck to have sex, and convinced them to take off their clothes, get out, and rub snow on themselves as foreplay. She then drove off with their wallets.

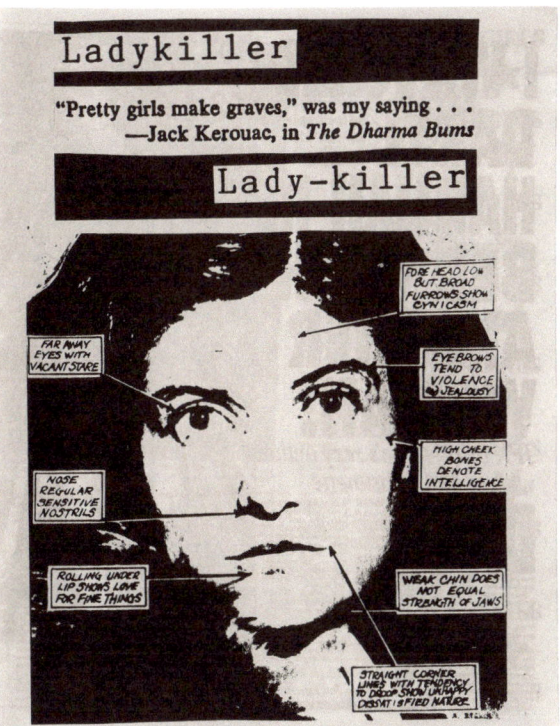

I ♥ Amy Carter, no. 4, January 1994
Photocopy, saddle stitched, pastel pink paper wrappers,
8 ½ × 7 in. (21.6 × 17.8 cm)
Collection Philip Aarons and Shelley Fox Aarons

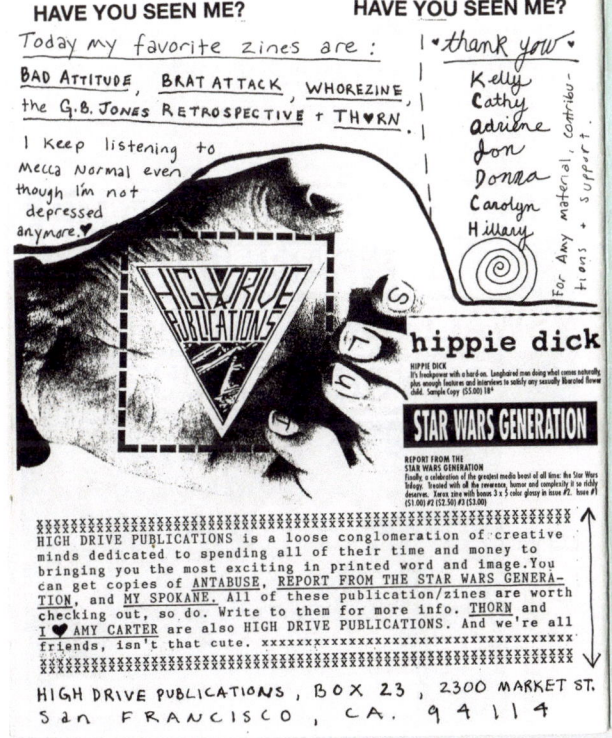

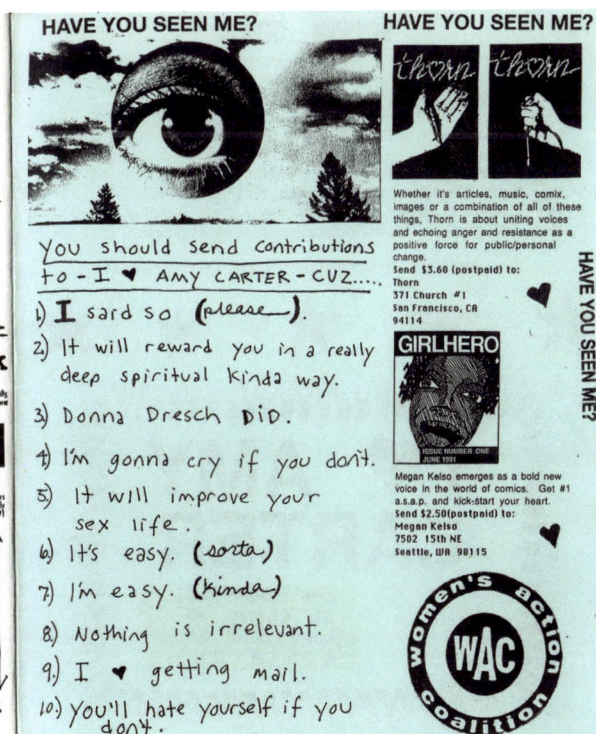

I ♥ Amy Carter, no. 2, 1993
Photocopy, saddle stitched, pastel pink paper wrappers,
8 ½ × 7 in. (21.6 × 17.8 cm)
Fales Library, New York University

★   ★   ★   ★ December 5th, 1992

Dear sweet readers, friends + future dates,

I ♥ (HEART) AMY CARTER has been a long time in the making.
The very first issue of this zine came out in the Fall of 86'
and despite my good intensions and serious desires and devo-
tions to it's existence, I just haven't been able to channel
my juices in this direction. As a matter of fact I don't
even have a copy of the first (now ancient and historic) zine.
So if by chance there's any one out there coverting one of
the precious few (there were only 25 of them made) pretty
please do send me a copy. Anyways, this time it's going to
stick, I mean I feel like I have a lot of AMY STUFF stored up
and ready to share. And the other day her name came up on
3 seperate occasions, so I figured that somehow, somewhere,
someone was trying to tell me something. Maybe even AMY herself. Also there are two other reasons for starting this zine
again: 1) I recently moved to southern CAL and I'm feeling
isolated, bored, lonely, and wanting to meet rad dorky egghead kinda girls...2) I moved here for graduate school and
I need a solid procrastination project to provide me with
an escape, and excuse to not constantly be feeling like all
I do is create fodder for the art world (one of my bigger
fears). And of course the most important of all reasons is
AMY and my commitment to AMYness. More on this later. I would
love it if you would send me any AMY STUFF, and I mean anything; sightings, stories, memories, drawings, comix, photos,
paraphernalia, ANYTHING........also if you want you could
send me info on your favorite AMY TYPE PERSON - whoever this
may be. In general I just love mail. I am a self confessed
mail junkie. So until next time..........★ XO Tammy Rae

I ♥ Amy Carter, no. 1, December 1992
Photocopy, saddle stitched, 8 ½ × 7 in. (21.6 × 17.8 cm)
Fales Library, New York University

→   *Random Letters to Ransom Girls*, 1998
     Photocopy, saddle stitched, cream paper wrappers,
     8 13/16 × 7 in. (22.4 × 17.8 cm)
     Collection the artist

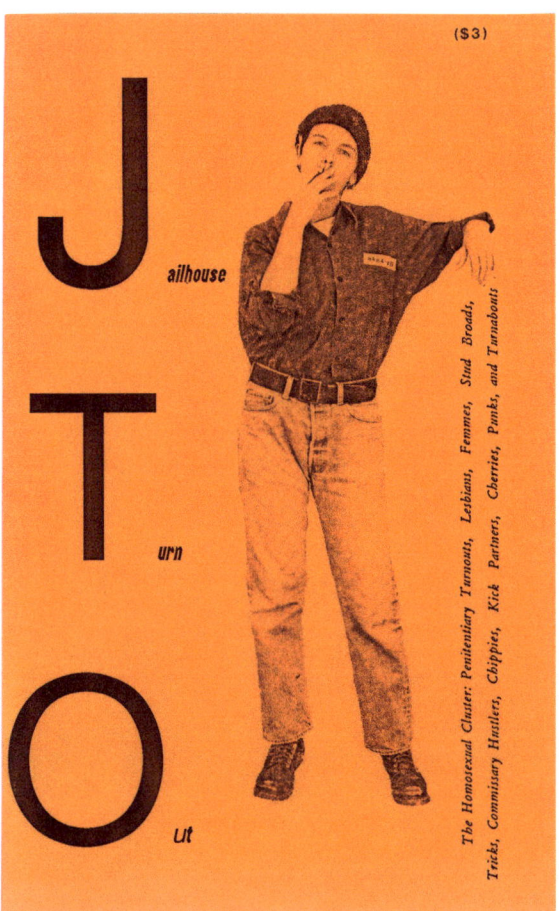

Jailhouse Turn Out, 1996
Photocopy, saddle stitched, illustrated orange wrappers,
8 ½ × 5 ½ in. (21.6 × 14 cm)
Fales Library, New York University

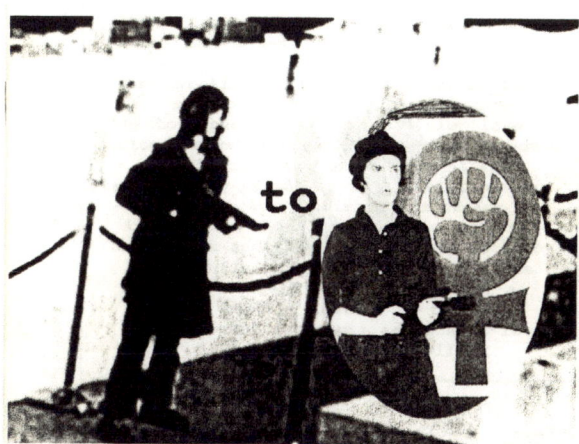

On Becoming: Billy and Katie 1964, 1998
Eight gelatin silver prints, 24 × 20 in. (61 × 58.1 cm) each
Collection the artist

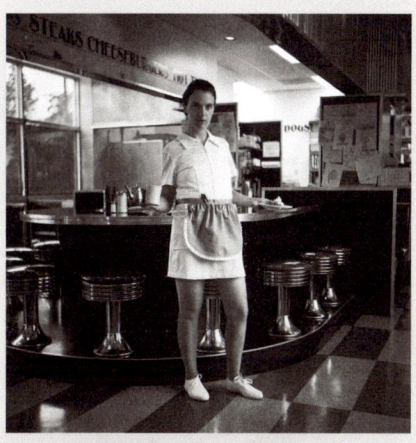

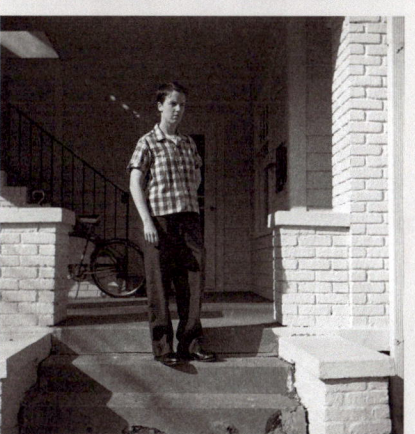

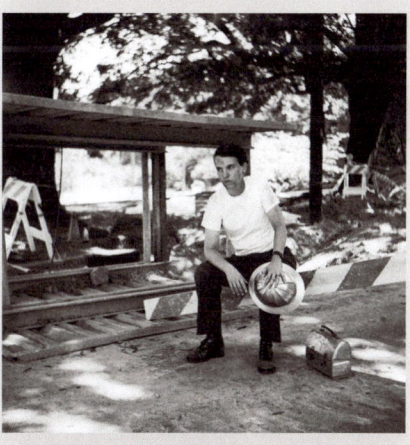

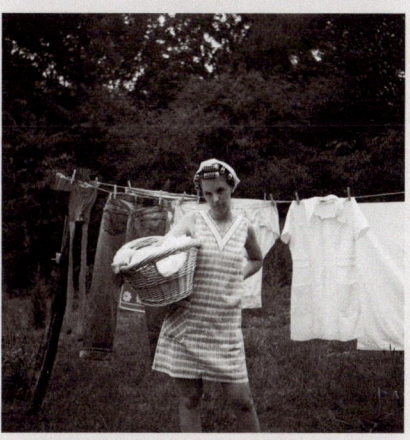

Allyson Shaw and Laura Splan

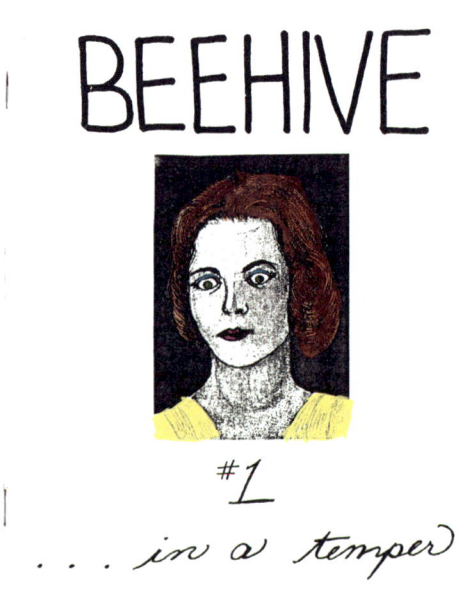

Beehive, no. 1, 1993
Photocopy, saddle stitched, gouache painted cover,
8 ½ × 7 in. (21.6 × 17.8 cm)
Fales Library, New York University

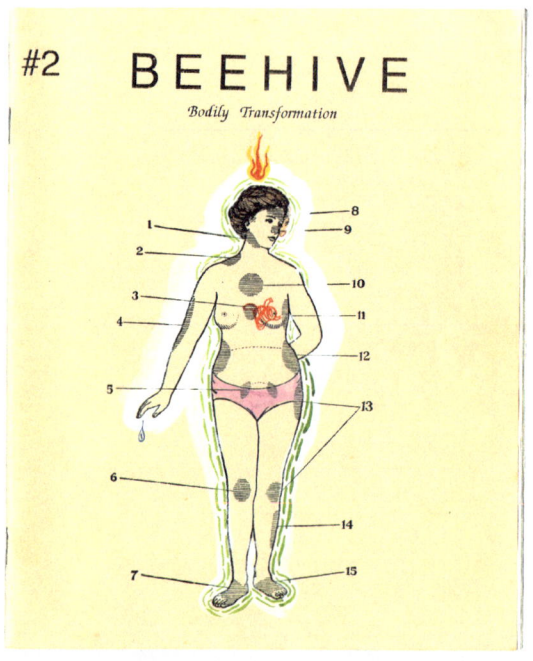

Beehive, no. 2, 1994
Photocopy, saddle stitched, gouache painted cover,
8 ½ × 7 in. (21.6 × 17.8 cm)
Fales Library, New York University

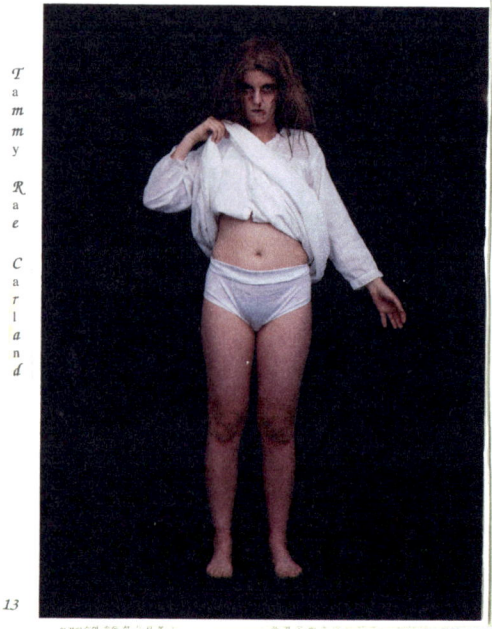

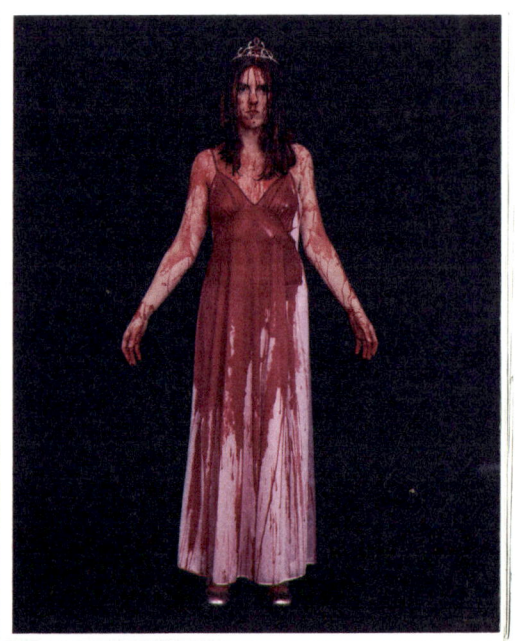

Paste-up for *Beehive*, no. 2, 1994
Chromogenic prints, paper, glue, 8 ½ × 7 in. (21.6 × 17.8 cm)
Fales Library, New York University

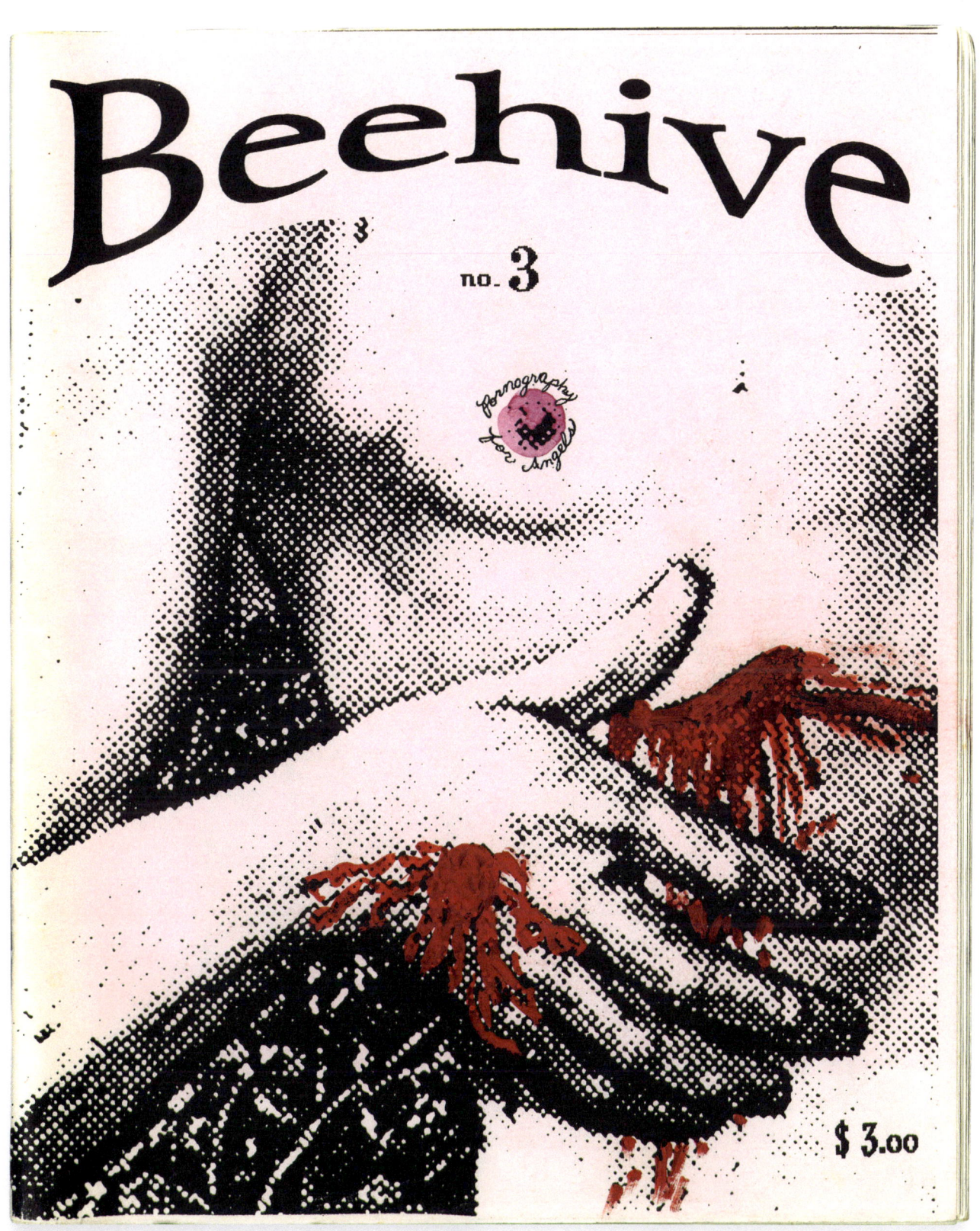

Beehive, no. 3, 1994
Photocopy, saddle stitched, gouache painted cover, 8 ½ × 7 in. (21.6 × 17.8 cm)
Fales Library, New York University

Kelly Marie Martin

→   *Thorn*, no. 2, 1992
      Color and black-and-white photocopy, saddle stitched,
      11 × 8 ½ in. (27.9 × 21.6 cm)
      Fales Library, New York University

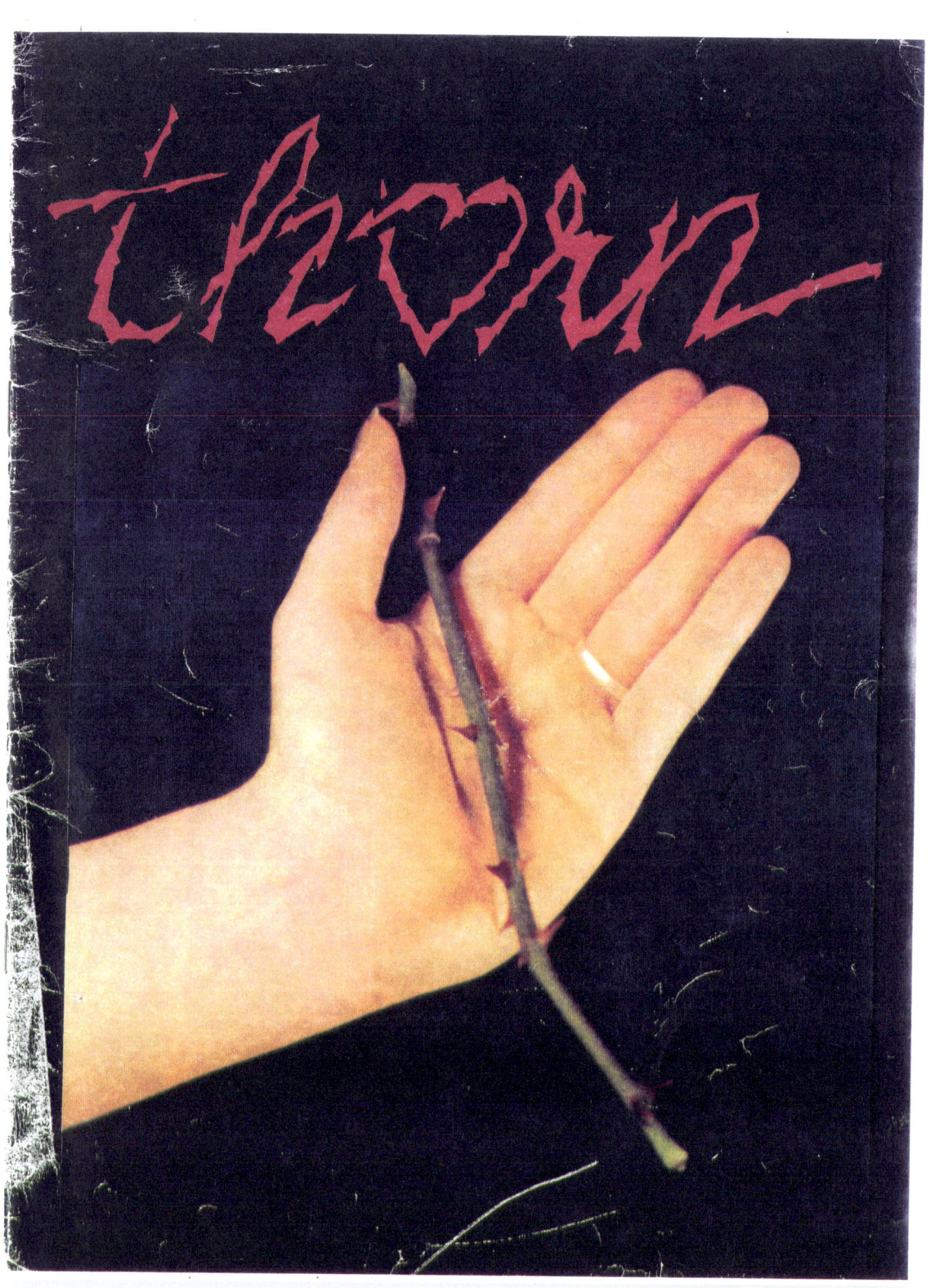

Thorn, no. 1, 1992
Color and black-and-white photocopy, saddle stitched,
11 × 8 ½ in. (27.9 × 21.6 cm)
Fales Library, New York University

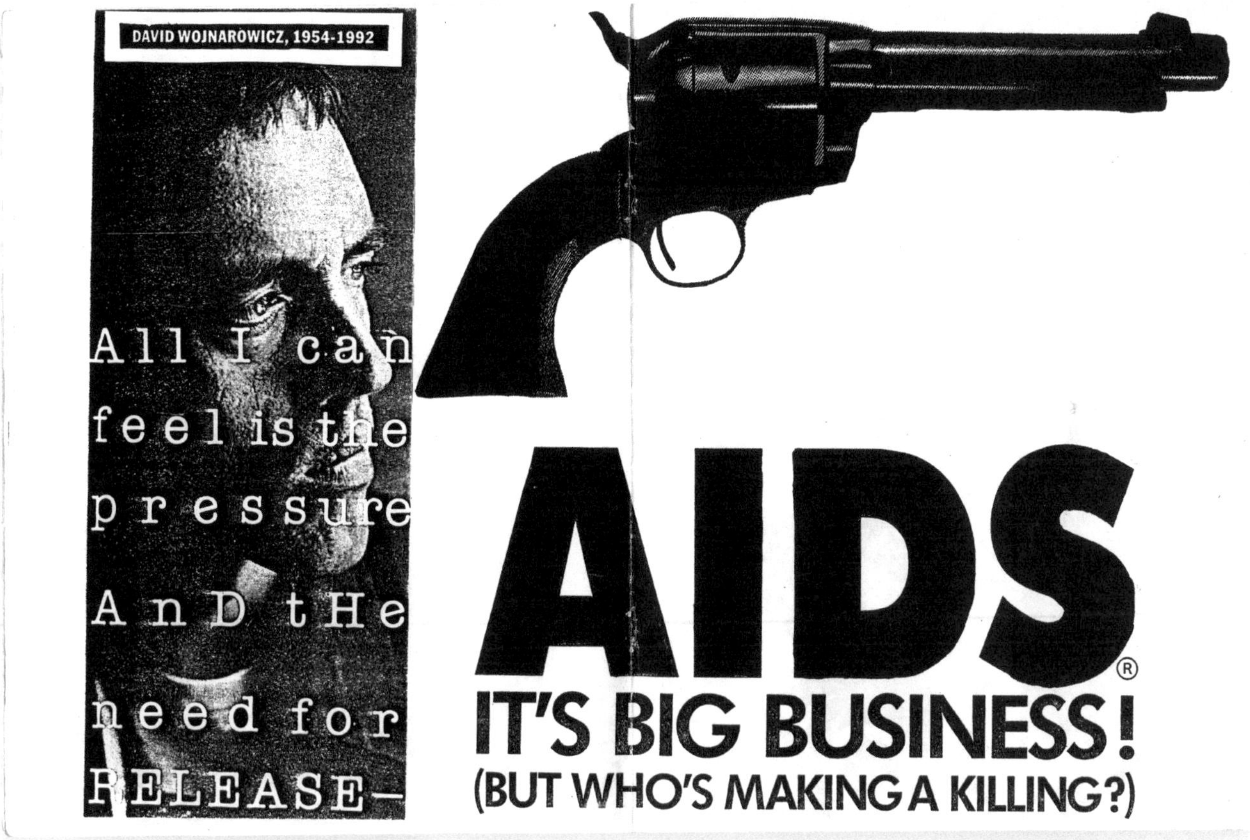

DAVID WOJNAROWICZ, 1954-1992

All I can feel is the pressure AnD tHE need for RELEASE—

AIDS®
IT'S BIG BUSINESS!
(BUT WHO'S MAKING A KILLING?)

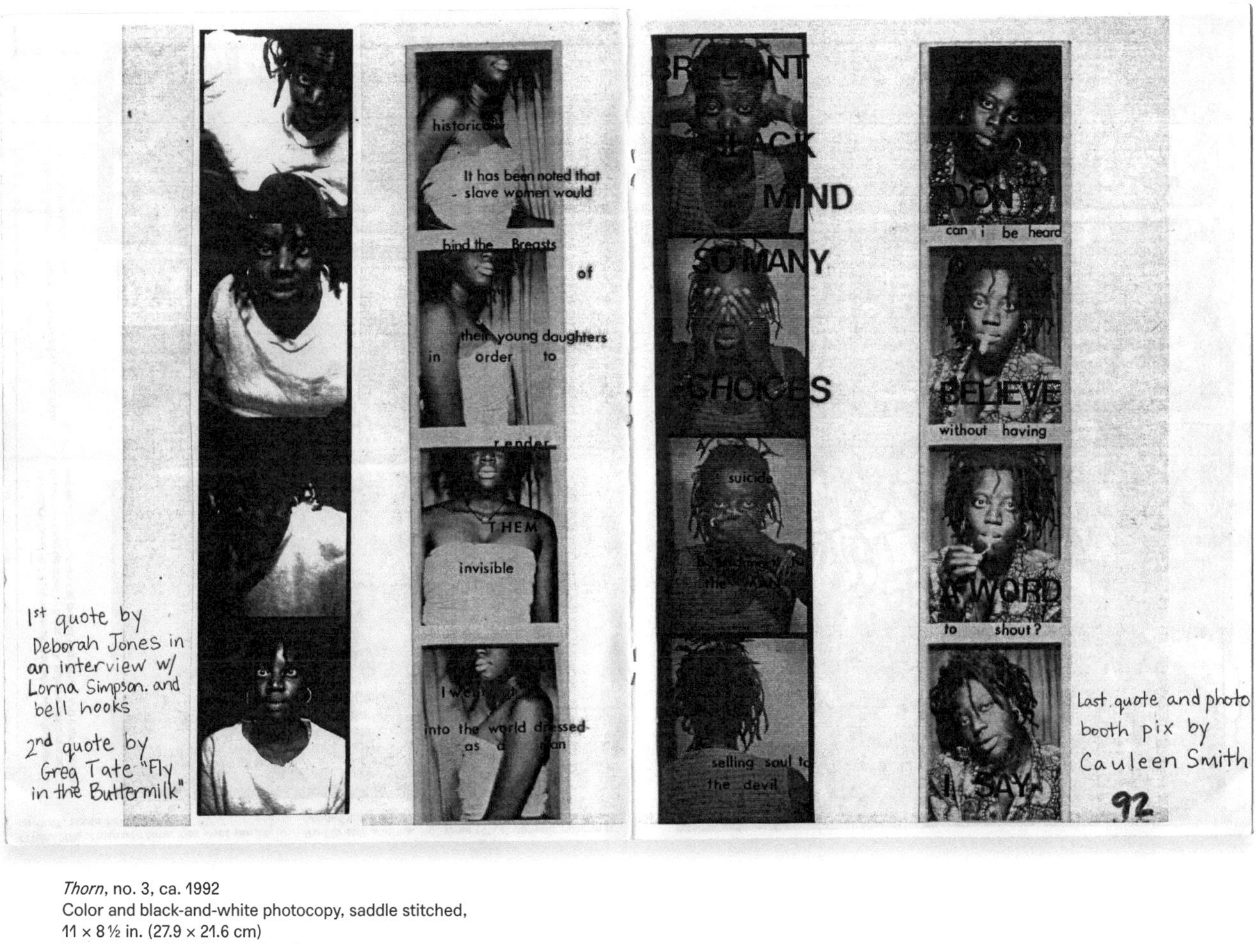

historically
It has been noted that slave women would bind the Breasts of their young daughters in order to render THEM invisible

i went into the world dressed as a man

BRILLIANT
BLACK
MIND
SO MANY
CHOICES

suicide

selling soul to the devil

DON'T
can i be heard

BELIEVE
without having

A WORD
to shout?

I SAY

92

1st quote by Deborah Jones in an interview w/ Lorna Simpson. and bell hooks

2nd quote by Greg Tate "Fly in the Buttermilk"

Last quote and photo booth pix by Cauleen Smith

Thorn, no. 3, ca. 1992
Color and black-and-white photocopy, saddle stitched,
11 × 8½ in. (27.9 × 21.6 cm)
Fales Library, New York University

Gene Barnes

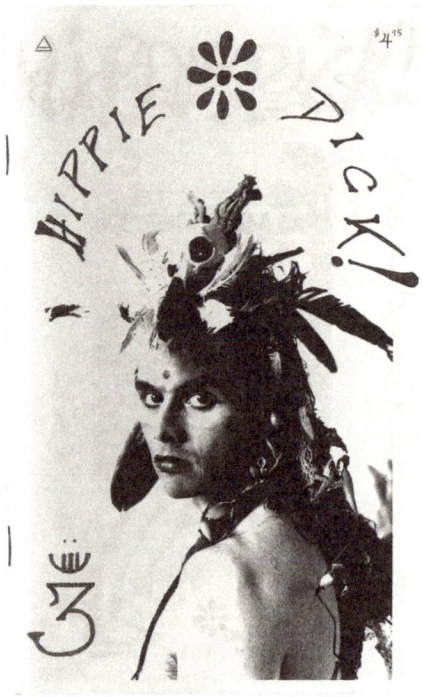

Hippie Dick!, no. 3, ca. 1992
Photocopy, saddle stitched, 8 ½ × 5 ½ in. (21.6 × 14 cm)
Collection Philip Aarons and Shelley Fox Aarons

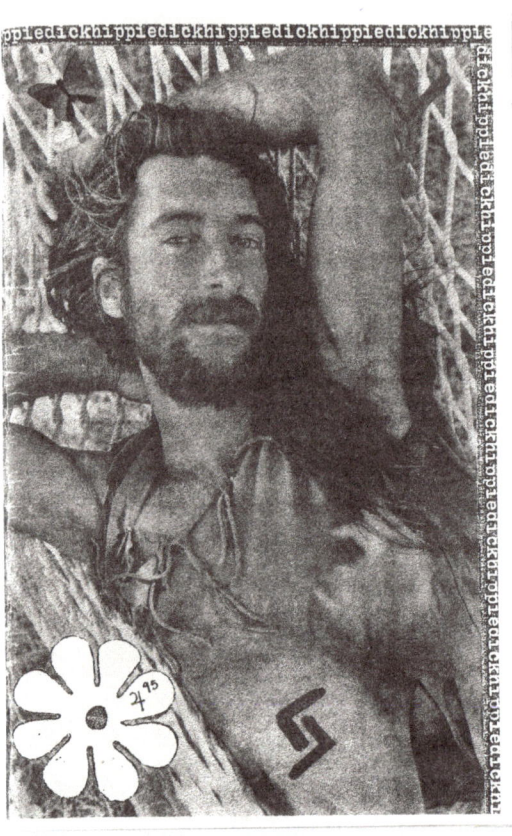

Hippie Dick, no. 1, 1991
Photocopy, saddle stitched, 8 ½ × 5 ½ in. (21.6 × 14 cm)
Collection Steve Lafreniere

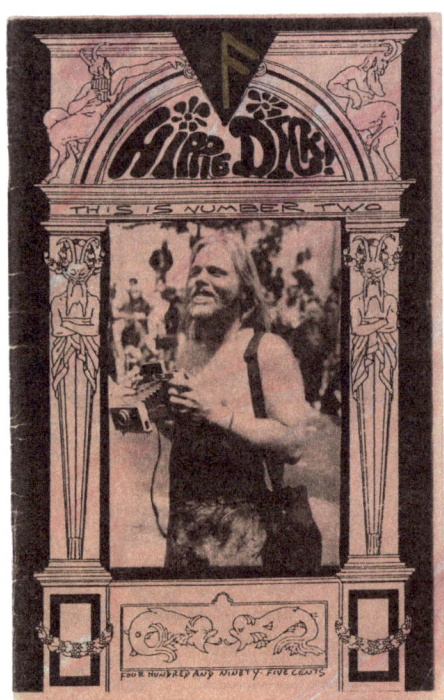

Hippie Dick!, no. 2, ca. 1991
Photocopy, saddle stitched, 8 ½ × 5 ½ in. (21.6 × 14 cm)
Collection Philip Aarons and Shelley Fox Aarons

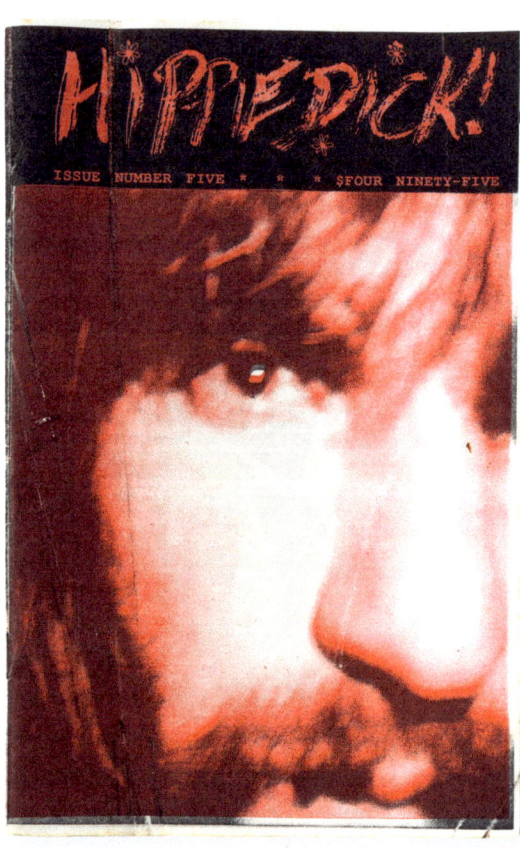

Hippie Dick!, no. 5, 1993
Color and black-and-white photocopy, saddle stitched,
8 ½ × 5 ½ in. (21.6 × 14 cm)
Collection Philip Aarons and Shelley Fox Aarons

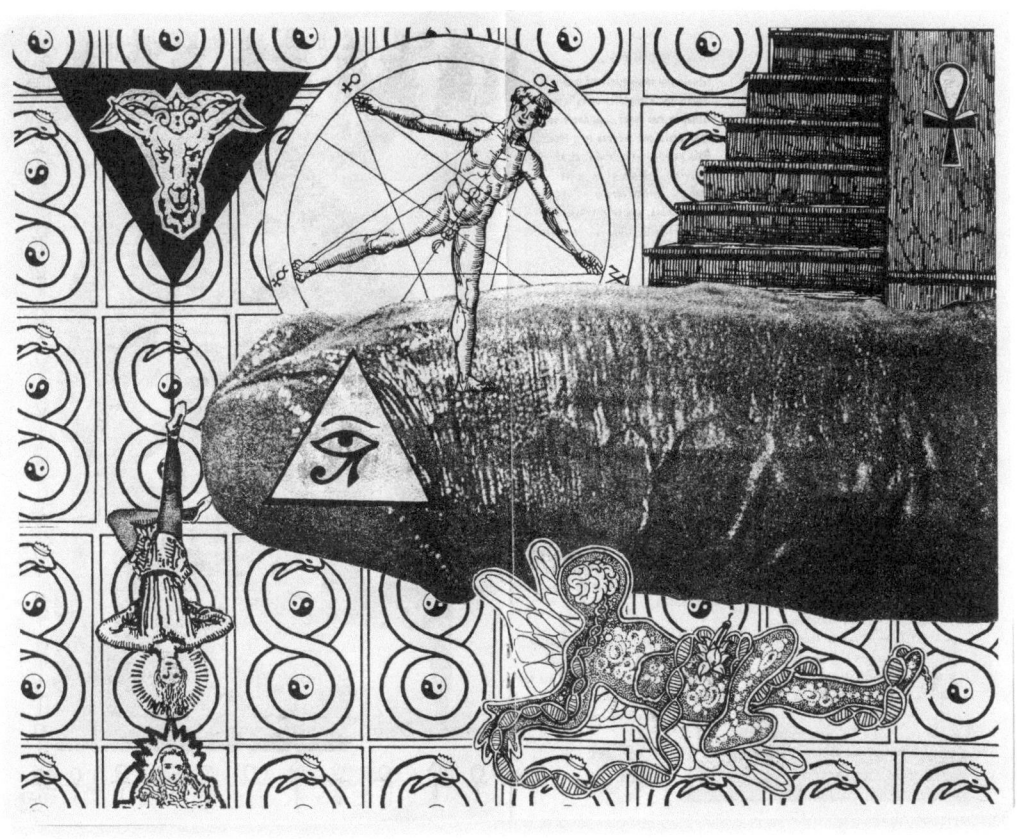

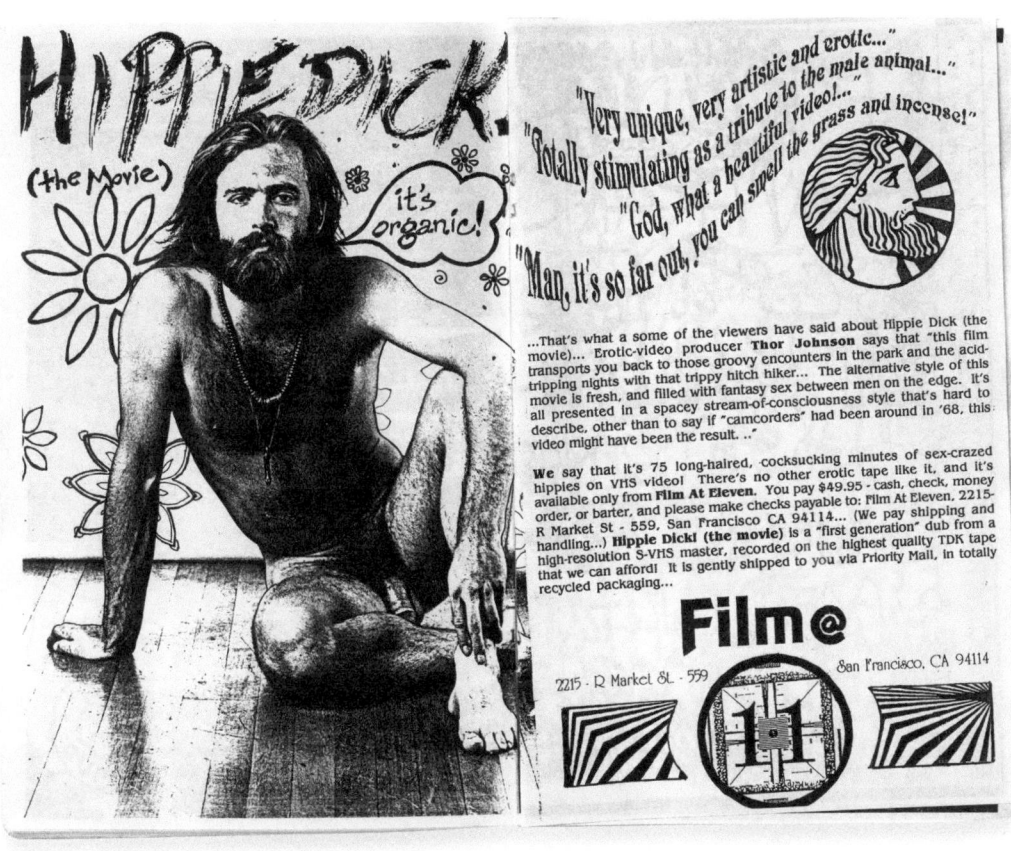

For
Portia
Manson.
xO

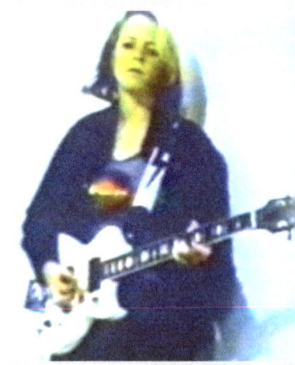

Kelly Marie Martin
Stills from *Motor Baby, Roar Roar*, 1995
Video; color, sound; 7 min., 11 sec.
Collection the artist

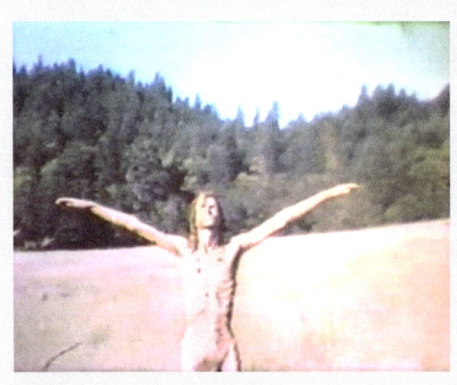

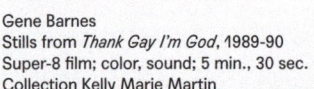

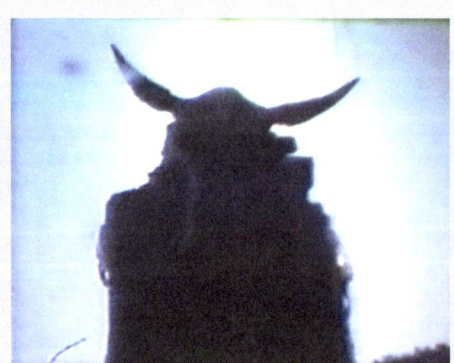

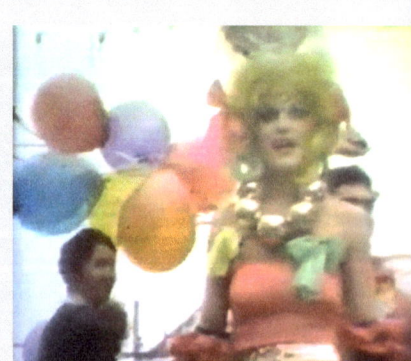

Gene Barnes
Stills from *Thank Gay I'm God*, 1989-90
Super-8 film; color, sound; 5 min., 30 sec.
Collection Kelly Marie Martin

Félix Endara

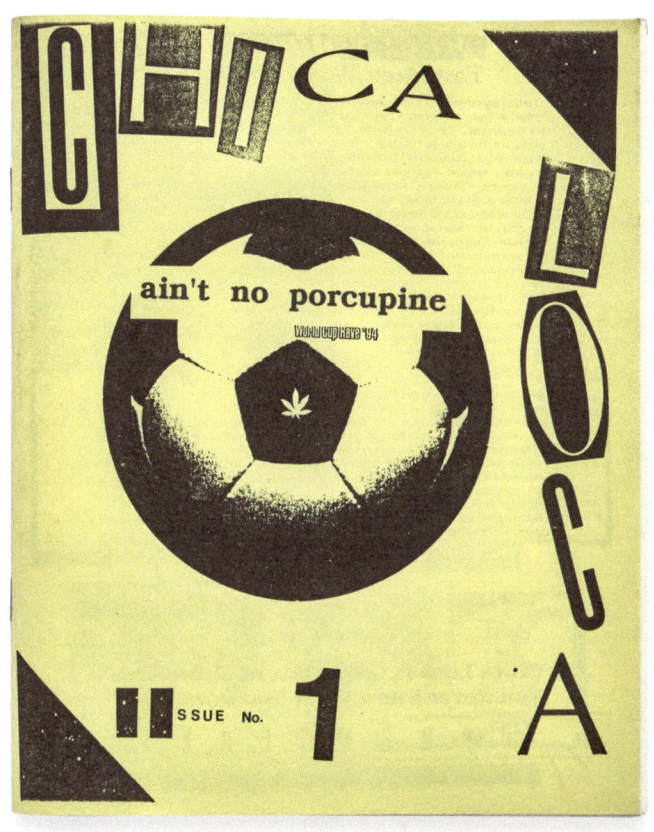

Chica Loca, no. 1, 1994
Photocopy, saddle stitched, yellow paper wrappers,
8 ½ × 7 in. (21.6 × 17.8 cm)
Collection the artist

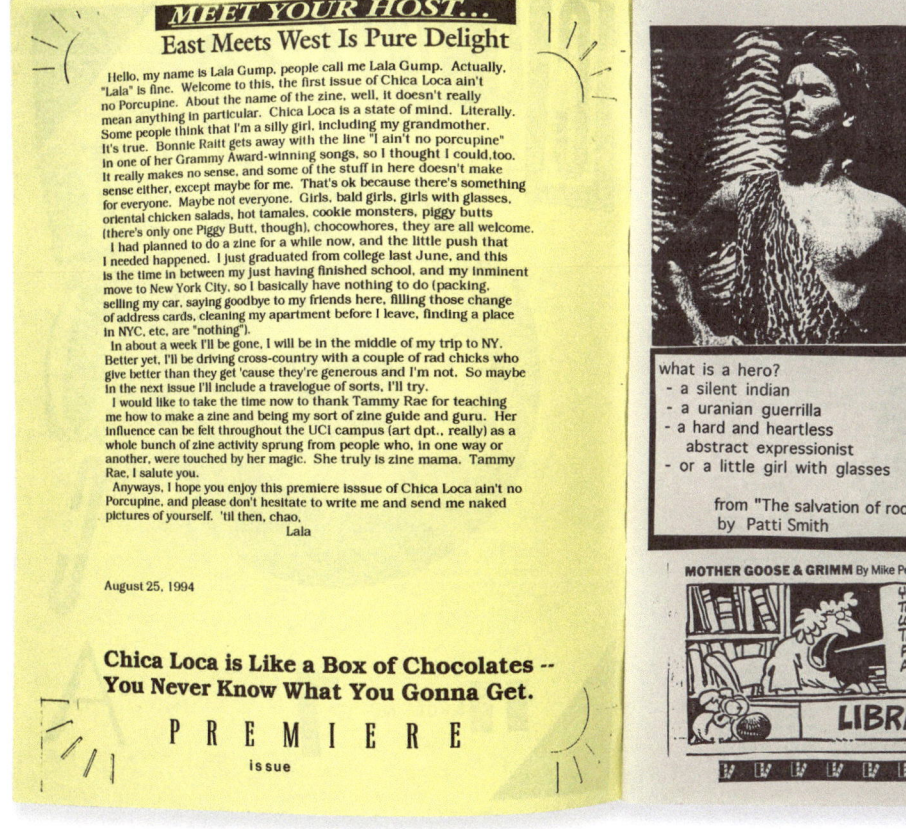

MEET YOUR HOST...
East Meets West Is Pure Delight

Hello, my name is Lala Gump, people call me Lala Gump. Actually, "Lala" is fine. Welcome to this, the first issue of Chica Loca ain't no Porcupine. About the name of the zine, well, it doesn't really mean anything in particular. Chica Loca is a state of mind. Literally. Some people think that I'm a silly girl, including my grandmother. It's true. Bonnie Raitt gets away with the line "I ain't no porcupine" in one of her Grammy Award-winning songs, so I thought I could, too. It really makes no sense, and some of the stuff in here doesn't make sense either, except maybe for me. That's ok because there's something for everyone. Maybe not everyone. Girls, bald girls, girls with glasses, oriental chicken salads, cookie monsters, piggy butts (there's only one Piggy Butt, though), chocowhores, they are all welcome.

I had planned to do a zine for a while now, and the little push that I needed happened. I just graduated from college last June, and this is the time in between my just having finished school, and my imminent move to New York City, so I basically have nothing to do (packing, selling my car, saying goodbye to my friends here, filling those change of address cards, cleaning my apartment before I leave, finding a place in NYC, etc, are "nothing").

In about a week I'll be gone, I will be in the middle of my trip to NY. Better yet, I'll be driving cross-country with a couple of rad chicks who give better than they get 'cause they're generous and I'm not. So maybe in the next issue I'll include a travelogue of sorts, I'll try.

I would like to take the time now to thank Tammy Rae for teaching me how to make a zine and being my sort of zine guide and guru. Her influence can be felt throughout the UCI campus (art dpt., really) as a whole bunch of zine activity sprung from people who, in one way or another, were touched by her magic. She truly is zine mama. Tammy Rae, I salute you.

Anyways, I hope you enjoy this premiere issue of Chica Loca ain't no Porcupine, and please don't hesitate to write me and send me naked pictures of yourself. 'til then, chao,
                                                                Lala

August 25, 1994

Chica Loca is Like a Box of Chocolates -- You Never Know What You Gonna Get.

PREMIERE
issue

This issue is dedicated to River Phoenix

what is a hero?
- a silent indian
- a uranian guerrilla
- a hard and heartless abstract expressionist
- or a little girl with glasses

    from "The salvation of rock"
    by Patti Smith

同性愛者是一個廣大的「少數民族」

在本書中所引用的同性愛者，係指那些與生俱來，自然地對同性發生興趣的人仕，而所謂異性愛者，同指那些對異性發生興趣的人仕。

從教養或環境的設計中指出：約有百分之十的人口是同性愛者，他（她）們與絕不同的地理環境，人種及社會階級的界限，他（她）們的腦筋更包括各行各業，如教師、醫生、牧師、文員、商人、軍官、運動員、及會計師等等。

我們同性愛的子女喜歡被稱為「同性愛者」（GAY），而不喜歡被叫「同性色情者」（HOMOSEXUAL）或「是歧視」的稱號，這就如同黑人不喜歡被稱為「黑鬼」，日本人被稱為「東洋鬼子」比較含有侮辱和成風的名詞相同。

MOTHER GOOSE & GRIMM By Mike Peters

YOU AGAIN?... WAIT, DON'T TELL ME, YOU'RE STILL LOOKING UP YOUR FAMILY TREE AND SEARCHING FOR YOUR ROOTS, HUH? ALWAYS YOUR ROOTS.

LIBRARY

Chica Loca, no. 2, *The Dream Girls Issue*, 1995
Photocopy, saddle stitched, yellow paper wrappers,
8 ½ × 7 in. (21.6 × 17.8 cm)
Collection the artist

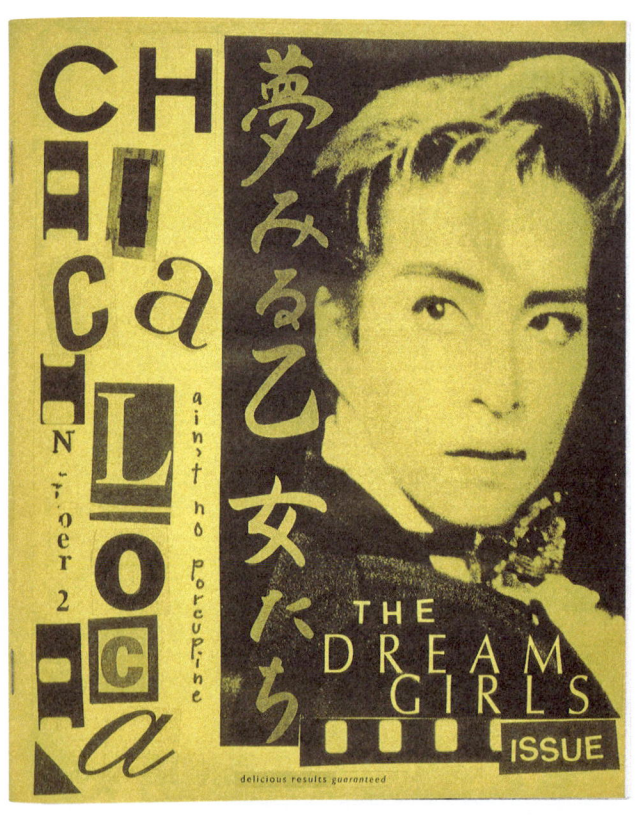

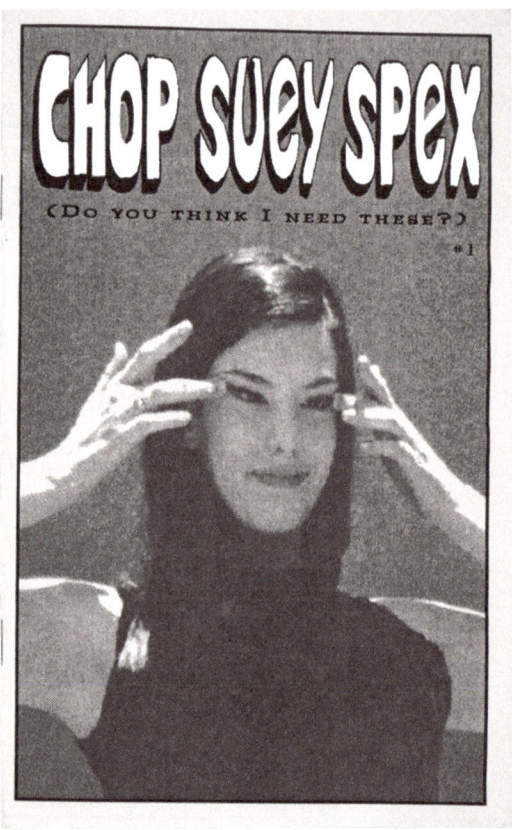

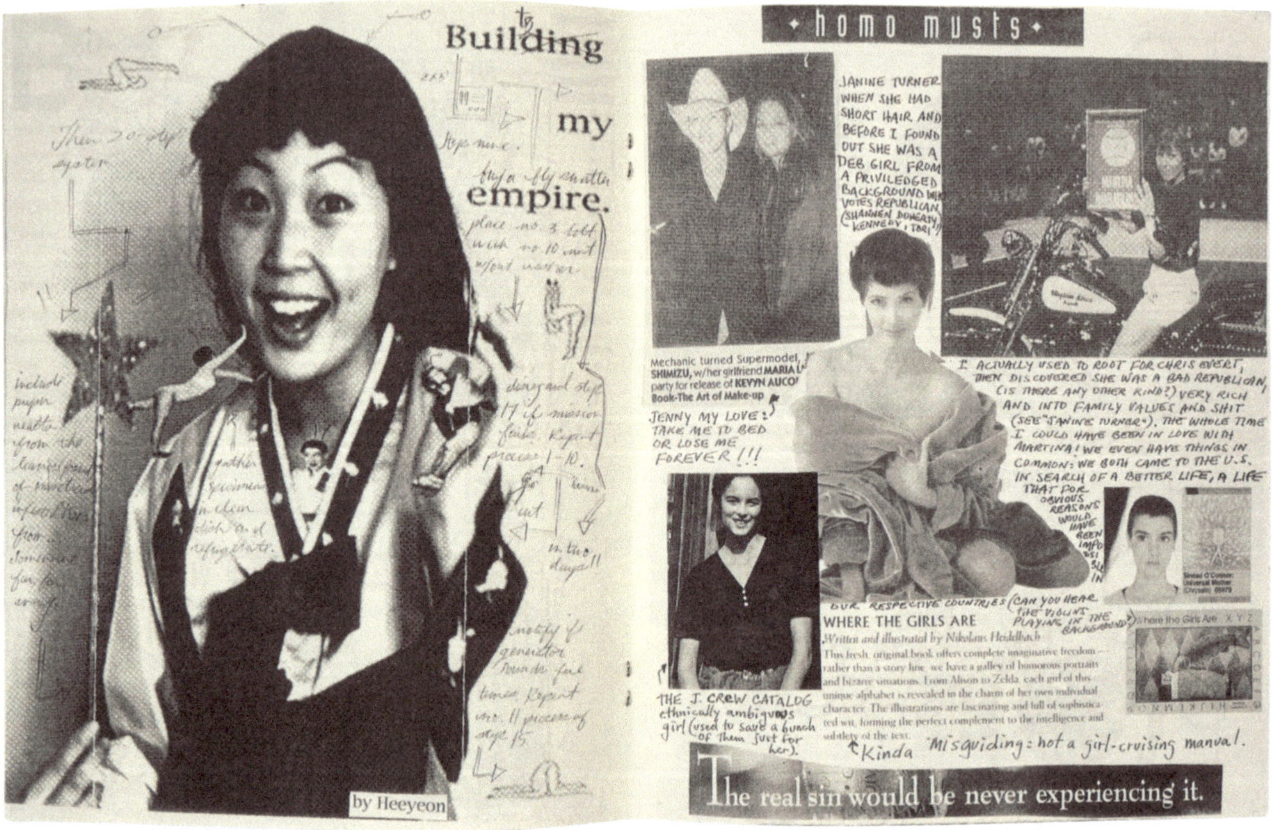

246

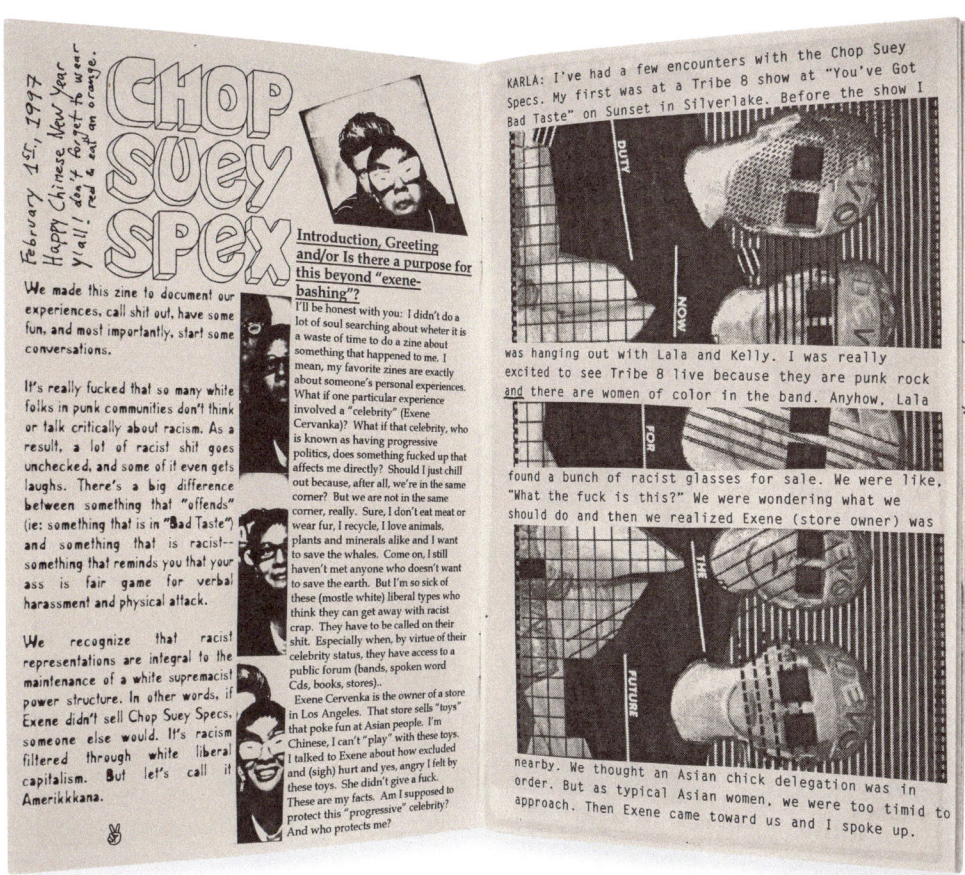

February 1st, 1997
Happy Chinese New Year Y'all! don't forget to wear red & eat an orange.

CHOP SUEY SPEX

We made this zine to document our experiences, call shit out, have some fun, and most importantly, start some conversations.

It's really fucked that so many white folks in punk communities don't think or talk critically about racism. As a result, a lot of racist shit goes unchecked, and some of it even gets laughs. There's a big difference between something that "offends" (ie: something that is in "Bad Taste") and something that is racist— something that reminds you that your ass is fair game for verbal harassment and physical attack.

We recognize that racist representations are integral to the maintenance of a white supremacist power structure. In other words, if Exene didn't sell Chop Suey Specs, someone else would. It's racism filtered through white liberal capitalism. But let's call it Amerikkkana.

Introduction, Greeting and/or Is there a purpose for this beyond "exene-bashing"?

I'll be honest with you: I didn't do a lot of soul searching about whether it is a waste of time to do a zine about something that happened to me. I mean, my favorite zines are exactly about someone's personal experiences. What if one particular experience involved a "celebrity" (Exene Cervanka)? What if that celebrity, who is known as having progressive politics, does something fucked up that affects me directly? Should I just chill out because, after all, we're in the same corner? But we are not in the same corner? Sure, I don't eat meat or wear fur, I recycle, I love animals, plants and minerals alike and I want to save the whales. Come on, I still haven't met anyone who doesn't want to save the earth. But I'm so sick of these (mostle white) liberal types who think they can get away with racist crap. They have to be called on their shit. Especially when, by virtue of their celebrity status, they have access to a public forum (bands, spoken word Cds, books, stores)..

Exene Cervenka is the owner of a store in Los Angeles. That store sells "toys" that poke fun at Asian people. I'm Chinese, I can't "play" with these toys. I talked to Exene about how excluded and (sigh) hurt and yes, angry I felt by these toys. She didn't give a fuck. These are my facts. Am I supposed to protect this "progressive" celebrity? And who protects me?

KARLA: I've had a few encounters with the Chop Suey Specs. My first was at a Tribe 8 show at "You've Got Bad Taste" on Sunset in Silverlake. Before the show I

was hanging out with Lala and Kelly. I was really excited to see Tribe 8 live because they are punk rock and there are women of color in the band. Anyhow, Lala

found a bunch of racist glasses for sale. We were like, "What the fuck is this?" We were wondering what we should do and then we realized Exene (store owner) was

nearby. We thought an Asian chick delegation was in order. But as typical Asian women, we were too timid to approach. Then Exene came toward us and I spoke up.

Chop Suey Spex, no. 1, 1997
Photocopy, saddle stitched, 8 ½ × 5 ½ in. (21.6 × 14 cm)
Collection the artist

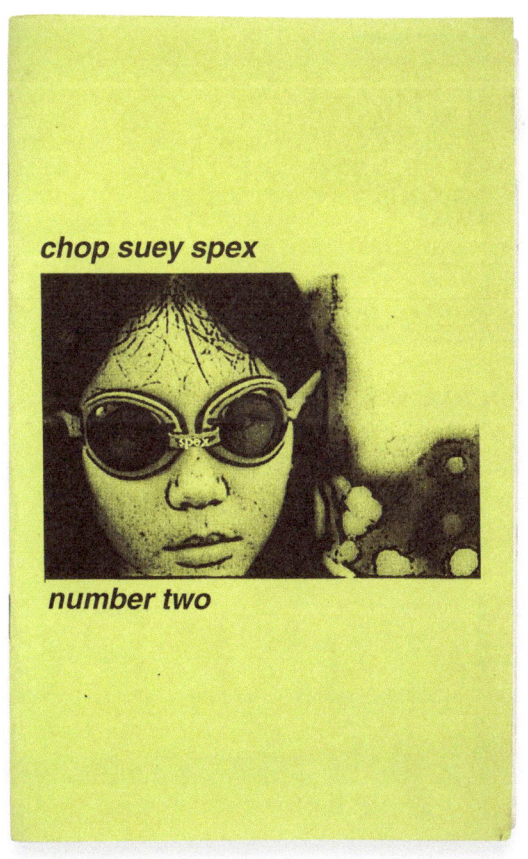

chop suey spex

number two

Chop Suey Spex, no. 2, 1998
Photocopy, saddle stitched, yellow paper wrappers,
8 ½ × 5 ½ in. (21.6 × 14 cm)
Collection the artist

Kathleen Hanna

Kathleen Hanna with Billy Karren, Tobi Vail, Kathi Wilcox
Bikini Kill, no. 2, 1991
Photocopy, saddle stitched, 8 ½ × 5 ½ in. (21.6 × 14 cm)
Collection Philip Aarons and Shelley Fox Aarons

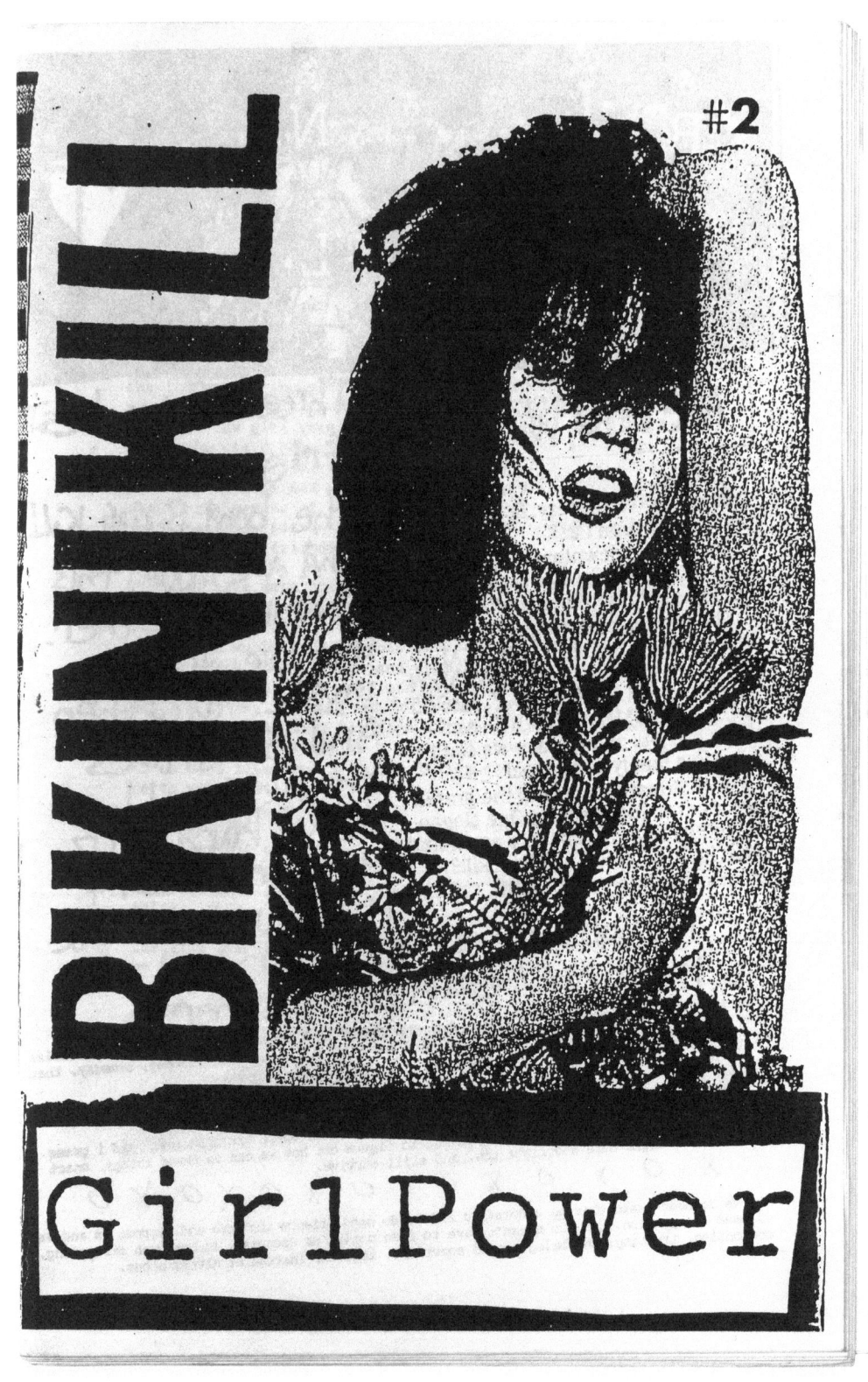

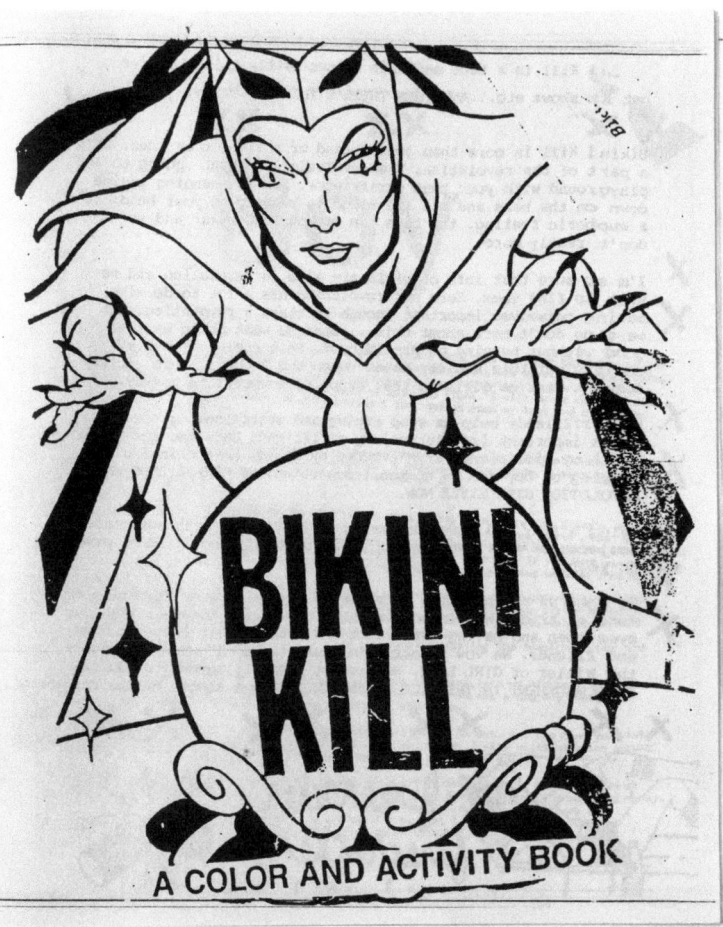

Kathleen Hanna with Tobi Vail and Kathi Wilcox
Bikini Kill, no. 1, ca. 1990
Photocopy, saddle stitched, 8 ½ × 7 in. (21.6 × 17.8 cm)
Collection Philip Aarons and Shelley Fox Aarons

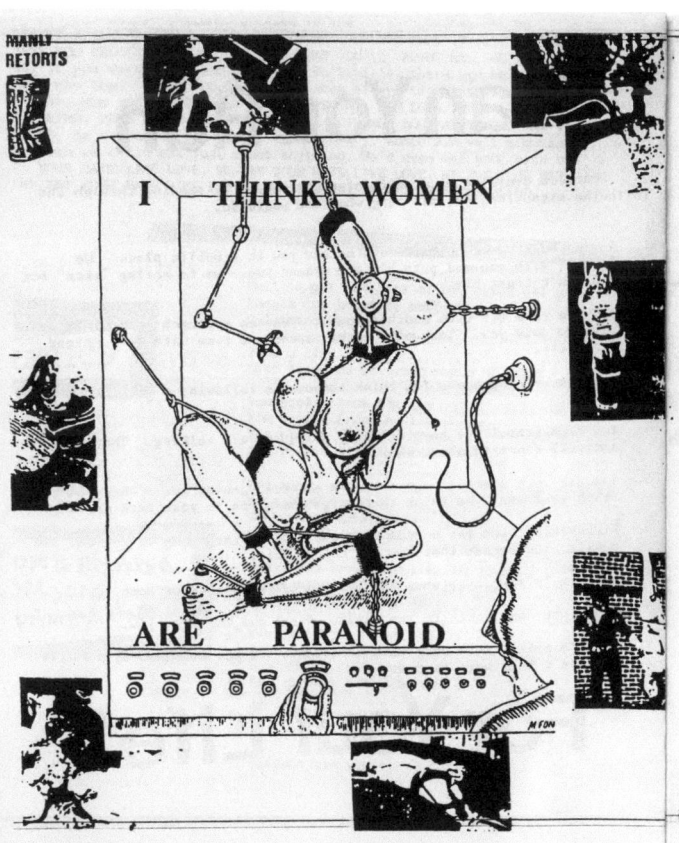

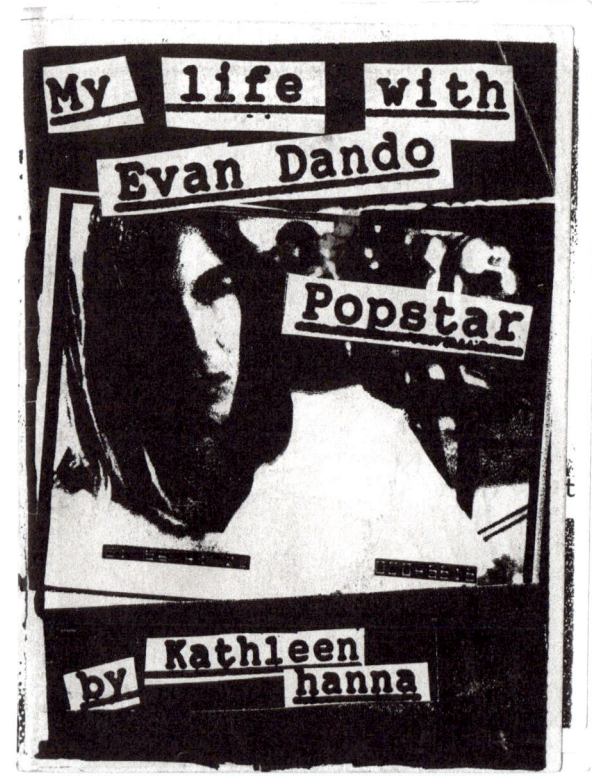

My life with Evan Dando Popstar

by Kathleen hanna

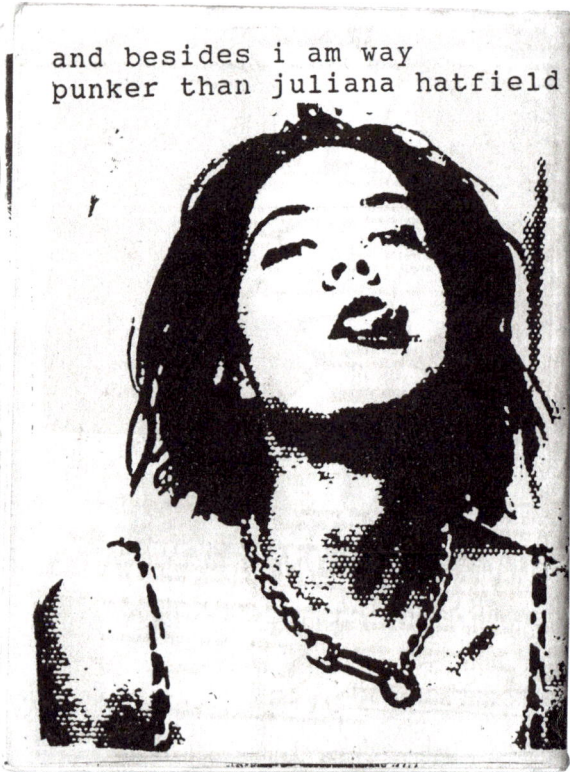

and besides i am way punker than juliana hatfield

REAL / FAKE

~~fred vs wilma~~

truth / lie

FRED VS. wilma

Fiction [Non-Fiction]

Feeling so spectated myself. I get pleasure from looking

at this bare chested boychild.

Writing creepy letters to Evan helps me to understand why men go to stripbars.

This understanding is

crucail to my reality

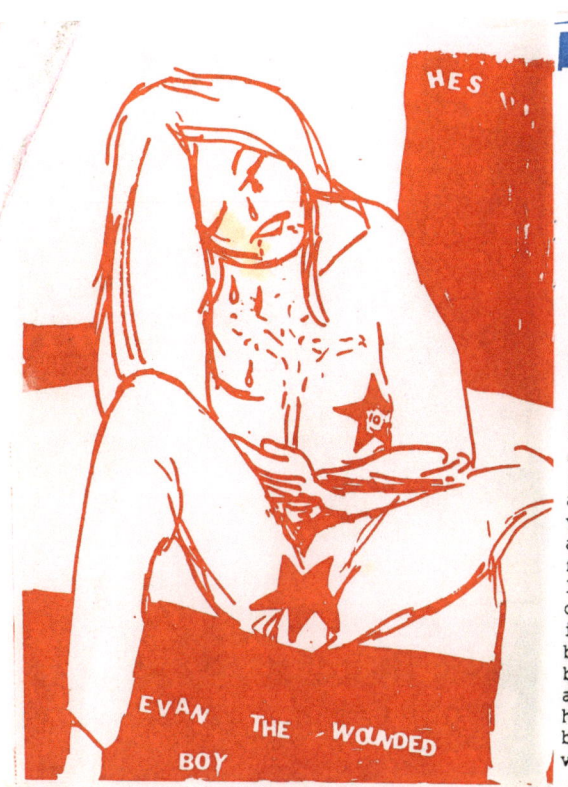

I fell in love with Evan because it
seemed like the worst thing i could
do at the time. I fell in love with
Evan because it was totally uncool
and pathetic which is how i felt inside. I fell in love with Evan because
the band i am in started getting all
this weird attention and i felt like
he was the only one who would understand. I fell in love with Evan because sometimes i wish i was a boy and
that the worst thing that ever happened to me was having too many girls
like me. I fell in love with Evan because i wanted him to die and thought
if i could get him to love me i would
show him what a broken heart really was.
I fell in love with Evan because he is
a total slut and everyone thinks its
very cute, unlike when i was in jr hi
and high school and the word "slut"
followed me everywhere at arms length.
I fell in love with Evan because i don't
do drugs and so i need other destruct-
ive pasttimes. I fell in love with Evan
because i can't deal with real boys
barely at all and yet am wildly attracte
attracted their flat chests and strait
hips (sometimes) and Evan is my perfect
boyfriend because i am allowed to invent him all by myself.

Confuse "truth"
with fiction
~~and~~ attempt to
de-centralize the
manufacturing of
"truth".

use Language as a weapon.

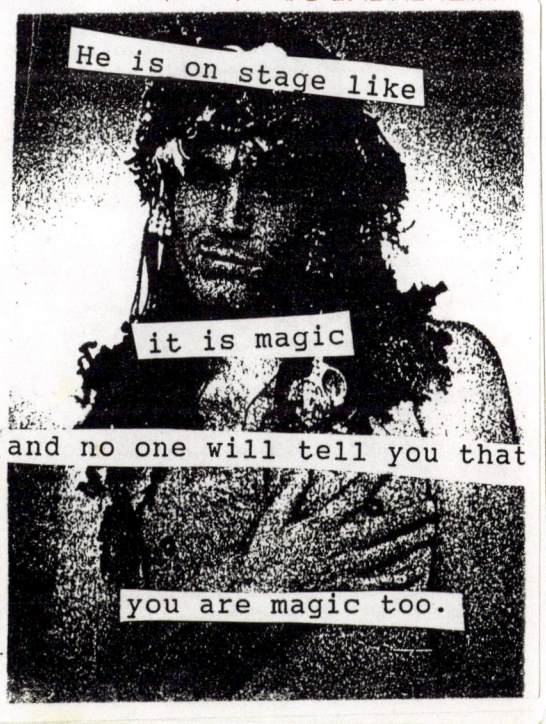

He is on stage like

it is magic

and no one will tell you that

you are magic too.

My Life with Evan Dando, Popstar, 1993
Photocopy, saddle stitched,
5½ × 4½ in. (14 × 11.4 cm)
Fales Library, New York University

Johanna Fateman and Miranda July

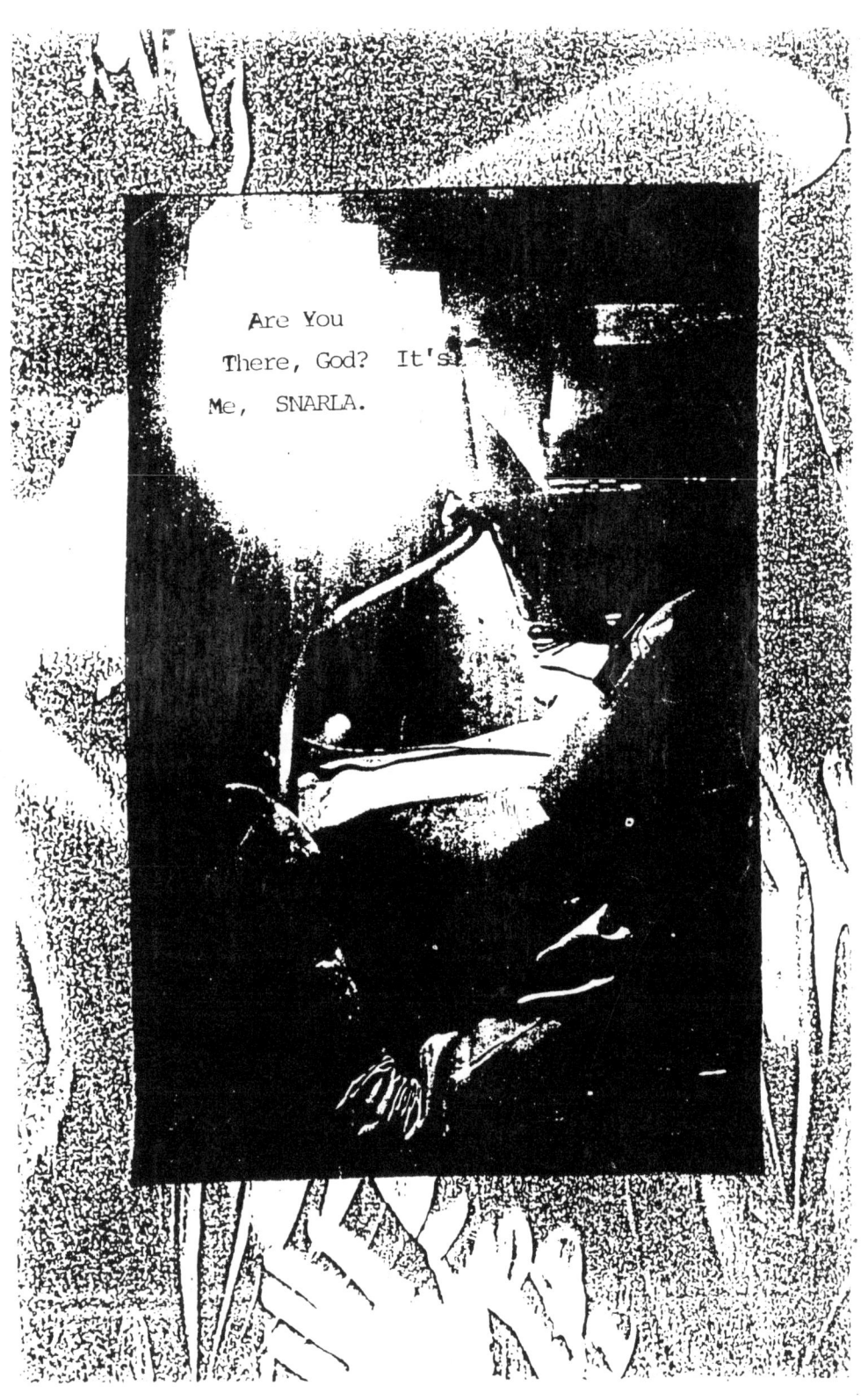

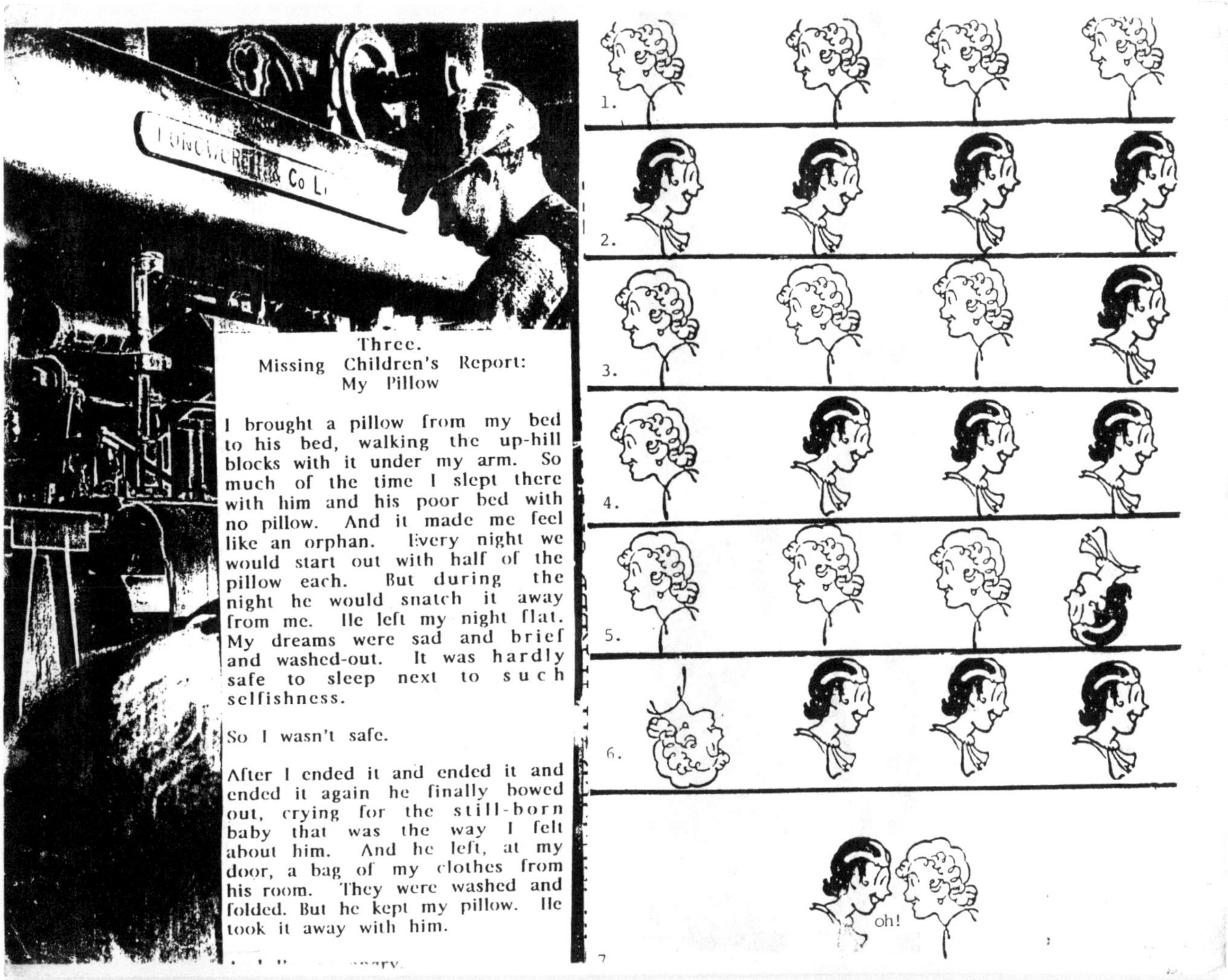

Three.
Missing Children's Report:
My Pillow

I brought a pillow from my bed to his bed, walking the up-hill blocks with it under my arm. So much of the time I slept there with him and his poor bed with no pillow. And it made me feel like an orphan. Every night we would start out with half of the pillow each. But during the night he would snatch it away from me. He left my night flat. My dreams were sad and brief and washed-out. It was hardly safe to sleep next to such selfishness.

So I wasn't safe.

After I ended it and ended it and ended it again he finally bowed out, crying for the still-born baby that was the way I felt about him. And he left, at my door, a bag of my clothes from his room. They were washed and folded. But he kept my pillow. He took it away with him.

oh!

Snarla, no. 2, ca. 1993
Photocopy, saddle stitched, 8 ½ × 5 ½ in. (21.6 × 14 cm)
Fales Library, New York University

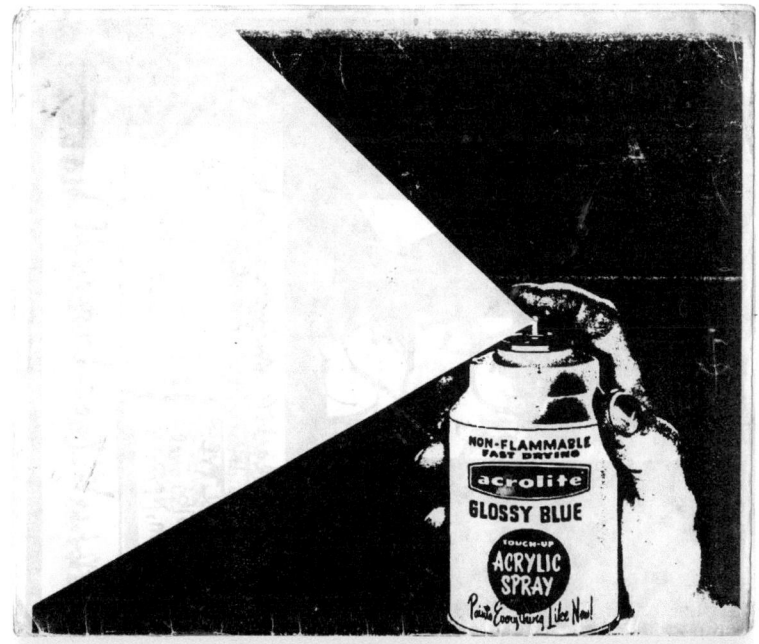

Snarla, no. 3, ca. 1993
Photocopy, saddle stitched, 8 ½ × 7 in. (21.6 × 17.8 cm)
Fales Library, New York University

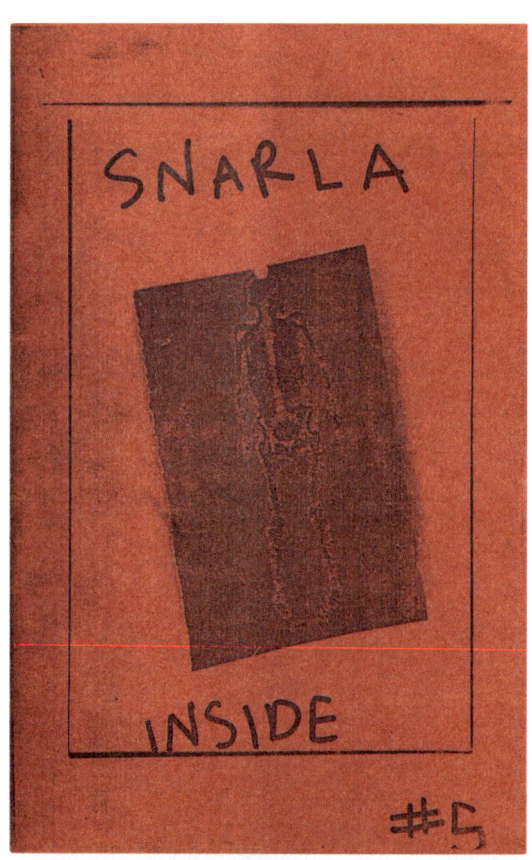

→ *Snarla*, no. 1, 1993
Photocopy, saddle stitched, 8 ½ × 5 ½ in. (21.6 × 14 cm
Fales Library, New York University

Snarla, no. 5, ca. 1994
Photocopy, saddle stitched, 8 ½ × 5 ½ in. (21.6 × 14 cm)
Private collection

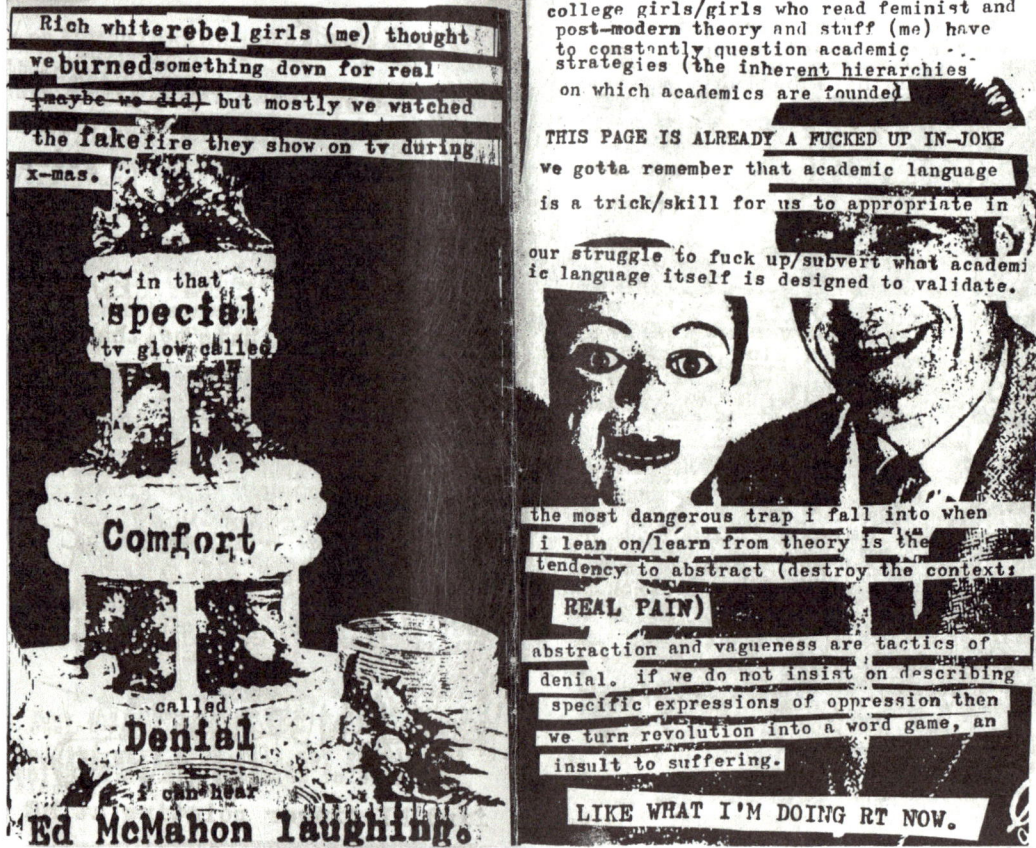

Rich white rebel girls (me) thought we burned something down for real (maybe we did) but mostly we watched the fake fire they show on tv during x-mas.

in that special tv glow called

Comfort

called Denial

i can hear Ed McMahon laughing.

college girls/girls who read feminist and post-modern theory and stuff (me) have to constantly question academic strategies (the inherent hierarchies on which academics are founded

THIS PAGE IS ALREADY A FUCKED UP IN-JOKE we gotta remember that academic language is a trick/skill for us to appropriate in our struggle to fuck up/subvert what academic language itself is designed to validate.

the most dangerous trap i fall into when i lean on/learn from theory is the tendency to abstract (destroy the context: REAL PAIN)

abstraction and vagueness are tactics of denial. if we do not insist on describing specific expressions of oppression then we turn revolution into a word game, an insult to suffering.

LIKE WHAT I'M DOING RT NOW.

XOXO. She

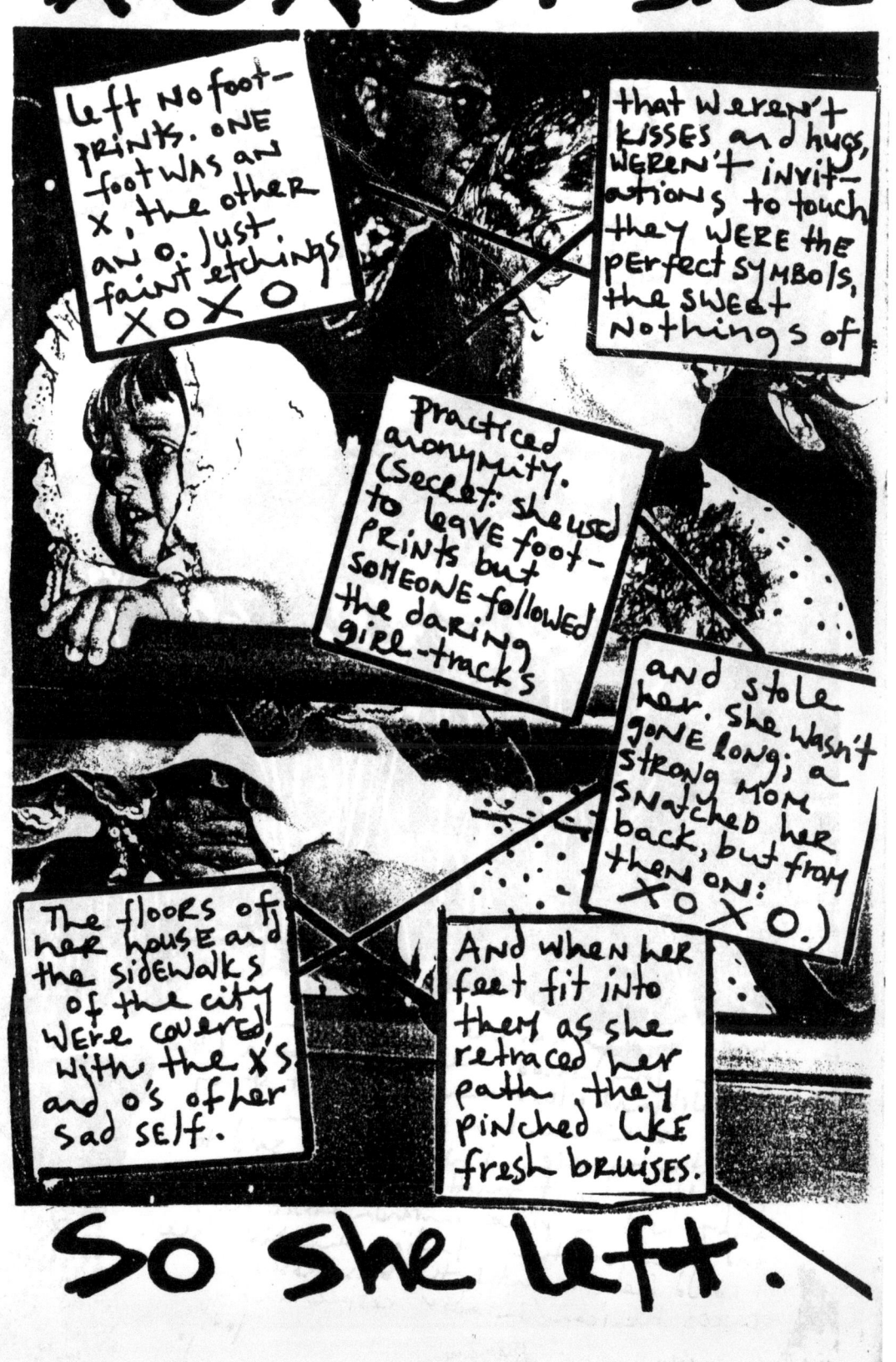

left no foot-prints. ONE foot WAS an X, the other an O. Just faint etchings XOXO

that weren't kisses and hugs, weren't invit-ations to touch, they were the perfect symbols, the sweet nothings of

practiced anonymity. (Secret: she used to leave foot-prints but someone followed the daring girl-tracks

The floors of her house and the sidewalks of the city were covered with the X's and O's of her sad self.

And when her feet fit into them as she retraced her path they pinched like fresh bruises.

and stole her. She wasn't gone long; a strong mom snatched her back, but from then on: XOXO.)

So she left.

Johanna Fateman

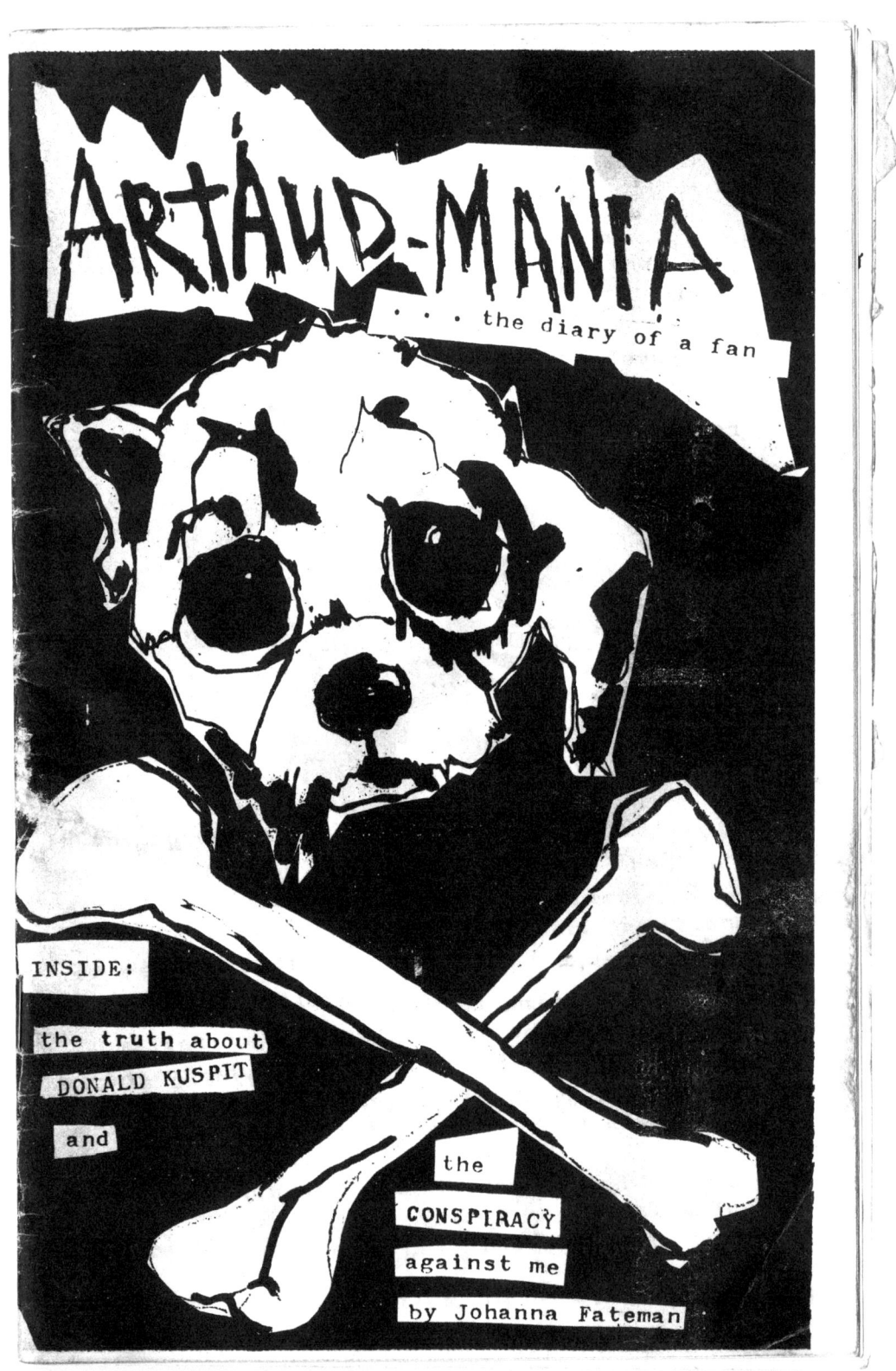

Artaud-Mania . . . the diary of a fan, 1997
Photocopy, saddle stitched, 8½ × 5½ in. (21.6 × 14 cm)
Fales Library, New York University

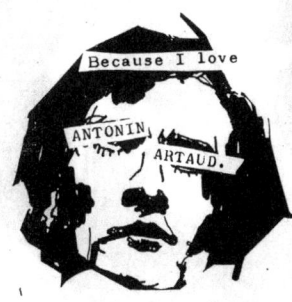

October 5 1996
Dear Diary,

I spent $50 on 6 tickets to various Artaud-related events at the Drawing Center and resolved to record my impressions.

Because I love

ANTONIN ARTAUD.

And because I had this idea that one way to get my writing to more explicitly mimic/depart from the disciplines of journalism and/or cultural criticism would be to choose as my subject this "subjectivity," Antonin Artaud, icon of Modern alienation.

It's a formal experiment: the application of a fanzine aesthetic to a subject outside the usual jurisdiction of my genre.

October 6 1996
Dear Diary,

I am writing to you because confessional writing is the self-effacing form most suited to the abject position of the fan.

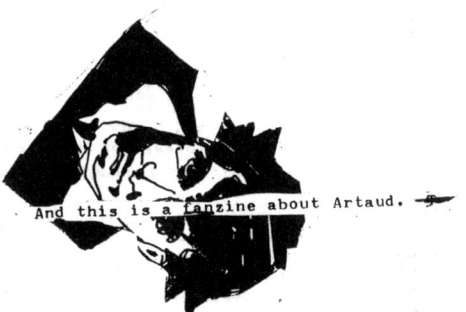

And this is a fanzine about Artaud.

But, transcribing these diary entries 3 months in the future I will add: this is a hateful pamphlet against the critic Donald Kuspit, a petty and vindictive strain of Institutional Critique most suited to the abject position of the student.

This is a letter to Antonin Artaud from written from Art School collapsed into

Dear Diary
cuz the pen is mightier than the sword, right?

11.

I am not without compassion for his bleak outlook on my generation and his generally depressive personality, but I do think he's got no business teaching a senior seminar if he can't deal with a 22-year old girl being a pain in the ass. ~~And it was infuriating to be called a cynic for caring enough to present a gesture of challenge or restitution to the endeavor of art-making in the face of his bitter nostalgia for a defunct idealism.~~

He
misread
my
sincerity
totally.

But because I really have no power in this situation to have him forcibly retired or whatever they do to big name academics without contemporary relevance who go nuts and become totally abusive to their students, the most strategic(self-preserving/interesting) use I have for him is as a period piece, a case study of embodied dogma for me to react to. ~~XXXXXXXXXXXXXXXXXXXXX~~

asshole

(Quite often, the need for revenge crystallizes my thoughts and results in a finished piece of writing But I want to Figure out a new way to work)

And this incident, ¶ Punctuates my consuming interest in Antonin Artaud and the N.Y. reception of his theorists, raising questions about my own critical approach to ▓▓▓▓ Artaud."

Kuspit selects artists and theorizes their artistic practice according to a taste-based promotional agenda justified by (ultimately conservative) notions about individual/authentic expression, using an artist and his or her work as the objectified and mute illustration or evidence of a theoretical model but of course this is precisely what I am doing with Artaud.

I couch this ~~rhetorically (facetiously)~~ in the underdog terms of the fan which always rely on mass media fiction, and which necessarily dehumanize their object, and it is through this facts of fandom that I ~~prepose×××critikquexfx~~ hold a mirror to my underlying intentions as "critic." That is to say that when I say "I love Artaud" I mean that I couldn't give a shit about Artaud beyond his usefulness within my personal aesthetic and political program. And my hope is that this honesty ~~×××××××××××××××~~ plus the content (values) of my agenda differentiates my project from normal-boring analyses routinely churned out and attached to specific ×××× cultural icons.

So as I walked downtown to the Drawing Center ~~still somewhat stunned and angry~~, attempting to invent myself as a cultural critic in direct and ~~explicit~~ opposition to the writing style and critical values of Donald Kuspit, I started to question my choice of Antonin Artaud as a subject. He is, after all, a figure of clinical "idiosyncracy" to say the least and a repository for various ▓▓▓ ~~×××××××××~~ distasteful × accounts of genius (pathological, supernatural, etc.).

I would like to say:"anything that could possibly interest Donald Kuspit could not possibly interest me..." But it is just not that simple.

→ *The Opposite, Part One*, 1996
Photocopy, saddle stitched, 8 ½ × 5 ½ in. (21.6 × 14 cm)
Fales Library, New York University

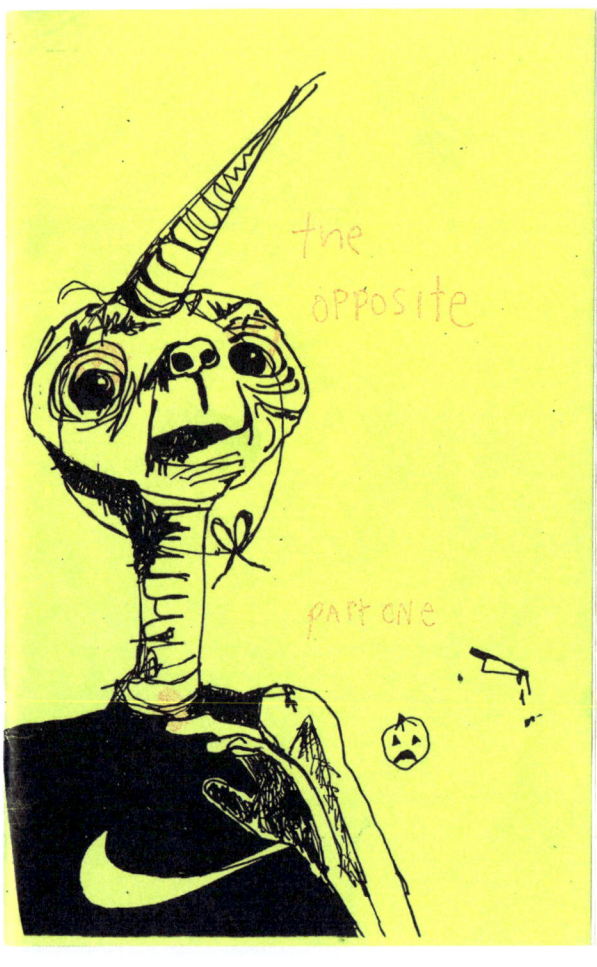

↓ *My Need to Speak on the Subject of Jackson Pollock*, December 1996
Photocopy, saddle stitched, 8 ½ × 8 9⁄10 in. (21.6 × 22.6 cm)
Fales Library, New York University

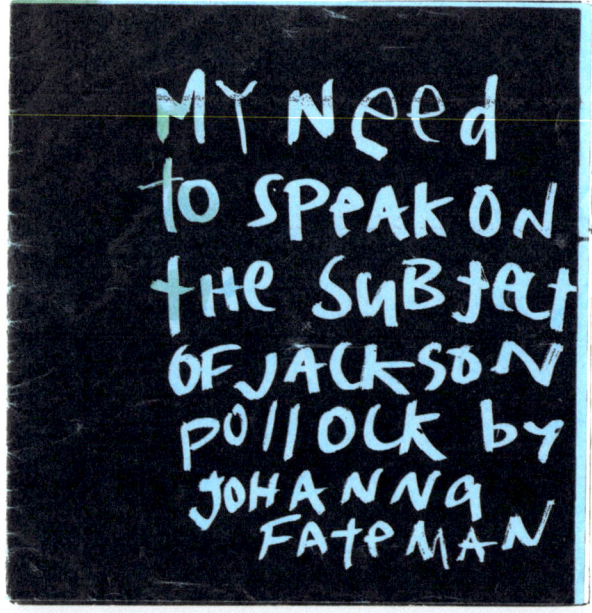

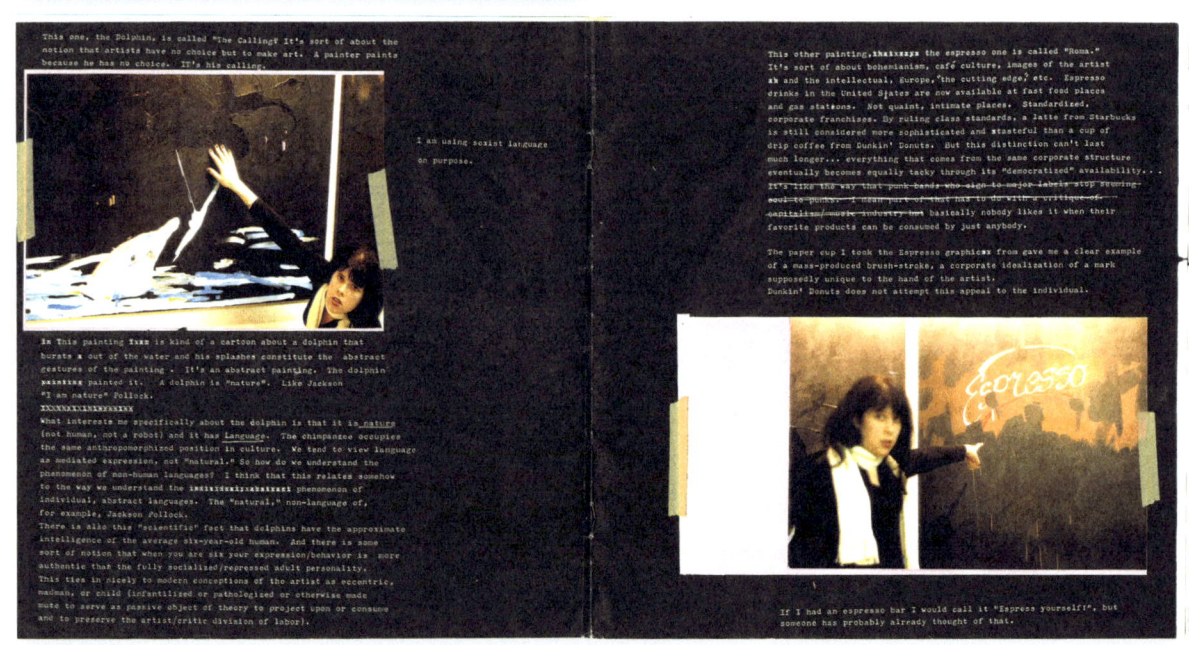

5 This is simplified and specific because it is a metaphor.

As a matter of ~~fxxx~~ fact, this is a parable.

What differentiates the Stains ~~XXX~~ from the skunks (their fans), is not their talent. The Stains have no talent, or they surpress it for ~~artisticxx~~ reasons.
any alleged virtuosity of theirs is not at issue.

The supposedly individually expressionistic content of their performance exists as a convention alongside their function as ~~fxxxxx~~ female placeholders of punk performance.

The Stains are special only because they are on stage, only because they thought of the idea to be on stage and figured out how to do it. They're fakes, they are urinals.

The skunks, having no guitars, no stage, no access to the apparatus are stars anyway. Because they dress up like stars they COULD be stars. Any Stain could be replaced by any Skunk.

THe Skunks, sensing the arbitrary designation of specialness, knowing that they could pessess the spotlight but don't, begin to hate the Stains.
It is the no-power love/hate longing of the fan, the groupie.

And it is the development of a political consciousness, a refusal to buy that which has rightfully belonged to you all along, the gag-reflect triggered by the commdification-murder of a creative/political impulse.

What a fucking disappointment ~~xxxxxxxxxxxxxxxxxgxxxx~~ when girls function identically to boys under capitalism, when a girl usurps a boy role and still you have nothing.
The Skunks realized that it was exploitation, what was happening: t-shirt sales, hierarchy.

A notion presents itself through the hot fog of frustration: I cannot ~~XXXXXXXXXXXXXXXX~~ hurt Guiliani or free Mumia, but I can make another girl cry. Watch me.
The Skunks take the lesson of the Stains to its logical conclusion by trying to destroy them. These are the patricidal tendencies which constitute the dialectic of the patrilineage, art historically speaking.

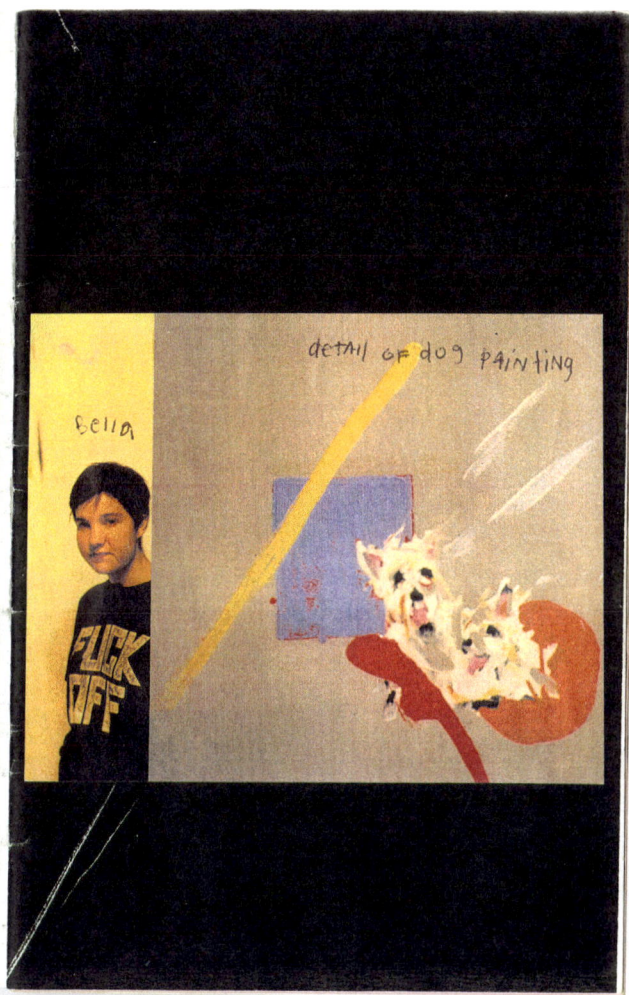

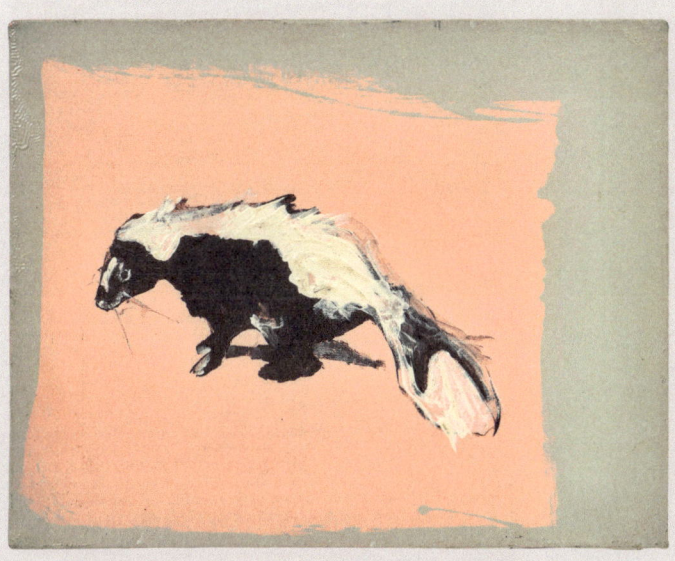

Skunk, 1996
Oil and acrylic on canvas, 11 × 14 in. (27.9 × 35.6 cm)
Collection the artist

Ramdasha Bikceem

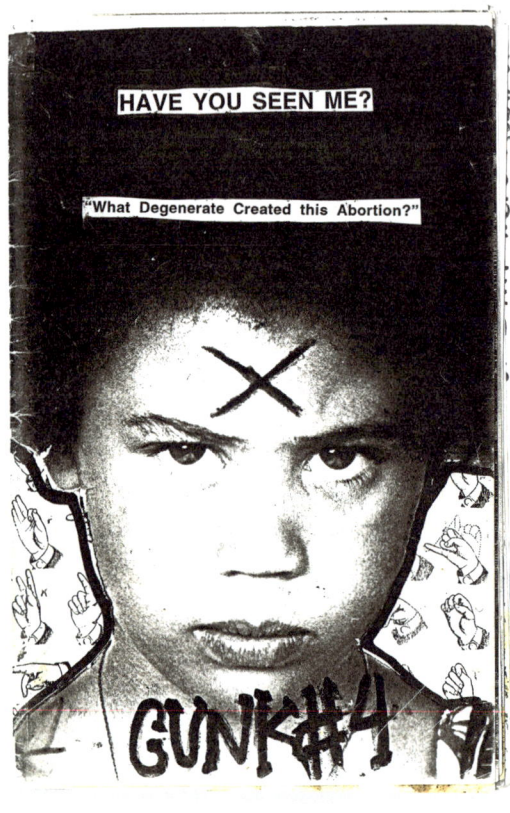

Gunk, no. 4, 1993
Photocopy, saddle stitched, 8 ½ × 5 ½ in. (21.6 × 14 cm)
Fales Library, New York University

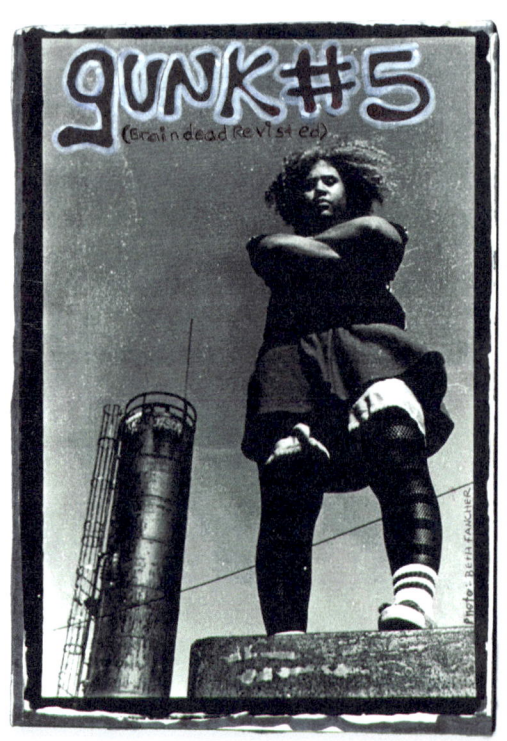

Paste-ups for *Gunk*, no. 5, 1994
Gelatin silver prints, photocopy, paper, glue, 8 ½ × 5 ½ in. (21.6 × 14 cm)
Fales Library, New York University

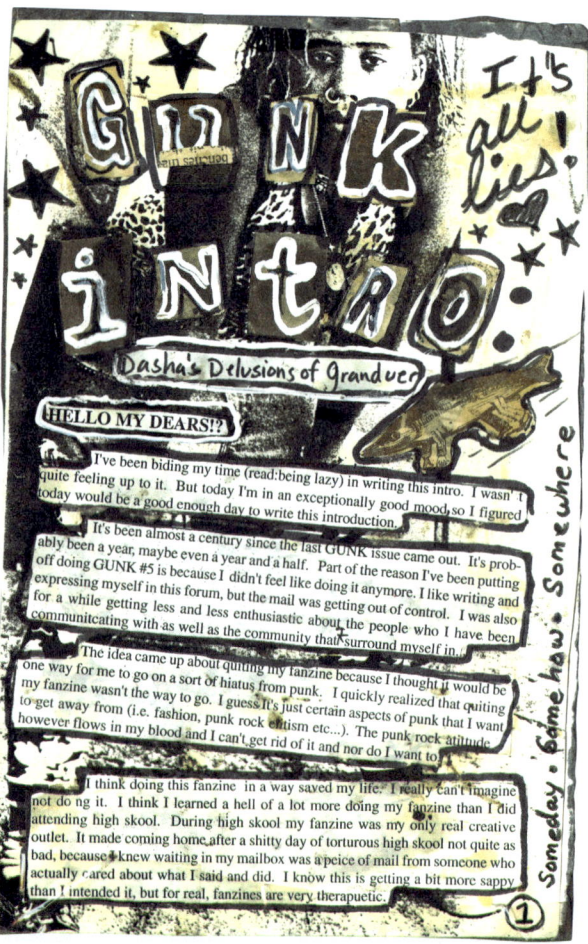

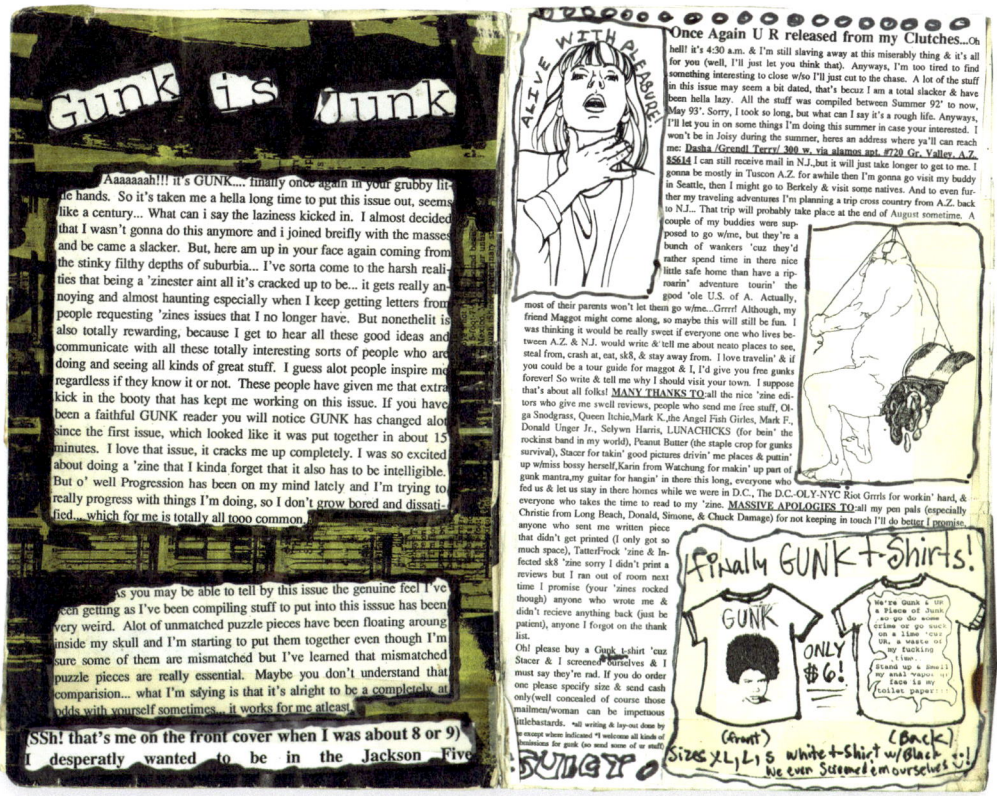

↑↓ Paste-up for *Gunk*, no. 4, 1993
Gelatin silver prints, photocopy, paper, glue, ink,
correction fluid, 8½ × 11 in. (21.6 × 27.9 cm)
Fales Library, New York University

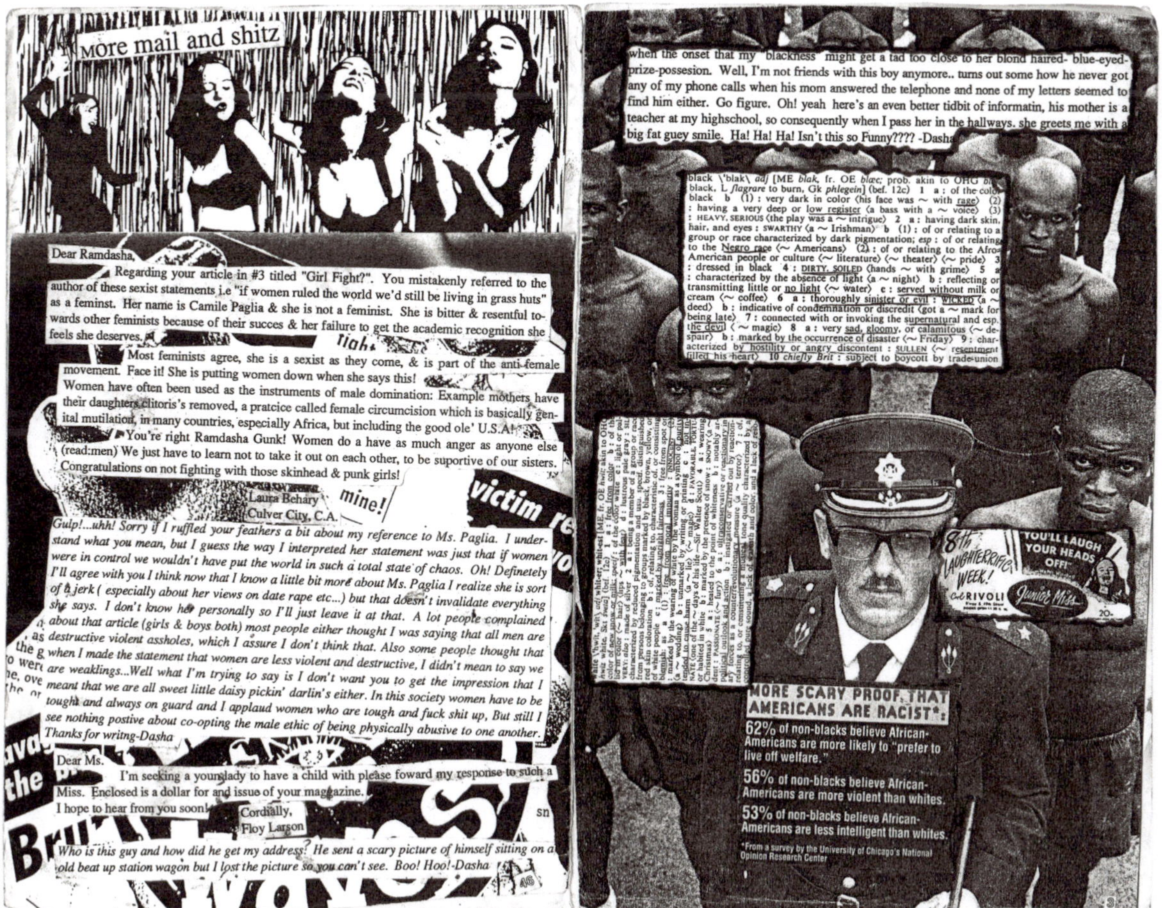

Sadie Benning

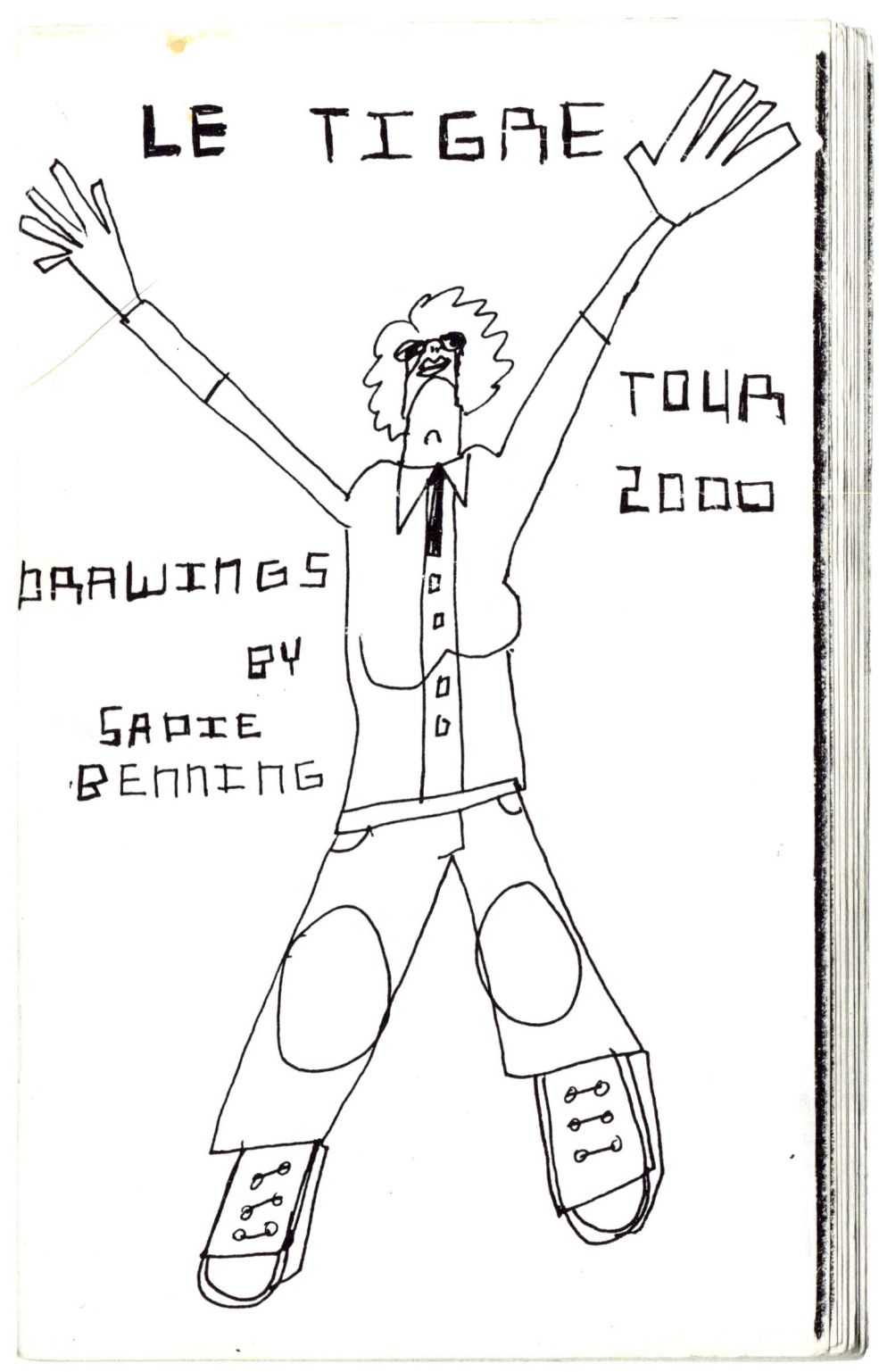

Le Tigre Tour, 2000
Photocopy, saddle stitched, 8 ½ × 5 ½ in. (21.6 × 14 cm)
Fales Library, New York University

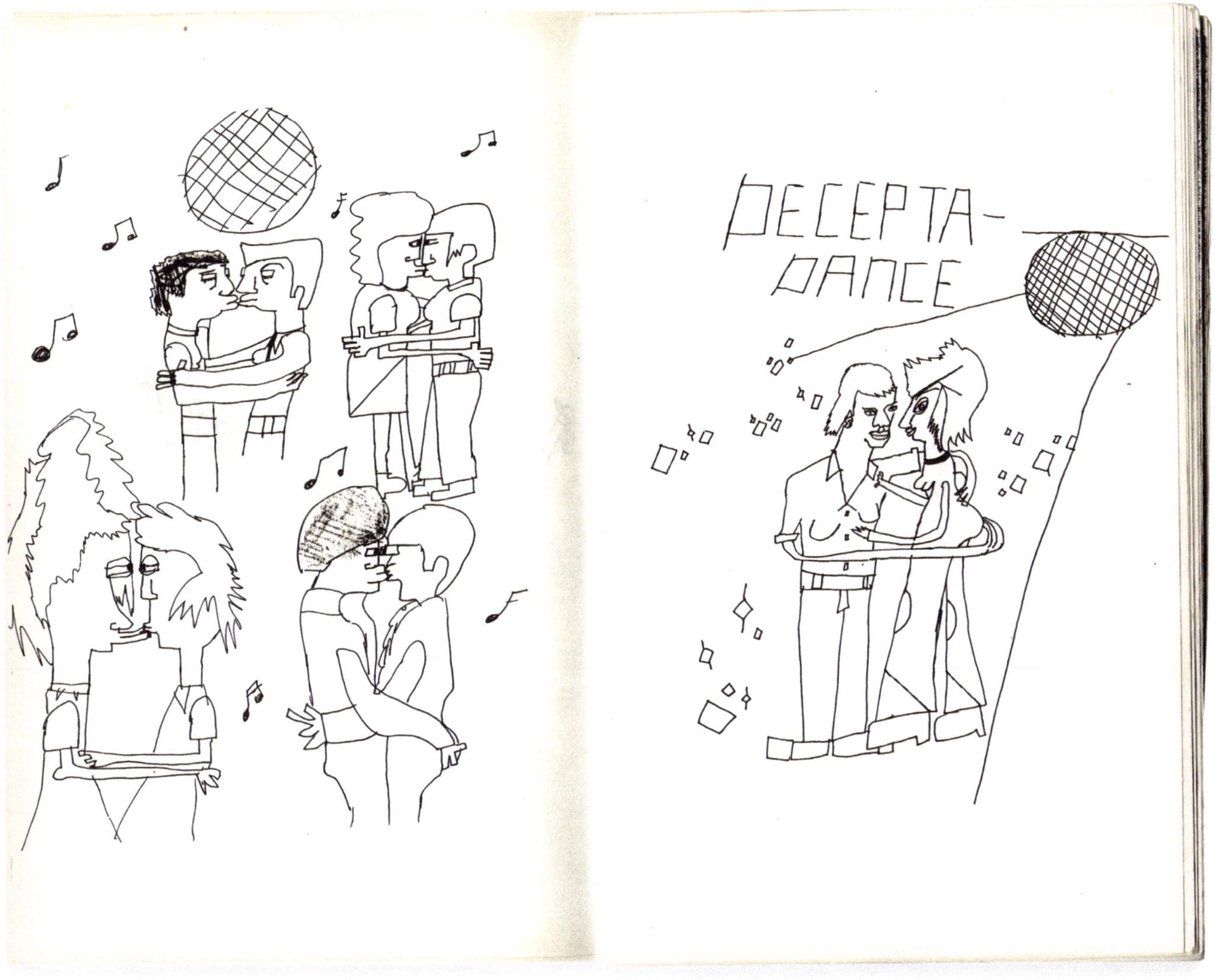

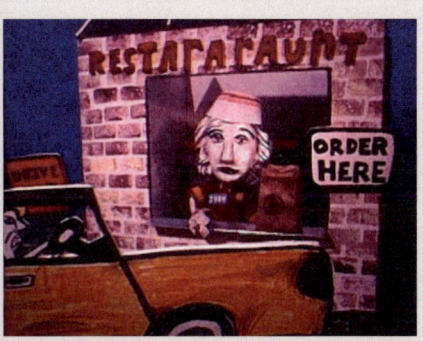
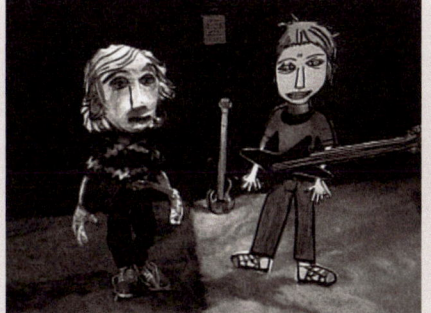
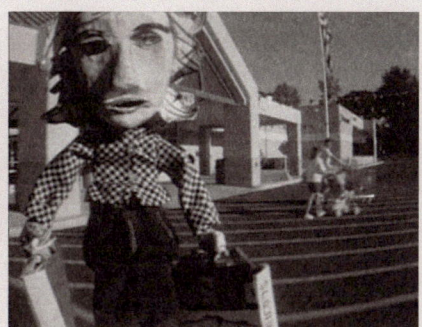

Stills from *The Judy Spots*, 1995
Video; color, sound; 12 min., 50 sec.
Video Data Bank; School of the Art Institute of Chicago

Miranda July

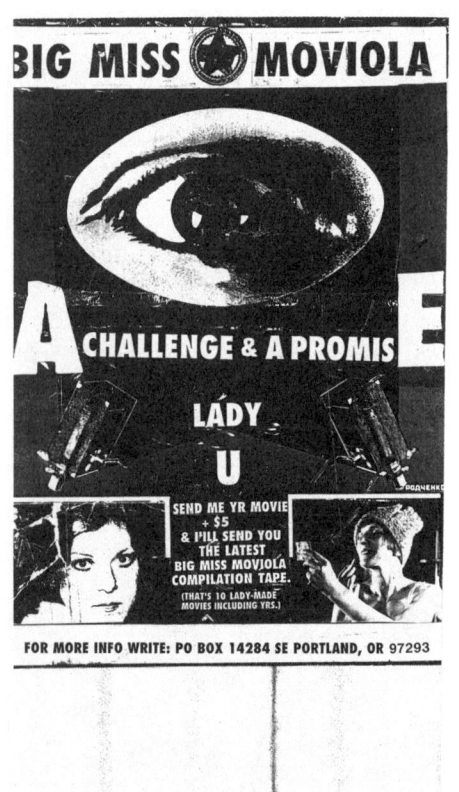

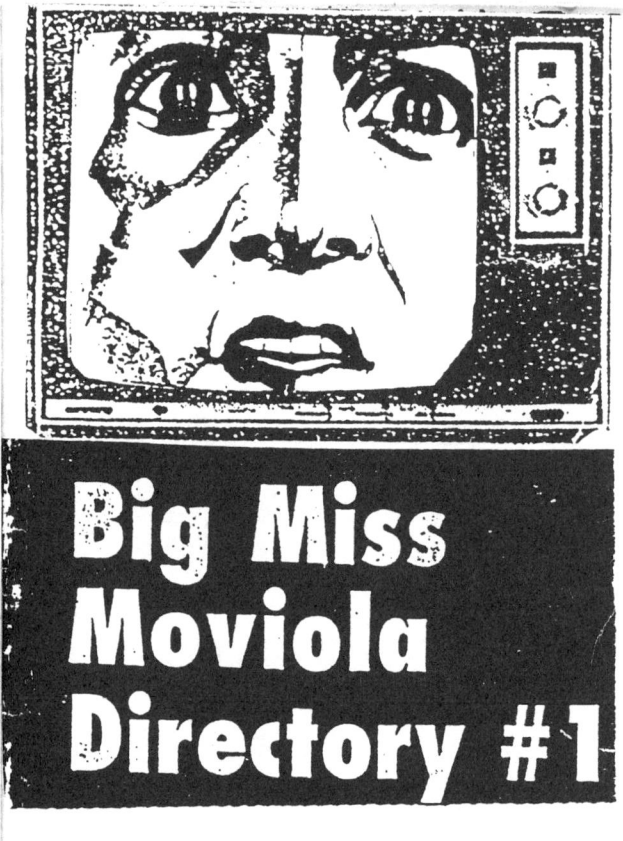

↑→ *Big Miss Moviola Directory #1 (The Velvet Chainletter)*, 1995
Photocopy, saddle stitched, 5 ½ × 4 ¼ in. (14 × 10.8 cm)
Getty Research Institute, Los Angeles, (2016.M.20)

↑↓ *Big Miss Moviola Chainletter #2: Directory (The Underwater Chainletter)*, 1996
Designed by Miranda July and Julia Bryan-Wilson
Photocopy, saddle stitched, 8 ½ × 7 in. (21.6 × 17.8 cm)
Getty Research Institute, Los Angeles (2016.M.20)

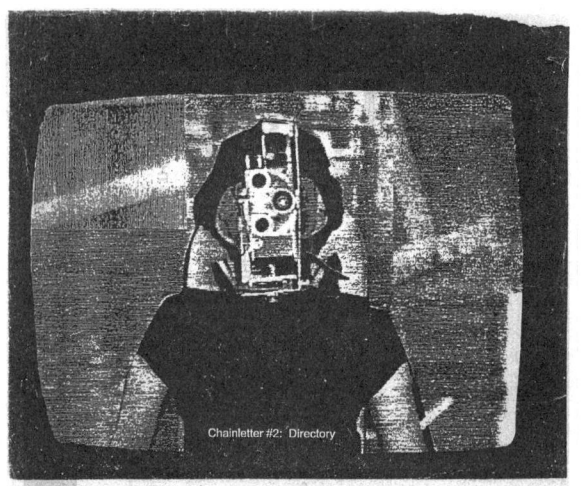

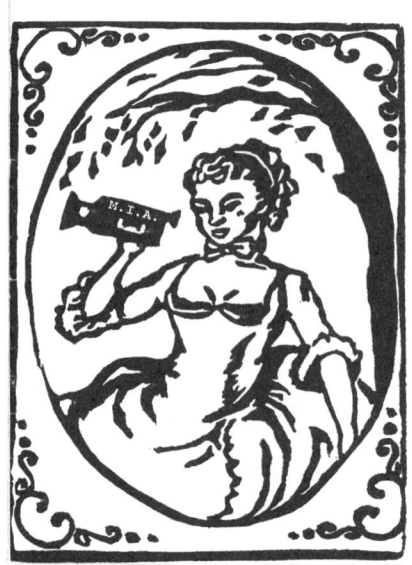

Big Miss Moviola, The M.I.A. Chainletter, 1999
Photocopy, saddle stitched, 5 ½ × 4 ¼ in. (14 × 10.8 cm)
Getty Research Institute, Los Angeles (2016.M.20)

Table of Contents:
1. OK
2. THIS TAPE
3. P-P-P-PUBLICITY
4. MEET THE FIRST 9 WOMEN TO WALK ON THE MOON!
5. THE MISSING MOVIE REPORT
6. JOANIE 4 JACKIE
7. THE CHAINLETTER

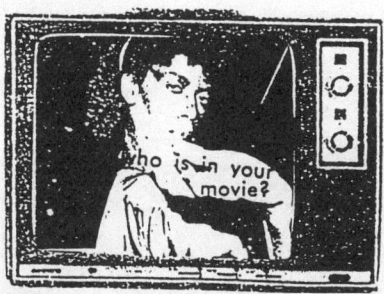

who is in your movie?

This is the second edition of this Directory. All adresses and "1-2-3-Go!" have been updated as of 7/8/97, but all of the actual content is as it was written in 4/96. For more current information about Big Miss Moviola, or to order other Chainletter Tapes write me at: P.O. Box 14284, Portland, OR.97293 or mjuly@europa.com.
A special thanx goes out to Co--whose endless support and technical assistence have radically upgraded this project -- and to Yariv: your visionary involvement and wild generosity has been SPINAL

1.OK:
It's April 11th 1996 and this is the Big Miss Moviola Directory #1. It goes with the Chainletter Tape #1. Big Miss Moviola isn't a film festival or contest. Every lady who sent a movie is either on this tape (#1) or will be on future tapes. Women of any age or skill level can send their movie and be garunteed that at least 9 other women will see her movie--or an infinite # of people, if she gives me the thumbs up to sell and screen her work. Everyone who sees her movie will also own this Directory. The Directory is important. It's the reason why Big miss Moviola is more about communication than presentation. The participants can give eachother feedback if they want and they will also get letters from non-participants who bought the tape for $15. This is possible because The Directory has all the moviemaker's adress' in it. Too bad this #1 Directory doesn't have more helpful hints and resources in it. If you (anyone) has information for #2 please do send it. And of course: send your movie. There's directions and a form to fill out in the back.

2. THIS TAPE:
These were the first 9 movies that were sent to me. It took a very long time to get these movies because I had no publicity. None of these ladies read about Big Miss Moviola in a magazine. They either got a flyer from me at some event I was at or they heard about it through word of mouth. Friends of friends. This means that these movies are all reflective of my crowd or scene (even though I only know 2 of the ladies). The tapes that I am recieving now that I've had some big publicity are totally different. That's the good/bad thing about publicity: it doesn't allow things to be private. For Big Miss moviola it's pretty much a good thing. Private=all your friends saying they really liked your movie (the one that they were in). Public=Ladies who really don't know where your coming from or who you are telling you what they think about your movie. I have spent the last few months scheming ways to bust this project out of it's designated (by the history) age & life experience slot. Bust out of: age 16-26, white, college-educated. This should make the feedback part more useful & interesting. [See: "P-P-P-PUBLICITY" & "JOANIE 4 JACKIE" & "THE MISSING MOVIE REPORT" FOR MORE ON THAT] Most of all I want to thank these 9 ladies b/c everytime I got a tape in the mail it was a huge event. Like driving by a billboard that says: This really happening: Go Go Go.

Elina Shatkin/ The Date
[16mm] P.O. Box 25013, Los Angeles, CA. 90025

I WANTED TO INCLUDE MY PO BOX/ ADDRESS AT THE END OF THE FILM SO THAT PEOPLE WHO WERE INTERESTED IN WHAT I WAS DOING COULD CONTACT ME + WE COULD HOOK UP & COMMUNICATE. I REALLY AGREE WITH WHAT YOU'RE SAYING ABOUT HOW MOST FILMS ARE A ONE WAY MODE OF COMMUNICATION: THEY MAKE THEM WE CONSUME THEM. I'D LIKE TO PUSH THESE WALLS OUT A LITTLE. I FUCKED UP WHEN I WAS FILMING THE PART W/MY ADDRESS SO OH WELL. I WOULD VERY MUCH LIKE TO CONNECT W/OTHER & DOING THEIR OWN SECRET COOL FILM SHIT. THIS FILM ("THE DATE) IS A ROUGH CUT: I'M GOING TO ADD SOUND TO IT EVENTUALLY + IM WORKING IN THE TIMING (QUICKER, SHARPER). IM IN FILM SCHOOL NOW WHICH CAN IS A GREAT RESOURCE IN SOME WAYS BUT CAN ALSO BE A REAL PISSER - ALL THE TARANTINO WANNA BES GET REAL OLD REAL FAST. NOW IM DOING SOME STUFF IN VIDEO & PIXELVISION (MUCH CHEAPER), ANYWAY. I VERY VERY VERY MUCH WANT TO SEE WHAT OTHER paper if you need to. UP TO. HAVE FUN.
ESP. QUEER. elina

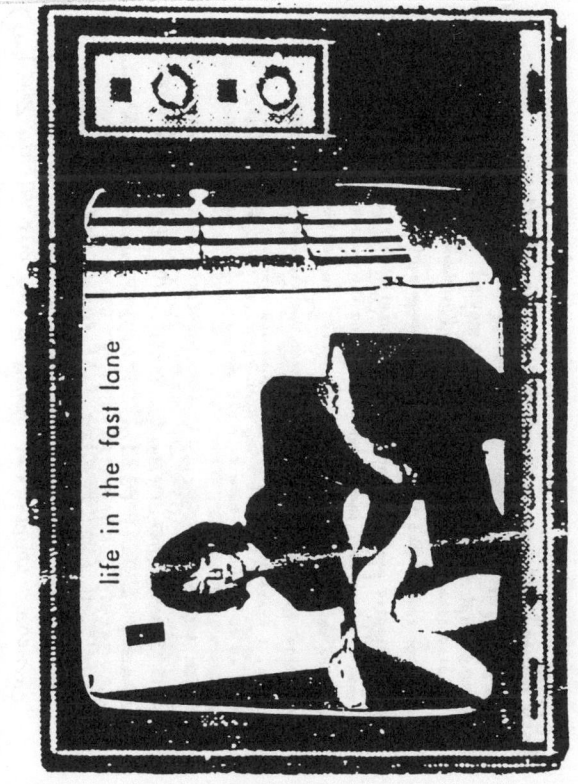

life in the fast lane

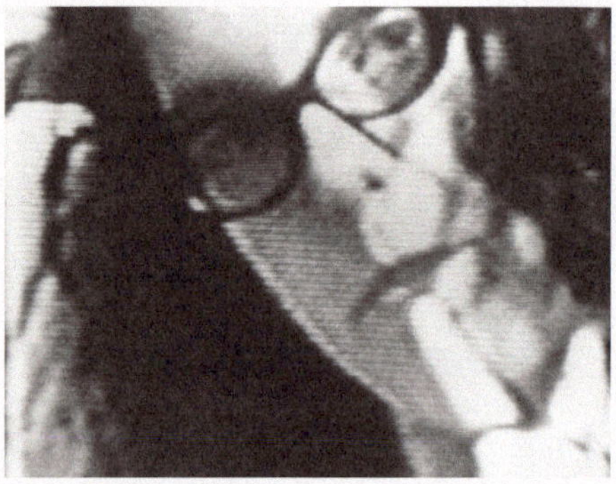

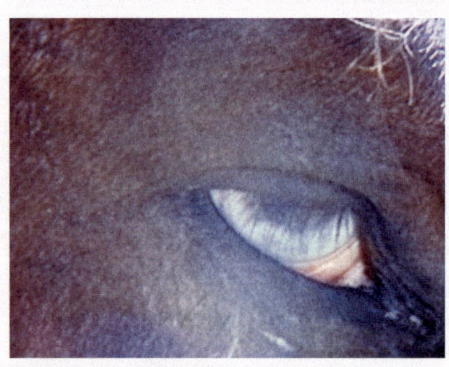

Still from Tammy Rae Carland's *Dear Mom*, 1995,
in *Big Miss Moviola, The Velvet Chainletter*, 1995
Video; color, sound; 3 min., 3 sec.

Still from Tammy Rae Carland's *Jug Town Road*, 1995,
in *Big Miss Moviola, The Velvet Chainletter*, 1995
Video; color, sound; 4 min.

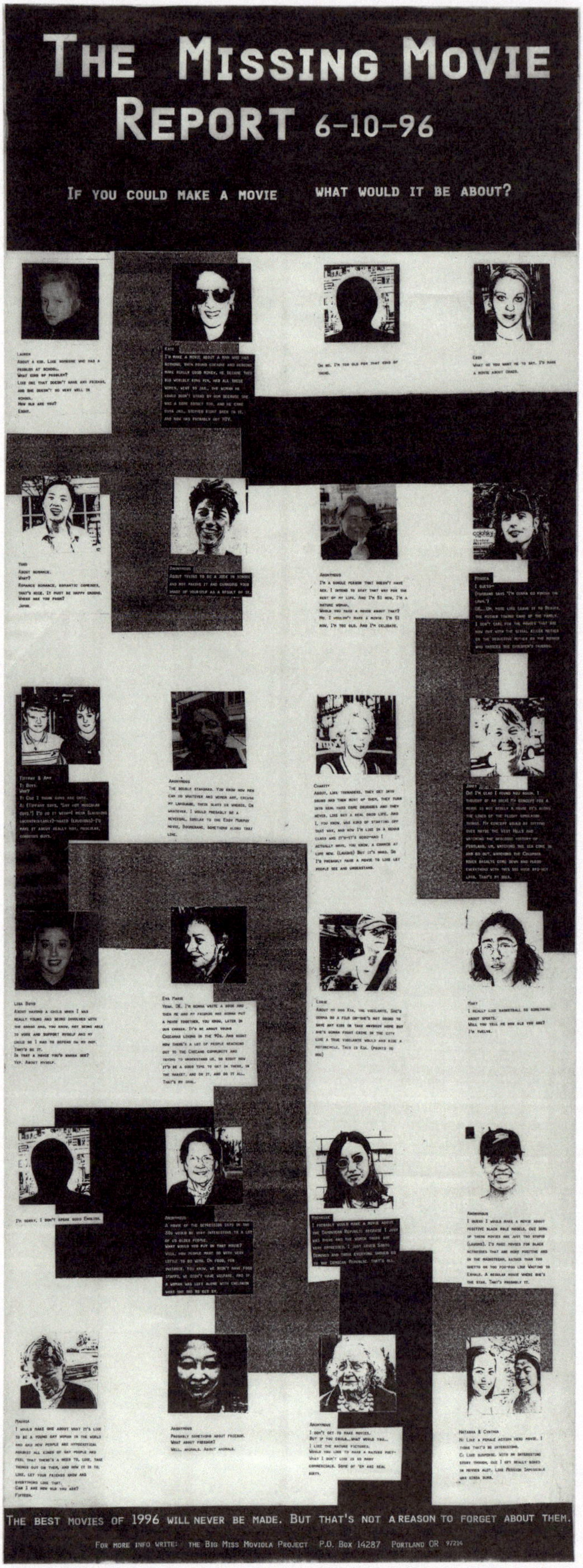

The Missing Movie Report, 1996
Photocopy, 48 ¼ × 18 ⁵⁄₁₆ in. (122.6 × 46.5 cm)
Collection the artist

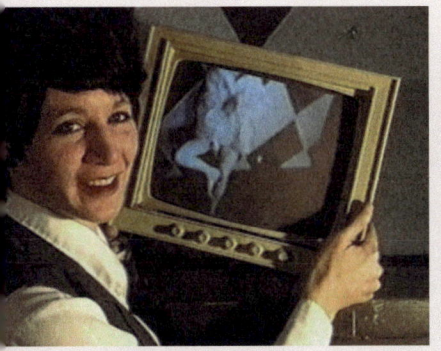
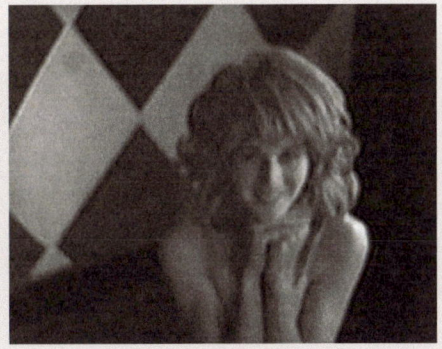
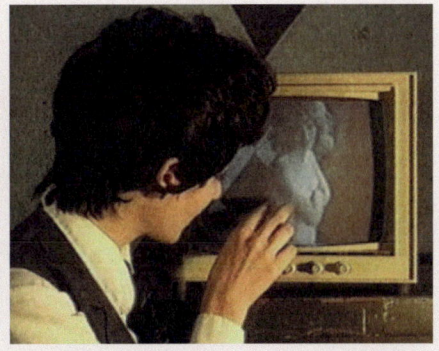

Stills from *The Amateurist*, 1998
Video; color, sound; 14 min.
Video Data Bank; School of the Art Institute of Chicago

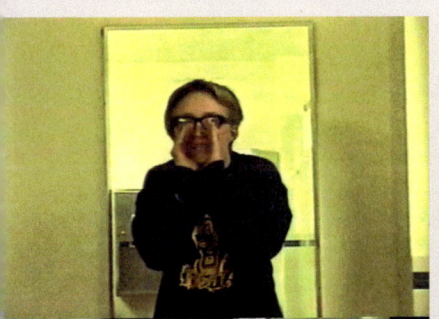
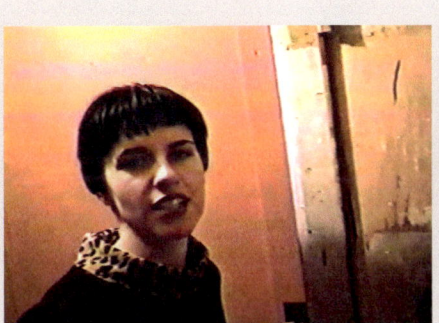
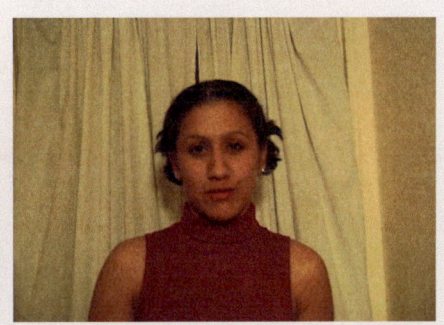

Stills from *Nobody Ever Told Me*, 1996–2001
Video; color, sound; 1 min. each
Collection the artist

4.

Subcultural Topologies, 1990–2010

While zines have often been associated with subcultures, the lines between "inside" and "outside"—or "center" and "margins"—were blurred by the mid-1990s as zines were becoming integrated into commercial art galleries, artist-run spaces, and museums. This section looks at zine makers and artists who drew upon or documented vernacular and subcultural practices. Aaron Rose's Alleged gallery, which opened in New York's Lower East Side in 1992, became a hub for self-publishing activities during this period, bringing together artists working in the worlds of graffiti, skateboarding, graphic design, film, photography, and fashion. While located in New York, Rose regularly collaborated with artists and cultural producers from his home state of California, including the renowned skateboarder Mark Gonzales, who around this time began making zines featuring his signature poetry and drawings.

Like the correspondence artists examined in section 1, Gonzales and others in this chapter began to understand the photocopy as a decentralized exhibition tool, often publishing zines in conjunction with exhibitions or to showcase new bodies of art. Other artists who exhibited at Alleged and sometimes produced zines with its publishing arm, Alleged Press, include Susan Cianciolo, Cameron Jamie, Harmony Korine, Ari Marcopoulos, Deanna Templeton, and Ed Templeton. Many of them translated the collage aesthetic of zines into their work in other media (or vice versa), from Cianciolo's garments for her Run fashion collection and related clothing kits to Marcopoulos's xeroxed photographs. The gallery also became an important antecedent for younger artists living or arriving in New York in the late 1990s, including members of Kunle Martins's IRAK graffiti group, such as Ryan McGinley and Dash Snow. Their zines, featuring provocative collages and voyeuristic photographs of themselves and friends, began circulating beyond their community, ultimately resulting in museum and gallery shows of their work.

This section situates these practices in conversation with other artists and zine makers who drew upon vernacular forms of cultural production typically outside or at the margins of contemporary art. The post-Minimalist artist Beverly Buchanan is perhaps best known for her sculptural "shacks"—loose interpretations of the dilapidated cabins that punctuate the southern US landscape. Buchanan also produced numerous zines throughout her career. Some of her photocopied publications from the 1990s and 2000s serve as archives of her photographic documentation of the architecture of Black communities in the South; others offer her conceptual and humorous takes on the art world. Frederick Weston, drawing upon his training in the fashion industry, became a dedicated archivist of mass media representations of men, amassing binders of magazine clippings—paper ephemera that he turned into zines and related collage works.

In the 1990s and early 2000s, artists in Mexico made use of the zine as a means to share their art, play with elements from popular culture, and disseminate difficult-to-find images and texts about avant-garde practices happening outside of Mexico. They defied both the traditionalism of the art world in their country as well as international copyright laws. Mexico City in particular was home to a thriving punk scene and several alternative magazines and spaces. There, a group of artists (among them Daniel Guzmán, Damián Ortega, and Luis Felipe Ortega), who had been members of the Temístocles 44 artists' collective in the early 1990s, initiated a series of self-publishing ventures, including the zines *Alegría* and *Casper*. Starting in 2000, inspired by *Casper*, a collective of thirteen (resolutely anonymous) artists in Guadalajara organized weekly gatherings during which they collaborated on making zines and homemade videos (and also partying). After the dissolution of the group, known only as El Chino, the collection of zines and videos was archived in *El mueble chino* (2000–2001), made from the large black cases used for moving the equipment of touring musical bands. Like the punk subcultures and fanzines that came before them, these artists used the model of the "bootleg" and the spirit of making do to engage in disrupting systems in Mexico as well as internationally.

Beverly Buchanan

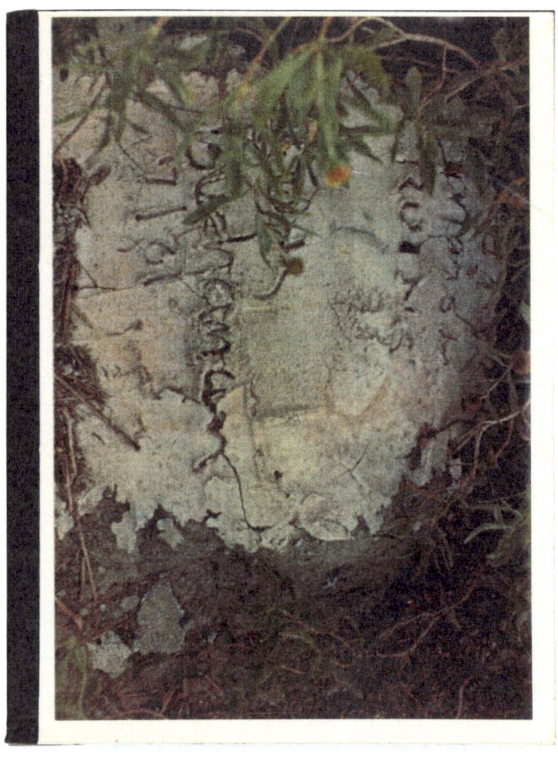

Marsh Ruins, 1981
Black-and-white and color photocopy, tape bound, 11 × 8 ½ in. (27.9 × 21.6 cm)
Beverly Buchanan papers, 1912–2017, bulk 1970s–1990s, Archives of American Art, Smithsonian Institution

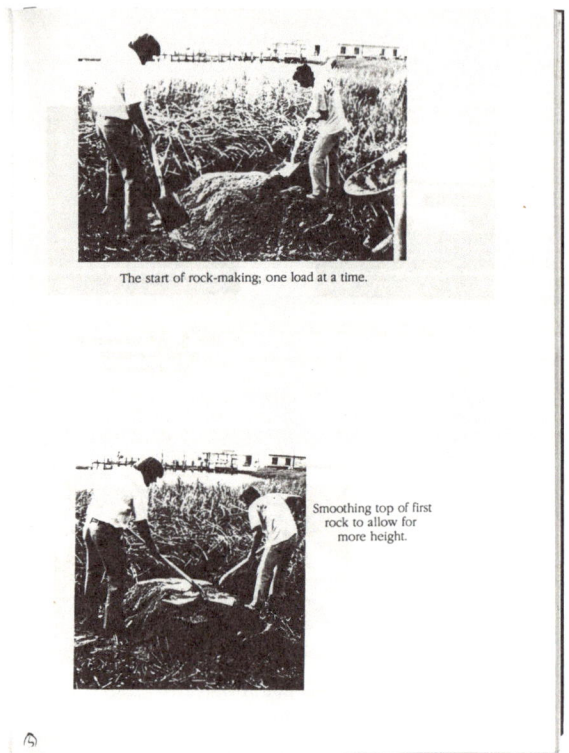

The start of rock-making; one load at a time.

Smoothing top of first rock to allow for more height.

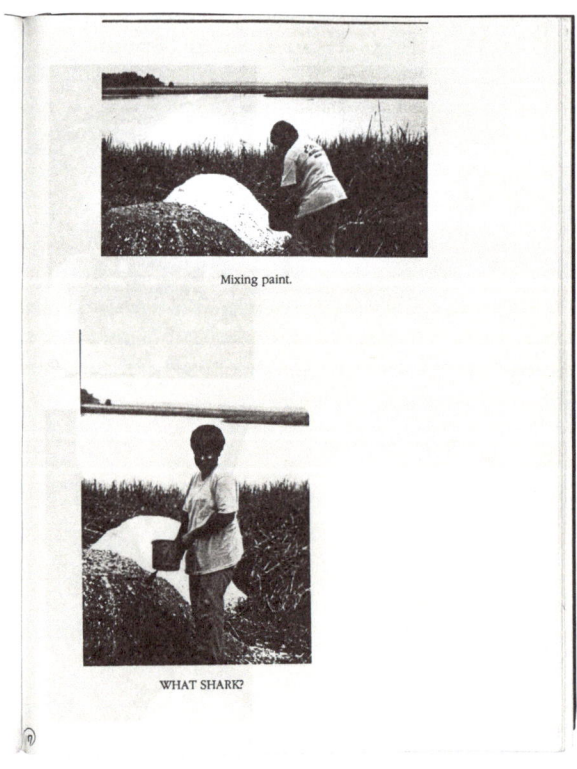

Mixing paint.

WHAT SHARK?

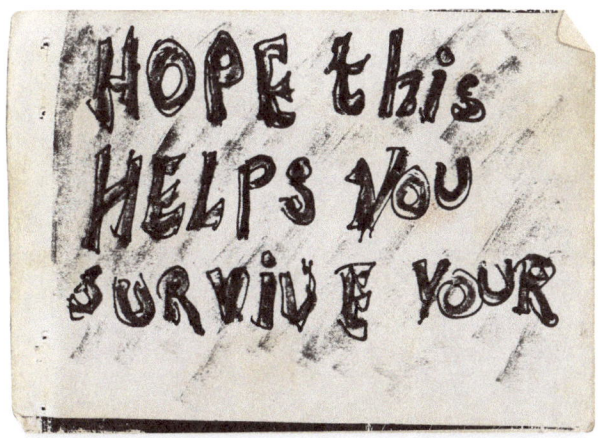

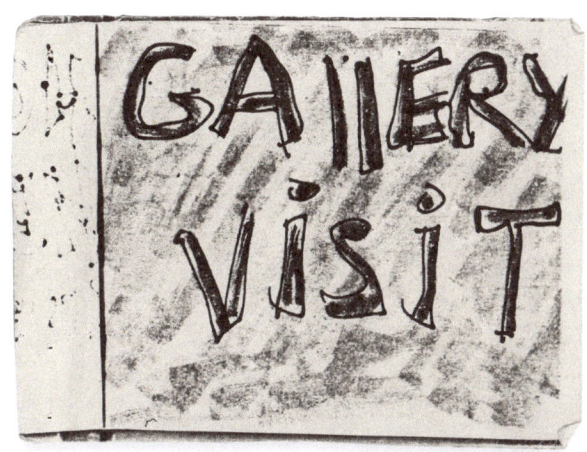

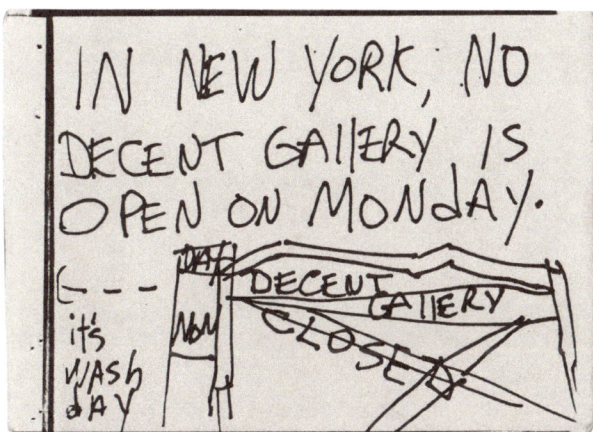

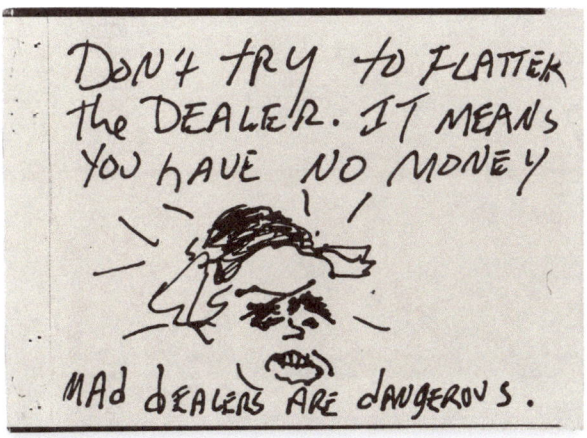

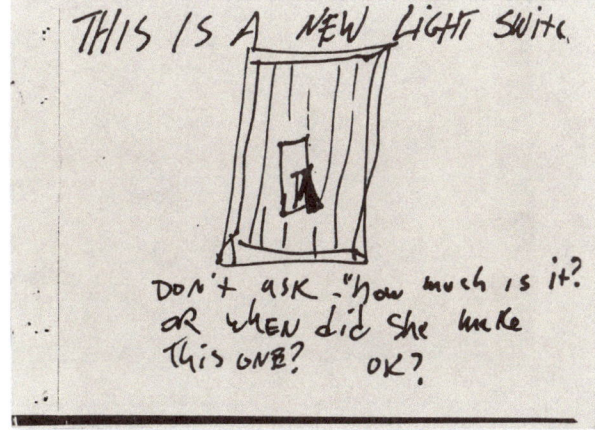

Hope This Helps You Survive Your Gallery Visit, n.d.
Photocopy, side stapled, 2 7/8 × 4 1/16 in. (7.3 × 10.3 cm)
Beverly Buchanan papers, 1912–2017, bulk 1970s–1990s,
Archives of American Art, Smithsonian Institution

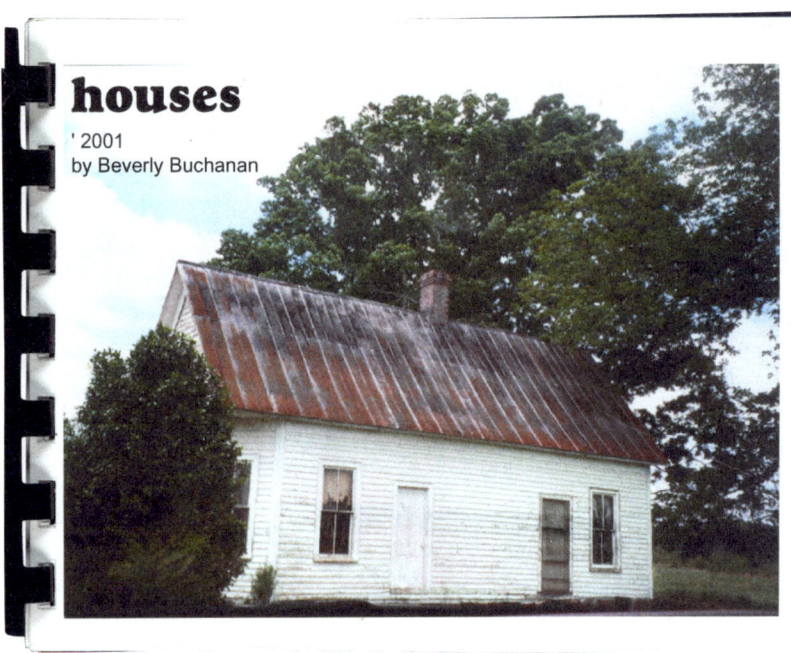

Houses, 2001
Photocopy, comb bound, 4 5⁄16 × 5 ½ in. (11 × 14 cm)
Beverly Buchanan papers, 1912–2017, bulk 1970s–1990s,
Archives of American Art, Smithsonian Institution

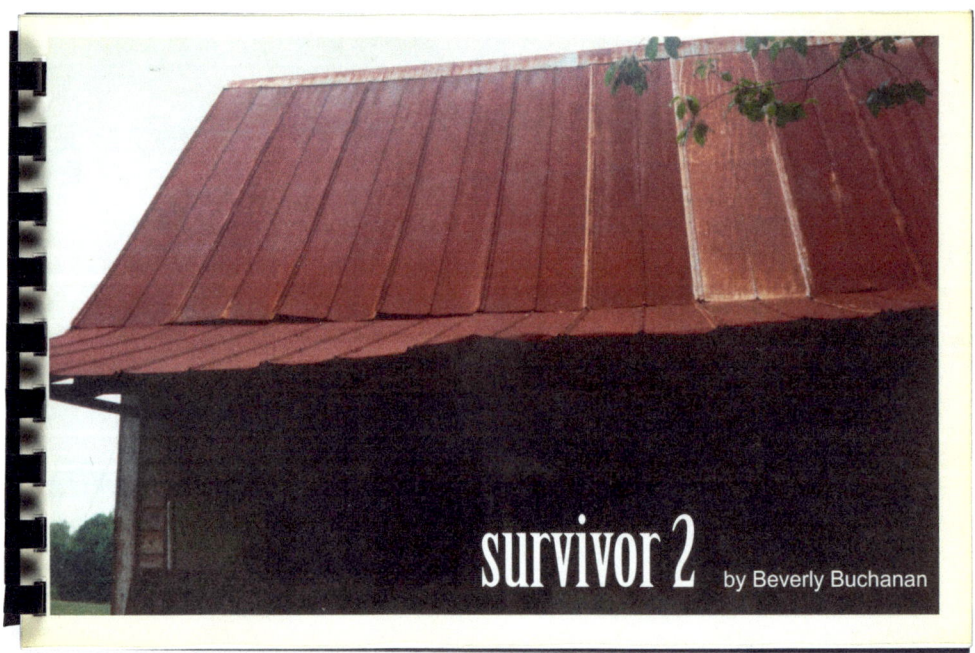

Survivor 2, ca. 2001
Photocopy, comb bound, 5 ¼ × 8 ½ in. (13.3 × 21.6 cm)
Beverly Buchanan papers, 1912–2017, bulk 1970s–1990s,
Archives of American Art, Smithsonian Institution

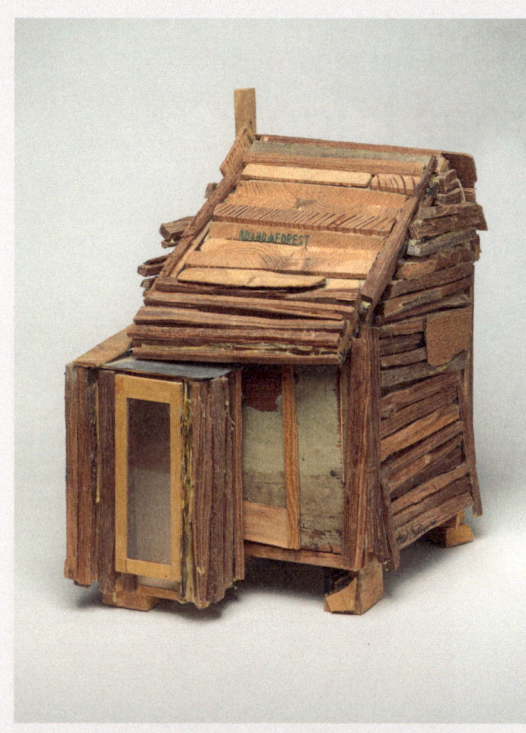

To Prudence Prop, n.d.
Metal, plastic, wood,
17 ⅞ × 10 ⅜ × 16 ½ in. (45.4 × 26.4 × 41.9 cm)
Brooklyn Museum

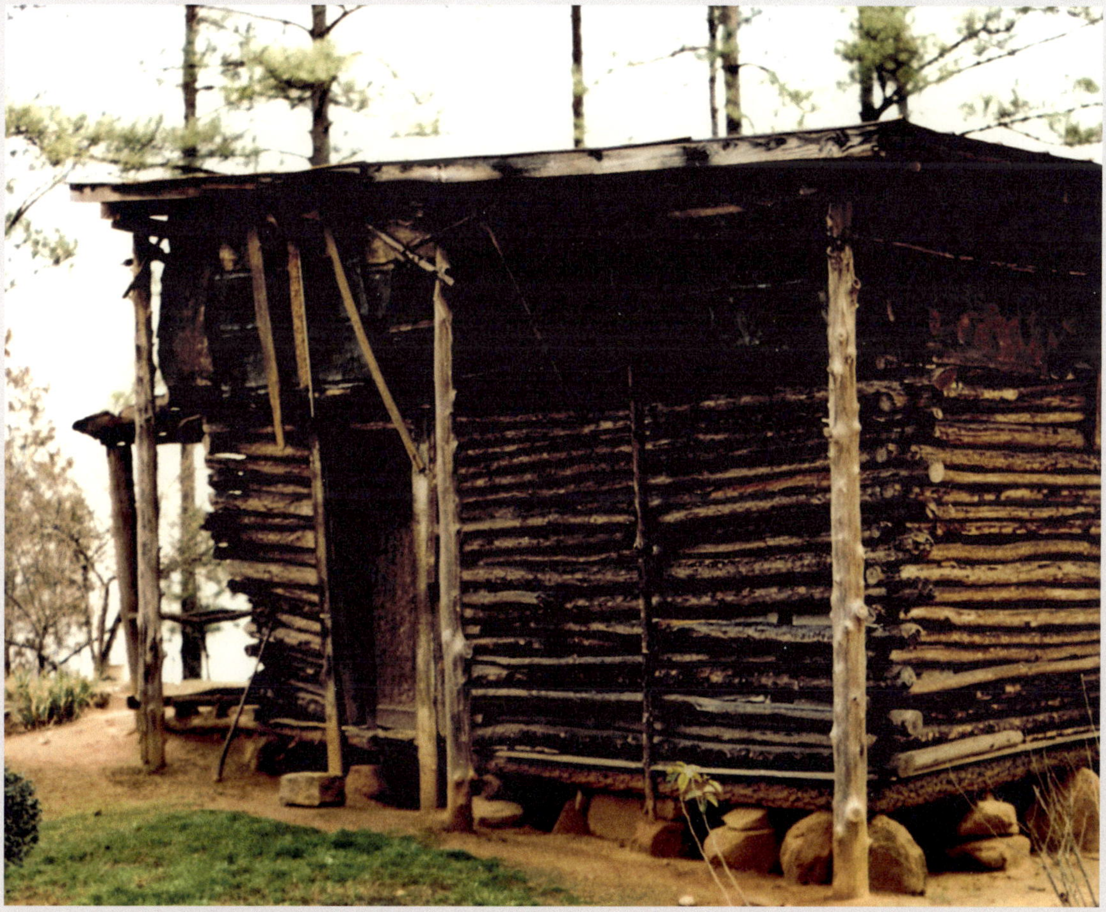

Mary Lou Furcron's House, 1989
Chromogenic print, 16 × 20 in. (40.6 × 50.8 cm)
Andrew Edlin Gallery, New York

Eduardo Abaroa, Damián Ortega,
Luis Felipe Ortega, Pablo Vargas Lugo

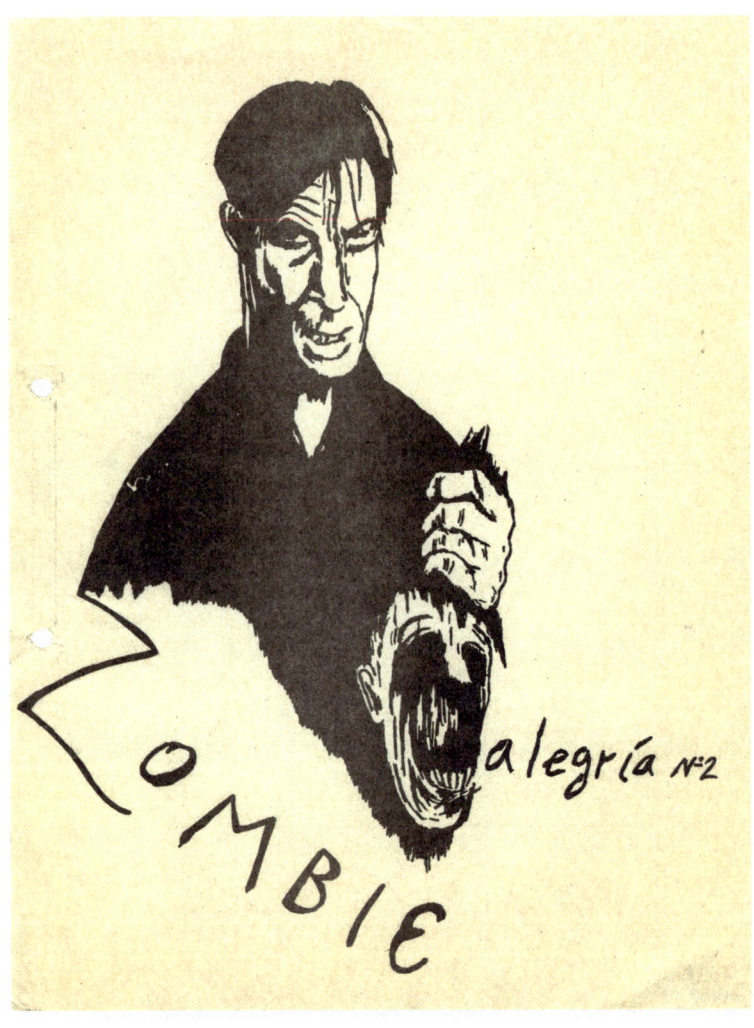

Alegría, no. 2, 1993
Editors: Damián Ortega, Luis Felipe Ortega
Photocopy, side stapled, 11 × 8 ½ in. (27.9 × 21.6 cm)
Collection Luis Felipe Ortega

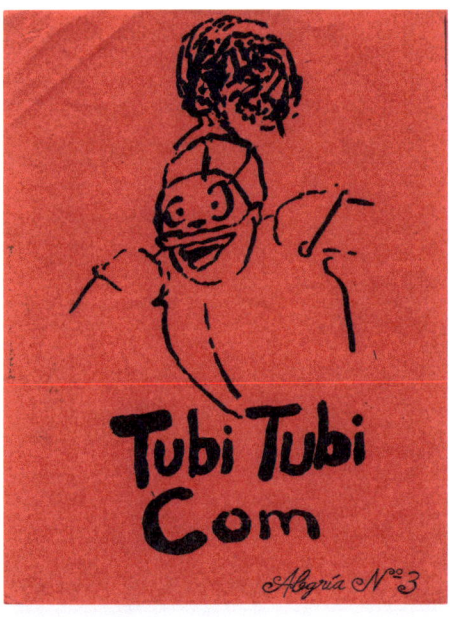

Alegría, no. 3, 1993
Editors: Fernando García Correa, Pablo Vargas Lugo,
Damián Ortega, Luis Felipe Ortega
Photocopy, 11 × 8 ½ in. (27.9 × 21.6 cm)
Collection Luis Felipe Ortega

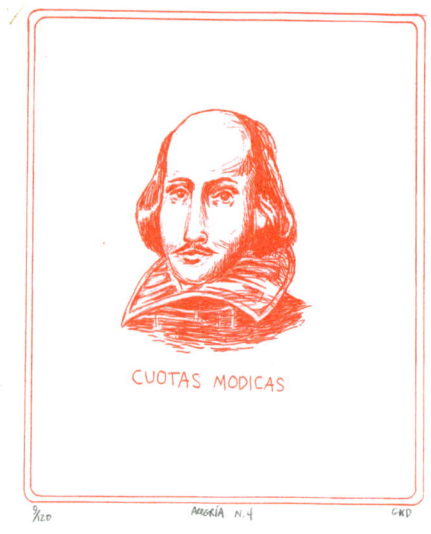

Alegría, no. 4, 1993
Editors: Fernando García Correa,
Pablo Vargas Lugo, Luis Felipe Ortega
Photocopy, 11 × 8 ½ in. (27.9 × 21.6 cm)
Collection Luis Felipe Ortega

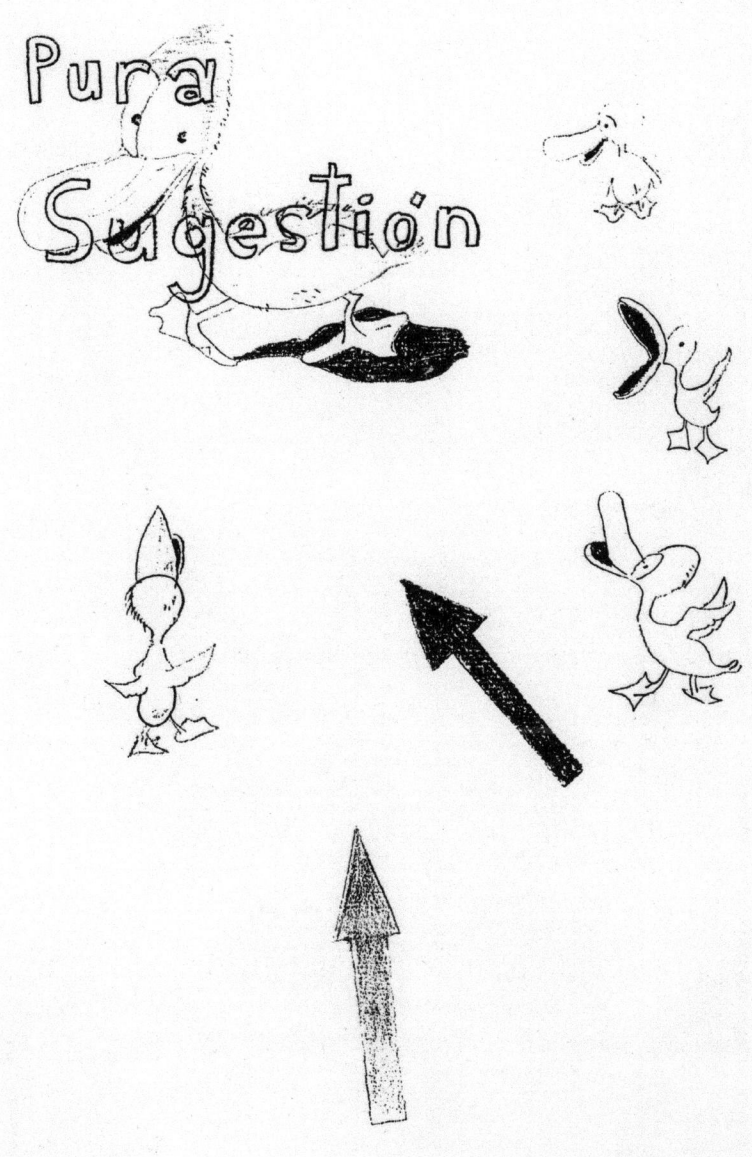

Alegría, no. 5, 1993
Editors: Eduardo Abaroa, Luis Felipe Ortega, Pablo Vargas Lugo
Photocopy, 11 × 8 ½ in. (27.9 × 21.6 cm)
Collection Luis Felipe Ortega

Daniel Guzmán, Gabriel Kuri, Damián Ortega, Luis Felipe Ortega

Note from the Editor

This is the pilot issue of Casper.
It is the first magazine with a mutating name ever recorded in Historical annals.
Writing our own History is not a duty that should concern us. This is why we invoque this organ: part organ, part material, part immaterial, part pastiche, part pun, to write it for us. And so we are able to devote ourselves to being performer almost spectators, sponsors, preachers, calumnists –and several other infamous occupations– of our own trade, to prevent ourselves from being the most infamous of all occupations, which is none other than reporters or journalists of that which does not concern us, be it that which we are meant to witness, but not only just to run and tell, but instead to give faith of our doubt, our confidence in chance (asisted by the sanest of nepotisms) and of our only certainty, which is that of being not so sure that we are, or even were there and then at the eye of the storm, ready with our credentials, and the necessary arrogance to affirm that this is this, was like that, or should be this way.

As it is costumary in publishing enterprise, the articles and other interventions that here appear, are responsibility of the authors, and even though the authors are responsibility of their own intricate genealogies, together with all of that which has formed, motivated and confused them, we would not want this to sound as a provocation, nor marking out of responsibilities, or ambiguity in matter of intelectual property.

Casper –and by this anima abbreviation, we mean to encompass all the names of its collaborators– is an organ that believes in the current validity of manifestoes. Understanding by currency, something like the life before expiry of seasonal fruit; and while fruit is, on one hand, a generous and reliable gift of the earth, we might have, on the other, the diverse advances in matter of Agrarian Reform Movements, (among them, printed manifestoes of technological and revolutionary struggle, that have the nobility of, having their contents expired, serving as wrapping device for housewives to take their produce back home) that have shown us that perpetuity and * (an asterisk) are practically synonymous when one is dealing with matter so immaterial as ideas, words, critique, point and line.

Casper is a publication in constant transformation. We gratefully encourage any criticism, as well as notes, articles, reviews, graphic work, original or plagiarised, at the enclosed adress. We will also be thankful if any of our readers –frequent or occasional– can put us in touch with anyone, or any organ that, they believe, should obtain or collaborate in the magazine.

Daniel Guzmán, Gabriel Kuri, Damián Ortega, Luis Felipe Ortega.

Ciudad de Mexico. May 1st, 1998. Labour Day.

Casper: Revista de título mutable, no. 0, 1998
Photocopy, saddle stitched; serigraph on Kraft envelope,
8 ½ × 5 ½ in. (21.6 × 14 cm)
Collection Luis Felipe Ortega

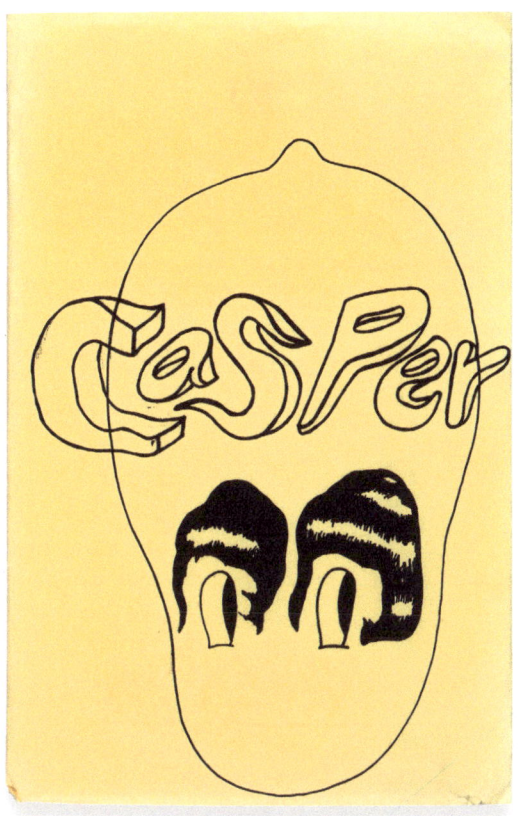

Casper: Revista de título mutable, no. 0, 1998
Photocopy, saddle stitched; serigraph on Kraft envelope,
8 ½ × 5 ½ in. (21.6 × 14 cm)
Collection Luis Felipe Ortega

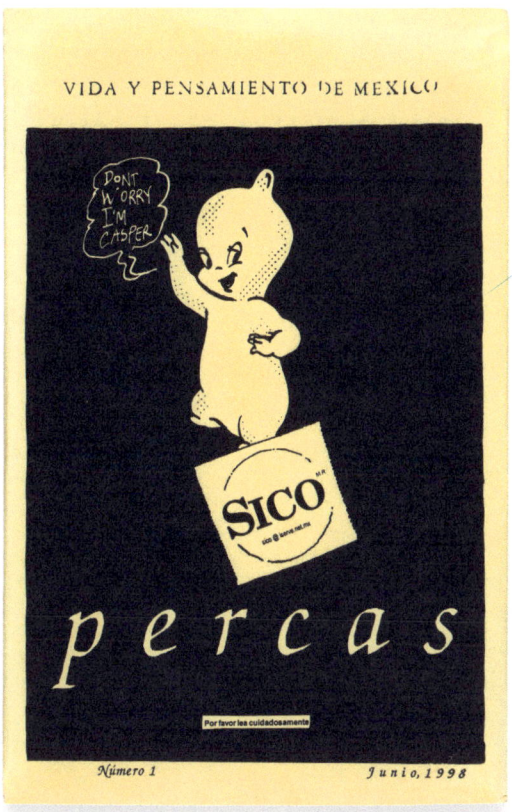

Casper: Revista de título mutable, no. 1, June 1998
Photocopy, saddle stitched, blue paper wrappers; with mixed media
inserts, serigraph on Kraft envelope, 8 ½ × 5 ½ in. (21.6 × 14 cm)
Collection Luis Felipe Ortega

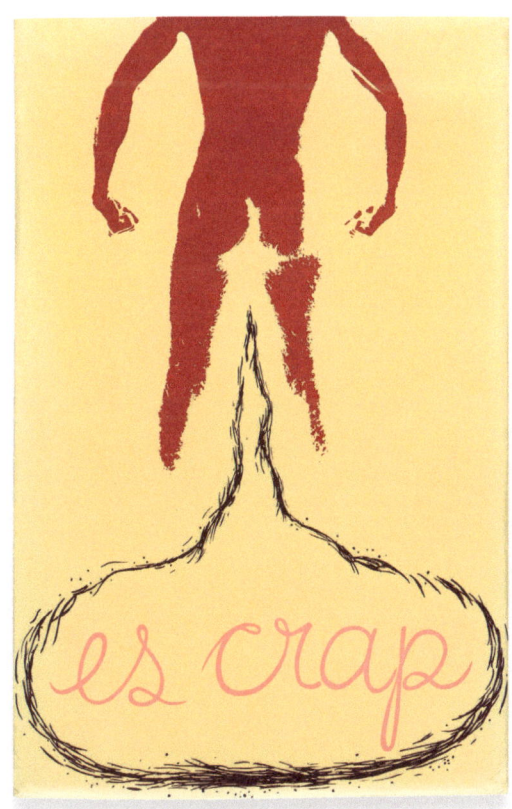

Casper: Revista de título mutable, no. 9, February 1999
Photocopy, saddle stitched, orange paper wrappers;
with mixed media inserts, serigraph on Kraft envelope,
8 ½ × 5 ½ in. (21.6 × 14 cm)
Collection Luis Felipe Ortega

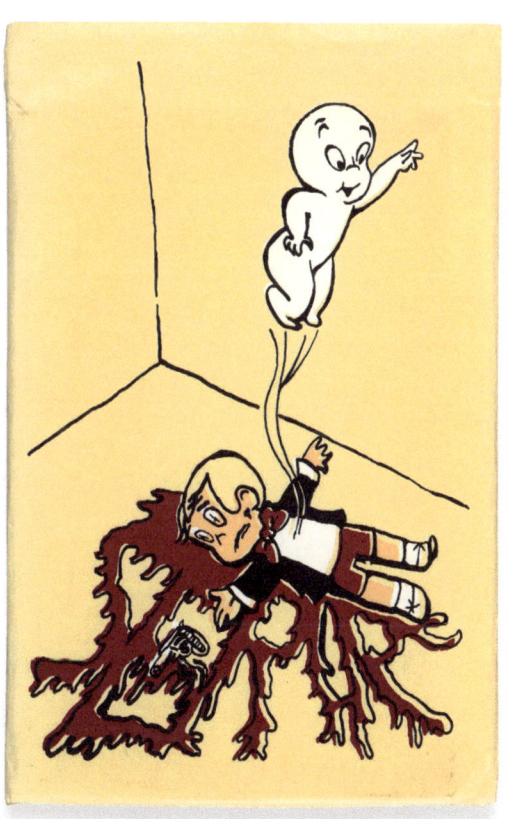

Casper: Revista de título mutable, no. 12, May 1999
Photocopy, saddle stitched, blue paper wrappers; with mixed media
inserts, serigraph on Kraft envelope, 8 ½ × 5 ½ in. (21.6 × 14 cm)
Collection Luis Felipe Ortega

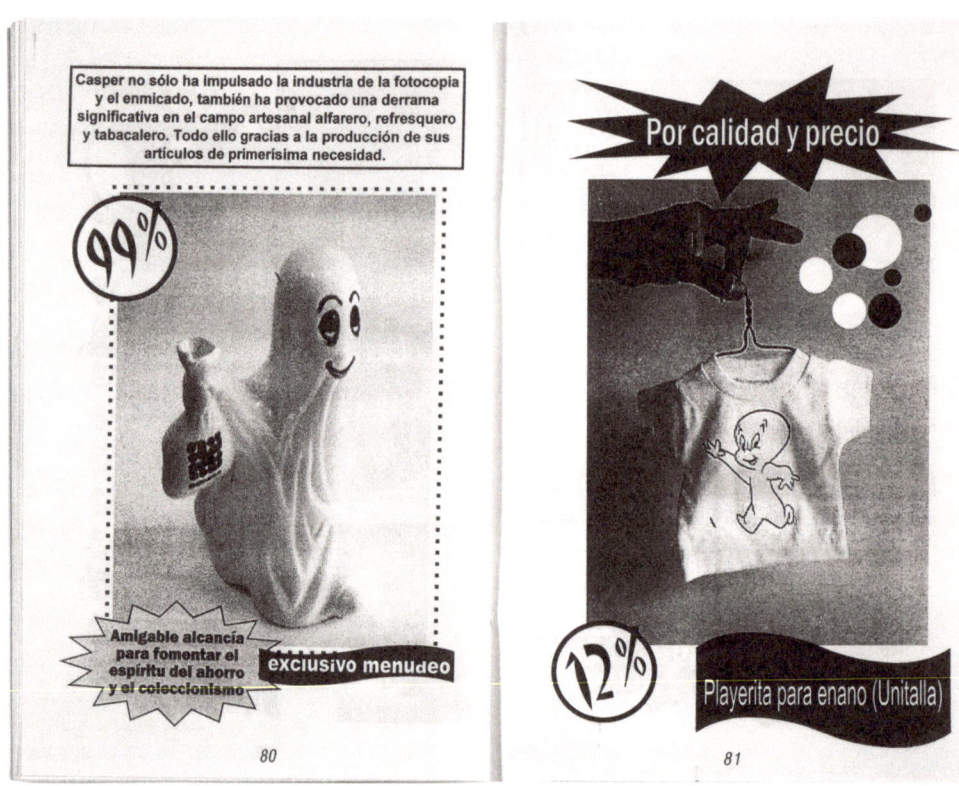

Casper: Revista de título mutable, no. 12, May 1999
Photocopy, saddle stitched, blue paper wrappers; with mixed media
inserts, serigraph on Kraft envelope, 8 ½ × 5 ½ in. (21.6 × 14 cm)
Collection Luis Felipe Ortega

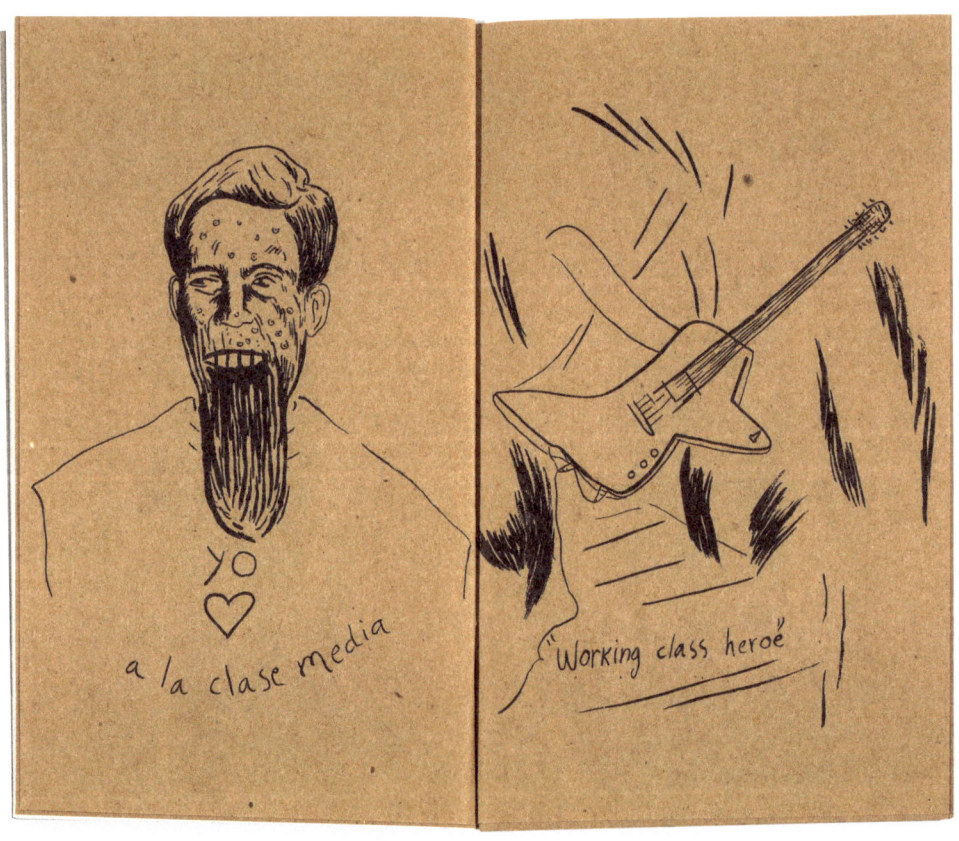

Casper: Revista de título mutable, no. 10, March 1999
Photocopy, saddle stitched, blue paper wrappers; with mixed media
inserts, serigraph on Kraft envelope, 8 ½ × 5 ½ in. (21.6 × 14 cm)
Collection Luis Felipe Ortega

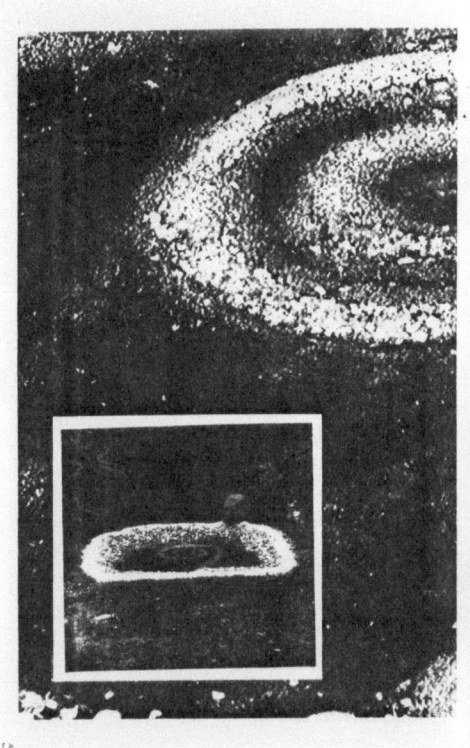
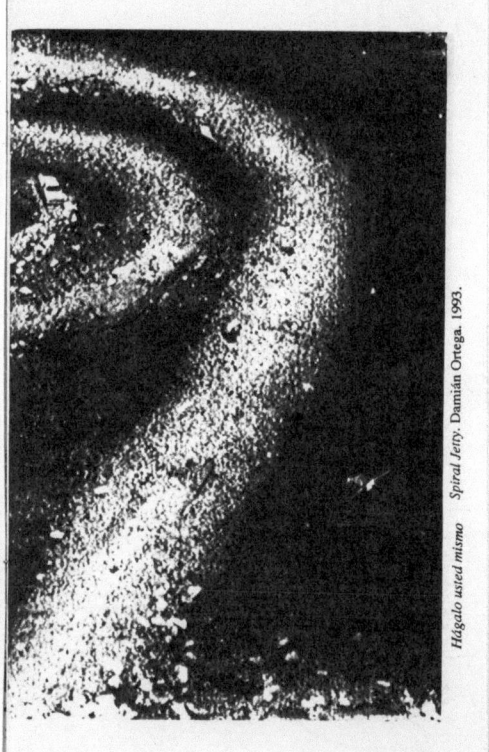

Hágalo usted mismo · *Spiral Jetty*. Damián Ortega. 1993.

"HAGALO USTED MISMO"
(Spiral Jetty)

Esta pieza fue parte de la segunda muestra que organizamos en Temístocles 44, una vieja casona de Polanco que nos habían prestado para hacer instalaciones *in situ*.

La pieza se trataba de una versión miniatura del "Spiral Jetty" de Robert Smithson. La realicé con material de jardinería en el patio de la casa. Al final de la reducida espiral hecha de piedritas, había un pequeño camión materialista de juguete, tirando una última carga de piedra.

La intención de la obra era bastante contradictoria, por una parte había una parodia de un niñito jugando a hacer arte radical en una casa prestada gentilmente por algún familiar millonetas; el espacio y la obra de arte monumental domesticado, vuelto un accesible jardincito interior decorativo en Polanco.

Por otra parte, había una ironía implícita al minimizar una obra tan grandilocuente y hacer una versión austera de aquel mamotreto multimillonario.

El juego era muy divertido porque yo invitaba a la gente a entrecerrar los ojos y a imaginarse que estaban viendo el auténtico "Spiral Jetty" desde un helicóptero… era algo bastante ridículo.

En una ocasión le preguntaron a Jimmie Durham si le gustaba Robert Smithson, él respondió que conocía mejores Robert Smithson.

Damián Ortega

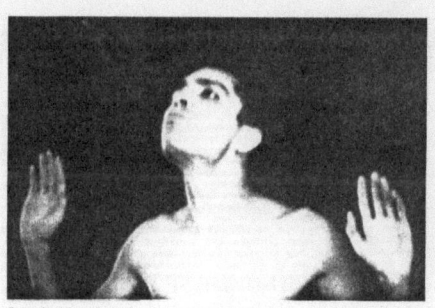

Remake (6 acciones)
Video, 9 min.
1994.

Cuando realizamos *Remake* (1994), habíamos estado investigando sobre algunos performances de los años 70's, particularmente en artistas que incidían en nuestra forma de realizar acciones, trabajar con textos o registrar ciertos momentos. Entonces nos dimos cuenta que no conocíamos (directamente) ninguno de los videos que nos gustaban. Solamente teníamos referencias fotográficas y, en los mejores casos, descripciones de la obra: en qué consistía, qué materiales se usaban y tiempo de duración. Así que decidimos hacer nuestras propias versiones, apegadas a las referencias que teníamos.

Luis Felipe Ortega
Daniel Guzmán

Casper: Revista de título mutable, no. 8, January 1999
Photocopy, saddle stitched, orange paper wrappers; with mixed media inserts, serigraph on Kraft envelope, 8½ × 5½ in. (21.6 × 14 cm)
Collection Luis Felipe Ortega

Mark Gonzales

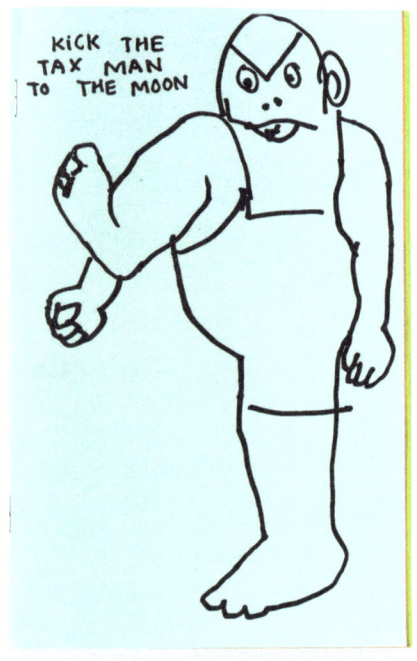

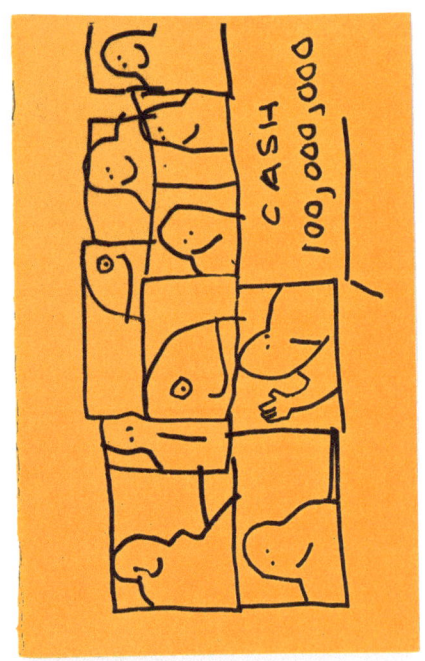

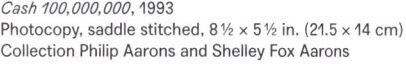

Kick the Tax Man to the Moon (Non Stop Poetry), 1993
Photocopy, saddle stitched, 8 ½ × 5 ½ in. (21.5 × 14 cm)
Collection Philip Aarons and Shelley Fox Aarons

Cash 100,000,000, 1993
Photocopy, saddle stitched, 8 ½ × 5 ½ in. (21.5 × 14 cm)
Collection Philip Aarons and Shelley Fox Aarons

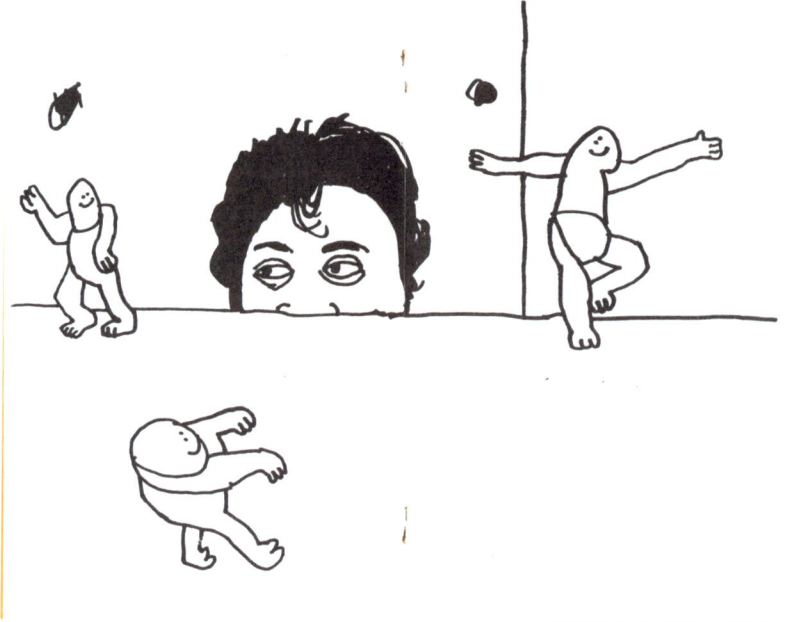

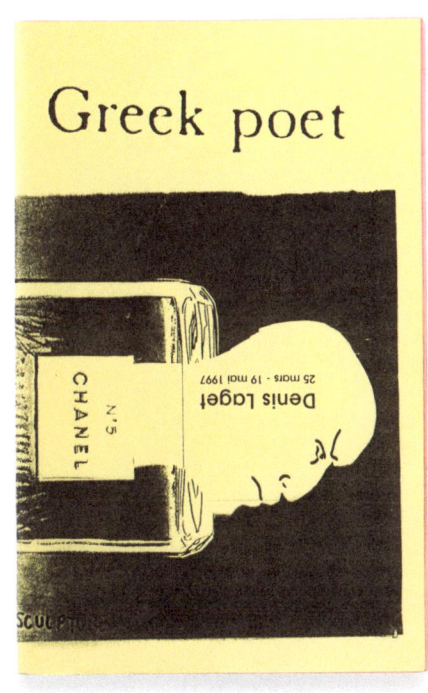

Greek Poet, 1997
Photocopy, saddle stitched, 8 ½ × 5 ½ in. (21.5 × 14 cm)
Collection Philip Aarons and Shelley Fox Aarons

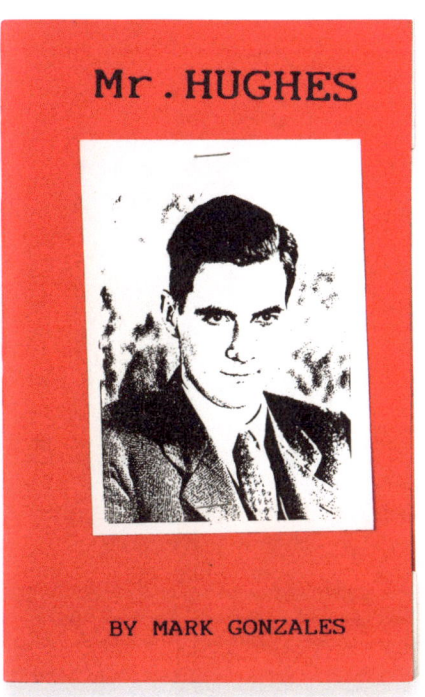

Mr. Hughes, n.d.
Photocopy, saddle stitched, 8 ½ × 5 ½ in. (21.5 × 14 cm)
Collection Philip Aarons and Shelley Fox Aarons

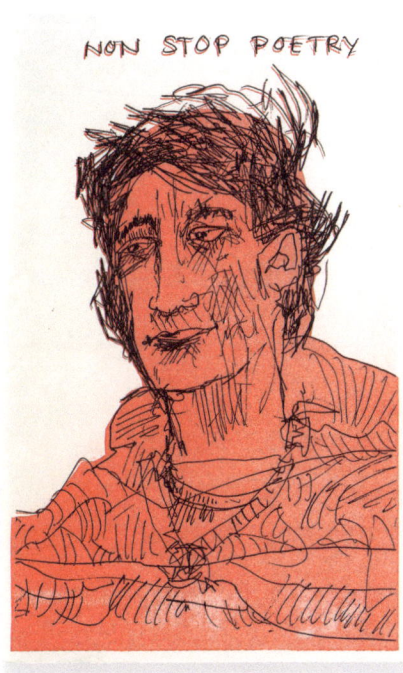

Non Stop Poetry (Portrait in Red), n.d.
Photocopy, saddle stitched, 8 ½ × 5 ½ in. (21.5 × 14 cm)
Collection Philip Aarons and Shelley Fox Aarons

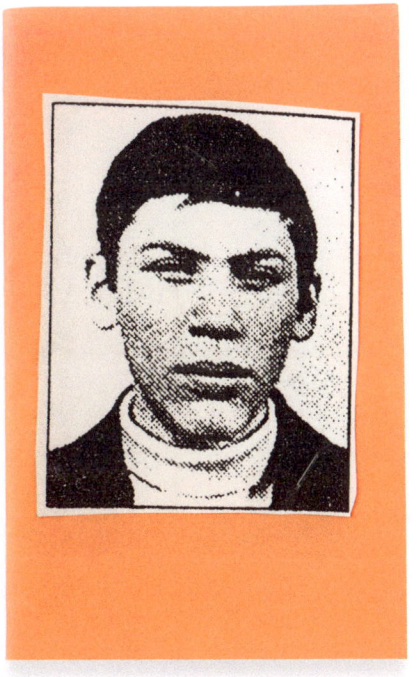

Untitled (Vladimir Levin Photo), n.d.
Photocopy, saddle stitched, 8 ½ × 5 ½ in. (21.5 × 14 cm)
Collection Philip Aarons and Shelley Fox Aarons

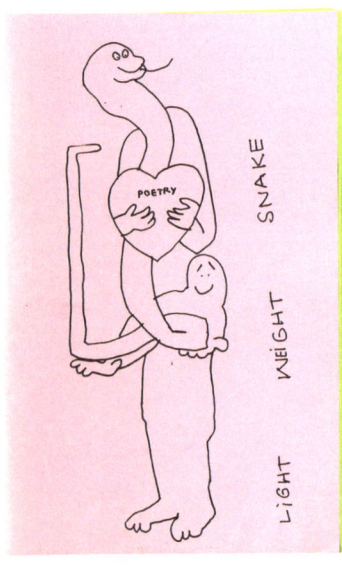

LIGHT WEIGHT SNAKE

POETRY

LIGHT

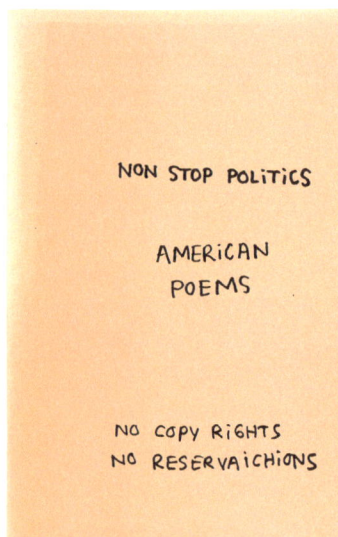

NON STOP POLITICS

AMERICAN
POEMS

NO COPY RIGHTS
NO RESERVAICHIONS

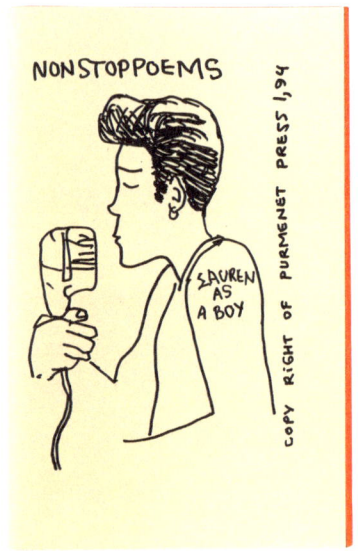

NONSTOPPOEMS

SAUREN
AS
A BOY

COPY RIGHT OF PURMENET PRESS 1,94

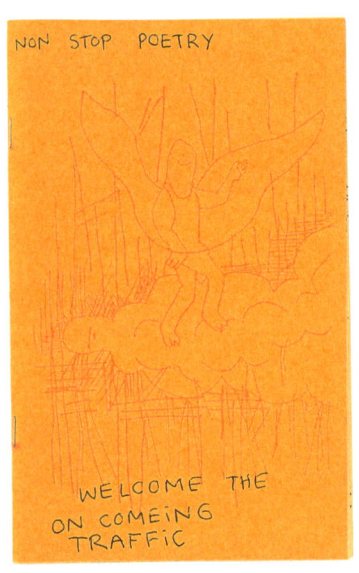

NON STOP POETRY

WELCOME THE
ON COMEING
TRAFFIC

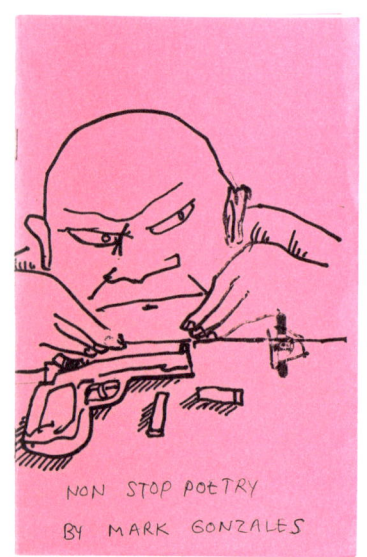

NON STOP POETRY
BY MARK GONZALES

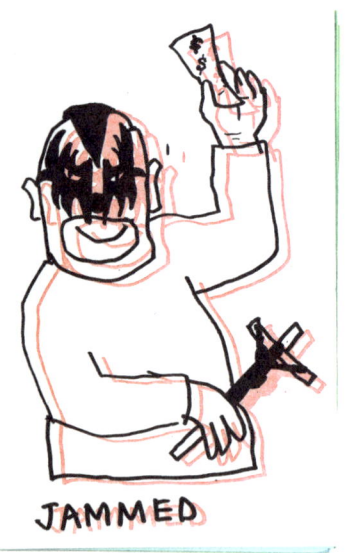

JAMMED

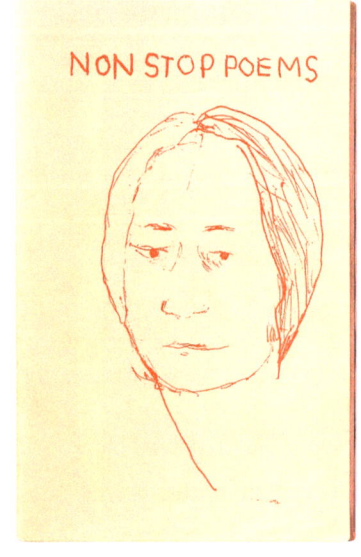

NON STOP POEMS

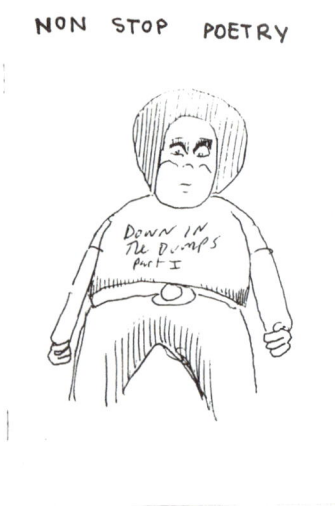

NON STOP POETRY

DOWN IN
THE DUMPS
PART I

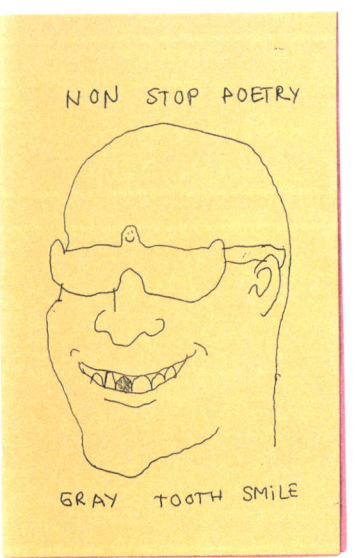

NON STOP POETRY

GRAY TOOTH SMILE

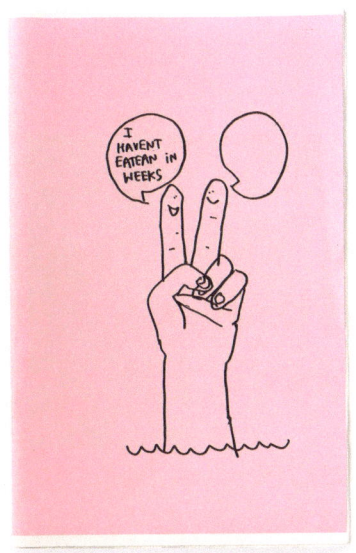

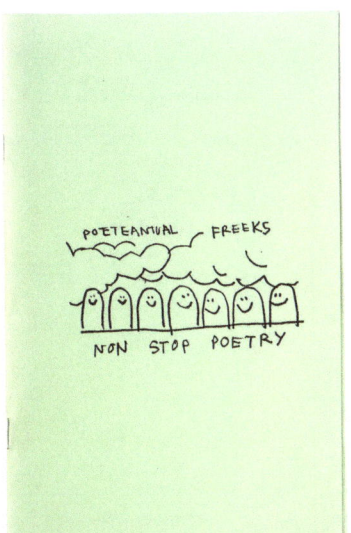

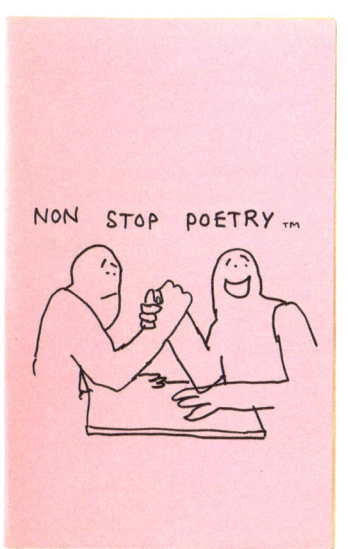

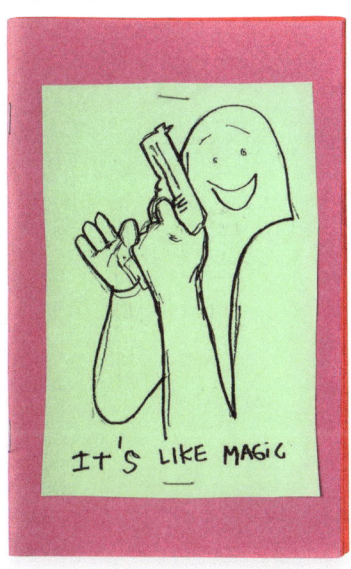

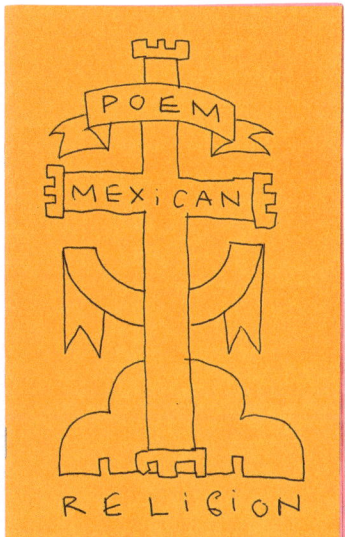

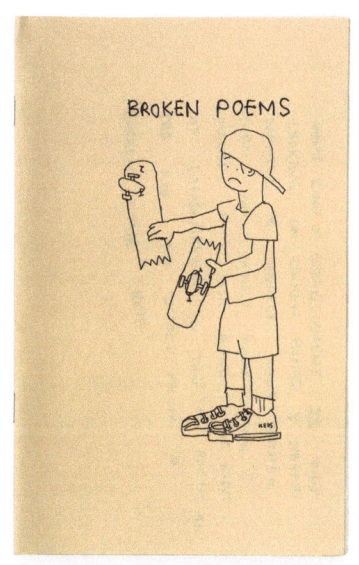

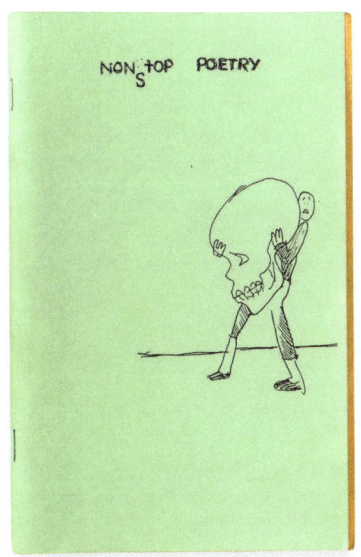

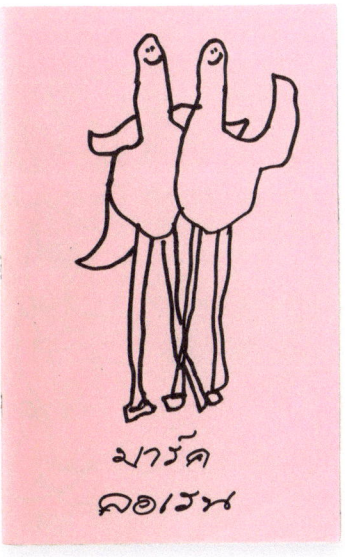

Various zines, ca. 1992–2000
All photocopy, saddle stitched,
8 ½ × 5 ½ in. (21.5 × 14 cm)
Collection Philip Aarons and Shelley Fox Aarons

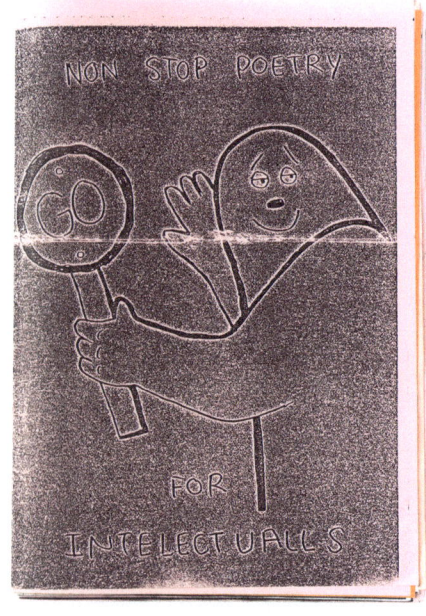

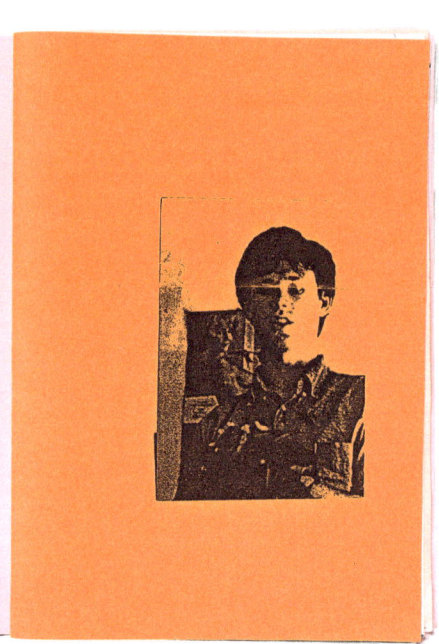

BIRDS NEST
RATS FEAST
CRIPALED
CHILDRENE
EATING PIG'S FEET

Non Stop Poetry For Intellectuals, October 1992
Photocopy, saddle stitched, 8 ¼ × 5 ⅞ in. (21 × 15 cm)
Collection Philip Aarons and Shelley Fox Aarons

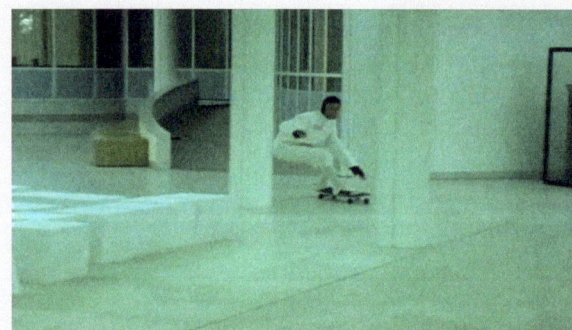

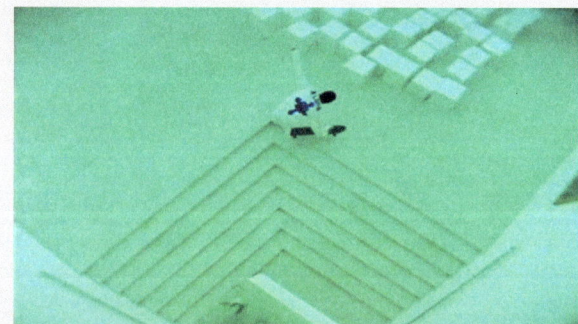

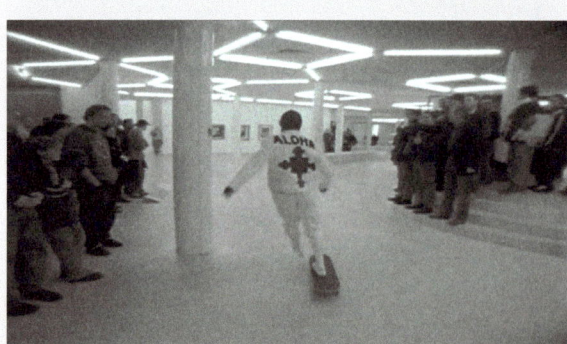

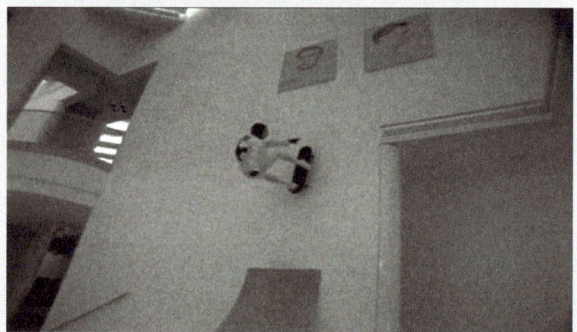

Cheryl Dunn
Stills from *Back Worlds for Words*, 1998
Film; black and white, sound; 3 min., 55 sec.
Collection the artist

Tod Swank

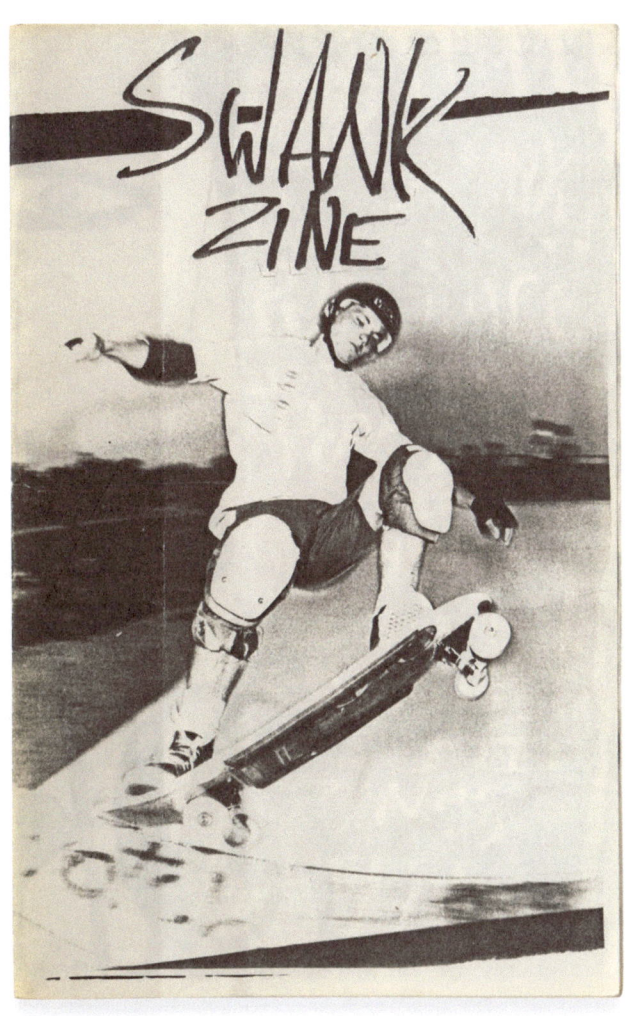

Swank Zine, no. 3, ca. 1984
Photocopy, saddle stitched, 8½ × 5½ in. (21.5 × 14 cm)
Collection Philip Aarons and Shelley Fox Aarons

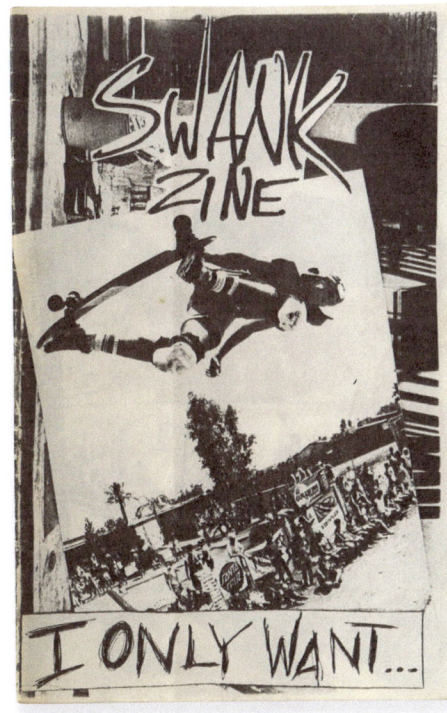

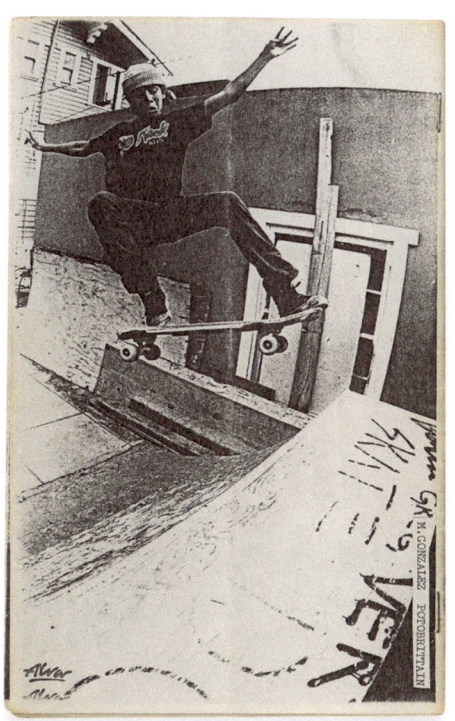

Swank Zine, no. 9, Summer 1985 (front and back covers)
Photocopy, saddle stitched, 8½ × 5½ in. (21.5 × 14 cm)
Collection Philip Aarons and Shelley Fox Aarons

Mark Gonzales and Harmony Korine

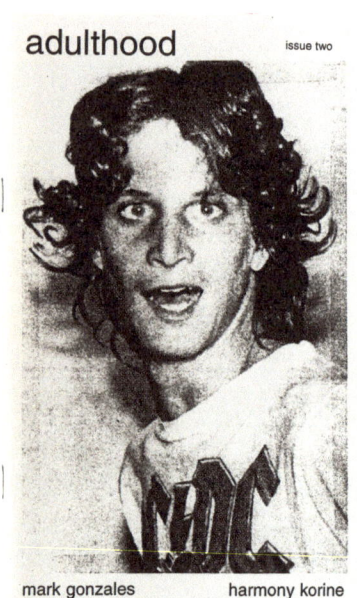

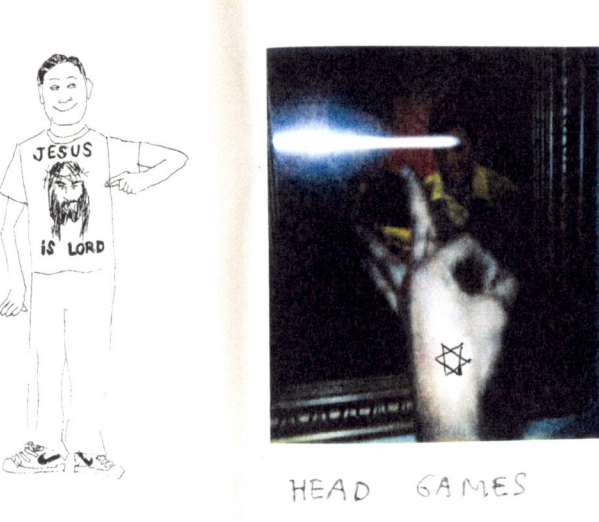

Adulthood, no. 2, 1995
Photocopy, saddle stitched, 8 ½ × 5 ½ in. (21.5 × 14 cm)
Collection Philip Aarons and Shelley Fox Aarons

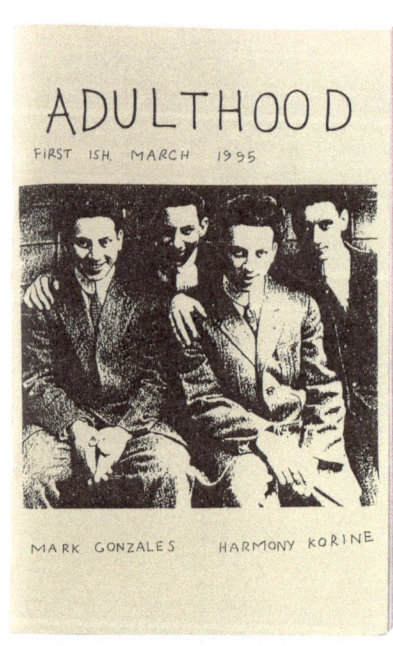

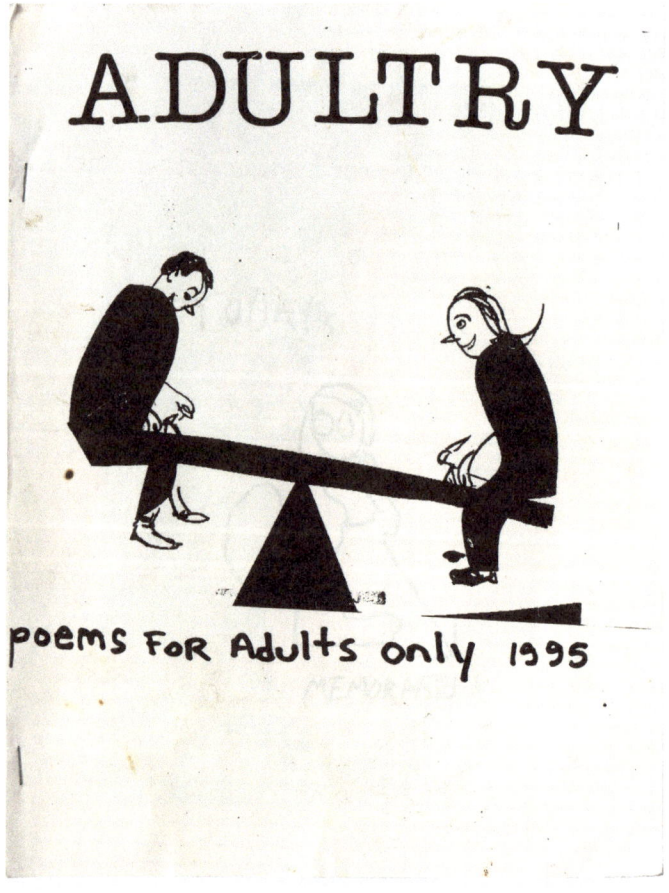

Adulthood, no. 1, March 1995
Photocopy, saddle stitched, cream paper wrappers,
8 ½ × 5 ½ in. (21.5 × 14 cm)

Collection Philip Aarons and Shelley Fox Aarons

Adultry: Poems for Adults Only, 1995
Photocopy, side stapled, 11 × 8 ½ in. (27.9 × 21.6 cm)
Collection Philip Aarons and Shelley Fox Aarons

Mark Gonzales and Cameron Jamie

→ *Scram*, no. 3, 2001
Photocopy, saddle stitched, 8 ¼ × 5 ⅞ in. (21 × 15 cm)
Collection Philip Aarons and Shelley Fox Aarons

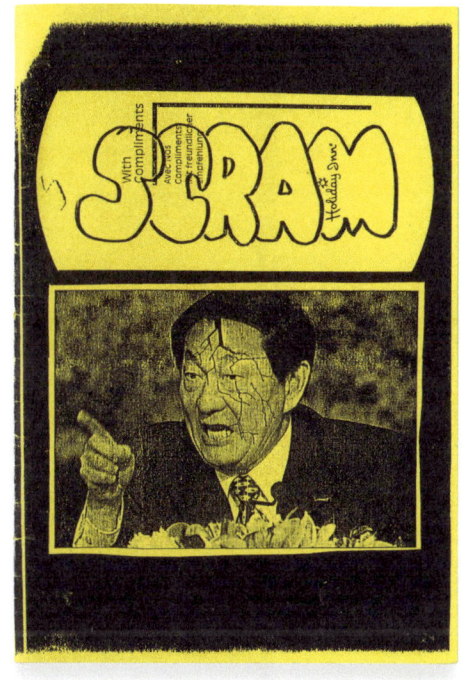

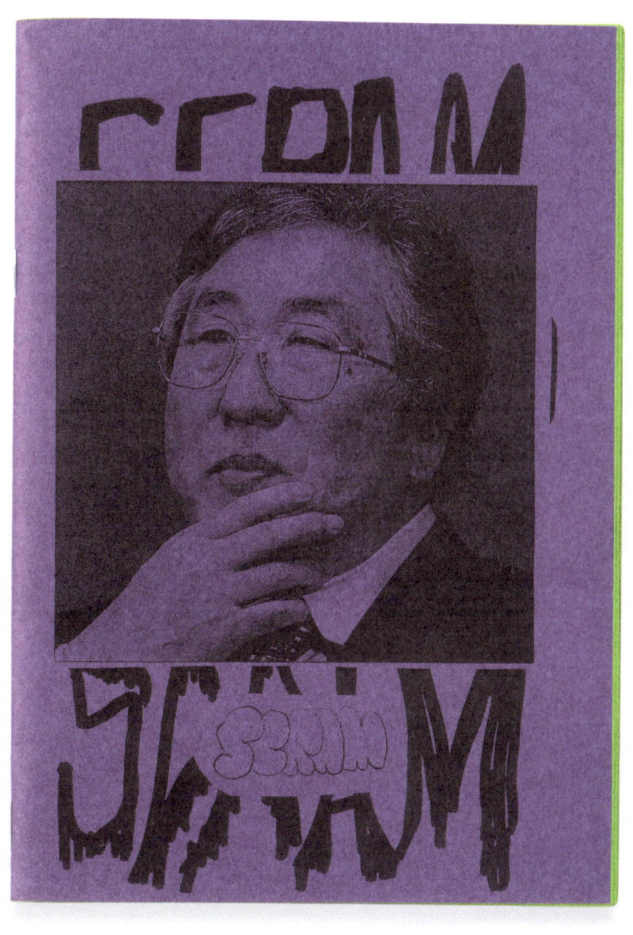

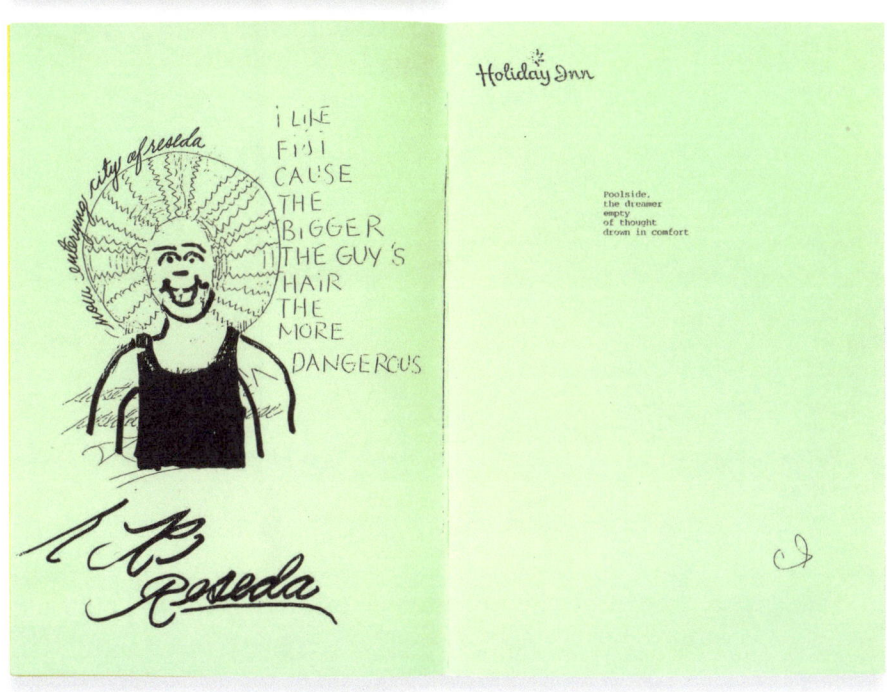

Scram, no. 1, 2000
Photocopy, saddle stitched, 8 ¼ × 5 ⅞ in. (21 × 15 cm)
Collection Philip Aarons and Shelley Fox Aarons

Susan Cianciolo

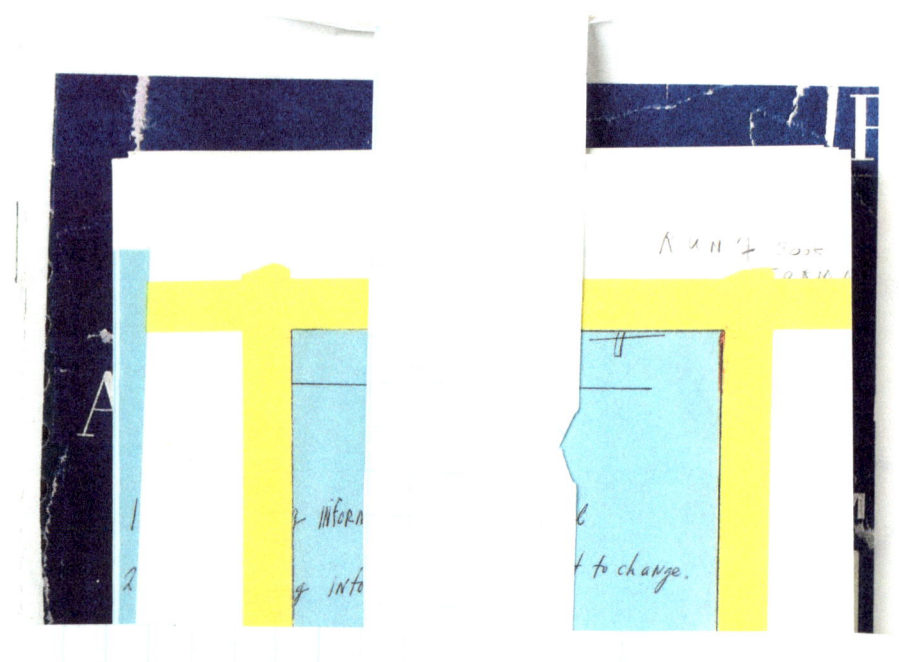

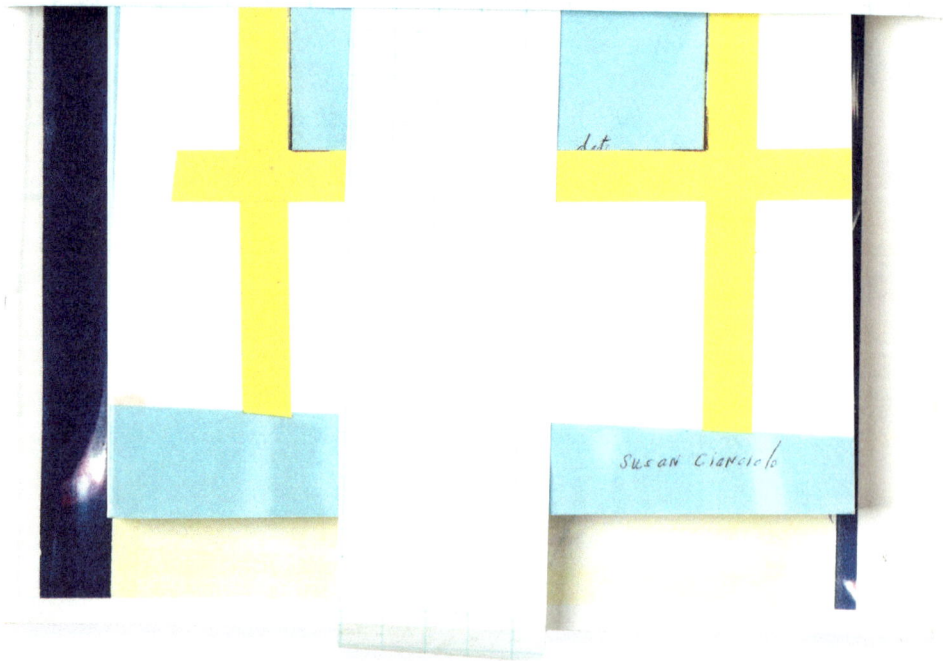

Run 7 Book/Run 8 Fanzine Set, 1998
Two booklets wrapped in printed paper strips, offset, perfect
bound, 7 × 4 5/16 in. (17.8 × 10.9 cm) / photocopy, saddle stitched,
8 ½ × 5 ½ in. (21.6 × 14 cm)
Collection Philip Aarons and Shelley Fox Aarons

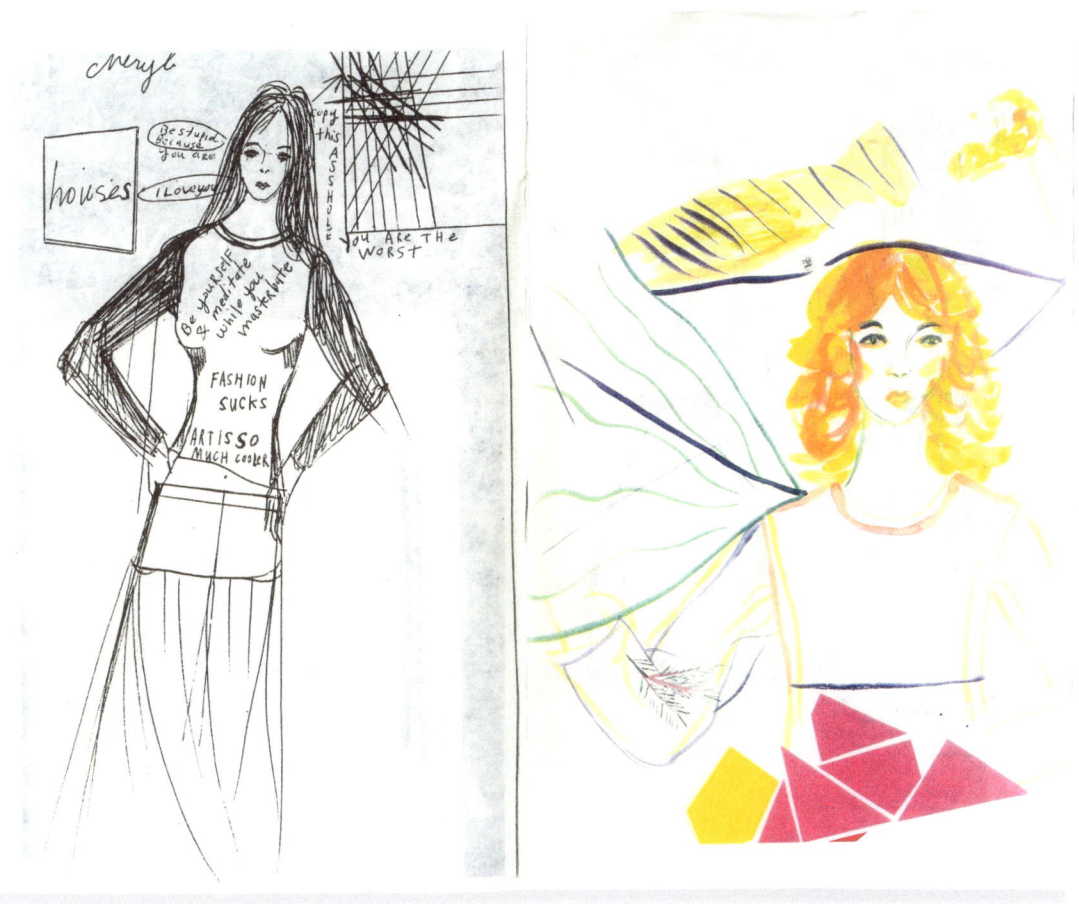

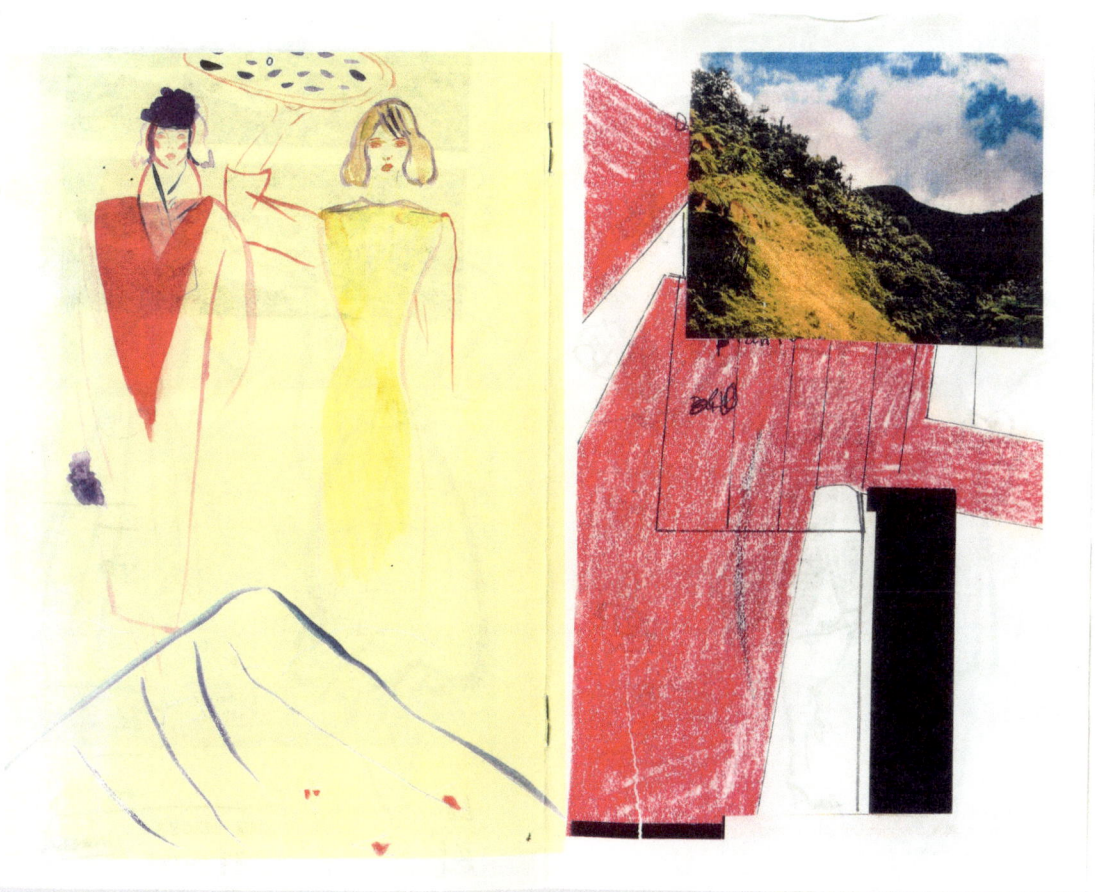

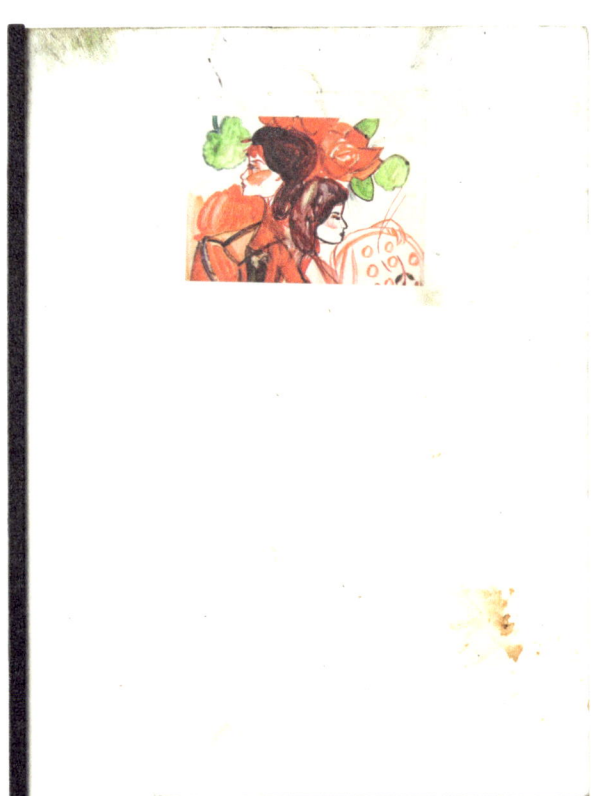

Pro-Abortion/Anti-Pink, 1995
Photocopy, tape bound, 11 × 8 ½ in. (27.9 × 21.6 cm)
Collection Philip Aarons and Shelley Fox Aarons

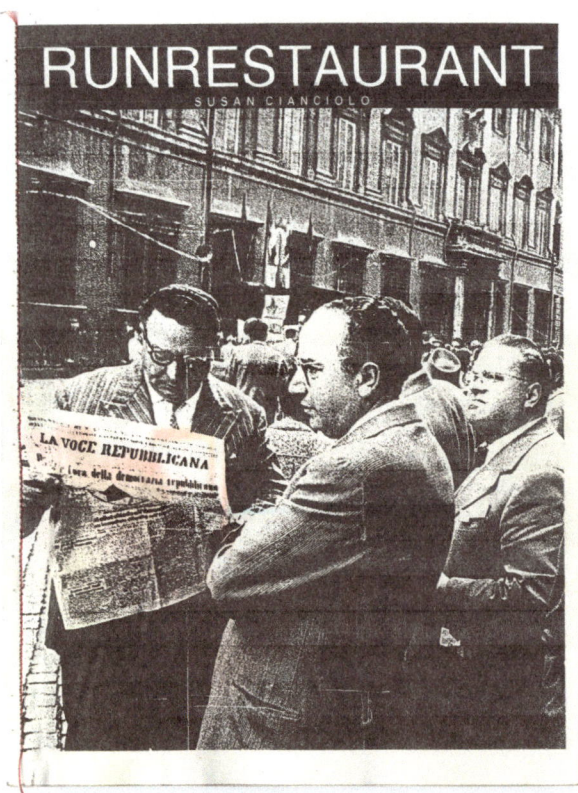

Run Restaurant, 2001
Photocopy, sewn binding, 11 × 8 ½ in. (27.9 × 21.6 cm)
Collection Philip Aarons and Shelley Fox Aarons

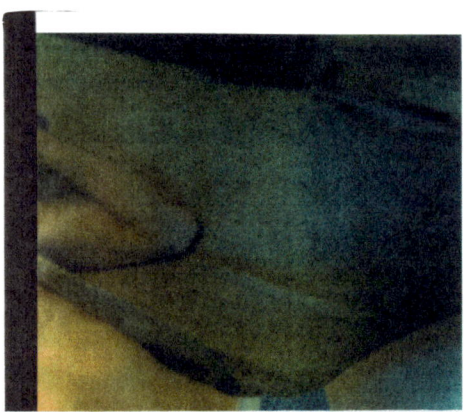

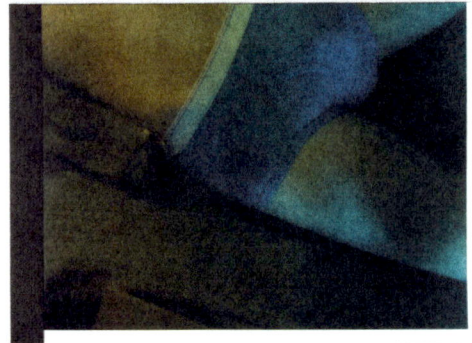

All Women Photography Show, curated by Susan Cianciolo, 1998
Photocopy, tape bound, with white elastic band,
11 × 8 ½ in. (27.9 × 21.6 cm)
Collection Philip Aarons and Shelley Fox Aarons

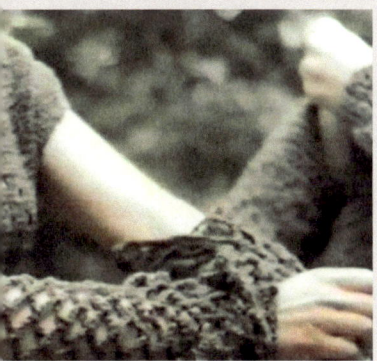 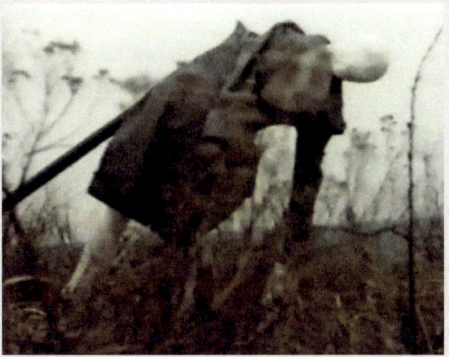 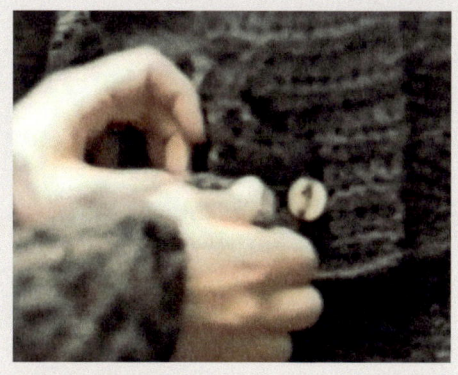

Stills from *Diadal*, 1997
Video; color, sound; 9 min.
Collection the artist

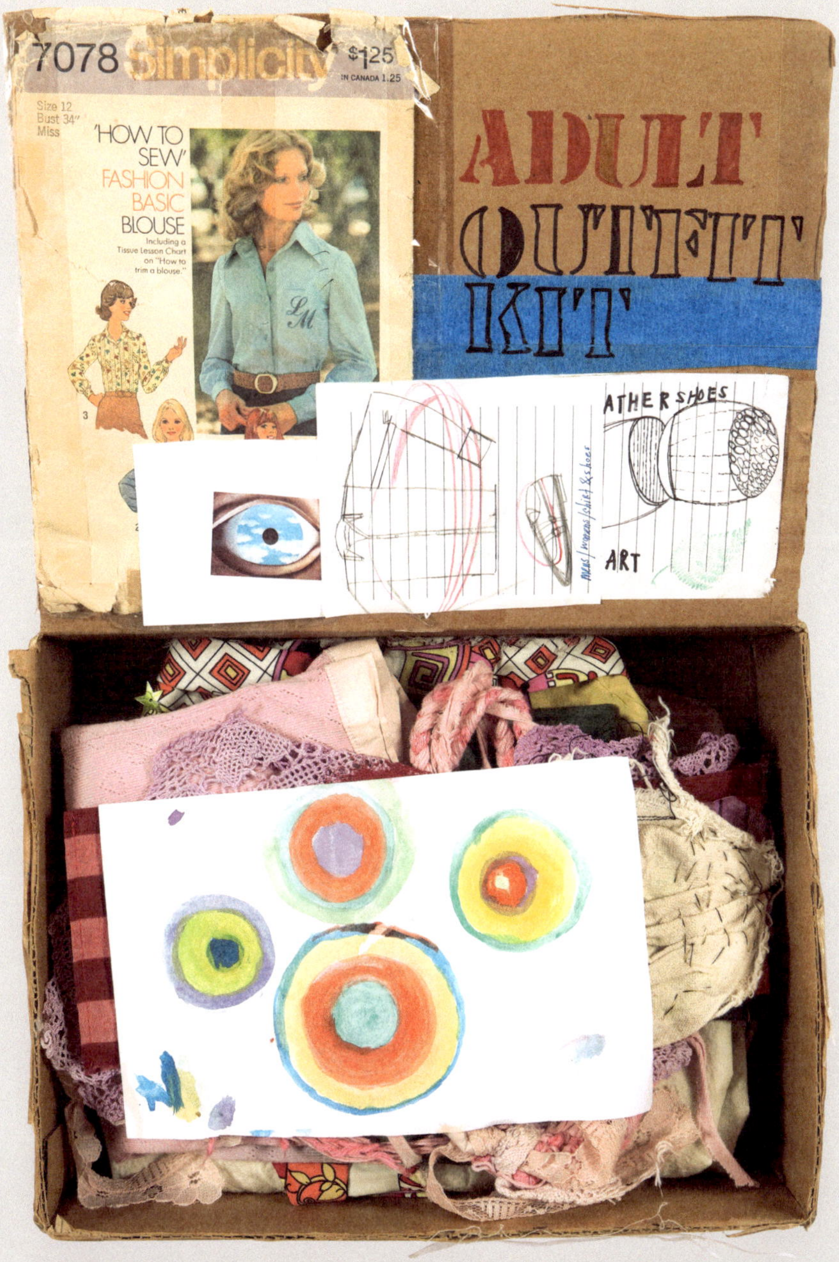

Adult Outfit Kit, 2012
Cardboard box with *Run 7* shoes, pants, top, flower corsage,
painting, 39 ½ × 56 ½ × 8 in. (100.3 × 143.5 × 20.3 cm)
Collection the artist

Friendly Specters:
Casper and Other Mexico City–based Artists' Zines and Projects

Alexis Salas

REPRODUCTION, PUBLISHING, AND POWER

In the mid-1990s a group of artists in Mexico City began showing their own "*versiones*" of iconic works by European and US artists at the artists' space they had founded in 1993, known as Temístocles 44. Abraham Cruzvillegas's 1993 *Sin título* (Untitled) recalls Marcel Duchamp's 1913 *Bicycle Wheel* through an invocation of patriarchs (Duchamp as well as Cruzvillegas's artist father); Eduardo Abaroa's 1991–93 *Obelisco roto portátil para mercados ambulantes* (Broken Obelisk for Ambulatory Street Markets) remakes Barnett Newman's 1963–69 Cor-Ten steel *Broken Obelisk* in pink plastic; Damián Ortega's 1993 *Hágalo usted mismo, Spiral Jetty* (Do It Yourself, Spiral Jetty) turns Robert Smithson's monumental 1970 Earthwork into a miniature garden sculpture; and Daniel Guzmán and Luis Felipe Ortega's 1994 *Remake* takes on 1970s performance art pieces, restaged in their bathrooms. Collectively the *versiones* underscore how materiality, circumscribed by economics, looks on markers of sublime modernity through unauthorized copies of them. In 1998, a few years after Temístocles 44 closed, the artists featured photographs of the *versiones* in issue 8 of their zine, **Casper**. These appropriations exemplify how Mexico City–based visual artists have used zines and affiliated projects to playfully and collectively challenge Euro- and US-centric concepts of intellectual property, appropriation, and copyright.

→ 276–79

    Mexico is second only to China and Russia in quantities of unauthorized reproduction; the country sustains a thriving extra-legal market of reproduction of cultural goods ostensibly sequestered under intellectual property law.[1] Just as they do today, in the 1990s a privileged few received international deliveries of original materials from elite vendors, file sharing websites, department stores, family members who traveled abroad, or megacorporations that adeptly navigated customs duties. For everyone else, there were unauthorized copies. Public markets—El Chopo, Tepito, San Cosme, and the Centro Histórico are but a few hubs—offered films, music, and texts that were largely unavailable if they were not reproduced through extra-legal means.[2] Now, online sharing forums have made the need for physical reproductions (CDs, DVDs, photocopies)—and therefore the markets that trafficked in them—largely obsolete, but the disparity of access to the often foreign, inaccessible "original" continues to be vexed.

    Working from this cultural context, Mexico City–based visual artists have used zines to defy intellectual property rights law as both a practical matter—a means to distribute materials that would otherwise be inaccessible—and to critique the capitalist commodification of cultural goods. Through their use of unauthorized reproduction, these artists highlight inequities of access between what theorist Shahidul Alam has named the Minority World (Europe and the United States) and the Majority World (everywhere else) while confronting stereotypes of scarcity, both cultural and material, and at the same time generating their own cultural products and networks. Underscoring the failures of capitalist strategies, zines (and projects adjacent to them) offer other ways of understanding culture through sharing, collaboration, and exchange.

ALTERNATIVE PUBLICATIONS IN MEXICO

The culture of alternative publications in Mexico provides a kind of counterintelligence to mainstream publishing venues, opening new discourses but also aligning with discussions underway in the art community.[3] Publisher, editor, and artist Rogelio Villarreal is a giant of the underground press, with publications such as *La regla rota* (The Broken Rule[r], 1984–87, launched with Ramón Sánchez Lira) and *La pus moderna* (The Pus-Modern, a play on "post-modern," 1989–96). Villarreal created editorial projects that focused on the taboo in relation to "high culture," setting the tone for alternative-publications culture in Mexico. Homegrown, local expressions, these periodicals—which frequently took form as "little magazines," or zines—did not have a place in other publishing practices of the time. Created and distributed through circulation systems that bypassed critics and censorship, the zines offered commentary on the political world and on the art scene in ways that were otherwise difficult to circulate.

    Then as now, the readership of these little publications tended to extend far beyond the initial release numbers; they were often exchanged among friends, and sharing them has been important because, until relatively recently, access to information was limited by conventional publishing practices. Throughout the 1990s the Mexican government continued to hold a near monopoly on information: it de facto controlled national television networks, newspapers, and even book publishing.[4] In terms of the everyday experience of purchasing books, this meant that the most economically accessible Spanish-language material was Mexican government-sponsored, and thus was usually exclusively about Mexican subjects. Imports from countries such as Spain and Argentina, while economically accessible in their homelands, were much pricier when they reached Mexico. In short, this meant that in order to read about topics other than those selected by the Mexican government, one needed to spend exorbitant sums on books imported from abroad. Or readers could look to alternative publications, which offered an antidote to the capitalist commodification of knowledge in the commercial publishing world.

CASPER: A FRIENDLY GHOST

Distinguished by irony and framed as a necessary antidote to commercial publishing, the artists' zine *Casper*, in the spirit of its title and mascot, haunted capitalism, in particular through its use of *plagio* (roughly, "plagiarism"). In 1998 *Casper*'s editorial board—Daniel Guzmán, Gabriel Kuri, Damián Ortega, and Luis Felipe Ortega—decided to make thirteen issues—the number, of course, associated with the unlucky and the occult, as witnessed in a whole subgenre of campy horror films (e.g., the *Friday the 13th* series). This choice was just one manifestation of the simultaneously pop-culture and Conceptual-art tenor of their project. *Casper* began and ended on International Workers' Day: its first issue was released May 1, 1998, and its last May 1, 1999; on the first day of every intervening month, a new issue appeared. The Temístocles 44 artists printed the zine themselves at a copy shop. *Casper*'s structure was basic: each issue was a stapled booklet, 8½ × 5½ inches (21.6 × 14-cm), with a colored paper cover and an interior of standard 8½ × 11-inch (21.6 × 27.9-cm) photocopier sheets, folded lengthwise and adding up to between fifty and eighty pages.

Casper had antecedents, both by the same artists and by contemporaries in other parts of Mexico. The 1992–93 zine **Alegría** (Joy or Happiness) was produced by some of the Temístocles 44 collaborators, primarily Eduardo Abaroa, Fernando García Correa, Damián Ortega, Luis Felipe Ortega, and Pablo Vargas Lugo, with regular contributions by Abraham Cruzvillegas and Daniel Guzmán. As the artists characterized it, *Alegría* was the "official organ" of the artists' space Temístocles 44. The 1999 Ediciones **El Chino**, a zine- and video-production project made by artists and curators in Guadalajara, was nearly contemporaneous with *Casper*.

When asked in 2008 why he and his co-editors created *Casper* three years after the dissolution of Temístocles 44, Luis Felipe Ortega observed that his past projects, such as *Alegría*, felt incomplete to him and that he felt *Casper* needed to be made.[5] This sense of unfinished business, of the past coexisting with the present, may have inspired the title *Casper*. (Should there be any doubt as to which Casper the artists were referencing, the cover of issue 1 featured a line drawing of the pop-culture-comic-turned-cartoon-turned-film-character Casper, the Friendly Ghost.) The publication was, like its cartoon namesake, envisioned as a "friendly ghost"—that is, a phantom with unfinished business that impedes it from moving to the beyond.

The zine's full title, *Casper: Revista de título mutable* (the subtitle means "Magazine with a Changeable Name"), took an element of pop culture, the "Casper" name, and persistently brought it back to life by rearranging its six letters, c-a-s-p-e-r, to make issue titles: "Sep Car," "Pescar," "cPersa," "Pacers," "Sperca," "scrape," "a-e-c-s-p-r," and "sercap." This break with the past in each issue—a form of reincarnation, or a raising of the dead—allowed the zine to invade and control the corpus of society and its different bodies of knowledge, just as a ghost might occupy different human bodies, giving them new life through possession.

Indeed, *Casper* functioned as a possession of multiple bodies, a collectivity, while maintaining individual voices. As Luis Felipe Ortega observed about the articles and art pieces included in the zine:

> They were equally important projects in terms of sharing interests—even those that were collective projects. At the same time, there was always a commitment that the voices have their own personality, their own weight and identity. . . . All the articles were always signed

274–75 ←

298–99 ←

[by their authors], there was always someone—even if it was a proposal for a translation, or was a translation by such and such person, or "I-choose-this-text"—because to *select* a text is an opinion, right?[6]

Sustained by various opinions, *Casper* became a space of confluence for many artists. The creators tailored it to their interests, and certain artists took charge of particular sections of the zine—but they also opened *Casper* to the work of others, reproducing existing texts that the artist-editors selected, as well as publishing new texts submitted by local artists and writers. Some of the Temístocles 44 artists content-managed specific sections (Guzmán, for example, oversaw the music section and "Toros y deportes" [Bulls and Sports]). The contents of the magazine ranged from art projects to lists of the editors' favorite records, excerpts from key contemporary art texts to self-referential contributions from artists, curators, and cultural agents.

Casper appealed to mass culture *and* served as an antidote to mass culture—*and* was a product of mass culture. Vacillating between the occult and the cult, *Casper* inserted itself into the Mexican cultural scene as a discrete and specific intervention. Every issue of the zine included an insert—a serigraph in the form of a poster or a sticker—enabling the project to contaminate and invade: these small artworks were designed to extend the reach of the zine, as they would be placed on bookshelves or hung on walls, or even plastered on surfaces in public spaces.[7]

EXPERTS IN *PLAGIO*

The artists' multisited approach was based in their work with multiples. As Luis Felipe Ortega put it: "We were experts in making copies. We were experts in *plagio*."[8] *Casper* infiltrated capitalist logic concerning intellectual property by its use of *plagio*—the unauthorized use of others' writing and images—throughout its thirteen issues. The editorial page of the pilot issue (number 0) sets forth ground rules, stating: "*Casper* is a work in progress; we gratefully accept *notas* (short essays), *gráficas* (illustrations), and *plagios* (plagurisms)."[9] Placing *plagios* on par with *notas* and *gráficas*, *Casper* posited the shifting of a text, image, or idea from one context to another as a creative act in itself.

The editors' commitment to *plagio* continued throughout *Casper*'s run, all the while clearly distinguishing *plagio* from plagiarism. In the editorial page of issue 5 they declared their resolve to make a place for themselves in the historical canon: "We deliver our battle cry to the myopia of historians . . . they can say whatever they will about us." Yet this "battle cry" intervened in the canon not through originality but rather through *plagio*: the artists' editorial is followed by an asterisk, leading to brief and quirkily conveyed "instructions" about how to restore the text to its original form:

> replace the word casper, with estridentismo. attribute it any artist of the movement.
> dedicate it to Germán List Arzubide, 1898–1998.

With this, the *Casper* artists clearly informed readers that they were reproducing one of the most famous art manifestos of twentieth-century Mexico, that of the avant-garde movement known as Estridentismo, a manifesto that was issued in multiple versions by the Estridentista artists, each time copying previous iterations of their manifesto.[10] In this way, the *Casper* artists' editorial rip-off of the canonical 1921 manifesto evidences how *plagio* pays homage to its source, rather than erasing it (as conventionally understood plagiarism would).

On the editorial page of *Casper*'s final issue, the artists proudly listed the zine's accomplishments (among them, "92 articles plagiarized").[11] These starkly stated achievements stand in opposition to the over-the-top branding in the back pages of the same issue. In a spread titled "¡¡Caspermanía!!," the artists displayed products, from **T-shirts for little people** to lighters to → 278 ghost-shaped paperweights, all emblazoned with the *Casper* "brand." Like fake designer products often sold by street vendors, the *Casper* crew's riffs on "designer" originals were rip-offs. Yet these *plagios* of exclusive products are proposed as rarer than the originals. The artists have taken mass-culture objects and brought them into the realm of art.

The *plagios* in *Casper* are not "plagiarisms" as the term is conventionally understood in English—that is, copied works whose origins are hidden in order to be passed off as original intellectual creations. Rather, *Casper*'s creators cited—explicitly or implicitly—the sources from which they were lifting their references in order to transfigure them. Therefore, the artists' *plagio*, as seen in *Casper*, is an act of citational invocation paired with contextual modification. Their admission to—in fact repeated *insistence* on—*plagio* evidences their strategy not only to critique how intellectual creations have been rendered private property, but also to embrace alternatives to prevailing powers.

ZINES AS EXAMPLES IN SHARING POWER

In Mexico City, artists continue to use zines to interrogate Minority World/Majority World power dynamics. While zines, as objects, have become, to some extent, institutionalized and commodified, current generations of artists draw from the legacy of these endeavors, often resulting in print publications but sometimes also taking form as social actions, public events, or even theoretical frameworks. In line with zines and through collaborative projects whose very structures challenge industrial publishing and distribution processes, a number of Mexico-based artists have turned to alternative modes of information distribution.[12]

Mexico City is home to many alternative spaces for public encounter and dialogue. Aeromoto, a nonprofit public library, specializes in contemporary art, circulating zines, artists' books, and independent publications. Casa del Ahuizote has run an archive, museum, cultural center, and printing press since 2015. Gato Negro Ediciones, founded in 2013, publishes challenging titles, including artists' books and art theory. Cráter Invertido, established in 2011, is an artists' and activists' collective using printed matter to reflect social struggles and construct community through self-production and knowledge sharing. These projects offer strategies that decentralize social dialogue, while conscientiously networking publics.

416–17 ←

Since 2016, **RRD** (Red de Reproducción y Distribución / Reproduction and Distribution Network) has served as an independent space for public encounter. Stewarded by five Mexico City artists—Joel Castro, María José Cruz, Anuar Portugal, Bruno Ruiz, and Sergio Torres—RRD uses a production studio and a kiosk, where print and audiovisual formats are combined and distributed through a range of channels.[13] In a project initiated in 2020, early in the COVID-19 pandemic, RRD sent out a "*caja paquete*" (box package) via "RedEx" (a faux delivery service) containing a miniature RRD kiosk. A video on RRD's website shows a person literally unpacking the project (recalling the unboxing videos that are so popular on social media) while wearing latex gloves, in the mode of early COVID-19 practices. "Are you frustrated by communicating and creating only through likes, comments, chats, and long-distance calls?" a voiceover in the video asks. "*RedEx es la red*" (RedEx is the network).[14] Through the video, RedEx points out the limitations of social media and counters it with alternative modes of distribution. The name "RedEx," a play on "FedEx," also invokes the "*red*," or network, especially as pandemic reluctance to do anything in person meant that megashipping corporations such as Amazon came into even more widespread use in Mexico City. RRD's video subversively concludes with a provocation that encapsulates alternative publications and their distribution: "*No odias a la máquina, sé la máquina*" ("Don't hate the machine, *be* the machine").

POWER PLAY AND NETWORK: A DIFFERENT MACHINE

RRD prompts us to "*be* the machine"—that is, to become a multipart apparatus working as a unit to perform a task. A strategic intervention into systems of power, RRD's call is to not reinvent the machine, but rather to make "*versiones*" of it that place a "ghost in the machine," bedeviling the publishing body with a spirit that animates it differently. Several of the artists who produced or contributed to *Casper* would, after the zine came to an end, pursue publishing projects that haunt the publishing machine by challenging its bases through their engagement with intellectual property, appropriation, and copyright. Cruzvillegas's 1999 book, *Ruta de la enemistad* (Route of Enmity), for example, is a takedown of iconic works of Mexico City architecture.[15] Around 2004 Cruzvillegas, Dr. Lakra, and Luis Felipe Ortega drafted a second (unfinished) iteration of *Casper* that, had it been produced, would have revived art historical components of the original zine.[16] Luis Felipe Ortega's 2011 *Informe para una academia* (Report to an Academy) gathered together, in republished form, newspaper and article clippings he has collected over the span of his career.[17] Damián Ortega founded the publishing house Alias (its name alluding to working under an assumed or fake name) in 2006; in the years since, it has published translations into Spanish of canonical texts by European and US artists, usually for the first time.[18] Through collaborative zine-inspired publications and projects, these artists retool the machine, enlivening it with friendly specters of the commercial publishing world.

NOTES

[1] See Kurt Hollander, *Several Ways to Die in Mexico City: An Autobiography* (Port Townsend, WA: Feral House, 2012), 204.

[2] Many of the artists that made *Casper* would, in 1999, install their works in a public market, Mercado de Medellín, in an exhibition titled *Economia de mercado* (Market Economy). For more on this, see the author's forthcoming book *Disparity at Play: The Artists and Projects of Temístocles 44 (Mexico City, 1991–2003)*.

[3] For a list of Mexican publications about art produced since the 1990s, including both periodicals and alternative publications, see Bárbara Perea, "Una mirada a las publicaciones periódicas y alternativas de arte en México," in *Ediciones: Estrategia legitimadora en el arte contemporáneo*, ed. Janitzio Alatriste Tobilla, Marengla León Álvarez, and Álvaro Villalobos Herrera (Toluca, Mexico: Universidad Autónoma del Estado de México, 2012), 61–72.

[4] For example, in the 1990s the private publishing sector in Mexico was smaller than the government publishing sector. See Giulia Trentacosti, "LBF 2015: A Close Look at the Mexican Publishing Market," *2 Seas Agency* (February 24, 2015); 2seasagency.com/mexican-publishing-industry.

[5] Luis Felipe Ortega, interview with the author, October 13, 2008.

[6] Luis Felipe Ortega, quoted in Alexis Salas, unpublished research conducted for the exhibition and catalogue *Below the Underground: Renegade Art and Action in 1990s Mexico*, sponsored by the Getty Foundation as part of the initiative Pacific Standard Time: LA/LA. (This passage and all others in this essay trans. the author.)

[7] It is of note that the poster and the sticker packaged with each copy of *Casper* did not display any information linking them to the zine. Thus, the cultural infiltration that was being facilitated was not a factor of the magazine entity, but of art. Note that my reading of *Casper* on the whole (and of the poster and the sticker packaged with the zine in particular) differs from that of Bárbara Perea. While I write of *Casper* in terms of alternative publications, Perea links *Casper* to "collectibles," calling it "a collectible object" ("un objeto coleccionable") with "small treasures like stickers and posters." While her comments make sense in the larger scope of the commodification of zines, I do not know of a collectors' market for the magazine (yet). Her comment may understand *Casper* as a collectible among its readers at the time of its production. See Perea, "Una mirada," 65.

[8] Ortega, quoted in Salas, unpublished research for *Below the Underground*.

[9] The *plagios* of the magazine are reiterated in a number of instances by the publication itself, the magazine's creators, and even the sole published article and short summary of the magazine.

[10] Florence Oliver notes that each of the four Estridentista manifestos cites sentences or sections from past manifestos. See Oliver, "Ludismo y dinamismo en el movimiento Estridentisa de German List Arzubide," in *Modernidad, vanguardia y revolución en la poesía mexicana, 1919–1930*, ed. Anthony Stanton (Mexico City: Colegio de México, 2014), 195–96.

[11] The claims and products on the "¡¡Caspermanía!!" pages stand in opposition to the starkly stated, if not minimalist, editorial page of the same final issue. The list includes "13 issues published (13 different names used) . . . 3,100 issues distributed . . . 82,000 photocopies printed . . . 72 occasional and regular contributors . . . \$36,200 Mexican pesos spent . . ." and "92 articles plagiarized," firmly grounding the zine in the theoretical spirit of Conceptualists in its attempt to calculate, or at least put into measurable terms, cultural interventions.

[12] For more on these and other contemporary editorial projects, see the "Radical Publishing in CDMX" speaker series, organized in 2020–21 by T-Kay Sangwand at the University of California, Los Angeles Libraries as part of the California Rare Books School, which includes a number of recorded Zoom discussions; see youtube.com/watch?v=qYkUEk_37KM.

[13] From RRD's website: "RRD is a platform for the production and distribution of printed and audiovisual content. This project is supported by a production studio and a magazine stand located in Mexico City. The RRD booth serves as a public meeting place, where artists, independent publishers, and passers-by exchange and present site-specific, multidisciplinary projects"; erreerrede.org/acercaes.

[14] See the video for "RedEx" on the RRD website; erreerrede.org /prodbes/redex?pgid=l6q34kz2-f6a57e_0fbf3219ffa7438d9597911ed e6f8e1b.

[15] Abraham Cruzvillegas, *Ruta de la enemistad* (edition of 100) (Mexico City: Ediciones Casper, 1999). "Antes de la Resaca" exhibition archive, courtesy Sol Henaro.

[16] Around 2004 Abraham Cruzvillegas (who was part of Temístocles 44 and a regular contributor to the zines associated with it), Luis Felipe Ortega (who was also part of Temístocles 44 and a major figure in the zines associated with it), and Dr. Lakra (who did not take part in Temístocles 44 but participated in Gabriel Orozco's Taller de los viernes workshops with many of the other Temístocles 44 artists) would begin working on a second *Casper* magazine. The artists compiled six pages but stopped production at the editing stage. The draft includes a Spanish translation, "La estructura del mito y la potencia de la magia," of art historian Kellie Jones's text on artist David Hammons's work (including a reproduction of his 1983 performance *Bliz-aard Ball Sale*), indicating that the zine would have revived the art historical components of *Casper*. Like Damián Ortega's future publishing house, Alias, this zine draft featured important texts that were otherwise unavailable in Spanish. The draft also indicates the artists' commitment to showing their own work: it features Dr. Lakra's 2003 colored ink and synthetic polymer paint on magazine page *Untitled (Betty González)*. This work was acquired by the Museum of Modern Art a year later, demonstrating that elite art institutions were collecting the work of this group. With expanded forums and greater access to institutional funding, the artists have pursued individual publishing projects but have not collectively produced another publication.

[17] Luis Felipe Ortega, *Informe para una academia*, Seminario de Investigación sobre la Universidad Desconocida Departamento de Humanidades (Mexico City: LAST, Desiré Saint Phalle, 2011).

[18] Alias publications include translations of works by Anni Albers, Lina Bo Bardi, Marcel Broodthaers, John Cage, Marcel Duchamp, Eva Hesse, Lucy R. Lippard, and Francis Picabia, among others. A list of Alias publications is available for consultation at aliaseditorial.com.

El Chino

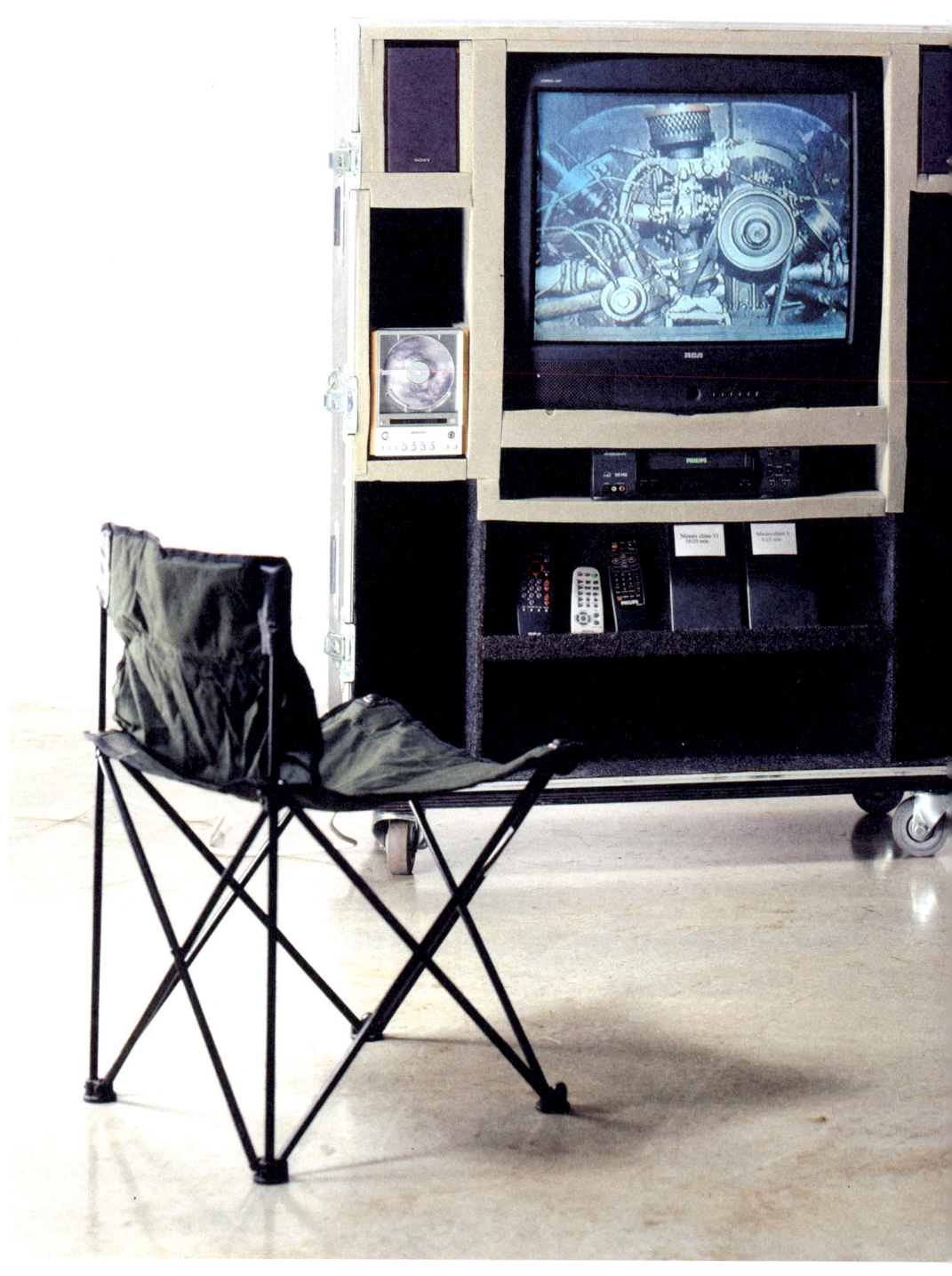

El mueble chino, 2000–2001
Mixed media, 55⅓ × 45⅓ × 27½ in. (140.5 × 116 × 70 cm)
La Colección Jumex, México

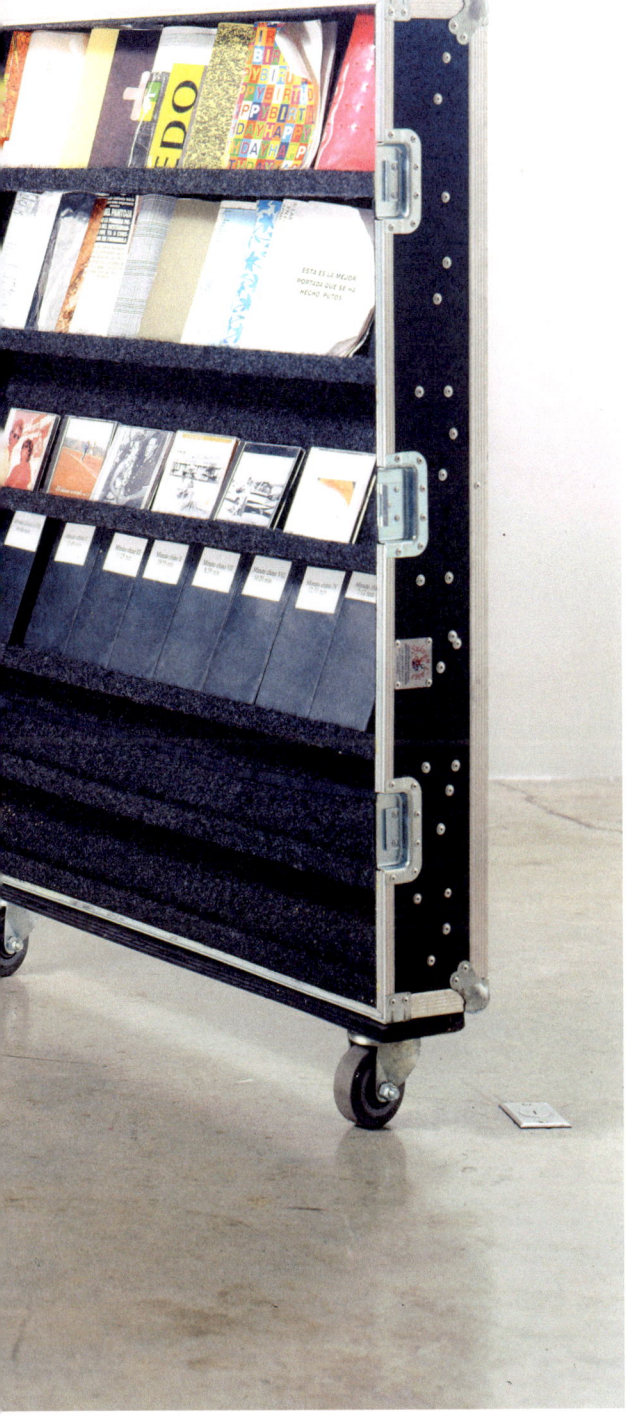

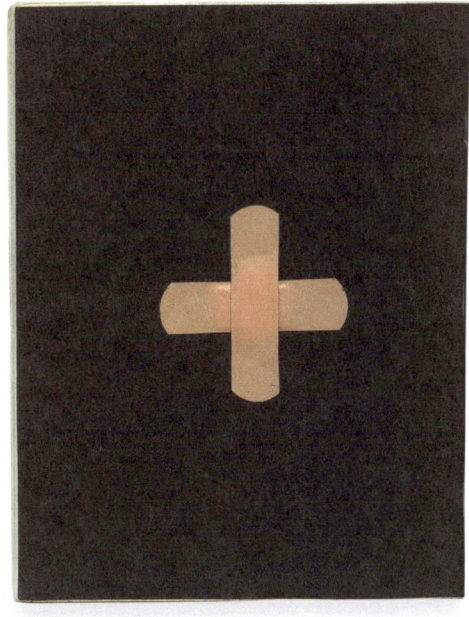

March 13, 2000, 2000
Photocopy, saddle stitched, 8½ × 6½ in. (22 × 17 cm)
Collection the artists

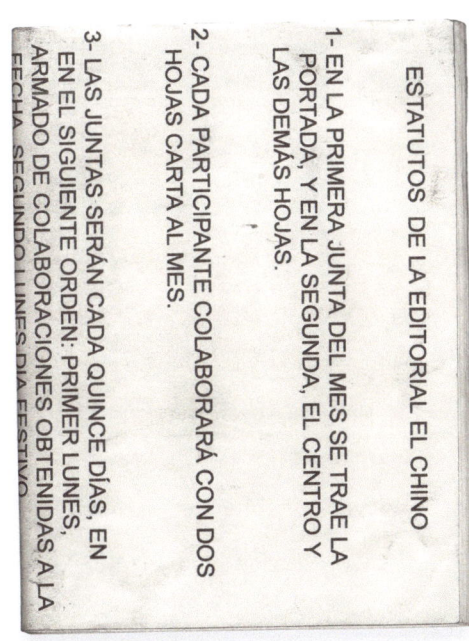

February 21, 2000, 2000
Photocopy, saddle stitched, 8½ × 6½ in. (22 × 17 cm)
Collection the artists

Tom Sachs

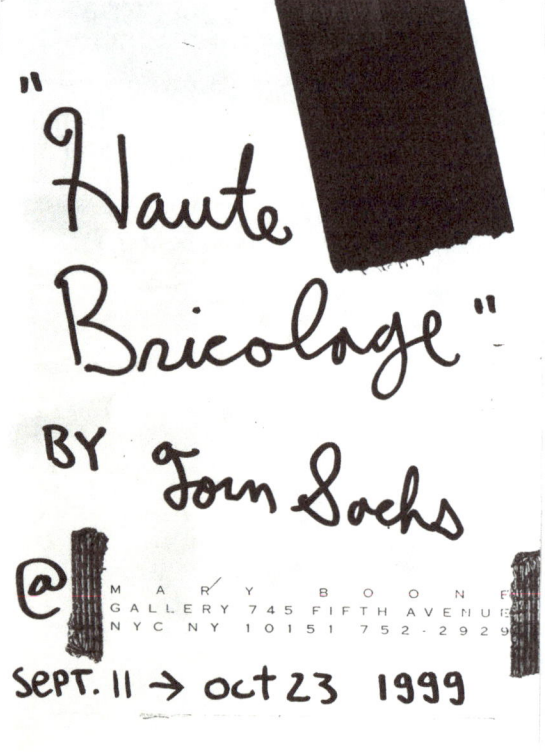

Haute Bricolage: Coach Class Version, 1999
Photocopy, saddle stitched, 8 ½ × 5 ½ in. (21.6 × 14 cm)
Collection Philip Aarons and Shelley Fox Aarons

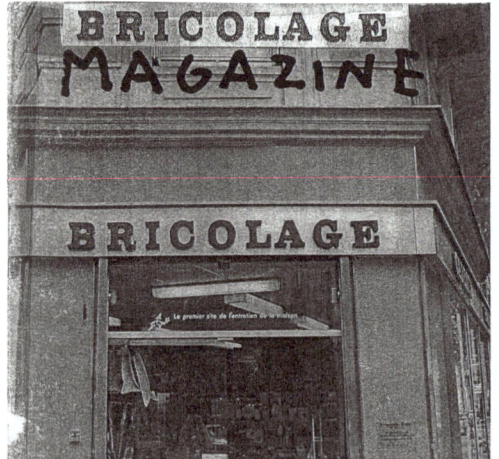

Bricolage Magazine, no. 1, November 2009
Photocopy, saddle stitched, 8 ½ × 5 ½ in. (21.6 × 14 cm)
Collection Philip Aarons and Shelley Fox Aarons

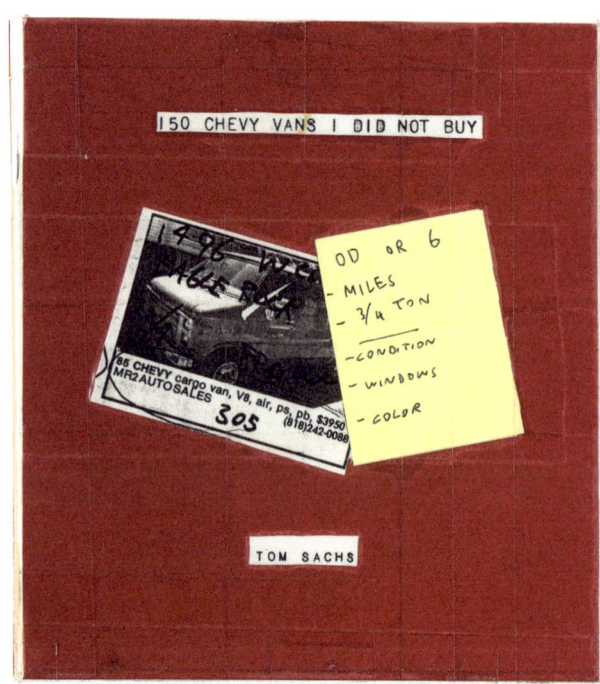

150 Chevy Vans I Did Not Buy, 1990
Photocopy, casebound with tape, 5 ¾ × 5 ¼ in. (14.5 × 13.2 cm)
Collection Philip Aarons and Shelley Fox Aarons

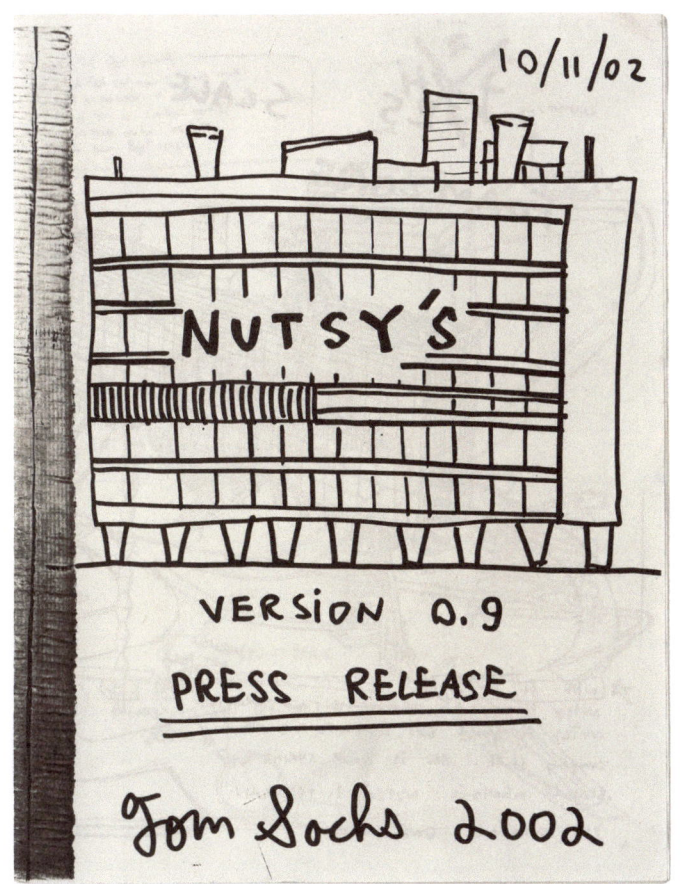

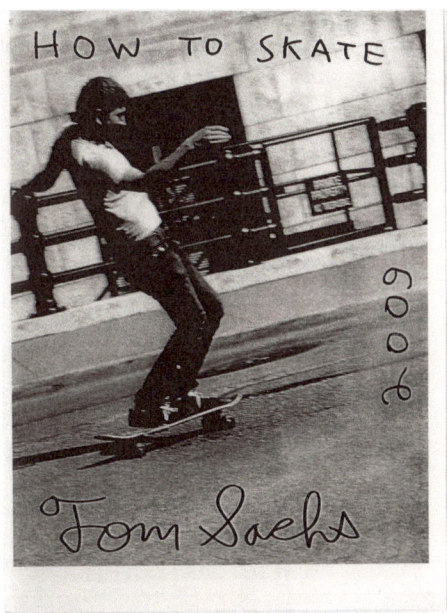

How to Skate, 2009
Photocopy, saddle stitched, 8 ½ × 5 ½ in. (21.6 × 14 cm)
Collection Philip Aarons and Shelley Fox Aarons

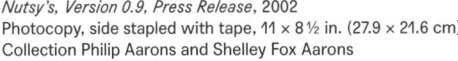

Nutsy's, Version 0.9, Press Release, 2002
Photocopy, side stapled with tape, 11 × 8 ½ in. (27.9 × 21.6 cm)
Collection Philip Aarons and Shelley Fox Aarons

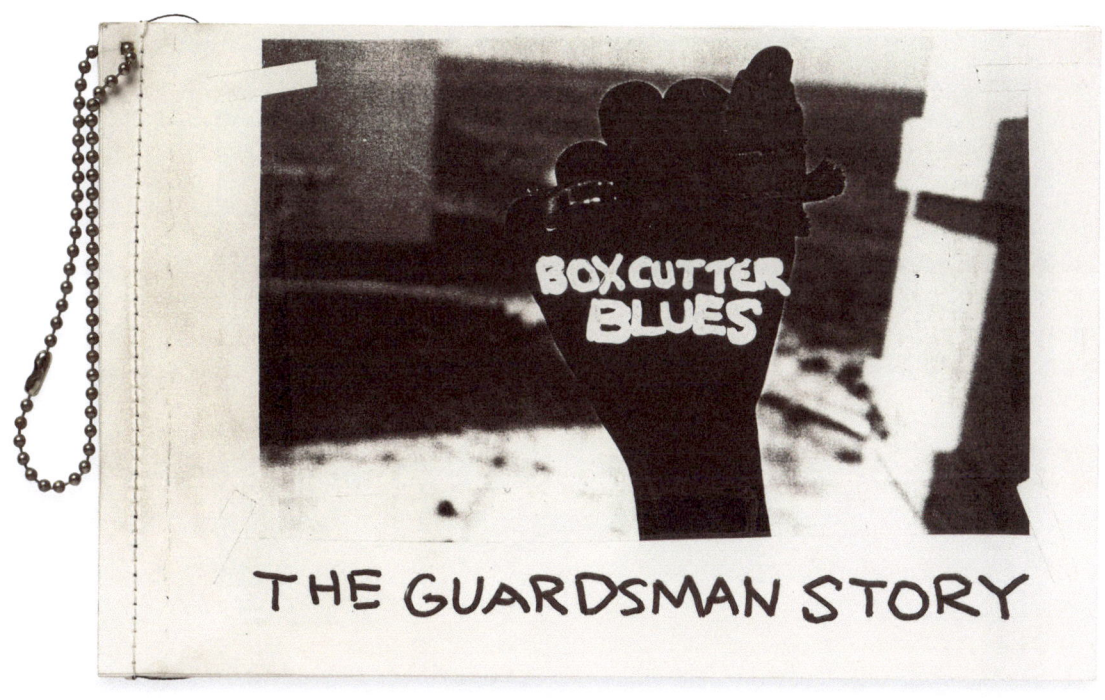

Boxcutter Blues: The Guardsman Story Version 1.0, October 2001
Photocopy, sewn binding, metal chain, 6 ⅛ × 9 ⅝ in. (15.5 × 24.5 cm)
Collection Philip Aarons and Shelley Fox Aarons

Ari Marcopoulos

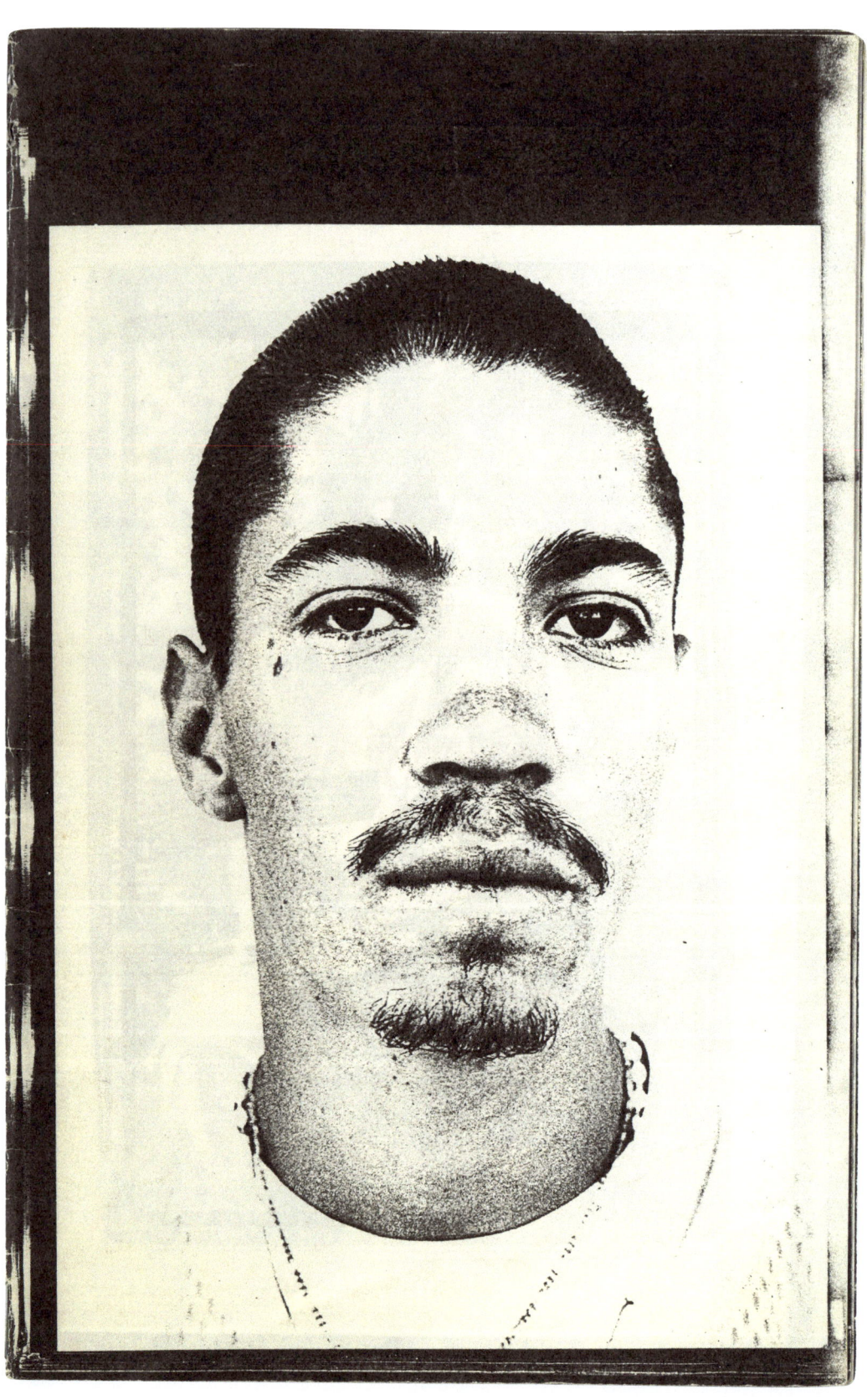

Untitled, 1995
Photocopy, saddle stitched, 8 ½ × 5 ½ in. (21.6 × 14 cm)
Collection Philip Aarons and Shelley Fox Aarons

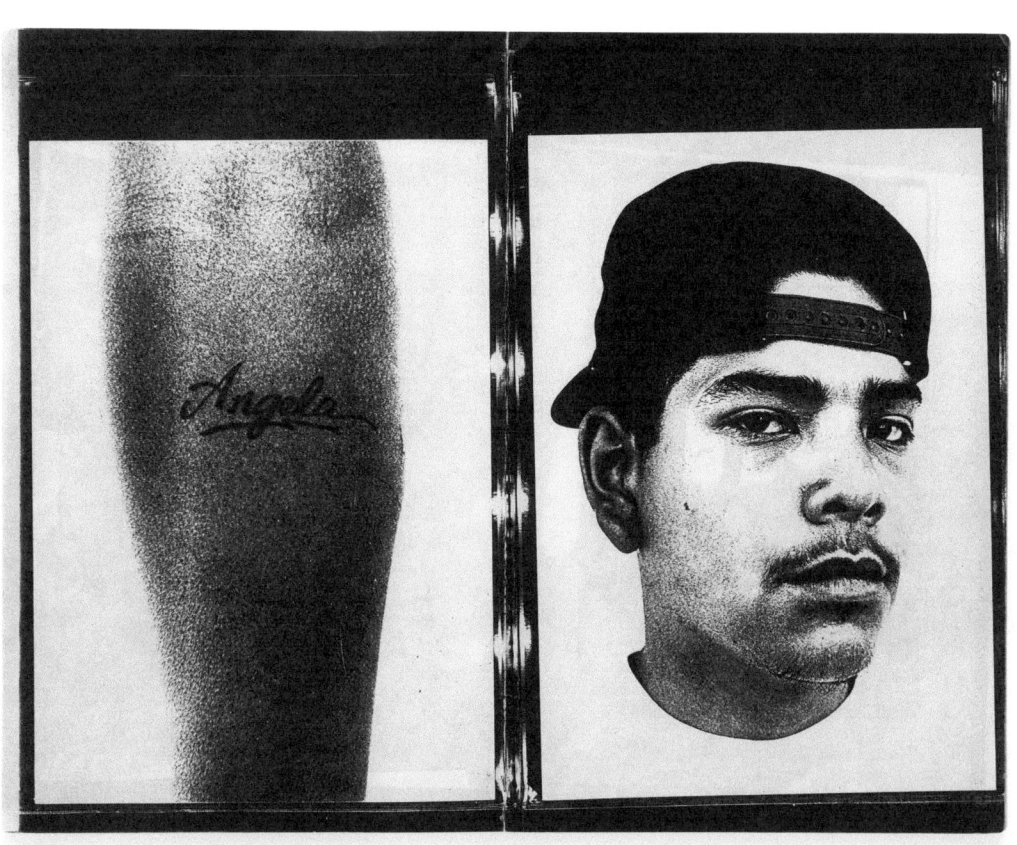

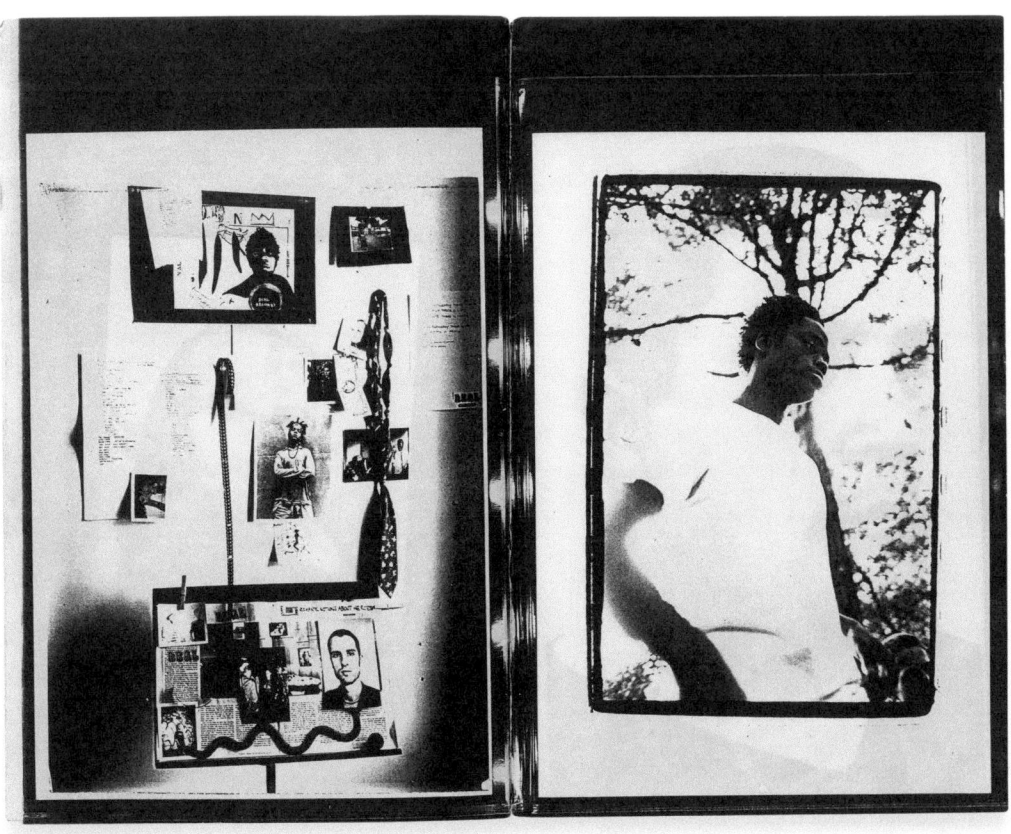

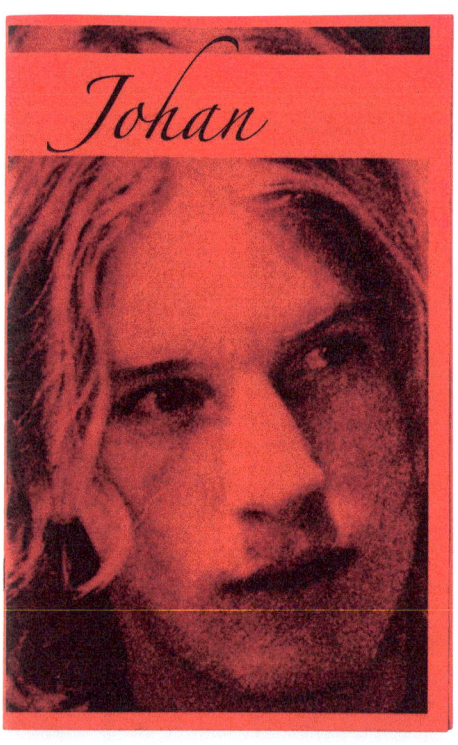

Johan, 2006
Photocopy, saddle stitched, 8 ½ × 5 ½ in. (21.6 × 14 cm)
Collection Philip Aarons and Shelley Fox Aarons

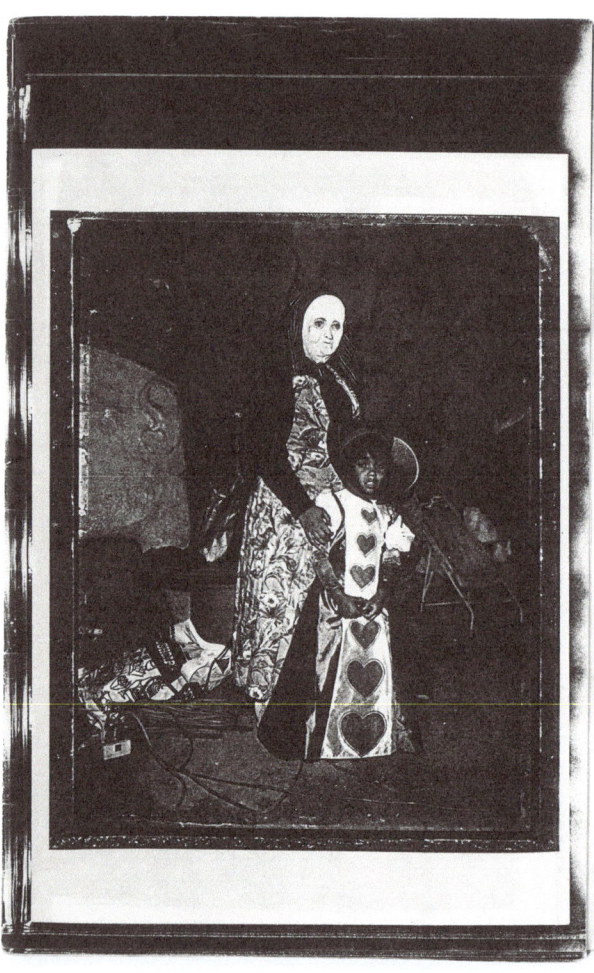

Untitled, 1994
Photocopy, saddle stitched, 8 ½ × 5 ½ in. (21.6 × 14 cm)
Collection Philip Aarons and Shelley Fox Aarons

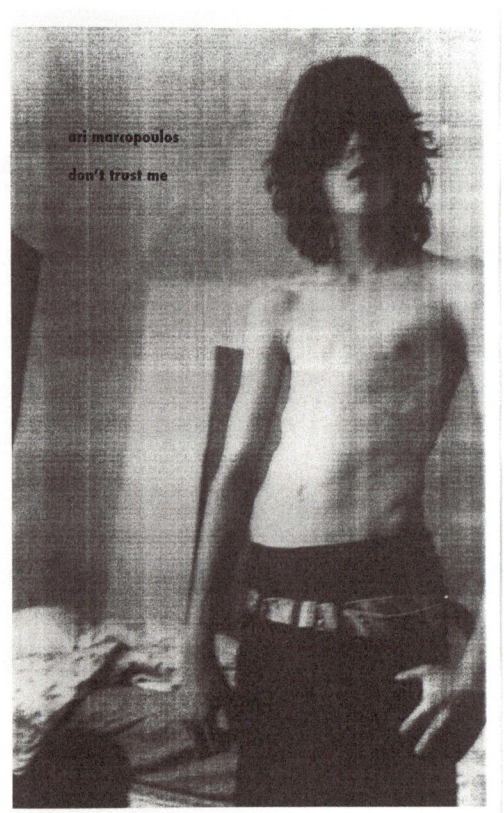

Don't Trust Me, 2009
Photocopy, saddle stitched, 8 ½ × 5 ½ in. (21.6 × 14 cm)
Collection Philip Aarons and Shelley Fox Aarons

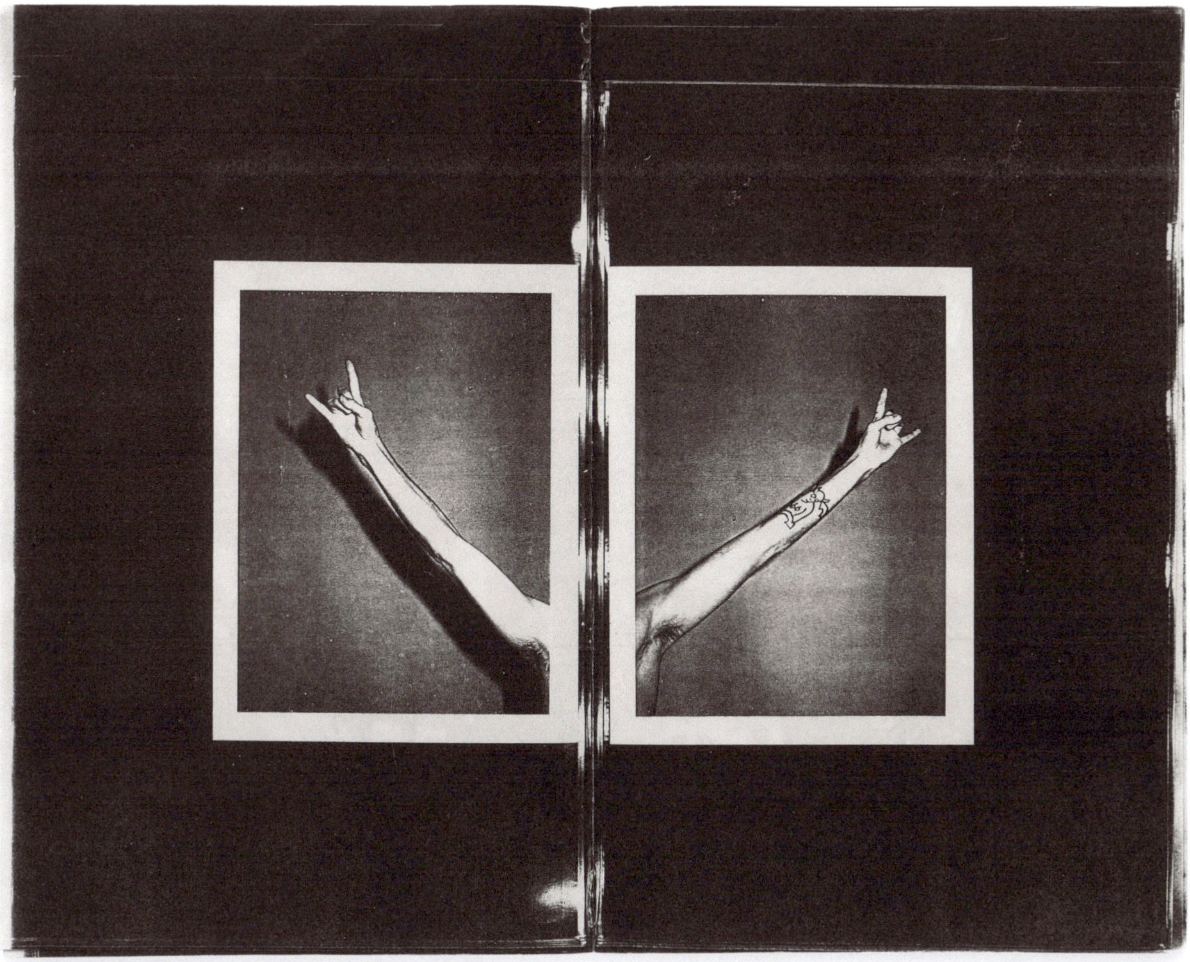

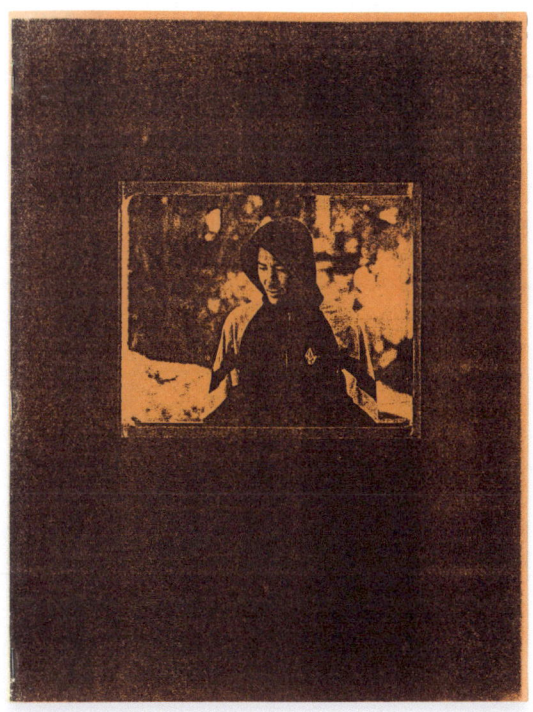

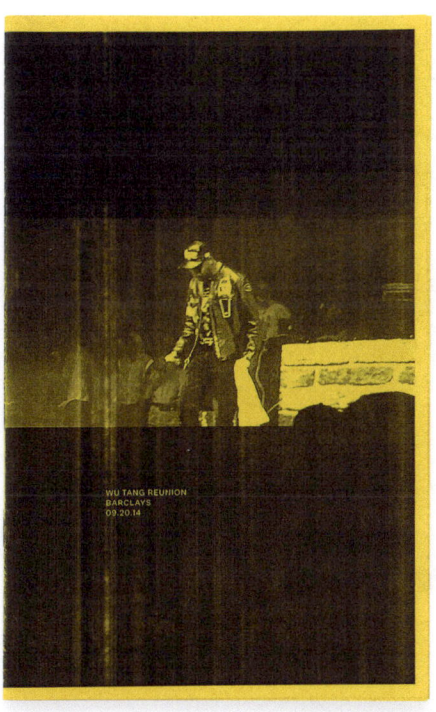

Transitions and Exits, 2001
Photocopy, saddle stitched, 11 × 8 ½ in. (27.9 × 21.6 cm)
Collection Philip Aarons and Shelley Fox Aarons

Wu Tang Reunion, 2014
Photocopy, saddle stitched, 8 ½ × 5 ½ in. (21.6 × 14 cm)
Collection Philip Aarons and Shelley Fox Aarons

Ed Templeton

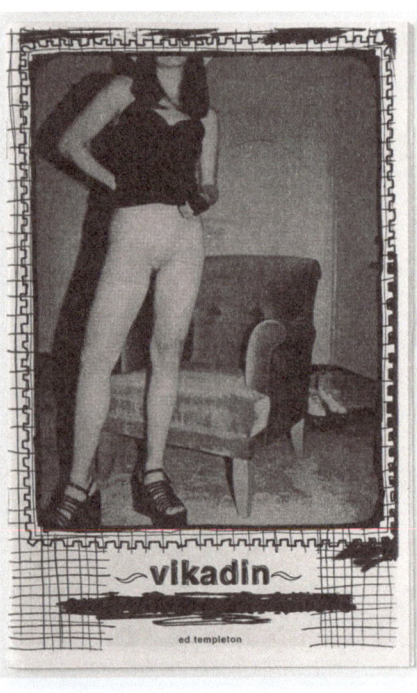

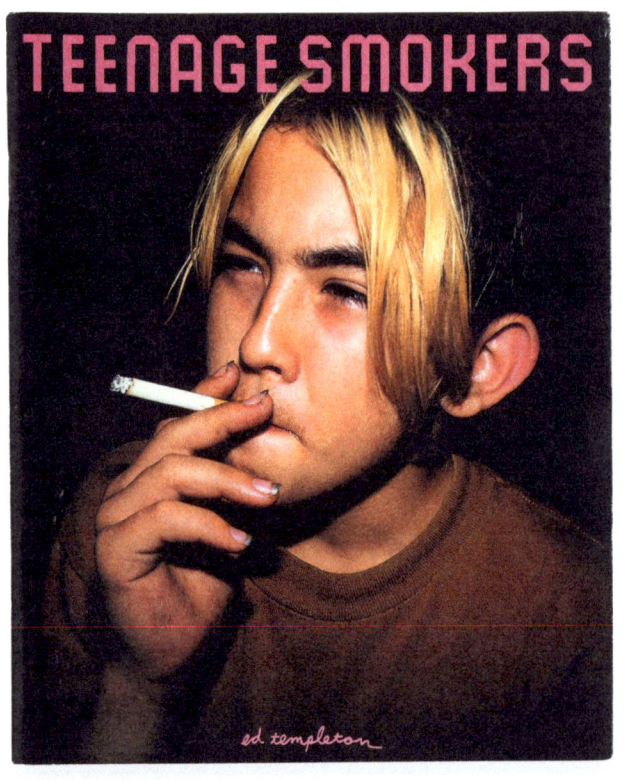

Vikadin, 1998
Photocopy, saddle stitched, 8 ½ × 5 ½ in. (21.6 × 14 cm)
Collection Philip Aarons and Shelley Fox Aarons

Teenage Smokers, 1999
Laser print, saddle stitched, 8 ½ × 7 in. (21.6 × 17.8 cm)
Collection Philip Aarons and Shelley Fox Aarons

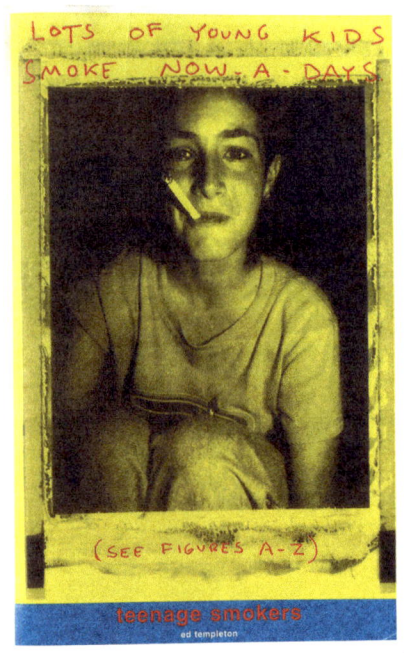

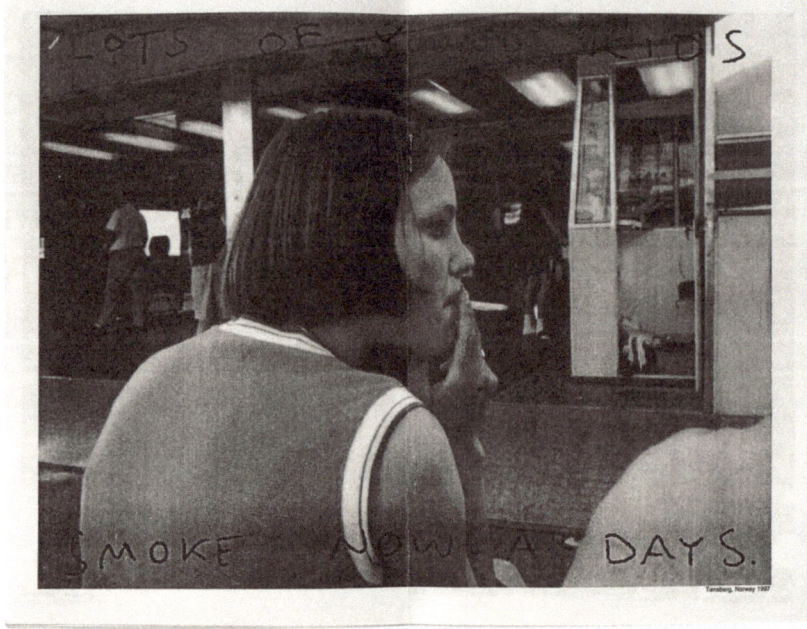

Teenage Smokers, 1998
Photocopy, saddle stitched, 8 ½ × 5 ½ in. (21.6 × 14 cm)
Collection Philip Aarons and Shelley Fox Aarons

Deanna Templeton

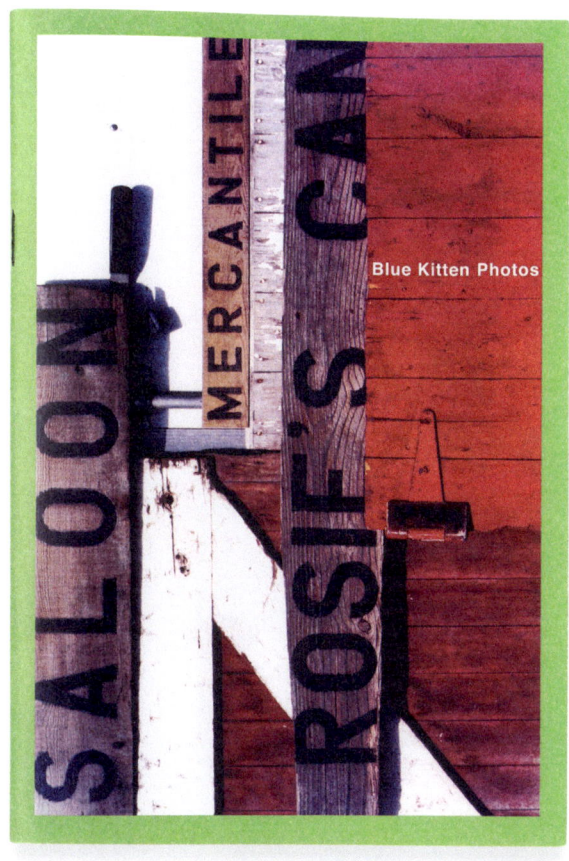

Blue Kitten Photos, no. 1, 2002
Photocopy, saddle stitched, 7 ¼ × 5 ⅛ in. (18.4 × 13 cm)
Collection Philip Aarons and Shelley Fox Aarons

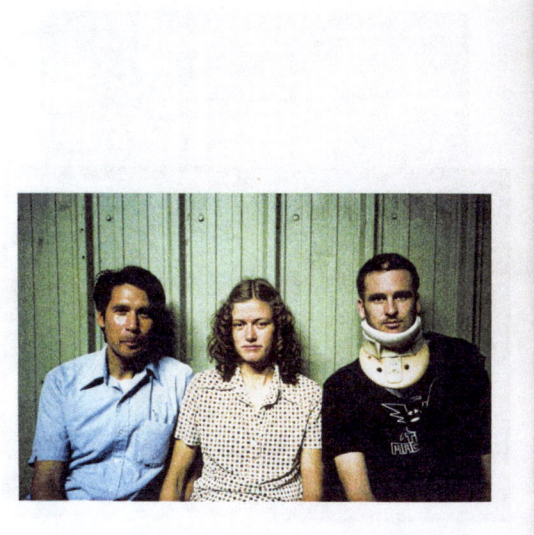

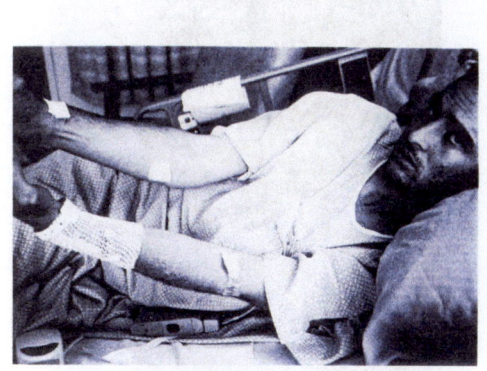

Ryan McGinley

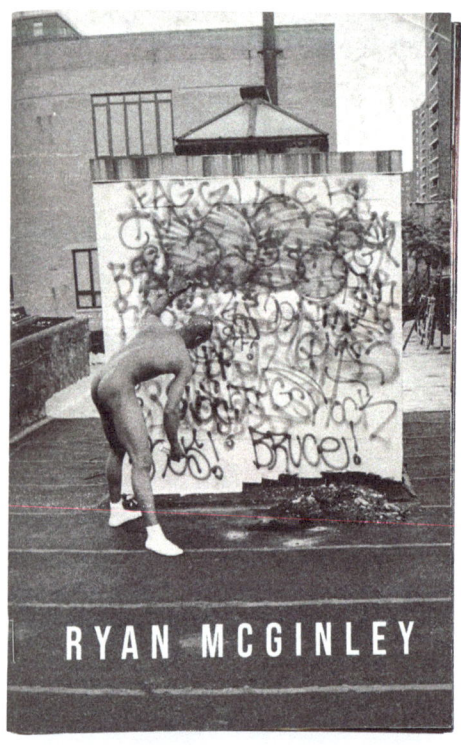

Ryan McGinley, 2002
Photocopy, saddle stitched, 8 × 5 ¼ in. (20.3 × 13.3 cm)
Collection the artist

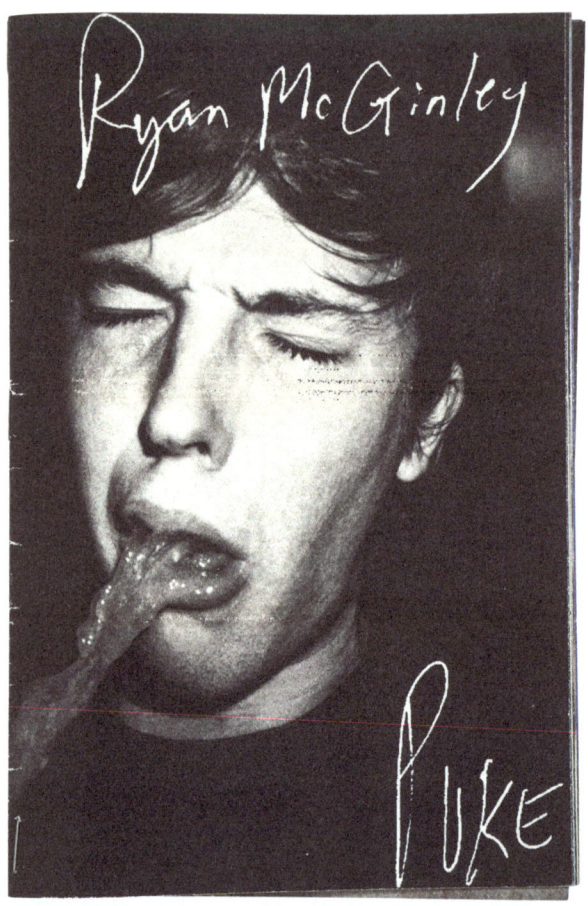

Puke, 2001
Photocopy, saddle stitched, 8 × 5 ¼ in. (20.3 × 13.3 cm)
Collection the artist

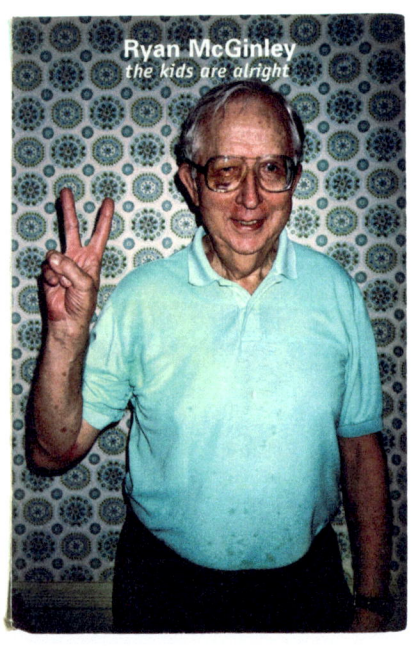

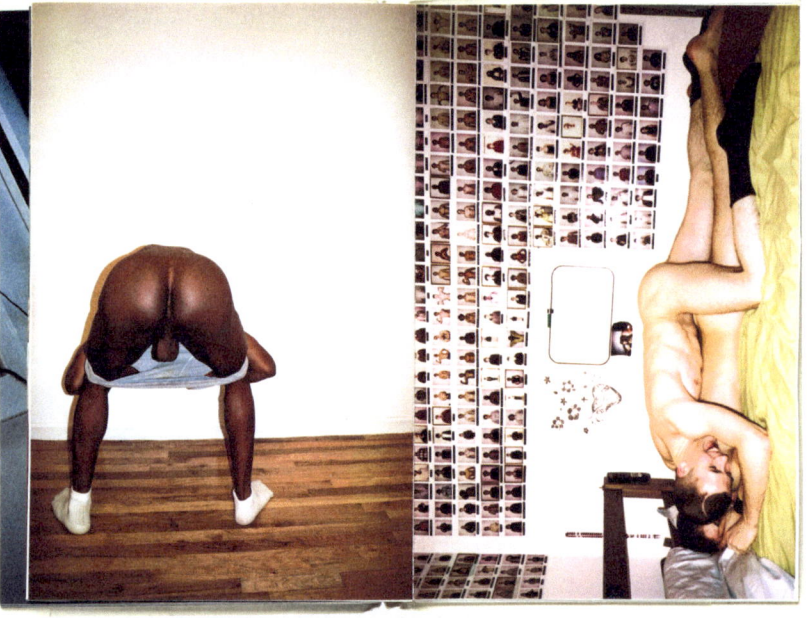

the kids are alright, 1999
Photocopy, saddle stitched, 8 ½ × 5 ½ in. (21.6 × 14 cm)
Collection Philip Aarons and Shelley Fox Aarons

Ryan McGinley
and Dash Snow

Suck a Dick Up till You Hik-Up, 2002
Photocopy, saddle stitched, 7 ½ × 4 ¾ in. (19.1 × 12.1 cm)
Collection Ryan McGinley

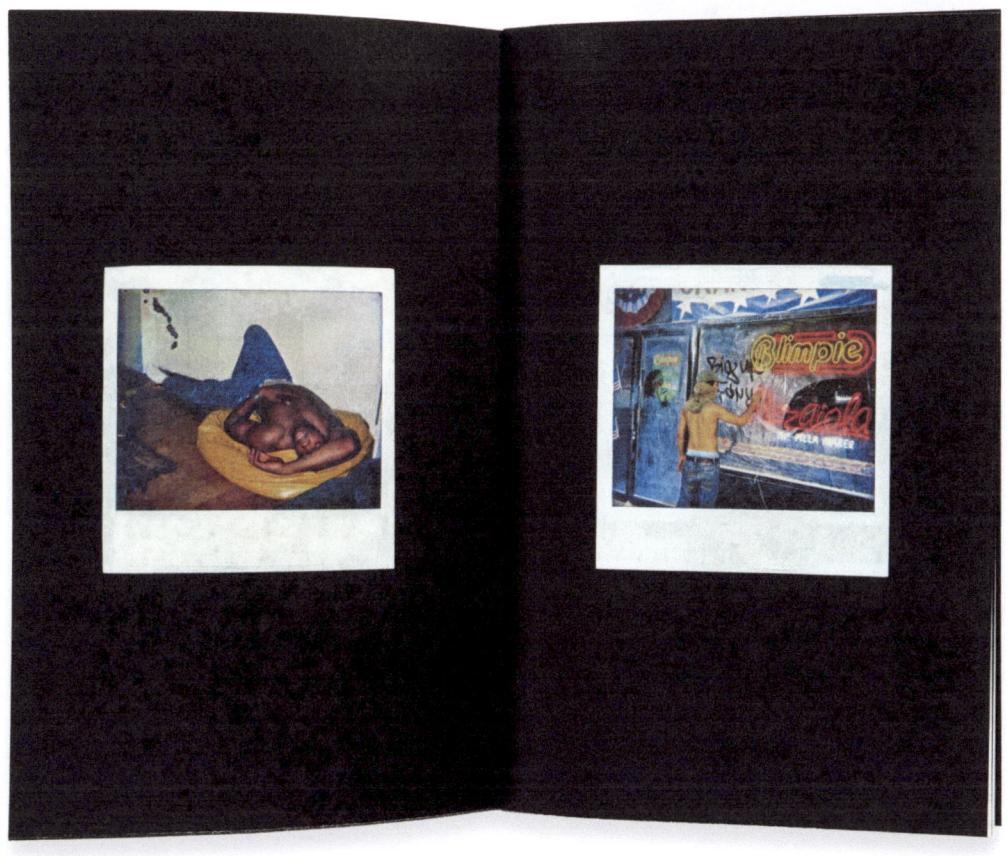

Dash Snow

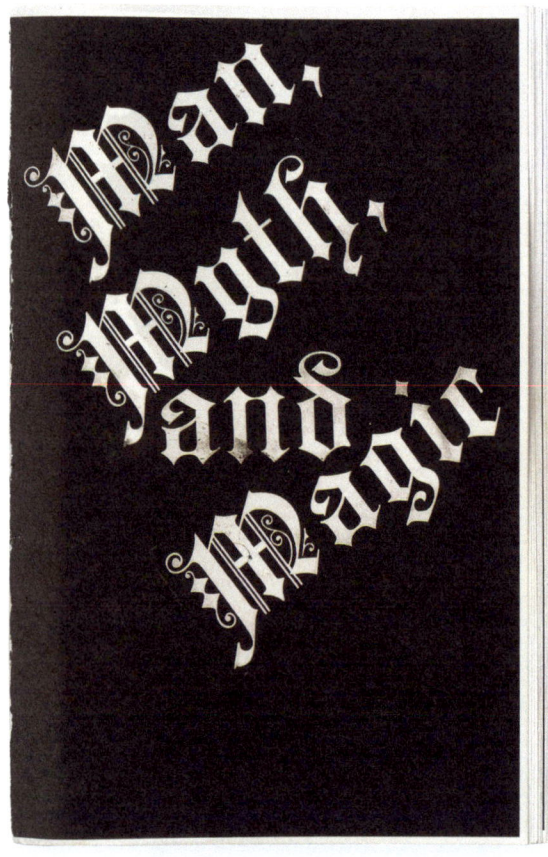

Man, Myth, and Magic, n.d.
Laser print, bound with rubber band, 8 ½ × 5 ¾ in. (21.6 × 14.6 cm)
Collection Philip Aarons and Shelley Fox Aarons

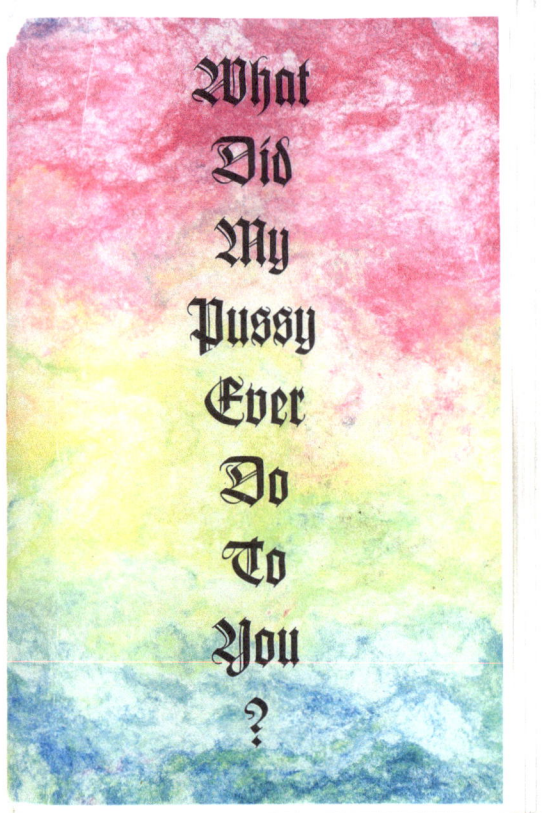

What Did My Pussy Ever Do To You?, 2006
Laser print, bound with rubber band, 8 ½ × 6 in. (21.6 × 15.2 cm)
Collection Philip Aarons and Shelley Fox Aarons

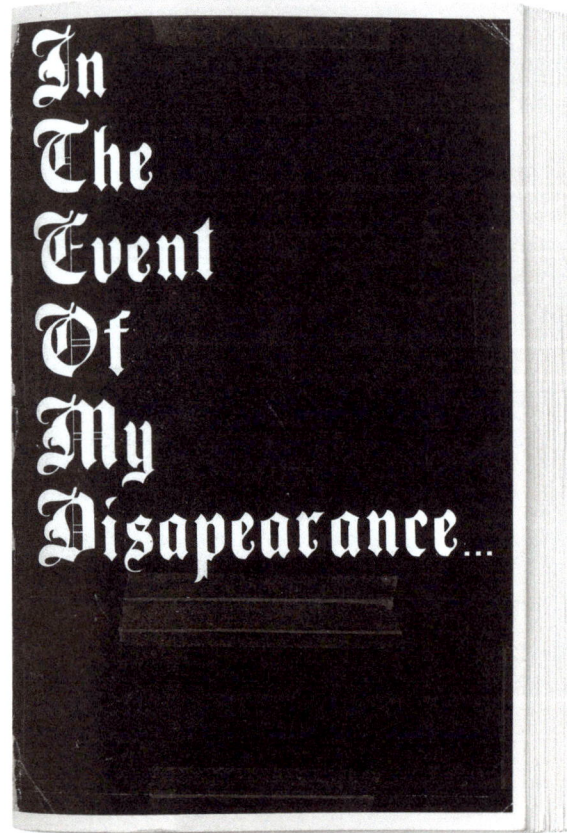

In the Event of My Disappearance, 2005
Laser print, folded, 8 ½ × 6 in. (21.6 × 15.2 cm)
Collection Philip Aarons and Shelley Fox Aarons

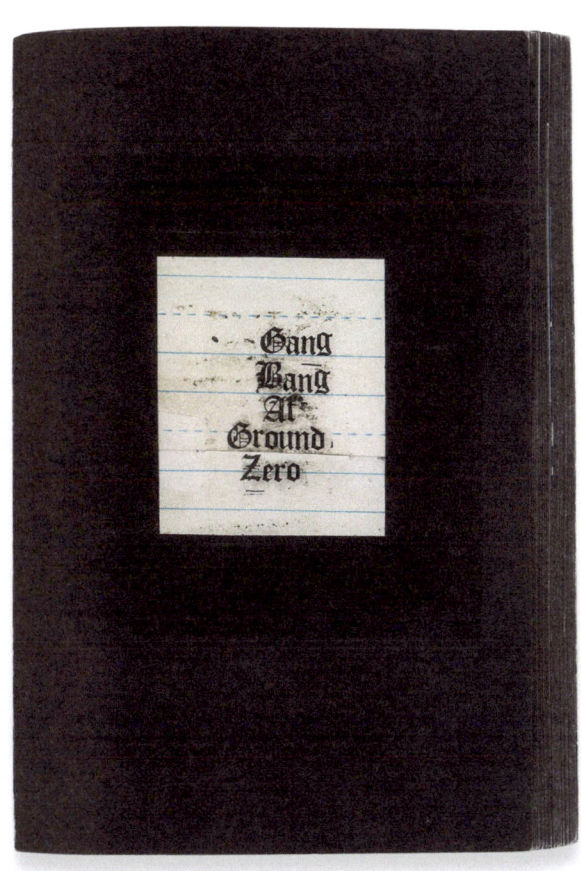

Gang Bang at Ground Zero, 2007
Photocopy, folded, 8 ½ × 5 ⅞ in. (21.5 × 15 cm)
Collection Philip Aarons and Shelley Fox Aarons

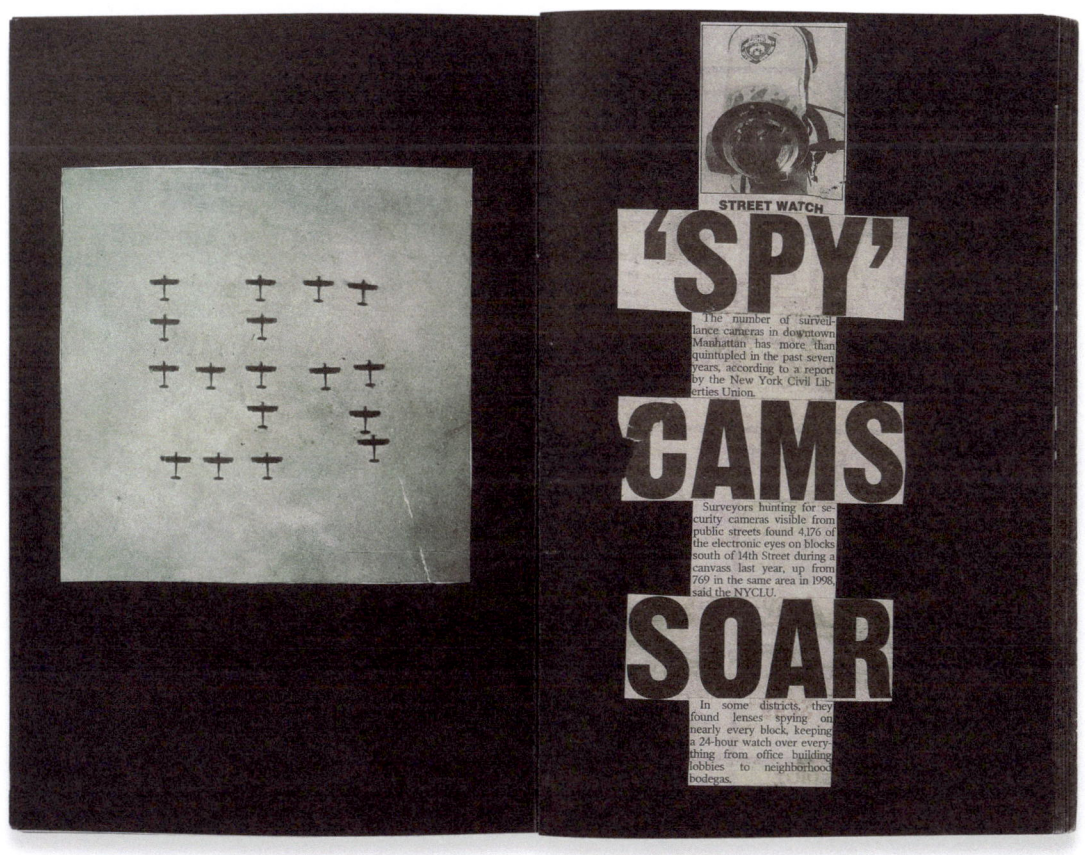

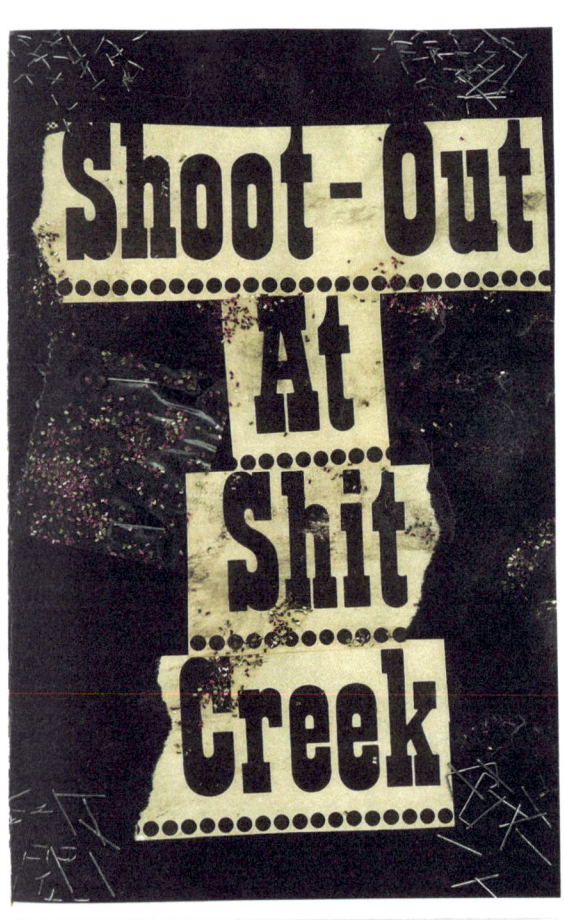

Shoot-Out at Shit Creek, n.d.
Laser print, folded, 8 ½ × 6 in. (21.6 × 15.2 cm)
Collection Philip Aarons and Shelley Fox Aarons

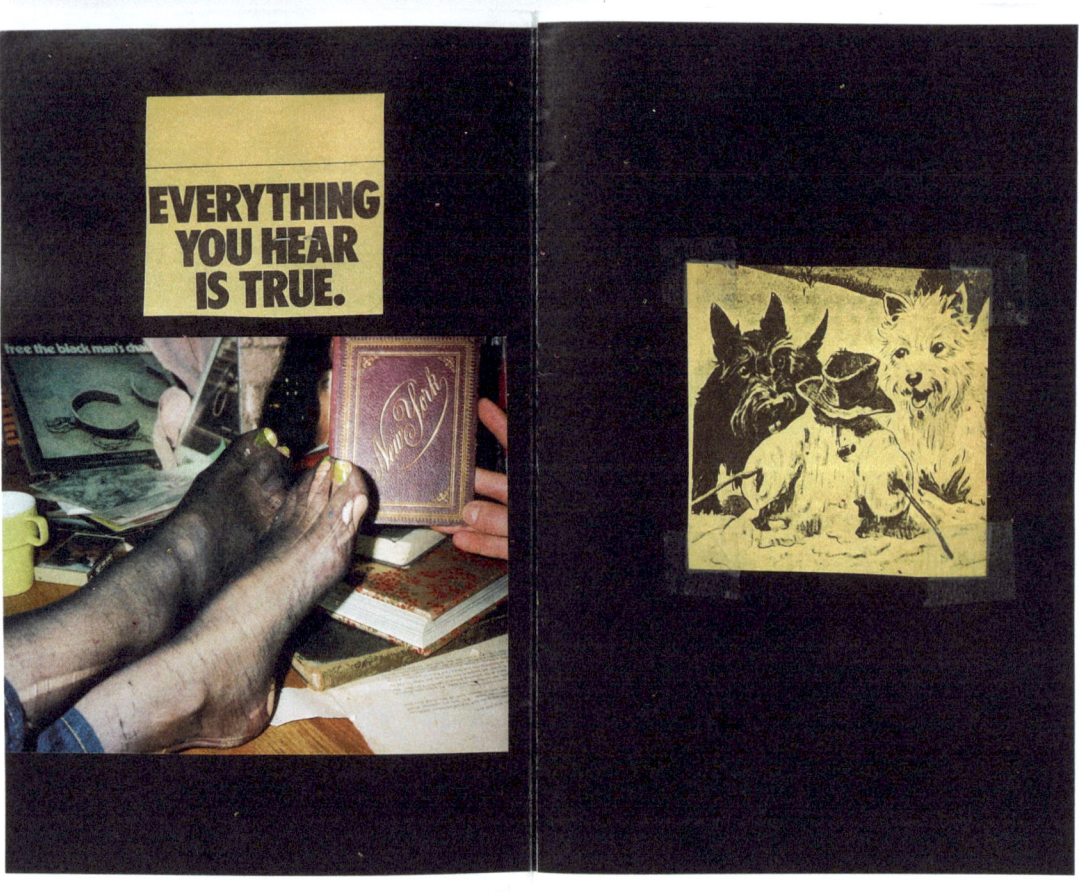

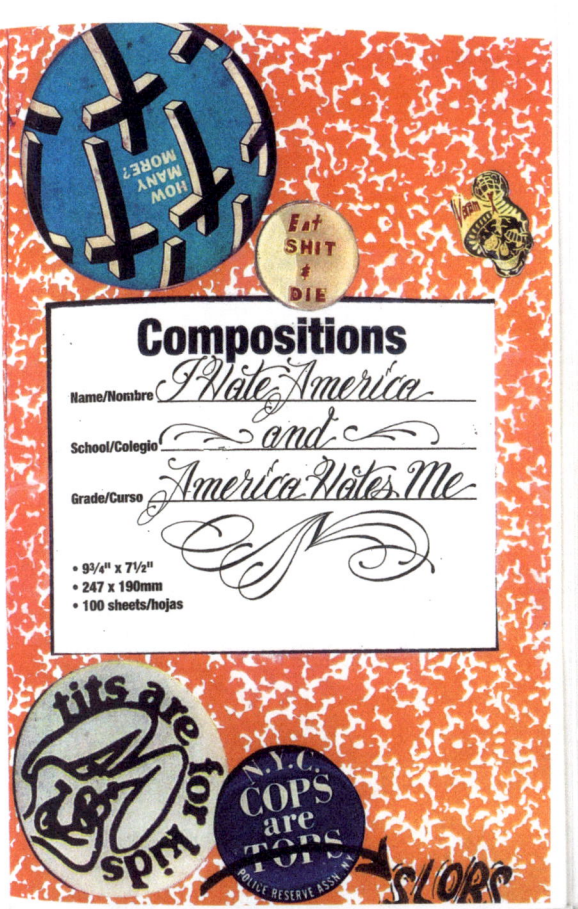

I Hate America and America Hates Me, 2005
Photocopy, folded, 8 ½ × 5 ⅞ in. (21.5 × 15 cm)
Collection Philip Aarons and Shelley Fox Aarons

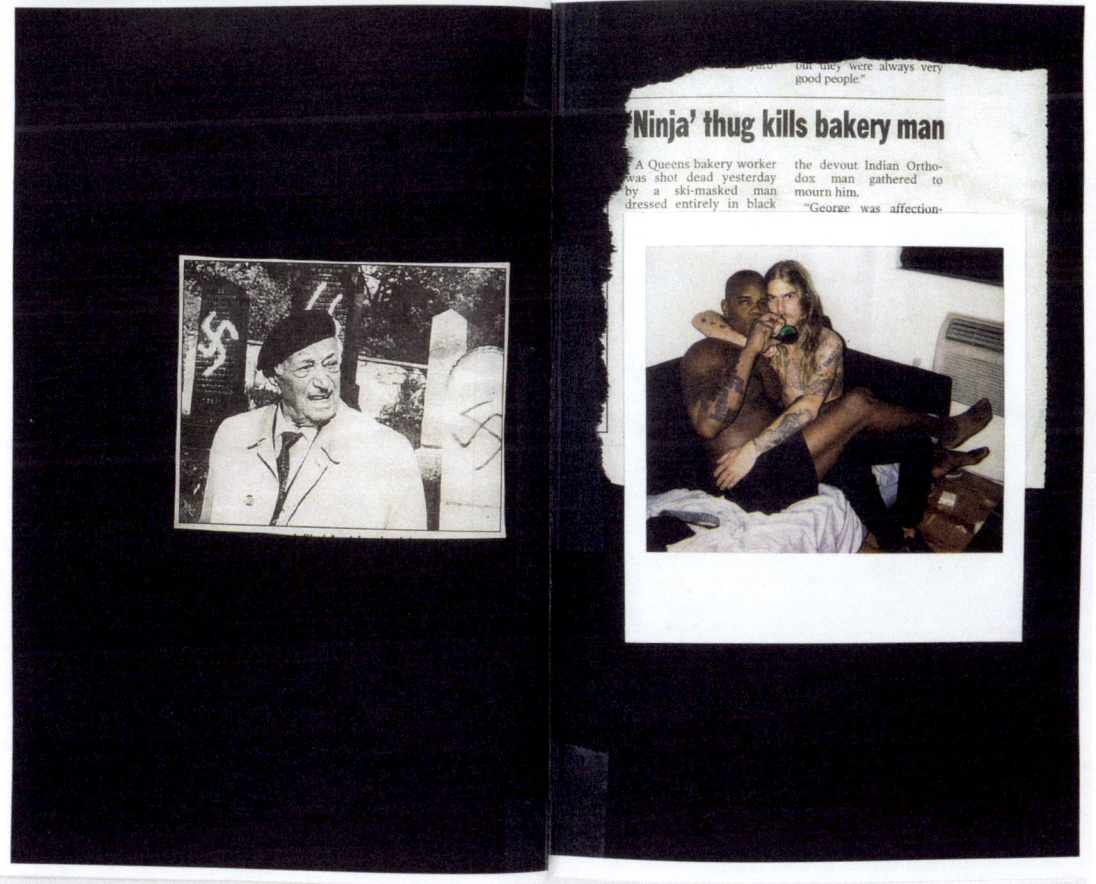

Kate Huh

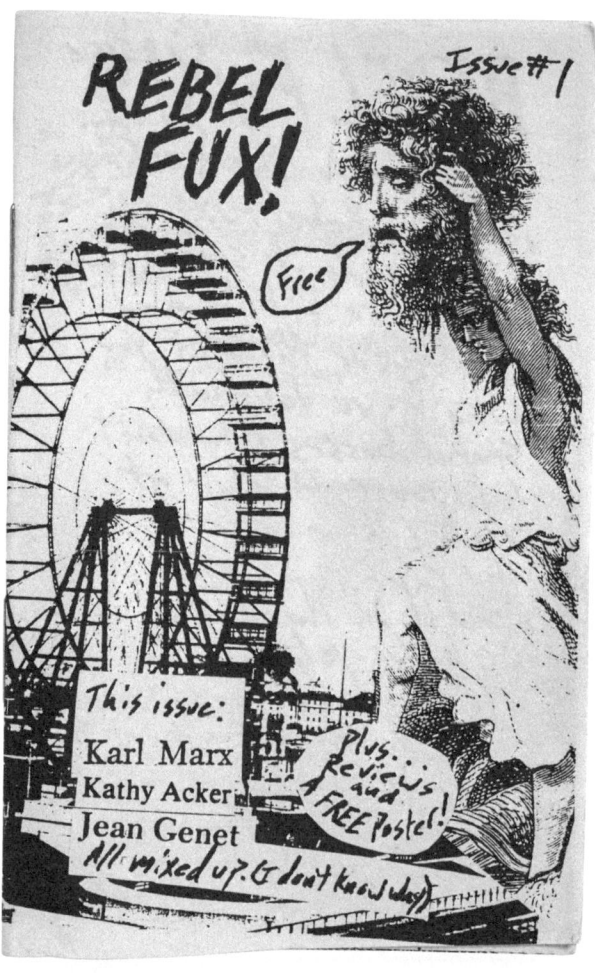

Rebel Fux!, nos. 1, 9, and 25, 1996, 1997, and 2002
All photocopy, saddle stitched, 4 ⅛ × 2 ⅝ in. (10.5 × 6.7 cm)
Collection the artist

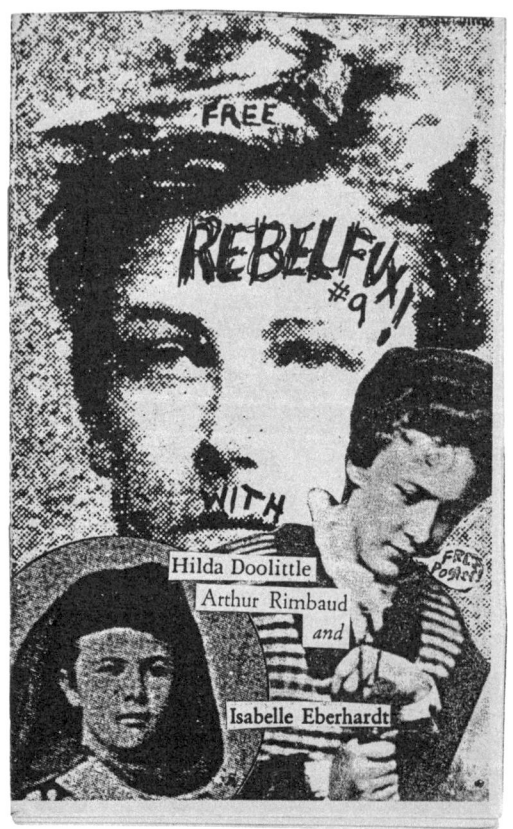

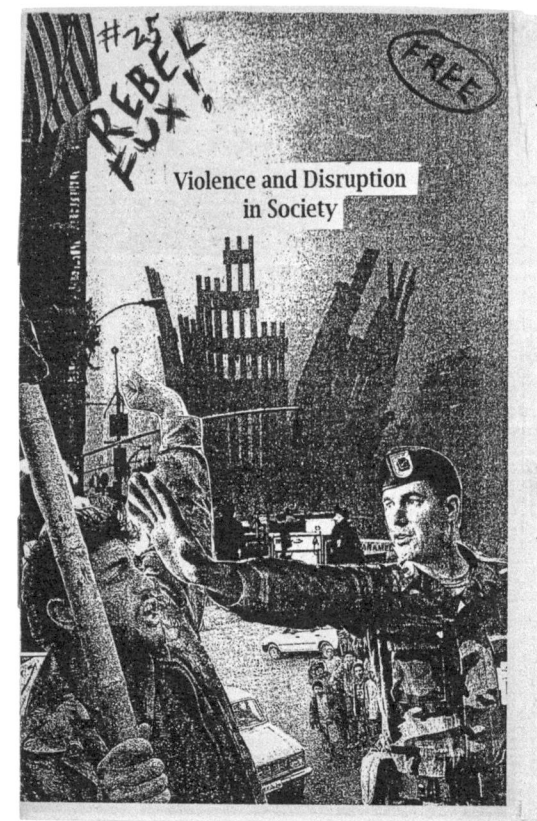

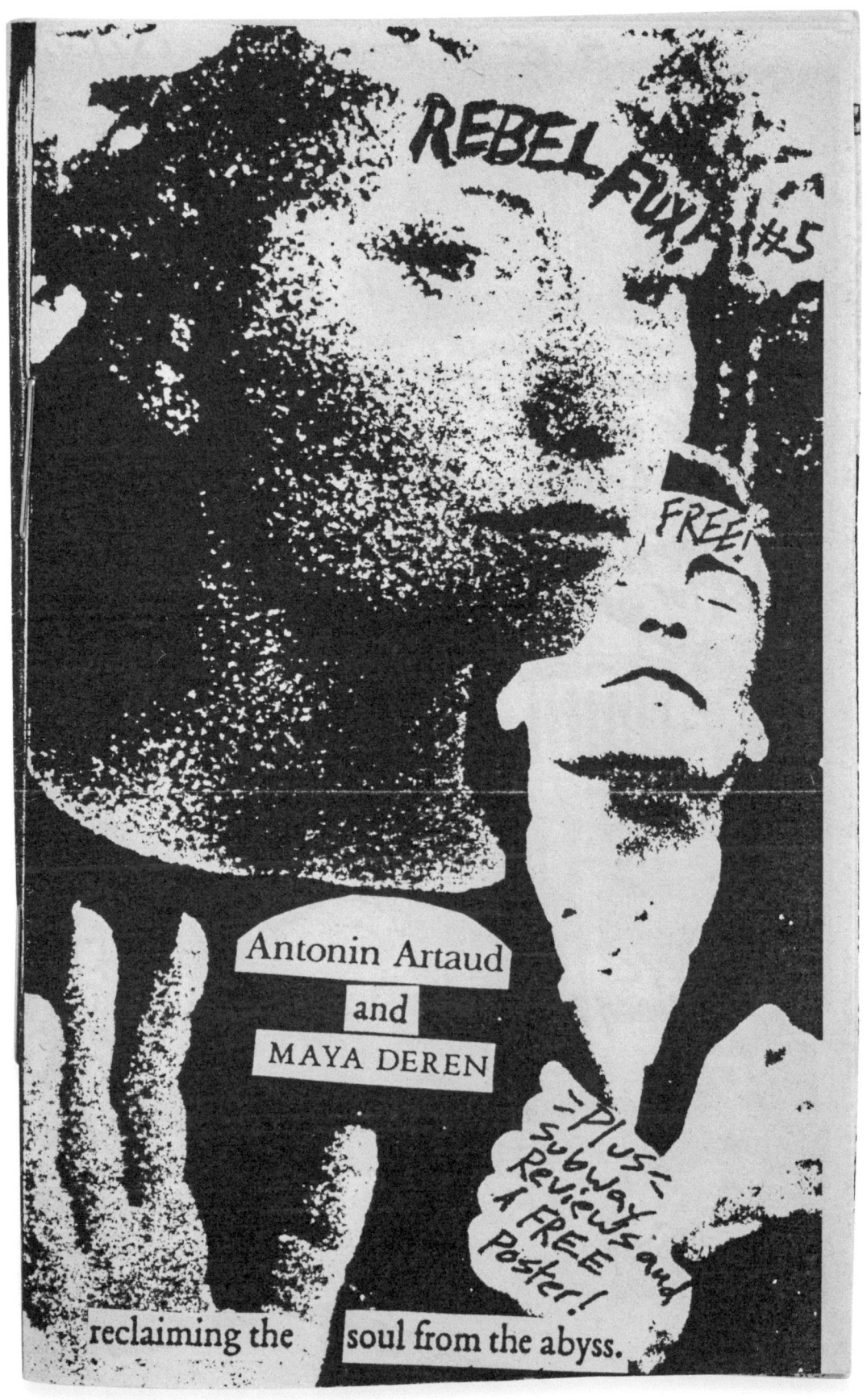

Rebel Fux!, no. 5, 1996
Photocopy, saddle stitched, 4 ⅛ × 2 ⅝ in. (10.5 × 6.7 cm)
Collection the artist

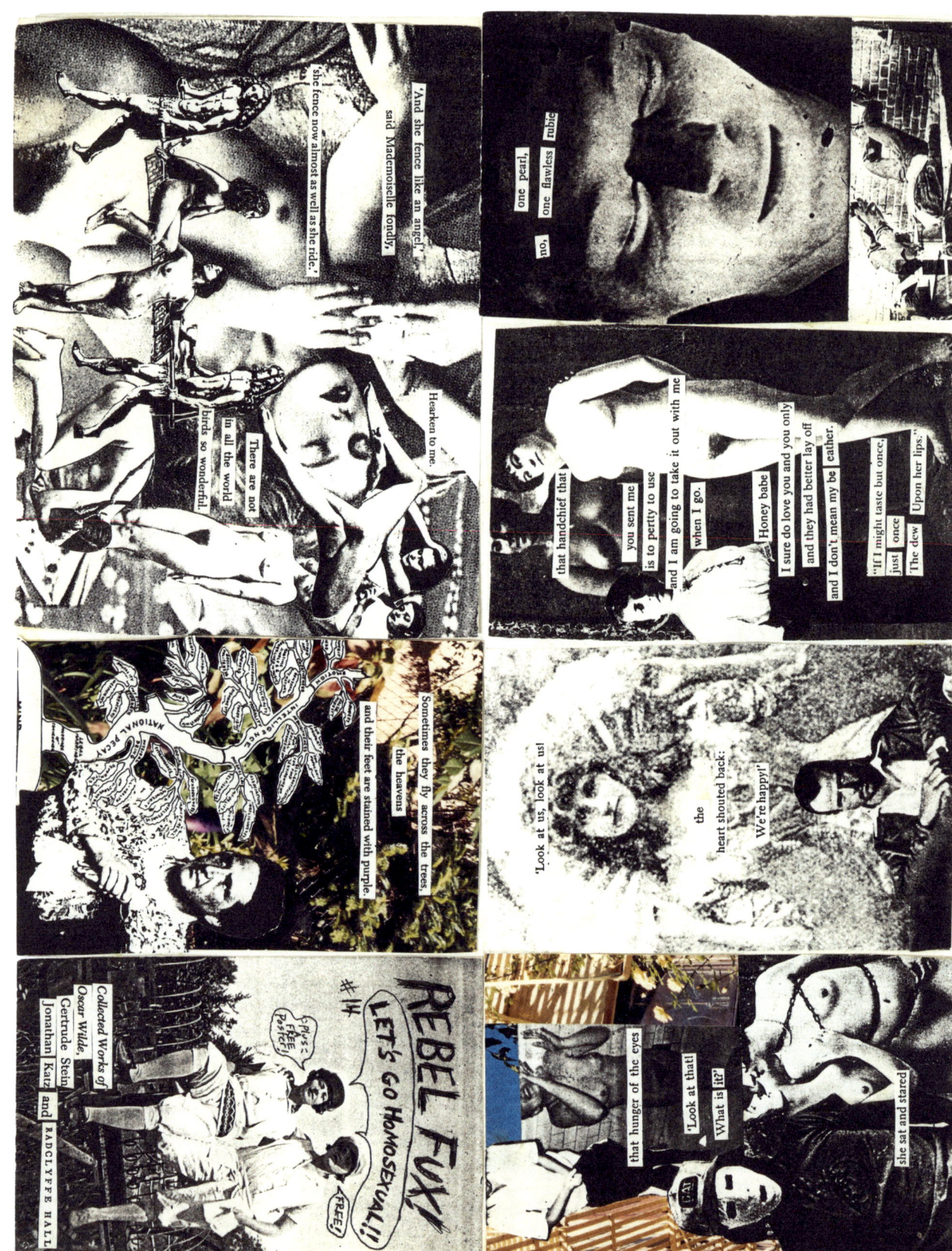

Paste-up for *Rebel Fux!*, no. 14, 1997
Collage of photomechanical prints, glue, 11 × 8 ½ in. (27.9 × 21.6 cm)
Collection the artist

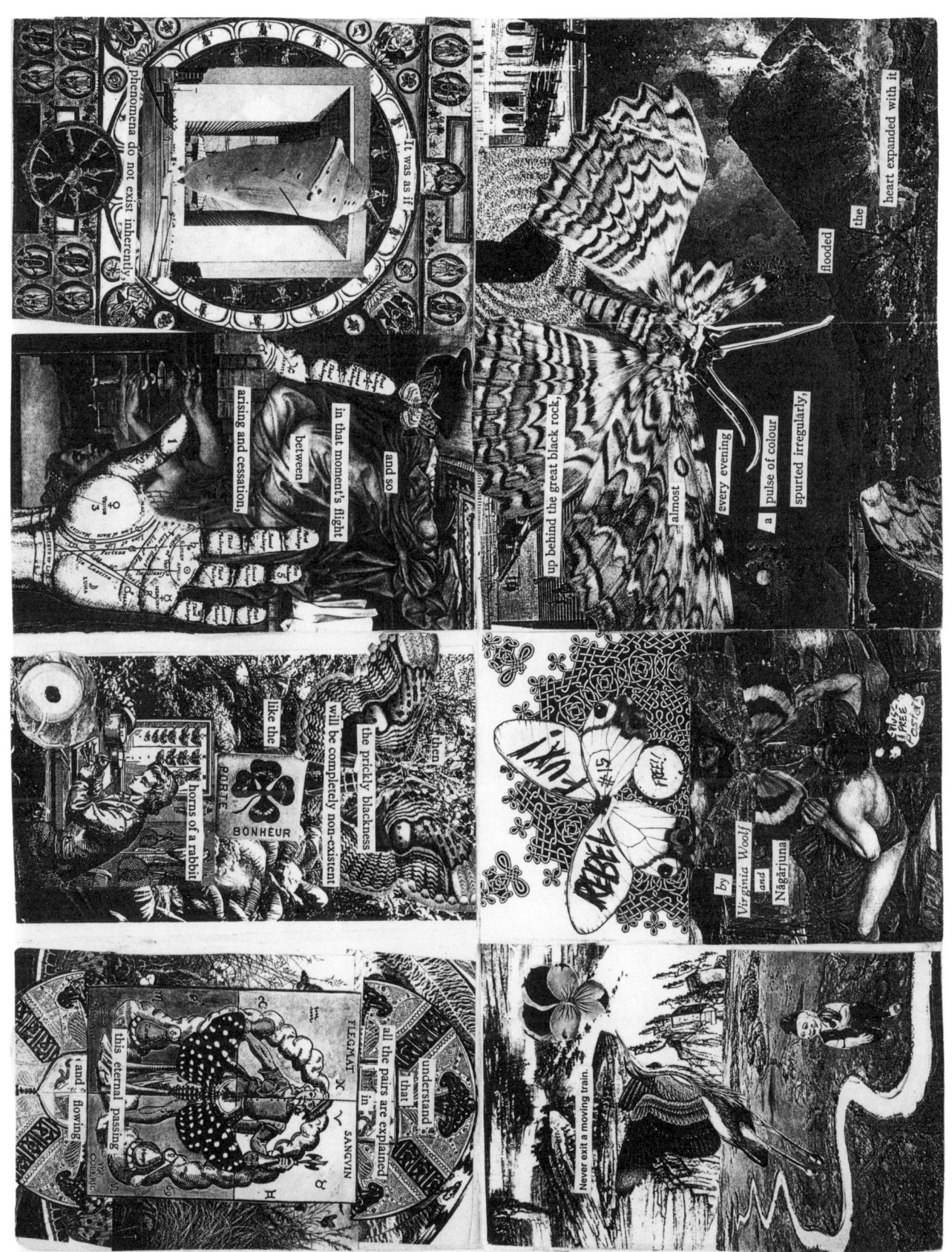

Paste-up for *Rebel Fux!*, no. 15, 1997
Collage of photomechanical prints, glue, 11 × 8 ½ in. (27.9 × 21.6 cm)
Collection the artist

Frederick Weston

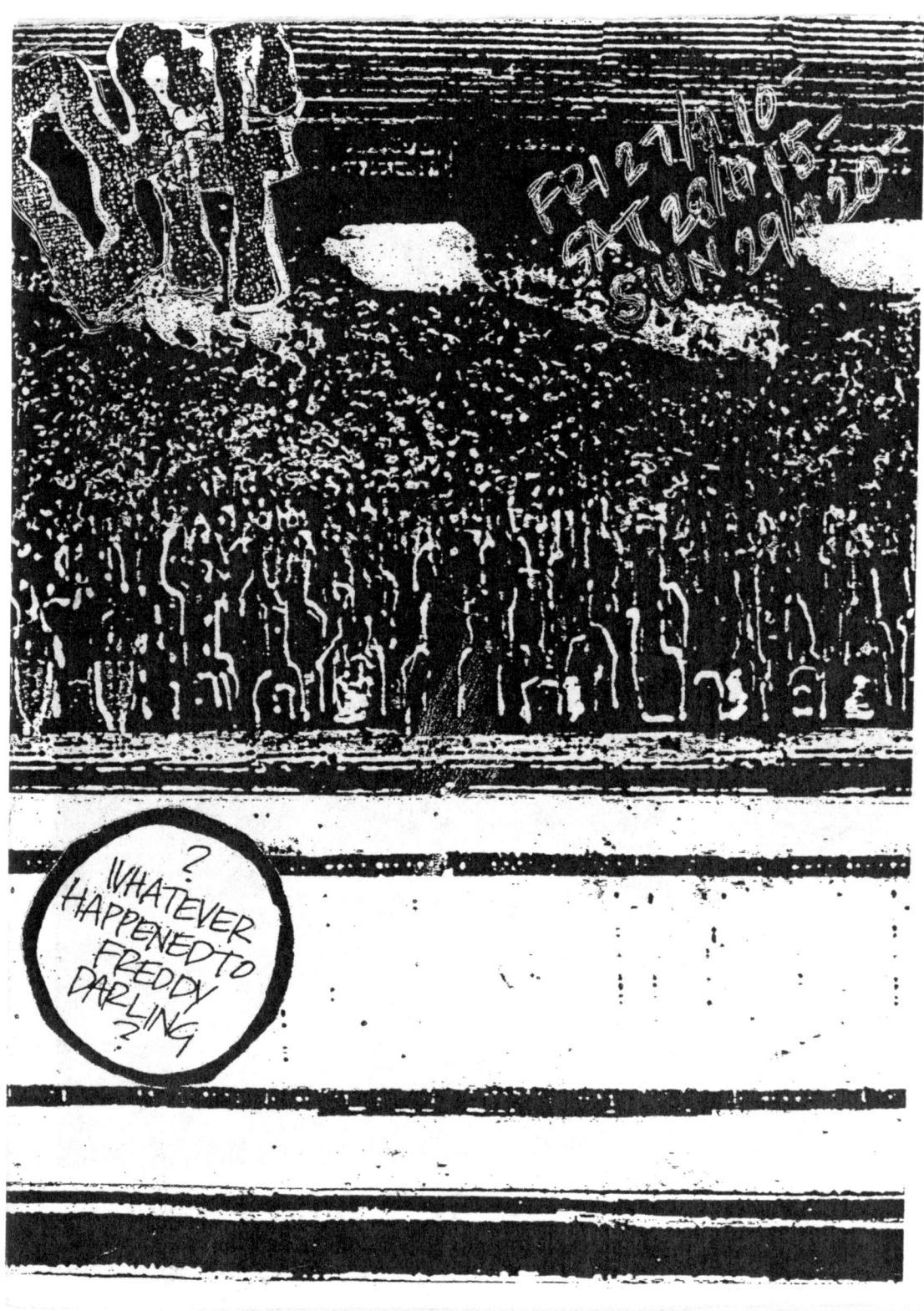

Whatever Happened to Freddy Darling?, 2003
Photocopy, saddle stitched, 5 ½ × 4 ¼ in. (14 × 10.8 cm)
Visual AIDS, New York

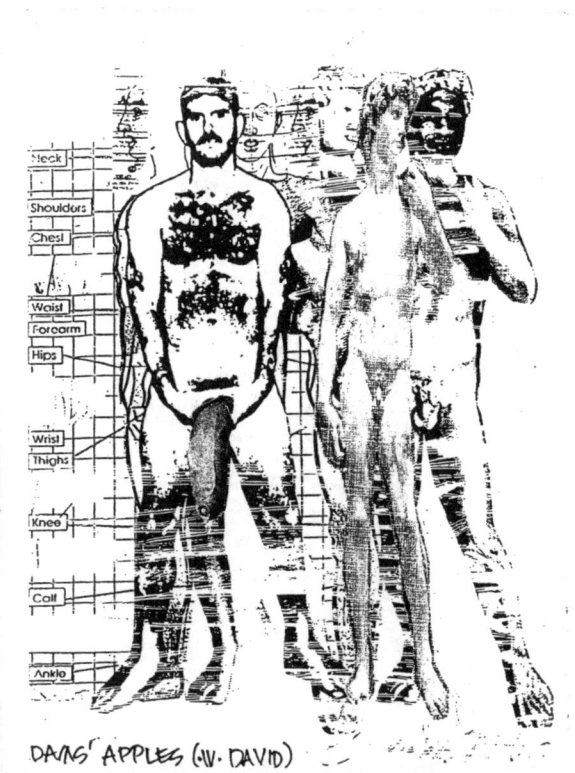

DAVIS' APPLES (IV. DAVID)

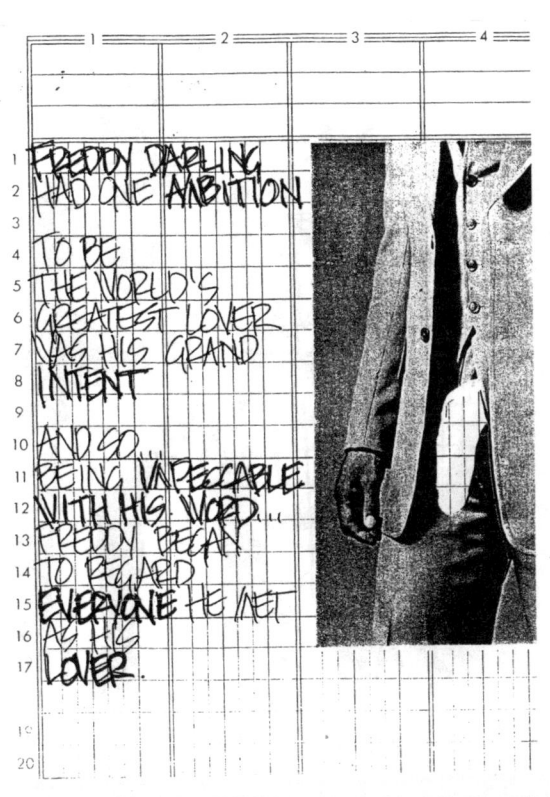

FREDDY DARLING
HAD ONE AMBITION

TO BE
THE WORLD'S
GREATEST LOVER
WAS HIS GRAND
INTENT

AND SO...
BEING IMPECCABLE
WITH HIS WORD...
FREDDY BEGAN
TO REGARD
EVERYONE HE MET
AS HIS
LOVER.

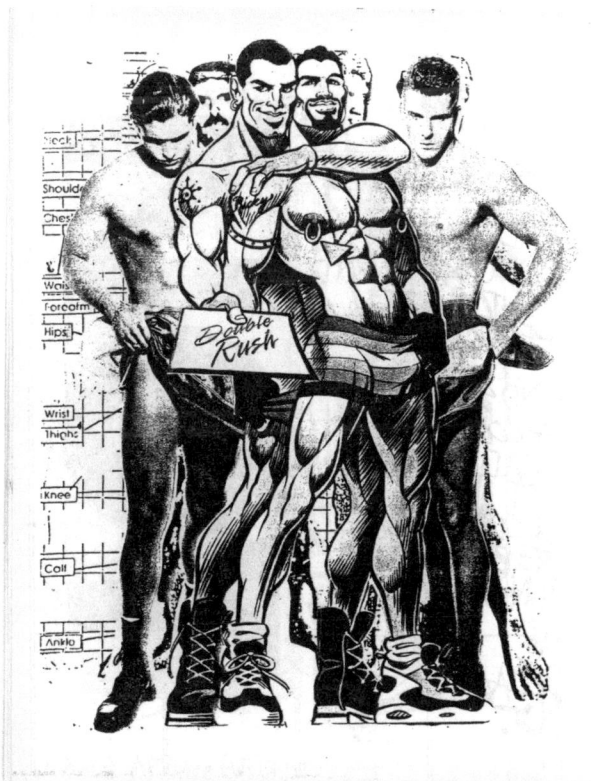

Double Rush

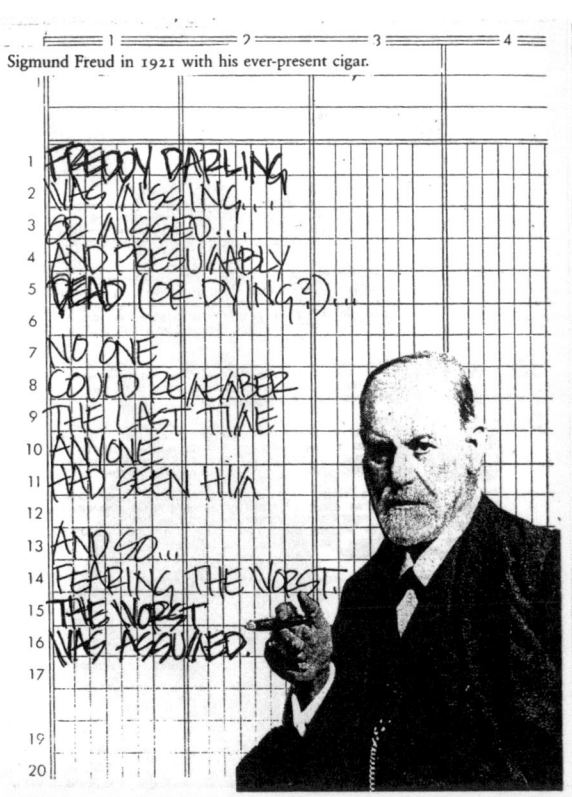

Sigmund Freud in 1921 with his ever-present cigar.

FREDDY DARLING
WAS MISSING...
OR MISSED...
AND PRESUMABLY
DEAD (OR DYING?)...

NO ONE
COULD REMEMBER
THE LAST TIME
ANYONE
HAD SEEN HIM

AND SO...
FEARING THE WORST...
THE WORST
WAS ASSUMED.

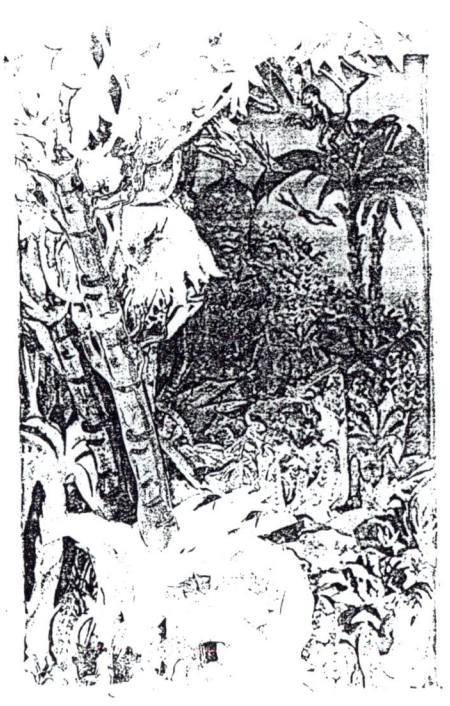

Once
upon a time
there was a story
about a little black boy,

but that story is not told
anymore
because people found the little black boy
to be an embarrassment.

Over time the little black boy had become
a reminder of slavery,
and over time he had become
a negative
racial stereotype.

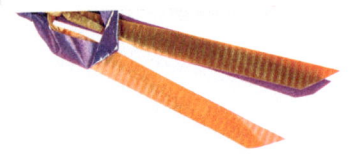

The Story of Little Black Sambo, September 2000
Photocopy, saddle stitched, with plastic foil ribbons,
5 ½ × 4 ¼ in. (14 × 10.8 cm)
Visual AIDS, New York

I would like to
redeem, reclaim, restore
my name.

I would like to speak
on my own
behalf.

I am that little black boy.

I am Sambo.

I was made fun of .
I came to be misunderstood .

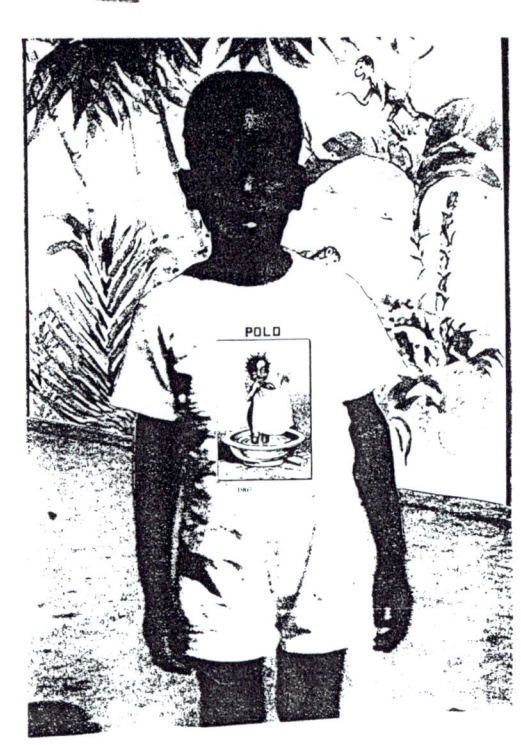

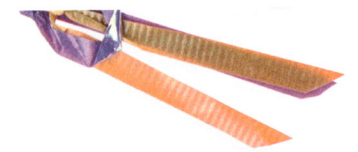

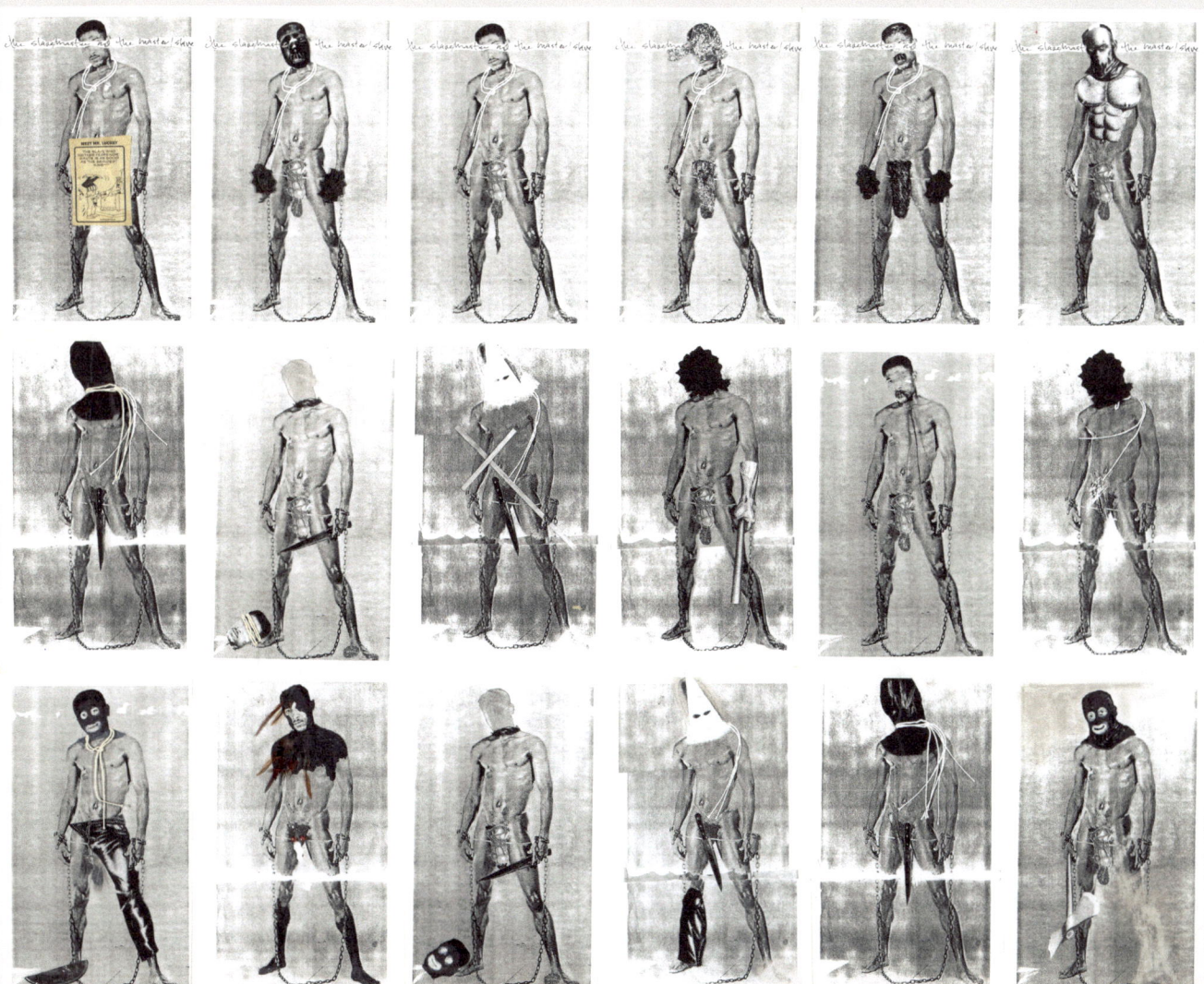

Nobly Nude (The Slave Master and the Master Slave), ca. 2000
Collage of photomechanical prints, newspaper, woven paper,
tape, string, staples, feathers, beads, with fiber-tipped pen and
metallic inks, 32 × 40 in. (81.3 × 101.6 cm)
The Art Institute of Chicago, purchased with funds provided by
Eric Ceputis and David W. Williams

5.

Critical Promiscuity, 2000–2020

The proliferation of queer and feminist zines that began in the late 1980s had subsided by the end of the 1990s—in part due to new publishing opportunities provided by the internet. Many artists, however, who had participated in these communities as young adults incorporated zine making into their studio practice during the first decade of the twenty-first century. K8 Hardy, who made zines as a teenager in Texas during the mid-1990s and later worked as an intern on Miranda July's *Joanie 4 Jackie* project, brought these countercultural energies and forms into her own artistic practice when she moved to New York in 2001. While participating in the Whitney Museum of American Art's Independent Study Program, Hardy co-founded, with Ginger Brooks Takahashi and Every Ocean Hughes (f.k.a. Emily Roysdon), the collective LTTR, which produced five issues of an eponymous zine between 2002 and 2006. The art historian Julia Bryan-Wilson has used the term "critical promiscuity" to describe *LTTR*'s collaborative and shapeshifting format as well as its capacious representations of sex and gender. In addition to collectively editing and producing *LTTR*, the group (joined by Ulrike Müller in 2005) also organized screenings, exhibitions, performances, read-ins, and workshops.

Many of the zine makers in this section used their publications to distribute art among their peers as well as to wider audiences. Paul Mpagi Sepuya's zine *Shoot* showcases his intimate photographs of mostly young gay men (one issue is dedicated to pictures of the artist himself), images that, soon after their publication, circulated on social media networks such as Myspace and Friendster. Several artists from Toronto continued to build on the legacy of *J.D.s.* Painter Paul P. and musician Joel Gibb's *Gay Goth Scene* zine comprises appropriated photographic images from 1970s gay porn magazines, collaged and altered with white correction fluid to depict a flourishing (if imaginary) queer Goth subculture, featuring bats, fangs, balaclavas, and witches' hats.

This period also witnessed projects aiming to distribute zines more widely and to assemble archives of zines by artists. While co-editing *LTTR*, Brooks Takahashi joined a group of Canadian and US artists to create the Projet Mobilivre-Bookmobile: an Airstream trailer transformed into a traveling exhibition of artists' books and zines. In an effort to challenge the localism and community-specificity of zines, Brooks Takahashi and her collaborators offered free public access to a rotating collection of more than four hundred works, as well as zine-making workshops and artists' talks.

New York proved to be a particularly fertile hub for such activities. From 2004 to 2010 AA Bronson led Printed Matter—the nonprofit organization dedicated to artists' publications—and in 2005 initiated the Printed Matter Art Book Fair; both have been crucial venues for promoting zines and establishing a canon of zines by artists. In 2008 Bronson and artists' book and zine collector Philip Aarons produced the pioneering compendium *Queer Zines*; the publication (which was expanded in 2013 to two volumes) features many of the zines in this chapter and is an important archive of these ephemeral and rare objects. This increased recognition continued with the migration of zines and related materials from closets and basements to archives and libraries at universities—such as the Riot Grrrl Collection at New York University's Fales Library— where many individuals who participated in zine cultures in the 1990s were now employed.

Terence Koh

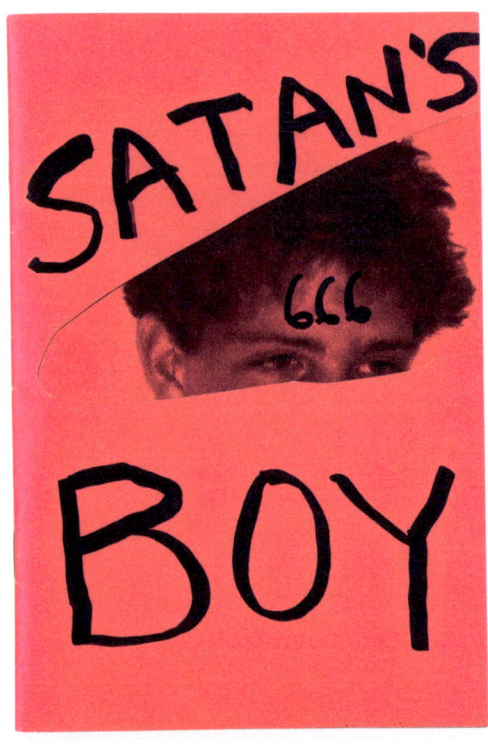

Satan's Boy, December 2004
Offset, saddle stitched, 7 ³⁄₁₆ × 4 ⁷⁄₈ in. (18.2 × 12.4 cm)
Collection Philip Aarons and Shelley Fox Aarons

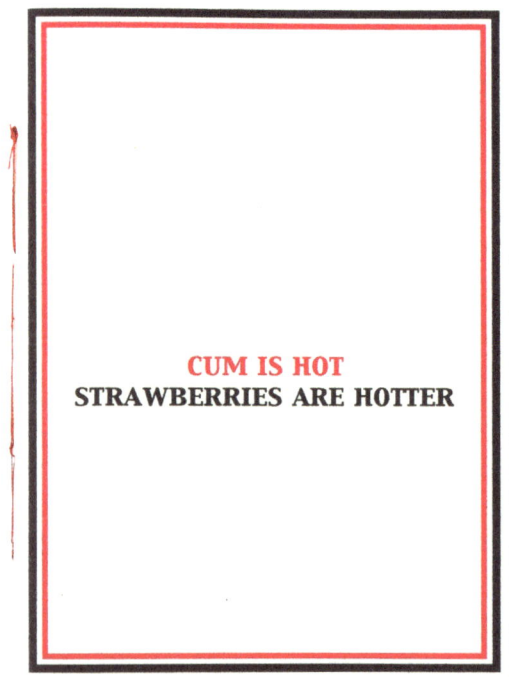

Cum Is Hot, Strawberries Are Hotter, 2003
Inkjet, hand stitched, 5 ¹⁄₁₆ × 3 ¹¹⁄₁₆ in. (12.9 × 9.4 cm)
Collection Philip Aarons and Shelley Fox Aarons

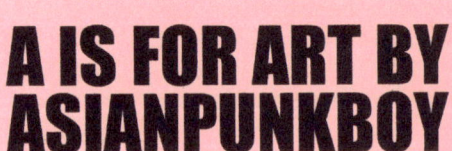

A Is for Art by asianpunkboy, January 2003
Inkjet, saddle stitched, 5 ½ × 4 ³⁄₁₆ in. (14 × 10.7 cm)
Collection Philip Aarons and Shelley Fox Aarons

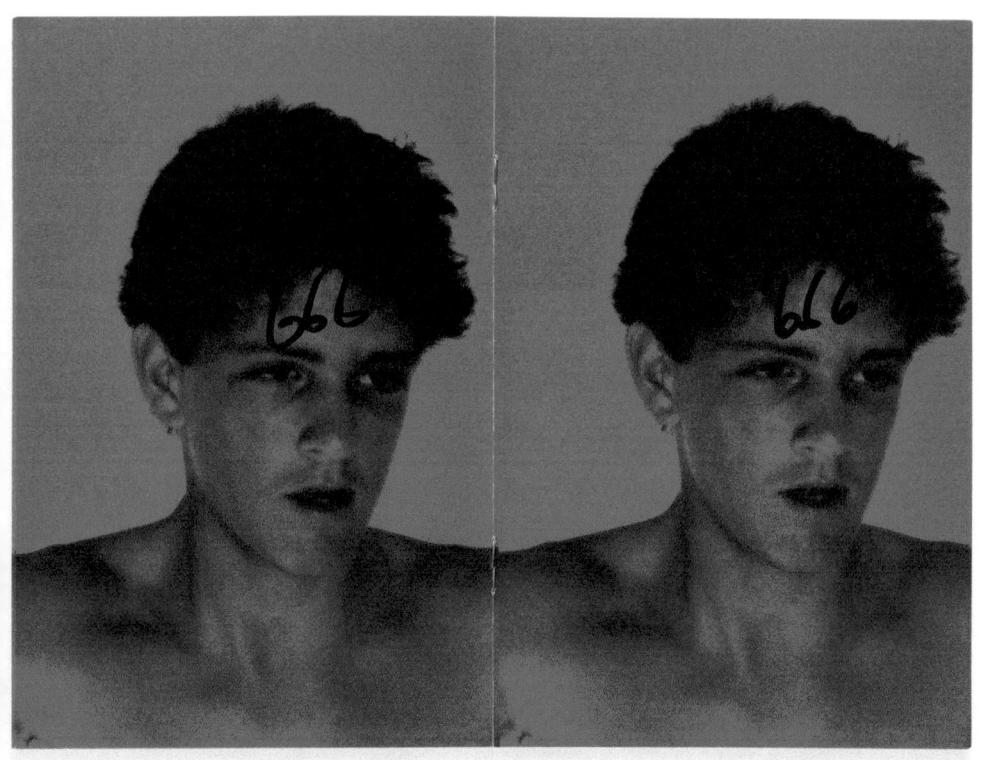

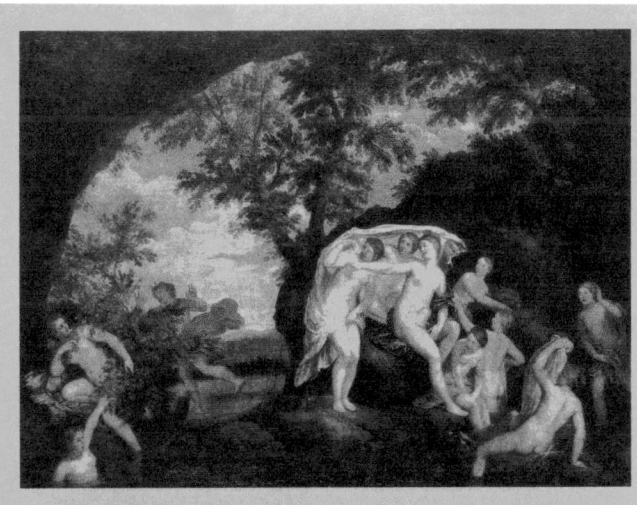

A IS FOR ALBANI.
A IS FOR ARC OF JUNIPER.
A IS FOR ALMOND MILK.
A TORN GRASP, ACCUMULATIVE ROOTS.
A JUMP TO FILL.

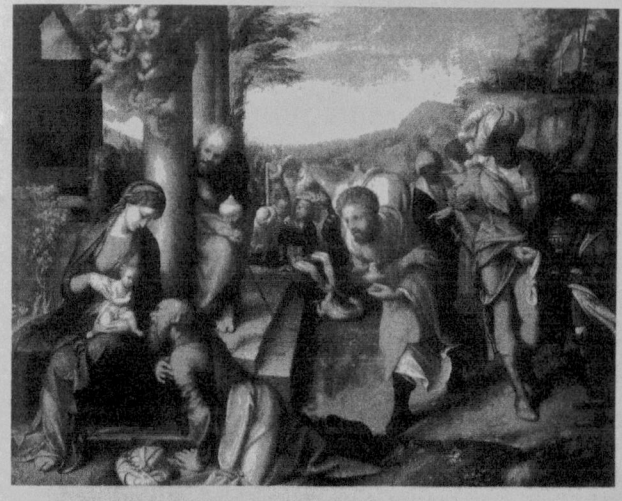

A IS FOR ALLEGRI
A DESTRUCTION ON MOUNT NYPTON.
A STRANGLED REED.
ANOINTED PEARL.
A BORROWED FLUTE.
A YELLOW RIVER.

Paul P. and Joel Gibb

→ *Gay Goth Scene*, no. 2, 2003
Photocopy, saddle stitched,
8 ½ × 5 ½ in. (21.5 × 14 cm)
Collection Philip Aarons and Shelley Fox Aarons

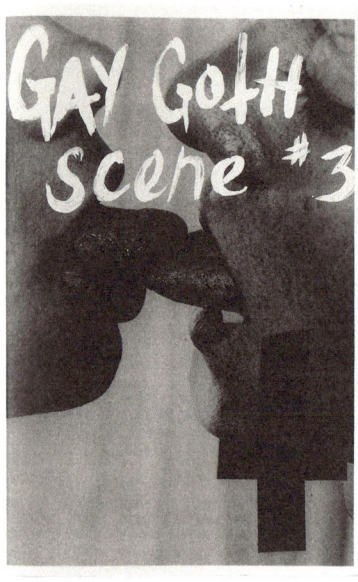

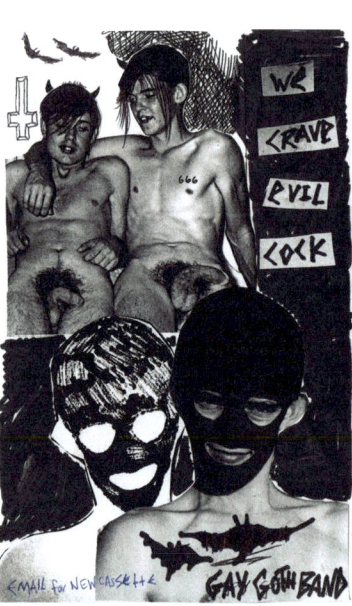

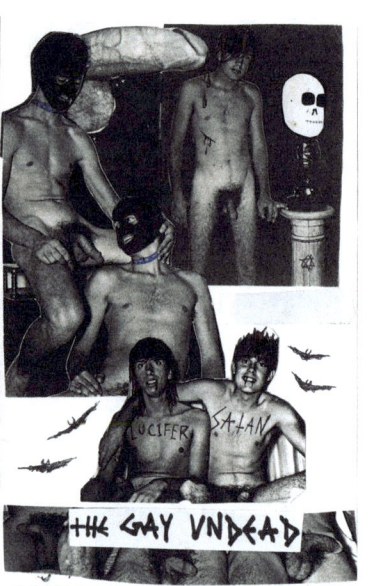

Gay Goth Scene, no. 3, 2016
Photocopy, saddle stitched,
8 ½ × 5 ½ in. (21.5 × 14 cm)
Collection Philip Aarons and Shelley Fox Aarons

Paste-up for *Gay Goth Scene*, no. 2, 2003
Photocopy, paper, glue, ink, correction fluid,
8 ½ × 11 in. (21.6 × 27.9 cm)
Collections the artists

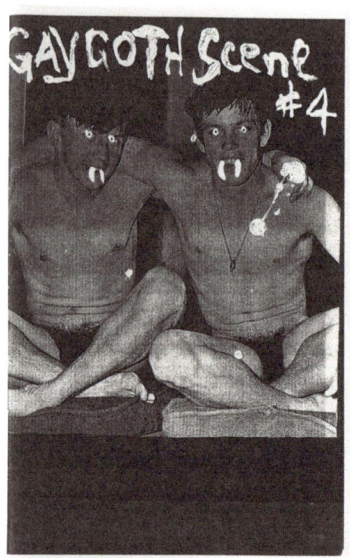

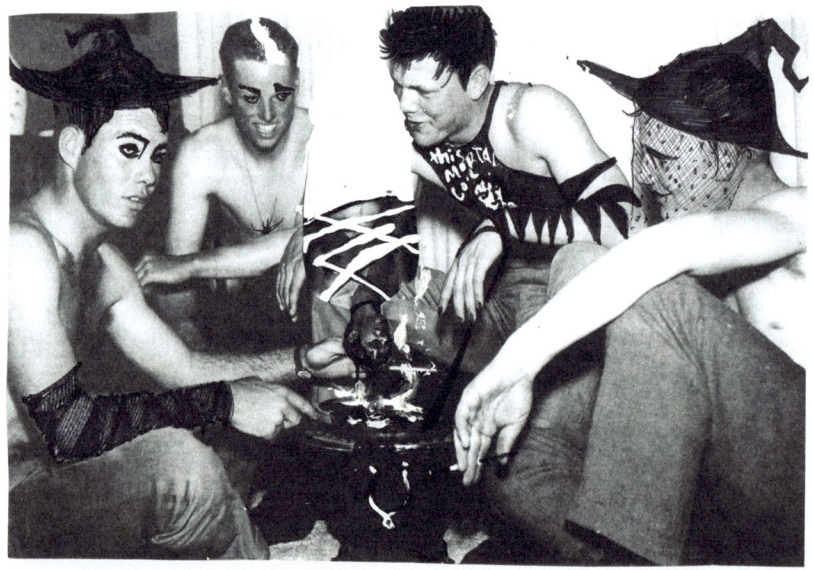

Gay Goth Scene, no. 4, 2016
Photocopy, saddle stitched,
8 ½ × 5 ½ in. (21.5 × 14 cm)
Collection Philip Aarons and Shelley Fox Aarons

Paste-up for *Gay Goth Scene*, no. 4, 2016
Photocopy, paper, glue, ink, correction fluid,
8 ½ × 11 in. (21.6 x 27.9 cm)
Collections the artists

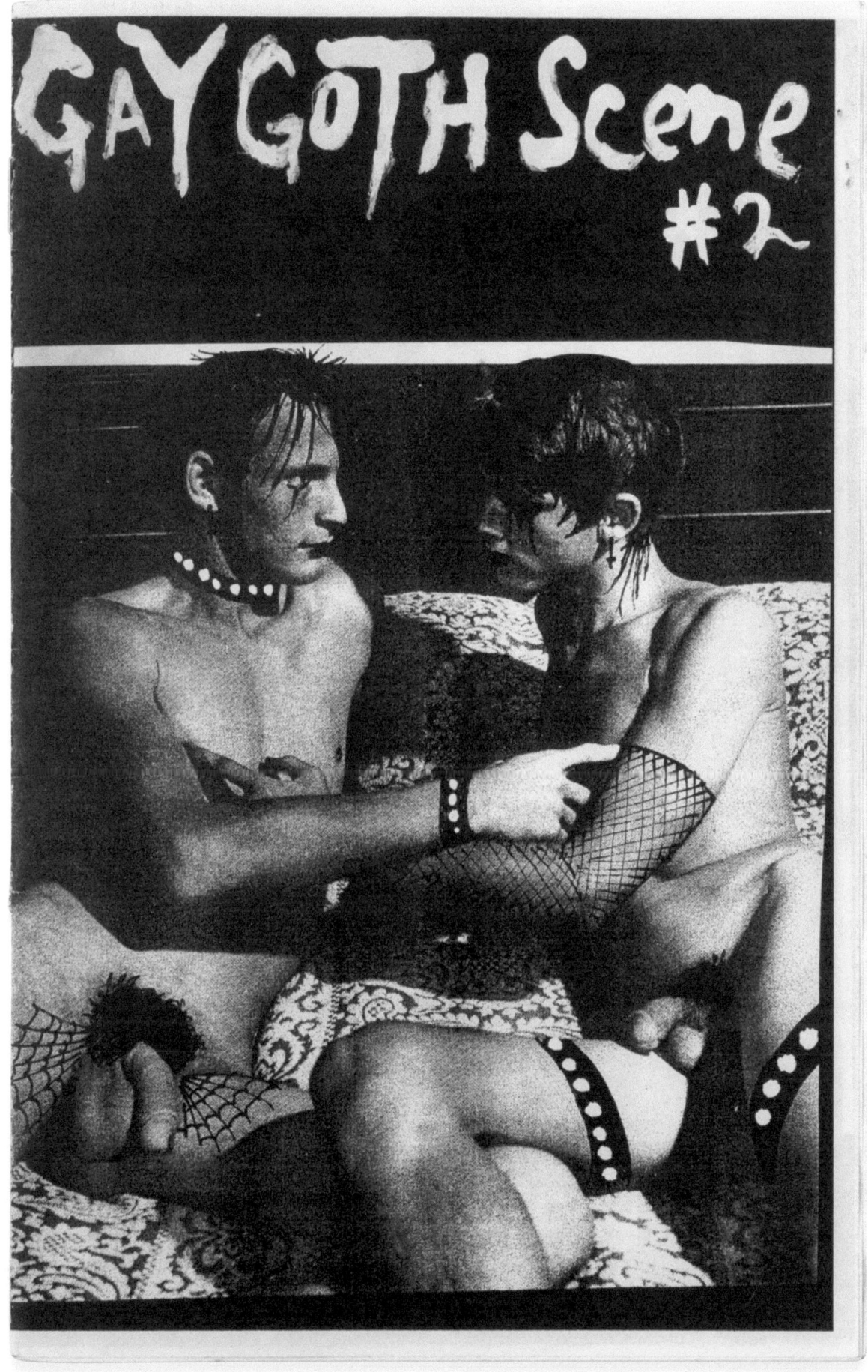

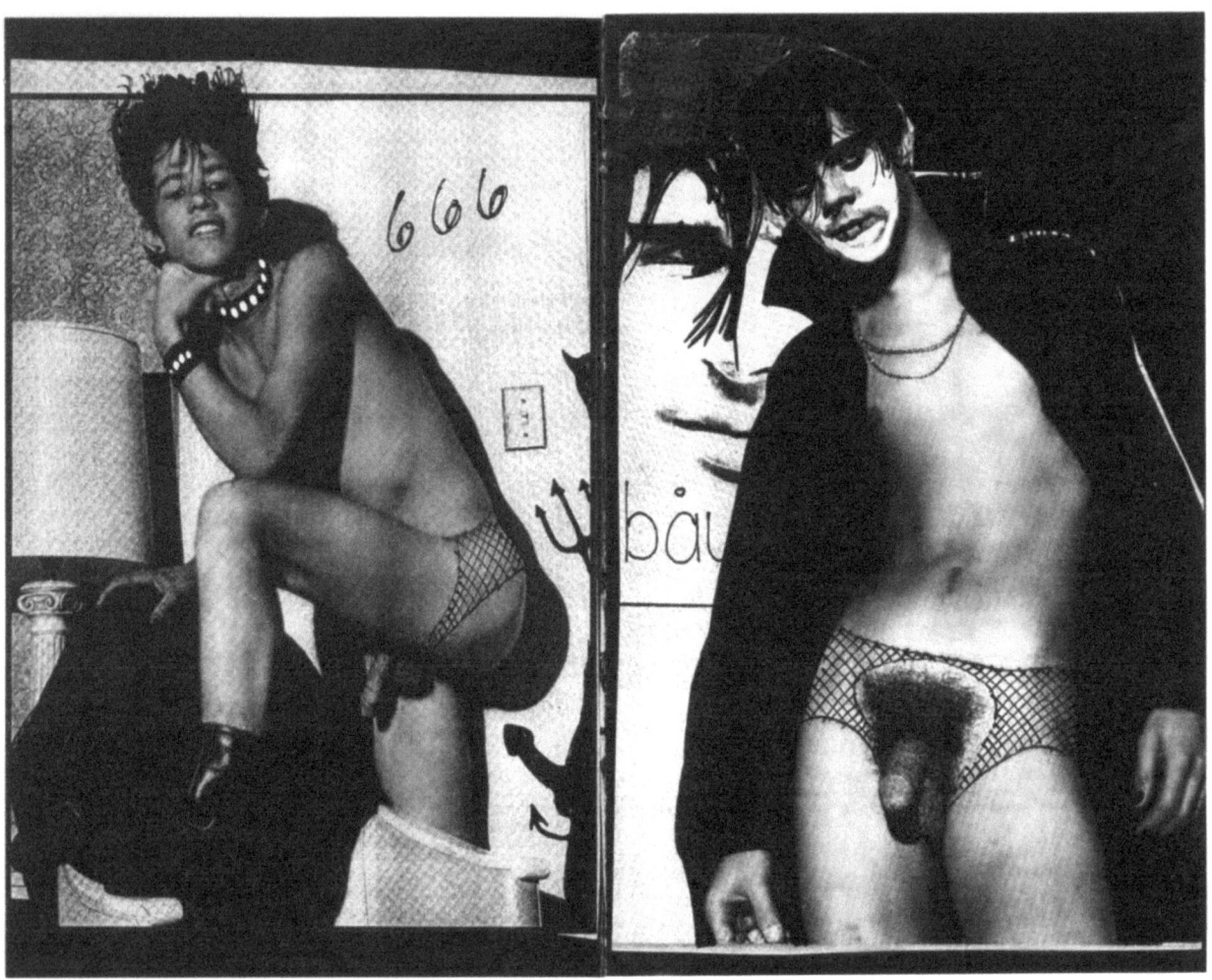

Gay Goth Scene, no. 2, 2003
Photocopy, saddle stitched,
8 ½ × 5 ½ in. (21.5 × 14 cm)
Collection Philip Aarons and Shelley Fox Aarons

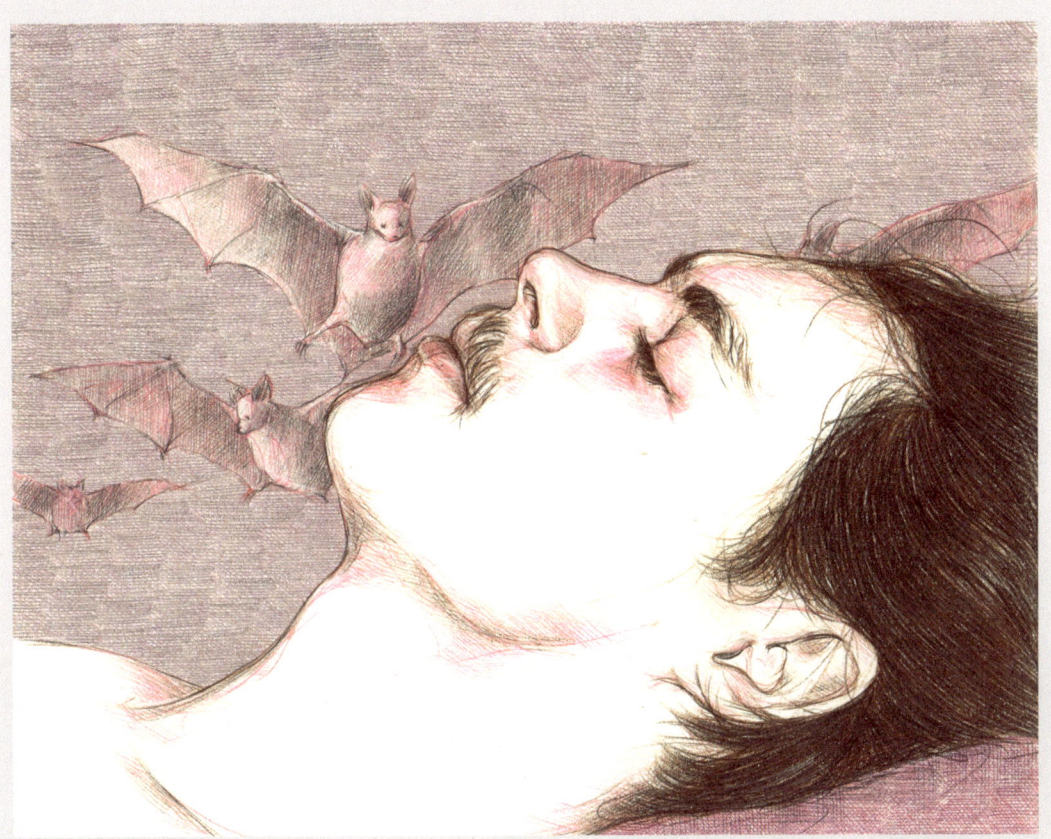

Paul P.
Untitled, 2003
Pencil and colored pencil on paper, 8½ × 11 in. (21.6 × 27.9 cm)
The Museum of Modern Art, New York. The Judith Rothschild
Foundation Contemporary Drawings Collection Gift

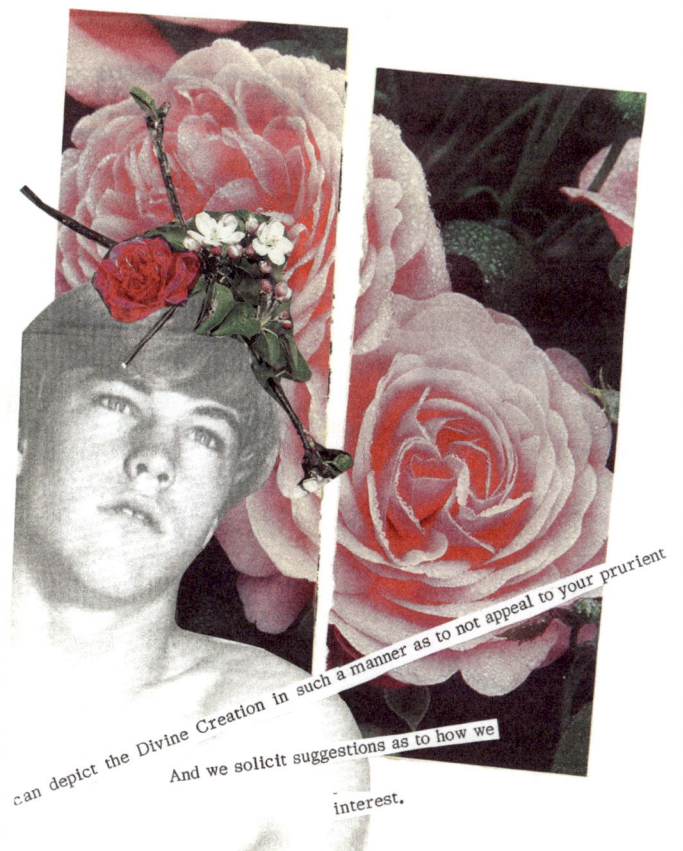

G. B. Jones and Paul P.
Untitled, 2002
Collage on paper, 11 × 8½ in. (27.9 × 21.6 cm)
Collection Paul P.

329

LTTR (Ginger Brooks Takahashi, K8 Hardy, Every Ocean Hughes, Ulrike Müller)

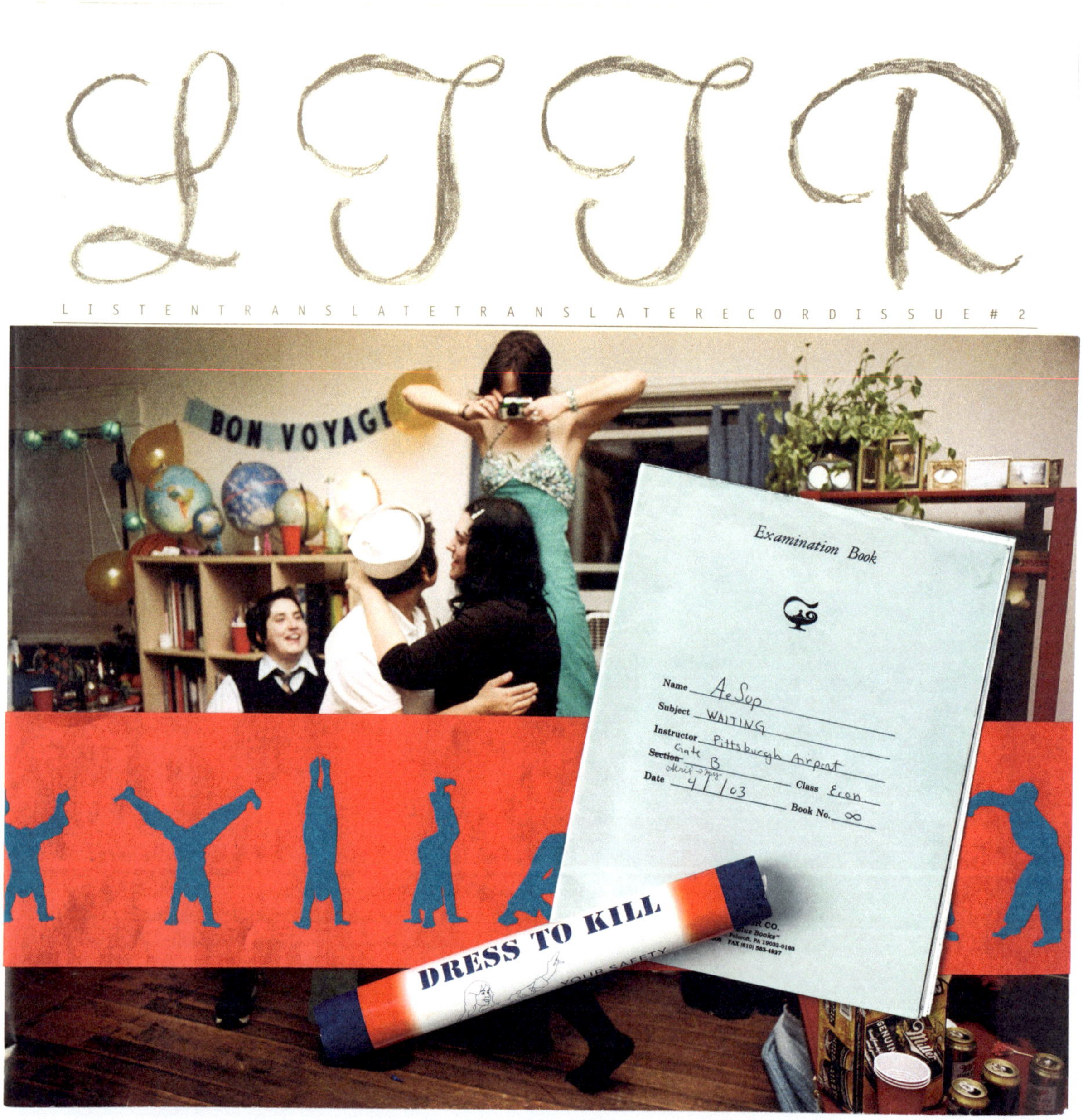

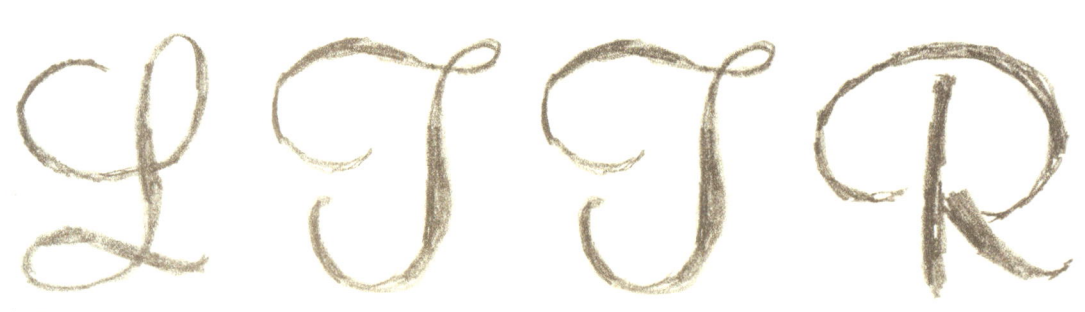

LTTR, no. 2, *Listen Translate Translate Record*, August 2003
Editors: Ginger Brooks Takahashi, K8 Hardy, Every Ocean Hughes
Offset, folded; with 1 booklet, 1 screenprinted band, 1 altered
tampon, compact disc, 12 ½ × 12 ½ in. (31.8 × 31.8 cm) overall
Collection Philip Aarons and Shelley Fox Aarons

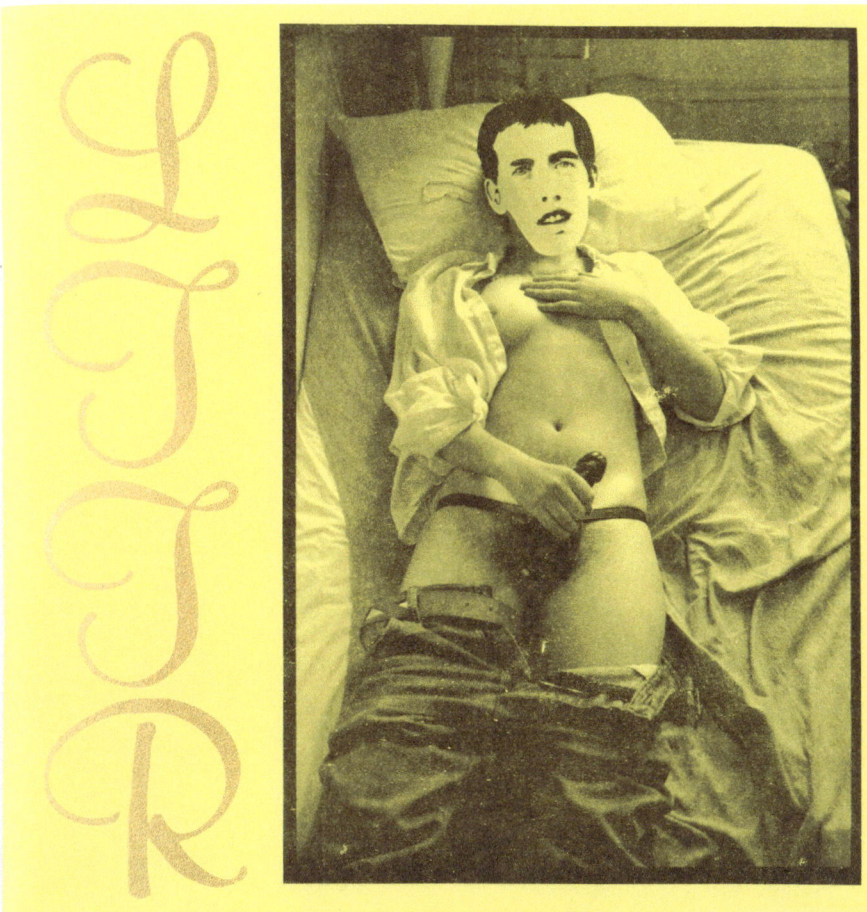

LTTR, no. 1, *Lesbians to the Rescue*, September 2002
Editors: Ginger Brooks Takahashi, K8 Hardy,
Every Ocean Hughes
Offset, saddle stitched, photocopy and letterpress on
yellow paper wrappers; with screenprinted door hanger,
bookmark, photocopied insert,
9 × 8½ in. (22.9 × 21.6 cm) overall
Collection Philip Aarons and Shelley Fox Aarons

LTTR, no. 3, *Practice More Failure*, July 2004
Editors: Ginger Brooks Takahashi, K8 Hardy, Every Ocean Hughes
Offset, thermal bound on cardboard; 1 poster, 1 pamphlet, and
1 envelope of printed cards; silkscreened manila envelope with
lavender ribbon, 10 × 7½ in. (25.4 × 19.1 cm) overall
Collection Philip Aarons and Shelley Fox Aarons

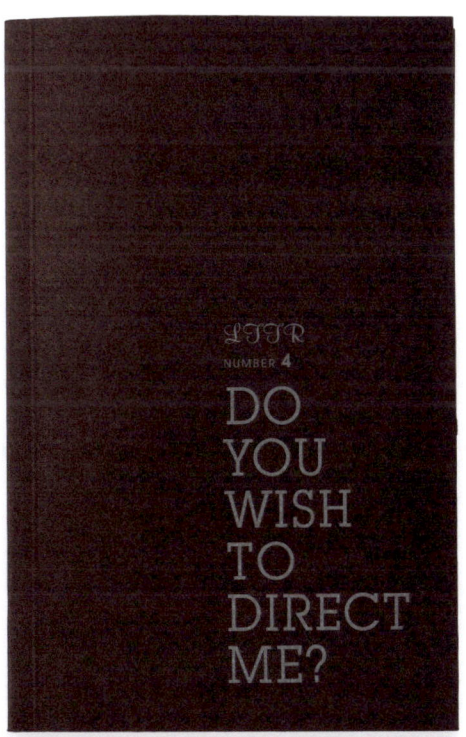

LTTR, no. 4, *Do You Wish to Direct Me?*, September 2005
Editors: Ginger Brooks Takahashi, K8 Hardy, Ulrike Müller,
Every Ocean Hughes, Lanka Tattersall
Offset, sewn binding, brown paper wrappers; with 1 glove,
1 bookmark, 1 silkscreen print, 3 painted pennies in bags,
8½ × 5½ in. (21.6 × 14 cm) overall
Collection Philip Aarons and Shelley Fox Aarons

LTTR, no. 5, *Positively Nasty*, October 2006
Editors: Ginger Brooks Takahashi, K8 Hardy, Ulrike Müller, Every Ocean Hughes
Offset, spiral bound, cardboard covers with gold stamping; resealable plastic bag
with 2 booklets, 2 cards, 2 posters, 1 belt, 12 × 9 in. (30.5 × 22.9 cm) overall
Collection Philip Aarons and Shelley Fox Aarons

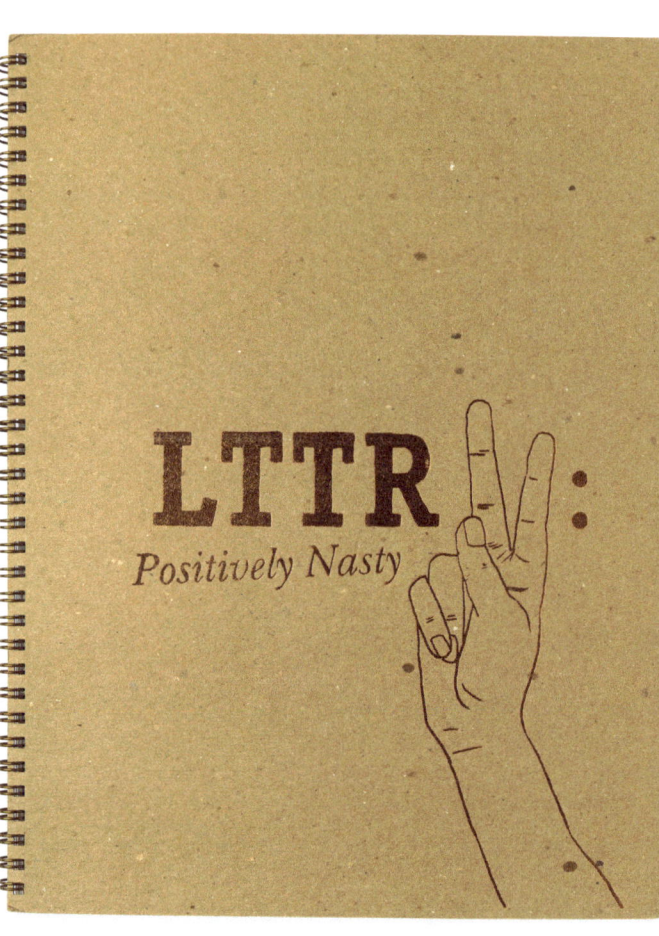

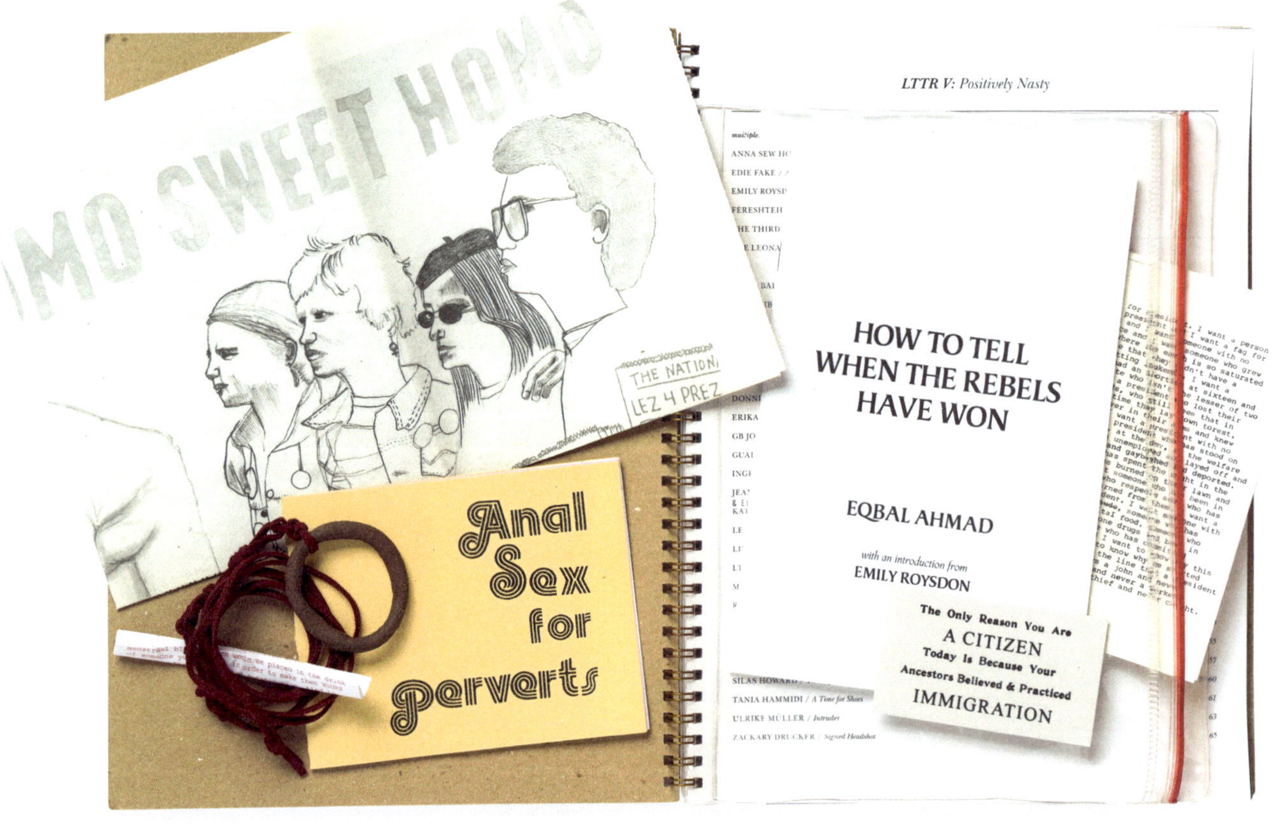

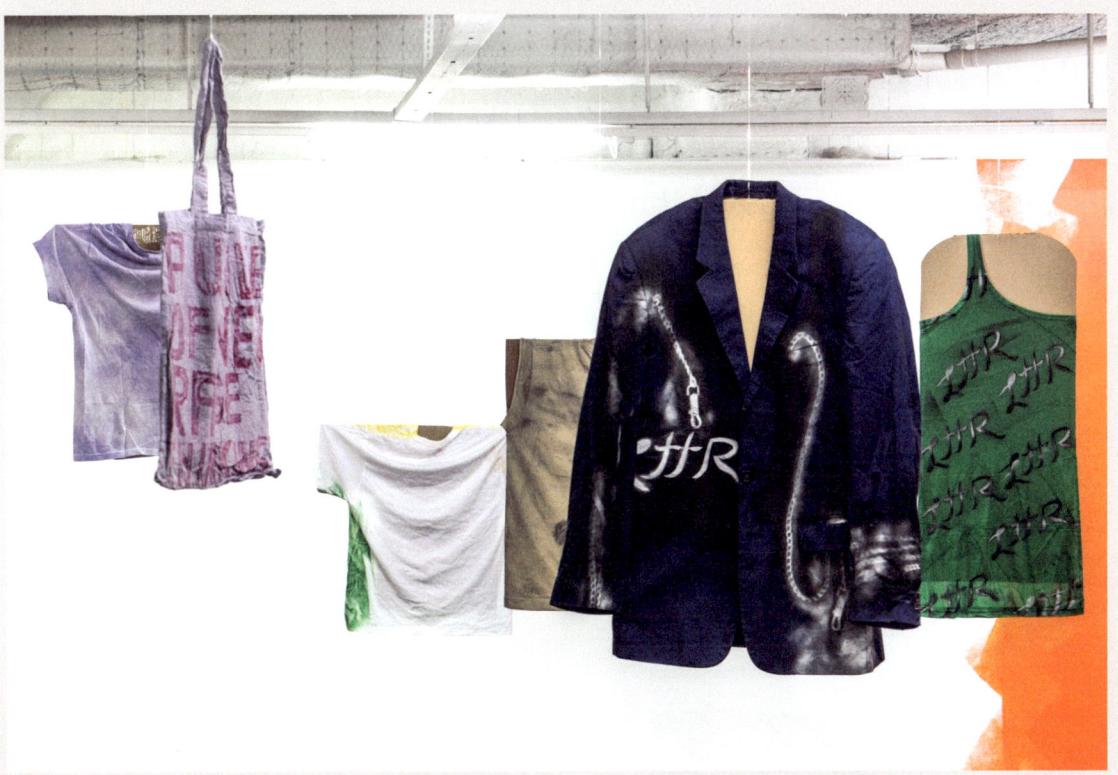

LTTR and friends (Ginger Brooks Takahashi, K8 Hardy, Ulrike Müller, Every
Ocean Hughes, Lanka Tattersall, with A. K. Burns and Dean Daderko)
Untitled collection of customized garments, 2015
Spray paint and screenprinting ink on various garments, dimensions variable
Collection the artists

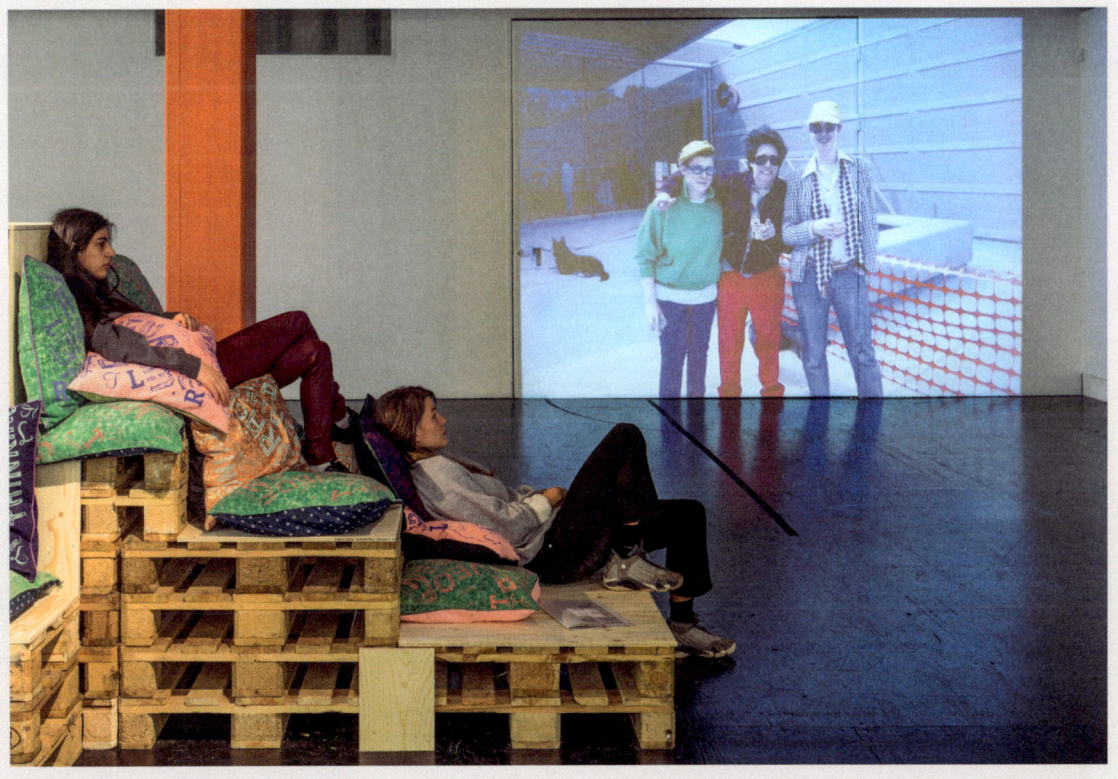

Untitled slideshow created for *Here We LTTR: 2002–2008*,
exhibition at Tensta Konsthall, 2015
Video made from digital photos, dimensions variable
Collection the artists

Bookmobile Collective (Ginger Brooks Takahashi, Courtney Dailey, Onya Hogan-Finlay, Leila Pourtavaf, Rebecca Watt)

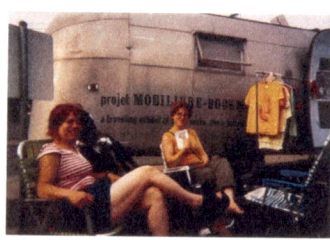

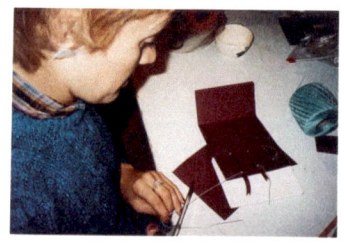

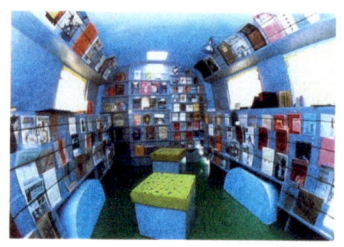

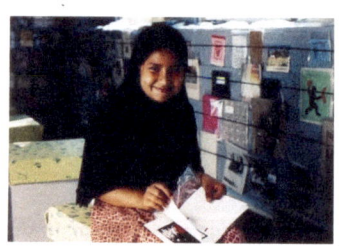

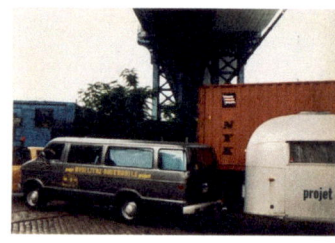

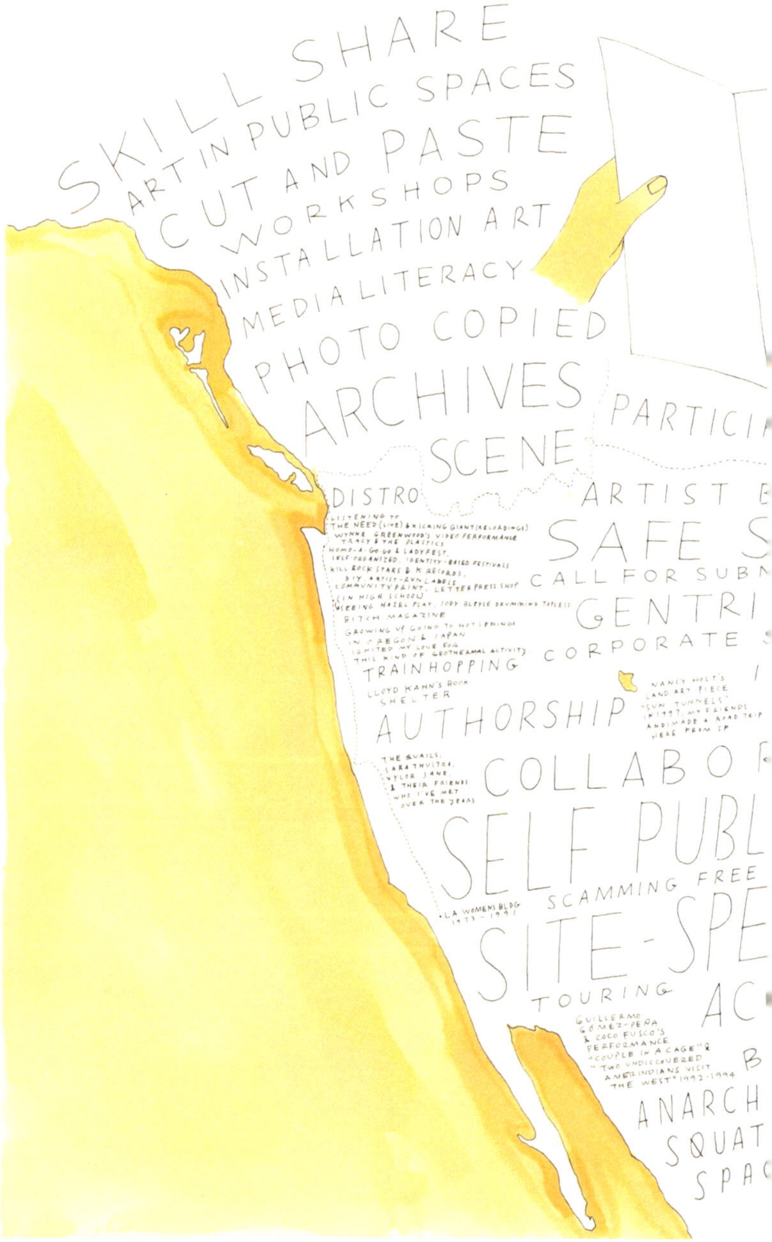

Ginger Brooks Takahashi
Map of Collected Influences, 2013
Ink on paper with chromogenic prints,
29 ¼ × 50 ¼ in. (74.3 × 127.6 cm)
Collection the artist

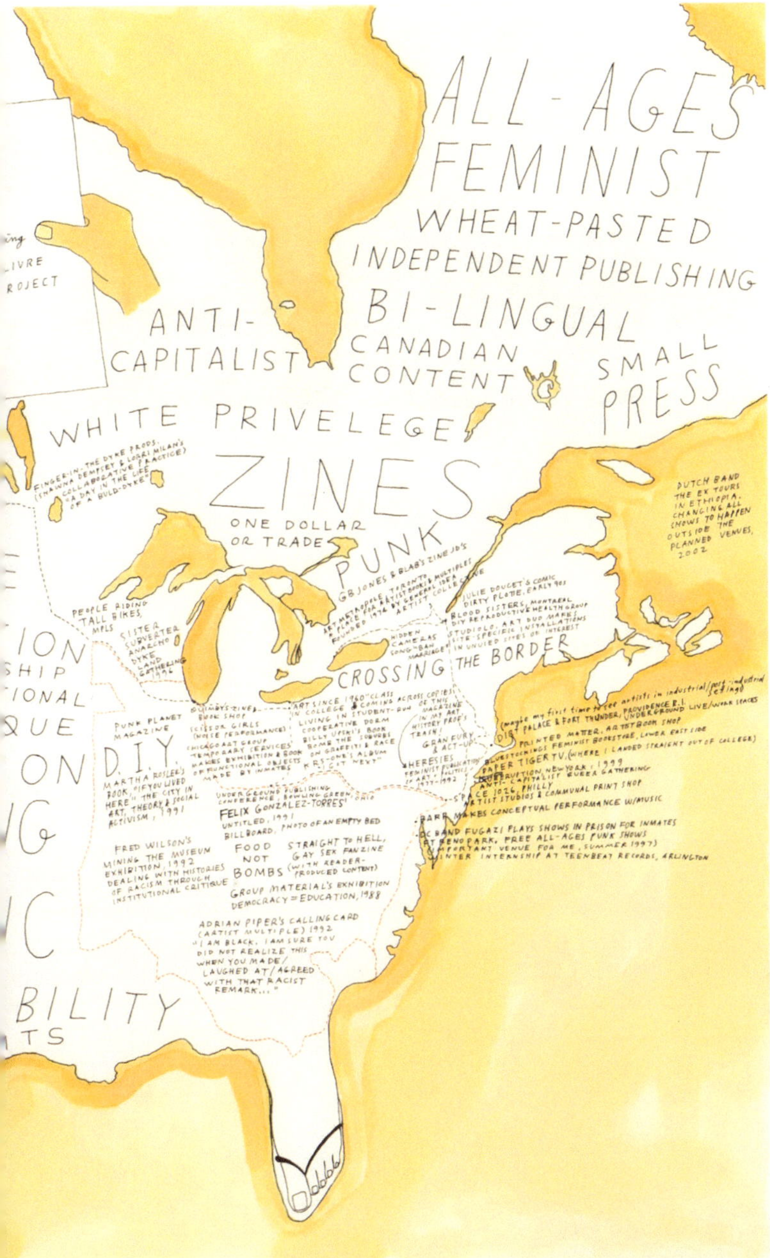

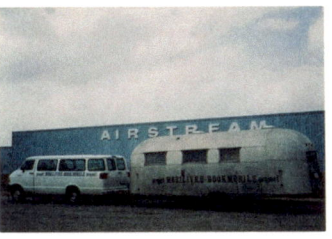

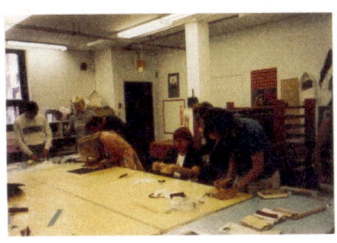

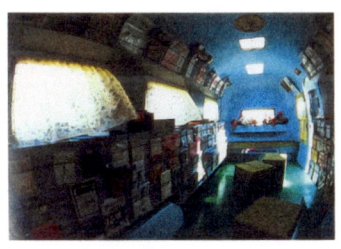

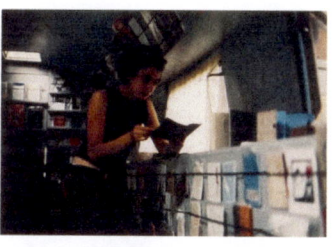

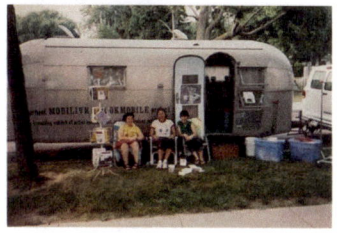

K8 Hardy

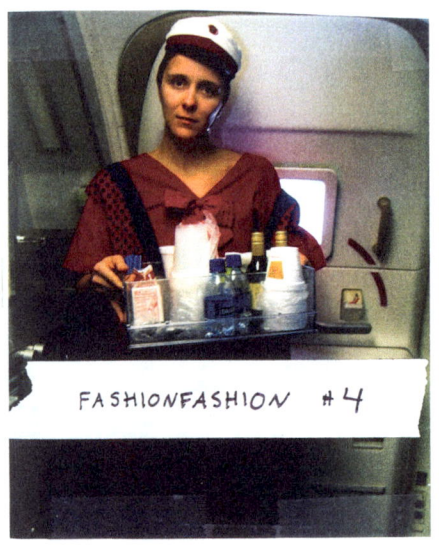

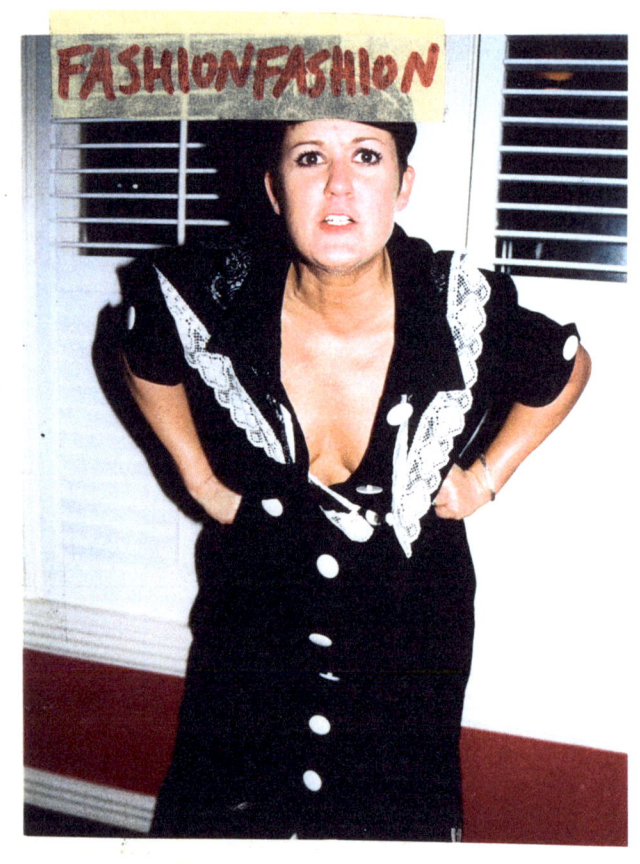

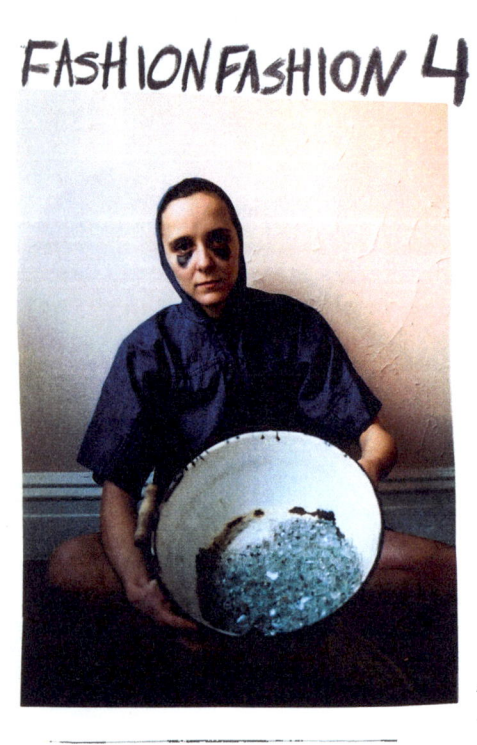

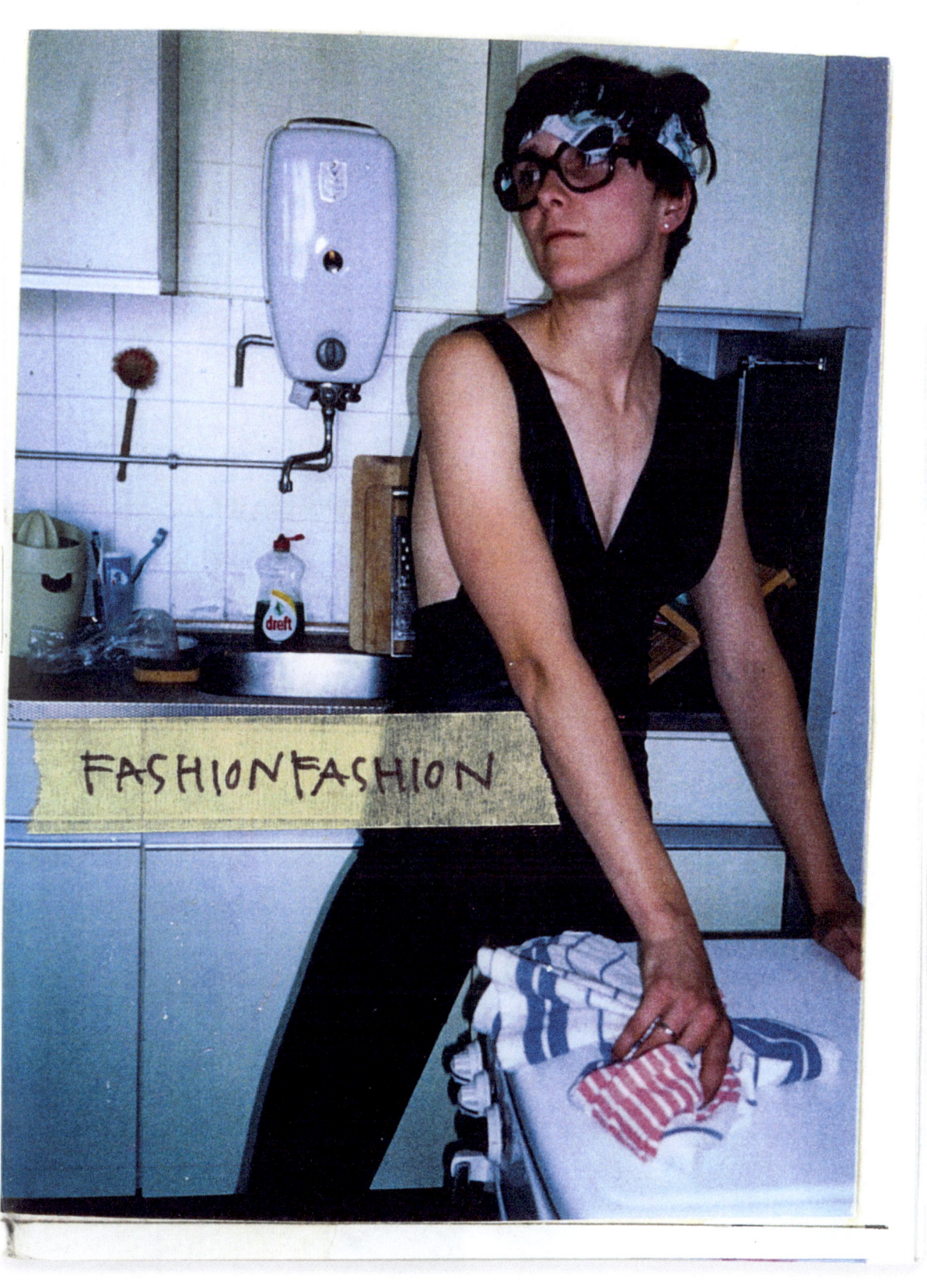

FashionFashion, nos. 1–4 (issue 3 misnumbered as 4), 2002–6
Photocopy, saddle stitched,
5 ½ × 4 ¼ in. (14 × 10.8 cm)
Collection Philip Aarons and Shelley Fox Aarons

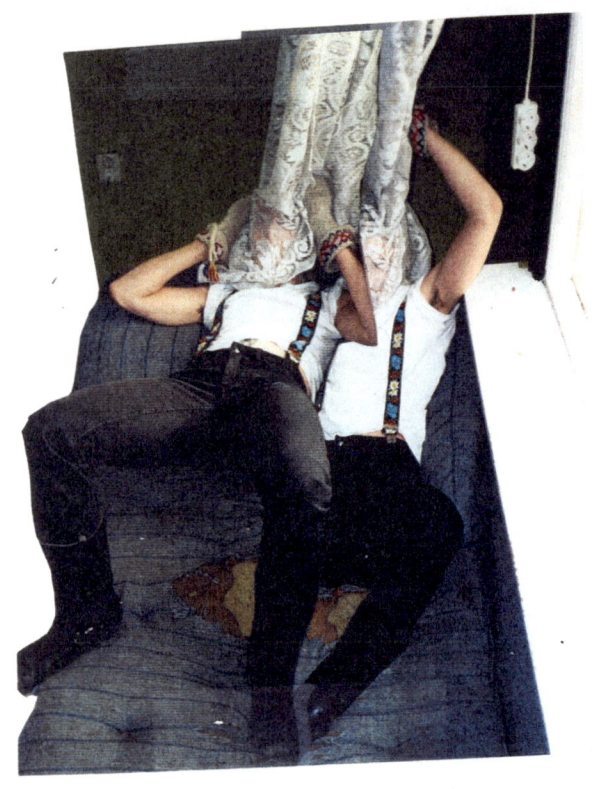

I CAN'T
VOMIT THE
RAZOR BLADES
of
~~Suiciety~~
society.

i can't get it. i can
sometimes reach.

TOPIC

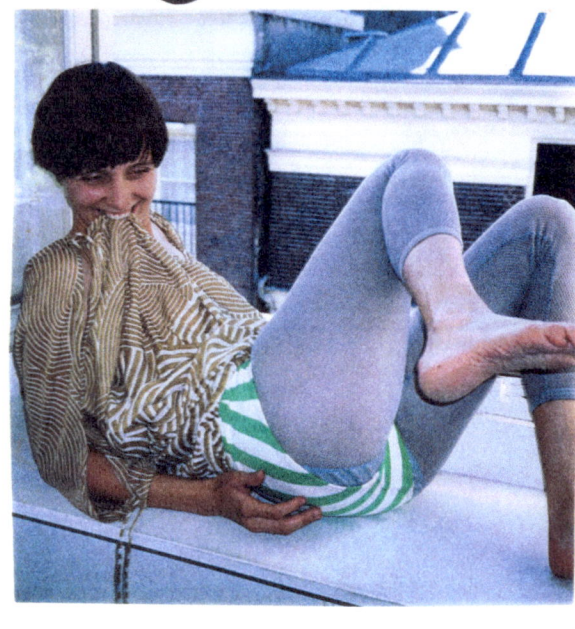

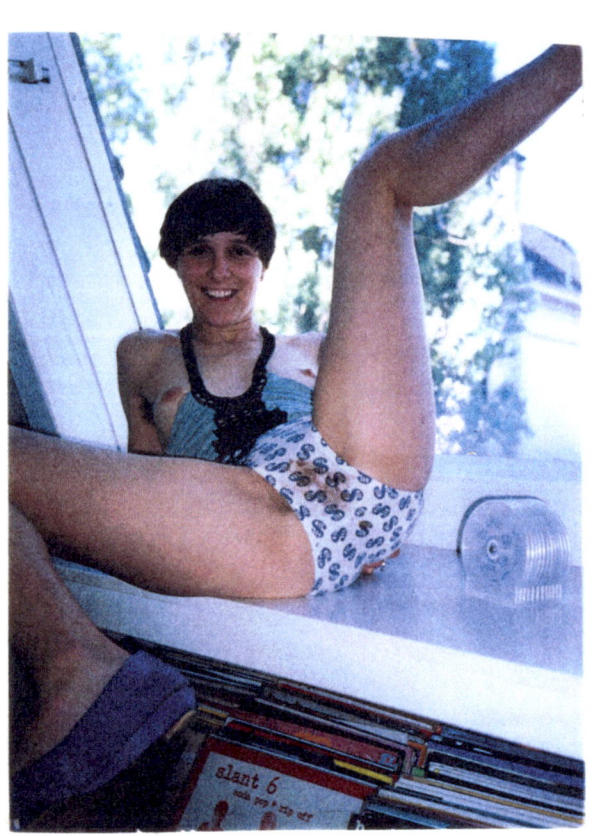

FashionFashion, no. 1, 2002
Photocopy, saddle stitched, 5½ × 4¼ in. (14 × 10.8 cm)
Collection Philip Aarons and Shelley Fox Aarons

FashionFashion, no. 4, 2006
Photocopy, saddle stitched, 5 ½ × 4 ¼ in. (14 × 10.8 cm)
Collection Philip Aarons and Shelley Fox Aarons

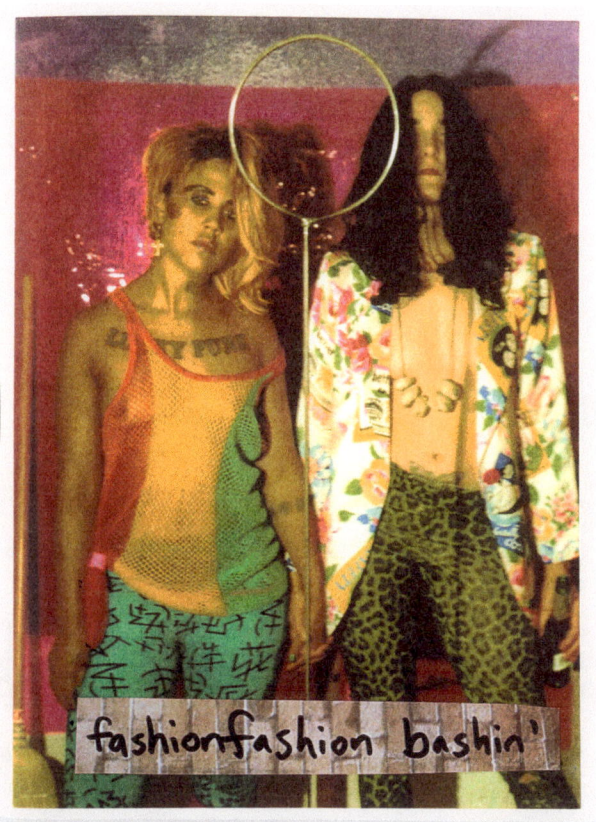

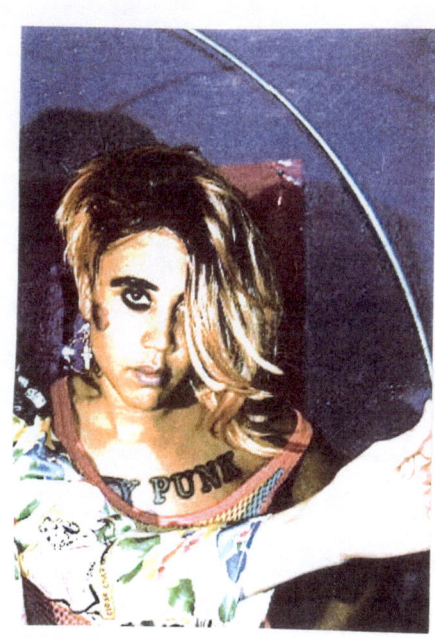

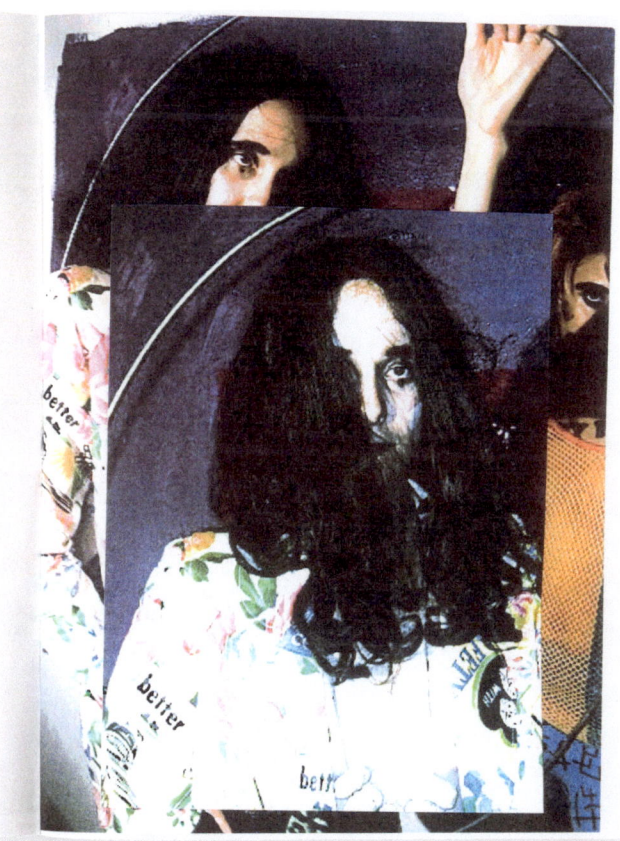

FashionFashion Bashin', 2010
Photocopy, saddle stitched, 5 ½ × 4 ¼ in. (14 × 10.8 cm)
Collection Philip Aarons and Shelley Fox Aarons

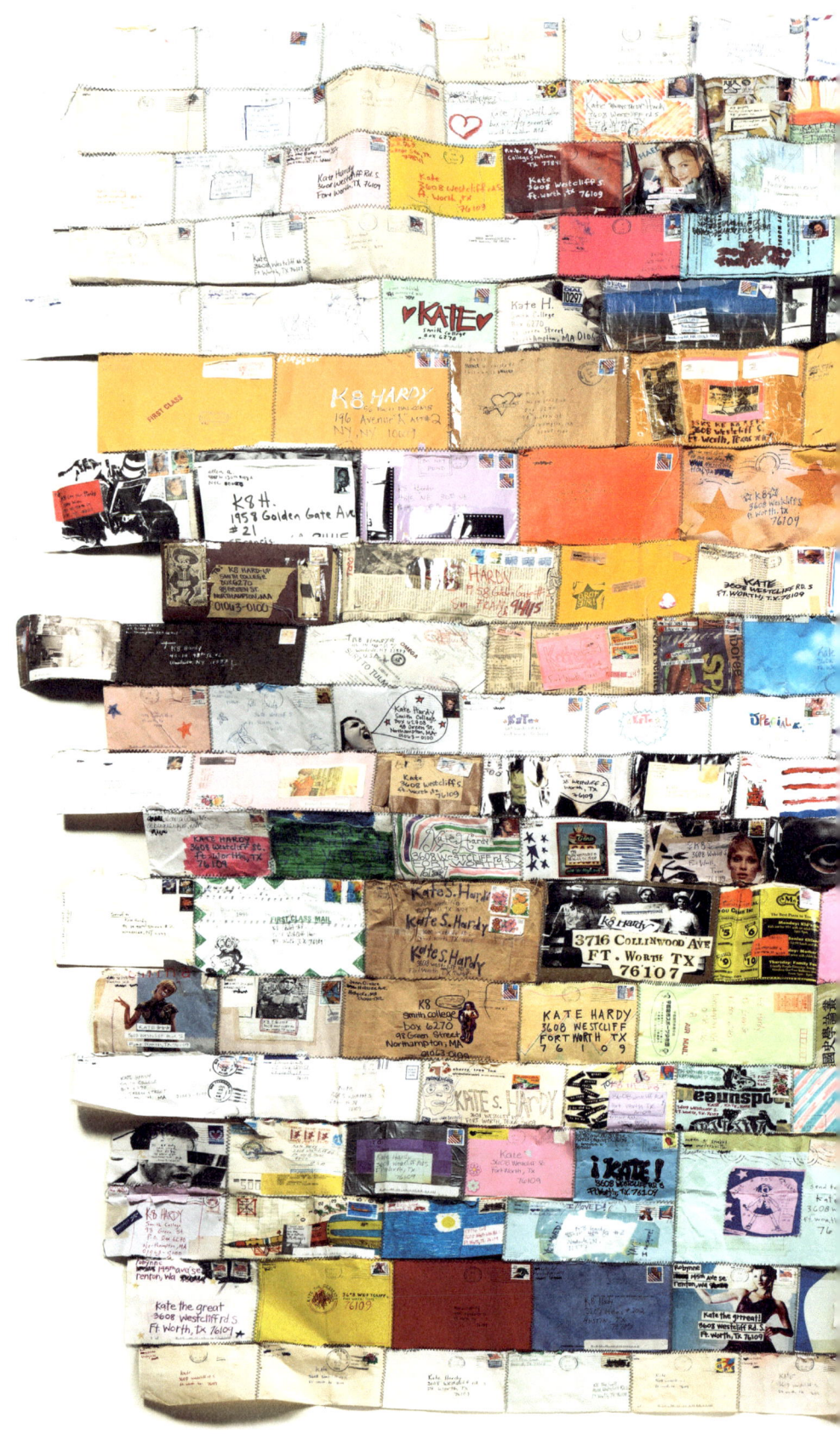

340

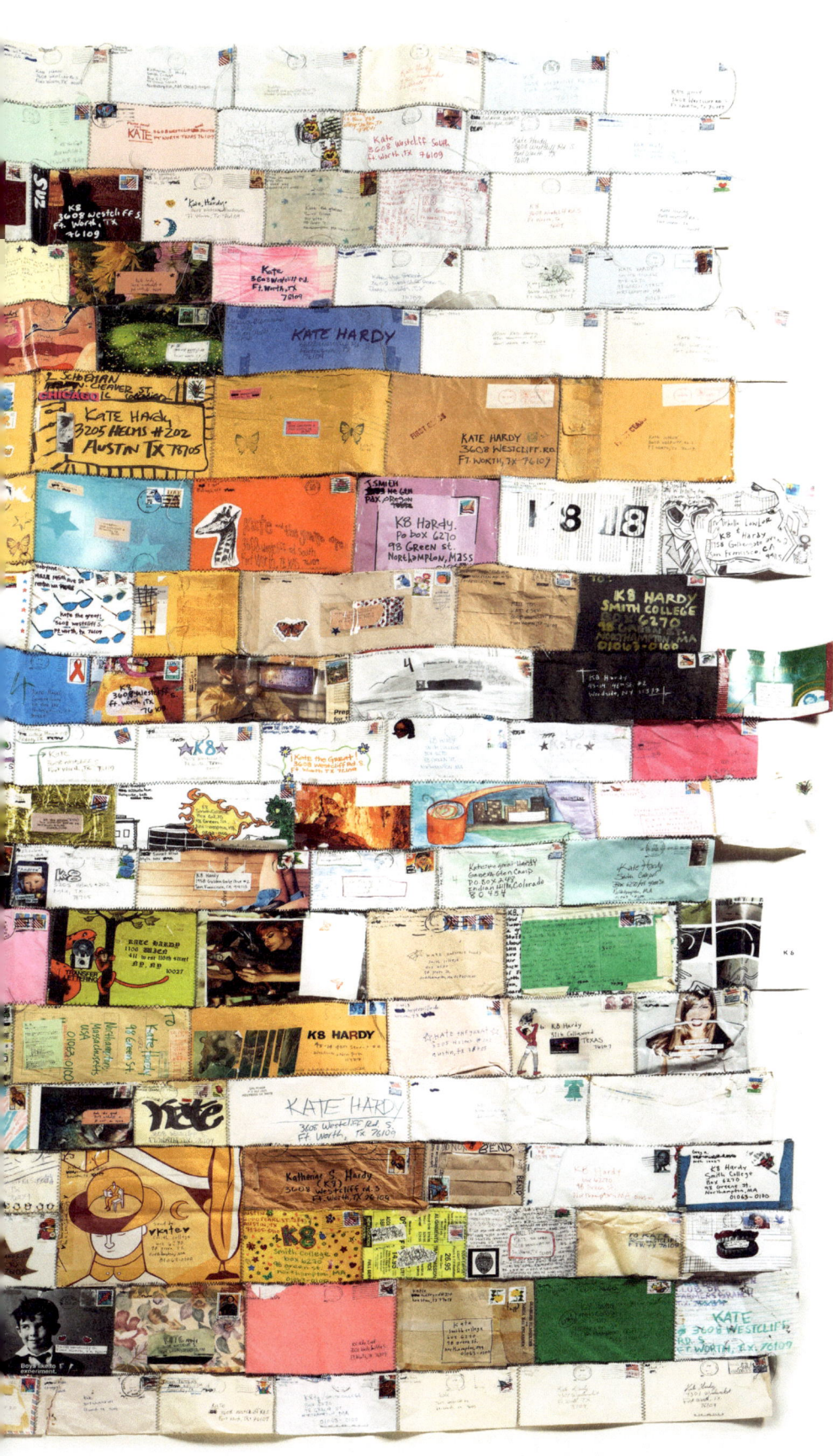

Envelope Quilt, 1994–2002
Paper, envelopes, tape, thread, glue, 96 × 60 in. (243.8 × 152.4 cm)
Collection the artist

In Love and Rage: The Revolutionary Counter-Mood of Zine Culture

Tavia Nyong'o

Punk has a hundred origin stories and all of them are true. As a community, it begins both developmentally and historically with adolescence, a stage of life that became newly salient in the post–World War II era, as punk historian Jon Savage observes in *Teenage: The Creation of Youth Culture*.[1] Before it was alchemized into a subcultural style that could be exploited for commercial gain, "punk" simply referred to anything juvenile, misshapen, of little or no account.[2] Punk graduated into a career. Punk writers today receive laureates; punk music is sold in deluxe boxed sets; and museum retrospectives of punk-era art are mounted. Some punks have even grown old enough to become cranks and reactionaries. But in the ephemeral archive of punk zines are told stories of punk's genesis that defy any single summary narrative or telos. Genealogy, Michel Foucault teaches us, promises origin but reveals dispersal.[3] The faith of punk lies in the intention and imperative always to begin again.

To begin again, one must free oneself from the tyranny of veracity. After all, the archive was established by the powerful in order to monopolize access to the past, as Jacques Derrida has shown.[4] Modern times have dispelled the "aura" of the work of art—to cite Walter Benjamin— and the work of art can now freely and cheaply circulate by means of its reproduction.[5] In the wake of the anti-systemic movements of the 1960s, the stage was set for the liberation of creative inventiveness from the constraints of state, religion, and social elites.[6] Punks are born free, and yet everywhere they are in chains. The ephemeral evidence of zines establishes an anti-systemic "counter-archive" of protest against this bondage and offers a road map with which to escape oppression—for all who are brave (or desperate) enough to find and follow it.[7]

It may seem implausible to present a tradition of punk aesthetics for current and future generations to emulate. Karl Marx warned that "the tradition of all dead generations weighs like a nightmare on the brains of the living."[8] Some histories of punk are indeed that kind of nightmare, just as some forays into the zine archive produce an infinity of broken links, undated documents, and contradictory or worthless information. The punk spirit of revolt and refusal would appear to be badly served by the very effort to preserve, systematize, and transmit that spirit. And yet to simply identify punk with rebellion for the heck of it would be to succumb to an anti-intellectualism that is both oedipal and normative: zines form one of the "thousand plateaus" that Gilles Deleuze and Félix Guattari associate with the anti-oedipal politics of resistance they heralded in their 1970s-era writings.[9] If we understand the genealogy of punk zines in the terms of Deleuze and Guattari: that is to say, as *rhizomatic* rather than arborescent, we may sidestep the weight of tradition, authority, and even veracity, and embrace this queer counter-archive as a set of tools and techniques for anti-fascist living.

Vaginal Davis is a paragon of punk performativity, and the lore of her zine archive offers an approximation of what I am getting at here.[10] Davis named herself in homage to the Black lesbian communist revolutionary Angela Davis, and has modeled her drag persona on the take-no-prisoners spirit of her own mother, a community activist who was inspired by Black power and liberation theology in the 1960s. "I'm so intertwined with my mother,"[11] Davis has said. "My whole career as an artist, and all of my visual art, is basically co-opting my mother." I have elsewhere sought to characterize Davis's mode of fabulation as projecting her audiences into a space of unverifiable possibility: the space of Black revolutionary queer utopia does not exist on any map, nor can it be located with the help of any GPS.[12] Beginning with *Dowager* (1972–75) and rising to a certain apogee of notoriety with **Fertile La Toyah Jackson Magazine** (1987–91), → 172–75 Davis's zines have long provided me with my own personal origin myth for zine culture.

In 2015 Davis discussed how her art pedagogy is grounded in the queercore movement of the 1970s and its analogue mode of production:

> When you're in one of my seminars, I sort of art-direct your entire life. You start learning how to do analogue things instead of [being] focused on gadgetries, and writing letters via post, the old-fashioned way. Because that's how everyone in the queer-core scene throughout the whole world communicated with each other: through these weird letters—we had photos and drawings and paintings and ephemera. Introducing that to younger people, it's such a different world.[13]

Valorizing the weird, the queer, the old-fashioned, and the handmade, Davis thus offers a set of clues as to how a trans-revolutionary "counter-mood" is made. Let's begin here, with Davis's potent stew of punk attitude, Black revolutionary mothering, and the utopian project of imagining and enacting a different world through scrawled drawings, cheap instruments, and transgressive lyrics. Beginning the story of punk zines with *Dowager* brings to the fore fabulation, transgender aesthetics, and genealogies of Black radicalism. This is my origin story, and I'm sticking to it.

II

In his valuable 2012 essay "How a Revolutionary Counter-Mood is Made," Jonathan Flatley writes:

> Only within a mood or by way of mood can we encounter things in the world as mattering to us. In an important sense, a mood creates our world at a given moment. Thus, in some moods collective political action might not even enter one's consciousness except as something impossible, futile, foolish, or obscure. But then, with a shift in mood, organized political resistance all of a sudden seems obvious, achievable, and vital, and it makes urgent and complete sense to storm the Winter Palace, to occupy Wall Street, or to strike. How do we get from one mood to another? Inasmuch as moods are a fundamental mode of being for Heidegger, we are never not in a mood. Our moods do, however, shift and change, and indeed Heidegger asserts that the only way we can "master" mood is by way of what he calls "counter-moods."[14]

In this passage Flatley describes a process by which our individual and collective attunement to the world can be altered by ourselves and others.[15] Over the course of the essay, Flatley shifts from Heidegger—who, he laments, "did not offer many tools to help us see how counter-moods might be invoked or directed"—to a close visual and textual analysis of the radical publication *DRUM*, "a modest, weekly factory newspaper or newsletter" produced and distributed by the Dodge Revolutionary Union Movement (DRUM) of Black autoworkers in Hamtramck, Michigan (the publication ran from 1968 to around 1975).[16] Flatley concludes that *DRUM* did not seek to instill a revolutionary counter-mood among Black autoworkers— oppressed by both racism and class exploitation—through standard "political education," or by disseminating Marxist-Leninist ideology. It was not through "understanding" but through "feeling" that the editors and writers of *DRUM* aimed to reach their fellow workers.[17] Instead of translating theory into praxis, Flatley argues, *DRUM*'s makers sought to create a "shift in mood" through close descriptions of everyday instances of humiliation, abuse, and exploitation at the hands of the Dodge Main auto plant owners, managers, and guards. The nuance to this account of *affect* (a field that encompasses feeling, mood, counter-mood, and taking action) is that "affects" are not inner, psychological states, but more subjective, coming to the subject (in this case, the reader) from without.

The kernel of Flatley's aesthetic theory is his contention that the experience of "reading-with" others can galvanize subjects, solidify community, and generate action, as seen in the Dodge workers' response to reading in *DRUM* about a coworker's humiliation and firing:

> The reading experience brings one into contact with these other readers, whose *reading-with* may contribute to the transformative thrill or shudder that, in some accounts, characterizes one kind of "aesthetic feeling." Readers might find an image of this transference of feeling from the person one is reading *about* to the others one is reading *with*, and its transformative effect, in the description of the workers on the line who, [once] a revolutionary counter-mood is made after witnessing the mistreatment of [their coworker] Willie Brookins, rally to his support, refuse to work, and greet the Hamtramck police with "a hail of washers, bolts and nuts and cat calls." Sharing a feeling with Brookins and expressing solidarity with him becomes solidarity with the other workers, a solidarity that leads directly to action.[18]

DRUM, although a hand-distributed underground publication, belonged to a recognizable tradition of leftist print culture. Flatley's focus is on the traditional setting of radical or revolutionary politics: a worksite. His aim is to show how action and solidarity, however autonomous or "spontaneous," relies on a process by which "the transformative thrill or shudder" of reading—the aesthetic encounter of *someone like us*—is required in order to produce the realization that the ostensibly bearable is in fact unbearable, that the compulsory can be rejected, that the master can be overthrown and the tools of production reclaimed and redistributed. Simply by describing an event from a new standpoint, that event can be shifted. Through reading the account of the mistreatment and firing of Willie Brookins, readers of *DRUM* experienced both *love* (which is, in the words of Black feminist theorist bell hooks, "an act of will, both an intention and an action") and *rage*.[19]

Love and rage. Rage and love. These are the key affects for approaching zines, a media form that is adjacent to and entangled with the tradition of leftist publications that Flatley is examining. In his useful study of zines, Stephen Duncombe lauds them as "a novel form of communication and creation that burst with an angry idealism"—an anger and a novelty that he later associates with their status as "amateur" media:

> If pushed to come up with a single defining attribute I would have to say this: zines are decidedly *amateur*. While this term has taken on a pejorative cast in a society that honors professionalism and the value of the dollar, the roots of amateurism are far more noble: *amator*, Latin for *lover*. While other media are produced for money or prestige or public approval, zines are done . . . for *love*: love of expression, love of sharing, love of communication.[20]

And, Duncombe makes the point of adding, "in protest against a culture and society that offers little reward for such acts of love, zines are also created out of rage."[21]

The eclectic world of zines that Duncombe surveys differs in its social basis from Flatley's analysis of *DRUM*: the arena Duncombe is examining is white rather than Black, youthful rather than adult, middle class rather than working class. Above all, zines are not rooted in a single community, but are meant to circulate rhizomatically: they do not map onto a given territory but are nonlinear. "Any point of a rhizome can be connected to anything other," Deleuze and Guattari write, "and must be."[22] When we consider the counter-mood that the aesthetic experience of reading, creating, and circulating zines can instate, we are faced neither with the vertical model of leftist organizing (Duncombe freely contrasts the vitality of zines with the output of "fringe groups hawk[ing] their ridiculous papers") nor with the horizontal spontaneity of atomized subjects.[23] Instead, what the distribution matrix affords is the circulation of counter-moods through the aesthetics of "transversal activism." Transversal activism, as Gerald Raunig observes, enacts assemblages or concatenations of art and politics.[24]

A quick perusal of any old-fashioned photocopied zine will telegraph this point. Zines are literally assembled—cut, copied, and pasted—out of new and preexisting media. Text is arranged in juxtaposition with art (hand-drawn or appropriated) in an idiosyncratic, sometimes slapdash manner. Even zines wholly devoted to images tend to rely on the low-fi, grainy aesthetics of the "poor image," Hito Steyerl's name for the image whose seeming deficiencies of quality allow it to bear the scars of its reproduction, as a kind of counter-provenance.[25]

These formal qualities amount to an insurrectionary projection of the *forces of production* against the dominant *relations of production*. While there are many valid histories of zines, the kind of zine we are most familiar with today took shape in the heyday of the photocopy machine. Beginning in the early 1960s, when the Xerox corporation's Model 914 became an overnight success, photocopying permitted anyone to duplicate anything en masse. Like the Polaroid camera (also introduced in the 1960s, and popularized in the 1970s), photocopying allowed media to be created and reproduced without censorship, surveillance, or oversight. Menial jobs that were generally assigned to women, youths, and minorities—in the secretarial pool, at the copy store—offered unsupervised access to technologies and resources that could be pilfered and the results redistributed. Punks, queers, feminists, vegans, antinuclear activists, mail art enthusiasts, and others all took advantage of the Xerox machine. Vaginal Davis, for example, helped herself to her employer's photocopier to publish *Fertile La Toyah Jackson Magazine* while working at the University of California, Los Angeles. Many a Kinko's copy center has inadvertently subsidized the local punk scene, courtesy of its underpaid and overworked staff. In the space of creative dispossession that Stefano Harney and Fred Moten call "the undercommons," a revolutionary counter-mood is copied, collated, stapled, and stuffed in a backpack.[26]

III

Earlier I suggested that zines were trans-local rather than community based. I'll qualify that: zines are often grounded in place, but through the mechanism of a *scene* rather than a worksite, family, or community in a traditional sense.[27]

Let me tell the story of my relationship to one such zine and the scene it recorded. I began researching the queer archive during the summer of 1994, when I was still in college. The Black and Brown queer and transgender house ball culture in New York City was in vogue in those years (thanks in large part to the external gazes of Jennie Livingston, Madonna, and Malcolm McLaren), and I received support from one of the first grants available for queer studies to spend the summer between my junior and senior years observing and participating in the scene.

As the saying goes, I was never the same again after that summer. When plans for my living arrangements in New York fell through, I ended up squatting in Columbia University housing; I managed to get into gay bars underage with a fake ID; I tried to negotiate condoms with a boyfriend who had a Prince Albert piercing; and I almost got recruited into the Latino Fan Club (a club for white daddies who enjoy taking photos of Black and Brown twinks). I did not, however, consider myself in any way to be a wild child. The previous spring I had taken one of the first college-level courses in queer theory ever to be offered.[28] On campus, we thought ourselves to be part of a generation that was going to invent queer culture with the help of some core principles: intersectional analysis of race and gender, direct action against corrupt authority, a sex-positive ethos, and a deep hatred of sexism and the patriarchy. I tried to put all these heady theories into practice as a twenty-year-old trying to get laid in New York, which was a source of occasional bemusement to my friends and informants, who didn't quite get why I was trying to understand my life at the same time as I was living it.

The AIDS crisis weighed on everything in those years and supplied a rationale for linking theory and practice. Books and articles by Douglas Crimp, Lisa Duggan, Cindy Patton, and Eve Kosofsky Sedgwick were dog-eared reminders of how to have theory in an epidemic. For my own research, which was oriented toward Black and Latinx queer and transgender folk, my point of entry into the New York ballroom scene was the House of Latex, an annual ball that had been launched in 1989 by the AIDS service organization Gay Men's Health Crisis (GMHC). Mentors at GMHC and GMAD (Gay Men of African Descent) provided introductions, allowed me to volunteer at the ball, and, in an almost offhanded way, made photocopies for me of a publication that introduced me to the ephemeral archive of queer counter-modal reading.

"Grandfather Marcel Princess Christian" (born Herman Michael Williams) was an artist and historian who wrote and self-published, and distributed an important queer-of-color zine called the *Idle Sheet* from the mid- to late 1980s. Produced and distributed by hand, the *Idle Sheet* provided the evidence I was seeking of the existence of ballroom history—a history, furthermore, told by a participant in the scene who understood himself as coming from a lineage of people who were stitching together an underground legacy for an oppressed minority. The Black queer community that Christian's publication served was dealing with both the AIDS epidemic and the spread of crack cocaine, a substance-abuse crisis that was used to wage a horrifying "drug war" upon Black communities and to intensely vilify and criminalize addicts. Ronald Reagan was in power as president of the United States, and inequality had been elevated from vice to virtue. Sodomy was illegal in many jurisdictions, marriage equality was hardly conceivable, and transgender rights were considered a bridge too far even for many lesbian and gay organizations.

It was against this recent history that I began my research into the ballroom scene as an art form created by the ghettoized. The legendary vogue balls—the "Marathon Circuit," as Christian called them—were such performances. They took place anywhere and nowhere, it seemed to me (although most regularly in the Marc Ballroom off Union Square that summer), and they provided a regular escape from hectic reality into a world of gender illusion and sexual fantasy. Christian was a self-designated documentarian of the scene as well as the founder of a small press, Widows Nails Media, which released hand-stitched poetry chapbooks and other transgressive literature, as well as copies of *Idle Sheet* that were handed out as program booklets at the balls.

One edition of the *Idle Sheet* was created for the Harlem "Fantasy Breakfast" Ball that took place in late June 1986 at the Imperial Elks Lodge Ballroom in Harlem, the weekend before Pride. On its cover are Christian's drawings of queens Dorian Corey and Pepper LaBeija, a man twerking his juicy butt, a variety of symbols and graphic decorations, and the face of a mime. Following the work of José Esteban Muñoz and Jayna Brown, we can see this *Idle Sheet* as providing images of a then-and-there that infuses the here-and-now with the spirit of utopia.[29] These drawings—some of them doodles, others sharply observed portraits—embellish and adorn the everyday. The artist has signed the work not in the corner, but dead center, displacing even Dorian and Pepper, the belles of the ball, to the left quadrant of the page. The impulse to inscribe oneself into the scene as both a witness and a participant can be a utopian one when it protests the constant diminishment and demeaning of ordinary life and the people who live it.

For the novice researcher I was when I first read it, the *Idle Sheet* educated my desire for a richer description and interpretation of the balls as art, as culture, and as history. Like many other young queers in desperate search for the path that might lead to my future, I was obsessed with Jennie Livingston's documentary film *Paris Is Burning* and drawn into the furious debates that followed its 1990 premiere—specifically, about the propriety of a Yale-educated white lesbian making a documentary about a trans and queer Black and Brown community. The *Idle Sheet* was evidence that this community possessed its own internal documentarians, historians, and theorists. It alerted me to the fact that the balls I was attending were in themselves a living archive of this history, and that the system of iconography that Christian was creating was infused with deep meaning not in spite of the fact, but *because* they were images created out of idleness—images that registered for the viewer, if at all, not deeply, but as part of an *ambience*. The *Idle Sheet* offered a revolutionary counter-mood through a series of startling and gentle distractions.

Christian's drawing of the mime on the cover of *Idle Sheet* may be an oblique reference to two Marcels: Marcel Christian and the iconic mime Marcel Marceau (after whom Christian chose his adopted name). The mask is the universal symbol of theater; the will to adorn and embellish the face with paint is at the heart of masquerade—drag queens call it "beating a face." In the drawing, Christian beats a face that adorns and embellishes the tradition of French mime, inventing his own ancestry in the process.

The idea of an underground tradition hiding in plain sight was important to Christian, as was the idea that his handmade, hand-distributed pamphlets were part of a heritage of balls in the Black community going back at least to the nineteenth century.[30] Christian understood himself to be working in the tradition of Gilded Age queens like William Dorsey Swann when he founded Widows Nails Media in the 1980s, a small press dedicated to continuing a tradition of "ornate program booklets" handed out "with a smile" at balls "from the early twentieth century" onward.[31] Christian published his own memoir under the Widows Nails imprint,[32] as well as a chapbook of poetry by his friend Assotto Saint, another key figure in the 1980s Black gay literary renaissance and AIDS activism.[33]

Widows Nails Media's memorable name was taken from a "hauntingly durable Singer sewing machine" that originally belonged to Bonnie Clark, an impresario of the Harlem Renaissance–era balls. The device was passed down to Crystal LaBeija, founding mother of the House of LaBeija, who bequeathed it to Pepper LaBeija, one of the icons of the film *Paris Is Burning*. The sewing machine was housed in the changing room of famed transgender performance spot Sally's Hideway on New York's West 43rd Street until that venue's tragic demise. As a history of Widows Nails Media puts it: "This sewing machine was a living symbol of a small, private cultural heritage that passed from the late 19th century to the end of the 20th century. The memory of the widows nails sewing machine lives on in the words and images created by Widows Nails Media."[34]

Although I never met Christian, reading his *Idle Sheets* provided me with an apprenticeship in queer archiving as a practice of care for the self and others. His zine contains a strategy that has been adopted by many minoritarian performers: techniques for creating a revolutionary counter-mood, to electrify the present with gestures of refusal. The use of style as a mode of self-assertion is a paradoxical one, in that it relies on the dramatic truism that you must give someone a mask to get them to tell the truth. "Marcel Christian," as noted, was a chosen name—a name selected to be used within the specific context of the "Marathon Circuit." Self-naming was not about the individual, but about the *being singular plural*, a *me* that exists only because a *we* exists.[35]

I knew little of this history when I began studying the queer archive of Black and Brown sex/gender transgression. But I'd had an "apprenticeship" of sorts in women-of-color feminism—a field in which the importance of the kitchen table as a gathering space for nurturing, fellowship, political discussion, and community organizing had long been recognized.[36] This apprenticeship prepared me to recognize how Widows Nails Media—and that beat-up sewing machine in the changing room at Sally's Hideaway—belonged to an inclusive tradition of women-of-color feminism that understood trans and femme people to have always been central to the movement. Femme cultural workers stitched together a fugitive lineage that connected past, present, and future through objects like this hand-me-down tool, powering the will to adorn across multiple generations. Armed with a sturdy sense that the costume of "queer researcher" into which I was stepping had been sewn together with the skill and care of hands unknown to me, I pored over the copies of the *Idle Sheet* I had been given as if they were hieroglyphs of my future.

As a form of communication from the undercommons, and as an expression of the punk spirit of revolt, zines have played a critical role in sustaining revolutionary counter-moods in today's reactionary times. The paradox of their aesthetic form—radical accessibility combined with cryptic content—has equipped zines both to document and to generate subcultural scenes. Elsewhere in this volume, the fate of the zine in the era of its digital reproducibility is taken up more extensively.[37] What I will say here, by way of conclusion, is that such a shift has represented a real subsumption of the cognitive and affective labor of handmade publishing by capital-intensive technologies, with the result that the capacity of zine culture to evade surveillance and cultivate sustained counter-moods has come under an onslaught the likes of which we have not seen before.

Here, in the desert of the digitized real, we must begin again.

Starting with Marx and Engels, the left has often sought to dismiss and patronize utopianism as an unrealistic and irrelevant distraction from "real" politics. Punk performativity—with its aesthetics of the counter-mood—suggests that, on the contrary, no map of the world without a place for utopia is worth looking at. Zines contribute to the queer counter-archive. That queer counter-archive is not something distant, remote, official, or institutionalized in a university, museum, or state facility. It is nearby—as near as a leaflet passed to you as you enter the club, ball, march, or parade. It should be a one-to-few message sent out and received in a moment of danger.

NOTES

1 Jon Savage, *Teenage: The Creation of Youth Culture* (New York: Viking, 2007).

2 For more on punk's genealogy, see Tavia Nyong'o, "Punk'd Theory," *Social Text* 23, no. 3–4 (84–85) (December 1, 2005): 19–34; doi. org/10.1215/01642472-23-3-4_84-85-19.

3 Michel Foucault, "Nietzsche, Genealogy, History," in *Language, Counter-Memory, Practice: Selected Essays and Interviews*, ed. D. F. Bouchard (Ithaca, NY: Cornell University Press, 1977), 139–64.

4 See Jacques Derrida, *Archive Fever: A Freudian Impression* (Chicago: University of Chicago Press, 1998).

5 Walter Benjamin, *The Work of Art in the Age of Its Technological Reproducibility, and Other Writings on Media*, ed. Michael William Jennings, Brigid Doherty, and Thomas Y. Levin (Cambridge, MA: Harvard University Press, 2008).

6 See Giovanni Arrighi, Terence K. Hopkins, and Immanuel Maurice Wallerstein, *Antisystemic Movements* (New York: Verso, 2011).

7 See José Esteban Muñoz, "Ephemera as Evidence: Introductory Notes to Queer Acts," *Women & Performance: A Journal of Feminist Theory* 8, no. 2 (January 1996): 5–16; doi.org/10.1080/07407709608571228.

8 Karl Marx, "The Eighteenth Brumaire of Louis Bonaparte (1852)," in *Later Political Writings*, ed. Terrell Carver (Cambridge, UK: Cambridge University Press, 1996), 31–127.

9   See Gilles Deleuze and Félix Guattari, *Anti-Oedipus: Capitalism and Schizophrenia* (New York: Viking Press, 1977); and Deleuze and Guattari, *A Thousand Plateaus: Capitalism and Schizophrenia* (Minneapolis: University of Minnesota Press, 1987).

10 Davis's queer counter-archive of her zine can be found at her self-maintained internet blog, "Speaking from the Diaphragm": www.vaginaldavis.com.

11 Vaginal Davis, in Nicole Disser, "Vaginal Davis Returns to New York, Taking on Sculpture and Mozart," *Bedford + Bowery* (November 23, 2015); bedfordandbowery.com/2015/11/vaginal-davis-returns-to-new-york-taking-on-sculpture-and-mozart.

12 I am drawing here on the work of queer scholar Marc Siegel: see his "Vaginal Davis's Gospel Truths," *Camera Obscura* 23, no. 1 (2008): 151–59; and Tavia Nyong'o, *Afro-Fabulations: The Queer Drama of Black Life* (New York: New York University Press, 2018).

13 Davis, in Disser, "Vaginal Davis Returns to New York."

14 Jonathan Flatley, "How a Revolutionary Counter-Mood Is Made," *New Literary History* 43, no. 3 (2012): 503–4.

15 For more on affect theory, see Jonathan Flatley, *Affective Mapping: Melancholia and the Politics of Modernism* (Cambridge, MA: Harvard University Press, 2008); Lauren Berlant, *Cruel Optimism* (Durham, N.C.: Duke University Press, 2011); Brian Massumi, *Parables for the Virtual: Movement, Affect, Sensation* (Durham, NC: Duke University Press, 2002).

16 Flatley, "How A Revolutionary Counter-Mood Is Made," 504.

17 Ibid., 509.

18 Ibid., 518–19 (emphasis mine).

19 bell hooks, *All About Love: New Visions* (New York: William Morrow, 2000).

20 Stephen Duncombe, *Notes from Underground: Zines and the Politics of Alternative Culture* (New York: Verso, 1997), 3.

21 Ibid., 14–15.

22 Deleuze and Guattari, *A Thousand Plateaus*, 7.

23 Duncombe, *Notes from Underground*, 3.

24 Gerald Raunig, *Art and Revolution: Transversal Activism in the Long Twentieth Century*, trans. Aileen Derieg (Los Angeles: Semiotext(e), 2007).

25 Hito Steyerl, "In Defense of the Poor Image," *E-Flux* (2009); e-flux.com/journal/in-defense-of-the-poor-image/#_ftn1.

26 Fred Moten and Stefano Harney, *The Undercommons: Fugitive Planning & Black Study* (Wivenhoe, UK: Minor Compositions, 2013).

27 For a queer critique of communitarianism, see Miranda Joseph, *Against the Romance of Community* (Minneapolis: University of Minnesota Press, 2002).

28 The professor of that course at Wesleyan University was Henry Abelove, who went on to co-edit the *Lesbian & Gay Studies Reader*.

29 See Jayna Brown, *Black Utopias: Speculative Life and the Music of Other Worlds* (Durham, NC: Duke University Press, 2021); and José Esteban Muñoz, *Cruising Utopia: The Then and There of Queer Futurity* (New York: New York University Press, 2009).

30 Historian Channing Joseph has recently brought to light the story of William Dorsey Swann, the formerly enslaved drag queen and political activist who threw masquerade balls during the Gilded Age. See Channing Gerard Joseph, "The First Drag Queen Was a Former Slave," *Nation* (January 31, 2020), thenation.com/article/society/drag-queen-slave-ball.

31 Digital oral history.

32 Digital oral history.

33 See Tavia Nyong'o, "The Crypt of Blackness: Or Assotto Saint with Gilles Deleuze," in *We Travel the Space Ways* (Transcript Verlag, 2019), 175–98; doi.org/10.1515/9783839446010-012.

34 Digital oral history.

35 Jean-Luc Nancy, *Being Singular Plural* (Stanford, CA: Stanford University Press, 2000); Fred Moten, "Black Op," *PMLA [Publications of the Modern Language Association]* 123, no. 5 (2008): 1743.

36 See Cherríe Moraga and Anzaldúa, Gloria, *This Bridge Called My Back: Writings by Radical Women of Color* (New York: Kitchen Table, Women of Color Press, 1983).

37 See Aria Dean, *Bad Infinity, Selected Writings* (Cambridge, MA: MIT Press, forthcoming).

Nicole Eisenman and A. L. Steiner

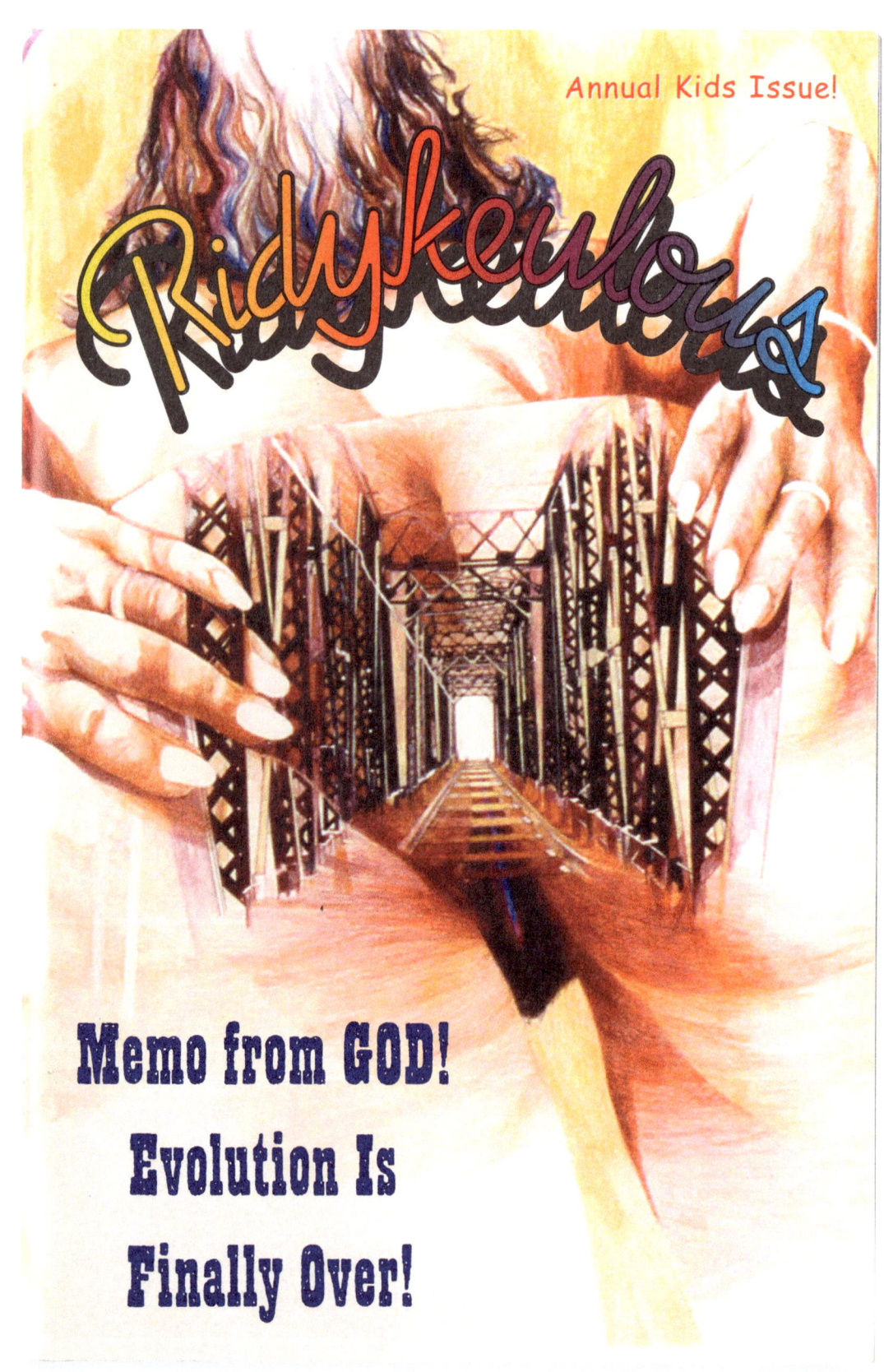

Ridykeulous: Memo from God, 2006
Offset, saddle stitched, 9 × 6 in. (22.8 × 15.2 cm)
Collection Philip Aarons and Shelley Fox Aarons

A. K. Burns and Sophie Mörner

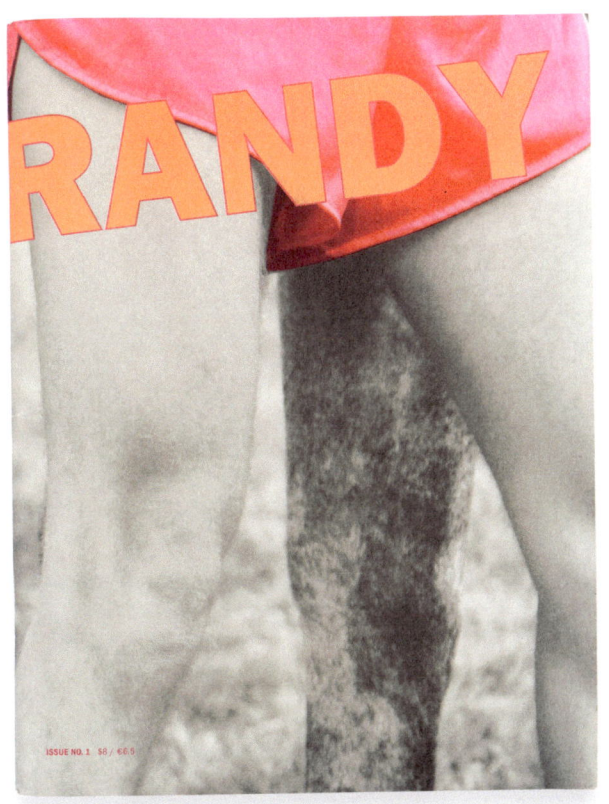

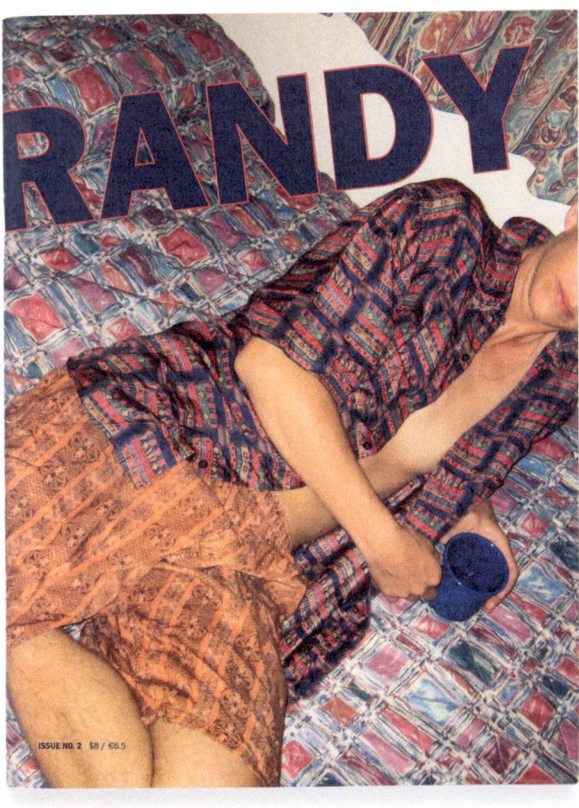

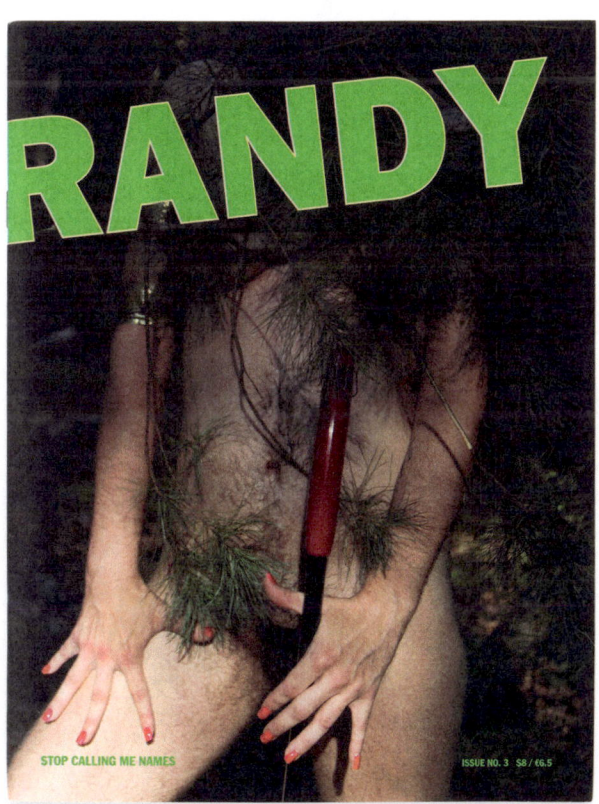

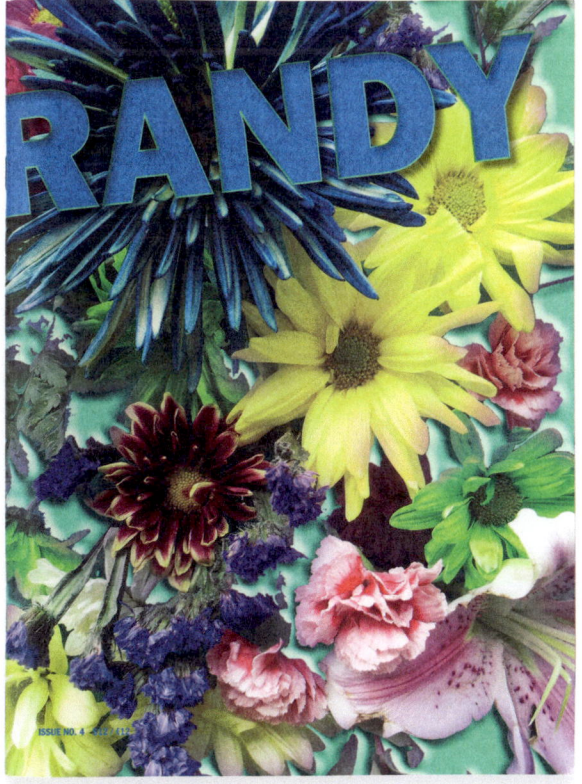

Randy, nos. 1–4, 2010–13
(Clark Solack is co-editor for issues 3 and 4)
Offset, saddle stitched, 10 × 7 ¾ in. (25.4 × 19.6 cm)
Collection Philip Aarons and Shelley Fox Aarons

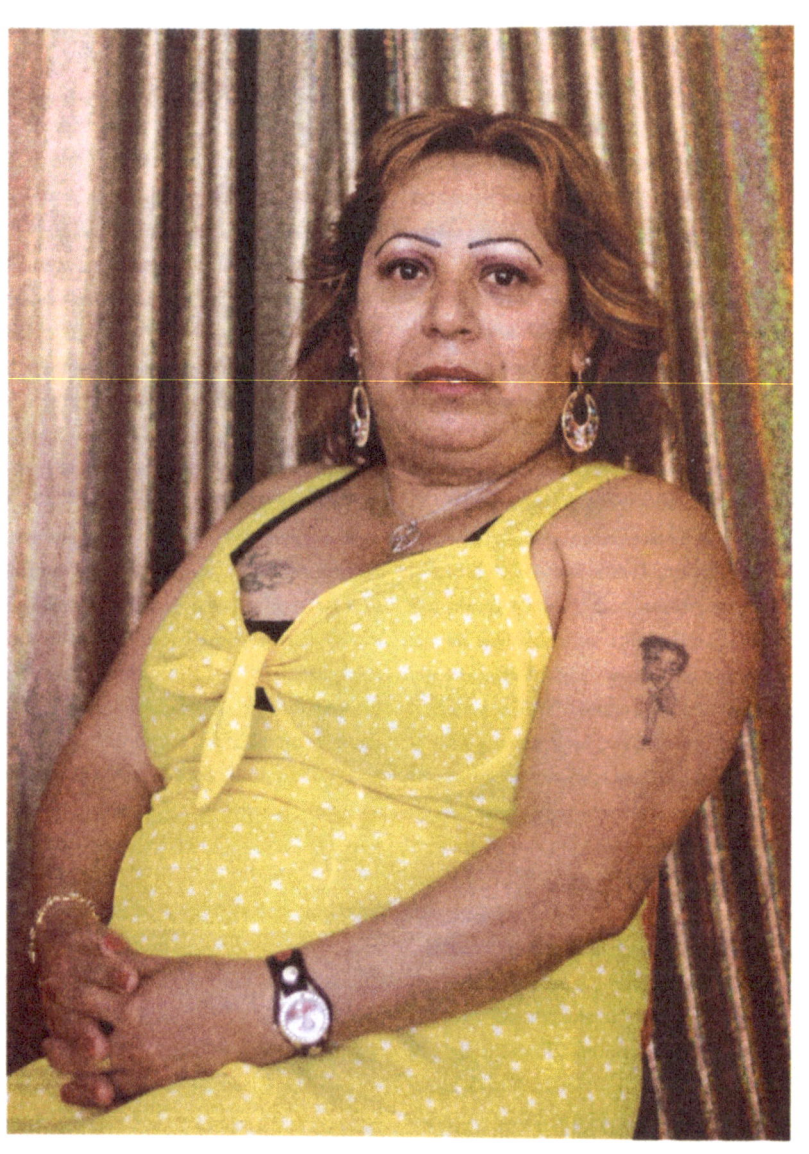

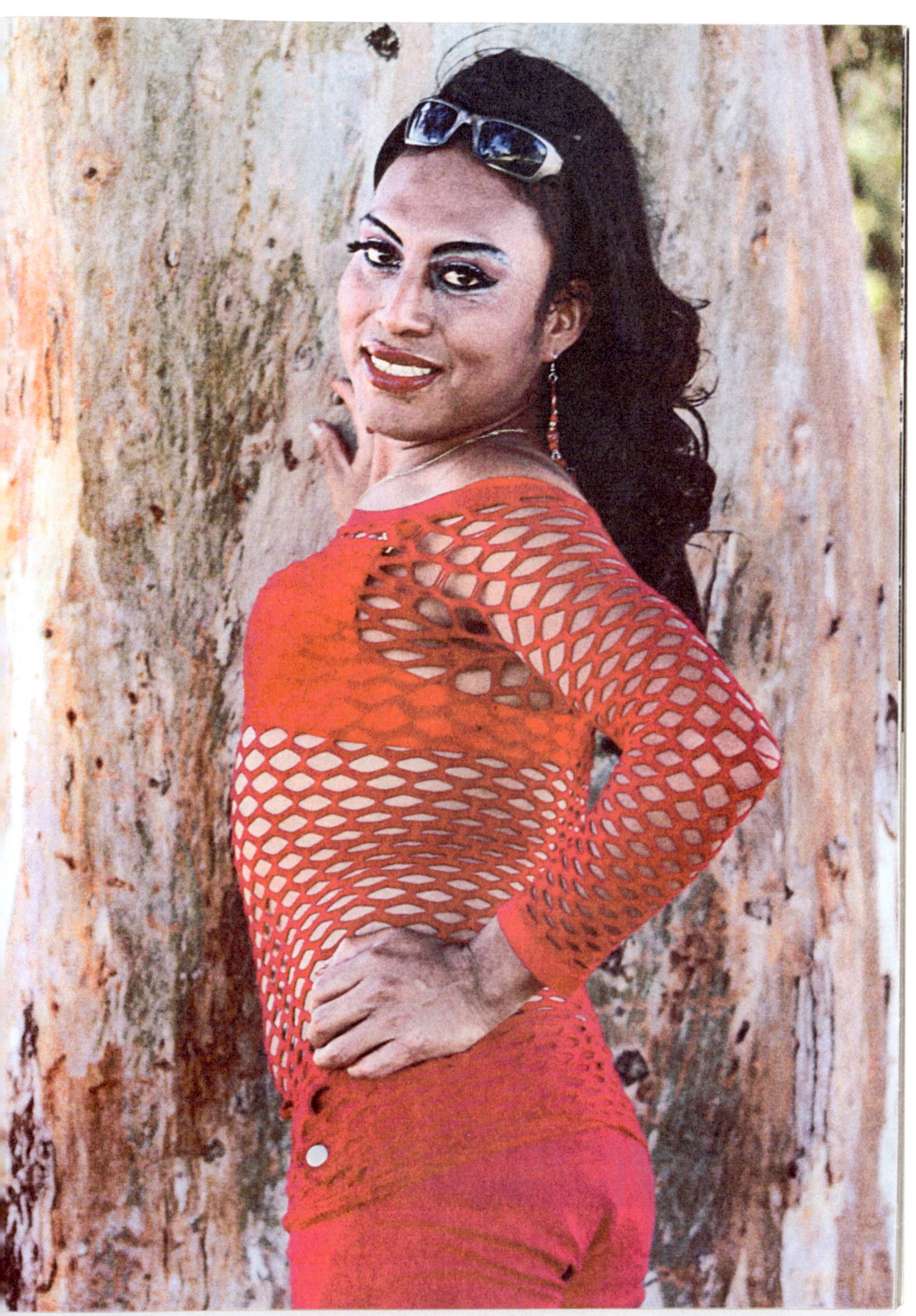

Randy, no. 1, 2010
Offset, saddle stitched, 10 × 7¾ in. (25.4 × 19.6 cm)
Collection Philip Aarons and Shelley Fox Aarons

Paul Mpagi Sepuya

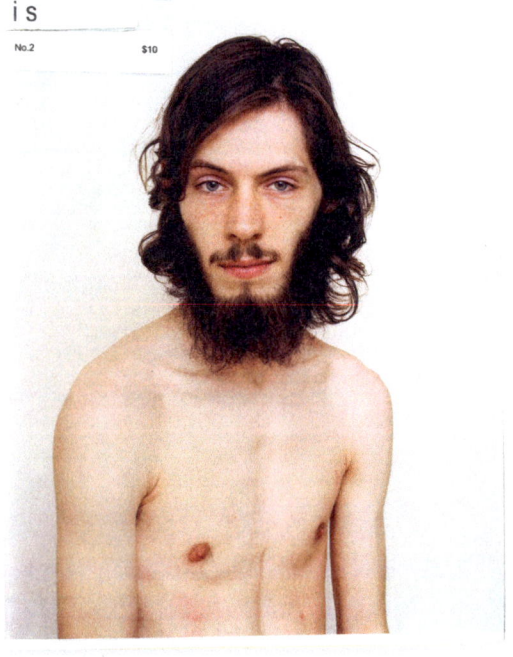

Shoot, no. 2, 2005
Photocopy, saddle stitched, 8 ½ × 6 in. (21.5 × 15.3 cm)
Brooklyn Museum

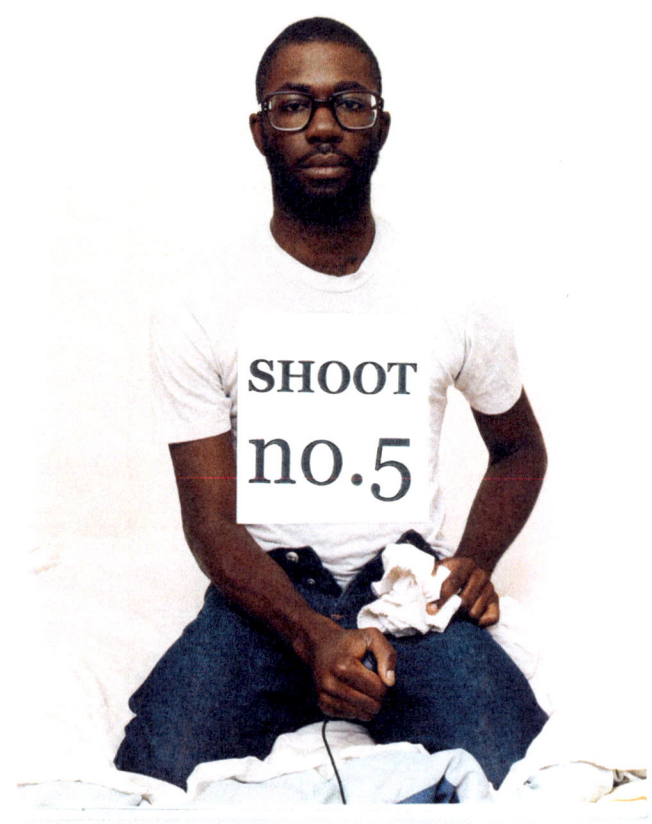

Shoot, no. 5, 2006
Photocopy, saddle stitched, 8 ½ × 6 in. (21.5 × 15.3 cm)
Brooklyn Museum

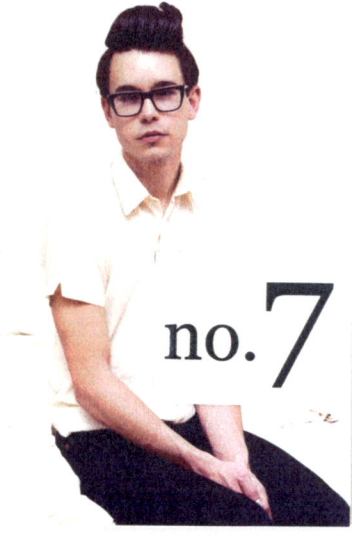

Shoot, no. 7, 2007
Photocopy, saddle stitched, 8 ½ × 6 in. (21.5 × 15.3 cm)
Brooklyn Museum

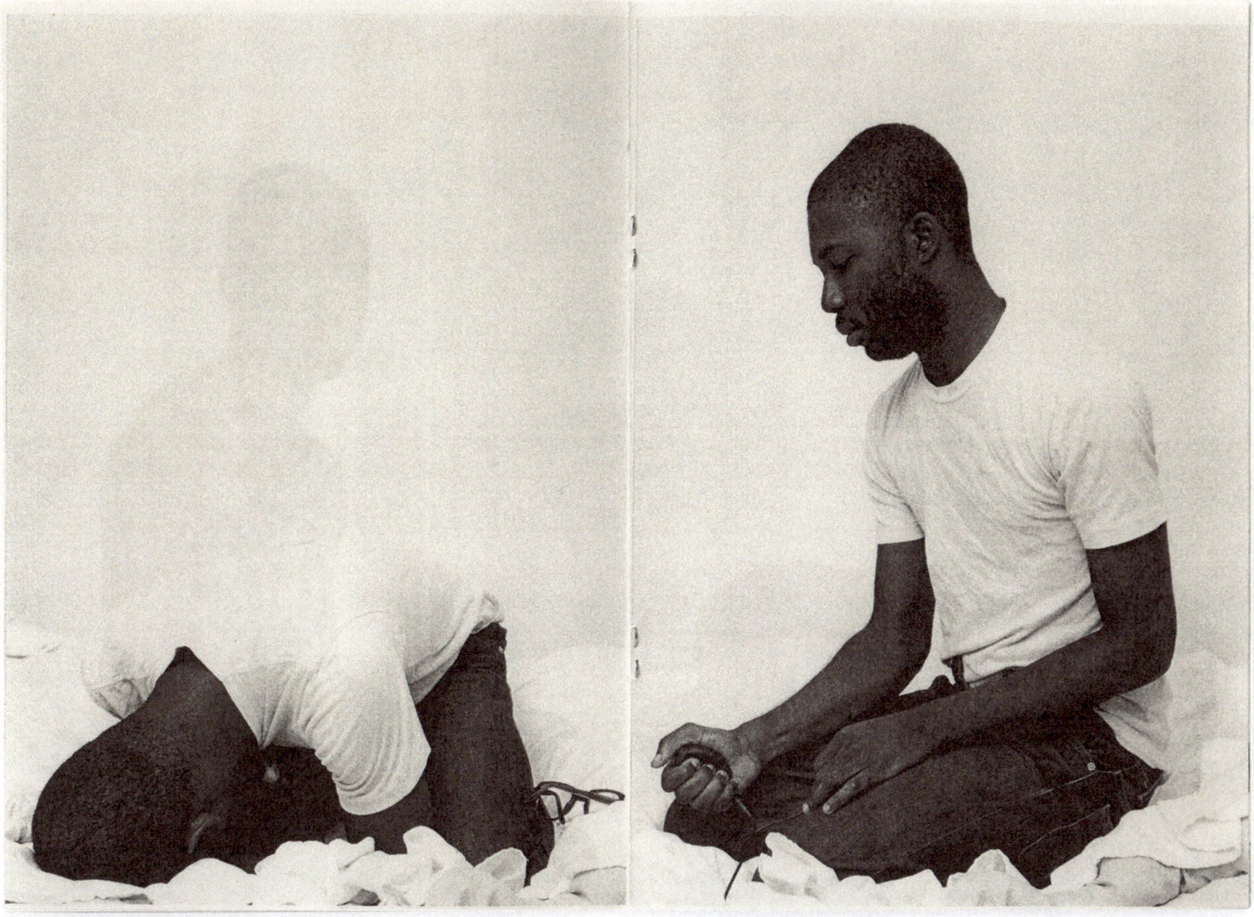

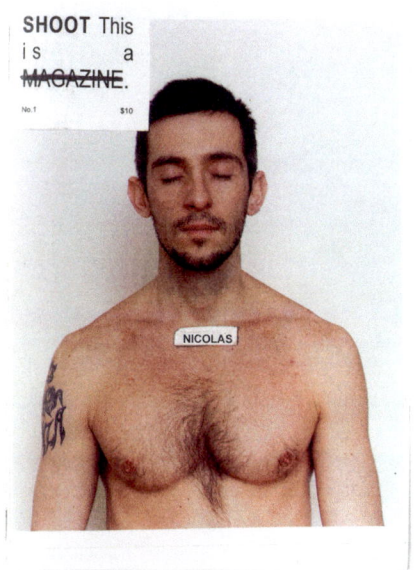

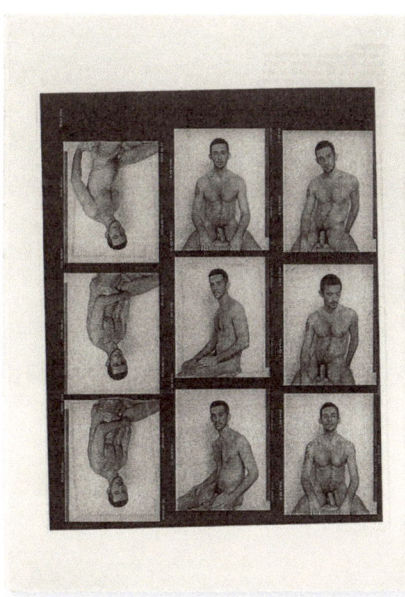

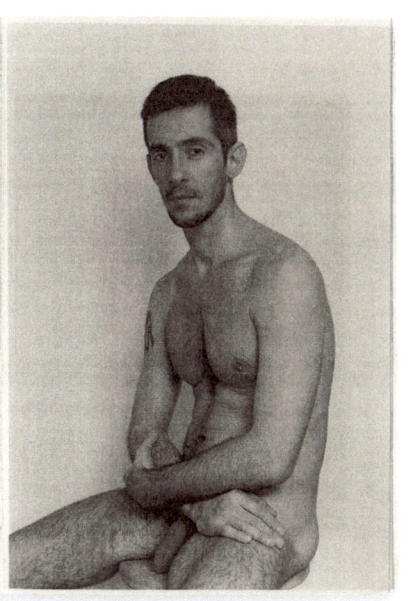

Shoot, no. 1, 2005
Photocopy, saddle stitched, 8 ½ × 6 in. (21.5 × 15.3 cm)
Brooklyn Museum

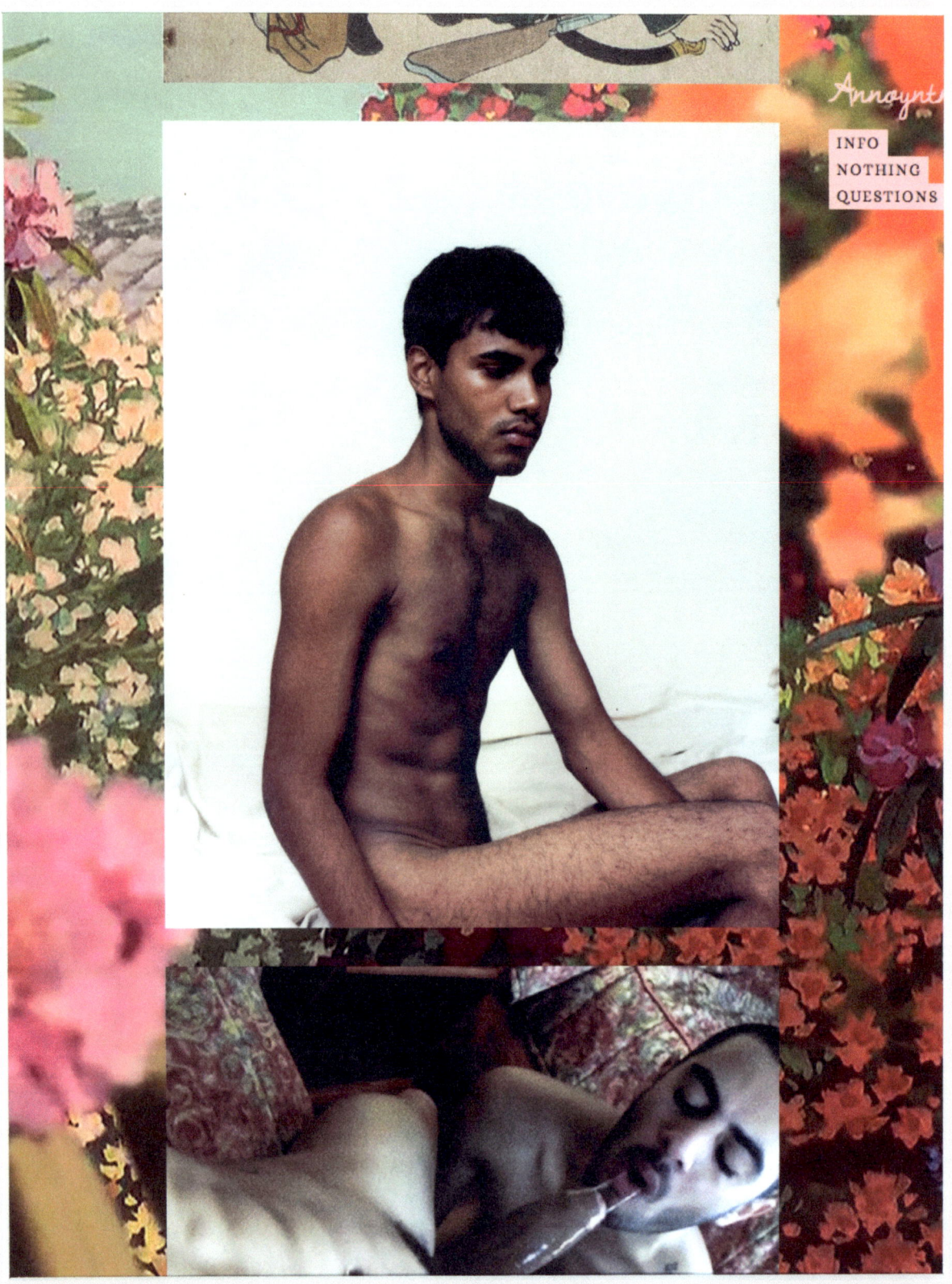

Rafi (annoyntment.tumblr.com), 2013
Inkjet print, 24 × 18 in. (61 × 45.7 cm)
Collection the artist

Mockup for *Seven Portraits*, 2005 (unpublished)
Laser print, 8 ½ × 6 in. (21.5 × 15.3 cm)
Collection the artist, courtesy Bortolami Gallery, New York

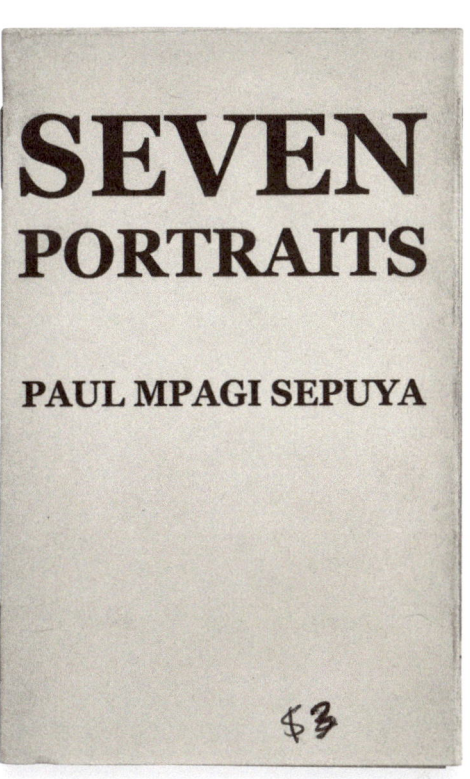

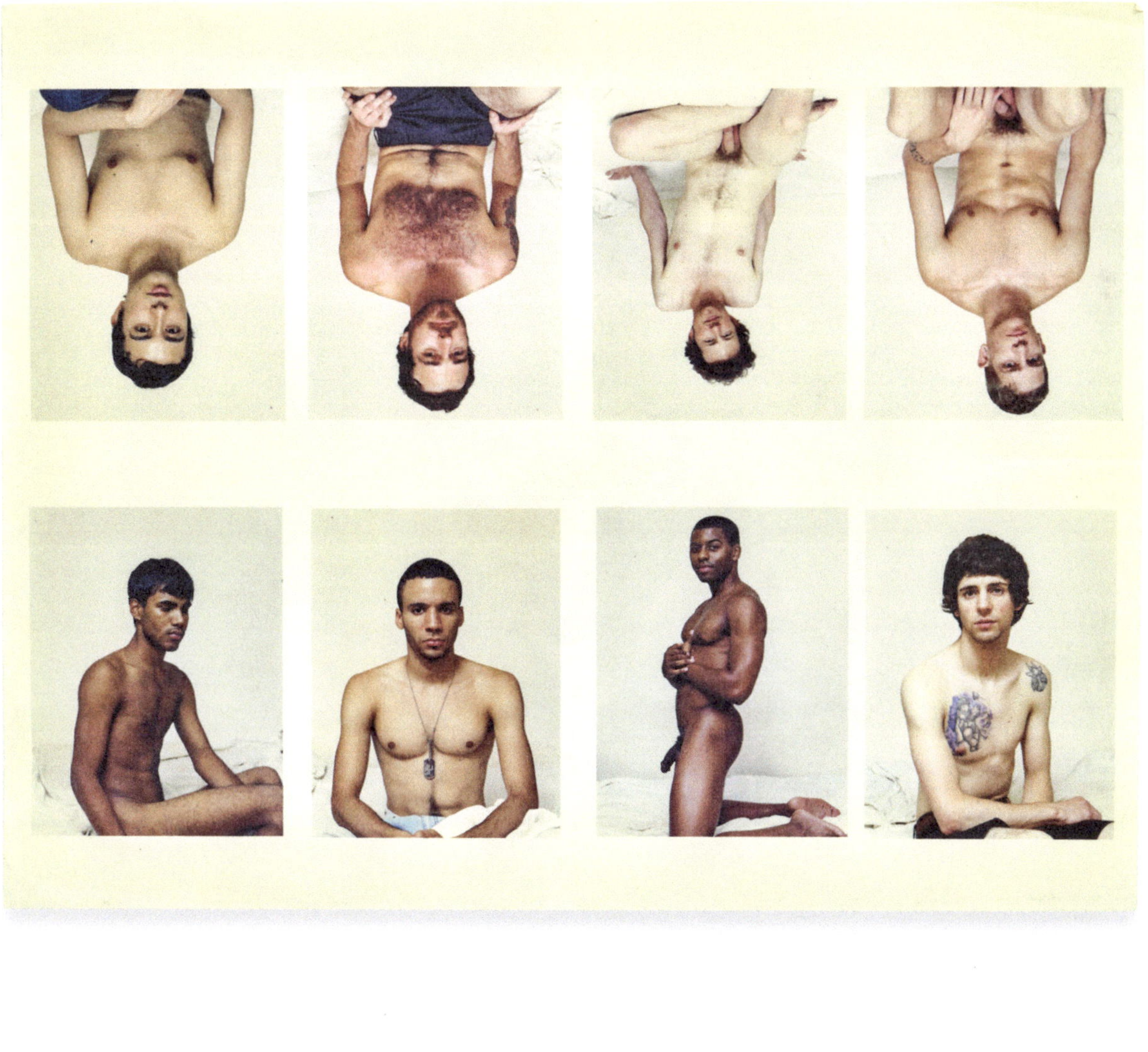

Futoshi Miyagi

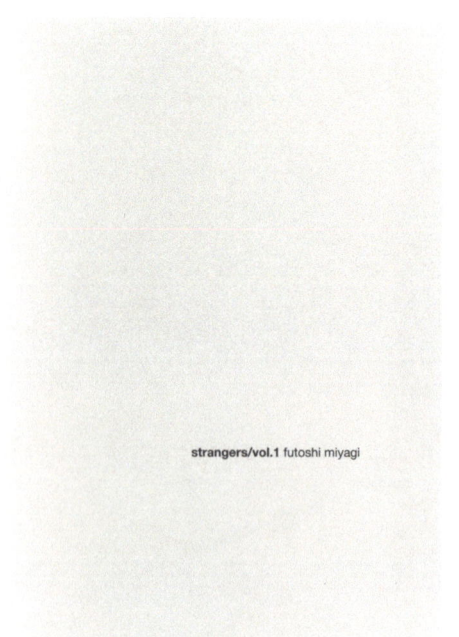

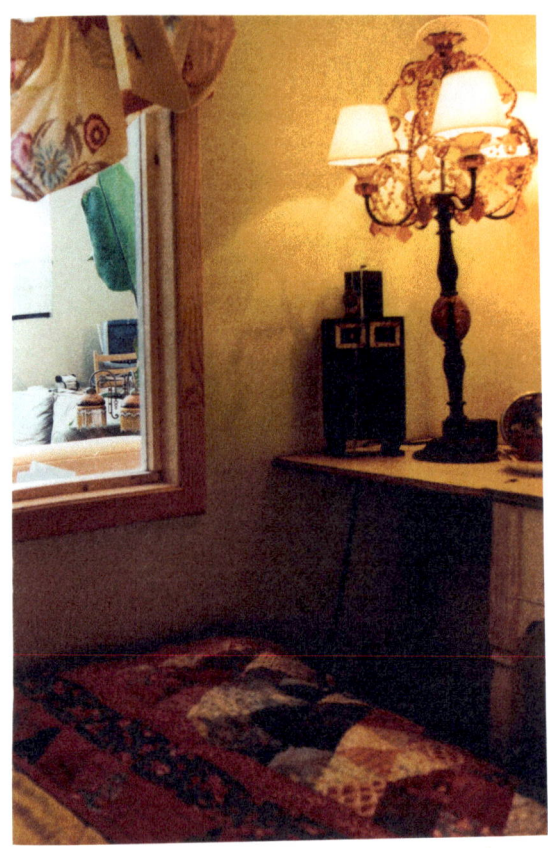

Strangers, vol. 2, 2006
Inkjet, saddle stitched, loose wrappers, 8 3/16 × 6 1/4 in. (20.8 × 15.8 cm)
Collection Philip Aarons and Shelley Fox Aarons

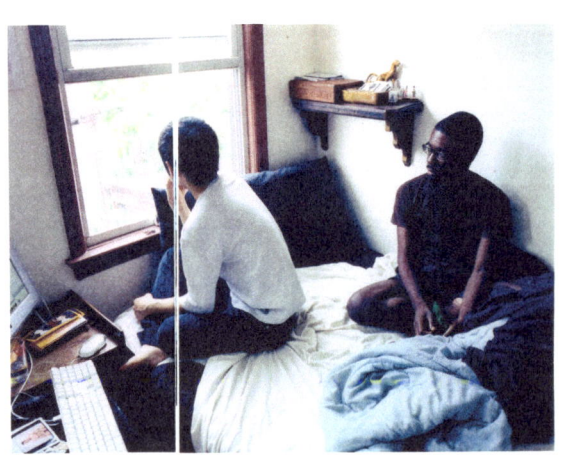

Strangers, vol. 1, 2006
Inkjet, saddle stitched, 8 3/16 × 6 1/4 in. (20.8 × 15.8 cm)
Collection Philip Aarons and Shelley Fox Aarons

Zackary Drucker
and Amos Mac

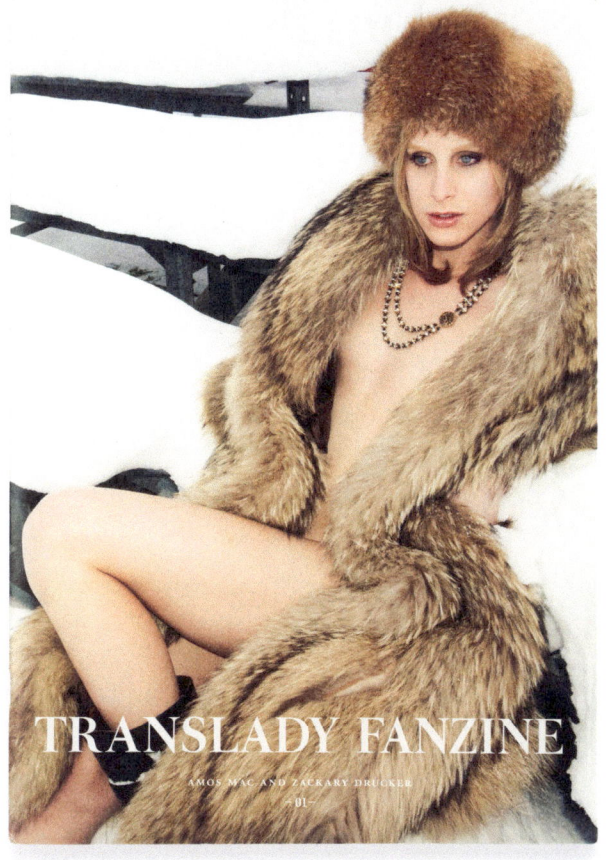

Translady Fanzine, 2011
Offset, saddle stitched, 13 ⅓ × 9 ¾ in. (33.9 × 24.8 cm)
Collection Philip Aarons and Shelley Fox Aarons

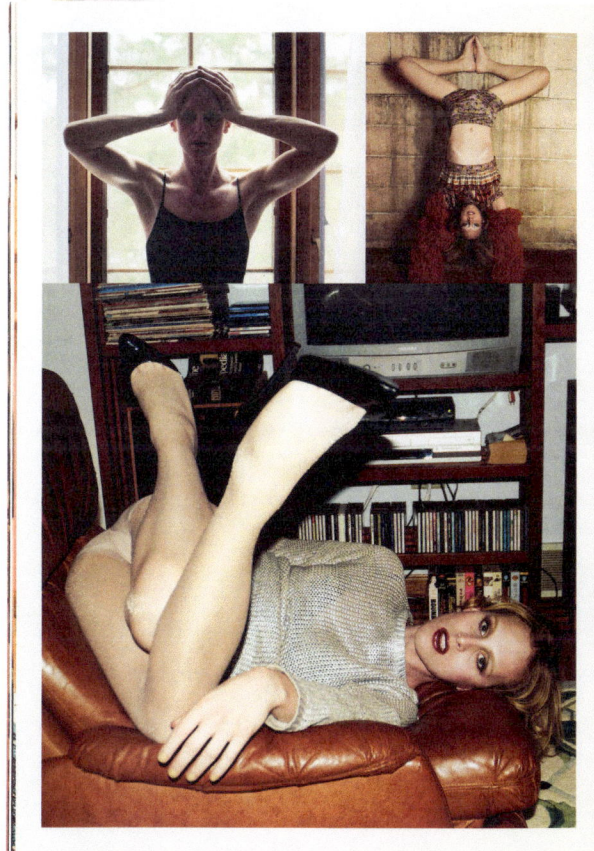

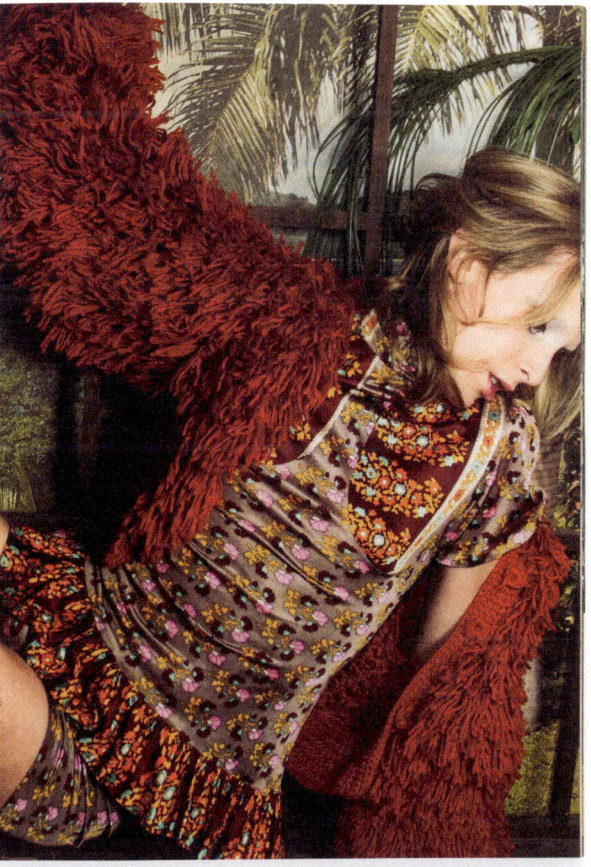

Brontez Purnell

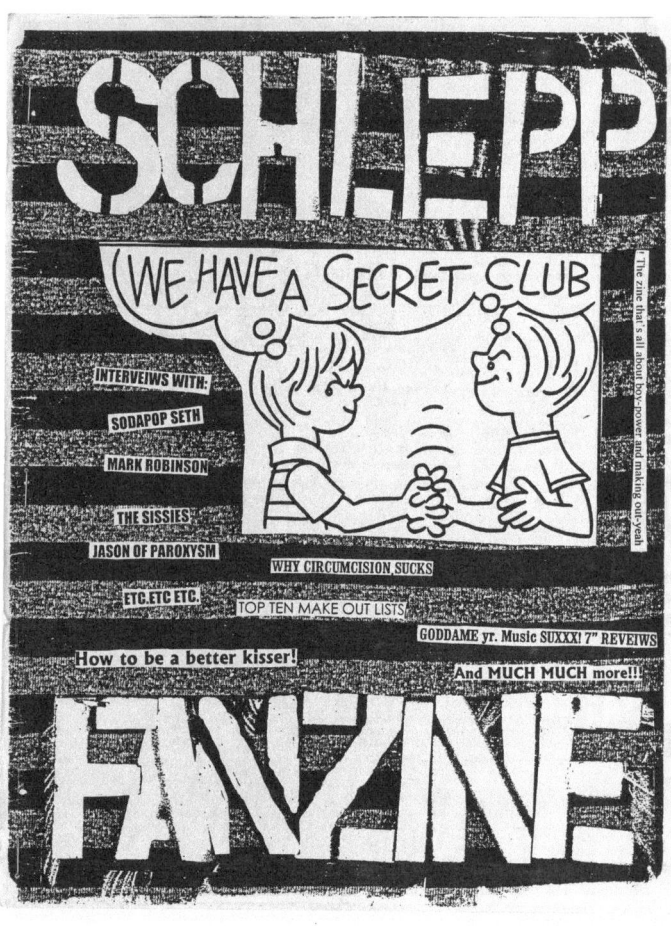

Schlepp Fanzine, no. 1, ca. 2000
Photocopy, side stapled, 11 × 8½ in. (27.9 × 21.6 cm)
Collection Philip Aarons and Shelley Fox Aarons

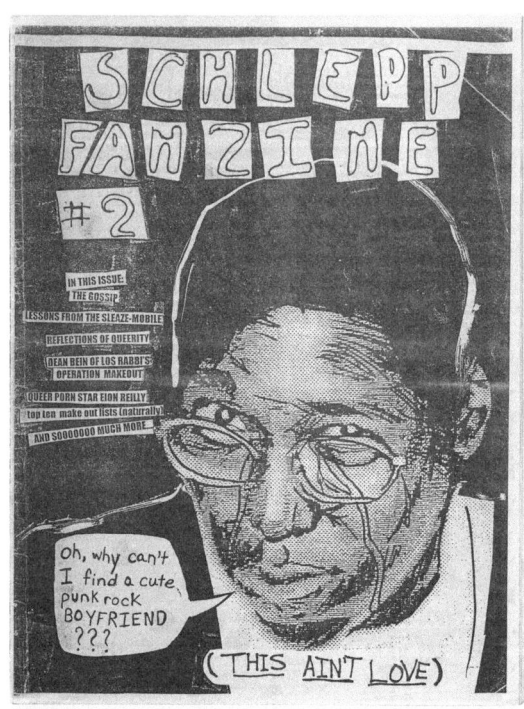

Schlepp Fanzine, no. 2, ca. 2000.
Photocopy, saddle stitched, 11 × 8½ in. (27.9 × 21.6 cm)
Collection Philip Aarons and Shelley Fox Aarons

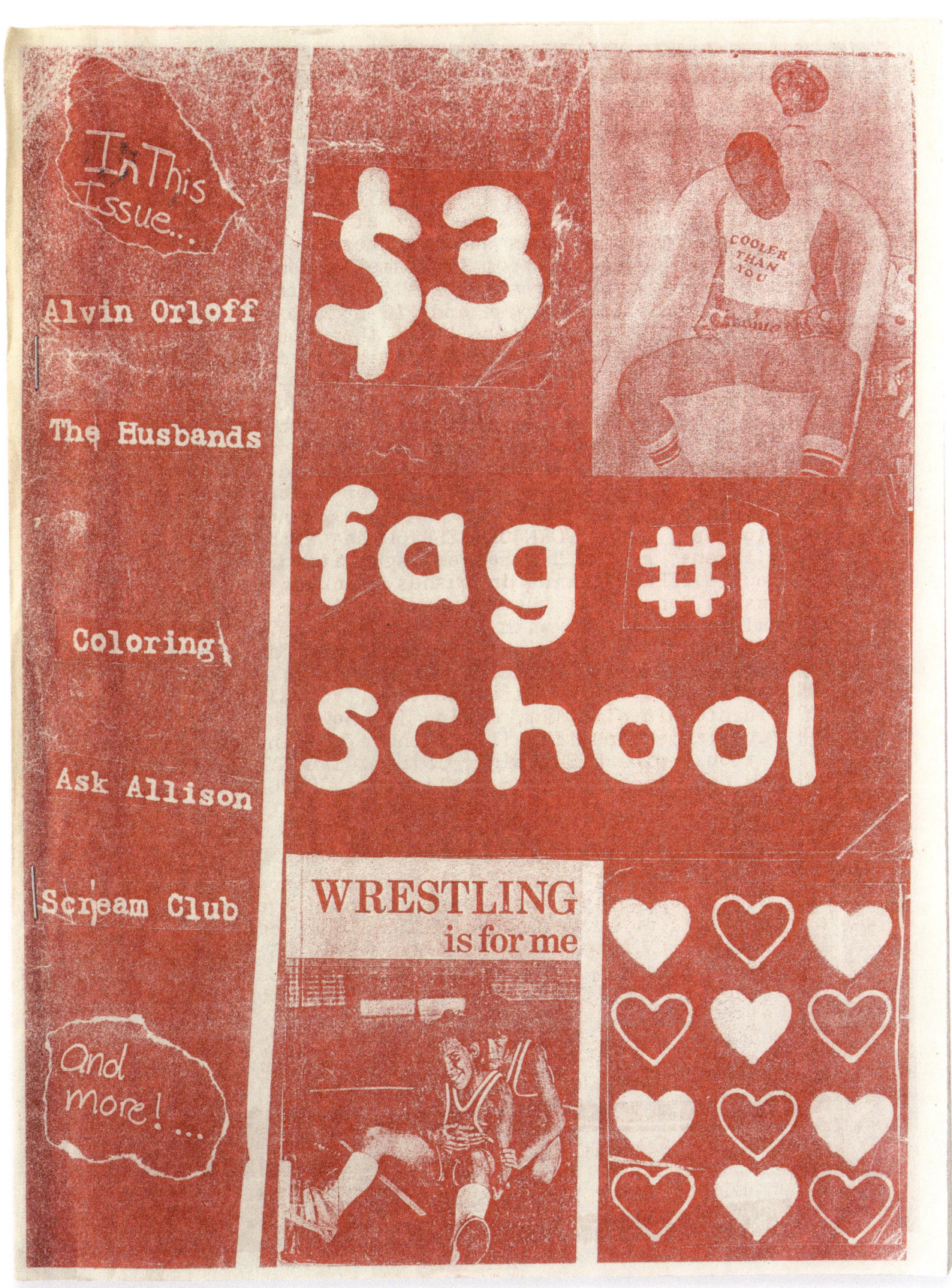

Fag School, no. 1, 2003
Risograph, folded and side stapled,
11 × 8 ½ in. (27.9 × 21.6 cm)
Collection Philip Aarons and Shelley Fox Aarons

Reviews (cont'd)

BRATZ-THE VIDEO BRONTEZ AND I RENTED ⟨...⟩ AND then Got HEXA STONED. GO GET THIS RIGHT N⟨...⟩

GOOD MUSIC TO BU⟨...⟩

THE OKMONIKS THIS BAND is Like A LESS-Retarded ver⟨...⟩ of SOUTH CITY, CA's **BRENTWOODS**. My record player is bu⟨...⟩ and plays records over and over. One time I let My OKMONIKS 45 play like 23 times in a Row... something tha⟨...⟩ hasn't happened since **TEACHER'S PET**. I partied with them ⟨...⟩ a BBQ and Sammy threw a fart bomb at me and made my ⟨...⟩ feedback on a handheld tapeplayer/microphone thing. Th⟨...⟩ SINGER has hot hair and is killer on the organ.

HARD PLACE BRONTEZ <u>hates</u> when I play their so⟨...⟩ "Sexy." I want to have violent sex with the singer, F⟨...⟩ Cristy. They sound like a more punk, more new wave ve⟨...⟩ of **STEELY DAN**. I like their adult contemporary songs best⟨...⟩ They sing about "Denim Boys". **Courtney Love** hates 'em⟨...⟩

LIPSTICK PICKUPS I have this teenybopper toy ⟨...⟩ called **BOPPIN' ROCKERS**. It's 2 black girls who have cool ou⟨...⟩ and have a band and they dance. The song <u>totally</u> rips o⟨...⟩ Lipstick Pickups. Total bubblegum pop w/ the cutest h⟨...⟩ pitched girl chipmunk vocals. I heard **BOMP!** wants to sign ⟨...⟩

S'COOL GIRLS If you're cool you love Hello, Bay Gi⟨...⟩ Rollers, Gary Glitter and now... **S'COOL GIRLS!!!** ½ Swedish, ½ ⟨...⟩ alifornian. The Swedish half are stone cold foxes. I wi⟨...⟩ more mens wore makeup & sung sweet glitter music!

GARY VALENTINE This "hottie" got kicked outta ⟨...⟩ BLONDIE after their first LP cuz he was annoying. His sol⟨...⟩ tunes are some of the best power pop songs ever. Get t⟨...⟩ CD that just came out. It is SO GOOD you'll bop every ti⟨...⟩

WILL POWER At first WILLPOWER gamme a case o⟨...⟩ ⟨...⟩ugs but now <u>I'm into it huge</u>. Like a gay **Justin Timbe⟨...⟩** moves like a sailor, COMING SOON to a RADIO STATION NEAR y⟨...⟩

5,6,7,8's they played BRONTEZ's house and used his room ⟨...⟩ a dressing room and I kept walking in on 'em making their ⟨...⟩ hair <u>SO</u> enormous. Too bad his bed was covered in dildos ⟨...⟩ and gay porno. I am pretty into them!! They are FAMOUS ⟨...⟩

CRUISING REVIEWS

...is dude was a SWEET TALKER. "Your soooo handsome, are you a real mailman?"
"No sir" I replied, "I got these shorts at the thrift store." He wanted to
take me home, fuck me AND buy me beer. This was WAAAY better than I ever did
at the bar on Saturday night, the fact that it was Tuesday morning in the park
bothered me NONE. No cover charge, no walk of shame...PERFECT. I went to his
house where he had pictures of his wife and kids everywhere and every solo
male jack-off film ever. We spent three hours in the shower pissing on each
other and he bought me a burritto later. PERFECT DATE.

...elt a sense of mission accomplished when i finally got down in the bathroom
Gilman St. Getting it on at Gilman is problematic. Everyone is 14 years old
screwing to thrash bands takes alot of concentration. I took the easy way
and partiexd with a balding (i.e. post-puberty) member of the staff betwee
ds. We kept being interrupted by a line of kids waiting for the stall so
could do drugs. I later found out this same dude wrote a detailed account
ur encounter FOR HIS GIRLFRIEND! AND THEN left me out of 90% of the text!
ry time i'm in the Gilman bx i still scratch my head (and balls) in confusio

...hours into my friends wedding party, I found myself in the bathroom with
der Cuban guy, SCORE! "I only like you cause your young and you get big
" This was the HOTTEST thing an old dude i was blowing had said to me, so
REALLY hot and started going double-time on his dang (he-he). He told me
a "big load for a little gun", jxjizzed all over my glasses and hair and
left my drunk ass to wander the party putting on my "oh, that wasnt ME
g slammed in the bathroom" face (everyone saw right through me). And then
lked home in the rain. It was by far the hottest sex exver and i would
amend it to a friend.

...mally as a rule of thumb type thing I try not to fuck dudes with
rry beamrds, cops, or men with kids because it is understood that axll
ese things are fuckin GROSS. I thought I'd cover the bases with this dude
little did i know! So i was at a party and decided to bring him to the
hroom. I kept reaching for the "D" but was being denied. He finally explained
ick southern accent) "I cant screw ya i get genital warts...LOOK!" And sure
ough, he did. I had NEVER gotten a non-erection SO FAST. He continued, "I
puttin' cream on um, but they wont go away." Some might applaude him for
honesty but frankly, I HATED HIS ASS. No decent person should have to endure
, wxxWould he pull this shit with his grandmother? He made me say things
never thought i would (p"put it away!). And just when i thought i could be
aumatized no more "Um yeah, I should hurry up and pick up my kids, its late."
wanted to vomit. "Oh MY GOD! Yoxu're a father?!! THAT'S DISGUSTING!" I took
hint and left.

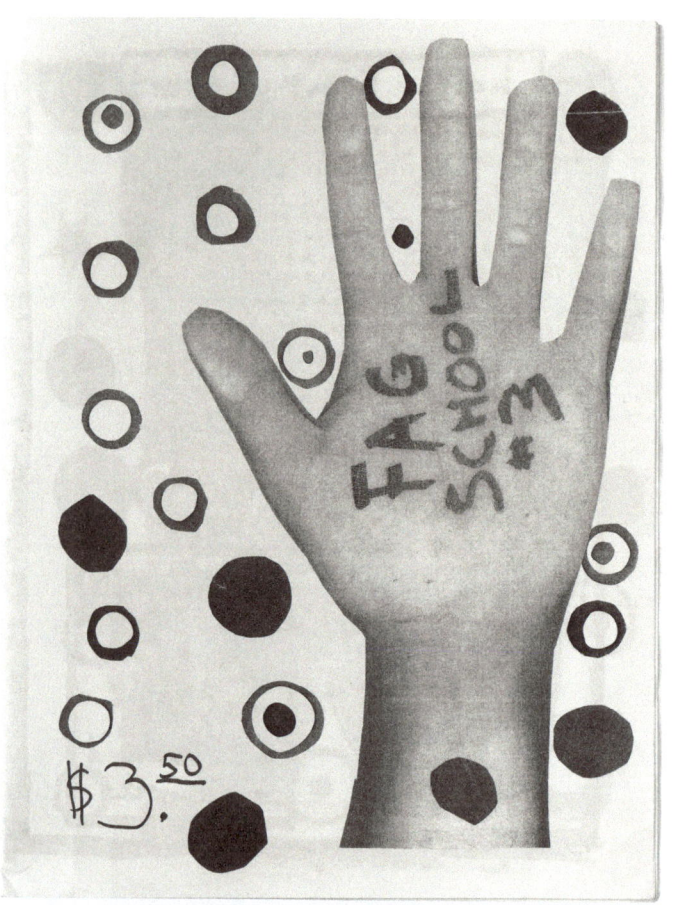

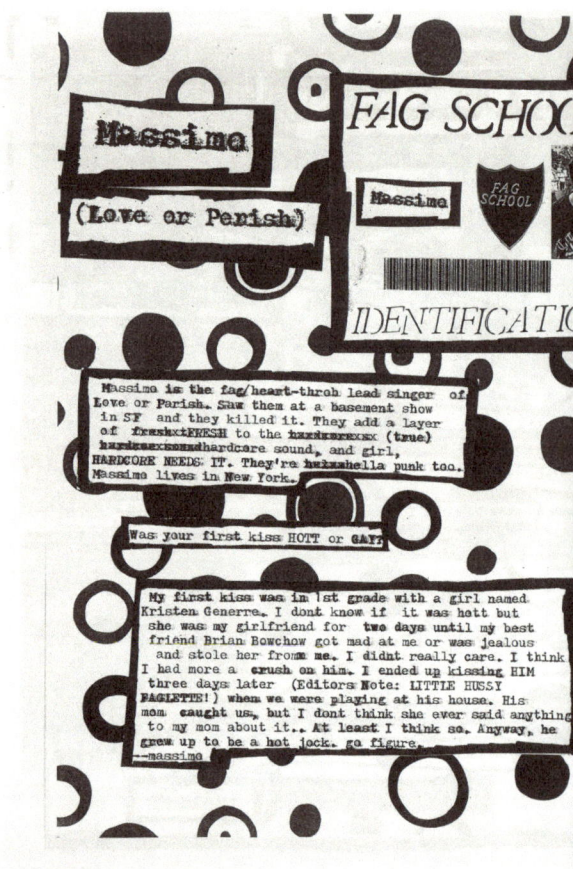

Fag School, no. 3, 2008
Photocopy, saddle stitched, 11 × 8 ½ in. (27.9 × 21.6 cm)
Collection Philip Aarons and Shelley Fox Aarons

FAG SCHOOL #4 JOIN THE PROFESSIONALS

Fag School, no. 4, 2012
Photocopy, saddle stitched, 8 ½ × 7 in. (21.5 × 17.7 cm)
Collection Philip Aarons and Shelley Fox Aarons

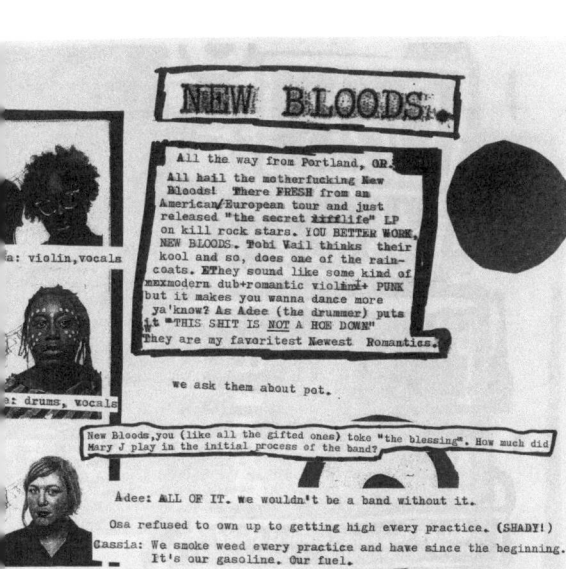

NEW BLOODS:

All the way from Portland, OR.

All hail the motherfucking New Bloods! There FRESH from an American/European tour and just released "the secret life" LP on kill rock stars. YOU BETTER WORK, NEW BLOODS. Tobi Vail thinks their kool and so, does one of the rain-coats. EThey sound like some kind of mxmodern dub+romantic violin+ PUNK but it makes you wanna dance more ya'know? As Adee (the drummer) puts it "THIS SHIT IS NOT A HOE DOWN" They are my favoritest Newest Romantics.

we ask them about pot.

New Bloods,you (like all the gifted ones) toke "the blessing". How much did Mary J play in the initial process of the band?

Adee: ALL OF IT. we wouldn't be a band without it.

Osa refused to own up to getting high every practice. (SHADY!)

Cassia: We smoke weed every practice and have since the beginning. It's our gasoline. Our fuel.

Why do so many musicians refuse to, own up to being stoners?

Adee:People don't want to look like hippys , but thats sad. Im black, I got dreadz and I'm Jaimaicain so I can get away with it. Cause I ain't some dirty white hippy. I smell like mango butter. and my dreads aren't nasty. I'm carrying coccoa butter with me RIGHT NOW.

Cassia: I dont know, I dont worry. Maybe they worry that their music wont be taken seriously or be "drug fueled" I dont care bout that.

Osa: I dont admit to,it because I dont want to break my parents hearts. They asked me if I did drugs and i said no.

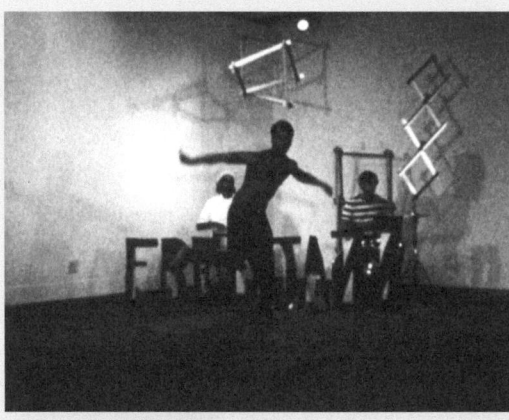

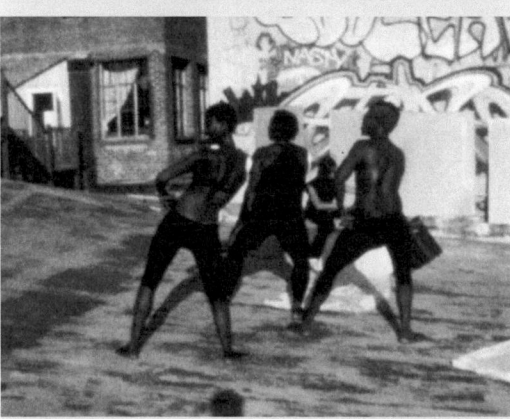

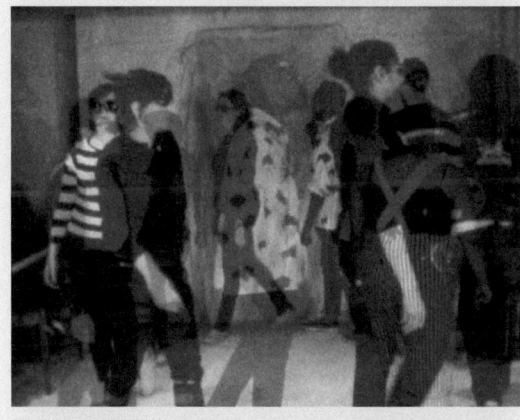

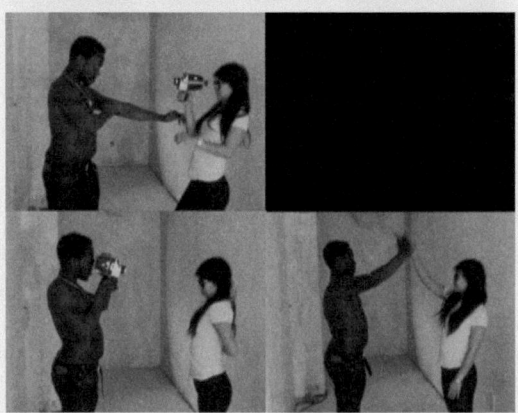

Brontez Purnell Dance Company
Stills from *Free Jazz*, 2013
Cinematographer: Gary Fembot
16mm film; black and white, sound; 23 min., 50 sec.
Collection Gary Fembot

Osa Atoe

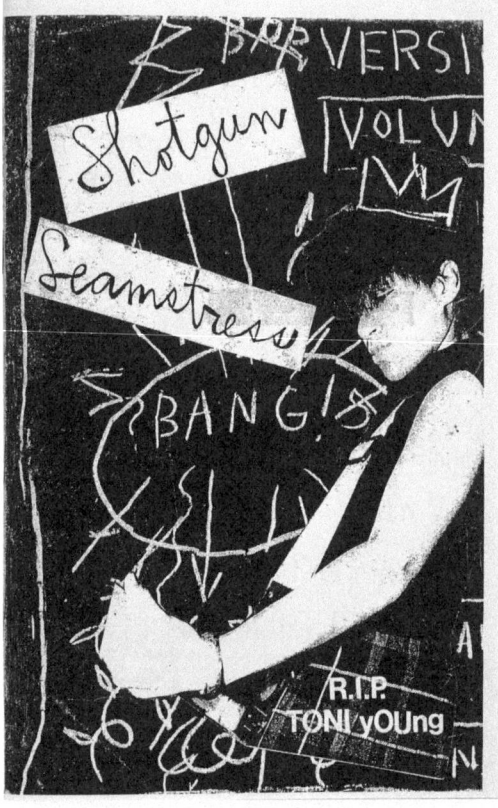

Shotgun Seamstress, no. 1, August 2006
Photocopy, saddle stitched, 8 ½ × 5 ½ in. (21.6 × 14 cm)
Private collection, New York

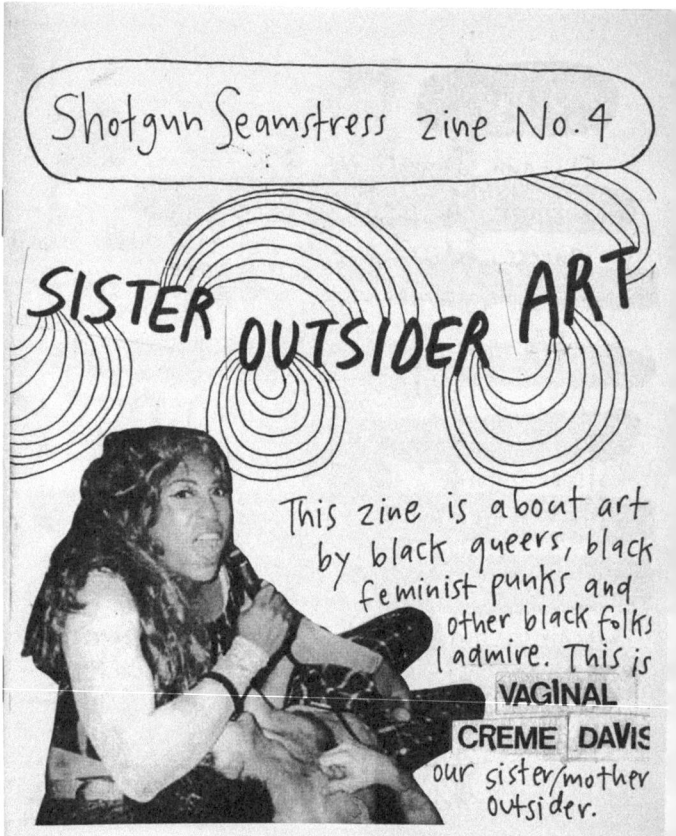

Shotgun Seamstress, no. 4, March 2010
Photocopy, saddle stitched, 10 ¾ × 8 ⅝ in. (27.3 × 21.9 cm)
Private collection, New York

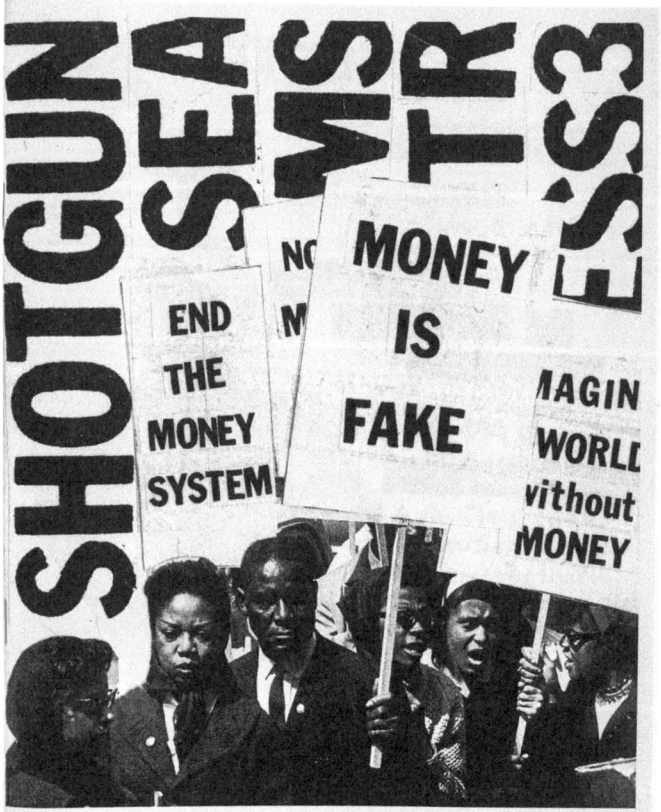

Shotgun Seamstress, no. 3, February 2009
Photocopy, saddle stitched, 10 ¾ × 8 ⅝ in. (27.3 × 21.9 cm)
Private collection, New York

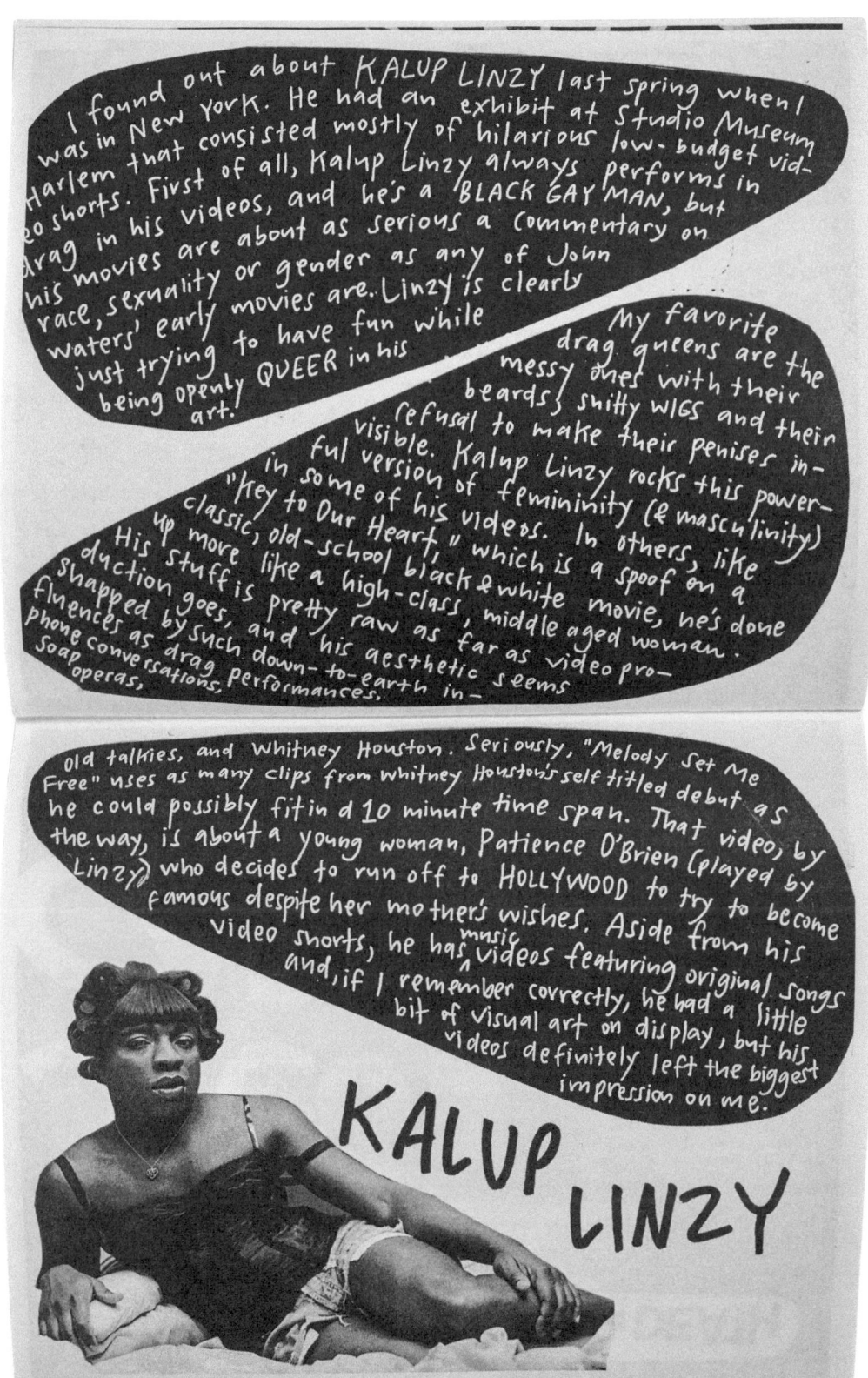

I found out about KALUP LINZY last spring when I was in New York. He had an exhibit at Studio Museum Harlem that consisted mostly of hilarious low-budget video shorts. First of all, Kalup Linzy always performs in drag in his videos, and he's a BLACK GAY MAN, but his movies are about as serious a commentary on race, sexuality or gender as any of John Waters' early movies are. Linzy is clearly just trying to have fun while being openly QUEER in his art!

My favorite drag queens are the messy ones with their beards, shitty WIGS and their refusal to make their penises invisible. Kalup Linzy rocks this powerful version of femininity (& masculinity) in some of his videos. In others, like "Key to Our Heart," which is a spoof on a classic, old-school black & white movie, he's done up more like a high-class, middle aged woman. His stuff is pretty raw as far as video production goes, and his aesthetic seems shaped by such down-to-earth influences as drag performances, phone conversations, soap operas,

old talkies, and Whitney Houston. Seriously, "Melody Set Me Free" uses as many clips from Whitney Houston's self titled debut as he could possibly fit in a **10** minute time span. That video, by the way, is about a young woman, Patience O'Brien (played by Linzy) who decides to run off to HOLLYWOOD to try to become famous despite her mother's wishes. Aside from his video shorts, he has music videos featuring original songs and, if I remember correctly, he had a little bit of visual art on display, but his videos definitely left the biggest impression on me.

KALUP LINZY

Shotgun Seamstress, no. 4, March 2010
Photocopy, saddle stitched, 10¾ × 8⅝ in. (27.3 × 21.9 cm)
Private collection, New York

6.

A Continuing Legacy, 2010–2023

Since 2010, the increasing popularity of art book and zine fairs has given artists' zines new levels of visibility. While the internet and social media have provided more affordable and faster means of publishing and networking, printed zines continue to offer physical relations with viewers and readers, material connections to an artist's oeuvre, and a sense of intimacy that rarely exists in online spaces. This chapter looks at a selection of artists whose zines and related practices draw from and expand the legacies found in preceding sections of this book.

For many, zines have become integral to their exhibition practice. Jordan Nassar, for example, has produced numerous zines that relate to his interests in Palestinian cultural heritage and the textile practices featured in his other artworks. Pat McCarthy's zines likewise relate to other components of his oeuvre, such as those documenting his pigeon-keeping projects, which also nod to the genre of hobbyists' zines. Since 2009, Amy Sillman's *The O-G* has supplemented her painting practice, allowing for explication, historical contextualization, and critical rejoinders to existing artistic discourses in often humorous ways. And Cameron Jamie's colorful, multilayered zines translate techniques found in his drawings and sculptures into print.

Crossing Indigenous activism with the legacies of 1990s queer and feminist punk cultures, the zines of Demian DinéYazhi'—both solo authored and as part of the initiative R.I.S.E. (Radical Indigenous Survivance and Empowerment)—contend with complex issues, including settler colonialism, environmental criminality, and queer intimacy. Maggie Lee's work also draws on the feminist punk legacy of Riot Grrrl as well as the aesthetics of the Alleged gallery generation, with explorations of adolescent girlhood, millennial subcultures, and the self as a first-generation Taiwanese American.

Several artists have made work that incorporates zine distribution in the vein of Projet Mobilivre-Bookmobile (seen in section 5). Between 2013 and 2014 Lele Saveri and his 8-Ball Community collaborators curated *The Newsstand*, a pop-up zine shop in a Brooklyn subway station. As a means of bringing visibility to artists of color underrepresented at the larger art book fairs, Devin N. Morris started the Brown Paper Zine & Small Press Fair in 2017. His *3 Dot Zine* highlights his experience in the Baltimore house music scene and interrogates the personal impact of police violence against Black Americans, among other issues. The Mexico City–based collective RRD (Red de Reproducción y Distribución / Reproduction and Distribution Network) utilizes a kiosk as a hub for their artistic activities. Their work has played with the issue of circulation, as in the 2020 project RedEx (a parody of FedEx), which was partly inspired by Mexican mail artist Ulises Carrión, who corresponded and collaborated with Anna Banana and Bill Gaglione (featured in section 1).

The zine's pedagogical potential and relation to political pamphlets continues to be important for many artists. Dominican Republic–born Lizania Cruz's *We the News* (2016–2022) speaks to issues of diaspora and displacement by gathering immigrants' stories in zine-like brochures distributed via a custom-made kiosk/snack cart. Cassandra Press, started by Kandis Williams with Nassar and Taylor Doran, quickly became the pedagogic arm of Williams's artistic project. It publishes both zines and "readers"—ad hoc photocopied textbooks once ubiquitous in university education. In their stark juxtapositions of texts on such theoretical topics as misogynoir, Cassandra's readers form the intellectual equivalent of collage (a practice often literalized in wall-sized works of appropriated photographs that relate to the texts), and are used in educational workshops under the auspices of Cassandra Classrooms.

Founded in 2018 by Yusuf Hassan (and now co-led with Kwamé Sorrell), BlackMass Publishing serves community building, archival, and pedagogic functions around Black diasporic cultures and histories. Juxtapositions of appropriated imagery honor artistic predecessors like Beverly Buchanan, feature African crafts, disseminate discographies of Black musicians, and more. The BlackMass Publishing Mail-in Program, initiated during the 2020 COVID-19 lockdown, harkens back to the correspondence practices of the 1970s. Neta Bomani's "100 Days of Zines" comprises innovatively designed zines dedicated to Black American histories and figures, from librarians to punks. With her *Dark Matter Objects*, Bomani produced a multimedia zine/video interrelating the legacies of racial oppression and computational history, proving that the zine can both inhabit and speak back to our increasingly digitized and electronic environment.

Cameron Jamie

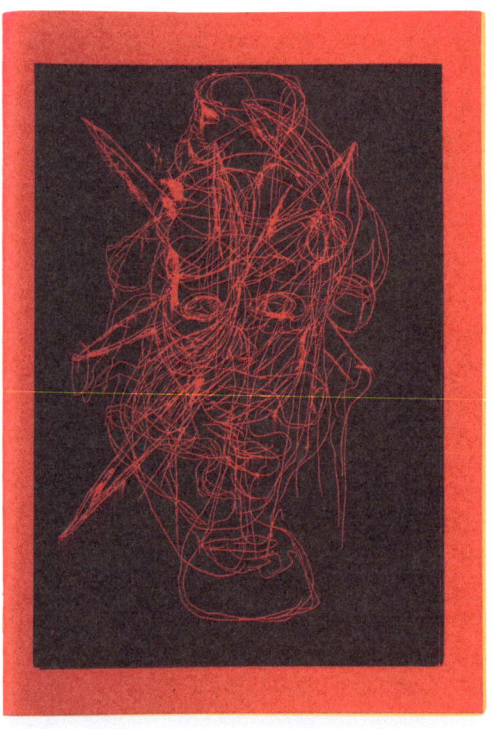

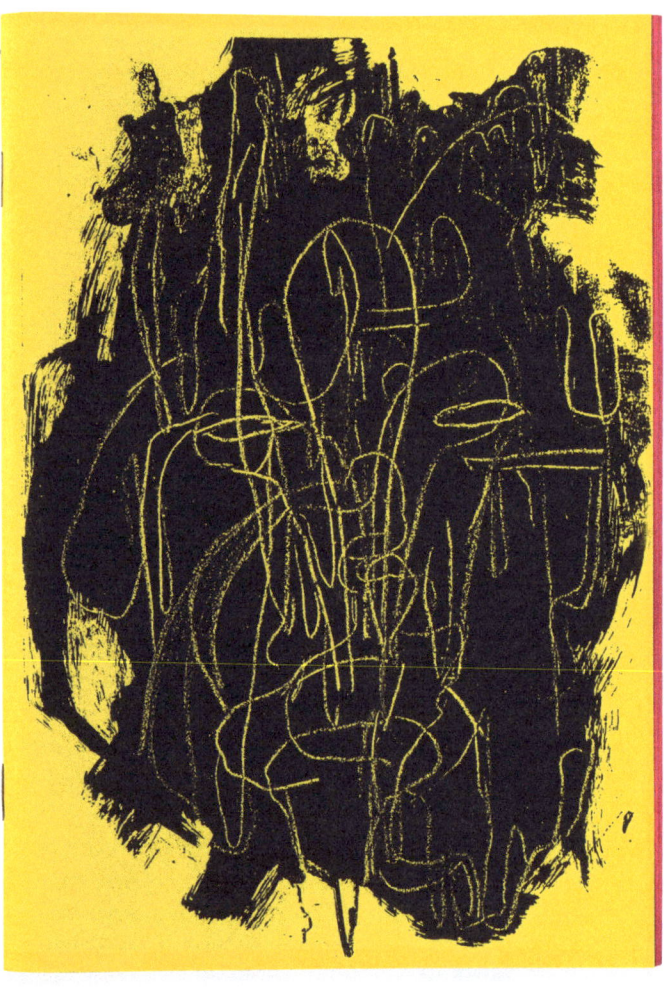

KOPBF Book III, 2005
Photocopy, saddle stitched, 8 ¼ × 5 ⅞ in. (21 × 14.9 cm)
Collection Philip Aarons and Shelley Fox Aarons

KOPBF Book I, 2002
Photocopy, saddle stitched, 8 ¼ × 5 ⅞ in. (21 × 14.9 cm)
Collection Philip Aarons and Shelley Fox Aarons

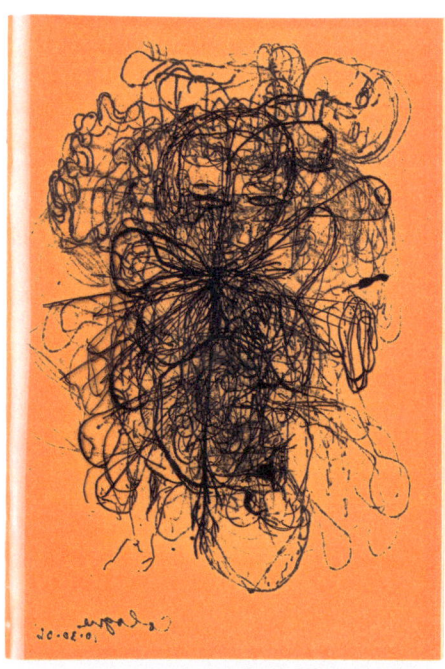

KOPBF Book V, 2007
Photocopy, saddle stitched, Mylar wrappers,
8 ¼ × 5 ⅞ in. (21 × 14.9 cm)
Collection Philip Aarons and Shelley Fox Aarons

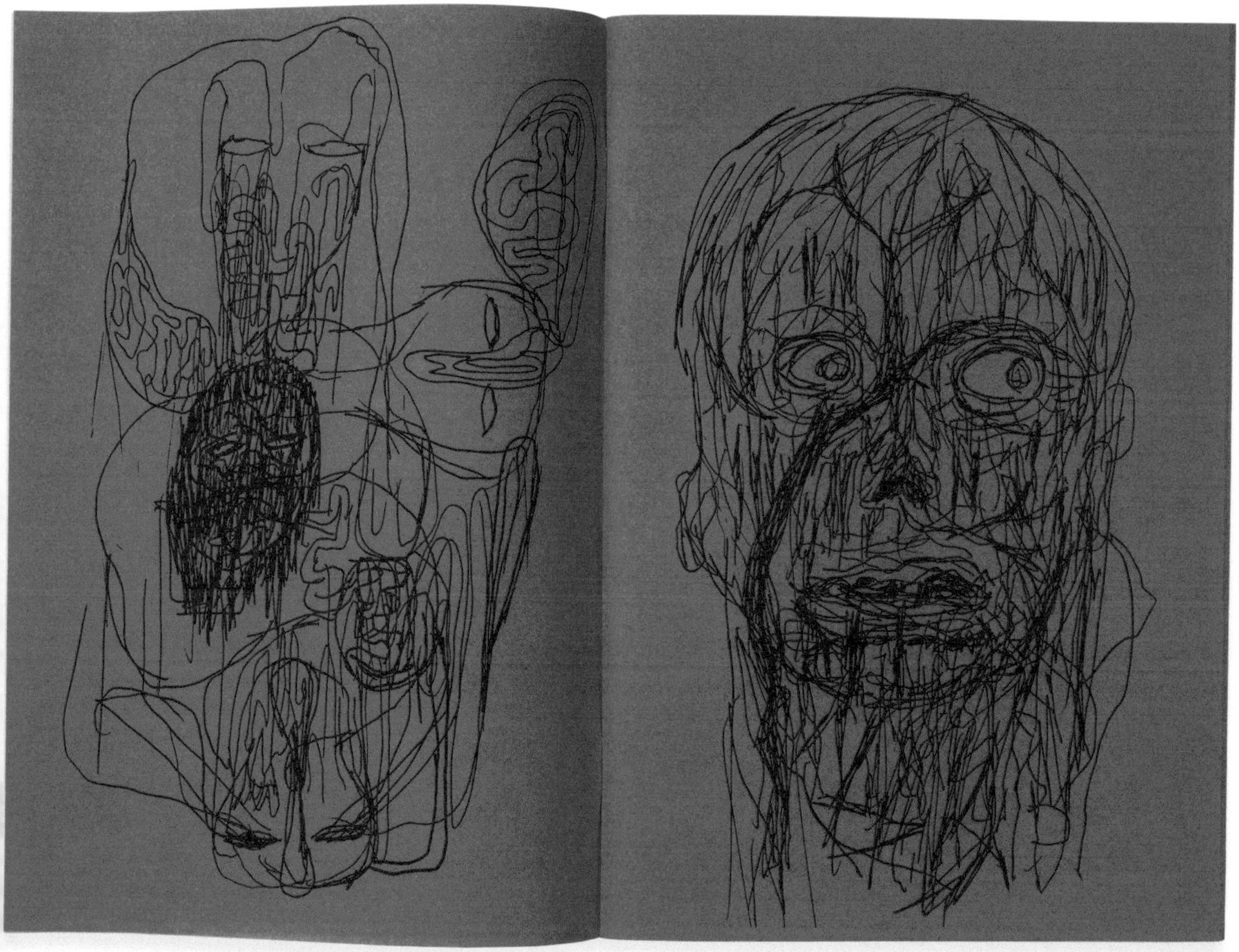

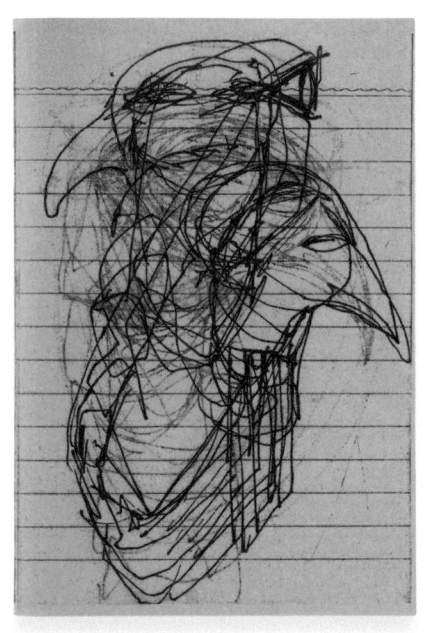
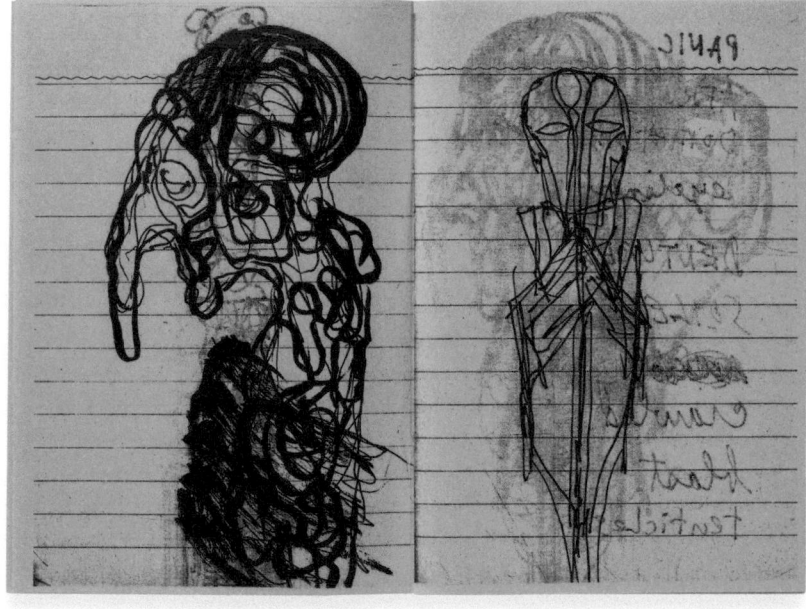

Clutch Fang Bush Toe, 2011
Photocopy, saddle stitched, 5 ⅞ × 4 in. (14.9 × 10.2 cm)
Collection Philip Aarons and Shelley Fox Aarons

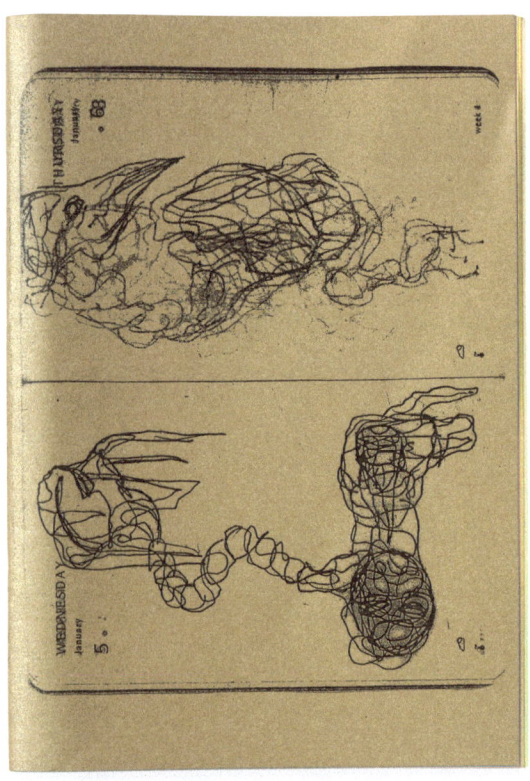

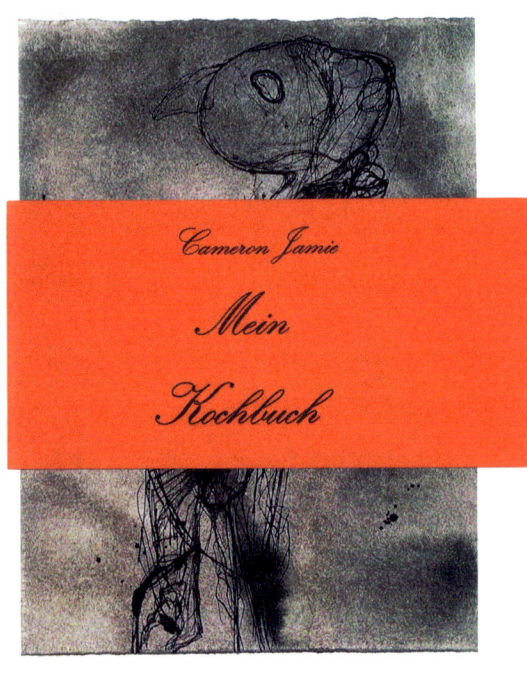

Orphan's Prayer, 2011
Photocopy, saddle stitched, 8 ¼ × 5 ⅞ in. (21 × 14.9 cm)
Collection Philip Aarons and Shelley Fox Aarons

Mein Kochbuch, 2011
Laser print, saddle stitched, red wrappers 8 ¼ × 5 ⅞ in. (21 × 14.9 cm)
Collection Philip Aarons and Shelley Fox Aarons

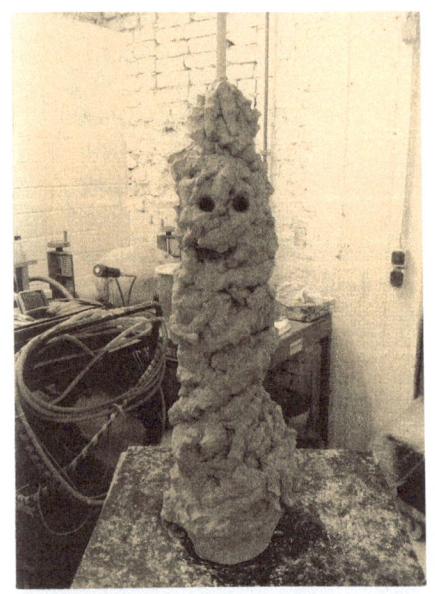

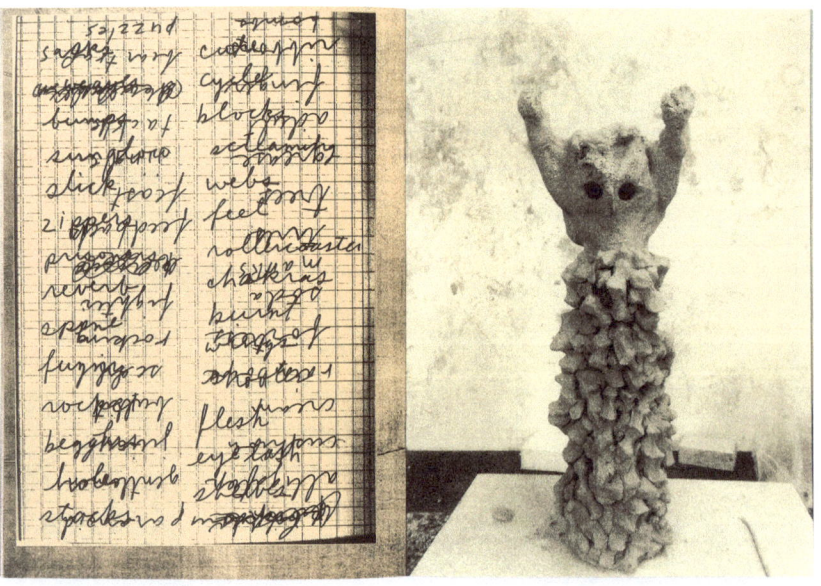

Bunka, 2012
Photocopy, saddle stitched, 7 ½ × 5 ½ in. (19.1 × 14 cm)
Collection Philip Aarons and Shelley Fox Aarons

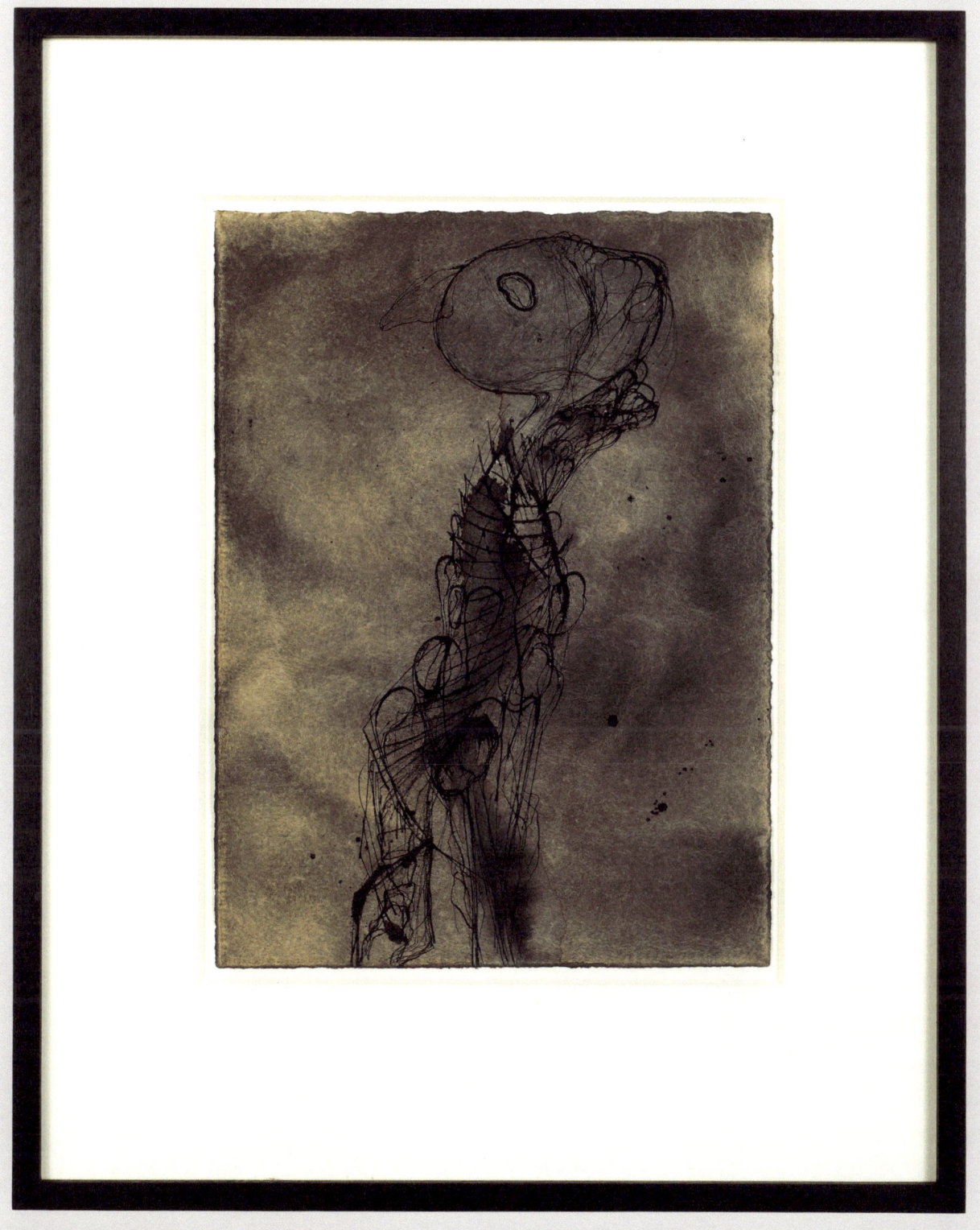

Ain't Gonna Cry No More, 2011
Ink and coffee on paper, 13 × 10 in. (33 × 25.4 cm)
Collection the artist

Maggie Lee

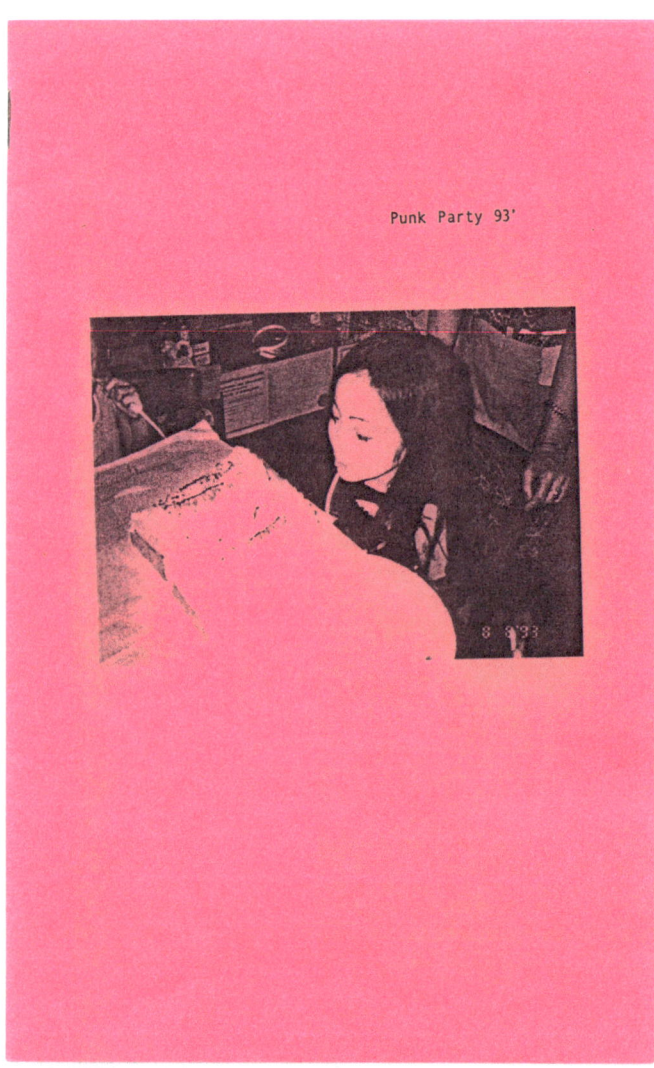

Punk Party '93, 2020
Photocopy, saddle stitched, 8 ½ × 5 ½ in. (21.6 × 14 cm)
Collection the artist

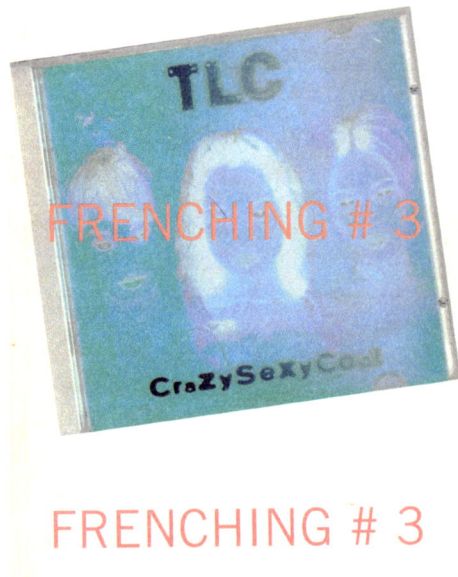

Frenching #3, 2009
Photocopy, saddle stitched, 9 × 6 in. (22.9 × 15.2 cm)
Collection the artist

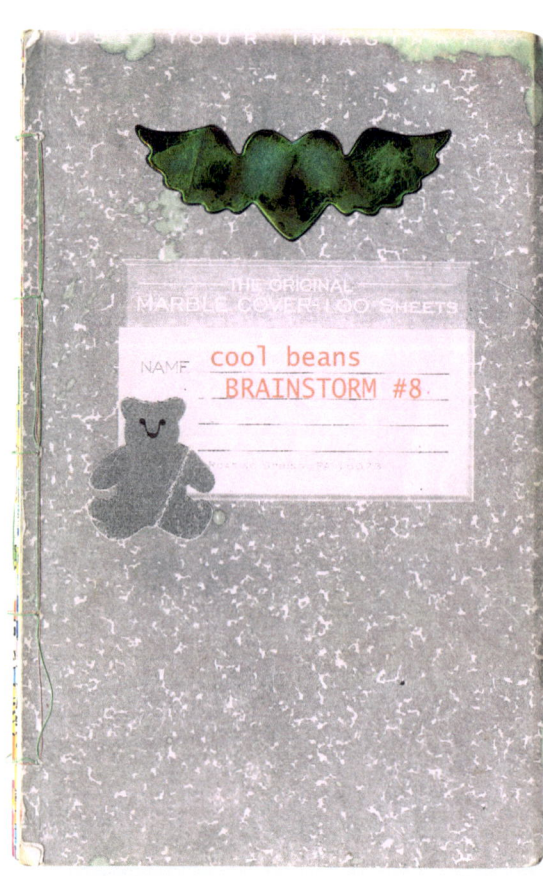

Cool Beans/Brainstorm, no. 8, 2008
Photocopy, Japanese stab binding,
8 ½ × 5 ½ in. (21.6 × 14 cm)
Collection the artist

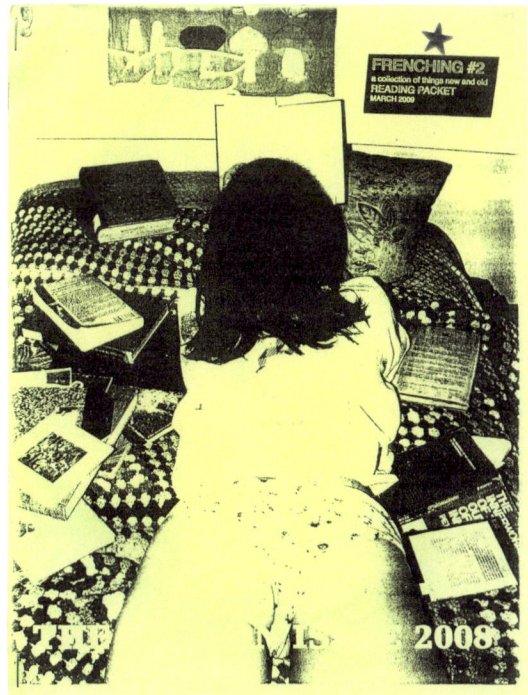

Frenching #2, March 2009
Photocopy, side stapled, 11 × 8 ½ in. (27.9 × 21.6 cm)
Collection the artist

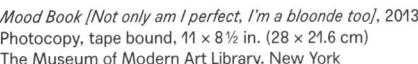

Mood Book [Not only am I perfect, I'm a bloonde too], 2013
Photocopy, tape bound, 11 × 8 ½ in. (28 × 21.6 cm)
The Museum of Modern Art Library, New York

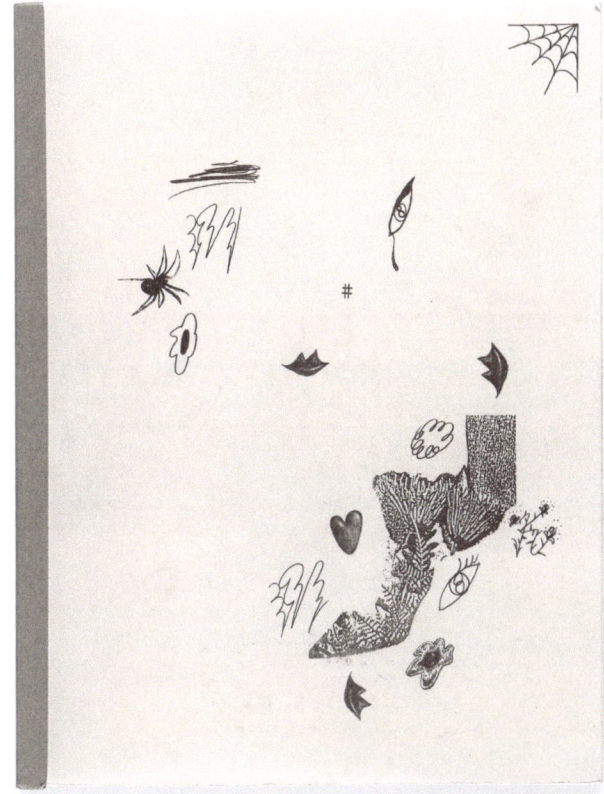

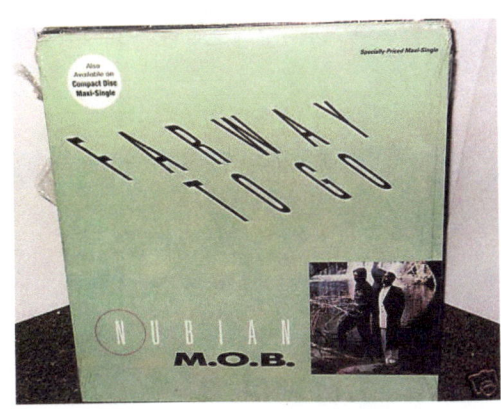

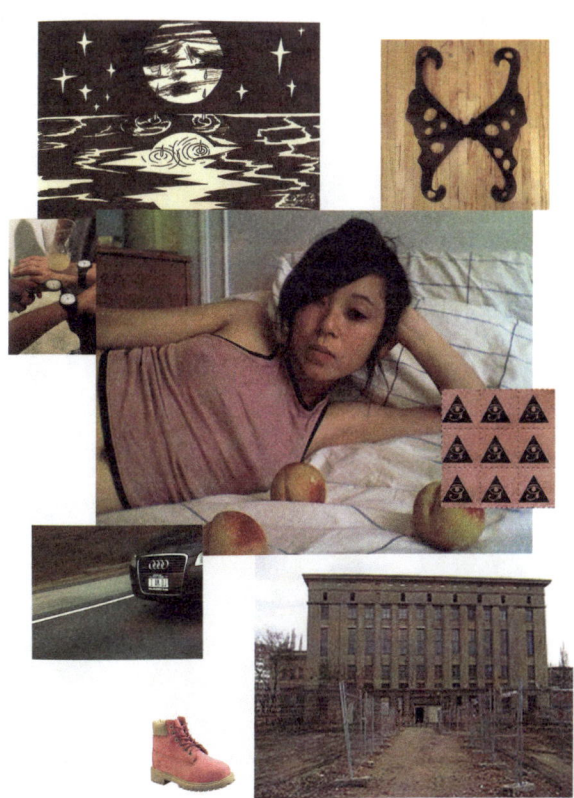

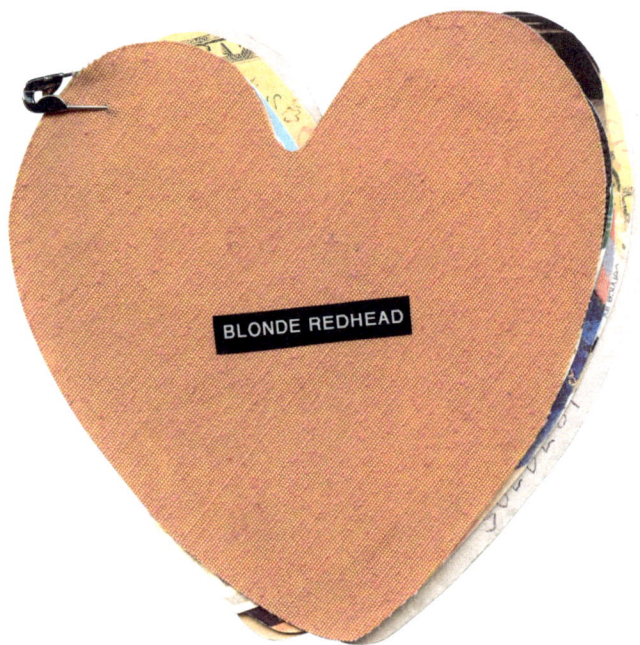

Blonde Redhead, 2015
Photocopy, bound with safety pin,
5 ½ × 5 ½ in. (14 × 14 cm)
Collection the artist

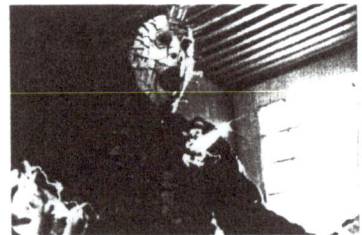

MAGGIE LEE
AND

FUCK
THIS
LIFE

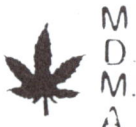

M
D
M
A.

Maggie Lee and Weirdo Dave (a.k.a. FTL)
MDMA, 2012
Photocopy, saddle stitched, 5 ¼ × 4 ¼ in. (13.3 × 10.2 cm)
Collection the artist

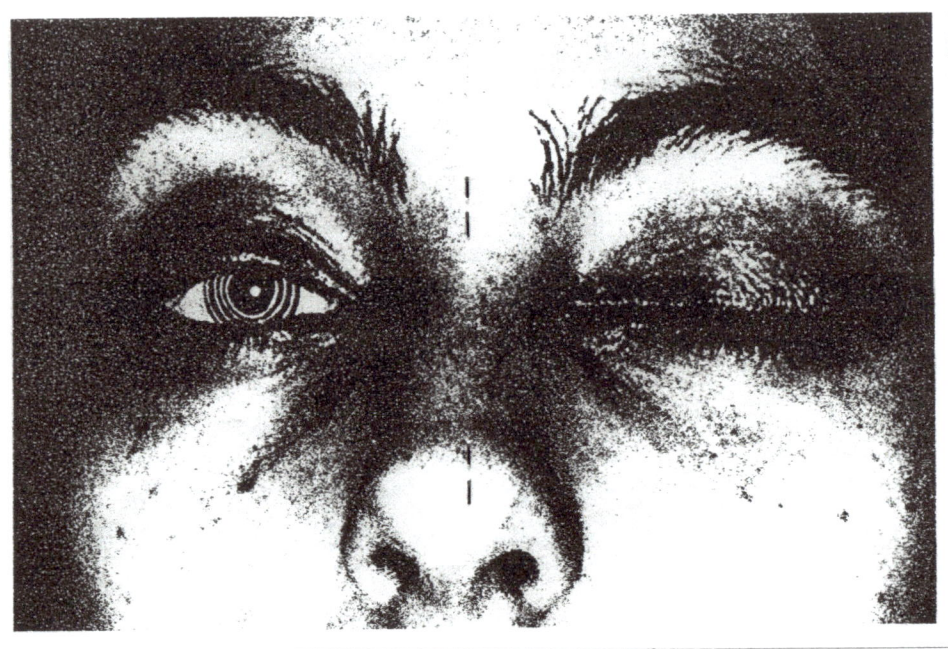

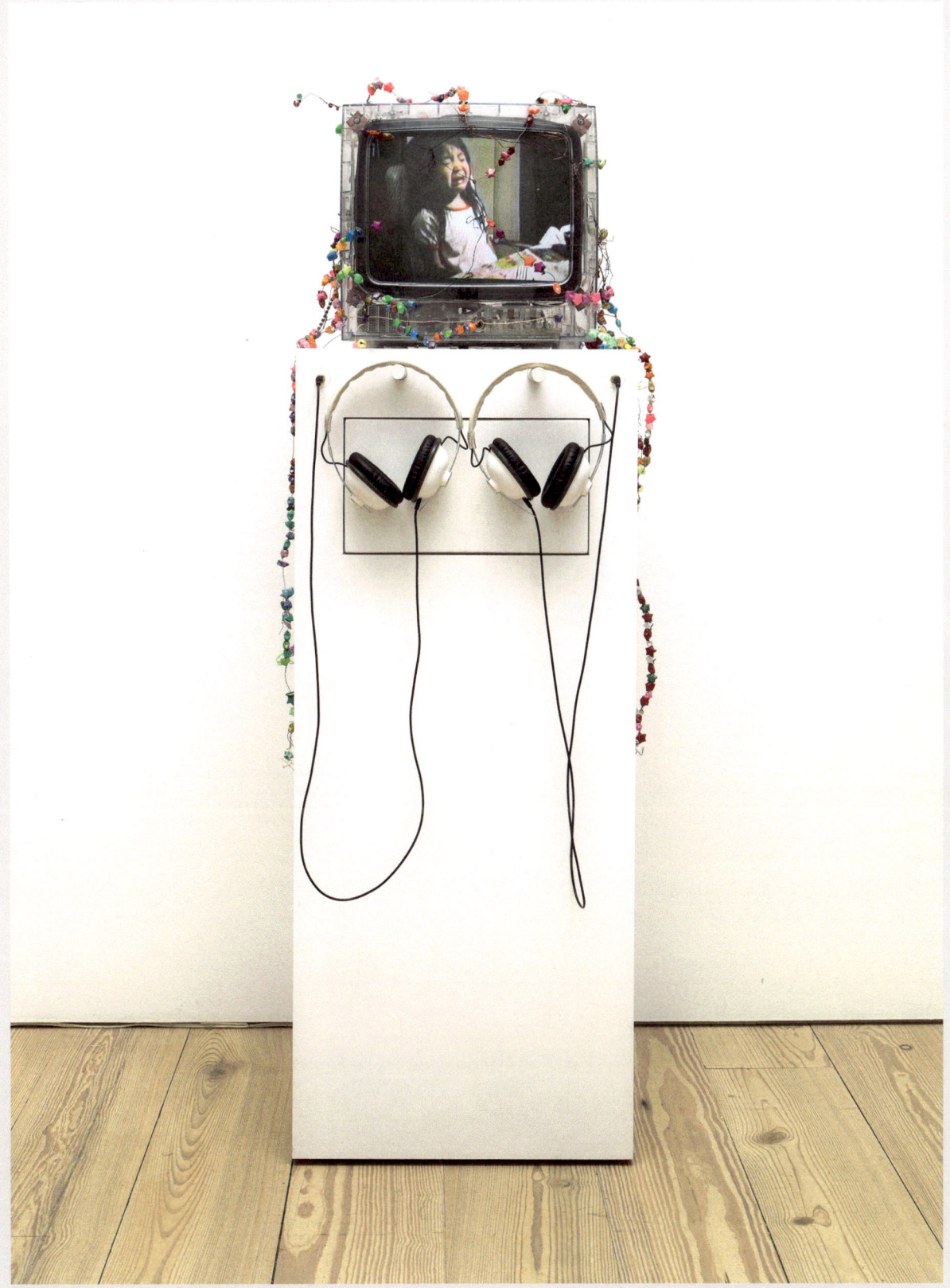

Maggie TV, 2017
Single-channel video on clear vintage Sony television, wire, epoxy-
covered paper stars, beads, mixed media, dimensions variable
Collection Bobby and Eleanor Cayre, New York

Amy Sillman

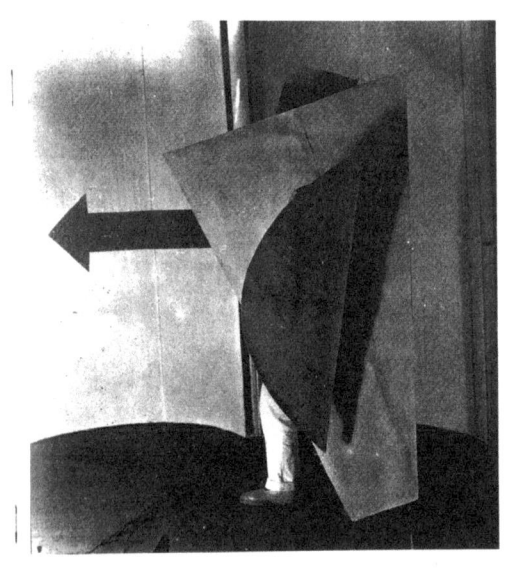

The O-G, vol. 1, 2009
Offset, saddle stitched, 8½ × 5½ in. (21.5 × 14 cm)
Collection Philip Aarons and Shelley Fox Aarons

The O-G, vols. 1–2, American Edition, 2009
Offset, saddle stitched, 8½ × 5½ in. (21.5 × 14 cm)
Collection Philip Aarons and Shelley Fox Aarons

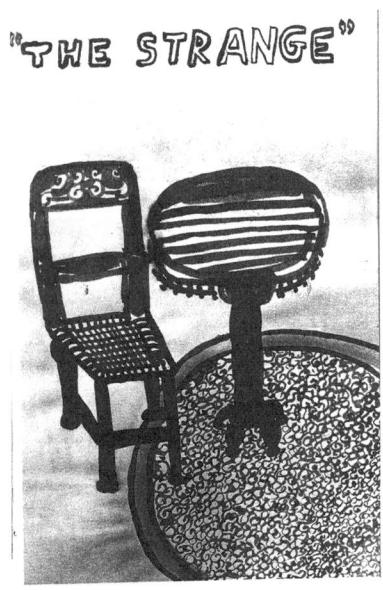

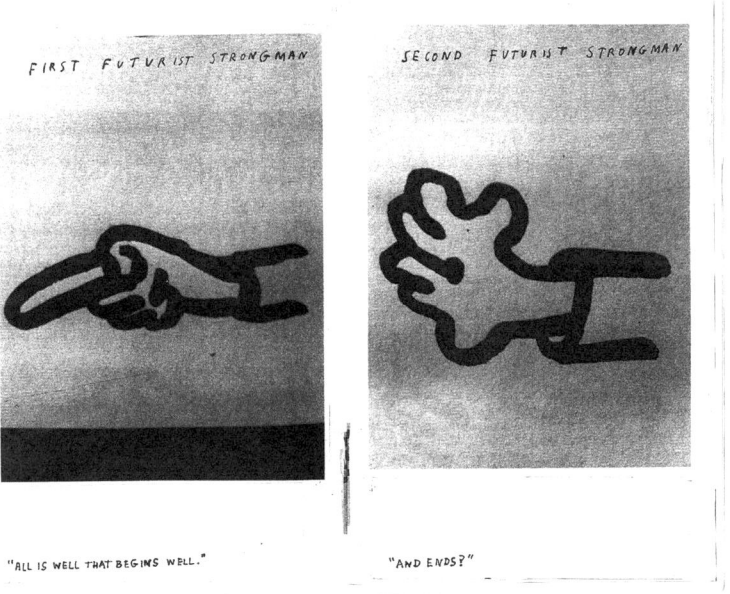

The O-G, vol. 4, The Strange, 2010
Offset, saddle stitched, 8½ × 5½ in. (21.5 × 14 cm)
Collection Philip Aarons and Shelley Fox Aarons

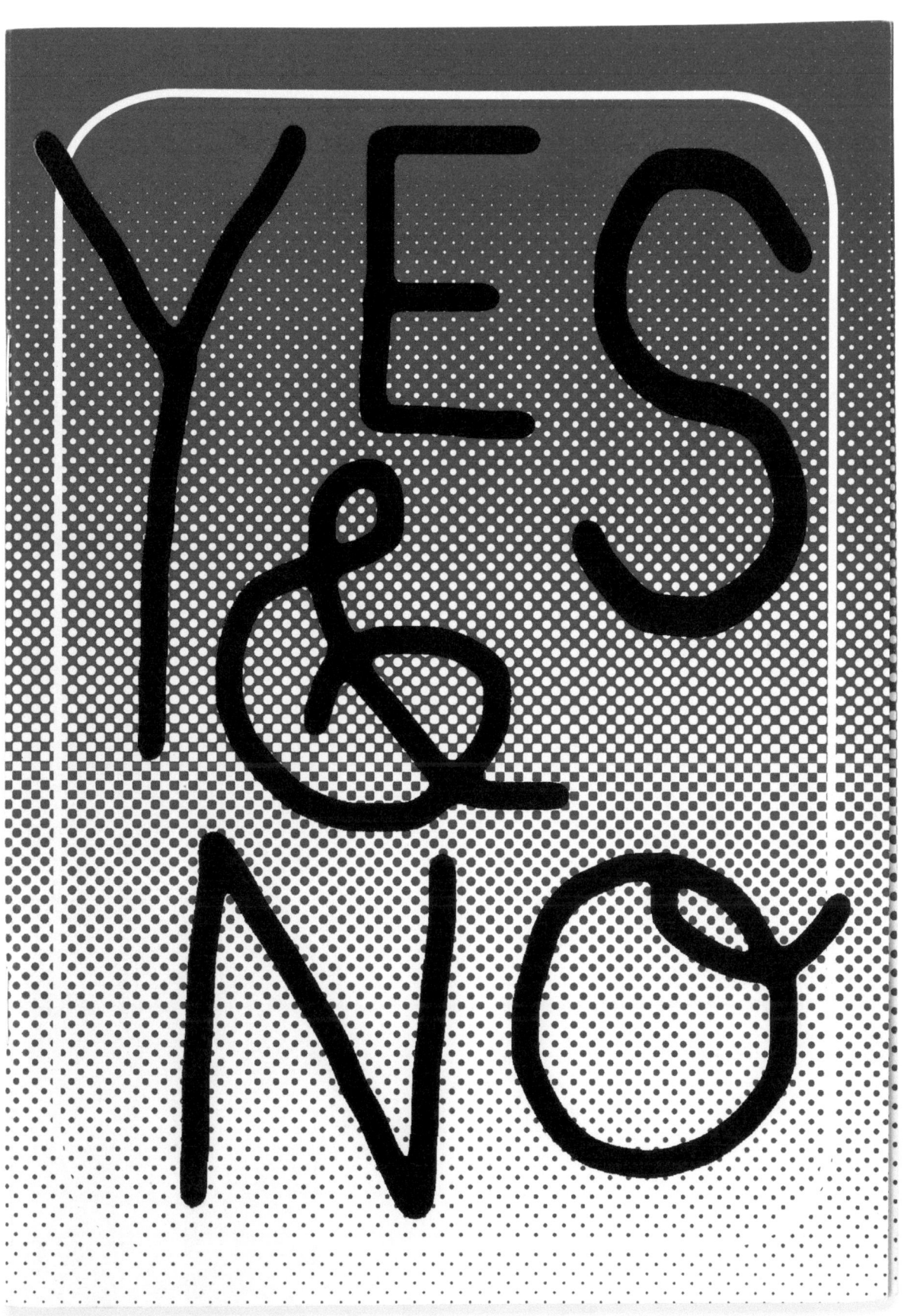

The O-G, vol. 9, *Yes & No*, 2016
Produced in collaboration with Rob Giampietro
Offset, saddle stitched, with foldout,
8 ½ × 5 ½ in. (21.6 × 14 cm)
Collection Philip Aarons and Shelley Fox Aarons

the All-Over
Amy Sillman

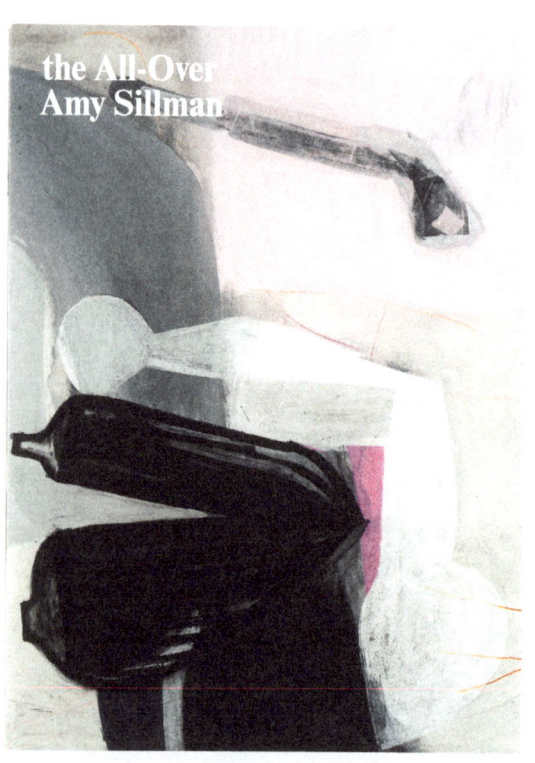

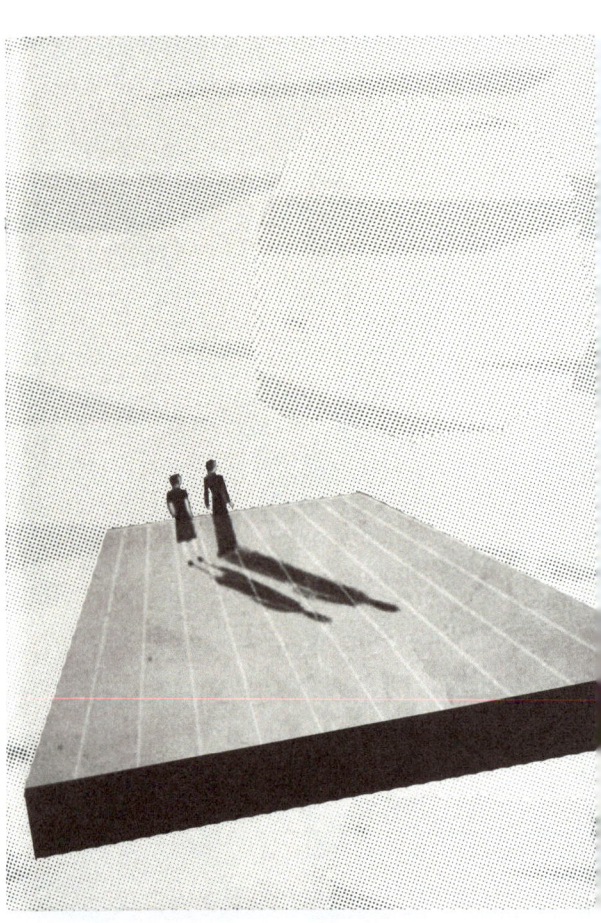

The O-G, vol. 10, *The All-Over*, 2016
Offset, saddle stitched, 8 ½ × 5 ½ in. (21.5 × 14 cm)
Collection the artist

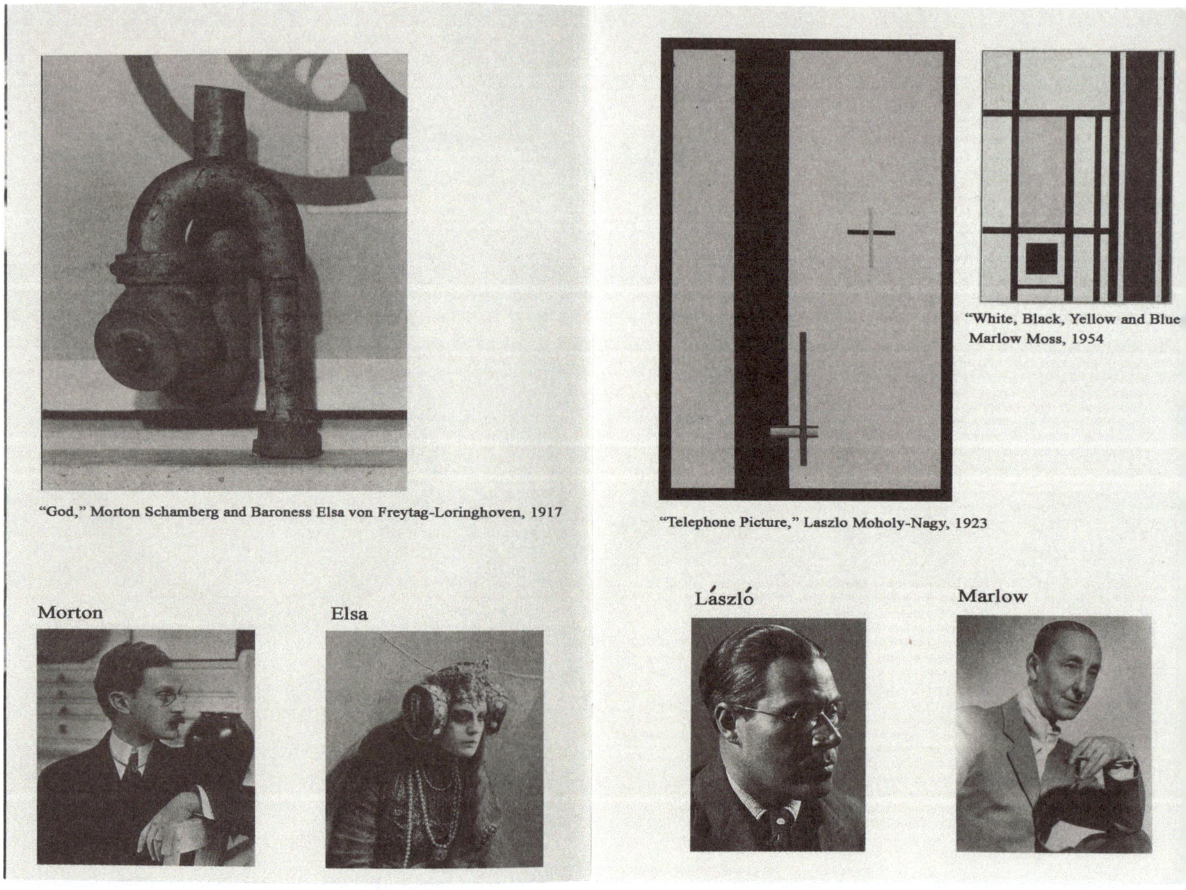

"God," Morton Schamberg and Baroness Elsa von Freytag-Loringhoven, 1917

"White, Black, Yellow and Blue
Marlow Moss, 1954

"Telephone Picture," Laszlo Moholy-Nagy, 1923

Morton

Elsa

László

Marlow

The O-G, vol. 13, *Shape*, 2018
Offset, saddle stitched, 8 ½ × 5 ½ in. (21.6 × 14 cm)
Collection Philip Aarons and Shelley Fox Aarons

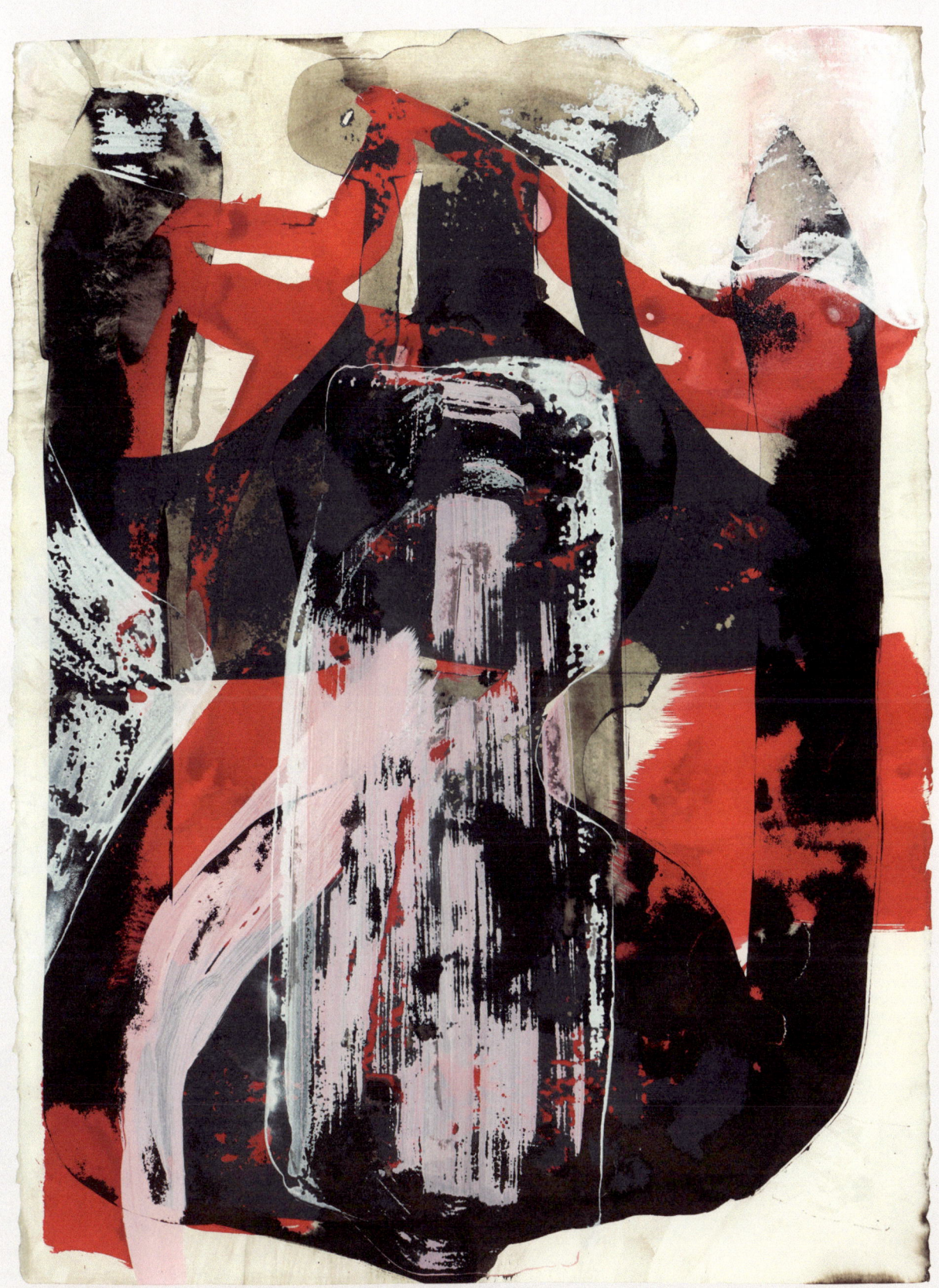

Pink Drawing #56, 2016
(published in *The O-G*, vol. 11, *Metamorphoses*, Winter 2017)
Acrylic, gouache, ink on paper, 30 × 22 ¼ in. (76.2 × 56.5 cm)
Collection the artist

Lele Saveri and
8-Ball Community

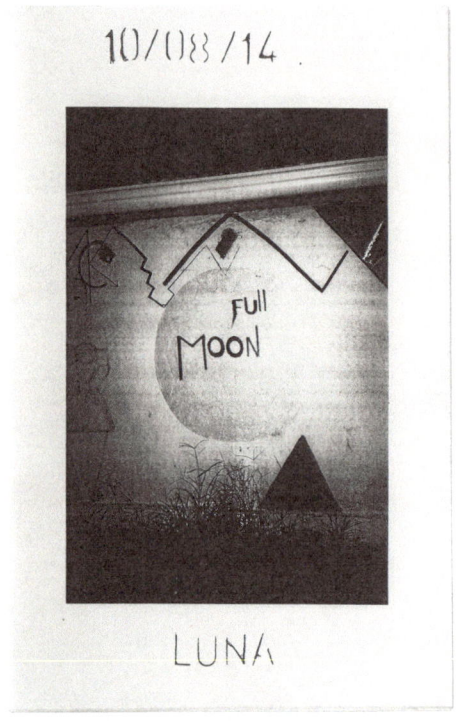

Lele Saveri
Luna, no. 1, 2014
Photocopy, saddle stitched, 8 ½ × 5 ½ in. (21.5 × 14 cm)
Collection Philip Aarons and Shelley Fox Aarons

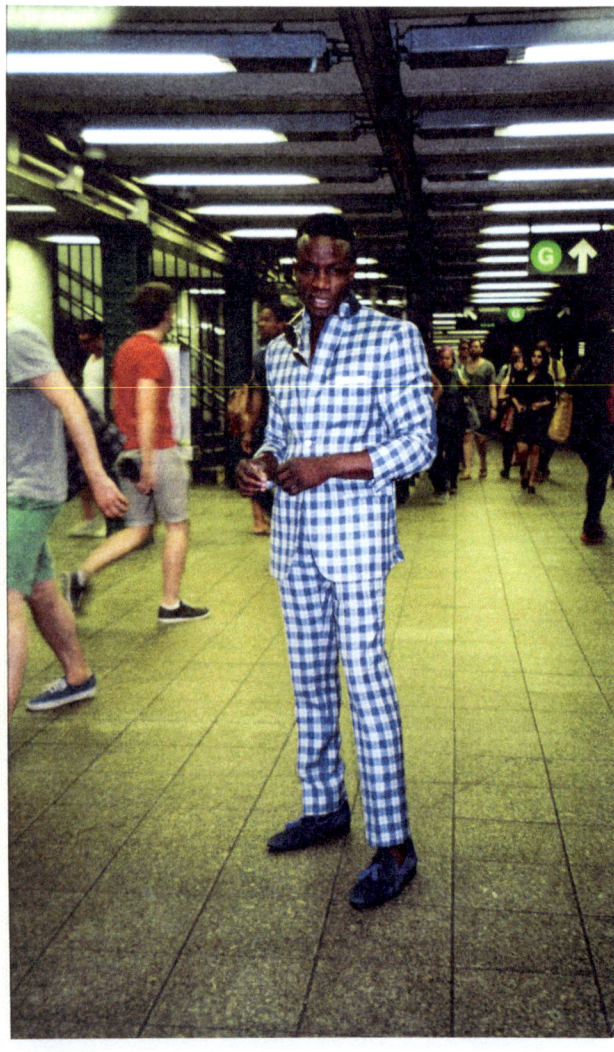

Lele Saveri
Commuters, January 2014
Published by Pau Pau and 8-Ball Zines
Offset, tape bound, 7 ½ × 4 ⅞ in. (19 × 12.5cm)
Collection Philip Aarons and Shelley Fox Aarons

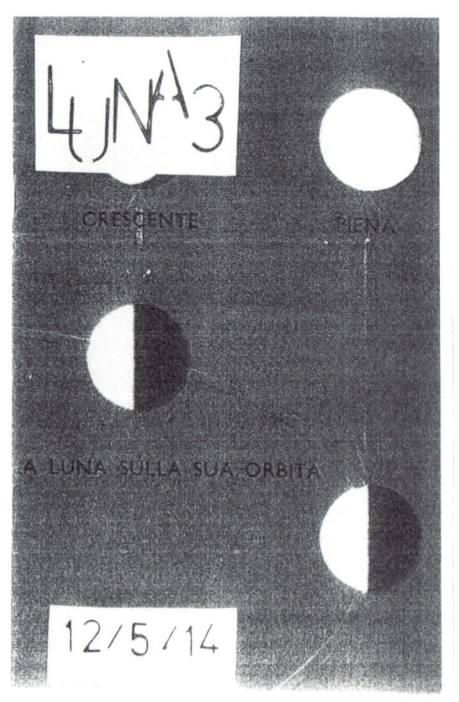

Lele Saveri
Luna, no. 3, 2014
Photocopy, saddle stitched, 8 ½ × 5 ½ in. (21.5 × 14 cm)
Collection Philip Aarons and Shelley Fox Aarons

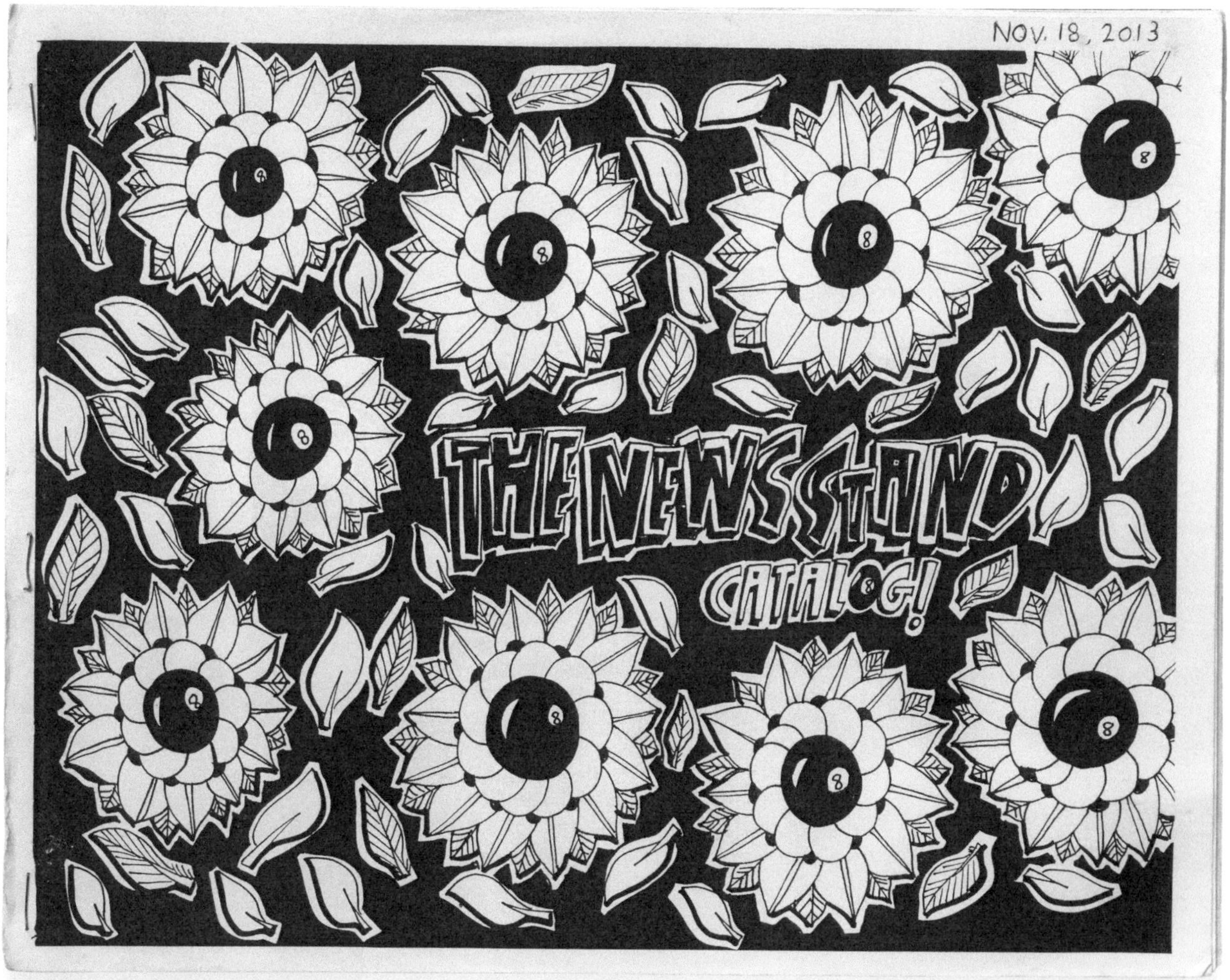

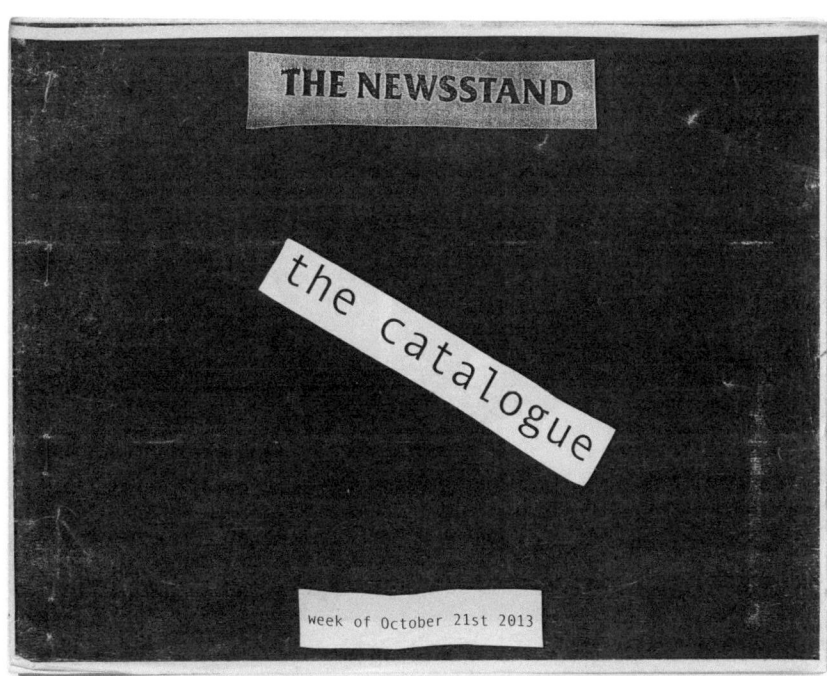

Ray Martinez
The Newsstand Catalog! Week of Nov. 18, 2013, 2013
Photocopy, side stapled, 8½ × 11 in. (21.5 × 28 cm)
Collection Philip Aarons and Shelley Fox Aarons

Lele Saveri
The Newsstand, The Catalogue,
Week of October 21st 2013, 2013
Photocopy, side stapled, 8½ × 11 in. (21.5 × 28 cm)
Collection Philip Aarons and Shelley Fox Aarons

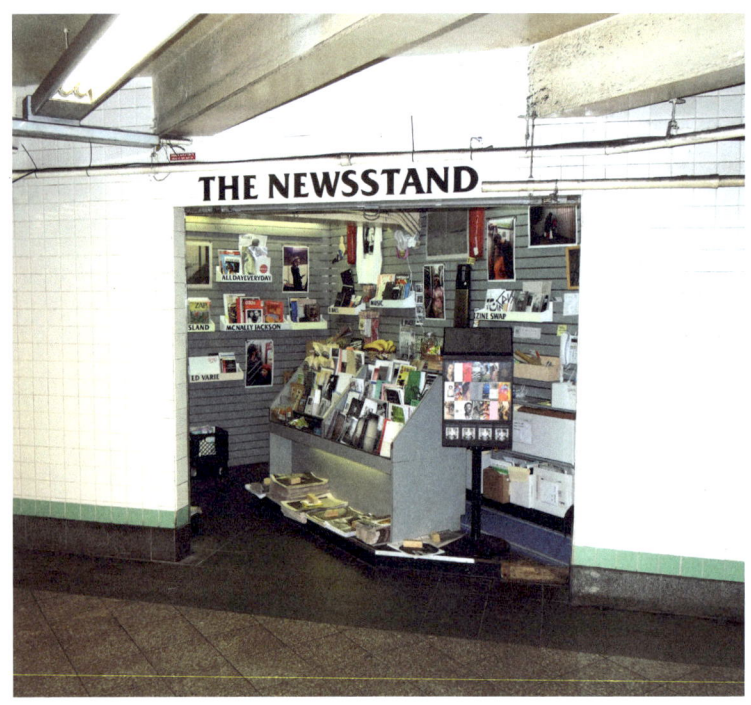

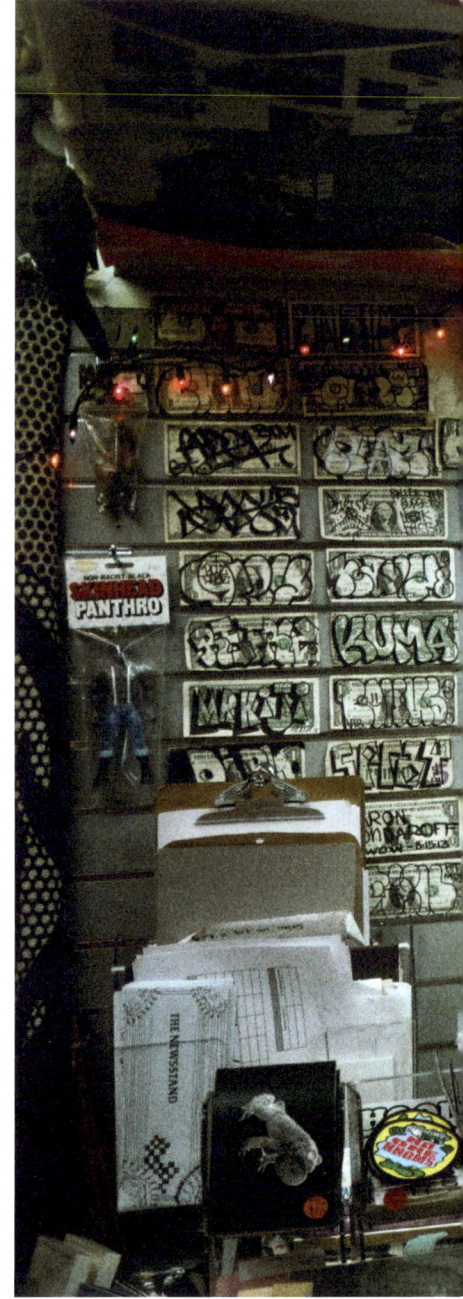

Documentation of Lele Saveri
The Newsstand exterior and interior, 2013–14
Chromogenic prints, 4 × 6 in. (10.2 × 15.3 cm)
Collection the artist

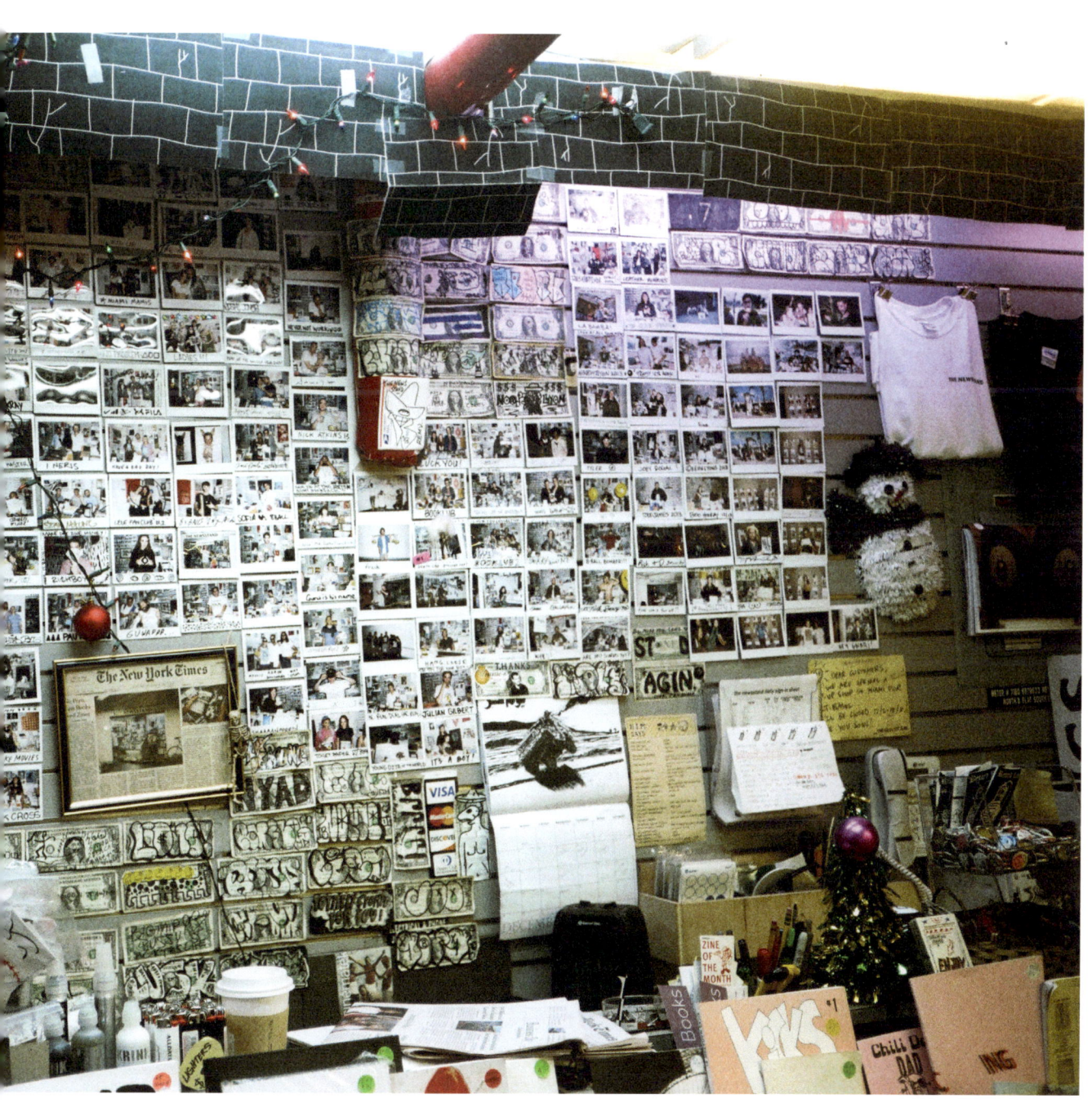

Pat McCarthy

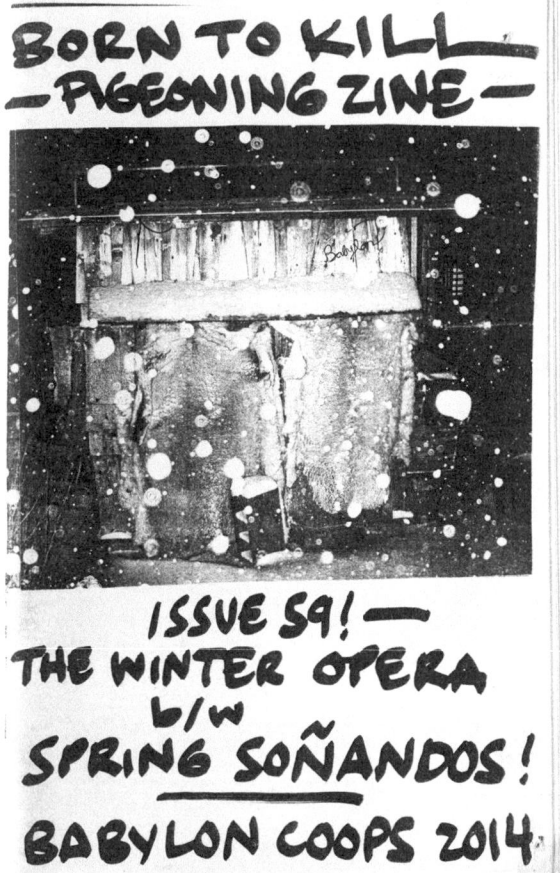

Born to Kill, no. 59, *The Winter Opera*, 2014
Photocopy, saddle stitched, 8 ½ × 5 ½ in. (21.6 × 14 cm)
Collection Philip Aarons and Shelley Fox Aarons

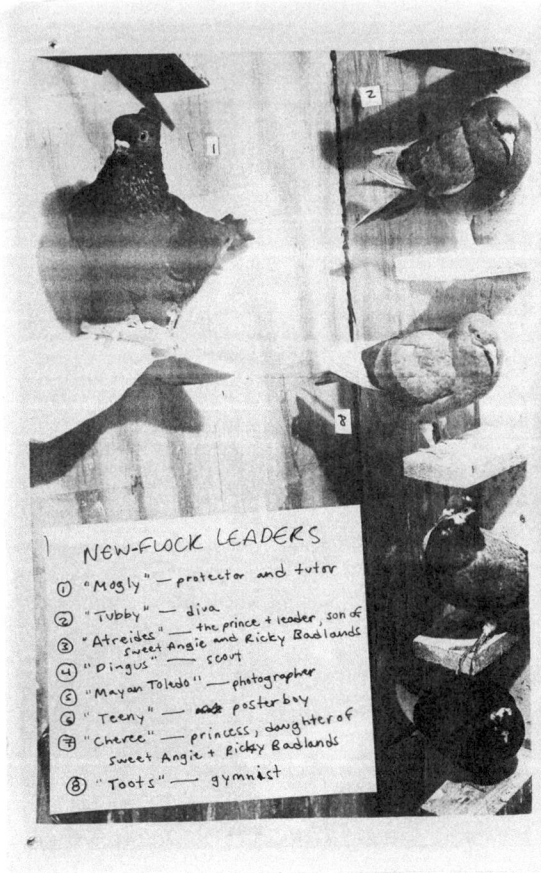

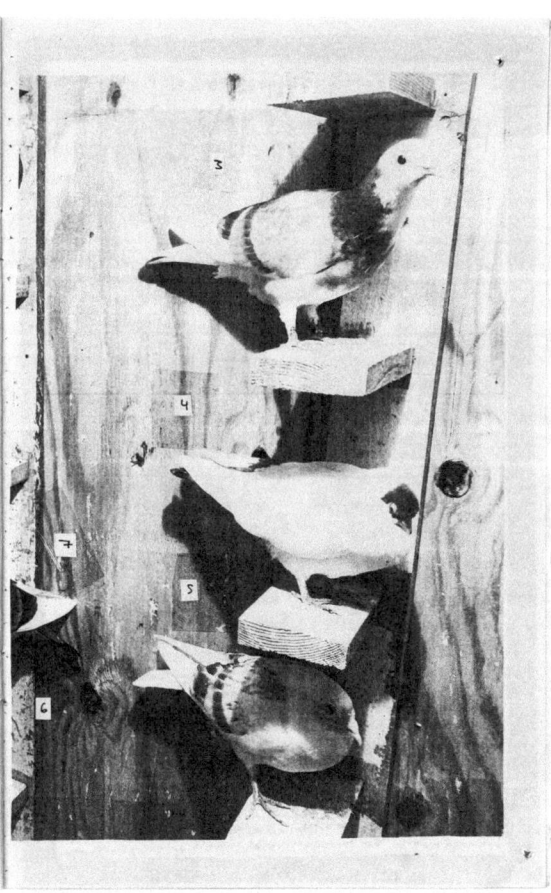

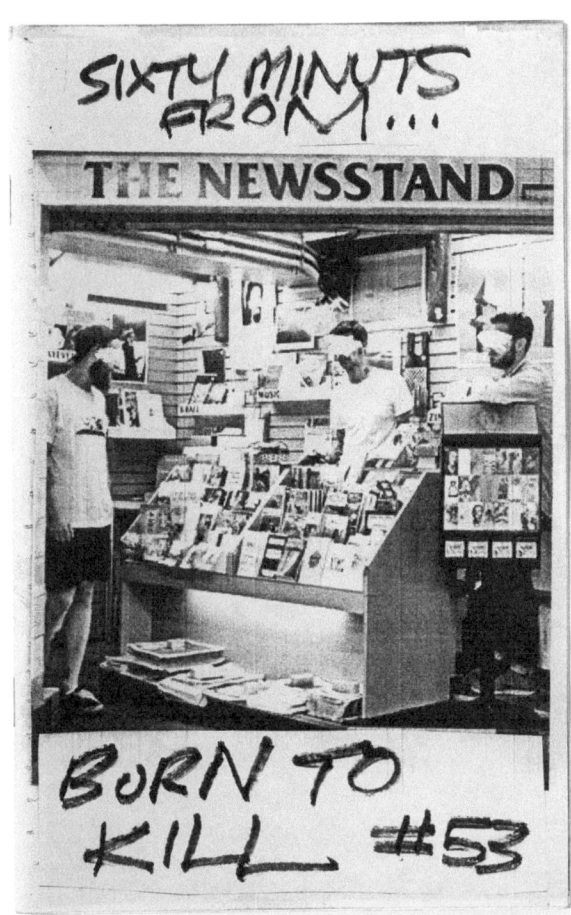

Born to Kill, no. 53, *Sixty Minuts from . . . the Newsstand*, 2013
Photocopy, saddle stitched, 8 ½ × 5 ½ in. (21.6 × 14 cm)
Collection Philip Aarons and Shelley Fox Aarons

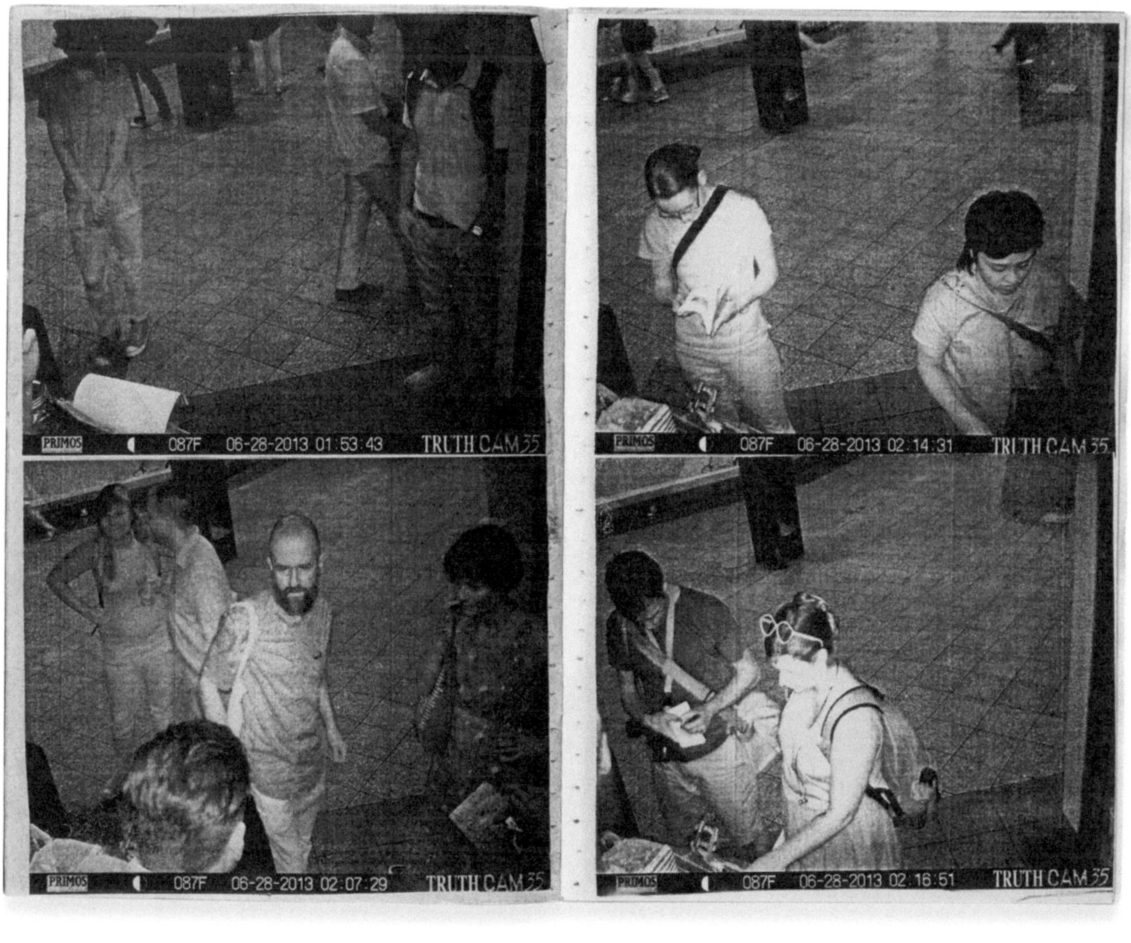

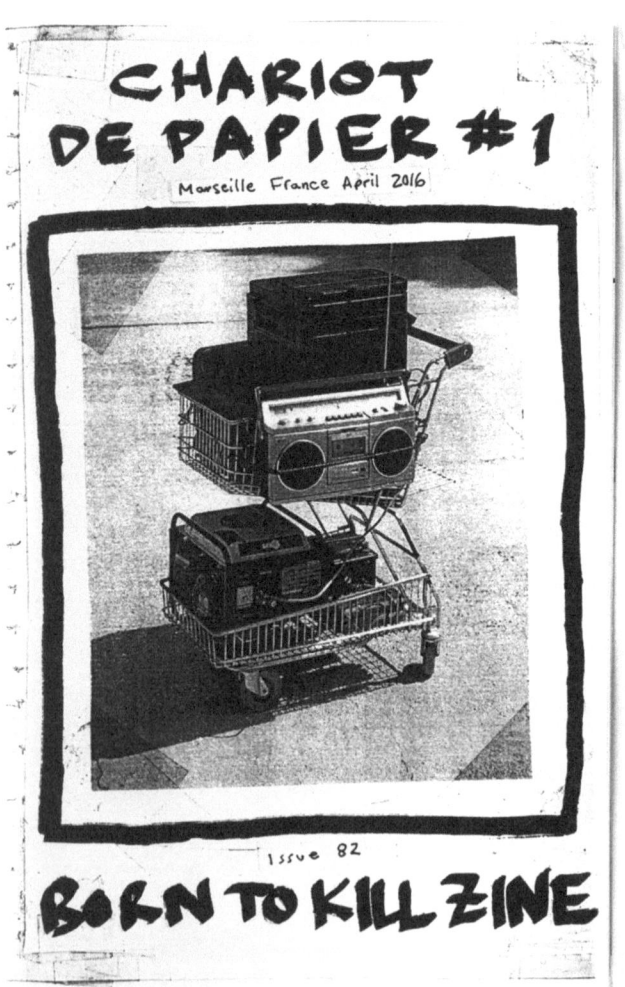

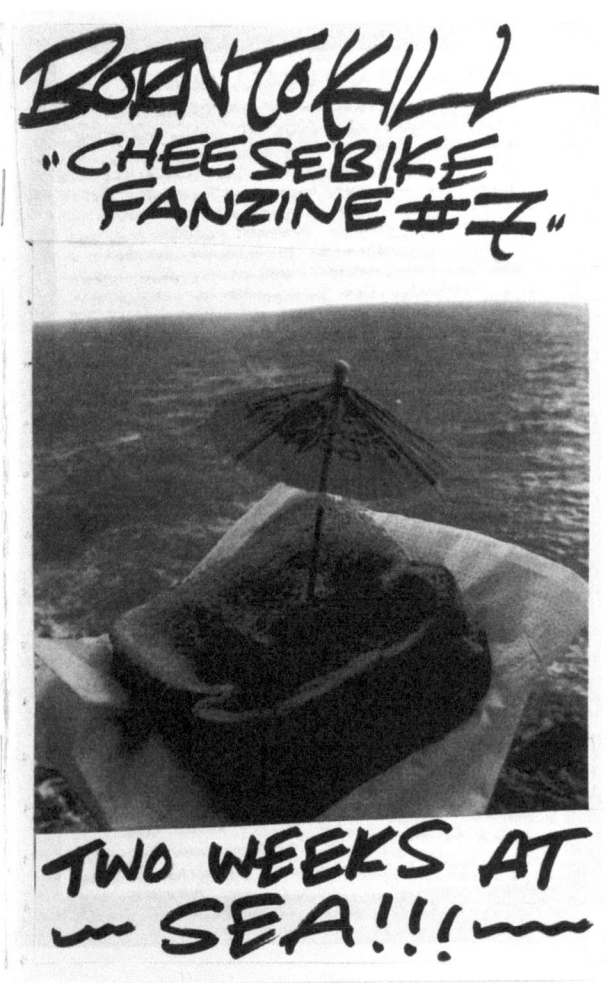

Born to Kill, no. 82, *Chariot de papier*, no. 1, 2016
Photocopy, saddle stitched, chromogenic print
taped to back cover, 8 ½ × 5 ½ in. (21.6 × 14 cm)
Collection Philip Aarons and Shelley Fox Aarons

Born to Kill, no. 7, *CheeseBike Fanzine*, January 2014
Photocopy, saddle stitched, chromogenic print
taped to back cover, 8 ½ × 5 ½ in. (21.6 × 14 cm)
Collection Philip Aarons and Shelley Fox Aarons

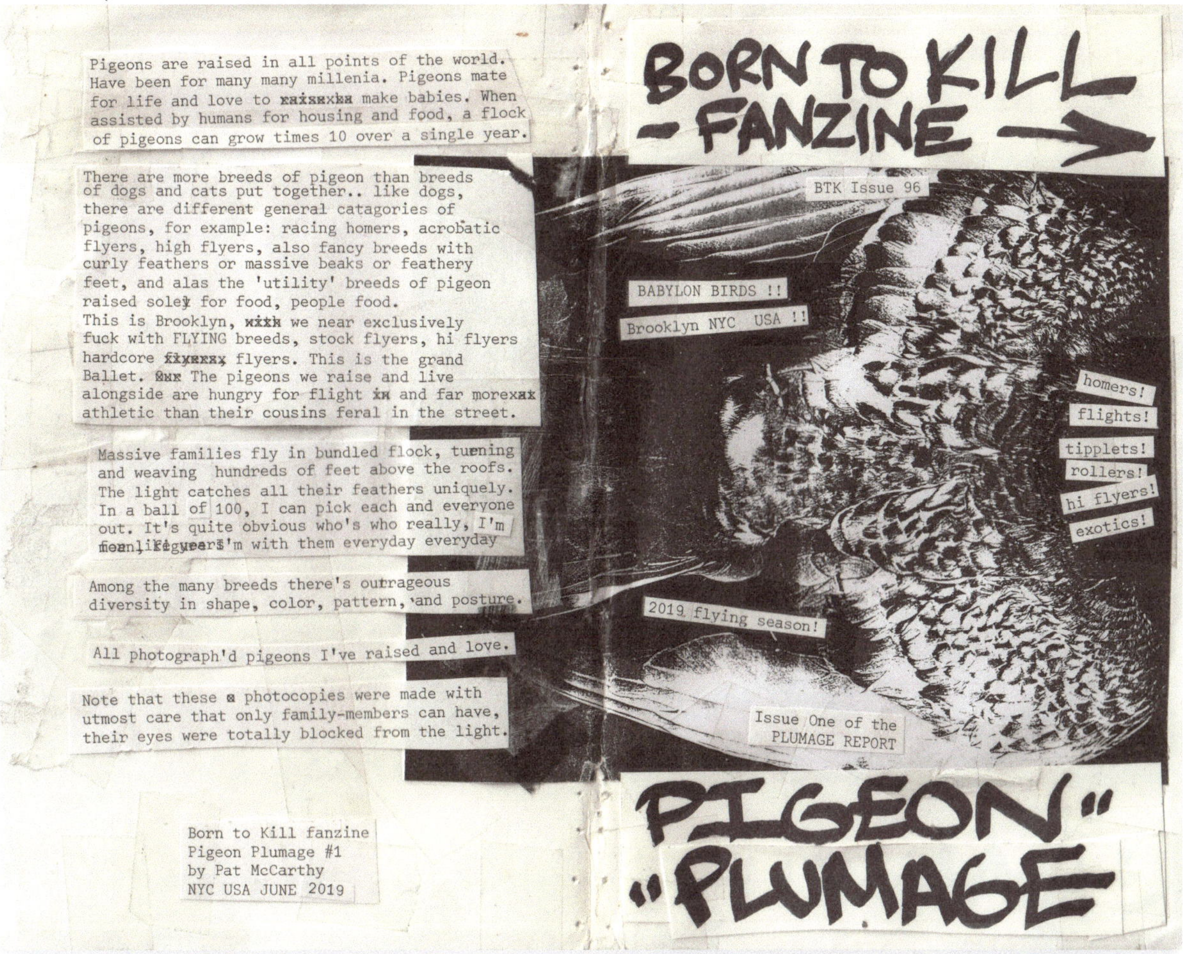

Pigeons are raised in all points of the world.
Have been for many many millenia. Pigeons mate
for life and love to xxxxxxxx make babies. When
assisted by humans for housing and food, a flock
of pigeons can grow times 10 over a single year.

There are more breeds of pigeon than breeds
of dogs and cats put together.. like dogs,
there are different general catagories of
pigeons, for example: racing homers, acrobatic
flyers, high flyers, also fancy breeds with
curly feathers or massive beaks or feathery
feet, and alas the 'utility' breeds of pigeon
raised solex for food, people food.
This is Brooklyn, xxxx we near exclusively
fuck with FLYING breeds, stock flyers, hi flyers
hardcore flxxxxx flyers. This is the grand
Ballet. &xx The pigeons we raise and live
alongside are hungry for flight xx and far morexxx
athletic than their cousins feral in the street.

Massive families fly in bundled flock, turning
and weaving hundreds of feet above the roofs.
The light catches all their feathers uniquely.
In a ball of 100, I can pick each and everyone
out. It's quite obvious who's who really, I'm
mean likeyears I'm with them everyday everyday

Among the many breeds there's outrageous
diversity in shape, color, pattern, and posture.

All photograph'd pigeons I've raised and love.

Note that these a photocopies were made with
utmost care that only family-members can have,
their eyes were totally blocked from the light.

Born to Kill fanzine
Pigeon Plumage #1
by Pat McCarthy
NYC USA JUNE 2019

BORN TO KILL
- FANZINE ->

BTK Issue 96

BABYLON BIRDS !!

Brooklyn NYC USA !!

homers!
flights!
tipplets!
rollers!
hi flyers!
exotics!

2019 flying season!

Issue One of the
PLUMAGE REPORT

PIGEON"
"PLUMAGE

Paste-up for *Born to Kill*, no. 1, *Pigeon "Plumage,"* June 2019
Photocopy, tape, glue, ink, 8 ½ × 5 ½ in. (21.6 × 14 cm)
Collection the artist

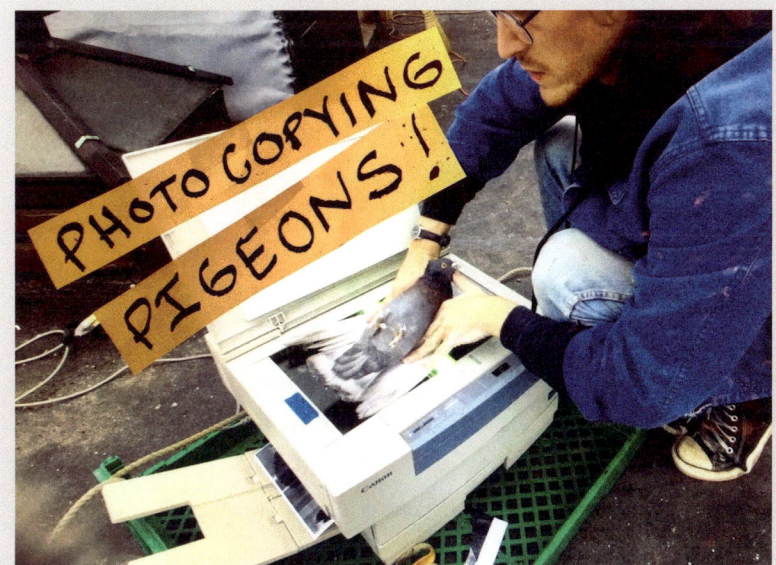

Still from *Babylon Pigeons*, no. 13,
Photocopying Pigeons, April 2019
Video; color, sound; 9 min., 43 sec.
Collection the artist

Devin N. Morris

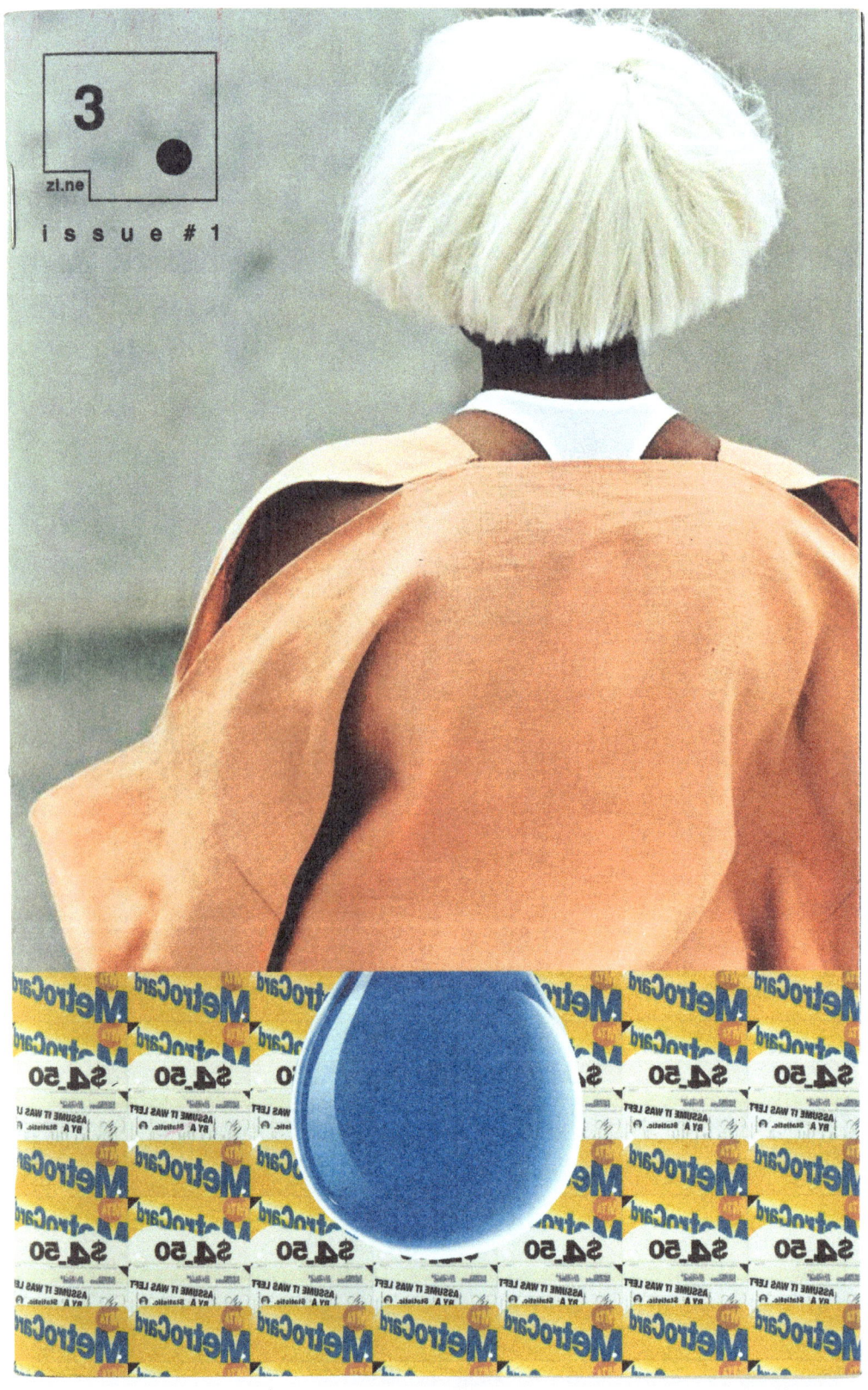

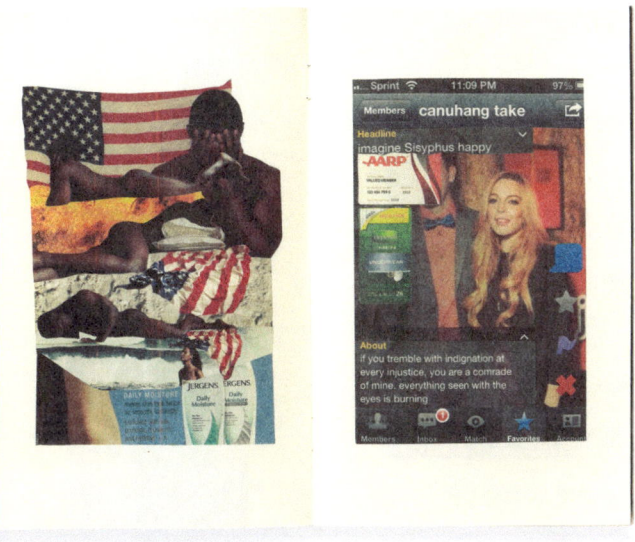

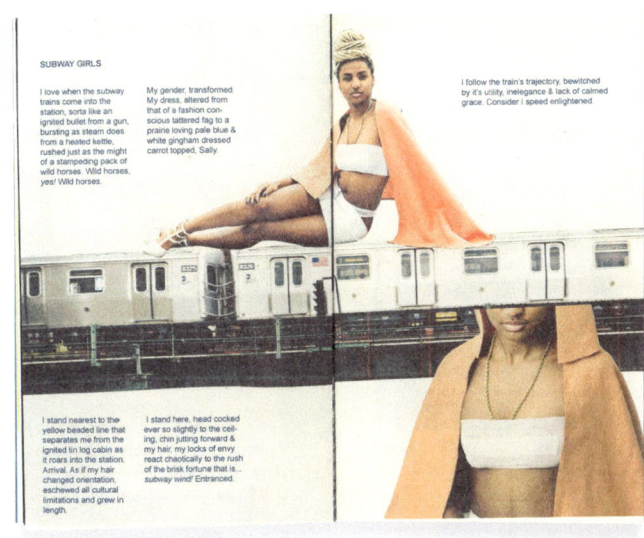

←↑ *3 Dot Zine*, no. 1, 2014
Design by Theresa Chromati
Inkjet, saddle stitched, 7 ¾ × 4 ⅞ in. (19.7 × 12.4 cm)
Collection Philip Aarons and Shelley Fox Aarons

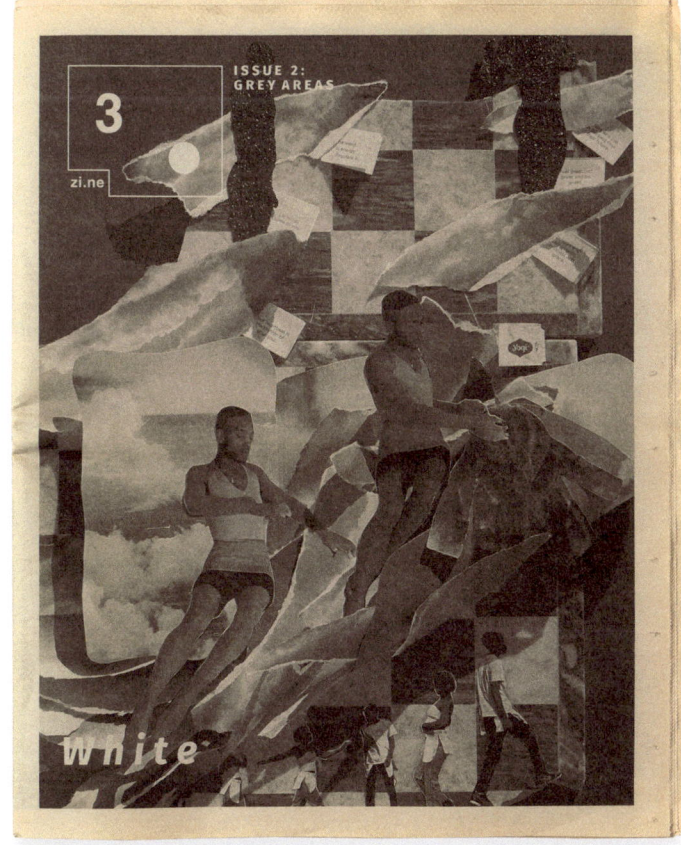

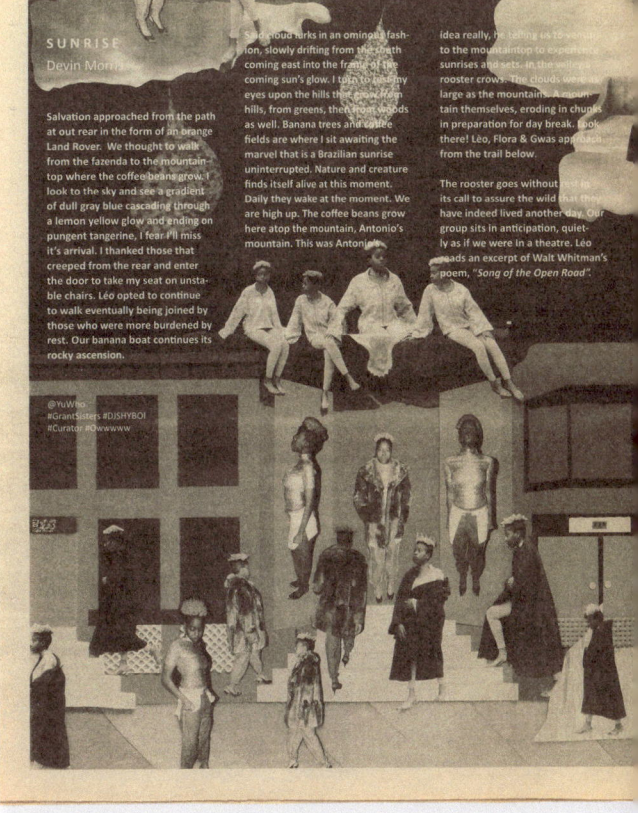

3 Dot Zine, no. 2, *Grey Areas*, 2015
Offset, folded, 14 × 11 ½ in. (35.5 × 29.2 cm)
Collection Philip Aarons and Shelley Fox Aarons

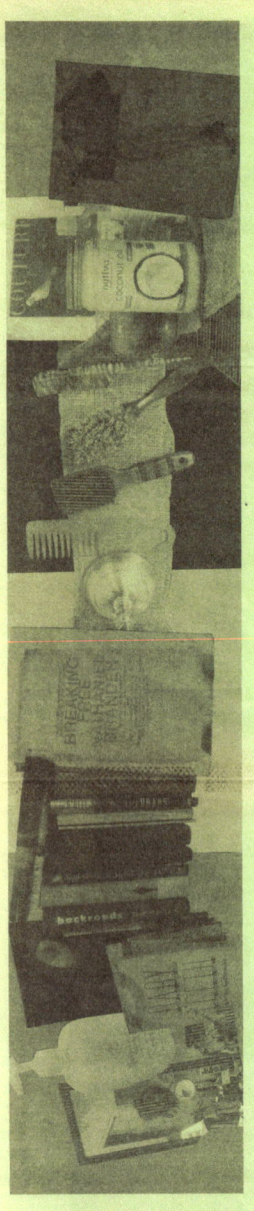

Waking Up Black

Why is ferguson acceptable? Because I'm hungry and I'm gonna stay that way unless I figure a way out. The only way up is to get out the ghetto, escape the afternoon sun that falls east on dingy walls. Escape the boisterous sounds of curious youths running everywhere and bellowing as loud as the passing dump truck's engine. Escape the tears that fall from my eyes as I read yet another story of racial injustice in the states' united. Direct your fire extinguishing hose right here! Hit me in the chest and turn me into mush. My inside is an ocean crashing against New England shores. Broken & frenzied I dissipate to bubble & foam, wave crashed all to be release with the departing tide and yet the net comes and drags me in again. Kill me, please, it's easier than waking up and looking at you and knowing you don't know what black life is. "All my life I had to..." That phrase shouldn't exist but it does because all my life I been black! So for all my life I will always, alongside the morning sun even when risen at one in the noon hour, face the mirror of my existence, a color. I hate that we hate the difference in being different from then to now still no scholar or holy man has healed the divide. But we could try to see it and not be it. "But I like to wax & wane ignorant," shut up.

Autumn is beautiful again, as it is every year. Exhale heap of fallen leaf and fill my lungs with the last wakings of life you shall muster. Dew it and take me back to being a poor young boy on the long trek home through a precise root of back alleys I tumbled through. I'm going home, alone and I'm trying to feel safe. I'm hungry. But it's hard to cook in this kitchen in the autumn because I lose light like-really fast and that candle's wax always burns me when I bend it slightly over the skillet to check the brown of my rue made w/ hamburger grease, flour, onions and hope. I'm hungry and I want change, I want to not be sad upon returning home from my Grandparent's house. They have luxuries I like; cars, clean carpets and three bathrooms, plus I get a snack before bed, an unsupervised snack of 3 bowls of strawberry ice cream if I want.

The saxophone player from the L train (10:54pm) scared away the two girls who are in the throes of detailing the life of college student visiting college academic adviser, the true tamer of the West come East. More like tamer of the Midwest. The education convents can be the worst kind of tourists. For their first 5 years at least. The problem, an educated tourist with an extended visa and a foreign identity complex ripe with an expiration date reeks havoc on what was once known.

I'm lost and looking for value that doesn't scorn because my wants are human and simple. Fear is a dangerous drug. & yet everyday I join you, the sea of you who hath displaced I. Bringing with you your lack of culture and a handy eraser to sweep any culture left in your wake. Your way. It is interesting that the culturally depressed suppress and then appropriate culture. It wouldn't be so bad if you assimilated for once. Lived amongst as opposed to moving in only to move me out. The plague of bad guests.

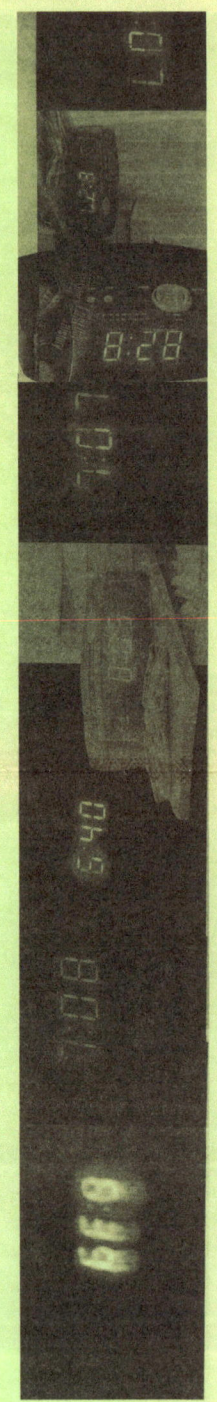

3 Dot Zine, special edition, *Waking Up Black*, 2015
Offset, folded, 14 × 11 ½ in. (35.5 × 29.2 cm)
Collection Philip Aarons and Shelley Fox Aarons

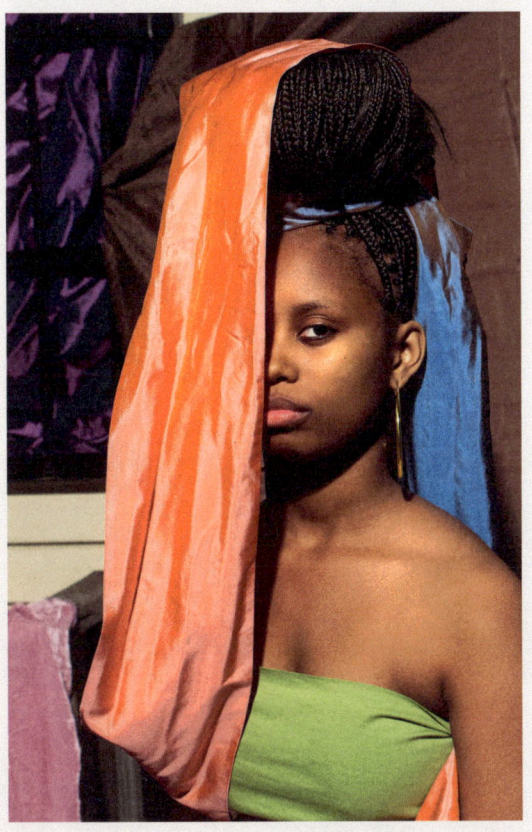

Nyla At 16, 2016
Archival pigment print, 36 × 24 in. (91.4 × 61 cm)
Collection the artist and Deli Gallery, New York,
Mexico City

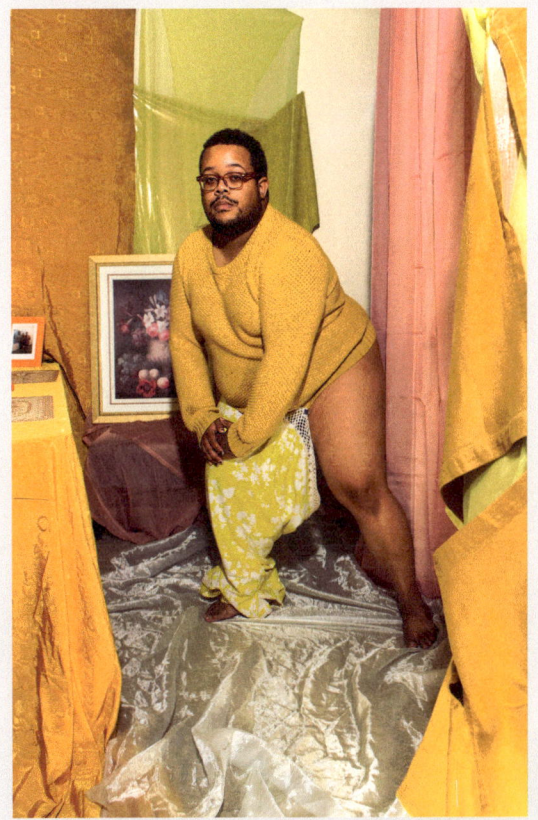

Jonny Gold, 2016
Archival pigment print, 36 × 24 in. (91.4 × 61 cm)
Collection the artist and Deli Gallery, New York,
Mexico City

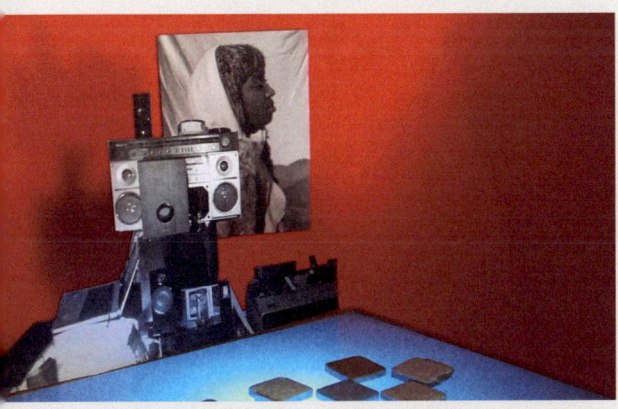

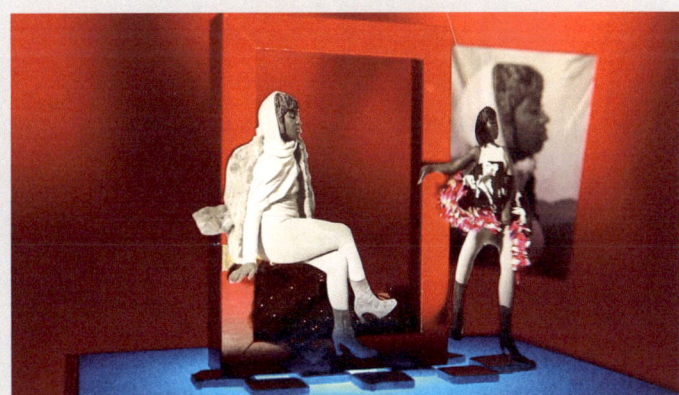

Stills from *3 Dot Mix*, 2016
Video; color, sound; 5 min., 32 sec.
Collection the artist and Deli Gallery, New York, Mexico City

Jordan Nassar

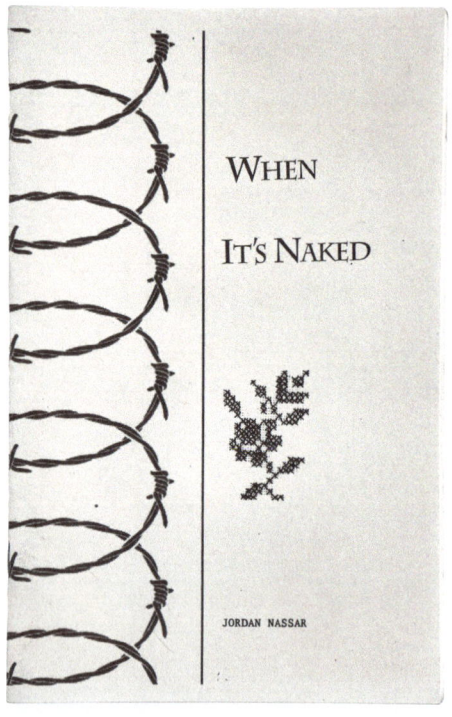

When It's Naked, 2015
Photocopy, saddle stitched, 8 ½ × 5 ½ in. (21.6 × 14 cm)
Collection the artist

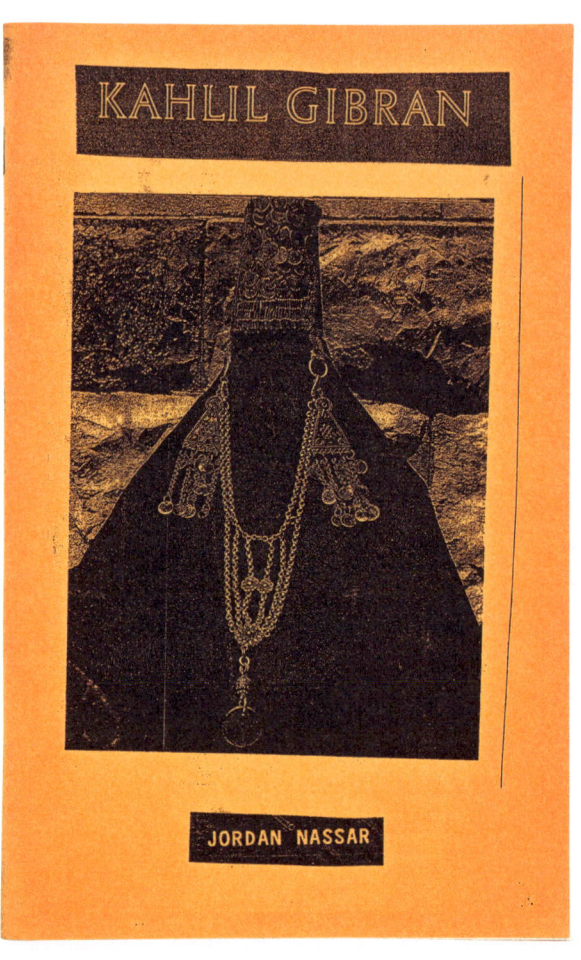

Kahlil Gibran, 2015
Photocopy, saddle stitched, orange paper wrappers,
8 ½ × 5 ½ in. (21.6 × 14 cm)
Collection the artist

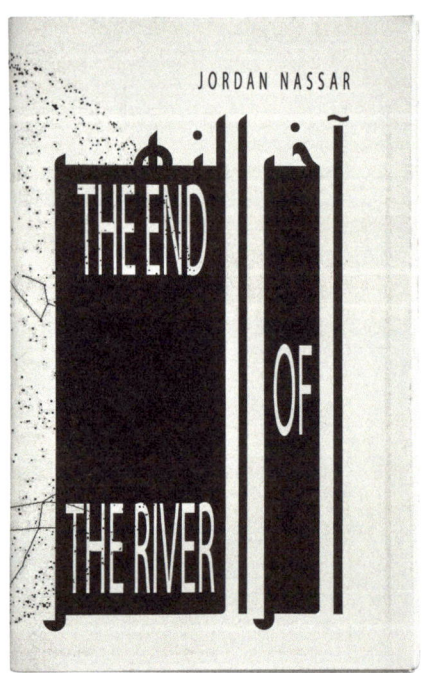

The End of the River, 2015
Photocopy, saddle stitched, 8 ½ × 5 ½ in. (21.6 × 14 cm)
Collection the artist

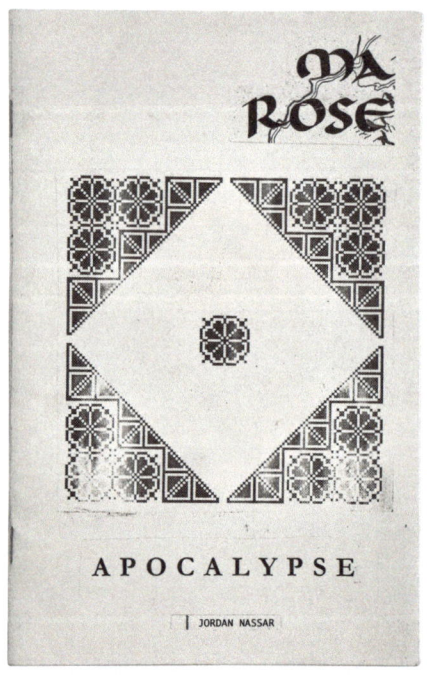

Ma Rose Apocalypse, 2015
Photocopy, saddle stitched, 8 ½ × 5 ½ in. (21.6 × 14 cm)
Collection the artist

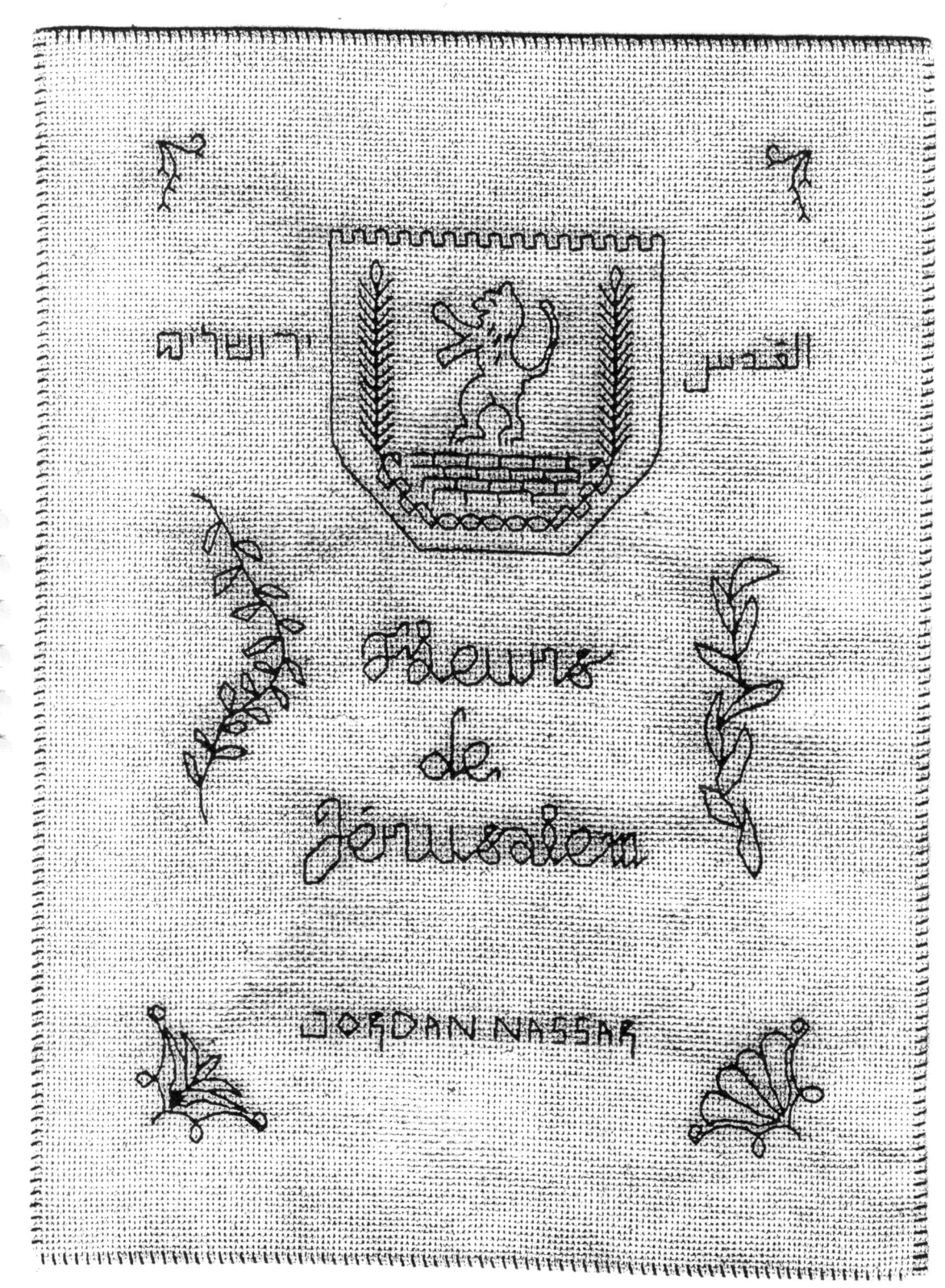

Fleurs de Jerusalem, 2017
Photocopy, crochet bound, 11 × 8½ in. (27.9 × 21.6 cm)
Collection Philip Aarons and Shelley Fox Aarons

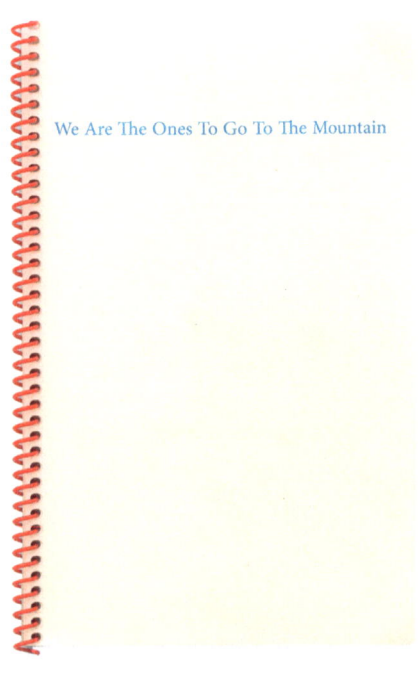
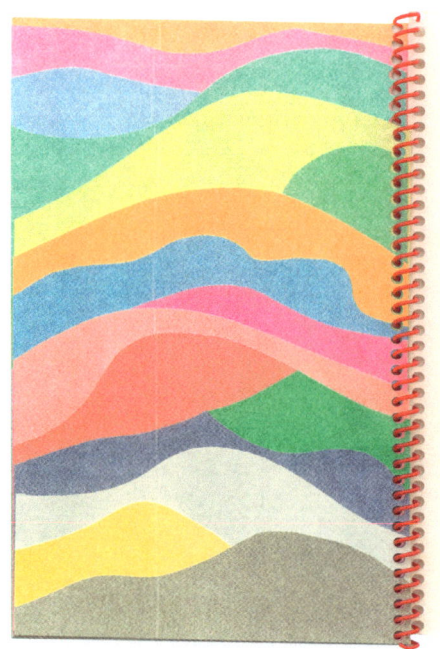

We Are The Ones To Go To The Mountain, 2020
Published by Endless Editions
Risograph, spiral bound, 10 × 6 in. (25.4 × 15.2 cm)
Collection the artist

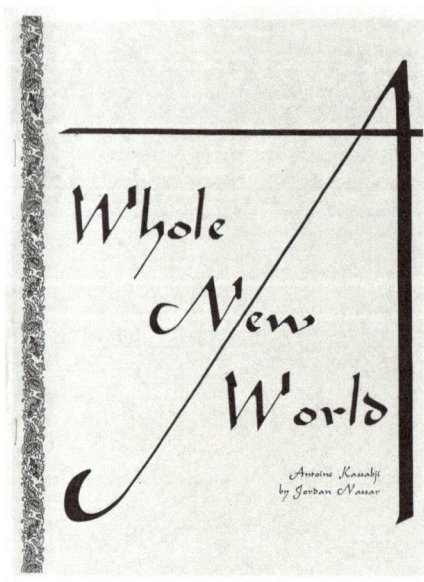
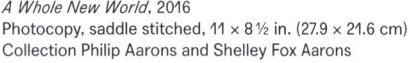
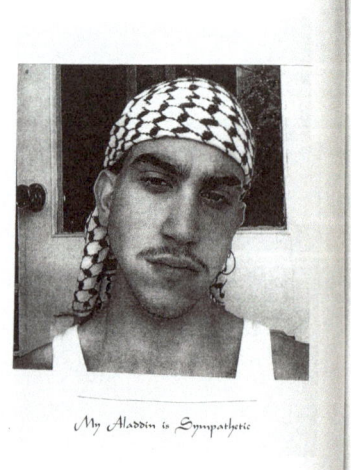
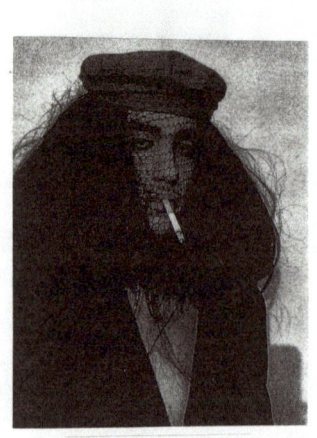

A Whole New World, 2016
Photocopy, saddle stitched, 11 × 8 ½ in. (27.9 × 21.6 cm)
Collection Philip Aarons and Shelley Fox Aarons

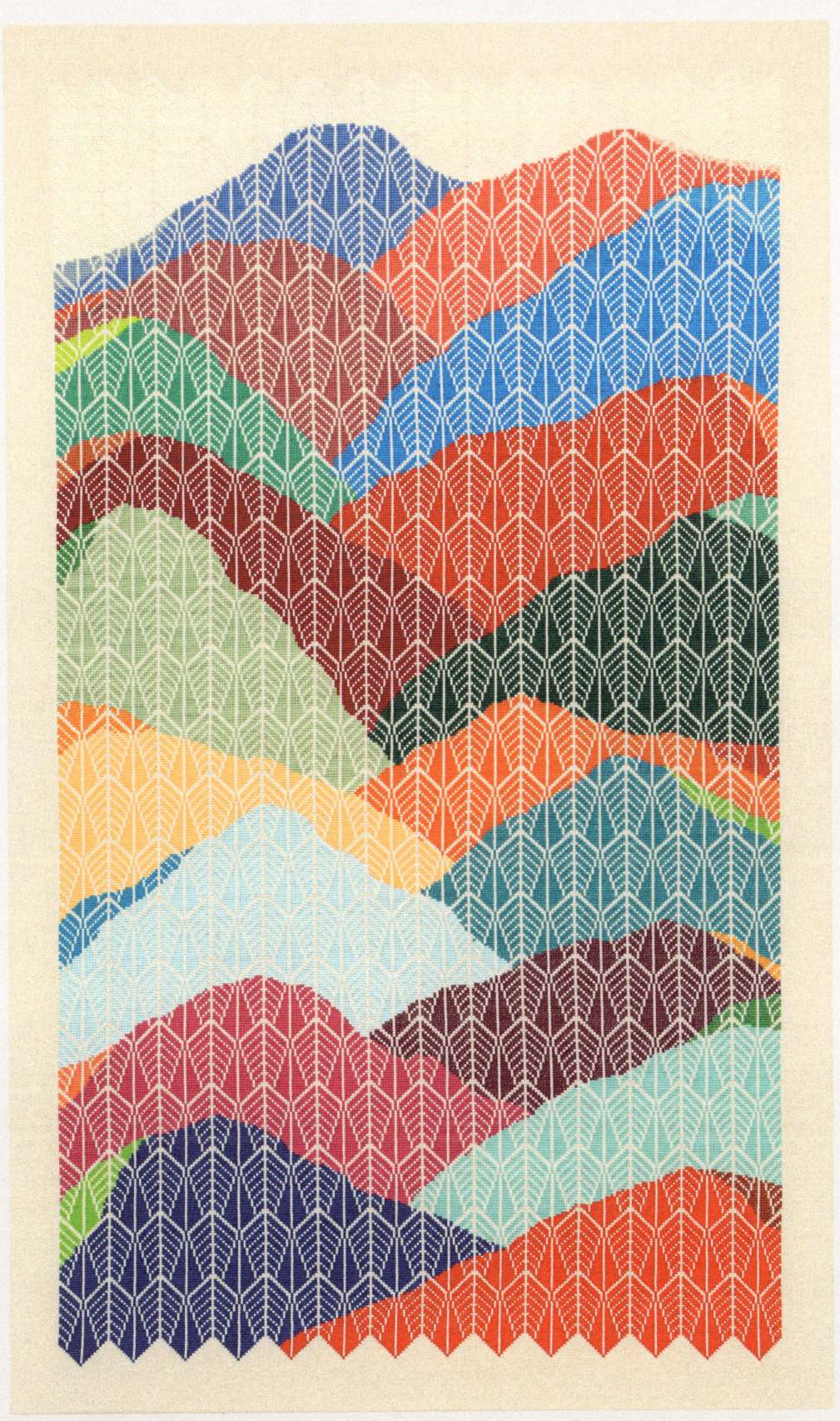

To Climb, To Walk, To Breathe, 2020
Hand-embroidered cotton on cotton,
49 × 30 in. (124.5 × 76.2 cm)
Private collection

The Eventfulness of Incomplete Presence, or No One Turned Away for Lack of Future

Mimi Thi Nguyen

Ask a punk/You're already late

—Beck Levy

Wheat-pasted onto wooden boards cut to fit the windows and doors of a used-books store in Brooklyn, a flyer announces the commemoration ceremony of first contact (an encounter that has yet to happen) over a blurry surveillance photograph of a possible UFO, as another proclaims the 2060 Punk Raft Fest ("Now that Miami's underwater it's time for . . . ") featuring "ottercore" bands and straight-edge breatharians, alongside advertisements for "Man with a Van" and dog walkers. Yet another flyer stages "A Local Fair in the World Forest Over the Bus Station" where slow blimps, solar commons, and linear urban farms comprise a "carnaval of necessities," coming in 2026, while one more invites us to "meet me in the crux of the time-space continuum," found in a "scissor portal" of legs emerging from a colorful void.

Each of these incongruous events—the UFO commemoration, the punk show on a floating barge, the future fair, and the tryst at the crux of the time-space continuum—gestures toward an asynchronous splice in time in the aftermath of something momentous, even calamitous, that *will have happened*. But we cannot know where we are in the history of its consequences, although we might guess we are further along than we might wish. Curated by musician and writer Erica Dawn Lyle and posted in the summer of 2022, *No One Turned Away for Lack of Future* is a provocation about our alienation from history at a moment in which its sense and significance breaks down or is perceived to be at its limit. And yet, as the queer portal advises, *the only way out is through*.

At first glance (sometimes the only glance), the form of the show flyer seems simple and straightforward. It promises eventfulness, inasmuch as something is happening or will happen that interrupts the meantime. The event itself promises a relational sense of presence in the experience of a space, a mood, an atmosphere, a person, or a collectivity in a here and now that is imminent, conditions (as both circumstance and stipulation) permitting. But how might a flyer signify such conjunctures when our sense of time and place is wrought (or wrecked) anew through waves of democratic and ecological collapse? *No One Turned Away for Lack of Future (NOTAFLOF)* asks us to witness this moment (or moments, because none of us occupies a moment in the same manner) when the lack of future, as a point of view or a judgment about impending catastrophe, seems inevitable. If crisis is so often the condition of thinking ourselves as subjects who might, or must, act on history—where *crisis* is anything we must survive, whether a virus, a bad situation, a war, a relationship, or a regime—it often presents itself, per the late cultural critic Lauren Berlant, as "a glitch [that] appears in the reproduction of life."[1] As I have argued elsewhere, the usual story about crisis establishes crisis as the condition for more perfectible form (whether as personal growth or the moral arc of the universe) or more terrible immiseration (whether as generational trauma or civilizational collapse) immanent to the structural contradictions of history.[2]

However, the *crisis* concept is not an ontological description of historical time but an interpretation of its sense or significance. Or, as anthropologist Janet Roitman observes, crisis is apprehended as history itself, as "the means to 'access' history and to qualify 'history' as such: crisis marks history and crisis generates history."[3] *No One Turned Away for Lack of Future* does not claim to know a future to come, or even to diagnose a history of the present. Instead, its fictional events establish the contingent or partial quality of claims of knowledge about history itself, hinting only at the suppositions, premises, and causal relations in these fragments of imagined time. These events are not turning points at which decisive action might alter the course of history; those points (global pandemic, climate cataclysm, aspirational fascism) have already happened in the past of the future, which is to say, in our present. Set into motion in our present are circumstances that establish arcs and with which—or against which—the future unfolds. In this redoubled time, the future haunts the present and the present haunts the future; or, as artist Beck Levy puts it in her entry (borrowing a convention used to avoid providing an address for an advertised gig in order to thwart police from shutting down the show): "Ask a punk/You're already late." How should we broach the future in the absence of alternative possibilities? What are the possibilities for remembering the future from here and now?

Nestled in Brooklyn's Punk Alley, a public arcade made from shipping containers, the shipping-container-cum-bookstore known as Better Read Than Dead staged a confrontation with futures that were not knowable a moment before—except as possibility—and that may never come to be. Lyle had originally been invited by booksellers Dave Morse and Matty D'Angelo (themselves old punks) to put together a retrospective show comprising thirty years' worth of ephemera, including her own zines, flyers, and handouts. Instead, she thought to invite a coterie of artists, writers, filmmakers, outcasts, and friends each to create a flyer for the future. It is worth lingering with Lyle's pitch:

> The prompt is just to make a flyer inviting people to or announcing a fictional event that takes place at any time and any place in the future that you can imagine. I would say from my own experience making flyers, that I've always considered flyers a form of potential prefigurative community building. If I had exhibited my thirty years of flyers, there would have been many for ordinary punk shows, sure. But the flyers were mostly for events like inviting people to join me in pushing a huge radio that was blasting Black Flag's *Damaged* LP in a shopping cart through downtown Miami or seeing if anyone wants to hang out at Monday night at midnight at Hunt's Donuts or seeing who wants to come help take over an abandoned building in downtown San Francisco to turn it into a squat or seeing who wants to ride bikes around SF, drinking beers in those weird public pay toilets that they put in tourist locations, or who wants to come do an anti-war parade in the Mission against the Gulf War. In those instances, four other humans came on a 90 plus degree Miami day to watch the spectacle of me and the cart and *Damaged*; Hunt's Donuts became a regular spot for like 30–50 kids to hang out and plot protests and shows and draw graffiti for 5 years every Monday at midnight; hundreds of people helped take over the building and the squat became an illegal autonomous show space and free café for 4 months; dozens of people wanted to go on that weird ass drunken bike ride and in fact did it every year for like 5 years; and a couple hundred folks showed up to march in costumes passing out anti-war literature in English and Spanish and throwing candy to kids behind a band on a flatbed truck.[4]

Flyers like this were once much more common, papering bulletin boards, construction scaffolding, and lampposts, and calling for real events and fake scenarios, impromptu protests, and underground shows. In a manila folder somewhere are still more flyers I made, or someone else made, for record-store shows, semi-spontaneous confrontations with neo-Nazi historians, and the celebratory march through San Francisco's Mission District on the occasion of Ronald Reagan's death, printed on sticker paper and featuring his headshot with a hand-scrawled "See You in Hell!" (the headshot includes an addendum to his dates: "1911–JUNE 5th, 2004—A DAY OF REJOICING").

Especially where and when human and other biological life is contracting, continues to contract, as stochastic right-wing terror, ecological collapse, unpayable debt, and captive labor come to define the life of so many, the disordering of our habits of sense-making feels like a necessity. Media scholar Rox Samer posits a historiographic concept called "lesbian potentiality," a form, a mood, or a habit (enacted by feminist and lesbian media workers and fans) that gestures beyond what the lesbian was, toward what the lesbian signifies and could come to be. Or, as Samer puts it: "Valuing the present-tense nature of same-sex romantic, sexual, and kinship relations while also looking ahead to the futures its sociality and politics could make possible."[5]

This is something that so many zines do well—create spaces of communion and possibilities for cohabitation across time or distance. In her column published in 2009 for the punk magazine *Maximum Rocknroll*, musician and writer Osa Atoe wrote about revisiting her zine collection to read again ten-, fifteen-year-old zines including *How to Stage a Coup*, *Mala*, *Quantify*, *Race Riot*, and *Slander*, and how these helped her and other Black and Brown punks who came later to imagine what forms of being-together could be conjured from a wish, a hope,

Mimi Thi Nguyen

a chance encounter. "What all of these early POC punk zines did for me was put me in touch with other brown punk kids. I remember meeting this queer Asian girl, Celeste, at a BBQ/B-day party because I saw a copy of *Race Riot* sticking out of her bag. Later, we started a Queer People of Color (QPOC) group together made up of about six brown queer kids."[6] Atoe's own zine, **Shotgun Seamstress** (first published in 2006)—which she described as "a zine by & for Black PUNKS, QUEERS, MISFITS, FEMINISTS, ARTISTS & MUSICIANS, WEIRDOS and the people who support us"[7]—documented the traces of Black punk presence to create an archive, and a genealogy, around which Black punks now could rally.[8] Earlier zines, such as G. B. Jones and Bruce LaBruce's **J.D.s** (1985–91) and Tom Jennings and Deke Nihilson's **Homocore** (1988–91), conjured queer punk scenes from Toronto to San Francisco through grit and spit—acting as catalysts for what had not yet come into being, in order to create it into the present.

→ 366–67

→ 160–64, 180–81

Similarly, *No One Turned Away for Lack of Future* might be said to enact such potentiality as an endurable form for what could be (or could have come to be: punk time is asynchronous), a shape for prefigurative community building from the present moment.[9] As Lyle explained to me:

> Making magazines has always been a way for me to imagine who I would like to be in conversation with, and to make a piece of writing that, I hope, will not just somehow bring them to me but will offer a place where perhaps the people who become that audience can see each other. It's important and useful to name a politics or sensibility this way, I think. It can prefigure actions or a movement by creating this place where the people who long for it can imagine it into being. But I have always felt that flyers actually can do that work too.[10]

Rather than offer specific or coherent ideological arguments, which might be more observable in fanzines or liner notes, the flyer is an often-dispersed array of rhetorical material (invitation, polemic, manifesto) that aims to call a collectivity into being. In Lyle's words: "We could just proclaim on a flyer that a gravel lot on the edge of civilization was a punk venue and, if people came to see a show there, then it really just was one! It was very democratic and wide open and had a lot of possibilities beyond just promoting ordinary shows."[11]

In *No One Turned Away for Lack of Future*, the flyers refer to disparate events, each of which stages a moment to *think history* itself, collectively if not cohesively. Each is a document of an (sometimes impossible) encounter in which emergence and emergency are both present. What do these events record about the present *from* the present, and what do they predict about futures?

Some flyers in *No One Turned Away* announce the inevitable reunion shows with geriatric punks basking in their former glories, such as Jacob Berendes's flyer for the Terribles' "30 Year Anniversary Show," promising "every song we can remember, twice." Others promote shows occurring in near-future dystopian scenes of landfills and floating barges, a reference perhaps to the 1995 postapocalyptic film *Waterworld* that finds Kevin Costner's drifter inhabiting a future Earth where sea levels have risen dramatically, swallowing all landmasses beneath endless oceans. At the compost heap, a contributor by the name of stoLen invokes early 1990s attempts as cross-scene solidarity: "Paper punx and fruit skins unite," while another artist, Chuck Loose, warns: "Get there early to avoid mutant sharks, C.H.U.D.S., and the marine cops." Other impossible show flyers comment wryly on the uselessness of currency in the aftermath of mercenary extraction and subsequent depletion. Admission is set at "free entry for trade of any food and water," "1 liter petrol or 1 edible plant," or "16 oz. water or ¼ gallon gas." Foreshadowing disaster as inevitable, these flyers are mired in the melancholic loss of the future already felt in the present.

Some artists engage tensions between present and future, past and present, lingering with the living who have endured somehow and sometimes mourning those who will have been lost, and what we are losing now, in our present. Anandi Wonder puts together a show flyer that parodies punk genres—"NOISE BAND WITH A NAME THAT NO ONE KNOWS HOW TO SAY OUT LOUD! (local queers making screeching noises)"—while also observing changes required for gatherings to be safer in a world where pandemics spread, barely checked, as one did in the United States the summer of this show, as vaccine availability trumped public health mitigation for vulnerable populations. Following from the eventfulness of crisis as condition (in this case the mass disabling event of the COVID-19 pandemic), Wonder does not assign meaning to either crisis or condition, but instead references shattered norms for a life that can be lived where the continuation of the present *as it is* corrodes the future.

In this way, each flyer in *No One Turned Away* posits a historical consciousness about probable futures in response to anterior events that happened, are still happening, or are likely to happen. We all know, for instance, that what critical geographer Ruth Wilson Gilmore calls "the state-sanctioned or extralegal production and exploitation of group-differentiated vulnerability to premature death" will continue to wreak havoc in the present, whether through brute and terrible violence or by deliberate neglect.[12] If, as philosopher Reinhart Koselleck observes, crisis is a cognate of critique because it is the judgment of history, and the determinations of the limits of reason and knowledge, *No One Turned Away* is not necessarily diagnostic (how could it be?) but instead takes as a given that crisis will not be curbed in time.[13] In that event (or nonevent), what is to come? In answer, some flyers draw on our present, in which do-it-yourself presses, abortion funds, shipping-container bookstores, art and video collectives, and mutual-aid campaigns build upon an anarchist political and ethical imaginary. Using humor and affection, abstraction and survival skills, these flyers articulate a felt sense of the world as it is, as it will be, and as it ought to be. Street Rat's flyer calls for a free school for DIY skill shares, with possible workshops including "tincture making, cooking, book club, soldering and electronics, instrument instruction, painting, sewing, farming," and more. More speculative is Sy Wagon's invitation: "Join us for a . . . refugee camp pro-enactment." This crudely hand-drawn notice shows a tent and a group of people gathered around a giant pot that is set atop some stones (I am guessing), as steam billows from a simmering stew. Someone in knee-high boots waves a ladle, near a table holding other bowls heaped with foodstuffs. The flyer invites an audience to "Come party down and practice!!!"—"how to be organized to cohabitate for an indeterminate amount of time," "best health + hygiene in desperate circumstances," "cooking + cleaning for 300+ with varying materials, fuels, setups," "temporary structures + infrastructure, problem solving, puzzles with materials," and "how not to contaminate the land + water." We do not know to what event or events this refugee "pro-enactment" responds, but the fact is that there are many possible disruptions—forever war, climate catastrophe, authoritarian regime—that might beget refugee masses.

Found here is a politics of futurity that speculates on what will follow from the failures of the present, including the US government's organized neglect and violence, creating mass death and chronic disability, refugees and outlaws. Camila Álvarez's flyer calls to us from our post-Roe present, in which abortion access and reproductive healthcare are increasingly precarious and under threat by Christian fascisms. Featuring collage and an abstract line drawing of a distorted body in parts, she stages a free live menstrual extraction (with fake bands Cellular Chaos and Deep Douche) at the De-Fertilization Station (presumably, a venue).

While an anticipatory politics of urgency suffuses some of these flyers, they do not offer a teleological history or narrative horizon but a glimpse of another world. Longtime Lyle collaborator, musician, muralist, and anti-gentrification activist Ivy Jeane announces the grand opening of the Undercommons Archives, a utopian space of radical collection (timespan: "1960–the PRESENT") based in the Mission District of San Francisco—once a space of Central American refugees and punks, increasingly pushed out. In this, perhaps the most hopeful entry in the show, I am reminded of Craig Willse and Dean Spade who, in reviewing *Born in Flames*, Lizzie Borden's 1983 speculative feminist science fiction film featuring a near-future after a socialist revolution, invite us to consider "the possibility that we do not know, cannot know, where we are in the history of the transformations we seek."[14]

Others stage occasions that resemble Happenings, or performances that obscure the lines between several genres of art but feature improvisation and audience interaction, and that convene presence as a relational concept or experiential quality. Also summoned are histories of cultural and media activism, including antiwar demonstrations and ACT UP protests: reminders of the potentials of earlier "artivist" practices that dreamed of other futures. In blue

Mimi Thi Nguyen

crayon font on a neon green background, MPA calls for "FEMINIST STRIKE NOW/LOCATION: EVERYWHERE." In a callback to the 1967 march to ritually exorcise the Pentagon of its warmongering, Ethan Swan announces a similar collective action to destroy BlueTriton, a former Nestlé subsidiary, guilty of water profiteering: "PUSH! IN THE SPIRIT OF ABBIE HOFFMAN AND GODZILLA WE ARE GOING TO PUSH OVER THE BLUETRITON HEADQUARTERS IN STAMFORD CONNECTICUT ON MARCH 31 2024." Using colored pencils, E. Conner and Jolie M-A mysteriously invite us to "stomp on the beating heart of the last living pig with the kindness of strangers," over a watermelon painted onto a blue flag. Sarah Kirby's flyer for "The Annual Moon Year Collecting Festival B.Y.O.B. (Bring Your Own Bucket)" feels like a throwback to a utopian countercultural moment. The artist RIDER/Kriss cut out letters and pasted them like a ransom note: "One hour of refusal"; "Don't look/Don't talk/Don't act/Don't react"; "Wherever you are at 11th hour next Wednesday." RIDER/Kriss requests also, "Report back: Transmit one sentence of written observation to—DROP OUT MILITIA/PO Box 666." (Of course, without further specification—*where* is this postbox?—any such communication is cut short.) Chris Johanson offers a simple black-and-white watercolor painting with the headline "Happening today is energy exchange," and illustrated with abstract figures with elongated arms and no discernable features, standing stiffly. The flyer further reads: "i am bringing a large amount of salad + come bring yourself and whatever else." And banning nefarious technologies that suggest future advances in increasingly intrusive surveillance, Dushko Petrovich and Mark Greif call, in hand-lettered scrawl, for a "Physical reality meetup/No video, no surrogates, no mindhole, no tracers." However, this impossible event is scheduled for "tomorrow at sunset"—in other words, it is an event perpetually pushed further into a mortgaged future.

In this way, *No One Turned Away for Lack of Future* generates a cluster of unpredictable encounters with others across times; all the more in the event in which future wreckage is staged here and now. As Lyle reflects:

> The *NOTAFLOF* flyers for future free clinics and cryogenically preserved punk bands were mounted in this utterly timeless place where kids who look very much like punks from 1977 were still doing almost literally the same things together. And it was a miracle to me how the act of covering with wheatpaste, say, a flyer about a UFO encounter in the future, somehow seemed to turn the event immediately into The Past. The effect for me finally was that the simulated walls I made all actually looked archival, as if all of the future events proposed had already taken place in that dim netherworld of the very recent past. (Nothing seems as forgettable or quotidian as an event that just happened the other day.) The mythical pasts and alternative futures seemed to fuse at a single temporal point, perhaps when the wheatpaste layer got slathered over the top of the flyer.[15]

In this meantime, *No One Turned Away* produced chance encounters through incomplete presence. "Presence" commonly denotes a *thereness*, the affirmation of an existence (of a person, an object, a situation), but it does not come from nowhere. American philosopher Charles Sanders Peirce named a footprint, a weathervane, thunder, the word "this," a pointing finger, and a photograph as indices of thereness, of historical circumstances or substances that presence requires as the grounds for its own possibility (and impossibility).[16] These grounds cohere as an arrangement of time and place, which is to say, presence anticipates an emptiness that can be filled only in specific dependent situations. An assemblage of variables must align in order for presence to permeate the spaces between you and me and others, whether as an intensity, a mood, an instant, a principle, or its index (*this is it*). The flyer promises the presence of someone, or something—bearing the imprint of a singular moment, person, object, or history, whether a dogwalker, a lost item, or a punk show—but such presence belongs to a speculative future, one in which that presence is immediately divided from itself (*it has been there*).

The experience of any event (whether real or fake) set in the future is wrought through incompleteness, especially when our sense of it is seized through its prefigurative presence. Even as a material object, the flyer is all impermanence. While some surfaces are papered in layers of announcements and proclamations, so thick that a staple gun might catch on its substratum, others are stripped bare in a day. At other times, the rain pulps them, the sun curls them or bleaches their details to the point of illegibility; we might drag a hand across them (to rip them, or to tuck them into a pocket) or avert our eyes, sensing them as only obstruction or noise. As Lyle reflected on the show for Layla Gibbon's *122 Hours of Fear* (2022)—a zine about shows during the COVID-19 pandemic, when there were no shows:

> The grey scrim of wheatpaste hardened The Future into The Past before my eyes, which was maybe in the end I think what the show was about for me, what I was trying to figure out, a way of thinking about the social reproduction of reality, you know, like asking how can we get capitalism out of our bodies if we are indeed made out of capitalism? I mean, where is the jump cut, where is the rip in the sky?!?[17]

This is the incomplete presence that suffuses *No One Turned Away for Lack of Future*; each flyer is a representation of a thing (the energy exchange, the feminist strike), a conduit to access a relation to that thing (the prefigurative "we" who gathers), but the flyer is all that is present as the promise of something else. It is *here and now* through reference to what is not and might never be.

Familiar to dharma potlucks, house shows, free clinics, tarot readings, and grassroots fundraisers, the phrase "No one turned away for lack of funds" most commonly describes a donation-based event or service requesting "pay what you can." An archivist friend (also a punk) found among the phrase's earliest iterations a 1921 advertisement for a quack cancer cure and a 1927 article on the YMCA. (For the quack cure: "Price according to severity of case, but no one turned away for lack of funds.") To this end, Lyle's wordplay observes so well that what is called a "lack of funds" is too often tantamount to a *lack of future* in an extractivist hellscape like ours. Against this, Lyle locates a necessary politics (or a politics of necessity) that has emerged and is still emerging from those (seen as) lacking a future—the punks, queers, weirdos, friends, lovers, and trans seers among us. "You are receiving this email," Lyle wrote in her invitation, sent out early in the summer of 2022, "because you have made flyers I love over the years, because I know you have a strong commitment to DIY subculture, activism, and community building, because you care about art outside of institutions, because I love the art you make, because you are a friend who I know is thinking deeply about the future, or because you are a rad trans woman I know and I want to see a world where trans women decide what the future should look like." Or as Lyle puts it in Gibbon's *122 Hours*: "The No Future subculture asked to imagine one."[18]

No One Turned Away for Lack of Future grants feeling and form to events and phenomena that are somehow inaccessible, or unsettling, precisely because we are not yet sure what feelings or forms of life will be possible. The end of the world is coming, but as the subway graffiti promises, *another end of the world is possible*. It might end otherwise with a feminist general strike, an energy exchange, a refugee pro-enactment, or a party on a floating barge, beneath a rip in the sky.

NOTES

NB: The epigraph that opens this essay is drawn from Beck Levy's flyer for *No One Turned Away for Lack of Future*, 2022.

[1] Lauren Berlant, "The Commons: Infrastructures for Troubling Times," *Environment and Planning D: Society and Space* 34, no. 3 (June 2016): 393.

[2] Mimi Thi Nguyen, *The Promise of Beauty* (Durham, NC: Duke University Press, forthcoming 2024).

[3] Janet Roitman, *Anti-Crisis* (Durham, NC: Duke University Press, 2014), 20.

[4] In her original call for contributions to the show, Erica Dawn Lyle sent the flyer out to a collection of friends in June 2022. She shared it with me later, when I told her I wanted to write about *NOTAFLOF*.

[5] Rox Samer, *Lesbian Potentiality and Feminist Media in the 1970s* (Durham, NC: Duke University Press, 2022), 15.

[6] Osa Atoe, *Maximum Rocknroll*, no. 313 (2009): n.p.

[7] Osa Atoe, tagline for *Shotgun Seamstress*, no. 2 (2007).

[8] See Mimi Thi Nguyen, "Minor Threats," *Radical History Review*, no. 122, "Queering Archives" special issue, ed. Kevin Murphy, Daniel Marshall, and Zeb Tortorici (May 2015): 11–24.

[9] Punk Alley is itself a place built from the detritus of the global supply chain: a speculative reuse of industrial materials.

[10] Erica Dawn Lyle, email to the author, September 29, 2022.

11 Ibid.

12 Ruth Wilson Gilmore, *Golden Gulag: Prisons, Surplus, Crisis, and Opposition in Globalizing California* (Berkeley: University of California Press, 2006), 28.

13 See Reinhart Koselleck, *The Practice of Conceptual History: Timing History, Spacing Concepts*, trans. Todd Samuel Presner, Kerstin Behnke, and Jobst Welge (Stanford, CA: Stanford University Press, 2002).

14 Craig Willse and Dean Spade, "Introduction: We Are Born in Flames," *Women & Performance* 23, no. 1 (2013): 3.

15 Lyle, email to the author, September 29, 2022.

16 Charles Sanders Peirce, *Philosophical Writings of Peirce*, ed. Justus Buchler (New York: Dover, 1955) 109.

17 Erica Dawn Lyle, "Untitled," *122 Hours of Fear: A Zine About the Show Going Experience* (2022): 83.

18 Ibid.

Kandis Williams

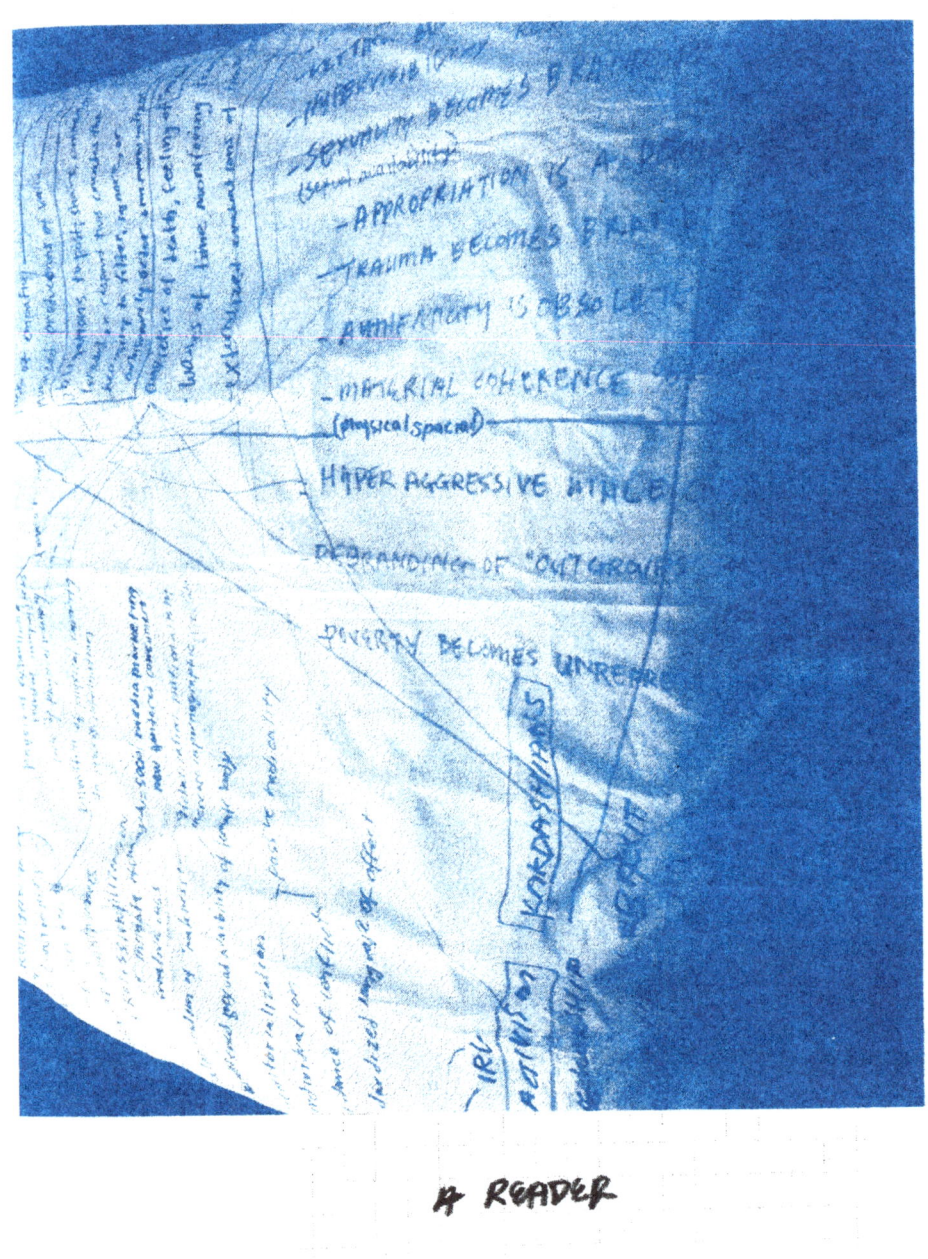

The Culture of the Fuccboi: A Reader, 2016
Photocopy, folded, risograph wrappers,
8 ½ × 5 ½ in. (21.6 × 14 cm)
Collection Philip Aarons and Shelley Fox Aarons

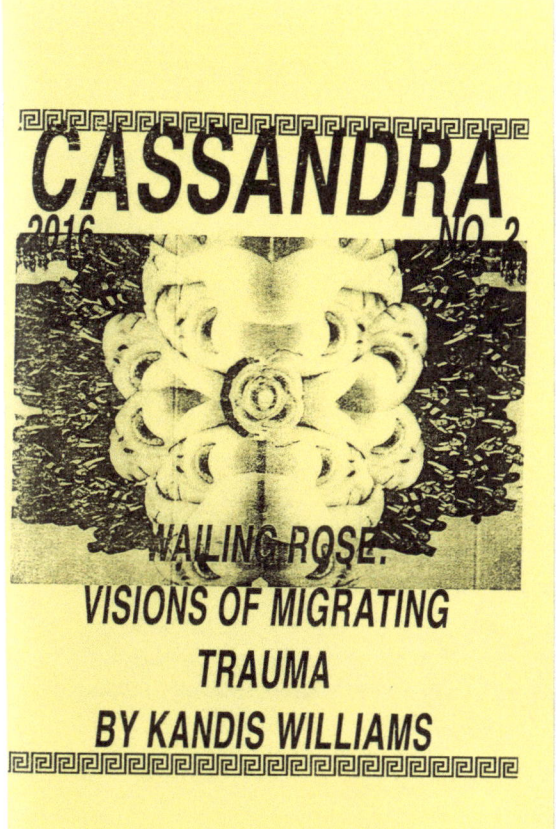

The Wailing Rose: Visions of Migrating Trauma, 2016
Photocopy, folded, yellow paper wrappers,
8 ½ × 5 ½ in. (21.6 × 14 cm)
Collection Philip Aarons and Shelley Fox Aarons

Marcel rolls in with a crew of clowns. Like psycho clowns, and drunkenly starts fights and makes love to the paintings and other works in the show. His every lean and touch of the walls leaving a smeared mark of clown makeup. Alcala's work feels like it opens an autonomous space within space. His looks, his text, the performativity of his work is unquestionably interesting, but what is outstanding to me is that he manages to create a space for himself to be in a full affective reality of his own making, while creating a platform for other bodies to access their own affectivity.

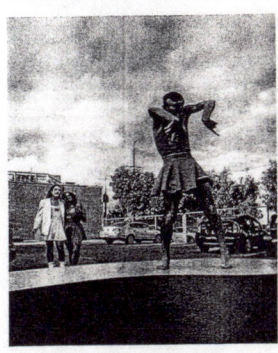

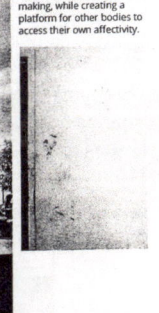

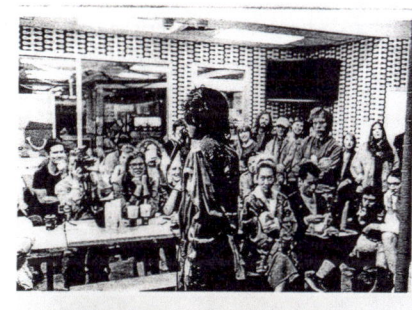

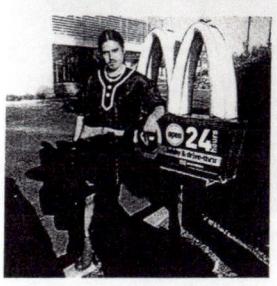

15

16

READER ON

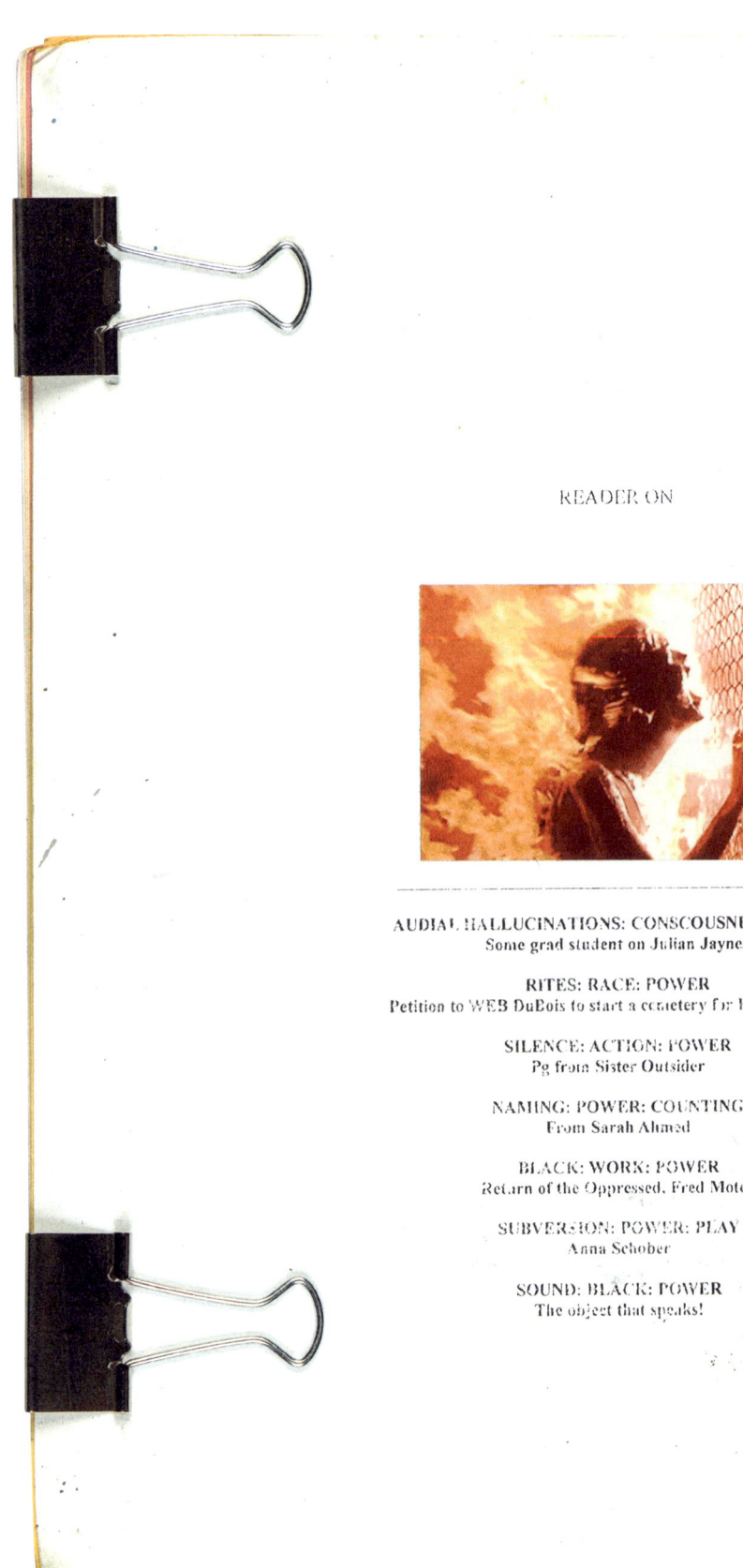

AUDIAL HALLUCINATIONS: CONSCOUSNESS: POWER
Some grad student on Julian Jaynes

RITES: RACE: POWER
Petition to WEB DuBois to start a cemetery for Famous Blacks

SILENCE: ACTION: POWER
Pg from Sister Outsider

NAMING: POWER: COUNTING
From Sarah Ahmed

BLACK: WORK: POWER
Return of the Oppressed, Fred Moten

SUBVERSION: POWER: PLAY
Anna Schober

SOUND: BLACK: POWER
The object that speaks!

Reader On, 2016
Photocopy, bound with binder clips, 11 × 8¼ in. (27.9 × 21 cm)
Collection the artist

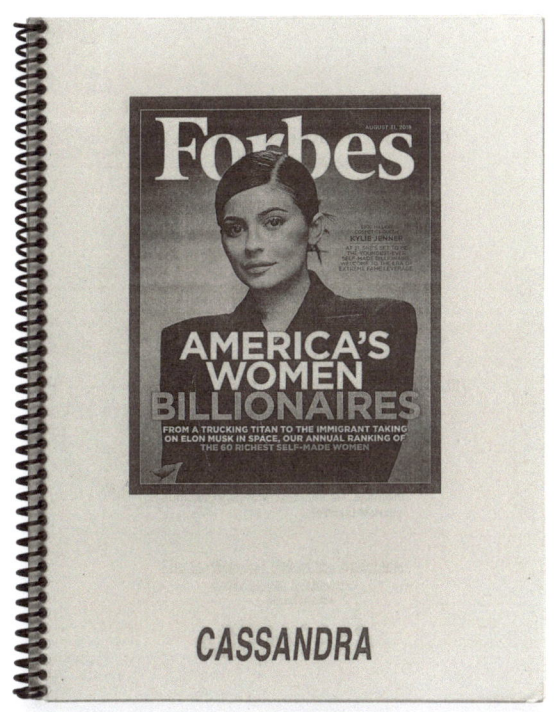

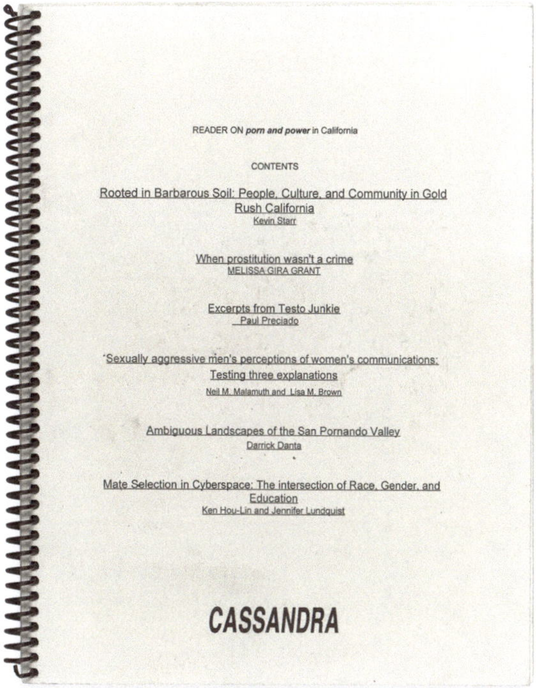

Reader On Porn and Power in California, 2018
Photocopy, spiral bound, 11 × 8 ¼ in. (27.9 × 21 cm)
Collection the artist

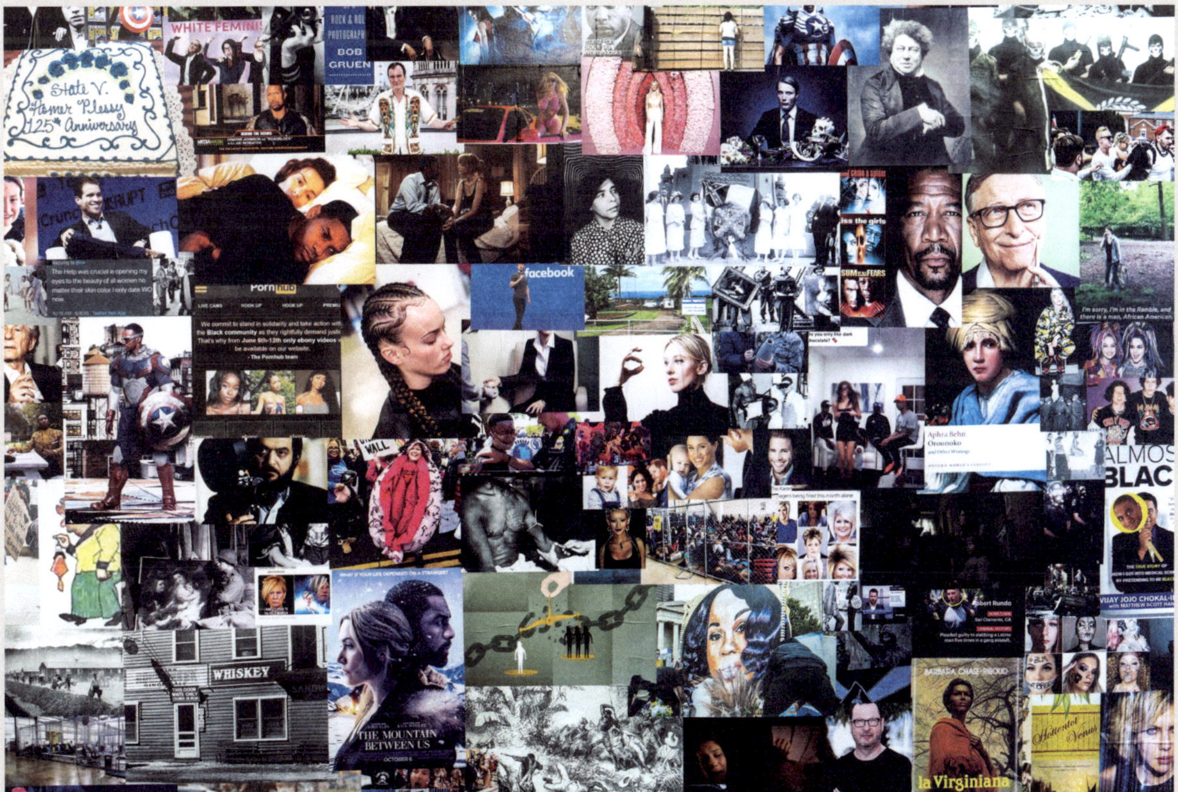

Detail of wall collage in the exhibition *The Absolute Right to Exclude:*
Reflections on and Implications of Cheryl Harris' Whiteness as Property,
LAXART, Los Angeles, May 28–July 31, 2021

Demian DinéYazhi'

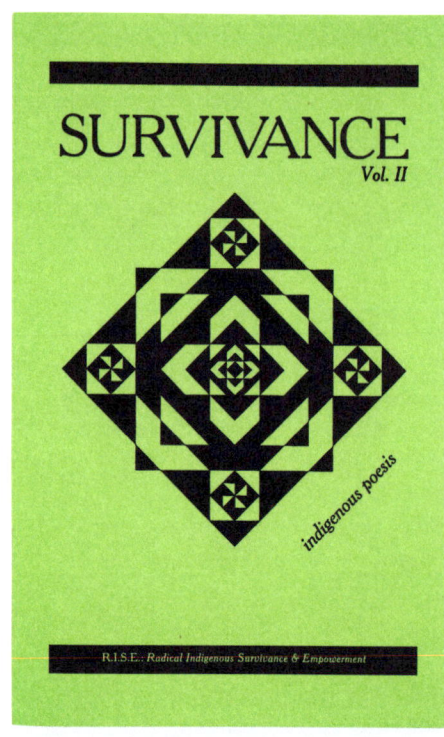

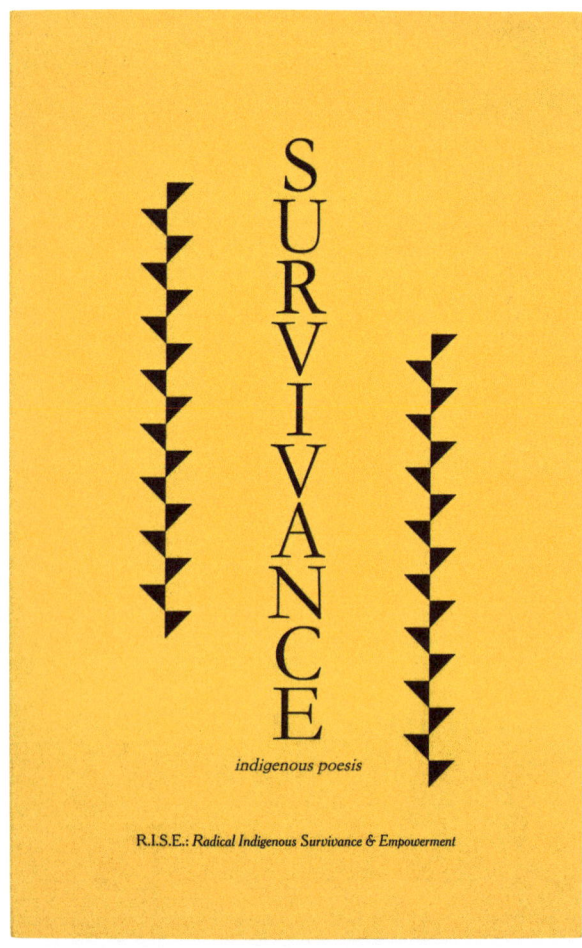

Survivance: Indigenous Poesis, vol. 1, 2015
Letterpress, saddle stitched, 8 ½ × 5 ½ in. (21.6 × 14 cm)
Collection the artist

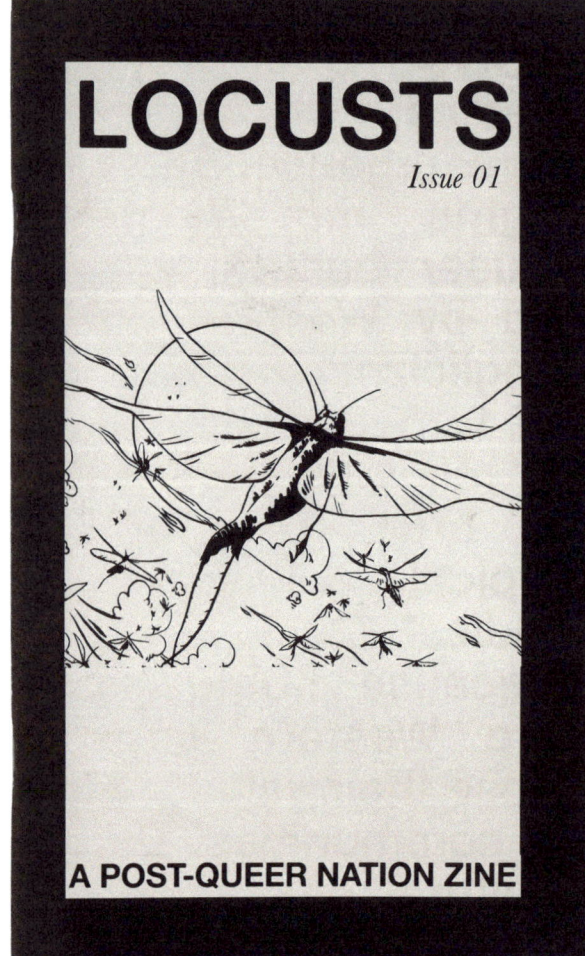

Demian DinéYazhi' and Kevin Holden
Locusts, no. 1, *A Post-Queer Nation Zine*, 2017
Letterpress, saddle stitched,
8 ½ × 5 ½ in. (21.6 × 14 cm)
Collection the artist

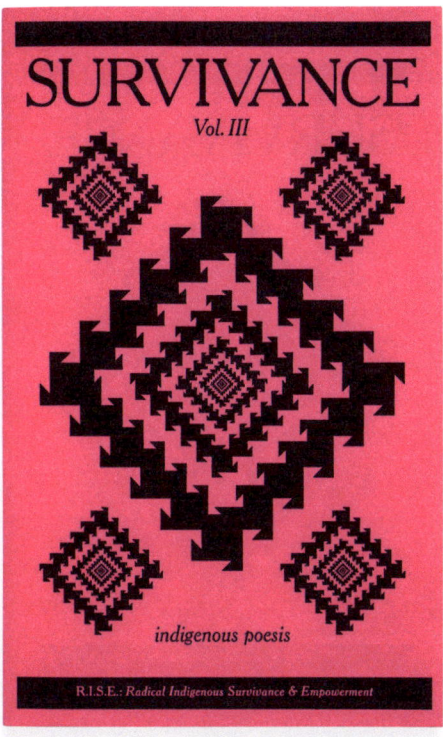 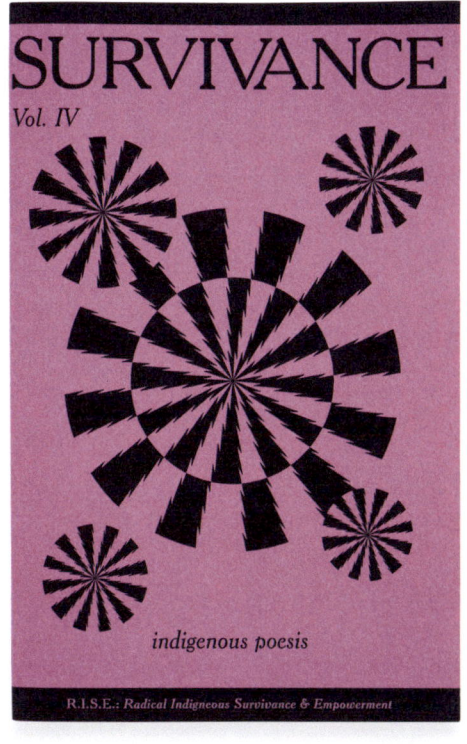

Survivance: Indigenous Poesis, vols. 2–4, 2016–19
Letterpress, saddle stitched,
8 ½ × 5 ½ in. (21.6 × 14 cm)
Collection the artist

LOCUSTS is a post-dedicated to art, cultu & resurgence. Because rights movement is Queer cultural repres ed by Western persp anglicized & propoga of forced assimilation, & religious persecutio in order to promote typical & normative radical Queer politics Because homosexuali are Western constru pose their values & po & communities. Becau cultural diversity & res Queer Nation zine re, literature, critique, the contemporary gay not enough. Because entations are dominat-ectives that have been ted through centuries colonization, political n, & societal pressures conformity to stereo-gender roles. Because will never be enough. ty & the gender binary cts that shouldn't im-litics on other cultures se we understand that pect begets revolution.

411

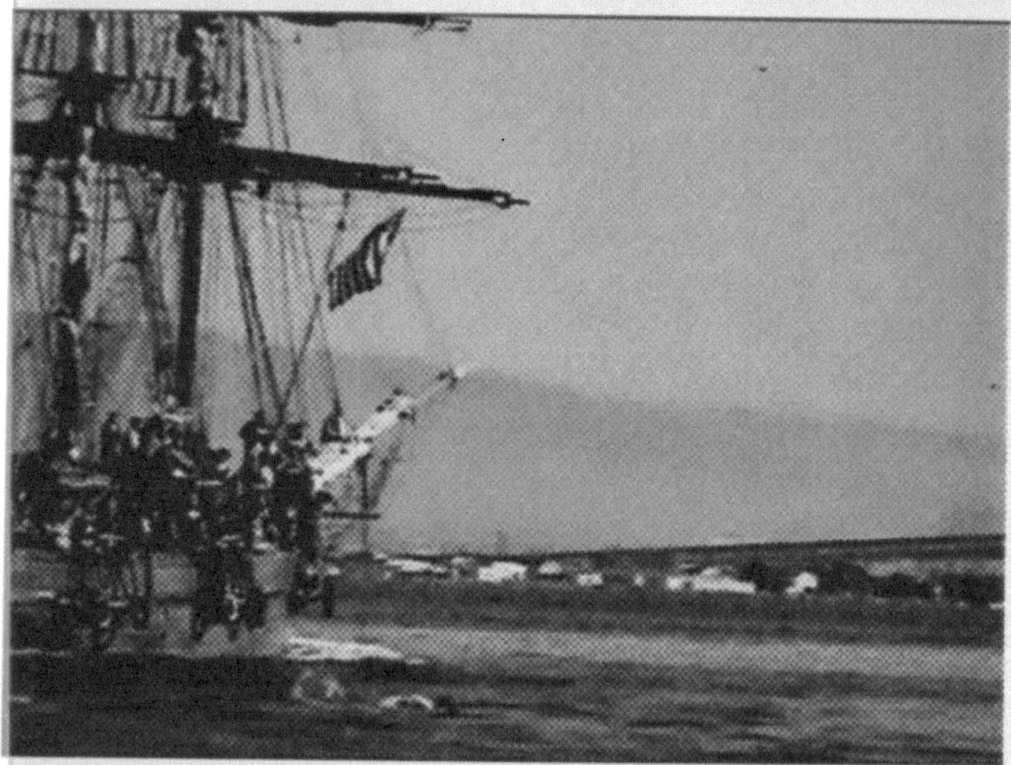

SWIMMING TO THE ISLAND:

PERFORMANCE ART & THE OCCUPATION OF ALCATRAZ

DEMIAN DINÉYAZHI'

R.I.S.E.: *Radical Indigenous Survivance & Empowerment*

Swimming to the Island, 2016
Letterpress, saddle stitched, 8½ × 5½ in. (21.6 × 14 cm)
Collection the artist

Swimming to the Island:
Performance Art
& the Occupation of Alcatraz

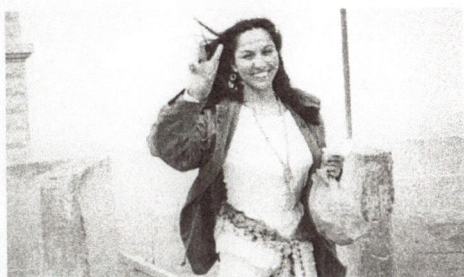

Among the varied roles embraced by contemporary, living artists, it is important to consider that one of those roles would be to present honest, radical perspectives that aim to challenge the viewer, the art institution, and the integrity of the art world through ongoing creative exchange. It comes as no surprise then when the role of the artist enters into the realm of social activism through the actions initiated by various forms of political resistance. More often than not, both spaces support similar missions and ambitions addressed through revolutionary political ideology, and in doing so, influence the aesthetics that are eventually adopted by the other. That is to say, the art that is propagated through politically charged art and socio-political movements impulsively inform and empower one another.

By entering this space you have an ethical responsibility to acknowledge that all Indigenous intelligence, creativity, fantasy, activism, and existence is grounded in revolutionary acts of Survivance.

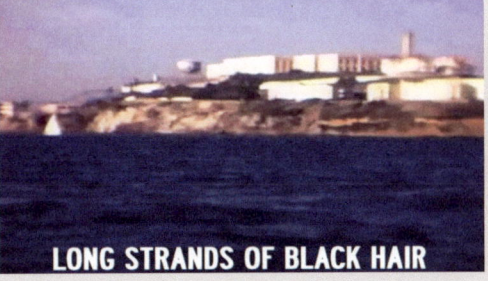

LONG STRANDS OF BLACK HAIR

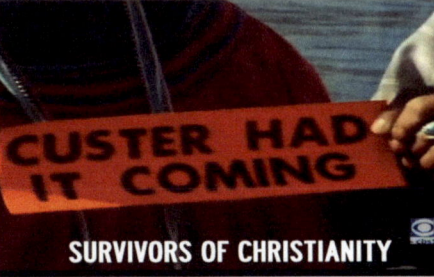

CUSTER HAD IT COMING

SURVIVORS OF CHRISTIANITY

Stills from *By Entering This Space*, 2020
Video; color, silent; 7 min., 29 sec.
Collection the artist

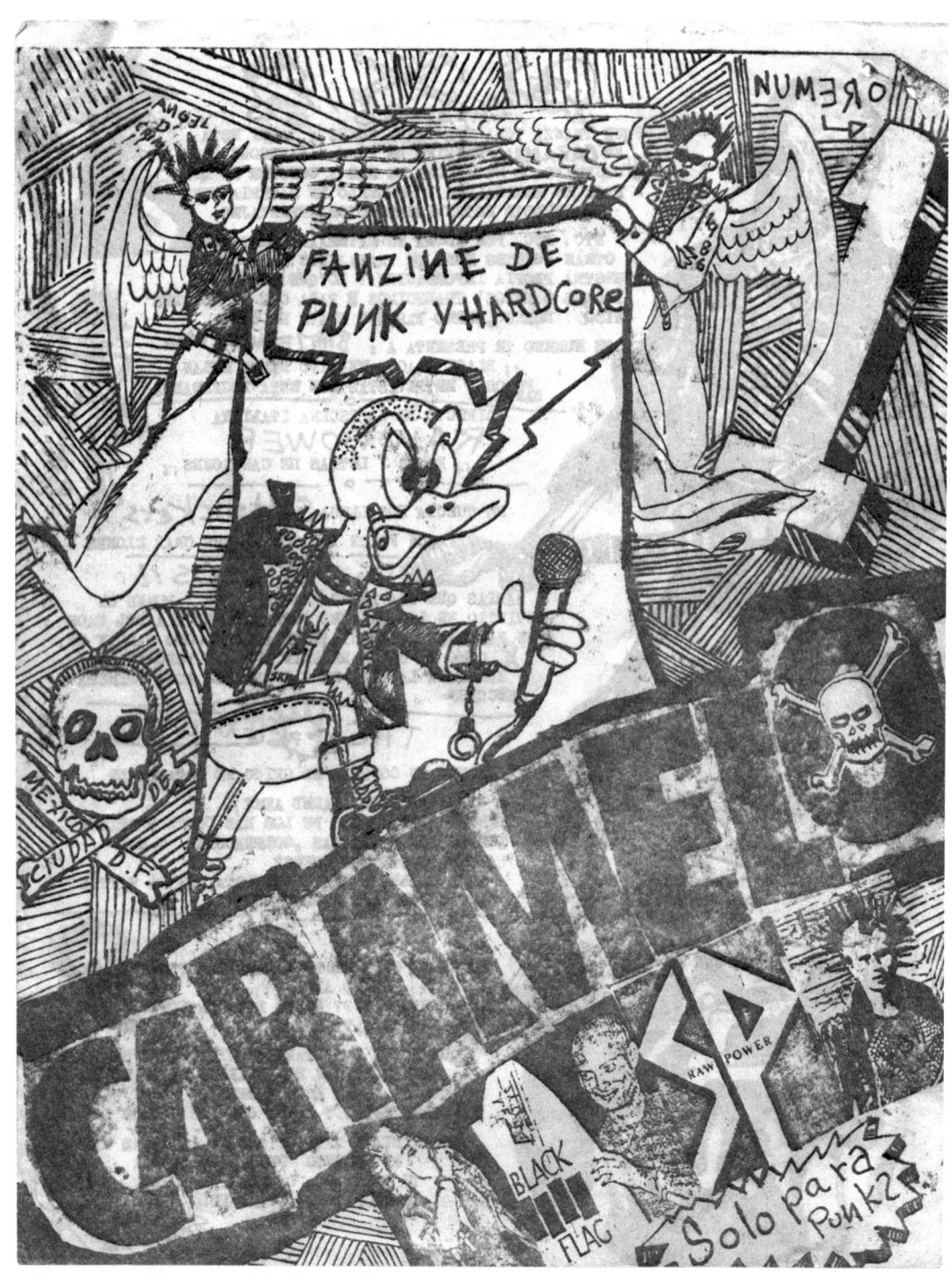

Archival materials for *PUNXDEFEKTUOZOZ*, 2014–ongoing
Collection the artist

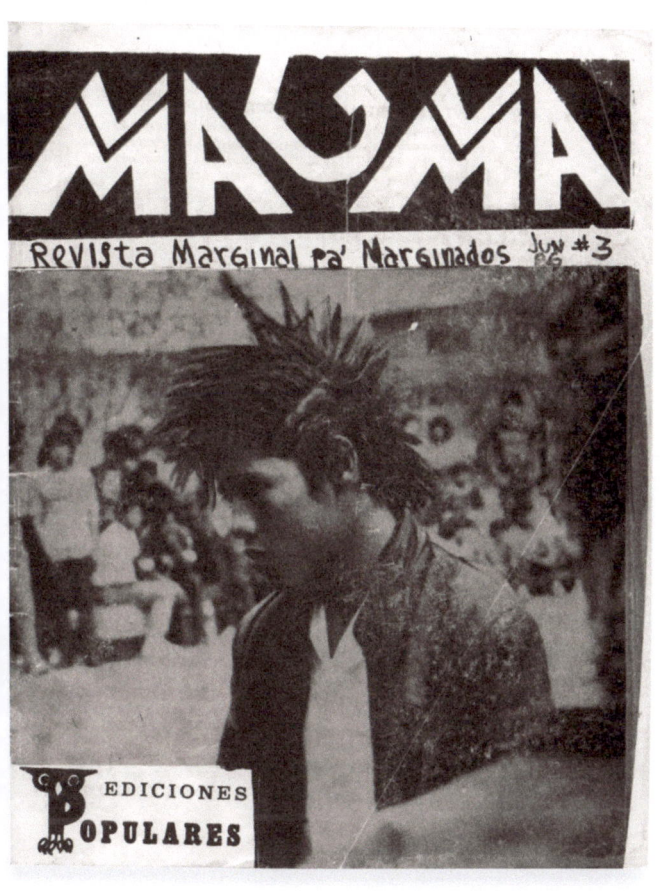

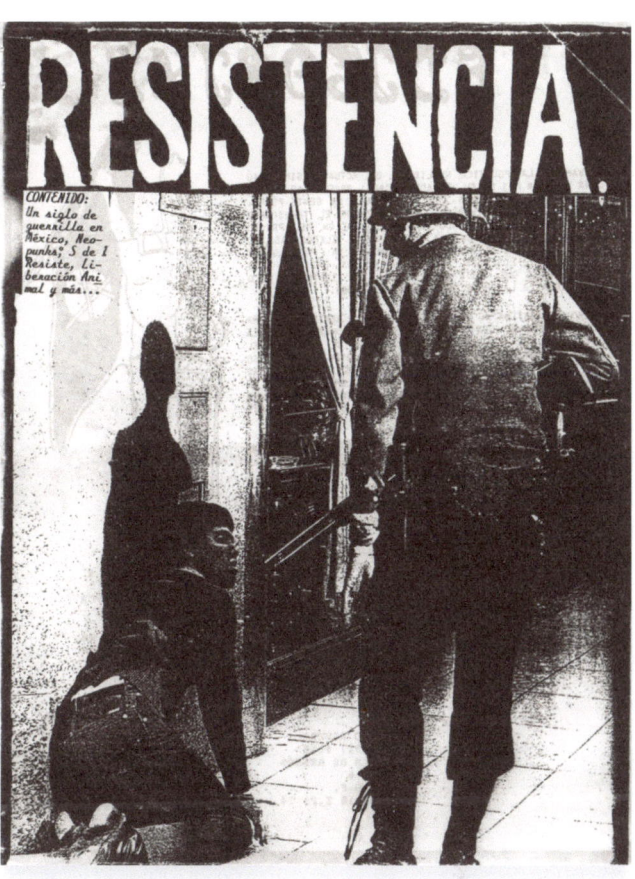

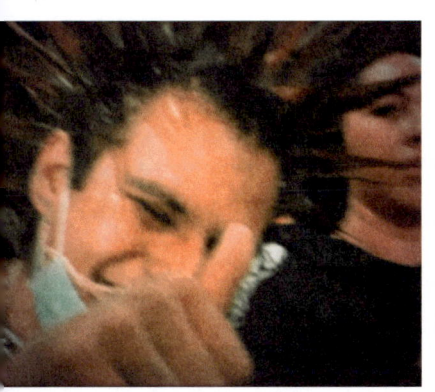

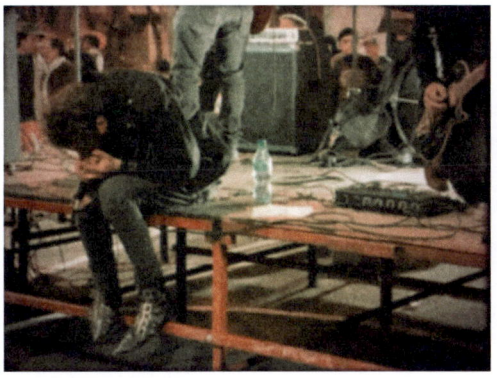

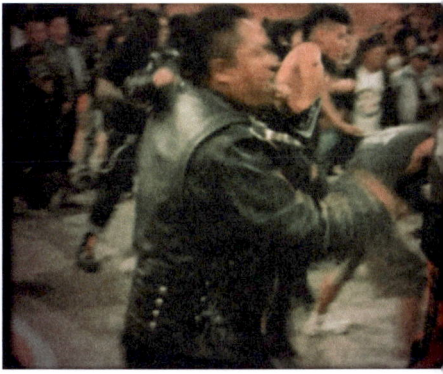

415

RRD (Joel Castro, María José Cruz, Anuar Portugal, Bruno Ruiz, Sergio Torres)

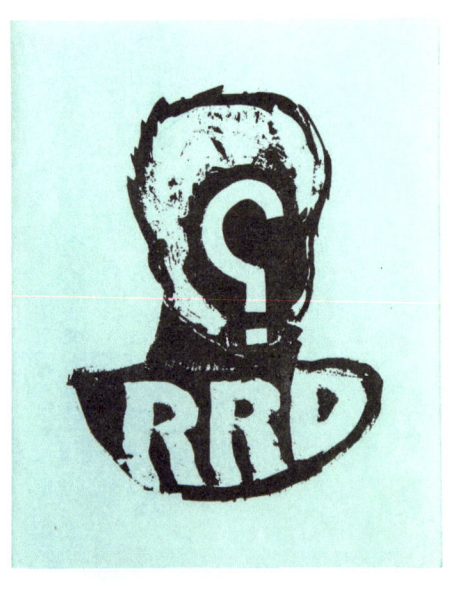

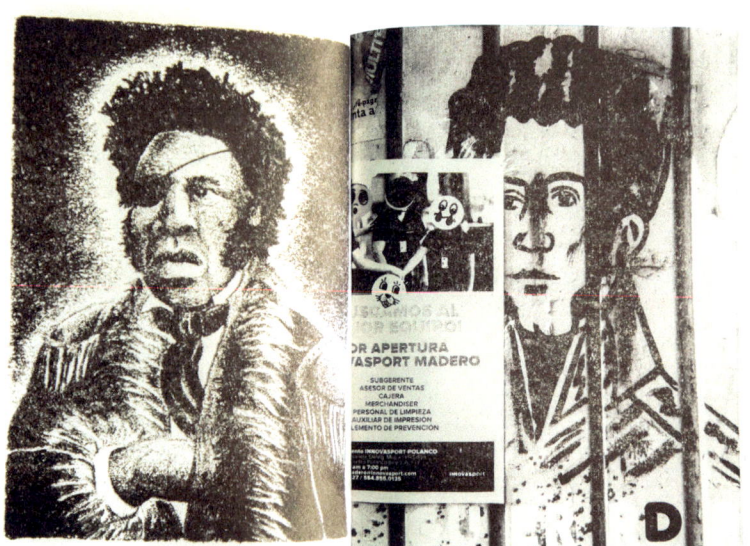

Vicentes, October 2018
Risograph, saddle stitched, 8½ × 6⁹/₁₀ in (21.7 × 17.5 cm)
Collection the artists

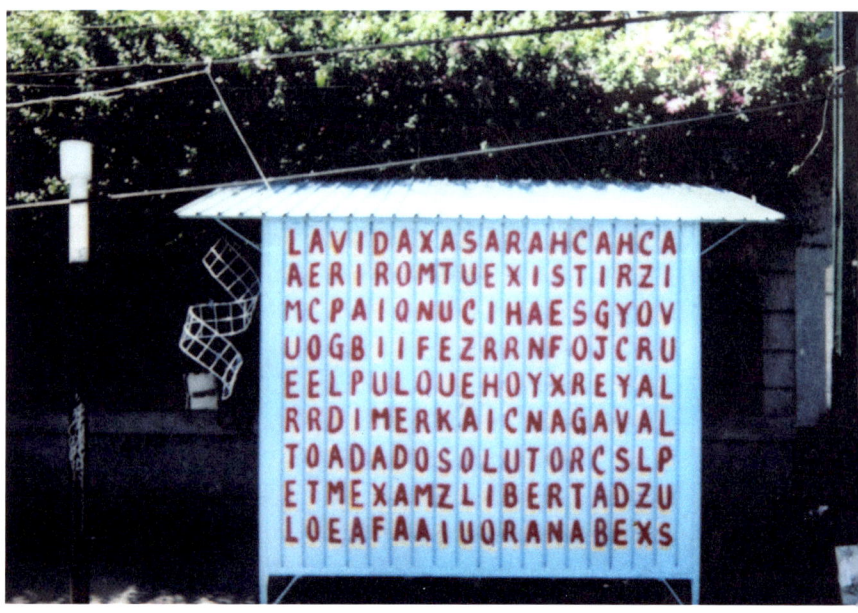

RRD kiosk, Mexico City, 2022

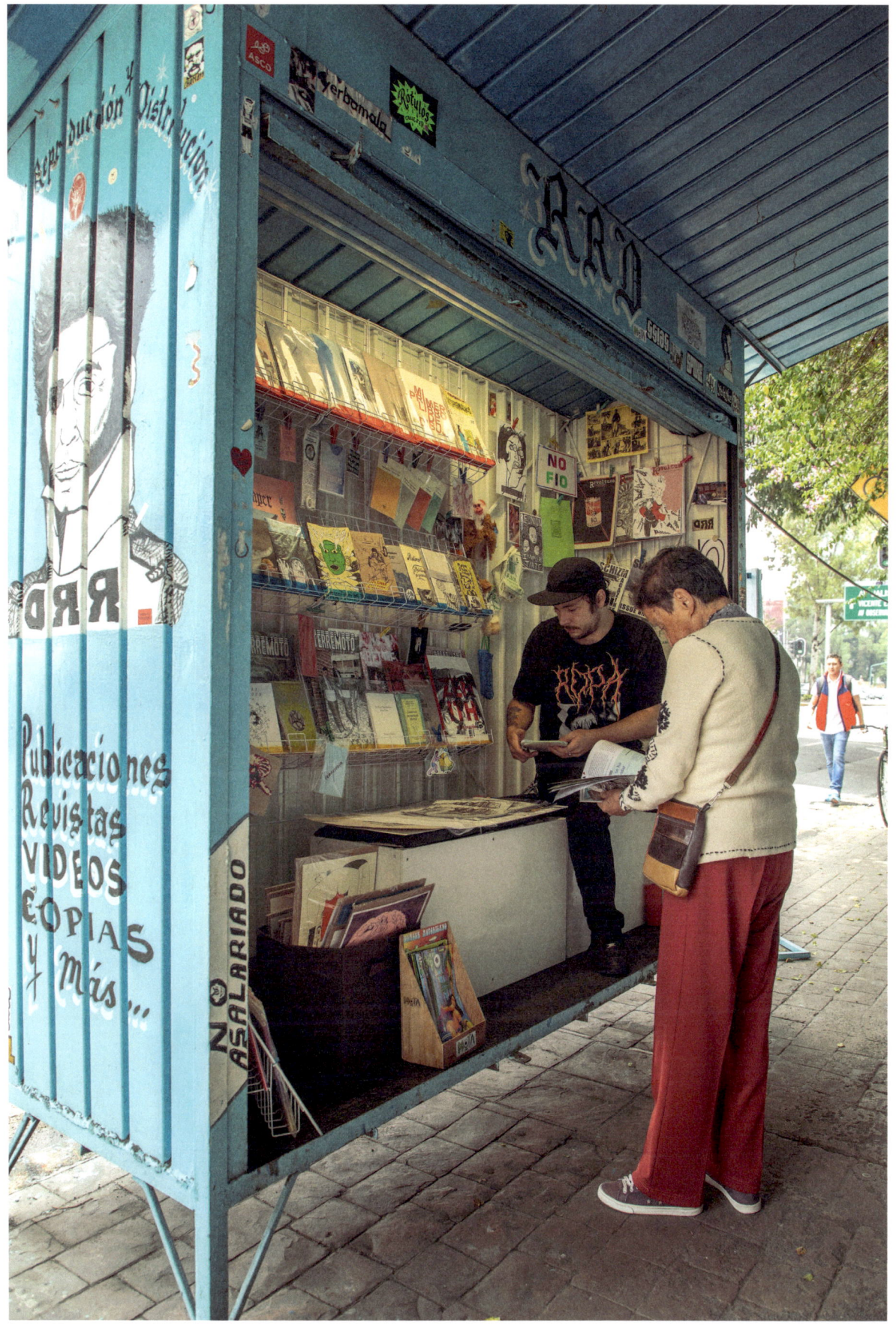

Lizania Cruz

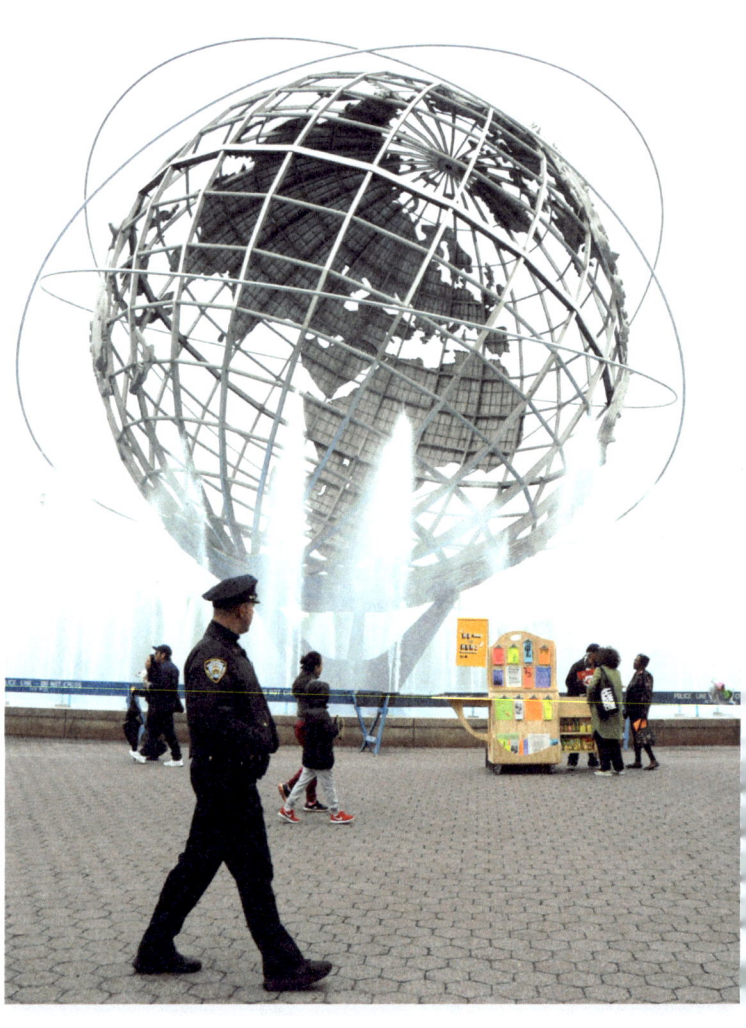

We the News newsstand, Flushing Meadows, Corona Park, Queens, 2018

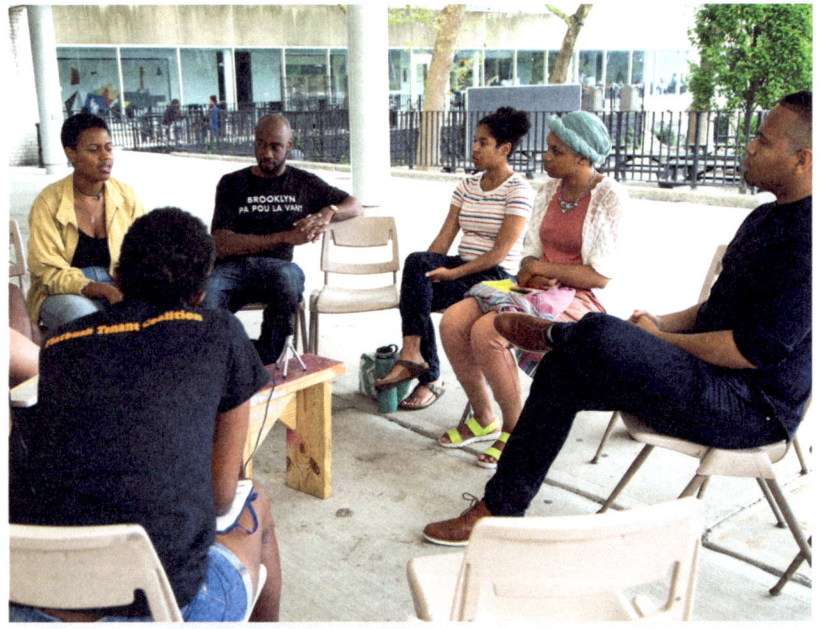

We the News story circle, Brooklyn Museum, part of Caribbeing House residency, 2017

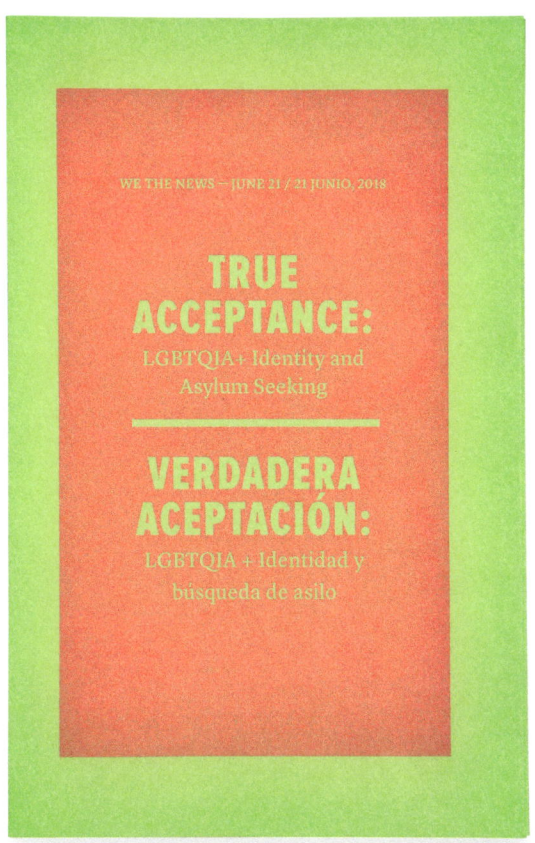

*True Acceptance: LGBTQIA+ Identity and Asylum Seeking | Verdadera
Aceptación: LGBTQIA+ Identidad y búsqueda de asilo*, June 21, 2018
Risograph, folded, 8 ½ × 5 ½ in. (21.6 × 14 cm)
Collection the artist

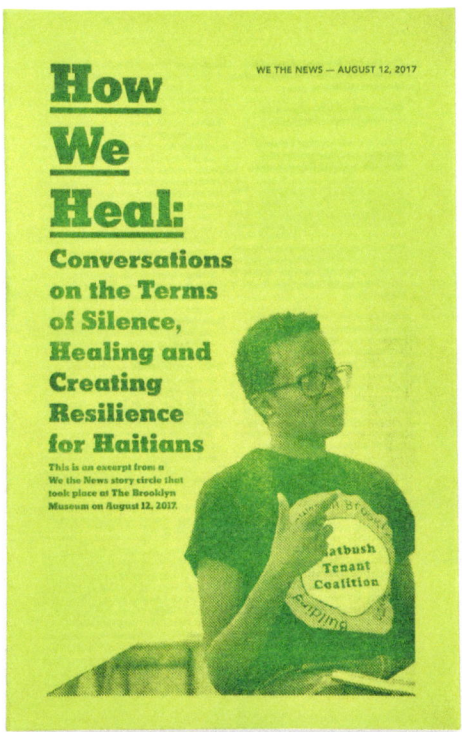

*How We Heal: Conversations on the Terms of Silence, Healing
and Creating Resilience for Haitians*, August 12, 2017
Risograph, folded, 8 ½ × 5 ½ in. (21.6 × 14 cm)
Collection the artist

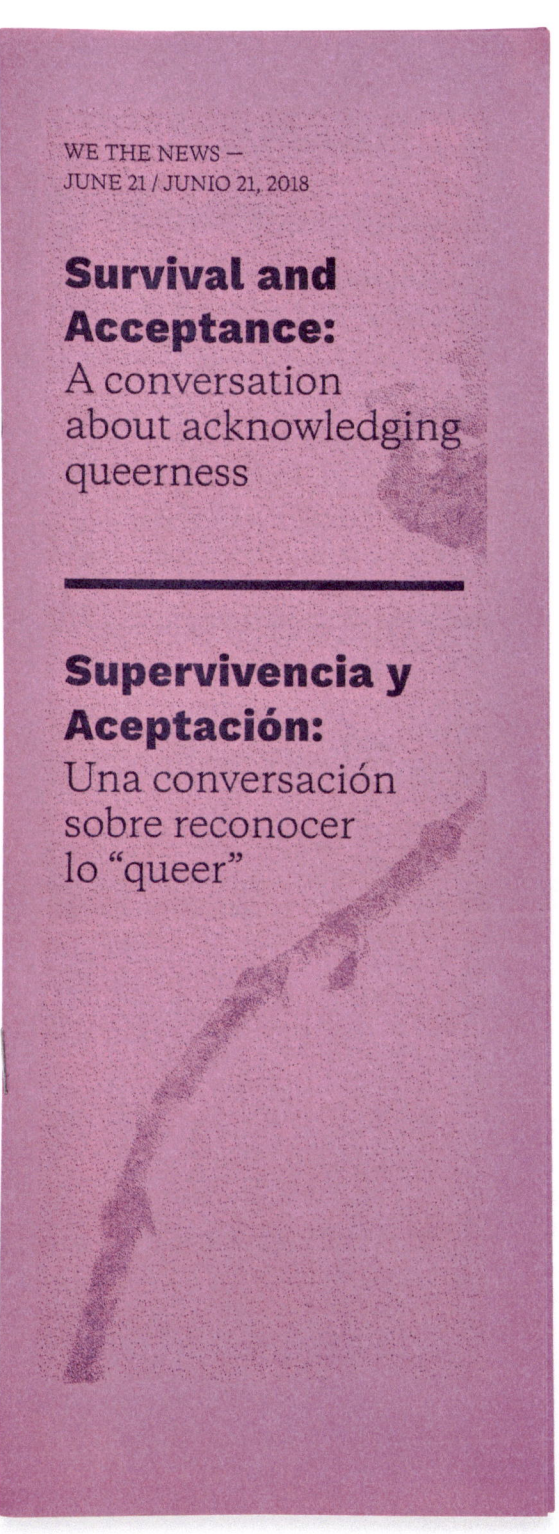

*Survival and Acceptance: A conversation about acknowledging queerness |
Supervivencia y Aceptación: Una conversación sobre reconocer lo "queer,"*
June 21, 2018
Laser print, saddle stitched, 11 × 4 ¼ in. (29.9 × 10.8 cm)
Collection the artist

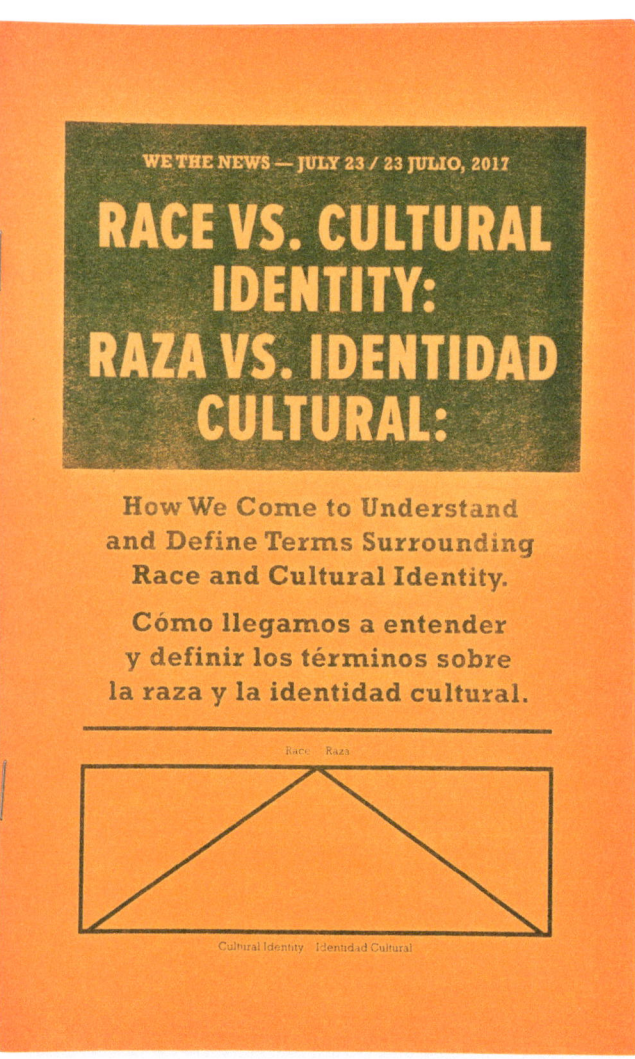

Race vs. Cultural Identity: Raza vs. Identidad Cultural, July 23, 2017
Laser print, saddle stiched, 8 ½ × 5 ½ in. (21.6 × 14 cm)
Collection the artist

→ *Crossing Borders: Conversations on Blackness and Seeking Asylum*, July 16, 2017
Laser print, side stapled, 11 × 8 ½ in. (27.9 × 21.6 cm)
Collection the artist

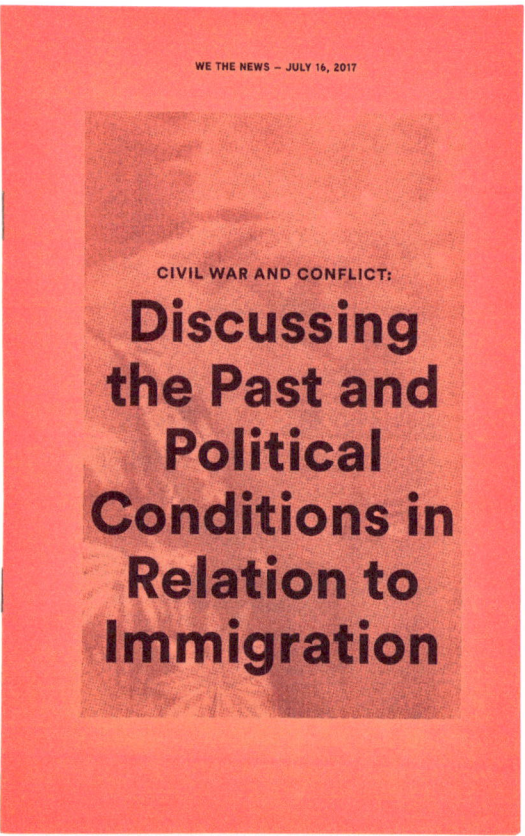

Civil War and Conflict: Discussing the Past and Political Conditions in Relation to Immigration, July 16, 2017
Laser print, saddle stitched, 8 ½ × 5 ½ in. (21.6 × 14 cm)
Collection the artist

Crossing Borders:
Conversations on Blackness and Seeking Asylum

Cruzando fronteras: Conversaciones sobre la negritud y buscando asilo

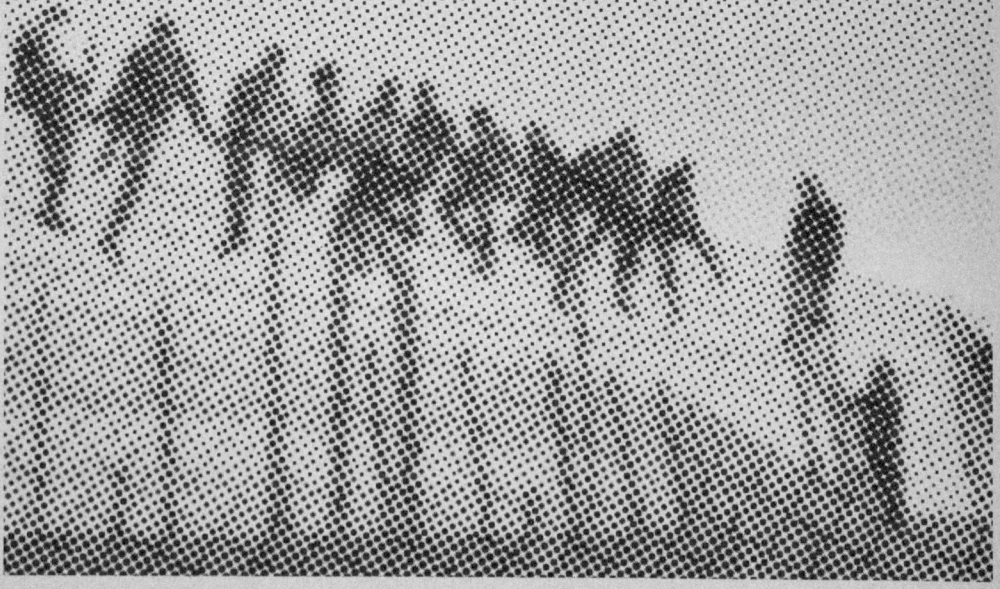

Este es un extracto de un ciclo de historias de We the News que tuvo lugar en Hancock Community Backyard Garden Park el 16 de julio de 2017.

El círculo de la historia exploró preguntas sobre de las fronteras, buscando asilo y racismo.

This is an excerpt from a We the News story circle that took place at Hancock Community Backyard Garden Park on July 16, 2017.

The story circle explored questions around borders, seeking asylum and racism.

BlackMass Publishing (Yusuf Hassan and Kwamé Sorrell)

Yusuf Hassan
Butchmorris, 2019
Photocopy, saddle stitched,
8 ½ × 5 ½ in. (21.6 × 14 cm)
Collection Philip Aarons and Shelley Fox Aarons

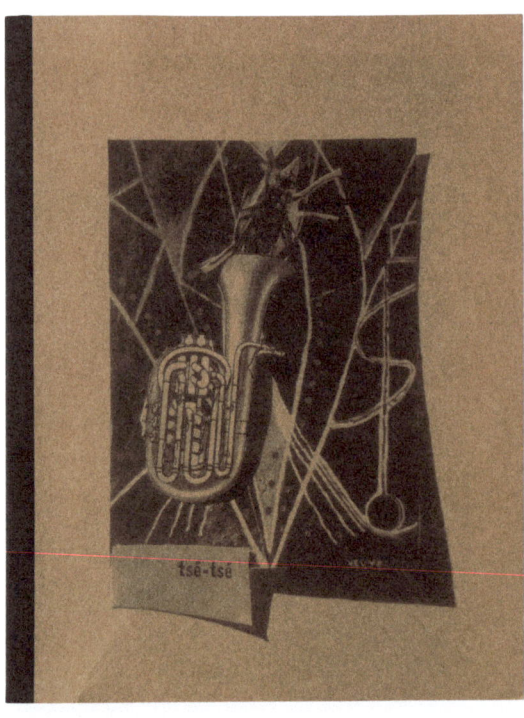

Yusuf Hassan (with Kwamé Sorrell)
tsé-tsé, 2019
Photocopy, tape bound,
11 × 8 ¼ in. (27.9 × 21 cm)
Collection Philip Aarons and Shelley Fox Aarons

Kwamé Sorrell
Je suis en face, 2020
Laser print, tape bound, 8 ½ × 5 ½ in. (21.6 × 14 cm)
Collection Philip Aarons and Shelley Fox Aarons

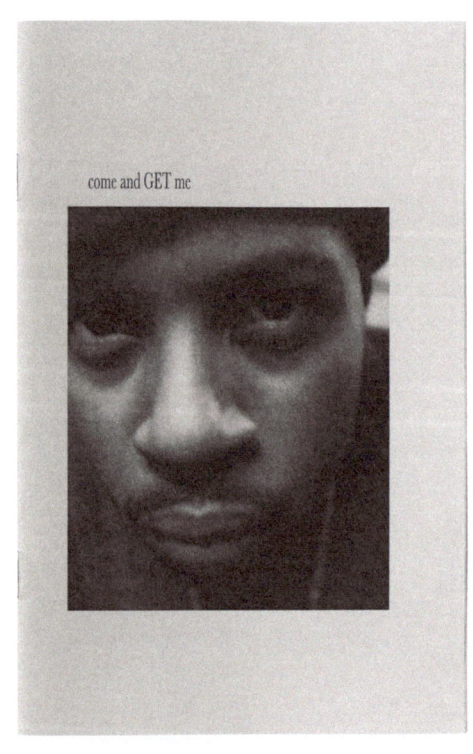

come and GET me, 2021
Photocopy, saddle stitched,
8 ½ × 5 ½ in. (21.6 × 14 cm)
Collection Philip Aarons and Shelley Fox Aarons

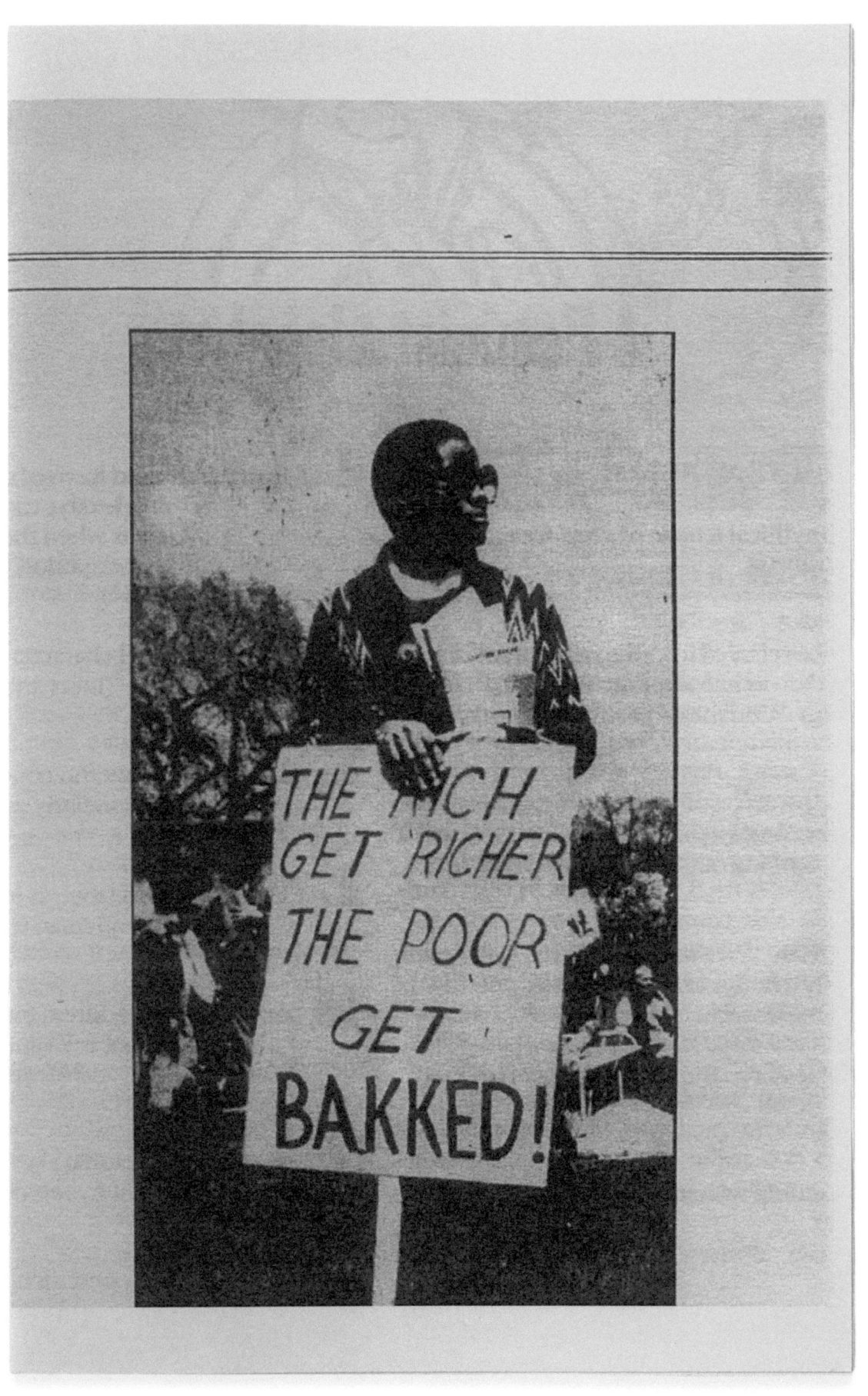

Yusuf Hassan
The Rich Get Richer the Poor Get Bakked!, 2019
Photocopy, saddle stitched, 8 ½ × 5 ½ in. (21.6 × 14 cm)
Collection Philip Aarons and Shelley Fox Aarons

→ Kwamé Sorrell
Kreyòl Homes/Southern Homes, 2020
Two booklets, photocopy, saddle stitched,
5 ½ × 4 ¼ in. (14 × 10.8 cm) / 8 ½ × 5 ½ in. (21.6 × 14 cm)
Collection Philip Aarons and Shelley Fox Aarons

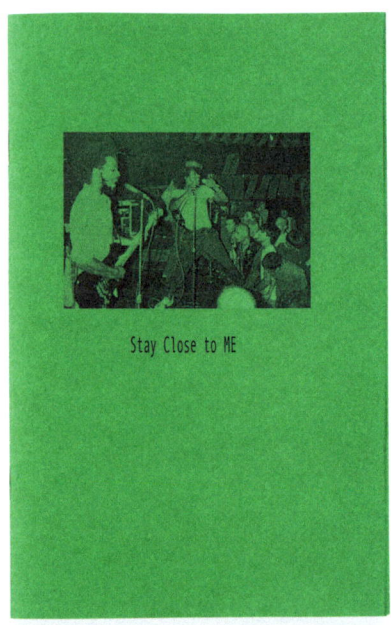

Stay Close to ME, 2021
Photocopy, saddle stitched, green paper wrappers,
8 ½ × 5 ½ in. (21.6 × 14 cm)
Collection Philip Aarons and Shelley Fox Aarons

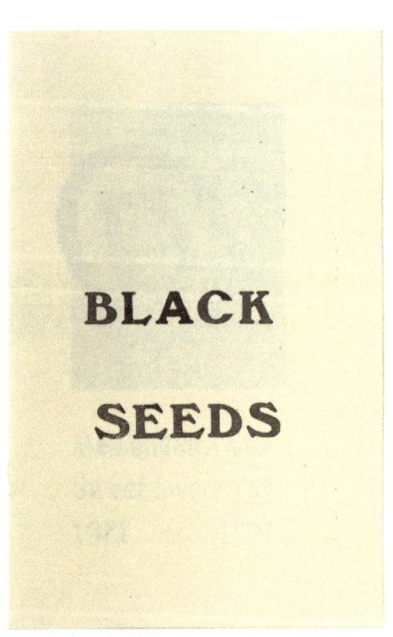

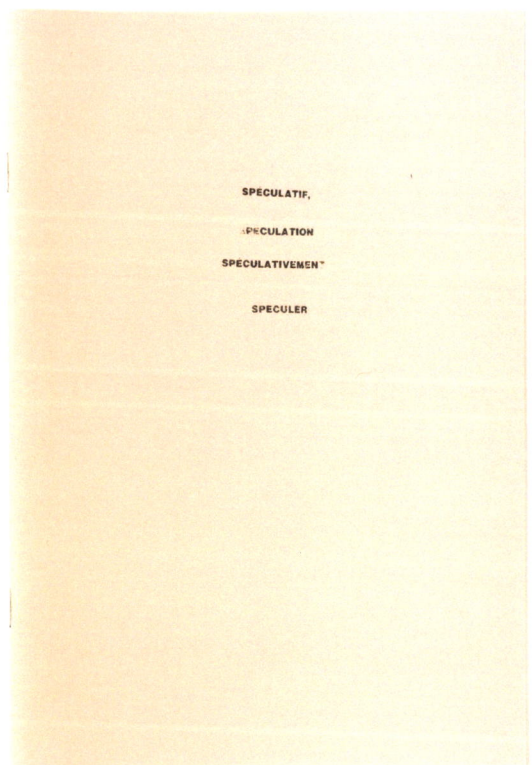

K. Omari (Kwamé Sorrell)
Spéculatif, Spéculation, Spéculativement, Spéculer, 2022
Photocopy, saddle stitched, 8 ¼ × 5 ¾ in. (21 × 14.6 cm)
Collection Philip Aarons and Shelley Fox Aarons

Yusuf Hassan
Black Seeds, 2019
Photocopy, saddle stitched, 8 ½ × 5 ½ in. (21.6 × 14 cm)
Collection Philip Aarons and Shelley Fox Aarons

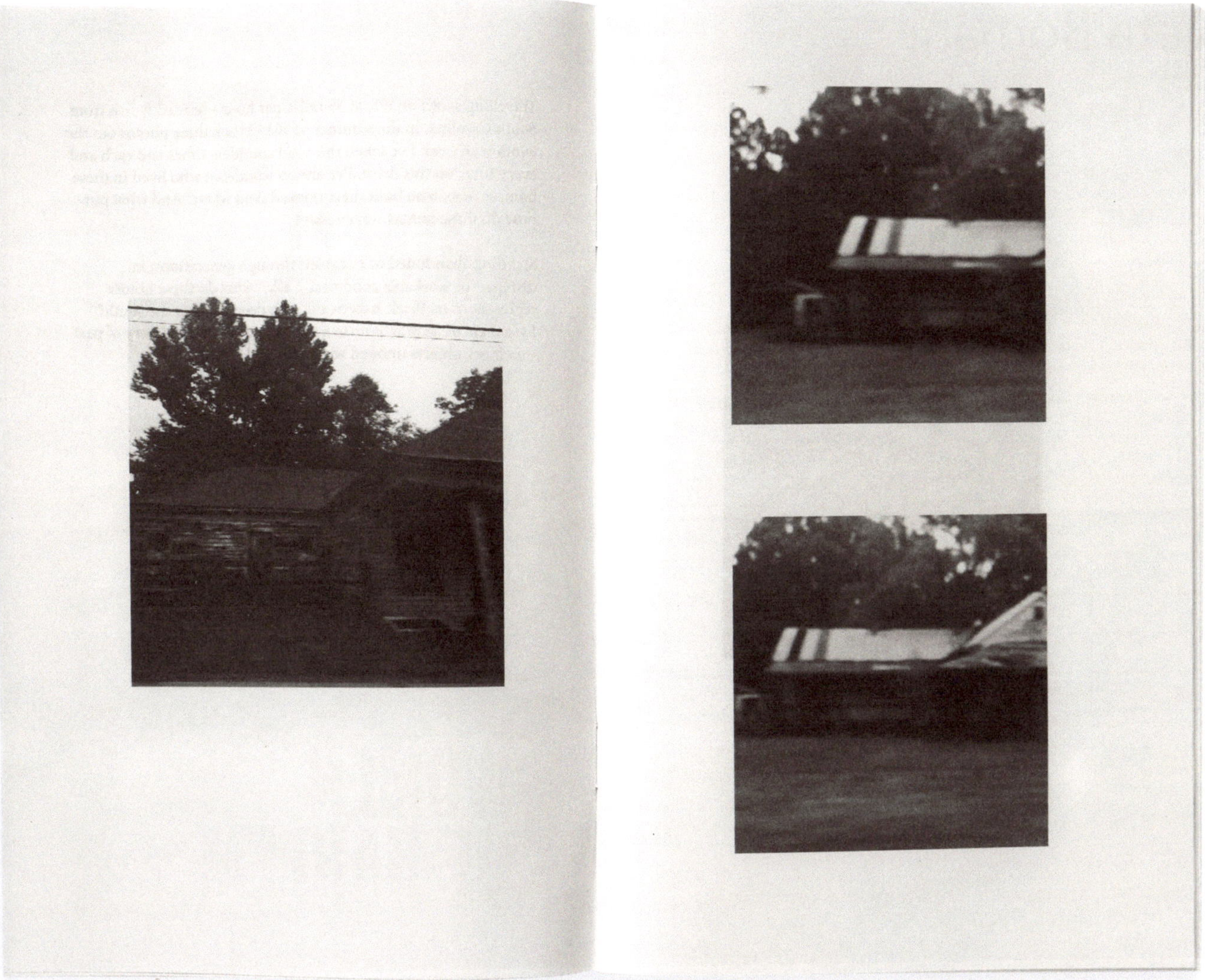

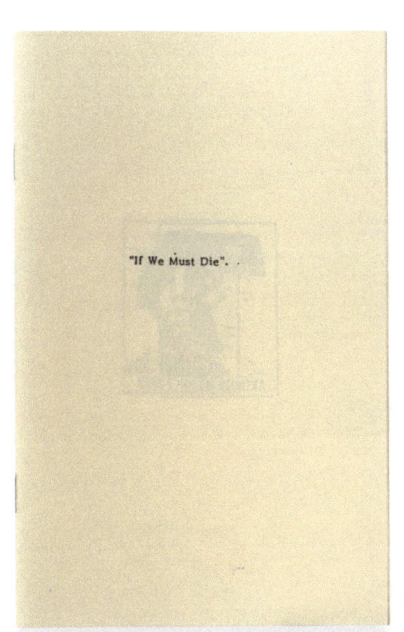

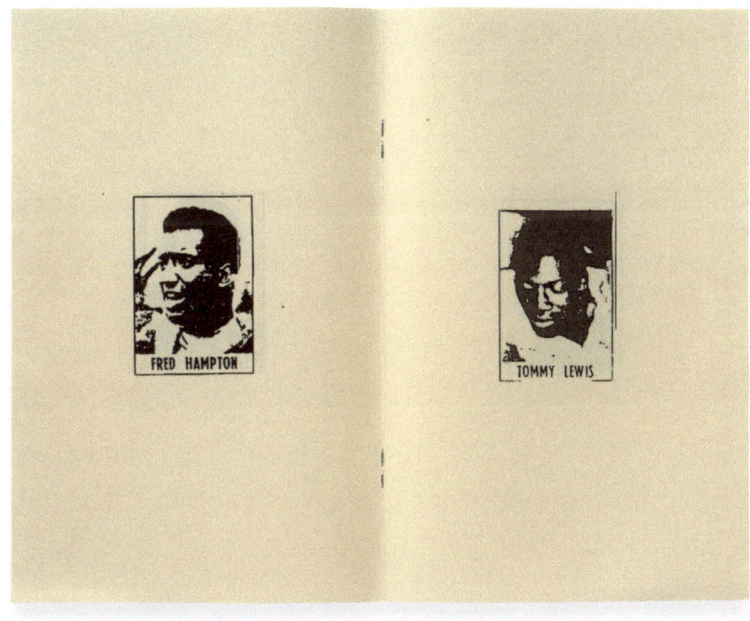

Yusuf Hassan
"If We Must Die," 2020
Photocopy, saddle stitched, 8 ½ × 5 ½ in. (21.6 × 14 cm)
Collection Philip Aarons and Shelley Fox Aarons

Neta Bomani

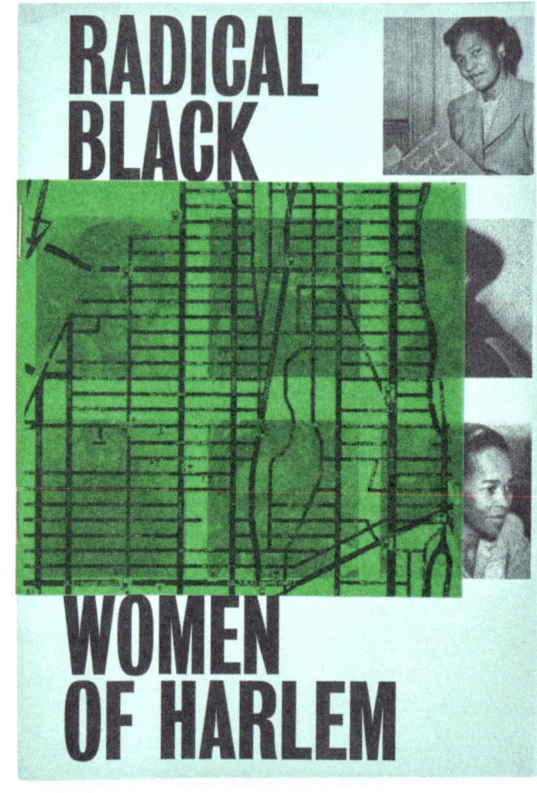

Radical Black Women of Harlem, 2021
Laser print, saddle stitched, green vellum and
blue wrappers, 7 × 4 ⅞ in. (17.8 × 12.4 cm)
Collection the artist

Black Women Librarians, 2021
Laser print, loose-leaf in sleeve, 5 ³/₁₆ × 3 ⅜ in. (13.2 × 8.6 cm)
Collection the artist

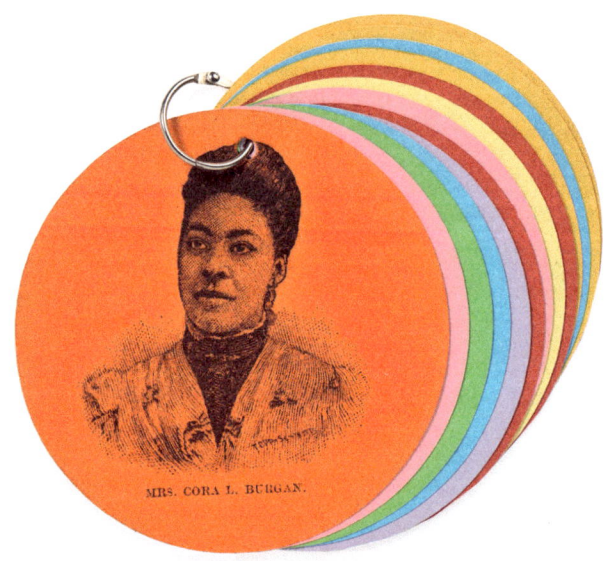

Noted Negro Women, 2021
Laser prints, bound with loose-leaf ring, 5 ⅝ × 5 in. (14.3 × 12.7 cm)
Collection the artist

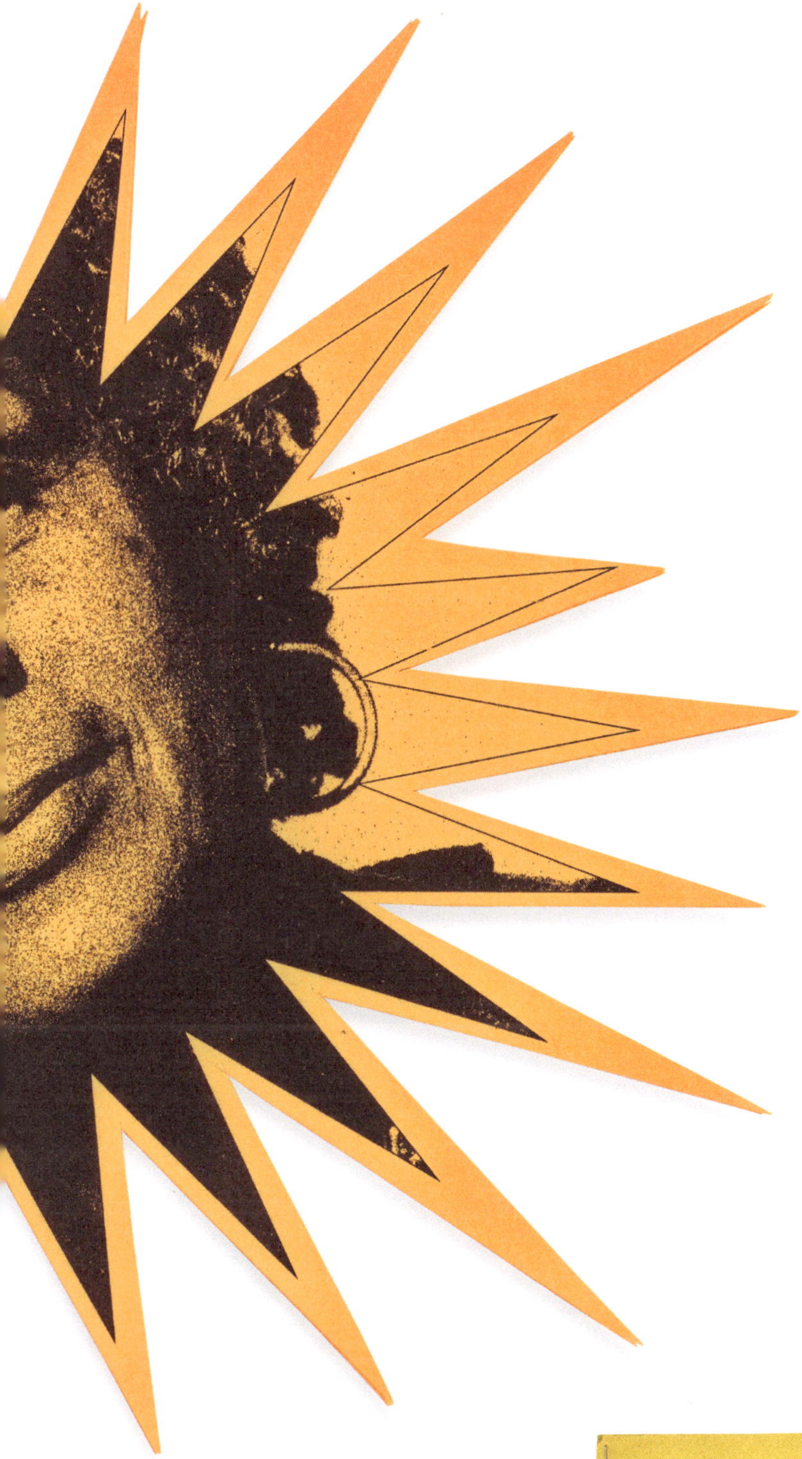

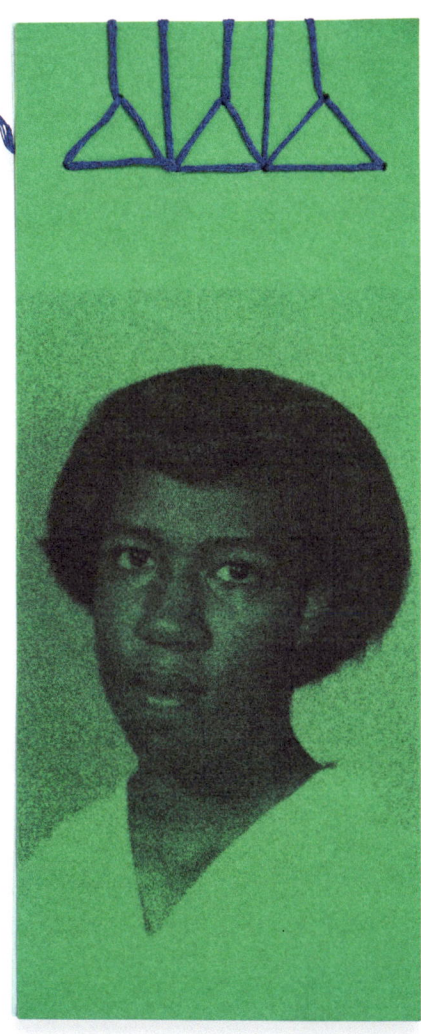

Octavia, 2021
Laser print, bound with embroidery thread,
7 15/16 × 3 3/8 in. (20.2 × 8.6 cm)
Collection the artist

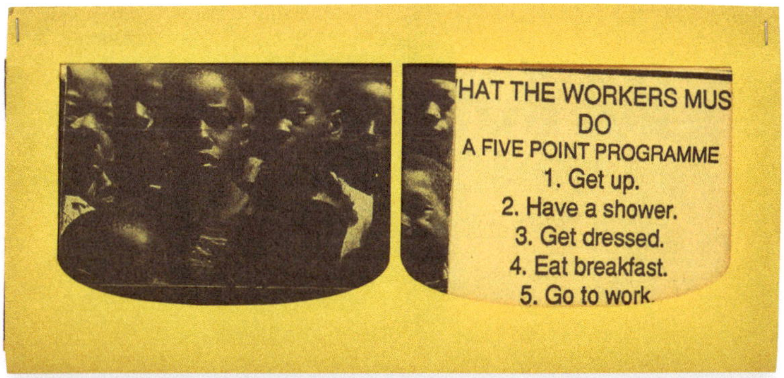

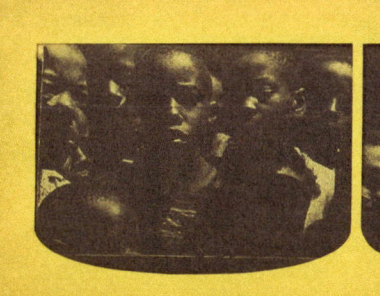

Two Story Images, 2021
Laser print, with envelope, 4 ¼ × 9 ¼ in. (10.8 × 23.5 cm)
Collection the artist

↑   *sonia sanchez: a sun woman for all seasons*, 2021
Laser print, saddle stitched, 8 ½ × 5 ¼ in. (21.6 × 13.3 cm)
Collection the artist

427

BLACK? WOMAN? PUNK?, 2021
Laser print, folded, red velum wrappers,
4 11/16 × 3 7/8 in. (11.9 × 9.8 cm)
Collection the artist

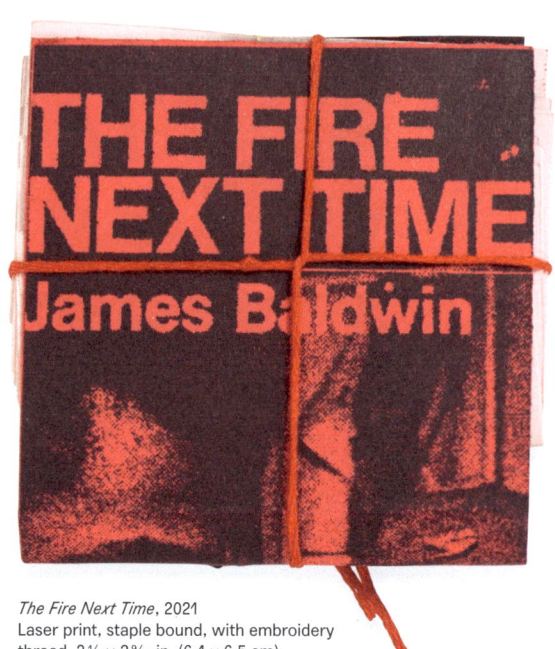

The Fire Next Time, 2021
Laser print, staple bound, with embroidery
thread, 2 1/2 × 2 9/16 in. (6.4 × 6.5 cm)
Collection the artist

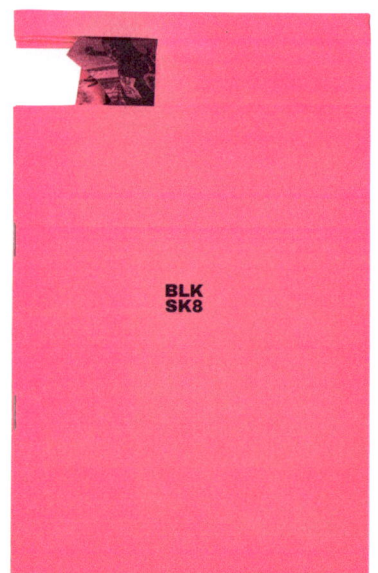

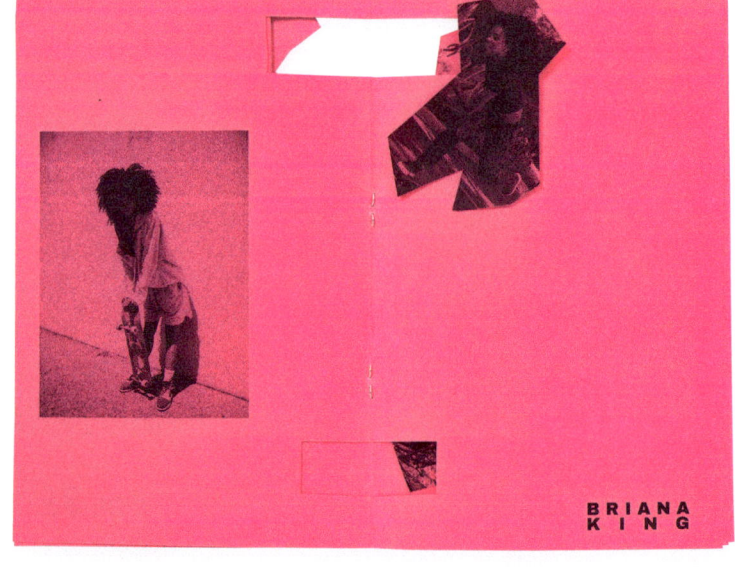

blk sk8, 2021
Laser print, saddle stitched,
8 × 5 1/4 in. (20.3 × 13.3 cm)
Collection the artist

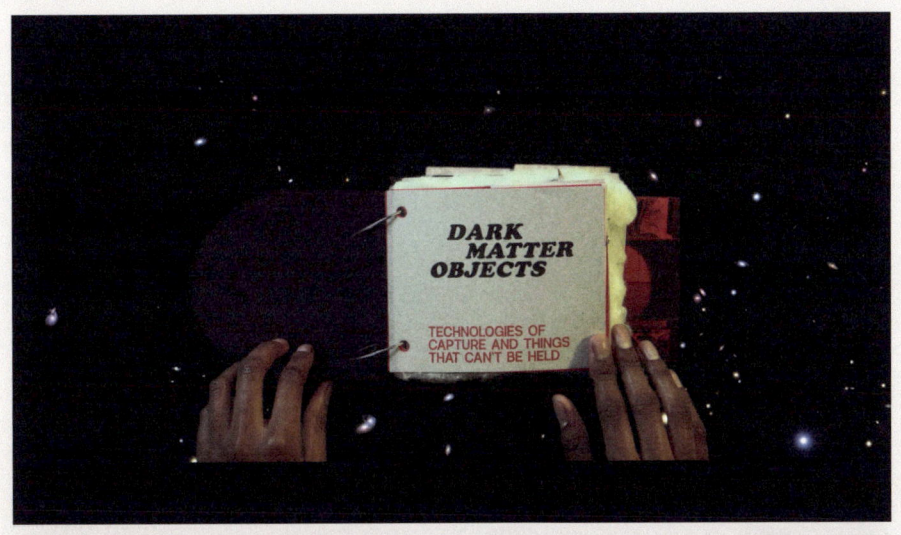

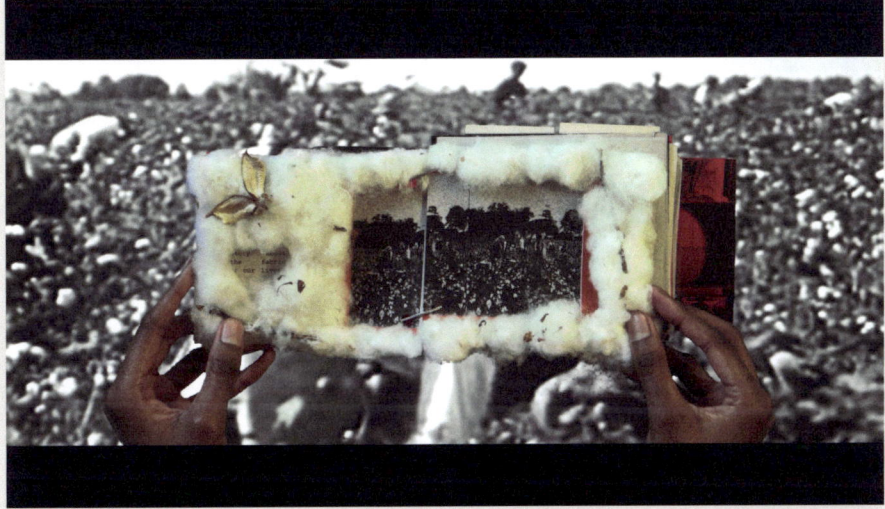

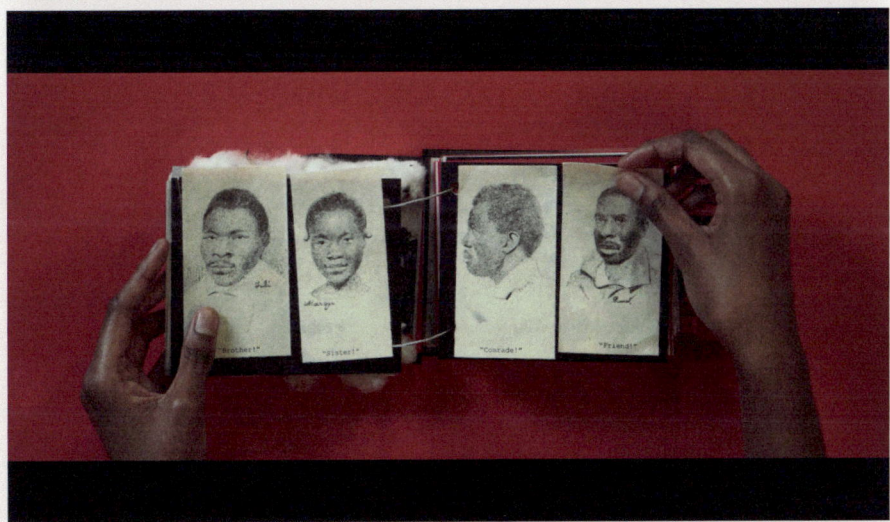

Stills from *Dark Matter Objects: Technologies of Capture and Things that Can't Be Held*, 2018–ongoing
Video; color, sound; 24 min., 55 sec.
Collection the artist

Selected Artists and Collectives

A

ARMSTRONG, SKOT (a.k.a. Skot Armst) (b. 1955, Montgomery, West Virginia, lives in Cerritos, California)

Armstrong's art practice began while he was a student at Immaculate Heart College in Los Angeles, where he became friends with the artist **Joey Terrill** and began participating in the international mail art network. In 1974, with financial assistance from the college, Armstrong began his own publishing enterprise, Science Holiday, as a way to produce artists' zines, including *Fetish Confidential* (1975), *Fist Fuck* (1975), *Masterbirthday* (1975), and *Jockstrap* (1976), the last of which featured drawings by Terrill. In the late 1970s and early 1980s, Armstrong was involved in the LA punk scene, notably designing flyers for **Gerardo Velázquez's** group Nervous Gender. → **76–78**

ATOE, OSA (b. 1978, Blacksburg, Virginia, lives in Sarasota, Florida)

A musician and zine maker who now works primarily in ceramics, Atoe began producing *Shotgun Seamstress* in 2006 (eight and a half issues, 2006–16). Initially subtitled "A zine by and for Black punks" (issue 1, 2006), the publication was intended to "support Black People who exist within predominantly white subcultures, and to encourage the creation of our own" (issue 2, 2007). Inspired by the zines of the Riot Grrrl movement, *Shotgun Seamstress* featured essays, reading lists, personal writing, and interviews. It not only highlighted contemporary bands such as **Brontez Purnell's** Gravy Train!!!!, but also pioneering Black punks from the 1970s to the 1990s and visual artists such as Alvin Baltrop, Kalup Linzy, and **Vaginal Davis**. The success of *Seamstress* eventually led Atoe to contribute a regular column to *Maximum Rocknroll*, disseminating her mission into the wider punk press. → **366–67**

AUSTIN, BRYN (b. 1966, Urbana, Illinois, lives in Boston, Massachusetts)

Austin was an editor, with **Adriene Jenik** and **Pam Gregg**, of the queer zine *Screambox* (three issues, 1990–92). → **232**

AZAR, CAROLINE (b. 1961, Beirut, Lebanon, lives in Toronto, Ontario, Canada)

As co-founder and co-lyricist of the band Fifth Column with **G. B. Jones**, Azar was a key figure in Toronto's queercore movement. In 1981 she joined **Candy Parker** in publishing *Hide* (five issues, 1981–85), an early and influential Toronto film and music zine co-founded by Parker and **Kathleen Pirrie Adams**. After the first issue, Jones joined Azar and Parker as an editor of *Hide*, remaining until the publication's dissolution in 1985 (Pirrie Adams left before completion of issue 1; Parker would leave after issue 3 to produce the zine *Dr. Smith*). Beginning with issue 2, *Hide* appeared with accompanying cassettes anthologizing

independent bands from Toronto and beyond, including Fifth Column. Azar appeared in several of the Toronto scene's films, including Jones's *The Troublemakers* (1990) and *The YoYo Gang* (1992), and **Bruce LaBruce's** *No Skin Off My Ass* (1991). → **156–57**

B

BANANA, ANNA (born Anne Long) (b. 1940, Victoria, British Columbia, Canada, lives in Roberts Creek, British Columbia)

Banana adopted her moniker while living and working at the Esalen Institute in Big Sur, California, in the late 1960s. Her career as a performance artist was initiated in 1971–72 when she designated herself the "Town Fool" of Victoria, Canada. Banana became involved in mail art in 1971, after sending a copy of her newsletter, *Banana Rag* (1971–ongoing), to artist Gary Lee-Nova, who connected her with the Vancouver-based artists' group Image Bank. In 1974, after moving to San Francisco, Banana launched *Vile*, a zine whose title played on that of the Toronto-based group General Idea's *File* "megazine" and featured work by many members of *File*'s coterie. Running for eight issues, three of which were edited by **Bill Gaglione**, *Vile* was a significant platform for mail artists in North America and beyond. Throughout the 1970s, Banana orchestrated the "Banana Olympics" and restaged historical Futurist performances, including the Futurist Sound tour of 1978, which she undertook throughout Europe with Gaglione. → **50–54**

BARNES, GENE (a.k.a. Portia Manson, born James Eugene Barnes) (b. 1964, Montgomery, Alabama, d. 1995, San Francisco, California)

A filmmaker and performer who lived primarily on the US West Coast, Barnes produced the Radical Faeries– and counterculture-inspired zine *Hippie Dick* (1991–94), encompassing both a print publication and related pornographic films distributed through the publication's network. Barnes also performed and made a series of experimental films under the name "Portia Manson," including *Thank Gay I'm God* and *Mercury Rising* (both 1989–90). Barnes's art practice originated while he was a student at Evergreen State College in Washington State, where he met friends and fellow zine-makers **Tammy Rae Carland**, **Kathleen Hanna**, and **Kelly Marie Martin**. Barnes died of complications from HIV/AIDS at the age of thirty-one; Hanna memorialized him in the Bikini Kill song "R.I.P." → **242–44**

BAUMGARDNER, LISA (a.k.a. Deena Schwartzbaum, born Lisa B. Falour) (b. 1957, Cleveland, Ohio, d. 2015, France)

Baumgardner started the zine *Modern Girlz* in 1977, while a student at Kent State University in Ohio, and continued its production after her move to New York City in the same year. In New York, she enrolled in film classes and

established herself as a bondage model and dominatrix, a career that would span two decades. She published five issues of *Modern Girlz* before launching *Bikini Girl* in 1978; it ran for ten issues, concluding with a special video issue in 1990. Printed on pink paper, *Bikini Girl* was characterized by its use of appropriated imagery that recalled "nudie-cuties" and girl gang films by Russ Meyer and Doris Wishman. It was published out of Baumgardner's apartment in the East Village, and profiled the neighborhood's art, music, and writing scenes, regularly documenting goings-on at the Mudd Club and Club 57. Baumgardner was also a filmmaker, whose movies highlighted themes such as girl gangs (*Girl Pack*, 1978) and bondage-discipline-sadomasochism (*Lisa in Bondage*, 1981). → **104–7**

BAY AREA DADAISTS (a.k.a. Bay Area Daddaists) (active 1970s, San Francisco Bay Area, California)

The Bay Area Dadaists was a loose group of performance and correspondence artists whose members included **Anna Banana**, **Monte Cazazza**, **Charles Chickadel**, **Irene Dogmatic**, **Bill Gaglione**, and **Tim Mancusi**. The group's artistic practice encompassed self-published "dadazines" and mailers, Happenings, and performances inspired by the historical avant-garde, Fluxus, and the work of Ray Johnson, whom Gaglione and Mancusi met as art students in New York (and with whom they corresponded). Key zines of the movement included *Dadazine* (six issues, 1970–78), *Nitrous Oxide* (two issues, 1973 and 1977), *New York Correspondence School Weekly Breeder* (or *NYCS Weekly Breeder*, with ca. twenty-five issues, 1971–74; an additional issue, titled simply "Weekly Breeder" was produced by Buster Cleveland, Gaglione, and Robert Rockola in 1980); *Vile* (eight issues, 1974–79); and the *West Bay Dadaist/Quoz?* (twelve issues, 1973–76). → **38–55, 86**

BAYLIN, JOHN JACK (a.k.a. Count Fanzini, Bum Bank) (b. 1948, Ottawa, Canada, lives in San Diego, California)

In 1971, while living in rural Garden Bay, British Columbia, Baylin initiated the homoerotic correspondence persona "Bum Bank" as an offshoot of the Vancouver-based Image Bank group (founded by artists Michael Morris and Vincent Trasov), whose image-request lists appeared in General Idea's *File* "megazine." In 1972 Baylin started the "John Dowd Fanny Club," named for New York artist and bartender **John Dowd**. Subsequently, Baylin and Dowd produced *John Dowd Fanny Club Fanzine* and several issues of *Fanzini*, including *Fanzine/Fanzini* (ca. 1972), "Fanzini Three" (1973), *Fanzini Goes to the Movies* (1974), and "Fanzini '75" (1975). The final issue of *Fanzini*, "Fanzini/America," edited by Baylin, was commissioned by and exhibited at California's Long Beach Museum of Art in 1976. → **30–35**

BECKMAN, LAUREL (b. 1953, Honolulu, Hawai'i, lives in Santa Barbara, California)

From 1988 to 1990 Beckman and Kate Sorensen, based in Los Angeles, edited *Lucky*, a "metazine" that blurred distinctions between a zine, an artists' magazine, and an artist's book. Three issues were produced, each organized loosely around a theme (such as issue 1's "Love and Pets," 1988) and featuring original contributions by women artists and writers, including Beckman and Sorensen, along with Meg Cranston, Laurie Haycock Makela, Catherine Lord, Catherine Opie, Judith Williamson, and Millie Wilson. Produced at the print workshop of LA's Woman's Building (where Beckman had taught and made books), each issue of *Lucky* was designed without pagination, with works appearing on fold-outs, in relatively nonhierarchic fashion. In 1994 Beckman, Sorenson, and Ryan Hill collaborated on the thematically organized publication *Joy*, which ran for three issues, until 1997. → **222–23**

BELASCO (b. 1964, Gary, Indiana, lives in Los Angeles, California)

Belasco's erotic illustrations and comics began appearing in the early 1990s in small-press periodicals in and around Chicago, where he met writer and editor **Robert Ford**, eventually becoming a regular contributor to Ford's zine-cum-magazine *Thing* (1989–93). Concurrently, Belasco used a photocopier to self-publish his comics: the general theme was erotic representations of relationships among Black gay men. Belasco's comics have been collected in the publications *The Brothers of New Essex: Afro-Erotic Adventures* (2000) and *Belasco's Boo and the Bruthas* (2011). → **189**

BELVERIO, GLENN (a.k.a. Glennda Orgasm) (b. 1966, Belleville, New Jersey, lives in New York, New York)

As the drag persona "Glennda Orgasm," Belverio wrote, produced, and co-hosted (with Duncan Elliott, a.k.a. Brenda Sexual) the *Brenda and Glennda Show*, presented on Manhattan public access cable television from 1990 to 1993. Often filmed on the street, the guerrilla-style talk show mixed the politics and activist strategies of AIDS Coalition to Unleash Power (ACT UP) with the satire and humor of drag performance. Concurrent with the production of the television show, Belverio and **Emily Nahmanson** (a.k.a. Annie Thing) co-edited three issues of the zine *Pussy Grazer* (1991–92). In 1992 and 1993, Belverio curated a series of film and video programs for the MIX festival and for SPEW New York; riffing on his column "My Fanzine Friends," they featured works by zine-makers **Sadie Benning**, **Rick Castro**, **Vaginal Davis**, **Richard Kern**, **Bruce LaBruce**, **Steve Lafreniere**, **Candy Parker**, **Linda Simpson**, **Greta Snider**, and others. In 1993 his television program evolved into *Glennda and Friends*, with host Belverio and a rotating cast of co-hosts, including zine-makers Davis, LaBruce (as "Judy" or "Fonda" LaBruce), and Simpson, among many others. → **198–201**

BENNING, SADIE (b. 1973, Madison, Wisconsin, lives in Los Angeles, California)

Benning began making videos when they were fifteen years old, in 1988, using a Fisher-Price Pixelvision toy camera. Reminiscent of journal entries and filmed mostly in their bedroom, Benning's early video work has been likened by them to zines associated with Riot Grrrl and queercore. Their video *Girl Power* (1992) features music by **Kathleen Hanna's** band Bikini Kill, and Benning and Hanna collaborated on the 1995 video *The Judy Spots*. In 1998 Benning became a founding member of the band Le Tigre, with **Johanna Fateman** and Hanna, and produced zines of their drawings. → **192, 262–63**

BIKCEEM, RAMDASHA (a.k.a. Designer Imposter) (b. 1975, Morristown, New Jersey, lives in Los Angeles, California)

Bikceem is an artist and musician who has exhibited work under both her own name and the DJ moniker "Designer Imposter." She started producing the zine *Gunk* in 1990, at age fifteen. Named after her skater group and band, *Gunk* ran for five issues until 1994, engaging a range of topics including skateboard culture, feminism, punk, and race. In 1993 Bikceem moved to Brooklyn to attend Pratt Institute and became more directly involved with Riot Grrrl–associated artists. She appeared in **K8 Hardy's** zine *FashionFashion* and contributed additional vocals to the 2000 album *From the Desk of Mr. Lady* (2000) by Le Tigre, with **Sadie Benning**, **Johanna Fateman**, and **Kathleen Hanna**. → **260–61**

BLACKMASS PUBLISHING (founded 2018, New York, New York)

Named after Amiri Baraka's 1966 play *A Black Mass*, this independent publishing venture was founded by **Yusuf Hassan** in 2018 with *Project BlackMass*, a spiral-bound publication with contributions from artists Arthur Jafa, Devin B. Johnson, Jacob Mason-Macklin, Frida Orupabo, **Kwamé Sorrell**, and others. Hassan and Sorrell, who continue as BlackMass's publishers today, have produced dozens of zines both separately and together, among them *tsé-tsé* (2019), a wide-ranging collection of imagery from African diasporic cultures, which are presented in different orders in each edition, drawing on the improvisational nature of jazz music. Although the majority of work is produced by Hassan and Sorrell, BlackMass also publishes zines by other artists, musicians, and writers, such as Timothy Yanick Hunter's *No More Important Time than the Present* and Keiyaa's *On Returning My Quikest Language Back to My Mouth* (both 2020). → **422–25**

BLAKE, NAYLAND (b. 1960, New York, New York, lives in New York, New York)

Blake is an interdisciplinary artist known for their work in sculpture, video, installation, and photography that explores sexual subcultures and the intersections of race and gender. While living in San Francisco in the early 1990s, Blake produced the zines *Brains: A Journal of Egghead Sexuality* (1990, with D-L Alvarez) and *Bunny Butt* (1994), the latter featuring an animal that would become a hallmark in Blake's subsequent artwork. In 1995 they co-curated the exhibition *In a Different Light: Visual Culture, Sexual Identity, Queer Practice* with Lawrence Rinder at the University of California, Berkeley, Art Museum, contributing a catalogue essay that posited the importance of both punk and queer zines in establishing queer sensibilities. → **205–7**

BOMANI, NETA (b. 1994, Berrien Springs, Michigan, lives in New York, New York)

A self-described abolitionist, learner, and educator, Bomani creates zines, both digital and in print, that consider Blackness, technology, and archives. With activist Mariame Kaba, she co-directs Sojourners for Justice Press (an imprint of Haymarket books), and she and Kaba collaborated on the zines *Black Photo Booth* and *Groundhog Day: The Killing of Bonita Carter* (both 2020). From January 28 to May 7, 2021, Bomani enacted "100 Days of Zines," creating one zine each day for the allotted period; the project led to *Dark Matter Objects: Technologies of Capture and Things that Can't Be Held*, a multimedia zine and video examining computational history and its societal implications for understanding race, gender, politics, and economics. Bomani is a co-director at the School for Poetic Computation, which in 2018 launched the New York Tech Zine Fair. → **426–29**

BROOKS TAKAHASHI, GINGER (b. 1977, Huntington, West Virginia, lives in Pittsburgh, Pennsylvania)

Brooks Takahashi is an interdisciplinary artist whose practice centers on collaboration. In 2000 she and Courtney Dailey, Onya Hogan-Finlay, Leila Pourtavaf, and Rebecca Watt co-founded the Projet Mobilivre-Bookmobile, an interactive touring exhibition of artists' publications housed in an Airstream trailer. Exhibiting some three hundred curated artists' zines and books at a time, the Mobilivre ran until 2005, traveling throughout the United States and Canada, visiting community centers, artist-run centers, libraries, and universities, often far from large urban settings. In 2001 Brooks Takahashi co-founded the queer feminist collective **LTTR**, which published five issues of its eponymous zine (2002–6). From 2008 to 2011 she was in JD Samson's electropop band MEN, alongside Michael O'Neill; the group also included, at times, **Johanna Fateman** and **Every Ocean Hughes**. → **330–35**

BUCHANAN, BEVERLY (b. 1940, Fuquay-Varina, North Carolina, d. 2015, Ann Arbor, Michigan)

Buchanan had an extensive career as a sculptor, photographer, Conceptual artist, and documentarian of the vernacular architecture of Black communities in the US South, and also produced a number of photocopied zines. One of the earliest, *Marsh Ruins*, was created in 1981 (and served as a report to the Guggenheim Foundation, which had awarded her a fellowship the previous year); the zine documented her site-specific work of the same title, installed in the marshes of coastal Georgia. Among Buchanan's other photocopied publications are *The Artist: A Visual Journey* (1997) and *Hope This Helps You Survive Your Gallery Visit* (n.d.), both wittily satirizing aspects of the New York art world in which she operated from the 1960s to 1977, when she moved to Macon, Georgia. Other photocopied booklets, including *The Shack Book* (2000), *Survivors* and *Survivor 2* (both ca. 2001), *Lila's Story* (2001), and *Houses* (2001), document the vernacular dwellings she observed throughout rural Georgia, relating to the celebrated series of "shack" sculptures she produced at the time. → **270–73**

BURNS, A. K. (b. 1975, Capitola, California, lives in New York, New York)

An artist working in video, installation, sculpture, and drawing, Burns closely examines societal structures and the body as a center point of social and political issues. In 2009 Burns launched the queer-feminist publication *Randy* (four issues, 2010–13) with Sophie Mörner, and later Clark Solack, who served as a co-editor of issues 3 and 4. Produced by Capricious Publishing (founded by Mörner in 2004), *Randy* celebrated an intergenerational dialogue on queer arts and engaged intersections of sexuality, gender, and visual culture. Burns collaborated with **A. L. Steiner** on *Community Action Center* (2010) and was a contributor to **LTTR** (and designed issues 4 and 5) and to Steiner's *Ridykeulous* (2006). In 2008, with Steiner and **K8 Hardy**, Burns formed Working Artists and the Greater Economy (W.A.G.E.), an activist and advocacy group focused on the rights of artists to be fairly compensated for their labor by art institutions. → **351–53**

C

CARLAND, TAMMY RAE (b. 1965, Portland, Maine, lives in Oakland, California)

As a student at Evergreen State College in Washington State in the late 1980s, Carland was at the center of the punk and queer feminist scene that gave rise to the Riot Grrrl movement. At Evergreen, she met fellow students **Gene Barnes** and **Kathleen Hanna**, and opened the Reko Muse Gallery (with Hanna and Heidi Arbogast). Reko Muse served as a performance space for their band, Amy Carter (named after the daughter of former US President Jimmy Carter), as well as such acts as the Go Team, Babes in Toyland, and Nirvana. In 1992, after Amy Carter broke up, Carland revived / ♥ *Amy Carter*, a fanzine she had started as a teenager; five issues were produced before it came to an end in 1994. She subsequently made single-issue artist's zines, such as *Jailhouse Turnout* (1996) and *Random Letters to Ransom Girls* (1998). Carland's photography appeared on the cover of Bikini Kill's album *Pussy Whipped* (1993) and in zines such as **Kelly Marie Martin's** *Thorn* (1992–95) and **Allyson Shaw** and **Laura Splan's** *Beehive* (1993–96). Carland received her MFA in 1994 from the University of California, Irvine, where **Adriene Jenik** was teaching (among Carland's fellow students were **Félix Endara**, Martin, and Splan). Carland's videos *Becky 1977* (1994), *Dear Mom* (1995), and *Jug Town Road*

(1995) were featured in **Miranda July's** *Big Miss Moviola*/*Joanie 4 Jackie* video "chainletters" (which started in 1995). In 1996 Carland co-founded Mr. Lady Records and Videos with her partner, Kaia Wilson (a member of the band Team Dresch); they distributed music by Le Tigre and **Vaginal Davis's** band Pedro, Muriel, and Esther (PME), as well as videos by **Sadie Benning** and others. → **233–38, 266**

CASTRO, JOEL (b. 1984, San Luis Potosí, Mexico, lives in Mexico City, Mexico)

Castro is a member of the Mexico City–based artists' collective **RRD**. → **416–17**

CASTRO, RICK (a.k.a. Beulah Luv) (b. 1958, Los Angeles, California, lives in Los Angeles)

Castro's work explores the worlds of fetish, as seen in his zines *Zack* (1991) and the *Bondage Book* (four issues, 1992–96), as well as in videos such as *Automolove* (1992) and *45 Minutes of Bondage* (1993). In 1996 he co-directed the feature film *Hustler White* with **Bruce LaBruce**, starring fashion model and actor Tony Ward, with appearances by artists Ron Athey and **Vaginal Davis**. As "Beulah Luv," Castro provided photographs for Davis's *Fertile La Toyah Jackson Magazine* (1987–91). In 1993–94, he worked with Davis on two issues of the *Fertile La Toyah Jackson Video Magazine*, hourlong VHS recordings made in the style of the television news show *60 Minutes*, with segments on such topics as "Streetwalker Fashions" and the West Hollywood haunt Eat a Pita. → **178–79**

CAZAZZA, MONTE (b. Philadelphia, Pennsylvania)

Cazazza is a performance and correspondence artist, filmmaker, and musician who played a key role in both the **Bay Area Dadaist** and industrial music scenes. He contributed frequently to the *New York Correspondence School Weekly Breeder* (or *NYCS Weekly Breeder*), the *West Bay Dadaist*/*Quoz?*, *File*, and *Vile* (a photograph of Cazazza appeared on the cover of *Vile*'s first issue). He produced two issues of the zine *Nitrous Oxide* (1973 and 1977) and contributed (with Tana Emmolo-Smith) to issue 6 of **Jim Jocoy's** zine *Widows and Orphans* in 1978. In California, Cazazza met Genesis P-Orridge and Cosey Fanni Tutti of the British performance-art collective COUM Transmissions and would collaborate closely with them when they formed the band Throbbing Gristle. In 1979 he co-edited (again with Emmolo-Smith) the second issue of *Industrial News*, the zine-like platform of Throbbing Gristle's Industrial Records, with which Cazazza also recorded the singles *To Mom on Mother's Day* (1979) and *Something for Nobody* (1980). Cazazza's films include *SXXX-80* (1980, with Emmolo-Smith), *Pierce* (1985, with P-Orridge), and *Catscan* (1989, with Michelle Handelman). → **40, 44–45, 49–50, 52, 55**

CHICKADEL, CHARLES (a.k.a. Arthur Cravan, born Carlo Giovanni Cicatelli) (b. 1943, Delaware, d. 2002, San Francisco, California)

Chickadel founded the "dadazine" *West Bay Dadaist* in San Francisco in 1973, publishing five

issues before changing the zine's title to *Quoz?*, under which seven more issues were published before 1976. After purchasing a secondhand printing press, Chickadel and fellow Bay Area Dadaists **Bill Gaglione** and **Tim Mancusi** formed Trinity Press. Publishing contributions from North America, Europe, and Latin America, the five-and-a-half-inch-high *West Bay Dadaist*/*Quoz?* served as an important, if diminutive, organ of the international mail art scene. → **46–49**

CIANCIOLO, SUSAN (b. 1969, Providence, Rhode Island, lives in New York, New York)

Zines have been part of Cianciolo's creative practice since the mid-1990s. After graduating from New York's Parsons School of Design in 1992, Cianciolo started the fashion line Run while working at artist and musician Kim Gordon's streetwear design company and boutique, X-Girl. From 1995 to 2001 Run produced eleven collections that were shown in alternative spaces, including a parking garage, a makeshift restaurant, Andrea Rosen Gallery, and Alleged gallery (Alleged was run by Cianciolo's one-time partner and collaborator, Aaron Rose). For these presentations, Cianciolo created garments, DIY kits (including printed matter, found items, and other ephemera), zines, and films that she made in collaboration with family members and friends, among them artists **Mark Gonzales**, **Harmony Korine**, and **Ari Marcopoulos**. In 1998 Cianciolo worked with Alleged to produce *The Run Book 7*, a zine featuring drawings and collages by Cianciolo as well as contributions from Rita Ackermann, Gonzales, Chris Johanson, and Margaret Kilgallen. → **288–91**

CONNOR, ANNE (b. 1954, Burbank, California, lives in Santa Monica, California)

Connor was a member of the art collective **World Imitation**. → **112–13**

CRUZ, LIZANIA (b. 1983, Santo Domingo, Dominican Republic, lives in New York, New York)

Cruz is an artist and designer who focuses on issues of migration and its many repercussions. In 2016 she began her project *We the News*, a traveling newsstand that distributes zines focused on the stories of Black immigrants and first-generation Black Americans, including titles such as *Crossing Borders: Conversations on Blackness and Seeking Asylum* (2017). Cruz produced the zines in collaboration with participants in story circles, which she often held in collaboration with other organizations (among them the Brooklyn Museum in 2017). Until 2022, when the project was retired, *We the News* traveled to locations throughout New York City as well as Pittsburgh and Miami. → **418–21**

CRUZ, MARÍA JOSÉ (b. 1994, San Cristóbal de las Casas, Mexico, lives in Mexico City, Mexico)

Cruz is a member of the Mexico City–based artists' collective **RRD**. → **416–17**

D

DAVIS, VAGINAL (alternately Vaginal Creme Davis) (b. Los Angeles, California, lives in Berlin, Germany)

Artist and performer Davis launched *Fertile La Toyah Jackson Magazine* in 1987. Named for a member of Davis's band the Afro Sisters (and a play on the name of pop star La Toya Jackson), the zine was published (according to an editorial in its second issue) "whenever Fertile becomes so indignant, so frustrated with the goings on of our critical times [in] which we live that she feels it's time for her to make comment." With recurring columns such as "What Makes Fertile La Toyah Mad?," "What Fertile Sez," and "La Toyah Talk," the fanzine gathered gossip, cruising stories, and reviews of performances alongside photo editorials by artists, including **Rick Castro** (as "Beulah Luv"). Five issues of the fanzine were produced before it came to an end in 1991; in 1993 it was revived and transformed into the *Fertile La Toyah Jackson Video Magazine* (two issues, 1993–94), hourlong VHS-tape recordings of varied segments made in the style of television news programs like *60 Minutes*. The character of Fertile was a feature in Davis's work beyond the publication as well, including in the play *Fertile LaToyah Salami Jackson's Last Dance* (1986) and the video *That Fertile Feeling* (1988). During the course of *Fertile La Toyah*'s run, Davis performed and recorded in several bands, including ¡Cholita! The Female Menudo; Pedro, Muriel, and Esther (PME); and Black Fag. Davis produced other one-off zines, including *Shrimp* (1993) and *Yes, Ms. Davis* (1994). → **172–77, 192–93, 199, 366**

DESTROY ALL MONSTERS (founded 1974, Ann Arbor, Michigan)

Destroy All Monsters was founded as a Detroit area–based art collective and music group by **Mike Kelley**, **Cary Loren**, **Niagara**, and **Jim Shaw**. In 1976 Kelley and Shaw left Michigan for graduate studies at the ArtCenter in Pasadena, California, subsequently becoming prominent and influential art world figures. After their departure from Michigan, guitarist Ron Asheton (formerly with the Stooges) joined Loren and Niagara in a more rock-oriented version of the band, before Loren, too, eventually left the band. *Destroy All Monsters Magazine* (six issues, 1976–79), edited, designed, and produced primarily by Loren, assembled contributions from the group's four original members, including drawings by Kelley and Niagara, Xerox collages by Shaw, and Niagara's costumed posing for Loren's photographs. In addition to documenting and reflecting upon the collective's work and history, *Destroy All Monsters Magazine* also invoked Loren's other interests and influences, such as Antonin Artaud, Virgil Finlay, Bettie Page, Jack Smith, and Andy Warhol. → **114–18, 120–21**

DINÉYAZHI', DEMIAN (b. 1983, Gallup, New Mexico, lives in Portland, Oregon)

Artist, poet, activist, and zine-maker DinéYazhi' was born to the Naasht'ézhí Tábąąhá and Tódích'íí'nii clans of the Diné, and is an enrolled member of the Navajo Nation. DinéYazhi' works across mediums and forms, often combining images and text, to address relationships between the land, Native cultures, and colonial, capitalist systems. In 2010 DinéYazhi' founded the organization R.I.S.E. (Radical Indigenous Survivance and Empowerment), which provides tools for Indigenous peoples to engage in resistance against colonialism and capitalism, and a voice for land and identity. R.I.S.E. published *Survivance* (four issues, 2015–19), a zine comprising Indigenous poetry and art. DinéYazhi' edited *Solastalgia: Queer Eco-Feminist Poetry Zine* (2016, co-edited with Jess X. Snow) and the Indigenous Two-spirit zine *Locusts: A Post-Queer Nation Zine* (2017, co-edited with Kevin Holden). → **410–13**

DOGMATIC, IRENE (born Nancy Maass, now Nancy Maass Mosen) (b. 1945, Sioux Falls, South Dakota, lives in Berkeley, California)

Dogmatic is a painter, performer, and correspondence artist, who was introduced to the concept of mail art in the early 1970s by artist Patricia Tavenner. A contributor to the Bay Area "dadazines" such as *New York Correspondence School Weekly Breeder* (or *NYCS Weekly Breeder*) and *West Bay Dadaist/ Quoz?* in the 1970s, Dogmatic also produced her own correspondence zines, such as *Rover's Romances* (1975), and pun-filled, canine-themed illustrational zines with titles like *Dogarithms* and *Dogmatic Attitudes* (both 1973). After forming the punk band SST with guitarist Ted Falconi (later of the band Flipper), Dogmatic produced the punk correspondence zines *Insult* and *Insults* (both 1979), with contributions by artists including **Lisa Baumgardner** and **Bill Gaglione**, and by musician Joe Potts. Dogmatic later contributed short fiction to issues 5 and 6 of **Richard Kern's** zine *Dumb Fucker*. → **86, 91**

DOWD, JOHN (b. 1940, Rensselaer, New York, d. 1988, San Francisco, California)

Dowd was a correspondence artist and painter, most active in the 1970s through his participation in the mail art networks surrounding General Idea's *File* "megazine," Michael Morris and Vincent Trasov's Image Bank group, and Ray Johnson's New York Correspondance [*sic*] School. Beginning in 1970, Dowd self-published numerous broadsheet publications, which he called "supplements," using appropriated content to produce collages loosely focused on specific topics—e.g., *Wristwatch Supplement*, *Performance Supplement*, *Sun Supplement*, and *Summertime Supplement* (all 1970). In 1972 Dowd was celebrated through the establishment of the "John Dowd Fanny Club" by artist and friend **John Jack Baylin**. That summer, a gathering of "club" members in Vancouver, Canada, spawned the *John Dowd Fanny Club Fanzine*, the first of a series of publishing collaborations between Baylin and Dowd. The issue featured a cover image by Dowd of Donald Duck and his nephews (Disney cartoons are a recurring trope in Dowd's work) and included contributions by Kate Craig (a.k.a. Lady Brute), Image Bank, and General Idea. Baylin and Dowd followed the fanzine with several issues of *Fanzini*, including *Fanzini/Fanzini* (ca. 1972), "Fanzini Three" (1973), *Fanzini Goes to the Movies* (1974), and "Fanzini '75" (1975). During its run, *Fanzini* published contributions by writer Vince Aletti, photographer Peter Hujar, and numerous mail artists. → **4, 26–35, 68**

DREVA, JERRY (b. 1945, Milwaukee, Wisconsin, d. 1997, Milwaukee)

Dreva's artistic practice spanned performance, photography, and mail art, often strategically manipulating mass media and other information networks. In 1971 he formed the radical queer collective Les Petites Bon-Bons in Milwaukee, with **Robert Lambert**, Chuck Betz, and others. Dreva and Lambert moved to Los Angeles (1973 and 1974, respectively), where the Bon-Bons were regulars at venues such as Rodney Bingenheimer's English Disco, and were featured in the pages of *Creem*, *Interview*, *Newsweek*, *People*, and *Rock Scene*—clippings they circulated as elements in ersatz press kits. In 1974 they participated in *Decca-Dance*, the gathering in Los Angeles of correspondence artists and zine makers. Dreva's 1978 zine, *Jerry Dreva and Friends at 33-⅓*, documented his interest in punk music and aesthetics. → **53, 73–75**

DRUCKER, ZACKARY (b. 1983, Syracuse, New York, lives in Los Angeles, California)

Drucker is an artist, actor, director, and producer, whose work across various mediums has often addressed gender representation, trans experiences, and body transformation. Over the years, Drucker has used her body to elicit desire, judgment, and voyeuristic shame from viewers. She has often worked collaboratively on films, performances, and photographic series—for example, contributing to issue 5 of *LTTR* (2006) and producing a booklet of photographic postcards with **A. L. Steiner** titled *Before + After* (2009). In 2011 Drucker and **Amos Mac**, photographer and publisher of the trans male zine *Original Plumbing* (2009–19), produced the large-format *Translady Fanzine*, which features photographs of Drucker performing in various states of dress in her childhood home. → **359**

E

EISENMAN, NICOLE (b. 1965, Verdun, France, lives in New York, New York)

Working across several mediums since the 1990s, Eisenman is best known for her figurative paintings and sculptures that often humorously explore queer communion and love. In 2005 she and the artist **A. L. Steiner** co-founded Ridykeulous, an artist-run collective that focuses primarily on queer and feminist art and produces exhibitions, performances, and publications, including an eponymous zine in 2006. → **350**

EL CHINO (active 2000–2001, Guadalajara, Mexico)

El Chino was a shifting collective of artists and curators based in Guadalajara in the early 2000s that produced zines via a structured procedure: they met weekly on Monday nights; each member contributed one zine page, while the week's designated editor selected the cover material and organized (by means of a vote) the sequence of spreads. Later meetings extended the collaborative practice to one-minute films and audio works. Eventually, the group collected each week's output into a musician's travel trunk, dubbed *El mueble chino* (2000–2001), which housed a CRT monitor and CD/DVD player alongside shelves holding the zines and folding chairs for easy viewing. The members of this group agreed never to name themselves in any exhibition or publication; thus any author or producer of Ediciones El Chino is known simply as "El Chino." → 298–99

ENDARA, FÉLIX (b. 1971, Guayaquil, Ecuador, lives in New York, New York)

Artist and filmmaker Endara studied art at the University of California, Irvine, alongside **Tammy Rae Carland**, **Kelly Marie Martin**, and **Laura Splan**. Endara began making zines after moving to New York in 1994: the publications *Girls on the Verge* (1994), *Chica Loca* (1994–95), *Chop Suey Spex* (1997–98), and *I Lie Like a Rug* (1997) told of personal experiences including incidents of racism, sexism, and homophobia. Endara also contributed to other artists' zines, such as Carland's / ♥ *Amy Carter* (1992–94) and Mimi Thi Nguyen's *Evolution of a Race Riot* (1997). Endara's films and videos, including *Saul Searching* (2006), *Bro Crush* (2006), *Grit & Grind* (2013), *Untitled Trans Names* (2016), and *Invert You* (2018), focus on queer histories and spaces. → 245–47

ESS, BARBARA (born Barbara E. Schwartz) (b. 1944, New York, New York, d. 2021, Elizaville, New York)

Ess was a photographer, publisher, and musician who launched the multimedia publication *Just Another Asshole* in 1978, producing seven issues before the zine came to an end in 1987. The first two issues were photocopied zines with duct-taped spines and titles scrawled in red nail polish. Issue 3 (co-edited with J. M. Sherry) took form as an offset-printed folio; issue 4, an insert in *Artforum* magazine; issue 5, a vinyl LP; issue 6, a paperback fiction anthology; and issue 7, a catalogue-like perfect-bound book titled *Thought Objects*. (Issues 5 through 7 were co-edited with composer Glenn Branca.) *Just Another Asshole* was one of the signature publications of downtown New York's No Wave music scene, to which Ess contributed as a singer and guitar and bass player in bands such as the Static (with Branca) and Y Pants. In the early 1990s, Ess produced the zine *Drum Core*, about women drummers. → **103, 108–11**

F

FATEMAN, JOHANNA (b. 1974, Berkeley, California, lives in New York, New York)

Artist, writer, and musician Fateman co-edited five issues of the graphically sophisticated zine *Snarla* with artist and filmmaker **Miranda July** in 1993–94, while attending Reed College in Portland, Oregon. Subsequently, as an MFA student at the School of Visual Arts in New York, Fateman extended her practice into zines that self-reflexively engaged with conventions of art criticism and the legacies of abstract painting and Pop, Conceptual, and performance art, including *My Need to Speak on the Subject of Jackson Pollock* (1996), *The Opposite, Part One* (1996), and *Artaud-Mania . . . the diary of a fan* (1997). In 1998 Fateman formed the band Le Tigre with

Kathleen Hanna and Sadie Benning (adding JD Samson after the departure of Benning). → 252–59

FORD, ROBERT (b. 1961, Chicago, Illinois, d. 1994, Chicago)

Ford was the publisher of *Thing* (ten issues, 1989–93), a zine he described (in a video made by Mary Patton at the 1991 SPEW conference in Chicago) as a "black gay and lesbian underground arts journal and magazine kind of thing." Initiated with Trent Adkins and Lawrence Warren as an inexpensively produced reconfiguration of their earlier publishing project *Think Ink* (1987–89), *Thing* ultimately evolved into a somewhat glossier magazine. It reported on other zines and featured interviews, writings, and photography by and about artists, musicians, writers, activists, and performers, including Joan Jett Blakk, **Vaginal Davis**, Lyle Ashton Harris, Essex Hemphill, Willi Ninja, Marlon Riggs, and RuPaul. At the height of its readership, *Thing* reached a circulation of nearly three thousand. In the summer of 1993, as his health declined, Ford stopped publishing *Thing* and turned to chronicling his struggle with HIV/AIDS in the column "Life During Wartime" in *Babble* magazine. → **186–89, 192**

FRIEDMAN, KEN (b. 1949, New London, Connecticut, lives in Kalmar, Sweden)

At the age of seventeen, in 1966, Friedman met Fluxus artist George Maciunas, and soon thereafter established himself as "Fluxus West," based in San Diego. He became involved in the newly active international mail art network, and in 1971 launched the photocopied, single-page zine/mailer the *New York Correspondence School Weekly Breeder* (or *NYCS Weekly Breeder*), which looked toward both Maciunas's *cc V TRE* newspaper and the products of Ray Johnson's New York Correspondance [*sic*] School. Friedman would produce eight issues of the *Breeder* before turning it over to Philadelphia-based correspondence artist **Stu Horn**. → 36

G

GAGLIONE, BILL (a.k.a. daddaland) (b. 1943, New York, New York, lives in Knoxville, Tennessee)

Gaglione, a central figure in the Bay Area Dadaists and international correspondence scenes, was featured frequently in such publications as *File*, the *West Bay Dadaist/Quoz?*, and the *New York Correspondence School Weekly Breeder* (or *NYCS Weekly Breeder*), as well as in international publications like Raúl Marroquin's *Fandangos* and Ulises Carrión's *Ephemera*. Gaglione edited three issues of **Anna Banana's** *Vile* zine, including issue 6, "Fe-Mail Art," and issue 7, "Stamp Art." He also produced six issues of *Dadazine* (1970–78). Gaglione was a prolific performance artist, concentrating especially on the revival of Futurist performance, collaborating often with Anna Banana. → **38–43, 48–49, 51, 54–55, 86**

GONZALES, MARK (b. 1968, South Gate, California, lives in New York, New York)

A widely influential figure in skateboarder culture, Gonzales began making zines in the early 1990s. Over the years he has made more than one hundred small publications, typically produced with a photocopier in editions of ten or fifteen copies, often under the rubric *Non Stop Poetry*, bringing his comic-like drawings and handwritten poetry together with appropriated photographs. From the start, Gonzales made use of the photocopier as a decentralized exhibition tool, producing entire shows transmitted through fax machine at New York City's Alleged gallery, which from 1992 to 2002 served as a hub for zine makers, skater and graffiti cultures, photographers and filmmakers, as well as the fashion demimonde. Gonzales has collaborated with other artists in the production of zines, including **Harmony Korine** on *Adulthood* (1995), *Adultry: Poems for Adults Only* (1995), and *Pocahontas Monthly* (1999), and with **Cameron Jamie** on *Scram* (2000–2001). → **280–84, 286–87**

GREGG, PAM (now Pamela Gregg Flax) (b. 1966, Phoenix, Arizona, lives in Santa Fe, New Mexico)

From 1990 to 1992, Gregg co-edited the zine *Screambox* with **Bryn Austin** and **Adriene Jenik**. In 1991 she collaborated with **Nayland Blake** on the exhibition *Situation* at New Langton Arts in San Francisco, a show that anticipated the subsequent exhibition *In a Different Light: Visual Culture, Sexual Identity, Queer Practice*, curated by Blake and Lawrence Rinder, exploring queer experiences, art, zines, and visual culture in America, and presented in 1995 at the University Art Museum of the University of California, Berkeley. → **232**

GUZMÁN, DANIEL (b. 1964, Mexico City, Mexico, lives in Guadalajara, Mexico)

Since the early 1990s Guzmán has worked in drawing, sculpture, video, and installation, engaging a range of references, from punk rock and pulp comics to pre-Hispanic iconography and sensational press clippings. In 1993 he co-founded the artists' group Temístocles 44 in Mexico City. Members of the group produced six issues of the photocopied zine *Alegría* (1992–93), in which Guzmán's drawings appeared alongside other Temístocles 44 artists' writings and work, as well as manifestos and essays by artists from abroad. Around 1995 Guzmán and **Luis Felipe Ortega** collaborated on a prototype (never published) for *Khurti*, a fanzine inspired by Nirvana front man Kurt Cobain after his death in 1994. In 1998–99, Guzmán was a co-editor of *Casper* with **Gabriel Kuri**, **Damián Ortega**, and Luis Felipe Ortega. Taking its title from the cartoon ghost of the same name, *Casper* ran for thirteen issues. → **276–79**

H

HANNA, KATHLEEN (b. 1968, Portland, Oregon, lives in New York, New York)

Hanna is the lead singer of the pioneering Riot Grrrl band Bikini Kill, with Billy Karren, Kathi Wilcox, and Tobi Vail (who produced the zine *Jigsaw* beginning in 1988), and of the band Le Tigre, with **Johanna Fateman** and **Sadie Benning** (who was later replaced by JD Samson). Hanna attended Evergreen State College in Washington State, where she met Heidi Arbogast and **Tammy Rae Carland**, who together founded the feminist art gallery Reko Muse and the band Amy Carter. Hanna produced zines both as part of Bikini Kill (*Bikini Kill*, no. 1, ca. 1990; and *Bikini Kill*, no. 2, 1991) and on her own (*My Life with Evan Dando, Popstar*, 1993; *April Fool's Day*, 1995; and *The Official Kathleen Hanna Newsletter*, 1996). → **248–51**

HARDY, K8 (b. 1977, Fort Worth, Texas, lives in New York, New York)

Hardy works in photography, film, painting, and performance. As part of the emerging Riot Grrrl movement in the early 1990s, she made the zines *Glitter Days* (1994) and *Move On* (1995). In 1998, while a student at Smith College in Massachusetts, she produced *A Cinezine by K8 Hardy*, a videozine comprising three of her films, *The Red Envelope*, *Believe Me*, and *A Little Off*. After graduating from college, she interned with **Miranda July** at the Northwest Film Center in Portland, Oregon, compiling *The Cherry Cherry Chainletter* (1998) videozine for July's platform *Joanie 4 Jackie* (which also featured Hardy's *The Red Envelope*). In 2001 Hardy co-founded the queer feminist collective **LTTR** with **Ginger Brooks Takahashi** and **Every Ocean Hughes** (later joined by **Ulrike Müller**); the group published five issues of the multimedia zine *LTTR* (2002–6). In the same period, Hardy created the zine *FashionFashion*, featuring photographs of herself (and occasionally family or friends) in various guises that challenge and satirize the fashion industry's presentation of women. → **330–33, 336–39**

HASSAN, YUSUF (b. 1987, New York, New York, lives in New York, New York)

Hassan, who founded BlackMass Publishing in 2018, explores the book as both form and idea. His work is primarily focused on the concept of an ongoing archive of Black cultural production, which is featured in his prolific zine-making practice via loosely associational compilations of texts (as with the 2019 zine *Black Seeds*), appropriated images (as in *Trife Life*, 2021), and compendia of poetry and music (such as *Selected Poems of Mikey Smith* and *Butch Morris Selected recordings and performances*, both 2022). → **422–25**

HORN, STU (b. 1946, d. 2008, Philadelphia, Pennsylvania)

Horn was a prolific mail artist whose early 1970s one-page mailer *Northwest Mounted Valise* (a title that also served as his correspondence moniker) consisted of gridded appropriations of words and images drawn from the popular press. In 1972 he took over from **Ken Friedman** as editor of the *New York Correspondence School Weekly Breeder* (or *NYCS Weekly Breeder*). Horn turned the single-page publication into a two-page stapled mailer, before passing the editorship over to **Tim Mancusi**. Horn's distinctive collage style appeared in various correspondence zines, including later issues of the *Breeder* and the *West Bay Dadaist/Quoz?*. → **37**

HOSIER, TOM (b. 1951, Waterbury, Connecticut, d. 2013, Farmington, Connecticut)

Hosier's *Modern Correspondence Magazine* (six issues, 1974–76) combined mail art with aspects of early proto-punk zines. With covers featuring the likes of Iggy Pop and MC5, it contained submissions by **Lisa Baumgardner**, the **Bay Area Dadaists**, **Stu Horn**, Clemente Padin, Genesis P-Orridge, Cosey Fanni Tutti, and more. Hosier was a member of the Connecticut-based punk band Disturbance, before relocating to New York. He also worked on the early mini-comic *Purple Warp* (sixteen issues, 1972–73) with Allan Greenier. → **87**

HOUSTON, MONTANNA (born Monte Hewson) (b. ca. 1952, Houston, Texas, d. 1990, Houston)

Houston was a writer, artist, and musician active in New York's East Village arts scene from 1979 to 1986. His fiction, such as the multipart "Crankcase Cronnikles," and poems composed of roughly cut out and reconstituted newspaper and magazine headlines, were featured in **Richard Kern's** *Heroin Addict, Valium Addict*, and *Dumb Fucker* zines in the late 1970s and early 1980s. In 1981 Kern and Houston collaborated on the more visually oriented zines *A Key for the Streets of Fear and Other Stories*, *You Should Taste What Happens to: You*, and *How Magic Works*. A series of wall-mounted, photocopied works combining grids of Kern's photographs and Houston's collage poetry (similar to what the pair were posting in the streets of New York) was mounted in 1981 at the Upstairs gallery in Tryon, North Carolina. Houston appeared in Kern's underground films *You Killed Me First* and *Stray Dogs* (both 1985) and contributed illustrations and news-clippings to **Tommy Turner's** zine *Redrum* (1985). → **142, 144–45**

HUDSON (b. 1950, New Haven, Connecticut, d. 2014, New York, New York)

Performance artist Hudson founded the gallery Feature in 1984 in Chicago, where he was a close friend and collaborator with **Steve Lafreniere**. After moving to New York in 1988, Hudson and Feature began publishing the zine *Farm* (seven issues, 1990–94), which complemented the gallery's program and showcased the work of numerous zine makers including **Vaginal Davis**, **Mark Gonzales**, **Richard Kern**, **Raymond Pettibon**, and **Jim Shaw**. Issue 7 of *Farm* (jointly published as issue 8 of Lafreniere's zine *Gentlewomen of California*) was dedicated to the work of **G. B. Jones**. → **191**

HUGHES, EVERY OCEAN (born Emily Roysdon) (b. 1977, Easton, Maryland, lives in Stockholm, Sweden)

Hughes is a co-founder of the queer feminist collective **LTTR**. → **330–33**

HUH, KATE (b. 1963, New York, New York, lives in New York, New York)

Huh is an artist, activist, and filmmaker who has been based in New York's Lower East Side

since the early 1980s. Working in a print-shop, she produced a number of intimate photocopied artists' books as well as larger-scale photocopied wall works (the latter were represented in the 1983 Ward Line Pier Project, organized by Mike Bidlo and **David Wojnarowicz**). Between 1996 and 2001, Huh published twenty-six issues of the small-scale zine *Rebel Fux!*; issues were characterized by meticulously crafted collages, loosely oriented around incongruous pairings of people (such as Mary Shelley and J. Robert Oppenheimer in issue 4; Maya Deren and Antonin Artaud in issue 5) or themes ("Violence and Disruption in Society," issue 25). In 2000, to accompany issue 25, Huh produced the animated film *Rebel Fux!: The Movie*. She also contributed to issue 5 of the queer feminist zine *LTTR*. In 2022 Huh launched *Fux de Rebel!* zine. → **314–17**

J

JACOB, LUIS (b. 1971, Lima, Peru, lives in Toronto, Ontario, Canada)

Jacob is an artist, writer, musician, and DJ who was associated with the Toronto queer-core movement through the zine *Salmon Hut* (four and a half issues, 1987–88). Collectively produced by a group of high school students working under the name Us Fish, *Salmon Hut* was retitled with each issue: themes ranged from gastronomy and diet-crazes ("Salmon Gut") to the celebration of same-sex desire ("Salmyn Hut"/"Salmen Hut"). In 1999 Jacob curated the exhibition *The J.D.s Years: 1980s Queer Zine Culture from Toronto* for Art Metropole in Toronto. → **169**

JAMIE, CAMERON (b. 1969, Los Angeles, California, lives in Paris, France)

Best known for a series of short films exploring modern rituals, including *BB* (1999–2000) and *Kranky Klaus* (2002–3), both set to music by the Melvins, Jamie has also created zines since the 1990s. His first artist's publication was the booklet *Retrato con Bart Simpson* (Portrait with Bart Simpson, 1994). Produced by a streetside printer in Mexico City, the publication was featured in the 1994 group exhibition *Chronologías* at Temístocles 44, a space run by a collective of Mexico City–based artists including **Damián Ortega** and **Luis Felipe Ortega** (who published the zine *Alegría* in 1992–93). Jamie's later publishing works bridge the gap between zines and artists' books, utilizing materials such as translucent paper or adjusting the photocopier's toner and exposure levels to create complex, multilayered effects. Jamie has also collaborated on other zines, such as *Scram*, made with artist and skateboarder **Mark Gonzales** in 2000–2001. → **287, 370–73**

JENIK, ADRIENE (b. 1964, East Orange, New Jersey, lives in Twentynine Palms, California)

Educator and artist Jenik has worked in a variety of mediums, including zine making, computer art, interactive cinema, and televised performance (she was an early member of the Paper Tiger Television collective in New

York, 1985–91). With **Bryn Austin** and **Pam Gregg**, Jenik edited the feminist lesbian zine *Screambox* (three issues, 1990–92), which published contributions by **Laurel Beckman**, Pat Califia, Catherine Opie, Kate Sorensen, Millie Wilson, and others. In this period, Jenik taught in the art department of the University of California, Irvine, which fostered several artist–zine makers, including **Tammy Rae Carland**, **Félix Endara**, **Kelly Marie Martin**, and **Laura Splan**. → 232

JENNINGS, TOM (b. 1955, Boston, Massachusetts, lives in Los Angeles, California)

Jennings was the co-editor, with **Deke Nihilson**, of the queer zine *Homocore* (eight issues, 1988–91). With its title borrowed from the pages of **G. B. Jones** and **Bruce LaBruce's** zine *J.D.s*, *Homocore* became an essential promoter of US queercore. Produced out of a San Francisco warehouse squat known as "Shred of Dignity"—a space Jennings established in 1986 with Nihilson, **Greta Snider**, and others—*Homocore* encapsulated an editorial style based on punk anarchism, Discordianism (a philosophy concerned with order and disorder), and gay separatism. Under the publication's banner, Jennings and Nihilson organized Bay Area performances for such bands as Fugazi and MDC. In 1984 Jennings launched the BBS network FidoNet, a progenitor of the internet that had more than forty thousand international users by the early 1990s; the platform's HIV/AIDS forum was a key resource for people living with AIDS in regions with little access to information about the condition. → 180–81

JOCOY, JIM (born Hyoung Su Lee) (b. 1952, Chuncheon, South Korea, lives in San Francisco, California)

While an undergraduate student at the University of California, Santa Cruz, in the late 1970s, Jocoy became immersed in the Bay Area punk scene. He began documenting his friends and bands with color slide film, which he was able to print at the copy shop where he worked in Palo Alto. He also began producing the xeroxed zine *Widows and Orphans* (six issues, 1977–78), which featured his photographs alongside contributions by artists and musicians such as **Monte Cazazza** and Genesis P-Orridge. → 88–89

JONES, G. B. (b. 1965, Bowmanville, Ontario, Canada, lives in Toronto, Ontario, Canada)

Jones is an artist, photographer, filmmaker, and musician whose work has been central to both the queercore and Riot Grrrl movements. She worked on the music and cinema zine *Hide* (five issues, 1981–85) beginning with issue 2, as well as on the accompanying cassettes, with co-editors **Caroline Azar** and **Candy Parker** (Parker left after issue 3 to create the zine *Dr. Smith*). With **Bruce LaBruce**, Jones produced the queercore zine *J.D.s* (eight issues, 1985–91), which featured her photography and signature "Tom Girl" drawings, depicting lesbian women in the style of Tom of Finland's iconic renditions of gay men. In 1981 Jones founded the band Fifth Column with Azar, Beverly Breckenridge, and Anita Smith. Their first two LPs, *To Sir with*

Hate (1986) and *All-Time Queen of the World* (1990), were issued on their own Hide record label. Jones's films, including *The Troublemakers* (1990), *The YoYo Gang* (1992), and *The Lollipop Generation* (2008), starred other zine makers and collaborators, including Anonymous Boy, **Vaginal Davis**, LaBruce, **Johnny Noxzema**, **Paul P.**, **Scott Treleaven**, and **Jena von Brücker**. The zine *Double Bill* (1991–2001), co-edited by Jones with Azar, Noxzema, Rex Boy, and von Brücker, poked fun at the cultish interest in the writer William S. Burroughs by zines like *Homocore* by unflatteringly comparing him to actor William Conrad. Jones continues to produce zines in collaboration with Paul P.
→ 156–57, 160–68, 175

JULY, MIRANDA (b. 1974, Barre, Vermont, lives in Los Angeles, California)

In 1995, after dropping out of the film school at the University of California, Santa Cruz, July moved to Portland, Oregon, where her friend **Johanna Fateman** was attending Reed College; the two of them had already launched the zine *Snarla* (1993–94). In Portland, July began the influential videozine *Big Miss Moviola* (later renamed *Joanie 4 Jackie*); from 1995 to 2000 she compiled seven issues, or "chainletters." The zine anthologized film and video works by a coterie of women artists (some of them zine makers in their own right, such as **Tammy Rae Carland**, **K8 Hardy**, and **G. B. Jones**), along with an accompanying zine-like program providing participants' bios and synopses of the films. Beginning in 2000, the chainletters were compiled by interns; in 2007 the work of making the videozine was turned over to film students at Bard College in New York State. The project was the first outlet for July's own videos before she turned to feature-length films in 2005 with *Me and You and Everyone We Know*. → 252–55, 264–67

K

KELLEY, MIKE (b. 1954, Wayne, Michigan, d. 2012, Los Angeles, California)

Kelley was a member of the Detroit-based artists' collective and music group **Destroy All Monsters**. → 114–18, 121

KERN, RICHARD (b. 1954, Roanoke Rapids, North Carolina, lives in New York, New York)

Kern published the first issue of his punk zine the *Heroin Addict* (seven issues, 1978–81) as a student at the University of North Carolina, Chapel Hill. After he moved to Philadelphia and then New York, he started the *Valium Addict* (three issues, 1981–82), changing the title to *Dumb Fucker* for an additional three issues (1982–83). All the zines featured fiction by Kern and by New York–based artists and writers **Montanna Houston**, **Tommy Turner**, **David Wojnarowicz**, and others, including Bay Area Dadaist-turned-punk **Irene Dogmatic** and Chicano poet and activist Ronnie Burk. Interspersed among the texts were Houston's magazine- and newspaper-headline poetry collages, and photographs by Kern, Turner, and punk photographer Ruby Ray. Kern also produced artists' zines, including *Car and Truck: The Pinup and/or Coloring Poster Book for the*

Motor Vehicle Fan (1980) and collaborations that paired Houston's collages with Kern's photographs: *You Should Taste What Happens to: You*, *A Key for the Streets of Fear and Other Stories*, and *How Magic Works* (all 1981). In the same period, Kern produced photocopied wall works using imagery that appeared in the zines, which he exhibited (with Houston) at the Upstairs gallery in Tryon, North Carolina, in 1981, and in the Ward Line Pier Project in New York, an exhibition organized by Mike Bidlo and Wojnarowicz in 1983. Kern would subsequently become a central figure in the downtown film movement known as the Cinema of Transgression, alongside filmmakers **Casandra Stark**, Turner, and **Nick Zedd**, among others. → 142–45

KOH, TERENCE (a.k.a. asianpunkboy) (b. 1977, Beijing, China, lives in Los Angeles, California)

Utilizing a range of mediums, Koh's practice often centers on self-portraiture and mythmaking. Starting around 2002, under the pseudonym "asianpunkboy," Koh produced dozens of zines, including *A Is for Art by asianpunkboy* (2003) and *Satan's Boy* (2004), which continued Koh's themes of self-mythologizing. Living in New York during these years, he became associated with a circle of downtown artists that included **Ryan McGinley** and **Dash Snow**. → 324–25

KORINE, HARMONY (b. 1973, Bolinas, California, lives in Miami, Florida)

Filmmaker, artist, and author Korine came to prominence with his script for Larry Clark's film *Kids* (1995) and for writing and directing his own early features *Gummo* (1997) and *Julien Donkey-Boy* (1999). Throughout the 1990s Korine produced a number of zines, including *My Friend or Sheep Boy* (1992), *Oh Death Where Is Thy Sting* (1996), and *Humor* (1997), combining irreverent texts with appropriated imagery. Collaborations with **Mark Gonzales**, including *Adulthood* (two issues, 1995), *Adultry: Poems for Adults Only* (1995), *Foster Homes and Gardens* (1996), and *Pocahontas Monthly* (1999), are filled with punning in-jokes and celebrity putdowns—a written dialogue conducted in the two artists' distinct handwriting styles. → 286

KURI, GABRIEL (b. 1970, Mexico City, Mexico, lives in Brussels, Belgium)

Since the 1990s Kuri's practice has centered on sculptures and collage that employ elements from everyday life, such as lottery tickets, receipts, cigarette butts, and other found objects. From 1998 to 1999 Kuri co-edited the zine *Casper* with **Daniel Guzmán**, **Damián Ortega**, and **Luis Felipe Ortega**. As a group, they published thirteen issues, made with serigraph and photocopies, featuring (and sometimes producing unauthorized translations of) texts and artworks by artists both local and from the international ambit. → 276–79

L

LABRUCE, BRUCE (b. 1964, Southampton, Ontario, Canada, lives in Toronto, Ontario, Canada)

Filmmaker and artist LaBruce was, with **G. B. Jones**, one of the founders of the queercore movement in music and film. After working as a go-go dancer for Jones's band Fifth Column, he and Jones launched *J.D.s* (eight issues, 1985–91), a Toronto-based zine that mythologized a semi-fictional community of queer punks, skinheads, musicians, and filmmakers, igniting what zine-maker Larry-Bob Roberts termed the "queer zine explosion" of the late 1980s and 1990s. LaBruce also produced the zine *Dumb Bitch Deserves to Die* (with **Candy Parker**, 1989), a parody of sexist tropes in horror movies, and *Monstar* (1992), which turned the satire on himself. LaBruce's early short films, shot during the period of editing *J.D.s*, include *Boy, Girl* (1987), *I Know What It's Like to Be Dead* (1987), and *Bruce and Pepper Wayne Gacy's Home Movies* (with Parker, 1988). LaBruce went on to direct numerous feature films, including *No Skin Off My Ass* (1991), *Hustler White* (co-directed with **Rick Castro**, 1996), and *Saint-Narcisse* (2020). → **160–64, 166, 169**

LAFRENIERE, STEVE (b. 1953, New Iberia, Louisiana, lives in Eugene, Oregon)

From 1989 to 1994, Lafreniere published eight issues of the *Gentlewomen of California*, featuring essays, illustrations, and photographs both appropriated and original, and often homoerotic. In 1991 he was one of the main organizers of SPEW, the first queer zine convention in North America. Held at the Randolph Street Gallery in Chicago on May 25, 1991, the gathering featured more than twenty publishers and zine makers from across the United States and Canada, and included performances by Dennis Cooper, **Vaginal Davis**, and the band Fifth Column. Subsequent SPEW festivals were organized in Los Angeles, New York, and Toronto. → **190, 192–93**

LAMBERT, ROBERT (a.k.a. Bobbi Bon-Bon) (b. 1948, Milwaukee, Wisconsin, lives in Kewaunee, Wisconsin)

Throughout his career, Lambert has continuously reinvented his public image through a performative practice that spans diverse mediums: publishing, performance, mail art, and media interventions. As "Bobbi Bon-Bon," he and fellow artist **Jerry Dreva** formed part of the conceptual queer collective of glam-rock groupies/correspondence artists known as Les Petites Bon-Bons, which they founded in Milwaukee in 1971. After relocating to Los Angeles in 1974, Lambert launched *Egozine* (three issues, 1975–79), a glossy fanzine that initially presented and self-reflexively theorized his own practice as a "life artist." Later issues of *Egozine* expanded to incorporate the work of **Skot Armstrong**, the art group Asco, **Anna Banana**, **John Jack Baylin**, Gronk, Genesis P-Orridge and Cosey Fanni Tutti (of COUM Transmissions), Teddy Sandoval, and others. → **70–73**

LEE, MAGGIE (b. 1987, Westfield, New Jersey, lives in New York, New York)

Multidisciplinary artist Lee has been producing zines since she was in middle school in the late 1990s. Much of her copious zine production explores personal memory, the aesthetics of youth subcultures, popular music, and contemporary fashion. Lee's publications range from small handmade staple-bound titles such as *Frenching #3* (2009) to more standard-format publications such as *MDMA* (2012, produced with Weirdo Dave, a.k.a. FTL) and *Star Zine* (2017), substantial readers like *Mood Book* (2013), and cast-off packets of silica gel (*Silica Zine*, 2021). Throughout, Lee has drawn material from her personal life and childhood, as in the two versions of *Punk Party '93* (both 2020), which document a punk-themed costume party held for her sixth birthday. Lee's film *Mommy* (2015) closely relates to her zine practice, exploring her coming of age and relationship with her deceased mother through a collection of home videos, cell-phone recordings, photographs, and Web 1.0 aesthetics. → **374–77**

LOREN, CARY (b. 1955, Detroit, Michigan, lives in Detroit)

Loren is a visual artist, photographer, musician, and writer, and was a member of the Detroit artists' collective and music group **Destroy All Monsters**, founded in 1974 with **Mike Kelley**, **Niagara**, and **Jim Shaw**. In addition to being the primary editor, designer, and publisher of *Destroy All Monsters Magazine* (six issues, 1976–79), Loren produced zines including *Lobster World* (1978), *Lust for Blood* (two issues, 1978–79), and *The Secrets of Photography* (1980). → **114–21**

LTTR (founded 2001, New York, New York)

With an acronym of mutable meaning—e.g., "Lesbians to the Rescue," "Listen Translate Translate Record," "Lacan Teaches To Repeat"—LTTR is a feminist genderqueer collective co-founded in 2001 by **Ginger Brooks Takahashi**, **K8 Hardy**, and **Every Ocean Hughes**. In addition to organizing events, screenings, and exhibitions, the collective's chief production was the zine *LTTR* (five issues, 2002–6; **Ulrike Müller** became co-editor in 2005 and Lanka Tattersall was an editor and collaborator for issue 4). While the publication varied in size and format—incorporating inserts and artists' multiples—its editorial rules remained consistent: each issue resulted from an open call to an international queer feminist community, with contributions edited by consensus. Contributors to *LTTR* included zine-makers **A. K. Burns**, **Tammy Rae Carland**, **Zackary Drucker**, **Johanna Fateman**, **Kate Huh**, **G. B. Jones**, and **A. L. Steiner**. → **330–33**

M

MAC, AMOS (b. 1981, Augusta, Georgia, lives in Los Angeles, California)

Mac is a photographer, writer, producer, and publisher who, with Rocco Kayiatos, co-founded *Original Plumbing* (2009–19), a fanzine devoted to trans men; the zine's look was inspired by teen magazine aesthetics and vintage physique pictorials. Mac and **Zackary Drucker** collaborated on a series of photographs of Drucker that became the basis for the 2011 publication *Translady Fanzine*. → **359**

MACKAY, XANTHRA PHILLIPPA (d. 2014, Toronto, Ontario, Canada)

MacKay was a video artist, activist, organizer, and radio host who collaborated with her partner, **Mirha-Soleil Ross** (a.k.a. Jeanne B), to produce the zine *Gendertrash* (four issues, 1993–95). As noted in issue 1, the zine was "devoted to the issues and concerns of transsexuals" and "any . . . systematic oppression by those who are in positions of power." As an activist in the Toronto area, MacKay organized mutual aid groups that assisted low-income and unhoused trans populations in the city, while also hosting the weekly radio show *Psychopathia Transsexualis*. Her films and video works include *Gender Troublemakers* (1993, with Ross) and *Rupert Remembers* (2000). → **208–11**

MANCUSI, TIM (a.k.a. dada processing) (b. 1950, Levittown, New York, lives in Santa Rosa, California)

Correspondence artist Mancusi played a key role in the Bay Area Dadaist network. In 1972 he became the editor of the *New York Correspondence School Weekly Breeder* (or *NYCS Weekly Breeder*)—a position that had first been held by the zine's founder, **Ken Friedman**, and then by artist **Stu Horn**. Mancusi expanded the publication from a two-page mailer into a full-fledged zine (six issues, 1972–73). Often working in collaboration with his cousin **Bill Gaglione**, Mancusi filled the *Breeder* with submissions from the international mail art scene and neo-Dadaist collages that prefigured Bay Area punk graphics. In 1975 Mancusi produced the diminutive zine *Punks*, which commemorated Canadian artist Jorge Zontal's visit to San Francisco through a series of photobooth portraits (the title preceded the widespread adoption of the term "punk" in the music community). Mancusi, an underground cartoonist, contributed the striking scatological cover image for the third issue of **Charles Chickadel**'s zine *West Bay Dadaist* and produced the minicomic *Sin City* (two issues, 1972–73). → **38–41, 43, 55**

MARCOPOULOS, ARI (born Aristos) (b. 1957, Amsterdam, Netherlands, lives in New York, New York)

Marcopoulos is a photographer, filmmaker, and videographer. A prolific zine maker, he has produced work on his own and with publishers including Alleged Press (which also published zines by **Susan Cianciolo**, **Mark Gonzales**, **Harmony Korine**, and **Ed Templeton** in the 1990s). Along with his volumes on such subcultures as skateboarding, snowboarding, urban graffiti, street basketball, and hip-hop, Marcopoulos has produced intimate, semi-diaristic depictions of his life and friends. While he has published several conventional photobooks, he also exhibits his photographic work as relatively low-grade printouts in keeping with the aesthetic of his zines. → **302–5**

MARTIN, KELLY MARIE (a.k.a. Keroscene) (b. 1969, Fort Wainwright, Arkansas, lives in Los Angeles, California)

Martin, an artist, writer, and musician, became involved with the queercore and Riot Grrrl movements while attending Evergreen State College in Washington State from 1987 to 1991 with fellow zine-makers **Gene Barnes**, **Tammy Rae Carland**, and **Kathleen Hanna**. Under the moniker "Keroscene," Martin published and edited the zine *Thorn* (six issues, 1992–95), featuring her own writing and work by artists including Carland, Trina Robbins, and Cauleen Smith, along with photographs, letters, comics, interviews, and other submitted content. Martin's work also appeared in the pages of Barnes's zine *Hippie Dick* and Carland's *I ♥ Amy Carter*. During her zine practice in the 1990s, Martin made several video works, including 1995's *Motor Baby, Roar Roar*, a tribute to Barnes after his death from AIDS-related illness. → **240–41, 244**

McCARTHY, PAT (b. 1987, Danbury, Connecticut, lives in New York, New York)

McCarthy's art often involves seemingly makeshift and mobile sculptures that provoke public interaction—such as his 2010 project *CheeseBike*, a moped rigged with a Coleman stove from which he served one-dollar grilled-cheese sandwiches, or *Chariot de papier* (2016), a shopping cart outfitted with a boombox and a gasoline-powered photocopier on which passersby could produce their own zines. Such works are documented throughout McCarthy's copious zine production, most notably *Born to Kill* (2009–ongoing; more than a hundred issues have been produced). Other zine titles include the softcore *Skirts* (six issues, 2012–14) and *American Cream* (four issues, 2012–15), the latter composed of erotic writing and the artist's nude self-portraits. McCarthy's recent art and zine practice has revolved around pigeon-keeping, with *Born to Kill* issues such as "Pat's Pigeon Club" (issue 60, 2014) and "Pigeon Bus" (issue 84, 2017), and the videozine *Babylon Pigeons* (2018–ongoing). → **386–89**

McGINLEY, RYAN (b. 1977, Ramsey, New Jersey, lives in New York, New York)

From the late 1990s to the mid-2000s, photographer McGinley compiled selections of his work, principally intimate and irreverent images of his downtown New York circle of friends and lovers—including **Dash Snow** and Kunle Martins (a.k.a. Earsnot), who were both members of the IRAK crew of graffiti artists—into zines such as *The Kids Are Alright* (1999). McGinley was frequently the subject of his own photographs during these years, as evident in zines such as *Puke* (2001), in which he documented himself vomiting. Snow and McGinley collaborated on the zine *Suck a Dick Up till You Hik-Up* (2002). These early endeavors were factors leading to McGinley's solo show *The Kids Are Alright* at the Whitney Museum of American Art in New York in 2003. → **308–9**

MIYAGI, FUTOSHI (b. 1981, Kumejima, Okinawa, Japan, lives in Tokyo, Japan)

Artist and writer Miyagi works in photography, film, printed matter, and installation. After graduating from City University of New York in 2005, he initiated a project photographing himself alongside other young queer men whom he met through friends, at bars, or on the internet. The scenes of intimacy, staged and yet triggering a sense of affection, were published in the zine *Strangers* (two issues, 2006). Photographer **Paul Mpagi Sepuya**, who began making his own zine *Shoot* in 2005, appears as one of the subjects in issue 1 of *Strangers*. → **358**

MORRIS, DEVIN N. (b. 1986, Baltimore, Maryland, lives in New York, New York)

Morris, who works in painting, sculpture, and photography, initiated *3 Dot Zine* (three issues, 2014–16) as a means (as he described it in his 2016 zine *Baltimore Boy*) to "center and elaborate on marginalized concerns and celebrat[e] the futurity of minorities." The zine featured contributions by visual artist Theresa Chromati (who designed the first issue), musician Abdu Ali, photographer Ian Lewandowski, and others; the collaborators were often profiled in the pages of *3 Dot Zine* with Morris's photographs and photocollages. Although dedicated to imaginative invention, the contents of *3 Dot Zine* also reflected on more somber issues, such as the death of poet Maya Angelou, the uprisings in Ferguson, Missouri, and the difficulties of "Waking Up Black" (a special insert to issue 2). *3 Dot Zine* eventually evolved into two other zines, *Baltimore Boy* (2016) and *.r zine* (2017), and the films *3 Dot Mix*, which animated the zine's photographic collages to a soundtrack of Baltimore house, and *3 Dot Zine Issue 3 Trailer* (both 2016). Morris also organized two iterations of the Brown Paper Zine & Small Press Fair (2017 and 2018) and the Zine and Self-Published Photo Book Fair (2017, a collaboration with photographer Elliott Jerome Brown Jr.). → **390–93**

MORRISROE, MARK (b. 1959, Malden, Massachusetts, d. 1989, Jersey City, New Jersey)

Photographer Morrisroe is known for his distinctive atmospheric gum prints, cyanotypes, and multiple negative C-prints that he termed "sandwich prints." While still in high school, Morrisroe and **Lynelle White** put out the scandal rag/punk fanzine *Dirt* (five issues, ca. 1975–77), which, despite its self-identification as "the magazine that *DARES* to print the truth," was generally filled with campy faux-gossip about musical acts and television and movie stars (such as Farrah Fawcett's alleged sex change, issue 4). *Dirt* was the earliest outlet for Morrisroe's exploration of photography and text and fostered a practice of self-mythologizing that would continue until the end of his life. → **94–99, 102**

MÜLLER, ULRIKE (b. 1971, Brixlegg, Austria, lives in New York, New York)

Müller is a member of the queer feminist collective **LTTR**. → **330–33**

NAHMANSON, EMILY (a.k.a. Annie Thing) (b. 1971, New Haven, Connecticut, lives in Northern California)

With **Glenn Belverio** (a.k.a. Glenda Orgasm), Nahmanson co-edited three issues of the queer zine *Pussy Grazer* (1991–92) and co-curated a screening of videos and films for the 1992 MIX festival in New York; the show was titled "Our Fanzine Friends" (the title borrowed from their column in *Pussy Grazer* "My Fanzine Friends"). Nahmanson directed one episode of Belverio's *Brenda and Glennda Show: The Drag Queen Starter Kit Infomercial* (1991), featuring **Vaginal Davis**, **Bruce LaBruce**, and Chris Teen. → **198–201**

NASSAR, JORDAN (b. 1985, New York, New York, lives in New York, New York)

Nassar is a Palestinian-American artist whose zines and related artworks draw on Palestinian traditions, histories, and popular culture, employing a variety of mediums—textiles, ceramic, wood, and other elements. Selected titles include *Ma Rose Apocalypse* (2015), *A Whole New World* (2016), *Nudity* (2017), *Dunya* (2017), *To Carry the Moon* (2020), *To Climb, To Walk, To Breathe* (2020), and *We Are the Ones to Go to the Mountain* (2020). From 2013 to 2017 Nassar worked with Shannon Michael Cane, overseeing the Printed Matter Art Book Fair in New York and Los Angeles. In 2016 Nassar co-founded and briefly worked on Cassandra Press with Kandis Williams and Taylor Doran. → **394–97**

NIAGARA (born Lynn Rovner) (b. 1956, Detroit, Michigan, lives in Detroit)

Niagara was a member of the Detroit artists' collective and music group **Destroy All Monsters**. → **114–21**

NIHILSON, DEKE (born Daniel Frontino Elash) (b. 1968, lives in Portland, Oregon)

Nihilson is an activist, zine maker, musician, filmmaker, and historian who participated in the San Francisco anarchist squat known as "Shred of Dignity" beginning in 1986. He was the editor of *Homocore* (eight issues, 1988–91, produced with Tom Jennings) and *Three Dollar Bill* (two issues, 1991–92). Nihilson also appeared in the queercore films *Shred of Sex* (1991) by **Greta Snider**, and *The YoYo Gang* by **G. B. Jones** (1992). → **180–81, 192**

NOXZEMA, JOHNNY (born John Richard Allan) (b. 1966, Toronto, Ontario, Canada, lives in Toronto)

Noxzema, a prominent member of the Toronto queercore scene, edited the gay-separatist zines *Bimbox* (seven issues, 1989–94, produced with Rex Boy) and *SCAB* (two issues, 1990s); the latter was styled after Valerie Solanas's infamous 1967 *SCUM Manifesto* ("SCAB" is an acronym for Society for the Complete Annihilation of Breeding). Noxzema co-edited *Double Bill* (five issues, 1991–2001) with **Caroline Azar**,

G. B. Jones, Rex Boy, and **Jena von Brücker**. Noxzema appeared in Jones's film *The Lollipop Generation* (2008) and shot a Doris Wishman-esque science fiction film titled *Project 36-C*, featuring Azar, Jones, and von Brücker. → **168**

O

O'CONNELL, LAURIE (b. 1955, Hawthorne, California, lives in Redding, California)

O'Connell was part of the zine-making art collective **World Imitation**. → **112–13**

ORTEGA, DAMIÁN (b. 1967, Mexico City, Mexico, lives in Mexico City)

Damián Ortega is a multimedia artist known for his sculptures of exploded everyday objects suspended in space. He and some of his collaborators from the artists' group Temístocles 44, Eduardo Abaroa, Fernando Garcia Correa, Pablo Vargas Lugo, and **Luis Felipe Ortega**, founded the zine *Alegría* (six issues, 1992–93). The zine featured writings about their own work and appropriated texts and unauthorized translations of writings by non-Mexican artists (among them Bruce Nauman and Robert Smithson) that had yet to be published in Spanish or widely taught in Mexico. (Ortega continues this mission via his publishing house, Alias, founded in 2006.) Ortega co-edited the zine *Casper* (thirteen issues, 1998–99) with **Daniel Guzmán**, **Gabriel Kuri**, and **Luis Felipe Ortega**. In 1999 Art & Idea, an independent art space in Mexico City, invited Ortega and his *Casper* collaborators to make a project room at the ARCO Madrid art fair. They created a project incorporating *Casper*: a display of the zines and "¡¡Caspermanía!!" objects, including pens, ashtrays, glasses, T-shirts, and posters. → **274–79**

ORTEGA, LUIS FELIPE (b. 1966, Mexico City, Mexico, lives in Mexico City)

Luis Felipe Ortega's work, across video, photography, drawing, sculpture, and installation, engages art historical references and philosophical discourse. Together with other artists associated with Temístocles 44—Eduardo Abaroa, Fernando Garcia Correa, Pablo Vargas Lugo, and **Damián Ortega**—he founded the zine *Alegría* (six issues, 1992–93). The publication included reprints of manifestos and articles on avant-garde practices that were not widely known in Mexico, such as the Conceptual work of Bruce Nauman, whose iconic *Self-Portrait as a Fountain* (1966–67) was appropriated in Ortega and **Daniel Guzmán's** video *Remake* (1992–95). Ortega and Guzmán also produced a prototype for *Khurti* (ca. 1995, but never officially published), a fanzine inspired by the late Nirvana front man, Kurt Cobain. Ortega was also an editor of the zine *Casper* (thirteen issues, 1998–99), along with Guzmán, **Gabriel Kuri**, and Damian Ortega. → **274–79**

P

P., PAUL (b. 1977, Hamilton, Ontario, Canada, lives in Toronto, Ontario, Canada)

Paul P. came to prominence in the early 2000s with watercolors and pencil drawings of young men that combined elements of 1970s gay male erotica with nineteenth-century gothic aesthetics. In 2003—partly in response to **Scott Treleaven's** Toronto zine *This Is the Salivation Army*—Paul P. and musician Joel Gibb (of the group Hidden Cameras) launched the zine *Gay Goth Scene*, working under the pseudonyms "Raven" (or "Rayven") and "Bones." Using imagery appropriated from gay porn magazines, they worked with white correction fluid and black pen, adding eyeliner, fishnet stockings, lipstick, and black hair to the figures, creating a queer analogue of the contemporary goth subculture. They printed *Gay Goth Scene* late at night at the Toronto copy shop where both Gibb and Paul P. worked, and distributed it among friends. Two issues of *Gay Goth Scene* were produced in 2003; it was revived in 2016, resulting in two more. Since 2013 Paul P. has collaborated with **G. B. Jones** on collages and collage-based zines, including *Born Yesterday* (2017) and *Tough Stuff* (2020). → **326–29**

PARKER, CANDY (b. Saint Louis, Missouri, lives in Toronto, Ontario, Canada)

Parker founded the film and music zine *Hide* (five issues, 1981–85) with **Kathleen Pirrie Adams**; Adams stepped down soon after the zine was launched, and **Caroline Azar** joined Parker on the publication. After **G. B. Jones** joined *Hide*'s editorship (with issue 3), Parker left to form the pioneering queer zine *Dr. Smith* (six issues, 1984–88) with artist and filmmaker **Jean Young** (a.k.a. Jean Mean). Other zines by Parker include *Fist in Your Face* (two issues, 1988–90, produced with her brother, Dr. Joe) and *Everything You Wanted to Know about Anita but Were Afraid to Ask* (ca. 1986), dedicated to Anita Smith, bassist for Azar and Jones's band, Fifth Column. As Candyland Productions, Parker directed the films *Sexbombs* (1987–88) and *Bruce and Pepper Wayne Gacy's Home Movies* (1988, produced with **Bruce LaBruce**). → **156–59, 167–69**

PETTIBON, RAYMOND (b. 1957, Tucson, Arizona, lives in New York, New York)

Pettibon is world renowned as a creator of artist's zines. After producing the comic book *Captive Chains* (1978) and the mimeographed first issue of the serialized title *Tripping Corpse* (1981), he settled on the more familiar offset-printed or photocopied, folded-and-stapled format, making more than one hundred publications by 1992. Known for their suggestive and sometimes enigmatic text/image juxtapositions that draw on the conventions of film noir and 1960s California counterculture, Pettibon's zines also occasionally contain writings and interviews or drawings by his then young nephew Nelson Tarpenny. Associated with the Southern California hardcore scene, and particularly with his brother Greg Ginn's record label, SST (through which his zines were distributed), Pettibon lent his distinctive imagery to posters, flyers, and record covers for such bands as the Minutemen, Sonic Youth, Supersession

(Pettibon's own group), and Ginn's band, Black Flag. Since the 1990s, as Pettibon's prominence in the art world has grown, he has continued occasionally to produce zine-like publications, such as *Let Us Compare Mythologies*, with Marcel Dzama (2016). → **124–29**

PHASE 2 (born Michael Lawrence Marrow, a.k.a. Lonny Wood) (b. 1955, New York, New York, d. 2019, New York, New York)

Phase 2 was a prolific "aerosol artist" (the term he preferred to "graffiti artist") beginning in the early 1970s, and an early member of the United Graffiti Artists collective. He served as the art director of *IGTimes* (*International Graffiti Times*, founded by **David Schmidlapp** in 1983) beginning with issue 8 in 1986. Around the same time, Phase 2 and Schmidlapp began an educational slideshow performance produced by *IGTimes* called *Aerosol Art Armada*, combining visual documentation of the development of aerosol street art with live dialogue between Phase 2 and fellow graffiti artist Vulcan. → **154–55**

PIRRIE ADAMS, KATHLEEN (b. 1958, Kingston, Jamaica, lives in Toronto, Ontario, Canada)

From 1980 to 1982 Pirrie Adams was the bassist for the Toronto post-punk band Fifth Column, led by **G. B. Jones** and **Caroline Azar**. In 1981 Pirrie Adams helped found the zine *Hide* with **Candy Parker**, working briefly on the first issue before ceding her place on the editorial team to Azar. → **156–57**

PORTUGAL, ANUAR (b. 1991, Xalapa, Mexico, lives in Mexico City, Mexico)

Portugal is a member of the Mexico City–based artists' collective **RRD**. → **416–17**

PURNELL, BRONTEZ (b. 1982, Triana, Alabama, lives in Oakland, California)

Writer, musician, dancer, and visual artist Purnell published his first zine, *Spandex Press*, in 1997–99, while still in high school in his Alabama hometown. At age eighteen, he published two issues of *Schlepp Fanzine* (2000), with the second issue documenting his move to Chattanooga, Tennessee. After relocating to Oakland, California, in 2002, Purnell began work on the zine *Fag School* (five issues, 2003–ongoing), containing humorous, and sometimes explicit, features on topics such as cruising, bad jobs, and Bay Area performances. His writing is often featured in *Fag School* and, starting in 2008, he contributed a column to *Maximum Rocknroll*. Purnell's books include *Since I Laid My Burden Down* (2017) and *100 Boyfriends* (2021). In addition, he has performed in the bands Gravy Train!!!! and the Younger Lovers. He co-founded the Brontez Purnell Dance Company in 2010 with Sophia Wang. → **360–65**

R

RANKIN, JEFF (b. 1954, Culver City, California, lives in Santa Monica, California)

Rankin formed part of the art collective **World Imitation** and the band Monitor. → **112–13**

ROBERTS-AULI, CORY (b. 1963, Puerto Rico, d. 1996, Los Angeles, California)

Roberts-Auli was a painter, performance artist, activist, and writer, and a co-editor, with W. Wayne Karr, of *Infected Faggot Perspectives* (fourteen issues, 1991–93). The zine focused primarily on problems of access to health care for people with HIV/AIDS, particularly minorities who experienced the systemic injustice of the health industry acutely. Roberts-Auli's art highlighted the AIDS crisis by sometimes incorporating HIV-positive blood and other bodily fluids into paintings and performances. → **202–5**

ROSS, MIRHA-SOLEIL (a.k.a. Jeanne B) (b. 1969, Montreal, Quebec, Canada, lives in Toronto, Ontario, Canada)

Ross is a Métis trans videomaker, performance artist, sex worker, and activist. With her partner, **Xanthra Phillippa MacKay**, she co-edited the zine *Gendertrash* (four issues, 1993–95), which compiled art, fiction, poetry, practical advice (such as "Safe Electrolysis"), features, and resource lists, with the aim of giving (as stated at the top of the zine's masthead) "a voice to gender queers, who've been discouraged from speaking out and communicating with each other." In the same period, in addition to producing the zine, Ross and MacKay's Genderpress distributed literature on trans rights and health advocacy and collaborated with local organizations. Ross's early videos include *An Adventure in Tucking with Jeanne B.* (1993) and *Gender Troublemakers* (1993, produced with MacKay), both addressing their experiences as trans women. → **208–11**

RRD (Red de Reproducción y Distribución / Reproduction and Distribution Network) (founded 2016, Mexico City, Mexico)

Founded in 2016 and now run by artists **Joel Castro**, **María José Cruz**, **Anuar Portugal**, **Bruno Ruiz**, and **Sergio Torres**, the collective RRD is a platform focused on the creation and distribution of audiovisual and printed content. The group's projects, which are often accompanied by zines, have explored histories of piracy and distribution of information in Mexico and globally; among them are the mimeograph workshop Copycat (2019–22) and RedEx (2020), a mail art project initiated during the COVID-19 pandemic that entailed sending recipients a miniature RRD kiosk, expanding the boundaries of digital social media. RRD has collaborated with other collectives and artists on zine projects, such as 2017's *La calle es de quien la trabaja: Ciudad neo-liberal y trabajo informal* (The street belongs to those who work it: Neo-liberal city and informal work), created with the publishing collective Pensaré Cartoneras. → **416–17**

RUIZ, BRUNO (b. 1990, Mexico City, Mexico, lives in Mexico City)

Ruiz is a member of the Mexico City–based artists' collective **RRD**. → **416–17**

S

SACHS, TOM (b. 1966, New York, New York, lives in New York, New York)

Sachs started making zines as a teenager in the 1980s. *Haute Bricolage* accompanied his first major solo show in New York, at Mary Boone Gallery in 1999. Between 2009 and 2014 Sachs produced four issues of the photocopied zine *Bricolage*—the title refers to the sculptural mode for which Sachs is known: repurposing consumer goods or fabricating new versions of them out of other materials. He has also experimented with other publication formats: he produced a zine in the form of a Swiss passport (*Swiss Passport Office Zine*, 2018) and another featuring small prints encased in a cassette tape (*TDK Cassette Zine*, 2021). → **300–1**

SAVERI, LELE (b. 1980, Rome, Italy, lives in New York, New York)

Saveri began making zines incorporating his own photographs in the early 2000s. In 2012 he launched a zine fair at a billiards hall where he was working in Brooklyn; the event led to the formation of 8-Ball Community, named for the pool tables on which the publishers at the gathering showed their wares. 8-Ball has since developed into an artists' collective, community space, library, publishing house dedicated to zines, and platform for independent radio and television. In 2013–14 Saveri and other members of 8-Ball, in collaboration with the agency Alldayeveryday, created *The Newsstand*, a zine-centered pop-up shop located in the Metropolitan/Lorimer subway station in Brooklyn. Saveri's many zines include *Luna* (more than one hundred issues, 2013–ongoing), which is compiled on the advent of every full moon and features photographs taken since the last full moon, and a number of collaborations with photographer Ray Potes and his publication *Hamburger Eyes*. → **382–85**

SCHMIDLAPP, DAVID (b. 1949, Piqua, Ohio, lives in New York, New York)

In late 1983 Schmidlapp, a photographer active in New York's downtown scene, started *IGTimes* (*International Graffiti Times*, later *International Get-Hip Times*, and finally *InterGalactic Times*), the first publication dedicated to graffiti art and culture. It began as a xeroxed mailer and evolved into an offset-printed broadsheet that continued the photomontages Schmidlapp was contributing at the time to the *SoHo Weekly News*. Starting with issue 8, Schmidlapp brought in the artist **Phase 2** as art director of the publication; they would work together for seven more issues, until the publication's dissolution in 1994. Building on Schmidlapp's live slideshow performances at underground spaces such as Club 57, *IGTimes* produced a slideshow of graffiti art to educate audiences about street art and its culture. They called their presentation the *Aerosol Art Armada* and toured it to schools, community centers, and other cultural venues

in the 1980s and early 1990s, combining visual documentation of the development of aerosol street art with live dialogue between Phase 2 and fellow graffiti artist Vulcan. → **154–55**

SCHNEEMANN, CAROLEE (b. 1939, Fox Chase, Pennsylvania, d. 2019, New Paltz, New York)

Schneemann is well known for her experimental multimedia works, often engaged with themes of the body, sexuality, society, and gender. Recognizing the political context and impact of the punk movement, she adopted its signature print format, the zine, as a vehicle to bring attention to the First Lebanon War in 1982. Schneemann was already an accomplished producer of artists' books (including *Parts of a Body House Book*, 1972; *Cézanne, She Was a Great Painter*, 1975; and *ABC—We Print Anything—In the Cards*, 1977) when she produced the zine *The Recent History and Destruction of Lebanon: A Research Extract* in 1983. It was published and distributed on its own and as an accompaniment to Schneemann's exhibition of the video-sculpture *War Mop* (1983) and other works from her *Lebanon Series* at New York's Max Hutchinson Gallery in 1983. → **152–53**

SEPUYA, PAUL MPAGI (b. 1982, San Bernardino, California, lives in Los Angeles, California)

Sepuya's photo-based work often addresses the relationship between photographer and subject in the confines of an intimate interior space, whether a studio, a bedroom, or elsewhere. He produced his first zine *Shoot* (seven issues, 2005–7) while living in Brooklyn after graduating from New York University. Each iteration of the zine focused on one subject or a pair of subjects, usually nude or partially clothed men in a bare room. Other zines from around this same time include *Beloved Object* (2005), *Seven Portraits* (2006), and *The Difference Between Memory, a Portrait, a Resolution* (2006), all likewise composed of portraits. During this period, Sepuya also appeared in **Futoshi Miyagi's** zine *Strangers* (2006) and contributed to *BUTT* and other zines. → **354–57**

SHAW, ALLYSON (b. 1969, Illinois, lives in northeastern Scotland)

Writer Shaw collaborated on the zine *Beehive* (five issues, 1993–96) with **Laura Splan**, a classmate at the University of California, Irvine (UCI), with whom she also created experimental poetry and videos. The two of them produced issues 1 through 4 of *Beehive* on a photocopy machine in the office of a UCI parking garage where they worked; issue 5 took form as an e-zine on a website coded by Splan. The zines feature contributions by various UCI classmates, including **Tammy Rae Carland**, **Félix Endara**, **Kelly Marie Martin**, and others. → **238–39**

SHAW, JIM (b. 1952, Midland, Michigan, lives in Los Angeles, California)

Shaw is a visual artist and founding member of the artists' collective and band **Destroy All Monsters**. → **114–21**

SILLMAN, AMY (b. 1955, Detroit, Michigan, lives in New York, New York)

Sillman produced the first iteration of her zine, *The O-G* (thirteen issues, 2009–ongoing), in Berlin as a means of exploring and expanding her art practice in a foreign context. Since then, her exhibitions have often been supplemented by publications combining humorous illustrations, philosophical and aesthetic speculations, and reproductions of paintings and drawings. Around the same time that she created her first zine, Stillman also began producing short, animated videos to accompany her larger paintings and drawings. → **378–81**

SIMPSON, LINDA (a.k.a. Les Simpson) (b. Gaylord, Minnesota, lives in New York, New York)

A fixture in the downtown New York drag scene since the early 1980s, Simpson launched the publication *My Comrade* in 1987 (eleven issues, 1987–94). Mixing the sensibility of an underground queer zine with production and editorial values closer to those of a glossy magazine, *My Comrade* featured gossip and reportage alongside commissioned editorials and work by artists including David Armstrong, Jack Pierson, and Tabboo! From issue 4 (in fall 1988) through issue 9 (summer 1992), *My Comrade* added the lesbian-centric *Sister!* to its flip side. Simpson revived *My Comrade* from 2004 to 2006 and again in 2022. → **194–97**

SNIDER, GRETA (b. 1962, Youngstown, Ohio, lives in San Francisco, California)

Experimental filmmaker Snider edited *Mudflap* (six issues, 1991–94), a zine ostensibly about bicycling in San Francisco, but which also covered such topics as train hopping, cultivation of food and psychedelic and aphrodisiac botanicals, reviews of local bars, and reflections on living communally as a punk. In 1986 Snider co-founded the anarchist squat known as "Shred of Dignity," along with **Tom Jennings**, **Deke Nihilson**, and others. Snider's film work is characterized by its combination of personal and archival materials. Among her films are *Hard Core Home Movie* (1989), *Our Gay Brothers* (1993), *No-Zone* (1993), and *Portland* (1996); she screened her work at the SPEW queer zine fair in Los Angeles (1992) and New York (1993). → **182–85**

SNOW, DASH (b. 1981, New York, New York, d. 2009, New York, New York)

Snow was a self-taught artist who worked in photography, collage, assemblage, and installation. He first became known as a member of the IRAK crew, a group of graffiti artists founded by Kunle Martins (a.k.a. Earsnot) and associated with artists Dan Colen and **Ryan McGinley**. Snow's zines, such as *I Hate America and America Hates Me* (2005), *In the Event of My Disappearance* (2005), *Gang Bang at Ground Zero* (2007), and *Shoot-Out at Shit Creek* (n.d.), are characterized by their irreverent archiving of post-9/11 New York City through text collages pieced together from newspaper and magazine clippings as well as his Polaroids and photographs of friends' debaucheries. Snow's zines led him to exhibit

his collages and photographs; his first show was presented at New York's Rivington Arms in 2006. → **309–13**

SORRELL, KWAMÉ (a.k.a. Kwamé Omari) (b. 1990, New York, New York, lives in Marrakech, Morocco)

Sorrell is an artist, poet, researcher, and publisher with BlackMass Publishing. Among his many zines are *African Pottery Forming and Firing* (2019), *Je suis en face* (2020), and *A Study on Asante Traditional Buildings* (2022). His publications *Kreyòl Homes/Southern Homes* (2020) and *Quotidien Acts of Minimalism (a lecture)* (2021) draw inspiration from the publications of artist Beverly Buchanan. → **422–25** ·

SPLAN, LAURA (b. 1973, Memphis, Tennessee, lives in New York, New York)

Splan is a transdisciplinary artist working at the intersections of science, technology, and culture. Between 1993 and 1996, with **Allyson Shaw**, she published five issues of the Riot Grrrl zine *Beehive*. The zine featured Splan's photographs and stills from videos she made while a student at University of California, Irvine, alongside work by UCI classmates, including **Tammy Rae Carland**, **Félix Endara**, and **Kelly Marie Martin**. → **238–39**

STARK, CASANDRA (a.k.a. Casandra Mele, Casandra Stark Mele) (b. 1964, New Haven, Connecticut, lives in south Florida)

Painter, writer, and filmmaker Stark was part of the No Wave film movement known as the Cinema of Transgression; among her films are *Dead on My Arm* (1985), *Wrecked on Cannibal Island* (1986), and *We Are Not to Blame* (1989). She produced a number of chapbook-like zines, including *Your World, Not Mine* (1986), *A Quiet Little Singing of Terror* (1991), *Clara* (1993), and *In Case of a Storm* (1994). A portrait drawing of her was featured on the cover of issue 9 of **Nick Zedd**'s *Underground Film Bulletin* (1990). → **147**

STEINER, A. L. (b. 1967, Miami, Florida, lives in New York, New York)

Steiner works in a wide range of mediums including collage, video, installation, and printed matter. In 2005 Steiner and painter **Nicole Eisenman** co-founded the collective Ridykeulous; the following year they published a zine of the same name. Steiner contributed to the zine *LTTR*, and organized several exhibitions focused on feminist and lesbian art. With **K8 Hardy** (co-founder of **LTTR**) and **A. K. Burns** (co-founder of *Randy*), Steiner formed Working Artists and the Greater Economy (W.A.G.E.) in 2008. In 2010 she collaborated with Burns to create *Community Action Center*, an installation, lecture, and video project exploring queer sexuality through the participation of artists and performers. As part of the endeavor, they published the zine *Cliffs Notes: Community Action Center*. → **350**

SWANK, TOD (b. 1966, Detroit, Michigan, lives in San Diego, California)

Swank is a professional skateboarder, photographer, and founder of Tum Yeto skateboard company. In the 1980s, he worked as a darkroom tech and a photographer for *TransWorld Skateboarding* magazine. During this time, he also published *Swank Zine*, which featured his photographs of skaters in action, including **Mark Gonzales**. → **285**

T

TAM, HO (b. 1962, Hong Kong, lives in Toronto, Ontario, Canada)

Tam is a multidisciplinary artist who has been producing zines since the early 1990s. His first was *Yellow Pages* (1993), a publication exploring stereotypes and clichés about Asian cultures in North America. In 1994 he adapted *Yellow Pages* into an eight-minute video, and has subsequently reformulated it as a wall work, an offset-printed edition, and an issue of his zine *Ho Tam* (fifteen issues, 2013–17). Tam's multifaceted art practice includes Pop art–inflected, often homoerotic painted portraits of Asian men, playing on notions of masculinity and femininity; among these projects are *Icones* (1993–94) and *Matinee Idols* (1994). Tam's spiral-bound artist's book *Idol + Worship* (1995) relates to this period of his work. Other publications include *Poser* (seven issues, 2013–16), a series of photographic street portraits of strangers based on the format of the zine *Monks* (2012), which he produced for his own imprint, XXX Zines. → **212–15**

TEMPLETON, DEANNA (b. 1969, Huntington Beach, California, lives in Huntington Beach)

Photographer Deanna Templeton began documenting punk shows at age fifteen. She is known for her depictions of female adolescence and young women in predominantly male subcultures such as the world of skateboarding. She published three issues of the zine *Blue Kitten Photos* (2002–5). → **307**

TEMPLETON, ED (b. 1972, Garden Cove, California, lives in Huntington Beach, California)

Ed Templeton is a photographer and painter who came to prominence as a professional skateboarder in the late 1980s and early 1990s. In 1992 he and fellow skateboarder Mike Valley produced two issues of the zine *TV Guide* for their short-lived skateboard company. Templeton's own photographic zines, such as *Vikadin* (1998), *North American Youth* (1998), and two versions of *Teenage Smokers* (1998 and 1999), focus on skateboarding, youth culture, and images of his partner and collaborator, **Deanna Templeton**. → **306**

TERRILL, JOEY (b. 1955, Los Angeles, California, lives in Los Angeles)

Terrill is known for his Pop art–inflected paintings of queer Chicano friends and associates.

He began his artistic career in the 1970s, as a student at Los Angeles's Immaculate Heart College, where he met **Skot Armstrong**, who introduced him to Ray Johnson's New York Correspondance [sic] School network and to zine-making. In 1978 Terrill started his own zine, *Homeboy Beautiful* (two issues, 1978–79), a satirical take on lifestyle magazines that also critiqued the machismo and homophobia of East Los Angeles Chicano culture; it included contributions by such artists as Willie Herrón and Teddy Sandoval, along with mail art solicitations from **John Dowd** and Ray Johnson. After being diagnosed as HIV-positive in 1989, Terrill focused increasingly on themes of public health and AIDS activism, leading to his Spanish-language series of HIV/AIDS educational comic pamphlets, *Chicos modernos* (1989–92). → **80–85**

THOMSEN, STEVE (b. 1953, Glendale, California, lives in Fredonia, Arizona)

Thomsen was a member of the art collective **World Imitation** and the band Monitor. → **112–13**

TOLEDO, LAUREANA (b. 1970, Ixtepec, Oaxaca, Mexico, lives in Mexico City, Mexico)

Toledo is a photographer and Conceptual artist whose projects explore histories of Mexican rock music and subcultures in relation to colonial powers through films, publications, collages, and installations. Since 2014, Toledo and her brother, Dr. Lakra (Jerónimo López Ramírez), have been working on the film-in-progress *PUNXDEFEKTUOZOZ*, which looks at the origins of punk in Mexico City. As members of the punk scene themselves, they have interviewed friends and contacts and have amassed a substantial archive of fanzines, flyers, and records to investigate punk's effects on broader socioeconomic contexts. → **414–15**

TORRES, SERGIO (b. 1987, Mexico City, Mexico, lives in Mexico City)

Torres is a member of the Mexico City–based artists' collective **RRD**. → **416–17**

TRELEAVEN, SCOTT (b. 1972, Toronto, Ontario, Canada, lives in Toronto)

Treleaven is a visual artist whose practice encompasses painting, collage, and filmmaking. In 1996 he directed the film *Queercore: A Punk-u-mentary*, about queer dynamics in punk music and zine subcultures. In the same year he launched the zine *This Is the Salivation Army* (eight issues, 1996–99, with a ninth produced as a video-issue in 2001, and a tenth *hors série* issue commissioned by Toronto's Art Gallery of York University in 2004). Treleaven's zine presented a unique mix of punk, queer, and occult aesthetics, drawing from the industrial music movement pioneered by Cosey Fanni Tutti, **Monte Cazazza**, and Genesis P-Orridge. Treleaven collaborated with P-Orridge on the 2008 short film *Last Seven Words*. → **216–21**

TURNER, TOMMY (b. 1959, New York, New York, lives in New York, New York)

Photographer and filmmaker Turner edited the zine *Redrum* (two issues, 1985); its title evokes the backward spelling of "murder" in a scene from Stanley Kubrick's 1980 film *The Shining*. Alongside copious press clippings of sensationalized deaths, *Redrum* featured Turner's photographs, drawings by **Montanna Houston**, faux-gory photographs by **Richard Kern**, writing by Lisa Carr (a.k.a. Lung Leg), and more. Each issue came with a reconfigured *Archie* comic attributed to "Norman Rockwell Jr." (actually the artist **David Wojnarowicz**), in which the Archie gang appears as a group of heroin addicts or serial killers. In 1983 Turner and Wojnarowicz collaborated on a series of double-exposed "Ghost Photos" made in cemeteries late at night. Two years later they co-directed the film *Where Evil Dwells*, loosely based on the story of the teenage murderer Ricky Kasso of Northport, Long Island (the subject of *Redrum*'s second issue). → **148–51**

U

UHLENKOTT, MICHAEL (b. 1954, Moscow, Idaho, lives in Los Angeles, California)

Uhlenkott was a member of the art collective **World Imitation** and the band Monitor. → **112–13**

V

VALE, V. (a.k.a. Vale Hamanaka) (b. 1944, Jerome War Relocation Center, Arizona, lives in San Francisco, California)

Vale is a writer, editor, and musician who published the Bay Area punk fanzine *Search & Destroy* (eleven issues, 1977–79). In 1980 he launched the zine *RE/Search*, which helped to define the aesthetic of the underground Industrial Culture movement, and took on such topics as sadomasochism and body modification. Among the contributors to *RE/Search* were Tana Emmolo-Smith and **Jim Jocoy**, and the zine published features on **Monte Cazazza** and Throbbing Gristle. Vale and his associate Andrea Juno expanded *RE/Search* into a series of perfect-bound publications, including the *Industrial Culture Handbook* (1983). → **90–91**

VARGAS, JACK (a.k.a. Le Club for Boys) (b. 1953, Santa Paula, California, d. 1995, Los Angeles, California)

Vargas was a multifaceted artist whose work interrogated connections between his identities as queer and as a Chicano man. He initiated the correspondence art network known as Le Club for Boys (and often worked under that name himself), collaborating closely with other artists in Los Angeles's queer Chicano community, such as Teddy Sandoval and **Joey Terrill**. Around 1975 Vargas produced the zine-like, color photocopy newsletter *Suburban J.* Vargas's poem *The New Bourgeois "I Want" with Gay Male Suggestiveness* (1976–79)—originally published as a twenty-seven-page photocopied document—inventories the intersections of queerness, race, and class. → **79**

VELÁZQUEZ, GERARDO (b. 1958, Mexico, d. 1992, Los Angeles, California)

Multimedia artist and musician Velázquez founded the queer synth-punk art band Nervous Gender in 1978 with Michael Ochoa, Phranc (Susan Gottlieb), and Edward Stapleton; the group was notorious for its aggressive and elaborately staged performances. In 1981 Nervous Gender released the album *Music from Hell* and produced the zine-like chapbook *Nervous Gender: never to be released lyrics*. After receiving an HIV-positive diagnosis in 1990, Velázquez began publishing a series of caustically humorous zines that tackled the AIDS crisis and critiqued the machinations of the art world; among the titles: *First the Fags*, *The Annals of Selective Annihilation*, and *The Gay Death List* (all 1990). → **122–23**

VON BRÜCKER, JENA (b. 1969, Prince Edward County, Ontario, Canada, lives in Toronto, Ontario, Canada)

Von Brücker appeared frequently in the pages of **G. B. Jones** and **Bruce LaBruce**'s zine *J.D.s* (notably on the cover of issue 7), as well as in Jones's films *The YoYo Gang* (1992) and *The Lollipop Generation* (2008), and LaBruce's *No Skin Off My Ass* (1991). She was co-editor of the zine *Double Bill* (five issues, 1991–2001), along with **Caroline Azar**, Jones, **Johnny Noxzema**, and Rex Boy. Von Brücker also produced the zines *Don't Tell Jane and Frankie* (1989), *Jane and Frankie's Joy o' Sex* (1990), and *Jane Gets a Divorce* (1993). → **168**

W

WESTON, FREDERICK (b. 1946, Memphis, Tennessee, d. 2020, New York, New York)

Weston arrived in New York City in 1973 with aspirations of working in the fashion world—hopes that were stifled by the industry's racism. Over the following decades he worked at expansive, often multi-panel collages relating to fashion, sexuality, and the male body, drawn from a vast archive of clippings he had collected that were housed in his apartment. His zines critically interrogated racial stereotypes (*The Story of Little Black Sambo*, 2000), featured his poetry (*E-Z on the Eye*, 2004), and served as invitations to performances and social events (*Formerly Off, Proposal for a Happening*, 2001, and *Whatever Happened to Freddy Darling?*, 2003). → **318–21**

WHITE, LYNELLE (b. Boston, Massachusetts, lives in Joshua Tree, California)

Starting as a high school student in Boston, White co-edited the punk fanzine *Dirt* (five issues, ca. 1975–77) with her friend and schoolmate **Mark Morrisroe**. According to White, after the two came up with ideas, she contributed most of the writing, while Morrisroe did the collaged layouts. She later attended the School of the Museum of Fine Arts in Boston with Morrisroe and assisted on a number of his films. → **94–99, 102**

WILLIAMS, KANDIS (b. 1985, Baltimore, Maryland, lives in New York, New York)

Williams works in a range of fields, from collage and assemblage to choreography, publishing, and curating. In 2016 Williams co-founded Cassandra Press with Taylor Doran and **Jordan Nassar**; the imprint produced a series of zines including Doran's *Who Is Cassandra* and Williams's *The Wailing Rose: Visions of Migrating Trauma* (both 2016). Now under Williams's direction, Cassandra Press has become an educational platform that produces artists' books, courses, exhibitions, and a variety of printed matter and other materials. Since 2016 Williams and Cassandra Press have published more than thirty photocopied readers, which are compendia of theoretical, historical, and literary texts primarily by Black thinkers, each focused on a different theme, from "misogynoir" and fetishism to cultural cannibalism and Black Twitter. The publication *Reader on Water and Power in California* (2018), for example, explores the political structure surrounding California's water system, while *Reader on Whiteness, Dissonance, and Horror* (2020) looks at the horror film genre in relation to race. → **406–9**

WOJNAROWICZ, DAVID (b. 1954, Red Bank, New Jersey, d. 1992, New York, New York)

Wojnarowicz was a writer, painter, filmmaker, photographer, and AIDS activist. He contributed stories, a drawing, and an altered comic to **Richard Kern**'s zine *Dumb Fucker* (three issues, 1982–83). Using the pseudonym "Norman Rockwell, Jr.," Wojnarowicz also contributed stand-alone reformulated *Archie* comic books to **Tommy Turner's** zine *Redrum* (two issues, 1985), in which the wholesome cartoon character and his friends are shown taking drugs and committing Manson-style murders. Wojnarowicz and Turner collaborated further on a series of "Ghost Photos" (1983; double exposures shot in cemeteries at night) and the feature-length film *Where Evil Dwells* (1985). → **149, 151, 241**

WORLD IMITATION (a.k.a. World Imitation Productions) (active 1977–82, Northridge, California)

World Imitation was an art collective whose membership consisted of **Anne Connor**, **Laurie O'Connell**, **Jeff Rankin**, **Steve Thomsen**, and **Michael Uhlenkott**. Before taking the name "World Imitation," the group operated as an offshoot of **Skot Armstrong's** publishing project Science Holiday. World Imitation produced more than two dozen zines characterized by collages of mid-century Americana, sourced from such publications as *National Geographic*, *Popular Mechanics*, *Look*, and *Life*; their publications had campy titles such as *The "Kooky" World of Magnets* (1978), *Surf Rules* (1978), *Tesla-Rama* (1978), *Really Twins* (1978), *Hula Dance* (1978), and *Computer Buddy* (1978–79). In 1978 the group (with the exception of Connor) joined Los Angeles's burgeoning punk music scene as the band Monitor, with O'Connell on bass and vocals, Rankin on percussion, Thomsen on synthesizer and keyboards, and Uhlenkott singing and playing guitar. (In 1979 Rankin left Monitor and was replaced by drummer Keith Mitchell.) As a member of Los Angeles's loose consortium of experimental punk groups known as "Associated Skull Bands," Monitor played on bills with the Bags, Bpeople, Human Hands, the Meat Puppets, and Gerardo Velázquez's band Nervous Gender, among others. Monitor released the single *Beak/Pet Wedding* (1979) and the LP *Monitor* (1981), as well as the single *Surfadelic* (1981, recorded under the band name the Tikis). → **112–13**

Y

YOUNG, JEAN (a.k.a. Jean Mean)

Young is a filmmaker and photographer who, with **Candy Parker**, co-edited the pioneering queer zine *Dr. Smith* (six issues, 1984–88), established out of frustration with the limitations of the more mainstream gay publication *Pink Ink* (of which Young was a co-publisher). As "Jean Mean," she frequently appeared and was mentioned in the pages of **G. B. Jones** and **Bruce LaBruce**'s zine *J.D.s*, as well as in films such as Jones's *The Troublemakers* (1990) and Suzy Richter's *Cross Your Heart* (1990). Young also directed her own films, *Suburban Bus Ride* (1985) and *Colonnade* (1986). → **158–59**

Z

ZEDD, NICK (born James Harding) (b. 1958, Takoma Park, Maryland, d. 2022, Mexico City, Mexico)

Artist and filmmaker Zedd was best known for his shocking and humorous ultra-low-budget films including *They Eat Scum* (1979) and *Police State* (1987). In 1985 he coined the term "Cinema of Transgression" to define his own work and that of filmmakers such as Manuel DeLanda, **Richard Kern**, **Casandra Stark**, and **Tommy Turner**. Working under various pseudonyms (such as "Orion Jeriko"), Zedd published the fanzine-like *Underground Film Bulletin* (1985–90), which featured the work of Kern, Stark, and Turner, among others. → **146**

Picture Credits

Copyright:
All rights reserved, Capricious Publishing: 351, 352–53; © Luke and Noel Dowd: 4, 26, 27, 28, 29, 30, 31 top left, 31 top right, 31 bottom left, 32, 33, 34; © Andrew Edlin Gallery, New York, and the Beverly Buchanan Estate: 270, 271, 272, 273; © Feature Hudson Foundation: 191; © IGTimes: 154, 155 top; © Mike Kelley Foundation for the Arts. All Rights Reserved / VAGA at ARS, New York: 121 top; © Harmony Korine. Courtesy the artist and Hauser & Wirth: 286; © Bud Lee Picture Maker Inc.: 68; © The Estate of Mark Morrisroe (Ringier Collection) at Fotomuseum Winterthur: 94, 95, 96, 96, 98, 99; © Raymond Pettibon, courtesy the artist and David Zwirner: 124, 125, 126–27, 128, 129; © 2023 Carolee Schneemann Foundation / Artists Rights Society (ARS), New York. Courtesy Hales Gallery and P·P·O·W, New York: 152, 153; Used by permission. © Dash Snow Archive, NYC: 310, 311, 312, 313; © Frederick Weston Estate and Gordon Robichaux, New York: 318, 319, 320, 321

Photo by:
Jean-Baptiste Beranger: 333

Marc Brems Tatti: 291 bottom

Brooklyn Museum, Sarah DeSantis: 100 top left, 266 right

Brooklyn Museum, Jonathan Dorado: 95, 114, 120 bottom, 340–41, 356, 357

Brooklyn Museum, Evan McKnight: 4, 29, 43, 44 bottom right, 45 bottom, 74, 77 top left, 78 bottom, 86 top right, 87 top left, 87 bottom, 88, 89 top, 94, 96, 97, 98 top, 99, 101, 112, 113, 147, 150, 156, 157, 158, 159, 168 top left, 168 top right, 169 top left, 169 bottom, 172 top, 173 top, 176, 178 bottom left, 178 bottom right, 179, 186, 187, 189 bottom right, 190, 193, 194, 195, 196, 197 left, 222, 223, 245, 246, 247, 259 bottom right, 308 top, 309, 314, 315, 316, 317, 366, 367, 394, 410, 411, 412, 413, 426, 427, 428

Brooklyn Museum, Danny Perez: 32, 33, 38 bottom left, 39, 86 top left, 86 bottom, 98 bottom, 99, 100 top right, 100 bottom, 232 top right, 232 bottom, 408, 409 top

Matt Grubb/Object Studies: 103 bottom

Tom Little Photography, 2013: 334–35

Rachel Topham Photography: 28 bottom right, 31 top left, 31 top right, 31 center right, 36, 44 top, 44 bottom left, 45 top, 46, 47, 48, 49, 55, 87 top right

David Vu: cover, 26, 27, 28 top left, 28 top right, 28 bottom left, 30, 34, 35, 38 top, 38 bottom right, 40–41, 50, 51, 52–53, 70, 71, 73, 82, 83, 90, 91, 104 bottom, 105, 106 top right, 106 bottom left, 109, 110 bottom, 111 top, 115, 116–17, 118, 119, 124, 125, 126–27, 128, 129, 142, 143, 144, 145, 146, 148, 149, 160, 161, 162–63, 164, 168 bottom right, 169 top right, 172 bottom, 173 bottom, 174, 175, 178 top, 180, 181, 182, 183 left, 184–85, 188, 191, 198, 199, 200, 201 left, 212 top, 216, 217, 218–19, 220, 221 left, 242, 243, 248, 249, 280, 281, 282, 283, 284 top, 285, 286, 287, 288, 289, 290, 300, 301, 302, 303, 304, 305, 306, 307, 308 bottom, 310, 311, 312, 313, 324, 325, 326, 327, 328, 330, 331, 332, 336, 337, 338, 339, 350, 351, 352–53, 354–55, 358, 359, 360, 361, 362–63, 364, 365 left, 370, 371, 372, 378, 379, 380, 382, 383, 386, 387, 388, 389 top, 390, 391, 392, 395, 396, 406, 407, 422, 423, 424, 425

Images courtesy:
The Art Institute of Chicago / Art Resource, New York: 321; Boo-Hooray: 108, 110 top, 111 bottom; Galerie Isabella Bortolozzi, Berlin: 177 bottom; Canyon Cinema Foundation: 183 right; Tammy Rae Carland and Jessica Silverman, San Francisco: 233, 234, 236, 237, 266 left; Centro de Documentación Arkheia MUAC (DiGAV, UNAM): 274, 275; Susan Cianciolo and Bridget Donahue, New York: 291 bottom; Susan Cianciolo, Nieves, Zurich, and Bridget Donahue, New York: 291 top; Arthur Fournier: 242 top right; G. B. Jones and Cooper Cole, Toronto: 165; Cameron Jamie and Gladstone Gallery: 373; Mike Kelley Foundation for the Arts: 121 top; Kurimanzutto: 276, 277, 278, 279; Matthew Marks Gallery: 121 bottom; Devin N. Morris and Deli Gallery, New York, Mexico City: 393; The Museum of Modern Art/Licensed by SCALA / Art Resource, New York: 42, 104 top, 106 top left, 106 bottom right, 107, 329 top; Jordan Nassar, Anat Ebgi, Los Angeles, James Cohan, New York, and The Third Line, Dubai: 397; The Estate of Barbara E. Schwartz (a.k.a. Barbara Ess) and Magenta Plains, New York: 103 top; Brent Sikkema: 102 top; Joey Terrill and Ortuzar Projects, New York: 84–85; Tommy Turner, Estate of David Wojnarowicz, and P·P·O·W, New York: 151; TBW Books: 89 bottom

Author Biographies

GWEN ALLEN is Professor of Art History at San Francisco State University. Allen has written extensively on the role of publications in contemporary art. She is the author of *Artists' Magazines: An Alternative Space for Art* (MIT Press, 2011) and editor of *The Magazine* for the Whitechapel Gallery's series "Document of Contemporary Art" (MIT Press, 2016).

JULIA BRYAN-WILSON is Professor of LGBTQ+ Art History and core faculty in the Institute for the Study of Sexuality and Gender at Columbia University in New York. Her research interests include feminism, queer theory, craft, and collaborative practices, among other topics. She is the author of *Louise Nevelson's Sculpture: Drag, Color, Join, Face* (Yale, 2023), *Fray: Art and Textile Politics* (Chicago, 2017), and *Art Workers: Radical Practice in the Vietnam War Era* (University of California, 2009), and editor of *OCTOBER Files: Robert Morris* (MIT Press, 2013). Among her many articles and catalogue essays, she has written on the work of Sadie Benning, LTTR, and Miranda July, with whom she collaborated in the mid-1990s.

BRANDEN W. JOSEPH is Frank Gallipoli Professor of Modern and Contemporary Art at Columbia University in New York. He has published widely in the areas of modern and contemporary art, paying particular attention to artists and practices that cross traditional boundaries between visual art, music, and film. In addition to numerous articles in magazines, journals, and exhibition catalogues, he is author of five books, including *Experimentations: John Cage in Music, Art, and Architecture* (Bloomsbury, 2016), *Beyond the Dream Syndicate: Tony Conrad and the Arts after Cage* (Zone Books, 2008), and *Random Order: Robert Rauschenberg and the Neo-Avant-Garde* (MIT Press, 2003). He is also editor of Carolee Schneemann, *Uncollected Texts* (Primary Information, 2018) and Kim Gordon, *Is It My Body? Selected Texts* (Sternberg, 2014). He served as consulting curator on the exhibition *Carolee Schneemann: Kinetic Painting* (2016) and co-curator of *Tony Oursler, UFOs, and Effigies* (2013).

MIMI THI NGUYEN is Associate Professor of Gender and Women's Studies at the University of Illinois, Urbana-Champaign. Nguyen has made zines since 1991, including *Slander* and the influential compilation zine *Race Riot*. As a scholar and theorist, she has continued to engage the existing historiography of the Riot Grrrl movement, most notably in the texts "Riot Grrrl, Race, and Revival" (2012) and "Minor Threats" (2015). She is the author of *The Gift of Freedom: War, Debt, and Other Refugee Passages* (Duke, 2012) and co-editor (with Thuy Linh Nguyen Tu) of *Alien Encounters: Pop Culture in Asian America* (Duke, 2007).

TAVIA NYONG'O is Chair and Professor of Theater and Performance Studies, Professor of American Studies, and Professor of African-American Studies at Yale University. He is the author of *The Amalgamation Waltz: Race, Performance, and the Ruses of Memory* (University of Minnesota, 2009) and *Afro-Fabulations: The Queer Drama of Black Life* (NYU Press, 2018). In these and other publications, Nyong'o has written extensively on queer artists of color whose work intersects with punk and performance, including zine-makers Vaginal Davis and Brontez Purnell, as well as on the photography and zines of Linda Simpson.

ALEXIS SALAS is Endowed Assistant Professor of Arts of the Americas at the University of Arkansas School of Art. Her first book project, *Disparity at Play: The Artists and Projects of Temístocles 44 (Mexico City, 1991–2003)*, looks at how an artist collective in Mexico City used the conditions of neoliberalism to produce subversive collective projects, including zines.

DREW SAWYER is Sondra Gilman Curator of Photography at the Whitney Museum of American Art (formerly Phillip and Edith Leonian Curator of Photography at the Brooklyn Museum). Sawyer has curated exhibitions and published on the social role of photography and its intersections with other media. His exhibitions with accompanying catalogues include *Jimmy DeSana: Submission* (Brooklyn Museum/DelMonico Books, 2022), *Art After Stonewall, 1969–1989* (Columbus Museum of Art/Rizzoli, 2019), *The Sun Placed in the Abyss* (Columbus Museum of Art/DAP, 2016), and *'Social Forces Visualized': Photography and Scientific Charity, 1900–1920* (Wallach Art Gallery, Columbia University, 2011).

Brooklyn Museum Board of Trustees

Published by

Phaidon Press Limited
2 Cooperage Yard
London E15 2QR

Phaidon Press Inc.
111 Broadway
New York, NY 10006

Phaidon SARL
55, rue Traversière
75012 Paris

phaidon.com

in association with

Brooklyn Museum
200 Eastern Parkway
Brooklyn, NY 11238-6052

brooklynmuseum.org

This publication accompanies the exhibition *Copy Machine Manifestos: Artists Who Make Zines*, on view at the Brooklyn Museum, New York, November 17, 2023–March 31, 2024; and the Vancouver Art Gallery, May–September, 2024.

Copy Machine Manifestos: Artists Who Make Zines is organized by Branden W. Joseph, Frank Gallipoli Professor of Modern and Contemporary Art, department of Art History and Archaeology, Columbia University, and Drew Sawyer, Sondra Gilman Curator of Photography at the Whitney Museum of American Art (formerly Phillip and Edith Leonian Curator of Photography, Brooklyn Museum), with Marcelo Gabriel Yáñez, Research Assistant, and Imani Williford, Curatorial Assistant, Photography, Fashion and Material Culture, Brooklyn Museum.

Leadership support for this exhibition is provided by Shelley Fox Aarons and Philip E. Aarons, the Phillip Leonian and Edith Rosenbaum Leonian Charitable Trust, and by

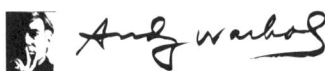

The Andy Warhol Foundation for the Visual Arts

Major support is provided by the Brooklyn Museum's Contemporary Art Committee.

First published 2023
Reprinted 2024, 2025
© 2023 Phaidon Press Limited
Text © 2023 Brooklyn Museum

ISBN 978 1 83866 708 5

Printed in the United Kingdom

Printed on paper that is FSC certified

For Phaidon
Commissioning Editor: Deborah Aaronson
Project Editor: Maia Murphy
Production Controller: Andie Trainer

For the Brooklyn Museum
Director of Publications, Interpretation, and Editorial Services: Audrey Walen
Head of Digital Collections and Services: Sarah DeSantis
Image Licensing Specialist: Taylor Catalana

Edited by: Diana Stoll
Designed by: Garrick Gott

Cover: *J.D.s*, no. 8, 1991 (detail, p. 164)

Every effort has been made to contact the owners and photographers of illustrations reproduced here whose names do not appear in the captions or in the picture credits listed on p. 444. Anyone having further information concerning copyright holders is asked to contact the Brooklyn Museum so this information can be included in future printings.